AUSTRALIAN DICTIONARY

OF BIOGRAPHY

General Editors
BEDE NAIRN
GEOFFREY SERLE

AUSTRALIAN DICTIONARY OF BIOGRAPHY

VOLUME 8 : 1891-1939

Cl-Gib

General Editors
BEDE NAIRN
GEOFFREY SERLE

Section Editors
G. C. BOLTON
K. J. CABLE
R. J. O'NEILL
J. R. POYNTER
HEATHER RADI

MELBOURNE UNIVERSITY PRESS

First published 1981
Printed in Australia by Wilke and Company Limited,
Clayton, Victoria 3168 for
Melbourne University Press, Carlton, Victoria 3053
U.S.A. and Canada: International Scholarly Book Services, Inc.,
P.O. Box 1632, Beaverton, OR 97075
United Kingdom, Ireland and Europe: Europa Publications Limited
18 Bedford Square, London WC1B 3JN

National Library of Australia Cataloguing in Publication data

Australian dictionary of biography. Volume 8. 1891-1939, Cl-Gib.

ISBN 0 522 84219 4.

1. Australia – Biography. 2. Australia – History – 1891–1939. I. Nairn, Bede. II. Serle, Geoffrey, 1922-.

920'.094

PREFACE

This volume of the *Australian Dictionary of Biography*, containing 672 entries by 465 authors, is the second of six for the 1891-1939 section. The two volumes of the 1788-1850 section and the four of the 1851-1890 section have already been published. The late Douglas Pike was general editor for volumes 1 to 5 and Bede Nairn for volume 6 and Nairn and Geoffrey Serle for volume 7. The chronological division was designed to simplify production, for more than 7000 entries will be included in volumes 1-12. (Volumes 1-2, for 1788-1850, had 1116 entries; volumes 3-6, for 1851-1890, 2053; and 4000 are planned for volumes 7-12). The placing of each individual's name in the appropriate section has been determined by when he/she did his/her most important work (*floruit*). A general index volume will be prepared when the three sections are completed.

The selection of names for inclusion required prolonged consultation. After quotas were estimated, working parties in each State and the armed services working party prepared provisional lists, which were widely circulated and carefully amended. Many of the names were obviously significant and worthy of inclusion as leaders in politics, business, the armed services, the professions, the arts, the labour movement, etc. Many others have been included as representatives of ethnic and social minorities and of a wide range of occupations, or as innovators, notorieties or eccentrics. Many had to be omitted through pressure of space or lack of material, and thereby joined the great mass whose members richly deserve a more honoured place; however, many thousands of these names, and information about them, are accumulating in the biographical register at the *Dictionary* headquarters in the Australian National University.

Most authors were nominated by working parties. The burden of writing has been shared almost equally by university staff and by a wide variety of specialists in other fields.

The *Australian Dictionary of Biography* is a project based on consultation and co-operation. The Australian National University has borne the cost of the headquarters staff, of much research and of some special contingencies, while other Australian universities have supported the project in various ways. Its policies were originally determined by the national committee, composed mainly of representatives from the departments of history in each Australian university. At Canberra the editorial board has kept in touch with all these representatives, and with the working parties, librarians, archivists and other local experts, as well as overseas correspondents and research assistants in each Australian capital. With such varied support the *Australian Dictionary of Biography* can truly be called a national project.

ACKNOWLEDGMENTS

Special thanks are due to Professor K. S. Inglis for his guidance as chairman of the editorial board. Those who helped in planning the shape of the work have been mentioned in earlier volumes.

Within Australia the *Dictionary* is greatly indebted to many librarians and archivists in Canberra and in each State; to the secretaries of many historical and genealogical societies; to the Australian War Memorial, Department of Transport library and Department of Veterans' Affairs, in Canberra; to the Metropolitan Water Sewerage and Drainage Board, Public Trustee, New South Wales Police Department, East Sydney Technical College, Australian Broadcasting Commission Archives, and Commercial Banking Co. of Sydney Ltd, in Sydney; to Australian National Railways, central division in Adelaide, the Public Service Board in Queensland, and the history section, Education Department, in Melbourne; to the registrars of probates, in the various States, and of Supreme and Family Courts, whose generous co-operation has solved many problems; and to the Department of Defence for authenticating many details. Warm thanks for the free gift of their time and talents are due to all contributors and to all members of the national committee, editorial board, and the working parties. For particular advice the *Dictionary* owes much to M. Austin, Sir Stanley Burbury, Eileen Duncan, B. Gandevia, A. C. Gray, A. J. and Nancy Gray, G. McKeown, H. S. Williams, M. Shaw, Sir Harold Wyndham and Sir John Young.

Essential assistance with birth, death and marriage certificates has been provided by the generous co-operation of registrars in New South Wales, Queensland, South Australia, Tasmania, Western Australia, the Northern Territory and the Australian Capital Territory and by the government statist, Victoria; by the Alexander Turnbull Library, Wellington, New Zealand; by the General Register Office, Edinburgh, Scotland; by Bureaux of Vital Statistics in State Health departments in California, Florida, Illinois, Maine, Maryland, Massachusetts, New Jersey, New York, Ohio, Rhode Island, Tennessee and Washington in the United States of America; by registrars general in Fiji and in Mauritius; by the Vital Statistics Department, Alberta, the prothonotary, Superior Court, Sherbrooke, and the registrar general, Toronto, in Canada; by the mayors of Boulogne-sur-Mer, Cannes, Pau and Romorantin-Lanthenay in France; by the mayors of Amsterdam and Delft in Holland; by the mayor, Belmont-sur-Yverdon and the state archivist, Neuchâtel, in Switzerland; by the director of tourism in Monaco; and by the South African and Royal Danish embassies in Canberra.

For assistance overseas, thanks are due to Diana Killen, liaison officer of the National Library of Australia in London and to her staff; to Léonie Glen and Deirdre Pescott, London, and Margery Walton, New Zealand; to the archives and/or libraries of the universities of Bristol, Cambridge, Durham, Exeter, Liverpool, London, Oxford and Reading and of the Imperial College of Science and Technology and King's College, London, in England; of the universities of Aberdeen, Edinburgh and St Andrews in Scotland, the New University of Ulster, Londonderry, in Northern Ireland, and the National University of Ireland, and Trinity College and All Hallows College, Dublin, in Ireland; to the archives and/or libraries of Columbia University, New York, Johns Hopkins University, Baltimore, and the universities of Chicago, Michigan and Oregon in the United States of

America; the University of Ottawa in Canada; Albert Ludwig's University Freiberg, and Heidelberg University in the Federal Republic of Germany. Thanks are also due to the Anglican Consultative Council, the Chamberlain's Court, Guildhall, the General Synod of the Church of England, the Geological Society of London, Guildhall School of Music and Drama, the Honourable Society of the Inner Temple and the Honourable Society of the Middle Temple, Jews' College, London College of Music, the Ministry of Defence, the Public Record Office, the Royal Academy of Dramatic Art, the Royal Academy of Music, the Royal College of Music, the Royal College of Veterinary Surgeons, the Royal Horticultural Society, the Royal Society of Arts, the Society of Authors, the United Society for the Propagation of the Gospel and Westminster School, all in London, and to the Bishop of Woolwich, the Chancellor, Lincoln, the General Registry, Isle of Man, Salisbury Diocesan Registry and Woolwich Garrison, in the United Kingdom; the Hochschule für Musik und darstellende Kunst, Vienna, in Austria; the archives of the Ministry of the Interior, and the general state archives, The Hague, in Holland; the Swiss National Library, Bern, in Switzerland; the Chicago Historical Society, the Chicago Public Library, Cohoes Public Library, New York, the Library of Congress, Washington D.C., the Museum of Comparative Zoology, Harvard, the National Museum of Natural History, Washington D.C., Newberry Library, Chicago, and the New York Historical Society, all in the United States of America; the Alumni Association of Queen's University, Kingston, Ontario, in Canada; the Dictionaries of Canadian and South African Biographies; and other individuals and institutions who have co-operated with the *Dictionary*.

The *Dictionary* deeply regrets the death of such notable contributors as Ellinor Archer, Marnie Bassett, G. F. J. Bergman, Irene Crespin, Sir Lorimer Dods, E. M. Dollery, H. J. Finnis, S. M. Gilbert, J. C. Jaeger, Patricia Keep, H. C. Lewis, W. E. Pidgeon, G. W. Symes, H. R. Thomas, D. H. Tribolet and Sir Kenneth Wheare who in their several capacities, greatly assisted the work of this and previous volumes. In this volume there appear articles on Sir John Cleland and Sir Hudson Fysh, the first time that former contributors to the *Dictionary* have been in turn included.

Grateful acknowledgment is due to the director and staff of Melbourne University Press; to Nan Phillips and Dorothy Smith (both recently retired after long service); to the editorial staff in Canberra: Martha Campbell, Sally O'Neill, James Gibbney, Suzanne Edgar, Chris Cunneen, Frank Brown, Merrilyn Lincoln, Ann Smith, Margaret Steven, Alan Fewster and Helga Griffin; to Barbara Dale, Ruth Frappell and Naomi Turner in Sydney, Betty Crouchley in Brisbane, Joyce Gibberd in Adelaide, Wendy Birman in Perth, Margaret Glover in Hobart and Mimi Colligan in Melbourne; and to the administrative staff: Ivy Meere, Frances Dinnerville, Dorothy McBride, Betty Newman, Judith Ly and Marion Consandine.

COMMITTEES

COMMITTEES

AUTHORS

ABBOTT, Jacqueline:
Davidson, E.
ADAM-SMITH, Patsy:
Clapp.
ALLEN, C. W.:
Duffield.
ALLEN, Judith:
Devine, M.
ALLINGHAM, Anne:
Cunningham, A.; Deane, J.
ANDREWS, B. G.:
Cobb, C.; Collins, H. L.; de Rougemont; Donovan.
ANTILL, J. M.:
de Burgh; Franki; Gibson, A.
ARCHER E.*:
Gaunt, M.
ARMSTRONG, John Brian:
Coyne, J.; Crampton.
ARTHUR, J. L.:
Ferguson, D.
ATCHISON, John:
Cramsie; Duncan, W. J.; Falkiner, Gibson, R.
AUDLEY, R. M.:
Eddy.

BAIN, Mary Albertus:
Drew.
BAKER, John S.:
Dunkley.
BARTLETT, Peter:
Downer.
BARWICK, Diane:
Cooper, W.
BATE, Weston:
Cooke, S.
BAUER, F. H.:
Cooper, R.
BAUER, J. B.:
Cooper, R.
BAYTON, John:
Dawes.
BAZLEY, A. W.*:
Gellibrand.
BEASLEY, A. W.:
Dunn, E.
BECHERVAISE, John:
Davis, J. K.
BEEVER, E. A.:
Cooch; Cooke, J.; Elder; Emery.
BELSHAW, Jim:
Drummond, D.
BENNETT, J. M.:
Cullen, W.
BENNETT, Robert:
Clendinnen.

BENNETT, Scott:
Ewing, N.
BERESFORD, Quentin:
Fysh, P.
BERGMAN, George F. J.*:
Cohen, G.
BIRMAN, Wendy:
Drake-Brockman, F.
BLACK, David:
Collett; Collier, P.; Davy, T.
BLAINEY, Geoffrey:
Crotty.
BLAKE, L. J.:
Cockerill.
BOLAND, T. P.:
Duhig, J.
BOLGER, Peter:
Davis, C.
BOLLEN, J. D.:
Clark, G.
BOLTON, G. C.:
Connolly, J.; Crowder; Draper, T.; Durack, M.; Ellis, H.; Emanuel; Forrest, A.; Fowler, J.
BONNIN, Nancy:
Cumbrae-Stewart, Z.
BOTTRELL, Arthur E. E.:
Forbes, A.
BOURKE, D. F.:
Clune.
BOYER, Peter:
Davies, J. & C.
BRANAGAN, D. F.:
David, T.; Dun, W.
BRIDGE, Carl:
Davidson, James E.
BROOME, Richard:
Dill Macky.
BROOMHILL, Ray:
Daly, J.; Dickinson, E.
BROWN, Julie K.:
Friström.
BROWN, Margaret:
Cowan, E.
BROWNING, T.:
Davidson, J., ecologist.
BRUCE, Candice:
Davies, D.
BRYAN, Harrison:
Cumbrae-Stewart, F.
BRYDEN, William:
Flynn, T. & E.
BUCKNALL, Graeme:
Flynn, J.
BURKE, Janine:
Cumbrae Stewart, J.

* deceased

xi

BURNESS, Peter:
Cope; Costello; Davey, P.; Geake.
BYGOTT, Ursula:
Dakin; Fawsitt.

CABLE, K. J.:
Dakin; D'Arcy-Irvine; Eddy; Fawsitt;
Fehon; Flower; Garrett.
CAIN, Neville:
Giblin, L.
CALLAGHAN, V. E.:
Gibney.
CARMENT, David:
D'Arcy, W.; Ferguson, John, builder.
CARNELL, I. G.:
Dunstan, T.
CARR, Barrett J.:
Deacon; Farrell.
CARRON, L. T.:
de Beuzeville.
CHAMBERLAIN, W. M.:
Conrick.
CHAMBERS, T. C.:
Ewart, A.
CHAPPELL, W. F.:
Floyd.
CIGLER, Michael J.:
Daneš.
CLARK, Manning:
Franklin, R; Furphy.
CLARK, Rex*:
Ewen.
CLARKE, E.:
Fewings.
CLARKE, Ron:
Flack.
CLAYDON, Robyn:
Clarke, M.
COATES, H. J.:
Foster, W.
COLLINGS, A. F.:
Fitzsimmons.
COLLINS PERSSE, Michael D. de B.:
Collins, J. W.; Fairbairn, G. C. & F.;
Fairbairn, J.; Fairbairn, S.
CONNAH, Margaret II.:
Connah.
COOK, B.:
Dixson.
COOK, Jenny:
Cussen.
CORBETT, Arthur:
Corin; Davis, J.; Freeman, A. & W.
COULTHARD-CLARK, C. D.:
Currey; de Mole; Ewen; Finn.
COURSE, L. J.:
Frater.
COURTNEY, James W.:
Freame.
CRIBB, Margaret Bridson:
Cribb.
CROUCHLEY, Betty:
Donaldson, St C.; Dunstan W. J.; Forrest,
E.; Fihelly.

CROWLEY, F. K.:
Cook, J.; Forrest, J.
CUBIS, Richmond:
Edwards, P.
CUNNEEN, Chris:
Clark, H.; Cleary, P.; Collins, R.; Comino;
Corbett, W.; Davidson, W. E.; Day, R.; de
Chair; Denman; Desmond, A.; Donohoe;
Dooley, J. T.; Dudley; Durack, E.; Flegg;
Forster, H.
CUTHBERT, D. D.:
Dickson, J. R.

DALY, John A.:
Creswell, J.
DANIELS, Kay:
Duncan, A.
DARLING, D. K.:
Darling, J.
DAVIDSON, Jim:
Dyer.
DAVIS, R. P.:
Culley; Dwyer-Gray.
DAVISON, Graeme:
Dyson, E.
DAWES, J. N. I.:
Dyett.
DE GARIS, B. K.:
Colebatch; Fowler, J.
DE SERVILLE, P. H.:
Connibere.
DEXTER, David:
Dexter.
DODS, Lorimer*:
Clubbe.
DOLLERY, E. M.*:
Dobson, H.
DONCASTER, E. W.:
Collick.
DONOVAN, Margaret M.:
Daly. A.
DOUGAN, Alan:
Ferguson, John, minister.
DRYEN, R. G.:
Duesbury; Fell.
DUFFECY, James A.:
Field, E. P.
DUNCAN, Ross:
Conacher.
DUNKLEY, Graham:
Crofts.
DUNPHY, E. A.:
Dwyer, W.
DYER, S. W.:
Field, E.

EARLAM, Malcolm S. S.:
Craig.
EASTWOOD, Jill:
Doorly.
EDGAR, Suzanne:
Coles; Craigie; Davey, C.; Edwards, A;
Ewing, J.

*deceased

AUTHORS

HALL, Richard J.:
Fuller, C.
HALLER-GRIFFITS, A. E.:
Dechaineux.
HAMMETT, A. W.:
Fletcher, J. L.
HANCOCK I. R.:
Cook, J. N.
HANNAH, Wilma:
Fink.
HARPER, Norman:
Elkington, J. S.
HARRISON, Peter:
Daley, C.
HICKS, Neville:
Claxton; Coghlan.
HILL, A. J.:
Cox, C.; Dodds; Downes; Elliott, H.
HOLDER, R. F.:
Davidson, A.; French, J.
HOLT, H. T. E.:
Cohen, J.
HOPLEY, J. B.:
Denham, H.
HORAN, John:
Devine, H.
HORNER, D. M.:
Eames.
HORNER, Jack:
Ferguson, W.
HOWELL, P. A.:
Cudmore; Galway.
HUDSON, W. J.:
Fuhrman.
HUTCHISON, D. E.:
Cooke, W.
HUTCHISON, Noel S.:
Cowan, T.
HUTLEY, F. C.:
Cobbett.
HYSLOP, Anthea:
Cuthbertson.
HYSLOP, Robert:
Creswell, W.; Garsia.

IKIN, Van:
Davis, A.
IRVING, Baiba:
Devine, M.
ISAACS, Keith:
Cobby.

JACKSON, Hugh:
Fletcher, L.
JACOBS, Marjorie:
Fidler.
JAENSCH, Dean:
Coombe; Copley.
JAMES, Bob:
Fleming, J.
JONES, Alan:
David, C.
JONES, Barry O.:
Cohen, I.; Deeming; Elmslie.

JONES, Helen:
de Lissa; George, M.
JONES, Joseph:
Gay.

KAYE, Geoffrey:
Embley.
KEEL, G. D. Ailwood:
Daley, V.
KENDALL, F. J.:
Duigan.
KENNEDY, B. E.:
Gepp.
KENNEDY, K. H.:
Corbould; Craven; Dash.
KENNETT, John:
Fraser, C.
KENNY, M. J. B.:
Curnow, W.
KENNY, Susan:
Finlay.
KEON-COHEN, B.:
Cussen.
KERR, Ruth S.:
Forsyth, J.
KING, C. J.:
Cobb, N.
KING, Hazel:
Day, E.
KING, Helen:
Durack, S.
KIRKPATRICK, Rod:
Dunn, A., A. & W.
KIRSOP, Wallace:
Dymock.
KUIPER, J.:
Darnell-Smith.

LACK, John:
Coates, J.; Cuming.
LAIRD, J. T.:
Gerard, E.
LAKE, Marilyn:
Earle.
LAND, William A.:
Clayton.
LANSBURY, Coral:
Edwards, G.
LARACY, Hugh:
Couppé.
LARMOUR, Constance:
Foster, A.
LAURENCE, John H.:
de Bernales.
LAWRY, J.:
Edwards, L.
LAWSON, Sylvia:
Edmond.
LEGGETT, C. A. C.:
Cooper, L.; Duhig, J. V.
LEOPOLD, Elisabeth:
Claxton.
LETTICE, M. N.:
Clarke, G.

NAIRN, Bede:
Coningham; Cotton, F., L. A. & F. S.; Crick,
W.; Cusack; Dacey; Davis, T.; Dunn, W.;
Fitzgerald; Flowers; Garden; Garvan.
NAYLOR, Bruce:
Dodd, J.
NELSON, H. N.:
Donaldson, J.
NEUMANN, C.:
Edwards, J.; Elliott, G.
NICHOLLS, Mary:
Cullen, J.; Delany.
NOLAN, J. G.:
Cran.
NORRIS, R.:
Deakin.
NOTT, R. E.:
Cobb, V.

OATS, William N.:
Clemes.
O'BRIEN, Joan M.:
Evans, A. E.
O'DONNELL, E. J.:
Denehy; Du Faur.
O'FARRELL, Patrick:
Dryer.
O'HAGAN, M. D.:
Evans, G.
O'HARA, John:
Collins, G.; Cropper.
O'NEILL, Sally:
Collier, F.; Cox, E.; Cronin; Fowler, T.;
Fullerton; Gaunt, C., E. & G.; Gibson, W.
OSBORNE, Graeme:
Delprat.
OSMOND, Warren:
Eggleston.
O'SULLIVAN, David M.:
Cole, F.
O'TOOLE, Silvia:
Davy, R.

PAGE, K. R.:
Collins, J. R.
PALMER, Imelda:
Derham; Flynn, J.T.
PARKER, R. S.:
Garran.
PARSONS, George:
de Bavay.
PAUL, J. B.:
Dunstan, A.
PEARCE, C. G.:
Dixon, H.
PEARCE, Ian:
Giblin, R.
PEDERSEN, P. A.:
Cooke, T.; Coyne, D.
PEOPLES, Kevin:
Curnow, J.
PERCIVAL, J.:
Fysh, W.
PERKS, Murray:
Coates, J. F.

PERRY, Warren:
Coxen; Foott; Foster, H.
PERVAN, Ralph:
Cunningham, J.
PESCOTT, R. T. M.:
French, C. & C. H.
PHILLIPS, Nan:
Cusack.
PHIPPS, Jennifer:
Colquhoun, A.
PIGGIN, Stuart:
Fleming, W.
PIKE, A. F.:
Crick, S.; Gibson, W. A.
PLAYFORD, John:
Cockburn.
PRIMROSE, B. N.:
Clarkson; Colvin.

QUINN, Rodney K.:
Elliott, C.

RADI, Heather:
Cox, E. J.; D'Arcy, C.; Fowler, E.
RADIC, Maureen Thérèse:
Ewart, F.
RAYMOND, Ira D.:
Clucas.
REID, John:
Conyers.
REYNOLDS, I. A.:
Dobson, E.
REYNOLDS, John:
Clark, E.
REYNOLDS, Peter:
Clamp.
RICHARDS, Eric:
Cohen, Lewis.
RICHARDS, Michael J.:
Cotton, A.
RICHARDSON, Alan:
Fowler, H.
RIDDEL, R. J.:
Dods.
RITCHIE, John:
Connolly, E.
ROBERTS, A. R.:
Connell, H.
ROBERTSON, J. R.:
Fenton.
ROE, J. I.:
Franklin, S.
ROE, Michael:
Cumpston; Elkington, J. S. C.
ROENNFELDT, Peter:
Dalley-Scarlett.
ROSS, Barbara:
Cottrell.
ROWSE, Jennifer:
Garvin.
RUNDLE, H. E.:
Clark, A.
RUTLAND, Suzanne D.:
Cohen, F. L.; Falk.

AUTHORS

RUTLEDGE, Martha:
*Cohen, S.; Connell, C.; Cottrell; Crick, W.;
Davidson, C.; Deamer; Dean, G.; Duff;
Fairfax, R.; Ferry, M.; Fox, F.;
Fuller, B. J. & J.*
RYAN, J. A.:
Farnell.

SACK, P. G.:
Flierl.
SALMOND, John:
Cunningham, E.
SANKER, I. G.:
Dunstan, B.
SANTAMARIA, Catherine:
Gabriel, C. L.
SAUNDERS, Kay:
Cowley.
SAYERS, Stuart:
Collins, C.
SCARLETT, Ken:
Cohn.
SCHEDVIN, C. B.:
Gibson, Sir R.
SCOLLAY, Moira:
Dooley, J. B.
SEMMLER, Clement:
Dalley; Fletcher, C.
SERLE, Geoffrey:
Croll.
SERLE, R. P.:
Dunstan, W.
SHARP, Ian G.:
Dethridge, G.; Drake-Brockman, E.
SHAW, Mary Turner:
Cockram; Currie, H. & J.
SHIRLEY, Graham:
Doyle, S.
SHORTEN, Ann R.:
Corby.
SIDNEY, Neilma:
Edments.
SIMINGTON, Margot Z.:
Dibdin; Dove.
SIMPSON, Caroline:
Fairfax, J. R. & J. O.
SIMPSON, Pat:
Draper, T.
SIMS, Eric B.:
Fiveash.
SKELSEY, W. C.:
Fletcher, J. W.
SLIGO, C. E.:
Crowther.
SMART, Judith:
Daley, J.
SMITH, Ann G.:
Collins, R.; Crawford, T. W.; Edwards, W.
SMITH, A. O.:
Cook, R.
SMITH, Bernard:
Dickinson, S.
SMITH, Brian J.:
Dendy; Gabriel, C. J.; Gatliff.

SMITH, Howard, J.:
de Largie.
SOLOMON, G. D.:
Easterbrook.
SOUTHCOTT, R. V.:
Cleland, J.
SOUTHERN, Roger J.: .
Coane.
SOUTHEY, R. J.:
Clarke, R.
SPATE, O. H. K.:
Collingridge.
SPEARRITT, Peter:
Clark, R.; Dunningham.
STAPLES, A. C.:
Clement.
STARKE, Monica:
Corbett, J.
STEPHENS, David:
Duncan, W. L.; Dunn, J.
STEVEN, M. J. E.:
Dixon, G.
STEWART, Ken:
Dorrington; Dwyer, J. F.
STEWART, M. F.:
Clemens.
STEWART, Noël:
Clutterbuck.
STOPS, Peter:
Gant.
STORE, Ron:
Devanny.
SUNTER, Anne Beggs:
Duggan, B.
SUTTON, R.:
French, G.; Gibb.
SWEETING, A. J.:
Cutlack.

TANNER, L. G.:
Crawford, T. S.
TEALE, Ruth:
Cramp; Crommelin; Dunstan, E.
TERRY, Martin:
Fullwood.
THOMAS, Alan:
Cleary, W.; Conder.
THOMAS, Daniel:
de Maistre; Fizelle.
THWAITES, John B.:
Emmett.
TIPPING, M. Borgia:
Forbes, C.
TOFLER, O. B.:
Freedman.
TOWNSLEY, W. A.:
Evans, J.
TRETHEWEY, Lynne:
Fenner.
TUCKER, Maya V.:
Dyason.
TURNER, Ann:
Earsman.

TURNER, I. S.:
Cole, P.
TURNER, Ken:
Farrar.
TURNEY, Cliff:
Cohen, F.

UNDERHILL, Nancy D. H.:
Gibson, E.

VALENTINE, Barbara:
Eady.
VALLANCE, T. G.:
David, T.; Dun, W.
VALLEE, Peter:
Ferguson, E.
VEALE, R. S.:
Cumberlege.
VELLAR, Ivo D.:
Dunhill.
VILLAUME, John:
Francis.
VOCKLER, , John Charles:
Frodsham.
VOGT, A. E.:
Forsyth, S.

WALKER, D. R.:
Esson.
WALKER, J. D.:
Deane, H.
WALKER, Mary:
Dumolo.
WALKER, R. B.:
Denison.
WALSH, G. P.:
Cotter; Davidson, J., shearer; Davis, W.;
Dunlop; Edgerton; Etheridge; Ewing, T.;
Farleigh; Fiaschi; Fletcher, J. J.; Follett;
Foy; Freeman, A. & W.
WALSH, Maureen:
Gibbs.
WARD, Edna:
Furber.
WARD, John M.:
Fuller, G.
WARDEN, Alan:
Gatty; Gardner; Gerard, A.

WARHURST, John:
Crowe, W.; Dickson, J.
WATERHOUSE, Jill:
Collier, J.; Fitzpatrick.
WATERS, K. H.:
Dunbabin, R.; Dunbabin, T.
WATERSON, D. B.:
Crombie; Forrest, W.; Foxton.
WHEELER, D.:
Darling, H.
WHITE, K. R.:
Donnelly; Dun, P.
WHITELAW, J.:
Daly, C.
WILKEY, Don:
Colquhoun, P.
WILLIAMS, J. G.:
Forsyth, J. K.; Forth; Fowles, H.; Frost;
Gale, C. & W. A.
WILLIAMS, Margaret:
Duggan, E.
WILLIS, Elizabeth:
Collick.
WILSON, Paul D.:
Gall.
WIXTED, E. P.:
Dallas.
WOOD, Christine:
Crisp.
WOOD, Harley:
Furber; Gale, W. F.
WOOD, Ronald:
Gibson, J.
WOOD, S. R. C.:
Creswick.
WOODMAN, Stewart:
Docker; Garland, J.
WRIGHT, Andrée:
Geach.
WRIGLEY, C. W.:
Farrer.

ZAINU'DDIN, A. Thomson:
Fitchett.
ZELLING, Howard:
Cleland, E.
ZUBANS, Ruth:
Fox, E.
ZWILLENBERG, H. J.:
Clare; Dean, G. H.

A NOTE ON SOME PROCEDURES

Among our authors and readers and, indeed, on the editorial board, there is strong disagreement on whether certain facts should normally be included — such as cause of death, burial or cremation details, and value of estate. In this volume our practices have been as follows:

Cause of death: include, except usually in the case of the very old; in practice we include in about two-thirds of the entries.

Burial/cremation: include when details available.

Value of estate: normally include for certain categories such as businessmen, and when the amount is unusually high or low. In recent years, when the practice developed of early distribution of assets in order to avoid estate and probate duties, the sum is not always meaningful; moreover it is not always possible to ascertain the full facts. Hence we have resorted to discretionary use.

Some other procedures require explanation:

Measurements: as the least unsatisfactory solution, we have used imperial system measurements (as historically appropriate), followed by the metric equivalent in brackets. Round metric figures are used when the number is clearly approximate, e.g., 500 miles (800 km).

Money: we have retained £ for pounds for references prior to 14 February 1966 (when the conversion rate was A£1 = A$2).

Religion: stated whenever information is available, but often there is no good evidence of actual practice, e.g., the information is confined to marriage and funeral rites.

[q.v.]: the particular volume is given for those included in volumes 1-7, but not for those in this and future volumes. Note that the cross-reference [q.v.] now accompanies the names of all who have separate articles in the *Dictionary*. In volumes 1-6 it was not shown for royal visitors, governors, lieut-governors and those Colonial Office officials who were included.

Small capitals: used for relations and others when they are of substantial importance but not included in their own right.

Five-year rule: a few men and women, whose *floruit* was pre-1940 but who lived to an advanced age, have been excluded on the ground that they died too recently for proper historical consideration. No one is included who died less than five years before date of publication, except some sportsmen whose years of fame were long ago.

CORRIGENDA

Every effort is made to check every detail in every article, but inevitably a work of the size and complexity of the *Dictionary* includes some errors.

Corrigenda have been published regularly with each volume and a list is included with Volume 8 showing corrections made since the publication of Volume 7 (1979).

Only corrections are shown; additional information is not included; nor is any reinterpretation attempted. The only exception to this procedure is when new details become available about parents or births, deaths and marriages.

Documented corrections are welcomed. Additional information, with sources, is also invited and will be placed in the appropriate files for future use.

A copy of cumulative corrigenda up to Volume 7 is available from the publishers at cost of postage.

REFERENCES

The following and other obvious works of reference have been widely used but not normally acknowledged:

Australian encyclopaedia, 1-2 (Syd, 1925), 1-10 (1958)

Biographical register for various Australian parliaments: (A. W. Martin & P. Wardle *and* H. Radi, P. Spearritt & E. Hinton—New South Wales; G. C. Bolton & A. Mozley—Western Australia; K. Thomson & G. Serle—Victoria; D. B. Waterson—Queensland; S. & B. Bennett—Tasmania; and J. Rydon—Commonwealth)

D. Blair, *Cyclopaedia of Australasia* (Melb, 1881)

B. Burke, *A genealogical and heraldic history of the colonial gentry*, 1-2 (Lond, 1891, 1895)

O'M. Creagh and E. M. Humphris (eds), *The V.C. and D.S.O.: a complete record* . . . 1-3 (Lond, 1934)

Dictionary of national biography (Lond, 1885-1971)

H. M. Green, *A history of Australian literature*, 1-2 (Syd, 1961, 2nd edn 1971)

C. A. Hughes and B. D. Graham, *A handbook of Australian government and politics 1890-1964* (Canb, 1968); *Voting for the Australian House of Representatives 1901-1964*, with corrigenda (Canb, 1975), for *Queensland Legislative Assembly 1890-1964* (Canb, 1974), for *New South Wales* . . . (1975), *Victoria* . . . (1975), and *South Australian, Western Australian and Tasmanian Lower Houses* . . . (1976)

F. Johns, *Johns's notable Australians* (Melb, 1906), *Fred Johns's annual* (Lond, 1914); *An Australian biographical dictionary* (Melb, 1934)

A. McCulloch, *Encyclopedia of Australian art* (Lond, 1968)

E. M. Miller, *Australian literature . . . to 1935* (Melb, 1940), extended to 1950 by F. T. Macartney (Syd, 1956)

W. Moore, *The story of Australian art*, 1-2 (Syd, 1934)

P. C. Mowle, *A genealogical history of pioneer families in Australia* (Syd, 1939; 5th edn Adel, 1978)

P. Serle, *Dictionary of Australian biography*, 1-2 (Syd, 1949)

Who's who (Lond), and *Who's who in Australia* (Syd, Melb), present and past editions.

ABBREVIATIONS USED IN BIBLIOGRAPHIES

AAA	Amateur Athletic Association	ed	editor
A.A.Co.	Australian Agricultural Company	edn	edition
		Edinb	Edinburgh
AAO	Australian Archives	encl	enclosure
A.B.C.	Australian Broadcasting Commission		
		Fr	Father (priest)
Ac no	Accession number		
ACER	Australian Council for Educational Research	G, Geog	Geographical
		GB	Great Britain
ACT	Australian Capital Territory	Gen	Genealogical, Genealogists
Adel	Adelaide	gen ed	general editor
Adm	Admiralty, London	Govt	Government
Agr	Agriculture, Agricultural		
AIF	Australian Imperial Force	HA	House of Assembly
AJC	Australian Jockey Club	HC	House of Commons
AMA	Australian Medical Association	Hist	History, Historical
		HL	House of Lords
ANU	Australian National University, Canberra	H.M.C.S.	Her Majesty's Colonial Ship
		HO	Home Office, London
ANU Archives	ANU Archives of Business and Labour	Hob	Hobart
		HRA	*Historical Records of Australia*
ANZAAS	Australian and New Zealand Association for the Advancement of Science	HSSA	Historical Society of South Australia
A'sian	Australasian	*IAN*	*Illustrated Australian News*
Assn	Association	Inst	Institute, Institution
Aust	Australia, Australian	*ISN*	*Illustrated Sydney News*
AWM	Australian War Memorial, Canberra	*J*	*Journal*
Basser Lib	Adolph Basser Library, Australian Academy of Science, Canberra	LA	Legislative Assembly
		LaTL	La Trobe Library, Melbourne
		Launc	Launceston
Battye Lib	J. S. Battye Library of West Australian History, Perth	LC	Legislative Council
		Lib	Library
Bd	Board	Lib Congress	Library of Congress, Washington, D.C., U.S.A.
BHP	Broken Hill Proprietary Co. Ltd	Lond	London
bibliog	bibliography		
biog	biography, biographical	*Mag*	*Magazine*
BM	British Museum, London	Melb	Melbourne
Brisb	Brisbane	MDHC	Melbourne Diocesan Historical Commission (Catholic), Fitzroy
CAE	College of Advanced Education	Mgr	Monsignor
Canb	Canberra	*MJA*	*Medical Journal of Australia*
cat	catalogue	ML	Mitchell Library, Sydney
Cmd	Command	MS	manuscript
CO	Colonial Office, London	mthly	monthly
C of E	Church of England		
Com	Commission	nd	date of publication unknown
CSIRO	Commonwealth Scientific and Industrial Research Organization	NL	National Library of Australia, Canberra
		no	number
cttee	committee	np	place of publication unknown
Cwlth	Commonwealth	NSW	New South Wales
		NSWA	The Archives Authority of New South Wales, Sydney
DNB	*Dictionary of National Biography*	NT	Northern Territory

xxiii

ABBREVIATIONS

NZ	New Zealand	RWAHS	Royal Western Australian Historical Society (Perth)
NZNA	New Zealand National Archives	1st S	First Session
Oxley Lib	John Oxley Library, Brisbane	2nd S	Second Session
		2nd s	second series
p	page, pages	SA	South Australia
PAH	*see* RPAH	SAA	South Australian Archives, Adelaide
pc	photocopy		
PD	*Parliamentary Debates*	Sel	Select
PMB	Pacific Manuscripts Bureau, Research School of Pacific Studies, ANU	SLSA	State Library of South Australia
		SLT	State Library of Tasmania
PMG	Postmaster-General's Department	SLV	State Library of Victoria
		SMH	*Sydney Morning Herald*
PNGA	Archives Office of Papua and New Guinea, Port Moresby	SOAS	School of Oriental and African Studies, London
PP	*Parliamentary Papers*	Soc	Society
PRGSSA	*Proceedings of the Royal Geographical Society of Australasia (South Australian Branch)*	supp	supplement
		Syd	Sydney
priv print	privately printed	TA	Tasmanian State Archives, Hobart
PRO	Public Record Office		
Procs	*Proceedings*	Tas	Tasmania
pt	part, parts	*T&CJ*	*Australian Town and Country Journal*
PTHRA	*Papers and Proceedings of the Tasmanian Historical Research Association*	tr	translated, translation
		Trans	*Transactions*
Q	*Quarterly*	Univ	University
QA	Queensland State Archives, Brisbane	UPNG	University of Papua New Guinea
Qld	Queensland		
		V&P	*Votes and Proceedings*
RAHS	Royal Australian Historical Society (Sydney)	*VHM(J)*	*Victorian Historical Magazine (Journal)*
rev	revised, revision	v, vol	volume
RGS	Royal Geographical Society	Vic	Victoria
RHSQ	Royal Historical Society of Queensland (Brisbane)	VRC	Victoria Racing Club
RHSV	Royal Historical Society of Victoria (Melbourne)	WA	Western Australia
		WCTU	Woman's Christian Temperance Union
RMIT	Royal Melbourne Institute of Technology	Well	Wellington, New Zealand
Roy	Royal	wkly	weekly
RPAH	Royal Prince Alfred Hospital	WO	War Office, London

Cl

CLAMP, JOHN BURCHAM (1869-1931), architect, was born on 30 November 1869 at 743 George Street, Sydney, son of John Clamp, a London-born hairdresser, and his wife Sophia, née Hunt, from Dublin. Known as Burcham, he was educated at Christ Church St Laurence School, and won the Mort [q.v.5] scholarship in 1882. Next year he was articled to H. C. Kent, a leading Sydney architect, and attended evening classes at the University of Sydney and the Sydney Technical College. In 1886 he received honourable mention in the student design competition of the Institute of Architects of New South Wales, and in 1889 was awarded its gold medal; that May he was the first student admitted to its membership. On 22 June 1893 he married Susie Young at Auburn; they later lived at Cremorne and, from about 1914, at Greenoaks Avenue, Darling Point.

Clamp worked for Kent until he joined T. M. Smith in partnership in 1899. In 1901 he set up on his own and became known for efficient planning, competent design and secure construction. By 1910 he had been responsible for St James's Hall, Phillip Street; Victoria Hall, Manly; Lister Private Hospital and nurses' home, Darlinghurst; and such major projects as the enlargement of Winchcombe [q.v.], Carson [q.v.7] Ltd's Pyrmont wool store, and Wyoming and Castlereagh chambers in the city. His most controversial commission was to rebuild Farmer [q.v.4] & Co. Ltd's Victoria House in Pitt Street – obliterating J. Horbury Hunt's [q.v.4] 1874 building which had been acclaimed as 'our finest example of street architecture'. Clamp's meeting with Walter Burley Griffin [q.v.] in the United States of America led to a brief partnership with him in Sydney in 1914. Later he was joined by C. H. Mackellar and they designed several factories and other buildings in 1918-24.

An active Anglican and prominent Freemason, Clamp was building surveyor for the diocese of Sydney, and exercised considerable influence in ecclesiastical architecture: among other projects he designed the Sydney Church of England Grammar School (Shore) chapel, North Sydney, St Matthew's Church, Manly (with Wright and Apperly) and converted a two-storey house at Rushcutters Bay into St Luke's Hospital. He was also a founder and councillor of Cranbrook School, altering the house after its use as the residence of the State governor in 1901-15, designing new buildings and landscaping its grounds.

Clamp and (C. H.) Finch were the architects between 1927 and 1930 of Tattersall's Club, Castlereagh Street, the Buckland [q.v.7] Memorial Church of England Boys' Home, Carlingford, Canberra Grammar School and the Ainslie Hotel in Canberra. Early in 1930 Clamp's son John replaced Finch.

An active and outspoken member of the local Institute of Architects, Clamp urged the federation of the separate State bodies and in 1907 had strongly backed the admission of Florence Parsons [q.v. Taylor] as an associate. He had a forthright but tactful manner, self-reliance and boundless energy. He was a member of the Town Planning Association of New South Wales, the Martin Place extension committee and of Tattersall's, the Millions and the National clubs. Fortunate to practise during two boom periods in 1901-14 and 1920-28, Clamp provided a bridge between the nineteenth-century romantic and twentieth-century functionalist styles, presenting an originality of design which combined character with sound commercial possibilities.

Survived by his wife, son and three daughters, Clamp died of acute bronchopneumonia on 7 July 1931 at his Cremorne home and was buried in the Anglican section of South Head cemetery.

Cyclopedia of N.S. W. (Syd, 1907); J. M. Freeland, *Architect extraordinary* (Melb, 1970), and *The making of a profession* (Syd, 1971); D. L. Johnson, *The architecture of Walter Burley Griffin* (Melb, 1977); *Building* (Syd), 12 Apr 1910, 13 July 1931; *Syd Diocesan Mag*, Aug, 1931; J. B. Clamp papers (held by Mr B. Clamp, Wollstonecraft, NSW); family information.   PETER REYNOLDS

CLAPP, SIR HAROLD WINTHROP (1875-1952), railway administrator, was born on 7 May 1875 at St Kilda, Melbourne, fourth child of Francis Boardman Clapp [q.v.3] and his wife Isabella Pinnock, née Pierce, both American-born. He was educated at Brighton Grammar and Melbourne Church of England Grammar schools, where, according to his sisters, he resisted discipline and 'escaped whenever his ingenious plotting and planning could manage it'. On leaving school he served his apprenticeship in 1893-95 at the Austral Otis Co.'s engineering works at South Melbourne. For four years he was superintendent of motive power for the Brisbane Tramway Co. Ltd of which his father was a founder and shareholder.

In 1900 Clapp went to the United States of America for experience, and spent six years with the General Electric Co., Schenectady, New York. He was then engaged by the Interborough Rapid Transit Co., and among other work was in charge of electrification of the West Jersey and Seashore division of the Pennsylvania Railroad Co. On 19 September 1906 at Providence, Rhode Island, he married Gertrude Vivien, daughter of Judge Arthur Noel of Brisbane.

Clapp joined the Southern Pacific Railroad Co. in 1908 and took charge of electrification of the suburban railways of Oakland, Alamedo and Berkeley, California. Then based at Columbus, Ohio, he was manager and later vice-president of the Columbus Railway Power and Light Co., and vice-president of the East St Louis and Suburban Railway Co., Illinois.

Despite a promising future in the United States, Clapp applied for and in April 1920 was appointed to the position of chairman of the Victorian Railway Commissioners, at a salary of £5000. He arrived in Melbourne on 15 September and began work two days later. Few Australian public servants have been so closely identified with their departments as Clapp; to many, he *was* the railways. On the technical side, he introduced many reforms. By mid-1922 the electrification of the suburban lines, begun ten years earlier, was complete. Clapp extended the network further, regraded and improved tracks, redesigned standard locomotives, introduced welded rails for smooth running, speeded up timetables and transformed railway storekeeping methods.

Clapp extended departmental control over a wide range of railway affairs. He gave particular attention to passenger amenities. By 1923 a model bakery provided 'wholesome goods', especially those containing dried fruit, for sale in refreshment rooms. To encourage the citrus fruit industry he opened a kiosk at Flinders Street station in 1924, set up stalls at other stations, and sold much fruit in times of glut. In November 1926 Clapp began selling pure orange and lemon juice drinks at a stall in Flinders Street station, the first, he claimed, in the Commonwealth. By then the department had its own butchery, bakery, laundry and poultry farm, and ran the book- and tobacco-stalls at city stations. He improved dining car facilities and introduced new steel buffet cars, the first being used during the visit of the duke and duchess of York in 1927.

Clapp's measures aimed both to promote the use of railway passenger and freight services and to help primary producers. His preoccupation with country interests led to the institution in 1924 of the Victorian National Resources Development Train,

known as Reso, which took city businessmen on tours of regional centres. The Better Farming Train, completed in 1925 as a joint venture with the Department of Agriculture, was equipped to demonstrate latest techniques to farmers.

In his pursuit of business for the railways Clapp showed both flair and innovation. He made a film of the Victorian railways at work, which was shown in Australia and overseas. From 1 July 1923 he took over the whole railway advertising business, previously leased to a private company. He produced pamphlets and posters, and by 1924 had begun in earnest his famous campaign of slogans, which included such watchwords as 'Citrus fruit is nature's way To keep you fit for work and play'; 'Grow more grass – topdress your pastures'; 'Cross crossings cautiously'; 'Go up into Brightness on the Buffalo Plateau'; other posters exhorted the public to travel by train to the zoo, the Royal Show, the seaside. In 1925 Clapp introduced weekly radio talks. He also keenly promoted tourism, especially within Victoria for Victorians. In October 1924 the department took over the Mount Buffalo chalet and made it one of the best-known resorts in the State. In 1929 Clapp was first chairman of the Australian National Travel Association.

Other innovations included a children's nursery at Flinders Street, opened in 1933, and the 'Man in Grey' at Spencer Street to answer travellers' queries. Sunday excursion trains had been running for many years but in 1929-30 Clapp persuaded the government to authorize Sunday trains from Melbourne to centres such as Bendigo and Geelong, and then between country towns.

The Depression curtailed many of Clapp's schemes. The railways made a profit in 1924-25 but in the following years deficits grew, with a record loss in 1931. Some of the costs were attributed to pay increases under Arbitration awards. But to Clapp the most serious problem, with which he became increasingly obsessed, was the competition of road transport. In an attempt to undercut road freights he reduced rail rates to what has been described as 'absurd levels'.

In 1934 Clapp toured America, Britain and the Continent investigating developments overseas including the use of diesel engines. Next year he introduced air-conditioned carriages to the service. By 1937 his pet project, the 'Cor-ten' steel passenger train, was nearing completion at the Newport workshops. Clapp was reportedly involved in every detail of its construction, from automatic couplings to interior fittings. The 'Spirit of Progress', as the train was named, was placed on the Melbourne-Albury run on 23 November 1937; after this journey, Clapp

2

trudged the length of the Albury platform to shake hands with the driver and thank him for 'a very good trip'.

In an interview on arrival in Melbourne in 1920 Clapp had announced: 'I am all for efficiency and team work and want to know my men and my men to know me'. With his grasp of detail he learnt the names and faces of thousands of railway employees. He welcomed suggestions from the staff: (Sir) Frederic Eggleston [q.v.] recorded that Clapp was in almost constant session with his colleagues, especially the technical officers, and that he was approachable and 'on cordial terms' with railway union officials. He took a close interest in the education of apprentices and encouraged pupil engineers and architects to complete studies at the University of Melbourne; in 1921 he introduced training classes for junior clerks and lad porters.

Clapp was sometimes lampooned for his passion for cleanliness: 'Clever Mary' was a nickname, and his penchant for running a finger along a high shelf in country stations was well known. He dressed carefully, and polished his shoes several times a day. In appearance he was 'a tall, gaunt, loose-limbed figure, with deep-set eyes and a sharp nose'; he never lost the accent and vocabulary he picked up in America. He had a sardonic turn of phrase, a brusque manner and a habit of ending an interview which was boring him with a barked 'I'm not hearing you'. He watched his diet carefully and drank sparingly. Horse-riding was a hobby, and he enjoyed football as a fervent Richmond barracker. Home life gave him pleasure: the family lived at Toorak and had a holiday house at Frankston.

On 30 June 1939 Clapp left the railways to become general manager of the Aircraft Construction Branch of the Commonwealth Department of Supply and Development, set up after the government decided to assemble Bristol Beaufort Bombers in Australia. He was made chairman of the new Aircraft Production Commission in March next year. In January 1941 he was knighted. When Menzies created the Department of Aircraft Production in June 1941 the commission continued to function but under the administration of the new department, and in January 1942 Curtin replaced it altogether by the Aircraft Advisory Committee. Clapp was not appointed to the new body. Instead, in February he became director-general of land transport to co-ordinate Commonwealth and State road and rail transport.

In February 1944 he was asked to prepare a report on plans for the standardization of Australia's railway gauges. This was printed in March 1945 and its recommendations were accepted in principle by the Com-

monwealth government, but ratifying legislation by all the States was not passed. Clapp argued for the change to uniform standard gauge on grounds both of defence and national prosperity. His report was used as a basis for further recommendations in 1956, after which projects to convert major routes were launched.

In September 1951 Clapp resigned for health reasons but continued to act as a consultant to the Department of Shipping and Transport. On 21 October 1952 he died in hospital at East Melbourne, survived by his wife, two sons and a daughter. He was cremated after a Methodist service conducted by Rev. (Sir) Irving Benson. A few months earlier he had ridden in the driving cabin of the Victorian Railways' first diesel-electric locomotive, named the 'Harold W. Clapp'. Many tributes were paid to him. Menzies spoke of his 'superb honesty as an adviser and administrator'; Eggleston described him as the 'ablest public servant' with whom he came in contact, with a 'genius for administration'. 'A remarkable man', summed up C. R. Bradish, 'with curiosities and vanities of personality which were probably responsible for the charge that he was wholly a "showman". But he had sufficient power and imagination to give the Victorian Railways a reputation they had never known before'.

D. P. Mellor, *The role of science and industry* (Canb, 1958); G. McInnes, *Goodbye, Melbourne town* (Lond, 1968); Vic Railway Commissioners, Annual reports, *PP* (LA Vic), 1921-39; Roy Com into . . . the Victorian railways, *PP* (LA Vic), 1928, 2 (32); *PP* (Cwlth), 1956-57, 3, 1103; P. Adam-Smith, 'Harold Clapp's railways', *VHM*, 44 (1973), no 3-4; *Argus*, 30 Apr, 1 May, 16 Sept 1920, 26 Feb 1942, 22, 23 Oct 1952; *Smith's Weekly*, 26 Sept 1926; *Courier Mail*, 18 May 1939; *Herald* (Melb), 28 June 1939, 21, 23 Oct 1952; *Daily Telegraph* (Syd), 25 Aug 1945; *SMH*, 22 Oct 1952, 21 Aug 1954; *Age*, 14 June 1975; F. W. Eggleston, Confidential notes: some great public servants (Menzies Lib. ANU).

PATSY ADAM-SMITH

CLARE, CHAPMAN JAMES (1853-1940), naval captain, was born on 23 June 1853 in the Bay of Biscay on the *Matilda Wattenbach*; his father was James Coughron Clare, master of the ship. Educated at Cheshunt and Edmonton in England, at 15 he began a merchant marine apprenticeship with Smith, Fleming & Co. of London, and worked on sailing ships until 1873 when he became a mate on a steamer of the Belgian Royal Mail Line.

In 1875-80 Clare served on the opium steamers of Apcar & Co., Calcutta, trading between Hong Kong and Calcutta. Resigning in 1880, he came to South Australia where on 15 June he joined the Marine Board. Four years later he was given command of the steamer *Governor Musgrave* which was used to service lighthouse installations and navigational aids along the coast. He married Ellen Minnie Cotgrave at Semaphore on 5 April 1885; they had two sons and a daughter.

After a period in the colony's naval reserve Clare was commissioned as a lieutcommander in the South Australian Naval Forces on 1 December 1886. He remained nominally in charge of the *Governor Musgrave* until 1900, although he was often involved with naval reserve training and other duties in the cruiser H.M.C.S. *Protector*. He was promoted commander in May 1900, was transferred to the *Protector,* and in July was appointed naval commandant in succession to Captain W. R. Creswell [q.v.].

In December he was promoted captain and from 1901 was second in seniority in the Commonwealth Naval Forces. During the Boxer Rebellion the South Australian government offered the British government the *Protector;* it was accepted on condition that it be commanded by an officer of the Royal Navy. This problem was overcome by Clare's agreeing to serve as executive officer under the command of Creswell who had served in the Royal Navy. For his services during the rebellion Clare was appointed C.M.G. in 1902 and from then until 1910 commanded the *Protector* in home waters.

On the formation of the Royal Australian Navy in 1911 Clare became district naval officer in Western Australia. During World War I he was awarded the Japanese Order of the Rising Sun in recognition of his association with the Japanese Navy, then engaged in convoying Australian troops to Europe. He returned to South Australia in 1918 and was district naval officer until he retired in July 1919.

In retirement Clare lived at Glenelg, Adelaide. Survived by his wife and children, he died there on 28 September 1940 and was cremated. His estate was sworn for probate at £5217.

H. T. Burgess (ed), *Cyclopedia of South Australia,* 1 (Adel, 1907); H. M. Cooper, *A naval history of South Australia and other historical notes* (Adel, 1950); R. H. Parsons, *The navy in South Australia* (Lobethal, SA, 1974); J. J. Atkinson, *Australian contingents to the China Field Force 1900-1901* (Syd, 1976); *Observer* (Adel), 15 May, 28 July 1900, 5 July 1902; *Advertiser* (Adel), 30 Sept 1940; file 1047/136 (SAA).   H. J. ZWILLENBERG

CLARK, ALISTER (1864-1949), rosarian and sportsman, was born on 26 January 1864 at Brighton, Victoria, second son of Walter Clark and his second wife Annie, née Cooper. Walter Clark, born in Argyllshire, Scotland, in 1803, arrived in Sydney on 23 January 1838 in the *Minerva,* sponsored by Rev. J. D. Lang [q.v.2]. He became a partner with Sir William Macleay [q.v.5] in Kerarbury station on the Murrumbidgee River, and made money out of stock during the gold rush. He overlanded stock to Melbourne, took up land at Bulla and built Glenara in 1857.

After Walter Clark was killed at Glenara on 18 March 1873, Alister and his brother and sisters were cared for by a kinsman, John Kerr Clark. Alister was educated in Hobart, at Sydney Grammar School (1877-78) and later at Loretto School in Scotland under the care of relatives. In 1883 he entered Jesus College, Cambridge (B.A., 1886); he was called to the Bar at the Middle Temple on 6 November 1885. He acquired in these years a lifelong interest in plants and flowers.

Clark returned to Australia after graduating and in 1892 for £18 375 he bought Glenara, then 1030 acres (413 ha), from his father's estate. On the ship travelling back from England he had met Edith Mary, daughter of wealthy New Zealander Robert Heaton Rhodes, and they were married at St Mary's Church, Christchurch, New Zealand, on 9 July 1888. They had no children. They maintained a gracious way of life at Glenara where Clark divided his interests between sport and his garden, which he developed as a place of great charm and beauty and as a vast nursery for the propagation of roses and daffodils.

A fine horseman, Clark served as master of Oaklands Hunt Club in 1901-08. He was chairman of the Moonee Valley Racing Club from its foundation in 1917. Although never very wealthy, he raced a few steeplechasers until 1907, with modest success. The Alister Clark Stakes is his memorial at Moonee Valley. He played polo in Melbourne and New Zealand which for many years he visited annually with his wife. He was also a keen golfer, having been introduced to the game at Musselburgh, Scotland.

Clark was best known as a rosarian. He was a foundation member of the National Rose Society of Victoria in 1900 and served as its president. He put great effort and skill into developing new varieties, and his 'Lorraine Lee', 'Black Boy', 'Sunny South', 'Nancy Hayward' and many others were grown throughout Australia; they were highly regarded in the United States of America. He supplied his new varieties without charge to State rose societies for propagation and sale. He won many awards but his greatest triumph was the 1936 Dean Hole Memorial Medal of the National Rose Society (England). His rose garden survives at Glenara and a selection of his roses grows in a memorial garden in Blessington Street, St Kilda.

Clark contributed also to the development of new species of daffodils. In 1948 he received the Peter Barr Memorial Cup from the Royal Horticultural Society (England), of which he was a fellow, and vice-president in 1944-48. He believed his pink daffodil to be the world's first.

Clark was a Bulla shire-councillor for many years until 1910, and served as president several times. He was a trustee of Bulla Presbyterian Church. Very handsome, he won people with his great charm, and he had many friends. At the same time his failings were easily recognized. He was totally impractical. Money meant little to him and he never seriously applied himself to any productive business activity. But this allowed him to grace his long era in a way which would scarcely be possible in a later generation. Survived by his wife, he died at Glenara on 20 January 1949 and was buried in Bulla cemetery, leaving an estate valued for probate at £22 073.

Aust and NZ Rose Annual, 1949; *Daffodil and Tulip Year Book* (Lond), 1949; *Table Talk,* 30 Oct 1930; Clark family papers (held by Lady Johnston, Brighton, Vic).   H. E. RUNDLE

CLARK, DONALD (1864-1932), educationist, was born on 17 February 1864 at Ashby, Victoria, son of John Clark and his wife Jessie, née McRae, both of whom had been born at Inverness, Scotland. Clark was the third of seven children, and at the time of his birth his father was working as a labourer on the Geelong-Ballarat railway. It was a strictly Presbyterian home. Donald was tutored by Rev. A. Stewart, 'an old student of Lord Kelvin's'. He early decided on an engineering career, but apprenticeship was irksome, and in 1883 he found employment as a surveyor's assistant. In 1886 he enrolled as an engineering student at the University of Melbourne, doing some coaching to help with his fees, and was active in the Science Club and the Engineering Students' Society. Clark graduated B.C.E. in 1889.

Professor W. C. Kernot [q.v.5] advised him to apply for the foundation directorship of the Bairnsdale District School of Mines at £300 a year. In January 1890 Clark commenced a long and spirited struggle to establish the school, combating both local indifference and what he saw as the 'antagonistic' attitude of the Department of Education. The mining and science classes which were supposed to be the school's *raison d'être* languished, as did Clark's experimental farm. But he succeeded in establishing a multi-purpose school of some distinction in a period of great stringency for technical education, teaching long hours himself. Perhaps most remarkable was his success in eventually developing a core of studies in mining and metallurgy, together with a treatment plant for refractory ores. Some of his students moved into positions of responsibility in the mining industry.

Clark became personally acquainted with all the major minefields of Australia and New Zealand, acted as a consultant and expert witness to the industry, and wrote extensively for the mining press; he published *Australian mining and metallurgy* in 1904 and *Gold refining* in 1909. In 1905 he patented a process for the treatment of gold slimes by the nitre cake method; he carried out experimental work on the 'flotation process', and received his university's first master of mining engineering degree in 1907 for a thesis on the refining of gold.

Clark was restless in Bairnsdale, and applied for the directorship of the Geological Survey in Victoria in 1904, without success. In 1907 he was appointed director of the Bendigo School of Mines and Industries. In his three years there he reorganized and raised the level of courses, doubled enrolment of full-time students and brought a treatment plant into operation. He also established successful junior classes to bridge the gap between elementary schools and the school of mines.

In 1909 Clark asked the director of education Frank Tate [q.v.] to support his application for a position in Queensland. Tate replied: 'We have reached the stage when all parties in the Assembly are pledged to technical education', adding that when the key position became available 'you have a remarkably strong record both as a University man, a practical man, and a teacher'. In 1910 Clark held a lectureship in metallurgy in the University of Melbourne, and in 1911 was appointed as the first chief inspector of technical schools.

'My first visit to our Technical Schools filled me with something akin to despair', Clark wrote in one of his three important booklets on technical education: *Reminiscences of technical education in Victoria* (1923), *The future of technical and industrial training in Australia* (1927) and *Some notes on the development of technical instruction in Victoria* (1929). At first happy to collaborate with Tate in developing a system of state high schools, which would incorporate an 'industrial' stream to feed his technical schools, Clark quickly became disillusioned. He objected strongly to the development within the high schools of a dichotomy, 'the professional and the industrial, the sheep and the goats'. He fought for, and obtained the attachment of junior technical schools to nearly all senior schools. Subsequently junior technical schools were established as alternatives to high schools in many areas, an extension Clark had not had in mind. Though only partly successful as 'feeder' schools, the 'junior techs' became an integral part of the Victorian post-primary education structure, and have increasingly developed a reputation as an 'alternative' system, less centralist and less educationally constricted than the high schools. This is as Clark would have wished it, and is his most significant memorial. Although periodically under challenge, the system flourishes in Victoria, alone among the Australian States to have a bipartite system of state secondary education. On Clark's retirement in 1930 there were twenty-six junior technical schools with 6600 students.

Clark firmly believed that the nation's prosperity rested on the education of its workers, and his regime also saw a considerable expansion of senior technical education, from eighteen schools with enrolments of 4300 in 1911 to twenty-nine with 18 000 in 1930. Clark accomplished much in rationalizing courses within and between institutions, and encouraging full-time and day courses. He also expanded trade courses, established specialized trade schools and was always an effective propagandist for technical education. Perhaps the most impressive tribute to his uncompromising stance in defence of vocational education and for recognition of technical education as a system in its own right was the freedom of action he won for himself within the department. He has been called a 'bonny fighter', would not abandon a cause even if it had ceased to be ministerial policy, and was prepared to go outside normal public service channels, to politicians or pressure groups. Tate had misgivings about Clark's policies, but he judged it wiser to accept his area as a detached command.

Clark was increasingly acrimonious in debate with opponents but an effective and tireless leader of his own troops, and he built into technical education in Victoria a sense of morale and mission. However, his last years in the department were clouded by bitter internal disputes, first with Tate but especially with Tate's successor, M. P. Hansen [q.v.], with whom there was no meeting-ground. Clark retired in 1930, a year later than he should, for his year of birth he always gave as 1865. In 1916 he had been appointed to the Advisory Council of Science and Industry, and in the same year he reported to the South Australian government on technical education in that State.

Donald Clark had married on 29 Sep-

tember 1890 a young teacher Robina Stodart; there were seven children, all born at Bairnsdale. He was remembered as an undemonstrative, morally strict but affectionate father, and the family as happy and close-knit. His friends were mostly from the mining world, his interests in natural history, golf and shooting. He much enjoyed getting away for brief periods with his dog to his farm at Thorpdale. Healthy and a non-smoker, he liked his Scotch, was a keen clubman and was regarded as fair but austere on the job, relaxed and fond of a good story outside.

Clark died on 7 April 1932 at his home in East Malvern, three months after his wife, and was buried in Brighton cemetery.

L. J. Blake (ed), *Vision and realisation,* 1 (Melb, 1973); *Industrial Aust and Mining Standard,* 14 Apr 1932; S. Murray-Smith, A history of technical education in Australia ... (Ph.D. thesis, Univ Melb, 1966); G. A. Reid, Teachers and bureaucracy ... (Ph.D. thesis, Univ Melb, 1974); Bairnsdale School of Mines, Reports to council, 1891-1906 (Bairnsdale Technical School); Bendigo School of Mines, Reports to council, 1907-09 (Bendigo College of Advanced Education).

S. MURRAY-SMITH

CLARK, SIR ERNEST (1864-1951), governor of Tasmania, was born on 13 April 1864 at Plumstead, Kent, England, third son of Samuel Henry Clark, schoolmaster, and his wife Ann, née Leaver. Educated privately and at King's College, London, he entered the civil service in 1881 and was appointed assistant-surveyor of taxes in 1883. Called to the Bar at the Middle Temple in 1894, he joined the Treasury legal staff. In 1904-05 he was seconded to the government of Cape Colony to assist in planning new taxation procedures and similarly served the Union of South Africa government in 1910-11.

A Treasury liaison officer with the War Office and Ministry of Munitions during World War I, Clark was appointed C.B.E. in 1918 and assistant secretary of the Board of Inland Revenue and deputy chief inspector of taxes next year. He was secretary of the 1919-20 royal commission on income tax. Knighted in 1920, he served as assistant under-secretary of Ireland in 1920-21 and secretary of the Northern Ireland ministry of finance and head of the civil service in 1921-25. His congenial manner made him both popular and influential. It was largely due to his skill that the severance of financial relations between Dublin and Belfast was so amicably achieved; and his friendship with the leading Northern Irish peer and governor of Northern Ireland, the third duke of Abercorn, assisted in easing relations between the new government and Downing Street. He was appointed K.C.B. in 1924. His expertise was again called on in 1930 when he became a member of the Joint Exchequer Board of Great Britain and Northern Ireland.

Clark visited Australia in 1928-29 as a member of the British economic mission invited by the Australian government to examine the economy. As an author of the subsequent report he deeply impressed the premier of Tasmania, J. A. Lyons [q.v.]. It may well have been due to the prompting of Lyons, as prime minister, in 1933, that Clark was offered the governorship of Tasmania, an office which lack of funds had kept vacant for the previous three years. The Federal government was seeking a return to the overseas loan market and Clark, already favourably known in Australia, was prominent in London business circles as a director of Martin's Bank, the London General Omnibus Co., the Pacific Steam Navigation Co., and the shipbuilding firm of Harland and Wolff. In accepting the position Clark agreed to the unusual condition of spending within the State a considerable sum from his private resources as well as part of his salary.

He proved an efficient and hard-working governor whose term was extended three times, although his first few years were marred by a lack of rapport with the premier A. G. Ogilvie [q.v.]. During his period in office Clark acted on occasion as unofficial adviser in regard to financial adjustments between the Tasmanian and Commonwealth governments. He developed an interest in Tasmanian history and visited every accessible district. A Freemason, he was installed Grand Master in 1935. While he cared little for 'social time-wasters' his door was always open to philanthropic groups. A photo of Clark as chief scout of Tasmania was requested by King George V.

He married Mary Winkfield, daughter of a London merchant, on 13 April 1899 at St Margaret's Church, Westminster, England. She shared his concern for community welfare, having before her marriage undertaken social work in the East End of London for the Ragged School Union and the Church Army. The greatest of her interests in Hobart was the Red Cross Society, in connexion with which she started a convalescent home, later named the Lady Clark Memorial Home, at Claremont; but she was patron or president of many other organizations including the Country Women's Association, State Council for Voluntary Aids, Tasmanian Sanitorium, Victoria League, National Council of Women of Tasmania, and Girl Guides' Association. A keen gardener and dancing enthusiast she was skilled in putting visitors to Government House at their ease. She died in 1944.

The children's library service in Tasmania is known as the Lady Clark Memorial Children's Library.

After his retirement in 1945 Clark returned to England to settle at Tasmania, Seaton, Devon. On 8 January 1947 at the parish church, Seaton, he married Harriet Jessie Constance McLennan. He was active in local affairs as a member of the Devon County Council and was deeply interested in Ryalls Court Probationary School. Appointed K.C.M.G. in 1938 and G.C.M.G. in 1943 he died on 26 August 1951 at his home. He had no children. His ashes were sent to Hobart for interment in Cornelian Bay cemetery.

SMH, 15, 16 Dec 1928, 13, 14, 15 Apr 1933; Chronicle (Adel), 20 Apr 1933; Mercury, 6 Sept 1944, 27 Aug 1951, 16 Jan 1952; The Times, 27 Aug 1951.
                                          JOHN REYNOLDS

CLARK, GEORGE DANIEL (1848-1933), politician and prohibitionist, was born on 30 July 1848 at Colchester, Essex, England, son of Daniel Clark, labourer, and his wife Mary Ann, née Clark. Financial troubles cut short his schooling and he went to sea; he arrived in Australia about 1871 and was employed in Australasian Steam Navigation Co.'s ships. After he married Rosannah Jane Druce with Congregational forms on 27 August 1875 at Woolloomooloo, he settled in Sydney and was a messenger at the Sydney Observatory. A determined self-improver, he already had three loyalties: temperance, Methodism and the cause of labour.

About 1873 Clark had joined the International Order of Good Templars, which he chose for its clear commitment to prohibition. He edited the New South Wales Good Templar (Australian Temperance World from 1896) in 1883-1917, and in 1925-32 held high office in the New South Wales Grand Lodge; for many years he was electoral superintendent. The Templars were close knit: Brother Clark, tireless and single-minded (he had no hobbies and only once took a holiday), helped to make the order the most determined and impatient contingent of the State's temperance cause. In 1887 Clark was also a member of the Independent Order of Rechabites and the Local Option League.

In 1891 Clark was elected to the Legislative Assembly for Balmain for the Labor Electoral League as one of the original Labor members: for him the drink problem was a labour problem and temperance legislation a means of social reform; he wrote extensively for the Labor press and later was a foundation member of the New South Wales

Institute of Journalists. His manoeuvring as grand electoral superintendent attempted to attract the temperance vote to Labor. However in 1893 he was unwilling to 'hand over to caucus his religious convictions, his temperance principles, and his freedom of action on moral questions'. He refused to sign the pledge and in 1894 was defeated for Leichhardt as a free trader.

Although he was a member of its executive, Clark's relations with the New South Wales Alliance for the Suppression of Intemperance were often strained. When reform was blocked by the Lyne-See [qq.v.] ministry, he helped to patch over differences with proposals for a distinct temperance political party 'to force the pace a bit', but the alliance refused to make prohibition its immediate goal. The connexion between the temperance and the Liberal parties after 1900 and the rift between Labor and the Churches made Clark's position awkward. A Labor candidate again, he put the best face possible on the party's vague liquor policy and commended its record to Protestant voters but was defeated for Leichhardt in 1898, Newtown (St Peters) in 1901, Botany in 1904 and Queanbeyan in 1907. He discounted the worth of a local option measure passed by the Carruthers [q.v.7] government in 1905. He was guided by the American Prohibition Party, but when the chance came for a State vote in 1928 prohibition was linked with compensation to the liquor trade. Clark declined to fight on such terms and led criticism of the alliance's ambiguous and, as it proved, disastrous stand. In 1928 he published the *Good Templar movement, its history and work*.

A lay preacher, he was a member of the Methodist Conference's social questions committee. Though not a leading figure in the denomination he was valued as a symbol of its earlier links with organized labour. As temperance reform lost momentum, Clark's energy and optimism were unaffected. 'Prohibition means prosperity': it was the simple creed, even naive, of a self-taught man. His closest ties were with the Good Templars and in 1932 he was made a patriarch.

Clark died on 21 February 1933 at Lakemba and was cremated with Methodist forms. He was survived by his wife, four sons and a daughter.

T. R. Roydhouse and H. J. Taperell, *The Labour Party in New South Wales* (Syd, 1892); J. D. Bollen, *Protestantism and social reform in New South Wales 1890-1910* (Melb, 1972); *Aust Temperance World*, Mar 1933; J. D. Bollen, 'The temperance movement and the Liberal Party in New South Wales politics, 1900-1904', *J of Religious History*, 1 (1960-61), no 3; A. Fairley, The failure of prohibition in New South Wales ... 1913-28 (B.A. Hons thesis, Univ NSW, 1968).   J. D. BOLLEN

CLARK, HUBERT LYMAN (1870-1947), zoologist, was born on 9 January 1870 at Amherst, Massachusetts, United States of America, son of William Smith Clark, president of Massachusetts Agricultural College, and his wife Harriet Kapuolani, née Richards. Educated at Amherst College (A.B., 1892) and Johns Hopkins University (Ph.D., 1897), in 1899-1905 he was professor of biology at Olivet College, Michigan. However, with his hearing impaired from an earlier bout of yellow fever, he was forced to retire from teaching and concentrate on research and field-work. In 1905 he joined the Museum of Comparative Zoology, Harvard University, where in 1910 he became curator of echinoderms and in 1927 curator of marine invertebrates and associate professor of zoology. He was acting associate professor at Stanford University, California, in 1936 and research associate, Hancock Foundation, University of Southern California, in 1946-47.

Though he wrote on pterylography, on variations in snakes and on flowers, Clark's most notable work was on echinoderms. He made his first expedition to Australia in 1913, collecting and later classifying all classes of sea-stars and their relations, and the Carnegie Institute published his book, *The echinoderm fauna of Torres Strait* (No. 214, Washington, 1921); he believed that its coloured plates, prepared by E. M. Gosse of Sydney, were unequalled. Clark returned in 1929 and 1932, visiting major museums and collecting on the north-western coast, especially at Darwin and Broome. His wife Frances Lee, née Snell, whom he had married in 1899, often accompanied him on these field trips and illustrated his research papers. In 1938 the Museum of Comparative Zoology published his *Echinoderms from Australia* as No. 55 of its *Memoirs*. The climax to his work was *The echinoderm fauna of Australia* ... (Carnegie Inst., No . 566, Washington, 1946) which recorded all known species (including fossils) and discussed the origins and composition of the fauna in relation to adjacent areas. Next year the Royal Society of New South Wales awarded him the (W.B.) Clarke [q.v.3] Memorial Medal 'in recognition of his distinguished contributions to natural science, particularly in regard to the elucidation of Echinodermata of Australia'.

Clark was a Republican. Described by an obituarist as having a 'charm of natural grace seldom met', he was an intensely religious Congregationalist, and always set aside the Sabbath for worship. A keen stamp collector and a lover of all sports, he considered none more fascinating than 'dredging under pleasant conditions on good bottom'. He died at his home in Cambridge, Massachusetts, on 31 July 1947.

Nature (Lond), 24 Sept 1938, 20 Sept 1947; *Aust Museum Mag*, 30 Aug 1947; Los Angeles: Univ Southern California, *Allan Hancock Pacific Expedition*, 8 (1948), no 5; *Science*, 19 Dec 1947; Roy Soc NSW, *J*, 82 (1948); *New York Times*, 1 Aug 1947; information from Dr F. Rowe, Aust Museum, Syd.   CHRIS CUNNEEN

CLARK, JAMES (1857-1933), pearler and pastoralist, was born on 2 October 1857 on Spit Island, Hunter River, New South Wales, son of Adam Clark, fisherman, and his wife Louisa, née Sheaff. Adam was drowned before James was 3, leaving his large family in poverty. James acquired two years of elementary education in Brisbane. At 14 he became a plasterer's boy with James Campbell [q.v.7] & Co.; he won promotion to the office and in nine years with the firm learned accountancy and commercial methods and achieved some minor business successes. Inspired by pearling stories, he went to Somerset on Cape York Peninsula in 1881 and entered into a partnership with Frank Jardine [q.v.4]. When they later split, Jardine stayed at Somerset and Clark transferred his half of the fleet to Friday Island. One of his first boats was the *Amy*, which was sailed from Brisbane to Thursday Island in 1882 by a crew which included P.P. Outridge, later managing partner in James Clark & Co. Robert Philp [q.v.] was later a partner in several ventures.

In March 1886 Clark moved his fleet to Broome, Western Australia; his enemies alleged that he had stripped the Thursday Island beds. He became a busy spokesman for a group of Queensland pearlers, seeking unsuccessfully to evade Western Australian duties. He claimed to have introduced diving apparatus and the 'floating station' system which became standard. Attracted by reports of revival in Torres Strait after 1890, he returned and participated in a successful campaign by European fleet-owners against the issue of pearling licenses to Japanese – this activity led to the Pearl and Beche-de-Mer Fishery Act of 1898. The growth of Clark's business was described at the 1897 royal commission: in 1896 his fleets had raised £31 500 worth of shell and £5000 worth of pearls and he was a substantial producer of edible oysters in Moreton Bay. Experiments in shell culture by his Pilot Cultivation Co. in Torres Strait provoked hostility, but were defeated by natural predators.

Clark lost heavily in the great cyclone of 1899 but recovered rapidly. Like others he was dissatisfied with the innovations in the Federal Immigration Restriction Act of 1901, and what he considered the lavish granting of pearling licenses by Queensland. In 1905 he took 115 of his boats from Thursday Island to the Dutch-owned Aru Islands. There he secured a concession and, since Dutch law required leasing companies to be founded in Holland or the Netherlands Indies, formed the Celebes Trading Co. (1904) with E. E. Munro. The concession was extended for 10 years in 1908. In 1905 Clark was appointed consul for the Netherlands in Queensland.

The Aru grounds proved disappointing. Only 130 boats could work there and the company had the right to use 115 – half the total number of boats licensed in Queensland. Clark told the royal commission of 1908 that his firm had £100 000 invested in plant and stores and wished to bring some boats back to Torres Strait. Applications in 1907 and 1909 were refused on the ground that no more boats could work the depleted beds.

Clark went to England in 1910 to investigate market conditions, and featured in negotiations for an Australian pearling combine in 1913. He secured permission in 1915 to transfer some of his Aru Islands fleet and, to the consternation of local operators, established thirty-five boats in Broome. Next year the Celebes Trading Co. was sold to a Dutch firm. Pressure from other pearlers led to new regulations designed to restrict the number of licences held by one firm, and Clark's Broome fleet was sold in October 1918 mainly to relatives and associates. He ceased to be a major factor in the industry.

In 1898 Clark had bought Boongoondoo station with Peter Tait, and they later acquired some of the largest and most highly improved sheep properties in Queensland. In 1915 nine of their stations were stocked with 497 947 sheep. Clark had joined the Central Queensland Pastoral Employers' Association. He took a keen interest in the problems of the wool industry, and from 1913 attended council meetings of the United Pastoralists' Association, representing the Pastoral Employers' Association of Central and Northern Queensland. He became a trustee for the United Graziers, and from 1919 was a Queensland delegate on the Australian Woolgrowers' Council. He attended conferences with the National Council of Woolselling Brokers, and joined deputations to the prime minister and to Sir John Higgins [q.v.], chairman of the Central Wool Committee. In 1922 he represented the council on the Wool Appeal Board of the

British Australian Wool Realisation Association. He campaigned for control over wool prices, submitting a stabilization scheme to the 58th convention of the Graziers' Federal Council in May 1925. But in August, feeling his views were not heeded, he resigned from both the Woolgrowers' Council and the United Graziers' Association. However, in 1932 he was invited to join the Wool Enquiry Committee as a producers' representative. Profoundly irritated by the cost of shipping wool, he chartered a vessel to move 10 000 bales to London in 1932 and saved his firm £7000.

Clark amassed a wonderful collection of pearls of all shapes and sizes and would pay as much as £5000 for one. Australia's finest pearl, 'The Star of the West', sold for nearly £6000, was found by an employee off Broome. In the 1890s he settled permanently in a fine house on the Brisbane River, kept his own yachts and won races all over Australia. During his pearling days he took cricket teams from Thursday Island to Normanton, and from Darwin to Port Hedland. A committee-member of the Queensland Turf Club, he paid high prices for racehorses. He was renowned for his kindness and generosity to many people and causes. A very heavy cigar smoker, he damaged his heart while gardening and died at his home on 9 July 1933 of a coronary thrombosis. He was survived by his wife Jessie, née Smith, whom he had married on 2 September 1885 at St John's Presbyterian Church, Paddington, Sydney, and by their son and daughter. He was buried in Toowong cemetery with Anglican rites and left an estate valued for probate at £80 896.

Handboek voor Cultuur-en Handelsondernemingen in Nederlandsch-Indië, jrg 27 1915 (Amsterdam, 1914); *Encyclopaedie van Nederlandsch-Indië*, 2nd edn ('s-Gravenhage, 1917), vol 1, p 62, vol 3, p 231; G. C. Bolton, 'The rise of Burns, Philp — 1873-93', A. Birch and D. S. Macmillan (eds), *Wealth & progress* (Syd, 1967); *V&P* (LC WA), 1888 (26), (LA Qld), 1897, 2, 1273, 1908, 2nd S, 2, 395; *PP* (Cwlth), 1913, 3, 645; J. P. S. Bach, 'The pearlshelling industry and the "White Australia" policy', *Hist Studies*, no 38, May 1962; N. S. Pixley, 'Pearlers of Northern Australia – the ... diving fleets', *JRHSQ*, 9 (1969-75), pt 3; *West Australian*, 5 Apr 1916, 12 Oct 1918; *Brisbane Courier*, 12 July 1933; J. P. S. Bach, The pearling industry of Australia, DS 33 (AAO, Canb); Graziers' Assn of NSW, E256/56, 57, 1373, 1374 (ANU Archives); records of pastoral employers' organizations (Oxley Lib, Brisb); Registers A30, 1903-09, *and* correspondence files, A461, A325/10/1, A3932, SC430 (6 and 9), *and* A468 AM500/11 (AAO, Canb); CSO 2100/18 (Battye Lib, Perth); PRE/A38 no 7999, TRE/30 5378, A20245 (QA); family papers (held by Mr J. W. Clark, Hamilton, Brisb); information from Algemeen Rijksarchief, Schaarsbergen, Holland.   PATRICIA MERCER

CLARK, JAMES PURCELL (1876-1971), soldier, barrister and solicitor, was born on 2 February 1876 at Hobart, son of Alexander James Clark, cabinetmaker and later undertaker, and his wife Sarah Bennett, née Purcell. Educated at The Hutchins School and Christ's College, Hobart, he was articled to Dobson, Mitchell & Allport, barristers and solicitors, and admitted to practice by the Supreme Court of Tasmania on 5 March 1897. On 18 September 1902 at St George's Anglican Church, Hobart, he married May Rowland.

By 1902 Clark was in practice at Scottsdale where, in 1908-09, he was chairman of the town board and in 1911 a municipal councillor. He was commissioned second lieutenant in the 12th Australian Infantry Regiment (Scottsdale Company) in 1906, was promoted lieutenant two years later, and was made captain in the 92nd (Launceston) Regiment in 1913. On the outbreak of World War I he was given command of the garrison at Fort Nelson, then in July 1915 entered Claremont Camp for enlistment in the Australian Imperial Force. From September to February 1916 he commanded the A.I.F. camp at Ross and on 7 March was appointed captain in the newly formed 40th Battalion; he was promoted major and second-in-command in May and embarked for overseas service in July.

The 40th reached France in November and served in the Armentières-Bois Grenier sector until March 1917; during this period Clark was intelligence officer. By April he was at Ploegsteert, Belgium, then in June commanded the battalion in the battle of Messines. Promoted lieut-colonel in August, he was transferred to the 44th Battalion as commanding officer and led the unit in the battle of Broodseinde on 3-4 October; he was wounded in action when a shell exploded in his headquarters. Resuming duty late in November, he commanded the battalion throughout 1918, seeing action at Morlancourt, Villers-Bretonneux, Hamel, Péronne and the final battles of the Hindenburg Line. He was awarded the Distinguished Service Order in the King's Birthday honours in June and was also mentioned in dispatches. From February 1919 he commanded the Australian Base at Le Havre until he embarked for Australia in August.

After demobilization Clark kept up a part-time association with the Australian Military Forces. In 1920 he was lieut-colonel in temporary command of the 5th Battalion, 40th Regiment, and he later led the 51st Battalion until June 1922. That year he was awarded the Long Service Decoration, and in 1923 the Volunteer Officers' Decoration; he was transferred to the reserve of officers in 1927. In 1920 he had joined the Solicitor-

General's Department in Hobart; from 1930 he held appointments as police magistrate, commissioner of the courts of requests, chairman of licensing courts, coroner and warden of mines. In 1940-45 he was police magistrate at Hobart and then went into private practice.

Survived by two daughters, and predeceased by his wife and their only son, he died on 6 February 1971 at the Repatriation General Hospital, Hobart, and was cremated with Anglican rites.

F. C. Green, *The Fortieth* . . . (Hob, 1922); C. E. W. Bean, *The A.I.F. in France*, 1917-18 (Syd, 1933, 1937, 1942); *London Gazette*, 28 May, 3 June 1918; *Mercury*, 8 Feb 1971; J. P. Clark file (AWM); information from Mrs J. P. Seager, Taroona, and Mr G. Sorell, Sandy Bay, Tas.   JAMES B. GALE

CLARK, JAMES WILLIAM (1877-1958), soldier, shipping merchant and company director, was born on 7 September 1877 at Wickham, New South Wales, son of James Blyth Clark, an English-born ship's chandler, and his wife Sarah Jane Clarinda, née Potter. Educated at Maitland High School, he went into his father's business at Newcastle. On 2 April 1902 at Chalmers Presbyterian Church, Hobart, he married Dora. Malvina Hood.

In July 1897 Clark joined the militia as a second lieutenant in the 4th Australian Infantry Regiment; by 1912 (with his unit renamed the 16th A.I.R.) he was a major and second-in-command. Promoted lieut-colonel just before the outbreak of World War I, he became commanding officer of the regiment and of Newcastle Defended Port; on 22 July 1915 he was appointed to the Australian Imperial Force in command of the 30th Battalion and embarked for Egypt in November.

Clark reached France in June 1916 and went into the line at Bois Grenier; on 19-20 July his battalion fought in the ill-fated battle of Fromelles. In September he temporarily commanded his brigade (the 8th), which spent the winter of 1916-17 in raiding and patrol work on the Somme. He was awarded the Distinguished Service Order in the New Year honours of 1917 and was also mentioned in dispatches. He resumed temporary command of the brigade in January; next month it advanced towards the Hindenburg Line and in March Clark's battalion played a vital role in the capture of Bapaume and the occupation of Beaumetz — remembered as the two most interesting of his wartime experiences. In mid-May his brigade took over a section of the Hindenburg Line near Lagnicourt; its next major service was in the Passchendaele offensive,

where Clark commanded the 30th Battalion in the battles of Polygon Wood and Broodseinde Ridge. Late in October he was again made temporary brigade commander and was mentioned in dispatches in December.

In March-April 1918 Clark's battalion returned to the Somme where the 5th Division was preparing for the Villers-Bretonneux offensive. Clark acted as commanding officer of the 5th Division nucleus, then resumed leadership of his battalion for operations at Morlancourt in July. Next month he was transferred to the 3rd Battalion, Overseas Training Brigade, as commanding officer, and from January 1919 commanded the brigade itself. He remained in England until October and before embarking for Australia attended a course on the manufacture of paints and oils. After demobilization he became a manufacturer's agent for a British paint firm. He lived with his family at Killara, Sydney, in the 1920s and early 1930s, by which time he had become a director of his company. Little is known of his career over the next twenty years — he worked for some time in London and New Zealand before retiring to Terrigal, New South Wales, about 1951.

Survived by his wife, a son and a daughter (all resident in England at the time of his death), he died on 8 February 1958 and was cremated. His estate was sworn for probate at £35 000. Tall, well-built, always impeccably dressed and well-spoken, he had been affectionately known by his men in France as 'Cissy Clark'; however, his fine qualities of leadership and concern for his men had made him respected and popular.

A. D. Ellis, *The story of the Fifth Australian Division* (Lond, 1920?); C. E. W. Bean, *The A.I.F. in France*, 1916-18 (Syd, 1929, 1933, 1937, 1942); H. Sloan (ed), *The purple and gold . . . 30th Battalion, AIF* (Syd, 1938); *London Gazette*, 1, 2 Jan, 28 Dec 1917; *Gosford Times*, 11 Feb 1958; J. W. Clark file (AWM).   MERRILYN LINCOLN

CLARK, SIR REGINALD MARCUS (1883-1953), retailer, was born on 9 November 1883 at Newtown, Sydney, son of Henry Marcus Clark, draper, and his native-born first wife Martha Annie, née Day. His father was born at Liverpool, England, and migrated to Victoria in 1880. He soon moved to Sydney and in 1883 started a small drapery shop at Newtown; the firm prospered, becoming universal distributors, and in 1902 Marcus Clark & Co. Ltd was registered as a public company.

Reginald was educated at Sydney Grammar School and at 19 went to London to undertake a surrogate apprenticeship in wholesaling and retailing. He returned to

Sydney in 1907 and next year became a director of Marcus Clark's. On 23 June 1909 at the Church of Christ Tabernacle, Enmore, he married Frances Hanks Rogers, the London-born daughter of a journalist. On his father's death in 1913, Clark became chairman and managing director of the family firm and its subsidiaries — Hobsons Ltd, its North Sydney store; Bon Marche Ltd, Railway Square (1900); and Marcus Clark (Victoria) Ltd (1923), which managed Craig, Williamson Pty Ltd in Melbourne and, from 1927, Miller Anderson Ltd in Adelaide. He was also a director of Hipsleys Ltd and on the Sydney board of the London and Lancashire Insurance Co. Ltd. The firm was hard hit by the Depression and failed to pay dividends from 1931 until after writing down its capital in 1937.

In 1916-18 Clark was president of the Master Retailers' Association (Retail Traders' Association of New South Wales from 1921) and of the Sydney Chamber of Commerce in 1933-36. He was a director and later vice-president of Royal Prince Alfred Hospital, and a life governor of the Women's Hospital, Crown Street, and the Alfred Hospital, Melbourne; in 1934-36 he was a member of the Board of Health. His war service was strictly commercial: he served as an adviser to the Commonwealth prices commissioner in 1918-19 and 1939-48 and was vice-chairman of the Requisitioned Cargoes Committee in 1942-48.

Like his business rival (Sir) Charles Lloyd Jones [q.v.] Clark was a noted, if conservative, collector of English and Australian works of art; in 1939 he became a trustee of the National Art Gallery of New South Wales. Knighted that year, he became known as Sir Marcus. He had a passion for collecting coins, and to a lesser extent, antique china, and was president of the Australian Numismatic Society. Actively interested in golf and racing he was a member of the Killara Golf Club and the Australian Jockey and Victoria Racing clubs; he was a member of a number of others including the New South Wales, National and the Melbourne Savage.

A staunch monarchist, Clark was a fellow of the Royal Empire Society and was also State vice-president of the Royal Society of St George and a member of the Royal Society of New South Wales. As president of the Associated Chambers of Commerce of Australia and a vice-president of the Federated Chambers of Commerce of the British Empire in 1939-41 and 1943-45, he emerged as a leading opponent of the Federal government's attempts to regulate retail trade. In 1944 he attacked 'regulation by dictators', alleging that the government was using 'gestapo methods' to control busi-

ness. In 1948-49 he was vice-president of the Citizens Reform Association, Labor's opponent in Sydney Municipal Council elections.

Clark died in Royal Prince Alfred Hospital with hypertensive vascular disease on 13 July 1953 and was cremated after a service at St John's Church of England, Gordon. Predeceased by his son, he was survived by his wife and daughter. His personal estate was valued for probate at £80 475. In 1948 his portrait by William Dargie won the Archibald [q.v.3] prize and in 1973 he was featured on a seven-cent stamp.

Stanton & Son Ltd, *Marcus Clark & Co. Ltd., sale of premises* (Syd, 1927); D. B. Copland and R. M. Clark, *Profits and price control* (Syd, 1941); *Commerce* (Syd), June 1919, May, Sept 1929; *R.P.A.*, Mar 1939; *T&CJ*, 19 Mar 1913; *SMH*, 2 May 1944, 14 July 1953; *Daily Telegraph* (Syd), 14 July 1953, 30 June 1954; Marcus Clark & Co. Ltd papers (ANU Archives).   PETER SPEARRITT

CLARKE, CHARLES JAMES (1894-1973), soldier and farmer, was born on 1 October 1894 at Launceston, Tasmania, son of John Clarke, labourer, and his wife Rebecca, née Wright. When he was in his early teens his family began farming at Kialla, Victoria, and he was shearing at Euroa when he enlisted as a private in the Australian Imperial Force on 15 October 1914.

Clarke was allotted to the 14th Battalion and sailed for Egypt in December. They reached Gallipoli on 25 April 1915 and served throughout the Peninsula campaign, including several major actions, among them Courtney's Post and Hill 60. Clarke was wounded at Durrant's Post on 12 November, was evacuated and rejoined his unit in Egypt on 19 January 1916. He was promoted lance corporal on 26 May and five days later embarked for France as a signaller. The battalion moved into the line near Armentières in mid-June and in August fought in the battle of Pozières Ridge. Clarke was awarded the Military Medal for gallantry: as a runner he delivered a message from the front line to reinforcements and, under heavy fire, guided them to their position. Later that year he served at Mouquet Farm and, after a brief period in Flanders, spent the winter of 1916-17 on the Somme.

In 1917 the 14th Battalion fought at Bullecourt, Messines and Polygon Wood. Clarke was promoted corporal on 27 February 1918 and was made acting sergeant in June. For 'conspicuous gallantry' in the battle of Amiens he was awarded the Distinguished Conduct Medal. The citation praised his assistance in maintaining communication lines 'over bare ground swept by field-gun fire'. He 'worked for 48 hours mending breaks and remained four hours after the unit was relieved' helping the incoming unit 'under shell fire of all calibres'. He was made a lance sergeant in August and from then until November fought in the battle of the Hindenburg Outpost-Line, receiving a Bar to his Military Medal for distinguished service as a signaller. He was made a temporary sergeant in January 1919.

Clarke returned to Australia in November and was demobilized in June 1920. Soon afterwards he began farming at Barmah East in Victoria and on 20 December, at St John's Anglican Church, Narioka, married Elizabeth Schier. He remained on the same farm for the rest of his life. Between the wars he helped to raise and train a local light horse squadron and was commissioned lieutenant in the 20th Light Horse Regiment in 1928; by 1938 he was a major. During World War II he served with the second A.I.F. in several training and administrative posts until failing health caused his retirement in 1942. Survived by his wife, two sons and two daughters, he died on 10 November 1973 at Mooroopna and was buried in Nathalia Anglican cemetery.

Clarke, known throughout the Nathalia district as 'Nobby', was a popular and colourful personality with a lively sense of humour and a reputation for spinning yarns. Though proud of his military awards he was modest about his achievements and is known to have used his medals on occasion to weight his fishing lines. His estate was sworn for probate at $59 210.

N. Wanliss, *The history of the Fourteenth Battalion, A.I.F.* (Melb, 1929); *London Gazette,* 14 Nov 1916, 5 Dec 1918; *Nathalia Herald,* 3 June 1970; *Southern Riverina News,* 9 Nov 1976; information from Mr W. J. Clarke, Yarroweyah North, Vic.

R. D. MANLEY

CLARKE, SIR GEORGE SYDENHAM, 1st BARON SYDENHAM OF COMBE (1848-1933), governor, was born on 4 July 1848 at Swinderby, Lincolnshire, England, eldest son of Walter John Clarke, vicar, and his wife Maria Frances, née Mayor. He was educated at Repton and Rossall schools, Haileybury College and Wimbledon House School and topped entrance and final examinations of the Royal Military Academy, Woolwich. In 1868 he joined the Royal Engineers. In 1871-80 he lectured on practical geometry and engineering drawing at the Royal Indian Engineering College near Staines, publishing five books and numerous articles. On 1 June 1871 he married Caroline Emily,

eldest daughter of General Peregrine Henry Fellowes.

Clarke served in Egypt in 1882, examining the Alexandria fortifications after the British bombardment. His significant report was followed by his appointment to the War Office staff in 1883. Seeking a wider audience for his ideas on both military science and Imperial organization and defence, he published in 1883 the first of many articles in *The Times* and other publications. In 1885 he served in the Sudan and was afterwards promoted major. Thereafter his promotion was slower and, although he undertook many technical missions abroad, his novel views and his use of the press did not appeal to his more traditional superiors. His appointments as secretary to the Colonial Defence Committee (1885-92) and the royal commission on army and navy administration (1888-90) provided scope for his interests in Imperial federation and defence and army reform. He was appointed C.M.G. in 1887, K.C.M.G. in 1893 and elected fellow of the Royal Society in 1896. He was superintendent of the Royal Carriage Department at Woolwich 1894-1901, being promoted colonel in 1898.

Clarke sat on the War Office reorganization committee in 1901. In that year Chamberlain offered him the governorship of Victoria, following the post-Federation decision to appoint career men rather than peers to State governorships. Clarke accepted, viewing the appointment as a step towards a more important civil post; he arrived in Melbourne on 10 December. In Victoria he and his wife were generally popular and respected. However he found the position, with its constitutional restraints, frustrating. With the temporary seat of the Commonwealth government in Melbourne he was overshadowed by the governor-general and drew the Colonial Office in to arbitrate on several Federal-State controversies. He was criticized twice for commenting on delicate political issues but committed no serious constitutional indiscretions. His grant of a dissolution of parliament to (Sir) W. H. Irvine after (Sir) A. J. Peacock's [qq.v.] ministry had resigned in August 1902 was uncontroversial.

A Liberal free trader, privately Clarke was critical of the influence of labour, democratic processes, protectionist and racial policies and the parochialism of Australian society. He claimed in his memoirs, *My working life* (London, 1927), that in Australia 'the faith of a Liberal was destroyed and too sanguine hopes for closer union [of the Empire] evaporated'. In November 1903 he was recalled to serve on the committee for the reconstitution of the War Office, and in 1904 he became secretary of the Committee of Imperial Defence. Lord Haldane's army reforms achieved many of Clarke's earlier aims but he attacked details and opposed naval reforms. In 1906 he supervised the preparation of a general defence scheme for Australia.

Clarke was appointed governor of Bombay in 1907. He first supported greater participation of Indians in the administration; however, disturbed by growing political violence, he became preoccupied with law and order. His prosecution and conviction in 1908 of the Brahman leader Tilak for sedition led to riots in Bombay and reproaches from the secretary of state for India, John Morley. He continued to repress sedition and agitation by western-educated Indians, causing concern in London. But he promoted elementary and technical education, and improved medical care and irrigation. His wife and daughter both died in India in his second year of office; in 1910 in Bombay he married a widow Phyllis Angelina Rosamond Reynolds, née Morant.

On his retirement in 1913 Clarke was raised to the peerage. He chaired a royal commission on venereal diseases (1913-15) and the central tribunal which heard appeals from local committees administering the National Service Act (1915-16). He spoke frequently in the House of Lords and continued writing, becoming increasingly reactionary.

Able but opinionated, Clarke did not gain the high military or civil posts he coveted. As a pro-consul his achievements were limited. As a truly professional military officer his ideas were ahead of his times and many – especially on fortifications, submarines, camouflage and army reform – proved remarkably prescient. His later distinctions included G.C.M.G. (1905), G.C.I.E. (1907), G.C.S.I. (1911) and G.B.E. (1917). Survived by his wife, he died in London on 7 February 1933; he left no issue and his peerage lapsed.

D. C. Gordon, *The Dominion partnership in Imperial defense 1870-1914* (Baltimore, 1965); R. A. Preston, *Canada and Imperial defense* (Durham NC, 1967); S. A. Wolpert, *Morley and India, 1906-1910* (Lond, 1967); *Daily Telegraph* (Lond), and *Morning Post* (Lond), and *The Times*, 8 Feb 1933; Balfour, *and* Campbell-Bannerman, *and* Sydenham (Clarke) papers (BM); records, Colonial Defence Cttee, Cab 7, *and* Cttee of Imperial Defence, Cab 2-6 (PRO, Lond); Tennyson papers (NL); Australian file, CO418 (PRO, Lond).

M. N. LETTICE

CLARKE, HENRY LOWTHER (1850-1926), Anglican archbishop, was born on 23 November 1850 at Firbank Vicarage, Westmoreland, England, son of the Reverend William Clarke and his wife Sarah, née Lowther. He was educated at home, and at near-by Sedbergh School, and St John's College, Cambridge, graduating B.A. (7th wrangler) 1874 and M.A. 1877.

Clarke was ordained deacon in 1874 and priest in 1875 by Archbishop Thomson of York; he served his title at St John's, Kingston upon Hull, under Canon H. W. Kemp whose daughter, Alice Lovell, he married on 10 August 1876. After two years in Hull he was appointed vicar of Hedon. He went in 1883 to York, first as a housemaster at St Peter's School, then as vicar of St Martin's, Coney Street, beginning an interest in educational administration which he continued when he moved to Dewsbury in 1890. He was appointed an honorary canon of Wakefield Cathedral in 1893, rural dean of Dewsbury in 1898, and vicar and rural dean of Huddersfield in 1901, and elected as proctor for the clergy of Wakefield Diocese in the York Convocation in 1902.

That year Field Flowers Goe [q.v.], bishop of Melbourne, retired and, for the first time, the Bishopric Election Board determined not to delegate the appointment to an English committee; they sent representatives to England to investigate and Clarke was eventually nominated. His knowledge of Victoria was limited, but he accepted the offer and was consecrated bishop in St Paul's Cathedral, London, on 1 November 1902. He arrived in Melbourne in February 1903 and was installed on 3 March. Following the organization in 1905 of an ecclesiastical province, comprising the five Victorian dioceses, Clarke became archbishop of Melbourne.

The diocese of Melbourne had been reduced in area by the creation of the dioceses of Bendigo, Gippsland and Wangaratta in 1901, but still contained half the population of Victoria. Clarke quickly saw the urgent need to improve the training and conditions of the clergy and the effectiveness of the parishes. St John's College was opened in St Kilda in 1906 under Reginald Stephen to train non-graduate ordinands. Lectures were shared with Trinity College, University of Melbourne; students based on a Clergy House at Fern Tree Gully served the recently settled Dandenong ranges. However, Clarke's hopes for a central college were torpedoed in 1910 when a group of evangelical clergy and laity opened Ridley College, and when Alexander Leeper [q.v.] in 1912 restored the teaching of theology at Trinity. Enrolments fell during World War I and St John's closed at the end of 1919. More successful were Clarke's efforts to raise the teaching standard: since the University of Melbourne remained opposed to the granting of degrees in divinity, he persuaded the Victorian parliament in 1910 to establish the Melbourne College of Divinity to examine for and grant degrees.

Clarke had found a variety of arrangements for clergy superannuation. Under pressure from him these were consolidated and in 1906 General Synod established the Australian Clergy Provident Fund, membership of which Clarke made compulsory. Suburban expansion caused a vigorous programme of parochial extension; in 1914 St James' Old Cathedral was moved to West Melbourne and a mission district of St James and St John established.

From Clarke's arrival he urged the adoption of a vigorous educational policy by his diocese. He supported undenominational Bible teaching in schools, and when a referendum on it was defeated in 1905 he backed a voluntary system in state schools. He also strengthened the existing boys' schools at Melbourne and Geelong, and established more secondary schools, especially for girls, and free kindergartens in industrial areas. Enrolments in Anglican schools increased fivefold during his episcopate. As well, the Sunday school system was improved; services to seamen and immigrants begun; the Church of England Men's Society introduced and other organizations encouraged; the Sisters of the Community of the Holy Name were recognized. In 1906 a synod Social Questions Committee was established to focus Anglican concern on community issues.

Clarke's term saw two major controversies. He was pressed to proceed against E. S. Hughes [q.v.] for alleged ritual excesses at St Peter's, Melbourne. Clarke disclaimed any party allegiance himself and in 1906 declined to prohibit Hughes's services and practices 'provided they did not replace the regular Prayer Book rites or contradict its spirit'. In 1907 Canon C. H. Nash [q.v.], vicar of Christ Church, Geelong, resigned following complaints to the archbishop. Many of his friends and parishioners believed that he had not received justice and Clarke was much criticized for his alleged harshness. In 1909 John Norton [q.v.] made a vicious attack in *Truth* against 'Clarke the Nark', castigating him as a 'contemptible cowardly conspirator'. Clarke sued Norton and won substantial damages and a public apology. But the incident was damaging both to Clarke and to the Church of England. During the war he gave wholehearted support to recruiting and to the 'Yes' vote in the conscription referenda.

Clarke was tall and handsome in appearance. Beneath a rather blunt north-country manner he concealed considerable shyness and tenderness. He enjoyed a joke against himself, and with family and intimates revealed a softer, even sentimental, side. His style of life was simple and he went to all his engagements by tram or train or bay steamer, carrying his robes in a basket suitcase.

Clarke maintained his scholarly interests, particularly in historical and constitutional fields, throughout his life. His significant publications include *Constitutions of the general provincial and diocesan synods of the Church of England in Australia* (1918) and *Constitutional church government in the dominions beyond the seas* (1924). He received the honorary degrees of D.D. (Cambridge, 1902; Oxford, 1908; and Melbourne College of Divinity, 1913) and D.C.L. (Durham, 1908).

His wife's sudden death in 1918 affected him greatly and in 1919 he announced that he would retire on his seventieth birthday. He left Melbourne in March 1920, and after attending the Lambeth Conference he settled at Melbourne House, Lymington, Hampshire. He failed rapidly after his housekeeper-daughter's death in 1924 and died at Filkins, Oxfordshire, on 23 June 1926. He was survived by a daughter and two sons, of whom Kemp, a noted theological scholar, was a canon of Chichester Cathedral (1945-68). A portrait by G. A. J. Webb is in the Chapter House of St Paul's Cathedral, Melbourne.

L. Gardiner, *Tintern School and Anglican girls' education 1877-1977* (Ringwood, 1977); *Church of England Messenger* (Vic), 1 July, 7 Oct 1926, 11 Nov 1932; *Argus*, 25, 28 June 1926; scrapbook (Mollison Lib, Trinity College, Melb); information from Canon B. Clarke, Reading, Eng.

JAMES GRANT

CLARKE, MARIAN (1853-1933), headmistress, was born on 27 March 1853 at Banbury Mill, Neithrop, Oxfordshire, England, daughter of Thomas Clarke, miller, and his wife Elizabeth Ann, née Staley. One of thirteen children, she finished her education in Germany, and went to University College, Bristol, where in 1880 she passed the Cambridge higher local examination with honours in political economy, history and logic. In 1880-84 she taught at the High School for Girls, Manchester.

Marian Clarke arrived in Sydney in December 1884 to assist at Normanhurst, a school run by her sister Ellen. On 20 July 1885 she opened her own school, Abbotsleigh, in a small terrace house at Mount Street, North Sydney, and soon acquired a second house. She suffered from chronic laryngitis and, on medical advice, she moved the school to Parramatta early in 1888. By December 1895 she had eighty pupils.

Miss Clarke was a strict disciplinarian and her pupils soon took pride in belonging to a well-run school. She had advanced ideas on education, including design, gymnastics, carpentry and geometry in the curriculum, despite protests from parents. She taught languages and mathematics; whatever the subject, she insisted on a thorough grounding, and Abbotsleigh became very successful in public examinations. Unobtrusively religious herself, she encouraged her pupils in charitable work. She had a keen sense of humour, with a love of literature, music and painting. Aided by her 'beautiful, vibrant voice', she was 'one of the very few who knew how to read aloud, which she made a practice of doing', from English, French and German masterpieces.

Miss Clarke spent 1896 in England for family reasons, leaving her partner Miss Pringle in charge. On her return she found the number of pupils had dwindled to twenty-four. She dissolved the partnership in May 1897 and next year bought 1¼ acres (.5 ha) at Wahroonga and moved the school, 13 boarders and 10 day girls, there in October; numbers grew rapidly and additions were made to the original building. On 14 October 1901 a games field was formally opened and in 1910 Abbotsleigh was one of the first schools to celebrate Empire Day. In December 1913 she sold the school, which then had 40 boarders and 100 day girls, to Miss Margaret Murray.

Dr Agnes Bennett [q.v.7], a pupil at North Sydney, recollected Marian Clarke as a brisk woman, 'liked rather than loved', and her old friend Sir Mungo MacCallum [q.v.] wrote that 'with the warmest of hearts she had the sharpest of tongues'. Only her large black dog, Nero, was completely unafraid of her.

Marian Clarke was in England at the outbreak of World War I. She worked for the British Red Cross Society in hospitals and in 1916-19 was in charge of a hostel in Somerset for nurses recovering from fatigue. Her favourite relaxation had always been sketching. After the war she spent much time in Austria, North and South Africa, Spain, France and Italy, and studied painting under distinguished masters. Her talent flowered and at 71 she had the first of several of her pictures accepted by the Salon de la Société des Artistes Français, Paris. On her return to Sydney in 1928 she held an exhibition at a Bond Street gallery. She sold many of her pictures for charity.

Miss Clarke died on 2 July 1933 at her Macleay Street flat and was cremated with Anglican rites. She left her estate, valued for probate at £23 046, to her sisters. Her portrait by Tom Roberts [q.v.] is held at Abbot-

sleigh, which is now owned by the Church of England.

D. Burrows, *History of Abbotsleigh* (Syd, 1968); *SMH*, 15 July 1933; records and reminiscences (Abbotsleigh Library Archives, Wahroonga, NSW).   ROBYN CLAYDON

CLARKE, SIR RUPERT TURNER HAVELOCK (1865-1926), 2nd BARONET OF RUPERTSWOOD, pastoralist and entrepreneur, WILLIAM LIONEL RUSSELL (known as Russell) (1876-1954), pastoralist and member of parliament, and SIR FRANCIS GRENVILLE (Frank) (1879-1955), member of parliament, pastoralist and company director, were sons of Sir William John Clarke [q.v.3]. Rupert was born on 16 March 1865 at Rupertswood, Sunbury, Victoria, eldest son of Sir William and his first wife Mary, née Walker. He was educated at Hawthorn Grammar School, Wesley College, Melbourne, and Magdalen College, Oxford, but took no degree.

In 1891 he leased his father's Cobran station, near Deniliquin, New South Wales, and later inherited the Sunbury properties of Bolinda Vale, Red Rock and Rockbank, totalling some 130 000 acres (52 500 ha). He sold these over a period, except for a reduced holding at Bolinda Vale and 800 acres (320 ha) near Rupertswood named Kismet Park, on which, after the sale of Rupertswood to Russell, he built a house. Rupert successfully carried on his father's stud of English Leicester sheep and Derrimut Shorthorn cattle. As his holdings in Victoria diminished, he developed pastoral and other interests elsewhere, notably in Queensland, where he later owned Isis Downs in partnership with R. S. Whiting.

Succeeding to the baronetcy on his father's death in May 1897, Rupert followed him into the Legislative Council of Victoria as member for Southern Province, retaining the seat until 1904. Early that year he addressed a meeting of some 10 000 in support of his kinsman Dr William Maloney [q.v.], the Labor candidate, who was challenging the validity of Sir Malcolm McEacharn's [q.v.] return to the Federal seat of Melbourne.

Rupert took his father's place as governor of the Colonial Bank of Australia. Other business interests over the next thirty years, not all successful, included a rabbit cannery and a butter factory at Sunbury, gold-mining at Coolgardie, Western Australia, 1895, banana and peanut farming, and a rubber and coconut plantation (also with R. S. Whiting) in Papua. In 1914 he financed and led an expedition up the Fly River in his yacht *Kismet*. In the early 1900s with John Gunn and Clyde Meynell he leased the

Theatre Royal, Melbourne, and the Criterion, Sydney; in July 1911 Clarke and Meynell amalgamated with J. C. Williamson [q.v.6] Ltd, and Clarke became a director of the company.

Rupert had served in his father's Rupertswood Battery of horse artillery. At the outbreak of World War I he went to England and was commissioned a lieutenant in the (British) Army Service Corps in 1915; he served at Salonica, Greece, and was invalided out in 1917. He was a fine horseman, and horses which he owned won the Victoria Derby, Oaks and Caulfield Cup, though the Melbourne Cup eluded him. He was also a first-class shot.

On 22 December 1886 he had married Amy Mary (later she called herself Aimée), daughter of T. F. Cumming [q.v.3]. They had two daughters. The marriage ended in divorce in 1909 and on 6 November 1918 in Sydney he married 22-year-old Elsie (later Elise) Florence Tucker; by her he had two sons and a daughter. Apart from his country properties and 12 Bank Place, Melbourne, Clarke owned several houses in Sydney, two in England (Brockwood Park, Alresford, Hampshire; and Old Place, Sussex) and a villa in Monte Carlo, where he died on 25 December 1926.

Rupert Clarke was a controversial figure, showing from boyhood an unsettled temperament. He was 6 when his mother died, and his stepmother Janet Marion Clarke [q.v.3], née Snodgrass, was a dominant personality. In the words of Frank, who was fond of him, 'Rupert . . . did resent . . . his own mother's fading memory and in consequence he spent much of his time when young in England playing polo and in travel . . . When he did return to Rupertswood . . . he was obviously not happy in his surroundings'. His lifelong inability to remain anywhere for long necessarily precluded him from that part in Australia's public life suggested by his inheritance, and possibly by his talents. The same restlessness may also in part explain the instability of his first marriage; though the testimony of their daughter Phyllis Power suggests that Aimée Clarke shared some responsibility for a divorce which was damaging to Rupert's career.

His half-brother Russell was born on 31 March 1876 in Melbourne, third child of his father's second marriage. He was educated at Miss Templeton's school, South Yarra, Melbourne Church of England Grammar School and Scotch College; followed by Trinity College (University of Melbourne), where he passed the first two years of a three-year B.A. course in 1895-98; New College, Oxford (M.A., 1902) and Wells Theological College. With his half-brother

Ernest he owned portion of Dowling Forest, near Ballarat, later subdivided for closer settlement; he also owned Hawksview, Albury, New South Wales, and Rupertswood from 1910 to 1922, when he moved to Melbourne.

Russell was a member of the Legislative Council for Southern Province from 1910 to 1937. He was commissioned second lieutenant, Australian Imperial Force, on 1 September 1916 and served abroad in the 12th Brigade, Australian Field Artillery. Returning to Australia in February 1919, he was active in furthering ex-servicemen's interests; he was a strong advocate of the building of hospitals as the most suitable form of war memorial. He was a lay member of the Anglican Synod, a council-member of Trinity College, and a benefactor of that college, of its associated Janet Clarke Hall and of the Ballarat Art Gallery. Among many sporting interests he was vice-president of the Moonee Valley Racing Club.

He had married Florence Douglas (Lute) Mackenzie on 23 September 1908 at St John's Church, Toorak; they had two sons and a daughter. Russell Clarke died in Melbourne on 14 May 1954 and was cremated, leaving an estate valued for probate at £366 875. A retiring disposition made him less publicly known than Rupert or Frank, but his influence, especially on education and on the building of hospitals, was lasting.

His brother Frank was born on 14 March 1879 at Rupertswood, fifth child of his father's second marriage. He was educated at Scotch College, Trinity College (taking Latin I in 1896) and Exeter College, Oxford, where he did not graduate. He farmed at Port Fairy, at Thule, south-west of Deniliquin, and at Murchison, but as his political and business interests developed his farming activities waned. He was a director of the Colonial Bank and later (after an amalgamation) of the National Bank of Australasia, becoming its vice-chairman. Other directorships included those of Goldsbrough Mort [qq.v.4,5] & Co. and the Victorian board of the Australian Mutual Provident Society.

Frank was best known in politics. He was elected to the Legislative Council in 1913, representing Northern Province until 1925, Melbourne South Province until 1937, and Monash until his death. In 1915 he attended the Panama-Pacific International Exposition at San Francisco as honorary commissioner for Victoria. In 1917 he was appointed leader in the Legislative Council, minister for lands, minister for water-supply and minister for public works. In successive ministries and under changing nomenclatures he retained the lands portfolio until 1919, that of water-supply until 1921, and that of public works until 1923, when he was elected president of the Legislative Council – a position he held for twenty years.

The most controversial event of his political career occurred in October 1947 when, as a private member, he successfully led a move in the Legislative Council to deny supply to the Cain Labor government. The plan was to force an expression of public feeling on the Federal issue of bank nationalization by bringing about a State election. The Legislative Assembly was dissolved on 8 October 1947 and an election took place on 8 November, Labor fighting on the alleged abuse of power by the Legislative Council and the Liberals on the banking issue. The Cain government was swept from office, and though the Chifley government forced its bill through a second reading on 12 November, Victoria's revolt signalled the ebbing of the tide of nationalization in Australia. Though earlier Clarke had been regarded as a cool and non-partisan president, the events of 1947 earned him the enmity of the Communist Party and the left wing of the Australian Labor Party.

On 24 July 1901 he had married Nina Ellis Cotton, a cousin on his mother's side. They had three sons, of whom the eldest did not survive to manhood, and three daughters. Frank Clarke suffered from a congenitally dislocated hip, which caused his rejection for service in the South African War and precluded strong physical activity. He was devoted to his family, his books and his garden. He was a president of the Royal Horticultural Society of Victoria and designed a notable garden at Mount Macedon. His charming book *In the Botanic Gardens* (Melbourne, 1924) shows keen observation, humour and broad learning. The same cannot be said of his ephemeral *World air control board: a plan* (Melbourne, 1944). His privately printed *The Clarke Clan in Australia* (Melbourne, 1946) provides delightful sketches of Victoria in a more leisurely age, but unfortunately repeats the erroneous statement that Sir William Clarke was Australia's first baronet – Sir Charles Nicholson [q.v.2] and Sir Daniel Cooper [q.v.3] preceded him. Frank Clarke was president of the Melbourne Club in 1925 and was appointed K.B.E. in 1926. He was also chairman of the Felton [q.v.4] Bequest Committee. He died in Melbourne on 13 February 1955 and was cremated.

His brother Ernest Edward Dowling (1869-1941), lieut-commander, R.N., was a successful racehorse breeder; he imported the celebrated sire The Welkin and bred and owned Trivalve, which in 1927 won the Australian Jockey Club Derby, the Victoria Racing Club Derby and the Melbourne Cup.

J. Smith (ed), *Cyclopedia of Victoria*, 1, 3 (Melb, 1903, 1905); H. H. Peck, *Memoirs of a stockman* (Melb, 1942); L. G. Houston, *Ministers of water supply in Victoria* (Melb, 1965); R. Gibson, *My years in the Communist Party* (Melb, 1966); P. M. Power, *From these descended* (Kilmore, Vic, 1977); *Tocsin*, 28 Jan 1904; *Weekly Times* (Melb), 21 Aug 1909; *Punch* (Melb), 16 Apr 1914; *Age*, 14 Feb 1955; W. Howat, Annals of the Clarke family (LaTL).

                                            R. J. SOUTHEY

CLARKSON, SIR WILLIAM (1859-1934), naval officer, was born on 26 March 1859 at Whitby, Yorkshire, England, son of James Nicholson Clarkson, draper, and his wife Mary, née Dixon. Educated at a private school in Whitby, he was articled to the shipbuilding firm of R. & W. Hawthorn of Newcastle upon Tyne and later worked there as a marine engineer.

In May 1884 Clarkson joined the South Australian Naval Service as an engineer lieutenant, coming to the colony in H.M.C.S. *Protector*. On 24 August 1887 he married Louisa Clarissa Hawker at Christ Church, Adelaide. Serving under Captain W. R. Creswell [q.v.], he shared his enthusiasm for the development of an Australian naval force. Clarkson was a staff engineer aboard the *Protector* during the Boxer Rebellion in 1900-01, then transferred to the Commonwealth Naval Forces. Promoted engineer commander in October 1905, two years later he was selected to visit Japan, the United States of America and the United Kingdom to study naval dockyards and ship construction. In 1908-11 he remained in the United Kingdom overseeing the building of destroyers for the C.N.F. which became in 1911 the Royal Australian Navy Fleet Unit.

Clarkson was promoted engineer captain, C.N.F., in July 1910 and on the establishment of the Royal Australian Navy in 1911 was appointed third naval member of the Australian Naval Board; he held this post until his retirement in 1923. He was responsible for the construction and engineering of ships, for ships' repairs, and for control of naval dockyards and bases. In 1913 he was appointed C.M.G. and on the outbreak of World War I became controller of shipping for Australia as well as director of transports. He was promoted engineer rear admiral in 1916 and created K.B.E. in 1918; that year the Interstate Central Committee was established to operate coastal shipping requisitioned for Imperial service, and he was appointed chairman and controller. These responsibilities made him well known, but his work as third naval member was his most important. In 1918 he was without peer in Australian maritime affairs.

By the end of the war Clarkson had contributed much towards providing Australia with a considerable naval shipbuilding capacity. The royal commission on navy and defence administration in 1918 lamented the effect on Clarkson's naval duties of the many other activities with which he was entrusted, yet recommended that in a reconstituted Naval Board he be appointed business member with wider naval responsibility. Cabinet later refused to accept the commission's recommendation that he concentrate solely on his naval duties.

In 1919-22, under Clarkson's guidance, the R.A.N. developed a modernization programme, including construction of ships, submarines and a fleet air arm. The level of naval construction and engineering expertise over which he presided (relative to overall industrial development and to the complexity of naval ships) has not since been equalled. Clarkson was promoted engineer vice admiral in November 1922 and transferred to the retired list. On the formation of the Commonwealth Shipping Board in August 1923, he was appointed chairman, serving until 1927.

Survived by his wife and their two sons, Clarkson died at his home in Darling Point, Sydney, on 21 January 1934 and was cremated with full naval honours. His estate was sworn for probate at £14 511. He was remembered by his fellow officers as a dignified and reserved person who was held in high regard not only in Australia but in the United Kingdom. In senior technical circles at the Admiralty and on the Clyde, he was respected for his appreciation of modern engineering development. His acceptance by the Admiralty was no mean feat for an ex-colonial and R.A.N. officer during the period.

F. M. McGuire, *The Royal Australian Navy, its origin, development and organization* (Melb, 1948); G. L. Macandie, *The genesis of the Royal Australian Navy* (Syd, 1949); R. Hyslop, *Australian naval administration, 1900-1939* (Melb, 1973); J. P. S. Bach, *A maritime history of Australia* (Melb, 1976); *Australasian*, 4 Nov 1922; *Courier Mail*, 22 Jan 1934; *SMH*, 22-23 Jan 1934; H. J. Zwillenberg, Citizens and soldiers: the defence of South Australia, 1836-1901 (M.A. thesis, Univ Adel, 1971); MP178/2 2215/18/2, 2286/3/34, 39, MP472 8/20/2556, MP446/201/344 (AAO, Melb).

B. N. PRIMROSE

CLAXTON, NORMAN (1877-1951), sportsman and businessman, was born on 2 November 1877 at North Adelaide, South Australia, son of William Denton Claxton, auctioneer, and his wife Hannah, late Moyle, née Parr. By the late 1890s Claxton was showing promise as a batsman in the Adelaide Electoral (district) cricket competition. An elegant right-hander, he scored over 500 runs in 1900 and again in 1904, at averages of 48 and 72. After 1904 he also shone as a fast-medium bowler and played for the South Australian team in Sheffield Shield contests in 1903-10.

Claxton was a popular cricketer 'of sanguine temperament' who was said to 'bat and bowl hopefully'. His bowling lacked penetration at State level; but his batting yielded an aggregate of 2090 with averages of 40 or better in three seasons. He took 5 wickets for 129 in 1904 against New South Wales. In a 1906 match against Victoria he 'turned the game' in South Australia's favour, batting for over six hours for a 'splendid 199' not out which included twenty-two boundaries. He managed the South Australian team on its 1913 tour of the eastern States and was a selector with Joe Darling, Clem Hill [qq.v.] and George Giffen [q.v.4] in 1902-05 and 1907-09. A committee-member of the South Australian Cricket Association for twenty years, Claxton fostered the game among high school students.

Baseball, Australian football, cycling and athletics also interested him and provided opportunities for business and social contacts with other people of modest commercial standing. A 'brilliant cyclist', Claxton joined the North Adelaide Cycling Club in 1902 and captained it from 1917 until his death; he won the Bay Sheffield sprint, using the name F. Pierce, at Glenelg in 1900 and the Bendigo cycling championship in 1901. He played senior football and baseball for North Adelaide. He was president of the South Australian Baseball League in 1913-29 and patron from 1932 till his death, doing much to promote the game at junior levels. In 1934 he donated the Claxton Shield, which remains the trophy of a regular Australian championship.

Claxton had joined the Adelaide Stock Exchange in 1910: his varied business interests included Aileron station via Alice Springs and a partnership in the dredging of Darwin Harbour. A dapper dresser, 'the man with the buttonhole', he never married but had a fatherly relationship with W. C. Clarke. The latter and his family were the chief beneficiaries of an estate of £27 118 left by Claxton when he died in North Adelaide on 5 December 1951, survived by two sisters. After a private funeral with Anglican rites, he was buried in North Road cemetery, Nailsworth.

Wisden Cricketers' Almanack, 1907; *Advertiser* (Adel), 7 Dec 1951; records (SA Cricket Assn, Adel); personal information.   NEVILLE HICKS
ELISABETH LEOPOLD

CLAYTON, ARTHUR ROSS (1876-1963), medical practitioner, was born on 14 May 1876 at Yankalilla, South Australia, son of John Woods Clayton, storekeeper, and his wife Elizabeth, née Cornish. Educated at the Collegiate School of St Peter, Adelaide, and the University of Adelaide (M.B.,B.S., 1902) he was resident surgeon at the Adelaide Hospital in 1903, then went abroad for postgraduate study (L.R.C.P., London; M.R.C.S., England, 1905). After returning home he went into general practice at Moonta in 1907, and was appointed surgeon to the Wallaroo and Moonta Mining and Smelting Co. (1908) and medical officer of health for Moonta (1909). Three years later he was commissioned in the Australian Army Medical Corps, and before the outbreak of World War I was regimental medical officer to the 24th Light Horse.

On 10 September 1915 Clayton joined the Australian Imperial Force as a captain, and on reaching Egypt served at the 1st Australian General Hospital and the 3rd Australian Auxiliary Hospital at Heliopolis. He was transferred to the 7th and 6th Field Ambulances in March 1916 and then to the newly formed 12th Field Ambulance which reached France in June; from August his unit was based at Bécourt on the Somme, dealing with casualties from the battles of Pozières and Mouquet Farm. Clayton was promoted to major in November and transferred to the 8th Field Ambulance as second-in-command. He was placed in charge of the 5th Divisional Rest Station at Vignacourt and, early in 1917, of the 1st Anzac Corps Rest Station at Bellevue Farm during operations at Bapaume. During the battles of Bullecourt he served at the 5th Division's main dressing stations and from October to December was acting commander of his unit.

Early in 1918 the 8th Field Ambulance remained with the 5th Division on the Somme. Clayton resumed temporary command in February and, except for a period in April-May, retained command until the Armistice. He was slightly wounded in action in April and was mentioned in dispatches and made temporary lieut-colonel in May; in June he was awarded the Distinguished Service Order. After the A.I.F.'s final Hindenburg Line operations he was posted to 5th Division hospitals in northern France and Belgium; he was confirmed as lieut-colonel in November and from April 1919 was commanding officer of the A.I.F.'s remaining divisional field ambulances in Belgium.

Clayton returned to Australia in August 1919 and was discharged in December. He was made a lieut-colonel in the Australian Military Forces in 1920 and was area medical officer at Moonta and Kadina before being placed on the unattached list in 1922. After demobilization he had resumed medical practice at Moonta and on 12 September 1922 at St Mary's Anglican Church, Wallaroo, married Nellie Mabel Mary Harbison; they had no children. Clayton remained at Moonta until his death on 2 September 1963; his wife had predeceased him. He was among the community's most prominent citizens and was mayor of the Moonta Corporation in 1924-26 and 1939-40. He was a warden of the local Anglican church and a Freemason. Clayton was tall, well built and distinguished in appearance and in his youth was a keen sportsman.

C. E. W. Bean, *The A.I.F. in France*, 1916-17 (Syd, 1929, 1933); A. G. Butler (ed), *Official history of the Australian Army Medical Services . . . 1914-18*, 2 (Canb, 1940); *London Gazette*, 28 May, 3 June 1918; *People's Weekly* (Moonta), 6 Sept 1963; A. R. Clayton file (AWM); War diary of the 8th Field Ambulance, AIF (AWM); family information from Mrs H. Laughton, Walkerville, SA.

WILLIAM A. LAND

CLEARY, PATRICK SCOTT (1861-1941), journalist, was born on 13 September 1861 at Brunswick, Victoria, only child of Patrick Cleary, labourer, and his wife Anne, née Scott. Both parents were Irish-born. Educated by the Christian Brothers, Cleary was a clerk, living at South Melbourne, when he married Mary Tuohill (d. 1903) at Sandhurst (Bendigo) on 22 July 1885.

About 1901 Cleary moved to Sydney, where he opened a newsagency at Woollahra; he was district registrar of births, deaths and marriages, and official valuer for the local municipal council. At St Mary's Cathedral on 24 January 1906 he married Irish-born Ellen Carey. Cleary became a frequent contributor to the Sydney press, notably the *Daily Telegraph*, on public issues. Articles of his, published in the quarterly *Australasian Catholic Record* in 1909-12, reveal a wide reading on church history. Other pamphlets showed a pronounced anti-socialist leaning. In 1913 he was a founder (and the first and only president) of the New South Wales branch of the Catholic Federation, whose purpose was to advance 'the religious, civil and social interests of Catholics throughout Australia'. It aimed at organizing denominational support with the chief objective of obtaining state aid for church schools. In 1915 he became sub-editor on the weekly *Catholic Press*.

Cleary opposed conscription in World War I; he gave evidence for the seven internees of Irish descent suspected of membership of the Irish Republican Brotherhood at the inquiry conducted by (Sir) John Harvey [q.v.] in August 1918. Cleary was prominent among Catholics who spoke in the Sydney Domain; in October 1919, after the introduction of proportional representation to New South Wales, he was a founding member of the Democratic Party, formed by the Catholic Federation in an attempt to obtain its objects by contesting State elections. He was one of the party's nine unsuccessful candidates in March 1920. In December a papal knighthood of St Sylvester was conferred on him.

Upon the death of J. Tighe Ryan [q.v.] in 1922, Cleary became editor of the *Catholic Press*. Though he lacked the provocative brilliance of his predecessor, he 'wrote from behind a rampart of knowledge built on wide reading . . . his style was trenchant but unhurried, cool and logical'. Cleary's less bellicose manner was appropriate to the calmer though isolationist atmosphere of Catholic activism after the furore in 1921 over Sister Ligouri [q.v.] had capped fifteen years of dramatic confrontation, in which he had been an active participant.

In 1933 he published *Australia's debt to Irish nation builders.* He had been a delegate to the Irish Race Convention in Paris in 1922. Unlike Ryan, Cleary was distrustful of a democratic, pluralist society; his editorials on occasion were tinged with anti-Semitism. He approved of Mussolini. His last pamphlet, *Spain's civil war* (1937), in which he supported Franco, signified the beginning of a new period of Catholic political activity.

Cleary continued as editor until he died on 7 December 1941 at his home in North Sydney. He was survived by his wife, and by three sons of his first marriage. After a requiem Mass he was buried in the Catholic section of Waverley cemetery. Less than three months later the *Catholic Press* amalgamated with the *Catholic Freeman's Journal* to become the *Catholic Weekly*.

P. J. O'Farrell, *The Catholic Church and the community in Australia: a history* (Melb, 1977); *Bulletin*, 29 Aug 1918, 29 Jan 1925; *Catholic Press*, 24 Nov, 8 Dec 1921, 11 Dec 1941, 26 Feb 1942; *Freeman's J* (Syd), 11 Dec 1941.

CHRIS CUNNEEN

CLEARY, WILLIAM JAMES (1885-1973), brewery manager and administrator, was born on 29 December 1885 at Redfern, Sydney, second son of native-born parents Thomas Patrick Cleary, foreman, and his wife Elsie, née Rose. His father was later a cellarman at Tooth [q.v.6] & Co. Ltd's Kent Brewery. Cleary was educated at Blackfriars Public School and at Sydney Boys' High School on a scholarship. At 14, although he wanted to stay at school, he started work at Tooth's. On 20 April 1912 Cleary married Melanie Newton Lewis in Adelaide; they began married life in a 'tent city' at Balmoral Beach, Sydney, and later lived at Mosman. He also attended the University of Sydney part time, won several prizes and graduated Bachelor of Economics with first-class honours in 1918. In 1922-29, while still at Tooth's, he lectured on business principles and practice at the university and was elected a life member of the Workers' Educational Association. In 1934-39 he served on the university senate.

At Tooth's Jim Cleary showed administrative brilliance and was appointed assistant manager in 1920 and general manager in November 1923. He revolutionized the company's book-keeping system, piloted the amalgamation of Tooth's and Resch's [q.v.] Ltd in 1929 and 'never had a strike despite a highly unionised workforce'.

In 1927 Cleary refused an offer to become chief civic commissioner for Sydney, but in November 1929 he accepted appointment as chief commissioner for railways for New South Wales. In an effort to make the railways pay he was responsible for 'dismissals, wage and salary cuts, and short time', and managed to save some £2½ million a year. Money meant little to Cleary and as the Depression worsened, he gave up part of his salary, but he remained an outsider to the railwaymen. From October 1930 he clashed fiercely with the new premier J. T. Lang [q.v.] who countermanded his orders and opposed his proposals to reduce the railway deficit. When Cleary dismissed C. A. Goode, a senior official and protégé of Lang, for corruption, Lang retaliated by legislating Cleary out of office. In July 1932, after Lang's electoral defeat, Cleary's charges against Goode were largely upheld by a royal commission, and he returned as chief transport commissioner. He resigned in December on realizing that if he made the necessary drastic changes 'it would be impossible to avoid the suggestion of vindictiveness'.

On 3 July 1934 Cleary succeeded (Sir) Charles Lloyd Jones [q.v.] as chairman of the Australian Broadcasting Commission at a salary of £500; he treated it as a full-time position. He was cultivated and loved classical music and intellectual pursuits; he had even continued his singing lessons each morning at the height of his clash with Lang, and had taught himself French, German and Latin; widely read, he possessed a large library. Cleary saw that an independent A.B.C. could supplement the mass appeal of commercial radio with programmes meant to educate as well as entertain. With the aid of Herbert Brookes [q.v.7], with whom he forged a close personal bond, he helped to establish permanent A.B.C. symphony orchestras in each State by 1936, encouraged the holding of composers' competitions, and arranged for celebrity artists from overseas to give public concerts. He also promoted talk and commentary sessions and radio plays. After W. T. Conder [q.v.] was dismissed in 1935, Cleary acted as general manager until he had groomed (Sir) Charles Moses to take over the position.

On the outbreak of World War II, Cleary fought against the restrictions and suspicions of the press which opposed an independent A.B.C. news service. Throughout the war he had to contend with government interference and censorship. (Sir) Robert Menzies had ordered E. A. Mann [q.v.], 'The Watchman', not to criticize the government, and tried to prevent the launching of the *A.B.C. Weekly* (the newspapers refused to publish A.B.C. programmes); H. V. Evatt wanted the news slanted towards the war in the Pacific, and John Curtin complained of the lack of Australian content in programmes. Cleary was often called to Canberra for discussions and to give evidence to the Parliamentary Standing Committee (Joint) on Broadcasting. Unexpectedly, late in February 1945 he resigned, partly because of political interference, but mainly because 'he could no longer rely on the loyalty of those from whom he had a right to expect loyalty'.

Cleary thereafter played little part in public life. A director of Mark Foys [q.v.] Ltd from 1935, he was its chairman in 1943-49, and was also chairman of J. Ireland Ltd of Newcastle and president of the Industrial Building Society. He was an adventurous and accomplished bushwalker, covering hundreds of miles through parts of New South Wales and Victoria and in New Zealand. Small in stature, he was agnostic, impeccably honest, cool, decisive and strong-willed; described as an 'archbishop of commonsense' he had 'a sturdy independence of spirit'. He was always eager to serve the community and was deeply affected by newspaper criticism. By practising his belief that too personal a relationship with staff was to risk showing favouritism, he was regarded as aloof.

Survived by five daughters, Cleary died in a Sydney nursing home on 20 July 1973 and was cremated. During his last years he looked back to his days as chairman of the A.B.C. with bitterness despite the fact that he had been its main guiding influence.

G. C. Bolton, *Dick Boyer* (Canb, 1967); D. Aitkin, *The colonel* (Canb, 1969); M. F. Dixon, *Inside the ABC* (Melb, 1975); *Brewer and Bottler's Gazette*, 15 July 1920; *Wireless Weekly*, 3 Aug 1934; *SMH*, 30 Sept 1931, 17 Dec 1932, 7 July 1934, 28 Feb, 25 Apr 1945; *Sunday Sun and Guardian*, 7 Aug, 18 Dec 1932; *Smith's Weekly* (Syd), 3 Aug 1938, 14 Apr 1940; H. Brookes papers (NL); Cleary papers (NL *and* A.B.C. Archives, Syd); information from Mrs Pauline Watson, West Pymble, NSW.

ALAN THOMAS

CLELAND, EDWARD ERSKINE (1869-1943), barrister and judge, was born on 7 April 1869 at Beaumont, Adelaide, son of John Fullerton Cleland, registrar of births, deaths and marriages, and his wife Elizabeth, née Glen. Educated at Prince Alfred College and the University of Adelaide (LL.B., 1890), Cleland became associate to Judge (Sir) W. H. Bundey [q.v.3.]. In 1891 he became a partner in Fenn & Hardy; after seven years he entered partnership with Sir Josiah Symon [q.v.] and H. V. Rounsevell which lasted until 1914, when he branched out on his own after financial disagreements with Symon. In 1919 he took his son T. E. Cleland into the firm; Paul Teesdale Smith joined it next year. In 1921-27 it was Cleland (father and son), Holland & Teesdale Smith and in 1927-36 Cleland & Teesdale Smith.

Cleland was a fluent and able advocate. His first reported appearance before the Full Court in 1892 (*Hodgkins v. District Council of Burnside*) revealed his ability to pick the one point on which a case would turn. It was further illustrated by his argument before the High Court of Australia in *Sinclair Scott v. Naughton* (1929): after a prolix address by counsel for the appellant, Cleland rose at 12.30 on the second day, stated his Statute of Frauds point, answered one question from Judge Dixon and sat down at 12.35. The appeal was dismissed. Cleland's appointment in 1912 as a King's Counsel when there was already one in the firm (Symon), was one of only four similar instances in South Australia. He was retained in practically every 'heavy' case, and represented his State before the Privy Council in the South Australia-Victoria boundary case.

In 1925 Cleland lent £23000 to an investor, Vincent A. Zed, who was subsequently unable to repay the loan. This left Cleland jointly indebted with Zed to a bank for a sum which, if called up, would have rendered Cleland insolvent. For this reason he refused a second offer of a Supreme Court judgeship in 1927. But Cleland paid the debts and in 1936 went on the bench.

For many years Cleland had been 'recognised as the leader of the Bar', but he was 67 and not healthy. However his brain was still agile. In 1938 he was in dissent in two-thirds of the reported decisions in Banco in which he took part. Nevertheless his opinions were respected: claims for damages for collisions at intersections involving 'two way' roads were settled for years, until the relevant statute was amended, on the basis that Cleland's dissenting judgement in *Bond v. Goudie* (1937) was correct. During his last eighteen months on the bench he was ill and sat infrequently. It is regrettable that so fine an intellect had little time to influence the work of the court.

Cleland was a member of council of the Law Society of South Australia in 1912-17 and 1935-36. He was a noted bon vivant, a witty after-dinner speaker, and a master of the devastating reply delivered with a smile and without change of voice or manner. On 12 April 1893 in Adelaide he had married Edith Mary Auld (d. 1928); they had two daughters and a son, all of whom survived him when he died on 1 July 1943; he was buried in St George's cemetery, Magill. A nephew, Sir John Cleland [q.v.], was an eminent naturalist; another, Sir Donald Cleland, was administrator of Papua New Guinea in 1952-67.

SA Law Reports, 25 (1892), 37; *Cwlth Law Reports*, 43 (1929-30), 310; *SA State Reports*, 1937, 416; *Aust Law J*, 10 (1936-37), 46; *Register* (Adel), 27 Dec 1912; *Advertiser* (Adel), 6 Mar 1936, 2 July 1943; G. Loughlin, South Australian Queen's Counsel 1865-1974 (B.A. Hons thesis, Univ Adel, 1974); Deputy registrar, Note-book for 26-27 Sept 1929 (High Court of Aust); information from Mr M. Cleland, Stirling, SA.   HOWARD ZELLING

CLELAND, SIR JOHN BURTON (1878-1971), pathologist and naturalist, was born on 22 June 1878 at Norwood, South Australia, elder son of William Lennox Cleland, medical practitioner, and his wife Matilda Lauder Burton, daughter of John Hill Burton, historiographer royal for Scotland. He was educated at Prince Alfred College, Adelaide, and the universities of Adelaide and Sydney (M.B., 1900; M.D., 1902). The deadlock between the honorary staff of the Adelaide Hospital and the government in 1897 meant that students had to transfer to medical schools in Melbourne and Sydney. In January 1900 he became house surgeon at the Royal Prince Alfred Hospital and next year was second resident pathologist. His M.D. thesis was on 'Iodic purpura. Cirrhosis of the stomach and colon'. In 1903 he travelled to England and studied at the London School of Tropical Medicine, and in Glasgow. In 1904 he was cancer research scholar at London Hospital.

Next year Cleland went to Western Australia as government bacteriologist and pathologist. Bubonic plague was present in the State and he was able to study the internal parasites of *Rattus rattus* and *Rattus*

norvegicus, and the laterality of pregnancy in these mammals. In 1907 he investigated the trypanosomal disease 'Surra' in camels at Port Hedland. Commercial interests objected, but the disease was finally eradicated by the identification and slaughter of infected beasts. Cleland noted also that the camels carried parasitic flies (Hippoboscidae) and ticks. One of his celebrated cases in forensic pathology at this time concerned the 'spirits of salts murders': death had been caused by the painting of the throat of child victims with strong hydrochloric acid, simulating diphtheria.

In 1909 Cleland joined the Bureau of Microbiology, Sydney, and he eventually became principal microbiologist. He edited the *Australasian Medical Gazette,* and made his major contributions to experimental medicine, in collaboration with Burton Bradley and W. McDonald. The first was the proof in 1916, using human volunteers, that the virus disease dengue is transmitted by the culicine mosquito *Aedes aegypti.* The second was the defining of the newly discovered encephalitis, then called 'Australian X disease', and the proof that it was distinct from poliomyelitis, not only by its microscopic characteristics, but also by the experimental transmission of virus strains to monkeys, sheep and other herbivores.

In 1920 Cleland was appointed first Marks professor of pathology (which then included bacteriology) at the University of Adelaide. Although it ended his experimental studies in epidemiology it allowed him to begin a systematic study of what must be one of the largest series of meticulous autopsy examinations ever conducted by one person — over 7000. Cleland regarded each post-mortem examination as a voyage of discovery and never wearied, continuing to do routine autopsy work into his mid-80s. He was honorary pathologist at the Adelaide Hospital in 1920-38, and then honorary consultant. He was also honorary consulting pathologist to the Adelaide Children's Hospital. He had an unrivalled experience in macroscopic morbid anatomy and histopathology, and often diagnosed rare conditions almost at a glance. With each further 1000 autopsy records amassed, he would analyse and epitomize his findings and publish them in the *Medical Journal of Australia* or the Royal Adelaide Hospital's *Medical and Scientific Archives,* which he founded and edited in 1921-48.

Cleland's interest in anthropology culminated in a long series of papers on the diseases of Australian Aboriginals. He also found time to promote and undertake field work in anthropology. With T. D. Campbell and Frederick Wood Jones [q.v.] he formed the Board of Anthropological Research at the university, which he chaired for nearly thirty years. His early researches were in blood groupings and the general ecological aspects of Aboriginal life, such as the use of indigenous plants for foods and drugs. Some of these studies were made with Thomas Harvey Johnston [q.v.] and N. B. Tindale. Cleland was twice president of the Anthropological Society of South Australia and a member of the State's Aborigines Protection Board: he had a 'sincere interest and affection for the Aboriginal as a human being'. An appreciation of his work in anthropology has been made by T. D. Campbell (1959).

However, Cleland's botanical studies were probably more important. As a boy his father had given him M. C. Cooke's *Handbook of Australian fungi* (1892). After his return to Adelaide his interest in fungi expanded and he published two volumes (1934-35) on the larger fungi of South Australia which included many other Australian records. Today this is the only general Australian work on the subject. Although largely taxonomic, other general biological features were included. He wrote also a number of papers on local vascular plants. In this field he was mainly a collector and floristic surveyor. He presented a collection of nearly 30 000 plants to the South Australian Herbarium. His collecting included nearly 60 plant species new to science, described by John McConnell Black [q.v.7] and others. Constance Eardley, in her sensitive appreciation of Cleland's botanical work (1959) as 'a discriminating plant explorer', has emphasized that one of his most important contributions to botany was his support of Black. Cleland also gathered data on the harmful effects of plants which he incorporated in a series of papers in medical and other journals.

Ornithology was another of his major interests, particularly in reference to the distribution and general ecology, and he did much field collecting and observing during his anthropological and other surveys. He donated nearly 1000 bird-skins to Gregory Mathews [q.v.] for his book, *The birds of Australia* (1910-1927), a number of which became type specimens. In 1956 Cleland presented 450 skins to the South Australian Museum, together with valuable data. He also collected the birds' ectoparasites and endoparasites.

In a series of papers in 1912-69 Cleland amassed and evaluated data on the ill effects, from both ingestion and physical encounters, passed to man from animals: some later papers were in collaboration with R. V. Southcott. In one, the illnesses of (Sir) Douglas Mawson [q.v.] and Xavier Mertz in the Antarctic in 1911-14 were attributed to the poisonous effects of excessive vitamin A intake from eating dog liver, a hypothesis which has received support from other evidence.

Wildlife conservation absorbed Cleland in his later years: he was a commissioner of the National Park, Belair, South Australia, in 1928 and chairman in 1936-65. He chaired in 1922-68 the Flora and Fauna Handbooks Committee of South Australia, a body founded largely at his instigation. It has produced a continuing series of descriptive biological manuals, with some on geology. They are largely taxonomic and have provided an unparalleled body of work on local, and often more generally Australian, flora and fauna.

Cleland's scientific interests, pursued through prodigious committee work, have probably proved of more lasting value than his medical studies. He was president of the Royal Society of New South Wales, Royal Society of South Australia (twice), Royal Australasian Ornithologists' Union, Medical Sciences Club of South Australia, and the Western Australian Natural History Society. He retired from the Central Board of Health of South Australia aged 90.

The onset of blindness in his late 80s, stoically accepted, forced Cleland to curtail his activities. These had included a trip to New Guinea a few years before where his forensic interests were stimulated by a collection of recipes for the cooking of human flesh. Despite his great age his faculties were quite unclouded, but he regretted that he was prevented from his favoured reading: the early journals of exploration in Australia. He was also interested in Australian and Scottish history and literature. His collection of favourite quotations from the classical period down to modern times was edited by Dr E. B. Sims (1963). Cleland was part-author of *The first hundred years. A history of Burnside, South Australia* (1956), and wrote 'The village of Beaumont' for the Royal Geographical Society of Australasia, S.A. Branch, (Volume 50).

Cleland's biological collecting resulted in perhaps forty species or subspecies among fungi, vascular plants and animals being named after him, as well as a new genus *Clelandia* being erected in both the plant and animal worlds. Although discriminating he was not excessively pedantic or critical. It is probable that his enormous collections will leave a continuing legacy for future biologists. He was appointed C.B.E. in 1949 and knighted in 1964. He was awarded the Sir Joseph Verco [q.v.] medal of the Royal Society of South Australia (1933), the Clive Lord [q.v.] memorial medal of the Royal Society of Tasmania (1939), the Australian Natural History medallion (1952) and the

John Lewis [q.v.] gold medal of the Royal Geographical Society of Australasia, S.A. Branch (1964). He was elected an honorary fellow of the Royal Society of South Australia in 1949 and a life member of the South Australian Ornithological Association in 1961. Cleland Conservation Park in the Mount Lofty Ranges was named after him.

Although a staunch Anglican, Cleland had married Dora Isabel Paton in Adelaide on 25 April 1908 with Presbyterian forms; she predeceased him. Survived by his four daughters and a son, he died on 11 August 1971 and was buried in Walkerville cemetery.

A. Musgrave, *Bibliography of Australian entomology 1775-1930* (Syd, 1932); H. M. Whittell, *The literature of Australian birds* (Perth, 1954); *MJA,* 7 Dec 1918, 22 June 1968; Roy Soc SA, *Trans,* 82 (1958-59), 95 (1971); *South Aust Naturalist,* 46 (1971-72); *Emu,* July 1972; Roy Soc WA, *J,* 56 (1973); *Advertiser* (Adel), 12 Aug 1971; Hunt Inst biogs (Basser Lib, Canb); O. Pink, Correspondence (SA Museum, Adel); J. B. Cleland *and* R. V. Southcott papers (SAA); family papers (held by Mrs E. N. Paton, Beaumont, SA, and by author).

R. V. SOUTHCOTT

CLEMENS, SIR WILLIAM JAMES (1873-1941), public service commissioner, was born on 27 March 1873 at Spring Creek, Beechworth, Victoria, eldest child of James Clemens, miner, and his wife Catherine, née Nicholls, both from Cornwall. Educated at Beechworth State School, in 1889 he became a clerk in the General Post Office, Melbourne, at a salary of £50. His advancement was slow: he modestly recounted on retirement that in his first twelve years as a public servant he had failed to obtain any position for which he had applied. On 14 September 1899 at the Baptist Church, East Melbourne, Clemens married Lillie White; they had five children.

In 1901 he transferred to the Commonwealth Public Service and in December next year joined the staff of the Public Service Commissioner as clerk to the public service inspector, Victoria. In 1916 he became senior clerk; he progressed to registrar, secretary to the commissioner and public service inspector for Victoria and Tasmania. In May 1922 he was appointed a special commissioner to report on and classify the public service of the mandated territory of New Guinea.

In 1923 Clemens became secretary and chief inspector to the new Commonwealth Public Service Board. In June 1925 he was awarded the I.S.O. Appointed secretary to the Department of Home and Territories in June 1928, he became a commissioner and member of the Public Service Board on 1 January 1929. In 1933 he was made chairman of the board; he was appointed C.M.G. next year.

Clemens's term on the board was a most difficult one. Coinciding with the Depression, it involved him in retrenchments, reductions in wages and lowered conditions. With skill and delicacy he helped to obtain agreement with staff organizations, and they acknowledged the 'courtesy and helpfulness' with which he handled these tasks. He retired as chairman of the board in March 1937 and was knighted in the coronation honours in May.

Clemens's first wife had died in 1911 and on 20 August 1914 at Elsternwick he married Bella May Webster, a nurse; they had a son and a daughter. He moved to Canberra in 1928 and continued to live at his home in Wickham Crescent, Red Hill, after retirement. He was president of the Canberra Eisteddfod and the local division of the Red Cross Society, a member of the Canberra Bowling and Golf clubs and a keen horticulturalist.

While regarded as somewhat aloof and austere with his staff, Clemens was respected for his ability to sum up situations and his determination to make the public service an efficient instrument. His period in office was one 'of extraordinary development in the sphere of co-operation between staff and management'. He was willing to discuss problems frankly with staff associations and to concede claims whenever it seemed justified, but he detested compromise when it was simply an easy path to temporary agreement.

Friends and neighbours remember him as a tall, spare, gentle person whose statements 'never needed reiteration'. Clemens died of cancer in hospital in Melbourne on 4 September 1941, survived by his wife, four daughters and three sons; his youngest son was killed in action in Malaya shortly after. He was cremated after a service conducted by the vicar of All Saints, St Kilda. His estate was valued for probate at £6654.

G. E. Caiden, *Career service* (Melb, 1965); Public Service Board, *Report,* 1936; *Federal Public Service J,* 30 Sep 1941; *Canb Times,* 5 Sep 1941; *Age,* 6 Sept 1941.

P. D. GOURLEY
M. F. STEWART

CLEMENT, DIXIE PAUMIER (1879-1935), physician and obstetrician, was born on 23 December 1879 at Dungannon, County Tyrone, Ireland, elder son of Mildmay Thomas Charlton Clement, civil engineer, and his wife Lucy Clara, née Christie

(Cristy). He attended St Faughnan's College, Rosscarbery, County Cork, until 1895 when he accompanied his family to Western Australia. Clement joined the prospecting team which discovered the Lancefield mine at Laverton and worked there till 1902 when he returned to Perth to matriculate. Next year he entered Trinity College, Dublin (B.A., M.B., B.Ch., B.A.O.), where several members of his family had also attended. Clement then studied obstetrics at the Rotunda Hospital, Dublin, where he qualified Licentiate of Midwifery (1908).

In 1908 he returned to Western Australia and, after six weeks at Pingelly, entered partnership in West Perth with Dr Athelstan Saw. Next year, on 1 September, he married Ethel Burt; they had three sons and four daughters. Clement encouraged the Women's Service Guilds and Edith Cowan's [q.v.] committee, which was seeking a maternity hospital to improve the conditions of childbirth and to train midwifery nurses. The guilds' 1915 protest prodded Scaddan's [q.v.] government to convert the Subiaco Industrial School to the King Edward Memorial Hospital for Women. It was opened next year with two honorary physicians, Clement and J. L. Couch, to attend patients and Dr Officer to lecture and examine nurses.

Clement was sanguine, cheerful and impulsive, with a great capacity for work: he would attend three confinements in twenty-four hours, with anaesthetics sandwiched in between. To this would be added a long visiting list. He would spend the night at confinements and next day play off for a golf championship. At the hospital he earned the confidence and respect of the matron, nurses and mothers. Calls from colleagues in general practice needing specialist advice were always promptly answered. He was also honorary physician to the Perth Hospital, the Home of Peace for the Dying and Incurable, the Home of the Good Shepherd and St Brigid's Convent, West Perth. He was honorary secretary for four years and president in 1924 of the council of the Western Australian branch of the British Medical Association.

Survived by his wife, four daughters and two sons, Clement died of a stroke on 25 July 1935. In keeping with his belief that it was an inhuman custom to display harassed feelings at a graveside, he was buried privately in Karrakatta cemetery with Anglican rites. His estate was valued for probate at £1515. A commemorative bronze bust was placed in the entrance foyer of his old hospital.

R. Allen, *Life in her hands* (Melb, 1955); B. C. Cohen, *A history of medicine in Western Australia* (Perth, 1965); B. C. Cohen and R. L. Hutchison, *A history of King Edward Memorial Hospital for Women* (Perth, 1966); *MJA*, 31 Aug 1935; *West Australian*, 6, 18 July 1916, 26, 27 July 1935.

A. C. STAPLES

CLEMENTS, FREDERICK MOORE (1859-1920), pharmacist and manufacturing chemist, was born on 14 March 1859 at Witton, Erdington, Warwickshire, England, son of James Moore Clements, master tailor, and his wife Matilda, née Williams. He was educated at Birmingham where he was later apprenticed to a chemist. Strong links bound him to the area throughout his life.

In 1880 Clements visited South Africa and next year, while working in a pharmacy at Port Elizabeth, he 'discovered' the formula for 'Clements Tonic'. There he met another English pharmacist, T. B. Melhuish, later a prominent manufacturer in Sydney of galenicals and simple tonics; Clements followed him to Sydney in 1881 and worked in his pharmacy. In October 1884 Clements passed the Board of Pharmacy's qualifying examination and was elected to the Pharmaceutical Society of New South Wales. Two years later he opened the shop in Newtown where he began to manufacture his tonic. In its original form it was similar to the common compound syrup of hypophosphites which Melhuish was marketing within the trade; but Clements's tonic, a veritable 'twin brother of health and strength', enjoyed far greater commercial success because he advertised it widely as a splendid cure for many ailments – 'Nervous Breakdown in particular'. In 1894, despite the depression, he sold his pharmacy and opened a factory next door to his rambling Stanmore residence, Brahea, for the production of his tonic, 'Fletchers Pills' and 'Clements Certain Cure'. In 1905 he sold most of his interests in these nostrums to Elliott Bros Ltd, believing, incorrectly, that he retained certain rights.

In his retirement Clements travelled and indulged his many scientific interests. He had 'a good knowledge of medicinal plants', and his garden, with a catalogue of some 800 names, contained many rare plants and well-stocked aviaries. He also had an 'Electrical Laboratory' and proclaimed himself a 'Medical Electrician. Registered Dentist. Pharmacist and Theraputist. X Ray and Finsen Light Operator. Etc. Etc. Etc.' A former business associate, on seeing his book *Some faces and phases of Clem* (Sydney, 1921) commented: 'People who did not know him would suspect him of being a gentleman'. Apart from local pharmaceutical bodies, he also belonged to the Linnean Society of New South Wales, although he never attended its meetings; he was a freeman of the City of London (1910), and a fellow of the Zoological (1910), Linnean (1917) and Royal Geographical (1919) societies of London.

During World War I Clements gave generously to patriotic funds in Australia and overseas. He died a bachelor at Brahea on 17 August 1920 of Bright's disease and diabetes and was buried in the Anglican section of the Waverley cemetery. His Australian estate was valued for probate at £87 980; this and his English estate formed the F. M. Clements Trust for the benefit of charities in England, including the Blue Coat School, London, which had produced several of Sydney's early pharmacists. His library went to the local Linnean Society. His will was disputed in the Supreme Court by his sister Edith. He had disinherited her in 1920, and then arranged to leave her £150 a year 'until her death or until she makes complaint of or finds fault with or abuses me'. He was more generous with his English relations and friends.

G. Haines, *The grains and threepenn'orths of pharmacy* (Melb, 1976), *Chemist and Druggist of A'sia*, 1 Nov 1886; *Pharmaceutical J of A'sia*, July 1891; Linnean Soc Lond, *Procs*, 133 (1920-21); *A'sian Pharmaceutical Notes and News*, Oct 1920; Linnean Soc NSW, *Procs*, 46 (1921).

GREGORY HAINES

CLEMES, SAMUEL (1845-1922), educationist, was born on 25 December 1845 at Liskeard, Cornwall, England, son of Samuel Clemes, hatter, and his wife Jane, née Willis. Both parents became teachers at Ackworth Friends' School, Yorkshire. Samuel was orphaned at the age of 5 and brought up by his uncle at St Austell, Cornwall. He attended the Friends' Sidcot School, Somerset, in 1857-59, and worked in the drapery business, but his interest in teaching and mission work led to his acceptance by the Friends' Foreign Mission Association for training at the Flounders' Institute, Yorkshire, in 1870-71. After a year's teaching apprenticeship at Rawdon School he married an Ackworth teacher, Susannah Hall, and they went as missionaries to Tananarive, Madagascar. Susannah's ill health caused their return to Yorkshire in 1882, and she died at Sowerby. Clemes then became head teacher at Wigton Friends' School, Cumberland, and on 12 July 1884 in Neuchâtel, Switzerland, he married Susannah's sister Margaret.

In 1886 Clemes was appointed as headmaster of a proposed Friends' school in Hobart, Tasmania, and, with his family, sailed in the *Tainui* on 12 August. Friends' High School opened at Warwick Street,

Hobart, on 31 January 1887 with thirty-three students; it moved to larger premises at Hobartville, North Hobart, in 1889. The school was unique as a co-educational day and boarding establishment with pupils from all Australian colonies and New Zealand. His leadership and geniality did much to create its sense of community while Margaret Clemes's help gave a family atmosphere to the boarding house.

Clemes emphasized the teaching of science, an attitude stemming from his pioneering interest in chemistry as a subject at Wigton. He also stressed physical and technical education, believing the latter should be part of every student's programme, not for vocational reasons, but because manual skills had a moral value; his introduction of the Sloyd System was in advance of contemporary practice. A distinctive feature of the extra-curricular programme was 'Education for Leisure', and through the school's Natural History and Essay Society Clemes encouraged exploration of the countryside, collection of fossils, plants and specimens and systematic recording.

Clemes was a frequent public lecturer in chemistry and geology in Hobart. He travelled as far as Queensland as a minister of the Society of Friends. He was honorary secretary in 1897-1910, chairman in 1910-15 and president in 1915-22 of the Blind, Deaf and Dumb Institution; a member of the Royal Society of Tasmania from 1910; a foundation member of the Hobart Young Men's Christian Association and president of the Tasmanian Council of Churches.

Clemes resigned in June 1900 after misunderstandings with the committee of his school, and that year he established Leslie House School in Pirie Street, New Town — it moved to Boa Vista in Argyle Street in 1907. It also flourished as a 'family' school with an emphasis on character development. The kindergarten was based on Froebel's ideas and Madame Montessori's methods were later introduced. Clemes died on 25 October 1922 in New Town and was buried in the Society of Friends' section of Cornelian Bay cemetery. He was survived by his wife, two daughters and two sons, the elder of whom, William, had followed his father in 1915 as headmaster of Leslie House School, renamed Clemes College in 1922 — in 1946 it was amalgamated with The Friends' School.

Clemes was regarded by many as an innovator fifty years ahead of his times. He was outspoken in his opposition to prizes and marks, having faith that students would pursue learning for its own sake. His announcement in 1887 that no homework would be set drew much public comment. To hundreds of his pupils he was affectionately known as 'Old Sammy'. One of these wrote: 'The traditional relation of master and pupil did not exist between him and us, for we always felt that in him we had a sincere and approachable friend . . . With him, religion was not a creed to be believed, but a life to be lived. His constant advice to his pupils was that they should aim at growing up good, rather than great or clever'.

Cyclopedia of Tasmania, 1 (Hob, 1900); I. M. Shoobridge, *Samuel Clemes 1845-1922* (Hob, 1933); W. N. Oats, *The Friends' School, 1887-1961* (Hob, 1961); *Mercury*, 3 Nov 1886, 26-28 Oct 1922; *Weekly Courier* (Launc), 2 Nov 1922; W. N. Oats, The Friends' School Hobart: formation and early development (M.Ed. thesis, Univ Tas, 1976).

WILLIAM N. OATS

CLENDINNEN, FREDERICK JOHN (1860-1913) and LESLIE JOHN (1887-1954), radiologists, were father and son. Frederick John was born on 13 April 1860 at Emerald Hill, Melbourne, son of Joseph James Clendinnen, a jeweller originally from County Limerick, Ireland, and his wife Frances Mary, née Barfoot, widow of William Henry Ede.

Frederick Clendinnen was educated at South Melbourne Grammar School and Scotch College. He matriculated in 1879, in which year he was captain of the unbeaten 'twenty-a-side' school football team. After studying medicine at the university for three years he went overseas, where he attended the Middlesex and St Bartholomew's hospitals, London. He qualified L. and L. Mid., R.C.P. and R.C.S. (Edinburgh) in 1884; in 1885 he obtained the M.D. and also doctorate of midwifery at Brussels, with degrees also from Ireland and London.

In January 1886 Clendinnen returned to Victoria and on 9 June at Carlton married Charlotte Elizabeth Welchman with Wesleyan forms. He became a general practitioner at Hawksburn and developed a laboratory for the study of electrical phenomena. A gifted amateur photographer and a keen microscopist, he experimented with Geissler tubes before W. C. Röntgen made the famous discovery of X-rays on 8 November 1895. On 21 May 1896 Clendinnen purchased his first X-ray apparatus from W. Watson in Melbourne for £5 13s. 9d.; he is acknowledged to be the first medical man in Melbourne to take an X-ray photograph of a patient, though some say that Dr Herbert Hewlett [q.v.] contended for this honour. Both Clendinnen and Hewlett, together with Dr Laurence Herschel Harris [q.v.] of Sydney have their names on the select roll of honour in the hall of the Fondation Béclère in Paris.

Clendinnen wrote about the 'new photography' in the *Intercolonial Medical Journal*, 20 August 1896, and in October published a striking picture he had made of a seven-month foetus whose arteries had been injected with opaque material. An untiring experimenter and innovator, he soon devoted himself entirely to X-ray work and in 1898 gave up his general practice to become a medical radiologist, one of the first in the world.

Described as 'quiet, reticent, almost taciturn', Fred Clendinnen was a man of many talents. He had fitted up his house at Hawksburn 'like a great electrical museum' full of marvellous contrivances. Among his inventions were an electrical coin catcher for removing swallowed coins, an automatic telephone, a chloroform inhaler and a sound to aid in removal of stones from the bladder. He was also an exceptional marksman, and in 1898 was awarded a prize rifle made for the Melbourne gunsmith James Rosier; he had won the Rosier Trophy three times.

Clendinnen used radium for treatment as well as X-ray for diagnosis. At the end of 1896 he was appointed the first 'honorary skiagraphist' to the (Royal) Melbourne Hospital and also the Eye and Ear Hospital. His early demonstrations were invaluable in convincing the medical profession of the value of X-rays for diagnosis and treatment. Like many of the pioneers he was a martyr to the science, suffering mutilating injuries from radiation as protection was little understood. This led to loss of fingers and possibly contributed towards his death in London on 6 November 1913, a few weeks after an operation for gall-stones. He had been in Britain to attend the International Medical Congress.

His practice was continued by his son Leslie John. 'Jack' Clendinnen, as he was known, was born on 16 May 1887 at South Yarra. He received his secondary education at Melbourne Church of England Grammar School. He matriculated in 1903 and studied medicine at the University of Melbourne (M.B.; Ch.B., 1911). On 16 December 1916 at Long Gully, Bendigo, he married Nellie Winifred Dunstan.

He had been apprenticed to his father who was then practising in Collins Street, Melbourne; at that time there was no systematic instruction in radiology. Clendinnen had planned to proceed to London for surgical training but on his father's death he had to carry on the increasingly large Melbourne radiological practice. He volunteered for service in the Australian Imperial Force at the outbreak of World War I in 1914, but as there were then only four skiagraphists in Melbourne, only (Sir) Stanley Argyle [q.v.] and Charles E. Dennis were allowed to go overseas.

Clendinnen had succeeded his father as honorary skiagraphist at the Melbourne Hospital in 1914, the youngest honorary doctor to be appointed. During the war he also became increasingly involved in work at the Caulfield Military Hospital. At this time he was practising both in diagnosis and therapy; his appointment in 1929 as the first radiotherapist to the Melbourne Hospital showed the growing specialization in radiology. In 1933, at the completion of his term at Melbourne Hospital, he was appointed to a similar position at Prince Henry's Hospital, holding this post until 1953. He was elected a fellow of the Faculty of Radiologists (London) in 1938.

Clendinnen was a pioneer in Australia of the interstitial use of radium needles in the treatment of malignant tumours, but unfortunately he was not given to medical writing. He had first-hand experience of the medico-legal hazards of radiology, and for twenty-two years was an assiduous council-member of the Medical Defence Association of Victoria.

Clendinnen had many interests, but his two main hobbies were birds, particularly budgerigars and native parrots, and flowers. For many years every spare moment was devoted to his aviary, but this hobby became so time consuming that he eventually had to abandon it. He turned to gardening at his country home at Kallista in the Dandenongs. Here he developed a garden on some three acres (1.2 ha), specializing in hydrangeas, rhododendrons, azaleas and camellias. His interest in natural history was recognized in his appointment as a trustee of Wilson's Promontory National Park and later of the Sir Colin Mackenzie [q.v.] Sanctuary at Healesville. He was a fanatical bridge-player and a keen Rotarian. Like his father, he developed radiation injuries to his hands, with loss of fingers. He died suddenly on 29 January 1954, survived by his wife and two sons. He was cremated.

J. Smith (ed), *Cyclopedia of Victoria*, 1 (Melb, 1903); W. Watson & Sons Ltd, *Salute to the X-ray pioneers of Australia* (Syd, 1946); *Scientific Australian*, 20 Dec 1898; *Aust Medical J*, 22 Nov 1913; *VHM*, 36 (1965), p 136; *MJA*, 12 June 1954; Roy Melb Hospital, *Clinical Reports*, 24 (1954); *Argus*, 4 Mar 1896, 8 Nov 1913; *Table Talk*, 7 Apr 1904; *Punch* (Melb), 12 Nov 1908; *Age*, 8 Nov 1913; information from Dr R. Kaye Scott, Melb; family information.   ROBERT BENNETT

CLIMPSON, JOSEPH (1894-1973), soldier and policeman, was born on 23 May 1894 at Redfern, Sydney, second son of native-born parents Richard Climpson, labourer and later printer, and his wife Margaret, née Morris. Between 1911 and 1914 he completed three years compulsory military training while working as a letterpress printer.

Of medium height, with blue eyes, auburn hair and a fair complexion, Climpson enlisted in the Australian Imperial Force on 14 August 1914. He landed on Gallipoli on 25 April 1915 with the 1st Division Signal Company, and was promoted lance corporal next day. Mentioned in General Sir Ian Hamilton's dispatch of 11 December, he was transferred to 4th Division Signal Company on 12 March 1916. He sailed for France on 2 June, was promoted corporal on 16 June and saw action at Pozières in July. For his performance during this and later engagements on the Somme he was promoted to sergeant on 2 November and awarded the Military Medal in December.

In April and May 1917 the 4th Division was engaged in severe actions before the Hindenburg Line. Climpson was awarded a Bar to his M.M. and on 15 June was promoted to warrant officer class 2. On 4 October he was posted to the Signal Service Officers Cadet School in England; he was commissioned second lieutenant on 23 March 1918 and returned to the 4th Division.

On the night of 24 and 25 April 1918, during the great Australian counter-attack which recaptured Villers-Bretonneux, Climpson was in charge of the signallers at the headquarters of the 13th Brigade. All the brigade's communications had to be improvised in a very short time: 'this was accomplished by the energy with which he led his party of linesmen ... lines were laid under incessant fire and maintained almost continuously throughout the attack'. On 26 April he was evacuated suffering the effects of gas. His gallantry, cheerfulness and devotion to duty won him the Military Cross, thereby completing a rare series of decorations. He was promoted lieutenant on 23 June 1918.

Climpson returned to Australia in June 1919 and on demobilization he joined the New South Wales Police Force. After training at the Police Depot in Sydney he was stationed at Wagga Wagga. On 7 April 1920 at Surry Hills he married Dorothy May Stevens, whom he had met in Britain. Briefly at Whitton in 1921, he was at Adelong in 1921-25 and at Maude in 1925-29; he attained the rank of constable 1st class on 1 July 1928. Next year he was transferred to Tarcutta and was stationed at Tumbarumba in 1934-42, Grenfell in 1942-45 and promoted to sergeant 3rd class at Bourke in 1945-47. Returning to Sydney he served at Burwood, Auburn and Parramatta police stations. He retired as a sergeant 2nd class on 22 May 1954.

As as country policeman, Climpson was

involved with the Boy Scouts' Association and organized amateur concert parties. About 1968 he moved to Cooma where he died on 15 January 1973 and was buried in the Catholic cemetery. He was survived by his wife, two sons and two daughters.

C. E. W. Bean, *The story of Anzac,* 2 (Syd, 1924), and *The A.I.F. in France,* 1916-18 (Syd, 1929, 1933, 1937); *London Gazette,* 28 Jan, 8 Dec 1916, 16 Sept 1918; information from NSW Police Dept, *and* The Scout Assn of Aust (NSW Branch); family information.   N. S. FOLDI

CLOGSTOUN, HENRY OLIVER (1881-1958), officer, Royal Engineers, was born on 19 September 1881 at Madras, India, son of Herbert Frederick Clogstoun of the Indian Civil Service, Madras. Educated at Clifton College, Bristol, he entered the Royal Military Academy, Woolwich, in January 1898 and was commissioned in the Royal Engineers on 2 May 1900. After a course at the School of Military Engineering, Chatham, Clogstoun served five years with the 2nd (Fortress) Company in Cairo, and two years with the 42nd (Fortress) Company at Portsmouth, England. He was an instructor at the Royal Military Academy until April 1912, when he was seconded to the Australian Military Forces to help to reorganize the engineers.

Clogstoun arrived at Melbourne in the *Orsova* on 20 May. As director of works (later engineers) he threw himself into his work with keenness and enthusiasm: the efficiency of the corps of engineers at the outbreak of World War I was largely due to his influence and driving power. In August 1914 he was accepted into the Australian Imperial Force as the officer commanding 3rd Field Company, Australian Engineers, 1st Division. Shortly after arrival in the Middle East, the company was chosen to construct trenches, and floating bridges on the Suez Canal. It returned to Mena Camp on 25 February 1915 and took part in the Gallipoli landing on 25 April.

At Anzac Clogstoun had a great part in planning the defences on the southern flank, particularly to the front of Holly Ridge (June 1915) where he applied the new shallow tunnelling technique to the excavation of fire trenches in exposed positions. On 6 August he was shot through the windpipe in a daring attempt to discover what the Turks were doing to the front of Leane's Trench. He was mentioned in dispatches and promoted brevet major in November.

In July 1916 Clogstoun became commanding royal engineer of the 3rd Division, A.I.F. with the temporary rank of lieutcolonel. After supervising the field companies of the division at Salisbury Plain he crossed with them to Armentières, France, in mid-November 1916. He took part in the Messines and Passchendaele offensives, serving until 9 April 1918 when he reverted to the British Army as C.R.E. XIII Corps Troops.

During his service with the 1st and 3rd Divisions, Clogstoun's professional expertise was highly respected. Like many other British officers, he did not fully understand the Australian soldier, but his courage and ability won him the loyalty of his men, even though few were spared his caustic tongue. Bean [q.v.7] names him as one of the British officers for whom the diggers 'conceived deep admiration and regard'. 'Cloggie' was tall and strongly built, with a 'long, smooth, florid face'. At Anzac he is remembered as getting about 'in a battered slouch hat, torn shirt, very brief shorts, thick army boots with grey socks draped over them — and a monocle'. His eccentricities were the source of many anecdotes.

On 6 May 1919 Clogstoun was sent on special duty to Berlin in his substantive rank of major. He afterwards served in Ireland, Scotland and Malta, being promoted lieutcolonel on 1 October 1925. He was placed on half pay on 1 October 1929 and retired on 1 April 1930. In 1934-42 he was employed as a civilian under the director of fortifications and works, War Office, spending his last years at Blakeney, Norfolk, where he died on 23 April 1958. He was survived by his wife Norah Stanford, née MacIlwaine, whom he had married on 23 July 1910 at Holy Trinity Church, Kensington Gore, London.

History of the 11th Field Company Australian Engineers (Lond, 1919); C. E. W. Bean, *The story of Anzac* (Syd, 1921,1924), and *The A.I.F. in France* 1916-18 (Syd, 1929, 1933, 1937, 1942); T. H. Prince, *Purple patches* (Syd, 1935); G. Drake-Brockman, *The turning wheel* (Perth, 1960); *Reveille* (Syd), 1 Nov 1938; 10th Field Company Engineers: History (in the field), 1916-1918 (Monash collection, AWM).

P. J. GREVILLE

CLOWES, EVELYN MARY; *see* MORDAUNT

CLUBBE, SIR CHARLES PERCY BARLEE (1854-1932), surgeon, was born on 2 February 1854 in the vicarage at Hughenden, Buckinghamshire, England, son of Rev. Charles Wishaw Clubbe and his wife Emily, née Barlee; he was a nephew of Sir Frederick Barlee [q.v.3]. Charles spent a happy childhood in the small village of Hughenden and there occasionally met Disraeli, who was a friend of his father.

Educated at Uppingham School and later at St Bartholomew's Hospital, Clubbe was admitted as a member of the Royal College of Surgeons, England, in 1876 and as a licentiate of the Royal College of Physicians, London, in 1877. He was appointed as a house surgeon to the Kidderminster hospital, and in 1879 served as a civil surgeon with the Army Medical Department of Natal during the Zulu War. Next year he was appointed chief resident medical officer to the (Royal) Manchester Children's Hospital, where his lifelong interest in paediatrics had its beginnings.

On 12 April 1882 at Kidbrooke, Kent, Clubbe was married by his father to Ethel Marion Jeffreys Harrison (d. 1900). That year, because of a 'chest complaint' he decided to migrate to Australia. Arriving in Sydney in 1883 he quickly established a general practice at Randwick. Within a year he was appointed honorary surgeon to the Hospital for Sick Children, Glebe Point (later the Royal Alexandra Hospital for Children), and five years later he became an honorary assistant surgeon to the Royal Prince Alfred Hospital, then was honorary consulting surgeon to both hospitals until 1932. (Sir) Robert Wade [q.v.] later maintained that Clubbe 'was adored by his house surgeons for his lovable, equable nature, his prompt attendance at hospital in times of emergency ... it was, he thought, the duty of the honorary surgeon to teach his house surgeon, and in this he was unique in his day'.

By 1900 Clubbe had moved his practice to Macquarie Street; his surgical skill was widely recognized by his colleagues who became increasingly aware of his mastery over various problems of infancy and childhood. His world-famous textbook *The diagnosis & treatment of intussusception* was first published in 1907 (2nd edition, 1921): it emphasized the great importance of early diagnosis of intussusception (telescoping of the bowel) and a dramatic fall in the death rate from this condition was achieved in the Sydney region. His papers in the *Australasian Medical Gazette* in 1889-91 on the surgical treatment of club-feet and of bow-legs marked the beginnings of the development of orthopaedic surgery in Australia. He also contributed much to the treatment of infants and children suffering from diphtheria – he established the diphtheria department at Glebe, he performed urgent tracheotomies as early as 1888, and he demonstrated the recoveries which followed the use of the first supplies of diphtheria antitoxin to reach Australia.

Clubbe served his profession tirelessly. He was president of the New South Wales branch of the British Medical Association in 1897-98 and lectured in clinical surgery at the University of Sydney in 1895-1907. He presided over the board of management of the Royal Alexandra Hospital in 1904-32 and oversaw its dramatic growth from a small, converted school building at Glebe Point to a modern teaching hospital with 350 beds. Clubbe also served on the Medical Board of New South Wales in 1915-16, as consulting surgeon to the Coast Hospital and Sanitorium (later the Prince Henry Hospital), the Institution for the Deaf and Dumb and the Blind, and the Greycliffe (Lady Edeline) Hospital for Babies, and was president of the New South Wales Bush Nursing Association, the District Nursing Association and the Infantile Paralysis Committee of New South Wales. As chairman of the Baby Clinics, Pre-maternity and Home Nursing Board in 1914, then as president of the Royal Society for the Welfare of Mothers and Babies, he was a major pioneer of baby health centres and the first Tresillian mothercraft homes.

In 1907 Clubbe visited the Mayo Clinic, in Rochester, Minnesota, United States of America, and in 1924 was elected an honorary fellow of the American College of Surgeons. He was appointed K.B.E. in 1927 and next year became a foundation fellow of the College of Surgeons of Australasia (later Royal Australasian College of Surgeons). He was a member of both the Australian and Union clubs, Sydney. Kindly, equable, and with an engaging smile that 'inspired confidence', he was tall and erect.

Clubbe died of coronary vascular disease at his Rose Bay home on 20 November 1932 and was cremated with Anglican rites. He was survived by a son and two daughters of his first marriage, and by his second wife Gertrude Florence, née Edwards, whom he had married in Melbourne on 5 April 1902, and by their son and daughter. His eldest daughter Phyllis played hockey for New South Wales and was a founder with Winifred West [q.v.] of Frensham school at Mittagong. Clubbe's estate was valued for probate at £33 145. His portrait by John Longstaff [q.v.] is held by the Royal Alexandra Hospital.

D. G. Hamilton, *Hand in hand* (Syd, 1979); *MJA*, 14 Jan 1933, 4 Aug 1945; *SMH*, 22 Nov 1932; information from Mr M. Preston, Marlborough School, Eng.   LORIMER DODS

CLUCAS, ROBERT JOHN MILLER (1871-1930), librarian, was born on 22 December 1871 on the Isle of Man, eldest son of John Clucas, schoolmaster, and his wife. In 1882 the family migrated to Adelaide. Robert was a pupil-teacher in 1886-90. After studying at the Training College, he taught for eight years, mostly at Parkside Public School. He married Alice Mabel Wallace on 22 December 1897. Their only child, a daughter, died in infancy.

In 1900 Clucas became the first full-time librarian of the University of Adelaide. He had no staff and no experience or training in librarianship, and had made but a slow beginning in his arts course (B.A., 1908). Yet he had the enthusiasm and intelligence to develop professional competence and efficiency. He built up the library's holdings from about 10 000 volumes to about 80 000. In 1927 a new building was planned, and he opposed the architect W. H. Bagot's [q.v.7] visit to Europe, believing that 'It is to America we have to look for guidance in library planning'. Nevertheless Clucas co-operated in designing the building, which was unfinished when he died.

In 1901-24 he was responsible, on behalf of the university, for public examinations in South Australia, Broken Hill, and Western Australia: eventually one-third of his staff's time was taken up by the work. A lecturer in economic geography in 1904-28, Clucas believed that geography fostered 'a keen power of observation, a high standard of logical fitting of cause and effect, and the development of a disciplined individuality'. In 1929 he published a revised and enlarged edition of J. A. Haslam's *The Commonwealth Geography* .... Clucas had a strong interest in cartography and surveying, working in his leisure for many years on a contour map of the Adelaide hills, and each year introducing surveying to the university's engineering students.

A foundation member of the Library Association of South Australia, he was also a council-member of the State Branch of the Royal Geographical Society of Australasia and a member of the Royal Society of South Australia whose transactions he had indexed in 1907. He admired Theocritus as 'the true artist who draws the essential lines with the fewest possible strokes', and translated his Idyll XV; his friend G. F. Hassell [q.v.] published it as an elegant booklet, *The feast of Adonis* (1910), claiming it as the first Greek text with parallel translation to be published in Australia.

A reticent, retiring man, a Methodist, Clucas was upright, punctilious and kindly, with a whimsical sense of humour. Survived by his wife (d. 1952) he died of cancer after a long illness on 7 September 1930 and was buried in West Terrace cemetery. He bequeathed 1300 volumes from his collection to the university.

The Hassell Press, 1885-1935 (Adel, 1935); W. G. K. Duncan and R. A. Leonard, *The University of Adelaide, 1874-1974* (Adel, 1973); *Adelaide Univ*

Mag, 6 (1930); *PRGSSA*, 31 (1930); *SA Institute J*, 31 Dec 1930; *News* (Adel), 2 Jan 1924; *Advertiser* (Adel), and *Register* (Adel), 9 Sept 1930; records (Univ Adel); Education Dept, Teachers' history (SAA).
                                           IRA D. RAYMOND

CLUNE, PATRICK JOSEPH (1864-1935), archbishop, was born on 6 January 1864 near Ruan, County Clare, Ireland, son of James Clune and his wife Margaret, née Lynch. Educated locally and at St Flannan's College, Ennis, in 1897 he entered the Catholic Missionary College of All Hallows, Dublin, to study for the priesthood and was ordained in 1886 at the early age of 22. His first appointment was to St Patrick's College, Goulburn, New South Wales, where he taught English literature and developed a love for it which always influenced his style of public speaking. He was later the administrator of the Goulburn cathedral until his return to England to train as a Redemptorist missioner in 1893.

In 1895-98 Clune gave very successful parochial missions throughout England and Ireland and in 1898 went to Perth with the first band of Redemptorists obtained by Bishop Matthew Gibney [q.v.]. Here his eloquence and manliness had a remarkable influence on the men in the rough settlements. In 1905 Clune became superior of the Redemptorist monastery, Wellington, New Zealand, where he remained until 1909, when he went back to the Perth house as superior. Gibney used Clune freely for his appeals at the openings of churches, schools and convents. Next year he reached the heights of sacred oratory in two famous sermons: the panegyric on the death of King Edward VII and the dedication of the cathedral organ.

Because of serious financial troubles, on 21 March 1910 Gibney was requested by Rome to resign; he had mentioned Clune as a successor, and he was the first choice of the diocesan clergy, and of three bishops of the other provinces. Clune was consecrated by Cardinal P. F. Moran [q.v.] on 17 March 1911. The church had a huge debt of £204 039, and to reduce it he appointed a committee of experienced lay financial administrators. With their help within four years he had paid off over £97 000 – of which £82 000 came from the judicious sale of real estate that Gibney had acquired. In 1913 Perth was elevated to an archbishopric with Clune as its first incumbent. He continued to express himself on Home Rule for Ireland.

In World War I Clune was senior chaplain to the Catholic members of the Australian Imperial Force. In 1916 he visited troops in England and also those in the Ypres salient where he made a profound impression. At the end of his appointment in the A.I.F. in March 1917, he returned to Western Australia where he appealed for the Belgian patriotic funds, assisted the families of Yugoslav internees and expressed himself publicly but tolerantly in favour of conscription.

On a visit to Ireland in 1920 he was deeply shocked by the outrages perpetrated by the 'Black and Tans' in the name of the British government. In London he was invited to negotiate between the British government and the Irish Sinn Fein leaders; he conferred with Lloyd George and members of his cabinet and travelled between London and Dublin for several weeks, conveying the cabinet's terms to the Irish leaders and their replies to Lloyd George. The prime minister was reported as approving cordially of Clune's support for a temporary truce; but the 'Tory Wing of the Cabinet and especially Mr. Bonar Law and Mr. Winston Churchill' were opposed 'unless the Sinn Feiners delivered up all their arms': the negotiations failed on this question. In Paris in January 1921, on his way to Rome, Clune stated publicly that he believed Lloyd George 'sincerely yearned for peace', but unhappily several members of his government and other politicians did not share this view; he described the Sinn Feiners as 'the cream of their race'.

Clune's work for peace aroused public awareness in Europe and the United States of America as to the true state of Irish affairs, and in a speech at his official welcome back to Perth, he spoke fully and frankly of what he had seen in Ireland. Many in Australia had known only the partial reports of the newspapers, and also seemed to believe that 'loyalty' consisted in exhibiting conditioned reactions based on the English class system. The governor of Western Australia, Sir Francis Newdegate [q.v.], under the restrictions of his office, made no public statement. However, he had failed to have the Colonial Office intervene to delay Clune's return, and he promptly denounced Clune's speech to Downing Street as likely to revive bitterness all over Australia. The governor, blind to the significance of Clune's role, even as an Australian, but aware of his reputation for moderation, feared his 'full influence with the Roman Catholic Community'.

Clune now developed his expanding archdiocese: between 1921 and 1931 fifty-six new buildings were erected, including the foundling home at Subiaco, a home for the aged at Glendalough and a school for mentally handicapped boys at Castledare. Helped by Dr J. T. McMahon he supported the establishment of the 'Bushies' Scheme' in 1923, for the religious education of chil-dren in isolated areas, and the Newman Society of Western Australia, founded in 1925, for Catholic university students and undergraduates. Clune will be well remembered for the building of the beautiful present sanctuary and transept of St Mary's Cathedral for which he made the appeal for funds. The completed portion, opened on 4 May 1930, owed much to his taste and care.

In 1933 he chose as his coadjutor Redmond Prendiville who took over much of the administration as Archbishop Clune suffered from increasing infirmities. His last public speech indicated his dual interests: the Church he said, 'was striving to teach two things – truth and beauty'. He died on 24 May 1935 and was buried simply in the Redemptorist plot at Karrakatta cemetery. Glowing tributes were paid to his memory by prominent citizens of all religious beliefs who felt that his tolerance had contributed materially to Perth's lack of 'rancorous religious controversy'. A public-spirited citizen, Clune had been a peerless orator and a man of peace with a genius for making friends. (Sir) Walter Murdoch [q.v.] found him 'never an austere recluse', full of 'unaffected geniality' and with a conversation which was 'particularly witty and stimulating'; and Rabbi Feldman said that 'he held the respect of . . . the Jewish community [and] maintained peace in his time'.

J. T. McMahon, *One hundred years* (Perth, 1946), and *College, campus, cloister* (Perth, 1969); D. F. Bourke, *The history of the Catholic Church in Western Australia* (Perth, 1979); *Record* (Perth), 25 May 1935; *West Australian*, 25, 27 May, 1 June 1935; F. Clarke, A biography of 'Archbishop Patrick Joseph Clune (1963, Battye Lib, Perth); CO 537/1148-1151.   D. F. BOURKE

CLUNIES ROSS, WILLIAM JOHN (1850-1914), science teacher, was born on 31 March 1850 in London, son of Robert Clunies Ross, sea captain, and his wife Harriet, née Allen. Robert came from the Shetland Islands and, with his brother John, traded in their own ships with Australia, the Dutch East Indies and Singapore; both were involved in acquisition of the Cocos Islands in 1827, where John settled. In 1864 William visited Australia in one of his father's ships. After working in a counting-house in London, he studied science at the Royal School of Mines, South Kensington, and from 1878 at King's College, University of London (B.Sc., 1880); he became an associate of the college and a fellow of the Geological Society in 1882.

Clunies Ross migrated to Australia about 1884 and that year attracted attention with a popular lecture in Sydney on the *Metallurgy of silver,* published next year. On 1 February 1885, while in Hobart, he was appointed resident science master at Bathurst, New South Wales, by the Board of Technical Education. He had to establish a branch technical school and in the first year taught mineralogy, chemistry, geology, physiography and geometrical drawing; next year he added mathematics, physics and botany. Attendances improved in 1888 when a building was rented and all classes were held in one place. By 1890 a technological museum was opened. Clunies Ross also gave popular lectures on the Jenolan Caves and astronomy.

The vote for technical education was halved in 1893 and several classes were dropped briefly, but continued growth led to the erection of new buildings in 1898 and record enrolments in 1902. In January 1904 he became lecturer in charge of chemistry and metallurgy at Sydney Technical College. Total enrolments grew rapidly until 1913 when school pupils were removed from the courses.

When Clunies Ross moved to Sydney he joined the Royal and Linnean societies of New South Wales. He published over twenty scientific articles, many in the *Australian Technical Journal* and the *Technical Gazette of New South Wales.* He also addressed the Australasian Association for the Advancement of Science three times. His early articles were mostly on the geology of the Bathurst region and based on field-work and careful observation. He believed that chemistry was an art as well as a science, and his later articles revealed a deep interest in the whole field. His educational ideas were unashamedly old fashioned: he criticized excessive use of discovery and experimental techniques in instruction.

On 29 December 1887 Clunies Ross married Hannah Elizabeth Tilley with Congregational forms at her home in Sydney; her brother William, in the late nineteenth century, opened the Tilly Institute in Berlin for teaching languages. Their youngest son Ian left a warm reminiscence of their family life: his father sober, religious, widely read, pipe-smoking, bearded, scorning doctors and dentists, admiring Disraeli and Scott, and blending social egalitarianism with political conservatism; his mother Australian-born and proud of a supposed noble ancestry, admiring Gladstone and Dickens, fiercely status conscious and insisting on private schools for the children.

Clunies Ross died of cancer on 7 November 1914 at his Ashfield home and was buried in the Congregational section of Rookwood cemetery. He was survived by his wife and four sons.

I. Clunies-Ross, *Memoirs and papers,* F. Eyre ed (Melb, 1961); Roy Soc NSW, *J,* 49 (1915); *Technical Gazette of NSW,* 5 (1915), pt 2; Board of Technical Education, Correspondence register and minutes 1884-85 (NSWA); information from Col. A. Clunies-Ross, Duntroon, ACT.   BRUCE MITCHELL

CLUTTERBUCK, KATHERINE MARY (1861-1946), Anglican Sister, was born in Wiltshire, England, daughter of well-off county parents, Captain Clutterbuck and his wife. At 22 she joined the Kilburn Sisters and worked for seventeen years in London soup kitchens and shelters for the homeless. In 1901 Sister Kate and a colleague Sister Sarah answered a call from the Church in Western Australia. They arrived at Fremantle in December with twenty-two English orphans. It was very hot, they had to camp in a Fremantle hall, and money was scarce. However by the end of 1902 they had collected £250 and bought a 20-acre (8 ha) property at Parkerville in the Darling Ranges. This was partially cleared, well watered and close to a railway station; it had a shabby old barn to shelter them temporarily.

They cared for eight babies, rescued from baby farms, as well as their English charges; local people helped and cottages were built. By 1905 they were fostering forty-five children and next year a benefactor, Walter Padbury, built a large stone nursery. He also donated a carriage and horse, a 6000-gallon (27 270 L) tank and 120 acres (48 ha) of land partially planted with fruit trees. The government gave an annual grant and, by 1911, 100 children lived in the Parkerville Homes. Two more Sisters had been recruited from England and a dining-room, schoolhouse and kitchen were built.

Sister Kate pioneered the cottage home system of child care in Western Australia. Most of her foster-children were with her from babyhood to maturity: they called her 'Mum' (later 'Gran') and came 'home' for holidays or when in trouble. Her face, with its smooth English complexion, radiated kindliness, and though not a big woman, she had a quiet strength that won her respect and confidence from young and old. Her own cottage usually housed the most difficult boys and one or two sick babies in cots beside her bed. Retiring by nature, she nevertheless was full of sympathy, understanding and good advice for her children. By 1933 they numbered 800. Ten of the eleven boys who had come from England served in World War I, several were mentioned in dispatches and six never returned. Their medals were sent to Sister Kate and she mourned them till her death. Sixty of her boys served in World War II. She retired from Parkerville in 1933 and was appointed M.B.E. next year.

Retirement did not suit Sister Kate. Encouraged by the Department of Native Affairs, she gathered a group of part-Aboriginal children about her in a small suburban house but later, with financial help from her close friend and associate, Ruth Lefroy, she purchased a large block at Queen's Park where she provided a happy, healthy environment for her charges. Some of her old Parkerville children helped and soon there were cottages, a kindergarten, a church and other amenities. By 1945 over 150 children had been sent to her and the commissioner for native affairs wrote in his annual report: 'There is no more deserving home in the State'.

Sister Kate was in hospital for only four days and, aged 85, she died on 31 July 1946. She was cremated. The children's homes that she had established still flourish.

The story of the Children's Home at Parkerville (priv print, 1913; copy Battye Lib); Sister Rosalie, *Record of the work of the Sisters of the Church* (Perth, 1958); *PP* (WA), 1947, 2 (16); *Aust Women's Digest*, Oct 1946; *West Australian*, 1 Jan 1934, 20 Oct 1937, 19 Aug 1969; *Swan Express*, 8 July 1976.

NOËL STEWART

COANE, JOHN MONTGOMERY (1848-1923), surveyor and consulting engineer, was born in Ballyshannon, County Donegal, Ireland, son of Henry James Coane, barrister, and his wife Jane, née Montgomery. He was educated in Dublin apparently with a view to joining the Royal Engineers but instead came to Australia about 1867. For at least three years he worked in Queensland mining districts before going to Victoria. In November 1873 he joined the Victorian Education Department, teaching for a year at Napoleon, south of Ballarat, and then at Samaria near Benalla, from 1 January 1875 until 31 December 1878. On 1 January 1876 he married Emma Anna Hunt Collas at Wycliff Church of England, Learmonth.

In February 1879 Coane was authorized as a surveyor and was appointed to Benalla in August. Later that year, with George Hudson Grant, he established a general surveying and civil, hydraulic and mining engineering practice. They became one of the most distinguished consulting engineering partnerships of the era – their office was located in Melbourne from 1886. In the 1880s they undertook extensive land surveying, including selections, roads and townships for the Lands Department in the Yea and Seymour areas. New techniques for levelling in steep country were developed. The firm expanded into subdivisional work in Melbourne and country towns and into developmental works in rural Victoria. Projects included the 'improvement of private estates in Melbourne and elsewhere', the new Epsom race-course at Mordialloc, a survey of the Cape Otway Forest, the water-supply for Shepparton, Daylesford and other districts, municipal works and swamp reclamation. Coane advised the government on the rate of flow of the Goulburn River for irrigation and electric supply and laid out several private irrigation schemes. For some years he was a partner in a fruit-growing and exporting firm (until July 1903 known as Blacker's Orchard and Cannery Co.), at Toolamba in the Goulburn valley.

Coane's papers read to the Victorian Institute of Surveyors indicate his wide experience and high standing in the profession. While he was president in 1890-91 and 1905-06, the institute lobbied ministers on legislation and the surveyor-general on the scale of fees. Coane was often called as an expert witness in arbitrations and in engineering and property valuation disputes; he represented the institute on the Land Surveyors' Board in 1906-14. As chairman of the Mines Department's Sludge Abatement Board in 1905-17 he influenced the mining companies to accept it as an environmental authority.

Henry Edward Coane (1877-1923) joined his father in 1892 as an articled pupil, and at the turn of the century the firm became known as J. M. and H. E. Coane; Grant had left in the early 1890s. John Montgomery Coane junior (1884-1910) completed the talented and highly regarded partnership later. Before their early deaths, they with their father, won renown with their *Australasian roads*, a handbook on road construction, maintenance and administration, which ran to five editions between 1908 and 1937; later revisions were undertaken by B. M. Coutie. It was the first practical handbook relevant to Australian and New Zealand conditions.

J. M. and H. E. Coane designed the water-supply system for the coal mine town of Wonthaggi, and were consultants for railway construction in the New South Wales coal mining area of Newcastle, Maitland and Cessnock. They were also consulting engineers in 1907-08 to the Pacific Phosphate Co. Ltd of London for installations on Nauru; they did similar work on Ocean Island, and on Makatea where they acted for a French company. In 1912 Coane senior chaired the board which advised King O'Malley [q.v.] on designs for the new Federal capital. Coane disagreed with his fellow members who supported Burley Griffin's [q.v.] plan; his minority report recommended proposals by Griffiths, Coulter and Caswell. In June 1913 he read a paper at the International Road Congress in London before visiting Europe and the United States of America. In 1921-22 the Coanes were consulting engineers to the State Electricity Commission of Victoria.

Coane senior had lived in Brighton from the mid-1880s. In 1899-1921, when he was consulting engineer to the City of Brighton the area's roads, drainage and administration were much improved. Offered the post of city engineer in 1919, he declined because he earned more as a consultant. Active in local affairs he helped to found the Brighton Re-adaptation Society in 1919. Aged 75, he died at his daughter's home in North Sydney on 28 December 1923 and was buried in Melbourne in the Church of England section of Brighton cemetery. He was survived by his wife (d. 1924) and two daughters.

R. Southern, 'John Montgomery Coane . . .', *VHJ*, May 1978, and for bibliog.
                                    ROGER J. SOUTHERN

COATES, GEORGE JAMES (1869-1930), artist, was born on 9 August 1869 at Emerald Hill, Melbourne, son of John Coates, bookbinder, and his Irish-born wife Elizabeth, née Irwin. He attended St James's Grammar School and at 15 was apprenticed to the stained-glass firm, Ferguson and Urie. He first studied art under W. Dellit at the North Melbourne School of Design before attending evening drawing classes under F. McCubbin [q.v.] at the National Gallery School. He soon became one of the school's best draughtsmen. His father had died when George was 8 and, unhappy at home with his stepfather, he shared various studios in the city, living for a time with Lionel Lindsay [q.v.] and Hugh McLean in Elizabeth Street. Coates ran a drawing class in his Swanston Street studio where the students included Max Meldrum, Norman and Percy Lindsay [qq.v.], and George Bell [q.v.7]. A fine swimmer and amateur boxer, he was dubbed 'king' of the bohemian student group, the 'Prehistoric Order of Cannibals'.

In 1895-96 Coates studied painting under L. Bernard Hall [q.v.], acquiring both respect for the painter's craft and the approach of the Munich School — qualities that formed the basis for his later development. He won a travelling scholarship in 1896 and went to London next year before moving to Paris, where he worked at the Académie Julian and studied under Jean Paul Laurens. In Paris Coates renewed an acquaintance with a fellow art student, DORA MEESON (1869-1955), who arrived in 1898. She was born on 7 August 1869 at Hawthorn, Melbourne, daughter of John Thomas Meeson, schoolmaster, later barrister, and his wife Amelia,

née Kipling, and grew up in New Zealand. A student at the Melbourne National Gallery School, and later the Slade School, London, Dora studied in Paris under Benjamin Constant and Laurens. The couple were engaged in France but could not afford to marry until 23 June 1903, some three years after their move to London. They resolved not to have children but to devote themselves to their artistic careers.

Coates and Meeson established themselves in Chelsea where they became members of an extensive circle of Australian expatriate artists. To earn money they contributed black and white illustrations to Dr H. S. Williams's *Historians' history of the world* and the *Encyclopaedia Britannica*. Coates had exhibited 'on the line' at the Old Salon in Paris in 1898 and continued to show there and at the Royal Academy. Recognition did not come until after 1910, with an honourable mention at the Old Salon, prominent public notice at the 1912 Royal Academy exhibition and success at the 1913 New Salon when he was elected an associate (a member in 1927). Numerous commissions followed and soon established him as one of London's leading portrait painters. He was a member of the Chelsea Arts Club, the International Society of Sculptors, Painters, and Gravers and the Royal Society of Portrait Painters. Meeson had the distinction of being the first Australian woman artist elected a member of the Royal Institute of Oil Painters.

Despite physical prowess Coates lacked a strong constitution; when Meeson visited Australia alone in 1913 to accompany an exhibition his health collapsed and she had to return to nurse him in Italy. In 1915 he enlisted in the Territorial Royal Army Medical Corps and served as an orderly at the 3rd London General Hospital, attaining the rank of sergeant. He was discharged in 1919 as physically unfit. While never an official war artist, he produced many portrait commissions for the Australian War Memorial. These included portraits of World War I heroes and a large group portrait of Major General (Sir William) Bridges [q.v.7] and his staff in Egypt — on which Coates and Meeson worked after returning to Australia in 1921-22. Coates also painted portraits of Canadian war heroes.

Neither artist responded to developments in art after impressionism and their work remained firmly wedded to strictly representational modes. Primarily a portrait painter, the diffident and unassuming Coates was temperamentally disinclined to challenge accepted assumptions about art despite his admiration for Whistler, Dégas and Puvis de Chavannes. His realism emphasized a harmonious range of low tones and his approach was painstaking and obsessive. While able to handle large-scale works, his best portraits were more intimate such as 'Arthur Walker and his brother Harold' (1912) which reveal a sensitive response to character. Meeson is best known for her many fine impressions of the River Thames, a number of which were acquired after 1945 by the Port of London Authority.

Coates died suddenly in London of a stroke on 27 July 1930. A memorial exhibition of his work was opened in May 1931 at the New Burlington Galleries by Lord Birdwood [q.v.7]. His wife continued an active artistic career until her death in London on 24 March 1955. The two were buried together in Rye cemetery.

D. Coates, *George Coates* (Lond, 1937); L. A. Lindsay, *Comedy of life* (Syd, 1967); *Mail* (Adel), 23 Aug 1913; *Argus*, 27 Feb 1937.

RICHARD HAESE

COATES, JAMES (1901-1947), confidence man, was born on 29 June 1901 at Broken Hill, New South Wales, son of James Mann, miner, and his wife Ellen, née Doyle, both from Ballarat, Victoria. The family apparently moved to Western Australia when James was an infant. He came to Melbourne as a youth and began a life of crime as a pickpocket and card-sharper. Between 1918 and 1927 he served sentences in most States totalling three and a half years.

Deciding to enter the field of international confidence trickery, Coates left for England and with an accomplice 'Dictionary' Harry, who had the gift of the gab, worked ships in the Atlantic. In London he attended a school of deportment and etiquette. Impeccably dressed and groomed, gracious of character and speaking with an Oxford accent, Coates posed as grazier, surgeon or gambler among wealthy tourists in England, Belgium, Switzerland and France.

His most elaborate swindle occurred on a cruise from Alexandria to Marseilles in 1932. Coates assumed the identity of an engineer-inventor and distributed copies of a magazine containing an article in which his photograph had been substituted by a job-printer. He then ingratiated himself with Sir Michael Watson, who invested 3 750 000 francs (£54 000) in a scheme to revolutionize the docking of ships. Coates collected in Paris and vanished. He is also said to have swindled an Australian grazier of £40 000, an Austrian nobleman of £19 000, the King of Sweden's son of £15 000, and an Indian prince of £80 000. Certainly he was the bane of police throughout Europe.

By 1933 Coates had returned to Australia.

He built a mansion in Toorak, lived luxuriously, and became a heavy punter, but his reputation, associates and conduct led to his exclusion from most racecourses. At Randwick, Sydney, in May 1933, he was arrested and remanded for the Paris swindle. The charge was dropped.

Just before World War II Coates went abroad again and resumed his life as a confidence man. He fled London in 1939 for New York, but the liner was battered by a hurricane and authorities found him in hospital recovering from injuries. Extradition difficulties saved him. Arrested in Los Angeles and ordered out of the country, he chose to come home.

After 1940 Coates operated as a 'financier' from a comfortable South Yarra flat. He masterminded wartime rackets in Sydney and Melbourne, including blackmarket dealing in cars and the forging of petrol coupons, and he engaged in racing swindles and the flotation of bogus companies. By the end of the war he had spent most of his ill-acquired fortune. Too well known to operate internationally as a swindler, he was driven to blackmail, petty thieving and thuggery. He attempted to enter the protection racket by way of Melbourne's illegal baccarat gambling schools. Hated and feared as a double-dealer and possible informer, Coates was harassed, bashed and shot at. Few mourned when he was gunned down in a contract killing at Windsor on the night of Saturday, 19 July 1947. No arrest was ever made. He was survived by his wife Edith, née Mason, whom he had married at the age of 19; he was buried in Melbourne general cemetery.

Coates epitomized the international confidence man operating between the wars. Suitably conservative or natty in dress, retiring or flamboyant in his conduct, relaxed or lavish as a spender, he inspired trust and became a scourge of wealthy travellers. In his hey-day a doyen among swindlers, he died a petty criminal, penniless and universally detested.

H. Cox, *The Australians* (Philadelphia, 1966); *People* (Syd), 7 May 1952, 18 Sept 1957; *SMH*, 25 May, 1 June, 8 July 1933, 6 Nov, 9 Dec 1939; *New York Times*, 4 Nov 1939; *Age*, 21, 22 July 1947; *Argus*, 21-25 July, 6 Aug 1947; *Herald* (Melb), 21 July 1947; *Truth* (Melb), 26 July 1947, 20 Apr 1957.

JOHN LACK

COATES, JOSEPH FARRAR (1878-1943), trade unionist and politician, was born on 21 September 1878 at Bathurst, New South Wales, son of James Farrar Coates, commercial agent, and his wife Honorah, née Mahony. Educated at a Patrician

Brothers' school and St Aloysius' College, Sydney, he married Mary Teresa Hinchy on 17 March 1899.

Coates became a commercial traveller for the large Sydney firm of S. Hoffnung [q.v.4] & Co. Ltd and enjoyed a successful business career. In the 1890s he joined the local branch of the Australian Natives' Association and became active in Labor politics: he was a member of the committee of the Early Closing Association of New South Wales and was a foundation member of the Shop Assistants' Union of New South Wales in 1902-43. In 1910 he was defeated for the State seat of Bathurst. In April 1921 he was elected to the executive of the New South Wales branch of the Australian Labor Party despite opposition from Jack Bailey's [q.v.7] dominant faction. In August he was nominated by John Storey's [q.v.] government to the Legislative Council. He resigned from the State executive in 1923 in protest at its expulsion of James Dooley [q.v.], incurring the ill will of the new parliamentary leader J. T. Lang [q.v.].

In May 1925 Coates was elected by caucus to Lang's first ministry; however the premier gave him the post of honorary minister and 'told him he was to be honorary in every sense of the term'. Coates swallowed his disappointment when A. C. Willis [q.v.] became government leader in the council; he supported the government's unsuccessful efforts to abolish the Upper House. When Lang, at loggerheads with the caucus, reconstructed his ministry in 1927 he omitted Coates. In Opposition after the election that year, Coates was chairman and leader of the Labor Party in the council in defiance of Lang.

In 1931 he refused to support the 'Lang Plan', and broke away to lead an anti-Lang Labor Party supported by the Scullin [q.v.] Federal Labor government. He also acted as a State delegate on the A.L.P. Federal executive. Coates's own remedy for democracy was the creation of 'a vast system of private ownership ... in which there should be a large body of small capitalists'. Remaining parliamentary leader of a disparate and dwindling group united by little more than hostility to Lang, he embarrassed his colleagues by vociferously supporting (Sir) Bertram Stevens's [q.v.] government's proposal in 1933 to reform the Legislative Council. Nevertheless, Coates retained sufficent support to secure election to the reconstructed council, and was a member until 1943. He was vice-president of the New South Wales branch of the Empire Parliamentary Association and for the remainder of his parliamentary career, generally sided with the coalition ministries but retained Labor sympathies.

Coates was a government director of Amalgamated Wireless (Australasia) Ltd from 1931, managing director of Universal Publicity Pty Ltd, a committee-member of the Food for Babies Fund and Good Samaritan Association, and a prominent Catholic layman. In the 1930s he travelled abroad several times. He died of cerebro-vascular disease on 4 May 1943 at Haberfield, where he had lived for many years, and was buried in the Catholic section of Rookwood cemetery. He was survived by two sons and a daughter. His estate was valued for probate at £9784.

J. T. Lang, *I remember* (Syd, 1956); K. Turner, *House of review?* (Syd, 1969), *PD* (NSW), 1943, p 2860; *SMH,* 17 Feb, 25 May 1932, 12 May 1933, 5 May 1943.
MURRAY PERKS

COBB, CHESTER FRANCIS (1899-1943), novelist, was born on 8 June 1899 at Charing Cross, Waverley, Sydney, son of Joseph Septimus Cobb, chemist, from England, and his Geelong-born wife Rosalie Thomasina Kate Cockburn, née Smith. Interested early in fiction, Cobb left school to become a cadet and later a reporter on the Sydney *Daily Telegraph.* In 1921, on his mother's death, he came into a small inheritance; he left for England soon after, settled in Oxfordshire, and took up poultry-farming. On 31 March 1924 at Little Rollright near Chipping Norton, he married Barbara Anne Convy, twenty years his senior.

In 1925 Cobb's first novel, *Mr. Moffatt,* was published in England and favourably received; an American edition followed in 1926, the year in which *Days of disillusion* appeared. In both works Cobb drew on his Australian experiences. The title character in *Mr. Moffatt,* a chemist at 'Claverley' in Sydney in the 1890s who takes a painting to London to be valued and finds it a 'fake', is based on the life and experiences of Cobb's father. Similarly, *Days of disillusion,* a chronicle of the growth and development of Robert Watson over thirty-odd years, is also set in Claverley and opens in 1894. The spiritual odyssey of Moffatt and Watson, the central concern of each novel, derives from an interest in religion which led Cobb to question orthodox Christianity as a youth and ultimately to embrace theosophy in England.

Cobb wrote a third novel but it was never accepted for publication. In 1938 he became a sub-editor on the *Countryman,* a quarterly rural review and miscellany. He died on 17 February 1943 after an operation for gall-stones at Radcliffe Infirmary, Oxford. Although his literary career was brief and he never returned to Australia, he is significant as the first Australian-born novelist to employ a 'stream of consciousness' technique in his work.

C. Roderick, *20 Australian novelists* (Syd, 1947); S. Tick, 'Casebook for a novelist', *Southerly*, 4 (1961).
                                        B. G. ANDREWS

COBB, NATHAN AUGUSTUS (1859-1932), plant pathologist, was born on 30 June 1859 at Spencer, Massachusetts, United States of America, only child of William Henry Cobb and his wife Jane, née Bigelow. His father was at various times a carpenter, millwright, sawmill-manager, factory foreman and farmer; working for him, Nathan learnt manual skills, and was educated at local schools during the winter term. At 14 he worked as farm labourer, then qualified as a schoolteacher and taught for two years at Spencer. In 1878-81 he attended Worcester County Free Institute of Industrial Science and from 1881 taught science at Williston Seminary, Easthampton. On 8 August 1881, probably at Spencer, he married 27-year-old Alice Vara Proctor, who interested him in botany and shared his love of drawing and painting; later he illustrated many of his own articles. In 1887 he studied in Germany and received a doctorate of philosophy from the University of Jena, then worked in Italy for the British Association for the Advancement of Science at its Naples Zoological Station.

After borrowing their fares, Cobb arrived in Sydney on 7 March 1889 with his wife and three children. Penniless, he wasted a year in petty jobs, but early in 1890 was appointed temporary professor of biology at the University of Sydney and from 1 August that year became pathologist in the new Department of Agriculture. From the outset 'the Doctor', as he was known, was given a free hand by H. C. L. Anderson [q.v.7].

At a time of depression and drought Cobb was faced with immense problems – rust in wheat, and a multiplicity of diseases in sugar-cane, farm crops, vines and fruit-trees, which involved research into a whole range of fungous, viral, bacterial, insect and parasitical diseases. His most immediate problem was with wheat. After the second meeting of the Intercolonial Conference on Rust in Wheat, held in Sydney in June 1891, William Farrer [q.v.] wrote to the department expressing his views, and the horizons of Cobb's own work widened. From 1892 he and Farrer collaborated in an experimental programme, including the detailed examination and identification of some 600 wheats that Farrer had cultivated. Cobb also personally directed hundreds of experiments at Wagga Wagga Experiment Farm.

A member of the main committees on grain rusts, he contributed greatly to their published reports. As chairman of the conference's ancillary committee on nomenclature, Cobb vigorously tried to tackle a situation where not only was the same name applied to different kinds of wheat, but the same wheat was known under several different names. By laborious examinations and assessments, made partly with a microscope in the field (often in blazing heat) and partly in the laboratory, he reduced the confused nomenclature to some kind of order, describing many of his observations in the *Agricultural Gazette of New South Wales*. He was a councillor of the Linnean Society of New South Wales in 1892-94 and contributed to its *Proceedings*, often on nematodes.

In 1898 Cobb decided to seek experience abroad and resigned. However he was appointed special commissioner to report upon the agricultural and other industries of America and Europe. He travelled extensively and represented the New South Wales government at the 1900 Congrès Internationale d'Agriculture in Paris. He returned to Sydney in 1901 and resumed his old position. His paper 'Universal nomenclature of wheat', published in the *Agricultural Gazette* in 1901-04, attracted world-wide interest.

Cobb left Australia early in 1905, and until 1907 he organized, and was head of, the division of pathology and physiology at Experiment Station of the Hawaiian Sugar Planters' Association in Honolulu. He moved to Washington in 1907 and joined the United States Department of Agriculture as agricultural technologist with its Bureau of Plant Industry and was later principal nematologist. He published prodigiously on sugar-cane, cotton and, later, on helminthology. An able technician throughout his life, he built dark-rooms and cameras, laboratory apparatus and microscopes. With an international scientific reputation, he was sometime president of the American Microscopical Society, the American Society of Parasitologists, the Washington Academy of Sciences and the Helminthological Society of Washington.

Survived by a son and four daughters, Cobb died of heart disease at the Johns Hopkins Hospital, Baltimore, on 4 June 1932. He was an affectionate family man in whom 'an exquisite mastery of technique and artistic skill was matched only by the mirror-like all-embracing quality of his mind'. His work was of 'economic importance as well as of permanent scientific value'.

Dictionary of American Biography, Supp 1 (New York, 1944); Dept of Agriculture (NSW), *Annual Report*, 1890-1904; *Agr Gazette* (NSW), 1-15

(1890-1904), and for publications; *Asa Gray Bulletin*, Spring 1957, and for publications; Linnean Soc NSW, *Procs*, 58 (1933); Hunt Inst biogs (Basser Lib, Canb).
                                                          C. J. KING

COBB, VICTOR ERNEST (1876-1945), artist, was born on 14 August 1876 at Footscray, Melbourne, eighth child of John Frederic Cobb, a surgeon from Sussex, England, and his wife Mary Anne Elizabeth, née King, of New Zealand. When Cobb was 6 the family moved to the Gippsland town of Warragul for six years, a change which gave him an early appreciation of the countryside. In 1891-93 Cobb attended Melbourne Church of England Grammar School where he learned basic drawing. He became a student of the National Gallery School under L. Bernard Hall [q.v.], worked in oils and water-colours and met Lionel Lindsay, J. A. T. Shirlow and E. Moffitt [qq.v.], all with an interest in etching kindled by a recent exhibition of offprints by overseas masters. Enthusiastic, but lacking technical facilities and any relevant Australian tradition, Cobb and his friends were soon experimenting with hand-made tools and ingeniously contrived etching presses. Cobb produced his first print in the mid-1890s.

In 1899 he worked his passage as a ship's fireman to Durban, South Africa. He enlisted in the Johannesburg Mounted Rifles and fought with distinction through the South African War. After a brief visit to Melbourne he joined the Johannesburg Police Force and for a short time was a clerk in the Central South African railways. In 1905 he returned to Melbourne. With high hopes, but few opportunities for an artistic career, he filled several uncongenial occupations. While a mail order clerk in Cole's [q.v.3] Book Arcade he met Alice Bassett, daughter of an engineer; they were married on 23 November 1908 at St Mary's Church of England, North Melbourne.

Cobb carried out various commissions, such as designing the ball cards and menus for the 1920 visit of the prince of Wales to Adelaide and a series of etchings of Coombe Cottage for Melba [q.v.]. In November 1925 he began work under (Sir) Colin Mackenzie [q.v.] as science artist to the National Museum of Australian Zoology. In the next five years, until the museum moved to Canberra to become the Institute of Anatomy, Cobb made hundreds of detailed anatomical drawings of Australian marsupials and reptiles, and skulls and skeletons of Aboriginals and notorious criminals such as Deeming [q.v.] and Ned Kelly [q.v.5] — they are now in bound volumes at the institute. Subsequently he exhibited regularly, taught

etching and lectured in country centres, to art societies, schools and universities.

Cobb's reputation rests on a large *oeuvre* of etchings, built up during his lifetime and depicting with meticulous accuracy the architectural splendour of Melbourne's colleges and churches, vistas of the city, the tea-tree patterned foreshore and the outer areas of bush and countryside. State galleries hold many examples of his work.

Cobb was tall, spare and blue-eyed. In his younger days he was a keen sportsman, a first-class rifle shot and a renowned boomerang and cricket ball thrower. He was a member of the Bread and Cheese Club, Twenty Melbourne Painters and the Victorian Artists' Society. A fine craftsman and master printer, he was generous to fellow artists with his technical knowledge and skill. A somewhat melancholy man in later life, he died of cancer at his home in East Brunswick on 2 December 1945, survived by his wife and one son. He was buried in Melbourne general cemetery.

A. Colquhoun (ed), *The year book of Victorian art 1922-23* (Melb, 1923); R. H. Croll, *The etched work of Victor Cobb* (Melb, 1940); H. W. Malloch, *Fellows all* (Melb, 1943); *Art in Aust*, no 3, 1917, no 9, 1921; Presbyterian Church, Brunswick, *Church News*, 20 Oct 1944; *Herald* (Melb), 21 Nov 1928, 2 Dec 1931; *Age*, 25 Apr 1931; *Argus*, 3 Dec 1945; *Aust Financial Review*, 28 Apr 1977; family information.
                                                          R. E. NOTT

COBBETT, WILLIAM PITT (1853-1919), professor of law, was born on 26 July 1853 in Adelaide, son of Pitt Cobbett, wine merchant, and his wife Caroline, née Richards. Returning to England, his father was ordained priest in 1864 and, after filling various curacies, was vicar of the Church of the Holy Rood, Crofton, Hampshire, in 1874-1901. William Pitt Cobbett was educated at Alleyn's College of God's Gift (Dulwich College), London, in 1869-72, and played Rugby for the school. He matriculated in October 1873 and entered University College, Oxford (B.A., 1876; B.C.L., M.A.:, 1880; D.C.L., 1887); he won the university amateur middleweight boxing championship.

Admitted as a student of Gray's Inn on 4 May 1875 he was called to the Bar on 18 November 1878. Although he had chambers at 4 King's Bench Walk, Temple, he did not develop a practice but tutored at Oxford and in London — one of his pupils was Sir Edward Grey (Viscount Grey of Fallodon) — and was reputedly one of the best law coaches in London. He published *Leading cases and opinions on international law* in 1885, a second edition in 1892 and a third in two volumes; and *Peace* in 1909 and *War and neutrality* in 1913. Posthumous editions were produced by others.

On 3 February 1890 he was appointed to the Challis [q.v.3] chair of law at the University of Sydney; he arrived in New South Wales later that year. From September he was an *ex officio* member of the senate; he was chairman of the professorial board in 1900.

Pitt Cobbett, as he was known in Australia, was required to teach jurisprudence, Roman, constitutional and international law; in 1893 financial problems compelled the senate to reduce expenditure and, in order to assist the law school, he also lectured in real and personal property until 1901. He soon became the dominant figure in legal education in New South Wales. Besides being the only full-time teacher in law, he was president of the Solicitors' Admission Board in 1894-1909, and was examiner in various subjects; he also examined for the Barristers' Admission Board from 1891. In addition, in 1903-09, he edited and contributed to the *Commonwealth Law Review* and to the *New South Wales Weekly Notes*. The demise of the *Commonwealth Law Review* coincided with his retirement at the end of 1909.

As a teacher Cobbett was given to trenchant criticism of students' work and was unsympathetic to Ada Evans [q.v.], the only woman who entered the course during his professorship, but in 1902 he furnished the student common-room in the law school at his own expense. In his speech at the farewell dinner given him by the Sydney University Law Society, he indicated that in view of the progress of American law schools, changes of a drastic character were necessary in Sydney. In 1908 he had won faculty approval to incorporate the department of commerce, but the senate included it in the faculty of arts. Some changes did take place, but in many essential features the law school retains the imprint of Pitt Cobbett. He submitted written evidence to the 1908 Commonwealth joint select committee on privilege, and during World War I he advised the Commonwealth on international law; he also contributed letters and comments to newspapers in explanation of issues arising out of the conflict.

After Cobbett retired he moved to Hobart and worked on a book, to be entitled 'The government of Australia', dealing with the Constitution. However, before it was ready for publication he died of cancer at his home in Holebrook Place on 17 October 1919, and was buried in the Anglican section of Cornelian Bay cemetery. By his will he charged his trustees with Mr Justice W. Jethro Brown [q.v.7], to arrange for the book's completion if it were sufficiently advanced. Brown told the trustees that it would be a mistake to entrust it to someone else, and they presented the bound manuscript to the University of Sydney. Cobbett had given a systematic conspectus of the Constitution as construed by the High Court of Australia up to that time. But Chief Justice Sir Samuel Griffith [q.v.] resigned on 17 October 1919 and the High Court judgment in the *Amalgamated Society of Engineers* v. *Adelaide Steamship Co. Ltd* case in 1920 would have required major revision of the whole text, and it would no longer have been Pitt Cobbett's book. However, the manuscript gives valuable information about the perception of a learned lawyer of the meaning of the Constitution before the Engineers' case.

His gross estate was sworn at under £75 000, the net value in excess of £65 000. He left property in England, New Zealand, the Federated Malay States, Tasmania and several States of Australia. Pitt Cobbett purported to settle his residence successively on his brother and his cousin in tail male. Under the Real Property Act, no estate in tail could exist in Tasmania, as the Supreme Court and the High Court of Australia had decided. The terms of the will, and the problems which arose in administering his estate, produced another appeal to the High Court from a decision of the Full Court of the Supreme Court of Tasmania, and at least one application to a single judge of the Supreme Court. In his death he joined the large band of distinguished lawyers whose unsatisfactory testamentary dispositions benefited his profession.

In 1909, when the date of Cobbett's retirement was known, Mr Justice R. O'Connor [q.v.] had said 'It would be difficult to estimate what law and Bench of the States owes' to him; and (Sir) George Rich [q.v.] asserted that 'In Pitt Cobbett [the quality of distinction] was manifested in the stuff of the mind; intellectual energy, individuality of thought and utterance and intensity in the pursuit and dissemination of knowledge'.

T. R. Bavin (ed), *The jubilee book of the law school of the University of Sydney* (Syd, 1940); *Mercury*, 18 Oct 1919; *SMH*, 18, 21 Oct 1919; Senate and Faculty of Law minutes (Univ Syd Archives).

F. C. HUTLEY

COBBY, ARTHUR HENRY (1894-1955), airman and administrator, was born on 26 August 1894 at Prahran, Victoria, the second of four sons of Arthur Edward Stanley Cobby, tramway conductor, and his wife Alice, née Nash. Harry, as he became known, was educated at a state school and at University College, Armadale. He gained a commission with the 46th Infantry (Brighton Rifles) in 1912, while working as a clerk with the Commonwealth Bank, Melbourne. He joined the Australian Imperial Force in 1916 and was posted to the Central Flying School, Australian Flying Corps, Point Cook, and completed his initial instruction in December.

Lieutenant Cobby embarked with No. 4 Squadron, A.F.C., in January 1917 and arrived in England in March. The squadron flew its Sopwith Camel fighters to France in December, and Cobby shot down his first enemy aircraft on 3 February 1918. F. M. Cutlack [q.v.] considered that 'Cobby was one of the most daring spirits in the Australian air service', and describes in detail his many encounters with enemy aircraft. Cobby shot down 29 aircraft and 13 balloons between February and September 1918, and was the leading A.F.C. ace. He was awarded the Distinguished Flying Cross in June, two Bars to the D.F.C. in July, the Distinguished Service Order in August, and was mentioned in dispatches. He was then posted to England as an instructor. Captain Cobby returned to Australia in 1919 and was discharged from the A.I.F. on 24 July. He married Hilda Maude Urban on 24 April 1920 at Caulfield, Victoria.

Cobby joined the Australian Air Force on 31 March 1921 with the rank of flying officer, and was promoted wing commander on 1 May 1933. He left the R.A.A.F. on 6 May 1935, and became a member of the Civil Aviation Board and its controller of operations in March 1936. He had contributed a chapter on the psychology of flying to *Australian Airmen*, by E. J. Richards (Melbourne, no date), and an article to *Popular Flying* (London) in February 1935. His autobiography, *High Adventure* (Melbourne, 1942), was based on his World War I experiences.

Wing Commander Cobby rejoined the R.A.A.F. in 1939 on the outbreak of World War II, and was promoted to group captain and air commodore. He was director of recruiting (1940), air officer commanding headquarters North-Eastern Area (1942), commandant, R.A.A.F. Staff School, in 1943, A.O.C. No.10 Operational Group (1944) and of the 1st Tactical Air Force in 1944-45. He was awarded the George Medal in March 1944; although injured, he rescued two officers when a Catalina crashed at Townsville, Queensland, on 7 December 1943. He was also appointed C.B.E. for the direction of air operations in New Guinea in 1942-43.

A crisis arose in April 1945 when eight senior officers, who considered the high losses sustained by 1st T.A.F. operations to be militarily unjustifiable, tendered their resignations to Cobby at Morotai Island. He was relieved of his command on 10 May. An inquiry under (Sir) J. V. Barry, K.C., found that, *inter alia*, widespread discontent existed and that 'the A.O.C., 1st T.A.F., failed to maintain proper control over his command'. On 28 May 1948 Cobby was presented with the United States of America Medal of Freedom with bronze palm, for meritorious wartime service.

In 1946 Cobby returned to the Department of Civil Aviation, was appointed regional director, New South Wales, in 1947-54 and next year became director of flying operations. He died suddenly of hypertensive cerebro-vascular disease on 11 November 1955 in the Heidelberg Repatriation General Hospital, survived by his wife, son and daughter. He was accorded full military honours at St Mary's Church of England, Caulfield, and was cremated. His estate was declared for probate at £4858. Portraits by W. B. McInnes [q.v.] are held at the Australian War Memorial, Canberra, and by his son.

General Sir Thomas Blamey regarded Cobby as 'one of the most loved and most gallant of our airmen . . .'. Cobby also possessed a delightful sense of humour, and historian A. W. Bazley recalled that 'he was always an imp of mischief'. Air Marshal Sir Richard Williams [q.v.] paid tribute to him as 'a man whose personal story is threaded through the entire history of Australian service and civil aviation'.

F. M. Cutlack, *The Australian Flying Corps . . . 1914-1918* (Syd, 1923); O'M. Creagh and E. M. Humphris (eds), *The V.C. and D.S.O.*, 3 (Lond, 1924); L. A. Strange, *Recollections of an airman* (Lond, 1933); G. Odgers, *Air war against Japan, 1943-1945* (Canb, 1957); D. N. Gillison, *Royal Australian Air Force, 1939-1942* (Canb, 1962); K. Isaacs, *Military aircraft of Australia, 1909-1918* (Canb, 1971); A. W. Bazley, 'Celebrities of the A.I.F., Captain A. H. Cobby', *Reveille* (Syd), Nov 1937; *SMH*, and *Advertiser* (Adel), 12 Nov 1955; J. V. Barry, Com of inquiry into affairs relating to the R.A.A.F. (1945, AAO, Canb).   KEITH ISAACS

COCHRANE, GEORGE HENRY; *see* HERVEY, GRANT

COCKBURN, SIR JOHN ALEXANDER (1850-1929), premier, Federationist and medical practitioner, was born on 23 August 1850 at Corsbie, Berwickshire, Scotland, second son of Thomas Cockburn, farmer, and his wife Isabella, née Wright. His father died in France in 1855, and his mother migrated to South Australia in 1867 with three of the four children. John, educated at Cholmeley (now Highgate) School, remained behind to study medicine at King's College, University of London (M.R.C.S., M.B., 1871; M.D. and gold medal, 1874), although he briefly visited his family in 1871.

Believing the medical profession to be overcrowded in England, Cockburn settled in South Australia in 1875, and set up a lucrative practice in Jamestown. He was elected its first mayor in 1878 and held the office for three and a half years. In 1881 he was appointed a commissioner of the North Midland Road Board. He was also vice-president of the Rifle Volunteer Force and captain of the Jamestown company as well as a lay reader of the Anglican Church.

Cockburn's ambitions did not lie in medicine and in 1884 he won the House of Assembly seat of Burra. He immediately made his mark in parliament as a pictur-esque and eloquent speaker. As minister of education in Sir John Downer's [q.v.] min-istry in 1885-87, he was mainly responsible for the inauguration of arbor day. He also established an inquiry to report on the best means of developing technical education. Although he lost his seat at the 1887 election, he won Mount Barker, which he represented until his retirement.

In 1888 Cockburn was appointed chair-man of the council of the new School of Mines and Industries but he resigned when it opened in June 1889. In the same month the Thomas Playford [q.v.] government was defeated and Cockburn formed a ministry as chief secretary. In August next year Playford successfully moved a motion of no-confidence, Cockburn was again chief secretary in F. W. Holder's [q.v.] ministry, June-October 1892. He was one of three former premiers in the cabinet of C. C. Kingston [q.v.], formed in June 1893, and he remained as minister of education and agriculture until he resigned in April 1898 to become agent-general in London.

An advanced liberal, Cockburn was held by his critics to be an impractical visionary, easily swayed by the writings of reformers such as Henry George [q.v.4] and Edward Bellamy. His intellectual eclecticism was paralleled in practical politics by frequent changes of mind; he was not a strong leader in an era of faction politics. Nevertheless Cockburn initiated a number of notable pieces of reform legislation. He was active in the struggle to secure payment for members of parliament, and he helped to change Kingston's mind on adult suffrage. He also introduced unsuccessfully a bill for a pro-gressive land tax.

Cockburn was an ardent Federationist, representing South Australia at the 1890 conference, and the 1891 and 1897-98 con-ventions. He was also the only notable South Australian to attend the unofficial People's Federal Convention at Bathurst in 1896. At these conferences he supported moves for a more democratic constitution. At the same time he wanted a strong Senate, basing his case on 'State rights' – his decentralist sen-timents were declared at Sydney in 1891: 'Government at a central and distant point can never be government by the people'. He and Kingston were the only two delegates in 1891 to support Sir George Grey's [q.v.1] proposal that the governor-general and the State governors should be elected by the people. Cockburn argued the governor-general would be a dummy and the office useless; many other delegates believed that an elective governor-general would have pretensions to real authority. A collection of his articles and speeches was published in *Australian Federation* (London, 1901), dedicated to his close friend, Sir J. Langdon Bonython [q.v.7].

Fears were expressed when Cockburn was appointed agent-general in 1898. The con-servative *Register* wrote that 'the Doctor of Fanciful Notions would be more congenially employed in a library studying mystical lore and in resurrecting impracticable political schemes from "Plutarch's Lives"' than in directing the commercial and financial operations of the government in London. The outgoing incumbent of the office, Thomas Playford, in a letter to the under-treasurer Thomas Gill, pointed out Cockburn's lack of knowledge of finance but felt that 'if he holds his tongue and refrains from gassing upon socialistic fads he may do well'. As it turned out, Cockburn was a successful agent-general until 1901; he never missed an opportunity of advertising the State and its products.

He was appointed K.C.M.G. in 1900. Pat-rick McMahon Glynn [q.v.] noted with dis-belief in his diary that 'Mr. Cockburn, the political mystic and interpreter of the democratic spirit as understood by himself, the paper-disciple of Rousseau, the chief South Australian exponent of philosophic equality and scientific methods of social progress – has been made *a Knight*'. In 1901 Cockburn was appointed knight of grace of the Order of St John of Jerusalem. That year he hoped to enter Federal politics, but his friends failed to nominate him in time. Shortly afterwards he was placed in an em-barrassing position by the government of J. G. Jenkins [q.v.], which wished to down-grade the agent-generalship to that of a State agent, at a reduced salary. Cockburn's term of office was not extended, as had previously been the case, and his retirement reflected rather poorly on his former political col-leagues. The *Critic* commented sourly that electors 'would hardly recognise their old friend with the ultra-radical views . . . [who]

Cockburn

A.D.B.

dressed "carelessly", wore his hair long like the typical anarchist of the papers illustrated, [but is] now immaculately frocked and has somewhat changed his views'.

Cockburn remained in England for the rest of his life as a sort of unofficial ambassador for South Australia, many of whose citizens he entertained at Dean's Hill, Harrietsham, Kent. He made an unsuccessful attempt to enter the House of Commons at a by-election for West Monmouthshire in November 1904, standing as an Independent Tariff Reformer supported by Joseph Chamberlain and the local Conservatives; however, he had nothing else in common with them. He held directorships of the English, Scottish & Australian Bank, the Mount Lyell Mining and Railway Co. Ltd, the Australian Mutual Provident Society, and the Central Insurance Co. He also became chairman of the Australasian Chamber of Commerce in London, the Nature Study Association and the Swanley Horticultural College, and was vice-chairman of the court of governors of the London School of Economics and Political Science. Cockburn was president of the Entente Cordiale Society, the National Association of Manual Training Teachers, the London branch of the Child-Study Society, the Men's International Alliance for Woman Suffrage, and the International Philological Society, and a vice-president of the Royal Colonial Institute. He was also a member of the council of King's College, University of London, from 1900. In addition, he did prominent work for the London County Council on elementary education, and was a prolific writer on Australian, Imperial and educational topics. Greatly interested in freemasonry, he had been deputy grand master in South Australia, and in England he became president of both the International Masonic Club and the Society for Masonic Study, and wrote extensively on the symbolism of freemasonry.

Cockburn was a short and handsome man. His obituary in *The Times* described him as 'stamped with the zeal and courtesy of a past generation'. He was proud of his extensive library, and bookbinding was one of his hobbies. He died in London, at King's College Hospital, on 26 November 1929, survived by his wife Sarah Holdway (d. 1931), née Brown, whom he had married in 1875, and by a son and a daughter. His estate was valued for probate at £20442. A bust in bronze by Alfred Drury is in the possession of the Art Gallery of South Australia.

A. Deakin, *The federal story,* J. A. La Nauze ed (Melb, 1963); N. Robinson, *Change on change* (Leabrook, 1971); *British A'sian,* 9 Mar 1899; *Critic* (Adel), 4 Jan 1902; *Freemason* (Lond), 30 Nov 1929; *Observer* (Adel), 10 Dec 1904; *The Times,* 27 Nov 1929; *Advertiser* (Adel), and *Register* (Adel), 28 Nov 1929; *Recorder* (Port Pirie), 30 Nov 1929.

JOHN PLAYFORD

COCKERILL, GEORGE (1871-1943), journalist and author, was born on 13 July 1871 at Bendigo, Victoria, son of George Cockerill, a miner from Northamptonshire, England, and his Irish-born wife Mary, née Vance. He was educated at Specimen Hill State School and Bendigo Corporate High School. At 15 he began a five-year apprenticeship to the *Bendigo Independent* and studied at the Bendigo School of Mines. He gained promotion as chief reporter of the *Independent* and conducted a Saturday coaching school. Meticulous reporting of the Amalgamated Miners' Association conference at Creswick in 1893 led to his appointment later that year as chief of staff of the *Ballarat Star*. He studied further at the Ballarat School of Mines, then in 1898 accepted an invitation to join the Melbourne *Age* staff under David Syme [q.v.6]. Strong in support of Syme's protectionist policies, Cockerill emerged as a specialist writer on national needs and problems and a staunch protagonist for the development of a national sentiment.

As *Age* special representative in the thick of the Federation campaigns, Cockerill became privy to many political secrets. Politicians such as Barton [q.v.7], Deakin, Hughes, Lyne, Reid, Fisher and King O'Malley [qq.v.] knew him as 'The Thunderer'. In 1910 (Sir) Geoffrey Syme [q.v.] appointed him chief of staff of the *Age*, and in January 1914 editor G. F. H. Schuler [q.v.] made him chief leader-writer. In this position he brilliantly delivered trenchant judgment on public affairs. For fifteen years from 1912 he served on the board of examiners for licensed shorthand writers. At one time he edited the Empire Press Union's Australian letter.

In 1926 Cockerill left the *Age* to become editor-in-chief of the Sydney *Daily Telegraph*. When it became a pictorial he returned to Melbourne in 1928 and joined the Development and Migration Commission as editor of reports and chief of publicity. Next year he became leader-writer for the Melbourne *Herald*. After a heart attack in 1939, he retired to live at Abbotsford.

A tall, fresh-faced man, in his youth Cockerill enjoyed football, cricket, boxing, wrestling, rowing and running; in later life he became an ardent bushwalker and chess-player. A lover of Australian art and literature, he was a member of the Bread and Cheese Club (founded 1938). At St Kilian's Catholic Church, Bendigo, on 12 September 1893, he had married Mary Ellen

44

O'Halloran, daughter of a contractor; they had three sons and two daughters. He died in hospital at East Melbourne on 2 June 1943 and was buried in Melbourne general cemetery. He was predeceased by a son and a daughter.

Author of numerous pamphlets, Cockerill also wrote *Building the Commonwealth; the Australian policy* (Sydney, 1948), but died before completing 'Study of the growth of Australian manhood'. Historical novels included *Down and out: a story of Australia's early history* (1912), *The convict pugilist* (1912) and *In days of gold: a romance of the 'fifties* (1926). Memories of his youth on the goldfields found expression in the humorous tales of Cornish miners published in the *Age* Literary Supplement. Using a slight veneer of fiction, he wrote his memoirs, *Scribblers and statesmen* (1944).

H. W. Malloch, *Fellows all* (Melb, 1943); R. Bridges, *That yesterday was home* (Syd, 1948); *Newspaper News*, 1 Nov 1929; *Herald* (Melb), 4 June 1943; *Age*, and *Argus*, 5 June 1943.

L. J. BLAKE

COCKRAM, THOMAS (1831-1912) and his son THOMAS (1860-1920) were builders. Thomas senior was born on 10 April 1831 either at Derby or at Biddulph, Staffordshire, England, son of Thomas Cockram, carpenter, and his wife Phoebe May. Trained as a bricklayer, he came to Victoria in 1853 and for some years worked at his trade in Melbourne. He supported the eight-hour movement and marched on 21 April 1856 to celebrate the establishment of the eight-hour day; his name is one of the fifty-two enshrined in the Melbourne Trades Hall as pioneers of the movement. On 22 July 1858 at North Melbourne he married, with Wesleyan forms, Ann Walsh from Cork, Ireland; they had two sons and three daughters.

In 1861 Cockram began contracting on his own account and by 1867 had opened a builder's office in North Melbourne. His earliest jobs were for schools: among those still standing are the Brighton school (1875) for leading architects L. Terry [q.v.6] and Oakden, and the Faraday Street school (1876) for J. Reed [q.v.6] and Barnes. In the boom of the 1880s his business grew; in 1883 he successfully tendered for the 320-room Grand Hotel (later the Windsor) in Spring Street, designed by C. Webb [q.v.6] and in 1888 for the equally grand Federal Coffee Palace (demolished 1972) for William Pitt [q.v.]. In 1886, also for Pitt, he had built the Princess Theatre in Spring Street. As Melbourne's boom subsided, a last impressive contract in 1892 was for the Head Fire Station on Eastern Hill. All but the first named of these surviving buildings now hold National Trust classifications.

Thomas junior, born on 6 February 1860 at Bendigo Street, North Melbourne, was trained as a bricklayer and worked with his father. In 1896 Thomas Cockram and Son were the successful tenderer for the nave of the Cathedral of the Sacred Heart in Bendigo, but the completion of the first section was greatly impeded by problems arising from the quality of the stone. By 1904 Thomas junior was tendering under his own name but he was faced with lean decades with few large contracts offering. He had married first at Parkville on 3 November 1886 with Bible Christian forms, Eleanor Byford (d. 1892), and second at St Mary's Catholic Church, St Kilda, on 12 September 1893, Mary Laurent, daughter of a French college professor.

Despite the depletion of Cockram resources, the standing of both father and son remained high. In 1896 the elder had been elected president of the Master Builders' Association of Victoria and in 1899 the younger was elected to the office. Thomas senior died on 7 April 1912 at his home in Brighton, predeceased by his wife and a son, and was buried in Melbourne general cemetery. Thomas junior died of cancer in hospital at Brighton on 2 June 1920, survived by his wife, a son of his first marriage and four sons and a daughter of his second. He was buried in Booroondara cemetery, Kew.

A. Sutherland et al, *Victoria and its metropolis*, 2 (Melb, 1888), M. T. Shaw, *Builders of Melbourne* (Melb, 1972), and for bibliog.

MARY TURNER SHAW

COCKS, SIR ARTHUR ALFRED CLEMENT (1862-1943), merchant and politician, was born on 27 May 1862 at Wild Duck Creek, Heathcote, Victoria, fourth son of English parents Thomas Cocks, farmer, and his wife Elizabeth, née Adams. About 1873 his father moved to Melbourne and set up as a hosier and tailor. Arthur was educated at a state school at Richmond and started work at 14 in a softgoods warehouse. About 1880 he joined W. Wood & Co., wholesale opticians, and became a commercial traveller. On 17 September 1884 at Richmond he married Elizabeth Agnes Gibb. In 1886 he was sent to Sydney to establish a branch of the firm. He gradually gained financial control and in 1899 registered his own firm, Arthur Cocks & Co., wholesale jewellers and opticians; he remained managing director until 1939. In 1911 the company was reconstructed and by

1914 he had set up branches in Melbourne, Adelaide and Brisbane.

Cocks became active in commercial circles. He was a trustee of the Savings Bank of New South Wales and was a director of the City Bank of Sydney, Arthur Rickard [q.v.] & Co. (Extended) Ltd, and the Australian Alliance Assurance Co. He also invested in the film industry and was a director of Spencer's Pictures Ltd, Australasian Films Ltd, the General Film Co. of Australia Ltd and Union Theatres Ltd. In 1916-18 Cocks was president of the Sydney Chamber of Commerce. Several times chairman of the Importers' Association of New South Wales, in 1940 he was first president of the new Wholesale Importers' Association. He contributed to the standardization of optometry in New South Wales.

Cocks had represented Lang Ward on the Sydney Municipal Council in 1906-14 and was lord mayor in 1913; he was vice-president of its electric light committee in 1909-14. In 1911, with Sir William McMillan and (Sir) Thomas Henley [qq.v.], he started litigation, which went to the Privy Council in 1915, to force the State government to use Government House only as the residence of the governor. He chaired the 1913 royal commission of inquiry into the question of a greater Sydney, which proposed the creation of inner and outer zones. He was founding president in 1921 of the Citizens' Reform Association.

Cocks was elected as a Liberal to the Legislative Assembly, for St Leonards, in October 1910 and held the seat as a Nationalist from 1917 until 1920; in 1920-25 he was a member for North Sydney. In the House he showed particular interest in the development of Sydney and the growth of its industry and commerce. On 20 December 1921 he was treasurer in Sir George Fuller's [q.v.] seven-hour ministry. He held the same portfolio in Fuller's coalition ministry from 13 April 1922. Faced with a deficit, Cocks preached economy and recommended that cabinet should enforce the Board of Trade's decision to reduce public servants' wages by 3s. By a tax agreement with the Commonwealth government he abolished duplication of income tax returns. He produced small surpluses in his two budgets, despite reducing income tax (from 1s. 3d. to 9d.) as well as other taxes. He also negotiated loans for the State in London. In 1924 he ordered (Sir) Bertram Stevens and John Spence [qq.v.], Public Service Board inspectors, to reorganize the Government Printing Office; some employees were retrenched or demoted and both inspectors promoted.

From early 1923 Cocks had hinted he would not stand at the next election. He was appointed K.B.E. in June and next year there was speculation about his possible nomination to the Legislative Council, but he resigned on 14 February 1925 and became agent-general in London. Melbourne *Punch*, 5 February 1925, approved of his appointment because 'this large, silent, slow-moving man, with the dim eyes, the big head, and the poker face leaves nothing whatever to chance'. While in London he was executive commissioner at the British Empire Exhibition. Cocks resigned on 17 September, after J. T. Lang [q.v.], premier from June, had attacked him in the House. Lang later alleged that as treasurer Cocks 'had faked the public accounts'. On his return to Australia in December, Sir Arthur expressed his disgust with public life; in the early 1930s he praised the New Guard.

A leading Congregational layman, deacon, lay preacher and Sunday school superintendent, Cocks consistently contributed to charities. He was a director of the Benevolent Society of New South Wales in 1913-19, a member of the board of the Carrington Centennial Hospital for Convalescents, Camden, and president of the Young Men's Christian Association in 1924-34. His appeals for film censorship and temperance seemed incongruous with his film interests and persistent cigar-smoking habits. He lent members of his staff the money to buy their houses and during the Depression often called at needy homes with boxes of groceries.

Cocks was very much a family man. He enjoyed tennis and auction bridge and was a member of the New South Wales Club. Afflicted by blindness and bronchitis, he died at Mosman on 25 April 1943 and was buried in the Congregational section of Northern Suburbs cemetery. He was predeceased by his wife, son and daughter. His estate was valued for probate at £42 908.

J. T. Lang, *I remember* (Syd, 1956); *NSW Law Reports*, 13 (1913), 295; *Cwlth Law Reports*, 16 (1914), 404; *Attorney-General for NSW* v. *J. L. Williams, Law Reports, Appeal Cases* (HL and PC), 1915; *SMH*, 2 June 1923, 17 Feb 1925, 26 Apr 1943; Carruthers papers (ML); YMCA, Minutes, 81st annual business meeting 1935 (Syd); news-cuttings, vol 157, 18-27 (ML).   GRETA GERATHY

COCKS, FANNY KATE BOADICEA (1875-1954), policewoman and welfare worker, was born on 5 May 1875 at Moonta, South Australia, eldest child of Anthony Cocks, a Cornish miner, and his wife Elizabeth, née George, a schoolteacher. In 1885 the family moved to a farm near Quorn and Kate was educated at home; she taught for a year at Thomas Plains in 1900 and next year became schoolmistress and sub-matron at the Industrial School, Edwardstown.

In 1903 she entered the State Children's Council as a clerk where she was influenced by Catherine Helen Spence [q.v.6.]. In 1906, anxious to prove that women could deal with vagrant boys, Cocks was appointed as the State's first probation officer for juvenile first offenders. The job took her into the slums; she decided that prevention was better than prosecution and her work lessened the number of children on parole who were placed in institutions.

In December 1915 Cocks was appointed as the State's first woman police constable, concerned with female offences in the areas of adolescent sexuality and alcoholism, and the enticing for brothels of girls newly arrived from the country and overseas. She worked easily with male colleagues, and won respect and obedience from juniors in the women's branch which she headed. She combined stern efficiency with generous advice and help to needy women. Her originality, insight and kindness, especially in the Depression, led to a wealth of legends. Moral but not censorious, she never used a revolver or baton. She saw the equality of the sexes as 'a just conclusion', but believed in the sacredness of child-rearing. Her staff had to take a first-aid course which emphasized maternity care. Although slight and spare she was proficient in ju-jitsu, and once helped a woman whose husband was beating her, by tutoring her in self-defence.

In 1935 Cocks retired to nurse her dying mother and, already a justice of the peace, was appointed M.B.E. Before resigning she had cared for homeless girls in her house. In April her speech on the problem persuaded the Methodist Women's Home Mission Association to rent a cottage behind her home. That year she became voluntary superintendent of the Methodist Women's Welfare Department and served till 1951. In 1936 a property at Brighton was bought as a refuge for unmarried girls and their newly born babies and other infants needing care. Cocks found fulfilment in this work, moving to Brighton in 1937 to superintend the home. She gave and demanded much and restored people's self-esteem, but her intellectual and organizational ability is often obscured by stories of her kindness and strong religious faith. She died on 20 August 1954 and was buried in Payneham cemetery. Her home and estate, which was valued for probate at £3344, were left to her Church and the Methodist Homes for Babies, later renamed the Kate Cocks Babies' Home.

C. Owings, *Women police* (New York, 1925); L. Brown et al (eds), *A book of South Australia* (Adel, 1936); E. Abbott, *Everybody's friend* (Adel, 1939); *PP* (SA), 1916 (88), 1924 (53), 1935 (53); *Women's World*, 1 May 1925; *Advertiser* (Adel), 3 June 1935, 21 Aug 1954; *Aust Christian Cwlth*, 16 Aug 1935; *SA Methodist*, 9 June 1950, 14 Dec 1951; Brighton Babies Home (MS, Central Methodist Mission, Adel); C. Shapley, Miss Kate Cocks – her life and work (1964, SLSA); Police dockets 489, 788/1915 (Police Hist Soc, Adel); file 313 66/2, *and* GRG 18-90, 27-464 (SAA). MARIE MUNE

COCKS, NICHOLAS JOHN (1867-1925), Congregational minister, was born on 29 March 1867 in Brisbane, son of Cornish parents Nicholas Cock, labourer and later farmer, and his wife Elizabeth Ann, née Crago. His family probably moved to South Australia in the 1870s; he attended Prince Alfred College, Adelaide, in 1880-82 and later wrote the school song. He worked in an office but came under the influence of J. C. Kirby [q.v.5], who suggested he become a minister. From 1886 Cocks trained at Camden College, Sydney, and also attended the University of Sydney (B.A., 1890). In 1892 he graduated M.A. with the gold medal in logic and mental philosophy. Pastor at Kogarah in 1892-1901, he delivered the Livingstone Lectures at Camden College in 1892 and published them as the *Growth of the conception of natural law* (1893). He was chairman of the Congregational Union of New South Wales in 1899-1900; and tutored at Camden College until about 1910. On 13 June 1894 in Sydney he married Elizabeth Arrabella Proctor.

Cocks served in 1901-07 at North Sydney, where he continued to live; from 1907 to 1924 he was minister of the Pitt Street Congregational Church. He was again chairman of the Congregational Union in 1917-18. During World War I Cocks held widely attended united intercessory services at Pitt Street. His sensitive and imaginative preaching commended him as a personal counsellor to many intelligent seekers. He was concerned to relate idealist philosophy to the central affirmations of Christianity and to come to grips with psychology and post-Darwinian thought. His strength lay in the quality of his mind and his understanding of people in doubt and distress, but was a relatively poor administrator and organizer.

As chairman of the Christian union committee of the Congregational Union and of the Student Christian Movement's graduates' auxiliary, he was an early worker for church union between Congregationalists, Methodists, and Presbyterians. Cocks visited England in 1911 and met the philosophers Hastings Rashdall, A. L. Smith, and Friederich von Hügel who became his friend. As theologian he was Christocentric, but drawn toward mystical awareness of the relation between time and eternity. His numerous hymns and lyric poetry blended a love of Australian landscape and atmosphere with insight into the longings of ordinary men and women. His skill in music, mathematics, water-colour painting and chess brought him in touch with Sydney's intellectual and artistic life; during his ministry at Pitt Street, the church's fine organ was built. His books of verse include *Songs of the Dardanelles* (1915), the *Betty songs* (1920), *Australian songs and other poems* (1925).

Cocks died of cancer on 21 January 1925 in St Luke's Hospital, Darlinghurst, and was buried in Northern Suburbs cemetery. He was survived by his wife and by their two sons and two daughters. His estate was sworn for probate at £508.

J. A. Garrett and L. W. Farr, *Camden College, a centenary history* (Syd, 1964); Congregational Union of NSW, *Year Book*, 1892-1926; *Congregationalist* (Syd), 10 Feb, 10 Apr 1925; *Prince Alfred College Chronicle*, May 1925; *SMH*, 21, 23 Jan 1925; ML cats.   JOHN GARRETT

CODE, EDWARD PERCIVAL (1888-1953), musician, was born on 3 July 1888 at South Melbourne, son of Edward Thomas Code, picture-frame maker and bandmaster, and his wife Mary Ann, née Payne, both from Bendigo. His father, a trumpeter, conducted Code's Melbourne Brass Band from 1892; it was a frequent winner of competitions and won the championship of Australia in 1898-1900. The family included other bandsmen. Taught to play violin and cornet by his father, Percy won numerous cornet competitions while attending school at Faraday Street, Carlton. Following his win at the South Street competition, Ballarat, in 1910, he was invited to join the visiting English Besses o' th' Barn Band. Leaving Australia early in 1911 he studied with bandmaster Alec Owen, won the gold medal of the London College of Music and played as a soloist with the band on a world tour. Returning to Australia, he settled in Ballarat as a choir and band conductor and music teacher. On 23 March 1915 at Lydiard Street Methodist Church, he married Elsie Maude Miller; they had no children and lived apart from about 1930.

In 1921 Code went to the United States of America and played with the San Francisco Symphony Orchestra under Alfred Hertz in its 1922-23 season. He returned to Melbourne in 1924 and moved into radio work with station 3AR, also playing in theatre orchestras. In July 1929 he became principal conductor for the new Australian Broadcasting Co. When the Australian Broadcasting Commision replaced the company in 1932, he remained in command of the new and larger orchestra.

Senior conductor for the A.B.C., Code was transferred to Sydney in October 1936 and trained its orchestra for a demanding series of celebrity seasons; he also conducted broadcast operas and travelled extensively within Australia. Much of his work was hampered by World War II. In April 1947 he exchanged positions with Joseph Post and spent his last active years in Melbourne. He retired sick in November 1951 and died of cardiovascular disease on 16 October 1953. He was buried in Box Hill cemetery with Methodist forms. His estate was valued for probate at £11 333.

Short, solid and somewhat colourless, Code was modest, and very popular with his players, although there were complaints about his difficult beat and his tendency to stamp when emphasizing time. Nobody saw him as a great conductor but he was a master tradesman. He was devoted to the works of Elgar — his most notable performance was of the symphonic study, *Falstaff*, in Sydney on 21 June 1941. He published *Allan's modern method for cornet or trumpet* in 1936 and most of his many compositions for bands and solo brass are still well known.

G. W. Davey and A. E. Warne, *Memoirs: Edward Thomas Code* (np, nd); *Wireless Weekly*, 9 Oct 1931, 19 Apr 1941; *Aust Musical News and Musical Digest*, 9 Jan 1952, 2 Nov 1957; *Tempo* (Syd), Nov 1957; *Table Talk*, 5 Sept 1929; information from Miss M. Hetherington, East Malvern, Vic, and Mr R. Wood, Mittagong, NSW.   H. J. GIBBNEY

COGHLAN, SIR TIMOTHY AUGUSTINE (1855-1926), statistician and public servant, was born on 9 June 1855 in Sydney, second son of Irish parents Thomas Coghlan, plasterer, and his wife Dorcas, née Jordan. He was educated at the Cleveland Street Public School, and in 1867-69 at Sydney Grammar School on a scholarship. For six months in 1870 he worked in the woolbroking office of Edward Flood [q.v.4]. In October he became a pupil-teacher at Fort Street Public School, but resigned in December 1872; in April next year he joined the harbours and rivers navigation branch of the Department of Public Works as a cadet. Favoured by his supervisors, he advanced rapidly, becoming an assistant engineer on 1 January 1884 at £400 a year. The statistical and mathematical aspects of the work attracted him most. He became an associate member of the Institution of Civil Engineers, London, in 1882, but he did not regard engineering as suitable to his talents and ambition.

In 1886 Coghlan sought the patronage of (Sir) George Dibbs [q.v.4] to obtain the new position of government statistician. His appointment in July prompted some hostile comment, and the employment of a staff of twelve created dissension and caused Dibbs's temporary resignation from the Jennings [q.v.4] ministry. The controversy hampered Coghlan's work during the first six months. Nevertheless, that year he produced both the *New South Wales statistical register* for 1885 and a new companion *Handbook to the statistical register*. The former differed little from earlier issues, but the *Handbook* foreshadowed his initiatives in the elaboration and explanation of traditional statistics. The extent of these changes became clear with the issue of the first year-book, the *Wealth and progress of New South Wales*, in December 1887, which revealed his ability to aggrandize New South Wales through statistics, especially in comparison with Victoria. The publications also disclosed his theories about population growth as the reflection of prosperity and the influence of economic factors upon populations – both remained consistent elements in his statistical, social and historical commentaries.

From 1888 Coghlan diversified and expanded the work of his office and his own role. His personal ambition and emphasis on the progress of New South Wales as based on free trade, generated some criticism of his work, especially from protectionists. Nevertheless, he earned an enviable Australian and international reputation, indicated by the reception of the census of 1891, in which the new classification of occupations devised by Coghlan and the Tasmanian statistician, R. M. Johnston [q.v.], was adopted against the opposition of H. H. Hayter [q.v.4]. His work attracted the attention of Mulhall in Ireland, and Giffen in England, and he became a fellow of the Royal Statistical Society, London, in 1893.

In 1887 and 1890 Coghlan was consulted about direct taxation proposals and bills relating to banking and finance companies. Later in the 1890s successive governments sought his aid in electoral reform and in local government schemes. He co-operated often beyond the provision of statistics; he was involved in Dibbs's legislation to meet the 1893 banking crisis, and in (Sir) George Reid's [q.v.] 1894-95 land and income tax proposals. He claimed to be the principal architect of the important Public Service Act of 1895, and in January 1896 he became one of the first members of the Public Service Board, securing a reputation for fairness and efficiency, despite criticism of retrenchments. He was also adviser on the administration of the land tax and shared in its general unpopularity. In 1892-1905 he was registrar of Friendly Societies, and in 1900-05 chairman of the Central Board for Old-Age Pensions; he was involved in several inquiries, including royal commissions into the management of the Metropolitan Water Supply and Sewerage Board (1897), on the decline of the birth rate and on the mortality of infants (1903) and on electoral districts (1904).

Coghlan contributed substantially to the public debate on the financial aspects of Federation. His insistence on safeguards for New South Wales influenced Reid and (Sir) William McMillan [q.v.], and other members of the National Australasian Convention; but it alienated some 'ultra' Federationists – such as B. R. Wise [q.v.] – who favoured free trade, but were willing to 'sink the fiscal issue' if that would achieve Federation. Coghlan declined further public debate after Reid's declaration for Federation in March 1898; but the 'ultras' believed that his influence had helped in the defeat of the first Constitution referendum in New South Wales in 1898, and that Reid's reliance upon his advice at the premiers' meeting in January 1899 forced further concessions to New South Wales.

When Wise became attorney-general in 1899 he asked Coghlan to relinquish one of his two main offices. He responded rashly, offering his complete resignation and then refusing to indicate which position he would quit. As a result he did not resume duty as statistician until 8 January 1900. Despite the bitter controversies, new editions of his *Wealth and progress* and his *Statistical account of the seven colonies of Australia* were warmly received in London and Australia; he dominated the Conference of Statisticians held in Hobart in June 1902; and his efforts to co-ordinate the methods of compilation in all States were at least partially successful. In 1903 Sir Edmund Barton [q.v.7] invited his comments on the proposed Federal bureau of statistics, and from October 1904 he was importuned to become Federal statistician; he finally refused in December 1905. His reasons for the rejection are still obscure, but he implied later that the State government had threatened to withdraw his pension rights if he transferred to the Commonwealth, and that he sorely regretted the loss of the Federal position.

In October 1904 (Sir) Joseph Carruthers' [q.v.7] Liberal government took office and invited Coghlan in vain to become comptroller of finance. In December the premier commissioned him to reorganize the New South Wales agent-general's office in London. Coghlan's decision to accept an acting appointment as agent-general in 1905 (confirmed next year) may have been influenced by his personal ambitions in another direction. He had been in London in 1897 as a delegate to the Diamond Jubilee,

and had been received into London society.
There is some suggestion that his wife
Helena (Lena) Mary, née Donnelly, whom he
had married at St Patrick's Church, Sydney,
on 27 April that year, found the social life
congenial. During the 1897 visit Coghlan
had investigated the agent-general's office
on behalf of the Public Service Board and
recommended changes. He had developed
an interest and expertise in finance and was
attracted to London as the great money
market. He envisaged some responsible position in London for himself and was
tempted to covet the post of high commissioner for Australia. As he had predicted in
1905, however, that position became political and he was never to achieve it or any
other Federal office he sought later.

Unlike his work as government statistician, Coghlan's service as agent-general
secured him little lasting fame. The position
allowed him much latitude; he soon secured
the co-operation of the States' agents-
general, became their unofficial spokesman
and played aggressively the role of general
Australian representative. His ambition was
encouraged, intentionally or otherwise, by
Alfred Deakin [q.v.] who asked his advice
on several problems including migration,
advertising Australia and the role of the
high commissioner. He was not a success in
diplomacy, partly because of his own inexperience and partly because of weaknesses
in the New South Wales government,
compounded by friction between it and
the Federal authorities. Coghlan vigorously promoted emigration and, while his
methods were not universally approved,
his efforts did coincide with a marked
increase in migration from Great Britain to
New South Wales between 1905 and 1911. He,
was embittered in 1912 when control of the
immigration branch was put in other
hands without acknowledgment of his
efforts.

Coghlan's principal achievements were in
finance. In 1897 he had advocated inscription of the State's stock at the agent-
general's office, rather than by the Bank of
England, and he continued to press for it. He
tried to reduce the various loan charges
imposed on New South Wales by the banks
and to increase the interest given upon
short-term deposits. In 1906 he at last persuaded the treasurer to issue new stock
through the London County and Westminster Bank, which offered better terms than
the Bank of England. In 1908 on his own
authority he used the Deutsche Bank, which
offered higher interest than the London
County and Westminster. Many of his initiatives were nullified, either by the New
South Wales government or by vested
interests in London. Practically, his policies

were sound, but his single-minded pursuit of
the best deal alienated some London
financiers, and his individualism upset his
own government.

Coghlan attracted suspicion that he might
be benefiting personally, at least indirectly,
from some of his dealings. Friendship with
various brokers influenced his advocacy of
particular banks; his relations with Krupps
and expectation of a directorship on the
board of Siemens Bros & Co. Ltd were not
unrelated to his recommendations of steel
purchases from Germany. Coghlan and Raphael Bauer, broker for the London City and
Midland Bank, probably profited from the
1916 contract between the New South Wales
government and Norton Griffiths & Co.
which Coghlan had urged from 1912. Such
associations were at least ethically dubious.

Coghlan's pursuit of his own interests,
especially from 1910, is understandable. His
tenure was renewed for a succession of short
periods with little regard for his dignity or
long service — succeeded by B. R. Wise in
1915, he was acting agent-general again in
1916-17 and from 1920 (except for six months
in 1925). He showed little enthusiasm for his
official duties and sought directorships or
other positions. His ambition, zeal for secret
negotiations and self-esteem were not dead
and he intervened in the constitutional
struggle between the New South Wales
premier J. T. Lang and governor Sir Dudley
de Chair [qq.v.] in 1926, even daring to
believe that Lang would appoint him in de
Chair's place.

The lasting achievement of Coghlan's
years in London was a project begun while
government statistician — the monumental
Labour and industry in Australia, published
in 1918. This work was the culmination of his
long interest in literature, socio-political issues, statistics and finance, reflected from
1874 in his contributions to the Redfern
Literary Society manuscript magazine
'Phoenix', and pursued in articles written for
the *Suburban Times*, the *Bulletin*, the Sydney *Daily Telegraph*, his numerous official
publications and various monographs and
addresses to learned societies. His social
commentary was enriched and influenced
by his observations as government statistician and his experience as a public official.
His personal attitudes and the political
climate were demonstrated in the area of
demography — where he had publicized and
provoked public discussion about an apparent dramatic decline in the New South
Wales birth-rate — and in his views on fiscal
and financial policies. *Labour and industry
in Australia* reflects the themes developed
by him in the New South Wales year-books
and other publications from 1887; yet he also
presents a balanced view of both the specific

events and general developments in which he was intimately involved. Coghlan's was a complex character, sometimes defensive, often aggressive, but in the end — like his book — authoritative.

Coghlan was awarded the Imperial Service Order in 1903, knighted in 1914 and raised to K.C.M.G. in 1918. Survived by his wife, a son and a daughter, he died in London on 30 April 1926: a funeral service was held at St Mary's, Cadogan Street, and his remains are in a mausoleum at the Catholic cemetery, Kensal Green.

N. Hicks, *'This sin and scandal'* (Canb, 1978); J. M. Cordell, T. A. Coghlan, government statist of New South Wales 1886-1905 (1969, held by J. M. Cordell, Syd); Coghlan papers (NL).

NEVILLE HICKS

COHEN, FANNY (1887-1975), headmistress, was born on 9 June 1887 at Grafton, New South Wales, only daughter of Jewish parents Algernon Aaron Cohen, a native-born physician and surgeon, and his English wife Priscilla, née Cohen. Educated at Miss Emily Baxter's Argyle School in Sydney, she was taught Latin and mathematics as well as English, French, music and history. In 1904 she passed the senior public examination with first-class honours and medals for mathematics, algebra and French. At the University of Sydney she performed brilliantly, graduating B.A. in 1908 and B.Sc. in 1909 with first-class honours in mathematics and first-class honours with the university medal in geology.

In 1909-11 Fanny Cohen was a junior demonstrator in geology at the university and in 1911 won the Barker graduate scholarship. Her studies in mathematics at the University of Cambridge were cut short by the ill health of her mother, who had accompanied her to England. She returned to the University of Sydney and graduated M.A. in 1913 with a thesis on 'The application of spherical trigonometry to crystallography'.

Meanwhile in July 1912 Miss Cohen became assistant mistress of mathematics at Fort Street Girls' High School, Sydney. Although untrained as a teacher, she was strongly supported in her application by Professors Edgeworth David [q.v.] and Carslaw [q.v.7]; the latter wrote: 'I know of none of my women students who can compare with her as a suitable teacher of mathematics'. She was an immediate success and was promoted to mathematics mistress next year. In 1922 she was appointed deputy headmistress of North Sydney Girls' High School and next year head-

mistress of the Maitland West Girls' High School. Back in Sydney in 1926 as headmistress of St George Girls' High School, at the end of 1929 she returned to Fort Street as headmistress.

Miss Cohen was 'a teacher of exceptional ability, a highly efficient organizer and a strong disciplinarian'. Her striking personality and her educational ideals left an indelible impression on the members of staff and the thousands of girls who passed through the school. Tall, handsome with expressive brown eyes, charming manner and merry laugh, she was a dignified, self-confident, direct, frank and, at times, very determined woman. She was admired too for her modesty, fairness and impartiality. She had a genuine affection for her pupils, an understanding for their problems and a keen interest in their development. Her personal interest in the welfare of her staff inspired their co-operation and effort; although something of an autocrat, she delegated considerable responsibility and had confidence in their work; many went on to high positions.

Although Miss Cohen never gave detailed expression to her educational ideas, she left no doubt about the three main interrelated principles for which she stood: she emphasized the need to select the intellectual élite of students and to educate them in segregated schools; she held to the belief that 'girls of sufficient ability were capable of reaching the same high academic standards as boys and of entering the professions on an equal footing'; she advocated high standards of education and always admired excellence of performance. She had great expectations of her pupils and sternly reprimanded those who were slacking or whose behaviour was lax. She thought external examinations maintained standards, conveyed to employers an objective standard of the pupil's academic worth and encouraged students to strive harder.

In 1934-44 and in 1949-59 Miss Cohen was a fellow of the Senate of the University of Sydney, served on a number of its committees and represented it on the Women's College Council in 1936-44 and 1949-59, and was a director of the Sydney University Women's Union in 1953-59. In 1937-52 she represented the Secondary Teachers' Association of New South Wales on the Board of Secondary School Studies. In this capacity, as at Fort Street, she endeavoured to promote high standards.

Miss Cohen had a rather unusual range of outside interests: horse-racing and betting, contract bridge, theatre and ballet, motoring and travel. Soon after her retirement from Fort Street in 1952 she became active in the Royal Blind Society of New South Wales.

In 1955 she obtained a braille writer's certificate and for some years translated books, helped to produce a monthly magazine for the blind, and trained other people in braille transcription.

In 1962 Miss Cohen was appointed M.B.E. for services to education. She died on 21 August 1975 in St Vincent's Hospital, Sydney, and was cremated. She left the residue of her estate, valued for probate at $101 577 to a niece. Her portrait by W. A. Dargie is held at Fort Street Girls' High School, Petersham.

Fort Street Girls' High School Mag, 1949, 1952; NSW Board of Secondary School Studies, Minutes (ML); Fanny Cohen papers, *and* Senate minutes (Univ Syd Archives).   CLIFF TURNEY

COHEN, FRANCIS LYON (1862-1934), rabbi, was born on 14 November 1862 at Aldershot, Hampshire, England, eldest son of Woolf Henry Cohen, marine store dealer and later tobacco manufacturer, and his wife Harriett, née Phillips. Cohen was educated at Jews' College, London, from 1879 and attended lectures in arts at University College, London; in 1883 he passed the intermediate music examination of the University of London as a private student. He served as minister of Dublin Synagogue in 1885 and then of Borough (South London) Synagogue in 1886-1904. On 14 December 1886 at the Great Synagogue, London, he married Rose, daughter of Rev. Marcus Hast. An excellent musician, Cohen published a number of works on music including *The rise and development of Synagogue music* (1887) and *Traditional Hebrew melodies* (1896). In 1904 he was appointed chief minister of the Great Synagogue, Sydney. After obtaining his rabbinical diploma in London, he arrived in Sydney in 1905 with his family.

Rabbi Cohen was the first and, for most of his ministry, the only spiritual leader in Sydney with rabbinical qualifications. As head of the Beth Din (Jewish Religious Court) he made all the ecclesiastical decisions. Active in all facets of Jewish communal life, he was president of the New South Wales Board of Jewish Education, helped to found the New South Wales Jewish War Memorial, Darlinghurst, and to develop suburban synagogues. He also worked for such philanthropic institutions as the Chevra Kadisha, the Sir Moses Montefiore Jewish Home for the aged and the local branch of the Anglo-Jewish Association, and was also involved in the Jewish Literary and Debating Society of Sydney. In 1928 he published the *Jubilee history of the Great Synagogue, Sydney.* His qualities as a public speaker won him the admiration of the general community. He was an active Freemason.

Cohen emphasized synagogue dignity and decorum, and, to suit the Christian environment, he tried to modify Jewish observances with some practices unacceptable to more orthodox Jews. His sermons were considered very effective and were published on the front page of the weekly *Hebrew Standard of Australasia.* However he appeared to prefer well-established Anglo-Jews and his aloof manner alienated many migrants; his criticism of Zionism hindered its growth in New South Wales. Cohen contributed more to raising the status of Jews in the community than he did to increasing Jewish commitment.

His patriotism and love of English culture and the British Empire were a passion. Reared in the military atmosphere of Aldershot, Cohen had served as the first Jewish chaplain of the British Army (1892-1904), was a founder of the Jewish Lads' Brigade and in 1893 originated the annual military Chanukkah service. In Sydney he joined the Australian National Defence League. Appointed chaplain of the Australian Military Forces in 1909, during World War I he was a vice-president of the Universal Service League and campaigned for conscription. In 1929 he was awarded the Colonial Auxiliary Forces Officers' Decoration.

Cohen died of cancer in hospital at Potts Point on 26 April 1934 and was buried in Rookwood cemetery. His wife, who had been very active in communal and civic endeavours, died the same year. They were survived by a daughter, and by two sons who served overseas with the Australian Imperial Force. Cohen's portrait by Joseph Wolinski is held by the Great Synagogue.

I. Porush, *The house of Israel* (Melb, 1977); *Hebrew Standard of A'sia,* 18 Mar 1904, 16 June 1905, 10 Apr 1925, 4 May 1934; *SMH,* 27, 30 Apr 1934; S. D. Rutland, The Jewish community in New South Wales, 1914-1939 (M.A. thesis, Univ Syd, 1978); J. H. Watson scrap book, vol 1, 1904-05 (ML); minute-books 1904-34 (Great Synagogue office, Syd).
                                        SUZANNE D. RUTLAND

COHEN, GEORGE JUDAH (1842-1937), banker and financier, was born on 27 April 1842 in Sydney, eldest son of Samuel Cohen and his wife Rachel, née Nathan; both came from old-established Anglo-Jewish families. Samuel had migrated from London in the *Resource,* reaching Sydney on 19 April 1834, and, with his brother David and later his cousin Lewis Wolfe Levy [q.v.5], established the wholesale firm David Cohen & Co. in Sydney and Maitland in 1836; he represented Morpeth in the Legislative Assembly in 1860 and was a founder of the breakaway Macquarie Street Synagogue.

George was educated at Cleveland House under James Kean then at University College School, London, in 1857-60. He returned to Sydney in 1861, intending to study law; however after the death of his father on 4 November, he decided to enter the family business. After four years in Sydney, in 1865 he took charge of the firm's Maitland office. He was active in local affairs – chairman of the Maitland Gas Co., treasurer of the Northern Jockey Club, and helped the School of Arts, one of the finest in the colony. On 19 February 1868 in Sydney he married Rebecca (Rè) Levy (d. 1933), daughter of his father's partner, in the presence of (Sir) Saul Samuel and J. G. Raphael [qq.v.6]. With the coming of rail transport, he established a branch of the firm in Newcastle, but in 1879 moved back to Sydney.

Cohen was a financial wizard and an indefatigable worker. His acumen was soon recognized and in 1885 he succeeded his father-in-law as a director of the United Insurance Co. Ltd, the Australian Gas Light Co. and the Commercial Banking Co. of Sydney. As deputy chairman of the bank in 1891 and 1893-1901 and chairman in 1892-93 and 1901-33, he helped to guide it through the banking crisis of 1893 and the depressions of the 1890s and early 1930s; he celebrated fifty years as a director of the United Insurance Co. and was chairman in 1904-35; he was also chairman of the Australian Gas Light Co. in 1887-1932, Tooth & Co. Ltd in 1889-1929 and of the Sydney Exchange Co. (Royal Exchange of Sydney) almost continuously from 1887 to 1935. In 1912 David Cohen & Co. Ltd was registered as a public company.

At 'no time did get-rich-quick schemes' appeal to Cohen. If he had any vanity, it was for his good name in financial circles. He had a profound insight into the whole Australian economy – as early as 1903, whilst warning against excessive borrowing by State governments, he urged that all their debts should be taken over by the Commonwealth. Many inducements were offered to him to enter politics, but he dreaded the interference with the happiness of his family life, and his dislike of publicity was a byword in financial circles. In 1898 he refused a seat in the Legislative Council because the offer was conditional on his support of the Australasian Federation enabling bill. Nevertheless he supported such patriotic causes as the New South Wales contingents to the Sudan and South African wars, the Queen's Jubilee Fund in 1887 and World War I comforts funds; he also gave liberally and privately to charities.

In Maitland Cohen had been the leader of the small Jewish community. On his return to Sydney in 1861 he had joined the Macquarie Street Synagogue and in 1869 became a trustee. A Jewish patriarch, he soon became the acknowledged leader of the community after the two congregations had joined again in the Great Synagogue in 1878. During fifteen separate years between 1883 and 1921 he was president of its board of management and was made a life member of the board. He also held high office in such organizations as the New South Wales Board of Jewish Education, the Jewish Literary and Debating Society of Sydney and the local Anglo-Jewish Association. His wife was an active charity worker, especially for the Royal Alexandra Hospital for Children and the Infants' Home, Ashfield, and was a council-member of Women's College, University of Sydney. They celebrated their diamond wedding in 1928.

Cohen was a member of the Union Club from 1901, where his silk hat distinguished him from other members; he also enjoyed racing and was a member of the Australian Jockey Club. He furnished his house, Engadine, Elizabeth Bay, with antique furniture, European pictures and rare china and glass; one of his few hobbies was coin collecting.

Survived by five sons, including Sir Samuel Sydney Cohen [q.v.], and two daughters, Cohen died at Engadine on 22 January 1937 and was buried in the Jewish section of Rookwood cemetery. His estate was valued for probate at £510 910. After his death, his family gave his valuable collection of coins to the National Art Gallery of New South Wales and £1000 to the University of Sydney to provide for the George Judah Cohen Memorial Lectureship.

A portrait of him by George Lambert [q.v.] hangs in the head office of the Commercial Banking Co. of Sydney; two other portraits commissioned by the United Insurance Co. from R. H. Jerrold-Nathan are held by the Royal Exchange and Tooth & Co.

Cyclopedia of N.S.W. (Syd, 1907); Great Synagogue, Sydney, *Jubilee history* ... (Syd, 1928); *George Judah Cohen: a memoir* (Syd, priv print, nd); *SMH*, 25 Jan 1937; *Bulletin,* and *Sydney Mail,* 27 Jan 1937.   GEORGE F. J. BERGMAN*

COHEN, HAROLD EDWARD (1881-1946), soldier, lawyer, politician and businessman, was born on 25 November 1881 at St Kilda, Melbourne, only child of Montague Cohen [q.v.] and his wife Annie, née Cohen. He attended Xavier College, the first Jewish boy to do so. He completed the two-year articled clerks' course at the University of Melbourne in 1900, winning the Law and the

Bowen Essay prizes. In 1904 he gained the Supreme Court Prize and was admitted to legal practice in the family firm of Pavey, Wilson & Cohen. He gradually assumed duties in his father's business empire. On 4 December 1907 at the St Kilda Town Hall he married Freda, daughter of Samuel Pirani, a solicitor; they had four children.

In 1901 Cohen was commissioned in the Field Artillery Brigade, Australian Military Forces, and was promoted captain in 1905 and major in 1909. In 1915 he was appointed commanding officer of the 6th Army Brigade, Australian Field Artillery Regiment, Australian Imperial Force, with the rank of lieut-colonel, serving in the Middle East, England and France until June 1919. Twice wounded and twice mentioned in dispatches, he was awarded the Distinguished Service Order in 1917 and created C.M.G. in 1918.

After his return to Australia in September 1919, Cohen resumed practice in commercial and constitutional law, and became director of eight big companies in the brewing, paper and non-ferrous metals industries. He followed his father as president of the Liquor Trades' Defence Union and as chairman of directors of Swan Brewery Co. Ltd and the Carlton group. In 1929 he entered parliament as member for Melbourne South Province in the Legislative Council, and was minister without office in 1932-35 in the Argyle-Allan [qq.v.7] ministry. In March 1935, as United Australia Party candidate, he won the seat of Caulfield in the Legislative Assembly, and from 20 March to 2 April was minister of public instruction and solicitor-general. He was narrowly defeated in the election of June 1943.

Cohen continued his military involvement after 1919. In 1921-26 he commanded the 4th Divisional Artillery, A.M.F., and in 1926-27 the 2nd Infantry Brigade before transferring to the unattached list. In 1940-41 he went to the Middle East as honorary Red Cross commissioner. He became director of amenities, Land Headquarters, in July 1942 and was appointed adjutant-general in February 1943 with the rank of brigadier. Next year he was put on the reserve of officers with the rank of honorary brigadier.

Cohen was chief commissioner of the Boy Scouts' Association in 1922-25 and was its president for twenty years. He was first president of the Legacy Club of Melbourne in 1924, and in 1926 was president of the Melbourne Constitutional Club, and of Melbourne Rotary. He was chairman of the Jewish Returned and Ex-Servicemen's Association in 1937-46.

Cohen's rigorous Jesuit education and the tutelage of his father combined to produce a hard-working, thorough man, dedicated to duty as he saw it. His naturally romantic nature expressed itself in warm, informal, authoritarian leadership of fellow soldiers, co-workers and employees. While his frequent, highly articulate speeches in parliament revealed a distrust of 'socialist legislation', they combined legal knowledge with wide business experience. Military history was a hobby and he cultivated physical fitness. He represented Victoria at lacrosse, kept his horses in Malvern (he won the Caulfield Cup with Northwind in 1936) and played tennis and golf. The Harold and Freda Cohen prizes in education at the University of Melbourne were donated by him. He embodied many of the admirable qualities of the establishment Anglo-Jew, and made a contribution to his country which he considered with justification safeguarded and dignified the group from which he came.

On 29 October 1946 in South Melbourne Cohen died of a brain tumour; he was survived by his wife, two sons and two daughters. He was accorded a military funeral and was buried in Melbourne general cemetery.

L. J. Blake (ed), *Vision and realization* (Melb, 1973); G. Dening, *Xavier* (Melb, 1978); Aust Jewish Hist Soc, *J,* 2 (1944-48), pt 6; I. Anderson, 'The origin and growth of the Legacy movement in Australia', *VHM,* 38 (1967), no 3; *Punch* (Melb), 3 Nov 1921, 11 June 1925; *Age,* and *Argus,* 30, 31 Oct 1946; family and personal information.

BARBARA FALK

COHEN, ISAAC HENRY (1872-1942), barrister and politician, always known as Henry Isaac, was born on 21 February 1872 in Flinders Street, Melbourne, eighth child of David Cohen, outfitter and later financier, and his wife Rachael, née Marks, both of London. He attended St James' Grammar School, the Melbourne Hebrew School and, from 1885, Scotch College, where he was dux. A student of Ormond College, University of Melbourne, he graduated B.A. (1894) and LL.B. (1895) with honours, and was admitted to the Bar in April 1896. On 27 June 1901 at the Office of the Government Statist, Melbourne, he married Ethel Mary Keon of Launceston, Tasmania. Cohen retained Jewish associations but his wife was a Catholic; their three sons and two daughters, who adopted the name Keon-Cohen, were brought up as Anglicans and attended Presbyterian schools.

Cohen's career progressed slowly in the depressed 1890s: reputedly his one brief in his first two years netted him two guineas. He taught backward boys at night, mastered shorthand and became a court reporter.

However, after a widely reported case in 1906, he began to prosper, building up a large practice in all jurisdictions except the criminal. He became a King's Counsel in December 1920.

At a by-election in May 1921, Cohen succeeded Sir Henry Weedon [q.v.] as a Nationalist member of the Legislative Council for Melbourne Province. He held the seat until 1937 when redistribution made it a Labor stronghold. As the elected unofficial leader of the Legislative Council in 1922-23, 1924-28 and 1935-37, he examined and spoke on every bill before the chamber in what was ostensibly a house of review. He also held several ministries, mostly for very brief periods: he was an honorary minister from September 1923 to March 1924 in the Lawson [q.v.]-Allan [q.v.7] ministry; commissioner of public works, minister of mines and vice-president of the Board of Land and Works from March to April 1924 under Lawson. He held the same portfolios under (Sir) Alexander Peacock [q.v.] from April to July; he was also attorney-general and solicitor-general for one week in July. He was leader of the Legislative Council and minister of public instruction from November 1928 to December 1929 under Sir William McPherson [q.v.], and minister of water supply and in charge of electrical undertakings for a fortnight in March-April 1935 under (Sir) Stanley Argyle [q.v.7]. In 1937 he contested Higinbotham Province but lost to J. A. Kennedy.

Regarded as 'zealous and uncompromising' in considering the principles underlying proposed legislation, Cohen chaired the parliamentary select committee on racecourses and race meetings (1928) and in 1935 became first chairman of the parliamentary Public Works Committee. He was chairman of the Parliamentary Sports and Social Club in 1931-37.

Cohen was a trustee of the Melbourne Exhibition for twenty years from February 1922. Active in welfare movements during the Depression, he was a member of the Slum Abolition Council and the Big Brother Movement and was president of the Children's Welfare Association. He was widely read in the classics and mathematics, enjoyed music and followed sport avidly, particularly bowls, racing and golf. He was a foundation member of the Old Scotch Collegians' Club and was president of the Association in 1921-22. In the 1920s he held several company directorships. However, parliamentary service crippled his income at the Bar and prospects of judicial appointment, and he received no official recognition. Predeceased by his wife, he died at Armadale on 20 December 1942 and was cremated.

PD (Vic), 1942, p2324; *Punch* (Melb), 21 Apr 1921; *Table Talk*, 11 Apr 1929; *Herald* (Melb), 11 June 1937; *Age*, and *Argus*, 22 Dec 1942; S. Merrifield, Biog notes (Vic Parliamentary Lib).

BARRY O. JONES

COHEN, JOHN JACOB (1859-1939), architect, politician and judge, was born on 20 December 1859 at Grafton, New South Wales, third son of London-born parents Samuel Cohen, storekeeper and pioneer in the Clarence River district, and his wife Rosetta, née Menser. Aged 11 he would rise at 3 a.m., row his father and a heavy set of scales several miles to weigh bags of maize before walking to Ulmarra East Public School; at night he used to make out invoices for the maize. He later became dux at both Grafton Grammar School and Calder House, Redfern, under Dr J. D. Sly [q.v.6]. From St Andrew's College, University of Sydney, he won a blue for Rugby football and graduated B.A. in 1879 with first-class honours in mathematics, (M.A., 1881). He was articled to Norman Selfe [q.v.6], consulting engineer, and did practical engineering at Davy & Sands; at night he studied architecture.

In 1882 Cohen moved to Mackay, Queensland, and set up as an architect and engineer, planning and supervising water installations for the sugar industry. Two years later he moved to Brisbane, became a founder and treasurer of the Queensland Institute of Architects and in 1892 was elected a life member. On 12 March 1889 in Sydney he married Bertie (Bertram) Hollander. Soon afterwards the economic depression decided him to read law in Sydney.

Admitted to the Bar on 31 May 1894, Cohen devilled for (Sir) William Cullen [q.v.], acted as crown prosecutor and was engaged in arbitration cases involving building and engineering works. A hardworking supporter of Federation, he was a member of the Australasian Federation League's literary committee and in 1898 won the Petersham seat in the Legislative Assembly for (Sir) Edmund Barton's [q.v.7] National Federal Party. Cohen held the seat until 1919 as a Liberal and later for the National Party. In 1907-10 he was chairman of committees and Speaker in 1917-19. An ardent monarchist, he denounced in the House in 1912 the action of two Labor members who had refused to remove their hats during the playing of the national anthem; in 1917 Cohen castigated the Industrial Workers of the World and criticized Labor sympathy for them.

He resigned his seat on 30 January 1919 and next day was appointed to the District Court Bench. The translation brought protests from the Bar and other places on the grounds that Cohen's practice had been negligible. H. B. Bignold [q.v.7] said that in nineteen years 'he had never yet seen Mr Cohen in robes' and that there had been political bargaining. His supporters maintained that he had a fairly good practice at the Bar and that no other member of the assembly had upset so many bills on legal points. He sat in the northern district courts and from 1921 in the metropolitan district. In 1926 he shocked lawyers by permitting a layman to appear for an accused person at a criminal trial at Darlinghurst. On his retirement in 1929 tributes were paid to his fair-mindedness, ability, integrity, common sense and loyalty.

Cohen took a diverse interest in public affairs and was a director of the Hospital Saturday Fund of New South Wales in 1893-1936, a member of the board of management of the Great Synagogue from 1900, and of the Captain Cook's Landing Place and the La Pérouse monuments trusts for many years; he was a founder and director of the University Club from 1905. An honorary member of the Institute of Architects of New South Wales, he published a pamphlet, *Some of the legal aspects of an architect's practice* (1912). On the outbreak of World War I he joined the executive committee of the State division of the Australian branch of the British Red Cross Society. Both his sons served with the Australian Imperial Force — Cedric Keith (1890-1952) became a distinguished ophthalmologist in Sydney, and Colyn Keith (b. 1896) a well-known solicitor in Newcastle. In 1923 he chaired the Commonwealth royal commission to inquire into the supposed loss of the *Sumatra* and, next year, the royal commission into proposals for the establishment of new States.

Survived by his wife and two sons, Cohen died on 23 March 1939 at his residence in Ocean Street, Woollahra, and was buried in the Jewish section of Rookwood cemetery. His estate was valued for probate at £4824.

Cyclopedia of N.S.W. (Syd, 1907); *Judge John J. Cohen — memoirs* (np, priv print, 1940); J. M. Freeland, *The making of a profession* (Syd, 1971); *Daily Telegraph* (Syd), 14 Mar 1917, 10, 11, 15 Jan 1919; *SMH*, 18 Apr 1917, 9, 10, 15, 17, 31 Jan 1919, 27 Mar 1939; *Daily Guardian* (Syd), 26, 27 Mar 1926; *Evening News* (Syd), 27 Mar 1926.

H. T. E. HOLT

COHEN, LAURENCE (1874-1916), trade unionist, was born on 22 March 1874 at Paradise Point, Gaffney's Creek, Victoria, sixth child of John Cohen, miner, a London Jew, and his Parisian wife Louisa Clotilda, née L'Estrange. He was brought to Melbourne as a child where he became a boyhood acquaintance of John Wren [q.v.]. Leaving school early, he had various jobs until he came under the influence of George F. Atyeo, of a noted family of monumental masons. Apprenticed to Atyeo as a letter-cutter, he formed a close relationship with the family and three of his sisters married three of Atyeo's sons. Cohen became a fine tradesman. He later left an inimitable tribute to Donald Macdonell [q.v.] of the Australian Workers' Union when, alone under a blazing sun for two weeks, he carved the inscription on the granite memorial at Stuart Mill, Victoria.

Laurie Cohen's trade union career began in the select fraternity of his craft with the Marble and Stone Workers' Union. He was secretary from 1905 until 1913 and made his first appearances in the Trades Hall Council as a union delegate. A strong believer in the modern amalgamated union, he effected his union's amalgamation with the Operative Stonemasons' Society in 1913. He rose quickly through membership of the executive of the T.H.C. to the presidency in 1913. That year he was appointed to the salaried position of assistant secretary. Cohen established himself as a 'professional' in the Trades Hall: one of the most active members of the Industrial Disputes Committee, he became a shrewd, diplomatic and always well-prepared advocate. He eschewed histrionics and faction-fighting, seeming to understand better than many of his contemporaries the demands modern industrial capitalism placed on trade union leaders.

Convinced of the trade unions' need for a strong political arm, Cohen distinguished himself in the Political Labor Council with his organizational skill and dedication. He emerged as a powerful leader in 1914 when, as president of the P.L.C., he quashed the Catholic Federation's campaign to infiltrate the party. As he had earlier denounced the Socialists as electorally divisive to the labour movement, he now fought to keep the Labor Party secular and comprehensive. In 1915 the P.L.C. paid him the then signal honour of re-electing him to the presidency. He was a Victorian delegate to the Federal Conference that year.

In February 1916, as the most prominent Laborite outside parliament in Victoria, Cohen was sent on the delegation to negotiate Senator (Sir George) Pearce's [q.v.] offer of a forty-four hour week with the striking miners at Broken Hill. After a mixed reception and with the strike partially settled, he returned exhausted to Adelaide on 11 February. After speaking at a fund-raising meeting for the Broken Hill strikers, he retired to bed. At 12.45 a.m. he was found mortally injured in an alley, having apparently fallen eighteen feet (5.5m) from his bedroom window. His death remains a mystery. Cohen was survived by his wife Sarah, sister of John Lemmon [q.v.]; their marriage at the Trades Hall, Carlton, on 27 January 1909 was performed with Presbyterian forms. They had no children. Laurie Cohen was widely mourned and the T.H.C. erected a noble memorial on his grave in the Coburg cemetery.

G. Dale, *The industrial history of Broken Hill* (Melb, 1976 edn); C. Hamilton, 'Catholic interests and the Labor Party . . . 1910-1916', *Hist Studies*, no 33, Nov 1959; *Socialist* (Melb), 1 Dec 1906, 11 Feb 1910; *Labor Call* 13 Mar 1913, 17, 24 Feb 1916; *Aust Worker*, 17 Dec 1916; N. W. Saffin, History of the workingman in Victoria, 3, pt 3 (held by Dr Saffin); information from Mr F. Atyeo, and Ms L. Benham, Beaumaris, Vic.   JANET MCCALMAN

COHEN, SIR LEWIS (1849-1933), merchant and politician, was born on 23 December 1849 at Liverpool, Lancashire, England, son of Henry Cohen, outfitter and businessman, and his wife Elizabeth, née Harris. The family arrived in Sydney about 1853 and Cohen was educated there until, at 14, he went to school at Edmonton near London. Three years later he returned to Sydney and worked in his father's office for twelve months. With capital provided by his father, in 1868 Cohen entered partnership in Fiji with a school mate, Adolphus Meyer Brodziak, handling cotton, copra, trepang and tortoise-shell, in an expanding and profitable barter trade. He later recollected that he had contributed usefully to negotiations for constitutional government in Fiji. In 1872 he sat on the first municipal council at Levuka.

In poor health, Cohen returned to Sydney in 1873 and in Melbourne, on 9 April, he married Selina Marks. Three years later on medical advice he settled in Adelaide, opened a branch of the Melbourne-based London Loan & Discount Bank, and became a wealthy businessman. Soon active in the Adelaide Hebrew congregation, he was also associated with the Independent Order of Oddfellows, South Australian Ancient Order of Foresters' Friendly Society, the Freemasons, Australian Natives' Association, and the United Ancient Order of Druids, of which he became grand president.

In 1886 Cohen was returned for the MacDonnell ward of the City Council. He was mayor in 1889, six more times by 1911, and that year represented the city at King George V's coronation. He campaigned strongly for a lord mayoralty for Adelaide; this was achieved in 1919 – he was lord mayor in 1921-23. Proud of the city's development, he felt that it had 'no compeer

in the matter of parks, squares, roads, and the general municipal improvements'. He initiated the wood-blocking of King William Street and the asphalting of Rundle and Hindley streets. An elegant dresser, while mayor he gave several huge balls for the citizenry.

Cohen was a member of the House of Assembly for North Adelaide in 1887-93 and Adelaide in 1902-06. In 1893 and 1906 he failed in elections for the Legislative Council, and in 1915 for the assembly. Strongly protectionist, he advocated the sale of crown lands to eliminate government deficits. He supported free and compulsory education, closer settlement of pastoral lands, progressive income tax, payment of members of parliament, introduction of the totalisator, and eight-hour legislation for government employees. He feared that Federation would threaten local industry, thought that government expenditure for work should be placed with private firms and opposed coloured immigration. He declined a portfolio in (Sir) J. A. Cockburn's [q.v.] cabinet (1889-90) and also the position of agent-general in London. In 1917 and 1918 he campaigned strongly for the Liberal Union. In January 1924 he was appointed K.C.M.G. and in 1927 he retired.

Cohen died on 24 June 1933 survived by his wife, two sons and two daughters, two other sons having predeceased him. His estate was sworn for probate at £36 955. His portrait hangs in the Adelaide Town Hall.

The 'Register' guide to the parliament of South Australia (Adel, 1887); H. T. Burgess (ed), *Cyclopedia of South Australia*, 1 (Adel, 1907); *Cyclopedia of Fiji* (Syd, 1907); H. Munz, *Jews in South Australia, 1836-1936* (Adel, 1936); Universal Publicity Co., *The official civic record of South Australia* (Adel, 1936); *Aust Municipal J*, 30 June 1922; *Pictorial Aust*, Mar 1891; *Register* (Adel), 27 Mar 1893; *Observer* (Adel), 11 May 1889, 5 Jan 1924; *Gadfly*, 14 Mar 1906; *Mail* (Adel), 26 Aug, 30 Dec 1922; *Advertiser* (Adel), 26 June 1933; diary (held by Mr W. T. Bridgland, Glenelg SA).

ERIC RICHARDS

COHEN, MONTAGUE (1855-1931), lawyer and businessman, was born on 4 August 1855 at Collingwood, Melbourne, eldest child of Simeon Cohen, salesman and later merchant, from Devonshire, England, and his wife Esther, née Levi (Levy), from London. Educated by tutors and at Scotch College, Cohen studied law at the University of Melbourne. While serving articles he was a founder and secretary of a literary and debating society whose members included Alfred Deakin and Theodore Fink [qq.v.]. After admission in 1878, Cohen joined P. D. Phillips as a partner. Seven years later he became partner in Pavey, Wilson, and Cohen (Pavey's). He practised as a solicitor but made rare, shrewd appearances as an advocate. The Law Institute of Victoria elected him president in 1903.

Cohen's financial and political acumen led him to much business activity in the boom years, especially in the brewing and non-ferrous metals industries. He survived the 1890s depression although many associates became insolvent. The stabilization of the liquor industry owed much to him: a director in the 1890s of the Foster Brewing Co. Ltd, in 1903-07 with C. L. Pinschof [q.v.] he negotiated the merger of the main Victorian breweries under the name of Carlton and United Breweries Ltd – and in 1925 a further combination took place. Cohen put the Brewers' Association of Victoria on a sound footing; he was president of the Liquor Trades' Defence Union of Victoria for many years and a member of its federal organization. In 1887 he was a founder of the Swan Brewery Co. Ltd in Perth and remained its chairman of directors for forty years.

Through A. J. F. de Bavay [q.v.], who had been with Foster's, Cohen became involved in the non-ferrous metals industry and, with W. L. Baillieu [q.v.7] and other members of the Collins House group, used personal funds to subsidize long-term research to develop the de Bavay flotation process. Cohen's directorships included twelve major companies, among them Amalgamated Zinc (de Bavay's) Ltd, and Electrolytic Zinc Co. of Australasia Ltd.

On 23 February 1881 he had married Annie, daughter of Edward Cohen [q.v.3]. She had attended the Presbyterian Ladies' College in 1879. 'Mrs Monty' was supported by her husband in her life work of organizing and dispensing charity. Between 1897 and 1939 she served as committee-member, treasurer and, for nineteen years, president of the Victorian Infant Asylum (Berry Street Foundling Hospital, East Melbourne), and was an energetic and forceful committee-member of the Melbourne District Nursing Society. Charitable to her fingertips, she never spoke of what she did; she went into the homes of people in trouble – an 'angel on earth', albeit a tiny, imperious and strong-willed angel. The couple maintained links with the Melbourne Jewish community. 'Mrs Monty' was at one time vice-president of the Melbourne Jewish Women's Guild and occasionally worshipped with the Melbourne Hebrew congregation.

Cohen was a formidable man. A proficient pianist, he sometimes performed for charity. When young he played football and cricket and was a cross-country runner. Later he was a founder and trustee of the Amateur Sports Club of Victoria, and, as president of the Victorian Amateur Athletic Association, presented a shield to stimulate interest in the 10-mile (16 km) cross-country run. Cohen was generally respected for his attention to the realities of business and professional life and for his integrity. He died in Melbourne on 18 October 1931 and was buried in Melbourne general cemetery, survived by his wife and their only child, Harold [q.v.]. Cohen's estate was sworn for probate at £131 074 in Victoria and £79 076 in South Australia. His portrait by Longstaff [q.v.] is held by the family.

W. S. Robinson, *If I remember rightly*, G. Blainey ed (Melb, 1967); N. Rosenthal, *People, not cases* (Melb, 1974); *Aust Brewers' J*, 20 Nov 1906; *Table Talk*, 26 May 1888, 25 May 1893; *Age*, and *Argus*, 19 Oct 1931; History of the Carlton and United Breweries (NL, and Univ Melb Archives); Vic AAA papers (Melb); information from Berry Street Babies' Home & Hospital (East Melb); family information.   BARBARA FALK

COHEN, SIR SAMUEL SYDNEY (1869-1948), businessman, was born on 11 March 1869 at Darlinghurst, Sydney, eldest son of native-born parents George Judah Cohen [q.v.] and his wife Rebecca, daughter of L. W. Levy [q.v.5]. Brought up at West Maitland, he was educated there and at Royston College, Sydney. At 16 he joined the family company David Cohen & Co. and soon became a partner. He later visited China, Japan, the United States of America, England and Europe on behalf of the firm and on his return became manager of its Newcastle branch. On 18 April 1901 at her father's house in East Melbourne he married with Jewish rites Elma (d. 1946), daughter of Alfred Hart, a merchant.

Cohen soon became prominent in the Newcastle district – he was president of Royal Newcastle Hospital board, a founder and president of the board of management of the Newcastle Synagogue, a member of the board of the Newcastle Club, a committee-member of the Newcastle Jockey Club and patron of innumerable cricket and football clubs. He was also vice-consul for Greece from March 1905, 'anything but a sinecure', and later acting-consul in Sydney until 1923. He declined several requests to stand for parliament.

In 1915 the Cohens returned to Sydney and later lived at Ocean Street, Woollahra. His business acumen was soon recognized: he was sometime chairman of David Cohen & Co. Ltd, the Australian Gas Light Co. (1939-47), John McGrath Ltd (1919-39), agents for Chevrolet and Cadillac cars, Paul & Gray Ltd, ship's-chandlers, the Newcastle and Hunter Steamship Co. Ltd (1944-47) and North Western General Stores Ltd (1948); he was also a director of Tooth [q.v.6] & Co. Ltd in 1934-48, and the Royal Exchange of Sydney in 1936-48. As chairman of the Australian Gas Light Co. during World War II he contended with frequent shortages of coal causing threats to the gas supply. In 1947 he organized the merger between the Clyde Engineering Co. Ltd and Paul & Gray Ltd.

Concerned about the low standard of local government administration, Cohen was a foundation executive-member of the Citizens Reform Association from 1921, and until 1936 shared its presidency with Sir Arthur Cocks and Sir James Murdoch [qq.v]. As president of the Kindergarten Union of New South Wales he worked for the extension of free kindergartens in industrial areas. He was also a director and vice-president of Sydney Hospital, vice-president of the British Orphans Adoption Society, honorary treasurer in 1930-41 of the Women's College Council, University of Sydney, a trustee of the Queen's Jubilee Fund and an executive-member of the Lord Mayor's Patriotic and War Fund; he served on the board of the Big Brother Movement and the Council of Social Service of New South Wales. He was knighted in the coronation honours of 1937.

A devout Jew, Cohen sat on the board of management of the Great Synagogue from 1915 and was made a life member in 1939 when he resigned after seven years as president. He was founding president in 1937 of the Australian Jewish Welfare Society and gave liberally to the New South Wales Jewish War Memorial. From the mid-1930s he was deeply disturbed about Nazi treatment of Jews in Germany: he founded and was president of the Australian Fund for German Refugees, which by 1938 had helped 600 men and women to come to Australia where work had been found for them. He was also patron of the local Mizrachi Palestine Committee, a world-wide organization for the return of Palestine as a Jewish homeland.

As a young man Cohen was dark with a luxuriant moustache; in his later years he was clean shaven and totally bald. A horse-lover, he rode in Centennial Park and at his farm at Bowral. He was a member of the Australian Jockey Club and raced many horses. A voracious reader, he enjoyed the theatre. He frequently visited England and was a member of the Devonshire Club in London, as well as the Warrigal and New South Wales clubs, Sydney, and the Royal Sydney Yacht Squadron.

Sir Samuel died in St Luke's Hospital on 27 August 1948 and was buried in the Jewish section of Rookwood cemetery. He was survived by a daughter, and by two sons who served with distinction in World War II and took the name Cullen when they enlisted. His estate was valued for probate at £85 012.

Cyclopedia of N.S.W. (Syd, 1907); Aust Jewish Hist Soc, *J*, 2 (1944-48); *SMH*, 18 May 1935, 11 May 1937, 7 July 1938, 3 Aug 1939; family information.
MARTHA RUTLEDGE

COHN, CAROLA (OLA) (1892-1964), sculptor, was born on 25 April 1892 at Bendigo, Victoria, daughter of Julius Cohn, a brewer of Danish origin, and his wife Sarah Helen, née Snowball. After schooling from the age of 12 at Girton College, Bendigo, she attended art classes at the Bendigo School of Mines in 1910-19 and in 1920-25 studied at Swinburne Technical College, Melbourne. In 1926 she went to London and attended the Royal College of Art where her lecturers included Henry Moore for sculpture. She enrolled in night classes in bronze casting at the School of Arts and Crafts, studied Egyptian, Assyrian and archaic Greek sculpture at the British Museum and travelled in Europe. In 1928 she was awarded a Royal College of Art free studentship; in 1929 she became an associate of the Royal College of Art.

Influenced in London by Moore, Ola Cohn produced sculpture in stone, wood, terracotta and bronze in which the human form was reduced to very simple masses, seen in terms of the materials used. 'Head of a Virgin' (1926), now in the National Gallery of Victoria, was considered very modern in Australia at the time. On her return to Melbourne in late 1930 she set up a studio at 9 Collins Street, later moving to Gipps Street, East Melbourne. In March 1931 her first one-person exhibition established her as a leading modern sculptor in Australia; however, after the mid-1940s her work grew less experimental. In 1938 she produced two seven-foot (2.1 m) sandstone figures for the new Royal Hobart Hospital. Next year she executed nineteen panels for the Mutual Life and Citizens building in Sydney (fourteen were designed by Murray Griffin) and in 1940-41 carved the limestone Pioneer Woman memorial statue, Adelaide.

Briefly in 1933 Ola Cohn taught art at Geelong Church of England Grammar School. She was part-time lecturer in art at the Melbourne Kindergarten Teachers' College from about 1940 until 1954. In 1948 she won the Roman Catholic Diocesan Centenary Prize in Melbourne and in 1952 the Crouch Prize – the first time it had been won by a sculptor – for a wood carving. In 1964 she was appointed O.B.E. for 'services rendered in the service of art, especially sculpture'.

Ola Cohn exhibited her work frequently in

group shows held by the societies of which she was a member. These included the Victorian Artists' and Australian Sculptors' societies, the Melbourne Society of Women Painters and Sculptors (of which she was president in 1948-64), the Victorian Sculptors' Society and Melbourne Contemporary Artists. She also exhibited with the Society of Artists, Adelaide. Her work is widely represented in public collections in Australia.

Ola Cohn loved animals and kept a variety of pets. Her 'Fairies' Tree in the Fitzroy Gardens, Melbourne, was inspired by the Elfin Tree in London's Kensington Gardens. She wrote stories around the characters that she had carved on the tree stump, publishing *The Fairies' Tree* (1932), *More about the Fairies' Tree* (1933) and *Castles in the air* (1936). Her reminiscences, *Mostly cats*, appeared in 1964 while her manuscript 'Me in the making' (c.1941-48) is held in the La Trobe Library, Melbourne.

On 6 May 1953 with Presbyterian forms Ola Cohn married Herbert John Green, retired government printer, who died in 1957. On her death at Cowes on 23 December 1964 she left an estate valued for probate at £85 787. Her studio and a collection of her works were bequeathed to the Council of Adult Education.

Woman's World, 1 Apr 1926; *Manuscripts* (Geelong), Nov 1931; *Art in Aust*, 15 Aug 1932; *Aust Home Beautiful*, 1 Sept 1939; *People*, 22 July 1959; *Herald* (Melb), 16 Mar 1931; *Age*, 26 July 1952, 24 Dec 1964; O. Cohn papers (LaTL).

KEN SCARLETT

COLDHAM, WALTER TIMON (1860-1908), barrister and sportsman, was born on 19 November 1860 at Grassdale near Branxholme, Victoria, third son of John Coldham, an Anglican minister from Norfolk, England, and his wife Josephine, née Lane, of County Cork, Ireland. His father had migrated to Van Diemen's Land in 1839 and later turned to squatting in Victoria's Western District. Coldham was educated at Hamilton College and Melbourne Church of England Grammar School, where he excelled at sport and was dux in 1879. He entered Trinity College, University of Melbourne, in 1880; graduating LL.B. in 1884 he was admitted to the Bar that year. On 27 November 1885 he married Edith Lucy, daughter of J. D. Pinnock [q.v.2], and established a large home in Balaclava Road, St Kilda.

Coldham played tennis for Victoria in 1885-87, and with W. J. Carre Riddell [q.v.] was Victorian doubles champion in 1884 and 1886 and intercolonial champion in 1886. A talented sprinter, high jumper and hurdler, he became vice-president of the Victorian Amateur Athletic Association; he also served on the committee of the Melbourne Cricket Club. His skill with the gun was recognized along the length of the Murray River. He maintained ties with his old school and was president of the Old Melburnians Council in 1906-07.

Coldham read in the chambers of J. L. Purves [q.v.5]. They formed a close friendship and became a formidable forensic combination. After Purves took silk in 1886, Coldham's application and wide legal knowledge made up for his leader's brilliant but less industrious qualities; he appeared as junior to Purves in many notable cases such as *Speight* v. *Syme* [qq.v.6]. His defence of the accused in the Victoria Bridge murder trial in 1890 established his reputation and he became much in demand and acquired a wide practice. Important cases in which he appeared included the Premier Permanent Building Society actions (he represented the Crown in *Regina* v. *Mirams* [q.v.5] in 1890), *Peacock* v. *D. M. Osborne & Co.* in 1900 and the Wallace divorce case. His unusual facility for mathematics, engineering and science enabled him to specialize in the flourishing patent jurisdiction. Although Coldham contested the Legislative Assembly seat of St Kilda in 1894 and Geelong in 1897, he had no deep interest in politics.

He was very popular, full of *bonhomie*, with cheery smile and a hearty laugh. A splendid advocate, a brilliant conversationalist and after-dinner speaker, he allowed his wit 'to play and not to wound'. Some of Coldham's many witticisms have passed down to posterity: Chief Justice Sir Samuel Griffith [q.v.] once chided him that the High Court was not much the wiser for his lengthy exposition of a particular point. Coldham replied 'No, not wiser, your Honour, but better informed'.

In 1901 Coldham developed carcinoma of the foot and despite a number of operations the cancer slowly spread. In November 1907 he collapsed in court, never to return. He died at St Kilda on 29 May 1908 and was buried in St Kilda cemetery. Handsome public tributes were paid to him by Purves, who commented on Coldham's 'singular faculty of being able to work hard and play hard', and by Judge Moule in the Insolvency Court. He was survived by his wife, a son and a daughter.

P. A. Jacobs, *A lawyer tells* (Melb, 1949); A. Dean, *A multitude of counsellors* (Melb, 1968); *Table Talk*, 28 July 1893; *Australasian*, 15 Mar 1894, 9 May 1896, 20 Nov 1897; *Argus*, 20 May 1908.

CHARLES FRANCIS

COLE, FRANK HOBILL (1863-1934), paediatrician, was born on 2 February 1863 at Carlton, Melbourne, third child of John Richards Cole, importer from Cambridgeshire, and his wife Elizabeth, née Horton, widow of William Baines. After education at Scotch College, East Melbourne, he was apprenticed to P. McLean, pharmacist of Fitzroy, qualifying from the School of Pharmacy in 1884. He concurrently studied medicine at the University of Melbourne from 1882, graduating M.B., Ch.B. in 1887, and began as a resident medical officer at the Melbourne Hospital for Sick Children along with Dr Jeffreys Wood.

Cole maintained an interest in the three institutions from which he received his education. He was the medical officer to Scotch College boarders for twenty years; he introduced regular physical examinations and growth records and, as a member of the school council, was closely involved in the school's move to Hawthorn Glen. During the formative years of the School of Pharmacy and the Victorian College of Pharmacy, Cole was lecturer (1891-1903) and later examiner (1898-1920) in materia medica. He became a member of the Pharmacy Board and represented it on the faculty of medicine at the University of Melbourne. At the Children's Hospital he became out-patient medical officer in 1892 and in-patient in 1900, acting as both physician and surgeon. He retired to become honorary consultant in 1920.

Cole's private practice was conducted from 88 Rathdowne Street, Carlton, and from Lister House, Collins Street. His consultant practice was limited to children, thus he became one of Melbourne's first paediatricians. To become Cole's assistant in his private practice was an apprenticeship most sought: notable amongst these doctors were H. Douglas Stephens [q.v.] (who married Cole's daughter Eileen), Reginald Webster, (Sir) (Frank) Kingsley Norris, (Sir) William Upjohn and Alan McCutcheon. Undoubtedly Cole's greatest achievement was his influence on the teaching of paediatrics, both at the Children's Hospital, and more importantly to this growing coterie of young paediatric specialists, both physicians and surgeons, who themselves carried his clinical tradition for another generation.

Cole collected Australian paintings and literature with discernment. He was said to have the best local collection of books on the discovery and exploration of Australasia. His paintings were sold by auction in 1923, probably because his circumstances changed with the progressive development of Parkinson's disease.

On 31 October 1888 at Mornington Cole had married Alice Flude, daughter of C. J. Jenner [q.v.4]; she died aged 26 in 1891 after the birth of their second child. On 16 December 1901 at Rippon Lea, Elsternwick, he married her sister, Clara (Claire) Josephine by whom he had five children. He retired in the early 1920s to Mornington because of increasing debility and died there on 6 December 1934 of heart failure, survived by his wife and seven children. He was cremated. He had worshipped regularly at the Collins Street Independent Church before his retirement.

Cole was a gentle and humble man, greatly respected by his contemporaries for his superior knowledge and skill in medicine, surgery and therapeutics. He was a generous benefactor to many institutions and people in need. He was among the last who practised as a physician and surgeon with equal skill, and among the first in Melbourne to specialize in diseases of children.

MJA, 14 Mar 1959; *A'sian J of Pharmacy*, 30 Sept 1967; family papers (held by Mrs L. M. H. Skelton, South Yarra, Vic).   DAVID M. O'SULLIVAN

COLE, GEORGE HENRY (1859-1919), Methodist minister, was born on 7 December 1859 at Mickleham, Victoria, son of William Cole, a selector who had come from Gloucester, England, in 1849, and his wife Elizabeth, née Comley. He rarely attended school as he was needed on the farm, and he became expert at agricultural work. At 13 he was a boundary rider on a station two hundred miles (320 km) from home, and at 15 a bullocky. Away from his family he slipped into dissolute ways and took to drink. Although as a child he had witnessed Primitive Methodist cottage prayer meetings, it was not until he returned to live at Mickleham at 17 that he attended church regularly. Under the preaching of the fervent Rev. W. H. Walton he experienced a dramatic conversion: 'my sins began to roll up under me. I fancied that someone had been telling him all about me. Yes, every word was for me'.

Cole felt the call to the ministry but he was almost illiterate. By dint of laborious night study he progressed from prayer leader to lay preacher. After four years he renounced his recent selection of two hundred acres (80 ha) and placed himself under a private tutor until he was accepted as a probationer into the Primitive Methodist Church in 1882. Ordained in 1886, he served at Sale, Murtoa, Eaglehawk, Armadale and Geelong. At Condah on 6 April 1886 he married Elizabeth Maria Cowan, daughter of a farmer. She died in 1893 and on 3 April 1895 at Eaglehawk he married 26-year-old Mary Euphemia Marshall.

Cole became a powerful evangelist and temperance campaigner, yet remained a common man's pastor, humorous and down-to-earth. To a fellow minister: 'he was one of the most deeply spiritual men I have ever known ... He prayed about everything'. In 1897 he was secretary to the Primitive Methodist Annual Assembly for Victoria and Tasmania. That year the assembly decided to convert its flagging church in Lygon Street, Carlton, into a mission and appointed him as minister. Not long settled at Geelong, he accepted reluctantly. He and his wife were appalled at the plight of homeless and delinquent boys in Carlton and devoted themselves to rescue work with remarkable success. His own harsh boyhood gave him a rare sympathy with these children. The Methodist Union of 1902 enabled him to implement his brainchild – a boys' training farm where instruction in agriculture could complement spiritual reformation and general education.

An evangelical tour of New Zealand in 1903 by Cole helped to raise funds and the Church purchased thirty-eight acres (15 ha) at Tally Ho, Burwood, attaching it to the Central Methodist Mission. He was superintendent in 1904-19, teaching farm work to hardened delinquents while ministering to their spiritual needs. By 1919 the farm accommodated one hundred boys and flourished as a commercial venture. Under him, Tally Ho was a congregate institution and discipline was harsh. His successor, Edgar Derrick, abolished corporal punishment and introduced the self-governing family cottage system – then a radical innovation in child welfare practice.

Cole died of heart disease at Tally Ho on 11 July 1919 and was buried in Burwood cemetery. He was survived by his second wife, and by two daughters and a son of his first marriage.

T. W. H. Leavitt (ed), *Australian representative men*, 2nd edn (Melb, 1887); C. I. Benson (ed), *A century of Victorian Methodism* (Melb, 1935); *Gippsland Mercury*, 7 Aug 1886; *Spectator* (Melb), 7 May, 16, 23 July 1919.   JANET MCCALMAN

COLE, JOSEPH STEAR CARLYON (1832-1916), schoolmaster, was born in 1832 at Exeter, Devon, England, son of George Talbert Cole and his wife. Educated by his father and at Oakhampton Street Grammar School, he was a dreamy boy who enjoyed reading Scott, Byron and Burns. In 1848 he went to London to work for his uncle, a builder's manager. Cole is said to have read some law and attended Birkbeck Literary and Scientific Institution. In 1857 he migrated to Adelaide to join his uncle John

Cole at Penwortham. He taught at Auburn Public School and was 'factotum general to the district': as clerk of the local court and of the Upper Wakefield District Council, secretary of the Independent Order of Oddfellows, curator of the cemetery and correspondent for the *South Australian Register*.

In 1861 Cole was headmaster for three months at Pulteney Street School, Adelaide, but left to open a public school at Watervale. His salary was £100. On 29 November 1862 he married Hannah Peacock in Adelaide; they had a son and five daughters. Next year he built the first six rooms, for boarders, of his own Stanley Grammar School for boys and girls, on thirty acres (12 ha) of land at a cost of £4000. He taught in both institutions, with his wife as matron, until 1877 when he relinquished the public school.

The grammar school, a two-storied freestone building, advertised that 'the two main aspects of human life – the industrial and the ideal' would be catered for: 'whatever dignifies, ennobles, and enlightens'. Although the prospectus stated that corporal punishment was 'derogatory to the dignity, and inimical to the progress of rational nature', it was listed as the penalty for obscene language and lewdness, or for striking a blow in anger. Subjects included: chemistry, assaying, surveying, linear and perspective drawing, brokerage discount and commission, book-keeping, and field subjects. Night school was also provided. There were two large class-rooms, five dormitories and a library of 1000 volumes containing a prized set of the *Encyclopaedia Britannica*. A French clock was presented to Cole by his pupils in 1875; the master's response was that he had 'never mistaken himself for a hero nor his poor service as heroic'.

Although Stanley Grammar School graduates were not qualified to enter the University of Adelaide, many of them matriculated later and flourished at the university, in State parliament and among the professions. Ex-pupils included Sir David Gordon, Dr W. G. Torr [qq.v.], Sir John Duncan, Dr W. Jethro Brown [qq.v.4,7] and Emile Sobels. The school's mottoes were: 'Without learning, life to man is death' and 'Let the boy so learn that he may teach'. In 1904 Cole retired; the school closed in 1917, although the family continued to live there and the building still stands. Survived by his wife (d. 1928), Cole died, aged 85, on 15 October 1916 at Watervale; they are buried in St Mark's churchyard, Penwortham. Cole's estate was sworn for probate at £1565.

M. Meller, *The Stanley Grammar School, Watervale* ... (Adel, 1949); W. R. Ray, *Pulteney*

Grammar School 1847-1972 (Adel, 1973); *Evening J,* 10 Jan 1903; *Mail* (Adel), 31 Oct 1936; *Chronicle* (Adel), 22 Feb 1939; Stanley Grammar School ledger, M1441 (SAA).   JEAN V. MOYLE

COLE, PERCIVAL RICHARD (1879-1948), scholar and educationist, was born on 18 May 1879 at Muswellbrook, New South Wales, son of John Cole, an Irish-born schoolteacher, and his Tasmanian-born wife Mary Jane, née Teeson. Educated at Granville North (Rosehill) Public School in 1885-91 and Sydney Boys' High School in 1892-95, he became a pupil-teacher at Glebe Superior Public School in 1896. In 1900 he went to the Fort Street Training School where, in his last year, he won the Jones medal; and in 1901 was awarded a three-year scholarship to the University of Sydney. He graduated B.A. in 1903 with first-class honours in history and philosophy, winning the Frazer [q.v.4] scholarship in history and the University Medal in philosophy, and M.A. in 1905 with first-class honours in modern history and the Woolley [q.v.6] travelling scholarship for study overseas.

In England Cole attended the London Day Training College, and in 1906 was awarded the University of London Diploma of Education with first-class honours; he was elected a fellow of the College of Preceptors, London. Next year he went to the Teachers' College, Columbia University, New York (Ph.D., 1907), where he taught the history of education in 1908-09. He was an organizer and first president of the Cosmopolitan Club, New York.

In 1910 Cole returned to Sydney and became vice-principal and lecturer in education at the Teachers' College, Sydney, and, next year, lecturer in the history of education at the university; he held both appointments until he retired on 11 February 1944. He became one of a trio of educationists of whom it was said that Peter Board [q.v.7], director of education, was the architect, Alexander Mackie [q.v.], the first principal of the college, the builder, and Cole the writer and poet of a new era in education and teacher-training in New South Wales.

One of the earliest and best-equipped among Australians in the history and philosophy of education, Cole published widely, culminating in his *History of educational thought* (London, 1931). His comprehensive view of education and the catholicity of his interests helped him to contribute many valuable articles, mainly to the college journals, *Schooling* (1910-35) and its successor, the *Forum of Education,* (1940-), on such aspects as classroom practice, the curriculum, early childhood education, and the relation of the school to society and employment. Their significance lay in that the teaching profession had previously had to rely almost entirely on overseas publications for reading and stimulation. With Mackie, Cole wrote *Studies in the theory of education* (Sydney, 1925), the first book of its kind published in Australia. He also assembled the contributors for, and edited comprehensive discussions of educational problems in *The primary school curriculum in Australia* (Melbourne, 1932), *The education of the adolescent in Australia* (Melbourne, 1935) and *The rural school in Australia* (Melbourne, 1937). Meanwhile, in a less obvious fashion, Cole, by his own scholarship and personal influence, reinforced Mackie's determination that a teachers' college should be an institution where professional practice was taught in an atmosphere of recognizable scholarship.

Fresh opportunities for him to use his wider knowledge and experience came in the late 1920s and 1930s – Cole was a foundation member of the Australian Council for Educational Research in 1930-33, and Australian representative for the Carnegie Endowment for International Peace in 1928-47. In 1929 and in 1936-37 he visited the United States of America, the second time as visiting Carnegie professor of international relations. He was honoured with the award of the prized Columbia University Medal in 1929 and King George V's Silver Jubilee Medal in 1935, and by membership of the American fraternity Phi Beta Kappa in 1936 and a fellowship of the Royal Society of Arts, London, in 1937.

Cole was fundamentally shy, and few of his contemporaries were aware of his interest in poetry and literary criticism. He published privately a volume of *Poems* in 1930. However he was a clubbable man, a life member of the Sydney University Union and a high-ranking tennis-player, who later enjoyed golf. Dr C. H. Currey praised the quality of Cole's scholarship, his outstanding success as a seminar-leader and the encouragement he gave his students. About two metres tall and large in proportion, he was tone-deaf and spoke almost in a monotone. Cole himself wrote that in 'the course of his own travels, the writer regarded himself as a communicating cell within the educational organism of modern civilization. At every opportunity he has received and transmitted educational ideas; but . . . he did not originate many of those ideas'.

A diabetic, Cole died of pneumonia on 7 August 1948 at his Manly home and was buried in the Church of England section of the Frenchs Forest cemetery. He was survived by his wife Ida Jane Louisa, née Skinner, whom he had married at St Andrew's Cathedral, Sydney, on 26 April

1911. His portrait by Arthur Murch is held by the Teachers' College, Sydney.

Univ Syd Union, *Union Recorder*, 23 Sept 1948; K. D. Williams, The educational writings of P. R. Cole (B.Ed. Hons thesis, Univ Syd, 1967); P. R. Cole papers, MS 1355 (ML); ML printed cat for publications.   I. S. TURNER

COLEBATCH, SIR HARRY (HAL) PATESHALL (1872-1953), journalist and politician, was born on 29 March 1872 at Underley, Wolverflow, Herefordshire, England, one of seven children of George Pateshall Colebatch, farmer and chemist, and his wife Georgina, née Gardner. In 1878 the family migrated to Goolwa, South Australia, where Hal attended the local school; at 11 he took a job as office boy and printer's devil at 6s. per week with the *Norwood Free Press*. At Norwood he attended evening classes in shorthand, English literature and Latin. When the *Free Press* collapsed he worked with a succession of transient newspapers at Peterborough, Port Pirie and Laura; at 16 he moved to Broken Hill, New South Wales, as a journalist with the *Silver Age*. In the 1892 strike he took verbatim notes at meetings and was later subpoenaed as a crown witness at the leaders' trial. His involvement in the case was fortuitous but this close contact with trade unionism did not win his sympathies for the emergent labour movement.

In 1894 Colebatch went to the Western Australian goldfields and a job with the Coolgardie *Golden Age*. Next year he joined the *Kalgoorlie Miner* for a few months and in 1896 moved to Perth as mining editor of the *Morning Herald*, a new daily which he edited from 1904, but soon left to become proprietor-editor of a major provincial paper, the *Northam Advertiser*. A champion chessplayer, by this time he was tall and distinguished looking with a pale face, a brown, pointed beard and the slight stoop of a scholar. On 29 April 1896 he had married Maud Mary Saunders, a South Australian; they had two sons, one of whom, Harley, took over the running of the *Advertiser* in 1919. Although he knew little of farming, Colebatch was readily accepted into Northam's agricultural and commercial élite, becoming mayor in 1909-14.

In Northam he organized the election of local bank manager (Sir) James Mitchell [q.v.] to the Legislative Assembly. After two false starts, Colebatch entered the Legislative Council for East Province in 1912. He advocated improved rural education – a favourite subject – Legislative Council reform, and rapid development through land settlement and immigration. He was president of the Northam branch of the Liberal League and a member of its State executive. The league was not formally linked with the parliamentary Liberal Party and, despite his involvement in the organization, he prided himself, like most other councillors, on his independence.

Scaddan's [q.v.] Labor government had a large majority in the assembly but scant representation in the council, where much of its legislation was defeated, delayed or emasculated. Colebatch thrived on this situation: his retentive memory, fluent speech and incisive wit made him a formidable debater; within two years he was unofficial Opposition leader in the 'non-partisan' council and one Labor member complained, 'When Mr Colebatch makes a speech other members follow him in a manner which forcibly reminds one of the hymn, "Lead Kindly Light"'. When the government fell in 1916, the new Liberal premier Frank Wilson [q.v.] appointed Colebatch leader of the council, colonial secretary and minister for education. He played no part in the formation of the National Party in 1917, in the course of which Wilson was displaced by (Sir) H. B. Lefroy [q.v.], but retained his portfolios in the new cabinet and became deputy premier. Among his many legislative and administrative activities in this period, those which satisfied him most were the establishment of district high schools in four country towns; the transformation of Rottnest Island from a prison to a class 'A' reserve and holiday resort; a major revision of the Health Act; and the reorganization of the State's trading concerns.

In April 1919 following a cabinet crisis, Colebatch was elected by the Nationalists to succeed Lefroy as premier; his ministry resembled his predecessor's but he brought back Mitchell. To remain in office Colebatch had to find an assembly seat, but the Country Party refused to allow him to change places with one of their members. His opportunities to resolve this tangle were limited by his part in a major waterfront crisis which culminated in the 'Battle of the Barricades'. In 1917 the Commonwealth government had been using non-union lumpers to break a wharf dispute and guaranteed them continued preference of employment over unionists. By 1919 the Lumpers Union of Workers' resentment had been increased by the return of many ex-servicemen members. A trial of strength developed at Fremantle over the unloading of the *Dimboola*, which carried perishable goods much needed by a community isolated for several months by anti-influenza quarantine rules. On 4 May Colebatch supervised attempts to barricade the wharf so that the non-unionists could unload the *Dimboola*, but in the ensuing *fracas* a lumper was fatally injured and the plan was abandoned.

This contretemps, combined with the difficulty of finding an assembly seat, led Colebatch, after only a month, to resign the premiership in favour of Mitchell, himself reverting to the deputy premiership. Political stability was restored and in 1919-23 Mitchell and Colebatch harmoniously fostered the State's development, including the ill-fated Group Settlement Scheme. In 1923 Colebatch went as the State's agent-general to London, where he found himself implementing policies he had helped to frame: selecting migrants, promoting Western Australian products and negotiating loans. Appointed C.M.G. in 1923, at his term's conclusion in 1927 he was knighted.

On his return to Perth the government commissioned Colebatch to edit a history of Western Australia for the centenary of British settlement; this was published in 1929 as *A story of a hundred years*. He also joined the 1927-29 royal commission into the working of the Commonwealth constitution, on which he was the only small-State representative. A strong supporter of State rights, Colebatch signed the majority report which advocated preservation of the Federal system, since unification 'would be likely to produce paralysis at the centre and anaemia at the circumference'. This theme dominated Colebatch's years in the Senate in 1928-33, for he accepted Nationalist endorsement on the understanding that he would hold himself free of party ties. Although this anachronistic stance, plus the Depression, limited his effectiveness, the Senate gave Colebatch a platform from which to express his forthright views on Commonwealth-State relations and the economic crisis; he published pamphlets and contributed many articles to leading Sydney and Melbourne papers during these years. In particular, as president of the Melbourne-based Tariff Reform League, he was a notable critic of high tariffs, which he saw as doubly bad in their unfair impact on the less-developed States.

In 1933 Colebatch resumed the post of agent-general for Western Australia and although there were now fewer responsibilities he again enjoyed the role. He led the delegation which in 1934 presented Western Australia's secession petition to the British parliament. Warned in advance that the parliament was unlikely even to receive the petition, he used the episode as an opportunity to publicize Western Australia's grievances.

Colebatch returned to Perth in 1939 and in 1940 re-entered the Legislative Council, where he sat till 1948. His first wife had died in 1940 and on 21 December 1944 he married Marion Frances Gibson, nursing sister; this second marriage brought him a third son, Hal. He died on 12 February 1953 and was buried in the Anglican section of Karrakatta cemetery; his estate was sworn for probate at £2346. He had rendered unusually varied service to his adopted State.

D. S. Garden, *Northam, an Avon Valley history* (Melb, 1979); *Advertiser* (Adel), 26 June 1923, 27 Aug 1932, 22 Dec 1944; *SMH*, 29 Oct 1924; B. K. de Garis, A political biography of Sir Hal Colebatch (M.A. thesis, Univ WA, 1962); Colebatch papers (Battye Lib, Perth).   B. K. DE GARIS

COLEMAN, PERCY EDMUND CREED (1892-1934), union organizer and politician, was born on 23 October 1892 at Surry Hills, Sydney, son of Thomas Coleman, bricklayer, and his wife Ellen, née Creed. Orphaned when very young, Percy went to sea aged 13 after an education in New Zealand. Three years later he became a clerk with the Sydney branch of the Federated Seamen's Union of Australasia; in 1916 he was appointed general secretary of the United Clerks' Union of New South Wales. Though opposed to conscription, Coleman volunteered for the Australian Imperial Force in February 1918 and served in France and England with the Army Service Corps. Promoted temporary sergeant, on 1 July 1919 he was attached to Australia House as a lecturer. After his discharge in April 1920 he toured the United States of America, lecturing extensively on Australian conditions. Back in New South Wales he continued as secretary of the clerks' union, now the Australian Clerical Association, until 1922. He was also honorary secretary of the State Services' Confederation of New South Wales and founder and secretary of the Australian Alliance of Professional, Clerical and Government Employees' Associations.

In 1922 Coleman entered Federal parliament as Labor member for Reid. He spoke on a wide range of subjects and became well known as a supporter of the League of Nations. He was a member of the Public Works Committee in 1928-29. In June 1928 he was called before a royal commission inquiring into allegations that certain Labor members had been offered money to vacate their seats, but he overcame the bad publicity and easily held Reid in the next elections, and increased his majority in 1929.

Though not a minister in the Scullin [q.v.] government (1929-32), Coleman served in 1930 as Australia's representative at the International Labor Conference and the meeting of the Mandates Commission of the League of Nations in Geneva, and at the

British Commonwealth Labour Conference in London. Chairman of the Parliamentary Joint Committee on Public Accounts in 1929-31, he conducted a review of Australia House in London, recommending the merging of the State agents-general with the Australian high commission. In May 1930 it was alleged that he had accepted a £500 bribe during the inquiry into the compensation claims of the newly nationalized 'A' class broadcasting stations. The ensuing royal commission cleared him.

Coleman was loyal to Scullin in the factional struggles that led to the collapse of the Federal Labor government, and lost his seat to the Lang [q.v.] candidate, J. H. Gander, in December 1931. Appalled at the extremist posturing of the 'Lang dictatorship' in New South Wales he became a prominent organizer against the State Labor machine. Plagued by recurrent bouts of sickness he was forced to withdraw from the East Sydney Federal by-election in 1932, but shortly after, in the State elections which followed Lang's dismissal by Governor Game [q.v.], Coleman lost only narrowly to Lang in the contest for Auburn. In March 1933 he was admitted to the New South Wales Bar; he soon accepted the difficult post of president of the New South Wales (Federal) branch of the Australian Labor Party. He died unexpectedly on 25 May 1934 in a car at Concord, a victim of heart disease. Survived by his wife Elsie Allen Victoria, née Prince, whom he had married on 17 December 1921 at St James's Church of England, Sydney, and by a daughter, he was buried in the Anglican section of Rookwood cemetery. His estate was sworn for probate at £2313.

SMH, 1 Dec 1922, 27 Oct 1925, 10 May, 4 Aug 1928, 16-28 June, 9-24 July, 24 Dec 1930, 25 Jan, 9 Feb, 18-30 May, 13 June 1932, 26-29 May 1934; *Aust Worker*, 29 Nov 1922, 13-27 June, 4, 18 July, 8 Aug 1928, 18 Dec 1929; *Bulletin*, 1 June 1932; *Argus*, 26 May 1934.   FRANK FARRELL.

COLES, SIR JENKIN (1843-1911), auctioneer and politician, was born on 19 January 1843 at Liverpool, New South Wales, eldest son of Jenkin Coles, publican, and his wife Caroline. The family returned to England in 1849 and Coles attended Christ's Hospital, London. In 1854 they migrated to South Australia and Coles became a junior clerk with the River Murray Navigation Co. From 1859 he worked at the Adelaide Hospital; in 1861 he failed in an application to join John McDouall Stuart's [q.v.6] exploring party, but it led to a job as a mounted policeman at Overland Corner. From 1864 at Kapunda, Coles was an auctioneer and stock and station agent with a popular 'trick of

repartee'. Next year, on 9 May, he married Ellen Henrietta Briggs in St Francis Xavier's Cathedral, Adelaide; they had seven daughters and four sons.

Although not a single-taxer, Coles admired Henry George's [q.v.4] ideas on land reform. In 1875, as a free-trader and land reformer, he won a House of Assembly by-election for Light. Standing down at the 1877 elections, he wound up his business and in 1881 regained Light (Wooroora) and held it until his death. When campaigning, Coles was 'a strange mixture of nervousness and intrepidity', although he 'spoke fearlessly'. His policies were 'sober, and sane and safe' and in parliament he proved practical and diligent. In June 1884 he was rewarded with the lands and immigration portfolio in (Sir) John Colton's [q.v.3] cabinet.

Coles was a just and efficient minister. He ensured that rents were paid and resisted special pleading and indignant squatters' deputations; although 'forcible, often aggressive', he extended 'the greatest leniency where it was justified'. He carried the important Pastoral Crown Lands Act, 1884. Aimed at land speculation, it classified pastoral land, opened old leases to public competition and extended fixity of tenure to genuine settlers.

In 1885 the government fell, and for a time Coles led the Opposition. His 1886 no confidence motion against Sir John Downer [q.v.] forced a restructuring of the cabinet. When Thomas Playford [q.v.] formed a government in 1887 Coles resumed lands and immigration. He amended much legislation to further facilitate settlement. His 1888 Crown Lands Consolidation Act embodied the recommendations of the important commission on the land laws of South Australia of that year, on which he had sat. It divided the colony into land districts with local land boards.

The Playford government was replaced in 1889 and next year Coles was unanimously elected Speaker of the House. The *Register* commented: 'the best prizefighter makes the fairest referee'. He proved an 'alert, suave and wise' arbiter and avoided further active political participation. In 1894 he was appointed K.C.M.G. and moved to Adelaide. A member of the Savage Club, he had joined the Adelaide Club in 1890, and became a director of the Bank of Adelaide. By 1900 his friend C. C. Kingston [q.v.] found him 'not so Liberal as might be wished'. Averse to 'promiscuous society gatherings', he loved a rubber of whist, and was 'a thorough home bird'.

In 1910 Coles achieved a record term as Speaker. He was unwilling to retire when illness overtook him next year and his son relayed his resignation to parliament shortly before Coles's death of Bright's disease at his Glenelg home on 6 December. Eulogies extolling his impartiality and tolerance were extravagant and from all political groups. His family declined the offer of a state funeral as being incompatible with his unostentatious habits.

G. D. Combe, *Responsible government in South Australia* (Adel, 1957); *Gleam,* Oct 1900; *Register* (Adel), 30 June 1854, 7 Dec 1911; *Advertiser* (Adel), 13 Apr 1881, 6 June 1890, 17 Nov, 7, 8 Dec 1911; *Observer* (Adel), 27 Aug 1887, 7 June 1890, 27 May 1893; S. Godwin, The land for the people (B.A. Hons thesis, Univ Adel, 1961); Carruthers papers, vol 20 (ML); PRG 30/5(SAA).   SUZANNE EDGAR

COLLETT, HERBERT BRAYLEY (1877-1947), librarian, soldier and politician, was born on 12 November 1877 at St Peter Port, Guernsey, Channel Islands, son of Frank Collett, auctioneer, and his wife Laura Augusta, née Wedlake. The family arrived in Western Australia in October 1884 and he was educated at Perth Grammar School, joining the staff of the Victoria Public Library, Perth, in 1891. On 20 April 1904 he married Anne Whitfield at St George's Anglican Cathedral.

At 16 Collett had joined the Metropolitan Rifle Volunteers as a private. He rose rapidly to captain and in 1901 commanded a company in the Western Australian contingent to the Sydney ceremonies inaugurating the Commonwealth of Australia. Later that year he was adjutant to the 1st Battalion in the Western Australian Infantry Brigade and, in 1903-06, militia adjutant to the 11th Australian Infantry Regiment. He attended a senior officers' course at the University of Sydney in 1907 and assumed command of the regiment next year – a lieut-colonel at 31. From 23 April 1915 Collett commanded the 28th Battalion of the Australian Imperial Force which he organized and trained to become 'one of the finest in the force'. It embarked for Egypt on 9 June. He served with the battalion at Gallipoli, in Egypt and Sinai, and in France from March 1916. On 29 July he was severely wounded at Pozières. Recuperating in England, he commanded the 4th Training Brigade at Codford before returning to the 28th on 12 October 1917 during the battle of Passchendaele. He acted as brigade commander for several weeks. On 1 June 1918 he was promoted colonel in charge of No. 2 Command Depot at Weymouth where he remained until his discharge from the A.I.F. in September 1919. Collett was mentioned in dispatches, received the Distinguished Service Order in 1916, the C.M.G. in 1919 and was promoted brevet-colonel in the Australian Military Forces for 'specially meritorious service'. He published the first volume of his battalion's history, *The 28th: a record of war service . . .*, in 1922.

In Western Australia in 1915-33 Collett was assistant general secretary to J. S. Battye [q.v.7] at the combined Public Library, Museum and Art Gallery. He commanded the 22nd Brigade in 1920-21 and the 13th Infantry Brigade until 1927. He was aide-de-camp to the governor and to the governor-general and from 1929 honorary colonel of his old battalion (A.M.F.). In 1925-33 he was president of the State branch of the Returned Sailors and Soldiers' Imperial League; during his term, although hampered by government indifference, the R.S.L. built the State war memorial in 1929 and drew up plans for headquarters at Anzac House. He disagreed with (Sir) Gilbert Dyett [q.v.] over tactics and State autonomy, and opposed in vain Dyett's re-election as federal president in 1928, 1929 and 1930.

On 6 April 1933 Collett was chosen by the governor-in-council to fill a Senate vacancy; his election was confirmed by State parliament in July. At the 1934 and 1940 Senate elections he was returned as a Nationalist but in 1946 he was defeated, vacating his seat on 30 June 1947. His main policy interests were defence and ex-servicemen's welfare and he was unofficial spokesman for his State's R.S.L. branch. He was minister in charge of war service homes in 1939-41; vice-president of the Executive Council and minister in charge of scientific and industrial research from August to October 1940; and minister assisting the minister for repatriation from August 1940 to June 1941, after which he was minister for repatriation until the Fadden government fell in October. He chaired the Western Australian War Industries Committee in 1941 and sat on joint committees investigating ex-servicemen's benefits. In 1942-44 he presided over the National Party in Western Australia.

Collett was a Freemason, and patron of the Totally and Permanently Disabled Soldiers' Association of Australia. Survived by his wife and two sons, he died from heart disease on 15 August 1947 and was buried in the Anglican portion of Karrakatta cemetery. A reserved man who inspired respect rather than affection, he possessed a dry humour and had a great concern for his men's welfare: he did not hesitate to criticize inefficiency even when his superiors were involved.

J. S. Battye (ed), *Cyclopedia of Western Australia*, 1 (Adel, 1912); C. E. W. Bean, *The story of Anzac* (Syd, 1924), and *The A.I.F. in France*, 1916 (Syd, 1929); H. K. Kahan, *The 28th Battalion . . .*

(Perth, 1965); G. L. Kristianson, *The politics of patriotism* (Canb, 1966); *Listening Post*, 16 Feb 1923, 23 Oct 1925, 26 Oct 1928, 23 Sept 1932, Apr-Oct 1933; *Reveille* (Syd), 1 Oct 1933; *Nationalist* (Perth), Dec 1942, May, June 1944; *West Australian*, 6 Apr, 3 May 1933, 16 Aug 1947.

                                        DAVID BLACK

COLLICK, EDWARD (HENRY) MALLAN (1868-1959), Anglican priest, was born on 4 November 1868 at Hoxton, Middlesex, England, son of Charles Henry Hornfray Collick, lawyer, and his wife Rosetta, née Mallan. Educated at Christ's Hospital, London, in 1892 he obtained his diploma as a Theological Associate of King's College, London. Ordained deacon that year, and priest in 1893, he became assistant curate at St Andrew's, Hoxton, in the slums of London's East End. In 1894 the Society for the Propagation of the Gospel sent him as a missionary to the Western Australian goldfields; he arrived at Coolgardie in December.

During that summer's typhoid epidemic, his untiring work with the sick and dying won him repute for self-sacrifice. Collick pioneered church work in Coolgardie, then in Menzies and Boulder. For some time he was the only Anglican priest on the goldfields. He roughed it like his flock, and gave his money to the needy: when parishioners raised money for a holiday for him, he gave that away too. His churchmanship was modified in the face of great distances and needs. He established schools, tent hospitals and churches, and formed church-related debating societies, gymnasiums and sporting clubs so that the church could become a community centre. He remained unmarried and his parishioners became his family. He included Aboriginals in his flock — he visited their settlements, nursed their sick, and organized annual tribal Christmas feasts. His example was an uncomfortable one: in 1897 the *Coolgardie Miner* called him 'the white man's living apology . . . of whom we are not worthy'. The Aboriginals called all clergymen 'Mr Collick'.

In March 1901 he went as chaplain with the Fifth Western Australian Contingent to South Africa, and saw action. He worked in England before returning as curate of Kalgoorlie in 1905. He became rector of Boulder in 1907 and archdeacon of the Goldfields and rector of Kalgoorlie in 1912. He continued his habitual self-denial and charity and became a well-known figure in the community. In 1915-19 he was chaplain 4th-class with the Australian Imperial Force in Egypt, England and France, where he worked among stretcher-bearers at the front. He was nominated, probably without his consent, to become second bishop of Kalgoorlie in 1919, but he lacked administrative skills and his nomination received little support.

In 1924-50 Collick was canon of St George's Cathedral and rector of St John's, Fremantle. Congregations grew only slowly under his charge. He assisted ex-prisoners from Fremantle gaol and worked with the Mission to Seamen. He gave money, food and sometimes his own furniture to the port's poor. Contemporaries spoke of his tolerance, sympathy, broad-mindedness and love of laughter; he was a familiar sight on his bicycle around Fremantle. Despite some later eccentricities and an increasing irascibility he retained the respect and admiration of church people and the community and was a special favourite with children.

In 1950 Collick retired in Perth; he was appointed O.B.E. for his 'philanthropy, generosity and practical Christianity'. He died penniless in Mount Hospital, Perth, on 3 June 1959 and was cremated. That year St Andrew's Church at Coolgardie was rebuilt and renamed Canon Collick Memorial Church.

Church of England diocese of Perth, *Qtly Mag*, Jan 1895, Jan 1897, Oct 1898; *WA Church News*, Mar 1897, Mar 1901, May 1902; *Kalgoorlie Diocesan Qtly*, Apr, Oct 1915, Jan 1924; Church of England, *Diocese of Perth Year Book*, 1949, 1950; *Coolgardie Miner*, 3, 16 Mar 1897; *Westralian Worker*, 23 Dec 1910; *Kalgoorlie Miner*, 25 June 1924, 4, 5, 9 June 1959.   E. W. DONCASTER
                                        ELIZABETH WILLIS

COLLIER, FREDERICK REDMOND (1885-1964), singer, was born on 5 October 1885 at Collingwood, Melbourne, son of Daniel Henry Collier, London-born coachpainter, and his wife Catherine, née Redmond, from Kilkenny, Ireland. After education at Victoria Park State School, he joined the Victorian Railways in November 1901 as a 'lad porter' in the traffic branch.

Collier began singing at 10 in the choir of St Philip's Church of England, Collingwood, and later studied with A. E. H. Nickson. In 1907 he won the grand aggregate award at the Ballarat South Street competition, with further success next year. From 1909 to 1919 he was bass soloist at St Patrick's Cathedral, Melbourne. In the war years he took part in patriotic concerts including a series with Melba [q.v.] in aid of the Red Cross. He appeared frequently with the Melbourne Philharmonic and the Royal Victorian Liedertafel, and in 1917 he left the railways to become concert manager for Chappell & Co. Ltd's Melbourne office.

In January 1919 Collier joined the Rigo Grand Opera Company which was taken over later that year by J. C. Williamson's [q.v.6]; Collier toured Australasia as the company's principal baritone. His wife Elsie (Elsy) Louise, née Treweek, whom he had married on 12 January 1910 at St Philip's, Collingwood, was also a member.

In 1921 Collier, Elsy Treweek and their daughter Elva, left for London where Collier joined the British National Opera Company. He became known for his Wagnerian roles, both bass and baritone. His Escamillo in *Carmen* received excellent notices, and he played at various times almost all the bass and baritone roles in *La Bohème*. Collier also sang in three English operas: Holst's *Savitri* and *The Perfect Fool*, and Vaughan Williams's *Hugh the Drover*. Noted for his magnificent dignity of bearing, he was also a fine actor. He sang often on British radio but his few recordings were made under a pseudonym. In 1926 he studied in Milan, returning to sing in the international season of grand opera at Covent Garden in which Melba starred; he took part in her farewell performance of *La Bohème* in June. In 1928-34 he toured Britain as a member of the Carl Rosa Company.

Collier returned to Melbourne in April 1934. From September to April next year he was engaged for Sir Benjamin Fuller's [q.v.] season of grand opera. In 1935-36 he sang in the Australian Broadcasting Commission's grand opera season. On 26 December 1940 he joined the A.B.C's Melbourne Wireless Chorus (later Melbourne Singers), whose work – to 1960 – ranged from opera to light entertainment, and included the 'Village Glee Club' and 'In quires and places where they sing'. In 1940 and 1944 he was with the National Opera Company for short seasons. Collier's last stage appearance was in the 1961 season of *The Most Happy Fella;* in October 1963 he took part in the A.B.C.'s videotaped production of *Simone Boccanegra.*

Collier died on 14 October 1964 at South Yarra, survived by his daughter who also sang professionally for some years. He was cremated.

His wife Elsy, described as 'very beautiful, with fair skin and blue-black hair', had early success in South Street competitions as a soprano. She made her name in Melbourne and interstate as Marguerite in *Faust.* She joined the British National Opera Company but had mostly minor roles. Particularly good in character parts, such as the witch in *Hänsel and Gretel,* she also received acclaim as Venus in *Tannhäuser.* She died on 3 November 1953.

B. and F. Mackenzie, *Singers of Australia* (Melb, 1967); *Listener In,* 14 July 1934, 12 Oct 1935; *Brisbane Courier,* 3 Aug 1918; *Australasian,* 20 July 1921; *Argus,* 6 Apr 1934; A.B.C. Archives (Syd); information from Miss M. Hetherington, East Malvern, and Mrs R. Hickey, Brighton, Vic.

SALLY O'NEILL

COLLIER, JAMES (1846-1925), writer, was born on 12 July 1846 at Dunfermline, Fifeshire, Scotland, son of James Collier, handloom weaver, and his wife Janet, née Dickson. At 12 he became a clerk with Erskine Beveridge and in 1863 went to the University of St Andrews where he read classics and mathematics until 1867 but failed to pay the fee that graduation entailed. In 1868-69 he studied medicine at the University of Edinburgh. In 1870 he was a leader-writer and reviewer for the *Scotsman*. He soon moved to London where he wrote for newspapers and journals, including *Mind*. He impressed Herbert Spencer, who was embarking on his scheme of *Descriptive sociology* and in March 1871 employed Collier as an assistant. Puffing on a cigar, Spencer dictated for three hours in the mornings and in the afternoons directed him to compile and tabulate material. Collier was later relieved of his duties as amanuensis in order to take more responsibility for the *Descriptive sociology*, particularly for the sections published in 1873 and 1881.

Collier spent ten years with Spencer but through overwork and disappointment over an unsuccessful application for a professorship, his health broke down and in 1882 he migrated to New Zealand. In 1885 he was appointed parliamentary librarian at Wellington. There he compiled *The literature relating to New Zealand: a bibliography* (1889), using his knowledge of French and German to advantage in describing over 1200 works. In 1895 Collier settled in Sydney. He published in several journals, including 'The evolution of colonies' in *Appleton's Popular Science Monthly* (1898-99), and articles on sociology in *Knowledge* (1902-04) and on colonization in the *American Journal of Sociology* (1908). In 1904 he contributed his personal reminiscences of Spencer to a biography written by Professor Josiah Royce of Harvard.

On 18 May 1905 at St Andrew's Anglican Cathedral, Collier married Florence Elizabeth Wildbredt, eldest daughter of a baronet Sir William Durrant of Scotlow Hall, Norfolk; they later lived at St Helena, Manly.

Collier wrote on such contemporary events in Australasia as old-age pensions and the early 1900s land scandals for the New York *Nation*; in 1906 he contributed 'Phases of religious reconstruction in France and Germany' to the *Hibbert Journal*. Over the next few years works followed quickly: a spirited biography of an acquaintance Sir George Grey [q.v.1] (1909), introduction and notes to D. Collins's [q.v.1] *An account of the English colony in New South Wales* (Christchurch, 1911), *The pastoral age in Australasia* (London, 1911) and an introduction to E. G. Wakefield's [q.v.2] *A view of the art of colonization* ... (Oxford, 1914).

Collier had remained a disciple of Spencer. His writings reveal an encyclopaedic knowledge carefully structured to support his obsessive belief that evolution was a universal principle, applicable to poetry and politics as well as to protoplasm. Biological terminology is the hallmark of his work and references to Charles Darwin [q.v.1] and Herbert Spencer abound. Intensely interested in history, he saw endless comparisons between developments in nature and society. The ease and frankness with which he connected biological and social subjects were well suited to hold the attention of nineteenth-century readers of popular, scientific magazines, even if not all of them accepted his generalizations. Some of his opinions sprang from a survival-of-the-fittest view of society. He believed that the Aboriginal population's decline, although regrettably painful, was the inevitable consequence of white man's natural superiority. He was less extreme in dealing with other social and economic questions.

Survived by his wife but childless, Collier died at St Ronan's Private Hospital, Manly, on 21 June 1925 and was buried in the Presbyterian section of Manly cemetery.

H. Spencer, *An autobiography*, 1 (Lond, 1904); *SMH*, 22 June 1925.   JILL WATERHOUSE

COLLIER, PHILLIP (1873-1948), premier, was born on 21 April 1873 at Woodstock near Melbourne, son of Phillip Collier, farmer, and his wife Catherine, née Bourke. Collier left school at 16 to go goldmining in Victoria and New South Wales; he was later foreman on the Melbourne sewerage works at Northcote. As founding secretary of the local Political Labor Council branch, he acted as campaign director for State and Federal election candidates, including Frank Anstey [q.v.7]. On 27 June 1900 at Northcote he married Ellen Heagney; they had four children.

In 1904 Collier moved to Western Australia to work with the Perseverance Gold Mining Co. at Boulder. As a delegate from the Amalgamated Workers' Association, he was vice-president of the goldfields Trades and Labor Council in 1905. Aided by his Victorian reputation, Collier soon won preselection for the Boulder seat in the Legis-

lative Assembly. That year, when Labor lost ten seats, he narrowly defeated the sitting member J. M. Hopkins. In 1908 he easily retained the seat and was opposed in only four out of twelve elections in 1911-47.

In his maiden speech Collier attacked Hopkins's alleged favouritism in allocating crown land to selectors, but for six years he spoke rarely and usually briefly. His main interests were mining and State and Federal land tax; he won legitimation for children born out of wedlock, whose parents subsequently married. In 1910 he was prominent in a stormy debate on the Wilson [q.v.] government's electoral redistribution.

When Labor took office under John Scaddan [q.v.] in October 1911, Collier became minister for mines and railways. A capable administrator, he had his hands full with the railway unions who resented alleged opposition to their wage demands. While caucus always backed him in such disputes, he was relieved to hand the portfolio to Scaddan in 1914. He succeeded T. H. Bath [q.v.7] as second senior member of the cabinet and became minister for water-supply, sewerage and drainage. Collier avoided the opprobrium of the 1915 Nevanas scandal which helped destroy the government in mid-1916. That year he was increasingly forthright in his opposition to conscription. In September he rejected caucus requests to become temporary leader, while Scaddan, who was becoming vulnerable because of his support for conscription, was temporarily out of parliament; when he resigned, Collier took his place in May 1917.

In December, during the second conscription referendum, Collier was fined by magistrate W. A. G. Walter [q.v.] at Kalgoorlie for utterances 'likely to cause disaffection'. Although the High Court eventually quashed the sentence, it rankled and when Collier was premier in 1924 he arranged to retire Walter somewhat prematurely.

Under Collier the Western Australian Labor Party slowly overcame the effects of the conscription split. During the disturbances on the Fremantle waterfront in May 1919 which forced premier (Sir) Hal Colebatch [q.v.] to resign, Collier congratulated the workers and bitterly, and perhaps unjustly, attacked Colebatch for allowing the police to use firearms. Nevertheless, they worked harmoniously when Collier was premier and Colebatch agent-general; Collier also had a warm working relationship with (Sir) James Mitchell [q.v.] who succeeded Colebatch as premier.

A split in the Country Party helped Labor to a narrow victory in April 1924 and Collier's government was returned for a second term in 1927. As premier, treasurer and minister for forests and industries, he had a capable and efficient cabinet. Taxation was reduced and in mid-term the government budgeted for the first surplus in sixteen years. In its emphasis on rural development, the ministry differed little from its predecessor. Generous advances, through the Agricultural Bank, were continued to intending settlers and much loan money was spent on railways, water-supplies, roads and bridges. The government saw the area under wheat more than double, and output treble. After hesitating, it also continued Mitchell's scheme to establish a dairy industry in the south-west. Despite some Labor opposition group settlement was linked with an active programme of British migration. Collier's 1925 visit to England resulted in an agreement with the British and Australian governments to settle British migrants on the land; he secured low interest loans to cover the cost. Over 4000 migrants a year were assisted in 1925-28.

Throughout his career Collier, who possessed a certain charm, and his ministers dominated caucus. Close co-operation between the unions and the party reflected the unique structure of the Western Australian movement whereby the State executive also acted as a trades and labour council, and revealed the dominance of the Australian Workers' Union to which most leading government members, including Collier, belonged. Despite problems with a hostile Legislative Council the government also protected its industrial supporters. Substantial improvements were made to workers' compensation and industrial arbitration legislation; the first full-time president of the Arbitration Court was appointed; for the first time a State basic wage and a forty-four hour week were granted; preference for unionists was given to most government workers; the State Government Accident Insurance Office established. Other notable achievements of Collier's first administration included the State's first metropolitan Town Planning Act, the setting up of a main roads board, and further legislation on the protection of illegitimate children and married women.

The one rift in party-union harmony was a clash in December 1924 between the government and the Seamen's Union of Australia, when police were allowed on the waterfront to protect passengers on a ship that the union had declared black. After a protracted dispute the party in 1925 upheld the government's action by a large majority. The rise in unemployment in the late 1920s produced criticism within the labour movement about migration and the need for practical schemes of work provision. Collier

as treasurer also had to accept diminished independence for the State resulting from the end of per capita payments by the Commonwealth and the financial agreement of 1928. However, he presided over the centenary celebrations in 1929 with little apparent premonition of the economic troubles to come.

Collier's defeat by Mitchell in the 1930 election was a disguised blessing. In coping with the Depression, his sympathies were with the 'sound finance' policies of the prime minister, J. A. Lyons [q.v.], but as Opposition leader he could criticize the details and implementation of the Premiers' Plan. The local Labor Party thus avoided the split which shattered their Federal and some State counterparts, with Collier playing a crucial role. He lacked sympathy with the more militant unemployed – he warned the Labor premier of South Australia of 'reds' in their ranks – but Mitchell's government had to bear the brunt of mass demonstrations.

In April 1933 Collier led the party to a sweeping victory on the same day as the electors voted to secede from the Australian Commonwealth. With most Labor members opposed to secession, Collier skilfully defused the issue. He appointed a delegation of secessionist leaders, with Labor supporters conspicuously absent; its petition was rejected by the British parliament's 1935 select committee, but by then the economy had improved and the movement lost momentum. This achievement was not fully appreciated by a few of Collier's followers. They also resented his unilateral action (and misleading explanations) in appointing Mitchell as lieut-governor. Collier now held the posts of premier, treasurer and minister for forests. He had some success at conferences in the east, but his absences from his office became more frequent and he grew less tolerant of opposition within the party. From November 1934 to January 1935, at the suggestion of colleagues, he holidayed in New Zealand to restore his health.

Collier remained premier after Labor was returned in 1936 but on 19 August, after the expression of some concern within the government, he decided to step down. He realized that increasing ill health – aggravated, no doubt, over many years, by a personal failing – had made him lose confidence. After a record term of nearly nineteen years as Labor leader and nine years as premier, he was succeeded by his deputy J. C. Willcock [q.v.]. In the next twelve years as a backbencher he spoke only twice: once, while attacking a Labor government bill to legalize off-course bookmaking, he implied disloyalty from within the party during his final phase as premier; viewed dispassionately this was probably unfair. He died on 18

October 1948 after almost forty-three years continuous parliamentary service, a record not exceeded until 1976 (by J. T. Tonkin). Survived by his wife, two sons and two daughters, he was given a state funeral and was buried in the Roman Catholic section of Karrakatta cemetery. His estate was sworn for probate at £28 498.

At the peak of his powers Collier had been Labor's greatest Western Australian leader and could have shone in Federal politics. He was a man of wit and intellectual capacity, well read in humanitarian literature and poetry. Despite a lack of formal training he displayed great financial ability and developed into an effective speaker. A moderate, especially after 1924, he nevertheless possessed a stubborn, ruthless streak and could play politics hard. At the same time his balance, tolerance and ability earned him deep respect, and his personal friendship with Mitchell influenced the character of Western Australian politics. Loyal as he was to his party, Collier still had his own scale of values, as evidenced by his fervent anti-Communism, his encouragement of prospecting parties to solve unemployment and his support for capital punishment against party policy, when two policemen were murdered on the goldfields. He always remained something of a loner.

J. S. Battye (ed), *Cyclopedia of Western Australia*, 1 (Adel, 1912); J. G. Wilson (ed), *Western Australia's centenary, 1829-1929* (Perth, 1929); G. C. Bolton, *A fine country to starve in* (Perth, 1972); D. J. Murphy (ed), *Labor in politics* (Brisb, 1975); V. Courtney, *All I may tell* (Syd, 1956); *Univ Studies in History* (WA), 3 (1959), no 3; *To-day* (Melb), 1 Mar 1933; *Tocsin*, 16 Oct 1902; *Western Argus,* 26 Sept 1905; *Kalgoorlie Miner,* 10, 16, 30, 31 Oct 1905, 9, 13 Mar 1918; *West Australian,* 28 Oct 1905, 13, 22 Dec 1917, 26, 28 May 1924, 19, 20 Oct 1948; *Daily News* (Perth), 29 Jan 1935; *Record* (Perth), 21 Oct 1948; D. Black, The early administrations of Philip Collier (B.A. Hons thesis, Univ WA, 1959); R. F. Pervan, The Western Australian Labor movement, 1933-47 (M.A. thesis, Univ WA, 1966).

DAVID BLACK

COLLINGRIDGE DE TOURCEY, GEORGE ALPHONSE (1847-1931), artist and historian, was born on 29 October 1847 at Goddington Manor, near Bicester, Oxfordshire, England, son of William Collingridge, and his wife Louisa, née Maguire. He rarely used 'de Tourcey'. His parents moved to France in 1853 and he was educated at the Jesuit College, Vaugirard, and the Académie des Beaux-Arts, Paris, studying architecture under Viollet-le-Duc, wood-engraving and painting. Corot informally accepted him as a pupil, a very rare favour. In 1867, when Garibaldi invaded the Roman States, Collingridge joined the Papal Zouaves and took part in seventeen engagements, receiving no wounds but three medals, including the Mentana Cross.

In 1869-70 he was back in Paris, returning to England after Sedan before settling again in Paris in 1872. Although he continued to paint throughout his career — he held his last exhibition in 1926 — he now found his real *métier* in wood-engraving, then the staple form of graphics in such famous journals as the *Illustrated London News* and *L'Illustration*, for both of which he worked. Collingridge very probably engraved for Gustave Doré, and made many blocks from drawings by Daniel Vierge, especially in the great 1877-78 edition of Michelet's *Histoire de France*. In 1878 *Le Monde Illustré* sent him to Spain with Vierge to cover the marriage of Alfonso XII.

On the advice of his brother Arthur (1853-1907), also an artist, who was already in Australia, Collingridge migrated in 1879 to join the *Illustrated Sydney News*, in which he published the first picture of Jenolan Caves (1881), from Arthur's drawing; he also worked for the *Australian Town and Country Journal* and the *Sydney Mail*. He very quickly made his mark, gaining the first prize for xylography at the Sydney International Exhibition in 1879; his view of Bathurst in 1880 was thought to be the largest wood-engraving yet produced. Dissatisfaction with lay control of the existing New South Wales Academy of Art led the brothers to found the (Royal) Art Society of New South Wales in July 1880, and in 1888 they launched the short-lived *Australian Art*, the first such journal in the continent. Both brothers taught in schools and technical colleges — George, who wrote a manual *Form and colour,* at Sydney Technical College.

On 23 November 1882 at the Villa Maria Chapel, Hunters Hill, Collingridge married Lucy Monica Makinson, who bore him four sons and two daughters. He took up a small property on Berowra Creek; in *Berowra & the unsolved mystery of its amazing ridge* (1924) he told of finding that the Department of Lands had omitted four or five miles of foreshore from its maps. By 1895 he had settled at Jave-la Grande, Hornsby, where he published, irregularly, a journal called *Progress*, which combined real-estate boosting for the new northern suburbs of Sydney with articles on Australian maritime discovery.

This latter theme became an over-riding passion, and between 1890 and 1925 Collingridge devoted two books and some thirty articles to establishing Portuguese priority. He based himself largely, but far from solely, on the maps produced at Dieppe between 1536 and 1566 showing a large land mass,

Jave-la Grande, in the right latitudes for Australia, but wrong longitudes. Collingridge's *magnum opus* is *The discovery of Australia* (Sydney, 1895); the smaller *First discovery of Australia and New Guinea* (Sydney, 1906) was designed for New South Wales schools but, owing to a change in administration, not adopted. He amassed formidable documentation, especially cartographic, in support of his thesis that the Portuguese had charted all but the south coast of Australia before 1530, and he put forward his views with great vigour and ingenuity; his skill as a draughtsman provided sometimes quaint illustrations to a lively if not always well-organized presentation. The analysis of the nomenclature on the Dieppe maps is thorough and acute, and since his work hardly any serious student, even amongst those who discount the evidential value of the maps, has disputed their Portuguese origins. On the other hand, his enthusiasm led him too often into special pleading, even into gratuitous attempts to discredit undoubted Dutch discoveries, and such extravagances must have contributed to his failure to obtain general acceptance. Nevertheless, it is now increasingly recognized that the cartographical core of his argument deserves more serious consideration than it received from orthodox Australian historians, with the partial exception of G. A. Wood [q.v.]. He was a prophet not without honours in countries other than his own: knight commander of the Portuguese Order of St James of the Sword (1908) and the Spanish Royal American Order of Isabella the Catholic (1917). In 1909 he was made the first honorary member of the (Royal) Australian Historical Society.

Collingridge was a most versatile and active man, and the pseudonym he sometimes assumed, 'the Hermit of Berowra', was a distinct misnomer. He had six languages, plus Esperanto, and in 1908 founded the first Esperanto Club in Australia. His later writings, privately published at Hornsby in the 1920s, are a strange medley, abounding in plugs for Esperanto and Portuguese priority and in the most bizarre puns. They include children's books – *Alice in one dear land* (1922) and *Through the joke in class* (1923), which may have had some appeal in their time; *IT is principally a collection of woodcuts* (1924); *Round and round the world* (1925-33), good humoured rambling reminiscences of travel; and *Pacifika, the antediluvian world* (1928-30?), which seeks to show that 'Atlantis' was really in the Pacific and that all later civilizations were its offshoots.

Collingridge died on 1 June 1931 and was buried in the Catholic section of the Field of Mars cemetery. He was survived by three sons and one daughter. In his earlier days,

his reputation as a wood-engraver stood high, but with the advent of photo-processing the demand and the reward for such work rapidly dwindled away. He was untrained as a historian and there was thus no check to his uncritical zeal for his theories. The impression remains, however, of a genial and engaging personality and a lively if undisciplined intellect. His talents were doubtless dissipated through a lack of rigour and by the pressures of work for a living on a falling market; but he deserves respect as a pioneer in the history of one aspect of Australia's origins. With all its flaws, *The discovery of Australia* is certainly a remarkable work for its time and especially for its place, far from the great centres of palaeocartographical research.

K. G. McIntyre, *The secret discovery of Australia* (Medindie, 1977); *Lone Hand*, 1 Sept 1917; *T&CJ*, 21 Jan 1882; *Sydney Mail*, 31 Oct 1923; *SMH*, 2 June 1931; Collingridge MSS (Dixson Lib, Syd); ML printed cat for his publications; information from Miss W. Collingridge, Hornsby, NSW.

O. H. K. SPATE

COLLINGS, JOSEPH SILVER (1865-1955), party organizer and politician, was born on 11 May 1865 at Brighton, England, son of Joseph Silver Collings, shopkeeper, and Mary Ann, née Dyke, his Quaker wife. Educated at Brighton Board School and by his mother and free-thinking father, he read advanced books when young, and later reported for the *Sussex Daily News*. Collings came to Brisbane with his parents on the *Roma* in 1883 and became a farm labourer and an unsuccessful selector at Mooloolah. Later, he worked in the office of the boot manufacturer, E. T. Neighbour, and managed Hunter's shoe store in Fortitude Valley. A florid, melodramatic orator, he was a popular speaker in the Christian Socialist Brotherhood, the Social Democrat Vanguard and the Rationalist Society.

Collings was briefly secretary of the Queensland Boot and Shoe Manufacturers' Association and helped significantly to terminate a boot strike in May 1890. In a strike in 1895 his involvement with southern scabs was anathema to the union, but he became a member of the Bulimba Workers Political Organisation from about 1900. In the absence of Ernest Lane [q.v.], in 1903 Collings probably wrote his column in the *Worker*. After the Brisbane general strike of 1912 he was given a testimonial 'in consideration of his self-sacrificing services to the Labor cause', and the Boot Trade Union forgave his lapse in 1895. Editing the *Official Bulletin* for the strike, he wrote, 'it is a bigger sin to starve than to steal in a land of plenty'. His success as editor led to the publication of the *Daily Standard* and he became chairman of the provisional directors.

After the strike Collings founded and was president of the Queensland Federated Clerks Union. In 1908, 1909, and 1915 he lost in contests for the Legislative Assembly, but in 1910-13 he sat on the Balmoral Shire Council. In 1905 he began a long attendance at the annual Labor-in-Politics conventions, and was regularly elected to Labor's central political executive and the Queensland central executive from 1913 to 1928. In 1927-33, he was a Queensland delegate to the federal conference of the Australian Labor Party.

In 1914-15, Collings was an organizer for the central political executive, then probably spent several years in labour journalism. He was an organizer again, with the same salary as the secretary of the executive, from 1919 until 1931. During the early 1930s when the general secretary, Lewis McDonald [q.v.], was ill, Collings carried much of the administration. He recruited widely, often travelling by bicycle, and reported his own meetings in glowing terms in the press. In 1916 he was an anti-conscription leader, campaigning throughout Queensland and in Victoria.

Appointed to the Legislative Council in 1920, he loyally voted for its dissolution. About 1923 he made a speaking tour of New Zealand, and in 1931 served as organizing secretary for the provisional State executive set up in New South Wales by the federal party. Elected to the Senate in 1931, Collings became leader of the Opposition there in 1935 and government leader in 1941. He was minister for the interior from October 1941 to July 1945, then vice-president of the Executive Council to November 1946. In September, he had been leader of the Australian delegation to the International Labour Conference at Montreal, Canada.

As minister for the interior during World War II he worked closely with E. G. Theodore [q.v.] on the Allied Works Council, was president of the River Murray Commission and chairman of the board of management of the Australian War Memorial. As a teetotaller, he was unpopular with some Canberra residents because of liquor restrictions. In 1943 he prosecuted the secretary of the Victorian Building Trades Federation for inciting a strike at a war factory, and the unions unsuccessfully urged his dismissal. Collings bore his unpopularity with equanimity.

He retired to Brighton, Queensland, in 1950 and died there on 20 June 1955. His body was cremated after a state funeral at which Dr J. V. Duhig [q.v.] delivered the panegyric. On 26 December 1885 at the Oxley Registry he had married Kate McInerney; of their six children, one son and one daughter survived. An archetypal party bureaucrat, his abilities in writing and speaking were valuable, and he enjoyed ministerial rank as a reward for long years of dedicated work.

E. Lane, *Dawn to dusk* (Brisb, 1939); L. F. Crisp, *Ben Chifley* (Melb, 1961); D. J. Murphy et al (eds), *Prelude to power* (Brisb, 1970); D. J. Murphy, *T. J. Ryan* (Brisb, 1975); P. M. Weller (ed), *Caucus minutes*, 1-3 (Melb, 1975); *Worker* (Brisb), 24 Jan 1903; Aust Boot Trade Employees Federation (Qld), Minute-book, T49/1/4 (ANU Archives).

                                        JOY GUYATT

COLLINS, CUTHBERT QUINLAN DALE (1897-1956), author, was born on 9 April 1897 at Balmain, Sydney, third son of Michael John Collins, an Irish doctor who had been a ship's surgeon in the Royal Mail Steam Packet Co., and his English wife Esther, née Copeland. Michael died of typhoid at Launceston, Tasmania, on 31 May 1898, before the birth of Dale's younger brother John, the future vice admiral and chief of the Australian Naval Staff. The family moved to Melbourne where, after minimal schooling much interrupted by illness, Collins became an office boy in a music warehouse. He was a voracious reader and incessantly wrote stories.

After moving to a suburban newspaper as a jack of all trades, Collins joined the Melbourne *Herald* as a reporter. He wrote for *Table Talk*, contributed stories to the *Bulletin* and in 1922 wrote *Stolen or strayed*, a melodramatic crime novel, which the N.S.W. Bookstall Co. bought for £25 and published. The same year, with the blessing of the *Herald* and on his own recommendation as a 'brilliant writer' and the 'only man in Australia ideal for the job', he was engaged by A. Y. Gowen, an American millionaire then visiting Brisbane, to accompany him on a world tour aboard his motor yacht the *Speejacks*. The voyage provided a store of material from which Collins would draw repeatedly, but chiefly for the books that established his name: *Sea-tracks of the Speejacks round the world* (London, 1923) and his second novel, *Ordeal* (1924), a best seller which was produced as a play in 1925 and later filmed as *The ship from Shanghai*.

Collins made London his base in 1923 and travelled extensively until World War II. He wrote prolifically for British and American magazines, often completing a 6000-word story in a day. Between 1925 and 1936 he completed twelve novels, most of them sea romances pitched unashamedly at a popular readership. He is rightly criticized by H. M. Green for wasting the promise of his talent in 'mere thrillerism', although his gift for description, especially of the sea in its different moods, is impressive. In all, he wrote thirty-seven books, including the autobiographical *Bright vista* (London, 1946) and *Victoria's my home ground* (Melbourne, 1951), and ten novels for children, most as Dale Collins, but some as 'Stephen Fennimore'. He also used the pen name 'Michael Copeland'.

In 1948 he returned to Melbourne to settle in Malvern. A 'pudgy, friendly little man', described as 'rather innocuous-looking and owlish behind horn-rimmed glasses', Collins claimed no hobbies and few active interests. His first wife, Melbourne-born divorcee, Aileen Mayal Davies, née Edmondstone, whom he had married in London on 30 June 1927, had died in Jersey in 1933. On 16 August 1939 in London he married Kathleen Pratt, by whom he had two daughters. Collins died of hypertensive cardiovascular disease in the Alfred Hospital, Melbourne, on 3 March 1956 and was buried with Catholic rites in Melbourne general cemetery. His estate was sworn for probate at £4886. An inscribed set of his books is held by the La Trobe Library, State Library of Victoria.

C. Roderick, *20 Australian novelists* (Syd, 1947); M. Muir, *A bibliography of Australian children's books* (Lond, 1970); *People* (Syd), 20 Dec 1950; *Age*, and *Argus*, 5 Mar 1956; information from Vice Admiral Sir John Collins, Sydney.

STUART SAYERS

COLLINS, GEORGE THOMAS (1839-1926), lawyer and politician, was born on 10 May 1839 at Launceston, Van Diemen's Land, son of William Collins, publican, and his wife Martha Matilda, née Rolls. In 1843 five months before his father's death he, his mother and his brothers, William Anthony and Charles Percival, joined the household of (Sir) Adye Douglas [q.v.4] who subsequently married Martha in England in 1858. Educated at Launceston Church Grammar School and the Church of England Grammar School, Campbell Town, Collins was articled to Douglas, admitted to the Bar of the Supreme Court of Tasmania in 1861, and soon entered the partnership of Douglas and Collins in Launceston. On 29 April 1863 at St Andrew's Presbyterian Church Collins married Ursula Flora McEachern.

In May 1895, after thirty years as a leading equity and criminal lawyer, he won the Legislative Council seat of Tamar; the Launceston *Examiner* had attempted to discredit him as a vacillating anti-Federationist, but Collins dispelled these doubts in the council. In October 1899 the *Examiner* encouraged speculation that he might be called upon to form a government and then welcomed his appointment as chief secretary in the Lewis [q.v.] ministry. Collins retained this office until 1903, whilst also holding the portfolios of agriculture and, until 1901, defence; meanwhile his eyesight failed and it was not rectified by surgery in Germany in 1906. In 1919 he retired from both the parliament and his practice.

More significant than Collins's parliamentary contribution, was the range of Launceston organizations for which he worked. A director of several companies and president of the Launceston Chamber of Commerce in 1910-12, he chaired numerous sporting bodies including the Tamar Rowing Club (1878-1925), Northern Tasmanian Rowing (1912-19) Cricket (1879-1919) and Golf (1903-22) associations, Launceston Bowling Club (1893-1920), Tasmania Bowling Association (1902-19) and Turf Club (1906-22), continuing as patron of many of these groups until his death. Vice-chairman of the Launceston Technical School Committee, he was warden of the Marine Board (1909-18), president of the Northern Tasmanian Fisheries' Association (1898-1921) and of the Central Board of Health (1900-03) and chairman of the Northern Tasmanian division of the Red Cross Society (1914-23).

Perhaps Collins's main concerns were the Launceston General Hospital, of which he was board chairman in 1879-99 and 1909-22, and the Launceston Artillery which claimed his attention from 1862, when he joined as a gunner, till 1902 when he retired from the command, having received the Volunteer Officers' Decoration in 1898 for twenty years continuous service as an officer. An enthusiastic amateur violinist, he was also a prominent patron of the arts. Appointed C.M.G. in 1919, he died on 25 August 1926, survived by his wife, three sons and four daughters. He was buried in Carr Villa cemetery, leaving an estate valued for probate at £83421.

Examiner (Launc), 7, 8 May 1895, 7-11 Oct 1899, 26, 28 Aug 1926; *Mercury,* 26 Aug 1926; Douglas family papers (TA); MSS 75/909, and 71/41 (TA).

JOHN O'HARA

COLLINS, HENRIETTA WYSE; *see* GREVILLE

COLLINS, HENRY MICHAEL (1844-1928), Reuter's agent, was born on 22 January 1844 at North Savernake, Wiltshire, England, fourth of the twelve children of Francis Michael Collins, agent to the second marquis of Ailesbury, and his wife Mary Ann, née Woods. Collins was well educated but had to leave school before he was 16; his first work was as a private tutor. In 1861 he was assistant schoolmaster at a preparatory school at Streatham, where one of his pupils was Herbert, son of (Baron) Julius Reuter, founder of Reuter's Telegram Co. Ltd. Next year he joined the company.

In February 1866 Collins left London for Bombay to set up and maintain Reuter's Indian and Far East agencies. He returned to England on leave in July 1872, detouring via Alexandria to reorganize the mismanaged agency there. Impressed by Collins's talent, Julius Reuter seconded him to act as his special representative for a private speculation in Persia known as the Reuter Concession. From about March 1873 he was based in Teheran; at near-by Gulahek on 2 October 1875 he married Isabella Maria Baker. Collins was recalled to London in 1878. In July he accepted the new agency post of general manager for Australasia, with Melbourne as his base.

An agreement to supply news to major Australian dailies had taken effect from 21 October 1872, and Reuter's had first used the existing telegraphic services of E. Greville [q.v.4] of Sydney, but in June 1874 he was replaced by Reuter's own men: Ferdinand Linden in Melbourne and Collins's younger brother Ernest Edward in Sydney. Henry's appointment coincided with one of the recurrent periods of tension between Reuter's and the Australian press barons, which Reuter's accepted because profitability in Australia depended not so much on the news services but on commercial activities, especially private telegrams and, from 1891, cash remittances cabled at cheaper than bank rates.

Collins's reputation within Reuter's was always high. The flair and energy of his early years may have been lost, but his skill and tact as a special investigator was employed again during a crisis in the South African office just before and during the war of 1899-1902, when Reuter's reputation for impartiality came under scrutiny. On his retirement in December 1909, Collins regarded the tribute paid to him by his Australian staff (which had grown from three to over ninety) as the highest possible praise: 'you have made the name of "Reuter" a synonym for efficiency and honourable dealing'. Henry was succeeded by Ernest, who had to retire for health reasons on 30 June 1913.

Henry Collins had joined the Board of the Alfred Hospital in 1895 and his involvement in its affairs increased after his retirement; he was vice-president in 1911-24 and president in 1924-27. In 1925 he published his reminiscences, *From pigeon post to wireless*. He had lost money in the banking crisis of the 1890s but the set-back was temporary

and his home, Gracehill, Frankston, was built for him about 1910. Collins also had a small farm in the district. He maintained his business contacts as the Victorian agent for W. & A. Gilbey Ltd, liquor distributors. This interest was taken over by his eldest son Henry Edmund Julius. Mrs Collins died in England in 1917 while on a visit. Henry Collins, the last of Reuter's pioneer generation, collapsed and died in Swanston Street, Melbourne, on 11 June 1928, and was privately cremated. He was survived by three sons and four daughters; one son had been killed at Ypres in 1917.

J. Smith (ed), *Cyclopedia of Victoria*, 1 (Melb, 1903); G. Storey, *Reuters' century, 1851-1951* (Lond, 1951); F. Clune, *Overland telegraph* (Syd, 1955); A. M. Mitchell, *The hospital south of the Yarra* (Melb, 1977); information from Mr T. M. Collins, Greta South, NSW, Mrs L. Lempriere, Malvern, Vic, and Reuters' Limited, Lond.

ANN M. MITCHELL

COLLINS, HERBERT LESLIE (1889-1959), cricketer, was born on 21 January 1889 in Sydney, son of Thomas Jones Collins, accountant, and his wife Emma, née Charlton. Educated at Albion Street (Superior) Public School, he was promising at cricket and Rugby Union from his schooldays. He played for the Paddington District Cricket Club under M. A. Noble [q.v.], and transferred to Sydney in 1909-10, when he made his Sheffield Shield début. In 1911-12 he topped the first grade batting with 727 runs at 66; next season he became established in the State side and scored 282 against Tasmania. He toured the United States of America and Canada in 1913 and New Zealand in 1914.

In June 1915 Collins enlisted in the Australian Imperial Force and served in Palestine with 6th Company Army Service Corps, and from June 1916 with 10th Company as a driver in France. Invited to join the A.I.F. team formed in England in 1919 Collins, although only a lance corporal, was elected captain after Charles Kellaway disputed with officials and his fellow players. On the tour of England and South Africa Collins scored 2290 runs at 41, took 145 wickets and proved himself an astute leader: among his 'discoveries' were J. M. Gregory and W. A. S. Oldfield [qq.v.].

Collins was discharged from the A.I.F. in March 1920. Next summer he was vice-captain to W. W. Armstrong [q.v.7] against the touring English side, and forged a formidable opening partnership with Warren Bardsley [q.v.7], with whom he shared three century stands; Collins's 557 runs at 61 in the series included 70 and 104 in the first Test and 162 at Adelaide. A broken thumb and the superiority of the Australians restricted him to three test innings on the 1921 tour of England but his dour 40 in 289 minutes at Old Trafford made safe the only Test in which the visitors were extended.

En route home Collins deputized for the injured Armstrong in the three tests against South Africa, scoring 203 in a day at Johannesburg. He was appointed captain for the 1924-25 series against A. E. R. Gilligan's English side; although he did little with the bat after an obdurate 114 in the first Test, he led Australia to a convincing 4/1 victory in the series. On his last tour of England in 1926 he was hampered by neuritis, but scored a skilful 61 in the decisive Oval Test, in which his team lost the Ashes. Further injuries caused his retirement soon after returning to Australia.

As a batsman Collins was no great stylist: primarily an on-side player, he scored most of his runs from deft placements and glances, with an occasional over the shoulder hook. Adjectives such as 'stolid', 'imperturbable' and 'courageous' abound in descriptions of his play, which was based on defence and concentration. Whereas the 'big ship' Armstrong was the rumbustious authoritarian captain, the small, dapper, leathery Collins exuded a quiet control which won the respect and loyalty of team-mates and the affection of his opponents. 'Nerveless as a city window cleaner', he enhanced his reputation by a poker face and a lugubrious expression. In 19 tests Collins scored 1352 runs at 45, and in all first-class matches just under 10 000 at 40. He bowled a tidy left-arm orthodox spin from a run up of two paces, and was a fine field. He was elected a life member of the New South Wales Cricket Association in 1936-37.

A passionate gambler, Collins was known to his public as 'Horseshoe' or 'Lucky' and to his team-mates as 'Mauldy', 'Nutty' or 'Bert'. Towards the end of his playing career he became a bookmaker on the Associated Racing Clubs' pony courses, and was later a stipendiary steward and commission agent. In July 1940 he enlisted in the second A.I.F. and from November was a sergeant in Eastern Command's Salvage and Recovery Section of the Army Service Corps; he was transferred to the reserve in November 1941. On 30 October 1939 he had married Marjorie Warilda Paine, whom he divorced in 1953.

Survived by a son, Collins died of cancer in Prince Henry Hospital on 28 May 1959 and was cremated.

A. E. R. Gilligan, *Collins's men* (Lond, 1926); R. Barker and I. Rosenwater, *England v Australia… 1877-1968* (Melb, 1969); R. Mason, *Warwick Armstrong's Australians* (Lond, 1971); R. Robinson, *On top down under* (Syd, 1975); *Wisden Cricketers' Almanack*, 1910-15, 1920-28, 1960; *People* (Syd), 25 Feb 1953; *SMH*, 19 Apr, 14 Nov 1921, 3 Oct, 31 Dec 1925, 10 Jan 1952, 29, 31 May 1959; news-cuttings file (NL).   B. G. ANDREWS

COLLINS, JAMES RICHARD (1869-1934), public servant, was born on 14 March 1869 at Sebastopol, Victoria, son of James Richard Collins, London-born miner, and his wife Catherine, née Drummond, of Scotland. He was educated at state schools in Ballarat, and joined the Victorian Public Service as a clerk in the Treasury on 16 June 1886. In 1893 he was selected by G. T. Allen [q.v.7] to assist in the preparation of the colonial budget and in 1900 he organized and ran the first Victorian Old Age Pensions Office.

From 1 January until mid-April 1901 Collins worked in the accountant's branch in the dual position of serving both the State and Federal treasurers. He transferred to the Commonwealth Treasury on 18 April as a clerk, at a salary of £250, deputy to Allen. He held a series of positions between 1901 and 1916, acting as secretary during Allen's absence for a total of two years eight months. During periods of furlough in 1908 and 1915 he studied financial and departmental matters in Ottawa and Washington. On 14 March 1916, he replaced Allen as secretary to the Treasury and commissioner of war, invalid and old age pensions and maternity allowances, at a salary of £1000. His signature appeared on paper money issued in Australia between 1910 and July 1926.

From July 1920 to January 1921, Collins acted as temporary commissioner for the negotiation of the Nauru Island agreement in London, and was delegate to the International Financial Conference in Brussels and to the first meeting of the Assembly of the League of Nations at Geneva. He was appointed C.M.G. in 1920 and C.B.E. in 1923. In the reorganization of the Commonwealth Bank undertaken in 1923 he became a director of the Note Issue Board on 14 December and on 10 October 1924 was appointed a director of the bank itself. From 1923 he was national debt commissioner and a custodian of expropriated properties in what was formerly German New Guinea.

On 29 April 1926 Prime Minister Bruce [q.v.7] announced Collins's appointment as financial adviser to the high commissioner in London and member of the London Board of Advice of the Commonwealth Bank, with a salary and allowances of £2750; he took up the post on 3 August. Collins was to advise the Commonwealth on economic and financial matters in London and arrange the raising of loans for the Loan Council and the bank, a task which became increasingly onerous as the Australian overseas debt increased.

Collins also represented Australia on the Pacific Cable Board (1926-30), as a member of the Reparations Conference at The Hague (1929-30) and Lausanne (1932) and as leader of the delegation to the Assembly of the League of Nations in 1931. In August 1930 his term on the London board of the bank expired but he retained his position as financial adviser until 1933. His health, however, was not good. After a visit to Australia in December 1933 he died in London on 18 June 1934, leaving an estate valued for probate at £16430. He was survived by his wife Alice Ada, née Stephenson, whom he had married with Anglican rites at Warragul, Victoria, on 22 July 1891. They had no children.

Known as '"Wilkie" ... when out of hearing', Collins was described in 1916 as 'ruddy, chubby faced, round of figure'. He was an active Freemason. In his leisure he read voluminously, always on subjects related to his work. His long-time colleague, C. J. Cerutty, paid tribute in 1934 to his profound knowledge of public finance gained 'not only by experience, but by deep study'; he was 'indefatigable in his work and conscientious in his duty'. To S. J. Butlin, Collins was 'very influential in early legislation on banking and note issue', had 'a better, more original brain' that G. T. Allen, and was 'a dominant force in ... [Treasury] history for over a quarter of a century'.

Punch (Melb), 19 June 1916, 8 Oct 1925; *SMH,* 12 Apr 1926, 19 June 1934; *Herald* (Melb), 24 July 1926, 20 June 1934; *Argus,* 19 June 1934; correspondence with S. J. Butlin (ADB); Treasury files (AAO).   K. R. PAGE

COLLINS, JOHN WILLIAM FITZCLARENCE (1906-1941), pastoralist, skier, horseman and aviator, was born on 6 March 1906 in Brisbane, only son of William Collins [q.v.3] (d. 1909) and his wife Mary Adelaide Gwendoline (1870-1962), née Roberts. His birth occasioned his father's purchase of Nindooinbah, near Beaudesert, and the gift, in thank-offering, of the great rose window in St John's Anglican Cathedral, Brisbane.

On the death of his cousin Christopher in 1919 John was left the sole male Collins descendant of the Mundoolun pioneers. His mother, a true matriarch, of regal bearing and great charm and kindness, was the prime influence on him and his three sisters. Collins was educated in New South Wales at Tudor House, Moss Vale, and The King's School, Parramatta; and in England at Magdalen College, Oxford (B.A., 1928; M.A., 1932), where he read agriculture, and skied

for the university, proving to be the second-fastest Briton of his generation. His style was unorthodox but effective. After returning to Australia in 1929 he became in 1930 the first Australian amateur ski champion.

Collins had gained pastoral experience at Westgrove on the Dawson River, after leaving school. On his return from Oxford he was manager as well as owner of Nindooinbah, starting five dairy-farms, conducted on the share system, continuing to fatten cattle, and making it a thoroughly progressive property. He was increasingly a force in the Collins family interests, which included the North Australian Pastoral Co. Ltd, owner of Alexandria in the Northern Territory; John Collins & Sons, owners of Chatsworth and Coorabulka, in the Channel country; and Collins, White & Co., owners of Eulolo and Strathfield stations, near McKinlay, and of Glenormiston, near Boulia. Kind and considerate, he worked hard and demanded high standards of himself.

A keen horseman, he played polo for Sydney and won camp-drafts and other events with his stock-horses in Queensland and New South Wales. At Beaudesert, where a street was named after him, he was president and patron of the golf club. His other clubs included the Hurlingham and Marylebone Cricket in London, the Gridiron at Oxford, the Royal Sydney Golf, and the Queensland, and the Sydney Cricket Ground. He was an ardent motorist. Increasingly, however, aviation became the sphere in which his spirit sought fulfilment. He became a private owner in 1931, and by 1940 had achieved 1645 solo hours. He held an A licence; he completed courses in blind flying and aerobatics in England in 1933; was awarded the Qantas trophy in 1935 for the year's most consistent flying; and in his Vega Gull won the speed test in the Brisbane-Adelaide air-race in 1936. Collins used his aircraft extensively in supervising his various pastoral and other interests.

When war began in 1939, his attempts to join the Royal Australian Air Force were at first frustrated by deficiencies in his eyesight, but he was eventually commissioned on 26 March 1940. Collins served as an instructor, with the rank of flight lieutenant, until 21 May 1941, when with Squadron Leader R. C. Phillips, he was killed instantly when the aircraft in which they were taking off struck a tree at Archerfield aerodrome in Brisbane.

Collins was survived by his wife Margaret Eleanor, née Hagon, whom he had married in Sydney on 12 September 1933. St John's Church at Mundoolun, All Saints Church at Tamrookum, and ten windows in St John's Cathedral, Brisbane, commemorate the con-

tribution to Queensland of three generations of the Collins family. Female lines
continue among the descendants of De
Burgh Persse [q.v.5], Sir Simon Fraser
[q.v.4], Sir Robert Philp [q.v.] and under
other names.

P. Cox and W. Stacey, *The Australian homestead* (Melb, 1972); *Courier Mail*, and *Telegraph*
(Brisb), 22 May 1941; *Beaudesert Times*, 23 May
1941; J. W. F. Collins scrap-books, *and* family
papers (held by Mrs R. Persse, Nindooinbah,
Beaudesert, Qld).

                MICHAEL D. DE B. COLLINS PERSSE

COLLINS, SIR ROBERT HENRY MUIR-
HEAD (1852-1927), naval officer and public
servant, was born on 20 September 1852 at
Chew Magna, Somerset, England, son of
Charles Howell Collins, surgeon, and his
wife Henrietta Jane Heaven, née Grosett.
Educated at Taunton and as a cadet in
H.M.S. *Britannia*, he entered the navy in
1866, served in flying squadrons in 1868 and
1872 and on the Channel and Australian
stations to 1876. That year he was promoted
lieutenant.

Retiring from the navy in 1877, Collins
was appointed lieutenant in the Permanent
Victorian Naval Forces. In 1883 he was sent
to England to assist in bringing to Victoria
two gunboats and a torpedo boat. After
courses of instruction in gunnery and torpedo practice on the *Excellence* and *Vernon*
he returned in command of the gunboat
Albert in June 1884, offering his vessel for
service in the Sudan War at Suakim on the
way; he was promoted commander in
December. Becoming secretary for defence
on 12 April 1888, he continued as commander on the unattached list until 1896
when he was retired with the rank of captain.

For twelve years Collins presided over a
Defence Department which, though
affected by financial depression, was the
largest in the Australian colonies. In matters
of policy he was a 'navalist'; for example, in
February 1890 he opposed an increase in the
Victorian military forces, suggesting that
the money would be better applied to naval
preparations. An equally ardent Federalist,
he believed defence should be one of the
powers unreservedly given to a central
government. He argued for a reduction of
dependence upon England; and, against the
Admiralty's scheme of 1898 for a Royal
Naval Reserve in Australia, he proposed the
termination of the 1887 Naval Agreement,
whereby the colonies subsidized an Australian Auxiliary Squadron. He wanted a
locally manned and maintained fleet, with
continuing Imperial naval ties — basing his
plan on the implications of the Colonial

Naval Defence Act (1865). His ideas were
accepted at a conference of naval officers
from New South Wales, Victoria, South
Australia and Queensland in August 1899,
but it was not until 1907 that such principles
were adopted by the Deakin [q.v.] government.

On the foundation of the Commonwealth
in 1901 Collins became secretary to the new
Department of Defence. Under several
ministers, he ably administered the department in a time of rapid growth but financial
stringency: colonial forces were amalgamated and defence policy hammered out,
particularly under the direction of Sir John
Forrest [q.v.]. Melbourne *Punch* observed
that 'Officers did not love him because he
curbed expenditure, and steadfastly set his
face against vain display ... Widely read,
always posted up-to-date, wise with the
wisdom of experience and a shrewd judge of
human nature, he was a match even for Sir
Edward Hutton [q.v.]', with whom he quarrelled. *Punch* commented that 'His light,
ladylike figure is no index to his character
... dressed with the daintiness of a dandy
and the art of an artist ... a first-class clerk'.
He left behind him 'a smoothly working
Department on the clerical side' when, in
March 1906, he was seconded to London
as official representative of the Commonwealth.

The London position, which Collins had
sought as early as February 1901, was
planned to handle large orders for defence
stores, to obtain information on defence
matters, and to pave the way for an Australian High Commission. His appointment
was generally well received, the *Australasian* observing that 'he is an official with a
special aptitude for checking, criticizing and
organizing'. (Sir) Timothy Coghlan's [q.v.]
criticism of his social ambition was probably
stirred by jealousy of Collins's capture of the
plum job. In London Collins co-operated
with Coghlan and the other agents-general
and established a 'sound nucleus around
which the larger more complex office of
High Commissioner could be built'; but he
bemoaned his meagre allowances and regretted the disinclination of the government
to use him more as a supplier of naval
intelligence.

When Sir George Reid [q.v.] arrived as
high commissioner in 1910 Collins stayed on
as official secretary. In 1906 he was a
member of the British royal commission on
shipping rings and in 1913 as Commonwealth representative attended the international conference in London on safety of
life at sea. On Reid's election to the House of
Commons in 1916, Collins advocated abolition of the High Commission in favour of
permanent Australian representation in the

British cabinet. After his retirement in September 1917 he sat for a year on the committee for Australia of the Imperial Institute. From 1919 he resided at Bath, where he campaigned against litter and roundabouts. A Conservative, he bitterly opposed socialism. He had been appointed C.M.G. in 1904 for his administrative services during the South African War and was knighted in June 1919. In September he returned to Australia for a brief visit.

Collins died on 19 April 1927 at Bath. He was survived by his wife Elizabeth, née Brush, whom he had married on 30 July 1885 at All Saints Church of England, St Kilda, Victoria, and by one son, Major Howel Collins. Although his influence on government policy was minimal, and his social pretensions made him slightly ridiculous, Collins was a capable administrator in both the Colonial and Commonwealth service.

L. W. Matters, *Australians who count in London* ... (Lond, 1913); G. L. Macandie, *The genesis of the Royal Australian Navy* (Syd, 1949); *British A'sian,* 28 June 1917; *Australasian,* 19 May 1883, 21 June 1884, 14 Apr 1888, 3 Mar 1906, 1, 29 Sept 1917, 7 June 1919, 23 Apr 1927; *Argus,* 16 Feb 1906; *Punch* (Melb), 15 Mar 1906; *The Times,* 20 Apr 1927; L. D. Atkinson, Australian defence policy: a study of empire and nation (Ph.D. thesis, ANU, 1964); J. R. Thompson, The Australian High Commission in London ... 1901-1916 (M.A. thesis, ANU, 1972); Deakin, *and* Attlee Hunt, *and* Jebb papers (NL); A6/01/520, A8/02/41/77, *and* news-cuttings A59 (AAO).   CHRIS CUNNEEN
ANN G. SMITH

COLQUHOUN, ALEXANDER (1862-1941), artist and critic, was born, probably on 15 February 1862 in Glasgow, youngest child of Archibald Colquhoun, merchant, and his wife Margaret, née Wright. The family migrated to Australia, arriving in Melbourne in the *Loch Vennacher* in 1876; the oldest child Archibald was a resident surgeon at the Alfred Hospital.

Alexander attended the National Gallery School, Melbourne, in 1877-79, and in 1882-87; he qualified as a teacher of drawing in the Department of Education in 1881. At the gallery school he was taught by Thomas Clark and G. F. Folingsby [qq.v.3,4] and formed his lifelong friendship with John Longstaff [q.v.]. With the leading younger painters, most of whom like Colquhoun belonged in the early 1880s to the Buonarotti Club, he exhibited in the Australian Artists' Association in 1887, and next year he began showing at the Victorian Artists' Society. His paintings of landscape and interior, and portraits were impressionistic, but tempered by Folingsby's Munich style; his later work became more tonal, influenced by his friend

Max Meldrum's [q.v.] colour theory. At Prahran registry office on 15 September 1892 he married a former gallery school student, London-born Beatrix Hoile who had studied art in Paris. They lived for a while at Brighton as close neighbours of Longstaff and Frederick McCubbin [q.v.].

Colquhoun took private students as well as teaching drawing at the Working Men's College about 1910, and art at Toorak College for many years until 1930. He held many one-man exhibitions in galleries and in his studio; and, as well as at the Victorian Artists' Society, of which he was secretary in 1904-14, he exhibited with the Yarra Sculptors' Society, 1901, and the Australian Art Association in 1916-32. He was a foundation member of the Twenty Melbourne Painters group in 1919 and the Australian Academy of Art in 1937.

Apart from a visit to New Zealand as a young man, Colquhoun's interest in European art and literature was cultivated from Australia. He wrote and illustrated regularly for journals, including the *V.A.S.* and *Art in Australia,* and for newspapers. He was art critic for the Melbourne *Herald* in 1914-22, a correspondent to the Philadelphian *Christian Science Monitor* in 1916-17, and wrote art critiques and regular feature articles in the *Age* from 1926 until his death. Many *Age* articles ran in series such as 'Who's who in fiction', 'Australian artists of the past' and contemporary biographies of Melbourne artists including Mary Cecil Allen [q.v.7], A. E. Newbury and Norman MacGeorge [qq.v.].

Colquhoun remained aloof from the public controversy of Meldrumism versus post-Impressionism and was open-minded towards, if rather remote from, contemporary art movements. He did much to record the early history of Australian art and the Impressionists, writing the first critical monographs on McCubbin (1919) and W. B. McInnes [q.v.] (1920?), and also editing the *Year Book of Victorian Art* (1922-23), all published by Alexander McCubbin.

In 1936 Colquhoun was appointed a trustee of the National Gallery of Victoria. He died in East Malvern on 14 February 1941, and was cremated, survived by his wife and three of their four children.

Melba's gift book of Australian art and literature (Melb, 1915?); Madoline Brown (N. Murdoch), *Portrait in youth of Sir John Longstaff* (Syd, 1948); *V.A.S.,* 1 Aug 1898; Working Man's College, *College Qtly,* Mar 1910; *Tatler* (Lond) 14 May 1898; *Age,* 20 July, 17 Aug 1929, 7 Mar, 6, 18 June 1931, 2 July 1932, 31 Aug 1940; *Argus,* 10 Aug 1929; Gallery School records (Vic College of the Arts, Melb); Art Room cats and indexes (SLV); information from Aust Medical Assn (Melb); family information.   JENNIFER PHIPPS

COLQUHOUN, PERCY BRERETON (1866-1936), sportsman, lawyer and politician, was born on 28 September 1866 at West Maitland, New South Wales, third son of George Colquhoun (1830-1901), a solicitor from Kent, England, and his London-born wife Mary (Polly), née Poulton. George, a descendant of a prominent English legal family, migrated to New South Wales in 1853 and was crown solicitor from 1894. Percy was educated by a tutor until the family moved to Sydney in 1877, when he attended St Paul's School, Redfern, and, from 1881, Newington College, where he captained both the Rugby and cricket teams and was a sergeant in the cadet corps.

In 1886 Colquhoun was articled to his father (then a partner in Allen & Allen); he was a committee-member and librarian of the Articled Clerks' Association. On 6 June 1891 he was admitted as a solicitor. That year he and his Rugby team-mate H. H. Lee opened Lee & Colquhoun at Orange. In 1893 the business was extended to Blayney, but in 1896 Colquhoun returned to Sydney to open their head office. In the 1890s he was a second lieutenant in the 1st Infantry Regiment.

Colquhoun had joined the victorious University Football (Rugby) Club in 1885. Next year he was chosen for the New South Wales tour of New Zealand, and was the team's leading points-scorer. By 1887 he was rated as the outstanding three-quarter in Australia, with a magic game based on balance and poise, skilful footwork and brilliant running, and the ability to kick field goals as opponents were closing in on him. He played for New South Wales in intercolonial matches until 1896.

Also a first class tennis player, Colquhoun in May 1889 represented New South Wales against Victoria at the Sydney Cricket Ground, winning both his singles matches. He played fifty-five matches for New South Wales against Victoria between 1889 and 1899, with a last appearance in 1909. A dashing player, he was a pioneer of the modern school with great volleying and smashing and a fine service. He always played in knickerbockers and black stockings. He twice held the New South Wales men's doubles title (1893, 1896) and won the mixed doubles in 1895 and 1896 with Mabel Ann Shaw (d. 1914), whom he married in Melbourne on 30 April 1897. She was a second cousin of George Bernard Shaw and, with her sister Phenie, one of the foremost lady players; in 1885-96 they won eight Victorian and ten New South Wales titles.

After playing with the Killara Golf Club's 'A' team for two seasons, Colquhoun turned to lawn bowls. With a game distinguished by the ease and rhythm of his delivery, for almost two decades from 1907 he represented New South Wales against all the Australian States and New Zealand. In 1916 he defeated the former international cricketer Harry Moses 32-22 at the City Bowling Club to win the State singles title, in a game which was long remembered as the best ever seen in Sydney.

Colquhoun was a vice-president and president in 1911-12 of the New South Wales Lawn Tennis Association. In 1909 he became president of the Lawn Tennis Association of Australasia, and refereed Sydney's first Davis Cup challenge round final. He worked strenuously on the Davis Cup sub-committee and held together the shaky alliance with New Zealand until 1922. He was first president of the Lawn Tennis Association of Australia until 1926 when its headquarters were transferred to Melbourne.

In 1913-20 Colquhoun held Mosman in the Legislative Assembly as a Liberal-Nationalist. Chairman of committees in 1919-20, he was an excellent debater and was regarded as an authority in constitutional law. In later years he concentrated increasingly on his legal practice with George King, his partner from 1912. He retired in 1934. For many years he played district tennis for Mosman and Middle Harbour and later socially. He was an ardent cricket-lover, enjoyed surfing and often had century breaks at billiards. In his quieter moments he loved growing flowers and was a skilled carpenter. He was a trustee of Taronga Zoological Park.

Survived by a son and a daughter, Colquhoun died of cerebro-vascular disease at his Mosman home on 23 October 1936 and was cremated with Anglican rites. His estate was valued for probate at £424. He was one of the finest all-round athletes to have represented New South Wales. Few have been more popular — he was remembered as much for his charm, old-world courtesy and affability.

Newspaper Cartoonists' Assn of NSW, *Sydneyites as we see 'em, 1913-14-15* (Syd, 1915?); *T & CJ*, 11 Aug 1894, 1 Feb 1911; *Arrow* (Syd), 1909; *Referee*, 5 July 1916; *Sydney Mail*, 14 May 1919, 28 Oct 1936; *SMH*, 24 Oct 1936.

DON WILKEY

COLVIN, SIR RAGNAR MUSGRAVE (1882-1954), naval officer, was born on 7 May 1882 at Whitehall, London, son of Clement Sneyd Colvin, civil servant, and his wife Alice Jane, née Lethbridge. He joined the Royal Navy as a cadet in H.M.S. *Britannia* in 1896 and was commissioned lieutenant six years later. Qualifying as a gunnery specialist in 1904, he had various appointments ashore and afloat until 1913 when he was promoted commander. In World War I he served as executive officer in the cruiser *Hibernia* and in the battleship *Revenge*, seeing action in the battle of Jutland. Promoted captain on 31 December 1917, he was posted to the Admiralty as assistant director of plans and was appointed C.B.E. In 1918 he married Sibyl Kays.

After the war Colvin commanded the cruiser *Caradoc* in the Black Sea and the Mediterranean; in 1922-24 he was naval attaché in Tokyo. He rejoined the *Revenge* as flag captain to the commander-in-chief, Atlantic Fleet, and in 1927 became director of the Naval Tactical School, Portsmouth. Colvin was promoted rear admiral in 1929 and soon afterwards was made chief of staff to the commander-in-chief, Atlantic Fleet. In 1932 he was appointed C.B. and posted to the 2nd Battle Squadron. Vice admiral in 1934, he became president of the Royal Naval College, Greenwich, and commander of the Royal Naval War College. He was appointed K.B.E. in 1937.

In October that year Colvin became first naval member of the Australian Naval Board. During the early part of his term he was not able to change the illusively secure view of the international strategic situation and the leisured approach to naval problems taken by Australian governments, under Lyons [q.v.] and Menzies, following the 1937 Imperial Conference. Although in direct touch with the first sea lord, it is probable that the Admiralty did not inform him of its increasing secret fears about war in Europe; as a result the pace of Australian rearmament remained unrealistic until the Munich crisis in 1938.

G. H. Gill described Colvin as 'an outstanding administrator, of reliable judgment and quick decision' with the 'ability to strip unessentials and get down at once to the basis of a problem'. He was tall and 'of commanding appearance, albeit essentially human and approachable and with a ready wit'. During his term of office the navy expanded and maintained its high standard. It acquired three six-inch gun cruisers and began building Tribal Class destroyers, corvettes, frigates and motor torpedo boats which saw useful active service later in World War II. In April 1939 Colvin led the Australian delegation to the Pacific Defence Conference in New Zealand and also represented the Admiralty; in May he was promoted admiral. By late 1940 his health was failing and on 11 March 1941 he resigned from the Naval Board.

Colvin returned to London and in 1942-44 served as naval adviser to the Australian High Commission. Survived by his wife, a son and a daughter, he died on 22 February 1954 at the Royal Naval Hospital, Haslar, Hampshire.

G. H. Gill, *Royal Australian Navy, 1939-42* (Canb, 1957); *Reveille* (Syd), Nov 1937; *The Times*, 24 Feb, 2, 5 Mar 1954; *SMH*, 25 Feb 1954; B. N. Primrose, Australian naval policy 1919-1942. A case study in Empire relations (Ph.D. thesis, ANU, 1974); AA1971/216, A2031, A2585, MP124/6, MP692, MP981, MP1049 series 3, 5, 7, 9 (AAO).

B. N. PRIMROSE

COMINO, ATHANASSIO (1844?-1897) and JOHN (1858?-1919), oyster merchants, were born on the Ionian island of Kythera (Cerigo), Greece, sons of Demetrio Comino, farmer, and his wife Agapy, née Menego. In 1873 Athanassio arrived in Sydney, probably as a crew member on a sailing ship from New Zealand. For a time he worked in the Balmain colliery, but by 1878 had started an oyster saloon at 36 Oxford Street. About 1882 he took up the lease of an oyster bed at Onions Point, at the mouth of the Lane Cove River, which he used to revive New Zealand oysters. But it was a short-lived, unremunerative enterprise and by 1886 Port Jackson was closed for oyster leasing. In 1884 he had leased 2000 yards (1828 m) of foreshore on the Evans River, on the north coast. That year John arrived in the *Potosi* and in 1885 applied for oyster leases on the Bermagui River. Despite fluctuations in the industry's prosperity Athanassio remained in business. John was described as a mechanic in bankruptcy proceedings in 1892 when he was found to have unsecured liabilities of £160; he was discharged on 5 September 1895.

The Cominos had arrived at a time when the New South Wales oyster industry was unregulated, with unsuccessful attempts by the government to legislate for an orderly system. Gradually the method of dredging for natural oysters gave way to cultivation and organized harvesting. Athanassio reached a prominent place in the industry. He never married. Aged 53, he died of a strangulated hernia on 30 December 1897 at Darlinghurst, leaving an estate valued for probate at £5217 to John and to nephews and nieces.

Inheriting from Athanassio the title, 'Oyster King', John applied a formidable business aptitude to orderly expansion. In 1898 he was naturalized. With several others he was responsible for raising funds to erect the first Greek Orthodox Church in Australia, Holy Trinity Church, Surry Hills, where on 6 September 1901 he married Anna Phocas, born in Rhodes, Turkey; her father Seraphim Phocas [q.v.] officiated. At the time of his marriage John was living at Randwick; later he moved to Coogee. As chain migration brought more Kytherans, he was a mainstay of the Greek community in New South Wales, at the centre of a complicated web of family and business activities, owning and supplying restaurants, oyster saloons and fish shops. The Fisheries Act of 1902 reformed the oyster industry, forcing lessees to make improvements or suffer confiscation. Comino held numerous leases along the New South Wales coast. About 1906 he entered into partnership with three other large oyster merchants, Frederick John Gibbins, Charles Edward Woodward and John Moriarty, and the firm, known as Woodward, Gibbons & Comino, dominated oyster marketing in New South Wales.

In 1916, under the supervision and probably at the expense of Comino, *Life in Australia* was published. In the Greek language, it extolled the opportunities available to Greek immigrants and listed some of the 625 shops allegedly owned by Greeks in Australia 'Apart from 5 shops owned by Cominos, ten others owned by different individuals traded under the name of Comino and it is probable that in some of them John Comino owned a share'. By 1919 there were 'Comino' oyster saloons in Parkes, Maitland, Armidale, Gunnedah, Moree and Katoomba. For a time all Greeks in New South Wales were commonly known as 'Comino'.

John died of pneumonic influenza (Spanish flu) at Belmore Road, Randwick, on 21 June 1919, leaving to his wife and four sons an estate sworn for probate at £31872. The Cominos were the pioneers of Kytheran migration to Australia and it is estimated that by the late 1930s well over 3000 had come, mainly to New South Wales, from this one Greek island.

C. A. Price, *Southern Europeans in Australia* (Melb, 1963); V&P (LA NSW), 1883-84, 11, 519, 559, 1885-86, 2, 901-02; *J* (LC NSW), 1887-88, 4, 751-57, 821; M. P. Tsounis, Greek communities in Australia (Ph.D. thesis, Univ Adel, 1971); Bankruptcy papers (NSWA); Registers of certificates of naturalization, 1849-1904 (NSWA); information from Sir Nicholas Laurantos, Sydney.

CHRIS CUNNEEN

CONACHER, CHARLES WILLIAM DAVY (1881-1937), company manager, was born on 27 November 1881 at Terang, Victoria, eldest son of Robert Lawrence Conacher, bank manager, and his wife Ellen, née James. He was educated at George Watson's College in Edinburgh and the West of Scotland Agricultural College, Glasgow. In 1897-1911 he worked for a Glasgow flour importer, Hunter Craig & Co. Ltd, and then joined Vestey brothers' International Export Co. Ltd as an executive representative in China and in their Madagascar meatworks. In early 1916 he was transferred to Darwin, Northern Territory.

In 1913 Vesteys had leased large properties, both in the Territory and the East Kimberley district of Western Australia, beginning in 1914 the building of a meatworks at Paraparap, near Darwin. Conacher took control of these pastoral and business enterprises, under power of attorney from Vestey's North Australian Meat Co. Ltd. With no experience of the Territory he faced a heavy task. The meatworks, with the capacity to treat 500 cattle a day, was handicapped by the wartime shipping shortage, high costs, chronic labour disputes and a lack of accessible markets. The works closed in 1920; Conacher was transferred to Sydney where he served Vesteys as manager of their Australian Investment Agency whose major interests also lay in the meat industry. His last position, from 1934, was general manager in Australia of Vesteys' fleet of passenger and refrigerated cargo ships, the Blue Star Line.

The failure of the Paraparap meatworks and the popular, largely working-class 'rebellion' against the administrator of the Territory, J. A. Gilruth [q.v.] in December 1918, seriously undermined public confidence in Darwin. Conacher's few years in the Northern Territory began for him an intense interest in the problems of the Australian outback. For the remainder of his life he preached, perhaps over-optimistically, the high development potential of the North and devoted himself to improving the welfare of the people who lived there: 'Many a poor devil who was down got a fresh start through Conacher's unobtrusive help'. He became a strong supporter of the Australian Inland Mission and the Australian Aerial Medical Service.

Conacher emerges as an efficient, compassionate figure who did not share the unpopular image of his employers. Never spectacular, loyal to Vesteys, he can be seen, in his later years, as a slightly disappointed man whose dreams had not been realized. The North remained underdeveloped, while Vesteys, seemingly more intent on nurturing their Argentinian investments, failed to acknowledge his value. His salary, fixed at £3500 in 1924, was still at that level in September 1936 despite his newly acquired responsibility for Blue Star. Conacher died of cancer on 30 December 1937 at Sydney, survived by his wife Dorothy Jean McMaster whom he had married according to Presbyterian forms on 20 December 1916 at Wyuna, Point Piper, and by their two sons. A service was conducted by Rev. John Flynn [q.v.] at the Northern Suburbs crematorium. One obituarist was prompted to exclaim: 'A notable main had ridden off to the Last Big Muster'. Conacher's estate was valued for probate at £51260.

H. T. Dorling, *Blue Star Line* (Liverpool, Eng, 1948); N.T. Admin, Report, *PP* (Cwlth), 1920-21, vol 3; *Pastoral Review*, 15 Jan 1938; *Bulletin*, 5 Jan 1938; papers held by Dr C. J. R. Conacher, Mangerton, NSW.   ROSS DUNCAN

CONDER, WALTER TASMAN (1888-1974), prison governor and wireless station manager, was born on 18 October 1888 at Ringarooma, Tasmania, son of Jones Henry Conder, commercial clerk, and his Scottish wife Allison Mary Maxwell, née Gibb. 'Wally' Conder boarded at Launceston Church Grammar School in 1902-07. School captain and commander of the cadets, he not only distinguished himself at rowing, boxing, sprinting and horse-riding, but also represented Tasmania at football. He became a master at the school in 1908, studied part time at the University of Tasmania, and in 1914 moved to Victoria to teach French, history and mathematics at Melbourne Church of England Grammar School.

In August 1914 Conder enlisted in the Australian Imperial Force and was commissioned in February 1915. He was wounded at Gallipoli on 25 April and returned to Australia in June. After convalescence, in August 1916 he was appointed by Colonel R. E. Williams [q.v.] to take charge of Langwarrin Military Camp on the Mornington Peninsula. In October he was promoted captain, and major in September next year. Conder made many enlightened improvements in the routine of the camp's inmates, most of whom had venereal disease: the twenty-four hour guard was removed and Conder arranged for soldiers to receive their pay (hitherto withheld); he also established a military band and encouraged gardening. Langwarrin remained relatively free from diseases such as meningitis, so common in other camps.

On 1 April 1922 Conder was appointed governor of Pentridge Gaol and inspector of prisons for Victoria. His ideas of prison reform, at a time of prisoner strife in Victoria, provoked the wrath of some authorities, but he served a useful term as governor, and generally raised prisoner morale. He resigned on 31 October 1923 when the offer of a high salary by J. C. Williamson [q.v.6] Ltd proved irresistible.

Conder's initial task at J. C. W.'s was to 'clean up' the operations of the company, particularly ticket sale abuses; but his main job, in the first years of wireless in Australia, was to control the firm's new interest in the field – the Broadcasting Co. of Australia Pty Ltd, which later merged with Dominion Broadcasting Pty Ltd. He was totally dedicated and worked long hours from his office in His Majesty's Theatre or his room at the Athenaeum Club. He presided over a major technical innovation, the reduction of 3LO's wave-length, and helped to establish radio's popularity in Melbourne. It was said that 3LO owed its early success to Conder's 'genius for organisation, his vision, and enthusiasm for all things affecting . . . radio'. When the Australian Broadcasting Co. took over 3LO under government contract in 1930, he left to organize Melbourne's centenary celebrations. Failing to become the first general manager of the Australian Broadcasting Commission in July 1932 he got the job in April 1933 after the first manager, H. P. Williams, died.

Known as 'the major', Conder was superb as a showman and organizer of entertainment. His time as general manager saw the famous broadcast of the England to Melbourne air race, and the first A.B.C. national concert tours. But while he worked well with the first chairman, (Sir) Charles Lloyd Jones [q.v.], he clashed with W. J. Cleary [q.v.], chairman from July 1934. Conder believed that programmes should be arranged to suit the masses. He did not believe in many talk sessions or in controversial broadcasts. He wanted more sporting programmes, more entertainment for its own sake, or as he put it – 'everything on the air but hot air'. Cleary could not accept either Conder's outlook or his 'barrack-room standards'.

Early in 1935 Cleary alleged irregularities in Conder's expenditure of A.B.C. funds but the precise details remain unclear. The commission dismissed Conder but granted compensation equal to one half-year's salary. News of his 'resignation' came as a complete surprise to the public.

With the aid of his severance money Conder formed a company to run Ivan Brothers' International Circus but the enterprise failed. He was unemployed for some twelve months, before being appointed to Australia's 150th Anniversary Council in September 1937; next year he worked for the Tasmanian Tourist Bureau. From March 1939 he was unemployed. Declared bankrupt in February 1940, when he could not be located, a warrant was issued for his arrest for contempt of court. He was held at Pentridge for a few hours before his release was arranged. In April 1940 he was given permission to go to the Middle East with the 2nd A.I.F. as General Blamey's entertainment officer. In 1944 he managed a United States Army hostel in Rockhampton, Queensland, and in 1944-45 the Pitt Street American Red Cross Club, Sydney.

On 14 July 1945 at St Matthew's Church of England, Manly, Conder married Cora Jeanne, née Wood, a hospital matron, and they sailed to England. Conder joined the

Ministry of Information and lectured on 'A new life in Australia' throughout Britain. In 1947-51 he ran the Swan Hotel, Bedford. He went to New Zealand in 1952 where he managed some breweries, the Empire Hotel, Wellington, and, later, the Tattersall's Lottery. After organizing the Festival of Wellington in 1962, he suffered a coronary occlusion. Survived by his wife, he died at his home in Nelson on 3 November 1974 and was cremated.

PD (Cwlth), 1930, p 1575-1577; *Punch* (Melb), 13 Nov 1920; *Herald* (Melb), 9 Aug 1922; *Table Talk*, 29 April 1926; *SMH*, 1 Apr 1933; *Smith's Weekly*, 6 Mar 1940; *Argus*, 20 Mar 1940; H. Brookes *and* Conder papers (NL); A.B.C. Archives (Syd).

ALAN THOMAS

CONEYBEER, FREDERICK WILLIAM (1859-1950), trade unionist and politician, was born at Clifton, near Bristol, England, on 27 September 1859, fourth of twelve children of John Powsland Coneybeer, horse-collar maker, and his wife Mary, née Hobbs. In 1865 the family migrated to Orange, New South Wales, where Coneybeer attended primary school and the Rev. F. B. Boyce's [q.v.7] Anglican Sunday school; he learned horse-collar making in his father's shop. At the end of 1881 Coneybeer went to Adelaide and worked for James Holden [q.v.] & Co.; the depressed state of his trade encouraged him to join the Saddle, Harness and Collarmakers' Society. A delegate to the United Trades and Labor Council and a tactful and likeable negotiator, in 1888 he became council president.

Coneybeer held the House of Assembly seat of East Torrens in 1893-1921 and 1924-30 (for the United Labor Party 1893-1917). A Freemason and active in temperance and friendly societies, in 1894 he had a bill passed enabling women to benefit from the Acts relating to friendly societies. He held a wide range of offices and appointments, including secretary of the U.L.P., government whip, visitor to the Parkside Lunatic Asylum, member of the University of Adelaide council, and minister of education in the Price-Peake [qq.v.] coalition government in 1908-09, and again in the John Verran [q.v.] Labor government of 1910-12. After Price died in 1909 Coneybeer was selected to head the coalition as premier, but he was denied office by the withdrawal of Peake and the belief of the governor, Sir Day Hort Bosanquet [q.v.7], that his ministerial experience was too slight.

As minister of education, Coneybeer increased the number of high schools and scholarships; he opposed Bible reading in state schools. Twice he tried to reform the education system but was frustrated while a royal commission examined the question. The Education Act, 1915, owed something to Coneybeer, but by then he had become Speaker, an office he held until 1921. In 1917, with other 'old hands', he was expelled from the Labor Party for supporting conscription. He at once helped to form the National Labor Party, and in 1923-24 was a leading negotiator for its fusion with the Liberal Union to form the Liberal Federation. Though he had now moved a long way from what he had once called his Christian Socialism, he still supported arbitration, improved education, reform of the Legislative Council, White Australia and temperance. He was defeated at the 1930 election and retired.

Meticulous, genial and energetic as a politician, Coneybeer was noted for his presence as master of ceremonies or humorous singer at countless smoke socials and concerts. He was at his best on the hustings — both Labor and non-Labor parties appreciating his organizing ability, assessment of electoral mood, and vote-winning appeal. From 1881 Coneybeer documented his political life and times in a remarkable series of personal diaries, which he bound himself, and an important collection of related papers.

On 20 February 1886 Coneybeer had married Margaret Jane Thomas at Holy Trinity Church, Adelaide. Predeceased by his wife, he died on 30 May 1950, survived by one daughter and three sons. He was given a state funeral and buried in Mitcham general cemetery. The State hundred of Coneybeer is named for him.

PD (SA), 1894; *Observer* (Adel), 7 Sept 1895; *Aust Worker*, 18 Feb 1905; *News* (Adel), 29 Mar 1924; *Advertiser* (Adel), 31 May 1950; G. L. Fischer, The Hon. Frederick William Coneybeer, 1859-1950: a political biography (M.A. thesis, Univ Adel, 1968); PRG22 (SAA).

G. L. FISCHER

CONINGHAM, ARTHUR (1863-1939), cricketer and notoriety, was born on 14 July 1863 at Emerald Hill, Melbourne, son of William Coningham, brass-finisher, and his wife Jane Ann, née Wilson, both English-born. He became an all-round athlete, excelling at football, pedestrianism, rowing, pigeon-shooting and, especially, cricket — as a left-arm fast medium bowler.

Coningham played for the Melbourne Cricket Club and in December 1884 went to Queensland and represented it in 3 games from February 1885 to January 1889; between December 1892 and February 1895 he played 3 times for Queensland and twice for New South Wales. In 1894-95 he represented Queensland in 2 games and, from February

1896 to December 1898, New South Wales in 7. In March 1896 he was in Australia's 2nd XI, against the 1st XI. In all his intercolonial games Coningham scored 510 runs at 17 and took 60 wickets at 23.46. A member of the Australian team that toured England in 1893, he did not play in a Test match, but in other games he scored 260 runs at 12.8 and took 38 wickets at 25.6. His only Test match was against England at Melbourne, 29 December 1894 to 3 January 1895: his match figures were 13 runs and 2 wickets for 76.

Coningham claimed to have been a 'chemist', but in the late 1890s he had difficulty earning a living – one unreliable source was gambling at billiards. Brash and excitable, he was of medium build and sandy; he sported a handlebar moustache. On the day he left on the English tour, 11 March 1893, in St Matthew's Anglican Church, Bondi, Sydney, he married English-born Alice Stamford Dowling (d. 1959), a Catholic. In November 1896 insolvency proceedings revealed that in September he had failed as a tobacconist at Waverley and was then 'managing a shop' at Glebe; released from bankruptcy in July next year, in 1899 he was a bookmaker.

In that year Coningham sued for divorce, naming Fr D. F. O'Haran [q.v.], administrator of St Mary's Cathedral, as co-respondent, and claiming £5000 damages from him. At the hearing in December 1900, amid clamorous scenes inside the court and outside, Coningham conducted his own case; his wife admitted adultery and O'Haran denied it. The jury disagreed. Meanwhile the case had exacerbated entrenched colonial forces of bigotry and sectarianism; by March 1901, when it was reheard, Rev. W. M. Dill Macky [q.v.] had rallied support, including a revolver, for Coningham, and several Catholics, notably W. P. Crick [q.v.], had organized aid for O'Haran. Dan Green [q.v.] headed an undercover operation which, with Crick's help as postmaster-general, exposed collusion between Coningham and his wife. Their denials, against an uproarious public background, nation-wide, compounded the confusion. The jury found against Coningham.

He took his family to New Zealand and worked as a book salesman. In November 1903 at Westport he was sentenced to six months gaol for fraudulent conversion of £6.3s. He was an agent in Wellington from 1906 and on 24 January 1912 his wife divorced him for adultery. It is not known when he returned to Australia, but he was admitted to Gladesville Mental Hospital, Sydney, on 2 November 1937, died there on 13 June 1939 and was buried in the Anglican section of Rookwood cemetery. Air Marshal Sir Arthur Coningham, R.A.F., born in Brisbane on 19 January 1895, killed in an air crash near the Azores on 30 January 1948, was his son.

C. P. Moody, *Australian cricket and cricketers* (Melb, 1894); *The celebrated divorce case, Coningham v. Coningham* (Syd, 1901); 'Zero', *The secret history of the Coningham case* (Syd, 1901); C. Pearl, *Wild men of Sydney* (Lond, 1958), *Boomerang* (Brisb), 7 Mar 1891; *Catholic Press*, 22 Dec 1900, 13 Apr 1901; *Evening Post* (NZ), 4 Nov 1903, 25 July 1959; *Bulletin*, 12 Nov 1903; *SMH*, 15 June 1939.   BEDE NAIRN

CONNAH, THOMAS WILLIAM (1843-1915), public servant, was born on 2 November 1843 at Birkenhead, Cheshire, England, son of Thomas Connah, head of a Liverpool and New York mercantile and shipping house of that name, and his wife Emily, née Wrigley. Educated at Hawthorn Hall, Wilmslow near Manchester, he won junior certificates from both Oxford and Cambridge in 1858, then trained as an accountant in his father's firm, expecting eventually to manage the New York office. The American Civil War virtually ruined the business; smaller shipping lines were bought up by the Cunard line. At 22 Connah came to Australia instead, reaching Brisbane by the *Young Australia* in September 1866. Until his marriage he lived with his sister Anne, wife of Thomas Blacket Stephens [q.v.6].

After working as accountant and bookkeeper for Bright Bros & Co. from November 1866, he joined the public service as an Audit Office clerk in January 1873, transferred to the Treasury in October 1875, became under-secretary in January 1902 and returned to the Audit Office as auditor-general in November 1907. He was awarded the Imperial Service Order in June. A member of the Government Advertising Board and a commissioner of stamps for six years he was managing director of the Civil Service Co-operative Stores which he had helped to establish.

On 9 March 1871 Connah married Emma Barton Heywood who had come from England for the wedding. They had three sons and two daughters. While living at South Brisbane, the family attended the near-by Congregational Church where Connah held various offices. After moving to Langlands, Coorparoo, he became active in St Philip's Anglican Church, Thompson Estate, as lay reader, church warden and synodsman. When lack of sufficient funds for a stipend threatened closure of the church, he was licensed to conduct services there for a year until the appointment of a minister; after his death the church erected a belfry in his memory. He served on a number of Anglican synod committees from 1890, filling various positions including synod treasurer in 1893-96. He is said to have arranged reburial of Bishop Webber's [q.v.] body under the high altar of St John's Cathedral.

Staunchly British, Connah would proudly wear a red rose (for Lancaster) in his buttonhole every St George's day, saying that a Connah fought in the Wars of the Roses. He was equally proud of his family's ancient Welsh lineage. Enthusiastic about both tennis and cricket, he was a member of the Queensland Lawn Tennis Association and, after being a vice-president, became its president in 1905. He died of a heart attack in his office on 2 November 1915 and was buried in the South Brisbane cemetery with Anglican rites.

L. E. Slaughter, *Coorparoo, Stones Corner centenary* (Brisb, 1956); Church of England, *Diocese of Brisbane Year Book,* 1890-1916; Commercial Publishing Co. of Sydney, Ltd. *Annual Review of Qld,* 1 (1902); *Brisbane Courier,* 3 Nov 1915; Synod reports and parish records (Diocesan Registry, Brisb); family papers (held by author).

MARGARET H. CONNAH

CONNELL, CORNELIUS MYLES (1881-1958), jockey, was born on 2 January 1881 at Redbank, Araluen, New South Wales, son of native-born parents Cornelius Joseph Connell, farmer, and his wife Sarah, née Watt; both were champion show-riders. Brought up in the Cooma district, Myles learned his horsemanship helping his father to round up cattle in the high snow leases, like A. B. Paterson's [q.v.] 'Man from Snowy River'. Until he was 18 he rode at Cooma and local bush meetings; he instinctively adopted the crouch style of riding, before the famous American jockey Tod Sloan. In 1899 he went to Sydney and was licensed by the Australian Jockey Club, but got few mounts. Next year he switched to the unregistered 'pony' courses. Over the next six years he became a leading rider and between October 1901 and October 1902 rode 105 winners. On 19 December 1906 in Sydney he married Agnes Mary, daughter of Lewis Kuhn, trainer.

In 1907 the A.J.C. offered an amnesty to 'pony' jockeys and Connell was again licensed in June. By 1910 he had won most of the important 2-year-old races in Melbourne and Sydney. In October 1909 he rode J. C. Williamson's [q.v.6] Blue Book to a dead heat in the Caulfield Cup. That evening, dressed in the owner's colours, he appeared in a sketch in a Williamson production, *The catch of the season,* at Her Majesty's Theatre. He rode throughout World War I – among his most important wins were the Brisbane Cup, the Queensland St Leger twice and the

Randwick Doncaster. From 1917 he rode for trainer F. Williams and won eleven races on Greenstead. His best season was the spring of 1920: he won five feature races including the A.J.C. and Victoria Derbies on Salitros. He rarely used his whip and even in close finishes depended on hands-and-heels riding and 'scolding'.

By 1921 Connell was having weight problems, and that year he visited England. In May 1922 he settled at Glenelg, South Australia, where the climate suited his asthmatic son. He retired in 1924. All his life he had carefully recorded the details of his career: out of 5886 mounts he had ridden 1080 winners, 908 seconds and 742 thirds. He claimed to have made a fortune by not betting, and invested in real estate round Randwick and Clovelly in Sydney. After he retired he was registered as an owner-trainer until 1954 and exercised his horses with his daughter Gwen on Glenelg beach.

Connell was about 5 ft. 4 ins. (106 cm) tall, handsome, with blue eyes and straight brown hair. Utterly honest, he was a devout Congregationalist and a strict Sabbatarian; he enjoyed bowls and golf. He died at Glenelg on 11 April 1958 and was cremated. Predeceased by his wife and son, he was survived by his daughter. His estate in New South Wales and South Australia was valued for probate at almost £80 000.

H. Mitchell (ed), *Victoria's greatest races* (Melb, 1924?); M. Cavanough, *The Caulfield Cup* (Syd, 1976); *Australasian,* 23 Oct 1909, 24, 31 May 1919, 9 Oct, 6 Nov 1920; *T&CJ,* 28 May 1919; *Advertiser* (Adel), 14 Apr 1958; *Daily Mirror* (Syd), 18 May 1979; M. Connell note-book and information from Miss G. Connell, Adel.

MARTHA RUTLEDGE

CONNELL, HUGH JOHN (1884-1934), soldier, teacher and politician, was born on 12 June 1884 at Woollahra, Sydney, son of Hugh Connell, ironmoulder, and his wife Jessie, née Blumer. Educated at Woollahra and Paddington Public schools, he later joined the New South Wales Department of Public Instruction and in 1905 was posted to two half-time schools at Gongolgon and Tarcoon. He married Mary Elizabeth Woods at Broken Hill Baptist Church on 28 December 1910. Always interested in things military, Connell was commissioned in the Australian Military Forces in 1912 and on the outbreak of World War I, when he was teaching at Burwood, was called up for home service with the 16th Infantry Battalion.

After serving on the instructional staff in various Australian Imperial Force camps, Connell enlisted for overseas service on 8 March 1916 as a lieutenant in the 35th Battalion. He was promoted captain on 1 May, the day he embarked for England, and underwent a period of training on Salisbury Plain before his unit moved into the Armentières-Houplines sector, France, in November. Connell was given command of 'C' Company which he was to lead through most of its active service. In June 1917 the 35th Battalion took part in the battle of Messines and Connell was awarded the Military Cross for fine leadership, thoroughness and personal courage: during a reconnaissance of the assembly trenches on battle eve he showed 'great coolness and determination' and his was the only successful one of three parties. He was wounded in action on 17 July and resumed duty in September in the Zonnebeke sector. In October his battalion fought at Passchendaele, then in the winter of 1917-18 served in the Ploegsteert area.

After the great German offensive of March 1918 the 35th Battalion (part of the 9th Brigade) was rushed from Flanders in anticipation of an enemy thrust towards Amiens; it was in these critical days, while he was acting as staff officer to Lieut-Colonel H. A. Goddard [q.v.], that Connell's gallantry and devotion to duty were most evident. For his exemplary courage and determination during the German assault of 4 April he was awarded a Bar to his Military Cross. For further gallantry in this period he was promoted major in June and awarded the Distinguished Service Order. He later took part in operations at Morlancourt, Bray-sur-Somme and Curlu but was evacuated to England in September because of injuries received when his horse fell on him during a reconnaissance. In addition to his decorations he was also twice mentioned in dispatches.

Connell returned to Australia in May 1919. He had joined the Labor Party before the war, and in 1909 had been rebuked by the Department of Public Instruction for his public activity at Broken Hill. He resigned from the department on 29 March 1920. That month he headed the poll for Labor in the five-member seat for Newcastle in the New South Wales Legislative Assembly; he held his seat until 1927 when single-member electorates were restored. Member for Kahibah until 1930, from then on he represented Hamilton until his death. In 1930-32 he was deputy Speaker and chairman of committees during the last J. T. Lang [q.v.] government. He made a name for himself as a quick thinker, a keen debater and a hater of hypocrisy. Though a strong disciplinarian in parliament, he never allowed his strongly held views to disturb his friendships with those of different persuasions.

Survived by his wife and daughter, Connell died of heart disease on 31 January 1934

and was buried in Sandgate Methodist cemetery. His estate was sworn for probate at £1398.

C. E. W. Bean, *The A.I.F. in France,* 1917-18 (Syd, 1933, 1937, 1942); *London Gazette,* 25 Aug, 25 Dec 1917, 26 July, 31 Dec 1918, 1 Jan 1919; *Reveille* (Syd), March 1934, Sept 1937; *SMH,* 29 May 1925, 20 Oct, 4 Nov 1930, 1 Feb, 30 June 1934; Dept of Education, NSW, Records (Syd), *and* Records of service in two world wars, T. A. White ed (AWM); War diary, 35th Battalion, AIF (AWM).

A. R. ROBERTS

CONNIBERE, SIR CHARLES WELLINGTON (1864-1941), businessman and philanthropist, was born on 6 February 1864 at St Kilda, Melbourne, son of George Connibere, Devon-born draper and later mayor of St Kilda, and his wife Emma Joan, née Richards, from Somerset. Charles and his two brothers ERNEST WILLIAM RICHARDS (1862-1957), and FREDERICK GEORGE (1868-1945) started in a small way as softgoods merchants in 1889, under the name of Connibere, Grieve & Connibere. Their partner, John Grieve (father of Robert Cuthbert [q.v.]), died in 1899.

Charles Connibere went to London as the firm's agent about 1895; when he returned in 1920, the brothers sold the firm to Sargood's [q.v.6], formed Connibere Bros and invested their money in city property. Shrewd businessmen, they always sold out at the top of the market and, as Ernest later acknowledged, worked in great harmony. They were reputed never to make a mistake in a business deal or in a charitable gift. Neither they nor their sister Emma Eliza, married. They lived quiet, abstemious lives in Toorak, 'model bachelors, reserved, correct to the point of austerity'.

Their list of known benefactions was considerable. In 1929 the brothers built three wards at the Orthopaedic Hospital, Mount Eliza. They and their sister paid for the building of the Young Women's Christian Association headquarters as a memorial to their father. Charles supported the Melbourne City Mission, the Victorian Institute of Hospital Almoners, and with George, the Eye and Ear Hospital. At the same time the brothers gave £5000 to the Prohibition League and an unnamed amount to the Sunday Christian Observance Council.

Their gifts rarely took the public eye, one exception being the cheque for £30000 which Charles Connibere handed W. M. Hughes [q.v.] at a luncheon for the Jubilee Fund in 1935. He stipulated that the money be used to build a maternity wing at the Women's Hospital, and later gave a further £10000 to ensure that the building opened debt free. In January 1936 Charles Connibere was appointed K.B.E. Both Sir Charles and George were active in church affairs, the first on the council of the Melbourne Diocese, the second a member of synod.

The demands of war increased their philanthropy. They bore the expense of the Young Men's Christian Association restroom in Elizabeth Street, where any man in uniform could have free refreshments, and they built Y.M.C.A. huts at Balcombe and Puckapunyal camps. At the time of his sudden death at Toorak on 25 June 1941, Sir Charles was on the board of numerous hospitals and charities (including the Red Cross). That year Ernest and George gave the Royal Melbourne Hospital £138 860 for a nurses' wing as a memorial to their brother. Two years later they gave £23 750 to St Andrew's Hospital for a similar wing. On 10 August 1945 George Connibere died after a long illness.

In 1945 and 1946 Ernest gave £10 000 to the Food for Britain Fund, and a further £10 000 each to the Melbourne City Mission, Ormond College and St Andrew's Hospital. He put up the money for a kindergarten at Port Melbourne, yet he considered his religious work more important than his charitable interests. He paid for two religious programmes on commercial wireless stations, distributed Sankey's hymn-books and supported schemes for the advancement of religious instruction. Interviewed when he was 92, Ernest – still a dapper man in frock coat and butterfly collar – declared that his one hobby was 'service to my fellow man'. In pursuit of this aim, he and his brothers had donated well over £750 000 to charity and religion. Ernest died on 12 November 1957, leaving the remainder of his estate, valued for probate at £296 872, to charity.

Church of England Messenger, 25 July 1941; *Aust Storekeepers' J*, July 1899; *Argus*, 1 Jan 1936, 13 Aug 1945.   P. H. DE SERVILLE

CONNOLLY, ERIC ALFRED (1880-1944), punter and owner-trainer, was born on 17 April 1880 at Degamero, a sheep station on the King River near Wangaratta, Victoria, the sixth of eight children of Henry James Connolly, grazier, and his wife Elizabeth Sarah, née Bould. After his father's move to Melbourne in the 1890s as a racehorse trainer, Connolly determined to make his living from the turf. In 1903 he bought The General, an undistinguished sprinter, trained it as a jumper and netted £14 000 in 1904 when it won the Grand National Steeplechase. The General was to remain his favourite horse and Connolly had

it painted by Fred Woodhouse, senior. After a visit to India and Singapore, on 16 January 1906 Connolly married Ada Jane Webb in St Peter's Church, Eastern Hill; they had three daughters.

His horses won the 1910 Oakleigh Plate, the 1913 Williamstown Cup, the 1922 and 1923 Newmarkets (which he considered the toughest race to win) and the 1927 Metropolitan. In his heyday in the spring of 1929 he dished the noted New South Wales punter, 'Rufe' Naylor [q.v.], in one of the most intellectual feats of Australian turf history – Connolly took control of Nightmarch, a champion New Zealand stayer, backed him in the one-mile (1600 m) Epsom, bet against him in the 13-furlong (2600 m) Metropolitan and then supported him against the mighty Phar Lap in the two-mile (3200 m) Melbourne Cup: each time his judgment proved correct. By the end of the heady 1920s Connolly's winnings, with his income from investments, had earned him an estimated £250 000 and the reputation of being Australia's outstanding better. Though he sometimes enriched the bookmakers, especially Sol Green [q.v.], he abided by the motto: 'Money lost, nothing lost; courage lost, everything lost'. Late in 1929 he suffered a heart attack and was bedridden for three months; thereafter his activities became more restricted and his fortunes fluctuated.

To contemporaries, his punting seemed inspired and 'the luck of Eric Connolly' became part of the Australian idiom, but behind his good fortune lay hard work. He trained at dawn most of the horses that carried his colours of red and black. He developed a photographic memory, an instinct for pace and an eye for form; he became adept at setting horses for races months ahead; he had pluck and composure. Arriving long before the first event, he seldom ate or drank on the course; he was the cynosure of all eyes at Flemington and Randwick, and his sorties into the ring were followed by many eager punters.

Brown-haired, blue-eyed and purse-lipped, in his prime 'E.A.C.' stood 5ft. 11 ins. (108 cm) and weighed 11 stone (70 kg). A fastidious and conservative dresser, reserved, quietly spoken, devout and a disciplinarian, he drank moderately, smoked heavily, appreciated a joke and had many friends and acquaintances, among them the prince of Wales and John Wren [q.v.]. Operettas cheered him, as did Tivoli stageshows. He also found relaxation in following test cricket, in a game of billiards, in a hand at bridge and in listening to his wife play the piano. Comfortably housed with his family and servants, he donated money to the Anzac Buffet and repatriation programmes.

to churches and hospitals, and to the down-and-out.

Connolly died of coronary thrombosis on 9 October 1944 at his home in Toorak, and was buried in Brighton cemetery with Anglican rites. He left his estate, valued for probate at £5741, to his surviving daughters.

Punch (Melb), 16 Oct 1913; Herald (Melb), 9 Oct 1944; Daily Mirror (Syd), 1 Feb 1958; information from Mrs Iris Clarke, Toorak, Vic, and Mr J. Holledge, Hilltop, NSW.   JOHN RITCHIE

CONNOLLY, SIR JAMES DANIEL (1869-1962), politician, was born on 2 December 1869 at Allora, Darling Downs, Queensland, son of Denis Connolly, labourer, and his wife Johanna, née Callaghan. He was educated at Warwick State School and at the Christian Brothers' St Joseph's College, Brisbane. He trained as a quantity surveyor and in 1893 went to the Western Australian goldfields and became a successful building contractor at Kalgoorlie. Campaigning on abolition of brothels and a ward system, he topped the poll for the Kalgoorlie town council in 1899. In 1901 he entered the Legislative Council as a member for North East Province and, having shown himself a courteous and able debater in the ensuing years of political instability, was chosen colonial secretary and minister for commerce and labour when (Sir) Newton Moore [q.v.] formed his Liberal ministry in May 1906. He remained colonial secretary under the more congenial leadership of Frank Wilson [q.v.] until the Liberal débâcle of October 1911.

In a ministry mainly devoted to rural expansion Connolly was practically its sole social reformer. His purposeful handling of Western Australia's immigration policy, at a time when the wheat-belt was opening up, won him praise from the agent-general (Sir) Walter James [q.v.], as 'the new spirit which had come to the Colonial Secretary's office after ten years of deep sleep'. He was responsible for the remodelling of the Perth Public Hospital's board, for the creation of the Children's (now Princess Margaret) Hospital, and for the initiation of the specialist maternity hospital which later became the King Edward Memorial Hospital for Women. Largely through his influence, Western Australia acquired in 1911-12 what was then the most advanced pure foods legislation in Australia. His proudest achievement was the establishment of the first large Aboriginal reserves in the Kimberleys. Moola Bulla, an area of some 450 000 hectares, north-west of Halls Creek, was reserved as a hunting and cattle-raising property where Aboriginals might settle without molesting pastoralists' stock. It was difficult at first to persuade Aboriginals to remain on the property, but cattle-spearing diminished; so did the frequency of white punitive expeditions.

In 1914 Connolly resigned his seat in the council and later that year won the Legislative Assembly seat of Perth from the sitting Labor member (Sir) Walter Dwyer [q.v.]. In July 1916 Connolly was appointed minister without portfolio in the second Wilson ministry. Intrigues against Wilson were proliferating, and the Liberals had to come to terms with the rising Country Party, so next year Connolly was pleased to become agent-general in London. He served until 1923, during the establishment of the group settlement scheme and the renewal of British migration. An energetic and aggressive publicist of Western Australia, he refuted pessimistic estimates of the land's capacity. Probably his most substantial achievement was the re-negotiation of the terms for Western Australian London loans. Made a commander of the Order of Belgium in 1919 and knighted in 1920, Connolly settled in London for the rest of his life, accepting directorships in a number of companies and banks. In 1928-32 he was agent-general for Malta at a time of financial distress. In old age he retained a lively interest in Western Australian economic development.

Connolly had married Catherine Charlotte Edwards (d. 1948) on 17 November 1898 at St Arnaud, Victoria. They had five daughters. Connolly died in London on 12 February 1962. A loyal Roman Catholic, he donated generously to the University of Western Australia's St Thomas More College, where a fine window in the chapel commemorates him.

J. S. Battye (ed), Cyclopedia of Western Australia, 1 (Adel, 1912); P. Biskup, Not slaves, not citizens (Brisb, 1973); Kalgoorlie Miner, 21 Nov 1899; West Australian, 8 May 1906, 5 Dec 1921; SMH, 4 Feb 1919; correspondence and interview notes, BL 419A/424A (Battye Lib, Perth).

G. C. BOLTON

CONNOR, DANIEL (1832?-1898), merchant and pastoralist, was born in Cahersiveen, County Kerry, Ireland, son of Michael Connor, labourer, and his wife Mary, née Sweeney. He migrated to Western Australia in August 1853 and later peddled his wares in a small way and developed a trade as a stock-dealer around Newcastle (now Toodyay). He soon bought land at Guildford for a holding paddock. On 16 January 1859 he married Catherine Conway, a servant girl from Kerry; they had four daughters and five sons. Next year they moved to Newcastle where Connor ran a store and agency. By 1870 he owned several buildings including a flour-mill and hotel. He held mortgages over many farms and pastoral leaseholds and when drought, flood, or economic depression ruined his clients, Connor foreclosed on their stock and properties.

He belonged to the Newcastle Mechanics' Institute and Agricultural Society and, despite limited schooling, was elected in 1871 to the local board of education. From that year also Connor was a foundation member of the Toodyay Road Board which he chaired in 1879-81 and 1883-93. He sat on the Newcastle Municipal Council from 1877 until his death. Known as 'the King of Newcastle', his wishes, public and private, were rarely denied. He held gambling parties at his hotel and would flout the Road Board's by-laws to gain his ends. A newspaper correspondent once denounced Toodyay people for 'allowing the one oracle to work for his own advantage to the detriment of the general weal'.

In Perth in 1883 Connor bought the Shamrock Hotel which he leased to Timothy Francis Quinlan (1861-1927), who had come to Toodyay aged two and been orphaned soon after. Reared by a kindly Irishman, Quinlan worked in shops at Perth and Roebourne and returned to the city to manage Connor's hotel; he married Connor's daughter Teresa. In 1889 Quinlan became a member of Perth City Council; he represented West Perth in the Legislative Assembly in 1890-94 and Toodyay in 1897-1911. This political success gave Connor great satisfaction.

During the prosperous 1890s Connor was reputedly worth over a quarter of a million pounds. One of Perth's leading financiers and landholders, he sold land for its offices to the Australian Mutual Provident Society, of which he was a shareholder. He was a director of the Stanley Brewery Co., founder of the Port Brewery Co. Ltd, and a major shareholder in the National Bank of Australasia.

Connor was a benefactor of the Catholic Boys' Orphanage and his family endowed a convent at Newcastle for the Sisters of Mercy in whose care his wife ended her days. Aged 67, he died at Perth on 12 January 1898; Bishop Gibney's [q.v.] appraisal was: 'Be to his faults a trifle blind, and to his virtues ever kind'. Connor's estate was sworn for probate at £76 584.

R. Erickson, *Old Toodyay and Newcastle* (Toodyay, WA, 1974); Newcastle Municipal Council, Minutes, *and* Toodyay Road Board, Minutes (Battye Lib, Perth).   RICA ERICKSON

CONNOR, DAME JEAN; *see* MAC-NAMARA, JEAN

CONRICK, HORATIO VICTOR PAT-RICK (1882-1960), medical practitioner, was born on 27 May 1882 at Fitzroy, Melbourne, son of Michael Francis Conrick, bank manager, and his wife Christina, née Love, both of whom were native-born. Educated at the Christian Brothers' School, St Kilda, he worked as a bank clerk before studying medicine at the University of Melbourne (M.B., B.S., 1910); he then became resident medical officer at Mater Misericordiae Hospital, Brisbane.

In January 1914 Conrick was commissioned captain in the Australian Army Medical Corps; when war broke out he was appointed to the Australian Imperial Force and posted to the 3rd Field Ambulance, A.A.M.C. He embarked for Egypt in September, served throughout the Gallipoli campaign and was mentioned in dispatches in August and December 1915. In January 1916 he was appointed to the 2nd Australian General Hospital in Egypt and a month later was promoted major. He was then transferred to the 3rd Australian Auxiliary Hospital and left for the Western Front in April.

After a period as medical officer-in-charge, Anzac Base Details, he was attached to the Australian Voluntary Hospital in July, then for the rest of 1916 held appointments with the 2nd A.G.H. and the 5th and 7th Field Ambulances. He was serving with the latter unit when his award of the Distinguished Service Order was gazetted in July 1917: showing 'fearlessness and disregard for his personal safety', he had 'proceeded to the scene of an explosion under very heavy shell fire and personally directed the removal of the wounded'. Later that year he served with the 1st and 15th Field Ambulances, the 10th Casualty Clearing Station and the 24th Battalion. He was made temporary lieut-colonel and senior medical officer at the 2nd Command Convalescent Depot in November and was again mentioned in dispatches. From 3 April to 24 May 1918 he commanded the 8th Field Ambulance; his rank was confirmed on 1 May.

Conrick embarked for Australia in June 1918 and was demobilized in August. On 12 September, at St Mary's Catholic Church, North Sydney, he married Mary Frances Punch. They settled at North Sydney and Conrick resumed medical practice; concentrating on children's medicine, he held appointments at the Renwick Hospital for Infants, Sydney, from 1922 and was honorary consulting surgeon there from 1957 until his death. From the late 1940s he was honorary assistant physician at Mater Misericordiae

General Hospital and for several years was New South Wales representative on the council of the British Medical Association. He kept up an active interest in the A.A.M.C. until 1943 when he was placed on the retired list with the rank of lieut-colonel; in 1931 he had been awarded the Volunteer Officers' Decoration.

Survived by his wife and two daughters, Conrick died on 18 July 1960 and was buried in the Catholic section of Gore Hill cemetery. His estate was sworn for probate at £2442. Throughout his life his main hobbies were art collecting, music, tennis and swimming. Conrick was a tall, well-built man with a military carriage and a jovial manner. His gentleness and rapport with children were exceptional.

A. G. Butler (ed), *Official history of the Australian Army Medical Services. . . 1914-18*, 1 (Canb, 1930); *Univ Melb, Record of active service* (Melb, 1926); *London Gazette*, 28 Jan, 11 July 1916, 28 Dec 1917; *SMH*, 19 July 1960; records (AWM); information from Miss M. Brissenden, Strathfield, NSW.   W. M. CHAMBERLAIN

CONSIDINE, MICHAEL PATRICK (1885-1959), union militant and politician, was born probably on 26 January 1885, in County Mayo, Ireland, son of Michael Patrick Considine of the Royal Irish Constabulary, and his wife Margaret Josephine, née Lowney. Brought to New South Wales in September 1890 by his mother, Mick was brought up as a Catholic at Kempsey and later moved to Sydney where he became prominent in the 1908 strike of tramway workers. He was also a member of the Socialist Federation of Australia, but resigned after a dispute over the role of Henry Holland [q.v.] in the Broken Hill strike of 1909. Early next year Considine spent six months in gaol for demonstrating in Sydney against the Wade [q.v.] government's Industrial Disputes Act and the gaoling of Peter Bowling [q.v.7]. After his release Considine worked on the wharves and in March 1911 moved to Broken Hill where he found work as a greaser.

Considine rose rapidly in the militant Amalgamated Miners' Association and became its president during World War I. He was for a time a member of the Marxist Australian Socialist Party, but had to resign over his support for a union-controlled political party. In 1916 he helped to achieve a forty-four hour week for underground miners. On 23 January 1918 at Eaglehawk, Victoria, he married, with Baptist forms, Bessie Washington.

In 1917 Considine succeeded the moderate Josiah Thomas [q.v.] as Labor member for the Federal seat of Barrier in the House of Representatives, in the aftermath of the conscription split. With unruly, dark, wavy hair and a cleft chin, he attracted attention as a spokesman of the far left: conservative criticism of him reached a peak when he announced that he was acting consul for the new Bolshevik government of Russia. In July 1919 in Melbourne City Court he received three weeks imprisonment and was fined £100 for saying publicly, 'bugger the King, he is a bloody German bastard'. Next month he was suspended from the House for four weeks for refusing to withdraw an assertion that the Australian government was supporting the forces of Kolchak in Russia.

After the split in the New South Wales Labor Party in 1919 Considine came under increasing pressure from the right-wing executive and resigned from the party late in 1920. He was defeated in the 1922 election as an Industrial Socialist Labor Party candidate. After an attempt at poultry farming in Victoria, he was back at Broken Hill in 1926 and rejoined the Australian Labor Party but, despite strong support from mining and other left-wing unions, he failed to gain endorsement for the Darling seat then held by Arthur Blakeley [q.v.7].

From 1927 Considine lived at Bond Street, Ivanhoe, Melbourne, and described himself as an agent. He had various jobs until and during the Depression, then worked for the Melbourne and Metropolitan Tramways Board. In the 1930s he was a delegate for several unions on the Trades Hall Council, Melbourne, and was a proponent of Labor's 'socialisation units'. Secretary of the Ivanhoe branch of the Australian Labor Party for many years, he was a rebel at Labor conferences in the 1930s and 1940s. From 1942 he worked in Melbourne employment offices of the Department of Labour and National Service, then returned to the tramways as a checker.

Considine died suddenly on 2 November 1959 and was cremated after a Rationalist service. He was survived by his wife, son and two daughters.

All-Australian Trades Union Conference, *Official report* (Melb, 1921); G. Blainey, *The rise of Broken Hill* (Melb, 1968); B. Walker, *Solidarity forever* (Melb, 1972); B. Kennedy, *Silver, sin, and sixpenny ale* (Melb, 1978); Labor Hist, Melb, *Recorder*, Apr 1978; *Aust Worker*, 24 Feb 1910, 31 July 1919, 9 Jan, 13 Feb, 17 Sept, 1 Oct 1924, 14 Oct 1925; *Barrier Daily Truth*, 6 Jan, 7 Aug 1916, 16, 17 Jan, 30, 31 Oct, 7-28 Nov, 1-18 Dec 1922, 3 May 1954; *Sun*, 8 Feb 1916; *Labor Call*, 8 Aug 1918; *Australasian*, 2 Aug, 6 Sept 1919; Attorney-General's Dept, A456, W26/199 [405], and Dept of Labour and National Service, MP24/1, V3085 (AAO); family information.   FRANK FARRELL

CONYERS, EVELYN AUGUSTA (1870-1944), matron-in-chief, was born on 1 March 1870 at Invercargill, New Zealand, daughter of William Conyers, engineer, formerly of Leeds, England, and his wife Fanny, née Mainprize. She was educated privately and at Invercargill and Dunedin girls' high schools.

In the early 1890s Evelyn Conyers migrated to Victoria. She trained as a nurse, first at the Children's Hospital, obtaining a certificate in 1894, and then at the (Royal) Melbourne Hospital, finishing in 1896. In 1901 she was appointed matron of a private hospital in Melbourne and in 1904 foundation matron of the Queen's Memorial Infectious Diseases Hospital at Fairfield. Some three years later she opened a private hospital, Lancewood, in Glenferrie Road, Kew, in partnership with Sister Jessie MacBeth.

Miss Conyers had joined the Australian Army Nursing Service as a sister in 1903. She joined the Australian Imperial Force on 11 October 1914, as senior sister, 1st Australian General Hospital, sailing in the transport *Shropshire* on 20 October. On arrival in Egypt she was sent to Cairo for urgent duty in the Egyptian Army Hospital, Abbassia, nursing New Zealand troops. On 10 July 1915 she rejoined 1st A.G.H. at Heliopolis as night superintendent, before being appointed acting matron of 3rd Australian Auxiliary Hospital, also at Heliopolis, on 1 August.

Meanwhile Matron Jane Bell [q.v.7] was striving to clarify the status of Australian army nurses. In the subsequent reorganization Miss Conyers was appointed matron-in-chief of the Australian Army Nursing Service on 12 December. She was now responsible for all Australian Army nurses except those in India and Salonica, Greece.

She was transferred in May 1916 to A.I.F. headquarters in Horseferry Road, London. Her skill in negotiation reconciled differences between the nurses and medical officers while her appointment helped to diminish rivalry between the Australian and British nursing services. She was in constant consultation with Miss Maud McCarthy, matron-in-chief of the British Expeditionary Force, travelling with her to casualty clearing stations and auxiliary hospitals on the Western Front.

Matron Conyers took furlough in Australia from November 1917 to January 1918, finally returning to Victoria on 12 December, and to her private hospital. Her A.I.F. appointment was terminated on 6 March 1920, but she rejoined the militia. On 3 June 1916 she had been awarded the Order of the Royal Red Cross (1st Class) and on 21 June was mentioned in General Sir John Maxwell's dispatches. She was appointed O.B.E. in January 1919, C.B.E. in March and in December received a Bar to her Royal Red Cross. On 23 February 1921 she was awarded the Florence Nightingale medal and diploma by the International Red Cross Committee at Geneva.

Active in the organization of the profession, she had been a founder of the (Royal) Victorian Trained Nurses' Association in 1901. In June 1914 she represented it at a conference with the Sydney-based Australasian Trained Nurses' Association which agreed to establish a federated body. She was appointed to the board set up under the provisions of the Nurses' Registration Act (1923), remaining a member for ten years. A life member of R.V.T.N.A.'s successor, the Royal Victorian College of Nurses, she was a founder and director of the Victorian Trained Nurses' Club Ltd, a member of the Victorian branch of the Australian Nursing Federation and of the board of management of Fairfield Infectious Diseases Hospital, and a trustee of the Edith Cavell Trust Fund. She also belonged to the Returned Nurses' Club and took a keen interest in its activities.

Evelyn Conyers died in Epworth Private Hospital, Richmond, on 6 September 1944 and was buried with full military honours in Kew cemetery. She left her estate, valued for probate at £6007, to her brother and sister and upon their deaths to Church of England funds.

A. G. Butler (ed), *Official history of the Australian Army Medical Services . . . 1914-18*, 3 (Canb, 1943); *Reveille* (Syd), 31 July 1930, 1 Oct 1944; *Age*, 27 Apr 1935, 22 Apr 1937, 7 Sept 1944; *Herald* (Melb), 6, 7 Sept 1944; *Argus*, 7 Sept 1944; *Weekly Times* (Melb), 13 Sept 1944; information from Miss H. Adair, Roy Aust Nursing Federation, Melb, *and* Mrs Tregellis Smith, Hawthorn, Vic.

JOHN REID

COOCH, ALEXANDER (1865-1948), bank officer, was born on 6 May 1865 at Stawell, Victoria, son of Alexander Cooch, miner, and his wife Jane, née Quin, both from Ireland. He was educated at Stawell Grammar School and in 1880 joined the Commissioners' Savings Bank, forerunner of the State Savings Bank of Victoria. In 1893 he was appointed accountant at head office in Melbourne and next year became inspector of branches. After the amalgamation of the Commissioners' Savings and Post Office Savings banks in 1896-97, he became chief inspector and in 1914 deputy inspector general. On the retirement of George Emery [q.v.], Cooch became general manager of the State Savings Bank in 1929, serving until his retirement in 1937.

Although he had a long and distinguished career at the State Savings Bank, the range of his achievements was limited by the fact that for over thirty years he worked in the shadow of his immediate superior, Emery; when he finally succeeded Emery, any scope for initiative was severely checked by the onset of the Depression, but for which, it is believed, Cooch would have been a notable pioneer of bank mechanization. Nevertheless he can still take primary credit for the introduction of school banking to Victoria in 1912 and, through the creation of the service department, for the further extension of savings banking to the factory floor in 1927. While general manager, Cooch also wrote a substantial, if fairly obviously official, history of the bank (Melbourne 1934) with what W. W. Kerr [q.v.] described in the foreword as 'characteristic zeal, thoroughness and self-sacrifice'.

With his vast experience in one of Victoria's largest public organizations, Cooch was generally recognized as an authority on administration, especially accounting procedures. In 1907, at the invitation of the Tasmanian government, he investigated the organization and administration of the State Savings Bank of Tasmania, and in 1908 inquired similarly into the affairs of the government Savings Bank of New South Wales. Both institutions were substantially reorganized following his recommendations. Later, in 1916, he chaired a royal commission into the Victorian Public Service. It reported in great detail after eighteen months of research and deliberations.

In 1926 Cooch was chairman of the Australian group of representatives at an international conference of savings bank delegates at Philadelphia, United States of America; from there he returned with a vision of highly mechanized banking operations. From 1927 to 1930 he was president of the Bankers' Institute of Australia. After his retirement he became a director of the Colonial Mutual Life Assurance Society Ltd. Then, as earlier, bowls appears to have been his one major recreation.

Cooch had married Normana Augusta MacLeod, at St Andrew's Presbyterian Church, Ballarat, on 17 June 1902. He died at his Toorak home on 13 August 1948, survived by his wife, two of his three sons, and a daughter. His estate was valued for probate at £14 420.

T. Craddock and M. Cavanough, *125 years . . . the State Savings Bank of Victoria* (Melb, 1967); *Age*, 14 Aug 1948.   E. A. BEEVER

COOK, BERTIE STUART BAXTER (1877-1968), journalist, was born on 2 March 1877 at Prahran, Melbourne, son of John Baxter Cook, clerk, formerly of Yorkshire, England, and his wife Charlotte, née Chambers, of Chelsea, London. After education at state schools Cook joined the Melbourne *Herald* as a copy boy in 1889. His wage was 5s. for a six-day week; ten years later, when he had become a fully fledged reporter, his salary had risen to £3 for a 70-hour week. At that time there was no journalists' union, and while other employees could resort to wages boards all attempts by reporters to improve their wages and conditions had failed.

Cook was deeply concerned about the conditions of work and the low morale of journalists. In 1906 he and several colleagues formed the Press Bond, a group for journalists to discuss their problems, but it was ineffectual. By 1908 it was on the point of disbanding, and Cook concluded that journalists' associations would have to look to the law for protection if they were to survive. As Federal parliamentary correspondent for the *Herald* from 1901, he had followed the passage of the Commonwealth Conciliation and Arbitration Act (1904). In 1908 he lobbied the prime minister, Alfred Deakin [q.v.], for the legislation to allow journalists as well as manual workers to be registered. Unsuccessful, he decided to test the Act by forming an association and applying for registration. On 10 December 1910 he convened a meeting in Melbourne, attended by 100 pressmen, at which the Australian Journalists' Association was at last formed. Cook became its first secretary, a constitution was drawn up and branches were set up in each State; registration was granted in May 1911. Cook was general president of the federated body in 1916-18; in May 1917 the Arbitration Court gave its first award to the A.J.A. for claims based on the grading system for journalists, a system which has operated ever since.

In May 1918 Cook accepted an offer by W. M. Hughes [q.v.] to organize the first Federal press bureau in the Prime Minister's Department. Next year he resigned to assist his friend (Sir) Gerald Mussen [q.v.] as resident industrial officer at Broken Hill. The strike of 1919-20 upset their conciliatory plans, and Cook spent much of his time as the companies' representative on the distress committee which administered funds to needy miners.

After two years Cook returned to Melbourne and with Mussen formed the Victorian Central Citrus Association; Cook was secretary and for six years general manager. In 1929 he accepted (Sir) Edward Cunningham's [q.v.] invitation to join the *Argus* as financial editor. In 1935 he became organizer of the publicity branch of the

Royal Automobile Club of Victoria, retiring in 1939.

On 8 March 1899 at St Luke's Anglican Church, South Melbourne, Cook had married Harriet Ann Butler (d. 1960). By his early 40s he had grown a vandyke beard, and wore pince-nez. As a journalist he was respected for his facile pen and gentle sense of humour and especially for his 'absolute fairness'. Selections from his memoirs, which contained racy sketches of many leading Federal politicians, were serialized in the Sydney *Bulletin* from October to December 1959. He was appointed M.B.E. at the A.J.A.'s diamond jubilee in 1960 and remained active in the association's affairs until his death at Glen Iris on 2 September 1968. He was survived by his two daughters and was cremated.

Cook is remembered as the one who did more for the welfare of working journalists in Australia than any other figure. It is fitting that when he returned later to his profession as a distinguished senior reporter, he was able to enjoy the fruits of his battles.

Aust Journalists' Assn, *Crusade for journalism*, G. Sparrow ed (Melb, 1960); *Punch* (Melb), 30 May 1918; B. S. B. Cook papers (NL)

ROBERT MILLIKEN

COOK, JAMES NEWTON HAXTON HUME (1866-1942), politician, was born on 23 September 1866 at Kihikihi, New Zealand, eldest of the nine children of James Cook, then a private in the Waikato militia and originally from Walsall, England, and his wife Janet, née Mair, from Rutherglen, Scotland. James Hume Cook, as he was known, had an unsettled childhood: his father failed in farming, three sisters died of diphtheria and he had to leave school at 13 and work as a travelling book salesman. In November 1881 the Cooks migrated to Melbourne where the father, supported by his oldest son's cheap labour, manufactured harness mountings. His health impaired, and eager to leave his mean-spirited father, Cook struck out on his own in 1887 to sell real estate in Ascot Vale. He also joined the Australian Natives' Association and began to read widely and attend political meetings.

Hume Cook claimed that he owed 'almost everything' to the association. At his first meeting he was appointed branch auditor, within fifteen months he was branch president, in 1894 he joined the board of directors and in 1896 was elected president. Through the A.N.A. he gained the confidence to expand his public activities. He joined the Anti-Sweating League and several protectionist associations; won a seat on the Brunswick Town Council in August 1893 at the fourth attempt, helped to straighten out the council's finances, and became mayor in 1896. Elected with Sir Graham Berry [q.v.3] in 1894 to represent East Bourke Boroughs in the Legislative Assembly, he campaigned for Federation and helped to persuade the A.N.A. to support the proposed constitution at its Bendigo conference of 1897.

For all his energy Hume Cook was a light-weight in Victorian politics. Regarded by the *Age* as 'too inexperienced', he finished nineteenth among the twenty-eight candidates who stood for the 1897 Australasian Federal Convention. He dismissed himself as a 'comparative non-success', his most notable achievement being membership of the royal commission on state banking (1894-95). He was important for his support of liberal causes: protection, electoral, educational and land reform, state intervention into wage-fixing and working conditions. In 1894 he was one of the younger element who pushed the A.N.A. on to a similar platform. In parliament he attended meetings with Labor members claiming that only their pledge prevented him from joining them formally, his sympathies being 'entirely with the labouring classes'. He was convinced that there was a middle way between Conservatism and Labor.

Rejected by East Bourke Boroughs in 1900, Hume Cook won the Federal seat of Bourke in 1901 and held it in 1903 and 1906. He was a firm Deakinite, loyal enough to liberal principles to oppose Alfred Deakin's [q.v.] support for (Sir) George Reid [q.v.] in 1905, yet loyal enough to the man, and sufficiently afraid of losing his seat, to join Deakin in the fusion with the Conservatives in 1909. Between 1905 and 1908 he was party whip, cabinet secretary and honorary minister, and in June-December 1908 chaired the royal commission on postal services (1908-10): experiences which he thought much less interesting than his rescue by the police from an armed lunatic who had invaded his parliamentary office. His evident pleasure in recounting such stories, and his habit of self-denigration, reflected a liking for the absurd, an honest view of his own limitations, and a contempt for the self-important. Yet inside the House he was respected for his sharp political nose and critical if discursive mind. Labor regarded him as dangerous because of his popularity among small business and working-class families in Brunswick, and set out to destroy him in the 1910 election. After a campaign of 'extraordinary heat and venom', in which 'Bloom Chook' was denounced as an Orangeman, he was soundly defeated by Frank Anstey [q.v.7]. Rejected again in 1913 by the Maribyrnong electorate, Hume Cook left politics, certain that he had saved his health and his finances.

He remained a non-Labor man without ever feeling comfortable among the rich and conservative. During the first World War W. M. Hughes [q.v.] replaced Deakin as his hero, in a friendship enhanced by a common liking for nigger minstrel shows and humorous tales. In 1916 Hume Cook helped to bring Hughes together with the non-Labor premiers in the National Federation. He was federation secretary until unjustly dismissed in May 1919 for 'disobedience and insubordination' following a dispute with the conservative wing. In 1929-30 he assisted Hughes in forming the abortive Australian Party. By then, however, his major work was with the Australian Industries Protection League of which he was secretary from 1922 until his death. In 1932 he represented manufacturing interests at the Imperial Economic Conference in Ottawa and, to mark a 'life-long' commitment to protectionist causes, was made a fellow of the Royal Economic Society in 1936 on the initiative of J. M. Keynes. He had also been involved in orchard-growing, mining and insurance companies and charitable organizations. He published a book of Australian fairy tales and wrote hundreds of protectionist pamphlets, patriotic poetry, and several manuscripts, including his memoirs and an extravagant piece on Hughes. On 7 June 1941 he was appointed C.M.G.

On 26 March 1902 in the Presbyterian Church, Brunswick, Hume Cook had married 18-year-old Nellie Maine. He died at a Brighton private hospital on 8 August 1942 and was cremated. He was survived by his wife, a daughter and two sons.

J. A. La Nauze, *Alfred Deakin* (Melb, 1965); J. Rickard, *Class and politics* (Canb, 1976); *PD* (Cwlth), 1909, 49, 167; *Age,* 25 Feb 1897, 8 Aug 1942; *Australasian,* 3 Feb 1900; *Table Talk,* 25 Apr, 9 May 1901; *Punch,* 21 June 1906, 16 Jan 1908, 17 Mar 1910; *Labor Call,* 3, 24 Mar, 28 Apr 1910; M. Aveling, A history of the Australian Natives' Association, 1871-1900 (Ph.D. thesis, Monash Univ, 1970); Aust Industries Protection League *and* Hume Cook papers (NL).   I. R. HANCOCK

COOK, SIR JOSEPH (1860-1947), prime minister, was born on 7 December 1860 at Silverdale, Staffordshire, England, son of William Cooke, coalminer, and his wife Margaret, née Fletcher. He grew up in poverty. In 1873 his father was killed in a pit accident and he became the family wage-earner, a responsibilty which developed in him a high degree of self-confidence and a strong sense of obligation. During his teens he joined the Primitive Methodists, and marked his conversion by dropping the 'e' from his surname. He eschewed alcohol, gambling, sport and other forms of entertainment, and sought self-improvement through study at home. Solemn and humourless, he nevertheless enjoyed the company of other people, among whom he was invariably quiet and modest. He became a lay preacher and a successful public speaker. He also became involved in trade union affairs: before he was 25 he had been elected successively to all the executive positions in his union lodge, and had also become interested in political issues; he supported tariff protection as a method of improving working conditions in the coal-mining industry. By the early 1880s Cook had fulfilled his obligations to his family and, after being several times unemployed, he decided to migrate.

On 8 August 1885 at the Wolstanton Primitive Methodist Chapel he married Mary Turner, a Chesterton schoolteacher whose brother was one of a number of Silverdale miners already settled at Lithgow, New South Wales. Cook left for Lithgow shortly after his marriage and by January 1887 had established a home there and was employed at the Vale of Clwydd colliery. In his spare time, having abandoned earlier studies for the Methodist ministry, he learned shorthand and book-keeping, and helped manage the *Lithgow Enterprise and Australian Land Nationaliser;* he also audited the books of the *Lithgow Mercury* and, in 1890, those of the municipal council. He served in the important position of check-weighman in his mine, and as secretary and president of the miners' lodge. He also took part in the 1888 public demonstrations against Chinese immigration. Politically, he was then a republican and a supporter of the Land Nationalisation League which, under the influence of the single-taxer Henry George [q.v.4], strongly supported free trade. In August 1890, during the maritime strike, he served on the Labor Defence Committee while the Lithgow mines were worked by non-unionists under the protection of a contingent of the permanent artillery.

In May 1891 Cook was elected president of the Lithgow branch of the Labor Electoral League, and was subsequently endorsed as its parliamentary candidate. In June he won the seat of Hartley in the Legislative Assembly. He was elected leader of the Parliamentary Labor Party in October 1893. Party members were divided on the tariff issue, and many were also unwilling to accept the directions of those organizations which had made their election possible. He became spokesman for those who wished to retain their independence in parliament. At a conference in March 1894, however, it was resolved that members had to bind themselves to accept caucus direction. Cook was the leader of those who refused to sign the 'solidarity' pledge and it was as an independent Labor member that he was again returned to the assembly in July. His immediate acceptance of the position of postmaster-general in the Reid [q.v.] government at £1500 a year was seen by members of the official Labor Party as an act of opportunism never to be forgotten or forgiven. It was the beginning of Cook's long drift from Labor to Conservatism, and from Free Trade to Protection.

However, he was convinced that the Reid government's programme was close to his own, and that he could serve the cause of Labor better as a minister than as a backbencher. Conversely, his inclusion in the government assured Reid of reasonable support from the independent Labor members. Cook's Hartley electors again returned him with a huge majority at the ministerial by-election. He then built a large house in the centre of Lithgow, and came to be highly respected in the town because of his new role as head of the postal department, one of the most important of the colony's public services.

Although Cook had ceased to represent only the working classes he held Hartley easily at the snap election of July 1895. Thereafter, he was associated with the Reid government's social reforms. He had always thought it the moral duty of government to elevate the working classes, as 'some sort of parent to the people'. As postmaster-general until August 1898, then secretary for mines and agriculture until September 1899, he took pride in his departments, and got on well with Reid, to whom he was steadfastly loyal.

An administrator who gave close attention to detail, Cook carefully implemented the government's policy of retrenchment in the public service; he also expanded the telephone network, completed the line between Sydney and Newcastle, issued charity postal stamps, and introduced postmen to bicycles. As minister for mines he failed to get reforming legislation through parliament because of opposition in the Legislative Council, but he supervised an executive order which compelled all skips of coal to be weighed according to the provisions of the Coal Mines Regulation Act (1896). As minister for agriculture he appointed William Farrer [q.v.] to the position of government wheat experimentalist. However, as a private member, Cook was unable to persuade parliament to adopt local option for the control of public house licences, and his administrative action in preventing lottery tickets passing through the mails was revoked after he had left office.

He gradually came to admire the institution of the monarchy, and to value the ties which bound the Australian colonies to the mother country, and he gave strong support to Britain at the outbreak of the South African War. He was slower to see the practical value of Australian Federation, mainly because Reid's 'Yes-No' label did not give him the guidance he had come to expect of his leader. Cook opposed the constitution bill at the first referendum because it would give equal, and therefore undemocratic, representation to each State in the Senate, and because, more significantly, he believed it would disadvantage New South Wales. However, after Reid had obtained concessions, both he and Cook supported the bill at the second referendum.

The Reid government lost control of the assembly early in 1899 and the Labor Party gave its support to (Sir) William Lyne's [q.v.] Protectionist group. As a private member of the Opposition, Cook successfully persuaded parliament to pass a Truck Act (1901) to prevent wages being paid other than in money. At that time his political ambition was probably limited to succeeding Reid as leader of the New South Wales Free Trade Party. However, early in 1901 he was persuaded to contest the new Federal seat of Parramatta, which included Lithgow and most of the Hartley State electorate. Unopposed by Labor, he easily won. He then moved to a new home at Marrickville, and joined Reid on the Opposition bench in the newly assembled House of Representatives. Tom Roberts [q.v.], who recorded the occasion on canvas, noted that Cook was 5 ft. 9 ins. (175 cm) in height, weighed 12 stone (76 kg) and his hat size was 7.

In the new parliament, he excelled as a doggedly pugnacious Oppositionist and unsparing critic of the Barton [q.v.7] and Deakin [q.v.] Protectionist governments, especially during the debates on the first Federal tariff. Re-elected in December 1903 Cook was not invited to take office during the brief period of the Reid-McLean [q.v.] coalition in August 1904-July 1905, but he did help Reid to establish a Liberal League and an anti-socialist campaign. In July 1905 he was elected deputy leader of the Free Trade Party, his first official party position, and thereafter developed the pronounced conservative views which characterized the rest of his political career.

Cook had been fourteen years out of the mines and now believed that no one class in society ought to benefit at the expense of any other and that there should be no unnecessary restrictions on personal freedom. He saw social reform as a slow and laborious achievement. He declared that all Labor Party policies were sectional and socialist, while his own were liberal and in the national interest. He attacked the Labor pledge and its organization and, during the long absences of Reid from parliament, was strongly critical of its policies and sometimes rude to its members. He unsuccessfully led the fight against increased tariff protection and New Protection, but otherwise had much in common with Deakin's Protectionist government. He supported the encouragement of immigration, electoral reform, old-age pensions, the appointment of a high commissioner in London, and an Australian flotilla of the Royal Navy. Hardworking, physically tireless and shrewd, he was incisive and combative in debate, with a thorough grasp of parliamentary manoeuvring, but he could be irascible and was always humourless.

Cook was prominent in New South Wales during Reid's anti-socialist election campaign of late 1906, and was returned unopposed. He then moved house to the most exclusive part of his electorate, Baulkham Hills. But the election had not improved his party's strength; at the end of 1908, Cook had spent almost eight years on the Opposition bench and had held no ministerial office. Deakin's biographer wrote of him that 'if there had been roots of geniality in his nature their growth had been inhibited by years in opposition'. The adoption of the new protective tariff in May 1908 meant that the Free Traders had no future in national politics; it became imperative that they should join forces with the Protectionists so as to provide an effective counterforce to Labor's growing electoral strength.

Cook became leader of the Free Trade Party after Reid's retirement in November 1908 and next year accepted a position as' deputy leader and minister for defence in a fusion ministry led by Deakin. The government had the support of a majority in both Houses and enacted a substantial programme during its brief period in office. Cook did his most lasting work as minister at this time. His Defence Act laid down the principles of compulsory military training and the establishment of a military college; he also took charge of the visit of Lord Kitchener to report on Australian defence and concluded with Britain the agreement which established the Royal Australian Navy.

However, in April 1910 the electors passed a strongly adverse judgement on the opportunism of the new fusion by giving the Labor Party a landslide victory in both Houses. For the fourth successive election Cook was a member of the defeated party, and for the next three years again sat on the Opposition bench. The surviving fusionists formed themselves into the newly titled Liberal Party, and Cook took part in developing an effective extra-parliamentary organization. By January 1913, the Fisher [q.v.] Labor government had implemented many radical proposals to which Cook's vociferous opposition had been unavailing, in particular the introduction of a Federal land tax and the establishment of a Federal government bank.

By then Deakin had realized that his mental powers were failing and he resigned, suddenly, from parliament. At a party meeting held on 20 January, Cook defeated Sir John Forrest [q.v.] for the leadership of the Liberal Party by 20 votes to 19, a division which seemed to reflect the party split on the tariff question. Thus, at the age of 52, the former Labor leader and free trader had become the national leader of a political party which since the fusion had become both protectionist and conservative. In his public manner, his speech and his social activities there was no longer any trace of his working-class origins. In private he was still deeply religious, and a devoted husband and father to his wife and nine children. He continued as a lay-preacher.

At the Federal elections of May 1913 the Labor Party lost its majority in the House of Representatives, though it kept control of the Senate. In June Cook became Liberal prime minister of Australia, twenty-two years after his first election to represent Labor in the New South Wales parliament. As he could control the House of Representatives only by the casting vote of the Speaker or the chairman of committees, his government had little chance to sponsor new legislation; his only practical achievement was to provoke the Opposition in the Senate into creating the constitutional situation for a double dissolution: this was done by proposing to abolish preference to trade unionists in government employment, and to reintroduce postal voting at Federal elections. In the ensuing poll of September 1914 the Labor Party easily regained control of both Houses. Cook went into Opposition once again, though now as a member of His Majesty's Privy Council, his first public honour.

Meanwhile, war had broken out in Europe; one of Cook's last public acts as prime minister had been to pledge his government's full support for Britain, including the transfer of the Royal Australian Navy to the British Admiralty, and to offer to send a contingent of 20 000 volunteer troops overseas. After the election Cook and his colleagues endorsed the Labor government's war policy, as well as the recruiting drives to raise troops, though they were annoyed that the Labor Party had rejected their proposal to form an all-party national government, and Cook was displeased at the increased land tax and the introduction of a Federal income tax.

By May 1916 Cook and his Liberal Party colleagues were convinced that compulsory military conscription for overseas service was the only way in which Australia could meet its commitment to Britain. Although this view was entirely unacceptable to the majority of Labor members it was supported by the new prime minister, W. M. Hughes [q.v.], who organized a national plebiscite on the question in October 1916. After the proposal was narrowly defeated, Hughes left the Labor Party with a small following to form a minority government, hoping for support from Cook's Opposition. This was an unworkable situation, and a coalition was negotiated early in 1917 which kept Hughes as prime minister and made Cook his deputy. Cook chose to be minister for the navy in the new government, although the senior portfolio, defence, had been accepted by (Sir) George Pearce [q.v.]. Cook then moved house once more – to the inner Sydney suburb of Summer Hill.

In the election of May 1917 the Nationalist coalition government won a majority in both Houses. Soon afterwards the parties fused. Cook, who had often been the recipient in parliament of Hughes's most barbed phrases, loyally accepted him as leader, and became his efficient deputy, as he had been to both Reid and Deakin. Hughes thought Cook plodding and unimaginative, but valued the way in which he was scrupulously loyal to the government in public. Cook recognized Hughes's success as a wartime prime minister and approved of strong leadership. Despite the defeat of the proposal to introduce overseas military conscription at a second plebiscite in December, the Hughes government remained in office during the closing stages of the war.

In June 1918 Hughes and Cook represented Australia at the Imperial War Conference and in the Imperial war cabinet; next year they were delegates to the Peace Conference where Cook sat on the commission which gave the Sudeten Germans to the new Czechoslovakia. Appointed G.C.M.G., in 1918 he had a hero's welcome at his birthplace. However, Hughes delegated no real responsibility to Cook during the discussions in London on the war and the peace treaty, and Hughes's biographer has suggested that Cook was 'solaced for any neglect' by the knighthood.

The Nationalists won the election of December 1919. From July 1920 until November 1921 Cook served as treasurer during a particularly difficult economic period. He was opposed to wage increases and did nothing to control unemployment, though at the time the government did not have the constitutional power to deal with Australia's finances effectively on a national scale. Cook was acting prime minister from April to September 1921, while Hughes was at the Imperial Conference in London, and in November he resigned from parliament in order to become high commissioner in London. He represented Australia well, and immensely enjoyed London's social round; his wife was appointed D.B.E. in 1925 for her services to the Red Cross Society. Cook returned to Australia in 1927, and in 1928-29 was chairman of a Federal royal commission which inquired into the finances of South Australia. He retired from public life and built a large block of flats at Bellevue Hill, Sydney, where he died on 30 July 1947, survived by his wife, five sons and three daughters, and leaving an estate valued for probate at £23 269. He was cremated after a state funeral.

He had refused to compile his memoirs, but he told relatives and friends that he viewed his career with every satisfaction. He felt that he had always done his duty and had never avoided his responsibilities. Joe Cook was an eminently successful politician and an able parliamentarian during an eventful period of Australian political history, because he was able to adapt to changing circumstances and because his sense of duty, as he understood it, triumphed clearly over adherence to early principles. Unfortunately for his career, he was most frequently in opposition and represented minority interests; his only notable achievements were the Defence Act of 1909 and the double dissolution of 1914. A harsh critic might say that when in office Cook saved the taxpayers' money at the expense of the class from which he had risen, and when in opposition he was an unprincipled opportunist. A sympathetic admirer would stress that he was a self-made man who rose to the top with those very virtues of hard work, perseverance, self-improvement and a sense of duty which formed the central and uplifting message of the Primitive Methodists. A portrait of Cook by Norman Carter [q.v.7] hangs in Parliament House, Canberra, and another by Sir James Guthrie is held by the National Gallery in Edinburgh.

L. F. Fitzhardinge, *William Morris Hughes*, 1-2 (Syd, 1964, 1979); J. A. La Nauze, *Alfred Deakin* (Melb, 1965); B. Nairn, *Civilising capitalism* (Canb, 1973); J. Rickard, *Class and politics* (Canb, 1976); J. R. M. Murdoch, Joseph Cook: a political biography (Ph.D. thesis, Univ NSW, 1968).

F. K. CROWLEY

COOK, ROBERT (1867-1930), primary producer and politician, was born on 18 April

1867 at Lancashire Lead, Chiltern, Victoria, son of Henry Cook, splitter and later contractor, from Birmingham, England, and his wife Mary, née Wilkinson, from Cork, Ireland. Cook was mainly self taught, having received minimum education at state schools. At 18 he selected land at Tallangatta where he arrived, as he often recalled, 'with his sole worldly possessions – a chestnut horse and a pair of blue blankets'. A few years later he also acquired land at Porepunkah and supplied laths for the Chiltern and Rutherglen mines.

On 24 December 1894 at Porepunkah he married Sarah Anne Weston. They lived in Chiltern for some years before moving about 1905 to Oxley, south of Wangaratta, where Cook established a dairy farm with 'characteristic energy and thoroughness' on a property later known as Buffalo View.

Cook had been a councillor of Chiltern Shire in 1902-04. In 1908 he was elected to the Oxley Shire Council and was president in 1910-11 and 1916-17. He was a keen debater and always ready to learn more about the needs of the area; it soon became customary to appoint him as representative at conferences. He had boundless faith in the future of the Wangaratta district and became one of its most active public men. In 1906 he was a founder and first chairman of directors of the North Eastern Co-operative Society Ltd; shareholders acknowledged that his practical help and encouragement at the critical early stages of the society ensured its survival. Cook was a director of the Milawa Dairy Co., a member of the Victorian Dairy Council and chairman of the Butter and Cheese Factories Association of Victoria. He supported the local tobacco growing industry and was a board member of the Western and Murray Co-operative Bacon and Meat Packing Co. He was also a committee-member of the Wangaratta Agricultural Society and an executive councilmember of the Chamber of Agriculture, Melbourne.

Cook joined the Victorian Farmers' Union when the movement was first introduced in the district and in 1919 was selected as its candidate for the Federal seat of Indi. He defeated the sitting member J. W. Leckie [q.v.] and increased his majority in the 1922 and 1925 elections. However, in the elections of November 1928, he mistook the deadline for lodging his nomination paper, thinking that it was 6 p.m. instead of noon; the seat went by default to the Labor candidate Paul Jones [q.v.] thus giving J. H. Scullin [q.v.] an important extra vote in the House of Representatives. Cook stood again as one of three Country Party candidates for Indi in 1929; he was overseas at the time on a tour of war graves, and failed to regain the seat.

Even then his health had begun to deteriorate. He died of cancer in a private hospital in Melbourne on 21 May 1930, survived by three daughters and two sons; his wife's death on 26 June 1927 had been a severe blow to him. After a service at St Paul's Church of England, Milawa, where he had been a member of the vestry, Cook was buried in the local cemetery.

Tributes were paid to him in the House of Representatives where (Sir) Earle Page [q.v.] described him as a 'plain, blunt, matter of fact, commonsense man . . . always genial, and able to see a humorous side to even the most serious circumstances . . . His work for the producers of Australia will be a monument more durable than any edifice of stone'.

V&P (LA Vic), 1901, 1 (2); PD (Vic), 1930, p 2036-38; *Wangaratta Chronicle*, and *Wangaratta Despatch*, 24 May 1930; *Aust Worker*, 28 May 1930.

A. O. SMITH

COOKE, JOHN (1852-1917), meat exporter, was born at Belfast, Ireland, son of James Cooke, merchant, and his wife Elizabeth née Douglas. First apprenticed to a linen manufacturer, he migrated to Dunedin, New Zealand, in 1873 in search of better health. He found work in a warehouse, then as a journalist on the *Otago Guardian*, and finally in the office of the New Zealand Loan and Mercantile Agency Co. In 1878 he went back to Belfast where on 9 August he married Edith Marshall. On his return to New Zealand Cooke was appointed manager of the company's Christchurch office.

In 1880 news arrived of the successful shipment of frozen meat from Australia by the steamship *Strathleven*. Cooke was quick to see the possible benefits for a depressed New Zealand, and was prominent in the successful promotion of the country's frozen meat export trade. In November 1881 he arranged a meeting which led to the formation of the Canterbury Frozen Meat Co. In 1889, while still a director of that company, he secretly founded a rival concern, the Christchurch Meat Co. (now the New Zealand Refrigerating Co.). His action angered the chairman of directors of the C.F.M. Co., a valued customer of Cooke's employers. His sudden transfer to Australia was probably the loan company's response to their client's displeasure.

Cooke was relieving general manager for the N.Z.L. & M.A. Co. in Melbourne for two years before becoming the Australian manager for the Australian Mortgage (Mercantile), Land, and Finance Co. Particularly emphasizing ownership and control by producers, Cooke helped to form the large producer-sponsored Queensland Meat Export and Agency Co. in 1890 and a smaller producer co-operative at Geelong in 1894. Most ambitious of his early promotions were meatworks at Deniliquin, New South Wales, which began operations in 1895. In this, his pet project, Cooke extended the concept of producer control by trying to match production with export needs and by killing stock as close as practicable to the pastures.

While initially a champion of producer self-help, Cooke realized that this was a passing phase. Resigning from the A.M.L. & F. Co. in 1895, during the next decade he built up the largest meat export business in Australia. In 1896 he acquired freezing works at Newport, the largest in Melbourne until (Sir) William Angliss [q.v.7] opened at Footscray in 1905. In 1899 Cooke promoted a company to buy Sydney's largest freezing works, at Sandown near Parramatta, along with associated chilling works in the country. Four years later he took over works at Redbank near Brisbane. These three centres had been greatly expanded by World War I, and as well he treated large numbers of stock at other works. In a tribute to his undisputed leadership, a rival merchant assessed his own prospects quite simply: 'To be successful, we must supplant him'.

Cooke was an entrepreneur in the classic tradition. He speculated in shipments and in the shares of other meat companies. He pioneered new markets, notably in South Africa and later Japan. Above all, he operated an essentially one-man business. Not until 1913 was it incorporated as a company, and even then 80 per cent of the shares were held by him or his family, the balance being held by his junior partner (Sir) James Elder [q.v.]. But as a one-man business it was also ephemeral. Already suffering from ill health by 1914, Cooke was unable to dominate as he had, and in Elder's less dynamic hands the business declined.

Articulate and public-spirited, John Cooke played an active role in the affairs of chambers of commerce, in Christchurch and Melbourne. With E. M. Young [q.v.6] he helped to organize the Pastoralists' Union of Victoria and was later active in the Pastoralists' Association of Victoria and the Southern Riverina. His belief in free enterprise also led him to take part in the founding of the National Association, dedicated to uphold the principle of liberty and the rights of property against the threat from the Trades Hall. Cooke was an elder of Scots Church and took an active interest in the Young Men's Christian Association.

For the last months of his life he lived in England near his son who was in hospital recovering from war injuries. Cooke died aged 65 at Eastbourne, Sussex, on 12 December 1917, survived by his wife, a daughter and two sons. His estate in Victoria was sworn for probate at £100 919. After his death the decline of his company accelerated, and in the difficult trading conditions of the 1920s John Cooke & Co. liquidated; the meatworks of a once great business were closed or sold off piecemeal to more resilient operators.

J. D. Bailey, *A hundred years of pastoral banking* (Oxford, 1966); C. Loach, *A history of the New Zealand Refrigerating Co.* (Christchurch, 1969); *Pastoral Review*, Mar 1893; *Argus*, 15 Dec 1917; E. A. Beever, A history of the Australian meat export trade, 1865-1939 (Ph.D. thesis, Univ Melb, 1968); Borthwick papers (Univ Melb Archives).

E. A. BEEVER

COOKE, SAMUEL WINTER (1847-1929), grazier and politician, was born on 13 March 1847, son of Cecil Pybus Cooke [q.v.3], and his wife Arbella, née Winter; he was baptized at St Peter's Church of England, Melbourne, on 10 April. Both his parents were of Anglo-Irish gentry descent. Because his mother abhorred colonial schools Samuel went to England in 1854 to Mr Shapcott's school and then to Cheltenham College, where he was football captain in 1865. He took a B.A. at Trinity College, Cambridge, in 1870, studied at Lincoln's Inn, and was called to the Bar in 1872. He was admitted to the Victorian Bar in 1873 after his return to the colony, but only practised briefly.

In 1878, his uncle, Samuel Pratt Winter [q.v.6], who died shortly afterwards, chose him from among his less talented brothers to inherit Murndal, a property of 10000 acres (4000 ha) near Hamilton. There Samuel Winter Cooke bred Corriedales, Herefords and blood horses. He became a renowned host and generous employer, revered in the district. Samuel combined an aristocratic sense of duty and dignity with a democratic open-mindedness which he recognized and valued as Australian. A fervent Imperialist and frequent traveller overseas, he was yet bound strongly to Murndal and to Hamilton, where he presided at various times over the Pastoral and Agricultural Society, Race Club and Hunt. To accommodate numerous guests, many of whom were vice-regal, he enlarged and altered the homestead but retained its pioneer rooms and rambling charm. He was president of the Melbourne Club in 1896.

Cooke was a Portland Shire councillor in 1879-85 and president in 1882-84. He sat in the Victorian Legislative Council from 1888 to 1901 as member for Western Province. Minister without portfolio in 1893-94, he acted briefly then as minister of defence and minister of education; he was a member of the royal commission on the Mildura settlement in 1896, and of the commission on law reform in 1897. Member of the House of Representatives for Wannon in the first Federal parliament in 1901, he resigned to go overseas in 1903, then stood again in 1910 and was defeated, having put aside his strong free-trade principles in favour of Alfred Deakin's [q.v.] fusion. In Federal parliament he stressed the importance of the Empire, free trade and White Australia, and opposed votes for women. In supporting soldier settlement he made his own land available on easy terms. He was a sincere Anglican.

On 6 January 1883 at All Saints, St Kilda, he married Alice Margaret Werge Chambers. She died in 1903 and on 6 July 1910 at Tahara he married her cousin Margaret, aged 29, daughter of John Hawdon of County Durham. Both marriages were childless. When he died in London on 26 June 1929 about half the estate, valued for probate at £100 141, passed to a nephew William Lempriere Cooke. A portrait by E. Phillips Fox [q.v.] hangs at Murndal.

Aust Council of National Trusts, *Historic homesteads of Australia*, 1 (Syd, 1969); *Pastoral Review*, 15 Nov 1905; *Argus*, 28 June 1929; *Hamilton Spectator*, 29 June 1929; Winter Cooke papers (LaTL)   WESTON BATE

COOKE, THOMAS (1881-1916), soldier and builder, was born on 5 July 1881 at Kaikoura, Marlborough, New Zealand, son of Tom Cooke, an English-born carpenter, and his wife Caroline Ann, née Cooper. Educated at Kaikoura Demonstration High School, he later moved to Wellington with his family and became a carpenter. There, on 4 June 1902, he married Maud Elizabeth Elliott. Cooke's main hobby was band music: he was an excellent cornetist and belonged to the city's garrison band.

In 1912, with his wife and three children, he migrated to Victoria, settling in the Melbourne suburb of Richmond. Cooke worked as a builder until World War I. On 16 February 1915 he enlisted as a private in the Australian Imperial Force and after training at Broadmeadows and other camps was allotted to the 24th Battalion as a reinforcement. He embarked for Egypt in November on the troopship *Commonwealth* and on arrival was transferred to the 8th Battalion at Serapeum in the Suez Canal Zone. His unit sailed for France on 26 March 1916 and from April to July served in the Fleurbaix and Messines sectors of the Western Front.

In mid-July the battalion was moved south to the Somme where it took part in the furious fighting around Pozières. The task of advancing through the village itself had been allotted to the 8th Battalion and on 24-25 July 1916, as the men moved forward under an intense bombardment, Cooke was ordered, with his Lewis-gun team, to a dangerous part of the newly captured line. There was little cover, and heavy enemy fire killed all his companions, but he continued to hold out alone. When assistance finally reached him he was found dead beside his gun. For his gallantry he was posthumously awarded the Victoria Cross. His name is commemorated on the roll of honour at the Australian war memorial, Villers-Bretonneux. Cooke was survived by his wife, who later remarried, and by his three children.

O'M Creagh and E. M. Humphris, *The V.C. and D.S.O.* (Lond, 1924); C. E. W. Bean, *The A.I.F. in France*, 1916 (Syd, 1929); L. Wigmore (ed), *They dared mightily* (Canb, 1963); *London Gazette*, 8 Sept 1916; *Call* (Perth), 28 July 1932; War diary of the 8th Battalion, AIF (AWM).   P. A. PEDERSEN

COOKE, WILLIAM ERNEST (1863-1947), astronomer, was born on 25 July 1863 in Adelaide, son of Ebenezer Cooke [q.v.3], commissioner of audit, and his first wife Eliza Peyton, née Ogden. Cooke won a series of scholarships at the Collegiate School of St Peter in 1875-79 and at the University of Adelaide (B.A., 1882; M.A., 1889). Next year he won the South Australian scholarship but waived it to go to the Adelaide Observatory as assistant to Sir Charles Todd [q.v.6]. Cooke joined in surveys of the South Australian borders with Victoria, New South Wales and Queensland. He was especially interested in the international programme to map the heavens photographically.

Sir John Forrest [q.v.], premier of Western Australia, invited Cooke in 1896 to become the first government astronomer. He made Perth Observatory one of the best-equipped in Australia for the photographic mapping of stars. His work was acclaimed internationally; the astronomer royal's advice was to 'follow implicitly the lead of the Perth Observatory and copy their methods'. An international conference in Paris (1909) adopted his proposals for a more efficient international star-mapping programme. Until 1908, when weather services were taken over by the Commonwealth, Cooke was also government meteorologist; he established an efficient Weather Bureau. He was the first to plot the transit of a tropical cyclone across the State, and instituted warnings which reduced their hazards for the shipping and pearling industries. He promoted public interest in science, and was the first chairman (1902) of the State's Civil Service Association.

In 1912 Cooke became both government astronomer for New South Wales and professor of astronomy at the University of Sydney, with his salary paid by the government. He was promised a new observatory and equipment and helped select a site at Wahroonga, but World War I frustrated his plans, and he could not obtain support after the war. An incompetent Public Service Board inquiry criticized him for becoming involved in wireless experiments in 1918—most unfairly in the opinion of his colleagues. With his son Frank Basil, a pioneer amateur radio operator, he had received time signals from Lyons, France, and recognized that this new technique would fix longitude more accurately.

Cooke improved the observatory equipment and introduced new methods of observation and computation which led to markedly better output. In 1926 the Lang [q.v.] government proposed to close the observatory, but was persuaded to continue it with fewer staff; Cooke was forced into early retirement. He had been planning to co-operate with observatories throughout the Pacific to test the theory of continental drift. Cooke believed that he had detected systematic variations in observations which supported the theory. He retired in Sydney, but in 1936 returned to Adelaide. On 30 June 1887, in Adelaide, he had married Jessie Elizabeth Greayer in the Unitarian Christian Church; they had three sons and two daughters who survived infancy. Predeceased by his wife, he died of cardiac disease in Adelaide on 7 November 1947.

Cooke was a considerate and kindly man. He found the New South Wales experience humiliating and frustrating, and Australian astronomy was possibly deprived of the full benefit of his potentially richest years. He wrote numerous papers. His status as a fertile inventor will only be evaluated after further research, as few of his inventions, said to number more than one hundred, were patented. His ingenious 'heliochronometer', a sun-dial which could be used to determine local time and true north accurately, won a gold medal at Wembley exhibition in 1924. He was a fellow of the Royal Astronomical Society.

PD (NSW), 1926, 2ndS, p 165, 200; Sydney Observatory, *Papers*, no 31 (1958); H. B. Curlewis, 'The Perth Observatory' *and* G. P. Stevens, 'The Civil Service Association', *Civil Service J* (Perth), 20 July 1929; *SMH*, 28 Aug, 10 Nov 1926; *Advertiser* (Adel), 12, 13 Nov 1947; Observatory records (Perth); family papers (held by Mr M. G. Cooke, Point Piper, NSW).   D. E. HUTCHISON

COOMBE, EPHRAIM HENRY (1858-1917), journalist and politician, was born on 26 August 1858 at Gawler, South Australia, eldest son of Ephraim Coombe, a farm-labourer and shopkeeper from Devon, and his wife Mary, née Lock. Educated at St George's day school, Gawler, he worked as a grocery assistant in Gawler and at his father's general store at Willaston. On 1 March 1880 in Adelaide he married Sarah Susannah Fraser Heywood of Willaston.

Coombe was local literary correspondent and Hansard reporter for the *South Australian Register* in 1888. Two years later he became editor of the lively Gawler *Bunyip* and in 1897 was one of the few country journalists selected to be an official Hansard reporter for the Adelaide Federal Convention. Coombe was always active in temperance, the arts and education: in Gawler he belonged to many cultural, sporting and benevolent societies and was a keen Freemason. He represented South Australia in both cricket and chess. He was a governor of the Adelaide Public Library, Museum and Art Gallery in 1901-06, vice-president of the Institutes' Association and editor of its journal in 1904-08. In his patriotic *History of Gawler* (1908) he voiced satisfaction that his 'lot was cast in a community whose institutions and citizenship are so favourable to the development of a robust and intelligent manhood and womanhood'.

Coombe was president of the Barossa Political Reform League from 1888; twice defeated in attempts to enter parliament as an independent in 1896 and 1899, in 1901 he won Barossa in a by-election and held it till 1910. At first he was seen as a progressive but his politics changed. He had early allied himself with A. H. Peake [q.v.], and was his Opposition whip in 1904; next year Coombe was government whip and chairman of committees in the Price [q.v.]-Peake coalition of 1905-09. A founding member of the Liberal and Democratic Union in 1906, Coombe was its president in 1907-09. On the breaking of the Liberal-Labor coalition in 1909, in June-December he was commissioner of crown lands and immigration, and minister of agriculture, in Peake's cabinet. When the ministry was restructured to include the Opposition leaders Coombe stepped down. He was re-elected as L.D.U. member for Barossa in 1910, but when it amalgamated with the Liberal Union he refused to sign the new pledge. He re-formed the L.D.U. with the support of the Northern Democratic Association, but was defeated at Barossa in 1912. In 1908-09 he had chaired an important royal commission on wheat marketing.

In 1914 Coombe left the *Bunyip* and moved to Adelaide to edit the labour *Daily*

Herald where he was seen as 'rigidly truthful, singularly just, transparently honest'. He joined the United Labor Party, led the party ticket for Barossa in 1915 and re-entered the House of Assembly, alienating some friends. Within the party he lived down suspicion about his former ties and came to be looked upon as one of its leaders. He spoke out strongly against the closure of German schools and in October 1916 led public campaigns against conscription and the intimidation of male voters in the referendum in 1917. He was prosecuted under the War Precautions Act at Tanunda in March, fined £10 and bound over to keep the peace. Coombe did not oppose the war: his three sons were in the forces and he resented the stigma of disloyalty, which contributed to a 'heavy burden of worry' — several commentators wrote that 'incessant persecution' over this issue precipitated his early death. Coombe collapsed with a cerebral haemorrhage while addressing a U.L.P. meeting at Semaphore and died on 5 April 1917. Survived by his wife, four sons and two daughters, he was buried in Willaston cemetery. In 1930 a commemorative marble monument was erected at Tanunda, and the town of Coombe in the State's south-east district was named for him.

H. T. Burgess (ed), *Cyclopedia of South Australia*, 2 (Adel, 1909); *SA Institutes J*, June 1931; *Barossa Historic Bulletin*, 1969; *Quiz* (Adel), 20 June, 31 July 1901, 13 Mar 1903; *Observer* (Adel), 10 Aug 1901, 14 Apr 1917; *Barossa News*, 10 Nov 1916, 2, 16 Feb, 2, 9 Mar 1917; *Bulletin*, 8 Mar 1917; *Bunyip* (Gawler), 16 Mar 1917; *Advertiser* (Adel), and *Daily Herald*, 6 Apr 1917; *Aust Worker*, 12 Apr 1917; *Chronicle* (Adel), 6 Mar 1930; F. S. Wallis, Labour's thirty years 1893-1923 (SAA).

DEAN JAENSCH

COOMBES, RICHARD (1858-1935), journalist and sports administrator, was born on 17 March 1858 at Hampton Court, Hampton Wick, Middlesex, England, son of Richard Coombes, hotelkeeper, and his wife Ellen, née Parsons. Dick was educated at Hampton Grammar School. In his youth in England he was active as a harrier (captain of the Harefield Hare and Hounds Club), a sculler (captain of the Waldergrave Rowing Club) and as a walker, in which sport he became a champion of the London Athletic Club. He was also, in the days of penny-farthing cycles, captain of the Kingston-upon-Thames Bicycle Club.

Coombes arrived in Sydney in 1886 and, after a spell as a jackeroo, became involved in the foundation and management of a variety of sporting organizations, notably the New South Wales Amateur Athletic Association which he helped to form in 1887. He was vice-president until 1893 and thereafter president until 1935. He also founded, in 1888, the Sydney Amateur Walkers' Club, and the Sydney Harriers. As president of the Amateur Walking Union of Australia he drafted its rules which were widely adopted.

Coombes began to contribute articles to the Sydney *Referee*. Joining its staff in 1890, he was associate editor from 1919 to his retirement in 1933. Journalism gave Coombes an opportunity to indulge his other sporting interests. Under a variety of pen names, he wrote on athletics and rowing as 'Argus', coursing as 'Amesbury' and rifle shooting as 'Binocular'. At various times he also wrote for the *Arrow* and the Sydney *Sunday Times*.

As manager, Coombes took an Australian athletics team to New Zealand in 1889, the first of twenty visits. In 1891 he was interested by a proposal in the London *Greater Britain* that a 'Pan Brittanic and Anglo-Saxon Olympiad' be held. With R. J. Parkinson of Victoria, he arranged the first Australasian championships in Melbourne in 1892 with contenders from New South Wales, Victoria and New Zealand: they were intended to produce competitors for the Olympics, but the scheme fell through. In 1895 he took a team to Queensland, and helped to set up the Queensland Amateur Athletic Association. Next year he founded the Amateur Athletic Union of Australasia. Coombes became chairman of the Australian organizing committee for an 'Empire Sports Carnival' to celebrate the coronation of George V in 1910; next year, as honorary manager, he took athletes to London. A member of the International Olympic Committee for thirty-one years, he also managed the Australian team that went to Antwerp in 1922.

Possibly Coombes's fading skills were responsible for a row that broke out over his rulings against two Victorian walkers at the Adelaide Australasian championships of 1922. Coombes, who as 'Argus' had the advantage of being able to report on his own case, was never forgiven by the Victorians, who in 1924 and 1926 challenged his presidency of the Amateur Athletic Union.

Coombes was also responsible for the foundation of the New South Wales National Coursing Association and later of the Australasian Coursing Union. He was captain of the Sydney Rifle Club in 1907-24, and vice-president of the Metropolitan Rifle Clubs' Union. In 1924 he was described as 'a living fossil — a Corinthian, a blood' and in most respects, apart from a seeming lack of interest in boxing and horse-racing, he fitted the description. Tall and spare, with a beard in early years, a moustache later, he was a dignified figure. He never lost his English accent and in later years may have seemed out of tune with Australian ways. The Coombes Memorial Prize commemorates his interest in athletics, as does his familiar description, 'the father of Australian athletics'.

Coombes died on 15 April 1935 at his home at Bellevue Hill, Sydney, and was cremated with Church of England rites. He was survived by his wife Abbe May Talbot, née Teas, a governess whom he had married in Sydney with Presbyterian forms on 29 June 1895, and by one daughter Gretchen.

Referee, May-June 1893, 18 Apr 1935; *Sydney Mail*, 4 Feb 1899; *Smith's Weekly*, 26 Jan 1924; *SMH*, 16 Apr 1935; Davis sporting collection, Box 27 (ML).   W. F. MANDLE

COOPER, LILIAN VIOLET (1861-1947), medical practitioner, was born on 11 August 1861 at Luton, Kent, England, daughter of Henry Fallowfield Cooper, captain of Royal Marines, and his wife Elizabeth, née Shewell. Educated privately, she dedicated herself to medicine when young. Despite parental opposition, she entered the London School of Medicine for Women in 1886, completed the course in October 1890 and, after passing the conjoint examinations of the Royal College of Physicians, Edinburgh, the Royal College of Surgeons, Edinburgh, and the Faculty of Physicians and Surgeons, Glasgow, received a licentiate from Edinburgh.

Cooper worked briefly and unhappily for a practitioner in Halstead, Essex, then came to Brisbane in May 1891 with her lifelong friend Josephine Bedford, and in June became the first female doctor registered in Queensland. Induced to work for an alcoholic doctor, she finally secured a cancellation of her contract and was boycotted professionally for two years. She was allowed to join the Medical Society of Queensland in 1893, and later became an honorary in the Hospital for Sick Children and the Lady Lamington Hospital for Women. In 1905 she became associated with the Mater Misericordiae Hospital and stayed with it for the rest of her life.

In June 1911 Cooper returned to England. Travelling through the United States of America, she visited the Mayo Clinic in Minnesota and the Johns Hopkins Hospital in Maryland; she then went on to win a doctorate of medicine from the University of Durham in June 1912. With Miss Bedford she joined the Scottish Women's Hospitals in 1915, served for twelve months, including a time in Macedonia, and was awarded the Serbian Order of St Sava, fourth-class. Cooper settled again in Brisbane after the

war and, despite an unsuccessful action for damages against her in 1923, won a large and successful practice. A tall, angular, brusque, energetic woman, prone to bad language, she travelled first by bicycle but became an early motorist and did most of her own running repairs. In 1926 she bought a house called Old St Mary's in Main Street, Kangaroo Point, and settled there in semi-retirement, becoming a foundation fellow of the Royal Australasian College of Surgeons in 1928. She retired in 1941 and died in her home on 18 August 1947. She was buried in Toowong cemetery with Anglican rites; her estate, sworn for probate at £12315 in Queensland and £2896 in New South Wales, was left mainly to members of her family.

After Cooper's death Miss Bedford gave the site for the Mount Olivet Hospital of the Sisters of Charity, part of which was entitled 'the Lilian Cooper Nursing Home'. St Mary's Church of England in Kangaroo Point has memorial windows and an altar on the frontal of which is embroidered Dr Cooper's medal of St Sava.

Alcazar Press, *Queensland, 1900* (Brisb, nd); E. S. Morgan, *A short history of medical women in Australia* (Adel, 1970); H. J. Summers, *They crossed the river* (Brisb, 1979); *MJA*, 30 Aug, 11 Oct 1947; *Sunday Mail* (Brisb), 15 Nov 1970; Roy A'sian College of Surgeons Archives (Syd).
C. A. C. LEGGETT

COOPER, SIR POPE ALEXANDER (1846-1923), politician and judge, was born on 12 May 1846 at Willeroo Station, Lake George, New South Wales, son of Francis Cooper, a wealthy squatter, and his wife Sarah, née Jenkins. When his family began to grow up, Francis moved to Sydney seeking schooling for them. Pope was placed first with private tutors; later, at Sydney Grammar School, he was well grounded in classics and the mathematics which became a lifelong joy. At 18 he matriculated, and at the University of Sydney, as a friendly rival of both (Sir) Edmund Barton [q.v.7] and (Sir) Samuel Griffith [q.v.], won several scholarships. Graduating M.A. in 1868, he went to London, enrolled at the Middle Temple, passed the intermediate law examination of the University of London in 1871 and was called to the Bar on 6 June 1872. On 19 August 1873 he married Alice Frener Cooper at Kensington.

Cooper returned to Australia in 1874. Admitted to the Queensland Bar on 13 May he entered the Public Service and advanced to crown prosecutor in the northern district Supreme Court in 1878. After the death of Henry Rogers Beor [q.v.3], (Sir) Thomas McIlwraith [q.v.5] appointed Cooper his attorney-general. The appointment was ratified on 24 January 1881 when he won Beor's Bowen seat. Though unhappy in politics, Cooper held his office and seat until 5 January 1883 when he was appointed to the northern bench of the Supreme Court. He became noted for severity in criminal cases.

For much of Cooper's twelve years in the north, his ability was obscured by a long quarrel over his circuit travelling expenses which, because of his extravagant tastes, were often excessive. This was aggravated when new circuits to Mackay, Charters Towers, Cairns and Normanton, established during Cooper's incumbency, made the allowance of £400 inadequate. His threat to close a circuit before completion brought some relief. Northern service was a martyrdom to one of his cultured taste, but he spent as much long leave as he could arrange in Britain and the south.

He was elevated in October 1895 to senior puisne judge in Brisbane. When Griffith became chief justice of the High Court of Australia, the Morgan [q.v.] ministry appointed Cooper chief justice of Queensland on 21 October 1903. His colleague Patrick Real [q.v.] complained publicly when he was being congratulated, but was placated. Cooper was knighted in 1904. His judicial style has been described as 'grand, pompous and arrogant'. There had been objections to his exaggerated view of judicial dignity in 1888 when he censured a country policeman for disrespect, and in 1889 when he reacted savagely to a personal attack on himself. In 1903 he began trying to secure through legal processes the exemption of judges from income tax; the case failed before the High Court in June 1907.

Although Cooper had temporarily deputized for the governor in 1906, when the need to appoint a lieut-governor to succeed Sir Hugh Nelson [q.v.] arose in 1907, Lord Chelmsford [q.v.7] could not ignore the objections of Premier Kidston [q.v.] and he was passed over. Chelmsford described Cooper's K.C.M.G. awarded in 1908 as 'a kiss for the place to make it well'.

Since Cooper had publicly censured the Ryan [q.v.] ministry in November 1915 (he had complained also of other governments), and had publicly objected to its socialism, he was still regarded as unsatisfactory for the lieut-governorship; but with no alternative, Governor Goold-Adams [q.v.] had to appoint him as deputy for short periods in 1917-19. In November of the latter year the Theodore [q.v.] ministry decided to appoint William Lennon [q.v.] as lieut-governor. Seeing the appointment as a prelude to the abolition of the Legislative Council and the governing of Queensland 'on Bolshevik lines', Cooper objected bitterly. Early in January he made an emotional appeal for support to the governor-general, and refused to admit the validity of a commission for Lennon drafted locally on telegraphic instructions from London; he deputized himself from 27 January to 3 February 1920 until Lennon's commission as lieut-governor arrived.

That year while Lennon was on diplomatic sick leave in New South Wales, Cooper again became lieut-governor under his dormant commission. When asked, he refused to sign the executive council minute appointing Lennon president of the Legislative Council; he argued that the council was already over strength. On his return, Lennon was forced to appoint himself to the council and to its presidency. On 30 March 1922 a proclamation under the Judges Retirement Act of 1921 removed Cooper, Real and Chubb – all well over 70 – from the bench.

In 1912 Cooper joined the Senate of the University of Queensland and was chancellor in 1915-22. Described when young as 'an enthusiastic sportsman and capital shot', he enjoyed racing, bowls and golf and had a taste for wine and music. He was said to be one of the best judges of china in Australia. He speculated with Robert Philp [q.v.] and others in the Raub syndicate's dubious Malayan mines. Cooper was president of the Queensland Club in 1897, 1900, 1905 and 1910. Tall and handsome, with the pointed beard and manner of a Renaissance noble, he did not have a first-class mind but was a skilful politician. Predeceased by his wife, he died at his Chelmer home on 30 August 1923. He was survived by two daughters and a son. Most of his estate, valued for probate at £3142, was left to an unmarried daughter. He was buried in the Anglican section of Toowong cemetery by the archbishop of Brisbane after a state funeral.

Alcazar Press, *Queensland, 1900* (Brisb, nd); Univ Qld, *Report of . . . presentation of chancellor's robes to . . . Sir Pope Cooper* (Brisb, 1916); C. A. Bernays, *Queensland – our seventh political decade 1920-1930* (Syd, 1931); D. J. Murphy, *T. J. Ryan* (Brisb, 1975); A. P. Haydon, *Sir Matthew Nathan* (Brisb, 1976); W. R. Johnston, *History of the Queensland Bar* (Brisb, 1979); *Cwlth Law Reports,* 4 (1906-07), 1304-1334; *Brisbane Courier,* 22, 28 Oct 1903, 16, 19 Nov 1915, 1 Apr, 18, 31 Aug 1923; *Daily Standard,* 1, 3, 4 Oct, 22 Nov 1915; *Bulletin,* 6 Sept 1923; B. A. Knox, The Honorable Sir Arthur Morgan, Kt . . . (BA Hons thesis, Univ Qld, 1956); Novar papers (NL); Palmer-McIlwraith papers (Oxley Lib, Brisb); A21534, *and* COL/G52, 53, 57, *and* GOV 16, 36-39, 58, 68, 69, *and* JUS/G29, 41, *and* PRE 13 (QA); CO 418/103, 149, 179.

J. C. H. GILL

COOPER, ROBERT JOEL (JOE) (1860-1936), buffalo hunter, was born on 29 February 1860 at Fairview, near Riverton, South

Australia, son of George Cooper, farmer, and his wife Harriett, née Peverett. Sometime between 1878 and 1881, with a brother George Henry (Harry), he overlanded horses to the Northern Territory and for several years engaged in timber-getting and buffalo shooting on the Cobourg Peninsula and adjacent areas.

In May 1893 the brothers were among those who, despite hostile Aboriginals, made an exploratory foray into Melville Island with E. O. Robinson, the pastoral lessee. They found thousands of buffalo and Cooper, as Robinson's manager, set up camp there in 1895; in June he was speared in the shoulder, but managed to abduct four Tiwi Aboriginals, including two women, before escaping to the mainland. Cooper treated his captives kindly and learned their language. In 1905 he returned with them and twenty Port Essington Aboriginals to Melville Island. By sending the Melville islanders ashore first to establish contact he was able to land unopposed and become the first European settler since Fort Dundas was abandoned in 1828. He stayed for ten years, taking upwards of 1000 buffalo a year for their hides and horns, cutting cyprus pine and fishing for trepang. He shipped his products to Darwin in his lugger, *Buffalo*. His 'wife' Alice, a Port Essington Aboriginal, bore him three children, two daughters who predeceased him and a son Reuben (c.1898-c.1941) who was educated in Adelaide and became a well-known sportsman. Returning to Melville Island in May 1915 Reuben later established a sawmilling business at Mountnorris Bay, Cobourg Peninsula. He was drowned in the Alligator River while trying to raise a sunken lugger.

Cooper was a large man, slow and sparing of speech, temperate, intelligent and courageous. Protective of his own interests, he managed to divert Father Gsell's [q.v.] attention to Bathurst Island for a mission site in 1911, but proved a good neighbour. He befriended the Commonwealth administrator, J. A. Gilruth, and Professor W. Baldwin Spencer [qq.v.]; Spencer stayed with Cooper in 1911 and 1912 while studying the Aboriginals, as did the German physical anthropologist, H. Klaatsch, in 1906. Enjoying the confidence and respect of the local people whom he treated fairly but firmly, Cooper was appointed honorary sub-protector of Aborigines in 1911. Mainland Aboriginals addicted to alcohol or opium were placed in his care. Inspector T. J. Becket noted, 'a year or two on Melville Island works wonders in the regeneration of these aboriginal decadents'.

In November 1914, however, a sawmiller Sam Green complained of Cooper's cruelty towards the Aboriginals and of the intimidating practices of his armed 'bodyguard' of Port Essington 'boys'. In view of the impending inquiry, and the Melville Island lease having changed hands, Cooper resigned his sub-protectorship next March. By order of the Department of External Affairs the Port Essington Aboriginals were returned to the mainland by December and Cooper, although largely exonerated, followed them in 1916. He became associated with several pastoral leases at the Top End and in 1921 was trepanging in Trepang Bay. A legend in his own time, the patriarchal 'Jokupper' became known as 'The king of Melville Island'. He lived at Port Bremer for a while and by 1933 was in Darwin where he died on 7 August 1936.

W. B. Spencer, *Wanderings in wild Australia* (Lond, 1928); W. E. Harney, *North of 23°* (Syd, 1946); E. Hill, *The Territory* (Syd, 1951); D. W. Lockwood, *The front door: Darwin 1869-1969* (Adel, 1968); Northern Territory, *Annual Reports*, 1913, 1915; *People*, 14 Mar 1962; *Daily Mirror*, 2 Oct 1978; NT news-cuttings, 1893-95 (SAA); A3 item NT 16/245 (AAO).

F. H. BAUER
J. B. BAUER

COOPER, WILLIAM (1861?-1941), Aboriginal leader, was born in Joti-jota tribal territory about the junction of the Murray and Goulburn rivers, fifth of the eight 'half-caste' children of Kitty Lewis; his father was James Cooper, labourer. The Atkinson/Cooper family, with Kitty's mother Maria, settled at the Mologa Mission established in 1874 by Daniel Matthews [q.v.5]. William was one of many workers forcibly retained by the Moira and Ulupna station managers, and was later sent to the Melbourne home of Sir John O'Shanassy [q.v.5] as coachman. He worked as shearer and handyman for pastoral employers for much of his life, because the Maloga Mission and the near-by government-funded Cumeroogunga Aboriginal Station required able-bodied men to earn wages to support their dependants.

The last of his family to be converted to Christianity, Cooper settled at Maloga in 1884, where he married on 17 June the orphaned Joti-jota 'half-caste' Annie Clarendon Murri; she died in 1889, survived by one of their two children. Six more were born of his second marriage, at the Nathalia Methodist parsonage on 31 March 1893 to Agnes Hamilton (d. 1910), a 'quarter-caste' born at Swan Hill and reared at Coranderrk Aboriginal Station near Melbourne. Their daughter Amy (Mrs Henry Charles) became matron of the first Aboriginal hostel established in Melbourne in 1959; their son Dan died in World War I; another son Lynch was a champion runner, winner of the 1928 Stawell Gift and the 1929 World Sprint. There was no issue of his third marriage, at Nathalia on 4 August 1928 to Mrs Sarah Nelson, née McCrae, of Wahgunyah and Coranderrk.

Cooper had attended adult literacy classes; he read widely and wrote a good letter. His family connexions and membership of the Australian Workers' Union made him a spokesman for the dispersed communities of central Victoria and western New South Wales who were ineligible for any aid during the 1920s drought and the 1930s Depression. But officials ignored his complaints. In 1933, undeterred by age and deafness, he left Cumeroogunga to become eligible for the old-age pension, his only income for a campaign which lasted until his death: as secretary of the Australian Aborigines' League, formed by the Melbourne Aboriginal community, he circulated a petition seeking direct representation in parliament, enfranchisement and land rights. He led the first Aboriginal deputation to a Commonwealth minister on 23 February 1935, and with members of the Aborigines' Progressive Association, formed in Sydney in 1937, led the first deputation to a prime minister (to ask for Federal control of Aboriginal affairs) on 31 January 1938. Although Commonwealth and three State authorities had refused co-operation, he had collected 1814 signatures from Aboriginals all over Australia by October 1937; but in March 1938 the Commonwealth declined to forward his petition to King George VI or seek the constitutional amendment necessary to legislate for Aboriginals or form an Aboriginal constituency.

Bitterly disappointed, Cooper spent his last years vainly protesting State government alienation of Cumeroogunga, Coranderrk and other reserves, still citing the rights of Maoris and Canadian Indians as an example for Australia. In November 1940 he retired to Barmah. He died, aged 80, on 29 March 1941 at Mooroopna, Victoria, survived by his third wife and six children. His grave at Cumeroogunga is unmarked; his main achievement was the establishment of a 'National Aborigines Day', first celebrated in 1940.

D. Matthews, *Annual report of the Maloga Mission School* (Echuca, 1876-95, copy ML); M. T. Clark, *Pastor Doug* (Melb, 1965); D. E. Barwick, 'Coranderrk and Cumeroogunga ...', T. S. Epstein and D. H. Penny (eds), *Opportunity and response* (Lond, 1972); *Argus*, 5 Dec 1934, 29 Sept 1935, 26 Oct, 3, 13 Nov, 17, 24 Dec 1937, 17 Jan 1938, 29 Nov 1940, 1 Apr 1941; *Courier Mail*, 6 Nov 1937; D. Matthews papers (ML).

DIANE BARWICK

COPE, WILLIAM (1852-1933), solicitor, soldier and pastoralist, was born on 26 June 1852 at Windsor, New South Wales, eldest son of London-born Joseph Cope, pastoralist, and his native-born wife Mary Ann, née Parnell. He was educated privately and at Sydney Grammar School. In October 1869 he was articled to H. B. Bradley [q.v.3] and was admitted as a solicitor on 19 December 1874. He was briefly in partnership with William Smith in 1878, and in 1883-99 practised with Frederic Hart King at 14 Castlereagh Street as Cope & King.

A notable horseman and sportsman, Cope was captain of the Sydney Rowing Club for many years and was master of the Sydney Hunt Club in 1890-94. In 1893 riding Criterion he won the Intercolonial Hunt Club Steeplechase at the club's meeting at Randwick. In 1885 Cope had enlisted as a private in the New South Wales contingent to the Sudan. Soon after landing at Suakin on 29 March, he was commissioned temporary lieutenant and appointed transport officer. He took part in the advance on Tamai Wells and returned with the contingent in June.

On 12 February 1900 Cope was commissioned lieutenant in the New South Wales Citizen's Bushmen's Contingent and on the 28th left with 'A' Squadron for the South African War; before sailing, at a special Randwick race meeting he won the Commandeer Welter Plate on Uproar, wearing full uniform. Disembarking at Beira, Portuguese East Africa, he took part in operations in the Mafeking area and later at the relief of Rustenberg, entering the town on 7 July. In August he was present at the Eland's River post when it was besieged for thirteen days until relieved by Lord Kitchener on 15 August. Early in the action Cope was responsible for siting some of the main defensive positions. However, 'he was never very regimental in his orders. Usually one would hear, "Get mounted, boys" '. He later suffered an eye injury and on 27 September was invalided to Australia. In 1901 he transferred to the reserve of officers with the rank of honorary captain, and to the retired list in 1907.

On his return to Sydney, Cope founded and became senior partner of Cope & Co. at his old premises until the firm moved to Bligh Street in 1924. In 1914 he was in London as solicitor for the appellants, (Sir) Arthur Cocks [q.v.] and others, in the 'Government House case'. When World War I broke out he was rejected for active service. Until December 1914 he was attached to the French Red Cross, when he joined the Australian Voluntary Hospital at Wimereux, near Boulogne, France, as transport officer and censor. From August 1916 until September 1917 as assistant commissioner for the Australian Comforts Fund he was attached to the 1st Australian Division in France and Flanders. Until he was demobilized in June 1918 he worked with the French Red Cross, was attached to the French 43rd Chasseur Regiment and was awarded the Croix de Guerre for helping wounded near Ingelmunster, Belguim.

Although Cope returned to his practice in Sydney, he also extended his long-held pastoral interests: in New South Wales he grew wheat at Calala, and bred Percherons, sheep and cattle at Cana and Allendale, near Werris Creek, and in Queensland owned Dagworth and Banchory stations and with Donald Macintyre controlled the management of others. A bachelor, he lived at the Union Club when in Sydney.

Cope died in Quirindi District Hospital on 24 September 1933 and was buried in St Thomas's Church of England cemetery, North Sydney. His estate was valued for probate at £199 564; included in the bequests were flora and fauna, war service and charitable organizations.

Aust Defence Dept, *Official records of the Australian military contingents to the war in South Africa*, P. L. Murray ed (Melb, 1912); S. H. Bowden (ed), *The history of the Australian Comforts Fund ... 1914-19* (Syd, 1922); S. Brogden, *The Sudan contingent* (Melb, 1943); R. L. Wallace, *The Australians at the Boer War* (Canb, 1976); *NSW State Reports*, 13 (1913), 295; *Cwlth Law Reports*, 16 (1914), 404; *Reveille* (Syd), 1 Nov 1933; *SMH*, 26 Sept 1933, 21 Feb 1934.   PETER BURNESS

COPLEY, WILLIAM (1845-1925), farmer and politician, was born on 25 April 1845 at High Green near Sheffield, Yorkshire, England, eldest son of James Copley, miner, and his wife Elizabeth, née Redfearn. The family migrated to South Australia in 1849 and lived at Burra Burra. They visited the Victorian goldfields in 1851, but returned to settle in West Torrens. Copley was educated at Hindmarsh Public School and James Bath's school, North Adelaide. In 1867-1910 he was a wheat-farmer, lastly on the Black Rock plain near Orroroo, and then moved to Gawler and Adelaide.

Copley's central interest remained agriculture. He examined students at the Roseworthy Agricultural College and was president of the Farmers' Association in 1883-84. In 1884 he was elected to the House of Assembly for Frome and two years later became a commissioner for the Colonial and Indian Exhibition. In 1887 he lost Frome but in July won a Legislative Council by-election for the northern division. As 'a strenuous opponent' of socialism, he was a founding member in 1892 of the National Defence League, a 'counter' to the new United Labor Party.

Copley was commissioner for crown lands and immigration in Thomas Playford's [q.v.] 1890-92 ministry. But the appointment of a legislative councillor to the position was opposed in the Lower House and he was transferred to agriculture and education. He was a 'strong farmer's advocate' and introduced progressive probate and succession duties and 'homestead block' measures, based on New Zealand legislation. This led to the inauguration of 10-acre (4 ha) holdings at Gawler Blocks, Peterborough, Cottonville and Croydon. He sat on the 1891 and 1898-99 pastoral lands commissions. Copley was minister of agriculture and education in Sir John Downer's [q.v.] 1892-93 ministry, and chief secretary briefly in 1893 when he piloted the bill for free education through the council.

Defeated in 1894, he returned to farming and assisting the N.D.L. In 1896-1902 he sat again in the House of Assembly as member for Yorke Peninsula. In 1902 he stood for Barossa and lost, and also failed in a bid to enter the Senate for the Australasian National League. A founder member and president of the Farmers and Producers' Political Union from 1904, he led discussions on its amalgamation with the Liberal and Democratic Union and the A.N.L., resulting in the formation of the Liberal Union in 1910.

Survived by his wife and four daughters, Copley died at Henley Beach on 16 September 1925, leaving an estate sworn for probate at £5308. His adherence to what 'he believed to be fair and right' had showed particularly in the South African War; as an Imperialist, he disliked the South Australian emblem outside Government House, and it 'excited a good deal of public attention' when he removed the flag and demanded that the Union Jack be hoisted. He was reserved but kindly, described by the *Observer* as 'not a genius' but 'a good, capable, inflexibly honest legislator'. The town of Copley commemorates him.

H. T. Burgess (ed), *Cyclopedia of South Australia*, 2 (Adel, 1909); *PP* (SA), 1881, 4, 127; *Pictorial Aust*, Aug-Sept 1890, Oct 1892; *Observer* (Adel), 20 Dec 1890, 9 May 1896, 6 May 1899, 10 May 1902, 19 Sept 1925; *Advertiser* (Adel), 26 Apr 1919; *Register* (Adel), 3 Dec 1921, 17 Sept 1925.

DEAN JAENSCH

COPPLESON, SIR VICTOR MARCUS (1893-1965), surgeon, was born on 27 February 1893 in Sydney, eldest child of ALBERT ABRAM COPPLESON (1864?-1948) and his wife. Albert was born at Mitava, Courland, Russia (Yelgava, Latvia), son of David Coppleson, miller, and his wife Nessa née Michael. After the pogroms of 1881 he migrated, going to London, New Zealand and Victoria. In 1884 he moved on to New South Wales and became an itinerant hawker in the north-west. About 1890, with W. R. Cohen, a Polish Jew whom he had met in London, he opened a general store at Wee Waa. He was naturalized on 31 March 1891 and on 9 February 1893 at the Redfern Registry Office, married a widow Sarah (Siba) Middlemass, née Sloman, also of Russian émigré stock. By 1900 he was in business on his own.

In November 1893 Coppleson had given evidence on the route of the proposed Narrabri-Moree railway to the sectional committee of the Parliamentary Standing Committee on Public Works. From its proclamation in 1906, he served on the Namoi Shire Council for nearly thirty years, for thirteen of them either as president or deputy president. In 1911 he first advocated a major dam on the Namoi River and never lost his enthusiasm for the project. His contemporaries expected that its completion would be a fitting monument to his devotion but, at the 1960 opening of the Keepit Dam, his name was not mentioned. In 1919 he resigned from the council in protest against the transfer of the shire offices from Wee Waa to Narrabri. He was re-elected in 1922. He and his wife worked hard for the local hospital, of which he was a trustee and both were life members.

Coppleson suffered severe financial losses in the Depression through extending credit to many customers. When he retired to Sydney in 1936 he was presented with a testimonial and a purse. An acknowledged Talmudic scholar, he was also an unacknowledged Yiddish poet. A Freemason, he died aged 83 at his Bellevue Hill home on 24 January 1948 and was buried in the Jewish section of Rookwood cemetery. He was survived by his wife, three sons and a daughter.

Victor was educated at the Wee Waa Public School, Sydney Grammar School and St Andrews College, University of Sydney (M.B., Ch.M., 1915). In November 1915 he joined the Australian Naval and Military Expeditionary Force to New Guinea. In March 1916 as a captain he sailed for the Middle East and in June went to France with the 15th Field Ambulance. He had several spells as regimental medical officer in France and Belgium and on 12 May 1917 was wounded at Bullecourt. From August until July 1918 he was officer commanding the 5th Sanitary Section and was promoted major on 28 February 1918. Working as a house surgeon at St George's Hospital, London, from April 1919, he was demobilized in London at the end of the year. He had ex-

perience at Westminster and Middlesex hospitals; he became a fellow of the Royal College of Surgeons in 1921.

On his return to Sydney in 1922 Coppleson set up in practice in Macquarie Street as a general surgeon. On 3 December 1924 at St James Anglican Church, Sydney, he married Enid Bohrsmann, daughter of Judge Augustus James. Of Coppleson's honorary hospital appointments, St Vincent's was his first love: he was on its surgical staff from 1923 (consultant from 1953); in 1926-53 he lectured there in clinical surgery and in 1928 edited its *Clinical handbook for residents, nurses and students* (revised in 1936 and 1946). He was also an honorary surgeon at Royal North Shore Hospital in 1928-44 (consultant from 1954); a member of the boards of Prince Henry Hospital in 1938-40 and 1948-63 and the Benevolent Society of New South Wales in 1961-65; part-time lecturer in surgical anatomy at the university in 1923-34 and an honorary curator of its anatomy museum in 1923-56; and was a State committee-member of the Royal Australasian College of Surgeons in 1940-60 (a fellow from 1928). His general scientific interests led him to join the Royal Zoological Society of New South Wales and the Australian Marine Sciences Association; he was also a fellow of the Royal Society of Medicine, London, and a member of other international organizations.

A prodigious worker, Coppleson was Australian correspondent to the *Lancet* (London) in the 1930s. He had remained on the reserve of officers, and in January 1941, as a lieut-colonel, he arrived in the Middle East. In April-May he served in Greece and returned to Sydney in 2/1 Australian Hospital Ship. He was a special visiting senior surgeon to the 113th Australian General Hospital, Concord. From 1926 he had been an honorary medical adviser to the Surf Life Saving Association of Australia and wrote several articles on the shark peril before publishing *Shark attack* in 1958 (revised in 1962, 1968 and 1976): the book brought him world recognition. With Judge Adrian Curlewis he helped organize the first International Convention on Life Saving Techniques, held in Sydney in 1960: as a result mouth-to-mouth resuscitation was universally adopted.

Coppleson's support of postgraduate medical education dominated all his other activities. From 1932 he was a member of the New South Wales Permanent Post-Graduate Committee, which had been prompted by the British Medical Association. It was reconstituted in the university in 1935 as the New South Wales Post-Graduate Committee in Medicine and in 1945 as the Postgraduate Committee in Medicine of the University of

Sydney. Coppleson was honorary secretary in 1935-55, chairman in 1956-64 and director of postgraduate studies in 1948-65. Despite his strenuous efforts the postgraduate school at Prince Henry Hospital, started in 1938, was never resumed after its breakdown in 1942. He wanted to promote further studies among general practitioners as well as specialists and to provide grants to send Australians abroad and bring distinguished visitors to the country. Under his skilful guidance the Post Graduate Medical Foundation, set up in 1958 to put fund-raising on a systematic basis, was an immediate success. With justifiable pride, he said in 1962 that by stimulating research the foundation had raised Sydney's lagging medical standards until they were equal to those anywhere. He was knighted in January 1964.

Younger colleagues were occasionally frightened by Coppleson's authoritarianism, but even in those 'irritated by his vigorous personality and methods, he tended to inspire a curious affection'. A large man, balding in his later years, he had 'a wonderful physique', was an excellent swimmer and enjoyed golf. He was a member of the University, Imperial Service and Australian Golf clubs. He collected stamps but was better known as a successful gardener and for his collection of orchids. His wife's support made his incessant activities possible.

Sir Victor died of cancer at his home at Wunulla Road, Point Piper, on 12 May 1965, and was cremated after a service at St Mark's Anglican Church, Darling Point; (he had become an Anglican while at school). He was survived by his wife, son and daughter, to whom he left his estate, valued for probate at £19016. His wife gave money from the sale of his orchids to the fund for the Victor Coppleson Memorial Institute of Postgraduate Studies, at the University of Sydney, opened in February 1978.

W. J. Mulholland, *Narrabri jubilee celebrations* . . . (Newcastle, 1933); D. Miller, *Earlier days* (Syd, 1969); *MJA*, 23 Oct 1965; Aust Jewish Hist Soc, *J*, 2 (1947-48), no 7, 9, vol 7 (1971-74) no 4; *Aust Zoologist*, 10 Aug 1965; *SMH*, 26 Sept 1911, 26 Jan 1948, 5 Nov 1955, 14 June 1958, 5 Feb, 19 Mar 1959, 1 July, 29 Oct 1960, 27 Jan 1961, 25 Oct 1962, 13 May 1965; *North Western Courier*, 4 Sept 1933, 12 Feb 1948, 27, 31 Oct 1960; Namoi Shire Council Minute-books (Narrabri, NSW); Annual reports, Prince Henry Hospital, *and* Roy North Shore Hospital, *and* Surf Life Saving Assn of Aust (Syd); Roy A'sian College of Surgeons Archives (Melb); Univ Syd Archives; information from Mrs P. Okkerse, Bellevue Hill, Syd.   ANN M. MITCHELL

CORBASSE, LOUISE; *see* LOVELY

CORBETT, JAMES FRANCIS (1834?-1912), Catholic bishop, was born at Limerick,

Ireland, eldest child of James Corbett and his second wife Catherine, née Reeves. After secondary education in France at Cambrai, he studied for the priesthood at Bruges in Belgium and Le Mans in France. He was ordained 'for Limerick' on 29 May 1858. For the next five years he worked in his native diocese, earning golden opinions from his bishop who was reluctant to release him to answer Archbishop Goold's [q.v.4] appeal for priests in Victoria.

On arrival in Melbourne on 29 August 1863 in the *Lightning*, Corbett was appointed to the St Kilda mission and soon became Goold's right-hand man and private secretary. His parish extended over the municipalities of St Kilda, Prahran, Caulfield and Gardiner, and under his vigorous administration developed into one of the richest in Australia. In 1876 he received from Rome an honorary doctorate of sacred theology and in 1879 he was appointed chancellor of the archdiocese and vicar forane.

In 1887 Corbett was chosen as bishop of the newly created diocese of Sale; he was consecrated at St Mary's Church, St Kilda, on 25 August. Although no longer young, and not a born horseman, he applied himself to his rugged charge with undiminished vigour. He was handicapped by an acute shortage of priests. However, he established new parishes, built churches, presbyteries, convents and schools, introduced nuns, recruited priests, and organized Catholic education in Gippsland. Honours, clerical and secular, came to him: the Papal Order of the Holy Sepulchre, the Pilgrim's Cross of Jerusalem and, in 1889, the Freedom of the City of Limerick. After 1907 he was the senior priest in Victoria, and in 1911 Pope Pius X appointed him assistant bishop at the papal throne.

Corbett's foreign education was reflected in his appearance. Bearded, with immense dignity and a courtly manner when offering his snuff box, he impressed more as a polished man of the world than a missionary. He was, however, of ascetic habits, adding the discipline of a Tertiary of St Francis to that of a priest. He was a fine scholar with a nice appreciation of art and letters, a passion for clocks and a love of dogs. His knowledge of the rubrics was legendary and he was a recognized authority on ecclesiastical law.

The bishop was a very effective if not a great preacher, and an outspoken critic whenever he believed censure was deserved. In the debates on the Education Act, 1872, Corbett was an eloquent champion of the Catholic Church's stand against secularization of education in government-funded schools. His major contribution to the system of Catholic education, evolved in oppo-

111

sition to the 1872 Act, was the introduction to St Kilda of the Presentation Nuns (1873) and the Christian Brothers (1878), and to Sale of the Congregation of Our Lady of Sion (1890). He was a disciplinarian, but was beloved by his priests for the support and understanding he gave them in their difficulties.

Corbett died at Sale, aged 79, on 29 May 1912 after a hernia operation, and was buried in St Mary's Cathedral, which he had planned to consecrate to celebrate his silver jubilee as a bishop.

Austral Light, July 1912; *Footprints,* July 1976; *Advocate* (Melb), 26 Aug 1876, 20 Sept 1879, 18 June 1887, 14 Sept 1889; *Gippsland Times,* 30 May 1912; P. M. O'Donnell, History of the Catholic Church in the diocese of Sale (Bishop's House, Sale); information from Mgr J. Daley, Warragul, and Presentation Sisters, Windsor, Vic.

MONICA STARKE

CORBETT, WILLIAM FRANCIS (1857-1923), and CLAUDE GORDON (1885-1944), sporting journalists, were father and son. William was born on 5 February 1857 at Woolloomooloo, Sydney, son of Francis Corbett, coachman, and his wife Mary Agnes, née McCarthy. On 1 June 1874 he became a junior operator in the electric telegraphy section of the Postmaster General's Department at a salary of £52. On 10 July 1878, with Presbyterian forms (although he had been baptized a Catholic) he married Amelia Kate Bragg (d. 1917) in Sydney. A fine amateur swimmer, sculler and boxer and a champion bowler, he reported these sports to newspapers, including the *Referee,* whose full-time staff he joined in 1896. For the next seventeen years he helped make it the best sporting newspaper in Australia, becoming 'as well known among sporting people as the Post Office clock is to the general public'. He worked also for the *Sunday Times* and the *Arrow,* writing as 'The Amateur' and 'Right Cross' on boxing, as 'Natator' and 'The Diver' on swimming, and as 'Toucher' and 'Blackwood' on bowls.

Closely associated with boxing, Corbett was a founder of the Sydney Amateur Gymnastic Club, the venue for many championship fights; he was a friend and supporter of Peter Jackson [q.v.]. In July 1910 he travelled to the United States of America to report the Johnson-Jeffries fight for the *Referee* and for two American syndicates. He became sporting editor of the pioneer of modern popular journalism in Australia, the *Sun,* in January 1913, and brought his special knowledge and experience to the treatment of sport in Sydney

daily papers, a development which was to lead to the decline of quality sporting publications such as the *Referee.* But he returned to the latter as boxing editor in 1916, after its purchase by H. D. McIntosh [q.v.].

Survived by six daughters and four sons, Corbett died of heart disease and diabetes at Bondi on 29 October 1923 and was buried in the Catholic section of Waverley cemetery. His son Harold William, an able sportsman, was killed in World War I; another, William Francis (1900-1970), was a boxing and football reporter.

His eldest son Claude was born on 25 April 1885 at Botany. Educated at Cleveland Street Public School, at 14 he joined the *Evening News* as a copy-boy. He excelled at swimming and boxing and played first-grade Rugby for St George, Newtown and Eastern Suburbs. In 1911 he accompanied the Rugby League tour of Britain as *Daily Telegraph* correspondent. He was an informed reporter of the code and one of its most loyal supporters, making two more Kangaroo tours of England. In 1913 he was, with his father, on the *Sun*'s staff. On 27 January 1914 at St Mark's Anglican Church, Darling Point, he married Lily May Fowles, McIntosh's adopted daughter. Corbett was managing director of the *Sunday Times,* the *Referee* and the *Arrow* from 1916, and visited America to buy new machinery for the *Sunday Times.*

In 1923 Corbett returned to the *Sun* as sporting editor. The development of Saturday afternoon papers meant he was responsible for reports of sporting events rushed for inclusion in successive editions; for two seasons it was a family affair as he, his brothers Bill and Jack and son Harold McIntosh ('Mac') covered the four first-grade Rugby League games. His weekly column, entitled for a time 'Claude Corbett says', was a popular feature of the Sunday *Sun.* He died of cancer on 12 December 1944 and was buried in the Catholic section of Waverley cemetery after a requiem mass celebrated by Fr Jimmy Carlton [q.v.7]. He was survived by his son and two daughters. Corbett was a notable sporting reporter with, as Kenneth Slessor wrote, 'not only a specialist's knowledge ... but also a crisp and magnetic style which fascinated readers'. A shield presented at Sydney Rugby League Tests between England and Australia commemorates him.

R. B. Walker, *The newspaper press in New South Wales, 1803-1920* (Syd, 1976); *Sydney Mail,* 12 Sept 1906; *Sun* (Syd), 5 Jan 1913, 13 Dec 1944; *Referee,* 19 July 1916, 31 Oct 1923; *Sunday Times* (Syd), 4 Nov 1923; *SMH,* 16 July 1970; Bankruptcy files 3183/3, 4987/4 (NSWA); information from Mr H. M. Corbett, Wahroonga, NSW.

CHRIS CUNNEEN

CORBOULD, WILLIAM HENRY (1866-1949), mining engineer, was born on 4 November 1866 at Ballarat, Victoria, son of William Corbould, tailor, and his wife Julia Augusta, née Signall. An unenthusiastic student, Corbould left home at 12 but later returned and attended the Ballarat School of Mines where he obtained a certificate in practical chemistry. In 1885 he became an assayer and chemist at the Central mine, Broken Hill, New South Wales.

Around 1891 Corbould went to the United States of America, working both in and out of the mining industry. He moved on to England, the Continent and South Africa, then returned to Adelaide and Broken Hill. He was in Western Australia in 1895 as manager of Hannan's Reward mine; he was a foundation member of the Chamber of Mines of Western Australia. In 1896 Corbould went back to England and married Una Robina Dodds on 5 August at Folkestone, Kent. He returned to Kalgoorlie and about 1899 was managing Hannan's Reward again. He took charge of his first copper mine at Burraga near Bathurst, New South Wales, about 1902.

In 1909 Corbould became general manager of the Mt Elliott mines near Cloncurry, Queensland, which soon turned into one of the most profitable operations in the Commonwealth. Under its energetic but unconventional manager, the enterprise returned over £400 000 in dividends between 1910 and 1913. He methodically tackled the many problems that arose during the wartime copper boom and in return was appointed managing director of Mt Elliott Ltd. The post-war slump in metal prices retarded his efforts. Corbould retained his faith in Cloncurry but by 1920 only Mt Elliott was still working. Despite falling prices, strikes and the exhaustion of the rich surface ore bodies, he argued that improved smelting processes and railways to outlying mines would restore profits. Failure to attract additional capital from shareholders dashed his hopes and he resigned in 1922.

As a private engineering consultant, Corbould toured the Mount Isa field at the urging of Douglas MacGilvray who held options on a number of leases. Convinced by Mt Elliott that the future of mining in north-west Queensland lay in large-scale operations, he returned to Cloncurry brimming with enthusiasm. Noting that the ore bodies of Mount Isa resembled the silver-lead lodes of Broken Hill, Corbould secured an option on 400 acres (160 ha) and hurried to Sydney to float Mount Isa Mines Ltd in January 1924. As director and general manager, he was responsible for much of the exploratory work and the raising of capital. When additional funds for exploration were not forthcoming, he invested his own money. Almost single-handed, he removed competition by manipulating the acquisition of Randolph Bedford's [q.v.7] Mount Isa Proprietary Ltd and, more importantly, persuaded the Queensland government to extend the railway from Duchess to the mines in late 1925; his case was supported by ministers with shares in his company.

Corbould succeeded in attracting overseas capital from J. L. Urquhart's Russo-Asiatic Consolidated group which secured the large-scale development of the field. It was the first major capital input into Queensland mining for nearly twenty years. Corbould resigned in 1927 and departed overseas but his faith in the area was not vindicated until 1947 when the first dividend was declared; ironically it was copper, not silver-lead, that made Mount Isa's name.

Corbould retained his interest in mining, working at Edie Creek in New Guinea, Java and Japan and in Europe where his reputation was considerable. His services to mining were acknowledged in 1919 when he was admitted as an associate of the Australian Chemical Institute, and later by an award of the Legion of Honour of the American Institute of Mining, Metallurgical and Petroleum Engineers for fifty years service to the industry. Copies of a manuscript autobiography 'The life of Alias Jimmy' are held in both the Mitchell and Oxley libraries.

Although Corbould had three children, his marriage was impeded by his life-style and he and his wife lived together only intermittently. She died at Moss Vale, New South Wales, in 1948. Corbould died at Nice, France, on 16 March 1949. Beneficiaries of his Australian estate of £21 448 included the Australian Club, Sydney, the Weld Club, Perth, the Queensland Club, the Institute of Mining and Metallurgy and the Australian Chemical Institute. To the Ballarat School of Mines, he left £6000 for a scholarship in honour of his old teacher Alfred Mica Smith [q.v.6].

G. Blainey, *Mines in the spinifex* (Syd, 1960), and *The rush that never ended* (Melb, 1963); School of Mines (Ballarat), *Annual Report*, 1883-86; Chamber of Mines of WA, *Mthly Report*, 1902-03; *Qld Government Mining J*, 50 (1949), 51 (1950), 478; *Western Argus*, 16 Feb 1895; *Kalgoorlie Miner*, 1 Oct 1895, 3 July 1896; information from Mr E. H. Corbould, Surfers Paradise, Qld.

K. H. KENNEDY

CORBY, JOHN McKENZIE (1857?-1927), marine engineer, was born in Mauritius, son of John Corby, engineer, and his wife Janet, née McKenzie. He came to Australia probably not long before his marriage on 31

March 1883 at Pyrmont, Sydney, to 18-year-old Grace Wilson. His name first appeared in the list of members of the Sydney district of the Australasian Institute of Marine Engineers in 1884. At this time he held a first-class marine engineer's certificate and was employed by William Howard Smith [q.v.6] & Sons Ltd as chief engineer of the *Derwent.* He was chief engineer of the company's *Burwah* in 1889-90 and of the *Leura* in 1890-96.

Corby was prominent in the organization of marine engineers from 1889 when he was elected president of the Sydney district of the A.I.M.E.; in 1890-96 he represented Brisbane on its executive council. In 1896 he was elected secretary of the Victorian district of the A.I.M.E., holding this position unchallenged until his retirement on 30 June 1926. In his capacity as a leader of the profession, he was a member of the Marine Board of Victoria and the Court of Marine Inquiry from December 1900.

In that year the A.I.M.E. formed a federal council with the head office located in Melbourne, and Corby was elected general secretary. He remained in his two positions until 1919, when the federal office was moved to Sydney. After September 1924, when the New Zealand branches separated from the Australian organization (henceforth the Australian Institute of Marine and Power Engineers), the head office was relocated in Melbourne and Corby again became federal secretary.

As a senior administrator of the institute's affairs, Corby helped to resolve disputes between marine engineers and shipowners. As Victorian delegate to conferences held between 1899 and 1924, he took a leading part in developing the rules and traditions of the institute. He had a long record of zealous endeavour to advance the status of the Australian marine engineer. With other colleagues he fought against the Federal government's efforts to introduce a third-class engineer certificate, which would allow advancement to the imperially valid second and first-class certificates without prerequisite completion of apprenticeship. Corby argued unsuccessfully against the move in evidence to the royal commission on the navigation bill (1906). However, he later pointed out to colleagues that the engineer manning scales which he had helped to prepare and which had been accepted by the royal commission, would virtually wipe out any possibility of third-class engineers becoming a threat to holders of imperially valid certificates. Although a firm believer in the importance of apprenticeship, as a member of the Victorian Marine Board Corby was involved in negotiations to establish certificate and diploma courses in

marine engineering at the Working Men's College in 1907.

Corby was a well-known yachtsman, and in 1908-09 and 1915-16 was commodore of the Royal Brighton Yacht Club. His first wife died on 28 August 1907; on 8 June 1908 at Mosman Presbyterian Church, Sydney, he married her younger sister Hannah, aged 26. There were no children of either marriage. Corby died aged 70 at Toorak on 15 July 1927.

Register of Australian and New Zealand shipping (Melb, 1879-89, copy at Univ Melb Archives); Roy Com on the navigation bill, Evidence, *PP* (Cwlth), 1906, vol 3; Aust Inst of Marine and Power Engineers, *Annual Report,* 1881-1928 (A.I.M.P.E. Archives, Syd), *and* correspondence T19/23, T19/25 (ANU Archives), *and* Minute-books 1887-1933 (Vic Branch Archives, South Melb); Board minutes, 1900-25 (Vic Marine Board, Melb); information from Mr C. Murphy, Roy Brighton Yacht Club, Vic.   ANN R. SHORTEN

COREY, ERNEST ALBERT (1891-1972), soldier and labourer, was born on 20 December 1891 at Green Hills near Cooma, New South Wales, eighth child of Thomas Corey, selector, and his wife Ellen, née Burke, both of whom were native-born. He was educated at Thubergal Lake Public School and then worked as a labourer in the Cooma district. On 13 January 1916 he left his job as a blacksmith's striker to enlist in the Australian Imperial Force, marching to Goulburn with the 'Men from Snowy River' in a recruiting march.

Corey was allotted to the 55th Battalion and embarked for overseas service in September. He joined his unit in France on 8 February 1917 and in April, as a private in 'C' Company, took part in the capture of Doignies. On 15 May, in an action near Quéant, his brigade suffered heavy casualties and Corey volunteered to serve as a stretcher-bearer: showing 'great courage' he worked for seventeen hours in no man's land and was awarded the Military Medal. He became a regular stretcher-bearer and won a Bar to his medal for 'devotion to duty' in the battle of Polygon Wood on 26 September, carrying out his duties under 'very heavy artillery and machine-gun fire'. He was awarded a second Bar for 'conspicuous gallantry' at Péronne on 1-2 September 1918 and a third during the attack on the Hindenburg Line north of Bellicourt on 30 September. At Bellicourt, Corey, who had been promoted corporal nine days earlier, was in charge of the battalion's stretcher-bearers and, despite intense machine-gun and shell-fire, directed them 'with the utmost skill and bravery'; 'regardless of personal danger . . . he attended to men and carried them from the most exposed positions' until he himself was severely wounded and evacuated. He returned to Australia on 30 April 1919.

After demobilization Corey worked at. Cooma as a contract rabbiter, and in 1922 moved to Canberra as a camp caretaker. On 23 September 1924, at St Gregory's Catholic Church, Queanbeyan, New South Wales, he married Sarah Jane Fisher; there was one daughter of the marriage which was dissolved in 1935. In 1927-40 he worked in Canberra as an office cleaner with the Department of the Interior, then served with the 2nd Garrison Battalion in World War II. He was later employed as a caretaker, as cook for a departmental survey party and as leading hand at the Canberra incinerator. By 1951 he was almost crippled with osteoarthritis. Survived by his daughter, he died at Queanbeyan Private Nursing Home on 25 August 1972 and was buried with full military honours in Canberra cemetery.

Though small in stature Corey was powerfully built and had a lively personality. He is believed to be the only man to have won three Bars to a Military Medal. Corey Place in the Canberra suburb of Gowrie is named after him, also a fountain in Cooma Centennial Park.

London Gazette, 18 July 1917, 11 Jan 1918, 13 Mar, 17 June 1919; *Reveille* (Syd), Mar 1931; *Aust Army*, 3 June 1971; *SMH*, 30 Nov 1915, 25 Apr 1968; *Cooma Express*, 14 Jan-11 Feb, Dec 1916, June 1918; *Canb Times*, 13 Apr 1935, 26 July 1971, 28 Aug 1972; *Canb News*, 26 July 1971; War diary, 55th Battalion, AIF, 1916-19 *and* 14th Brigade, AIF, 1917-18 (AWM); information from Mrs P. Phelps, Downer, ACT.   JEAN P. FIELDING

CORIN, WILLIAM (1867-1929), electrical engineer, was born on 13 October 1867 at Forest Hill, Kent, England, fifth of twelve children of Edwin Paul Corin, importer, and his wife Eliza, née Knight. Educated at King's College School and University College, London, he graduated in engineering in 1885 with numerous prizes. He was employed in Glasgow by Dubs & Co., then by James Cleminson & Sons, civil engineers, until in 1891 he joined the London Metropolitan Electric Supply Co. Appointed as city electrician, he migrated to Launceston, Tasmania, on 26 November 1895. On 21 January 1896 at the Launceston registrar's office Corin married Kathleen Susan Sleeman whose family he had known in England; after the birth of their daughter in November, she died in April 1897. On 12 March 1900 at Scottsdale he married Ellen Louise Unwin: they had three daughters and two sons.

Corin had begun work in Launceston just before the opening of the hydroelectric scheme, developed by C. St John David [q.v.], and he controlled the Duck Reach power station; he later made preliminary surveys for the Great Lakes schemes. His safety standards in the installation of wiring in Launceston were exemplary; in 1904-07 his conversion of the wiring to the three-phase four-wire system was among the first in the British Empire.

In 1907 Corin entered private practice in Melbourne; he also acted as consulting engineer to the municipality of Launceston. On 1 July 1908 he was appointed chief electrical engineer to the New South Wales Department of Public Works and consulting electrical engineer to the Department of Mines. His major responsibility was the generation of thermal electricity for local distribution, but he foresaw the advantage of intrastate connexions, with links to adjoining States. In 1913 he was sent abroad to study developments in electrical engineering. He returned with renewed enthusiasm for hydroelectricity and in 1915 began a series of reports on a Snowy River scheme. During his lifetime, however, the only schemes completed in New South Wales were comparatively small ones at Burrinjuck, Mullumbimby, Dorrigo and Nymboida. To continue the consulting work which he found more congenial he resigned in December 1923.

Corin advised the British and French governments respectively on hydroelectricity in Fiji (1906) and New Caledonia (1920), and also reported to the New Zealand government on the Lake Coleridge scheme. He was consulted on the Queensland Barron Falls project in 1906 and 1923-24. A member from 1909 and president in 1917 of the New South Wales section of the Electrical Association of Australia, he became a foundation member of the Institution of Engineers, Australia, in 1919. He was also a member of the American Institute of Electrical Engineers and of the institutions of Electrical Engineers and Civil Engineers, London; the latter body awarded him the Telford Premium in 1911 for a paper on the water power of Tasmania.

In 1920 Corin estimated the cost of the Snowy River scheme at £2 million, and in 1927-28 he suggested to local councillors that they might install a small hydroelectric plant to meet shire needs. In his writings Corin advocated afforestation and the arrest of soil erosion to conserve all rainfall for the development of the hydroelectric potential. A practical engineer who 'saw hydro-electricity in every running stream', Corin was of distinguished appearance, possessing a great sense of humour and much personal charm, but outspoken about dishonest practice. He died of cancer on 2 March 1929 at Chatswood, Sydney, and was buried in the

general section of Northern Suburbs cemetery. His work is commemorated by the
Corin Dam, near Canberra, and by street
names in that city and in Launceston.

K. R. Shedden, *Pioneering hydro-electric
development in Australia: notes on the life and work
of William Corin* (np, priv print, nd); Inst of Engineers, Aust, *J*, 1 (1929); *Examiner* (Launc), 5 Nov
1895, 28 Apr 1897; *SMH*, 8 Mar 1929; family papers
(held by Dr K. R. Shedden, Port Macquarie, NSW).
ARTHUR CORBETT

CORLETTE, JAMES MONTAGU
CHRISTIAN (1880-1969), soldier and engineer, was born on 25 August 1880 at
Ashfield, Sydney, fifth son of Rev. James
Christian Corlette, a native-born and Ox-
ford-educated Anglican clergyman, and his
wife Frances Edith, daughter of Sir William
Manning [q.v.5]. He was educated at Sydney
Grammar School and the University of
Sydney where he graduated B.E. with hon-
ours in civil engineering in 1902 and mining
and metallurgy in 1903. For eighteen
months he demonstrated in the university
engineering school, then lectured at the
Kalgoorlie School of Mines, Western Aus-
tralia. In 1908 he returned to New South
Wales and joined the engineering staff of the
Hunter District Water Supply and Sewerage
Board.

A notable sportsman, Corlette rowed in
the Grammar crew and played Rugby football for his school and, in 1900-05, for the
university, which he also represented at
rifle-shooting. He captained the Western
Australian Rugby XV against a New South
Wales side in 1907 and next year played for
Northern Districts of New South Wales
against an Anglo-Welsh team. In his later
years he was prominent at bowls.

Corlette had been sergeant major in the
Sydney University Scouts Rifle Corps, and in
May 1906 was commissioned second lieutenant in the Goldfields Infantry Regiment
of Western Australia; in 1908 he transferred
to the 4th Australian Infantry Regiment,
Newcastle, New South Wales. Promoted
lieutenant, he joined the Australian Intelligence Corps in December and was in
charge of the survey and mapping of 750
square miles (1940 km^2) round Newcastle. A
captain from January 1910, he spent six
months training in India in 1911-12 and attended the coronation Durbar at Delhi. In
1913 he transferred to the Australian Engineers and was promoted major. On 28
August 1914 he was appointed to the Australian Imperial Force, as a captain. Before
sailing for Egypt, he married Ruby Saunders
(d. 1961), daughter of the editor of the
Newcastle Morning Herald, on 17 September

at St James Church, Sydney. She served for
two and a half years full-time duty with the
Voluntary Aid Detachment at St Dunstan's
Hostel for Blinded Soldiers and Sailors in
London during World War I, and was
awarded the British War Medal.

Corlette's own war record was both dis-
tinguished and gallant. He landed at Gal-
lipoli on 25 April 1915 and was promoted
major in July, commanding the 1st Field
Company. He was invalided with enteric
fever in October, eventually to Egypt; from
March 1916, as temporary lieut-colonel, he
organized and commanded the 4th Pioneer
Battalion and transferred in May to the
Engineering Training Depot at Tel-el-
Kebir; in July he joined the 2nd Australian
Engineers in France for the first battle of the
Somme. In September he joined the staff of
the chief engineer of the 1st Anzac Corps
Headquarters at Abeele, Belgium. Confirmed in rank, he was commanding royal
engineer of the 2nd Australian Division in
France and Belgium from 4 July 1917 until
he was demobilized on 31 August 1919. He
was five times mentioned in dispatches,
awarded the Distinguished Service Order in
1917 and the Croix de Chevalier of the
Légion d'honneur in 1919 and that year was
appointed C.M.G.

Corlette returned to the Hunter District
Water Supply and Sewerage Board, and was
chief engineer in 1925-45. He designed and
constructed Tomago Sandbeds water-supply for Newcastle, pioneered the use of 54 in.
(137 cm) continuously welded steel water-
mains and completed sewerage works for
Wallsend, Kurri Kurri, Belmont, Toronto,
Cardiff and Boolaroo. He was a foundation
member of the Northern Engineering Institute of New South Wales, and contributed
technical articles on military bridge-building and surveying to its journal. After it
became the Newcastle division of the Institution of Engineers, Australia, he was a
committee-member in 1920-69 and president
in 1927-28. He also served on the council of
the institution in 1927-59 and was president
in 1930.

Corlette was appointed C.R.E. of 2nd
Division, Australian Military Forces, as a
lieut-colonel, in 1921. Promoted colonel on 1
May 1926, he commanded the 1st Infantry
Brigade until 1932, and as a brigadier administered the command of 1st Division at
Victoria Barracks, Sydney, in 1932-33; he
was awarded the Volunteer Officers' Decoration in 1923. During World War II he
served with the Volunteer Defence Corps
and was on full-time duty in 1941-43 as group
commander of the Newcastle area.

Corlette was also a fellow of the Australian Planning Institute and president of
its Newcastle division in 1954; he strongly

advocated and carried out tree-planting for shade and environmental purposes. He took a keen interest in returned soldiers and in 1927-56 was president of the United Service Club, Newcastle. 'Monty', as he was known, was an alert, humane man whose grit, loyalty, co-operative spirit and quiet, commanding presence were an inspiration to all who came into contact with him. In 1945 he was awarded the Institution of Engineers' Warren [q.v.6] Memorial Prize for engineering, and in 1946 the Peter Nicol Russell [q.v.6] Memorial Medal for a 'notable contribution to the Science and Practice of Engineering'; in 1960 he was elected a fellow of the institution, and in 1966 was awarded an honorary doctorate of engineering by the University of Newcastle. He was also a member of the Institution of Civil Engineers, London.

Survived by his son, Corlette died in Sydney on 11 December 1969 and was cremated after a service in Christ Church Anglican Cathedral, Newcastle. The Corlette Fountain Court in the engineering school of the University of Newcastle was given in his memory in 1973.

A. H. Corbett, *The Institution of Engineers, Australia* (Syd, 1973); *London Gazette*, 28 Jan 1916, 1 June, 25, 28 Dec 1917, 31 Dec 1918, 29 Jan, 3 June, 11 July 1919; Inst of Engineers, Aust, *J*, 42 (1970); *Chartered Engineer* (Syd), 40 (1973); *Industrial Aust and Mining Standard*, 3 Apr 1930; *Morning Herald*, 7 July 1934; *SMH*, 13 Dec 1969, 18 Jan 1972.   P. J. GREVILLE

CORNELL, OLIVE; *see* WILTON

COSTELLO, JAMES JASPER (1858-1934), soldier, was born on 25 June 1858 in Dublin, son of John Costello, bootmaker, and his wife Elizabeth, née Murphy. He enlisted in the British Army, and was a sergeant in the 7th Regiment (Royal Fusiliers) when he married Ruth Hayes on 20 August 1881 at Farnham, Surrey. Next year as colour-sergeant with the 1st Battalion of the 87th Regiment (Royal Irish Fusiliers) he saw action in Egypt, receiving the Egypt medal with Tel-el-Kebir clasp and the Khedive's Bronze Star. He also served in India, and was discharged in December 1891.

On 1 April next year Costello became an instructor with warrant rank in the Tasmanian Rifle Regiment at Hobart. In 1894 his services were dispensed with due to financial restrictions. After working as a clerk in Melbourne he rejoined the Tasmanian Defence Force on 23 February 1898. When the Tasmanian Infantry Company (later mounted infantry) under C. St C. Cameron [q.v.7] was raised for service in the South African War, Costello was its sergeant major. The unit sailed on the *Medic* in October 1899 and formed part of the Australian Regiment serving in the De Aar-Modder River district. After operations around Colesberg, Bloemfontein and Pretoria, it took part in engagements at Diamond Hill and Belfast. In October it returned to Pretoria and on 3 November embarked at Cape Town for return to Australia. Mentioned in Lord Roberts's dispatches, Costello subsequently received the Distinguished Conduct Medal. For campaign service he received the Queen's South Africa Medal with five clasps.

Costello was appointed regimental sergeant major for the Australian Corps at King Edward VII's coronation in London. In 1903 he joined the Commonwealth Military Forces, and next year represented the 12th Australian Light Horse Regiment at the presentation on 14 November of the King's Banner to the Tasmanian Mounted Infantry for its South African work. In 1907 Costello and his family moved to Sydney and he transferred to the New South Wales administration and instructional staff, as an instructor for the large citizen force component of the Commonwealth forces. In 1910 he was awarded the Meritorious Service and in 1912 the Long Service and Good Conduct medals. Next year he was promoted honorary lieutenant and temporary adjutant and quartermaster of the 33rd Infantry Regiment (Citizen Forces).

Too old for active service, Costello served in New South Wales during World War I, but five of his eight sons enlisted in the Australian Imperial Force; two of them, James Albert (b. 1882) and Thomas (b. 1894) were killed in action on Gallipoli on 2 May 1915. In 1918 Costello was promoted honorary captain and his retirement age extended. On 1 November next year he retired with honorary rank of major and thereafter lived in Sydney. He died on 14 November 1934 and was buried in the Roman Catholic section of Randwick cemetery, survived by his wife, one son and three daughters. His estate was sworn for probate at £1665.

A long-serving and decorated soldier, Costello was one of the small number of regulars whose extensive experience provided a solid core of instructors and administrators for the early Commonwealth Military Forces.

J. Bufton, *Tasmanians in the Transvaal war* (Hob, 1905); Aust Defence Dept, *Official records of the Australian military contingents to the war in South Africa*, P. L. Murray ed (Melb, 1911); *South African War honours and awards, 1899-1902* (Lond, 1971); *London Gazette*, 16 Apr, 27 Sept 1901; *Weekly Courier* (Launc), 29 Nov 1934.

                                                    PETER BURNESS

COTTER, ALBERT (1883-1917), cricketer, was born on 3 December 1883 at 132 Phillip Street, Sydney, sixth and youngest son of English-born John Henry Cotter, butcher, and his Scottish wife Margaret Hay, née Pattison. When he was 6 his family moved to Glebe. He was educated at the Forest Lodge Public School, where fellow-pupils included the cricketers Charles Kellaway and Warren Bardsley [q.v.7], and at Sydney Grammar School in 1899-1900. In the annual matches between the Sydney and Melbourne Grammar schools in Melbourne in 1899 he took 6 for 53, including the wicket of S. M. (Viscount) Bruce [q.v.7] twice, and next year in Sydney took 7 for 57.

Known as 'Tibby', he joined the Glebe District Cricket Club in 1900 and established himself as a fine pace bowler and hard-hitting batsman. Successful for New South Wales against the English tourists in 1903-04, he enjoyed moderate success in the fourth and fifth Tests; he toured England with Joe Darling's [q.v.] team in 1905 where in all matches he took 124 wickets at 19.83 apiece, including 12 for 34 against Worcestershire. His tour batting average was 17.6. On the 1909 tour of England he obtained 64 wickets at 24.09 runs each, including 5 for 38 and 6 for 95 in the third and fifth Tests respectively. He took 22 wickets at 28.77 against the touring South Africans in 1910-11 but his Test career ended when he, Victor Trumper, M. A. Noble [qq.v.] and others split with the Board of Control in 1911.

In 21 Tests Cotter took 89 wickets, seven times taking five in an innings, at an average of 28.64 each, and in all first-class matches 440 wickets for 24 apiece and 2450 runs at an average of 16. In the Sheffield Shield he took 123 wickets at 23.45 each. Among his best performances for Glebe were 4 wickets in 4 balls and his highest score of 156 which included 16 sixes. He was also a very fine Rugby three-quarter for Glebe, the 'Dirty Reds', in his younger days.

Cotter was employed as a book-keeper by the Riverstone Meat Co. when in April 1915 he enlisted in the Australian Imperial Force. He served at Gallipoli with the 1st Light Horse; with the 12th Light Horse from February 1916, he was promoted lance corporal in May next year but soon reverted to trooper at his own request. While acting as a mounted stretcher-bearer he was killed on 31 October 1917 at the third Battle of Gaza; he was buried two miles south-east of Beersheba. He was unmarried.

'Tibby' Cotter was strikingly handsome and beautifully proportioned; always cheerful and modest, he was generous in his praise of others. Very fast, but often erratic, he had a slinging action and could make the ball lift high from a good length on the plumbest of wickets without recourse to bumping; he could keep his feet on a wet pitch (important in those days), bowl for long spells and was a good fieldsman. His happy nature and comportment on the field endeared him to all lovers of the game.

F. Laver, *An Australian cricketer on tour* (Lond,. 1905); A. G. Moyes, *Australian bowlers* . . . (Syd, 1953); D. Frith, *The fast men* (Lond, 1975); *Wisden Cricketers' Almanack*, 1919, 1978; *Cricket* (Lond), 4 May 1905; *Arrow* (Syd), 24 Feb 1906; *SMH*, 20 Nov 1917; *Referee*, 21 Nov 1917; *T&CJ*, 28 Nov 1917.

G. P. WALSH

COTTON, ALFRED JOHN (1861-1941), pastoralist, was born on 21 June 1861 at St Helier, Jersey, Channel Islands, son of Charles Nelson Cotton, landed proprietor, and his wife Sarah Mary, née Frost. His father's ruin in the pursuit of South African diamonds presaged the pattern of Cotton's later life. Educated privately at Brighton, he was apprenticed at 14 to the merchant marine and by 1879 was a third mate working chiefly between London and East Asia. At 22 he left the sea to settle in Australia, working first as a jackeroo and book-keeper on Yallaroi station, near Warialda, New South Wales. After four years he became a drover, and by 1890 employed sufficient men to have five mobs moving simultaneously between North Queensland and New South Wales. It was as a drover that he was most remembered in the pastoral industry after his death. His autobiography, *With the big herds in Australia*, was published in 1931.

In 1893 Cotton took over part of Bromby Park, near Bowen, occupied previously by F. R. Bode, father of Annie Isabel Jane, whom he had married at Bowen on 11 December 1891. When Cotton's attempts to buy the property in 1895 were hampered by the cattle-tick plague, he turned to exporting hides and tallow. Instead of selling to Sydney he dealt directly with London through family contacts. By 1900 he had begun to speculate in cattle properties. He had also secured important contracts to supply horses for South Africa and China, but he abandoned them at the end of the South African War to concentrate on pastoral speculation and on stud stock-breeding at Hidden Vale, near Grandchester, Queensland. He also contracted to dispose of some 85 000 head of cattle for the Bank of New South Wales. By 1912 he was able to retire to Mintoburn, near Hobart, Tasmania, where he gained some repute as an amateur yachtsman.

In 1913 Cotton formed a partnership with J. C. and F. J. White to take over Brunette

Downs on the Barkly tableland of the Northern Territory. When the Fisher [q.v.] government demanded major improvements before renewing the lease, he became deeply involved in the debate over land tenure in northern Australia. He employed W. Massy Greene [q.v.] as a lobbyist in 1922-23. Next year Cotton was one of the pastoralists denounced by Arthur Blakely [q.v.7] as being involved in 'one of the greatest boodling jokes ever put over any parliament in Australia'. Earlier in the same debate, he had been accused of having planned to cut Brunette Downs into 25-mile (40 km) blocks for sale at considerable profit if the lease was renewed under the proposed legislation. He tried unsuccessfully to make Brunette Downs pay by changing over from cattle to sheep to use fully the improvements required by the Federal government, but he finally withdrew from the partnership, reputedly at considerable loss.

In the *Brisbane Telegraph* in 1934 Cotton advocated closer settlement in the north; the government was to supply capital and half the initial stock for several hundred new properties at no rent. Three-quarters of the holdings were to be resumed over fifty years for more intensive development, and charges were to be levied on all products. Above all the new settlers had to be free of 'restrictive legislation and interference by politicians'.

Cotton was a convivial man, at home in the Queensland Club (to whose members he dedicated his autobiography), much admired for his energy, enterprise, and imagination. He operated on a national, at times international, scale. Though his biggest enterprise failed, he remained an optimist, but his prosperity had ended before the Depression; he retired to Southport and then to South Brisbane. He died at St Martin's Hospital, Brisbane, on 24 April 1941 and was cremated with Anglican rites. Of his four surviving children, Frederick Sidney (1895-1969) joined the Royal Naval Air Service in 1916, became prominent from his invention of the Sidcot flying suit and settled permanently in England. In 1938 he was involved in aerial espionage over Germany and commanded a special photo-reconnaissance unit of the Royal Air Force in World War II. He died in Surrey on 14 February 1969.

E. J. Brady, *Australia unlimited* (Melb, 1918); M. J. Fox (ed), *The history of Queensland*, 1 (Brisb, 1919); H. M. Barker, *Droving days* (Melb, 1966); *Pastoral Review*, 16 May 1941; *Graziers' Review*, 14 Sept 1921; *Sunday Telegraph* (Syd), 15 May 1960; *Courier Mail*, 31 July 1935, 15 Feb 1969; A3, NT13/11380, NT23/1677 (AAO).

MICHAEL J. RICHARDS

COTTON, FRANCIS (1857-1942), journalist and politician, **LEO ARTHUR** (1883-1963), professor of geology, and **FRANK STANLEY** (1890-1955), professor of physiology, were father and sons. Francis was born on 5 May 1857 in Adelaide, son of Richard Cotton, grocer, and his wife Esther Ann, née Payne. Leo Arthur was born on 11 November 1883 at Nymagee, New South Wales, and Frank Stanley was born on 30 April 1890 at Camperdown, Sydney.

Educated at Prince Alfred College, Adelaide, Francis later worked on a cattle station at Port Lincoln. At 17 he moved to western New South Wales, becoming a shearer, a farmer, a drover and a Methodist lay preacher. On 1 January 1883 at Forbes he married Evangeline Mary Geake Lane, born at Bathurst. Developing as a noted open-air orator, he became a social reformer with radical views on land taxation; in 1887 he founded a tax reform group in Forbes, and in 1889 he joined the Single Tax League in Sydney; he became a journalist and a leading supporter of single-taxer Henry George [q.v.4]. A firm free trader, in March-April he was active in the middle-class Liberal Association, trying to influence the founding of a free-trade party on Georgian lines. Next year he represented the Wagga Wagga shearers on the Trades and Labor Council, where mixed feelings were held about him. His eloquence and literary talents made him a valuable member of the Labour Defence Committee in the 1890 maritime strike. He was on the royal commission which inquired into the strike in 1890-91.

Although Cotton's importance was later exaggerated, he did take a prominent part in the council's planning in 1890-91 to form a political party. In February 1891, with T. J. Houghton [q.v.] and R. Boxall, he was on a sub-committee 'to draft a scheme of government of [the Labor] leagues'. The single tax was rejected but a compromise land tax plank was adopted; accused of disloyalty, Cotton survived a clash on the council with a protectionist, C. Hart. He was now editor of the *Democrat*, a single-tax paper, and was informing Sir Henry Parkes [q.v.5] by letter about the incipient Labor Party. At a by-election in April he ran as an independent for the Legislative Assembly electorate of East Sydney. By June he had joined the Labor Electoral League, and at the general election he won a seat at Newtown and was admitted to the party's first caucus.

In parliament Cotton's free-trade views soon produced tension with the developing solidarity system of the Labor Party. He attended the 'unity' conference of November 1893, but in April next year he joined (Sir) Joseph Cook [q.v.] in refusing to sign the party's pledge. At the 1894 general election he was returned as a free-trade candidate and held his seat (Newtown-Camperdown from 1895) until 1901. He continued as a reforming journalist and pacifist, writing for the *Australian Worker* among other publications; he developed an interest in science and invention. Predeceased by his wife and survived by three sons and three daughters, he died at Lindfield on 28 November 1942 and was cremated.

Leo Arthur was educated at Fort Street Model Public School and the University of Sydney, winning several prizes (B.A., 1906; B.Sc., 1908; M.A., 1916; D.Sc., 1920). In 1902 he became a draughtsman in the Department of Lands, undertaking his arts course as an evening student. On completing his science degree he went (on the voyage only) with Professor Edgeworth David [q.v.] to the Antarctic on the 1907 Shackleton expedition. On his return in 1908 he became a junior demonstrator in geology at the university and in 1909-11 was Macleay [q.v.5] fellow in geology of the Linnean Society of New South Wales; he was a demonstrator, assistant lecturer and lecturer in the department of geology in 1911-20. At Hornsby Methodist Church on 9 February 1910 he married Florence Edith Channon; she died on 7 October 1930, leaving three sons and two daughters.

Cotton was taught by David and was influenced by him. His main research fields were isostasy, diastrophism, polar wanderings and the strength of the earth's crust — geophysical studies that reflected his mathematical expertise. Acting head of the geology department in David's absence during World War I, in 1920 Cotton became assistant professor. In 1925 he succeeded David in the chair of geology and the W. H. Hovell [q.v.1] lectureship in physical geography. His heavy administrative responsibilities reduced his research work but several of his students achieved high academic distinctions. He served on many scientific committees and in World War II he was chairman of the Advisory Committee on Scientific Manpower (General). He was a member of the Linnean Society of New South Wales and a fellow of the Geological societies of London and America. Dean of the faculty of science in 1944-46, he retired in 1948.

Popular and respected, Cotton was a good chess-player and liked bowls. On 9 November 1946 at Artarmon he married Lilian Reed (d. 1980). He died at Newport on 12 July 1963 and was cremated after a Methodist service. The geology department of the University of New England is named after him.

Frank Stanley was educated at Sydney High School and the University of Sydney (B.Sc., 1912; D.Sc., 1931). He excelled in sport and developed a lifelong interest in its effects on the body; he won a blue for swimming, and in 1921 he took the New South Wales 440 yards and 880 yards championships; he held all university titles from 220 yards to one mile for over twenty years. He had become a lecturer and demonstrator in physiology in 1913, and married Catherine Drummond Smith with Presbyterian forms at Hornsby on 25 August 1917. He was made chief lecturer in 1923.

Cotton's doctoral thesis was on 'Studies in centre of gravity changes' and he published papers on the physiology of circulation and respiration. In 1932 he was awarded a Rockefeller travelling scholarship and spent eighteen months in the United States of America. Appointed reader in 1938, he was senior research fellow of the National Health and Medical Research Council in 1939-45. He became research professor in 1941 and was professor from 1946 until his retirement in 1955.

In World War II, with the Royal Australian Air Force, he was mainly responsible for the invention of the 'Cotton aerodynamic anti-G flying suit', which minimized the effects of high-speed flying on pilots. His research into the techniques of various sports and their physiological effects won international renown after the war. He devised machines and instruments to test the effects of strain on athletes, and his experiments made it possible to improve training methods and to predict the adaptability of competitors to certain sports. Friendly and congenial, he received cooperation from many men and women. Amongst the Australians he assisted were Denise Spencer, Judy Joy Davies and Jon Henricks in swimming, Peter Evatt in rowing and Edwin Carr in running. In 1949 he used his ergometer to help select the victorious university eight-oar crew, and in 1952 was scientific adviser to the Australian Olympic team at Helsinki.

Cotton died of coronary-vascular disease at Hornsby on 23 August 1955 and was cremated after a Methodist service. He was survived by two sons and his wife, who had graduated in 1911 with first-class honours and the University of Sydney medal in geology; in 1938 she published *Ludwig Leichhardt and the great south land*.

B. Nairn, *Civilising capitalism* (Canb, 1973); F. Picard, 'Henry George and the Labour split of 1891', *Hist Studies*, no 21, 1953, p 45; *Aust J of Science*, 18 (1955), p 21; Roy Soc NSW, *J*, 97 (1964), p 224; *People* (Syd), 25 Aug 1954; *Aust Worker*, 13 Aug 1930; *SMH*, 3 Dec 1942, 25 Aug 1955, 13 July 1963.   BEDE NAIRN

COTTRELL, IDA DOROTHY OTTLEY (1902-1957), writer, was born on 16 July 1902 at Picton, New South Wales, daughter of Australian-born parents Walter Barwon Wilkinson, mine-manager, and his wife Ida Constance, née Fletcher. Her parents moved to Ballarat, Victoria, where, aged 5, Dorothy contracted infantile paralysis and was thereafter confined to a wheelchair. When her parents separated she was brought up by her grandmother at Picton and later at Toowoomba, Queensland, and on her Fletcher uncles' stations, Elmina, near Charleville, and Ularunda, near Morven, where she trained sheep and cattle dogs to draw her wheelchair. She was taught at home by governesses until about 1915, then she lived with her aunt Lavinia Fletcher in Sydney, where she was taught by Theo Cowan [q.v.] and attended Dattilo Rubbo's [q.v.] classes at the Royal Art Society of New South Wales, becoming a competent black and white artist.

In 1920 Dorothy went to live at Ularunda; she had 'the sportsman's ardour for hunting' and became an excellent shot. She also swam, rowed and soon learned to drive a car. With dark hair and 'luminous brown eyes', she was a stimulating companion. On 23 May 1922 at the Ann Street Presbyterian Church, Brisbane, she married Walter Mackenzie Cottrell, book-keeper at Ularunda, where they returned without disclosing their marriage. In February 1923, taking 'two dogs, a large quantity of bulbs and plants and some 11 cwt of Dossie's belongings', they 'eloped' to Dunk Island where they lived with the beach-comber E. J. Banfield [q.v.7]. Later that year they went to Sydney, living for a time at the People's Palace, and Dorothy sold cartoons to several magazines. In 1924 they travelled round New South Wales in a truck, selling odds and ends. In the winter they returned to Ularunda and Dorothy started to write fiction.

She sent a manuscript to the American *Ladies' Home Journal*, which bought the serial rights for $5000 in April 1927. It later appeared in the *Sydney Mail* and the English *Women's Journal*. Published in Boston and London in 1929 as *The singing gold*, it achieved great success in Australia, Britain and the United States of America. It was largely autobiographical: in the *Sydney Morning Herald*, 27 October 1928, Mary Gilmore [q.v.] wrote: 'But genius rises above faults. Mrs. Cottrell writes Australia as it has never been written before'.

To avoid 'iniquitous taxation' on her American earnings, the Cottrells sailed for California on 19 October 1928. In 1930 she published *Earth battle* (*Tharlane*, in America), depicting the struggle to wrest a living from the outback. One critic wrote that few Australian novelists 'have drawn a more gripping picture of [the country's] barbaric beauty and its terror'. They led a vagabond life in America and took out American citizenship in 1939; from 1942 they lived in Florida. Dorothy became a successful journalist and wrote short stories, mainly on Australian themes, for magazines. She also published two children's books: one was filmed — *Wilderness orphan* (Sydney, 1936), about a pet kangaroo. In the early 1940s a serious back injury interrupted her writing.

Dorothy loved the small West Indian islands 'that still grow Elizabethan flowers and whose people use words that ceased to be part of normal English three centuries ago'. In 1953 she published *The silent reefs* (New York), a mystery adventure story set in the Caribbean: it was serialized in the *Saturday Evening Post* and made into a film in 1959. She confessed that she might have written more had she not been so deeply imbued with wanderlust. With an adventurous spirit and 'resolute recklessness', she would board any boat that would take her wheelchair — she once returned to Florida in a 24 ft (7.3 m) ketch. She also loved gardening.

In 1954 the Cottrells came back to Queensland to manage Ularunda until 1956 when they returned to Homestead, Florida, where Dorothy died of heart disease on 29 June 1957. She was survived by her husband and an adopted son.

C. Roderick, *20 Australian novelists* (Syd, 1947); *Wilson Library Bulletin*, 1 Sept 1955, *All About Books*, 15 July 1930; *SMH*, 27 Oct 1928, 23 Mar 1929; *Labor Daily*, 3 Nov 1928, supp; *Australasian*, 6 Apr 1929, 20 Dec 1930; *New York Times*, 17 Nov 1940; Cottrell papers (NL); M. Gilmore papers (ML); Palmer papers (NL); Fletcher Bros, Papers 14/3/12, 13 (ANU Archives); information from Mr W. M. Cottrell, Bowen, Queensland.

BARBARA ROSS
MARTHA RUTLEDGE

COUNSEL, EDWARD ALBERT (1849-1939), surveyor and administrator, was born at Piper's River, north-east Tasmania, son of Lawrence Counsel, farmer, who had migrated from County Louth, Ireland, in 1832, and his wife Zillah, née Jones. Counsel, educated at home, assisted on his father's selection near Ulverstone until, aged 20, he was articled to a local surveyor. An outstanding student, he qualified in 1872, and spent the next eight years on government mining and exploration surveys in the west and north-east of the colony, gaining much practical experience in track-cutting and bush field-work, and first-hand knowledge of the physical resources of Tasmania, and of the lives of the settlers. On 23 July 1879 at

Hobart he married Mary Stuart Simson (d. 1933).

In 1889 Counsel became the career head of the Surveys Department with his appointment as deputy surveyor-general for Tasmania. His recommendations on the Crown Lands Act (1890) were incorporated in an amending Act of 1894, which encouraged the disposal of crown land to industrious bona fide settlers without capital, and provided for the amalgamation of the Lands and Surveys departments. That year Counsel was appointed to the new position of surveyor-general and secretary for lands.

Throughout his long term of office he advocated an interventionist policy. He saw the prosperity of Tasmania as dependent on the stability of the small landholder, whom he believed the government should aid by extending credit, by developing roads and by undertaking exploration, with guaranteed titles established through accurate survey. Counsel's credit system substantially reduced the inherited departmental arrears, but met with only limited success in extending settlement owing to the scarcity of good agricultural land and the high cost of public works. The policy led, however, to the State Advances Act (1907) and to the establishment of several institutions — the Closer Settlement Board (1906), the Agricultural Bank of Tasmania (1907), the Scenery Preservation Board (1915) and the Forestry Department (1920) — with all of which Counsel was closely associated.

A popular departmental head who believed in the efficacy of administrative action in resolving disputes over land use, Counsel was a foundation member in 1897 of the Civil Service Association and a member of the nominated Civil Service Board in 1900-05. He successfully defended his department against twenty charges investigated by a royal commission in 1910. As president of the Institute of Surveyors, Tasmania, in 1898-1923, and chairman of the Surveyors' Board in 1909-24, he worked for the achievement of high standards in his profession and for reciprocity with other States.

A fellow of the Royal Geographical Society and of the Royal Society of Tasmania, he served on the Council of the University of Tasmania in 1907-11 and 1915-27. In 1911 he represented the Commonwealth and New Zealand at the London conference of surveyors-general of the Empire, and was appointed Companion of the Imperial Service Order in 1921. After his retirement in 1924 he was retained by the government as a consultant. He died, aged 90, on 9 August 1939 in Hobart and was buried in the Roman Catholic section of Cornelian Bay cemetery, survived by two sons and two daughters. Six physical features in Tasmania are named for him.

Cyclopedia of Tasmania, 1 (Hob, 1900); *Aust Surveyor*, Dec 1939, Sept 1967; *Tas Mail*, 9 June 1921; *Examiner* (Launc), and *Mercury*, 10 Aug 1939; *Advocate* (Burnie), 11 Aug 1939; CUS 30 (TA).

ANN ELIAS

COUPPÉ, LOUIS (1850-1926), missionary archbishop, was born on 26 August 1850 at Romorantin, department of Loir-et-Cher, France, son of Charles Couppé, locksmith, and his wife Margeurite Vinéraude, née Cougnet. Ordained in the diocese of Blois on 30 May 1874, he worked in the parish of Selles-sur-Cher before joining in 1880 the Missionaries of the Sacred Heart, recently expelled from France by the anti-clerical decrees. Couppé took his first vows in Holland in 1881 and made his final profession in Rome on 25 July 1884.

Aroused by the case of the Marquis de Rays [q.v.6], the Vatican appointed the Order in 1881 to evangelize the vacant vicariates of Melanesia and Micronesia. The first missionaries began work at Kokopo near Rabaul, New Britain, in 1882. Following the division of eastern New Guinea between Britain and Germany in April 1885, Melanesia was divided in 1889 into two new vicariates of New Pomerania and British New Guinea, coterminous with the new political jurisdictions.

Arriving in Sydney in January 1885 with three brothers of his Order and five nuns of the related Order of Our Lady of the Sacred Heart, Couppé was appointed by Fr Navarre to establish a house of the Order. At Cardinal Moran's [q.v.] request he also ministered to Botany and Randwick parishes. He landed at Yule Island, British New Guinea, in August 1886, joined Henri Verjus [q.v.6] in exploring the headwaters of the St Joseph River and in 1889 was appointed vicar apostolic of New Pomerania. Couppé was consecrated titular bishop of Lero at Antwerp, Belgium, in 1890 and returned to his vicariate in 1892. After 1897 his jurisdiction was restricted to New Britain, New Ireland, Manus and the Marshall Islands. The latter group was withdrawn in 1905.

The population was not always receptive. In 1904 ten missionaries were killed in the Baining Mountains and in 1919 a catechist and his wife were killed there. Nor was the government always helpful. In 1889 mission work was banned because of the anti-Jesuit laws then in force in Germany and the missionaries were threatened with expulsion from New Guinea. As soon as these impediments were removed in 1890 it was ordered that the Methodist and Sacred Heart missions should occupy separate districts to avoid tensions.

When Couppé appealed, the German Foreign Office agreed that each mission should retain its existing stations whether or not they were in the territory of the other. The 'spheres of interest' policy was abandoned as impractical in 1899. There were problems, too, over land. To provide for the future growth and financing of the mission, Couppé travelled widely and bought large areas, particularly those with good anchorages. Bitter wrangles with competing claimants such as 'Queen' Emma Coe and the New Guinea Co. ensued, but these became fewer after the German government assumed direct control of New Guinea in 1899.

Couppé was plagued by patriotic sentiment. Under German pressure, his French confrères were replaced by Germans in 1904. Although he urged them to behave correctly towards the occupying force in World War I, the mission remained under official suspicion; funds from Europe were cut off and after the end of the war, until 1924, there were continual deportation threats. His mission nevertheless became largely self sufficient and its headquarters at Vunapope near Kokopo was almost a town, with schools, workshops, a hospital, an orphanage, a printing shop, a church and various religious houses.

When Couppé retired in 1923 he was administering thirty-four mission stations, a school for catechists and an indigenous order of nuns, the Daughters of Mary Immaculate. He had also converted most of the Rabaul Chinese community. He retired to St Mary's Towers at Douglas Park near Sydney, and died there on 20 July 1926, six months after being named titular archbishop of Hieropolis. He was buried at Vunapope. Couppé was 'a very tall, strong, portly, energetic man with a long black beard and, though French, has little of that nationality about him'. His energy, determination, foresight and business acumen gave the Church in the islands a good start.

C. D. Mackellar, *Scented isles and coral gardens* (Lond, 1912); Michael, *75 glorious years, 1882-1957* (Vunapope, 1957); Sister M. Adela, *I will give them one heart* (Vunapope, 1968); P. G. Sack, *Land between two laws* (Canb, 1973); 'Missions', P. Ryan (ed), *Encyclopaedia of Papua and New Guinea* (Melb, 1972); J. Winthuis, 'Ein seltenes Jubiläum', *Hiltruper Monatshefte*, 32-33 (1915-16); *Aust annals of Our Lady of the Sacred Heart*, Sept 1926; *J of Pacific Hist*, 10 (1975), pt 1; *Freeman's J* (Syd), 29 July 1926.   HUGH LARACY

COWAN, EDITH DIRCKSEY (1861-1932), social worker and politician, was born on 2 August 1861 at Glengarry near Geraldton, Western Australia, second child of Kenneth Brown, pastoralist and son of early York settlers Thomas and Eliza Brown, and his first wife Mary Eliza Dircksey Wittenoom, a teacher and the daughter of the colonial chaplain, J. B. Wittenoom [q.v.2]. Edith's mother died in childbirth in 1868 and she went to a Perth boarding school run by the Misses Cowan, sisters of her future husband; she completed her education with Canon Sweeting, ex-headmaster of Bishop Hale's [q.v.4] School. Her adolescence was shattered in 1876 by the ordeal of her father's trials and hanging for the murder, that year, of his second wife. These experiences made her a solitary person, committed nevertheless to social reforms which enhanced women's dignity and responsibility and which secured proper care for mothers and children.

On 12 November 1879 in St George's Cathedral Edith married James Cowan, registrar and master of the Supreme Court. His appointment in 1890 as Perth police magistrate gave them permanent social and economic security and gave her an insight into the wider society's social problems. They had four daughters and a son between 1880 and 1891.

In the 1890s Edith Cowan became involved in voluntary organizations: she was the Karrakatta Women's Club's first secretary in 1894 and later vice-president and president. There Perth's leading women mastered public speaking and shared their reading on health, literature and women's rights: Cowan's included Olive Schreiner, J. S. Mill and Charlotte Perkins Stetson (Gilman). A state education advocate, she served several terms on the North Fremantle Board of Education, one of the few public offices then open to women. She worked with the Ministering Children's League (from 1891) and the House of Mercy for unmarried mothers (Alexandra Home for Women) from 1894. A foundation member of the Children's Protection Society in 1906, she pioneered its 1909 day nursery for working mothers' children. The society was instrumental in the passing of the State Children Act, 1907, which set up the Children's Court. She was among the first women appointed to its bench in 1915; also an early woman justice of the peace (1920), she constantly urged the appointment of women to such positions.

Cowan was an initiator of the Women's Service Guild in 1909 and was vice-president to 1917 when she resigned. Amongst other work, the guild undertook the fund-raising, public meetings and government lobbying, in which she was prominent, which led finally to the opening of the King Edward

Memorial Hospital for Women in 1916. She was secretary of the new hospital's advisory board. In 1911 she was prominent in the creation of the Western Australian National Council of Women; she was its president in 1913-21 and vice-president until her death. She was a foundation member of Co-Freemasonry in her State in 1916, and the first female member of the Anglican Social Questions Committee from 1916 and a co-opted member of synod from 1923.

Up to 1915 the many women's organizations co-operated confidently and harmoniously, with the same people prominent in several of them, like Cowan, Lady James, Jane ('Jean') Beadle [q.v.7], and Bessie Rischbieth and Roberta Jull [qq.v.]. After a bitter controversy that year over amendments to the Health Act concerning venereal disease, the movement split: the National Council of Women and a group around Cowan, who supported the clauses recommending compulsory notification; and a more radical group around Rischbieth and the Women's Service Guild. The rift between these two women was never healed.

Cowan went overseas in 1903 and 1912 to Britain and Europe, and in 1925 to the United States of America as an Australian delegate to the seventh International Conference of Women. During World War I, already heavily engaged in social welfare, she took on a wide range of war work for which she was appointed O.B.E. in 1920. Immediately after the war women's organizations renewed their efforts for civic rights, as part of 'the full democratic re-generation of the world', and in 1920 legislation ended the legal bar to women entering parliament. In the 1921 elections Cowan was one of five women candidates. As an endorsed Nationalist for the Legislative Assembly seat of West Perth, she opposed an independent Nationalist and T. P. Draper [q.v.], the sitting Nationalist attorney-general in Sir James Mitchell's [q.v.] government. The electorate had a majority of women on the roll, but was solidly wealthy with a few potential Labor voters. She campaigned on her community service record, the need for law and order, and for women in parliament 'to nag a little' on social issues. She narrowly defeated Draper to become the first woman member of an Australian parliament.

Cowan used her term to promote migrant welfare, infant health centres and women's rights: she 'was convinced of the necessity of motherhood endowment', even defended the idea, in parliament, of a housewives' union, and continued to press for sex education in state schools. The Women's Legal Status Act, which she introduced in 1923 as a private member, opened the legal profession to women. She had taken seriously the wartime Nationalist claim to be a non-party organization, and voted sometimes with the government and sometimes with the Opposition, impressing neither. In the 1924 elections West Perth business interests stood a strong candidate in T.A.L. Davy [q.v.]. A Labor candidate and the continuing conflict between the two major women's organizations further depleted her support and she lost. She failed again in 1927.

Cowan was a founder of the (Royal) Western Australian Historical Society in 1926 and contributed to its journal – her daughter Dircksey was its first keeper of records. She was active in planning the State's 1929 centenary celebrations. Until her last illness she maintained her committee and social work. Survived by her husband (d. 18 October 1937), she died on 9 June 1932 and was buried in the Anglican section of Karrakatta cemetery. She left an estate of £161. Colleagues erected a clock tower memorial at the King's Park gates to indicate her place as 'one of Australia's greatest women'. She had led a group of forceful articulate women who made the Western Australian women's movement a model; while she shared its concern with purity, temperance and ameliorative social work, she gave it her own rational analysis of issues and an austere dedication. Her portrait is in the Western Australian Art Gallery.

P. Cowan, *A unique position* (Perth, 1978); *PD* (WA), 1921, p1731; Children's Protection Soc, *Annual Report*, 1909-32 (copy, Battye Lib, Perth); *Western Women*, Aug 1915, Jan, Oct 1916, June 1917; Women's Service Guilds (WA), *Dawn*, 15 June 1932; *WA Times*, 13 June 1876; *Western Mail*, 12, 19 June, 2 Oct 1914; *West Australian*, 7 Sept 1919, 13 Mar 1920, 24 Feb, 29 Apr 1921, 20 Jan 1923, 22 Feb 1924, 11 Mar 1927, 10 June 1932; *Australasian*, 8 Apr 1922; R. Jull, Papers, *and* History of the Karrakatta Club 1894-1954, *and* Supreme Court (WA), files 741, 752a, *and* National Council of Women, Minutes, 1911-13, 1916-19, 1919-22, *and* Women's Service Guilds, Minutes, 1913-16, (Battye Lib, Perth).

MARGARET BROWN

COWAN, SIR JOHN (1866-1953), grazier and politician, was born on 6 December 1866 at Port Gawler, South Australia, third son of Thomas Cowan, farmer and politician, and his wife Mary Jane, née Armstrong. His grandfather John Cowan had arrived in Adelaide from Belfast, Ireland, on the *Epaminondas* in 1852 and pioneered the public transport system between North Adelaide and the city. After education at Whinham [q.v.6] College, North Adelaide, Cowan managed one of his father's Milang properties. In 1881 he bought Glen Lossie station near Murray Bridge and lived there until his death. On 10 February 1892 at

Murray Bridge he married Elizabeth Johnston Jones; they had three daughters and
two sons.

He became a member of the Mobilong
District Council in 1892 and chaired it in
1896-1912. Very active in local community
affairs, particularly education, Cowan took
an early interest in irrigation: he urged the
construction of locks and weirs on the River
Murray and at Goolwa and arranged a
deputation to the premier to induce the
government to reclaim the lower Murray
swamps. He entered the Legislative Council
in 1910 as a member for the Southern region.
His father had been the member for Yatala in
the House of Assembly in 1875-78 and his
uncle, James Cowan, was the member for the
same district in 1890, the year of his death.
Sir John's son John Lancelot was to be a
member of the Legislative Council in 1949-
59. During World War I Cowan was active in
the enlistment campaign. In 1923-24 he was
minister of agriculture, town planning, and
assistant minister of repatriation for the last
five months of Barwell's [q.v.7] government;
in 1927-30 he was minister of agriculture,
immigration, repatriation and irrigation in
Butler's [q.v.7] cabinet. He sat on the 1911-13
royal commission on education which
recommended increased finance for the
University of Adelaide, the empowering of
the university to grant bachelor's and
master's degrees in engineering, and considerable changes to the State's education
system.

Cowan's main contribution to legislation
was in the area of drainage of the South-East
and afforestation: he urged the purchase of
new milling plant to develop the economy of
that region's forests. He introduced the first
dairy legislation in the State in 1927, resulting in the Dairy Industry Act, 1928, and
claimed to have been the first person in
Australia to suggest adjustment of farmers'
debts. He also piloted through the council
the important 1928 legislation to ensure organized marketing in the dried-fruit industry. He was government whip for twenty
years, and when he retired in 1944 had the
longest continuous service of any member in
both Houses. That year he was knighted.

A Freemason, Cowan's other interests
included hunting, tennis and bowls. At 85 he
remained alert, riding a hack daily around
his property. Survived by his wife (d. 1958)
and children, he died on 8 March 1953 at
Murray Bridge and, after a Presbyterian
service, was buried in the local cemetery. His
estate was sworn for probate at £37 246.

H. T. Burgess (ed), *Cyclopedia of South Australia*, 2 (Adel, 1909); *Advertiser* (Adel), 5 Apr 1927,
13 Mar 1936, 1 Jan 1944, 25 Apr 1947, 23 Jan 1950.
                                      MARYANNE McGILL

COWAN, THEODORA ESTHER (1868-
1949), sculptor, was born on 13 November
1868 at Richmond Villa, The Domain, Sydney, daughter of Jewish parents Samuel
Cohen, a monetary broker from London, and
his English-born wife Elizabeth, née Marks.
Said to have 'dabbled in putty from the age of
six', Theo Cohen was taught drawing and
modelling by Lucien Henry [q.v.4] at Sydney
Technical College in 1887-88. On his advice,
confirmed by Percival Ball [q.v.7], her parents took her to Florence, Italy, in 1889.
There she was taught by Longworth Powers
and privately by Professor Augusto Rivalta
of the Academia di Belle Arti. She received
several commissions and in 1894 exhibited
at the Ladies' Gallery, London. She returned
to Sydney in the *Prinz-Regent Luitpold* with
her mother and sisters on 27 July 1895.
Working in the Strand Arcade, as Theo
Cowan she soon made a reputation with her
controversial bust of Sir Henry Parkes
[q.v.5], and became active in the Society of
Artists, Sydney – she was a council-member
in 1897-98.

During 1897 Cowan gave classes at her
studio and was invited to submit maquettes
in the sculptures competition for the Victoria Markets. James Green, the critic,
believed her work 'showed fertility of
imagination, power of composition and executive ability'. Later she told Frank Dolman that 'There is a good deal of prejudice
here against a woman sculptor. You see I am
in the position of a pioneer'. She was commissioned by the trustees of the National Art
Gallery of New South Wales to produce
marble busts of F. E. du Faur and E. L.
Montefiore [qq.v.4, 5]. In 1899 she showed
her 'strikingly realistic' bust of (Sir) Edmund Barton [q.v.7] at the Society of Artists'
Spring Exhibition.

In September 1901 Cowan went to London
and set up a studio in Grosvenor Street,
where in 1904 she held a private view. She
completed busts and statuettes of well-
known people and executed a medal for the
Hunterian Society. In 1906 she won first
prize at the Society of Women Artists' exhibition at the Austral Club with her bronze
Will-o-the-Wisp, and in 1908 a gold medal at
the Franco-British Exhibition in London for
the best piece of child portraiture. She exhibited at the Grafton, Doré, Chenil and
Suffolk Street galleries.

Cowan returned to Sydney in June 1913
and set up at Darlinghurst, before moving in
with her mother and sisters at their home,
Osiris, 84 Berry Street, North Sydney. She
now mainly exhibited with the Society of
Women Painters, and taught privately.
Much of her later work was poetic and
mystical, using children as the basis for
imagery. In the 1920s Cowan's artistic

career tapered off, though she exhibited water-colours of the Solomon Islands at Swain's Gallery in 1925. She set up the short-lived Koala pottery in 1933. She also wrote occasional articles for the *Sydney Morning Herald*. In April 1949 she was made an honorary life member of the Women's Club.

Cowan died, unmarried, in hospital at Vaucluse on 27 August 1949 and was cremated with Anglican rites. Her estate was valued for probate at £5047. In her prime she had a 'tall, stately figure, [with] dark handsome features . . . such as to impress the memory'. Showing a precocious talent in her early years, she suffered from the common antipathy to female artists, the failure to obtain a regular income from her work and a decline in her artistic powers as she aged. Her later years were spent in genteel penury.

F. Dolman, *Ladies of Sydney* (Syd, nd); L. W. Matters, *Australians who count in London* . . . (Lond, 1913); J. G. De Libra, 'The fine arts in Australia', *A'sian Art Review*, 1 July 1899; *Studio* (Lond), 22 (1901), 51 (1911); *A.A.A.*, 1 Aug 1904, 1 Oct 1906; *Society* (Syd), 1 Apr 1922; *SMH*, 29 July, 19 Aug, 20 Sept 1895, 10 Mar 1913, 30 Aug 1949; *Sun* (Syd), 30 Aug 1949; Theo Cowan papers (ML); Parkes papers (ML); Mary Gilmore's news-cuttings (NL).   NOEL S. HUTCHISON

COWARD, HARRY KEITH (1887-1971), soldier and grazier, was born on 20 November 1887 in Sydney, second son of William Gratus Coward, an English-born architect, and his wife Jane Ann, née Crossing. After his father's death in a railway accident at Glebe in 1894 he moved with his family to Mudgee (where his Crossing relatives lived) and attended the grammar school there. He joined the Commercial Banking Co. of Sydney on 13 January 1905 and was transferred in turn to Coolamon, Wagga Wagga and Kempsey.

In July 1909 Coward resigned to go into partnership with his brothers, William and Edwin, on a land-ballot block at Mungindi. He helped work the property, Comilaroy, until 20 May 1915 when he enlisted in the Australian Imperial Force as a private. Reaching Egypt in January 1916, he was posted to the 45th Battalion in March and sailed for France on 8 June. On 4 July he was attached to the 12th Light Trench-Mortar Battery and went into the line at Fleurbaix. He then fought at Pozières Heights and Mouquet Farm. On 15 October, while his trench-mortar crew was under heavy fire, a fragment from an enemy shell ignited the fuse of a mortar bomb in an ammunition pile

beside their gun-pit. Coward grabbed the shell and hurled it over the parapet where it exploded. For his promptitude, which saved many lives, he was awarded the Distinguished Conduct Medal.

Coward was promoted lance corporal in December and in April 1917 was commissioned second lieutenant in the field in the 45th Battalion; however, he remained attached to the 12th L.T.M.B. He served in the battle of Messines and for 'devotion to duty and courage from 7 to 11 June' was awarded the Military Cross: he followed the barrage in front of advancing Australian troops, destroying several enemy strong points and enabling the attack to proceed. Afterwards he 'commanded his guns under continuous heavy enemy bombardment, setting a fine example to his men'. He was promoted lieutenant in August. Early in 1918 his battery fought on the Somme and, at Dernancourt on 3 April, Coward was wounded in the face and right leg by shell fragments; he was evacuated and did not resume duty until late July. His leg injury was to plague him in later life. By August he was serving at Méricourt and on 18 September, during operations near Bellenglise, won a Bar to his Military Cross for using his mortars to silence German machine-guns which were holding up the Australian advance.

Demobilized on 14 July 1919 Coward returned to Comilaroy, then in 1922 moved to Newfarm, an adjoining grazing property. On 17 January 1923 he married Mary Roberta Curwen-Walker at All Saints Anglican Church, St Kilda, Melbourne. Three years later he took up Riversdale at St George, Queensland, and spent the rest of his working life there. He and his wife retired to a small property near Glen Innes, New South Wales, in 1953.

Tall and well made, Coward evoked C. E. W. Bean's [q.v.7] image of the bushman soldier. Though city-born, he had always preferred country life. In a letter written from the front in 1917, Kit, as his family called him, made light of the holocaust around him; rather, he questioned his brother about wool prices, sheep-crutching and shearing. Survived by his wife (who died only five days later), three sons and two daughters, he died at Glen Innes on 1 August 1971 and was buried with military honours in the Anglican cemetery.

C. E. W. Bean, *The A.I.F. in France*, 1916-18 (Syd, 1929, 1933, 1937, 1942); J. E. Lee, *A brief history of the 45th Battalion, A.I.F. 1916-1919* (Syd, 1962); *London Gazette*, 8 Dec 1916, 24 Aug 1917, 8 Mar 1919; Commercial Banking Co. of Sydney Archives (Syd); information from Mr G. and Miss J. Coward, Mungindi, NSW, and Messrs D. and R. Coward, St George, Qld.   ALAN FEWSTER

COWEN, NELLIE LOUISE; see LOVELY

COWIE; see LEE, BETSY

COWLEY SIR ALFRED SANDLINGS (1848-1926), sugar-planter, politician and company director, was born on 24 April 1848 at Fairford, Gloucester, England, son of Isaac Cowley, stonemason and Baptist preacher, and his wife Charlotte, née Coppin. His father went as a lay missionary to Natal where Alfred was apprenticed, specializing in the installation of sugar machinery. He became a sugar and coffee planter. After migrating to New South Wales in 1871 he managed a sugar mill on the Macleay River, then worked on a plantation near Maryborough, Queensland. In 1875 he started a small sugar farm on the Herbert River, but his capital was inadequate for a newly settled district, and when the venture failed he visited Natal. He married Marie Campbell at Pietermaritzburg on 24 July 1880; they had three children. She was the aunt of the South African poet Roy Campbell and his sister Ethel, who was called 'the angel of Durban' by Australian soldiers in World War I.

Returning to Queensland, in 1881 Cowley became manager of a plantation at Ingham owned by the Hamleigh Sugar Co. Ltd of Melbourne, which also owned Macknade on the Herbert River. In 1888 he was appointed as a royal commissioner to investigate the depression in the sugar industry. He and Henry King [q.v.5] both recommended the continued employment of black labour but W. H. Groom [q.v.4], in a minority report, advocated the abolition of non-European labour and criticized the experimental central mill system.

On 12 May 1888 Cowley was elected member for Herbert. An ardent separationist who quoted statistics prolifically, he supported Sir Thomas McIlwraith [q.v.5] and, despite his parliamentary inexperience, became secretary for public lands and secretary for agriculture in 1890-93. As Speaker from May 1893 until 15 February 1899 he was considered tactless. Sir Robert Philp [q.v.], whom he had once supported, complained that 'he spoke to me as I would not speak to a dog'. Appointed a commissioner to inquire into the liquor industry in 1900, he stood unsuccessfully for the Senate next year. His acceptance of the Speakership again from September 1903 to April 1907, which facilitated creation of the Morgan-Kidston [qq.v.] combination, was a piece of opportunism fuelled by a grudge. He was knighted in 1904. Defeated for Herbert in 1907 by William Lennon [q.v.], Cowley failed to win Burrum in 1908, and retired from politics. During World War I he was an ardent recruiter and conscriptionist. He was chairman of the Queensland Patriotic Fund.

Cowley was the last chairman of the Bank of Queensland, chaired the local boards of the National Bank of Australia and the Australian Mutual Provident Society and was a trustee of the Royal National Association. In 1920 he accompanied Philp and J. A. Walsh to London in a successful attempt to thwart E. G. Theodore's [q.v.] loan-raising plans. He died on 1 December 1926 at his Brisbane home and was buried after a Presbyterian service in Toowong cemetery. His estate, valued for probate at £8047, was left to his widow.

D. J. Murphy and R. B. Joyce (eds), *Queensland political portraits 1859-1952* (Brisb, 1978); *Brisbane Courier,* 11 Aug 1890, 18, 19 Sept 1903, 2 Dec 1926; *Telegraph* (Brisb), 2 Dec 1926.   KAY SAUNDERS

COWLISHAW, LESLIE (1877-1943), physician, medical historian and bibliophile, was born on 4 January 1877 in Sydney, eldest son of native-born parents Mahlon Clarke Cowlishaw, shipping merchant, and his wife Jane, née Gratton. He was educated at Sydney Grammar School and the University of Sydney (M.B., Ch.M., 1906); a 'delightful batsman' he captained his school first eleven and in 1903 won a cricket blue at the university. His early interest in history and books was nurtured by several visits to Britain and Europe with his family — in 1906-08 he collected early medical works throughout Europe, and laid an imposing foundation for his library. On his return to New South Wales in 1908 he settled in general practice at Cooma and there on 11 August 1909 he married Jessie Rose Ann Garnock, daughter of a grazier.

Commissioned captain in the Australian Imperial Force in March 1915, Cowlishaw was attached to the 12th Light Horse Regiment in June and served briefly at Gallipoli. He was invalided to England from Lemnos in October; from January to May 1916 he was officer-in-charge of invaliding in London, where he met leaders in medical history, notably Sir William Osler, who gave him help and encouragement, books, and the lasting title of 'the bibliophile from the bush!' After a voyage to Australia on transport duty he was promoted major in December and in 1917 served in France with the Australian Field Ambulance and at Rouelles and Etaples. His A.I.F. appointment ended in December 1917 and he returned to Sydney.

In 1918 Cowlishaw set up in practice at Hornsby, moving next year to Lindfield, where he worked as a family doctor for the rest of his life. His collecting and study continued; his publications were mainly in the *Medical Journal of Australia*. Sought after as a lecturer and widely recognized as a historian, he strove tirelessly to advance both professional and academic appreciation of his subject. In 1925 he was chief sponsor of a section on medical history and literature of the local branch of the British Medical Association, and of a similar group at the Australasian Medical Congress in 1929. From 1931 he was an honorary lecturer in medical history at the University of Sydney and consistently pressed for improved library facilities and organized teaching of the subject.

Cowlishaw was 'a friendly, courtly man' of wide culture, and an able physician revered by his patients. In 1939, after examination, he became a member of the Royal Australasian College of Physicians. He was a fellow of the Royal Society of Medicine, London, and an active member of the Returned Sailors' and Soldiers' Imperial League of Australia and of the medical committee of the Legacy Club of Sydney. The later years of his otherwise happy life were clouded by the loss, in a car accident, of his only child David, aged 20. Survived by his wife, he died of heart disease at Lindfield on 11 December 1943 and was cremated with Anglican rites. His library, rich in rare medical and surgical classics, is the most important of its kind in Australia; it now forms the Cowlishaw collection in the library of the Royal Australasian College of Surgeons.

K. F. Russell, 'Historical collections . . . of the Royal Australasian College of Surgeons', *Aust & New Zealand J of Surgery*, 36 (1966); *MJA*, 5 Feb 1944, *and* E. Ford, 'Three Australian medical historians . . .', *MJA*, 18 Nov 1967.

EDWARD FORD

COX, CHARLES FREDERICK (1863-1944), soldier, railway auditor and politician, was born on 2 May 1863 at Pennant Hills, Sydney, son of Frederick Charles Cox, butcher and later orchardist, and his wife Eliza, née Anderson. Both parents were native-born. He was educated at Parramatta and entered the State railways in 1881 as a clerk in the traffic audit branch. Over the next ten years he developed an increasing interest in the volunteer movement and joined the New South Wales Lancers in 1891. He was commissioned in 1894 and that year, on 7 March, married Minnie Elizabeth Gibbons at All Saints Anglican Church, Parramatta.

Cox was tall and had a fine presence. Showing himself to be a forceful and reliable officer, he was given command of the lancer detachment which went to London for Queen Victoria's Diamond Jubilee in April 1897; he was promoted captain in November. On returning home he resumed work with the railways then, two years later, commanded a squadron of lancers who went to England, at their own and their regiment's expense; to train with regular cavalry. On the outbreak of war in South Africa in October 1899, Cox and most of his men volunteered for active service and their offer was approved by the New South Wales government. They were the first colonial volunteers to land at Cape Town. From May 1900 Cox was attached to the Inniskilling Dragoons, serving under Major (later Field Marshal) E. H. H. Allenby who was to be his commander-in-chief in 1917-18. He took part in almost every major action including the relief of Kimberley, the battles of Paardeberg and Diamond Hill and in operations in the Eastern Transvaal.

He and his lancers returned to Sydney at the end of their year's service. There, as a major, he was appointed to command the newly raised 3rd New South Wales Mounted Rifles and was back in South Africa with this regiment in April 1901. In June he was made an honorary lieut-colonel and joined a force led by Colonel M. F. Rimington, perhaps the ablest of the British column commanders in the guerilla phase of the war. He remained in the field with Rimington until the end of April 1902, winning the respect and admiration of the British regulars. Rimington's glowing farewell order to Cox and his regiment reflected great credit on their commander: 'They have shown, by their dash in attack, steadiness in action and alert behaviour on outpost duties, that they are thorough good soldiers of whom the Empire may well be proud. Their cheerful conduct under privation and exposure is above all praise. Under splendid officers, their coolness, self-reliance and dash brought them out of difficulties where other troops might have suffered severely'. Thus Cox and his mounted rifles foreshadowed the great light horse regiments of 1914-18.

He was appointed C.B. while still a major, an uncommon decoration for so junior an officer, and was mentioned in dispatches. In two years in the field he had won a reputation as a spirited leader and had earned the affectionate nickname of 'Fighting Charlie'. Cox returned to the railways in June 1902 and in 1912 was appointed an inspector in the traffic and audit branch. His heart, however, remained with the Lancers, now named the 1st Australian Light Horse, which he commanded in 1906-11. On the outbreak of World War I he resigned from the railways and, in the rank of lieut-colonel, raised the 6th Australian Light Horse Regiment, Australian Imperial Force. They fought dismounted on Gallipoli in the 2nd Light Horse Brigade. Cox was wounded on 21 May and did not resume duty until 1 July. From late September to early November he was temporary commander of the brigade then, as an honorary brigadier general, succeeded Brigadier General H. G. Chauvel [q.v.7] in command of the 1st Light Horse Brigade which he led until the end of the war.

When Chauvel was forming the Australian and New Zealand Mounted Division in March 1916, Cox was far up the Nile around Minia patrolling against the Senussi; owing to the shortage of mounted troops he was not released to join the division until May. He then went to England on sick leave, thus missing the battle of Romani, when his brigade fought with great distinction. He resumed command on 26 August. At Magdhaba, on 23 December, Cox showed his quick grasp of a situation when, caught in the open by Turkish artillery, he handled the brigade with great flexibility, thereby saving heavy casualties. Later in the same fight, when a stalemate appeared to have been reached and no water was available for the horses, Chauvel sent an order for withdrawal just as Cox was preparing to assault a Turkish position. 'Take that damned thing away', said Fighting Charlie, 'and let me see it for the first time in half-an-hour'. The successful assault by his 3rd Regiment was the beginning of the end of Turkish resistance at Magdhaba.

In 1917-18 Cox commanded the brigade in Palestine and Syria. At Abu Tellul in the Jordan Valley on 14 July 1918, he again revealed his instinctive grasp of a battle situation when he launched his 1st Light Horse Regiment in a counter-attack against a strong German and Turkish force which had penetrated far into his position. His timing was exact; the enemy, caught between the 1st Light Horse and the fire from Cox's posts, surrendered in hundreds. In November he was evacuated to hospital in Cairo, resuming command on 10 December.

Cox was not without his critics, some of whom disliked what they saw as vanity and a seeking after popularity, even at the expense of discipline. Major (later Brigadier) W. J. Urquhart, an officer who knew him during the Sinai-Palestine campaign, provides an engaging picture: 'No academic soldier he, but a leader in battle whom his men would follow, a man of the sword and the warhorse, of the night march and the attack at dawn, a *beau sabreur*, who wore . . . an emu plume of large dimensions and had a roving eye'. If command of a brigade was the limit of his capacity it must be observed that, in this role, his record was one of unbroken success over more than two years of strenuous campaigning. He was appointed

C.M.G., awarded the Distinguished Service Order, and mentioned in dispatches many times.

Soon after his return to Sydney in 1919 Cox was elected to the Senate as a Nationalist, holding his seat until 1938. Although he made no mark in politics and never attained ministerial office, he found life as a senator more congenial than that in the railways. He did not speak often in debate, especially in his later years, but he travelled widely in New South Wales, becoming one of the best-known politicians of that State. His speeches reflect a sturdy nationalism balanced by firm support for the British connexion: if they lack weight they reveal a considerable range of interest, especially in defence, the development of trunk railways and the Federal capital.

For a time after the war Cox had continued to serve with the Australian Military Forces, commanding the 4th Light Horse Brigade in 1920 and the 1st Cavalry Division temporarily in 1921-23. He was placed on the retired list in 1923 as an honorary major general. In 1929 he was made honorary colonel of the New South Wales Lancers, now 1st/21st Light Horse. He devoted himself to the welfare of returned soldiers until age and failing sight restricted his activities, and was much in demand at soldiers' ceremonies and on public occasions. Survived by his wife and daughter, he died at Croydon on 20 November 1944 and was buried in the Anglican section of Carlingford cemetery with full military honours. Cox's portrait, by Longstaff [q.v.], hangs in the Australian War Memorial.

J. Watkins Yardley, *With the Inniskilling Dragoons . . . 1899-1902* (Lond, 1904); Aust Defence Dept, *Official records of the Australian military contingents to the war in South Africa*, P. L. Murray ed (Melb, 1911); H. S. Gullett, *The A.I.F. in Sinai and Palestine* (Syd, 1923); C. E. W. Bean, *The story of Anzac* (Syd, 1924); P. V. Vernon (ed), *The Royal New South Wales Lancers, 1885-1960* (Syd, 1961); *Reveille* (Syd), July 1937; *Cwlth Parliamentary Handbook* (1919-38); C. F. Cox papers (NL); contemporary letters (AWM).			A. J. HILL

COX, SIR EDWARD JOHN OWEN (1866-1932), businessman and politician, was born on 21 January 1866 at Langharne, Carmarthenshire, Wales, son of George Hugh Augustus Cox, commercial traveller, and his wife Elizabeth, née Owen. Educated at Christ's Hospital, London, he sailed as midshipman to New Zealand about 1880. He was a clerk with the Bank of Australasia, Wanganui, when at Christchurch he married Penelope Ealinor Mary, daughter of Thomas M. H. Johnston, an engineer, on 12 December 1888. Cox later set up as a produce merchant and gained experience in the New Zealand frozen meat trade. He returned to London in 1893 and joined Birt & Co. Ltd, merchants and shippers; in 1898 he came to Sydney as their local chairman, retaining that position until 1929.

Cox reputedly made money in the South African War. At his fine house, St Luke's, Darling Point, he had a good chef, and, though abstemious himself, he was a notable host. He enjoyed practical jokes and the company of women. His formal initiation into public affairs was as president of the New South Wales Justices' Association in 1914. When the Imperial government began chartering shipping in 1915, Cox became chairman of its Australian committee; he reorganized the packing of refrigerated carcasses by having them cut in half and packed one inside the other. A close friend of W. M. Hughes [q.v.], he joined the Commonwealth Shipping Board in 1917 and was appointed deputy controller of overseas shipping on 2 March 1918.

During World War I Cox served on the executive of the New South Wales division of the British Red Cross Society, on the New Zealand Soldiers' Reception Committee, Sydney, and as president of the Rejected Volunteers Association of New South Wales, which in addition to demonstrating its members' willingness to serve, also undertook to build six cottages for war widows. Cox was a vice-president of the Millions Club and in 1920 he was foundation president of the National Roads Association. Appointed K.B.E. in 1918 and K.G.B.E. in 1920, he was known as Sir Owen.

His friendship with Hughes probably prompted Cox's initiative in 1919 in reforming the businessmen's committee which supported the Nationalists; William Brooks [q.v.7] had allowed it to become inactive. Cox believed that the party should represent a 'federation of interests', enlisting support from employers' organizations for its financing which he controlled for several years. In 1922 he was appointed to the Legislative Council. He spoke rarely and his attendance fell off as he spent more time overseas. He was Australian agent for the 'Federal' and 'Shires' shipping lines and a local director of the Federal Steam Navigation Co. Ltd of London. He was a director of the Bellambi Coal Co. Ltd and of the British Australian Cotton Association Ltd, formed after the war in Queensland under the chairmanship of Sir Hugh Denison and later (Sir) Walter Massy Greene [qq.v.].

In 1927 Cox took leave of absence from the council and spent more time overseas; he resigned his seat in 1930. He died at Monte Carlo on 30 July 1932, leaving his estate, except for provision for his wife, to Gwladys Bonsor of the same address as himself. He was survived by his wife and daughter.

SMH, 15 Feb 1918, 1 Jan 1930, 1 Aug 1932; *Smith's Weekly* (Syd), 7 Oct 1922; *Punch* (Melb), 22 Jan 1925; *Sun* (Syd), 1 Aug 1932; Holman papers, uncat MS 111 (ML).   HEATHER RADI

COX, ERLE (1873-1950), writer and journalist, was born on 15 August 1873 at Emerald Hill, Melbourne, son of Ross Cox, teacher, part-time writer and later inspector of schools, from Dublin, and his wife Mary, née Haskell, of Melbourne. After education at Castlemaine Grammar School and a year at Melbourne Church of England Grammar School, Cox took up wine-growing at Rutherglen. Ten years later he went to Tasmania, where he was based in Launceston as a traveller for a tobacco firm. On 24 December 1901 he married Mary Ellen Kilborn, daughter of a Wahgunyah vigneron; the couple later settled in Melbourne where Cox worked as a 'mercantile agent'.

Cox's first published stories appeared in the *Lone Hand* in 1908 and 1909. In 1918 he won a *Bulletin* competition for a four-line epitaph on a fallen soldier. Regular contributions to 'The Passing Show' column in the Melbourne *Argus* led in 1921 to a post on the editorial staff. As 'The Chiel' and under his own name he wrote special articles, features on religion and the Churches, book reviews and from 1929, film critiques. He became well known as a champion of British movies; his pungent style, humour and unquestionable honesty won him a large following of readers and the grudging respect of the film industry. In 1946 with others he was given five days notice to leave the ailing *Argus*. He promptly joined the *Age*, taking his 'Chiel' nom de plume, and many of his readers with him.

Cox's main claim to fame is his novel *Out of the silence*, a classic work of science fiction. Set in rural Australia, it tells the story of a young vigneron who discovers, buried beneath his land, a huge sphere containing the culture and technology of a past civilization. Cox began to write the book about 1916 but had shaped the idea for it earlier – 'pacing up and down the St Kilda sands'. At first he was unable to find a publisher but in 1919 the *Argus* printed the story in weekly instalments between 19 April and 25 October. It created extraordinary interest: 'No more successful serial story has been published in Australia' claimed the *Australasian* in 1925, heralding its appearance in Melbourne in book form. That year it was also published in London and, in 1928, in New York. American reviewers placed it alongside the works of Jules Verne and Rider Haggard. A new edition appeared in 1932; in 1934 the *Argus* published a picture-strip version and 3DB broadcast the story as a 25-part serial. Two more editions were published: one in 1947 with a prologue added, and in 1974 a French translation entitled *La sphère d'or*.

In 1938 at the behest of the *Argus*, Cox wrote another book, designed to awaken Australians to the threat of an invasion from the north: *Fools' harvest*, serialized in the *Argus* in November 1938 and published next year, pictured Australia plunged into a grim struggle against occupation forces. *The missing angel*, a humorous piece, was published in 1947.

Tall, well-built, with silver hair and distinguished features, Cox was an avid reader with especial interest in the history of the French court. In August 1950 he retired because of ill health and on 20 November died at his home in Elsternwick; he was cremated after a Presbyterian service. He was survived by his wife, two daughters and a son, Erle Harold, who for many years represented the Melbourne *Herald* in Canberra.

H. W. Malloch, *Fellows all* (Melb, 1943); G. McInnes, *Goodbye, Melbourne town* (Lond, 1968); Melb Science Fiction Club, *Somerset Gazette*, Jan 1971; *All About Books*, 18 Apr 1929; *Australasian*, 1 Aug 1925, 3 June 1939; *Herald* (Melb), 20 Nov 1950; *Argus*, 21 Nov 1950; R. H. Croll papers (LaTL); family information.　　SALLY O'NEILL

COXEN, WALTER ADAMS (1870-1949), soldier, was born on 22 June 1870 at Egham, Surrey, England, son of Henry William Coxen [q.v.3], and his wife Margaret, née Morehead (Moorhead). His father, who owned several large pastoral properties in Queensland, brought his family back to Australia in 1880. Coxen was educated at Toowoomba and Brisbane Grammar schools and joined the Department of Railways as a clerk and draftsman on 18 August 1887; five years later he was retrenched.

In February 1893 he was commissioned in the Queensland militia garrison artillery and in June 1895 transferred to the Queensland Permanent Artillery as a lieutenant. Two years later he was sent to the School of Gunnery, Shoeburyness, England, for the long course in coast defence and siege artillery and, having completed it with honours, trained in field artillery at Aldershot in January-March 1898. On returning home he was appointed officer commanding Queensland's garrison troops on Thursday Island and in August 1899 was promoted captain. He married Adelaide Rebe White Beor at Chatswood, New South Wales, on 26 March 1901. After the post-Federation

reorganization of Australia's military forces Coxen, who was a proficient mathematician, became chief instructor at the School of Gunnery in Sydney in July 1902. He held this important post at a time when the artillery lessons of the South African War were being evaluated and when procedures were making gunnery more scientific.

In November 1907 Coxen went to England for further training, gaining an ordnance certificate at Woolwich, and qualifying as an inspector of warlike stores. He was promoted major in June 1908 and returned to Australia in February 1910. Next April he became a company officer in the Royal Australian Artillery and was posted to Queenscliff, Victoria, but soon afterwards was appointed inspector of ordnance and ammunition at army headquarters, Melbourne. From January 1911 he was director of artillery, Australian Military Forces, and on the outbreak of World War I was also made inspector of coast defences and promoted lieut-colonel. He was seconded in that rank to the Australian Imperial Force on 21 May 1915 to raise and command the 36th Heavy Artillery Group, commonly known as the Australian Siege Brigade. The only unit to leave Australia with its establishment manned exclusively by regular officers and men, it was the first A.I.F. fighting unit to reach France – in February 1916. It first saw action in the British XVII Corps area, north of Arras. For the rest of the year Coxen commanded the brigade on the Somme, taking part in operations at Serre, Hamel, Ovillers and Pozières.

Coxen was awarded the Distinguished Service Order on 1 January 1917. Promoted colonel and temporary brigadier general later that month, he left the siege brigade to command the 1st Australian Divisional Artillery and in January-July served during the German withdrawal to the Hindenburg line. He took part in the attacks on Bullecourt in April and May and in the German counter-attack at Lagnicourt on 15 April. Later he commanded the divisional artillery in the 3rd battle of Ypres. He was appointed C.M.G. in January 1918, and, with the creation of the Australian Corps that month, became the senior artillery commander of the corps, retaining this position until after the Armistice. It has been claimed that in the battle of 8 August he commanded the greatest aggregation of artillery in the history of warfare. On 16 November he was made director of ordnance in the A.I.F.'s Department of Repatriation and Demobilization in London. He was created C.B. in the New Year honours of 1919. During the war he was also awarded the Belgian Croix de Guerre and was mentioned in dispatches four times.

Coxen returned to Australia in August

1919. His first post-war appointment was that of chief of ordnance and fourth member of the Military Board. In January 1920 he was promoted.colonel and in April was made deputy quartermaster general. From May 1921 to December 1924 he was chief of artillery. He became quartermaster general and third member of the Military Board in 1925 and two years later also became adjutant general, temporarily. He reached his final rank of major general in March 1927 and in April 1930 was appointed chief of the general staff. At the time it was said of him: 'if he had not been a captain in arms he would have made a captain of industry. Good temper and a vivid sense of humour characterises this man of action. At the front he was known as "the boss gunner". Gifted with keen insight, and an outsize memory, he never forgets a face or a fact. Efficiency is his watchword'. Coxen's tenure of office in the army's top post was short; because of new governmental policy concerning conditions of retirement he was prematurely retired on 1 October 1931.

Known throughout the army as 'Wacky' Coxen, he was tall and well built, with strong features and a self-possessed and dignified manner. He was a good public speaker with a pleasing, well-modulated English voice and after his retirement sometimes gave radio talks for the Australian Broadcasting Commission. He was director of the council for Victoria's centenary celebrations of 1934, a role which he carried out with characteristic efficiency. His chief recreations were ornithology, gardening and cabinet-making. He enjoyed the social life of military society, in which he moved with ease and unpretentiousness. Survived by his wife, a son and four daughters, he died on 15 December 1949 at the Repatriation General Hospital, Heidelberg, and was cremated with full military honours. His portrait, by Longstaff [q.v.], hangs in the Australian War Memorial.

PP (LA Qld), 1893, 2, 731, 1894, 3, 367; *Reveille* (Syd), May 1930; *Emu*, Apr 1950; *Army J*, Mar 1975; *SMH*, 2 Mar 1929, 1 May 1930, 12 Sept, 3 Oct 1931, 12 Oct 1932; *Queenslander*, 8 May 1930; B. M. Morris, 'The Australian Siege Brigade', *Stand-To*, 1957-58, p9; G. E. Manchester, Australian Siege Brigade in the great war (AWM).

WARREN PERRY

COYNE, DAVID EMMET (1896-1918), soldier and farmer, was born on 14 March 1896 at Ballinrush, near Mackay, Queensland, eighth child of David Emmet Coyne, farmer, and his wife Anne, née Hughes, both of whom were Irish-born. He was educated at Marian State School and then joined his father on the land.

Coyne enlisted as a private in the Australian Imperial Force on 25 January 1916 and went into training at Fraser's Hill Camp, Brisbane. While there he showed considerable athletic prowess and figured in an incident which was perhaps a portent of the selfless act which resulted in his death two years later. After the horses of an express wagon had bolted, endangering several soldiers' lives, Coyne leapt on to the back of one of the horses and managed to bring the wagon to a halt. He embarked for France with reinforcements in May and on 24 December was taken on strength with the 31st Battalion. His unit spent the winter of 1916-17 on the Somme engaged in raiding and patrol work, then in March took part in the advance on Bapaume. On 21 April 1917 he was promoted lance corporal and for the next six months was absent from his unit qualifying as a bombing instructor and serving temporarily with the 67th Battalion. He was promoted sergeant in June and rejoined the 31st Battalion in October.

From November 1917 until March 1918 the battalion served in Flanders in the Messines-Wytschaete sector, then returned to the Somme. On the night of 15 May, while in the line at Vaire-sous-Corbie, Coyne was testing some Mills grenades which he believed had been affected by damp. He threw one of them but it rebounded off the parapet and fell into the trench in which he and several others were standing. Ordering his men out, he tried to find the grenade in the darkness; then, realizing that his companions were not clear, deliberately threw himself over the grenade's approximate position and received over twenty wounds when it exploded. At first it was thought that Coyne would survive and it was typical of his courageous and genial nature that he joked about the incident as he received preliminary medical attention. His wounds proved worse than expected and he died within hours. He was posthumously awarded the Albert Medal in Gold, the highest class of that decoration: he was the only member of the A.I.F. to gain such a distinction. Coyne's grave lies in the Vignacourt British cemetery near Amiens. He was unmarried.

A. D. Ellis, *The story of the Fifth Australian Division* (Lond, 1920?); *London Gazette*, 5 Dec 1918; Roy Qld Regiment, *'Crossed boomerangs', the historical journal of the Thirty First*, 1 (Ingham, Qld, 1971, copy AWM); *Sabretache*, Jan 1978; War diary of the 31st Battalion, AIF (AWM).

P. A. PEDERSEN

COYNE, JOHN HARRY (1865-1926), bushworker, unionist and politician, was born on 16 January 1865 in a tent about six miles from Melbourne, son of John Henry Coyne, teacher, and his wife Margaret, née Ryan. Leaving school before he was 16 he became a fencer, slab-splitter, drover, shearer, rouseabout, woolpresser, stationhand, miner and sawmiller. Searching for work, he humped his swag hundreds of miles and settled eventually at Eulo, Queensland, in 1890. He married a widow Mary Elizabeth Gordon, née Heath, at Cunnamulla on 22 March 1894; they had six children.

A member of the Australian Workers' Union from its inception, Coyne joined in the 1891 and 1894 shearing strikes. From 1901 when, for the first time, he became a delegate to the union convention, he was much more prominent in the Queensland labour movement. In 1902-08 he was an organizer for the union and also for the Political Labor Party; he exemplified the orthodox view that the political wing should be based on sound union organization.

In February 1908 Coyne stood for the Legislative Assembly seat of Warrego; he beat the sitting government member P. J. Leahy, secretary for public works and mines, and held the seat until 1923. He was a convention delegate for the Australian Workers' Union in 1910, 1913 and 1916 and went to its federal conference in 1912. He was a member of the central political executive of the Labor Party in 1910-16. Elected president of the Queensland provincial council of the Australian Labor Federation in 1910, he guided it through a temporary revival, but it died in 1913. In the sugar-workers' strike of 1911 he went to the southern States seeking finance and deterring scabs. He presided at the meeting of unions in January 1912 which decided to turn the tramway dispute into a general strike, and chaired the combined unions' defence committee, but his moderate advice throughout the dispute was frequently overridden by the militants. In 1915 he joined the board of the *Worker*.

Coyne was chairman of committees of the Legislative Assembly in 1915-16, then became minister for railways until April 1918. Because of his efforts in 1912, railway strikers in 1917 trusted him sufficiently to accept conciliation by E. G. Theodore, T. J. Ryan [qq.v.] and himself. In 1917-18 Coyne chaired the land settlement and the Anzac committees of the Queensland War Council. His influence with fellow unionists facilitated house-building. With a son on active service, he was at most lukewarm in his opposition to conscription but loyally followed the party decision. In the Theodore cabinet, Coyne was minister without portfolio in 1920 and secretary for public lands in 1920-23. His development of forestry projects and his attempts to convince the public and the government of the need to conserve timber resources were his most important works.

Coyne resigned from parliament in 1923 and was appointed to the Queensland Land Court bench from 1 August. He died on 12 June 1926 at Townsville from injuries received in a car accident and was buried in Toowong cemetery, Brisbane, with Presbyterian forms, after a state funeral – the attendance by people from all walks of life indicated the popularity of, and respect for, this bluff, direct and hard-working Labor stalwart.

The Labour government in Queensland (Brisb, 1915, copy Oxley Lib, Brisb); D. J. Murphy (ed), *Labor in politics* (Brisb, 1975), and *T. J. Ryan* (Brisb, 1975); *Courier Mail*, and *Daily Standard*, 14 June 1926; *Worker* (Brisb), 31 Mar 1906, 4 Jan 1908, 19 Feb 1910, 16 June 1926.

JOHN BRIAN ARMSTRONG

COZENS, DAPHNE; *see* AKHURST

CRAIG, ROBERT GORDON (1870-1931), surgeon, was born on 23 May 1870 at Ardrossan, Ayrshire, Scotland, eldest son of Robert Craig (d. 1917), sea captain, and his wife Elizabeth, née Brown. His father had earned enough to marry by running guns to Confederates during the American civil war, and later augmented the family income by running brandy from France to Belfast; in 1877 he decided to settle in Sydney.

Next year Gordon Craig joined his parents; he was educated at Sydney Grammar School and George Watson's College, Edinburgh. After a year in the faculty of arts, University of Sydney, in 1888 he contracted enteric fever; he spent 1889 in a shipping office. Back at the university next year, he was awarded a blue for distance running and graduated M.B., Ch.M. in 1894 with firstclass honours and the university medal. After a year as resident medical officer at Royal Prince Alfred Hospital, he bought a practice at Newtown. On 29 June 1895 at Pymble he married Maria Graeme Connon, a graduate of Canterbury College, New Zealand.

Craig became an honorary assistant surgeon at Royal Prince Alfred Hospital in 1901, honorary surgeon in 1911, honorary urological surgeon in 1926 and consultant in 1930. In 1908 he relinquished his practice to his brother Francis Brown Craig and visited England and the United States of America. On his return he began surgical practice in Macquarie Street, first at Craignish and later at Ardrossan, which he bought. From 1914 he lectured in surgery at the university.

In May 1915 he enlisted in the Australian Imperial Force and in July was commissioned lieut-colonel. He served in No. 1 Hospital Ship *Karoola* in the Mediterranean and Australia until the end of 1916, and from 1917 as surgeon at Randwick Military Hospital, Sydney.

Exceptionally gifted as a surgeon, Craig was full of confidence in his ability, and was thoughtful and unhurried: yet his speed in operating was surprising. He treated his public hospital patients with the same kindness and care as his private patients received. In 1927 he successfully operated on a boy (one of whose kidneys had been shattered by a bullet) in a small and almost inaccessible bush hut in the Burragorang valley. Craig presided over the surgical section at the 1928 session of the Australasian Medical Congress, was a councilmember of the New South Wales branch of the British Medical Association and president in 1917-18, and a foundation fellow of the College of Surgeons of Australasia in 1928.

In the early 1920s Craig endowed a urological fellowship (at the time unique in Australia) at the University of Sydney and at departments of Royal Prince Alfred Hospital and the Royal Alexandra Hospital for Children. In all he donated some £20000 in money, laboratory equipment and books to the university.

Proud of his Scottish descent, he spoke with a burr which varied in intensity with the importance of the occasion. Sailing was in his blood and he raced with the Royal Sydney Yacht Squadron and Royal Prince Alfred Yacht Club. He was a first-class golfer and a vice-president of the Australian Golf Club, a member of the Rotary Club of Sydney and the Australian and University clubs. Fascinated by motor cars, he had a small fleet and once built a steam car in the backyard of his home at Centennial Park. In the late 1920s he bought Ulinda station, near Binnaway, where he hoped to carry out research into the prevention of the break in wool caused by malnutrition.

Craig died suddenly at Ulinda of coronary thrombosis on 2 September 1931 and was cremated after a service at St Stephen's Presbyterian Church, Sydney. He was survived by his wife and two daughters. His estate was valued for probate at £115555; he left the residue, amounting to about £60000, to the Royal Australasian College of Surgeons, which holds his portrait in charcoal by George Lambert [q.v.].

MJA, 24 Jan 1959; *Aust and NZ J of Surgery*, 3 Dec 1973; *Reveille* (Syd), 30 Sept 1931; *SMH*, 7 Jan 1927, 14 Aug 1928, 3 Sept, 10 Oct 1931.
                                    MALCOLM S. S. EARLAM

CRAIGIE, EDWARD JOHN (1871-1966), single taxer and politician, was born on 5 December 1871 at Moonta, South Australia, son of Scottish parents Henry Cameron Craigie, miner, and his wife Jane, née Moyle. At 11 he left the local public school and worked in Adelaide for a baker and at Kithers', butchers. He became a rationalist and was interested in socialism. In 1900 he was converted to the single-tax theories of Henry George [q.v.4]. In 1904 he returned to Moonta, joined the United Labor Party and wrote on political topics for the *Plain Dealer* (Kadina) and the *People's Weekly* (Moonta). Like George he favoured a zealous evangelical style. In 1905-11 he sat on the Moonta Corporation, then went back to Adelaide to become secretary of the Single Tax League (later Henry George League) of South Australia. On 2 February 1912 at Mile End he married Beatrice Maud Sedgman, a shop assistant.

Craigie's career as a prolific pamphleteer probably began with his 1914 booklet, *Fallacies of protection*. Australian Georgians saw his output as 'an invaluable armoury of dialectical weapons'. He organized Statewide meetings, including soap-box harangues in Botanic Park; he campaigned against conscription for World War I. Bespectacled, he 'seemed a small, mild and rather insignificant man', but he argued clearly in a 'dry, matter of fact, unhurried style'. From 1921 he edited the League newspaper, the *People's Advocate*. In 1929 in Edinburgh at the fourth international conference to promote land value taxation and free trade, Craigie presented two papers. At the 1939 New York conference, celebrating the centenary of George's birth, he became president of the international union of single taxers.

A non-Labor parliamentary candidate from 1910, in 1930-41 Craigie held the seat of Flinders in the House of Assembly as an independent. He opposed income tax, stamp duties, probate and motor taxes and insisted that the correct and only source of revenue should be 'the rental value of land brought into existence by the collective presence and energy of the people'. In some campaigns he had been stoned and pushed off the platform by Labor Party supporters. After the 1938 elections T. C. Stott asked him to join in a government of independents, but Craigie 'preferred to stand alone'.

In 1948 Craigie retired as League secretary but remained a trustee of the Henry George Foundation (Aust). In 1954 he visited Britain. A 'health fanatic', his lifelong devotion to 'the cause' had meant that he was hardly a family man, but his son Tom worked for years as his secretary. Predeceased by his wife and survived by three sons, Craigie died on 17 January 1966 at his Rose Park home. He had prudently invested in stocks and shares, and his estate was sworn for probate at $58440.

NSW Public Service Board, *Progress*, Feb 1966; *Good Government*, Mar 1966; *Advertiser* (Adel), 24 Mar 1938, 25 Apr 1944, 18 Jan 1966; *Peoples' Advocate*, 21 Aug 1948; information from Mr T. E. Craigie, Rose Park, SA.   SUZANNE EDGAR

CRAMP, KARL REGINALD (1878-1956), public school inspector and historian, was born on 21 January 1878 at Reigate, Surrey, England, son of William Cramp, builder's foreman, and his wife Mary, née Christmas. In November 1887 he arrived in Sydney with his parents who settled at Newcastle. He was educated at Hamilton Public School and in September 1895 became a pupil-teacher with the Department of Public Instruction. In 1900 he entered Fort Street Training School and won a scholarship to the University of Sydney (B.A., 1904, with the Frazer [q.v.4] scholarship in history; M.A., 1906). He was appointed a lecturer at the Teachers' College in February 1906, an examiner in the chief inspector's branch of the Department of Public Instruction in May 1912 and chief examiner in 1922; he was a secondary schools inspector from 1923 to 1943 when he retired. He was an exacting inspector, feared by teachers.

With J. G. Bartholemew, Cramp published the *Australasian school atlas* (Oxford, 1915); his textbooks indoctrinated generations of schoolchildren in hero-worship, the Whig interpretation of English history and a jingoistic view of Australia bonded to Britain by a 'crimson thread of kinship . . . sealed by the blood of [her] bravest men'. In 1909-54 he examined in history at the university public examinations and in 1915-22 lectured for the University Extension Board (he was first vice-president of the Workers' Educational Association), and was sometime president and vice-president of the Teachers' Guild of New South Wales.

Cramp had joined the (Royal) Australian Historical Society in July 1910. An original fellow in 1916 and a life member in 1918, he was honorary secretary in 1915-20, 1922-27, 1930-36, 1943-44; president in 1921, 1928-29, 1937-39, 1953; and vice-president in 1941-42, 1945-52, and 1955. He augmented the society's membership, helped it to acquire its own premises and contributed extensively to its *Journal and Proceedings*. He published much Australian history including *The State and Federal constitutions of Australia* (1913), *William Charles Wentworth* . . . (1918), *Australian winners of the Victoria Cross* (1919), *Great Australian*

explorers (1926) and *The roar material of history: schoolboy howlers* (1946). His style was florid, his tone chauvinistic and moralizing.

Cramp was also a member of Captain Cook's Landing Place Trust and the La Perouse monuments, a section president at the Australian and New Zealand Association for the Advancement of Science conference of 1937 at Auckland, a member of Australia's 150th Anniversary Celebrations Council (1936-38) and convener of its historical exhibition, first vice-president (1947) and president (1949) of the New South Wales branch of the National Trust of Australia, and a director and vice-president of the New South Wales Institution for the Deaf and Dumb and the Blind. He was appointed O.B.E. in 1933.

Initiated into Lodge University of Sydney in January 1925, he was its worshipful master in 1934-35; with George Mackaness [q.v.] he published *A history of the United Grand Lodge of ancient, free and accepted Masons of New South Wales* (1938) and another volume in 1949. Invested a past deputy grand master in 1948, he equated his craft with the 'moral solidarity of a country'.

At Newcastle on 24 December 1901 Cramp had married Ethel May Neill. Survived by two sons and a daughter, he died on 19 July 1956 at his home at Bellevue Hill, and was buried in the Methodist section of Woronora cemetery. His estate was valued for probate at £26357. Though never modest about his scholarship, he did much to promote the study of Australian history.

JRAHS, 42 (1956), pt 5; *SMH*, 23 Feb 1921, 21 July 1956; *Daily Telegraph* (Syd), 24 July 1956; Australia's 150th Anniversary Celebrations Council, Files and papers (ML).   RUTH TEALE

CRAMPTON, WALTER RUSSELL (1877-1938), trade unionist and journalist, was born on 3 July 1877 at Redfern, Sydney, son of Walter James Crampton, boot finisher, and his wife Sarah, née Philips. Leaving school at 14, he humped his swag to western New South Wales and became a member of the Slaughtermen's Union in April 1892. At 21 he found work in a Townsville, Queensland, meatworks and on 2 February 1903 married Amy Maria Beadle. Soon afterwards they moved to Brisbane.

Crampton became a full-time organizer for the Australasian Federated Butchers' Employees' Union in 1908. On regular visits to the north he was able to secure the abolition of contract work and establishment of an industrial type of union organization with a workers' board of control in each plant. According to V. G. Childe [q.v.7],

'When the managers refused Crampton admission to the works he splashed across the tidal flats and crawled in through the thick jungle'. Energetic, audacious and a socialist militant in close communion with Ernie Lane [q.v.], he was committed to reforming both the political and industrial wings of the Queensland labour movement. His organizing skills assisted other unions: in 1911 he established the southern district branch of the Amalgamated Workers' Association and organized Mackay in the sugar workers' strike. President of the Brisbane District Council of the Australian Labor Federation in 1912 and a member of the central political executive in 1910-13, he was defeated in 1912 for the Legislative Assembly seat of Windsor, then became secretary of the Queensland branch of his union. He served as a foundation director of the *Daily Standard,* and of the *Worker* in 1913-16.

Crampton resigned from the union late in 1914 to become industrial writer on the *Daily Standard* under the pseudonym 'Jack Aster'. He was still a member of the Australian Journalists' Association when he died but his career in the profession was not continuous. Appointed as State director of labour in August 1915, he successfully reorganized his department in accordance with a new Act but resigned in 1917 to become general manager of the *Daily Standard* and stayed for ten years.

In 1916-19 he was a government representative on the university senate and chaired the Returned Maimed and Wounded Soldiers' Fund during the war. Appointed to the Legislative Council in 1917, he worked for its abolition in 1922. He was an alderman of the Brisbane City Council in 1922-24, deputized frequently for the mayor and led a sub-committee on municipal abattoirs visiting Sydney, Melbourne and Adelaide in 1924.

In the 'Greater Brisbane' election of 1925, Crampton did not stand, probably as a protest against proposals for paid aldermen. He bought shares in Perkins & Co. Ltd, brewers, became a director of the company (chairman 1932), and probably shared the management of hotels held in his wife's name. He had resigned from the *Daily Standard* in 1927. The couple were at Redland Bay in 1929-34 and in the Hotel Brisbane, Wharf Street, from 1935.

Elected unopposed for Paddington in a 1935 Brisbane City Council election, Crampton became chairman of the combined health and town planning committee and served on other committees dealing with works, water, sewerage and electricity. His principal achievement was the improvement of milk supply and distribution. Heavily built, he died of heart disease on 20 October 1938 and was cremated with Anglican rites. His wife, three sons and a daughter survived him.

F. J. Brewer and R. Dunn, *Sixty-six years of municipal government* (Brisb, 1925); D. J. Murphy (ed), *Labor in politics* (Brisb, 1975); *Courier Mail,* 21 Oct 1938; *Worker* (Brisb), 25 Oct 1938.

JOHN BRIAN ARMSTRONG

CRAMSIE, JOHN BOYD (1871-1944), meat expert, was born on 2 March 1871 at Balranald, New South Wales, second son of John Cramsie (1832-1910), storekeeper, and his Scottish wife Lilias, née Rankin. His father, who had migrated from Belfast, later became a pastoralist and represented Balranald in the Legislative Assembly in 1880-87. John Boyd was educated at Sydney Boys' High School and Queen's College, St Kilda, Melbourne. He gained proficiency in sheep management around Narrabri and on the family property, Glendon, Wellingrove.

In 1891 Cramsie became manager of Strathdarr station in western Queensland. As manager of the Longreach Wool Scouring, Extract & Boiling Down Co. from 1896, he built and developed its works at Clear Lagoon and Ilfracombe. On 30 June 1897 at Glendon, New South Wales, he married Jessie Halling McIntyre of Waterloo station. He left Queensland on medical advice and in 1902 with Edward James Comerford set up Comerford, Cramsie & Co., stock and station agents, at Moree, New South Wales, and invested in grazing, individually and in the Willarie Pastoral Co. Extensive travel made Cramsie optimistic on Australia's future and an enthusiast for the meat industry.

Leaving Moree in 1912 he visited England, Europe and the United States of America to study marketing. On his return in 1914 he began a short-lived meat export business. Next year in Sydney he founded Cramsie & Lethbridge Ltd, stock, station and financial agents.

Cramsie was deputy-chairman of the Metropolitan Meat Industry Board in 1919-24 and was chairman in 1926-31. He effectively reorganized and rebuilt the Homebush abattoirs, and in 1931 rebutted a report by A. G. Noble alleging irregularities. In 1922-24 he was first chairman of the Australian Meat Council, seeking a sound export system, helped by expanded mixed farming and closer settlement. He urged State governments to introduce standardized grading and meat encouragement bills, and also tested markets in Asia. In 1923 he became first chairman of the New South Wales State Meat Advisory Board and initiated improvements in transport methods and loading facilities. He was a vice-president of the Graziers' Association of New South Wales, a council-member of the Stockowners' Association of New South Wales and a life member of the Farmers and Settlers' Association; he was also general editor of *Management and diseases of sheep in Australia* (Sydney, 1920). In 1927 he chaired the royal commission on bushfires.

Late in 1924 Cramsie had resigned all his positions to study meat processing in North and South America and marketing in Britain and Europe. In London he gave evidence to the 1925 royal commision on food prices and to the Imperial Economic Committee. He returned to Sydney convinced of the need for capital investment and scientific research. Confident about the potential of northern Australia, he acclaimed Sir George Buchanan's 1925 report on Northern Territory development and administration. After the announcement of the 1932 Ottawa conference provisions, he lobbied the Lyons [q.v.] government to take advantage of them. In 1933 he reported the registration of a company to build a railway from Bourke, New South Wales, to Birdum in the Northern Territory.

In the 1930s Cramsie envisaged group settlement of a 'peasant population of British stock' on improved lands in eastern Australia, especially between Port Macquarie and Tweed Heads. As Australian representative of several Jewish organizations, he supported Jewish colonization in the Kimberleys and on Melville Island. To help rural unemployment, he suggested self-subsistence closer settlement schemes. Through the Millions Club in Sydney he advocated a register of unemployed and a list of jobs available for skilled migrants.

Cramsie was president of the Woollahra electoral conference of the United Australia Party, but failed to win pre-selection for the 1937 by-election. He was a council-member of the Royal Agricultural Society of New South Wales. In his spare time he enjoyed coursing, motoring and surfing, but liked best week-end cruising in his yacht, *Scot Free*.

Cramsie died on 26 November 1944 at his Edgecliff residence and was buried with Presbyterian forms in Waverley cemetery. He was survived by a son and two daughters, to whom he left his estate, valued for probate at £7166.

Agr Gazette (NSW), May 1924; *Agr Bureau Record*, 18 Apr 1934; *SMH,* 12 Apr 1919, 18 June 1924, 9, 23 Apr, 10 Nov 1925, 10 Nov 1931, 12 July 1932, 10 Jan 1933, 19 Mar, 8 Dec 1934, 2 Nov 1936, 29 May 1937, 22 Sept, 17 Nov 1938, 9 May 1939, 27 Nov 1944; E. A. Beever, A history of the Australian meat export trade, 1865-1939 (Ph.D. thesis, Univ Melb, 1968); information from Mr A. W. Cameron, Kalanga, Matheson, NSW.   JOHN ATCHISON

CRAN, ROBERT (1821-1894), JOHN (1848-1935), JAMES (1850-1922) and ROBERT (1856-1940) were sugar manufacturers in central Queensland. Robert senior was born on 6 August 1821 at Towie, Aberdeenshire, Scotland, son of John Cran, farmer, and his wife Jean, née Petrie. He married Elspeth Winks at Aberdeen in 1847 and John, the eldest of their nine children, was born there on 14 January 1848. The family migrated to Queensland in 1849.

Cran was a stockman at the Albert River in 1850. He was at Lagoon station, Myall Creek, in 1856 and next year was employed by Robert Tooth [q.v.6] on Jondaryan station. He was at Pikedale, near Warwick, as a superintendent in 1861, and became manager of Tooth's boiling-down works and abattoir on his property at Yengarie near Maryborough in 1865. It soon became a beef extract plant and Cran became a partner with Tooth and others in a firm known as Tooth & Cran. John, Robert junior and other members of the family became sub-managers in the Yengarie plant which soon won a sizeable export trade.

When sugar-growing started round Maryborough in the mid-1860s, the beef extract plant was adapted by experiment to sugar refining, thereby avoiding the consequences of increasing cattle prices. Yengarie superseded most of the pioneer sugar-makers, taking the juice from local crushing mills through a network of pipes. It was probably one of the first plants in the world to apply to cane the double carbonation process, used hitherto only for beet sugar.

When two of the Tooth family withdrew in March 1872, the firm became Robert Cran & Co. During 1880 it was accused of allowing excessive mortality among employed Melanesians by poor feeding, bad water, overwork and absence of proper care for the sick. Despite ten per cent mortality in 1879-80, the accusation was denied by the firm and the matter was not pursued.

When rumours reached the neighbouring town of Bundaberg that Crans were seeking other localities for investment, a leading businessman published an invitation in the *Bundaberg Star* in March 1875 for the establishment of a refinery which would help the district to change from maize to sugargrowing. John Cran and his brother Robert surveyed the district in April 1876 and were impressed by the rich volcanic soil of the Woongarra scrub. They returned next year to assess cane supplies and decided to open a plant. John Cran launched the building programme in June 1878. Financing the initial investment of about £310000, mainly from Victoria, took time and in the interim some growers unsuccessfully approached

the Colonial Sugar Refining Co. Robert Cran
senior went to England for machinery late in
1880, and in 1882 a ball hosted by the Cran
family launched the Millaquin refinery.
Within a decade it was unable to handle all
the local production; by 1887 there were five
new crushing mills, including one owned by
Cran Bros and Frederic Buss [q.v.7], and
twenty new plantations in the district.

The sugar industry underwent radical
structural changes in 1890-1915 and the
Cran properties were mortgaged to the
Queensland National Bank. Flood damage
and the financial crisis of 1893, followed by
the transition to white labour, upset the
solvency of the firm, and in 1896 the bank
foreclosed. Robert senior died of pneumonia
at Millaquin on 16 December 1894 and was
buried in Bundaberg general cemetery with
Presbyterian forms. His estate, valued for
probate at £223 540, was left in trust for his
family.

John was head of Robert Cran & Co. until
1896. In 1902 he joined Buss in launching the
Farleigh Estate Sugar Co. Apart from his
position as a director, he took little part in
management and lived in retirement. Initially prosperous, the company suffered
severely from the disruptive effects on the
industry of World War I; when it went into
voluntary liquidation in 1926, John Cran
stayed on the board of the co-operative
which succeeded it. He was a justice of
the peace in 1886-1919, an enthusiastic
Freemason, and a member of St Andrew's
Presbyterian Church, Bundaberg; but much
of his private time was devoted to local
government. Unmarried, he died in Bundaberg on 24 September 1935, was buried in
Bundaberg general cemetery and left an
estate valued for probate at £52 489.

James was born at the Albert River on 28
July 1850 and joined his father in Yengarie
while young. On 21 June 1876 at Tamworth,
New South Wales, he married Jane Irving;
they had five children. When the others went
to Millaquin, he stayed to manage Yengarie
and, when it finally closed down, he began
sugar-planting at Duncraggan near Bundaberg as a partner in Buss, Williams &
Cran. He was later on a plantation called
Mon Repos. He died at Maryborough of
bronchitis on 22 April 1922 and was buried in
Maryborough cemetery. He was widowed
about three years before his death and his
estate, valued for probate at £3922, was left
to his unmarried daughter.

Robert junior was born at Lagoon station,
Myall Creek, on 4 May 1856. Employed initially as a clerk by the Commercial Banking
Co. of Sydney, he left soon to join the family
enterprise and managed Yengarie for a time.
When it was lost he mustered sufficient
capital to move to Sydney in 1903 and set up

as a sharebroker. On 6 April 1887 at Brisbane, he had married Annie Mary, daughter
of Sir Charles Lilley [q.v.5]. Another
brother, Alexander, married her sister.
When Robert died on 16 December 1940, he
left a well-established business which still
survives and an estate valued for probate at
£39 992.

Inclined to be dour, the Crans were not
prominent public figures but were involved
in local government. John, James and
Alexander were members of the Woongarra
Divisional Board – John was a member in
1885-96 and chairman in 1886-87 and 1890-
94; his brothers were members in 1902.
James was a member of the Tinana Shire
Council in 1912-15 and chaired it in 1916-17.
All the principal members of the family
served on the Antigua Divisional Board in
1880-99.

J. Y. Walker, *The history of Bundaberg* (Brisb,
1890); N. Bartley, *Opals and agates* (Brisb, 1892); G.
E. Loyau, *The history of Maryborough* ... (Brisb,
1897); H. Turner, *Rural life in sunny Queensland*
(Bundaberg, 1955); C. T. Wood, *Sugar country*
(Brisb, 1965); Farleigh Co-operative Sugar Milling
Assn Ltd, *Golden Jubilee*, 1926-76 (Mackay, 1976);
J. Nolan, *Bundaberg history and people* (Brisb,
1978); *V&P* (LA Qld), 1880, 1, 71 *and* 2, 409; *Aust
Sugar J*, 6 Jan 1922, 8 July 1926, 10 Oct 1935, Sept
1975; *A'sian Insurance and Banking Record*, 21 Jan
1941; *Bundaberg Star*, 17, 19 Mar 1875; *Bundaberg
Reporter*, 6 Mar 1888; *Brisbane Courier*, 19 Dec
1894.
                                        J. G. NOLAN

CRAVEN, RICHARD (1845-1899), mining
entrepreneur, was born on 1 June 1845 at
Preston, Lancashire, England, son of
Thomas Craven, joiner, and his wife Ann,
née Townson. Trained as a millwright with
Colin, Mather and Platt, textile manufacturers at Salford, Craven migrated at the
age of 20 and settled at Maryborough in
Queensland. In 1866 he began prospecting at
Crocodile Creek, and during the next three
decades worked on nearly every major
goldfield in Queensland. He arrived at
Gympie three weeks after its discovery in
1867, and staked a profitable claim at
White's Gully. Over the next four years, he
prospected at Ridley's Rush, Cape River, the
Gilbert, Peak Downs, Normanby, Broughton, and on the alluvial field at Mount Ley-
shon where he met Mosman [q.v.5], Clarke
and Fraser only days before they discovered
Charters Towers.

By March 1872 Craven had moved there
and pegged the Mexican, and subsequently
took up the No. 2 St Patrick and the St
Patrick block, which yielded £250 000
worth of gold. Having established the Enterprise crushing mill, he rapidly acquired

other claims, including the No.2 Queen and Kelly's Queen block after the holders departed for the Palmer rush. Charters Towers' fortunes fluctuated until Craven discovered the Brilliant lodes. He supposed that the Day Dawn and Queen lines of reef intersected, and after leasing twenty-five acres (10 ha) and raising £12 000 to prove his theory spent three years sinking a shaft to 700 feet (213 m) with no result. Many derided his efforts until in 1889 a small drive some 200 feet (60 m) underground yielded the field's richest ore body. Craven announced his success to the world at a champagne celebration. His theory was actually erroneous as the Brilliant proved to be an extension of the Day Dawn line.

The fortunes of both Craven and Charters Towers were secured. The Brilliant Gold Mining Co. Ltd, of which he was chairman and major shareholder, and the Brilliant and St George United Gold Mining Co. Ltd, which he also controlled, thereafter invested heavily in many claims. His name soon carried unusual weight among Sydney and London mining investors, and his investments widened to include a sawmill, a cyanide works and a joinery. He founded and endowed the local hospital and sponsored the Charters Towers Jockey Club. In 1891, he moved to Waverley, Sydney, with his wife Kate, née Cummins, whom he had married with Presbyterian forms in Sydney on 30 June 1875, and their six sons and four daughters. He became a director of Burns [q.v.7], Philp [q.v.] & Co., and one of Australia's best-known horse-racing identities.

Despite substantial investments Craven's famous stud at Clarendon produced few winners, the most notable being Woodlark which finished third in both the Australian Jockey Club Metropolitan Stakes and Victoria Racing Club Derby in 1898. He died at his home, Preston, on 17 January 1899 of cirrhosis of the liver and was buried in Waverley cemetery with Roman Catholic rites. Craven's dogged persistence with his 'junction' theory and his enterprising investments in Charters Towers not only crowned his personal success, but more importantly gave impetus to gold-mining in North Queensland by restoring the town's fortunes. His estate was sworn for probate in Queensland at £62 933 and £54 838 in New South Wales.

W. F. Morrison, *The Aldine history of Queensland*, 2 (Syd, 1888); L. W. Marsland, *The Charters Towers gold mines* (Lond, 1892); Alcazar Press, *Queensland, 1900* (Brisb, nd); R. L. Jack, *Northmost Australia*, 1-2 (Lond, 1921); *Northern Mining Register*, Christmas no, 1891; *SMH*, 18 Jan 1899.

K. H. KENNEDY

CRAWFORD, ALEXANDER (1857-1935), agriculturist, was born on 5 May 1857 in Belfast, son of James Wright Crawford, starch manufacturer, and his wife Madge, née Mathews. His parents, devout Methodists, sent him to near-by Queen's College and then to the Albert Agricultural College, Glasnevin, Dublin.

Hoping that the climate would benefit his health, Crawford migrated to Australia, probably visiting Queensland first but later prospecting for gold, surveying possible routes through Western Australia for the transcontinental railway, and for a time managing a butter factory at Ballan, Victoria. In November 1881 he became part-owner of Moorarrie, a sheep run inland from Geraldton, Western Australia, but poor prospects induced him to move to Perth next year. On 3 March 1885 at Linton, Victoria, he married his cousin Eliza Jane Mathews. A trip home to Ireland was extended to include the dairying districts of Norway, Sweden and Denmark and nearly a year in North America visiting agricultural colleges. By this time Crawford claimed that he had 'given a good deal of attention to the dairying, read it up theoretically, and knew it practically'.

In 1888, as part of the Victorian government's programme to encourage the butter export industry, Crawford was appointed manager of a travelling dairy. For the next two to three years he visited by rail thirty-eight centres in Victoria giving practical demonstrations and lectures on butter and cheese production; hygienic operation of the cream separator was a feature. He also wrote more than a dozen articles on topics ranging from cool-chambers for transporting butter to breeds of dairy cattle.

In April 1891 Crawford became manager of the newly founded Victorian Creamery and Butter Co.; farmers were encouraged to establish creameries to supply cream for the manufacture of butter of a uniformly high quality. However the company, one of a group owned by Bartram & Sons, went out of business in December 1895.

By then Crawford had gone to Western Australia, and in 1896 he joined the Bureau of Agriculture in Perth. He rose to acting director of agriculture in 1903 and acting under-secretary in 1905 when a director was appointed. His career may have been adversely affected by the findings of the royal commission on the butter industry in Victoria (1905). This report alleged irregularities in the accounts of the Victorian Creamery and Butter Co. although Crawford, who appeared before the commission, claimed that he had joined the company on the understanding that he knew nothing about finance and was employed only for his practical skills. While no charges against him were laid, his reputation suffered from these reports. In 1909-19 he was chief inspector under the Rabbit and Vermin Acts. A lover of the outback, he enjoyed the trips by camel and vehicle to check the rabbit-proof fence across the State.

Crawford was a councillor of the Royal Agricultural Society of Western Australia in 1899 and president in 1916. An active Wesleyan layman, he is commemorated by a plaque in Wesley Church, William Street, Perth. He was a foundation member in 1905 of the Claremont Yacht Club and commodore in 1908-09.

Crawford's first wife had died in November 1891 leaving no issue. On 5 April 1893 at Dandenong, Victoria, he married her sister Martha Linton Mathews; she died of tuberculosis in Albany, Western Australia, in 1921 leaving two sons and a daughter. On 4 July 1923 at South Perth he married a 28-year-old widow Gladys Greenham, née Chatham. Crawford died at South Perth on 8 November 1935 and was buried in Karrakatta cemetery. His wife, their daughter and the children of his second marriage survived him.

J. Smith (ed), *Cyclopedia of Victoria*, 1 (Melb, 1903); Roy Com on the butter industry, *PP* (Vic), 1905, 2 (10); Dept of Agr (Vic), *Bulletin*, 1888-91, no 1-14; M. Morgan, Biog outline of A. Crawford, *and* Moorarrie correspondence (LaTL).   L. LOMAS

CRAWFORD, EMMA (1864?-1939), teacher and mother superior, was born probably at Woolwich, Kent, England, daughter of Lieutenant William Crawford, adjutant of the coastal brigade of artillery, and his wife Sarah, née Gregg. Well-educated and probably with some teaching experience, she came to Queensland shortly before her admission to the Anglican Society of the Sacred Advent in September 1896. Its founder, Sister Caroline, worked among the poor and neglected in Brisbane as she had in England; at the time of Emma Crawford's profession on 28 December 1897 the society had accepted Bishop Webber's [q.v.] invitation to manage an orphanage and a 'rescue' home for women and babies.

Under the provisions of the State Education Act of 1875, religious instruction was banned in Queensland state schools. To satisfy demands for Anglican teaching. Webber asked the society both to open a primary day school and to manage the Eton High School for girls. In becoming sister-in-charge of the latter (later St Margaret's) Emma Crawford made Anglican girls' schools in Queensland viable. Though she did not become superior until 1905, she was influential from the late 1890s when Mother Caroline sought money and helpers in England. After developing an industrial school for wayward girls in Brisbane, the community took charge of a school in Stanthorpe in 1909 which was later moved to Warwick and named St Catharine's.

During World War I Mother Emma accepted the invitation of Bishop Feetham [q.v.] to establish boarding schools for country girls in his diocese. St Anne's, Townsville, was opened in July 1917; St Mary's, Herberton, in 1918 and St Gabriel's, Charters Towers, in 1921. After the war she acquired All Saints Hostel, Charleville, for far-west children attending the local state school, and in 1922 she accepted responsibility for St Martin's War Memorial Hospital in Brisbane. Her last major Brisbane venture was the foundation of St Aidan's School at Corinda in February 1929. She took the society to the diocese of Rockhampton in 1932 by accepting an invitation to manage St Faith's School at Yeppoon.

When Mother Emma died of cancer on 9 March 1939, the society was working in three of five Queensland dioceses. Its schools, based on English models, formed a definite system with similar uniforms and badges, high academic standards and an insistence on trained staff. The society never had more than thirty professed sisters. Mother Emma commented ruefully in 1906 that 'responses to the call to the life of a sister are still very rare in Australia'. On her death, Bishop Feetham described her as 'the principal benefactress of this diocese'. Her most significant contribution was in moderating materialism and secularism in many aspects of Queensland life. A contemporary in the society described her as every inch a lady who could be icy if displeased, but always remained calm, even under great stress. Once, she managed to persuade Archbishop Donaldson [q.v.] to her point of view on issues on which his opinions had been equally firm.

A short history of the SSA 1892-1954 (Brisb, nd); E. C. Rowland, *The tropics for Christ* (Syd, 1960); *Courier Mail*, 10 Mar 1939; K. Rayner, The history of the Church of England in Queensland (Ph.D. thesis, Univ Qld, 1962); H. Amies, The Society of the Sacred Advent in Queensland 1892-1968, *and* A. Hayhoe, John Oliver Feetham ... (B.A. Hons theses, Univ Qld, 1968).   HELEN GREGORY

CRAWFORD, THOMAS SIMPSON (1875-1976), Presbyterian minister, politician and barrister, was born on 23 December 1875 at Bulli, New South Wales, eldest son and fifth child of James Crawford, coalminer, and his wife Ellen, née Simpson; both his parents came from Airdrie, Lanarkshire, Scotland. He left Bulli Public School at 14 and worked in the telegraph branch of the railways for some four years, then, influenced by Rev. Simpson Millar, decided to enter the Presbyterian ministry. He resumed his studies under the guidance of his ex-headmaster Joseph Bourke and a tutor in classics; later he went to Sydney Boys' High School and the Cooerwull Academy at Bowenfels, matriculating in 1897. At St Andrew's College, University of Sydney, he worked for the ministry and his degree (B.A., 1901; M.A., 1904). On 12 September 1900 at Nowra he married Hilda Victoria Eve Graham.

Ordained in November 1902, Crawford was briefly at Newcastle and Port Macquarie; he served at the Hunter Street Church, Newcastle, in 1903-05, where he implemented plans for a new church building in Watt Street (St Philip's, 1905). He was minister there until 1908, then at Berrigan in the Riverina; in 1909 he moved to a mission station at Campsie, a growing Sydney suburb.

Crawford was deeply concerned with the conditions of industrial workers and believed that the Political Labor League of New South Wales 'placed humanity above property'. In April 1910 he was narrowly defeated for the Federal seat of Lang. However, 'the fighting parson' campaigned vigorously and, 'helped by an enthusiastic band of women workers', was elected to the New South Wales Legislative Assembly for Marrickville in 1913 — he was on the party's executive in 1911 and 1913. He resigned from the Presbyterian ministry on 13 October 1914. A supporter of conscription, he joined the Nationalists and was defeated in the 1917 elections.

While in parliament Crawford had studied law and was admitted to the Bar on 29 August 1912. He set up in practice and in October 1917 he was appointed crown prosecutor for the western district, extending from Parramatta to Bourke. He published a book on practice, *Proofs in criminal cases* (1922), which was later updated. In 1924 he transferred to the southern and Hunter district, and in 1930 to the metropolitan district. He was appointed a K.C. in 1935 and was senior crown prosecutor in 1940-47.

Crawford remained active in retirement — he prosecuted for the Commonwealth in the Supreme Court of the Australian Capital Territory and was briefed in a royal commission in Sydney. In August 1948 he conducted an inquiry in Nauru into allegations of the excessive use of force by special guards at the gaol after a riot by forty-nine Chinese. On 25 November he was admitted as a barrister and solicitor of the Central Court of Nauru in order to prosecute in a murder trial. Next October he was appointed a judicial commissioner in the Solomon Islands during the absence of the chief magistrate.

Complete retirement was forced on Crawford by failing sight and hearing. He lived at the Newcastle suburb of Mayfield and was interested in bowls: the Soldiers Point Bowling Club, which he helped to found, celebrated Crawford's century by naming its main green after him in 1975. Predeceased by his wife in 1938 and by his son Carlyle Graham, a surgeon, he died in a Newcastle hospital on 20 April 1976 and was cremated. He was an uncle of Sir John Crawford and Professor R. M. Crawford.

C. A. White, *The challenge of the years* (Syd, 1951); *PP* (Cwlth), 1950-51, 2, 551; *Bowls in New South Wales,* Feb 1976; *Aust Worker,* 18 Aug, 1, 29 Sept 1910; *Illawarra Mercury,* 6 Dec 1963; *Newcastle Sun,* 22 Dec 1975; *SMH,* 23 Dec 1975, 21 Apr 1976; family papers (held by Mrs P. Everett, Lindfield, NSW).
                                           L. G. TANNER

CRAWFORD, THOMAS WILLIAM (1865-1948), sugar-grower and politician, was born on 31 January 1865 at East Collingwood, Melbourne, son of Thomas Crawford, an Irish storekeeper, and his English wife Helen, née Lawson. After spending his childhood on the farm which his father had acquired in Gippsland, Crawford served a printing apprenticeship with the *Gippsland Mercury*. He then spent two years with the Melbourne *Federal Australasian* and in about 1886 moved to Brisbane to work for the *Courier*. A unionist, he was elected permanent secretary of the Queensland Typographical Association in March 1889, although he appears not to have accepted the office; he became president in 1892 and was a delegate to the Brisbane District Council of the Australian Labour Federation in 1889-92.

The land, however, attracted Crawford's chief interest and in 1895, in association with William, Edward, George and Alfred Muntz whose sister Emily he had married on 17 September 1886 at the Bowen Hills Wesleyan parsonage, he obtained the 400-acre (160 ha) Brie-Brie estate in the Mossman district. He was to develop the property into one of the most successful cane-growing undertakings in Queensland. Crawford went to the area in anticipation of the erection of the Mossman Central Mill, one of the mills proposed under the 1893 Sugar Works Guarantee Act; on the formation of the Mossman Central Mill Co. Ltd he was elected to the directorate and was later chairman. He took an active part in the 1907 conference of sugar representatives convened by the Townsville Chamber of Commerce to discuss the replacement of Melanesian by white labour, and became vice-president of the subsequent Queensland Sugar Producers' Association. He was president in 1909-43, then again vice-president until 1945.

Although Crawford was a member of the Douglas Shire Council, public life did not hold great appeal for him and it was only after pressing requests from sugar-growers that he stood, unsuccessfully, as a Liberal candidate for Herbert in the Federal elections of 1910. He lost a bid for the Senate in 1914 but was elected a Nationalist senator in 1917 and held the seat until his retirement in June 1947. A member of the Standing Committee of Public Accounts in 1918-20, he was honorary minister in the Bruce [q.v.7]-Page [q.v.] government of 1923-28 and acting minister for trade and customs for much of this time. Described as a 'keen debater with a capacity for lucid and logical expression' Crawford spoke as an acknowledged authority on sugar matters. Early in his parliamentary career he was a strong advocate for a separate State to encompass the Australian tropical zone. Survived by his wife, four daughters and three sons, he died on 9 June 1948 at Indooroopilly, and was cremated. He left an estate valued at £21 066 for probate in Victoria and at £39 935 in Queensland. Two of his sons served in the Australian Imperial Force, the elder, William Hugh, receiving the Military Medal for bravery in the field.

A'sian Typographical J, Mar, Apr, July 1889, Jan, June, Dec 1890, June 1891, Feb 1892; *Aust Sugar J*, Nov 1975; *Brisbane Courier*, 20 July 1914; *Punch* (Melb), 19 Aug 1920; *Queenslander*, 19 Sept 1929.
                                    ANN G. SMITH

CREAL, ROSE ANN (1865-1921), nurse, was born on 3 November 1865 at Young, New South Wales, daughter of John Creal, miner, and his wife Ann, née Brady, both of whom were Irish-born. Her childhood was spent in the gold-mining districts of Young and Parkes. She was educated at home by her father and when 16 began work in a small hospital at Parkes. Recognizing the quality of her young assistant, the matron there arranged for her to be taken on as a probationer at Sydney Hospital and by about 1891 Rose Creal was head nurse of a ward.

When the hospital's matron, E. J. Gould [q.v.], resigned in 1898 Senior Sister Creal was made acting matron. Her appointment was confirmed in February 1899 and later that year she became a founding member and councillor of the Trained Nurses' As-

sociation of New South Wales. According to some of her nurses, she was a strict disciplinarian but did her utmost to promote the welfare of those under her care, thereby winning both respect and admiration. She was a large, handsome woman of extraordinary strength and could not understand why some of her staff found their twelve-hour shifts exhausting.

Before World War I Matron Creal was a member of the Australian Army Nursing Service Reserve, and in October 1914 she was appointed principal matron of the 2nd Military District (New South Wales), while remaining matron of Sydney Hospital. Her main military duty was the selection of nurses for active service, a role she fulfilled until 14 August 1916 when she too enlisted in the A.A.N.S., Australian Imperial Force. Embarking on the hospital ship, *Karoola*, on 19 August, she assumed duty on 23 September as matron of the 14th Australian General Hospital at Abbassia, Egypt. The casualties of the Australian Light Horse were treated almost exclusively there, and in November 1916 numbered about 570. Following heavy fighting at Magdhaba and Rafa the numbers rose to over 900 and by May 1917, after the battle of Gaza, to 1140. These increases placed great strains on the nursing staff and in her report for September 1917 Matron Creal paid tribute to their 'unselfish devotion to duty' after the first battle of Gaza when some nurses were on duty for eighteen hours at a time.

Conditions at Abbassia were primitive: for instance, primus stoves were the only means of obtaining boiling water for sterilization. In February 1918 the hospital moved to Port Said; in both locations the staff did their best to provide first-rate nursing care in an atmosphere as relaxed as military discipline would permit. H. S. Gullett [q.v.], the official historian, praised 'the service of the splendid band of Australian nursing sisters who, under the inspiration of . . . Miss Rose Creal . . . greeted the battered men from the front as they reached hospital and nursed them back to strength, or softened the close of their soldier-life'. 'No womanhood', he wrote, 'has ever presented a richer association of feminine tenderness and sheer capacity'.

For her services in Egypt Matron Creal was awarded the Royal Red Cross (1st Class) in the New Year honours of 1919. She returned to Australia in January 1920 and was demobilized in May; in April she had resumed her position as matron of Sydney Hospital. Next year, following an attack of appendicitis, she died on 7 August. One obituary described her as 'sympathetic, yet firm, and thoroughly capable and conscientious'. She was accorded a military funeral, her nurse's cap lying on the flag-draped gun-carriage. Hundreds of people had to be turned away from the memorial service in St James Anglican Church, and the funeral procession to Waverley cemetery was one of the most impressive seen in Sydney. The Rose Creal Medal, established in her honour, is the highest award made by Sydney Hospital to students of the Lucy Osburn [q.v.5] School of Nursing.

H. S. Gullett, *The A.I.F. in Sinai and Palestine* (Syd, 1923); A. G. Butler (ed), *Official history of the Australian Army Medical Services ... 1914-18*,3 (Canb, 1943); I. Brodsky, *Sydney's nurse crusaders* (Syd, 1968); *London Gazette*, 1 Jan 1919; *T&CJ*, 22 Jan 1919; *SMH*, 8, 10, 12 Aug 1921; *Sydney Mail*, 17 Aug 1921; *Aust National Review*, 22 Aug 1921; *Western Champion* (Parkes), Aug 1921; War diary of the 14th Australian General Hospital, A.I.F. (AWM).　　　　　　　FREDA MACDONNELL

CREED, MARIE LOUISE; *see* MACK

CREER, REGINALD CHARLES (FERRERS) (1881-1958), and HERBERT VICTOR (1881-1969), naval officers, were born on 21 September 1881 at Watsons Bay, Sydney, twin sons of Joseph Creer, a Manx mariner, and his second wife Sarah Needham, née Ferrers, a South Australian. They were educated at Sydney Boys' High School and in 1898 became cadets in the New South Wales Naval Brigade.

In August 1900 as a sub-lieutenant Reginald sailed with the New South Wales naval contingent to the China Field Force. In January 1902 he went to the South African War as a captain with the 3rd Battalion Australian Commonwealth Horse, but saw no action. His transfer to the Commonwealth Naval Forces was back-dated to 1 January 1901.

In 1899 Herbert had sailed as ship's boy in the *Balmore*. He claimed to have served in the South African War in 1900-02. Between May 1902 and August 1905 he made three voyages in the square-rigged *Mount Stewart*. On 30 December 1907 at Christ Church, North Sydney, he married 36-year-old Veronique Lilian Violet Greville (d. 1956), daughter of the second Baron Greville.

Between 1907 and 1911 the Creers obtained their mates' and masters' certificates for foreign-going steamships. Late in 1911 as sub-lieutenants they were among the first to join the Royal Australian Navy and a year later were made lieutenants.

In January 1914 Reginald joined the light cruiser H.M.A.S. *Pioneer*. After patrolling the north-west coast of Australia, he sailed for East Africa via the Cocos Islands, where he acquired the beached *Emden's* crest and

her captain's bridge table. He led a landing party in the capture of Bombamyo on 15 August 1916. From October that year to June 1917 he served in the *Brisbane* in the Mediterranean and the Indian Ocean. On 15 June at Carlton, Melbourne, he married Eulalie Henty, granddaughter of Stephen George Henty [q.v.1]. In July he transferred to the *Una*, and patrolled German colonial waters north of Australia. From December 1918 he was stationed at *Penguin*, the Sydney depot.

Herbert served in the *Melbourne* from August 1914 until April 1918 on patrol and convoy duty in the Indian and Atlantic oceans, and from 1916 with the Grand Fleet in the North Sea. In mid-1918 he joined the *Brisbane*. He was appointed to the first of his six commands, in the *Success*, on 19 July 1920. Both brothers were promoted lieutenant-commander late in 1920. Reginald's first command was the destroyer *Swordsman*, from 21 July 1921. He held five commands including the *Parramatta* (coinciding with Herbert's command of the *Yarra* for nearly four months) and the boys' training ship *Tingira* from December 1922 until November 1925. Herbert commanded the *Anzac* from December 1922 until January 1925. The twins retired as commanders in 1926 and contemplated operating a sea-transport business in the islands.

In 1927 Reginald was divorced, and his wife later changed her name to Henty-Creer and took her children to England. On 27 August that year at Darling Point, Sydney, he married Kathleen Marianne Silver. He was master of merchant ships off the China coast. In February 1938 he was commanding the *Asian* when she was captured by the Japanese and held for eleven days.

Meanwhile Herbert commanded a private yacht in Britain for some years. In 1938-39 he was master of the *Gemlock*, chartered to a Japanese company, and passed intelligence to the Royal Navy until he beached his ship in a blizzard; the officers reached the Manchurian coast in an open boat and were found by police; the British ambassador secured their release. In 1940 the twins joined the Royal Navy. Reginald in 1940-41 was senior officer in command of the gunboat flotilla, China Station, Hong Kong, sunk in the Japanese attack in December 1941. He was a prisoner of war from 21 January 1942 in Hong Kong Camp 'N' at Sham Shui Po until 19 September 1945, when he returned to Sydney. Herbert was senior naval officer at Shanghai and commanded a gunboat flotilla. He became naval officer-in-charge at Singapore, and supervised the embarkation of the Australian nurses in the ill-fated *Vyner Brooke*. Until his discharge on 31 March 1946 Herbert held several posts: naval officer-in-charge Addu Atoll in 1942, and in Ceylon as commandant, Duty Naval Camp, Diyatalawa, in 1942-44, resident naval officer at Jaffna in 1944-45 and officer-in-charge Ketti Camp in 1945-46. He returned to Sydney in H.M.S. *Indefatigable* in June and lived at the Imperial Service Club.

Reginald died on 29 June 1958 at the War Veterans' Home, Narrabeen, and was buried with Anglican rites in Northern Suburbs cemetery. He was survived by his second wife and two daughters of his first marriage. His son, Lieutenant Henty Henty-Creer, died commanding his midget submarine X5 after the attack on the German battleship *Tirpitz* in Altafjord, Norway, in 1943.

In October 1951 Herbert became master of the *Vila Star*. On 12 June 1957 at St Stephen's Church, Sydney, he married a divorcee Lynda Mary Martin, née Williamson. She died two months later. On 14 July 1960 he married a widow Bonita Allen, née Mackellaig. He died on 5 August 1969 at the War Veterans' Home, Narrabeen, and was cremated with Anglican rites. He was survived by a son of his first marriage.

As junior officers with identical looks and mannerisms, the Creer twins often stood in for each other at social functions, where their charm and gentlemanly manners made them very popular with the ladies. They were excellent seamen, good 'ship handlers' and highly regarded by their senior officers.

Aust Defence Dept, *Official records of the Australian military contingents to the war in South Africa*, P. L. Murray ed (Melb, 1911); A. W. Jose, *The Royal Australian Navy 1914-1918* (Syd, 1928); H. J. Feakes, *White ensign — southern cross* (Syd, 1951); A. S. Walker, *Middle East and Far East* (Canb, 1953); S. W. Kirby et al, *The war against Japan*, 1 (Lond, 1957); S. W. Roskill, *The war at sea, 1939-1945*, 1, 3, Lond, 1954, 1961); J. J. Atkinson, *Australian contingents to the China Field Force 1900-1901* (Syd, 1976); *London Gazette*, 10 Feb 1948, supp; *Naval Hist Review*, Dec 1972, 35, Mar 1976, 23; *Despatch*, Aug 1976; *The Times*, 21 Feb 1938, 4, 6 Mar 1939; *Sun* (Syd), 9 June 1946; Log, HMAS *Pioneer* (AWM); family information.

JEAN P. FIELDING

CRESWELL, JOHN (1858-1909), company secretary, was born on 8 December 1858 at Woodville, South Australia, son of John Thomas Creswell, pioneer merchant and shipping agent, and his wife Mary Ann, née Smith. Educated at the Collegiate School of St Peter, at 16 he joined the office of F. S. C. Driffield, local manager of the National Fire and Marine Insurance Co. of New Zealand.

Creswell played for and was secretary of the South Park Football Club in 1876-79, was a founder and early secretary of the South Australian Football Association, and was a representative in intercolonial matches. He played cricket for Norwood and was secretary of the Kensington and Norwood Cricketing Association in 1881-83. A 'fine shot', he was a poultry fancier and a bowls player, with his own private green. He was an authority on greyhounds and his dogs won many major coursing events; for ten years from 1895 he managed the company that built and controlled the racing arena at Plympton. On 4 June 1884 he had married Elizabeth Maria Kingsborough at Kent Town.

As a sports administrator Creswell became 'a household name' in South Australia. In 1883-1909 he was secretary of the South Australian Cricketing Association and, 'by foresight, judgement and capacity', greatly raised its status. This ability was recognized in 1892 with his election as secretary to the first, controversial Australasian Cricket Council.

Sometimes referred to as 'the busiest man in Adelaide', in 1889 Creswell had succeeded Driffield as manager of the insurance company and secretary of the Chamber of Commerce. He was the colony's representative on the English Board of Trade, and secretary to the Vinegrowers' Association, the Eastern and African Cool Storage Co. and the Farmers' Distress Fund. Although 'bluff and incisive', this 'prince of showmen' had a great capacity to inspire and enthuse and as secretary from 1900 of the Royal Agricultural and Horticultural Society of South Australia he altered its condition 'from one of debt to one of deposits'.

From 1892 until his death Creswell served on his old school's board of governors and in 1900-09 was a vigorous president of its Old Collegians' Association, a position he valued highly. In 1893 he was an unsuccessful independent candidate for the Legislative Council. Shortly after returning from one of his frequent trips to New Zealand, Creswell died of hypertensive cerebro-vascular disease at Unley on 24 March 1909. He was survived by his wife, four daughters and a son and was buried in Payneham cemetery. His estate was sworn for probate at £4645. The Creswell memorial scholarship at his old school recalls his influence and his peers' esteem, as do the Creswell scholarships for studies in commerce at the University of Adelaide. The City Council named the Creswell Park for him and the John Creswell Stand at the Adelaide Oval honours his contribution to cricket.

J. J. Pascoe (ed), *History of Adelaide and vicinity* (Adel, 1901); A. G. Price, *The Collegiate School of St Peter, 1847-1947* (Adel, 1947); S. Downer, *100 not out* (Adel, 1972); SA Cricket Assn, *Report*, 1909; *St Peter's College Mag*, May 1909; *Observer* (Adel), 5

Dec 1896; *Register* (Adel), 25 Mar 1909; St Peter's College Archives (Adel).   JOHN A. DALY

CRESWELL, SIR WILLIAM ROOKE (1852-1933), vice admiral, was born on 20 July 1852 at Gibraltar, son of Edmund Creswell, the colony's deputy-postmaster-general, and his wife Margaret Mary Ward, née Fraser. Educated at Aitken's Private School, Gibraltar, and Eastman's Naval Academy, Southsea, England, he entered the Royal Navy's training ship *Britannia* as a cadet in December 1865. Promoted midshipman in May 1867 he joined H.M.S. *Phoebe;* two of his four years on it were spent on a world training cruise, including Australia late in 1869.

Creswell's next posting was to H.M.S. *Minotaur,* flagship of the Channel Fleet. He was promoted sub-lieutenant in 1871 and later transferred to the *Thalia* on the China Station. He also served in the gunboat *Midge* and on 16 September 1873, during a skirmish with pirates on the Malay coast, was shot in the hip. However, he remained at his post and for his gallantry was specially promoted lieutenant. Invalided home, on recovery he studied at the Royal Naval College, Greenwich. His next sea-going appointments were with the *Topaze,* the *Undaunted*, flagship of the East Indian Station, and from 1877 the *London,* a depot ship at Zanzibar, East Africa. Here the navy was suppressing the slave-trade and Creswell, who quickly became an interpreter in Swahili, commanded a flotilla until fever invalided him. The foreign minister Lord Salisbury thanked him for his services at Zanzibar.

On resuming duty in April 1878 Creswell took a torpedo course on the *Vernon,* then commanded the *Lion,* a training ship at Devonport. Disappointed at the slowness and uncertainty of promotion within the Royal Navy, he retired on 6 September 1878. Next year, hoping to become a pastoralist, he migrated to Australia with his brother Charles, and until 1885 pioneered in the Northern Territory, exploring and cattle-droving. Despite his fine physique and determination he never came to terms with the outback. In 1885 while visiting Adelaide, he met an old shipmate, Commander John Walcot, naval commandant of the South Australian Defence Forces, who offered him an appointment as a lieut-commander. Creswell took up duty on 12 October as first lieutenant of the cruiser H.M.C.S. *Protector,* the only ship in the colony's defence force.

In 1886 Creswell began speaking out on the need for adequate Australian naval forces to supplement the Royal Navy squadron based at Sydney. In the *South Australian Register* in 1886 he argued that it would be better to develop local forces instead of subsidizing the British squadron. Though such views had been raised earlier by Rear Admiral (Sir) George Tryon [q.v.6], Creswell's articles stimulated much debate. On 29 December 1888, at St Jude's Anglican Church, Port Elliot, he married Adelaide Elizabeth, daughter of R. I. Stow [q.v.6].

Five years later, in the rank of commander, he succeeded Walcot as naval commandant. He was promoted captain in June 1895 and appointed C.M.G. in 1897. That year one of his reports was taken to the colonial conference by the South Australian premier. It recommended enlisting Australians in the Royal Navy and a Royal Naval Reserve in Australia for British squadrons east of Suez. The conference rejected these proposals and Creswell later abandoned them; in 1899, at a conference of Australian naval officers in Melbourne, he recommended instead the raising of an Australian force.

Creswell was appointed commandant of the Queensland Naval Forces on 1 May 1900. The *Protector* was offered to the British government on the outbreak of the Boxer Rebellion, and Creswell was released to take command of his old ship; he served from August 1900 to January 1901, impressing the commander-in-chief of the China Fleet, under whose command the ship carried out survey and dispatch work. In September Creswell, responsible to the minister for defence in the newly formed Federal government, reported on 'the best method of employing Australian seamen in the defence of commerce and ports'. He urged that Australia establish her own naval defence gradually, beginning with one modern warship, manned by Australians. However, the Colonial Conference of 1902 resulted in a naval agreement which provided for a financial subsidy and the acceptance of Australians for service as sailors (but not officers) in Royal Navy ships on the Australian Station. The Admiralty continued to insist on a free hand strategically, and on the restriction of colonial naval activity to local defence.

Parliamentary debate on this agreement showed that Creswell was not alone in wanting an Australian navy. He was being looked upon as the nation's chief spokesman on naval matters, and the government appointed him on 25 February 1904 to a newly created position of naval officer commanding the Commonwealth Naval Forces. This was additional to his duties as naval commandant in Queensland and, after 20 October 1904, in Victoria. In December he became director of naval forces, pending a board of administration, and in January 1905 he was made a member of the Council of Defence and of the Australian Naval Board, while remaining naval commandant in Victoria. Through frequent changes of defence ministers, Creswell consistently pressured and preached for new ships and increased manpower for the Commonwealth Naval Forces; he was indefatigable and in line with Australian national sentiment. He believed that adequate Australian naval forces were needed to open careers in which Australians could render that personal service necessary for the country to contribute to Empire naval strategy.

In 1906 Creswell urged in his annual report the creation of a torpedo and destroyer force. That year he was sent to England to study naval developments and especially to look into the destroyer question. He found himself *persona non grata* at Whitehall which considered that agitation for an Australian navy was largely due to personal self-interest. Creswell's proposed Australian navy was dismissed as having 'no strategical justification'. In his history of the navy in Australia Rear Admiral H. J. Feakes [q.v.] remarked that 'to one of Creswell's orthodox service upbringing and temperament the rejection by the Admiralty of both himself and all his works was the unkindest cut of all'.

Back home, supported by naval commandants in all the States, Creswell continued to press for a local naval force. Prime Minister Deakin [q.v.] accepted these views but in February 1907 the British naval commander, Vice Admiral Sir Wilmot Fawkes, urged him to abandon the destroyer scheme. Creswell wrote a comprehensive memorandum for Deakin to take to that year's Colonial Conference but his views were not acted upon. He followed up with memoranda to the minister for defence T. T. Ewing [q.v.] on destroyers, submarines and changes in the world naval situation. In October Deakin sent a message to the Admiralty proposing that Australia should provide a thousand seamen and purchase submarines or destroyers.

In a report presented in 1908 Creswell opposed the acquisition of submarines. He declared that 'the excellence or otherwise of a service rests first and last with the Legislature, who can have any service they desire'. And he added: 'Criticism of a Government proposal by a Government officer is of course unusual and I much regret the present occasion. There are however responsibilities impossible to disregard'. Later that year an Admiralty memorandum was issued, detailing a scheme for the acquisition by Australia of destroyers and submarines but nothing came of this. Creswell's patience was at its limit but on 5 February 1909 the

Fisher [q.v.] government decided to order three destroyers.

The 1909 Imperial Defence Conference, alarmed by the rapid increase of German naval power, recommended the acquisition of one battle cruiser, three unarmoured cruisers, six destroyers and three submarines. Creswell had never aimed so high, and the proposal adopted was, therefore, not written by the one man who had so persistently advocated an Australian navy. The proposal came from the Admiralty which now acknowledged Australia's needs in the existing international situation. It was pressed through in Australia by Deakin who brooked no delay in placing the order for construction of the new vessels.

Having been an advocate for a navy Creswell now found himself administering one. Following a report to the government by Admiral Sir R. Henderson, giving detailed advice on naval defence, he was promoted rear admiral and became first naval member of the Australian Naval Board on 1 March 1911. He was appointed K.C.M.G. in June. On 10 July King George V granted the title of 'Royal Australian Navy' to the Permanent Commonwealth Naval Forces and the work of building it up proceeded. Ships had to be constructed, stores and dockyard facilities taken over from the Royal Navy, recruits found and systems of manning and training worked out. Officer cadets had to be appointed and a naval college founded. In all this, Creswell worked closely with the minister, (Sir) George F. Pearce [q.v.].

The Australian Fleet assembled in Sydney on 4 October 1913 and Admiralty control of the Australian Station then ceased. That the Australian ships were ready for active service when war began in August 1914 was in large part due to Creswell's efforts, and this was the climax of his career. It was the pride of his later years that in 1914 Australia had a fleet, that it was the strongest British naval force in the Pacific, that it had effectively deterred the squadron of German cruisers in the Pacific, and that an Australian ship, H.M.A.S. *Sydney*, had destroyed the raider S.M.S. *Emden*.

Paradoxically, Creswell's influence now declined. His objective had been attained, and in greater measure than he had anticipated. The ships of the Australian Fleet were dispersed into various British squadrons and the naval board's orders for the fleet were controlled by the Admiralty. But the board remained a part of the Australian government and Creswell the government's naval adviser. This situation, so full of anomaly, might easily have been a source of conflict between the British and Australian governments; that it was not stands to the credit of those involved, including Creswell. His work during the war was concerned more with administration than with operations or strategy. He was involved in ship construction in Australia, the development of shore support and the arranging of convoys.

Creswell was active in formulating a postwar defence programme based on lessons of the war. To his mind that experience reaffirmed the importance of continued development of the Royal Australian Navy and not a return to reliance on one great Imperial navy. It also focused his attention and that of other members of the naval board on the strategic importance to Australia of the Pacific island groups near the Equator occupied by Japan. The naval board frequently urged the Australian government to counter Japanese claims to permanent occupation. There was substantial evidence in the closing years of his career that Creswell was acutely aware of the growing divergence of strategic priorities between Australia and Great Britian.

Creswell was appointed K.B.E. in 1919; he relinquished office on 14 August, was formally transferred to the retired list on 27 November, and was promoted vice admiral in September 1922. In retirement he engaged in farming at Silvan, near Melbourne, and kept up his interest in public affairs. Survived by his wife and three of their six children (two sons had been killed in action) he died on 20 April 1933 at Armadale, and was buried in Brighton cemetery after a state funeral.

Creswell combined a keen sense of humour with breadth of outlook, an appreciation of issues other than naval matters, an ability to get on well with politicians and the public, and patience with parliamentarians even when they disappointed him. It was 'a most effective combination'. Undoubtedly he played a major role in developing Australian naval policy. From the 1880s he had begun to press for Australia to take her naval defence seriously and to contribute adequately to it. And from 1901, when he accepted the principle that Australia needed her own navy, he strenuously advocated it until his hopes were realized by the decision in 1909. The rightness of this decision has not been disputed and much credit for it must go to him. His accomplishment as professional head in organizing and administering the new navy in 1909-19, with all that this responsibility involved, was no less outstanding. He has deservedly been called 'The Father of the Royal Australian Navy'.

H. J. Feakes, *White ensign – southern cross* (Syd, 1951); W. Creswell, *Close to the wind*, P. Thompson ed (Lond, 1965); *Reveille* (Syd), Dec 1938; *Punch* (Melb), 29 June 1911, 16 Oct 1918; S. D. Webster, Creswell, the Australian navalist: a career biography ... (Ph.D. thesis, Monash Univ, 1979); Deakin, and Jebb papers (NL); J. C. P. Walcot papers (ML); Chief Secretary, Correspondence 1884-99 (SAA).   ROBERT HYSLOP

CRESWICK, ALEXANDER THOMSON (1853-1939), pastoralist, was born on 28 July 1853 at The Hawthorns, Hawthorn, Victoria, second child and only son of Henry Creswick and his wife Jane, only child of Dr Alexander Thomson [q.v.2] of Geelong. Henry Creswick was one of three brothers who in 1842 had occupied the Creswick's Creek run and whose name was given to the town. In 1851-58 he was a partner in the wine and spirits business of D. S. Campbell & Co. and made a fortune from liquor during the gold rush.

Alexander was educated at Melbourne Church of England Grammar School, matriculating at the University of Melbourne in March 1872. In 1873 his father bought Liewah, and Alexander, much to his disgust, was taken away from university to manage it. The property comprised 35000 acres (14 000 ha) between the Edward and Wakool rivers in the Riverina. A run of bad seasons and rabbits troubled Creswick until 1893. In that year he owed Goldsbrough, Mort [qq.v.4,5] & Co. Ltd, much more than the value of his assets, and was threatened with foreclosure. With better seasons he improved Liewah's carrying capacity to 30000 sheep and by 1900 had £25000 at call and was out of debt.

The death of James Tyson [q.v.6] in 1898 gave Creswick the chance which was to gain him the reputation, after Sir Samuel McCaughey [q.v.5], as the largest individual sheep owner in the history of Australia. In 1900 and through the drought of 1902 he was financed by Goldsbrough's in the purchase of Tyson's Tupra-Juanbung complex near the junction of the Lachlan with the Murrumbidgee. Later he bought adjoining Tarwong for £100000 from the estate of Tyson's brother Peter. In all he acquired from the Tysons 681000 acres (275600 ha), of which 115000 acres (46000 ha) were freehold, with a carrying capacity of 5000 cattle and 85 000 sheep.

By 1924 Creswick, with Goldsbrough's backing, had bought and sold over thirty other stations and was shearing over 400000 sheep. His requirements for retention were river frontages and proximity to a railway, on which he could shift stock to his relief stations whenever drought threatened. In addition to Liewah and Tupra, stations which he retained in widely scattered districts of New South Wales included Moolpa, Mooloomoon, Gunbar, Yarrara, Copabella, Merribindinyah, Arthursleigh, Bedford Park, Combogalong, Bullagreen and Collaroy. In Victoria he had Bumbang, Bolinda Park and the Nook Stud. In Queensland he at one time owned Coongoola, Tomoo and St Helens.

A gifted horseman and only 5 ft. 5 ins. (165 cm) tall, Creswick was a very successful amateur jockey in his early years in the Riverina. After 1901 he bred and raced hundreds of horses and won over £70 000 in stakes. In 1919-30 he was the master and financial mainstay of the Melbourne Hunt Club and led the field up to his 74th year. Creswick was a director of the Bank of Victoria and of the Carlton Brewery group of companies. To Melbourne Grammar he gave Creswick House and land for tennis courts. To the Melbourne Hunt he gave land and buildings at Cranbourne.

Except on horseback, Creswick's light build was no help in the bush, and by way of protection he had grafted onto a naturally irascible nature a grumpy and forbidding manner. Despite frequent rages he was generally liked by his employees because of generous and open-hearted contrition.

On 7 July 1881 Creswick had married Helen (d. 1925), daughter of Rev. James Forbes [q.v.1]; they had three daughters and one son. Though he scorned public ostentation his house, Yarrien, with a porter's lodge, ballroom and footmen in livery, was one of the last Toorak establishments to be kept in the style which had made that suburb a byword for opulence. Survived by two daughters, he died there on 19 March 1939 and was buried in Kew cemetery. His estate was valued for probate at £190 726, but he had disposed of most of his assets during his lifetime. A portrait in hunting pink by W. B. McInnes [q.v.] is owned by a grandson, Sir Alec Creswick.

J. A. Graham, *Early Creswick* (Melb, 1942); H. H. Peck, *Memoirs of a stockman* Melb, 1942); R. B. Ronald, *The Riverina: people and properties* (Melb, 1960); H. B. Ronald, *Hounds are running* (Kilmore, Vic, 1970); *Pastoral Review*, 15 Apr 1939; *Age*, 20 Mar 1939; *Australasian*, 25 Mar 1939.

S. R. C. WOOD

CRIBB, THOMAS BRIDSON (1845-1913), JAMES CLARKE (1856-1926), and HENRY SMART (1864-1944), businessmen and politicians, were sons of Benjamin Cribb [q.v.3]. Thomas, second son of Benjamin and his wife Elizabeth, née Brideson, was born on 1 December 1845 in London and accompanied his parents to Moreton Bay aboard the *Chaseley* in 1849. James, born on 4 Oc-

tober 1856 at Ipswich, was the third child of Benjamin's second marriage in 1853 to Clarissa Foote; Henry, born on 5 April 1864 at Ipswich, was their youngest son.

Thomas was a foundation pupil of the Ipswich Boys' Grammar School, where his brothers were also educated. Like them he entered his father's mercantile and banking business, ultimately becoming senior partner and retiring in 1902. In religion, they continued the family tradition of staunch and devoted Nonconformism; Thomas in lifelong service to the Ipswich Congregational Church, much of it as a deacon, while James and Henry were for many years superintendents and teachers of the Sunday school. Family support for the grammar schools was maintained by Thomas and James, the former as chairman of trustees of the Ipswich Girls' Grammar School. His love of music was reflected in his presidency of the Blackstone-Ipswich Cambrian Choir.

On 23 May 1893 Thomas was appointed to the Legislative Council; he resigned three years later and won Ipswich in the Legislative Assembly. He served in the assembly during great political instability, including the fall of three ministries, a railway construction scandal and the worst drought on record. The Philp [q.v.] ministry was forced to drastically retrench the civil service and, as colonial treasurer in 1901-03, Cribb compounded the government's unpopularity with the first income tax in Queensland, causing its fall; he was defeated at the next election in 1904. With others who disliked the political bias of the *Brisbane Courier* he had launched the *Daily Mail* in May 1903.

Cribb was reappointed to the Legislative Council in June 1913, but was too ill to serve. He died at his Southport home on 4 September. Of his marriage on 3 June 1874 to Marian Lucy, née Foote, there were five sons and two daughters. His estate was valued for probate at £69 435. Slightly built, gently spoken and with a keen sense of humour, Cribb seemed happiest within his family. Asthmatic from youth, only a strong sense of duty propelled him into public life; deafness from middle age increased his problems.

James was member for Rosewood in the assembly in 1893-96. He devoted 1896-99 to the family business, then represented Bundamba in 1899-1912 and Bremer in 1912-15. A confirmed liberal, he easily held these working-class seats, perhaps because of his help to Ipswich coal-mining. He gained much credit for stabilizing the industry by persistent agitation for a schedule price scheme for railway coal in place of tendering; the loop-line to Bundamba and Blackstone mines was another success. He was also a skilful industrial conciliator.

James served on the Bundamba Shire

Council and on the Girls' Grammar School Board, while holding directorships, including the Queensland Woollen Manufacturing Co. Ltd and the Ipswich Gas and Coke Co. Ltd. On 20 February 1884 in Melbourne, he married Alice Elizabeth, daughter of Rev. F. H. Browne, of the Richmond Congregational Church. They had three sons and five daughters. He disposed of his interest in the family firm to relatives in 1904 and died at Ipswich on 23 May 1926 of arteriosclerosis.

The true inheritor of his father's entrepreneurial skill was Henry. Friendly and sociable, he was very much a man of the world and a sporting gentleman. He represented the colony in cricket, football and tennis. A foundation member of the Queensland Hunt Club, where his horse Parnell twice won the point-to-point steeplechase, he was also a fine horseman and polo-player. Breeding and exhibiting fox terriers, greyhounds, homing pigeons, Jersey cattle and horses, he was a councillor of the Royal National Agricultural and Industrial Association in 1920-40 and was active in other agricultural show societies. As a bloodstock breeder, notably of trotting horses, on his grazing property, Gulvallis, at Toogoolawah, he imported sires from New Zealand and America and helped to improve show trotting in Queensland. A lieutenant in the Queensland Mounted Infantry, he served during the 1891 shearing strike.

In 1917 Henry was closely connected with the Nationalist Party as president of the Ipswich and Bremer National Association, and as a financial backer and president of the National Democratic Council in 1919-21. Three sons and one daughter were born of his marriage on 2 May 1888 to Esther Elizabeth Gomez de Silva. By the death or retirement of other shareholders, he was able to acquire sole ownership of the family firm on 31 December 1924. On 22 June 1927 he and his family sold their interests, severing the last connexions of the Cribb and Foote families with the firm founded by Benjamin Cribb in 1849. Henry died at Ipswich on 16 July 1944.

The Cribbs made no outstanding or lasting contribution as members of parliament. Yet they were typical of those Queensland families who came to hold and to wield considerable local and regional power. For almost a century they dominated the cultural, sporting, economic and political life of the West Moreton district. Ipswich is still graced by their town houses, several of which are outstanding Queensland examples of the best of colonial architecture.

C. A. Bernays, *Queensland politics during sixty years* (Brisb, 1919); M. J. Fox (ed), *The history of Queensland*, 1 (Brisb, 1919); L. E. Slaughter, *Ips-*

wich municipal centenary (Brisb, 1960); *Brisbane Courier*, 6 Sept 1913; *Telegraph* (Brisb), 23 June 1937; *Qld Times*, 24 June 1937; family information.

MARGARET BRIDSON CRIBB

CRICK, STANLEY SADLER (1888-1955), film distributor, was born on 9 October 1888 at Launceston, Tasmania, son of William Throne Crick, accountant, and his wife Alice, née Sadler. His grandfather was Throne Crick, a prominent businessman in Leicestershire. While an infant Stanley was taken by his parents to England, and in 1895 returned with them to Hobart where he entered The Hutchins School; he won a prize for classics in 1901, distinguished himself at football and sang in the choir of St David's Cathedral. His first job was as a clerk with a Hobart auctioneer, J. W. Abbott & Sons, but he soon moved to Melbourne as an accountant for Lohmann & Co., before joining the new Melbourne branch of the film production and distribution company of Pathé Frères in 1908.

Crick rose rapidly in the organization and established branches in Queensland and New Zealand; in 1909 he became manager of the Sydney office. On 25 April 1910 at the Methodist church, St Kilda, Melbourne, he married Ruby Margaret Burman, a nurse. In 1911 he left Pathé to produce his own films, first with Herbert Finlay and from June in the ambitious Australian Photo-Play Co. Employing a large stock company of actors and technicians, Crick turned out some twenty feature films in about a year, including outdoor adventures such as *Moora Neya or the message of the spear* (1911), and melodramas based on topical events such as *The cup winner* (1911). The enterprise closed down because of distribution difficulties and the loss of negatives in a fire. Thereafter, although Crick invested in a few later productions such as Raymond Longford's [q.v.] *The mutiny of the Bounty* (1916), he concentrated on the distribution of imported films.

His wife, predeceased by their only child, died in Sydney in October 1918 and next year Crick travelled in Asia. On his return he joined the American Fox Film Corporation (Australasia) Ltd, as Victorian manager. On 26 April 1921 at St Kilda he married a divorcee, Eleanor Ida Turner, née Williamson. In November he moved to Sydney as general sales manager for Fox in New South Wales and became managing director for Australasia in June 1922. He travelled extensively to branch offices and often visited the United States of America. In 1930 Crick also became managing director of the large cinema chain, Hoyts Theatres Ltd, after Fox had bought a controlling interest.

From the early 1930s Crick devoted increasing energy to civic affairs: in 1931-32 he served on the Sydney Harbour Bridge Celebrations committee, and in 1934 on the management of Sydney Festival Week. The gardens of his luxurious home, Berith Park, Wahroonga, were often used to aid charities. He also served on the committees of the City of Sydney Eisteddfod, the Returned Sailors' and Soldiers' Imperial League of Australia, and, being a keen golfer, the Pymble Golf Club. In 1935 he was awarded King George V's Jubilee Medal for his civic contributions and, in November, as a Citizens Reform Association candidate, was elected to the Sydney Municipal Council for Gipps Ward. As an alderman he was closely involved in the 1938 sesqui-centenary celebrations in Sydney and chaired the pageant committee.

Crick resigned from Hoyts Theatres in September 1937 and from Fox in February 1938, but remained as joint managing director of Australian and New Zealand Theatres Ltd, a company controlling J. C. Williamson [q.v.6] Ltd, and was also a director of the Macquarie Broadcasting Services Pty Ltd. He was lord mayor of Sydney from December 1939 until December 1942, and concentrated his entrepreneurial skill on patriotic functions and fund-raising, particularly the Lord Mayor's Fund, for the war effort.

Crick had always liked racing and owned several horses including Sir Regent, winner of the Metropolitan Handicap in Sydney in 1937. He was also a member of Royal Sydney Yacht Squadron, the Royal Motor Yacht Club of New South Wales and the Athenaeum Club, Melbourne. In 1948 he bought the Navua stud farm at Richmond, New South Wales, and bred horses there until 1951 when he sold it for £50 000.

Crick died of a heart attack on 10 August 1955 while visiting Los Angeles; his body was flown back to Sydney and was buried in Northern Suburbs cemetery after a service at St Philip's Anglican Church. He was survived by his second wife and their son and two daughters. His estate was valued for probate at £72 583.

Gregarious and a lavish entertainer, Crick enjoyed his personal wealth in sports and social life, but always remained an adroit manager of his business affairs, with a talent for picking gifted people to work for him. He promoted both the showing of British films, and the development of an Australian film industry, although, ironically, he worked for an American company which was never involved directly in feature film production in Australia.

Everyone's, 12 Apr 1922, 3 Sept 1930; *Film Weekly*, 3 Sept 1931, 7 Nov 1935, 24 Feb 1938; *Photoplayer*, 16 Apr 1932; *Lumiere* (Melb), Mar 1973; *Smith's Weekly* (Syd), 25 Oct 1930, 14 Jan 1933; *SMH*, 2, 19 Nov 1935, 13 Dec 1940, 16 Dec 1942, 11 Nov 1945, 19 Aug 1955; *Sun* (Syd), 23 Feb 1938; S. S. Crick scrap-book (National Film Archive, NL).   A. F. PIKE

CRICK, WILLIAM PATRICK (1862-1908), solicitor and politician, was born on 10 February 1862 at Truro, South Australia, son of English-born William Crick, labourer later farmer, and his Irish wife Margaret, née Mungovern. About 1868 the family moved into western New South Wales, finally settling at Spicer's Creek near Wellington. Crick went to school at St Stanislaus College, Bathurst. Articled to R. J. Ryan in Dubbo in 1881, he continued in Sydney with T. M. Slattery and L. F. Heydon [qq.v.] in 1884 and next year with J. A. Cahill. In 1886 he was with H. Dawson and was admitted as a solicitor on 13 November. On 30 June 1890 at St Francis Catholic Church, Paddington, he married Mary Catherine Kelly. They separated in 1892 and had no children.

Paddy Crick grew into a stocky man with dark curly hair; he looked and moved like a middle-weight boxer and was handy with his fists, easily provoked. He belonged to the group of country Irish-Catholics who, sometimes with reason, saw themselves as even more deprived than the rest of the rural poor – though the Cricks became well off selectors. Crick's vision of himself as a grudgeful champion of his tribe was sharpened from the mid-1880s by his addiction to whisky. Sober, he spoke cogently and convincingly but without delicacy of language or grace of expression; drunk, he bellowed – either way he dominated the Police Courts, where he developed a lucrative practice. His outstanding intellectual gifts enabled him to perceive the law as more than a source of income, and to master the rules and procedures of parliament and comprehend their relationship to the constitution. But his talents did not modify his judgment that society was antagonistic to 'his people' and needed reform.

Colonial politics reflected the forms of social and economic power generated by free trade. Crick recognized the potential for change through parliament; he failed in election bids in 1887. In 1885 with another outsider, more tolerant, E. W. O'Sullivan [q.v.], he founded the Land and Industrial Alliance, aiming to combine, through protection, country selectors and city workers in political action; their hopes proved vain. In February 1889 he won the seat of West Macquarie as an independent protectionist; that year he made no headway as a legal reform legislator, but began to make his mark as a pugnacious parliamentarian. On 4 October he was found 'guilty of a contempt of this House' for having called certain members 'bloody Orange hounds and thieves'. On 12 November 1890 the sergeant-at-arms needed help to overcome Crick's violent resistance to removal, 'causing great disorder and scandal'. He was expelled, but was returned at the by-election on 6 December. His radicalism prompted his interest in the new Labor Party in 1891, but his independence prevented his acceptance of its discipline.

As early as 1890 Crick's perception of his role as vindicator was being befuddled by alcohol, but his spells of sobriety remained constructive, and he was usually prepared to admit his errors. His involvement with W. N. Willis [q.v.] in the ownership of *Truth* that year, instead of providing a newspaper forum for progress, led in 1892-95 to convulsive arguments and protracted legal action with J. Norton [q.v.] and to the exit of Crick. In parliament in 1890-93 he failed in attempts to improve legislation affecting juvenile crime; but his first offenders' probation bill, 1894, became law. His high professional reputation was enhanced in 1892 when he saved an innocent man, E. Buttner, from execution after he had been found guilty of rape. The same year he formed a partnership with his boyhood friend, R. D. Meagher [q.v.], and for a while he seemed likely to turn over a new leaf, but by 1894 he could not abide his partner's pretentious precocity. Next year Meagher was implicated in the Dean [q.v.] case and, while under the influence, Crick made a wild speech in parliament against Sir Julian Salomons [q.v.6] who was also involved; Crick was charged with conspiracy but was cleared.

He continued to bring down improving legislation but none of his bills, in 1894-97, were enacted. His attempt in 1896 to tighten control over the registration of stallions and racehorses suggested his great interest in the turf. By the mid-1890s he was reputed to be one of the biggest punters in Australia; he owned several horses, but only Collarit, in 1906, seems to have been profitable. As the number of his friends dwindled in the late 1890s he gravitated more and more to the racing fraternity and roistered with them in hotels in Randwick, where he lived, near the racecourse. Even in 1895 he could say that he had 'not been in a private home in Sydney or its suburbs for four or five years'. His honesty, truculence and mastery of procedure made him both respected and feared in parliament – even (Sir) George Reid [q.v.], premier in 1894-99, could not curb him when he was in full flight. He had become a senior and leading member of the Protectionists and played an important part in the defeat of

the Free-Trade government in 1899, becoming postmaster-general in (Sir) William Lyne's [q.v.] ministry.

Crick was far from pious, but he remained attached to the Catholic Church, although he had courted its disfavour in 1889-92 by supporting Sir Alfred Stephen's [q.v.6] divorce reform legislation. He saw it as an Irish institution, a bulwark against social privilege and affectation derived from England, which in a way could justify his defiant boorishness if not his excessive drinking. He had not been able to do much for it, but he seized the opportunity to help it in 1900-01 when the administrator of St Mary's Cathedral, D. F. O'Haran [q.v.], was cited as co-respondent in the Coningham [q.v.] divorce case. With the aid of his runner, Daniel Green [q.v.], Crick led the Catholics against the Protestants (under W. M. Dill Macky [q.v.]) in an uproarious contest to see justice done. He did not use his ministerial office to anything like the extent that has been alleged, but he did contribute much to the vindication of O'Haran. He had hoped to lift up many more.

Minister without portfolio from 1 March to 10 April 1901, Crick was minister for lands from 11 April 1901 to 14 June 1904, when the See [q.v.] government resigned. He expected to become premier, but instead became chairman of committees – until 27 June 1905. He was an alderman of the Sydney Municipal Council in 1904.

He was thoroughly versed in the State's complex land laws and had always held radical views on agricultural settlement. A very severe and lengthy drought still prevailed in 1901 and Crick responded benevolently, legislating to help lessees in the western division, and even effecting some procedural reforms in the labyrinthine department. But his liberal policy miscarried in the granting of some improvement leases, based on Carruthers' [q.v.] 1895 Land Act, to pastoralists whose leases expired in 1901-04. Judge (Sir) William Owen [q.v.] acted as a royal commissioner in 1905-06 to inquire into the administration of the Lands Department; he reported that Crick had overruled adverse official reports while approving improvement leases in thirty-five applications; of these Willis was agent in twenty-one, and P. C. Close, a rural consultant, was associated with nine. Large fees were paid to some agents for minor work that was unnecessary in terms of the minister's policy; the commissioner suspected bribery, and decided that Crick had received half of Close's fees of nearly £16000. But his affairs, including substantial betting for cash, were contorted; Close's firm had financed Crick and, when the latter faced criminal charges it was impossible to prove beyond reasonable doubt that he had acted corruptly. He resigned his seat on 6 December 1906, but some old scores were paid off when parliament formally expelled him on 11 December; likewise, on 23 August next year he was struck off the rolls. Now alienated from the country, he ran for the city seat of Surry Hills in 1907, but lost.

Although Crick had been reported in 1903 as about to give up smoking and drinking, from 1905 he suffered increasingly from cirrhosis of the liver. After a day at Rosehill races, in the night he had a severe attack of haematemesis and died, intestate, on 23 August 1908. He was buried in the Catholic section of Waverley cemetery. His wife inherited £5200 from him and his father £4700.

Report of the royal commission on ... Lands Department (Syd, 1906); H. V. Evatt, *Australian Labour leader ... W. A. Holman* (Syd, 1942); C. Pearl, *Wild men of Sydney* (Lond, 1958); B. E. Mansfield, *Australian democrat* (Syd, 1965); B. Nairn, *Civilising capitalism* (Canb, 1973); *V&P* (LA NSW), 1889, 1, 103, 1890, 1, 430, 525, 1901, 2, 852; *Catholic Press*, 27 Apr 1901; *T&CJ*, 22 June 1904; *Aust Worker*, 27 Aug, 3 Sept 1908; *Sydney Mail*, 26 Aug 1908; M. Rutledge, Sir Alfred Stephen and divorce law reform in New South Wales, 1886-1892 (M.A. thesis, ANU, 1966); Attorney-General and Justice Dept, Special bundle, 1895, 5/4702 (NSWA).   BEDE NAIRN
MARTHA RUTLEDGE

CRISP, SIR HAROLD (1874-1942), judge, was born on 27 July 1874 in Hobart, eldest son of David Henry Crisp, solicitor, and his wife Mary, née Burdon. Educated at the High School and Christ's College, Harold, following family tradition, studied law, and on 14 July 1891 was articled to his father. On 16 April 1896, after topping the examinations in general literature and law, he was admitted to the Bar of the Supreme Court and entered into partnership with his father. Next year Harold was in practice in Zeehan but returned to his Hobart partnership in 1898. On 21 March 1899 at Holy Trinity Church, Hobart, he married Harriette, daughter of A. Page, M.L.C.; they had two daughters and a son.

Crisp distinguished himself early at the Bar; he acquired repute for industry and brilliance, and by 1904 was appearing regularly in important cases. In 1904 and 1905 he acted for the plaintiff in the Supreme Court case of *Enever* v. *The King*, an attempt to establish the relation of master and servant between the Crown and a constable, and one of the few Tasmanian cases taken up as precedent case-law in other law jurisdictions. Tall, well-built and handsome, with a magnificent voice and great command of

language, he was witty but never unkind, and had a passion for accuracy and punctuality. He worked hard, but never to the neglect of his family. On 1 August 1914 he was appointed a puisne judge of the Supreme Court of Tasmania and on 2 November a member of the Executive Council.

In 1924 Crisp was acting chief justice when the centenary of the establishment of the Supreme Court was celebrated at a special sitting of the Full Court in Hobart, and he acted as administrator of the government in 1930 when the chief justice, Sir Herbert Nicholls [q.v.], was absent through illness. Appointed chief justice of Tasmania on 21 December 1937, he was knighted the following June. In July 1939 he was granted leave of absence due to ill health, and moved to Double Bay, Sydney, where he retired on 14 April 1940. He died there suddenly on 12 May 1942 and was cremated. His wife and younger daughter predeceased him.

In his youth Crisp had been a fine all-round sportsman, excelling in football and tennis. In his twenty-five years on the bench his integrity, courtesy and patience earned him a rare respect and affection both from the legal profession and the public. His successor as chief justice, Sir John Morris, stated, 'confidence was universal that in his Court, justice would be done'.

Cyclopedia of Tasmania (Hob, 1931); R. L. Wettenhall, 'A case of wrongful arrest', *PTHRA*, 19 (1972), no 4; *Mercury*, 9 June, 11 July 1938, 15 July 1939, 13 May 1942; *Examiner* (Launc), 9, 10 June 1938; *Advocate* (Hob), 11 July 1938, 13 May 1942; PD 1/616/164, and GO 98/1 (TA); family and other information.   CHRISTINE WOOD

CROFTS, CHARLES ALFRED (1871-1950), trade unionist, was born on 11 July 1871 at Bethnal Green, Middlesex, England, son of James Crofts, general dealer, and his wife Ann Rebecca, née Luxton. He left school at 12 to work in a sheet metal factory where he soon joined the Tinsmiths, Braziers and Gas Meter Makers' Society of London. On 6 August 1893 at Bethnal Green he married Agnes Humphreys in the Anglican Church, though in Australia the family became Presbyterian.

With his wife and daughter, Charlie Crofts came to Melbourne in 1898 on a two-year contract with the Metropolitan Gas Co. Working as a metermaker, he soon became active in the Sheet Metal Workers' Union which at that time covered the gas industry; he was vice-president in 1907 and president in 1908-09. He was a foundation member in 1911 of the national executive of the Federated Gas Employees' Industrial

Union (usually known as the Gas Employees' Union). In 1914 he was elected to the national executive of the Sheet Metal Workers' Union, and that year was dismissed by the Metropolitan Gas Co. for attending a meeting of the union in Sydney after being denied leave. Shortly afterwards, on 26 March, he was elected to the paid position of Victorian secretary of the Gas Employees' Union, and two months later was also elected national secretary. He retained these two positions for the rest of his life.

Crofts became one of the most active union leaders in the country, serving for many years on the executive of the Melbourne Trades Hall Council and on the T.H.C. Disputes Committee. He was T.H.C. president in 1924-25 and a member of the Gas Meter Makers' Wages Board in 1913-49. He was a delegate from his union to most of the major trade union congresses and a strong advocate of a national central body of the trade union movement. After involvement in the short-lived national Council of Action formed by the 1921 congress, he was secretary of the Commonwealth Council of Federated Unions while it existed from 1923 to 1927, and president of the ephemeral Commonwealth Industrial Disputes Committee in 1925.

In 1927 at the foundation congress of the Australasian (later Australian) Council of Trade Unions Crofts was elected secretary ahead of J. S. (Jock) Garden and R. S. Ross [qq,v,], his support coming mainly from the Victorian and the politically moderate sections. He held the position on an honorary basis until 1943, working from the Gas Employees' office. In 1930, as A.C.T.U. secretary, he travelled overseas, acting as the Australian trade union delegate to the Fourteenth Session of the International Labour Conference in Geneva, the Fifth Annual Congress of the International Federation of Trade Unions in Stockholm and the British Commonwealth Labour Conference in London. For a time he was a deputy member of the governing body of the International Labour Organization.

As A.C.T.U. secretary Crofts played a part in the long and bitter watersiders' and timber workers' strikes of the late 1920s and several other disputes of the period. He was the leading union advocate in the basic wage cases of the Depression period, and was in frequent contact with people at all levels of government, putting the union point of view. He relinquished the A.C.T.U. secretaryship when it became a full-time position at the 1943 congress, preferring to retain his post with the Gas Employees' Union, but remained a Victorian delegate to the executive until his death.

Crofts was active in the Labor Party for many years at both State and Federal levels, being a long-standing executive member of the Victorian branch and ten times a delegate to Federal conference between 1927 and 1945. He was president of the Victorian branch in 1926-27 and treasurer in 1942-44, and an unsuccessful Labor Senate candidate in 1934.

In the trade union movement Crofts supported stronger, more centralized union structures, a national trade union centre, the use of arbitration for settling industrial disputes, and greater co-operation between employers and unions. In the 1920s he set himself apart from many in the movement by supporting the Federal government's referendum for an extension of the powers of the Commonwealth Arbitration Court and by advocating tripartite industrial peace conferences on the 'Mondist' model in Britain. Partly because of his influence, the A.C.T.U. in its early years supported such conferences and was known among militant unions as 'the graveyard of strikes'.

As an industrial advocate Crofts had many successes. In his early years with the Gas Employees' Union, he was prominent in the attainment of a six-day week, alternate weekly changes of shifts and the raising of gas workers' wages to above the average levels for labourers. As chief advocate for the Commonwealth Council of Federated Unions in the 1926 standard hours case, he succeeded in having the 44-hour week accepted in principle by the Arbitration Court. He led the A.C.T.U. panel of advocates for the 1930-31 basic wage case in which it was reduced by 10 per cent, the unsuccessful 1932 and 1933 cases and the successful restoration case of 1934. Crofts was always well prepared with highly detailed economic material. However, he was at times unduly lengthy, taking several days when one would have been adequate, which often irritated members of the bench; during the tense Depression hearings he sometimes clashed with judges. His submissions to the court were always technically meticulous in questioning the current methods of calculating the basic wage and the price indices on which it was based, and he commonly argued for wage levels based on the standard set by the Piddington [q.v.] commission of the 1920s.

Crofts's early political education had begun in London listening to the speeches of Tom Mann [q.v.], Ben Tillett and Keir Hardie and took a dramatic turn when he once saw horses being used against strikers in a street march. He was never a militant unionist though he was capable of rhetoric bordering on the radical, such as at the announcement of the 10 per cent wage reduction in the Arbitration Court chamber, when he led the singing of *The Red Flag* and called for three cheers for the social revolution.

His position in both the union movement and the party was that of a moderate, though in Labor politics Crofts was a firm advocate of union control over the party machine; during the Depression he was prominent in the expulsion of Premier Hogan [q.v.] and other supporters of the Premiers' Plan. On the other hand, in the 1930s he incurred the wrath of many on the left, especially for his anti-communist activities in the party and the unions. Ideologically he regarded himself as a socialist, frequently publicly advocating greater government controls over banks and the money supply. But he was not anxious to enter parliament, claiming that ideals too often became tarnished there. He was a sometime member of the Council of the Melbourne Technical College, the Australian Council for Civil Liberties and the Victorian Fabian Society.

Crofts died at Caulfield on 25 March 1950 and was cremated, survived by his wife, three of his four sons and two of his three daughters. One daughter, Irene, worked for many years in the trade union movement. His estate was valued for probate at £3027.

Herald (Melb), 14 Feb 1948; G. Dunkley, The ACTU 1927-1950: politics, organization and economic policy (Ph.D. thesis, Monash Univ, 1974); information from, and news-cuttings held by, Miss I. Crofts, Armadale, Vic.

GRAHAM DUNKLEY

CROLL, ROBERT HENDERSON (1869-1947), author and public servant, was born about midnight on either 4 or 5 January 1869 at Pleasant Creek (Stawell), Victoria, fifth child of Charles Croll, goldminer, and his wife Janet, née Henderson, both Scottish-born. An introspective and sensitive boy, he was educated at Stawell State School and in September 1886, after passing the clerical examination for the Public Service, was appointed to the Public Library of Victoria. He remained there, reading voraciously, for five years until he transferred as junior clerk to the Education Department, where he stayed for over forty years. He revered Frank Tate [q.v.], became a firm administrator, and retired as senior clerk at 65, having been registrar of the Council of Public Education for thirteen years. He had also been secretary of two royal commissions and had occasionally written speeches and articles for premiers.

In his youth Croll was a founder of the East Melbourne Harriers and eventually became a senior official of the Victorian Amateur Athletic Association, managing several Victorian teams. He was an enthusiastic bushwalker who eventually claimed to have carried his swag for about 3000 miles (4800 km), to have tramped at least as far on short trips, and to have been an office-bearer of the Melbourne Walking Club for fifty years. Encouraged to write by David Blair [q.v.3], Croll began contributing in the early 1890s to *Bohemia*, then to the Sydney *Bulletin*, the Melbourne *Argus* and *Herald* and many other journals; at one stage he was writing three columns each week. His *The open road in Victoria* ... (1928) and *Along the track* (1930) were selections from his journalism; he possibly did more than anyone else in his time to encourage bushwalking. For some years he was associate editor of the *Emu*. He developed his talent for light verse and the composition of epigraphs, and helped his close friend Percival Serle [q.v.] compile his *Australasian anthology* (1927); he also produced editions of the works of the poets John Shaw Neilson and F. S. Williamson [qq.v.] in 1934 and in 1940 and, after his retirement, plunged into literary activity. He was generous in advising young writers, especially through the Bread and Cheese Club.

Bob Croll was equally prominent in art circles. He was author in 1935 of an important biography of Tom Roberts [q.v.], edited Streeton's [q.v.] letters to Roberts (1946), and in 1920 produced an edition of etchings by John Shirlow [q.v.]. He also organized the State Centenary Art Exhibition, was general secretary of the Australian Academy of Art and a councillor of the Victorian Artists' Society, and opened many exhibitions of paintings.

In 1929, with the psychologist S. D. Porteus [q.v.], Croll made the first of his six trips to Central Australia; he vigorously covered the field on camels, was jocularly granted 'honorary membership' of the Arunta tribe, and by broadcasting and in his *Wide horizons: wanderings in Central Australia* (1937) expressed his affection for Aboriginals. He also, with Charles Barrett [q.v.7], published in 1943 *Art of the Australian Aboriginal*.

During World War II Croll was acting chief censor for Victoria for five months in 1941 and relieving talks officer for the Australian Broadcasting Commission in Victoria next year. A classical product of the Victorian goldfields, he nowhere ran very deep, perhaps, yet few in his time made a more diverse contribution to cultural and intellectual life. He was president at various times of the Field Naturalists' Club, the Anthropological Society, and the Travel League of Victoria, and the Wallaby, P.E.N. and Book-plate clubs among others. Sympathetic to Labor in his youth, he became more conservative in later life when he was influenced by (Sir) Robert Menzies; his religious views were broad and tolerant. Croll was the most gregarious of men, an *habitué* of the Amateur Sports Club of Victoria and the Savage Club, with hundreds of friends. He had a 'facetious graceful manner' of unfailing pleasantness; many of his anecdotes are gathered in his reminiscences, *I recall; collections and recollections* (1939). In 1946 he published *An autobituary*.

He died at Camberwell on 18 October 1947, survived by his wife Grace Devereaux, née Croall, whom he had married at Hawthorn Presbyterian Church on 23 September 1914 and by their son; he was cremated. Several portraits of him were painted and he is commemorated by a bronze plaque in the Stawell Town Hall.

H. W. Malloch, *Fellows all* (Melb, 1943); S. D. Porteus, *A psychologist of sorts* (Palo Alto, 1969); L. J. Blake (ed), *Vision and realisation* (Melb, 1973); Croll papers (LaTL).   GEOFFREY SERLE

CROMBIE, JAMES (1834-1898), pastoralist and politician, was born on 8 June 1834 at Kilminning Farm, Crail, Fifeshire, Scotland, son of David Guillan Crombie, farmer, and his wife Jessie, née Webster. Educated at Madras College, St Andrews, he reached Melbourne on 4 March 1853 on the *Typhoon* and prospected with fair success at Bakery Hill, Ballarat.

Joined by his brother William (1836-1898), Crombie commenced mixed farming at Mount Prospect, Creswick, and developed a close relationship with the family of John Cameron [q.v.7]. Crombie was an active member of the Creswick District Road Board, the Bullarook Farmers' Common and the Smeaton, Spring Hill and Bullarook Agricultural Association. He embarked on a pastoral trek to Queensland with the Camerons in 1863. On 1 December 1869 at Springsure he married Isabella Harriet, Cameron's sister. They had four sons and three daughters.

The partnership stocked Barcaldine Downs in 1864-78 and later leased Kensington Downs and Greenhills, near Muttaburra in the Mitchell district. Crombie visited Britain in 1877-79 and, in 1881, the brothers took control of Greenhills. James moved to Brisbane and also purchased a large Fassifern farm. He became a director of the Royal Bank of Queensland and the Queensland Meat Export and Agency Co., and joined the Queensland Meat and Dairy Board. Representing Mitchell in 1888-93, and Warrego in 1893-98, Crombie was one of the last of the pioneer Central Queensland squatters to enter parliament. Publicly taciturn and blunt, he was uninterested in political advancement although privately

warm hearted and genial. He raised his widower brother's four children.

Crombie was foundation treasurer of the United Pastoralists' Association of Queensland (1891-96), and delegate to all conventions of the Pastoralists' Federal Council of Australia during the shearing strikes of 1891 and 1894. In 1889 he believed that 'the [trade] union had been a blessing to the district', but by 1891 he eulogized the role of the defence forces in the great confrontation. Similarly, in 1894, he was one of the more intransigent of the employers, a position he admitted had been forced upon him by falling prices, rising rents and militant unionists. He judged the pastoralists' victory as a logical triumph of commonsense over the 'threats and intimidation by certain union leaders' who were 'rightly rejected by the very bushmen they purported to represent'.

Like other Victorian 'gold rushers' but not his Queensland confreres, Crombie was a protectionist who advocated state assistance to create a sturdy section of western grazing farmers. But these views were subordinated to the efforts he made to preserve dwindling family-structured pastoral empires mired in the quicksands of post-1889 Queensland. His utterances during 1894-95 reflect both their and his bewilderment at the threat of radical change and the frustrations of pioneer aspirations forged a generation before. Still, he had contributed substantially to the 'establishment and diversification of sound, productive rural enterprise in Queensland, and his conservative opinions concealed a successful rearguard action. He preserved family properties, helped maintain the political *status quo* and successfully curtailed the 'socialist menace' before Federation.

Predeceased by a son and a daughter, Crombie died of heart disease at Oriel, Albion, Brisbane, on 17 September 1898, and was buried in the Presbyterian section of Toowong cemetery. His estate was valued for probate at £33 000.

PD (Qld), 1896, p 720; *Qld Heritage*, 3 (1978), no 3, p 6; *Pastoral Review*, 15 Oct 1898; *Creswick and Clunes Advertiser*, 29 Apr 1862, 17 Feb 1863; *Brisbane Courier*, 4 May 1893, 5, 10, 26 Mar 1896; *Queenslander*, 24 Sept 1898; R. E. Cameron, Pastoral organizations in Queensland, 1884-1900 (B.A. Hons thesis, Univ Qld, 1956); J. McCormack, The politics of expediency. Queensland government in the eighteen nineties (M.A. thesis, Univ Qld, 1975); Roy Bank of Qld, Chairman's speech 1899, A/RBQ/061 (National Bank of Aust Archives, Brisb); family information.

D. B. WATERSON

CROMMELIN, MINARD FANNIE (1881-1972), postmistress and conservationist, was born on 29 June 1881 at Aston station, near

Bombala, New South Wales, eldest daughter of George Whiting Crommelin [q.v.3], station manager, and his wife Frances Emily, née Dawson. At 12 Minard left Pipe Clay Creek Public School to help the postmistress at Burrawong who, to compensate for her tyranny, later sent her for a year to the Sydney Church of England Grammar School for Girls. After assisting in the post office at Moss Vale in 1906, Minard became acting postmistress at Woy Woy, where she remained five years. She then took public service examinations and over the next twenty years was relieving postmistress at over 150 towns. She was described in 1916 as 'tall and thin, with very thin features and very black hair'.

In 1936 on long service leave, Miss Crommelin visited England, Ireland and Europe, began buying antique furniture and rare books on Australia and its natural history and joined the International Society for the Protection of Nature, other conservation groups and the Royal Empire Society. In 1937 she inherited two legacies and retired from the public service. On a visit to Pearl Beach that year she saw for the first time a lyre bird displaying and determined to retire there. Unable to lease 2000 acres (810 ha) of crown reserve on the northern bank of the Hawkesbury River, she canvassed support from various societies to which she belonged, including the Royal Zoological and Naturalists' societies of New South Wales, for the proclamation of the Warrah Sanctuary, of which she was a founding trustee in 1938. In 1937 she had bought seven acres (3 ha) adjoining the sanctuary at Pearl Beach where she lived after 1939.

As a ranger, she constantly protested against thefts of wild flowers, shooting of native fauna, careless back-burning by local residents and 'improvements' such as a sewerage disposal plant and a rifle range on her 'waratah patch'. She tried beekeeping and cultivating native plants, but was hampered by floods and fires. Dispirited by loneliness and the hostility of local residents, she offered her property to the Commonwealth Council for Scientific and Industrial Research, which declined. In December 1946 the Senate of the University of Sydney accepted it as a biological and natural field station for research and named it after her. In return she received an annuity and 'undisturbed enjoyment' of her residence for life.

From 1948 Minard Crommelin unsuccessfully lobbied Federal and State politicians, government departments and newspaper editors with plans for a 'national botanic garden, fauna park and arboretum' and for a national ecological conservation authority. She was appointed M.B.E. in January 1959. Disturbed by the university's supposed non-fulfilment of the intent of her gift, between 1960 and 1966 she gave £3500 to the Australian Academy of Science, Canberra, to establish the Crommelin Ecological Conservation Fund, to which she bequeathed £10 768. An ardent bibliophile and litterateur, Minard Crommelin possessed much genealogical material about her family's Huguenot descent; unpublished manuscripts including 'Twinkle's Diary', an account of her pet sugar glider (possum), and privately printed pamphlets; she was a member of the Society of Australian Genealogists and the Huguenot Society, London. She helped to form local branches of the Australian Red Cross Society, the Country Women's Association of New South Wales and the Business and Professional Women's Club of Sydney.

Content with her simple life, yet single-minded in purpose, Minard Crommelin died at her home at Pearl Beach on 14 February 1972 and was cremated. Her estate was valued for probate at $12 605.

Business and Professional Women in Aust, Dec 1964; *Descent,* 6 (1972) pt 1; Crommelin papers (Univ Syd Archives).   RUTH TEALE

CRONIN, BERNARD CHARLES (1884-1968), author, was born on 18 March 1884 at Ealing, Middlesex, England, son of Charles Frederick Cronin (d. 1887), and his wife Laura, née Marshall. Cronin arrived in Melbourne on 28 March 1890 in the charge of the captain of the *Austral*; his mother and stepfather had preceded him. He was educated at The Grange, South Yarra, Surrey College, Surrey Hills, and Dookie Agricultural College from which he graduated dux and gold medallist and with a diploma of agriculture in 1901. After jackeroo experience in Gippsland and northern Victoria, he joined his brother Laurie cattle-farming at Marrawah in north-west Tasmania. On 11 March 1908 at Toora, Gippsland, he married Victoria Maud Ferres, daughter of a farmer.

About 1913 Cronin returned to Melbourne almost penniless. He worked as a salesman before joining the Department of the Navy as a clerk, but devoted his spare time to writing. In 1918 he published his first novel, *The coastlanders*, set in Tasmania. He went on to write some thirty full-length novels, countless short stories and several one-act plays, including the radio play *Stampede* (1937); he is also represented in anthologies of verse. Cronin wrote under several pseudonyms, including those of 'Hugh Bohun, Denis Adair, Tas East and Eric North'. His reputation rests mainly on his novels *Bracken* (1929) and *The sow's ear* (1933), both of which express his urge to expose what he termed 'wrong, stupid or uneconomic' in Australian life. E. Morris Miller [q.v.] described the latter as 'a novel of impelling interest, powerful handling and intimate characterization' but added that the characters were 'subordinated to the design of the story'.

In the 1930s Cronin worked for the Melbourne *Herald*. Later he set up a 'Literary Critical Service' in Flinders Lane, and freelanced. During World War II he was employed as a publicity censor in Victoria and Western Australia. After the war he ran correspondence courses in writing technique for the Melbourne Technical College. From the late 1950s he contributed regularly to the Melbourne *Sun*.

In 1920, with Gertrude Hart, Cronin had founded the Old Derelicts' Club for struggling authors and artists. Out of this in 1927 came the Society of Australian Authors; as first president in 1928-34, Cronin strove to improve conditions and win recognition for writers. The society was wound up in November 1936 because, according to Cronin, it was becoming 'infiltrated by politics'. In 1933 he founded the Quill Club. He was long a member of the International P.E.N. Club (Melbourne) and was accorded life membership in 1961.

From the early 1930s Cronin spent most weekends at his cottage at Upwey in the Dandenong Ranges, building with local stone and landscape gardening. In his 70s and 80s he took up painting and woodcarving. Craggy-faced with a thick mop of silver hair in old age, he remained vigorous until his last years, when asthma troubled him increasingly. Cronin was a keen student of the Bible and a supporter of the British-Israelite movement, though the family had been Anglican for generations. He died at his home in East Camberwell on 9 June 1968 and was buried in Springvale cemetery. He was survived by two sons and a daughter.

Police Life, 15 July 1968; *Wireless Weekly*, 4 May 1934; *Pix*, 26 Oct 1946; *Herald* (Melb), 20 Apr, 16 July 1927, 17 Mar 1931; *West Australian*, 18 Apr 1933; *Australasian*, 20 May 1939; *Sun-News Pictorial*, 10, 14 June 1968; B. Cronin papers (NL); family information.   SALLY O'NEILL

CROPPER, CHARLES WILLIAM (1859-1932), public servant and racing administrator, was born on 12 July 1859 in Sydney, elder son of Charles Michael Walsh Cropper, grazier, and his wife Mary Ann, née Howe. He was educated at Sydney Grammar School and in 1876-94 worked as an inspector of conditional purchases in the Department of Lands but failed to achieve any spectacular success. By 1894 he had made no progress up the public service ladder but had watched his salary drop from £350 in 1876 to £290. However, in the late 1880s and early 1890s he was a successful tennis player and in 1886 and 1887 he was New South Wales champion and captain of the Sydney Lawn Tennis Club.

Cropper, frustrated by his lack of advancement, resigned in 1894 and moved to Western Australia where the influx of gold seekers promised the chance of more rapid promotion. For a decade from 1900, as secretary of the Kalgoorlie Racing Club, he impressed his associates with his administrative abilities and earned the admiration of a wider audience by transforming the barren racecourse into an attractive garden where horse-racing was conducted at a high standard. The reputation he achieved resulted in 1910 in his appointment as successor to T. S. Clibborn [q.v.3] as secretary of Australia's premier racing body, the Australian Jockey Club in Sydney.

For twenty-two years Cropper supervised the administration of Randwick racecourse and the other affairs of the A.J.C., including the purchase of Warwick Farm racecourse in 1922. Cropper formed an admirable partnership with (Sir) Adrian Knox [q.v.]. Whilst Knox rewrote the rules of racing, Cropper reorganized the physical facilities: new tracks were designed and built, buildings relocated, grandstands extended, lawns and gardens were cultivated and the totalisater installed. These picturesque courses remain his monument.

During World War I Cropper was closely involved in the establishment and administration of Canonbury, Darling Point, bought by the A.J.C. as a convalescent home, at first for returned servicemen and later for children. This project provided an outlet for Cropper when further improvements to the Randwick course were prohibited by the War Precautions Act. In 1927 he was granted eight months leave to visit racing centres in Europe and North America, and was given £1000 by the A.J.C. committee and a valuable testimonial by bookmakers. During his last years, Cropper was plagued by ill health and gradually his administrative duties were assumed by his assistant George T. Rowe.

Cropper, a bachelor, was a member of the Union Club and the Presbyterian Church. He had a kindly and sympathetic, but somewhat private character – highly respected and conscientious but undemonstrative. He was well regarded by bookmakers, trainers and jockeys, who considered him to be more approachable and more considerate than the typical race club administrator.

Cropper died on 22 May 1932 at the Scottish Private Hospital, Paddington, and was buried in the Presbyterian section of Waverley cemetery. His name has been perpetuated in the C. W. Cropper Plate, a weight-for-age race (later changed to the C. W. Cropper Handicap), held on the third day of the A.J.C.'s Easter meeting. His estate was valued for probate at £24 608; he left his books and furniture to his favourite sister Ada, wife of Sir Alexander MacCormick [q.v.].

K. Austin et al (eds), *Racehorses in Australia* (Syd, 1922); D. M. Barrie, *Turf cavalcade* (Syd, 1960); H. Norton, 'Racing in Western Australia', *Leeuwin,* 1 (1910-11), no 6; *T&CJ,* 9 Feb 1889; *SMH,* 14 May 1924, 18, 19, 21 Jan, 28 May, 20, 23 Sept 1927, 23, 25 May 1932, 25 Feb 1933; *Sydney Sportsman,* 24 May 1932; *Referee,* 25 May 1932; Aust Jockey Club, Annual Report, 1911-32 (ML).

JOHN O'HARA

CROSS, ZORA BERNICE MAY (1890-1964), writer, was born on 18 May 1890 at Eagle Farm, Brisbane, daughter of Ernest William Cross, a Sydney-born accountant, and his wife Mary Louisa Eliza Ann, née Skyring, whose parents were early settlers at Moreton Bay. Zora inherited literary aspirations from both parents: a strong sense of poetic mission from her mother, and a strain of Celtic fantasy from her father, the son of an Irish printer. She was educated at Gympie and Ipswich Girls' Grammar School, and from 1905 in Sydney at Burwood Superior Public School and Sydney Girls' High School. In 1909-10 she attended the Teachers' College, Sydney. She started primary teaching but left the service to give birth to a daughter who died. On 11 March 1911 she married Stuart Smith, an actor, but refused to live with him and the marriage was dissolved on 10 September 1922. The child of a further mysterious love affair Norman Garvin (b. 1914) was adopted later by Zora's *de facto* husband David McKee Wright [q.v.], editor of the 'Red Page' of the *Bulletin;* they had two daughters.

With immense courage and enterprise, Zora Cross supported herself by acting in one of Philip Lytton's companies and teaching elocution, then by freelance journalism. She wrote drama criticism for the magazines *Green Room* and the *Lone Hand,* was a columnist for the *Brisbane Daily Mail,* sent poems to literary magazines, and after the outbreak of World War I, toured North Queensland with a concert party in aid of war funds.

In 1916 Zora Cross submitted her first novel, apparently on an Aboriginal theme, to T. C. Lothian [q.v.], who refused it. Her first book of poems, *A song of mother love* (1916), was published in Brisbane in answer to the German 'Song of Hate'. She was also corresponding about a long poem with Wright, who tried to impose some discipline on her life and her writing.

Zora returned to Sydney in 1917 and at the end of the year published *Songs of love and life,* some of which had already appeared in the *Bulletin.* The sixty love-sonnets in the book were the first sustained expression in Australian poetry of erotic experience from a woman's point of view, a fusion of sensuousness and religiosity, rather than sensuality; they attracted favourable if somewhat startled reviews. These sonnets, and similar poems in *The lilt of life* (1918) were a frank, passionate, if somewhat monotonous, expression of her love for Wright, with whom she later went through a form of private marriage in an empty church.

As the inspiration of the poems became known, the affair scandalized literary and journalistic circles in Sydney, mainly because it was mistakenly believed that Wright had abandoned his responsibility for his four sons by Margaret Fane, who had left him for the journalist Hilary Lofting; in fact he and Zora contributed generously to the support of the Lofting *ménage.* Nevertheless, Wright seems to have been gradually eased out of his editorship of the 'Red Page'; the strain on their combined resources was severe.

Wright's sudden death in 1928 left Zora in great financial difficulties. Her struggle to support her three children, mainly by freelance journalism, makes a painful story, though she remained cheerful, free of self-pity and simply got on with her work. Her younger daughter remembers her as 'a delightful and amusing parent, who never for one moment lost sight of her priority as a writer and a poetess'. In spite of a Commonwealth Literary Fund pension of £2 a fortnight from 1930, the family were often short of the bare necessities.

After Wright's death, Zora concentrated on a Roman theme which had surfaced from a previously unpublished novel, 'A story from Australia', or the complete education of Daisy Marsh', intending to write a trilogy of Roman novels. A legacy from her mother in 1953 enabled her to visit Rome for research, but the books were never completed. Faithful to her dream of love and poetry, she continued to work until she died of arteriosclerotic heart disease on 22 January 1964, at the cottage in which she had lived with Wright at Glenbrook, in the Blue Mountains: she was buried with Anglican rites in Emu Plains cemetery. She was survived by her son and her younger daughter April; her elder daughter Davidina died in 1941.

Zora Cross had a true lyric gift, revealed best perhaps in some of her children's verse: for example, the charming *The city of Riddle-mee-ree* (1918), and in more sombre tones in the fine *Elegy on an Australian schoolboy* (1921), in memory of her 19-year-old soldier brother, John Skyring Cross. The landscape of her verse is rarely Australian in character, but she could suddenly abandon romantic convention for lines of surprising dramatic strength. Her serialized novels have little artistic importance: those in book form, notably *Daughters of the seven mile* (1924) show a then unusual interest in Queensland settings and some awareness of developing social and economic stresses in Australia. Her pamphlet *An introduction to the study of Australian literature* (1922) has outlived its original usefulness, but her unpublished impressions of writers she knew still have value. So have the accounts left by members of her family of their relationships with tribal Aboriginals, of which she made some use in her novels.

Aussie, 15 June 1922; *Herald* (Melb), 15 Nov 1919; *Bulletin,* 14 June 1939; Z. Cross papers (LaTL, ML, and Fisher Lib, Univ Syd); W. P. Hurst correspondence (LaTL); D. McK. Wright papers (ML); information from Mrs A. Hersey, Glenbrook, NSW.
                                        DOROTHY GREEN

CROSSLEY, ADA JEMIMA (1871-1929), singer, was born on 3 March 1871 at Tarraville, Gippsland, Victoria, daughter of Edward Wallis Crossley, ironmonger, and his wife Harriette, née Morris, both from Northamptonshire, England. Ada was sixth surviving child in a family of twelve children: 'a regular rough bush youngster I was with my auburn pigtail'. She took piano lessons when 7 from Mrs Hastings of Port Albert, and between 12 and 15 played the organ and led the singing at the three village churches. Later Ada studied pianoforte with the elder Alberto Zelman [q.v.6] in Melbourne.

When it became apparent that Ada had a voice of great promise, her parents allowed her to take lessons with Madame Fanny Simonsen, on the condition that she never sang opera. One of her first public appearances in Melbourne was in November 1889 when she took part in the third Philharmonic Subscription Concert in the town hall. In the next four years she sang frequently at oratorios and concerts, including the popular promenade concerts organized by W. J. Turner, and was principal contralto in the choir of Charles Strong's [q.v.6] Australian Church. She became well known in Sydney after her début there in January 1892.

In March 1894 Ada left for London where she studied first with (Sir) Charles Santley and then for some seven months in Paris with Madame Marchesi. Her London début was at the Queen's Hall in May 1895 but her big opportunity came when she substituted at a moment's notice for Clara Butt at a concert in Manchester; she was soon singing at principal oratorio festivals throughout Great Britain. While her voice was admired for its rich velvet quality and steady purity of timbre — one reviewer described it as having the 'luscious richness of a Carlsbad plum combined with the translucent purity of rock crystal' — she was praised particularly for her interpretative skills. A favourite of royalty, she was commanded five times in two years to sing before Queen Victoria, and she sang on many important ceremonial occasions. In 1903 she claimed a repertoire of 500 sacred songs and ballads, ranging from Gluck and Handel to Richard Strauss, and she sang in English, German, French, Italian, Norwegian, Danish and Russian.

While on a successful tour of the United States of America in 1902-03, during which she recorded for the Victor Gramophone Co.'s Red Seal Celebrity series, Madame Crossley was engaged by J. C. Williamson [q.v.6] to visit Australia and New Zealand. She arrived in September 1903 and was received with acclaim. The young Percy Grainger [q.v.] was among her entourage. She returned to England in February 1904 via South Africa.

On 11 April 1905 at the parish church of St Marylebone, Ada married Dr Francis Frederick Muecke (1879-1945), son of H. C. E. Muecke [q.v.] of Adelaide. She revisited Australia in 1907-08, again with Grainger among her supporting artists. From 1913 she reduced her professional engagements but continued to sing at charity concerts, especially during World War I. As her husband gained eminence as a throat specialist, she withdrew from public life, but her London house remained a haven for newly arrived Australian artists.

Ada Crossley died on 17 October 1929 at Woodlands Park, Great Missenden, Buckinghamshire. After a memorial service at All Souls, Langham Place, she was buried in St Marylebone cemetery, East Finchley.

L. W. Matters, *Australians who count in London*... (Lond, 1913); B. and F. Mackenzie, *Singers of Australia* (Melb, 1967); *British A'sian,* 23 May 1895; *Critic* (Adel), 26 Sept 1903; *Australasian,* 23 Nov 1889, 20 Dec 1890, 21 Mar, 26 Sept, 10 Oct 1903, 2 Jan 1904, 20 May 1905; *Sydney Mail,* 17 Mar 1894; *Gippsland Standard,* 15 Jan, 1 Apr 1904, 14 June 1905, 4 July 1906, 15 Jan, 24 Mar 1909; *Argus,* 12 Apr 1902, 19 Oct 1929; *Herald* (Melb), 18 Oct

Crossley

1929; *SMH*, 19, 26, 29 Oct, 2 Dec 1929; Crossley clippings and letters (Percy Grainger Museum, Univ Melb).   MARGERY MISSEN

CROTTY, JAMES (1845?-1898), prospector, was born in County Clare, Ireland, and migrated when about 18 to the Victorian goldfields where he became a skilled miner and battery-man. About 1879 he went to the new goldfields in western Tasmania, worked as a digger near the Pieman River for several years and made prospecting trips up the Gordon River. In 1884 he camped at the new gold diggings at Mount Lyell and bought a one-third interest in the most promising mine, the Iron Blow. He paid £20 for his share which was to be worth £1½ million in 1897.

The Iron Blow was the cap of a massive deposit which was rich in gold near the surface and – unknown to the prospectors – valuable in copper at depth. Most grains of gold were difficult to extract, large boulders had to be levered or blasted in order to expose the gold-bearing ground, and progress was slow. In 1886 Crotty's syndicate found richer gold and Crotty walked about 100 miles (160 km) to Waratah to register the find. 'I'll be that rich', he said, 'I'll buy Ireland and make it a present to Parnell'.

Ireland remained unbought. The mine continued to puzzle geologists and metallurgists. It devoured so much money that Crotty, in order to pay calls on his shares, had to borrow £900, and work as a miner in Sydney's new sewerage tunnels. In 1890 he returned to the mine as a manager, and when it closed he remained as caretaker. He had virtually married himself to the mine.

In 1891 most of the shares passed to new Broken Hill silver kings. When they confirmed that the mine contained vast deposits of copper, they formed the Mount Lyell Mining and Railway Co. Ltd in 1893, opened copper smelters in 1896, and so made Crotty – still a minority shareholder – a rich investor. He was now living in Yallambee, a mansion in the Melbourne suburb of Auburn, and trying to float his large acreage on the borders of the main Mount Lyell mine. He was often seen in law courts – he was decidedly litigious – and at company meetings and Catholic gatherings: an eloquent, excitable man-about-town.

In January 1897 Crotty left Melbourne, intending to raise capital for the smaller Lyell mines on the London stock exchange. After a gale of publicity he floated the North Mount Lyell Copper Co. in September. A month later roadmakers accidentally found rich copper at the mine. Crotty harvested his luck, planning his own port and smelting town, and a railway from Macquarie Harbour to the mine. All were built after his death: the short-lived smelting town was named Crotty.

When after a brief illness Crotty died at Mayfair, London, on 16 April 1898, his death certificate mentioned cirrhosis of the liver. In London he had attracted so many friends and financial 'sea-gulls' that his requiem Mass in Regent Street and his burial at Kensal Green were largely attended.

Crotty had married in July 1889, when he lived in obscurity in Sydney. His bride, 22-year-old (Irene) Mary Gordon, later known as May Kathleen, was possibly a Protestant by background, was probably a barmaid, and was at least twenty years younger than him. In apportioning an estate of close to £200000 – a huge sum in the depressed 1890s – Crotty left her only £100 a year with the promise of another £500 a year if she entered a convent. As his will bequeathed £300 a year each to a Melbourne businessman and a priest, and £100 a year to each of Crotty's six sisters and brothers (and no bonus to tempt them into a convent or monastery), the young widow had clearly been out of favour. The largest share of the estate passed to the Catholic Church, and St Patrick's Cathedral in Melbourne was completed with the aid of dividends which continued to flow from Mount Lyell for decades after Crotty's death.

G. Blainey, *The peaks of Lyell* (Melb, 1954); *Mount Lyell Standard*, 28 Nov 1896, 20, 27 Apr 1898; *Tasmanian* (Launc), 12 Feb, 5 Nov 1887; *British A'sian*, 21 Apr 1898; MDHC Archives (Fitzroy, Vic).   GEOFFREY BLAINEY

CROUCH, RICHARD ARMSTRONG (1868-1949), politician and soldier, was born on 19 June 1868 at Ballarat East, Victoria, son of George Crouch, miner, storekeeper and later a wealthy boot-retailer from Tottenham, London, and his wife Selina Durham, née Marks, from Aberdeen, Scotland. The family was Congregationalist. Richard, from the age of 6, attended Mount Pleasant State School under the brilliant headmastership of W. H. Nicholls. In 1885 his father moved the family to Melbourne. In 1887 Richard began the two-year articled clerks' course at the University of Melbourne, winning the Bowen Prize for an essay on economic co-operation in 1889. He was awarded the Supreme Court Judges' prize in 1891; next year he was admitted as a barrister and solicitor and commenced practice as a solicitor in the city. He was both a member of the burgeoning Australian Natives' Association and an executive member of the waning Imperial Federation League, but after 1893 he gave firm support to 'Advance Australia', the motto of the A.N.A.

At the first Federal election in 1901 Crouch as a Protectionist won the seat of Corio in the House of Representatives. Only 32, he was the youngest member and was obliged to second the adoption of the address-in-reply. At this time he was a friend of Alfred Deakin [q.v.]. He retained his seat with good majorities in 1903 and 1906 but was defeated in April 1910 along with other supporters of Deakin. He had served briefly as a chairman of committees, gained recognition as a wit and a radical, and once was outspoken on the delicate matter of lavish allowances for the governor-general.

Crouch enthusiastically supported new trends in Australian defence policies. He had been commissioned in April 1892 in the 2nd Infantry Battalion. From July 1903 he was a captain in the 6th Australian Infantry Regiment and commanded the Prahran Infantry Militia. He approved of the Australian National Defence League which advocated compulsory military service and while overseas in 1911-12 contributed an important article on national service to the official British *Army Review* (1912). On his return to Australia his many articles on defence included warnings on the military might of Germany.

Crouch was promoted major in 1908 and in July 1912 commanded the 56th Infantry Battalion (Yarra Borderers). Promoted lieut-colonel in February 1913, on 16 March 1915 he was given command of the 22nd Battalion, Australian Imperial Force. The battalion landed at Gallipoli on 5 September 1915 but early in December Crouch was transferred to command the Base Camp at Mudros. He was compelled by illness to return to Australia in March 1916 and on 13 April his A.I.F. appointment was terminated.

Crouch, whose support for national service had stopped short of advocacy of compulsory overseas service, now set his mind to opposing conscription. As Victorian branch president of the Returned Soldiers' No-Conscription League he worked against W. M. Hughes [q.v.] during the referenda campaigns of 1916 and 1917. Encouraged by J. H. Scullin [q.v.], he joined the Labor Party and in 1924 was chosen to represent Australia at the International Federation of Trade Unions Education Conference in Oxford. On his return he became an active leader of the Labor movement in Victoria. His presidential address to the 1928 Easter conference of the Victorian party was a plea for national unity and a restatement of the concept most dear to his heart, 'Australia for the Australians'.

Crouch won the Federal seat of Coran-gamite in October 1929 but lost it in the resounding defeat of Labor in 1931. He decided to forsake politics for philanthropy, travel, writing, and encouraging Australians to take a greater interest in their history. A member of the (Royal) Victorian Historical Society, he was an executive-member from 1926 to 1935, and until 1940 contributed articles to the society's journal. He wrote a largely autobiographical novel, *The prime minister*, published in 1937 under the pseudonym 'Richard Greenhill', but it was not a success.

In 1926 Crouch began a long and generous sequence of gifts to Ballarat institutions and sporting clubs. These included bequests to the Ballarat Fine Art Gallery for awards in memory of his father and sister: the George Crouch prize for oils and sculpture (1926) and the Minnie Crouch Prize for water-colours (1944). His most generous benefaction to the gallery was also in 1944 when he presented his superb collection of medieval and Renaissance manuscripts. At the Ballarat Botanical Gardens he initiated the avenue of sculptures of Australian prime ministers and bequeathed funds for maintaining the project.

In his later years Colonel Crouch lived with his sister Gertrude at Point Lonsdale, where his father had built a house in 1882. He never married. He died on 7 April 1949, leaving an estate valued for probate at £43 490, and was buried at Point Lonsdale.

Biblionews, 3 (1969), no 3, 4 (1970), no 1; *Punch* (Melb), 4 Oct 1906; *Labor Call*, 28 May 1925; *Aust Worker*, 18 Dec 1929; *Ballarat Courier*, and *Geelong Advertiser*, 9, 11 Apr 1949. AUSTIN McCALLUM

CROWDER, FREDERICK THOMAS (1856-1902), businessman and politician, was born in Adelaide on 21 January 1856, son of William Nathaniel Crowder, a manufacturer of aerated waters, and his wife Emily, née Hayward. After working in his father's firm, W. N. Crowder & Co., he migrated to Western Australia in 1876, and in 1878 established at Fremantle a business which soon became the colony's leading manufacturer of aerated waters. Trading later under the name of Crowder & Letchford, the firm survived at Fremantle for a hundred years. In 1884 Crowder bought a part-ownership in the Fremantle *Herald;* it merged in 1886 with the Perth *Daily News.* He became a director of its publishers, Stirling [q.v.6] Bros & Co. Ltd, including a term as chairman in 1900-02 in which it was decided to close down the old-established weekly *Inquirer.* By 1895 he was also a member of the Perth stock exchange, speculating in the Coolgardie gold-mining boom. For many years he was chairman of the Perth Gas Co.

Crowder's political career began with service on the Perth City Council in 1885-91. When the Legislative Council became elective in 1894 he contested South-East Province and, although non-resident in the district, topped the poll. He generally supported (Sir) John Forrest's [q.v.] ministry, but he had all the small businessman's antipathy to government spending, and was an implacable critic of the engineer-in-chief C. Y. O'Connor [q.v.]. Even after disproof of his predictions that the centralized Fremantle harbour would be a failure, he continued to attack the Coolgardie pipeline scheme until O'Connor's suicide. A consistent foe of Federation, holding that intercolonial free trade would kill Western Australian agriculture, he nevertheless consented to serve as a delegate to the 1897-98 sessions of the Australasian Federal Convention when it became necessary for the Western Australian legislature to replace members whose parliamentary terms had expired. He spoke only twice at the convention, both times inanely objecting to the proposal to phase out Western Australian tariffs on a sliding scale.

On seeking re-election to the Legislative Council in 1900 Crowder was defeated, but was returned in 1901 at a by-election for East Province which he represented until his death from cancer at his residence in Cottesloe on 2 May 1902. By his wife Annie Imelda, née Fitzpatrick, whom he had married in Adelaide on 17 March 1877 he left a son and a daughter. A Roman Catholic, he was buried in Karrakatta cemetery. A decent, mediocre, local politician, Crowder's national importance was due solely to his membership of the Federal Convention, to which he was elected mainly to serve as a follower in the wake of Forrest, and in whose principles he had not the slightest faith.

Morning Herald (Perth), 3 May 1902; information from Letchford & Co., Fremantle, WA.

G. C. BOLTON

CROWE, ROBERT (1867-1955), dairy expert, was born on 7 June 1867 at Koroit, Victoria, second son of William Crowe [q.v.], farmer, and his wife Catherine, née Aldworth. Robert was educated to merit certificate standard at Koroit State School.

Crowe's working life spanned the period of the beginning and expansion of the export butter industry in Victoria; he greatly influenced its progress. In 1888 he attended the Centennial International Exhibition in Melbourne, saw the butter-making ma-

chinery at work and spoke with the manager David Wilson [q.v.]. Next year Crowe was appointed to control the new Koroit co-operative butter factory, which was the first to use the Babcock method of measuring the butter-fat content of milk – he had purchased an early model of the testing equipment from Germany. He was first secretary of the Victorian Institute of Dairy Factory Managers and Secretaries and its president in 1895 and 1896.

In the latter year Crowe joined the Department of Agriculture as a dairy expert; he later became officer-in-charge of the Government Cool Stores, Victoria Dock, and from October 1911 exports superintendent. As dairy expert he was responsible for training managers of Victorian butter factories and for providing and distributing information to farmers. Seeking to improve the life-style of dairying families, he urged them to abandon 'rule-of-thumb' routines and to adopt 'systematic' techniques, particularly herd-testing. He was a valued speaker at rural gatherings and contributed to farmers' papers and journals. A pioneer in radio broadcasting, he spoke to farmers in their own style about their practical problems. In 1924, after supervising the produce section of the Wembley exhibition, London, he visited Sweden and Denmark, returning home to praise the thoroughness of the Danes and to advise Victorians to follow their example. Crowe was in charge of the Produce Division of the Department of Agriculture from 1915. In 1931 he succeeded Dr S. S. Cameron [q.v.7] as director of agriculture, retiring in 1932 after two difficult Depression years.

An acutely observant and deep-thinking man, always searching for perfect solutions to problems, Crowe developed a wide range of interests. An amateur photographer, he was also interested in plants, particularly pasture species, and as a young man had been a friend of the botanist (Sir) Ferdinand Mueller [q.v.5]. From 1910, during leave, he pioneered two 500-acre (200 ha) blocks of forested land on King Island; after overcoming trace element deficiencies, he spent much of his long retirement there establishing a farm that exhibited his meticulous detail and systematic methods.

Crowe, who observed his Catholic faith throughout his life, was a tolerant, kindly man remembered familiarly as 'Bob Crowe' by his colleagues. On 10 October 1893 he married Agnes Mary Meagher, a schoolteacher from Camperdown and daughter of another Irish migrant family; they had four sons and two daughters. He died at his home at Preston on 17 June 1955 and was buried in Fawkner cemetery, predeceased by his wife and two sons.

K. Sillcock, *Three lifetimes of dairying in Victoria* (Melb, 1972); Roy Com on the butter industry, *PP* (Vic), 1905, 2 (10); *J of Agr* (Vic), 53 (1955); information from Mr D. Crowe, Glen Iris, and Mr J. Russell, Koroit, Vic.   L. LOMAS

CROWE, WILLIAM (1837?-1931), farmer, was born at The Glen, County Clare, Ireland, son of Thomas Crowe, farmer, and his wife Margaret, née O'Donnell. He was educated at the near-by town of Upper Kilbane, where he grew up with his maternal grandparents; he was still young when first his mother and later his father died.

Following the example of his uncle, Crowe migrated to Australia in 1855. After first landing in Adelaide, he sailed to the Western District of Victoria, and disembarked at Belfast (Port Fairy), before moving further east to Koroit where land was more easily available. Within two years he had purchased his first land — a single acre (0.4 ha). On 20 April 1863 at Belfast Catholic Church, he married Catherine Aldworth, Irish-born daughter of a Koroit farmer; they had nine sons and four daughters.

Crowe was an energetic and successful farmer. The Victorian gold rushes had raised the prices of primary produce, especially potatoes, and he travelled long distances in a dray to fields near Stawell and Ararat to market his crops. At a time when traditional methods were being displaced, he was noted for his innovative approach to agriculture, a skill inherited by his son Robert [q.v.]. He was reputedly the first in the district to introduce aids such as reapers and binders, milking machines, potato diggers and windmills. Several of his own inventions, including a system of watercooling were also used on his property. He was a keen businessman, remembered as hard but fair; in order to employ workers who would not need overseeing, he was said to have offered his employees five shillings per week above the going rate.

Crowe had a long career in local government. After the proclamation of the Borough of Koroit on 7 October 1870, he stood for election and was successful in November as one of nine new councillors elected from fourteen candidates, polling the second highest number of votes. He served until August 1910, with only one twelve-month break, and was mayor six times between 1878 and 1903. From all accounts he was a popular mayor. He was a founder of the Koroit Agricultural Society and of the town's butter factory. He supported a number of sporting clubs, and was a successful greyhound owner. There is no evidence of an interest in politics at the parliamentary level, although he agitated

for the continuation of the railway to Koroit after it had reached Warrnambool in 1890.

A Catholic, Crowe was a strong supporter of his church's charitable organizations. Aged 93, he died at Koroit on 3 January 1931 and was buried in Tower Hill cemetery. He was predeceased by his wife and two sons.

J. A. Allan, *The Victorian centenary book* (Geelong, 1936); H. A. McCorkell, *A green and pleasant land* (Koroit, 1970); *Koroit Sentinel*, 27 Jan 1892, 10 Jan 1931; family papers (held by Mrs M. Carey, Koroit, and Sister M. Crowe, St Jude's Primary School, Langwarrin, Vic); family information.   JOHN WARHURST

CROWTHER, GEORGE HENRY (1854-1918), educationist, was the father of GEORGE O'DELL (1882-1950), lawyer, and HENRY ARNOLD (1887-1966), schoolteacher and grazier. George Henry was born on 8 June 1854 in Jamaica, eldest of the six children of Joseph Crowther and his wife Mary Ann, née Bebb. His parents had migrated to the West Indies from Yorkshire in the 1840s. In 1857 the family went to Horsham in Victoria and later to Melbourne; his father taught in country schools at Lexton (1858-61), Carngham (1862-76) and Macarthur until his death there on 17 April 1877.

George Henry was educated at Lexton and Carngham, where he was a pupil-teacher from May 1868. With the help of Philip Russell [q.v.6] he completed his secondary education in 1872 as a day scholar at Wesley College, Melbourne, and went on to the University of Melbourne (B.A., 1876; LL.B., 1878; M.A., 1879; LL.D., 1884). He was licensed to teach on 1 July 1875 and after some time as a private tutor, became master of the matriculation form at M. H. Irving's [q.v.4] Hawthorn Grammar School in 1879. Gaining much repute as a schoolmaster, he moved to Brighton early in 1882 and opened his own grammar school, day and boarding; some two thousand boys passed through his classes in the thirty-seven years of his proprietorship. On 12 January 1882 at Christ Church, St Kilda, he married Alice Elizabeth, sister of T. H. Armstrong [q.v.7], later bishop of Wangaratta. She and her unmarried sister Eva, who was housekeeper and matron in 1882-1920, assisted in administering the school.

Crowther was a foundation member and later president of the (Incorporated) Association of Secondary Teachers of Victoria, formed in 1904 to counter the government's moves to establish its own secondary schools. In 1907 he led a committee which presented to the State government a plan for a comprehensive system of education in-

cluding all government and non-government educators and community leaders. He
was an antagonist of Frank Tate [q.v.], first
director of education in Victoria: his establishment of state secondary schools in 1910,
Crowther believed, hindered any effective
co-operation between government and
non-government schools in Victoria and
eventually closed most of the latter, about
337 of which had existed in Victoria between
1885 and 1910.

Crowther was deeply involved in many
community activities in Brighton and
beyond. He was founder of the Secondary
Schools Amateur Athletic Association, a
member of the councils of Trinity College in
the University of Melbourne and of Firbank
Church of England Girls' Grammar School,
and a founder of the Old Wesley Collegians'
Society. Among other interests he was
chairman of the Brighton Gas Co., a trustee
of the local cemetery and for thirty years a
churchwarden of St Andrew's Church,
Brighton. He was a member of the Anglican
Diocesan Synod. Crowther died of coronary
vascular disease at Brighton on 6 November
1918 and was buried in Brighton cemetery.
His estate was valued for probate at £12 712.
He was survived by his wife, two sons and his
daughter Elsie, who married the surgeon
(Sir) Victor Hurley.

George O'Dell was born on 17 November
1882 at Brighton and was educated at
Brighton Grammar School and Trinity
College, University of Melbourne (B.A.,
1904; LL.B., 1906; LL.M., 1917). He established a flourishing legal practice with W. F.
Weigall and became a director of several
companies. At Christ Church, South Yarra,
on 4 September 1912 he married Kathleen
Russell Daly. He died at his home in Toorak
on 3 November 1950, survived by his wife, a
son and two daughters. His estate was
valued for probate at £32 166.

Henry Arnold was born on 29 July 1887 at
Brighton and was educated at his father's
school and Trinity College (M.A., Dip.Ed.,
1911). He distinguished himself as a swimmer, footballer and marksman. He taught at
The Armidale School, New South Wales,
before returning to Brighton Grammar
School as second master and co-proprietor.
In May 1915 he was commissioned in the 21st
Battalion, Australian Imperial Force. He
received special mention for his work assisting the *Southland* into Mudros after being torpedoed in September 1915; in
December he was in one of the last parties to
leave Gallipoli and was promoted captain. In
March 1918 he became lieut-colonel commanding the 14th Battalion. He was mentioned four times in dispatches and was
awarded the Distinguished Service Order in
April 1917.

In December 1918 Crowther returned to
Australia to take charge of the school after
his father's death. He was headmaster until
the end of 1923, when he sold it to an association of friends and old boys. He then
went on the land at Hillston, New South
Wales, and later at Wildings, Flinders, Victoria. In 1941-42 he was assistant provost
marshal of Southern Command. He had
married Doris Douglas Umphelby at the
Presbyterian Church, Toorak, on 22 March
1927. Survived by his wife, a son and a
daughter, he died on 17 April 1966 at Hastings, and was cremated.

A. Sutherland et al, *Victoria and its metropolis*, 2
(Melb, 1888); W. Bate, *A history of Brighton* (Melb,
1962); *Brighton Grammarian*, Dec 1915, Dec 1966;
Argus, 7 Nov 1918; Inc Assn of Secondary
Teachers of Vic, Council minutes (Melb); private
papers on Vic non-government secondary schools,
1885-1950 (held by author).   C. E. SLIGO

CUDMORE, JAMES FRANCIS (1837-
1912) and DANIEL HENRY (1844-1913),
pastoralists, were born on 11 October 1837 at
sea between Hobart Town and Adelaide, and
on 7 February 1844 at Modbury, South
Australia, eldest sons of DANIEL MICHAEL
PAUL CUDMORE (1811-1891) and his wife
Mary, née Nihill, of Limerick, Ireland. D. M.
P. Cudmore, the younger son of a Quaker
Anglo-Irish landowner, applied for a free
passage to Australia in 1834 as his means
were 'very limited'. With his wife he migrated to Van Diemen's Land in June 1835
and, after a few months as schoolmaster at
Ross, worked in a brewery. He moved to
South Australia in 1837, and made enough
money building *pisé* houses to establish
breweries in Adelaide and later at Kapunda.
He also bought and farmed a section at
Modbury. In 1847 he inherited property in
Ireland but sold it to take up a pastoral lease
of 80 square miles (207 km²) at Yongala,
which carried 18 000 sheep. In the 1850s he
also leased Pinda, Beautiful Valley and Paringa stations. In the 1860s, after a 1700-mile
(2700 km) exploratory journey from Rockhampton, he acquired still larger leases in
Queensland and New South Wales. He then
began transferring his holdings to his sons,
and retired to his villa, Claremont, Glen
Osmond, where he died on 3 November 1891,
survived by his wife, four sons and four
daughters. In 1882 he had published *A few
poetical scraps from the portfolio of an Australian pioneer*.

James Francis was first educated by the
Jesuits at Sevenhill then at the Collegiate
School of St Peter, Adelaide, after the family
had transferred to the Anglican Church.
From 1859 he managed Paringa, 208 square

miles (530 km²), and in 1860 he leased Ned's Corner, further up the Murray. From these properties he overlanded sheep to Queensland and took up leases there.

On 26 March 1867 he married Margaret Budge. Three years later, with his wife's brother, he bought Gooyea (later Milo) on the Bulloo, Queensland, from Vincent Dowling [q.v.4]. In 1876 he enlarged Ned's Corner in partnership with Robert Barr Smith [q.v.6] and A. H. Pegler. By the end of the 1870s 130 000 sheep were being shorn at his stations on the Murray, and his Queensland prospects seemed excellent. But, tiring of travelling between his properties, he began to play the gentleman, left too many decisions to his managers, and spent £40 000 building and furnishing Paringa Hall at Somerton.

Cudmore overreached himself by buying Welford Downs on the Barcoo and amalgamating it with Milo, making a run of 5100 square miles (13 000 km²). He had to take as additional partners Sir Thomas Elder [q.v.4] and W. R. Swan, and establish the Milo and Welford Downs Pastoral Co.; they insisted on a change from cattle to sheep, requiring expensive improvements, and it was twenty years before the company paid a dividend. Meanwhile, a rabbit plague reduced his woolclip by 80 per cent, and by 1886 his debts exceeded £200 000. His creditors agreed to postpone insolvency proceedings for a year. An unsecured loan from the Bank of New Zealand helped pay his interest bills and he provided for his family by completing the transfer of Paringa Hall and other freeholds to his wife and his unencumbered Queensland leases, Tara, Dartmouth and Blackall, to his sons.

In 1888 Cudmore was forced to make a composition under the 1886 Insolvent Act. His secured creditors accepted all his mortgaged properties and investments at their conservative valuations. Other creditors had to accept 5s. in the pound. He died at Paringa Hall on 17 August 1912, survived by his wife and eleven of their children, and a natural son and daughter by Isabella Crowe, spinster, of Nailsworth, South Australia, whom he also provided for. An old life policy yielded more than enough to pay the debts he had incurred since 1888 and his estate was sworn for probate at £4859. His second son by his wife Margaret, Sir Arthur Murray Cudmore (1870-1951), was a leading Adelaide surgeon.

Daniel Henry Cudmore was educated at Sevenhill and the Collegiate School of St Peter; he managed Yongala from 1860. Unlucky in his sheep leases on the Clarke and Warrego rivers in Queensland, he was successful at Avoca station, New South Wales, acquired in 1870, with frontages of ten miles (16 km) to the Murray and twenty-five miles (40 km) to the Darling. He was fascinated by technology and spent many thousands draining the Darling's anabranch, making water storages and erecting fences. He used pumps to irrigate lucerne and other fodder crops, and 120 000 sheep were shorn at Avoca in 1888 with his new Wolseley [q.v.6] shearing machines.

An honorary magistrate, Cudmore served as sheriff of the county and chairman of the Wentworth district council and agricultural society, built St John's Church, Wentworth, and paid its vicar. He used Melanesian labour to grow sugar-cane on 3000 acres (1200 ha) his father had bought on the Herbert River, Queensland, and invested in the North Queensland Brewing Co. and urban property in Brisbane and Rockhampton. In Scotland in 1890 he stayed at the Trossach's Hotel, which inspired him to build his turreted seaside mansion, Adare, at Victor Harbour, South Australia, where he died on 14 December 1913. His estate was sworn for probate at £5752. On 20 February 1872 at Glen Osmond he had married Harriet Garrett Smedley who bore him two sons and a daughter before her death on 16 March 1879. On 15 November 1882 he married Martha Earle McCracken, by whom he had another four sons, the second of these being Sir Collier Robert Cudmore (1885-1971), who won a gold medal for rowing at the 1908 Olympics and was long prominent in South Australian politics.

Besides their numerous progeny (used as dummies in the free-selection era), the Cudmores left two abiding legacies: the improvements they effected on their Yongala and Riverland leaseholds paved the way for the later success of numerous smallholders; and their great houses, Tara, Avoca, Claremont, Paringa Hall, Popiltah and Adare, though now bereft of the elaborate formal gardens which once graced them, are still a wonder to behold.

W. R. H. Jessop, *Flindersland and Sturtland* (Lond, 1862); R. Cockburn, *Pastoral pioneers of South Australia*, 1, 2 (Adel, 1925, 1927); T. C. Borrow, *The Cudmore family in Australia* (Adel, 1945); M. H. Ward, *Some brief records of brewing in South Australia* (Adel, 1951); K. Sharp and B. Crump, *A history of Milo and Ambathala* (Adel, 1963); *Observer*, 7 Nov 1891, 24, 31 Aug, 2 Nov 1912, 20 Dec 1913; *Federal Standard*, 23 Nov 1895; *Advertiser* (Adel), 14 Dec 1913; *Chronicle* (Adel), 24 Aug 1912, 20 Dec 1913; *Sunday Mail* (Adel), 10, 17 Aug 1975; Cudmore papers (SAA); CO 201/244/129-30.   P. A. HOWELL

CULLEN, EDWARD ALEXANDER ERNEST (1861-1950), engineer, was born on 21 December 1861 at South Brisbane, son of

Edward Boyd Cullen, an accountant from Scotland, and his Irish-born wife Fanny, née Moore. His father subsequently became under-secretary of the Treasury. After leaving Brisbane Boys' Grammar School about 1875, Cullen joined the Royal Navy survey of the Queensland coast as a civil assistant in 1878-80. He was assistant to J. B. Henderson [q.v.4], the government hydraulic engineer, until 1883.

After his appointment as nautical surveyor to the Department of Harbours and Rivers in 1884, some of Cullen's early surveys were virtually voyages of discovery. He made the first survey of the Norman River in 1884, and was associated with H. H. Milinan in the discovery in 1887 of Port Musgrave, describing it as 'the best natural harbour in Queensland except Port Curtis'; its western promontory is still known as Cullen Point. He also surveyed in detail the northern half of Moreton Bay in 1890-91, securing a master's certificate in order to command his own survey vessels. On 26 November 1892, at Stanthorpe, he married Mary Margaret Robinson, née Cullen, a divorcee.

The Department of Harbours and Rivers was abolished in 1893 and Cullen was transferred to the Department of Marine as principal engineer. Here began his main work of transforming the shallow Brisbane River to a fourteen-mile (22 km) channel of usable depth. Because finance was so short, he spent much of his time sounding to estimate quantities dredged. Realizing the futility of only dredging, he proposed in 1897 that training walls be built to confine the tidal flow; his proposal was supported by the American expert L. W. Bates, but was not at once accepted.

Cullen went to the United States of America and Europe in 1900 to report on harbours and water power. He returned to become chief engineer of a new Department of Harbours and Rivers. Elected an associate member of the Institution of Civil Engineers, London, in 1895, he became a full member in 1902. When the government eventually accepted his river-control scheme, in 1912, he aligned the walls purely from his own intimate knowledge of the river and organized their construction to secure immediate benefits. In 1913 he obtained consent to the reclamation of land at Hamilton and, against considerable opposition, organized the progressive transfer of port facilities downstream. His continuing work on the river made Brisbane one of the few successful river ports of the era. By the time of his retirement in December 1931, his scheme, though by no means complete, offered a safe sixteen-feet (5 m) depth to Hamilton and beyond — a depth which is only just now becoming inadequate. In 1922 his paper,

'Improvement of the Brisbane River', won him the coveted Telford Premium.

Cullen's responsibilities ranged far beyond the Brisbane River. In one way or another he was involved in the development of all ports in Queensland, twenty of which were gazetted. When he became engineer in 1900, the only means of travelling to central and North Queensland was by coastal steamer. Since land travel beyond the railways was difficult and hazardous, every protected cove and river was used to transport local produce and supplies. Even in 1927 there was still a weekly express steamer to Mackay supplemented by calls from the Torres Strait mail service.

Because of the need to maintain these vital links, with larger ships needing deeper berths and wider turning-basins, Cullen was inevitably involved in bitter disputes between local factions. Sometimes the disputes involved adjacent ports such as Rockhampton and Broadsound, Gladstone and Port Alma, or Townsville and Bowen. Some of his decisions, such as the abandonment of the Flat Top Island port at Mackay, must have required great courage, but they were usually accepted without resentment. According to local opinion in Mackay, however, Cullen's Island, a large sand and gravel mass which built up in the Pioneer River, was the only explicit result of his director wall designed to increase depths at the town wharf.

After his retirement, Cullen became the Australian representative on the council of the Institution of Civil Engineers, and was awarded the Imperial Service Order in 1932. For a time he joined his son Edward Boyd in business as a consulting engineer. Predeceased by his wife, Cullen died on 13 April 1950 at St Helen's Private Hospital, South Brisbane, and was buried in South Brisbane cemetery with Presbyterian forms. His estate, valued for probate at £15 817, was left to his son and daughter.

G. Lewis, *A history of the ports of Queensland* (Brisb, 1973); *V&P* (LA Qld), 1885, 3, 393, 1887, 4, 3, 1900, 5, 1013; *Courier Mail*, 27 Nov 1950.

GORDON R. McKAY

CULLEN, JOHN HUGH (1883-1970), priest, was born on 14 June 1883 at Kilquade, County Wicklow, Ireland, son of Michael Cullen and his wife Mary, née Troy. He was educated by the Christian Brothers in Dublin, and at Mungret College, County Limerick, where he graduated B.A. in 1904 as an external student of the Royal University of Ireland. After four years at All Hallows College, Dublin, he was ordained priest on 24 June 1908 and at the instigation of Archbishop Delany [q.v.] of Hobart was sent to the University of Fribourg, Switzerland.

On arrival in Hobart in June 1910 Cullen became curate at St Joseph's parish, and remained in the position for almost twenty-four years. As an early executive-member of the Australian Catholic Federation he exercised a 'moderating and sensible influence'; in 1916 he debated with the *Mercury* the wartime relations of Pope Benedict XV and the Kaiser. But he gradually became absorbed in literary and educational affairs, and was the driving force behind the building of St Joseph's School, opened in April 1923; a new wing added to St Joseph's Orphanage for Girls (later Aikenhead House) in 1924; a two-storey convent for the Sisters of Charity in 1926; and the Church of St Francis Xavier in South Hobart opened in June 1933. He became parish priest on 6 February 1934. In June he was appointed diocesan consultor. In May 1944 he was made a domestic prelate (Monsignor) and in the following September became vicar-general of the archdiocese of Hobart.

Cullen contributed articles to *Austral Light, Australasian Catholic Record* and the Launceston published *Monitor*, chiefly on religious themes but incorporating much general historical material. In 1916 with A. E. Warne he established the monthly *Catholic Magazine*, in which appeared a series of articles which formed the basis of his *The Catholic Church in Tasmania* (Launceston, 1949). After twelve months leave of absence in Ireland and Europe in 1926-27, when he was presented with a silver chalice by the Catholics of Delgany and formed a lifelong friendship with Eamon de Valera, he published *Young Ireland in exile: the story of the men of '48 in Tasmania* (Dublin, 1928). Cullen's interest in the work of the Sisters of Charity led to *The Australian daughters of Mary Aikenhead: a century of charity* (Sydney, 1938), and in 1966 he published the history of the Presentation Sisters' hundred years in Tasmania.

Perhaps Cullen's finest historical work was the series of articles in the *Australasian Catholic Record* in 1949-54 on R. W. Willson [q.v.2], the first Catholic bishop of Van Diemen's Land. Cullen wrote for the *Catholic Standard* which superseded the *Monitor* in January 1921, and after that paper was taken over by the Church in October 1937 and renamed the *Standard*, he was editor in 1939-45. Keenly interested in education, both religious and secular, he was appointed to the Teachers' and Schools' Registration Board as the Catholic representative in 1923. Admitted B.A. *ad eundem gradum* at the University of Tasmania in 1911 he became the first chaplain to the Newman Society in 1930. In 1965-69 he was patron of the Tasmanian Historical Research Association.

Cullen retired from St Joseph's in July 1956 and was appointed chaplain to St Joseph's Orphanage where he could indulge his love for children. Although fluent in six languages and popular as a public speaker, he disliked publicity, and was reluctant to celebrate his diamond jubilee in 1968. His speeches and homilies were noted for clarity and brevity, and his writing also was a model of simplicity. In September 1967 he resigned as vicar-general of the archdiocese and died in his sleep on 17 November 1970 at Aikenhead House, Taroona, leaving, in his own words, 'neither debts nor debtors'. He was buried in Cornelian Bay cemetery. He had outlived two younger brothers, Arthur (1889-1939) and Joseph (1892-1951), who had followed him through All Hallows, the National University of Ireland and priestly service in Tasmania.

W. T. Southerwood, *Planting a faith in Hobart* (Hob, 1970); Catholic Church in Aust, *Official Year Book*, 1911-45; *Catholic Who's Who* (Lond), 1952; *Monitor* (Launc), 19 Feb, 9 July 1909, 26 Aug 1910, 17, 31 Mar 1916; *Catholic Standard*, 12 May, 21 July 1923, 31 Mar 1927, 9 Feb 1928, 19 June 1930, 19 Jan, 6 July 1933, 28 Oct 1937; *Standard* (Hob), 25 Nov 1937, 30 Mar 1939, May 1944, June, July 1968, Nov, Dec 1970; *Mercury*, 18 Nov 1970.

MARY NICHOLLS

CULLEN, SIR WILLIAM PORTUS (1855-1935), chief justice and politician, was born on 28 May 1855 at Mount Johnstone, near Jamberoo, New South Wales, seventh son of John Cullen, a farmer from Ireland, and his wife Rebecca, née Clinton. A natural student, Cullen defied his father's attempts to suppress his education, walked many miles daily to the nearest school at Kiama, and left home at 20. Persuaded by Professor Charles Badham [q.v.3] to enter the University of Sydney, he won a scholarship by examination, and graduated B.A. with first-class honours in classics in 1880, having taken other scholarships and prizes during his course. He went on to graduate M.A. (1882), LL.B. (1885), showing outstanding ability in equity and real property law, and LL.D. (1887). He was admitted to the Bar on 30 April 1883.

Torn between the Bar and an academic career, Cullen applied for a lectureship in mathematics (a subject he particularly enjoyed) at the University of Adelaide: the opinions of learned and influential referees were summarized by (Sir) Edmund Barton's [q.v.7] view that Cullen 'is much esteemed by his professional brethren as a highly educated gentleman and a very capable lawyer': but he did not receive the appointment. Except for part-time law lecturing he gave up ideas of academic life.

On 17 December 1891 at Carrington, Port Stephens, he married Eliza Jane (Lily), elder daughter of R. H. D. White [q.v.6] of Tahlee. Cullen and his wife were pioneer residents of the Sydney suburb of Balmoral where he acquired a large holding of land and built a stately home, Tregoyd. In the grounds he maintained natural vegetation and propagated Australian wildflowers, his botanical interests later being recognized by the naming after him of *Eucalyptus cullenii*. The Cullens had two sons and two daughters: one daughter died in infancy.

Strongly nationalist, Cullen was a vocal advocate of Australian Federation. He confessed that it was 'almost the only political question on which I feel with the whole strength of which I am capable of feeling'. He expounded those views as a member of the Legislative Assembly for Camden in 1891-94, and of the Legislative Council in 1895-1910. He also delivered many public addresses in which he urged that Australians learn from the experience of Switzerland, Canada and the United States of America, and settle intercolonial friction. He was an adviser to (Sir) George Reid [q.v.] when the final agreement on Federation was reached in Melbourne in 1899.

In the legislature Cullen was a skilled draftsman of bills and of amendments, and he took many initiatives about the reform of 'lawyers' law'. While respecting the continuance of English tradition, he allowed his nationalism to prevail. He was a vigorous supporter of the creation of the High Court of Australia, and an early proponent of abolishing appeals to the Privy Council.

From 1896 Cullen began a long association with the administration of the university when he was elected a fellow of its senate; he was acting dean of the faculty of law for some time in 1897. Professor (Sir) Edgeworth David [q.v.], a close friend, acknowledged Cullen's 'able, impartial and generous guidance in all our counsels' in the senate. Cullen was vice-chancellor in 1908-11 and chancellor in 1914-34. He served the university well during its post-war expansion, but attracted much criticism for remaining too long as chancellor.

At the Bar Cullen's career had prospered with the opening of the High Court of Australia. He became a K.C. in 1905. Although a sound practitioner, his unassuming manner had earlier tended to mask his outstanding command of the law. Sir John Peden [q.v.] wrote that 'Cullen's merits as a lawyer were not adequately recognized by the profession as a whole until the High Court of Australia was established in 1903, and it became known that its first chief justice, Sir Samuel Griffith [q.v.], regarded him as being in the first rank of the barristers then practising before the High Court'.

On 14 February 1910 Cullen was appointed chief justice of New South Wales in succession to Sir Frederick Darley [q.v.4]. His elevation, which commanded wide support from the legal profession and the community, was notable because he had neither solicited it nor taken any part in a sharp contest by other aspirants to the vacancy. Knighted in 1911, he was appointed K.C.M.G. in 1912.

Cullen was an ideal choice as chief justice. Sir Frederick Jordan [q.v.] considered him to have been 'courageous in his judgements, and rapid in his determination'. Cullen was obliged, however, to put aside many of the reforming ideas he had espoused as a politician and to accept, as a judge, the legal system as he found it. He also served as lieut-governor and administered the State on six occasions. He faced an awkward constitutional problem when, in 1911, he declined the McGowen [q.v.] government's advice to have the evenly divided Legislative Assembly dissolved.

Early in 1925 Cullen qualified for a judicial pension and retired at once because of gravely impaired health. He remained lieut-governor until 1930. Throughout his public career he was active in many charitable and patriotic bodies and was president of the Boy Scouts' Association and the Boys' Brigade. He was 'fond of simple pleasures, the mountain ramble, the billy tea, the camp fire and liked to hear and tell a good story'. Lady Cullen was a founding vice-president of the New South Wales division of the British Red Cross Society in 1914 and president in 1916-17 of the Australian Red Cross Society. She also served on various comfort funds and, among her many activities, was president of the Victoria League, vice-president of the Bush Book Club of New South Wales and chief commissioner of the State's Girl Guides' Association.

Lady Cullen died at Leura, where they had lived in retirement, on 10 June 1931 and Sir William on 6 April 1935; they were buried in the Anglican section of Wentworth Falls cemetery. Portraits of Cullen by Norman Carter [q.v.7] are held by the Supreme Court of New South Wales and by the University and Schools Club; one by Jerrold Nathan is held by the University of Sydney.

J. M. Bennett, 'Sir William Portus Cullen — scholar and judge', *Canb Hist J*, Sept 1977, and for bibliog; *Aust Law J*, 9 (1935); *SMH*, 11 June 1931, 9 Apr 1935; *The Times*, 8 Apr 1935; family papers (held by Mrs J. A. Bragg, Sutton, Sussex, England, and Mrs W. H. Cullen, Syd).   J. M. BENNETT

CULLEY, CHARLES ERNEST (1877-1949), trade unionist and politician, was born on 16 April 1877 at Broadmarsh, Tasmania, son of James Culley, shoemaker, who migrated probably from Ireland, and his wife Julia, née Smith. His father died while Charlie was young and his schooling was limited to the primary grades. A groom in a northern Tasmanian racing stable, Culley subsequently worked in the stables of private houses and on occasion rode as a jockey. In his early twenties he became a miner at Broken Hill, New South Wales, but soon returned to work at the Beaconsfield, Tasmania, gold mine and the North Farrell mine at Tullah. In 1913 he moved to Hobart where, after a spell as a farm labourer in Margate, he made his permanent home.

Culley gained union experience in the Amalgamated Miners' Association at Tullah and Beaconsfield, where he was in 1912 elected secretary. In Hobart he joined the Builders' Labourers' Union, becoming secretary in 1913 and subsequently secretary of the Tasmanian branches of the Federated Liquor and Allied Trades Employees' Union, the Female Confectioners' Union, and the Amalgamated Clothing and Allied Trades Union. When, in 1917, an attempt to establish a Tasmanian Labor Federation, integrating unions and political Labor branches, broke down, Culley represented his union at the re-established Hobart Trades Hall Council. Secretary to the council in 1918-29, and president for most of 1934-44, he played an important part in obtaining its recognition as the Tasmanian branch of the Australian Council of Trades Unions, of which he was an executive member.

Culley's political career complemented his trade unionist experience. Elected as a radical Labor member for Denison to the Tasmanian House of Assembly in 1922, he polled highest of the four Labor candidates elected for Denison in 1925; but three years later he lost his seat when the Lyons [q.v.] Labor government was defeated. As a back-bencher for his two parliamentary terms, Culley was required to mediate between the Lyons government and a frequently hostile Trades Hall Council and was subsequently highly critical of Lyons. In 1928 he won the Federal seat of Denison. On 3 March 1931, after the defection of Lyons and J. A. Guy from the Scullin [q.v.] government, he was elected an honorary minister to represent Tasmania. He resigned, however, on 24 June in protest against the cabinet's espousal of the Premiers' Plan; he lost his seat in December.

Culley regained Denison in the Tasmanian House of Assembly election of 1934, which established the ministry of Albert Ogilvie [q.v.] and inaugurated a period of 35 years of unbroken Labor government. The Hobart Trades Hall Council disapproved of a number of the Ogilvie ministry's actions, and Culley was often deputed to protest to the government. He was chairman of the Parliamentary Standing Committee on Public Works until 1943 and a member of the Executive Council in 1941-43. Under Robert Cosgrove he was minister for mines in 1942-43 when he was elected chief secretary and minister for transport. By 1946 his health was deteriorating, and though he narrowly regained his seat in November, he did not stand for cabinet, but remained a back-bencher until 1948.

Culley was appointed C.M.G. in 1947. He twice served, in 1927 and 1938, as Australian representative at the International Labor Office conferences in Geneva. He was president of the Tasmanian branch of the Australian Labor Party in 1944-47, and was appointed a justice of the peace in 1943. Keenly interested in sport he was a life member of the Hobart Amateur Cycling Club. Noted for his sincerity, forceful speech, and conciliatory manner in negotiation, he was lauded as a 'straight goer'. Especially during the Depression, he represented the socialist wing of the Labor Party and often clashed with right-wing Labor politicians. A member of the Church of England, he died on 10 June 1949 at New Town, survived by his wife Mary Jane, née Pope, whom he had married on 27 June 1906 at Beaconsfield, and by four sons and a daughter; three of his sons served in the Australian Imperial Force. He was cremated at Cornelian Bay cemetery after a state funeral.

Mercury, 17 Dec 1941, 11, 15 June 1949; *Voice* (Hob), 11 June 1949; Council minutes (Trades Hall, Tas); information from Mr J. W. Culley, Moonah, Tas.
                                                    R. P. DAVIS

CUMBERLEGE, CLAUDE LIONEL (1877-1962), naval officer, was born on 9 June 1877 at Marylebone, Middlesex, England, son of Lieut-Colonel Alexander Bulstrode Cumberlege of the Madras Staff Corps, and his wife Emily Florence, née Broadwood. On 15 January 1891 he entered the Royal Navy's training ship *Britannia* as a cadet, and in 1893 was posted as a midshipman to H.M.S. *Tourmaline* on the North American and West Indian Station. Over the next ten years he served with the Channel and Mediterranean fleets and was promoted sub-lieutenant in 1897 and lieutenant in 1899. He held commands in the Mediterranean in 1905-11, was promoted commander in June 1911 and returned to the Home Fleet. In

October 1912 he was appointed to the 4th Destroyer Flotilla in command of *Lurcher,* the navy's fastest destroyer.

On 7 November 1913 Cumberlege was transferred on loan to the Royal Australian Navy and appointed, in the rank of commander, to H.M.A.S. *Warrego* which, with the *Parramatta* and *Yarra,* constituted the R.A.N.'s first destroyer flotilla, which Cumberlege commanded from December. By temperament and personality he was well suited to destroyer command: he was handsome, unconventional, dashing and breezy, and his courage, initiative and lack of 'frill' inspired respect and affection. He expressed himself in very direct language and his letters and written reports were always precise and succinct.

When war was declared on 5 August 1914 the destroyer flotilla joined other ships of the Australian Squadron in a search for enemy warships in the Pacific. It was believed that German cruisers were based at Simpson Harbour, New Britain, and as A. W. Jose [q.v.], the official historian, has written, it was 'in expectation of almost certain battle' that Cumberlege's destroyers slipped into the harbour on the night of 11 August. No warships were found and next day Cumberlege made an armed landing at Rabaul in an attempt to locate the radio station; he then resumed the search for the German Squadron.

In September his destroyers escorted the Australian Naval and Military Expeditionary Force to German New Guinea. Cumberlege was commended for his services during the capture of the wireless station at Bitapaka on the 11th: when a party sent ashore under Lieutenant R. G. Bowen [q.v.7] came under fierce fire, Cumberlege landed a destroyer contingent, pending the arrival of reinforcements from the expeditionary force. In the summer of 1914-15 his flotilla patrolled the New Guinea coasts and surrounding islands and searched the Sepik River for German ships and installations. It left for Sydney in February after work which 'probably more than any other single factor, established British dominance in the huge area of scattered island-groups so recently taken from Germany'.

In 1915 the flotilla patrolled in eastern Australian waters and in the Timor and Arafura seas, then from November served with the Royal Navy in the Malay Archipelago. Cumberlege was promoted captain (R.A.N.) on 30 June. In January 1916 he was transferred to command the cruiser H.M.A.S. *Encounter,* which served in home waters. In October he took over the new light cruiser *Brisbane,* which joined the British Mediterranean Fleet in December, but early in 1917 was recalled to the East Indian Ocean. From October until January 1918 it patrolled in the Gilbert and Solomon Islands and Nauru and then in the Torres Strait.

Early in 1919 Cumberlege returned to the Royal Navy but in April was appointed to command the battle-cruiser *Australia,* flagship of the Australian Fleet. It sailed from Portsmouth, England, that month and on 1 June, at Fremantle, Western Australia, a mutiny occurred when Cumberlege refused a request from some of the ship's company to delay her departure by one day. Always imperturbable in a crisis, Cumberlege took firm action and after arrival at Sydney five of the mutineers were court-martialled. The incident caused considerable controversy but Cumberlege retained the *Australia* until September 1920 when he was appointed to command the *Melbourne.*

On 9 May 1922 he returned to the Royal Navy but soon afterwards retired. He was promoted rear admiral on the retired list in 1926. After 1922 he took paid command of a nobleman's steam-yacht which cruised the Mediterranean. He published his reminiscences, *Master mariner,* in London in 1936. Little is known of his later life, but he finally made his home on a sailing craft with a shifting postal address from Ostend via Biarritz to Gibraltar and the Mediterranean. He died on 22 November 1962.

A. W. Jose, *The Royal Australian Navy 1914-1918* (Syd, 1928); H. J. Feakes, *White ensign — southern cross* (Syd, 1951); *Public Administration* (Syd), 29 (1970), no 3; *SMH,* 13 Jan 1916, 17, 25 Apr, 26 Sept, 21 Oct 1919; Dept of Defence (Navy), MP1049, 1, 15/079, 18/070 (AAO, Melb); author's recollections.   R. S. VEALE

CUMBRAE-STEWART, FRANCIS WILLIAM SUTTON (1865-1938), lawyer, university administrator and teacher, was born on 27 January 1865 at Riversleigh, Canterbury, New Zealand, son of Francis Edward Stewart, grazier, who had been in the Gladstone colony in Queensland, and his wife Agnes, née Park. Another child was Janet Agnes [q.v.]. Educated at Melbourne and Geelong Church of England grammar schools, Francis junior took second-class honours in modern history at Christ Church, Oxford, in 1887, was called to the Bar at the Inner Temple in November, and returned to Melbourne next year. He took his B.C.L. with third-class honours in 1897, when he was known as Cumbrae-Stewart.

Stewart read with Henry Bournes Higgins and Sir Edward Mitchell [qq.v] in 1889; he practised at the Victorian Bar in 1890-92 and later as a country solicitor. Admitted to the Queensland Bar in September 1890, he practised in Brisbane in 1898-1903, then joined Thynne and Macartney [qq.v] as managing clerk. As a member of the Anglican diocesan council and the cathedral chapter, he helped draft a successful provincial constitution. At the same time he was the inaugural editor of the *Queensland State Report.* At St Andrew's Anglican Church, Brighton, Victoria, he married Zina Beatrice Selwyn Hammond [q.v. Z. Cumbrae-Stewart] on 24 January 1906; they had one son. Cumbrae-Stewart became the proud chief of part of the clan Stewart in 1908.

Appointed foundation registrar and librarian of the new University of Queensland in 1910, Cumbrae-Stewart also conducted the State public examinations and sometimes examined in French himself. He was an assistant district censor and interpreter in World War I. Universally known as Cumbrae, he was a commanding figure in the university. Severe, with an erect military bearing and a fiercely waxed moustache, he was always formal and pontifical in public. Though he mellowed with age, he attracted respect rather than affection. The thesis, 'Actio Pauliana; its origin development and nature', with which he won an Oxford D.C.L. in 1922, was admired by authorities.

Energetic and intensely curious, Cumbrae-Stewart was a voracious reader and an almost compulsive writer. By 1925 he was a founder and president of the (Royal) Historical Society of Queensland and editor of its journal. He was president of the Queensland branch of the Dickens Fellowship, chairman of the Queensland Place Names Committee, vice-president of the Queensland Authors and Artists Association, a founder and trustee of the Oxley Library and a member of both the Royal and the Royal Geographical societies of Queensland. For years he regularly contributed to the Saturday edition of the *Brisbane Courier* and gave short radio talks.

In January 1926 Cumbrae-Stewart became Garrick professor of law and was appointed K.C. in 1927. He gave eleven lectures a week, established law as a discipline in the university almost single-handed and laid the foundation for the full faculty that was set up when he retired in 1936. He settled in Melbourne to be near his son, died at South Yarra on 24 March 1938 and was buried in Burwood cemetery.

A fluent and sometimes witty writer, Cumbrae-Stewart published little substantial work, but his innumerable short pieces reached a wide audience, are still respected by historians, and enhanced the reputation of the university.

Australasian, 3 Feb 1906, 16 Apr 1927; *Courier Mail,* and *SMH,* 25 Mar 1938.

HARRISON BRYAN

CUMBRAE STEWART, JANET AGNES (1883-1960), artist, was born on 23 December 1883 at Brighton, Victoria, youngest of the ten children of Francis Edward Stewart, an early settler of Gladstone, Queensland, and his wife Agnes, née Park, of Wellington, New Zealand. The Stewarts had arrived in Victoria from New Zealand in 1870; Francis was chief inspector for the National Bank in Melbourne before becoming general manager of Goldsbrough, Mort [qq.v.4, 5] & Co. Ltd, resigning in 1891. He was then chairman and managing director of Younghusband, Row & Co. Pty Ltd until his death in 1904. Janet followed her brother, Francis William Sutton [q.v.], in adopting the surname Cumbrae-Stewart.

Janet grew up in the family home, Montrose, at Brighton Beach. She went on outdoor sketching trips with John Mather [q.v.] before studying at the Melbourne National Gallery School in 1901-07 under Bernard Hall and F. McCubbin [qq.v.]. In 1905 she was awarded second place in the National Gallery travelling scholarship competition. Elected to the council of the Victorian Artists' Society in 1914 she exhibited regularly with the society in 1909-19. In 1915 she was awarded a silver medal in the Panama-Pacific International Exposition, San Francisco. Between 1920 and 1937 several exhibitions of her work were held at the Athenaeum Gallery, Melbourne, as well as in Adelaide and Sydney.

In 1922 she went to London with her sister Beatrice and began exhibiting at the Galérie Beaux-Arts, Paris (1924-31), the Royal Academy and the Salon de la Société des Artistes Français (the Old Salon), Paris — in 1923 she received an honourable mention from the latter. In the same year she travelled through the Continent and to Canada. During her seventeen-year stay in Europe she lived at Avignon and Caen in France and at Laiguelia on the Riviera di Ponente, Italy, with Miss Argemore ffarington 'Bill' Bellairs, her companion. She returned to Australia in 1939 to visit her family and remained there after the outbreak of World War II. She lived at Margaret Street, South Yarra, from 1947 until her death on 8 September 1960. Her estate was valued for probate at £13 143.

Cumbrae Stewart (she dispensed with the hyphen and signed her work in this manner) devoted the most significant section of her *oeuvre* to studies of the female nude in pastel. Her nudes were the subject of a monograph by John Shirlow [q.v.] published in Melbourne in 1921. While influenced by the academic draughtmanship of Bernard Hall, Cumbrae Stewart imparted a sensuous and graceful quality to her rendering of women's bodies. While her *oeuvre* includes water-colour and oil studies of landscapes and portraits she is chiefly known for use of pastel.

J. Burke (ed), *Australian women artists: one hundred years, 1840-1940* (Melb, 1975); *Art in Aust*, no 6, 1919, Aug 1922; *Home*, June 1920, Aug 1925; *Brighton Southern Cross*, 8 June 1966.

JANINE BURKE

CUMBRAE-STEWART, ZINA BEATRICE SELWYN (1868-1956), community worker, was born on 30 August 1868 at Brighton, Victoria, daughter of Robert K. Hammond, stock and station agent, and his wife Jessie Duncan, née Grant. Her father died in 1875 leaving a widow and ten children. Archdeacon R. B. S. Hammond [q.v.] was a brother. Zina grew up in the lively social life of well-to-do Brighton society until the bank crash of 1893 ruined her mother. Educated at Mrs R. Sadleir Forster's Ladies School, St Kilda, she returned there to teach drawing. Janet Cumbrae Stewart [q.v.] was a pupil. On 24 January 1906 at St Andrew's Church of England, Brighton, she married Janet's brother Francis William Sutton Cumbrae-Stewart [q.v].

They lived in Brisbane and their only child was born in 1908. Her husband became registrar of the University of Queensland. A deeply committed evangelical Anglican, Zina undertook community and charitable service. She was an executive member of the Australian Red Cross in Queensland for twenty-two years and won its long service medal. She became an original member of the Mothers' Union and was its president for nine years. President of the National Council of Women of Queensland in 1926-35, she led campaigns against the exploitation of children and for domestic science education; she sought different sections for the sexes in community organizations. In 1931 she helped found the Queensland Social Service League to cope with Depression problems, joined its executive and became vice-president of the women's division. Through the National Council of Women she was on the Australian Broadcasting Commission's education committee for four years. A fluent speaker, she gave some radio talks.

Mrs Cumbrae-Stewart was usually on the executive of the twenty or more societies to which she belonged; they included the Mothercraft Association, the Traveller's Aid Society, the Bush Nursing Association and the Shakespeare Society. Brusque in public, she had a lively sense of humour in private. She regarded her own abilities as giving her a right to leadership and to the exercise of a formidable dignity. She enjoyed putting down pretentious or silly

people but believed none the less that her first responsibility was to be a good wife and mother. To her son 'she was like those grand old ladies whose pictures hang in the National Portrait Gallery in Edinburgh who plainly had no need of rights'.

On her husband's retirement in 1936, the Cumbrae-Stewarts visited Britain. Representing the Queenland Red Cross, she had planned a busy programme of public work which was cut short when his illness forced a hurried return to their new Melbourne home. After his death she lived with her bachelor son; when he moved to Hobart as deputy parliamentary draftsman, she joined him there, making her first flight in 1948. She died in Hobart on 31 July 1956 and her body was returned to Melbourne for burial in Burwood cemetery.

A biographical register of Queensland women (Brisb, 1939); National Council of Women (Qld), *The first fifty years...* (Brisb, 1959); Aust Red Cross Soc (Qld), *Annual Report*, 1935-36; *Brisbane Courier*, 15 Apr 1930; F. W. S. Cumbrae-Stewart papers (Fryer Lib, Univ Qld); family papers (held by Mr F. D. Cumbrae-Stewart, Hobart, Tas).

NANCY BONNIN

CUMING, JAMES (1861-1920), businessman, was born at Portland, Maine, United States of America, second son of JAMES CUMING (1835-1911) and his wife Elizabeth, née Smith, of Aberdeenshire, Scotland, who had migrated first to St John, New Brunswick, Canada. In 1862 the family went to Melbourne and Cuming senior prospered as a farrier. He worked on the construction of acid works, studied chemistry at the public library and in 1872 joined his brother-in-law George Smith and a fellow Aberdonian, the merchant Charles Campbell, in purchasing a chemical works at Yarraville. In 1875 Cuming Smith & Co. leased adjoining bone-mills and entered the fertiliser trade, manufacturing bone dust and bone and guano superphosphate. In the next twenty-five years they adopted overseas innovations in acid manufacture, substituted rock phosphate for bone in the production of fertiliser, and established a network of distributors in the Victorian wheat-belt. In 1881 George Smith left the partnership.

Cuming senior's eldest son, Robert Burns (1859-1910), established in 1882 the Adelaide Chemical Works Co., a joint venture of Cuming, Alfred Felton, F. S. Grimwade [qq.v.4] and Campbell. James junior, educated at Melbourne Church of England Grammar School in 1876-79, furthered his study of industrial chemistry with a tour of the United States, Europe and Great Britain in 1884. Admitted to partnership in Cuming

Smith, he became head chemist and later manager.

James senior retained a keen interest in the business, but his activities as a Footscray councillor and as a patron of societies, churches and charities absorbed much of his time. He also travelled extensively overseas. His other sons, George, Mari and William, attended Melbourne Church of England Grammar School and received a practical education at Yarraville, in technical institutes and on tour with their father. They were works managers at Yarraville, Port Melbourne and Yarra Junction.

James junior became general manager of the new company upon the amalgamation in 1897 of Cuming Smith & Co. and Felton, Grimwade & Co.'s acid and chemical works at Port Melbourne. He prevented ruinous competition with rivals Wischer & Co. (1895), Federal Fertilisers (1904), and Mount Lyell (1905) by securing adoption of gentlemen's agreements on prices and marketing, formalized in 1907 by the creation of the Victorian Fertilizer Association. He was a founder of the Society of Chemical Industry of Victoria and president in 1903 and 1914. During a world tour in 1904 he studied new developments in fertiliser and chemical plants; in 1907 he established at Yarra Junction a wood distillation works to produce chemicals previously imported. He also initiated sickness and retirement benefits for employees, but the increasing scale of business, the intervention of wage-fixing tribunals and militant unionism gradually eroded the old paternalist relations. His notes and addresses as president of the Victorian Chamber of Manufactures, 1917-20, and of the Old Melburnians, 1918-19, reveal the social and political fissures opened by the conscription and strike issues during World War I. He was not only angered by the disloyalty of militant unionists and political radicals but saddened by the collapse of the partnership of capital and labour.

Upon his death, aged 58, on 31 May 1920, James Cuming junior was acknowledged as one of Australia's foremost industrialists. On 3 February 1885 he had married Alice, daughter of W. M. Fehon [q.v.], and their daughter and four of their five sons lived to maturity — the eldest, William Fehon (1886-1933), became on his father's death general manager of Cuming Smith & Co., and subsequently of Cuming Smith & Mount Lyell Farmers Fertilisers Ltd and of Commonwealth Fertilisers and Chemicals Ltd, created as a result of amalgamation of the major fertiliser interests in Western Australia and Victoria in 1928 and 1929. The youngest son Mariannus Adrian (b. 1901) became manager in Western Australia in

1933 and in Victoria in 1943, and was subsequently chairman of the associated fertiliser companies. James Cuming senior, who died on 18 October 1911, is commemorated in Footscray by a marble bust, commissioned by public subscription and executed by Margaret Baskerville [q.v.7]; a portrait is in the possession of the City of Footscray. In memory of James junior, Cuming Smith & Co. Ltd financed a lecture theatre and research laboratory in the School of Chemistry at the University of Melbourne; a portrait is held by M. A. Cuming of Melbourne.

M. A Cuming (ed), *James Cuming: an autobiography* (priv print, 1916); J. R. Poynter, *Russell Grimwade* (Melb, 1967); J. F. Lack, Footscray: an industrial suburban community (Ph.D. thesis, Monash Univ, 1976), and for bibliog; Cuming Smith & Co. papers (Univ Melb Archives).

JOHN LACK

CUMMINS, JOHN (1857-1934), merchant, was born on 6 November 1857 on the Sofala gold diggings near Orange, New South Wales, son of John Cummins, storekeeper, and his wife Mary, née Halpin. Matriculating from St Stanislaus' College, Bathurst, Cummins avoided the University of Sydney and became a clerk in the firm of Dalton [q.v.4] Bros, Orange. He then moved to Sydney for a short stint on the staff of the Orient Steam Navigation Co. before beginning a long association with the mercantile firm of (F. A.) Wright [q.v.6], Heaton & Co. Ltd. As an auditor for that company, he made his first visit to Townsville in 1886 on a tour of inspection of its North Queensland operations. In Brisbane on the way to Sydney, he received instructions to assume management of Wright Heaton's Townsville branch. On 20 November 1895 at St Columba's Catholic Church, Charters Towers, he married Annie Flynn.

In April 1899 Cummins resigned and entered a partnership with Aylmer Campbell as general merchants. The business opened on 17 March 1899 and thereafter traded as Cummins & Campbell Pty Ltd. Like many another Irish Catholic, Cummins rapidly developed an independent and patriotic attachment to his region. He was a big North Queenslander, long and affectionately remembered for his remark that 'Tannymorel' was a healthy place but 'not-any-morelthy' than Townsville.

Not only big but bluff, Cummins was fond when young of social life, and in later years of ebullient companionability. Though tempered by the responsibilities of commercial and civic leadership, his warm humanity was reflected in the company practice of allotting shares to employees and managing 'C & Cs' as almost a co-operative concern. For many years the firm's house journal, *Cummins & Campbell's Monthly Magazine*, was almost the sole repository of writing on North Queensland.

The company filled the gap left in the north after the diversification of Burns [q.v.7] Philp [q.v.] and the removal of its headquarters to Sydney; its prosperity waxed initially through its dealings with the revived Charters Towers goldfield — Aylmer Campbell managed the first branch there but died before 1909. Branches were established at Cairns, Bowen, Innisfail and Ingham with agencies at Ayr, Hughenden, Yungaburra and Cloncurry and a depot at Mount Isa.

Cummins became one of a triumvirate of local merchants including James Burns and Samuel Allen of Samuel Allen & Sons who dominated the commerce of Townsville and North Queensland from the first settlement. The companies that they founded still do. As importers and exporters and agents, they provisioned the squatters, backed the teamsters and packers and stood behind the goldfields storekeepers when they sank their capital in prospecting ventures and re-couped it in grog selling.

Cummins was a member of the Townsville Harbour Board in 1908-17 and its chairman in 1910-12. He was president of the Chamber of Commerce and chairman of the Turf Club until just before his death on 1 August 1934 at Townsville. Flags throughout the city flew at half-mast as he was buried in Townsville cemetery. He was survived by his wife (d. 1935) and one of his two sons, and two daughters.

A. Donnelly (ed), *The port of Townsville* (Townsville, 1959); G. C. Bolton, *A thousand miles away* (Brisb, 1963); *Cummins & Campbell's Mthly Mag*, Aug 1934; *Townsville Daily Bulletin*, 2 Aug 1934; *SMH*, 3 Aug 1934; *North Qld Register*, 4 Aug 1934.   IAN N. MOLES

CUMPSTON, JOHN HOWARD LIDGETT (1880-1954), first director-general of the Australian Department of Health, was born on 19 June 1880 at South Yarra, Melbourne, son of George William Cumpston, warehouseman, and his wife Elizabeth, née Newman, a pioneer kindergarten teacher. Cumpston attended New College at Box Hill and Wesley College, although his adult faith was devout, conventional Anglicanism. He had a distinguished medical course at Melbourne, 1898-1902, and immediately committed himself to preventive and public medicine. 'The medical world', he recalled of that time, 'was afire with enthusiasm for the

new bacteriology, the new pathology, the new epidemiology, and these were beacons indicating the new road to the prevention of disease on a national scale'. After about a year as resident medical officer at the Melbourne Hospital and assistant medical officer at Parkside Lunatic Asylum, Adelaide, Cumpston left Australia in April 1905, intending to study public health throughout the world. An early highlight was to see American achievements, led by V. G. Heiser, in the Philippines. In London in 1906 he acquired a Diploma in Public Health and did research on scarlet fever and diphtheria which in 1907 won him an M.D. from Melbourne. He also served on the London Metropolitan Asylums Board.

In December 1907 Cumpston was appointed medical officer to the Central Board of Health, Western Australia. His interests soon ranged widely — schoolchildren's health, pulmonary disease among miners, historico-epidemiological studies of tuberculosis and diphtheria, quarantine, diet, housing, eugenics. Cumpston wrote well, if somewhat grittily, on these and broader topics. He called upon the profession to ponder 'the tendency towards nationalisation of medicine', and expounded his constant creed that 'it is certainly by sympathetic administration, but always through the people, that effective sanitary progress is obtained'.

Cumpston joined the Federal quarantine service, established by an Act of 1908 and operative from mid-1909, as general quarantine officer in Western Australia on 23 November 1910; he also retained his State duties until he left Perth next year after his appointment on 20 August as chief quarantine officer in Victoria. In September the director, W. P. Norris, travelled overseas, leaving Cumpston in charge of the Federal service until May 1912. At the end of that year Cumpston moved to Brisbane as supervisor in Queensland, a State made especially important by fear of Asian diseases. Now Norris transferred to London: Cumpston returned to Melbourne in May 1913 as acting director, being confirmed in that post from 1 July. Coincidentally there developed widespread, although mild, smallpox in New South Wales. Cumpston asserted Federal power in this very difficult and delicate area. The States, led by New South Wales, struck back. Cumpston survived, receiving support from his minister, E. L. Groom [q.v.]. He published one monograph (Melbourne, 1913) arguing that Australia's quarantine harmonized with general practice and community needs, and another on *The history of smallpox in Australia 1788-1908* (Melbourne, 1914). The latter witnessed his remarkably vigorous research, ranging from unpublished first fleet journals to interviews with Aboriginals in Western Australia. The quarantine service issued other material which attested Cumpston's concern to gather a store of facts on which to base purposeful policies. This was a palpable aspect in which he showed affinity with American Progressives and British Fabians, although he was never a party-political man.

Cumpston had often described quarantine work in military metaphors: in 1910 he had been a command sanitary officer in the Australian Army Medical Corps in Western Australia and World War I much enlarged his role. The quarantine service did remarkably well in checking the introduction of disease by returned servicemen. Cumpston himself advised the forces on sanitation. He sat too on a wartime Federal committee 'concerning causes of death and invalidity in the Commonwealth', which reported in favour of vigorous governmental activity in health matters. From these and other sources came pressure towards converting the quarantine service into a Department of Health, although Cumpston himself did not explicitly advocate that move until 1919. A minor wartime role was to serve, in 1917-19, on the first Commonwealth film censorship board.

The immediate post-war period saw stronger agitation for a Federal department, but also the influenza pandemic. Australia's quarantine resisted virulent flu notably long (until January 1919, at least), and the ultimate death-rate was much lower than, for example, in New Zealand and South Africa; still more impressive was the record pertaining to Australia's dependencies in the Pacific. Nevertheless the episode revealed the continuing strength of State claims to autonomy in health matters. The proponents of a Federal department waited until the Australasian Medical Congress at Brisbane, August 1920, for their major onslaught. Cumpston then spoke of himself as among those 'who dream of leading this young nation of ours to a paradise of physical perfection'. In January 1921 came the final decisive influence — an offer by Heiser, now director for the East of the Rockefeller Foundation's International Health Board, to provide skills and training for a department. The government at last agreed and Cumpston was appointed director-general of health and director of quarantine in March 1921.

The young department promised to realize its proponents' hopes. While quarantine remained the basic task, work was done too in tropical medicine, industrial hygiene, sanitary engineering, provision of laboratories and sera. Cumpston found time, between 1925 and 1927, to publish further massive histories of disease in Australia. The Federal royal commission on health (1925) endorsed the department's work, and promised to give it a broader role via the Federal Health Council, which first met in January 1927, and continued regularly to do so, under Cumpston's chairmanship. Thereby it appeared possible that he and his fellows could guide the States not only on the matters above but also on tuberculosis, cancer, venereal diseases, and infant and maternal care.

Yet even before 1927 and increasingly thereafter Cumpston and his department lost much of the earlier driving idealism. Several of the most able departmental officers left its service. The director himself became more pessimistic about mankind in general and the efficacy of bureaucratic action. The removal of the department to Canberra in 1928 symbolized its relative political unimportance. With the Depression its budget was much reduced, Cumpston seeming to acquiesce.

The later 1930s saw revival, burgeoning into new growth, especially of Cumpston's belief in the need to cherish health rather than treat illness. In 1937 the Federal Health Council transformed into the National Health and Medical Research Council. Subsidized with relative generosity, the council sponsored much inquiry and discussion on a very wide range of health and social matters. Beyond that, Cumpston promoted initiatives in pre-natal care (a jubilee fund raised in 1935 being directed thither), an advisory council and an inquiry relating to nutrition (1936-38), child education and welfare (notably through the Lady Gowrie [q.v.] centres opened in each capital), and the national council for physical fitness (1939). During World War II he played an important part, via a sub-committee of the N.H.M.R.C., in drawing up an elaborate scheme for a federally organized health and medical service. Cumpston supported this blue-print to his retirement in mid-1945. By then many portents had gathered to indicate that the scheme faced impassable obstacles.

As with his career generally, Cumpston's retirement had a mixture of elements. He had the honour and pleasure of advising on health services in Ceylon in 1949, and the next year travelled through South-East Asia on behalf of the United Nations Children's Emergency Fund. He now turned to narratives of Australian exploration, notably through biographies of Charles Sturt (Melbourne, 1951), T. L. Mitchell [qq.v.2] and A. C. Gregory [q.v.4], the two latter posthumously published in Melbourne, 1954, and Canberra, 1972. These studies attest feeling for adventure, effort, and Australian landscape. Cumpston also attempted more ambitious, never-published work, on Milton, Carlyle and Kipling. Meanwhile his attitudes to medicine and to man became increasingly sour. Within weeks of resigning he lost faith in a national health scheme, while a manuscript history he subsequently prepared of the Health Department (published in Canberra in 1978 as *The health of the people*) ended with a suggestion that preventive medicine had been 'biologically disastrous' in defying 'Nature's scheme for the survival of the fittest'.

Perhaps this pessimism sprang from Cumpston's rationalization for having failed to make Australia 'a paradise of physical perfection', or even to organize an effective programme of national medical care. By more mundane standards, the man achieved and merited much, as administrator, reformer, analyst and historian. He served infant Canberra, notably as chairman of the 'advisory council' in 1931-35 and a foundation member of the local historical society; the Australian Institute of Anatomy, administered by the Health Department, was the physical focus for much of the capital's early intellectual and academic life. Cumpston presented his extensive collection of medical Australiana to the National Library. The C.M.G. which he received in 1929 did but scant justice to his record. It might be said of him, as did he of Sturt, that his career exemplified 'the beliefs, ideals and aspirations which for centuries have inspired man's nobler efforts'.

Cumpston's personal standards always remained those of the upright, worthy, professional bourgeois. Tall, thin and bespectacled, he had a cool manner, at times sharpening into acerbity; those around him were expected to aspire, labour and achieve. He was a model pater familias. On 2 January 1908 at St John's Church of England, Fremantle, he had married Gladys Maeva, daughter of Dr G. A. Walpole of Gormanston, Tasmania. Mrs Cumpston survived her husband. Their seven children included Ina Mary, an academic historian of British imperialism, and John Stanley, diplomat, author and publisher. Cumpston died on 9 October 1954 at Forrest, Australian Capital Territory, and was cremated.

R. W. Cilento, *Blueprint for the health of a nation* (Syd, 1944); M. Roe, 'The establishment of the Australian Department of Health ...', *Hist Studies*, no 67, Oct 1976; *Health*, Dec 1954; *MJA*, 5 Feb 1955, 18 Nov 1967; *Punch* (Melb), 14 Aug 1913; *Herald* (Melb), 25 Feb 1939; C. Thame, Health and the state . . . (Ph.D. thesis, ANU, 1974); Cumpston papers (NL).   MICHAEL ROE

CUNNINGHAM, ARTHUR HENRY WICKHAM (1879-1942), pastoralist, was born on 29 June 1879 at Woodhouse station, near Ayr, Queensland, son of Edward Cunningham, grazier, and his wife Caroline, née Hann, niece of William and Frank Hann [q.v.4]. Harry Cunningham was educated at Barker College, Sydney, and returned to North Queensland; when his father died in 1898 he managed Woodhouse station, owned by Gilchrist, Watt [qq.v.1,6] and Cunningham. Much of the property was resumed and in 1902 the group purchased Strathmore on the Bowen River. Cunningham assumed management of both properties and settled permanently at Strathmore. On 12 May 1910 at Croydon, Sydney, he married Nellie Maud Wharton, of Birralee station. They had three sons and one daughter.

Cunningham was a member of the Wangaratta Shire Council from 1903 until 1942 and its chairman for twenty-six years; he was also involved in the Kennedy Stockbreeders and Collinsville Graziers associations, the Kennedy Hospital, Bowen Harbour Board, and the Townsville and Bowen show societies. A keen horseman, he was a long-time member and later patron of the Townsville Turf Club. During World War I his experience on the Bowen war council generated a scheme to assist returned servicemen by means of the profits from a cattle property.

Following negotiations with the Queensland government and the minister for repatriation in 1918-19, Cunningham inspected and purchased four properties on the lower Burdekin and consolidated them into Scartwater. The station was gradually stocked by donations of cattle and from funds contributed by sporting and other bodies. A board of five trustees included the local parliamentarian, the crown solicitor and Cunningham as managing trustee.

All returned servicemen and women resident in a defined area of North Queensland prior to enlistment were eligible, at first only for interest-free loans to establish themselves in business or on the land; the first grant of £500 was made in 1929. After 1936 the scheme was extended to help to educate dependants of ex-servicemen and women, and since then Scartwater and A. H. W. Cunningham scholarships have been awarded annually. The Returned Sailors' and Soldiers' Imperial League of Australia awarded Cunningham its certificate of merit and gold badge in 1933. Since his death, benefits of the trust, managed by his son, have extended to veterans of other wars. To the end of 1976 loans totalled $733 375, and scholarships had supported 690 secondary and 345 tertiary students, representing a total value of $621 665.

Cunningham died on 8 January 1942 in

Bay View Hospital, Townsville, of injuries received in a motor accident. He was buried in Townsville cemetery with Anglican rites. His estate was sworn for probate at £124129.

M. J. Fox (ed), *The history of Queensland*, 2 (Brisb, 1921); *The story of Scartwater* (priv print, 1956; copy, Oxley Lib, Brisb); G C. Bolton, *A thousand miles away* (Brisb, 1963); *Cummins & Campbell's Mthly Mag*, Feb 1942; *Telegraph* (Brisb), 17 Nov 1951; Cunningham and Scartwater Trust papers (held by Mr E. Cunningham, Strathmore, via Collinsville, Qld); Scartwater Trust records (held by Mr J. A. Sherriff, Hermit Park, Townsville).   ANNE ALLINGHAM

CUNNINGHAM, SIR EDWARD SHELDON (1859-1957), journalist, was born on 21 July 1859 at Battery Point, Hobart, son of Benjamin Marriott Cunningham, shipping manager, and his wife Jane Eccles, née Neilson. As a child, Cunningham lived in New South Wales and later Bendigo, Victoria. He went to private schools but owed his education mainly to his talented and cultivated mother. In 1874 he began his newspaper work as office-boy for the *Bendigo Advertiser*. After three years there, he went back to Tasmania to work on the Hobart *Mercury*, initially as a proofreader, but, after he had mastered shorthand, as a general reporter.

In 1879 Cunningham answered an advertisement for a parliamentary reporter for a 'mainland newspaper', which turned out to be the Melbourne *Age*. He was offered the job and accepted. Though hired as a political journalist, he also served as the paper's court reporter and police roundsman. Melbourne *Punch* remembered him as 'always the sedate, earnest young man, with more liking for work than for play'. His skill at seeking out a story soon became apparent. He was the only reporter present when Ned Kelly [q.v.5] was taken from the train bringing him to Melbourne after his capture; Cunningham had deduced correctly that the police would remove Kelly at the North Melbourne station rather than Spencer Street. His reports of the trial were masterpieces of meticulous, yet dramatic journalism.

In 1880, while covering the Melbourne exhibition of that year, Cunningham struck up a friendship with David Watterston [q.v.] of the *Argus*. In 1881 he was invited to join the *Argus* as its chief parliamentary reporter. In 1884-85, as special correspondent, he travelled to the United States of America with Alfred Deakin [q.v.]. On this tour he became convinced of the adaptability of American irrigation techniques to Victorian conditions, and it was partly as a result of his urging that the Chaffey [q.v.7] brothers came to the colony. In 1887 he accompanied Deakin to the first Colonial Conference in London.

In 1885 Cunningham was appointed chief of the reporting staff of the *Argus*. He made a name for himself as a good organizer and judge of men, with an ability to co-ordinate to the best advantage the output of the brilliant reporters working for him. As a man of energetic habits, who 'put a prodigious amount of go' into his work, he found the strain of a 4 a.m. publishing time too much for his health and in 1896 he resigned to take an extended holiday in the south of France. In London next year he was engaged by cable to represent the *Argus* at the Queen's Jubilee celebrations and to report the proceedings of the colonial conference. Editor F. W. Haddon [q.v.4], whom Cunningham greatly admired, said of these dispatches from London: 'you could hardly have had a better, more evenly balanced, concise, yet effective description'.

Cunningham rejoined the *Argus* in Melbourne in December 1897. Early next year he was appointed to assist the new editor Howard Willoughby [q.v.6], serving in the same capacity under Watterston from 1903 until July 1906 when he himself became editor. In 1909 he was one of six delegates at the first Imperial Press Conference in London chosen to receive the honorary degree of doctor of laws from the University of Glasgow. From then on he was always referred to in the *Argus* as Dr Cunningham.

Cunningham was not a 'literary editor' in the style of his predecessors; under his administration news assumed far greater importance. While some had mourned the demise of the *Argus* as an organ of culture, Cunningham was hailed on his retirement as editor in December 1928 as 'one of the best known and most highly respected figures in Australian journalism' who had 'kept the *Argus* abreast of the times without sacrificing dignity or decency'. (Sir) F. W. Eggleston [q.v.], however, criticized him for lack of enterprise. In 1929 Cunningham was appointed to the paper's board of trustees and as editorial adviser to the director. In 1936 he was knighted for his services to journalism. He retired in 1938 and became a trustee of the Edward Wilson [q.v.6] estate.

Cunningham was a member of the Melbourne and Australian clubs, enjoyed gardening, especially growing camellias, and was a fine amateur carpenter. He had married Maud Mary Jackson with Anglican rites at Sandhurst on 29 September 1886; they had no children. He died on 28 April 1957 and was cremated, having been predeceased by his wife in 1931. His estate was valued for probate at £28253.

C. McKay, *This is the life* (Syd, 1961); H. Gordon, *An eyewitness history of Australia* (Adel, 1976); *Newspaper News*, 2 Jan 1929; *Australasian*, 19 Sept 1896, 12 Mar 1898, 21 July 1906; *Punch* (Melb), 11 June 1914; *Argus*, 31 Dec 1928, 26 Mar 1929, 16 Nov 1931; *Age*, 21 July 1953, 21 July 1956, 29 Apr 1957; F. W. Eggleston, Confidential notes: journalists and press barons (Menzies Lib, ANU).

JOHN SALMOND

CUNNINGHAM, JAMES (1879-1943), politician, was born on 28 December 1879 at Warabraer, South Australia, son of James Cunningham, stonemason and farmer, and his wife Catherine, née Herrin, domestic servant. His parents could not write and Cunningham had little formal schooling. From about 1899 he was prospecting and mining on the eastern goldfields of Western Australia, and he later suffered severely from silicosis. On 29 October 1907 at Kalgoorlie he married Alice Daly. Active in the infant trade union movement, in 1914 he became full-time secretary of the Kalgoorlie and Boulder branch of the Goldfields Amalgamated Miners' Union of Workers of Western Australia.

Cunningham was a member of the Western Australian Legislative Council in 1916-22 and of the Legislative Assembly in 1923-36. Following Labor's 1924 victory, he was elected honorary minister and, in 1927, minister for goldfields and agricultural water supplies, a position he held until the government's defeat in 1930. In 1933 however, when Labor regained office, he was not re-elected to the ministry or even to other non-cabinet positions. This most unusual rebuff occurred largely because of his serious alcohol problem.

In 1936 Cunningham was defeated in the ballot for party re-endorsement. Subsequently it was announced that a number of voting papers had been discovered mixed in with those for other ballots: there followed a long intra-party struggle, in which it was clear that he had significant support from mining union officials. It was decided to allow all three candidates to contest the seat in the State election under the Labor banner. Thus he received a second and most favourable chance; however, he lost to H. H. Styants by a convincing margin and retired to his farm at Mullewa.

In 1937 Cunningham was elected to the Senate for Labor and in 1940 he became deputy leader of the party there. In July 1941 his remarkable come-back reached its zenith with his election as president of the Senate. The circumstances of the election were unusual: the absence of two non-Labor Senators (one on active service, the other unexpectedly admitted to hospital that very morning) resulted in a tied vote; in the draw

to resolve the deadlock, Cunningham won.

Throughout his life Cunningham remained part of the strong network of moderate views and personal loyalty which bound together the leading members of the Labor Party in Western Australia. He died of coronary-vascular disease on 4 July 1943 at Albury, New South Wales, and was buried in the Roman Catholic section of Karrakatta cemetery, Perth, following a state funeral. Significant among the tributes paid to him were those of his political opponents who lauded his friendliness and the common sense and fairness he displayed as Senate president. He was survived by his wife, daughter and two sons.

PD (Cwlth), 1941, 1st S, p 565, 1943, 1st S, p 11; *Westralian Worker*, 31 May, 5, 21 June 1935; *West Australian*, 21 Oct 1935; Aust Labor Party (WA), Styants's appeal file, *and* State executive minutes, 27 June, 1 July, 5, 19 Aug, 7 Oct 1935, *and* General council report, 1935, *and* Parliamentary Labor Party minutes, 19 Apr 1936 (Battye Lib, Perth); information from Messrs J. and M. Cunningham, Perth.   RALPH PERVAN

CURLEWIS; *see* TURNER, ETHEL

CURNOW, JAMES HENRY (1861-1932), businessman, was born on 21 March 1861 at Ludgvan, Cornwall, England, son of Sampson Curnow, tinminer and later mine-manager, and his wife Elizabeth Ann, née Pearce. He came to Australia with his parents when he was 2. The family settled at Long Gully on the Bendigo goldfield and he was educated at the local state school and St Andrew's College, Sandhurst (Bendigo). On 27 June 1883, with Congregational forms, he married Jane Ann Corbel.

In May 1881 Curnow joined the Postmaster-General's Department as a letter-carrier and stamper. Taking leave in 1887 he acted as secretary of the Australian Natives' Association exhibition at Geelong. Next year he became a clerk with Connelly and Tatchell's, Bendigo solicitors, leaving in 1894 to establish an accountancy and real estate business at View Point. Shrewd and hard-working, Curnow prospered; he later added an auctioneering section and formed the company J. H. Curnow & Son.

The A.N.A. provided the grounding for Curnow's public life. He joined the Sandhurst branch in 1881, became an executive-member that year and was secretary in 1883-91; he was on the board of directors in 1888, treasurer of the board in 1890-91, vice-president in 1891-92 and auditor in 1893. He helped to form new branches in northern Victoria. With (Sir) John Quick [q.v.] he set up the first Federation League in the colony in Bendigo (1893).

After failures in 1895 and 1897, Curnow was elected to the Bendigo City Council in 1901; apart from 1906-09 he remained a councillor for the rest of his life, and was five times mayor. His efficient and imaginative work in council expressed his dedication to the advancement of Bendigo; for fifty years he was associated with almost every progressive ·movement in the life of the town — including the leading role in the installation of sewerage; he was a founding member (1916) and later chairman of the town's sewerage authority. He represented the cities, boroughs and towns of Victoria on the Board of Public Health (1913) and was appointed to the Commission of Public Health in 1920. Favouring a practical decentralist policy, Curnow was an executive-member of the Municipal Association of Victoria and president in 1919. He was keenly interested in politics, but his four attempts to enter parliament failed. Curnow was managing director of the Bendigo Pottery, director of the Bendigo Gas Co. and the Bendigo and Eaglehawk Star Building Society, and chairman of directors of the Bendigo Boot and Shoe Factory.

Curnow (known locally as 'Cock-eyed' due to an eye defect) was an active, impetuous character bursting with energy; he had a sharp wit and his reputation as a hard businessman is probably justified. His family affairs were marred by tragedy. His father was killed in a mining accident in 1881; his first wife and three of their five children died in the measles epidemic of 1893. Curnow's second wife Mary, née Jordan, whom he married with Wesleyan forms on 27 March 1895, died in 1909 after spilling carbolic acid on her hip, leaving three young children. On 2 August 1911 at Malvern, Curnow married Amy Elizabeth McLean according to Presbyterian forms; they had one daughter.

Curnow died on 25 April 1932, survived by his wife, a daughter of the first marriage, two daughters and a son of the second, and a daughter of the third. He was cremated. His estate was valued for probate at £21 389.

G. Mackay, *Annals of Bendigo, 1921-35* (Bendigo, 1935); *Advance Aust,* 7 June 1899, 16 June 1900, 15 Mar 1901, 15 Dec 1902; *Age, Argus,* and *Bendigo Advertiser,* 26 Apr 1932; Council meeting minute-book, 1904-32 (Bendigo City Council).   KEVIN PEOPLES

CURNOW, WILLIAM (1832-1903), clergyman and journalist, was baptized on 2 December 1832 at St Ives, Cornwall, England, son of James Curnow, miner, and his wife Jane, née Hallow. He was educated for the Wesleyan Methodist ministry, which he entered at 21 and was soon sent to Australia. He arrived in Sydney on 23 May 1854 in the *American Lass* with Rev. William Kelynack [q.v.5] and other ministers. Briefly at Newcastle, he served at Maitland and Parramatta, where he married Matilda Susanna Weiss on 16 March 1858. After a year at Bowenfels, he was transferred to Queensland, serving in Brisbane and at Ipswich until he was recalled to York Street, Sydney, in 1862. After three years there and three at Bourke Street, he served at Goulburn in 1868-71, before returning to York Street.

Described as a 'prince of preachers', Curnow was much sought-after as a speaker on public affairs. His experiences as a co-editor of the *Christian Advocate and Wesleyan Record* in 1864-68 and 1871-73 interested him in journalism; from about 1873 he contributed articles to the *Sydney Morning Herald.* Suffering from a throat ailment, he visited England in 1874, but returned uncured. After two years at Forest Lodge he became a supernumerary minister in 1877. Meanwhile he had impressed the Fairfax [q.v.] family with his aptitude for journalism and he was appointed to the *Herald's* editorial staff in 1875. Ten years later he edited their *Sydney Mail* for five months and on 1 January 1886 he succeeded Andrew Garran [q.v.4] as editor; he resigned from the Wesleyan ministry on 22 January.

Curnow once claimed that 'when a man joins a newspaper he sinks his personality, and you don't know what he does', and he remains the least known of all the *Herald's* editors. Within this anonymity he guided its policies — it approved a properly constituted and representative Federal parliament; it was apprehensive about Labor and opposed the payment of parliamentarians because it would interfere with the independence of parliament and bring undesirables into politics. Curnow's policies were conservative and his language temperate. Although he and the paper believed in free trade Sir George Dibbs [q.v.4] found him 'a fair and open opponent'. An obituarist in the rival *Daily Telegraph* claimed that 'His judgment was sound, though if ever it erred it was on the side of caution. His methods were judicial rather than aggressive'.

Curnow loved music and was a frequent theatre-goer; at his country home at Eastwood he created a 'charming garden'. He retired early in 1903 in failing health, and died aged 70 of cerebro-vascular disease at his home at Newtown on 14 October 1903 and was buried in Rookwood cemetery. He was survived by his wife, two sons and two daughters.

Mrs Curnow, with Maybanke Anderson [q.v.7] and Louisa Macdonald [q.v.], helped to establish free kindergartens and was a founder of the Women's Literary Society and of the Women's College, University of Sydney. Lady Poore in her *Recollections of an admiral's wife* (London, 1915) described her as 'a light-hearted and intelligent lady of eighty' — in 1909 she founded the Optimists' Club of New South Wales with Lady Poore as president and Sir George Reid [q.v.] as patron. She died aged 92 on 15 September 1921.

A century of journalism. The Sydney Morning Herald (Syd, 1931); *Daily Telegraph* (Syd), 15 Oct 1903; *SMH*, 15, 16 Oct 1903; *Sydney Mail*, 21 Oct 1903; *Aust Worker*, 18 June 1908.

M. J. B. KENNY

CURREY, WILLIAM MATTHEW (1895-1948), soldier and politician, was born on 19 September 1895 at Wallsend, New South Wales, son of William Robert Currey, labourer and later miner, and his wife Mary Ellen, née Lang. Educated at Dudley and Plattsburg Public schools, he moved to Leichhardt, Sydney, and found employment as a wireworker. After the outbreak of World War I he twice attempted to enlist without his parents' consent, giving a false age, but was discovered and discharged. He was accepted for the Australian Imperial Force on 9 October 1916 and posted to the 4th Light Trench-Mortar Battery, embarking for France in November. On 1 July 1917 he was transferred to the 53rd Battalion; later that year he fought at Polygon Wood and then returned to the Somme.

Private Currey was awarded the Victoria Cross for his part in the Australian attack at Péronne on 1 September 1918. The 53rd Battalion began taking heavy casualties early in the day, Currey's company in particular suffering from a 77 mm field-gun firing at very close range. Currey rushed forward under machine-gun fire, killed the whole crew and captured the weapon. When in mid-afternoon the battalion encountered intense fire from a strong point, he worked round the flank of the position and opened fire with a Lewis-gun before rushing the post, inflicting many casualties and dispersing the survivors. His courageous action enabled the battalion attack to proceed. At 3 a.m. next morning he volunteered to warn a company which had become isolated to withdraw: moving out into no man's land he stood up and called out to the company, the sound of his voice attracting a torrent of enemy fire. After three attempts, during which his respirator was struck and he was gassed, he finally contacted the exposed company which then safely retired.

Despite his gas wound, Currey saw out the war with the 53rd Battalion, arriving back in Australia in March 1919. In September he joined the New South Wales railways as a storeman and next year, on 10 April, married Emma Davies at St Saviour's Anglican Church, Punchbowl. While employed with the railways he became active in the Australian Labor Party and on 16 May 1941 he resigned his post to stand as Labor candidate for Kogarah in the Legislative Assembly. He won the seat, thereby becoming the first V.C. winner to enter the New South Wales parliament. He was twice re-elected — in 1944 and 1947 — and made the interests of ex-servicemen his particular concern. In 1930-32 he had served with the 45th Battalion in the citizen forces, rising to warrant officer rank, and in 1940-41 with the Australian Instructional Corps.

Currey collapsed suddenly in Parliament House on 27 April 1948 and, survived by his wife and two daughters, died three days later of coronary-vascular disease. He was cremated after a Presbyterian service which was attended by four V.C. winners. His portrait by John Longstaff [q.v.] is in the Australian War Memorial collection.

A. D. Ellis, *The story of the Fifth Australian Division* (Lond, 1920?); C. E. W. Bean, *The A.I.F. in France*, 1917-18 (Syd, 1933, 1937, 1942); L. Wigmore (ed), *They dared mightily* (Canb, 1963); *London Gazette*, 14 Dec 1918; *SMH*, 12 May 1941, 1, 4, 13 May 1948; *Bulletin*, 11 June 1941, 5 May 1948; Public Transport Commission of NSW, Records (Archives section, Syd).

C. D. COULTHARD-CLARK

CURRIE, SIR (HENRY) ALAN (1868-1942) and JOHN LANG (1856-1935), pastoralists, were sons of John Lang Currie [q.v.3] of Larra, near Derrinallum, Victoria, and his wife Louise, née Johnston. Alan, the eighth child and sixth son, was born on 6 June 1868 at Osborne House, Geelong. Educated at Melbourne Church of England Grammar School, he graduated in civil engineering in 1891 from the University of Melbourne. In 1894 he was civil engineer for a contractor to the Melbourne and Metropolitan Board of Works' sewerage scheme at Werribee, and from April 1896 was assistant engineer in the Public Works Department of Western Australia, where he took some part in the water-supply project for the Kalgoorlie goldfields.

On his father's death in 1898 he returned to Victoria and, having inherited part of the Gala and Titanga estates, reverted to the family calling. Two years later he and his brother Edwin bought the 17 000-acre (6900 ha) southern part of A. S. Chirnside's [q.v.3] Mount Elephant run, with a homestead on Logan's Lake. There he began breeding merino sheep, Shorthorn cattle and racehorses. In 1906-14 he served as a councillor of the Shire of Hampden, and was shire president in 1909 and 1911.

In his university days Currie had been a gunner in the volunteer Rupertswood battery of horse artillery founded by Sir William Clarke [q.v.3]. After the outbreak of World War I he enlisted in 1915 in England, serving in Belgium and France as a lieutenant in the Royal Field Artillery. He was mentioned in dispatches and in January 1918 was awarded the Military Cross for making 'a most daring and gallant personal reconnaissance in order to secure forward positions for the guns'. In January 1920 he was demobilized with the rank of major.

Parts of Mount Elephant had been sold from time to time, and when in 1920 the last portion went to soldier settlement, Currie bought the 8000-acre (3200 ha) Ercildoune, near Ballarat, first settled by the Learmonth brothers [qq.v.2]: he carried on there the fine-wool merino stud the brothers had established under the guidance of the Thomas Shaws, senior and junior [qq.v.2,6], based on the original Camden Park strain, as his father's Larra merinos had also been. On the sale of the Shaws' Wooriwyrite station in 1923 Currie bought the small pure-bred Camden Park flock that had been preserved there, and maintained the breeding of what had become for the pastoral community a living museum piece.

After the war Currie had concerned himself with the interests of the man on the land, and introduced a group settlement scheme for ex-servicemen. In June 1928 he was elected a member of the Legislative Council of Victoria for the Nelson Province, and was an honorary minister in the 1928-29 Nationalist ministry of Sir William McPherson [q.v.]. He did not contest the seat after the redistribution in 1940. In the House he spoke rarely, but always on subjects with which he was thoroughly conversant. He was remembered for his 'fearless and lucid way of putting forward his views'.

Alan Currie was probably best known for his lifelong association with the Australian turf. He became a member of the Victoria Racing Club in 1899, and soon began importing English mares for his stud. His first win was at Caulfield in 1906, and one of his best horses, Mala, won the Newmarket handicap in 1909. He was also successful in steeplechases and hurdle races. In 1910-13 he was chairman of the Victoria Amateur Turf Club, resigning in 1914 to become a committee-member of the V.R.C., of which he was vice-chairman in 1920 and chairman in 1935. On 11 June 1902 at St John's Church of England, Toorak, he had married Muriel, granddaughter of Henry Miller [q.v.5]; they had no children. They entertained widely in the handsome old Ercildoune homestead where guests included the duke of Gloucester during his Australian tour in 1934. That year Currie became a director of the Equity Trustees, Executors & Agency Co. and in 1937 was knighted. He died on 10 October 1942 at Ercildoune and was buried privately in Learmonth cemetery. His estate was valued for probate at £123 768.

John Lang Currie junior was born on 21 May 1856 at Geelong. He was educated at Geelong College and trained as a pastoralist on Larra which, with his sister's husband Patrick Sellar Lang, he later leased from his father. After the rabbit plague of the late 1880s, which ate out the native grasses, Larra's pastures became too rich for the fine-wool merino; these were replaced by a Lincoln cross to produce a larger sheep of stronger wool.

In 1898 John Currie inherited the homestead portion of Larra. Under his ownership the property became known for its Corriedale stud and Currie himself as a judge at sheep shows. He was a councillor of the Pastoralists' Association of Victoria in 1908-23 and a vice-president in 1918-19. He also maintained the station's long-established Shorthorn dairy herd and developed its stable of thoroughbreds, which he raced with some success at district meetings and in Melbourne. Shooting and coursing were two other sports he enjoyed, and for many years the Commonwealth Cup, the major annual coursing meeting, was held on Larra.

On 5 September 1894 at All Saints, St Kilda, Currie had married Lorna Mary Box and they had one daughter. In 1898-1922 he was a councillor of the Shire of Hampden and was shire president in 1903 and 1916. He was also a director of the Derrinallum Butter Factory and a supporter of the Presbyterian Church. He died at Larra on 27 July 1935, and was buried in Lismore cemetery. His wife and daughter survived him. He left an estate valued for probate at £94 161.

A. Henderson (ed), *Australian families*, 1 (Melb, 1941); M. T. Shaw, 'Larra', *Historic homesteads of Australia*, Aust Council of National Trusts, 2 (Syd, 1976); *Pastoral Review*, 16 Jan 1930, 16 Aug 1935, 16 Nov 1942; *Camperdown Chronicle*, 30 July 1935, 13 Oct 1942; *Australasian*, 17 Oct 1942.

MARY TURNER SHAW

CURRIE, PATRICK (1883-1949), soldier and teacher, was born on 2 August 1883 at Petrie Creek, near Caboolture, Queensland, son of Daniel Currie, farmer, and his wife Bridget, née Neylon. Educated at Nambour State School, in 1898 he became a teacher with the Queensland Education Department. He resigned in 1908, spent two and a half years in Ellis Kadoorie College, Hong Kong, rejoined the Queensland department, and on 11 October 1911 married Kitty Gallwey in St Stephen's Cathedral, Brisbane.

With a strong interest in the militia, Currie was commissioned as a lieutenant in the cadets in 1906; he had attained the rank of captain on the eve of World War I. Joining the Australian Imperial Force on 28 April 1915, in May he was promoted major in 'B' Company, 26th Battalion, drawn from Queensland and Tasmania. They embarked in June and were placed in reserve at Anzac Cove until they relieved the 28th Battalion in the trenches; on 30 November Currie was appointed second-in-command, and next day he was wounded in the forehead while on an inspection tour and was sent to hospital.

Rejoining his battalion in Egypt in January 1916 Currie took command of 'A' Company. The unit went to France in March and on 7 June relieved the 28th in the line near Pozières. In a major allied attack on the night of 4–5 August, Currie jumped over the parapet to take his wave forward and, exposed to heavy enemy fire, led his men to seize their objective. Although wounded he displayed consistent gallantry for which he was awarded the Distinguished Service Order.

Currie was given command of the 7th Training Brigade in Britain until June 1917, and returned to the 26th Battalion. In March 1918 he took command of the West Australian 28th Battalion, with the temporary rank of lieut-colonel. During the Passchendaele and Somme operations his gallantry won him the C.M.G. He was also awarded the French Croix de Guerre and twice mentioned in dispatches. He returned to Australia in 1919. A very big man with snow-white hair and moustache, Currie looked much older than he was. Nicknamed 'Snow' or 'Snowy', his experience as a teacher had given him a good understanding of his men, most of whom he knew by name and ability. He was a popular commander who exercised firm but humane control and knew when to turn a Nelsonian eye.

Currie failed to win the Brisbane seat in the Legislative Assembly as a soldier-Nationalist in 1920. Appointed as brevet major, he commanded the 42nd Battalion in the militia from 1931 to 1934. He had resumed his career with the Queensland Education Department, taught in Brisbane primary schools and on 31 December 1948 retired as headmaster of New Farm primary school. In 1939-45 he served as assistant officer in charge of troops on the troopships *Queen Elizabeth* and *Aquitania* in the Middle East and Java, and later as officer-in-charge on the troopships *Taroona* and *Awkui* in New Guinea.

Currie died on 6 January 1949 from heart disease in Toombul, Brisbane, and was buried in the Catholic section of Lutwyche cemetery. He was survived by his wife, a daughter and two sons, of whom Neal Lincoln (1914-1975) became a professional soldier, was a prisoner of war in 1941-45 and died as a brigadier and deputy master general of the ordnance.

O'M. Creagh and E. M. Humphris, *The V.C. and D.S.O.* (Lond, 1924); C. E. W. Bean, *The A.I.F. in France*, 1918 (Syd, 1942), and *Anzac to Amiens* (Canb, 1946); H. K. Kahan, *The 28th Battalion . . .* (Perth, 1965); *London Gazette*, 26 Sept 1916, supp, 3 June 1919, supp; *Qld Digger*, Feb 1949; *Listening Post*, 15 Dec 1938; AIF war diaries, 26th Battalion, 1915-16, *and* 28th Battalion, 1918-19 (AWM).

DARRYL McINTYRE

CURTIS, GEORGE SILAS (1845-1922), auctioneer and politician, was born on 19 July 1845 at Tamworth, New South Wales, son of George Curtis, farmer, and his wife Suzanne, née Martin. Educated at Sydney Grammar School and Maitland High School, he went to Rockhampton with an overland party in 1863; he returned there in 1866 to enter Wormald's auctioneering firm, which he acquired in 1872 and developed as G. S. Curtis and Sons. As a prominent auctioneer, landholder and real estate speculator, Curtis became one of the city's most vigorous and influential public figures, first in campaigning through the Chamber of Commerce for railway extensions and a deep-water port, and from 1889 as the leading exponent of territorial separation in central Queensland.

When the Central Queensland Territorial Separation League was formed in 1889 with Curtis as chairman, the movement had entered its third and most active phase. In 1891 he attacked the 'act of gross injustice' contained in the draft constitution for Federation which prevented separation without the consent of the parliament affected. This was followed in 1893 by a petition to the Imperial government from householders of central Queensland, and by a letter from Curtis to Sir Henry Parkes [q.v.5] seeking his support. As with similar petitions in the 1860s and 1870s, that of 1893 and others of the decade were doomed to failure.

Curtis's fluent speeches demonstrated wide reading and the vigour of his campaign for separation helped in his return in 1893 as one of Rockhampton's two members in the Legislative Assembly. In 1898 he declined to join T. J. Byrnes's [q.v.7] ministry because it would have distracted him from his main purpose at a crucial period, and would have appeared to his voters as a compromise with irreconcilable 'Brisbane governments'. He was defeated in 1902, partly because of his bankruptcy and partly through the rise of the Labor Party.

Curtis failed in several bids to re-enter parliament, including the Federal seat of Capricornia in 1903. As a member of the Legislative Council in 1914-22 he became an extreme conservative and fought hard to save it from abolition. In 1920 he protested to Sir T. B. Robinson [q.v.], Queensland agent-general in London, about the swamping of the council by 'pledged partisans of the Labour Socialist Party, which is controlled by revolutionary extremists'.

On 25 May 1875 at Rockhampton Curtis married Dorinda Ann Parker, daughter of the city's first publican; they had three sons and five daughters. He was an expert horseman. A keen musician, he played the violin in the Orpheus Club orchestra and was a member of other musical societies in Rockhampton. Curtis died in Sydney on 6 October 1922 and was buried with Anglican rites in South Head cemetery.

C. A. Bernays, *Queensland politics during sixty years* (Brisb, 1919); *V&P* (Qld), 1891, 1, 1157-89, 1893, 3, 1029-51, 1894, 1, 505-65, 1898, 3, 823-30, 1899, 1st S, 121-26; *Capricornian*, 1 Aug 1891; *Morning Bulletin*, 6 Jan 1925; M. Walker, George Silas Curtis (held by Rockhampton & District Hist Soc); P. F. MacDonald papers (Rockhampton Municipal Lib); Parkes correspondence (ML); Philp papers (Oxley Lib, Brisb); information from Miss M. Walker, Rockhampton, Qld.

LORNA L. McDONALD

CUSACK, JOHN JOSEPH (1868-1956), coachbuilder, garage proprietor and politician, was born on 8 August 1868 at Bellevale near Yass, New South Wales, youngest of six sons of Irish-born parents Michael Cusack, farmer, and his wife Ann (Bridget), née Boan, late Kenny. His schooling at Yass was brief and at 15 he was apprenticed to a blacksmith at Berrima. He gained experience in Sydney in his trade and in coachbuilding; much of his spare time was spent in libraries. He returned to Yass and on 11 April 1898, in the Catholic Church, he married Minnie (Mary) Theresa Cassidy, a dressmaker.

Cusack built up a successful coachbuilding business; originally known as Cusack & Schofield, it later became Cusack & Palmer and retained that name after he became the sole owner. By 1910 he was the largest employer in Yass, with twenty-four workmen; apart from blacksmith services, the firm met a wide demand for vehicles and exported to South Africa.

Known as 'J.J.', he was elected to the Yass Municipal Council, was mayor in 1904, and represented the council at the State's first Local Government Convention in 1910. He was a member of the local hospital board and active in the Pastoral and Agricultural Association. A constant contributor to the local newspapers, he joined the Australian Journalists' Association.

Cusack was engrossed in politics and a founder of the first Labor League at Yass in the 1890s. In 1910 he won the Legislative Assembly seat of Queanbeyan, and held Albury in 1913-17. He was amongst those expelled from the Labor Party in November 1916 for failing to support a no-confidence motion against W. A. Holman's [q.v.] National government. Readmitted to the party, Cusack entered the House of Representatives in 1929 by winning Eden-Monaro from J. A. Perkins [q.v.] and surviving a High Court appeal. (Sir) Earle Page [q.v.] beat him in Cowper in 1931. His efforts to return to parliament as a Federal Labor candidate, opposed to J. T. Lang [q.v.], were unsuccessful in Monaro (State) in 1932 and in Riverina (Federal) in 1934; he also failed in the State elections at Yass in 1947 and Burrinjuck in 1953.

Outspoken, unpredictable and tenacious, Cusack enjoyed parliamentary debate, fought hard for his constituents and for improved conditions for all workers. Despite his expulsion, he opposed conscription, and was severely critical of Labor defectors. His entry into Federal politics was marked with the quip, 'I will not be surprised if I am the first Australian appointed as Governor-General': he said later that if he got the job he would use (Viscount) Bruce's [q.v.] spats as bowyangs. In October 1930 he made an 'amazing attack' on the banker Sir Robert Gibson [q.v.], whom he considered was interfering in the government.

Cusack had retained his business in Yass, adapted it to the motor car and owned one of the earliest service stations. He moved to Canberra in 1932 and opened a furniture store. His community interests were many and lively; he canvassed for election to the Advisory Council with placards and slogans hung around his old truck. Increasingly litigious, in January 1956 he proceeded against W. F. Sheahan, for obliterating slogans on the walls of his property in Yass.

Predeceased by a son, Cusack died in hospital on 8 September and was buried in Canberra cemetery. He was survived by two sons and a daughter, and by his wife who, until her death on 7 September 1962, aged 92, took an active interest in the expanding family business in Canberra. Dymphna Cusack, author, is his niece.

E. J. Lea-Scarlett, *Queanbeyan* (Queanbeyan, 1968); *SMH*, 15 Nov 1916, 23 Mar, 6 Dec 1917, 7 Nov 1929, 18, 31 Jan, 7 Oct 1930, 21, 24, 26, 30 Mar,

22 Apr 1931, 1 May 1932, 7 Jan 1936, 3 Aug 1937, 20, 21 Jan 1956; *Aust Worker*, 25 Dec 1929; *Canb Times*, 10 Sept 1956, 9 Sept 1962; *Yass Tribune*, 10 Sept 1956; information from Mr G. Cusack senior, Canb, ACT.

NAN PHILLIPS
BEDE NAIRN

CUSSEN, SIR LEO FINN BERNARD (1859-1933), judge, was born on 29 November 1859 at Portland, Victoria, fourth surviving son of Maurice Cussen (d. 1880) and his wife Margaret, née Finn. Maurice Cussen had been head tenant at Creveen House on the Rattoo estate in County Kerry, Ireland, before migrating to Sydney in 1841. He established himself as a grocer and provision dealer in Sydney and married in May 1850. In 1854 he joined his brother-in-law at Portland, Victoria, where he set up business as a grocer and general dealer. In 1860 the family moved to the near-by township of Merino.

Leo was educated at the local school and, after winning a scholarship, entered Hamilton College as a boarder in 1875. He became captain of the school next year, when he matriculated with credits in mathematics. In 1877 he entered the University of Melbourne, completing his certificate in civil engineering in 1879. Cussen played for the university football and cricket teams, and was awarded a full blue for cricket in 1879. He also played football for West Melbourne and took part in amateur athletics. On graduation he joined the Victorian Railways and after a year as a draftsman went into the field with assistant engineer W. Curtois. He worked on surveys of several important lines, including Ballan to Bacchus Marsh, and reported on the feasibility of a line from Alexandra to Mansfield through the Puzzle Ranges. Cussen later recalled: 'I liked the life, and the survey camps were comfortable. I grew as strong as a horse with the open-air life. The excessive walking spoilt me as a runner, but it seemed as if I had left athletics behind me'.

At 25 he decided to become a lawyer. He returned to the university, completing his B.A. in 1884 and the first and second years of his law degree in 1885-86 (LL.B., 1886; M.A., 1887). On 1 September 1886 he was admitted to the Victorian Bar. He read with (Sir) John Madden [q.v.] and occupied 35 Selborne Chambers. To supplement his earnings after graduation, he taught international law at the university; between 1890 and 1900 he also lectured in the law of obligations. He wrote legal articles and in 1897 was reputedly the first Victorian to have an article published in the London *Law Quarterly Review*. He also became a reporter for the

Australian Law Times and the *Victorian Law Reports*.

Working long hours, Cussen soon became one of the most sought after and highly paid barristers, renowned for thorough preparation, clarity of argument and sound knowledge of legal principles. He developed a wide-ranging practice, with the exception of criminal law; his engineering experience led him to specialize in local government, patent and engineering cases. He quickly emerged as a leading counsel among a strong Bar which included such men as Purves [q.v.5], Isaacs, Higgins, Frank Gavan Duffy, Irvine and Weigall [qq.v.]. In 1901 and 1902 Cussen was elected to the Bar committee.

He achieved a remarkable reputation for advocacy, opinion and wit. Anecdotes abound from this period. 'It almost became a maxim that if a solicitor had a difficult case and did not consult Cussen, he was guilty of negligence'. However he never took silk, preferring to remain a stuff gownsman along with others such as (Sir) Hayden Starke [q.v.]. While taking no part in the Federal constitutional conventions of the 1890s, he harboured some interest in politics and in 1901 stood for the House of Representatives seat of Wannon, his childhood country. S. W. Cooke [q.v.] soundly defeated him.

On 8 April 1890 at St Mary's Cathedral, Sydney, Cussen had married Johanna, daughter of John Bevan; they raised six sons and one daughter. In 1903 he took his wife and two sons for the first of his three trips to Europe, Great Britain and Ireland, and developed interests in church architecture, music and art.

In March 1906 (Sir) Thomas Bent's [q.v.3] government appointed Cussen to the Victorian Supreme Court. Cabinet was divided over the matter but the appointment was warmly welcomed by bench, Bar and the press, which noted that he was a popular and genial figure with the reputation of being the 'hardest worked and perhaps highest paid of present Melbourne barristers'. His salary of £2500 represented a considerable financial sacrifice; it was not reviewed or raised during his twenty-seven years on the bench. His work is recorded in many important judgments in the *Victorian Law Reports*. He was a judge for both the parties and the profession, deciding cases with insight and with just discrimination of fact and argument. He was a master at summing up to a jury and discussed and developed with precision and scholarly thoroughness legal principles involved in cases before him, thereby often setting the law on a solid basis for years ahead. In 1924, and again in 1931-32, Cussen was appointed chief justice in the absence of Irvine.

Apart from these judicial contributions, Cussen undertook massive projects of statutory consolidation for the Victorian parliament. This he did in his spare time, entirely gratuitously, and probably at the expense of his health. In 1908 he began working, almost single-handed, on the Victorian statutes. The task had twice previously been carried out by George Higinbotham [q.v.4], in 1865-66 and 1890, but much new legislation required attention. Cussen modernized the language of many provisions, and included many amendments and valuable and substantial annotations. The finished work, in five volumes, appeared in 1915. For this achievement, he was thanked by both Houses of the Victorian parliament.

Three years later Cussen began work on an even larger and more complex task of statutory consolidation, which culminated in the Imperial Acts Application Act of 1922. This project involved an exhaustive and definitive examination of over 7000 English and Australian Acts dating back to the thirteenth century, to determine exactly which English and colonial Acts were applicable in Victoria. He was assisted by Professor (Sir) Harrison Moore [q.v.], S. H. Z. Woinarski and G. Piggott. On completion of this work Cussen was given leave of absence to recover his health, for he had undergone surgery earlier in 1922 to remove part of the large intestine. Now Sir Leo Cussen – he had been knighted in January – he took his wife and daughter on an extensive tour of Europe.

In 1929 Cussen completed his second consolidation of Victorian statutes and presented them to the Victorian parliament for enactment. He was assisted by six barristers and acted as editor, taking responsibility for the whole work; as before, he was thanked by parliament for his services. The achievement was, however, marred by a squabble in parliament over whether an honorarium of £2500 be paid, in addition to granting him a year's leave of absence. In the end the government deferred the grant and it was not proposed again. His leave was lengthened to two years (from August 1929), because of illness.

Cussen was a trustee from October 1916 and from September 1928 president of the Public Library, Museums, and National Gallery of Victoria. He was a member of the Felton [q.v.4] Bequest Committee and prepared a report on the law of copyright and works of art, which unfortunately has been lost. He was a member of the law faculty of the University of Melbourne for forty-three years and from 1902 a member of the university council. He was also a member of the Council of Legal Education and vice-president of the Walter and Eliza Hall [qq.v.] Institute of Research. As president of the Melbourne Cricket Club from 1907 he was noted for his 'tact and kindliness as an administrator' and his ability to preserve harmony and goodwill. At the turn of the century he had regularly represented the Bar in annual cricket matches; as his sons grew up he enjoyed playing cricket with them and with their friends from near-by Xavier College in an adjacent paddock. He followed with interest his sons' sporting careers at school and university. He belonged to the Melbourne, Yorick and University clubs.

On 17 May 1933 Cussen died suddenly at his home in Hawthorn. He had been sitting in court only two days before. A huge public funeral and procession followed, with Archbishop Mannix [q.v.] presiding at pontifical Mass in St Patrick's Cathedral. He was survived by his wife and children. Of his six sons, one died in boyhood, one became a distinguished Melbourne physician and the others prominent lawyers. In 1964 the Sir Leo Cussen chair of law was created at Monash University and in 1972 the Leo Cussen Institute for Continuing Legal Education was founded in Melbourne. (Sir) Robert Menzies, at Cussen's death, described him as 'one of the great judges of the English-speaking world'. Members of the law profession stressed his deep learning 'unaccompanied by pedantry', his soundness of judgment, dignity of demeanour, humanity, natural courtesy and sense of public duty. Sir Owen Dixon considered it an extraordinary error by governments not to have appointed him chief justice of the High Court of Australia or of the Victorian Supreme Court.

Portraits by John Longstaff [q.v.] are held by the National Gallery of Victoria and by the Victorian Supreme Court Library, and another by W. B. McInnes [q.v.] by the Melbourne Cricket Club.

R. G. Menzies, *Afternoon light* (Melb, 1967); A Dean, *A multitude of counsellors* (Melb, 1968); W. Ebsworth, *Pioneer Catholic Victoria* (Melb, 1973); S. M. Ingham, *Enterprising migrants* (Melb, 1975); R. Campbell, *A history of the Melbourne Law School, 1857 to 1973* (Melb, 1977); *Aust Law J*, 15 June 1933; *Hamilton Spectator*, 26 Feb, 12, 14, 26 Mar, 2 April 1901; *Argus*, 14, 30 Mar 1901, 14, 21 Mar 1906, 2 Jan, 2 Feb 1922, 24 Feb 1928, 19 Sept 1929, 18, 19, 20 May 1933; *Age*, 15 Mar 1906, 22 Sept 1915, 18 May, 22 July 1933; *Sun-News Pictorial*, 23 Oct 1929, 18, 19, 30 May 1933; *Herald* (Melb), 15 July 1931; *Australasian*, 27 May 1933; family papers (held by Mrs Alice Morrissey, Hawthorn, Vic).
                                          JENNY COOK
                                     B. KEON-COHEN

Cuthbertson

A.D.B.

CUTHBERTSON, MARGARET GAR-DINER (1864-1944), factory inspector, was born on 6 September 1864 at Bacchus Marsh, Victoria, daughter of James Cuthbertson, contractor from the north of England, and his wife Jessie, née Watson, who had come to Australia from Edinburgh at the age of 7.

After gaining 'considerable experience in connexion with factory work', Miss Cuthbertson entered the Victorian Public Service in July 1888 as a telephone switchboard attendant in the Postmaster-General's Department. In March 1894 she was appointed to the newly created position of female inspector of factories, becoming the first woman in Australia to hold such a post. By that year there were 11 104 women in registered factories, and she supervised their general accommodation, ventilation and sanitary conditions, and investigated pay rates, hours of work and conditions of apprenticeship. A year later her appointment 'had fulfilled the most sanguine expectations', and soon she had two assistants.

In 1897 Miss Cuthbertson did valuable work as secretary of the Clothing Board, one of several wage boards introduced by the factories legislation of 1896 to regulate wages in sweated trades; the system later ramified and by 1907 she was secretary of six such boards. In 1898 she contributed to the investigation by Sidney and Beatrice Webb of Victoria's pioneering factory laws, and in 1900 she became a senior inspector. The government sent her to the United Kingdom in 1912 to find suitable female migrants for work in Victorian industry. In 1913, with Henrietta C. McGowan (Walker), she published *Woman's work* (Melbourne), a guide to the nature, terms and conditions of many kinds of work for women.

Miss Cuthbertson was first president of the Victorian Women's Public Service Association, formed in 1901, and represented it on the National Council of Women of Victoria, founded in 1902. She held office for some years on the council's executive and worked on sub-committees for improving prison conditions for women and for establishing the Talbot Epileptic Colony. She also supported the Free Kindergarten Union, founded in 1908, to provide kindergartens for slum children, and worked with Vida Goldstein [q.v.] to assist unemployed women during World War I.

Miss Cuthbertson resigned her inspectorship in 1920 to take up an appointment with a city firm, but continued to work for the welfare of women and children. From 1921 she was a council-member of the College of Domestic Economy (now Emily McPherson College) and from 1923 of the South Melbourne Technical School. She also served on the board and auxiliaries of the

Queen Victoria Hospital, and was for many years treasurer of the Yooralla Hospital School for Crippled Children.

On 17 November 1944, in Melbourne, Miss Cuthbertson died after a long illness, and was buried in the Presbyterian section of Burwood cemetery. She left an estate valued for probate at £24 312. The *Age*'s obituary described her as 'modest and retiring', yet a 'stimulating companion', cultivated and witty, and a 'capable public speaker'. It paid warm 'tribute to her 'valuable work in safeguarding the rights and well-being of woman and girl workers in the days when Victoria was becoming known as the leading industrial State in Australia'.

B. Webb, *The Webbs' Australian diary, 1898*, A. G. Austin ed (Melb, 1965); L. M. Henderson, *The Goldstein story* (Melb, 1973); National Council of Women (Vic), *Annual Report*, 1904-10 (Melb); *Aust Woman's Sphere*, 10 Oct 1902, May 1903; *Weekly Times* (Melb), 14 Aug 1897, 26 June 1909; *Argus*, 3 Oct 1905, 13 Nov 1913, 18, 20 Nov 1944; *Age*, 4 Oct 1912, 13 Nov 1913, 18 Nov 1944.

ANTHEA HYSLOP

CUTLACK, FREDERIC MORLEY (1886-1967), journalist, war correspondent and war historian, was born on 30 September 1886 at Upper Lancing, Sussex, England, son of Frank William Cutlack, dredging contractor, and his wife Elizabeth Swanwick, née Hall. His family migrated to South Australia when he was 5 and he was educated at Renmark and University College, North Adelaide. In 1904 he began newspaper work on the *Register*. He visited Germany in 1910 and next year joined the staff of the *Daily Chronicle* in London. He worked on other London newspapers and on the publicity staff of the Australian High Commission, and in 1913 was special correspondent on the H.M.A.S. *Australia* on her maiden voyage from England.

Cutlack was reading for the Bar in London when war broke out in 1914 and he soon enlisted in King Edward's Horse. Commissioned lieutenant, he served in France in 1915-16 with the Royal Field Artillery, then in April 1917 was attached to the 3rd Divisional Headquarters, Australian Imperial Force, as an intelligence officer. In October C. E. W. Bean [q.v.7] sought his services as assistant official war correspondent. In January 1918 he was appointed, relinquishing his existing office and rank and receiving the pay and allowances of a captain in the A.I.F., but without rank. He crossed to France on 4 January 1918 and took over the tasks Bean had performed, including the preparation and dispatch of cables and letters to Australia concerning the activities of the Australian force, instructions to the official photographer, and liaison with the British detachment of the Australian War Records Section in France. He also assisted in collecting records and trophies for the war museum which Bean had proposed and which the Australian government had already approved.

In March, when Bean returned to France, Cutlack remained as his assistant and thereafter the two worked together in harmony. Cutlack rapidly proved himself a relentless investigator, as concerned to discover the truth as Bean, not afraid of risks but not taking them needlessly. He narrowly escaped death near Morlancourt in July when a whizz-bang shell passed over his shoulder; before he reached shelter about twenty shells had been fired at him. Later that month he was seriously injured in a motor cycle accident and while convalescing wrote an account of the 1918 operations of the Australian divisions which was published in London late that year. The Australian Historical Mission, led by Bean, left for Gallipoli early in 1919 but Cutlack continued in his appointment with the Australian Corps. He was discharged in England on 20 March and later that year was called to the Bar at Lincoln's Inn, London.

In 1920 Cutlack returned to Australia with his English wife, Annie Isobel, née Dunlop, whom he had married at Ealing, London, on 25 October 1917; the marriage was annulled in January 1937. He joined the staff of the *Sydney Morning Herald* in 1920 but soon afterwards was commissioned to write the volume on the Australian Flying Corps for the official war history. Published in 1923, the work was reprinted many times and about 18500 copies were sold. Cutlack was on the staff of the prime minister, (Viscount) S. M. Bruce [q.v.7], for the 1923 Imperial Conference and then rejoined the *Herald*. After working as a leader-writer, he was given two years leave in 1925 to practise law in Renmark in the hope that the climate would hasten his recovery from tuberculosis. He then returned to the *Herald*, becoming one of its key men; his articles on defence in particular were highly regarded. He accompanied the (Sir) J. G. Latham [q.v.] mission to the Far East in 1934 as the paper's special representative, and that year his book, *Manchurian arena*, was published. *War letters of General Monash*, which he edited, appeared next year. During the abdication crisis in 1936 he wrote most of the *Herald*'s leaders, and their temperate, learned and thoughtful nature earned him the special commendation of the proprietors.

Cutlack married Helen Pauline Curr at Christ Church St Laurence, Sydney, on 5 August 1937; the marriage was dissolved in 1946. He was associate editor of the *Herald* in 1937-47, then worked with the *Bulletin* until retiring at the end of 1947. From the mid-1950s Cutlack lived in England. At Renmark in 1899 he had met H. H. Morant [q.v.]. Convinced that the execution of Morant and P. J. Handcock [q.v.] in South Africa in 1902 was a grave miscarriage of justice, he set out to vindicate them and in 1962 published *Breaker Morant.*

Survived by his third wife Mildred Mary, Cutlack died without issue on 27 November 1967 at his home at Burwash, Sussex.

British A'sian, 21 Jan 1915; *Home*, 1 Mar 1921; *Newspaper News*, 1 Feb 1947; *Stand-To* (Canb), Feb-Aug 1959; *SMH*, 31 July 1923, 21 Mar 1934, Dec 1936, 11 Dec 1937, 2 Jan 1947, 29 Nov 1967; *Bulletin*, 23 July 1925, 28 Mar 1934; records, including 782/34/1 (AWM).   A. J. SWEETING

D

DACEY, JOHN ROWLAND (1854-1912), politician, was born in June 1854 at Cork, Ireland, son of Thomas Dacey, barrister, and his wife Margaret, née Jamson. His father soon died and in 1858 he and his mother migrated to Victoria, settling at Kyneton; she died next year and Dacey was adopted by Dr Smith. Educated locally, he left school at 12 on Smith's death and became a butcher's assistant. Later he was a successful agricultural blacksmith and managed a branch for May & Miller. On 27 July 1878 he married Martha Ellen Douglass in St John's Church, Horsham. By the 1880s he had saved enough to start his own business and in 1883 he set up as a coachmaker at Alexandria, Sydney.

A protectionist, attracted by politics, Dacey was on the Alexandria council in 1886-96, and was mayor in 1888-89. He was returning officer at Redfern in 1889-91; in the latter year he joined the first Redfern Labor Electoral League and was narrowly defeated for pre-selection by J. S. T. McGowen [q.v.]. A Catholic, influenced by the papal encyclical *Rerum novarum*, he combined it with the Labor platform in campaigns for Botany in 1894 and 1895, when he won. He soon gained parliamentary repute for his integrity and debating skill, and emerged as one of the leaders of the Labor Party, especially interested in the problems of gaining suburban seats and attracting white-collar voters. He was not happy with the party's support of the Free Trade government of (Sir) George Reid [q.v.] and, according to W. A. Holman [q.v.], in 1899 was the spearhead of the 'solid six' who threatened caucus that they would resign their seats unless the party transferred its backing to (Sir) William Lyne [q.v.]. Lukewarm to Federation, at the 1899 Labor conference at Woonona, with Holman and W. M. Hughes [q.v.], he failed in an attempt to change party policy, which favoured the submission of the question to a referendum.

As an employer Dacey did not enjoy unanimous Labor support, though he helped to found the Wool and Basil Workers Union in 1901 and was its secretary until 1912; he was also the parliamentary party's treasurer in 1901-10 and was on the central executive in 1912. But he unexpectedly failed to be elected to Labor's first cabinet in 1910. He became an honorary minister next year and, following N. R. W. Nielsen's [q.v.] and A. C. Carmichael's [q.v.7] resignations, in November he became colonial treasurer. Ill health prevented him from fulfilling the promise of great administrative skill and financial acumen he had shown; he died of chronic nephritis on 11 April 1912 and after a state funeral, was buried in the Catholic section of Botany cemetery. He was survived by his wife (d. 1933), three of his four sons and five of his six daughters. His estate was valued for probate at £413. S. Hickey [q.v.] was his son-in-law.

From the 1890s Dacey had campaigned for the building by the government of low-cost housing for working-class people. His plans were matured by the time of his death and were partly carried out by the Holman ministries in 1913-20, chiefly by J. D. Fitzgerald [q.v]. The model suburb of Daceyville in South Sydney is a memorial to his sympathetic social insight.

S. Hickey, *Travelled roads* (Melb, 1951); B. Nairn, *Civilising capitalism* (Canb, 1973); *V&P* (LA NSW), 1889, 4, 917; *Daily Telegraph* (Syd), 12 Apr 1912; *T&CJ*, 17 Apr 1912; *Bulletin*, and *Freeman's J* (Syd), 18 Apr 1912.

BEDE NAIRN

DADSON, LESLIE (1884-1961), soldier, was born on 6 March 1884 at Sidmouth, Tasmania, son of John Dadson, farmer, and his wife Emily, née Flood. Educated at Bangor State School, he took up farming in the district. For nine years before 1914 he served in militia units, attaining the rank of sergeant.

Dadson enlisted in the Australian Imperial Force on 25 August 1914 and embarked in the *Geelong* with the 12th Battalion on 20 October. He became a corporal on 9 February next year while training in Egypt. The battalion landed at Gallipoli on 25 April and on 12 May he was promoted sergeant. In the bitter fighting at Lone Pine he led a platoon and on 16 August, while in hospital at Alexandria, was appointed second lieutenant, though he had earlier declined a commission, 'as he did not want to leave his cobbers'. After the evacuation from Gallipoli he remained with the 12th Battalion and moved with it to the Western Front, taking part in its major actions during 1916. He was promoted lieutenant on 25 May.

On 9 April 1917 the battalion attacked in the village of Boursies, which screened the Hindenburg line. Dadson led forward two platoons under heavy fire and captured two machine-guns; his bravery and initiative won him the Military Cross. On 15 April the enemy counter-attacked at Lagnicourt where he commanded 'B' Company. He took a small party forward to form a defensive

188

flank and, though hard pressed, refused to abandon his position, while narrowly escaping capture; he won a Bar to the M.C. for his fine example of tenacity and pluck.

After eight months as an instructor with a training unit, Dadson returned to his battalion in March 1918 and on 10 May was wounded in action. On 11 August the enemy line in the Lihons vicinity, near Auger and Crépey Woods, was heavily defended, but Dadson's company, led with great dash and courage, captured fifteen machine-guns and three field-pieces. Commended for his conspicuous gallantry and devotion to duty, he was awarded the rare distinction of a second Bar to the M.C. He sailed for Australia on 13 October with other 1914 men on 'Anzac leave'. On 23 February 1919 his A.I.F. appointment was terminated, though he continued militia service until country units were disbanded in 1924; in 1928 he was awarded the Volunteer Officers' Decoration.

Dadson returned to his farm at Bangor and in 1922 was appointed inspector to the Closer Settlement Board. He was the first president of the local sub-branch of the Returned Sailors' and Soldiers' Imperial League of Australia, and in 1921-24 was on the Lilydale Municipal Council. On 30 October 1923, at the Anglican Christ Church, Essendon, Melbourne, he married Margaret Ann Vaughan, of Oswestry, England. From about 1929 they lived in Launceston, where he was employed by the Agricultural Bank of Tasmania, retiring in 1950. In 1943 he was made a justice of the peace.

Survived by his wife and one of his three sons, Dadson died on 5 May 1961 at Launceston.

C. E. W. Bean, *The A.I.F. in France*, 1916, 1917, 1918 (Syd, 1929, 1933, 1942); *London Gazette*, 18 June 1917, 1 Feb 1919; *Reveille* (Syd), 1 June 1932; R. Clark, 'Australian winners of the Military Cross and two Bars', *Sabretache*, Apr 1976; *Examiner* (Launc), 10 May 1961.   N. S. FOLDI

DAGLISH, HENRY (1866-1920), public servant and politician, was born on 18 November 1866 at Ballarat, Victoria, son of William Daglish, engine driver, and his wife Mary Ann, née James. Educated in Geelong, he matriculated, and was apprenticed to mechanical engineering in Humble & Nicholson's foundry. On 28 July 1883 he joined the public service as a clerk in the Police Department. Nicknamed 'the lean and hungry', he was a teetotaller and protégé of Samuel Mauger [q.v.] in temperance action. He was also interested in the labour movement. By June 1895 he was temporary secretary of a new United Public Service Association and in September he went into business. Next year he was at the bottom of the poll in a South Melbourne by-election on a radical programme.

Daglish went to Western Australia in 1896 and joined the Police Department next year. He settled in Subiaco and soon became involved in local politics. He was a municipal councillor from 1900 and mayor in 1903-04 and 1906-07. He joined the Subiaco Political Labor League, and in 1901, after winning Subiaco with the biggest majority in the State, he became whip of the parliamentary Labor Party of six, all of whom, except Daglish, represented goldfields seats, and had no administrative experience. He first became prominent in a defiant statement to the labour congress of 1902, asserting the right of members of parliament to independent judgment. Party leader Robert Hastie then offered to stand down for him.

Withdrawal of Labor support from the (Sir) W. H. James [q.v.] ministry in August 1903 led to a general election in June 1904. The twenty-two Labor members were the biggest single party in the new House. After strong opposition Daglish became leader. He was described by a parliamentary official as 'tall and of fine presence with a powerful if not pleasing voice'; but Melbourne *Punch* thought him 'thin and consumptive' with 'big goo-goo eyes, cadaverous cheeks', long neck and 'floppy ears'. The government's attempt to include an expression of confidence in the governor's address was defeated; James resigned, and Daglish became the first Labor premier of Western Australia. With serious financial problems and an inexperienced ministry drawn mainly from warring goldfields unions, Daglish had no easy task and his aloofness made it more difficult. Fortunately caucus permitted him to choose his own colleagues: he administered the Treasury and the Education Department.

His keynote speech, delivered at Subiaco on 23 August without consulting anybody, was a blunder. Obsessed by financial difficulties, he forecast a 'mark time policy', an expression he was never allowed to forget. Militant supporters felt other aspects of the speech to be a rejection of the fighting platform. His appointment of James as agent-general was regarded by some as political dishonesty; the ensuing by-election was lost, but an agreement with a loose group of independents saved the day. A hostile Legislative Council rejected much of the government's programme and its one major success was a new Public Service Act. Radical supporters resented acceptance of the council's actions.

During the Christmas recess Daglish reconstructed his ministry. His replacement of George Taylor [q.v.] and John B. Holman by Thomas Bath [q.v.7] and Patrick J. Lynch [q.v.] was clumsily executed but in June 1905 he defeated a caucus vote of no-confidence. Though publicly rebuked by the State labour congress for the exemptions in his land tax legislation, Daglish won some support for deferring conflict with the Legislative Council, and for his refusal to accept non-alienation of crown lands. In the second session he sought a coalition with the Independents; when they proposed that C. J.' Moran [q.v.] replace him as premier, the scheme collapsed. In August there were further fruitless negotiations for a coalition with the Opposition. When faced with a no confidence motion, however, the Independents voted with the government.

The ministry had decided to offer £1 500 000 for the assets of the Midland Railway Co.: its opponents believed the price excessive. When Daglish sought parliamentary approval on 17 August, the motion was lost. On 22 August he announced his ministry's resignation and on 27 August resigned as party leader. In apologizing to his constituents, he said that he had never been happy about the party pledge but had temporarily accepted it and believed that it was cancelled with the dissolution; he had found caucus impossible to satisfy and experience had shown him that the party's policy of non-alienation of crown lands was impractical. In Kalgoorlie his deputy W. D. Johnson [q.v.] hinted that the resignation may have been partly a strategy that misfired when Opposition leader C. H. Rason [q.v.] was unexpectedly successful in forming a ministry.

At the next election in October Daglish won Subiaco as an Independent Labor candidate. When he urged in July 1907 that there was no need for party warfare in Western Australia, because there was no fundamental difference between the parties, old colleagues attacked him in the press. In August he was elected chairman of committees and, after winning his seat again in 1908, drifted into the Liberal camp. From September 1910 to October 1911, he was minister for works in the Frank Wilson [q.v] ministry.

Daglish was defeated in 1911 and became an estate agent. In March 1912 he was appointed employers' representative on the State Arbitration Court at £6 a week. He died of cancer on 16 August 1920 and was buried privately in the Congregational section of Karrakatta cemetery. His estate, valued for probate at £342, was left to his wife Edith, née Bishop, whom he had married at Carlton, Melbourne, on 20 August 1894. They had two children.

Hostility to Daglish in the Labor Party died quickly because he was consistent and sincere and never became a real opponent. In 1910 he was not contradicted when he claimed in the House that his political views were totally unchanged. When elected leader he was the only possible choice but he had no real understanding of the labour movement. The opposition of party radicals to him only hastened an inevitable outcome.

D. J. Murphy (ed), *Labour in politics* (Brisb, 1975); P. Loveday et al (eds), *The emergence of the Australian party system* (Syd, 1977); *Univ Studies in Hist* (WA), Sept 1955, 32-61; *Argus*, 11, 26 May 1896; *Bulletin*, 13 Oct 1904; *Punch* (Melb), 9 Feb 1905; *Southern Times* (Bunbury), 30 Mar 1905; *West Australian*, 10-12, 17 Oct 1905; *Western Argus*, 17 Oct 1905; *Labor Call*, 26 Aug 1920; E. S. Buttfield, The Daglish ministry 1904-5 (M.A. thesis, Univ WA, 1979); A. R. Grant memoirs, MS 280 (ML); CO 418/33/494, 40/521; CSO 3401/96, 1612/97 (Battye Lib, Perth); Files 1895/B7, 153, P1895/1786, 7153, P1896/3306 (PRO, Vic).

H. J. GIBBNEY

DAKIN, WILLIAM JOHN (1883-1950), zoologist, was born on 23 April 1883 at Toxteth Park, Liverpool, Lancashire, England, son of William Dakin, coal merchant, and his wife Elizabeth, née Grimshaw. Entering the University of Liverpool in 1901, he graduated B.Sc. with first-class honours in zoology in 1905 and M.Sc. in 1907. As an 1851 Exhibition scholar, Dakin spent 1907-08 at Christian-Albrechts-Universität, Kiel, Germany, with professors Brandt and Lohmann, partly at the biological station on Heligoland, where he furthered his already strong oceanographical interests. After a season in Italy at the British Association School for the Advancement of Science, at the Naples Zoological Station, where he declined a permanent appointment, Dakin in 1909 became assistant lecturer at Queen's University of Belfast. He returned to teach at Liverpool in 1910 under his old mentor Sir William Hardman, completing work on osmotic pressure and the blood of fishes for his D.Sc. (1911).

Dakin moved to a senior assistantship at University College, London, in 1912 but applied, almost at once, for the chair of biology in the new University of Western Australia. On the withdrawal of a more favoured candidate, Dakin, described by the electors as 'bright, keen and with a good manner', was appointed. Before taking up his post he married Catherine Mary Gladys Lewis on 15 January 1913 at the Welsh Calvinistic Chapel, West Kirby, Cheshire. His wife, who held a science degree and assisted his work, bore him a son Harvey.

Dakin entered on his Australian career zestfully. He introduced local material to his students and published for them *The elements of animal biology* (1918). He set up a biology club, chaired the extension committee (1917) and argued about the payment of fees. To further his physiological studies, he twice visited the Houtman Abrolhos archipelago; to widen the zoological impact, he became president of the local Royal Society in 1913-15. Refused permission to enlist, he was seconded for public health service in Colombo and Perth. In a city where a university was a novelty, Dakin helped to gain acceptance for it.

On leave in England in 1920, Dakin sought and was offered the Derby chair of zoology, at Liverpool — it did not fulfil his high expectations. Within eighteen months, he applied for the Challis [q.v.3] chair of zoology at the University of Sydney. Despite endorsement by British and local selection committees, Dakin lost out narrowly to a Sydney graduate, Launcelot Harrison [q.v.] whom he succeeded in 1929, having in the meantime published *Elements of general zoology* (London, 1927), using methods of comparative physiology. He reached Sydney on 24 January 1929.

Dakin's long professoriate at Sydney was distinguished by enthusiasm, diversity and great activity. Despite the Depression and World War II, he enlarged and enlivened his department, some of whose members did not approve of his wide range of interests or his teaching methods. A stimulating and innovative undergraduate lecturer, he gave postgraduate students much latitude but exacted great effort from them. He took little part in university administration.

Marine biology in many forms engrossed Dakin. With A. N. Colefax of Sydney, he published a pioneer study, *Plankton of the Australian coastal waters off New South Wales* (1940) and investigated the life cycle of commercial prawns. He turned to history in his *Whalemen adventurers* (1934). The fisheries laboratory of the Commonwealth Council for Scientific and Industrial Research at Cronulla was partly his creation and he served on the C.S.I.R. advisory panel for many years before becoming a councillor in 1948. Dakin, a trustee of the Australian Museum, Sydney, was a council-member and president of the Royal Zoological (1931) and the Linnean (1934-35) societies of New South Wales and received their fellowships. Intensely interested in science in schools, he constructed syllabuses in general biology and zoology for the State intermediate and leaving certificates. A daring new syllabus stressing a general approach to scientific education had been drawn up by 1950. Above all, Dakin took science into the market place. A few tentative radio talks developed into a long-term series, 'Science in the News', for the Australian Broadcasting Commission. His enormous knowledge,

simply presented in his Liverpool accent, gave him a large audience and brought his university direct to many people who otherwise scarcely knew of its existence.

During World War II Dakin in 1941 became technical director of camouflage for the Ministry of Home Security and built up a research institute and museum in his department at the university. His publication, *Art of camouflage* (1941), which drew heavily on his marine experience, summarized much of his work in this field.

Dakin received world-wide recognition, not least for the large number of his students who achieved prominence in zoology. In addition to his books he published over sixty papers on scientific subjects. He retired at the end of 1948 and was made emeritus professor next April. That same year the Hobart meeting of the Australian and New Zealand Association for the Advancement of Science awarded him its Mueller [q.v.5] medal. He was a keen photographer and yachtsman; these hobbies helped his marine work but were not simply a part of it. He tried his hand at painting and was a better musician, being a member of an academic string quartet, and a supporter of the A.B.C. symphony concerts. He was a member of the Australian Club, Sydney.

Despite a long illness, Dakin pressed on with a major book, *Australian seashores*, for, as he wrote, 'for over thirty years the study of the Australian seashores and seas has been my life work'. He received a large amount of help from his two long-term assistants Isobel Bennett and Elizabeth Pope, who saw the volume through to posthumous publication in 1952. Dakin died of cancer at his Turramurra home on 2 April 1950 and was cremated with Anglican rites. He was survived by his wife and son. His estate was valued for probate at £19 874.

F. Alexander, *Campus at Crawley* (Melb, 1963); Univ Syd Union, *Union Recorder*, 6 Apr, 8 June 1950; *Aust J of Science*, June 1950, p 208; Linnean Soc NSW, *Procs*, 76 (1951) p. iv; *SMH*, 3 Apr 1950; *Bulletin*, 12 Apr 1950; W. J. Dakin papers, *and* Senate and Professorial Board minutes (Univ Syd Archives).   URSULA BYGOTT
                                 K. J. CABLE

DALE, JOHN (1885-1952), medical practitioner, was born on 2 May 1885 at Coleshill, Warwickshire, England, son of James Francis Dale, grocer, and later chemist, and his wife Mary, née Grace. He was educated at Solihull Grammar School and the University of Birmingham, where he graduated M.B., Ch.B in 1908, also taking his M.R.C.S. and L.R.C.P. Next year he gained his B.Sc. (Public Health) in Birmingham where in 1911, after a two-year travelling studentship to Germany, he became assistant medical officer of health; he worked mainly in the depressed area of Smethwick. On 9 July 1914 he married Wynifred Mary Evans, a trained Montessori kindergartener. There were four children of the marriage.

Dale served with the British Army in 1915-19 as a major in the Royal Army Medical Corps and as deputy assistant director of medical services (sanitation) to the Second and Fourth Armies and the Army of the Rhine. He was appointed O.B.E. in 1918, and was awarded a French decoration for 'overcoming a typhoid epidemic'. On his return to Birmingham he took his M.D. (1919). After demobilization Dale and his family migrated to Australia and in February 1920 arrived in Perth where he had been appointed medical officer of health and assistant inspector of hospitals. Early in 1927 he left Western Australia to become medical officer of health to the City of Melbourne.

His first concern was for the children of the poor and for their mothers. When he took office, the infant mortality rate in the inner city was higher than that of any other municipality; five years later it was lower than that of any of the five adjoining, similarly depressed municipalities. When Dale retired in 1950 it was virtually the same as the State average. This improvement was partly due to the appointment, at Dale's instigation, of two assistant medical officers — Dr Hilda Kincaid to supervise child welfare, and Dr Hilda Bull (wife of Louis Esson [q.v.]) to take charge of the successful anti-diphtheria campaign. The building of more baby-health and pre-school centres, and the council's provision of free milk, and in the Depression years, of free vegetables, also improved city children's health. The only major health crisis was the poliomyelitis epidemic of 1937-38. Dale tried to improve the housing of the poor but the Depression, then World War II and the subsequent shortage of building materials delayed progress.

In 1929-50 Dale was lecturer in public health at the University of Melbourne, reputedly the only man who could pack a lecture theatre with undergraduates on a Saturday morning. He was a council-member of the Victorian branch of the British Medical Association and president in 1945, and a member of many committees connected with public health. In appearance he was tall, lanky and angular, with a rugged face, a charming smile and a 'deep resonant musical voice'. Outside his work his interests were cultural and his friends included many prominent musicians, writers and painters. He loved the theatre, especially opera, rarely missed an orchestral concert

and was himself a fine singer of German *lieder*. Other recreations included trout-fishing and duck-shooting.

Dale's first marriage ended in divorce in February 1951 and on 7 March he married Dr Hilda Bull. Shortly after, the couple left for Holland, where Dale spent eighteen months as a medical officer for the Commonwealth government, checking the health of prospective migrants. He was killed in a road accident at Venice, Italy, on 27 September 1952 and was buried near Verona. His wife returned to Melbourne, where she died of cancer on 29 June 1953.

WA Health Inspectors Assn, *WA J of Hygiene*, 1 (1928), no 3; *MJA*, 17 Jan 1953, p 81; *Age*, 29 Sept 1952; City of Melb, Health Dept annual report, 1927-49 (Council House, Melb).

LYNDSAY GARDINER

DALEY, CHARLES STUDDY (1887-1966), administrator, was born on 4 July 1887 at Maldon, Victoria, eldest son of Charles Daley and his wife Caroline Rose, née Bromfield. Charles Daley senior (1859-1947), a teacher with the Victorian Department of Education for forty-six years, was a prominent member of the Victorian Field Naturalists' Society. Specializing in the flora of the Bendigo district and the Grampians, he collected for Baron von Mueller [q.v.5]; two of his publications *The Grampians, Victoria* (1931) and *The history of 'flora Australiensis'* (1927-28) became standard works of reference. He was a notable member of the Royal Historical Society of Victoria, and author of several historical works.

Charles junior attended Harvard College, Stawell, in 1899-1903 and the Stawell School of Mines in 1903-04; he later went to the University of Melbourne (B.A., 1914; LL.B., 1921). On 27 January 1917 at the Australian Church, Melbourne, he married Henrietta Jessie Shaw Obbinson (d. 1943); they had two sons and three daughters.

Daley joined the Public Works Branch of the Commonwealth Department of Home Affairs in Melbourne as a clerk in 1905 and for several years was secretary to Colonel P. T. Owen [q.v.] who, with J. S. Murdoch [q.v.], encouraged him to attend classes in accountancy, architecture and engineering at the Working Men's College. Daley was later proud of his part in the construction of Australia House in London; but his career was centred on the development of Canberra. He closely observed the controversy preceding the selection of the site in 1909 and the conduct of the international competition for the design of the city in 1911-14. Sharing with many colleagues a suspicion and dislike of Walter Burley Griffin [q.v.] and disapproval of the eccentric King O'Malley [q.v.], he nevertheless comprehended Griffin's design and in later years became its principal and, on occasion, its sole protector.

In January 1921 when the Hughes [q.v.] government finally resolved that the development of Canberra should proceed on the basis of Griffin's plan, Daley was appointed secretary of the Federal Capital Advisory Committee which established an effective programme of construction until its replacement in January 1925 by the Federal Capital Commission. At his own volition and with a fine sense of prospective history, Daley prepared the committee's over-viewing final report. The committee added a recommendation that Daley be awarded a £500 honorarium for his 'absolutely indispensable and invaluable' services, but it was never paid.

Daley became secretary of the Federal Capital Commission in 1924 and took up residence in Canberra. Dedicated to the work of the commission which, under (Sir) John Butters [q.v.7], was responsible for the construction of the city and the administration of the Territory, Daley was appointed O.B.E. in 1927. During this period he also took a prominent part in community affairs. An accomplished musician, he encouraged the formation of a city band, was a founder in 1928 and president in 1932-53 of the local Musical Society, and was honorary organist for 17 years of the Presbyterian Church of St Andrew. He was a founding member of the Literature and Arts Society (1927) and the Rotary Club (1928) and later of the Young Men's Christian Association (1940). He was at some time president of each institution.

The Federal Capital Commission was abolished in 1930 and the Department of Home Affairs took over the administration of the Territory. Daley retained his key position as civic administrator, Federal Capital Territory Branch. From 1932 until he retired in 1952, he was assistant secretary, Department of the Interior. He was also a nominated member in 1930-52 and chairman for three terms of the Capital Territory Advisory Council; his primary concern was to alert the minister to proposals thought to conflict with Griffin's intentions. In 1939, at Daley's instigation, the National Capital Planning and Development Committee, with himself as executive member, was set up as a body of review and advice. The committee strengthened his protective role during the war and post-war years when the approved plan was under the threat of temporary buildings and other expedients. In his evidence in 1955 to the Senate's committee

inquiring into the development of Canberra Daley stressed the advantages of an independent commission; he described the period of the Federal Capital Commission as 'Canberra's golden age'.

Daley's community activities continued after his retirement. A member of the Interim Council of the Australian National University in 1945-50, he completed twenty-eight years on the Council of Canberra University College in 1958 and represented it at a university congress in Cambridge, England, in 1953. He was an early member of the Canberra and District Historical Society, founded in 1953, and president in 1958-61. In 1963 he was made an honorary associate of the Royal Australian Institute of Architects, and in 1965 represented Australia in Japan at a meeting of the World Council of the Young Men's Christian Association. With clear recollections of his unique experience at the centre of Canberra affairs Daley was ever willing to recount them to all who had time to listen. Disappointed at not being commissioned to write an official history of Canberra, he recorded his memoirs in a weekly series of articles, 'As I Recall', published in the *Canberra Times* in 1964-66. Other important publications include 'The Canberra plan and its development' in the 1951 Federal Congress on Regional and Town Planning *Record of proceedings* (Canberra, 1951) and 'The growth of a city' in *Canberra: a nation's capital*, edited by H. L. White (Sydney, 1954). These modestly impersonal accounts effectively disguise the importance of Daley's own role.

Daley died on 30 September 1966 at Canberra leaving an estate sworn for probate at £18 263. A service was conducted at the Anglican Church of St John the Baptist. The C. S. Daley Memorial Gardens were established at the Griffin Centre, housing the A.C.T. Council of Cultural Societies, in 1967. The C. S. Daley medal is offered annually by the A.C.T. Chapter of the Royal Australian Institute of Architects for meritorious design in domestic building.

Vic Naturalist, 64 (1947-48), p 1318; C. S. Daley papers (NL), *and* biog file (Canb & District Hist Soc).   PETER HARRISON

DALEY, JANE (JEAN) (1881-1948), political organizer, was born on 24 September 1881 at Mount Gambier, South Australia, daughter of Robert Dennis Daley and his wife Julia Ann, née Scott. Jane was educated at convents of Mercy in Mount Gambier and Adelaide, and then, when the family moved to Victoria, at Loreto Convent, Portland. Her father was one of the earliest members of the Amalgamated Shearers' Union and she was 'reared in a political atmosphere'. In 1906 in Melbourne she bore a child and returned to live with her parents at Wallacedale near Hamilton.

About 1909 Jean, as she became known, made her home in Melbourne, and became active in Labor politics. She joined the Women's Organizing Committee of the Political Labor Council of Victoria but after February 1914, when it was declared to have no official standing, she devoted herself to general industrial matters. In 1916 she was a delegate to the Trades Hall Council for the Hotel and Caterers' Union and was one of the earliest members of the Militant Propaganda League. She was also an executive member of the Victorian Socialist Party in 1916-17 and of its women's section, the Women's Socialist League.

Jean Daley was active in the No-Conscription Fellowship set up by R. S. Ross [q.v.] and organized the Labor Women's Anti-Conscription Committee formed in September 1916. However, she was not associated with the attempt in the following January to make this a permanent organization. She did not support Vida Goldstein [q.v.] as candidate for the Federal seat of Kooyong in 1917 but was a vice-president of the rival Labor Women's Campaign Committee. During 1917 Daley was one of the party's most effective speakers in campaigns against the high cost of living and conscription. Concerned also about problems such as alcohol consumption and venereal disease, she spoke out in favour of the P.L.C. policy of compulsory notification of V.D.

When the Women's Central Organizing Committee was formally recreated in March 1918, Daley was elected first president; she held this position until 1920 and for most of that time wrote 'We women' in *Labor Call*. Under her presidency, the W.C.O.C. firmly supported pacifism, efforts towards the industrial organization of women, and the protection and education of children.

At the State conference of the Australian Labor Party in 1919 Jean Daley was defeated by Mary Rogers for the new post of woman organizer but was elected a Victorian delegate to the next federal conference in 1921. With Mary Rogers and Muriel Heagney [q.v.] she called a conference of female delegates of all unions with women members in April 1921. Three months later she was elected to the central executive of the party and in July next year was one of two women delegates to the All Australia Trade Union Congress. At that time the *Union Record* of Seattle published a series of articles written by her on Australia's fight against conscription (later published as *A bird's eye view of the conscription campaign*).

In December 1922 she stood for Kooyong — the first woman in Victoria to stand for Federal parliament as an endorsed Labor candidate — but was defeated. Next year in March she and Muriel Heagney organized a maternity allowance conference for Australian women's organizations; two hundred delegates from all States attended.

In 1926 Daley became the woman organizer for the State. The fruition of her work was the formation of the Labor Women's Interstate Executive in 1929, of which she was secretary from 1930 until her retirement in 1947. From 1933 she was also State secretary for the W.C.O.C. and was thus responsible for organization and reports of activities at both State and Federal level. During the Depression much of her work was concentrated on the problems of unemployed women and girls and undernourished children.

While on the central executive of the Victorian branch of the A.L.P., Daley worked on the organizational committee, and, during the war years, on the social services and medical and health committees. In 1946-47 she was one of three W.C.O.C. representatives on the party's education committee.

It was a saying at the Trades Hall that 'when Miss Daley is not working for the A.L.P. she is dreaming about it'. When roused in debate she could 'flay an adversary' and often prevailed in verbal duels with the men. In 1947 ill health forced her to resign from the central executive. A month later she resigned her other posts, but not before finally lambasting the A.L.P.'s male leaders whom she accused of being uninterested in organizing women.

Jean Daley did not marry. In 1924 she ran a confectioner's shop at Northcote; from about 1926 she lived with her mother and other members of her family at Northcote, until the late 1930s, when she bought a house at Auburn which she divided into flats. She died of liver disease on 5 November 1948 at the Alfred Hospital and was cremated. *Labor Call* paid tribute to 'her ardent exposition of Labor policy [which] awakened in women a political consciousness and an awareness of the important role they had in national affairs'.

Labor Call, 15 June, 21 Sept, 30 Nov 1916, 8 Feb, 5 Apr, 10 May, 7 June, 23 Aug 1917, 28 Feb, 28 Mar, 16 May, 20 June 1918, 14 Dec 1922, 12 Nov 1948; *Sun-News Pictorial*, 10 Mar 1947; *Herald* (Melb), 23 May 1947, 6 Nov 1948; *Age*, 8 Nov 1948; S. Merrifield collection (LaTL).   JUDITH SMART

DALEY, VICTOR JAMES WILLIAM PATRICK (1858-1905), poet and journalist, was born on 5 September 1858 at Navan, County Meath, Ireland, son of John William Daley, soldier in the Indian Army, and his wife Maggie, née Morrison. He was educated by the Christian Brothers at Armagh, but his early schooling was sketchy as he preferred roaming the countryside and visiting the sites of history and legend as recounted by his grandfather. He claimed that many of his relations were Fenians and that as a child he had often helped to 'cast bullets at night'. After his mother remarried he completed his education at the Christian Brothers' school at Devonport, England, and about 1875 became a clerk in the Plymouth office of the South Devon (later Great Western) Railway Co.

About 1878 Daley set out for South Australia where he had connexions, but arrived in Sydney by mistake. He soon earned enough to go to Adelaide where he worked as a clerk and reputedly contributed to a small evening newspaper, the *Star*, edited by H. Allerdale Grainger [q.v.]. About 1880 he moved to Melbourne, *en route* for New Caledonia, but lost his money at the races. He wrote about racehorses for the Carlton *Advertiser* then joined its staff

About 1881 Daley set out to see Australia: in southern New South Wales, he worked on the *Queanbeyan Times*, then moved on to Sydney where he wrote for *Sydney Punch* and later the *Bulletin*. In March 1882 J. F. Archibald [q.v.3] described him 'as the rising poet of this country. For a long time we have not had more melodious and imaginative verses from an Australian writer'. Thereafter Daley's verse, much of it lyrical and often fashionably melancholic, appeared regularly in the *Bulletin*. In 1890, at the height of 'ballad fever', he was described in the *Bulletin* as 'one of the few Australian writers who are justified in styling their verse poetry'. That year Archibald gave more space to his verse in *A golden shanty* than to the work of any other poet.

On 5 September 1884 at Mosman, Daley had married Elizabeth Ann Thompson, who bore him six children over the next eight years. He returned to Melbourne, probably in the late 1880s and contributed, sometimes as 'Creeve Roe', verse, short stories and articles, to newspapers and magazines. He knew the Lindsay [q.v.] family, especially Lionel, and reputedly amused his friends while in his cups with sonorous recitations from English Romantic poets 'but frowned down the bawdy story'. 'Of medium height and build' and 'youthful appearance', in 1895 Daley wore a 'full brown beard' and spoke with a slight Northern Irish accent. In 1898 he returned to Sydney for the publication of his first book of verse, *At dawn and dusk*, which had been produced under the

guidance of A. G. Stephens [q.v.]. It was received most favourably and a whole *Bulletin* 'Red Page' was devoted to praise of Daley's verse by his contemporaries. As the 'symposiarch', he was chief participant in the Dawn and Dusk Club, named after his book and a light-hearted society of such artists and writers as Randolph Bedford, Fred Broomfield [qq.v.7], Henry Lawson, Nelson Illingworth, Norman Lindsay, Bertram Stevens and Frank Mahony [qq.v.].

Suffering from tuberculosis, Daley stayed with E. J. Brady [q.v.] at Grafton in 1902. Next year some of his friends got up a testimonial fund to send him to New Caledonia, but his health did not benefit. He died at his home at Waitara, Sydney, on 29 December 1905 and was buried in the Catholic section of Waverley cemetery. He was survived by his wife, two sons and two daughters, whom he left in financial difficulties. A fund was set up and on 3 March 1906 a memorial matinée held at the Theatre Royal was tendered 'by the entire Theatrical Profession of Sydney'. However Elizabeth Daley died on 22 November and their children were sent to relations overseas. Daley's *Poems* (1908) and *Wine and roses* (1911), with a memoir by Stephens, were published posthumously.

In his own day, Daley's literary fame rested on his lyric poetry, the best of which was written in the 1880s and early 1890s. From the late 1890s he was hailed as preeminently a Celtic poet – a view that reflected Australia's enthusiasm for the European Celtic revival and that has dominated critical assessment of his work. Only his verse from the mid-1890s and some late prose in fact belong to the historical Celtic revival. Daley's humorously satirical sociopolitical verse, most of it written as 'Creeve Roe', was not considered literature by his contemporaries, but attracted attention in the 1940s for its Irish revolutionary spirit and for its wit and skill. *Creeve Roe*, edited by Muir Holburn and Marjorie Pizer, was published in 1947. Another selection of his poetry appeared in 1963.

A. G. Stephens, *Victor Daley* (Syd, 1905); *Tatler* (Melb), 20 Aug 1898; *Aussie*, 4 Mar 1925; *Bulletin*, 11 Mar 1882, 23 Aug 1890, Red Pages, 11 June, 10, 17 Sept, 3 Dec 1898; *Table Talk*, 22 Feb 1895; *Tocsin*, 2 Oct 1897; *Aust Worker*, 4 Jan 1906; G. D. Ailwood Keel, Homespun exotic: Australian literature 1880-1910 (Ph.D. thesis, Univ Syd, 1976); V. J. Daley papers (ML, NL); A. G. Stephens papers (ML); ML printed cat.   G. D. AILWOOD KEEL

DALLAS, RODERIC STANLEY (1891-1918), airman, was born on 30 July 1891 at Mount Stanley station near Esk, Queensland, son of Peter McArthur Dallas, labourer, and his wife Honora, née Curry. The family moved to Tenterfield, New South Wales, and about 1898 to Mount Morgan, Queensland. Dallas attended the local school and in July 1907 joined the assay office of the Mount Morgan Gold Mining Co. At night he studied chemistry and technical drawing at the technical college.

Dallas led an active, mainly outdoor life. He became a sergeant in the school cadet corps and was later a lieutenant in the Mount Morgan Company of the 3rd (Port Curtis) Infantry Battalion. Other interests were gymnastics, Rugby Union and amateur theatricals. When his family moved to Brisbane in 1912, Dallas and his brother stayed at Mount Morgan.

In 1911 Lindsay Campbell, who had established the Queensland Aero Club in Brisbane, formed a similar club at Mount Morgan. Next year a visiting American aviator, Arthur Burr Stone, carried out the first powered flight in Queensland at Rockhampton. Dallas, who was already interested in flight and had studied the flight of birds for years, was inspired. He had built a frail glider but failed in an attempt to launch it. He corresponded with other enthusiasts abroad and, to raise the money required for travel, he and his brother worked as miners at the Mount Morgan Co.'s quarries on Iron Island. He built a large-scale seaplane there, but while experimenting with it at Marble Island he lost it in the sea.

By 1912 Dallas was 6 ft. 2 in. (279 cm) tall and weighed 16 stone (101 kg). He did not drink and smoked rarely. His voice, said by his father to be made for a bullocky, was useful on the stage but he usually spoke quietly, and was never heard to swear. His eyesight was exceptional. He paid his own way to England in 1915 but met with difficulties in trying to become an airman. He thought of an acting career in the United States of America, but advice from an Australian aviator, Sydney Pickles, and assistance from Australia House gained him entry to the Royal Naval Air Service. At the entrance examination he topped the eighty-four students, and on 5 August won pilot's licence No. 1512.

He became a flight sub-lieutenant with No. 1 Squadron, R.N.A.S., remained with it in 1916-17 and finally as a lieut-commander became its commanding officer. After a practical joke early in his career, he was known in the squadron as 'Breguet' Dallas. The squadron did reconnaissance and fighting patrols, sometimes with French airmen. His first dogfight took place in December 1915, and his first kill came in May 1916 in circumstances that won him the Distinguished Service Cross. Dallas exchanged his Sopwith Pup for a Sopwith

Triplane, the first of its type, little more than a test plane. In a later model he scored many victories against all types of enemy aircraft. With a fellow pilot he once tackled fourteen enemy planes at 18 000 ft. (5500 m); for 45 minutes the two kept the enemy formation split up, shot three of them down and forced the others to retreat.

In March 1918 Dallas was appointed major commanding No. 40 Squadron in the newly formed Royal Air Force. Because of his naval background, his men sometimes called him 'the admiral'. His official tally of 30 victories soon rose to 39, though in correspondence he claimed only 32 as certain. Unofficial estimates suggested there were over 50. All types of German aircraft fell to his superior skill, but in an instructional booklet he made it clear that impetuousness was not synonymous with agressiveness. He warned his airmen of traps set by the enemy and of the vital need to search the sky thoroughly. He frequently applied his dexterity to protect inexperienced pilots, and won some of his victories by manoeuvres based on a knowledge of structural flaws in enemy planes.

On 1 June 1918, while patrolling over the lines near Liévin, Dallas went to the assistance of another pilot though aware of enemy planes in positions of vantage. Thus pinioned, he was shot down by three triplanes. He was buried in the British cemetery at Pernes. At his death he was sixteenth on the list of allied aces and second only to R. A. Little [q.v.] among the Australians.

His awards included the Distinguished Service Order, a Bar to his D.S.C., the Croix de Guerre avec Palme and a mention in dispatches. He also won non-military recognition: the gold medal of the Acro Club de France (1918) and the medal of merit and honor of the Aero Club of America (1917).

An obituary notice in *Aeroplane* acknowledged not only his extraordinary skill and gallantry, but also his sense of humour and ability as a black and white artist; it revealed the opinion of his comrades that he was a great leader of men.

W. Raleigh, *The war in the air*, 3, H. A. Jones ed (Oxford, 1931); G. H. Lewis, *Wings over the Somme, 1916-1918*, C. Bowyer ed (Lond, 1976); E. P. Wixted, *Search the sky* (Brisb, 1978); *Aeroplane*, 3 July 1918; *Reveille* (Syd), 1 May 1935; *Brisbane Courier*, 7 June 1918; *Sunday Mail*, 20 Nov 1977.

E. P. WIXTED

DALLEY, JOHN BEDE (1876-1935), journalist and writer, was born on 5 October 1876 at Rose Bay, Sydney, second son and third of the five children of native-born parents William Bede Dalley [q.v. 4], barrister and politician, and Eleanor Jane, née Long. He began his education at St Aloysius College but after his father's death in 1888, despite his wish that his sons be educated in Sydney, John and his brothers were sent to England in 1889 by their uncle and principal guardian W. A. Long [q.v. 5]. John was educated at St Augustine's Abbey school at Ramsgate, and Beaumont College at Old Windsor, Oxford. He matriculated from University College, Oxford, on 1 November 1895, and later entered the Inner Temple, and was called to the Bar on 18 November 1901. The brothers enjoyed hunting; the youngest Charles (b. 1878) was killed in a fall in 1899. Returning to New South Wales in 1902 John practised for several years at Wigram Chambers. He joined the Union Club and enjoyed the pleasures of a young man-about-town. Standing as a protectionist, he was defeated for the Federal seat of Wentworth. He denied allegations that he traded on his father's name, except that 'I absolutely oppose sectarianism in politics as he did'.

On 20 August 1895 his brother William (1873-1942) had married Ianthe Pauline Lamonerie Fattorini; in 1900 John settled certain property on William, his sister-in-law and the two children. William gained a legal separation from his wife in London in 1903, but in 1905 in Sydney petitioned for divorce, citing his brother as co-respondent. The jury found the charges unproven, but Mrs Dalley's counter-charges proven. The case became a *cause célèbre*. Further litigation followed when she sought alimony and maintenance for her second child.

A fall from a horse left Dalley deaf; he turned to journalism and in 1906-07 edited the Bathurst *National Advocate*. In 1907 he became a sub-editor on the *Bulletin* and was a leader-writer from 1911. He contributed short stories, articles and verse, and was a superb writer of paragraphs, capturing the apparent ease of composition, pungency and ironic flippancy that characterized the *Bulletin's* style. He inherited his father's 'wit and command of language'.

Several times rejected for active service because of his deafness, Dalley pleaded with the government 'that no son of the man who had sent the first Australian troops abroad' should be denied entry to the Australian Imperial Force. He was commissioned second lieutenant in the Australian Field Artillery in March 1915 and, promoted lieutenant in the A.I.F. in November, he was allotted to the 2nd Divisional Ammunition Column. He served with the 5th Divisional Artillery until invalided to Australia in May 1916 after a bout of typhoid. He left again with reinforcements in September and served with the 6th Field Artillery Brigade

in France and was in and out of hospital until he was invalided home late in 1918. He defended many 'diggers' at courts-martial and contributed to *Aussie*, an A.I.F. monthly published in the field.

On his return to Sydney, he rejoined the *Bulletin*. On 7 May 1919 at Paddington registry office he married a New Zealand-born divorcee Sarah Anne Sharpe, née Bright, manageress of a costume business; he divorced her in 1925. Meanwhile in 1924 he edited Melbourne *Punch*, then spent several years in London as representative of the Melbourne *Herald*. In London in 1928 he published two novels, *No armour* and *Max Flambard*. Back in Sydney and on the *Bulletin*, at St Stephen's Presbyterian Church, Macquarie Street on 8 November, he married an artist Claire Campbell Scott, who had designed the dust-jackets for his books.

In 1930 Dalley's best novel, *Only the morning* (London), appeared; it ran to six editions. In all his novels he satirized the social life of upper-class Sydney, and in *Only the morning* English society as well. He sharply observed their peculiarities and shortcomings, drawing on his own experiences. To that extent he is in the interesting line of Australian novelists from Henry Kingsley [q.v. 5] to Patrick White, who combined an Oxbridge education with a sardonic or satirical view of Australian life and manners. Always immaculately dressed, perfectly spoken, and courteous, Dalley effortlessly transferred these qualities to his novels, which thus have the unusual value of faithfully depicting the metropolitan and more cultured phases of Australian life in the 1920s. His contemporary Frank Dalby Davison remembered him as 'the kindliest of men, markedly tolerant of views that opposed his own, charitable in his judgement of fools and sinners'. A notable graduate of the half-world of literature and journalism that produced writers like A. G. Stephens and A. B. Paterson [qq.v.], he was perhaps more distinctly cosmopolitan in his outlook.

Dalley was presumed to have been drowned while rock-fishing at Avalon Beach north of Sydney, on or about 6 September 1935. He was survived by his second wife and their daughter; his estate was valued for probate at £8515.

Home, 1 Dec 1921; *Aust Writers' Annual*, 1 (1936), p 61; *Bulletin*, 16 Feb 1889, 18 Sept 1935; *SMH*, 7-11, 15-18, 21-25, 28-30 Nov, 1, 2 Dec 1905, 15 Mar 1906, 13 Dec 1930; *Table Talk*, 15 Nov 1928; *Australasian*, 14 Sept 1935; *Smith's Weekly* (Syd), 28 Sept 1935.   CLEMENT SEMMLER

DALLEY-SCARLETT, ROBERT (1887-1959), musician, was born on 16 April 1887 at

Dalley-Scarlett

Darlinghurst, Sydney, son of Robert Campbell Scarlett, public servant, and his wife Emily Florence, née Hancock. The prefix to his surname was adopted on the insistence of his godfather William Bede Dalley [q.v.4], and was later hyphened. Educated at Sydney Grammar School, he was a clerk with the Sydney Municipal Council in 1905-12. He had learned piano from S. Gordon Laver and organ under Arthur Mason, city organist, while young, and was soon serving as organist in suburban churches, singing in choirs and conducting amateur choirs and orchestras. In 1912, he became organist and choral conductor to Christ Church Anglican Cathedral, Grafton.

Enlisting in the Australian Imperial Force in May 1916, Dalley-Scarlett embarked with reinforcements for the 21st Battalion in October. He was transferred to the Army Pay Corps early in 1917, returned sick to Australia in September and was discharged in November. While stationed in London, he studied church music with Sir J. Frederick Bridge and Dr Richard Terry.

After returning briefly to Grafton, Dalley-Scarlett was organist at St Andrew's Presbyterian Church, Brisbane, in 1919-32. He also conducted the South Brisbane City Choir in 1920-25 and the University (of Queensland) Musical Society in 1920-30 and 1938-41. He led many performances of works previously unknown to Brisbane, including particularly those of Renaissance composers and Bach; the university choir gave a Bach festival in 1930.

Although Dalley-Scarlett matriculated in the University of Queensland in 1920, he abandoned an arts course after one term and later enrolled for external study with the University of Adelaide (B. Mus. 1926; D. Mus. 1934); he majored in composition. With practical qualifications including Licentiate of the Associated Boards (1922), Licentiate of Music (Australia) (1924) and Fellow of Trinity College, London (1924), he maintained a teaching practice in piano, organ, singing, harmony and composition until 1941; successful pupils included Hugh Brandon and Herbert Cannon. A founding member of the Music Teachers' Association of Queensland (Musical Association), he became its president in 1935. He was an active member of the university's Music Advisory Board in 1924-37.

Dalley-Scarlett conducted at the Valley Methodist Church in 1932-34 and at All Saints' Church in 1934-41 but his main choir was the Brisbane Handel Society in 1932-59. After successful Handel festivals in 1933 and 1934, the society broadcast all his oratorios between 1934 and 1942. In the 1950s it gave annual unabridged performances of the *Messiah*, faithfully observing the composer's intentions.

In 1941-55 Dalley-Scarlett was employed full time by the Australian Broadcasting Commission as music presentation officer, acting music supervisor and music arranger, producing many broadcasts himself with the A.B.C. Brisbane Singers. One of his special projects was a programme of English coronation music, broadcast world-wide by the British Broadcasting Corporation in 1953.

Dalley-Scarlett was a prolific composer; many of his 300 works were broadcast or performed locally, although few were published. He was founding president of the Queensland Guild of Composers in 1940-53. His most notable contribution, however, was in musical scholarship. His 5000-volume library, now in the Fisher Library, University of Sydney, includes nearly 150 priceless first editions of Handel and other eighteenth-century composers. The library enabled him to produce arrangements specially designed for modern performance. His Handelian research was recognized in 1940 by award of the Hallé Medal. Besides his regular musicological articles in various journals, Dalley-Scarlett's most important publications were the 'Australia' article for *Grove's Dictionary* (5th edition) and a pamphlet on eighteenth century performance entitled *Handel's 'Messiah': how can we realise the composer's intentions?* (New York, 1955). As music critic for the *Australian Musical News* in 1934-37 and for the Brisbane *Courier Mail* in 1945-46 and 1952-59, he was a respected authority who continually encouraged all forms of music-making at both amateur and professional levels. His own indefatigable work inspired others with his initiative, untiring enthusiasm and dedication to high musical ideals.

On 8 September 1909 at Christ Church St Laurence, Sydney, Dalley-Scarlett had married Gertrude Alice Pier, who bore him two sons. She refused to go to Brisbane and after ten years separation the marriage was dissolved on 3 March 1930. On 11 March he married Joyce Buckham who, as a singer and music copyist, proved an asset to his work; they had no children. He died at his home of a heart attack on 31 July 1959 and was cremated. A triennial scholarship to his memory exists within the University of Queensland.

Descent, 1 (1961-62), pt 4, p 3, *and* 2 (1963-65), pt 1, p 3, and for bibliog; *Studies in Music*, 1971, no 5, p 87; *Sun* (Syd), 15 Mar 1921; P. Roennfeldt, Robert Dalley-Scarlett . . . (B. Mus. Hons thesis, Univ Qld, 1978); E. Briggs, 'The unappeasable mind', Dalley-Scarlett memorial lecture, Apr 1961 (Fellowship of Aust Writers, Qld); Dalley-Scarlett collection (Fisher Lib, Univ Syd, *and* Fryer Lib,

Univ Qld); news-cuttings (A.B.C. Archives, Syd).

PETER ROENNFELDT

DALRYMPLE, DAVID HAY (1840-1912), chemist, pastoralist and politician, was born on 14 December 1840 at Newbury, Berkshire, England, son of James Dalrymple, tea dealer, and his wife Georgina Hay, née Dalrymple (or Dalrymple-Hay). He was educated at the West of England Dissenters' Proprietary School at Taunton; his qualification as an associate of the Pharmaceutical Society, was followed by attendance at the Bristol Medical School. Dalrymple reached Melbourne in 1862; next year he went to Rockhampton, Queensland, and then to Mackay where he bought land at the first sales, opened in Gordon Street the town's first chemist shop and began his pastoral investments. He became a magistrate from 1870. In July 1878 he was in the second party to climb Mount Dalrymple.

An executive-member of the Mackay Hospital and the School of Arts, Dalrymple was the town's first mayor in 1869-71 and later served again. He was a member of the Road Board before the Divisional Boards Act of 1879, and then of the Pioneer Divisional Board until 1888 when he left local government and became a member for Mackay in the Legislative Assembly. At first he was a staunch advocate of northern separation, but in 1899, when speaking on the Federation enabling bill, he no longer identified himself with the northern separation bloc.

In 1895-1903 Dalrymple served in ministries under (Sir) Hugh Nelson [q.v.], T. J. Byrnes [q.v.7], (Sir) James Dickson, and (Sir) Robert Philp [qq.v.], holding successively public instruction, public works, public lands, agriculture and public instruction. Dalrymple was a middling administrator but succeeded in the Department of Public Instruction because of his own intellectual interests. He improved the system of grammar school scholarships and simplified the payment of teachers. His bill for a university in 1898 was lost in prorogation. In 1901 as minister for agriculture, he secured the Agricultural Bank Act which facilitated rural finance.

'Awkward, shy, ridiculously nervous and aggressively unkempt', Dalrymple yet became a notable debater. His parliamentary speeches and his pamphlet *Letters on Socialism* (Brisbane, 1894) illustrate his eclecticism and polished sarcasm. Although the *Worker* deplored 'Dal's' conservative politics, it described him as 'a man of wit, philosophy, intellectual dexterity and ingenuity and a certain nerve and vim'. He was respected but not especially popular in the House; but his real abilities were wasted in parsimonious conservative administrations.

Dalrymple lost his seat in August 1904 and lived in retirement at Hamilton; he died there on 1 September 1912. He was predeceased by his wife Euphemia Margaret, née McLean, whom he had married at Mackay on 23 December, 1880; his estate, valued for probate at £33719, was left to their four children. He was buried in the Anglican section of Toowong cemetery.

Alcazar Press, *Queensland, 1900* (Brisb, nd); C. A Bernays, *Queensland politics during sixty years* (Brisb, 1919); J. Kerr, *Pioneer to leader* (Brisb, 1980); *PD* (Qld), 1897, p 932, 1899, p 236, 690-708; *V&P* (LA Qld), 1898, 1, 917; *Echo* (Brisb), 20 Feb 1897; *Mackay Mercury,* 10, 12 Apr, 8 May 1888; *Worker* (Brisb), 25 Apr, 3, 10 Oct 1896; *Brisbane Courier,* 2 Sept 1912; J. Martin diary, MS617 (ML); C. Lack, 1, *and* Turner, 7, Cutting-books (Oxley, Lib, Brisb).

ROSEMARY HOWARD GILL

DALY, ANNE (1860-1924), founder of hospitals, known as Mother Mary Berchmans, was born on 28 May 1860 at Tipperary, Ireland, ninth child of John Daly, blacksmith, and his wife Mary, née Cleary. About 1865 the family migrated to New South Wales, settling at Jembaicumbene near Braidwood, but on 4 March 1867 John Daly died.

Annie was educated at home by tutors. As soon as she was old enough she applied to the Department of Public Instruction and in May 1877 was appointed assistant at Braidwood Catholic School. After further training she was appointed to Newtown Girls' School and later Grafton Primary, but she probably gained most of her experience at St Mary's Cathedral Girls' School, Sydney, run by the Sisters of Charity. In May 1881 she entered the Sisters of Charity at St Vincent's Convent, Potts Point; as Sister Mary Berchmans she continued to teach at St Mary's.

In December 1888 Sister Berchmans was appointed to the first foundation of her Order in Melbourne. Next year, on 21 January, she took charge of St Patrick's School in Victoria Parade. Under her guidance the school made rapid progress and the number of pupils trebled. In 1892 she was appointed superior of the Sisters of Charity in Melbourne and was responsible not only for St Patrick's but for four other primary schools established by the sisters between 1891 and 1897.

Meanwhile, on her visits to the sick poor in the inner city area, she had become convinced of the need for a hospital administered by the sisters, similar to St Vincent's, Sydney. She received practical encouragement and in 1893, as a temporary measure, she established the first St Vincent's

Hospital in a 'low roofed, old-fashioned boarding house' at 3 Albert Terrace. As rectress, she helped to prepare the young trainee nurses for examinations and arranged their practical work. When the building fund raised £10 000, she planned the new hospital (opened in 1905) and the re-siting of what became known as the Catholic Ladies' College. The hospital had been granted its first government subsidy in 1903, and that year its training school for nurses was established and affiliated to the Royal Victorian Trained Nurses' Association.

In 1910 Mother Berchmans successfully completed negotiations for the establishment of St Vincent's Clinical School in association with the University of Melbourne. That year she visited Europe to study ways of increasing the hospital's efficiency. She arranged to buy equipment and furnishings for the outdoor department, the nurses' home and a new private hospital. She continued to look for further land for expansion; Mount St Evin's private hospital was opened in 1913 on the site of a disused church.

In 1920 Mother Berchmans was elected superior-general of the Sisters of Charity, returning to St Vincent's Convent, Potts Point. She was now responsible for almost four hundred sisters in New South Wales, Victoria and Tasmania. Her powers of leadership and organization were clear to all. Equally obvious was the decline in her health; but she responded with courage to needs as they arose. In 1920 St Vincent's Hospital, Toowoomba, Queensland, was established. In 1921 she founded a hospital at Lismore, New South Wales, and another in 1922 at Bathurst. Her last great contribution to the care of the sick was her part in the recognition of St Vincent's Hospital, Sydney, as a clinical school in 1923.

Mother Berchmans died in Sydney on 4 March 1924. Her work as foundress of Melbourne's St Vincent's Hospital and of the clinical school is commemorated by a bronze bust by Paul Montford [q.v.]; at its unveiling in August 1935 tributes were paid to her vision, intuition, courage and charm. Sir Thomas Dunhill [q.v.] described her as 'unique in her day and generation or in any day and generation'. Her memory is perpetuated also in the Berchmans Daly wing of St Vincent's, opened in October 1960.

St Vincent's Hospital (Syd), *Annual Report,* 1923, and (Melb) *Annual Report,* 1893-1900, 1903, p 6, 1905, p 7, 43, 1910, p 7, 1919, 1920; *Argus,* 31 Aug 1935; *SMH,* 7 Mar 1924; Sisters of Charity Archives, (St Vincent's Convent, Potts Point, NSW); information from Roy Aust Nursing Federation, Vic Branch (Melb).
MARGARET M. DONOVAN

DALY, CLARENCE WELLS (1890-1918), soldier and bank clerk, was born on 5 May 1890 in Hobart, third son of William John Daly, businessman, and his wife Florence Eleonore, née Beckx. After his family moved to Canterbury, Melbourne, he was educated at Camberwell Grammar School and, from 1905, at Wesley College. He matriculated at the University of Melbourne and became a bank clerk.

Daly showed an early interest in military affairs, gaining a commission as second lieutenant in the 5th Australian Infantry Regiment, later renamed the 64th (City of Melbourne), in January 1911; he was promoted captain in March 1913. An early volunteer for overseas service, he was appointed to the 6th Battalion, Australian Imperial Force, on 19 August 1914 and embarked two months later on the *Hororata* as officer commanding 'D' Company. After training in Egypt his battalion served as an assault unit at the Gallipoli landing on 25 April 1915: after hours of severe fighting near Pine Ridge, during which they managed to repulse several Turkish attacks, Daly and his party were ordered to retire to 400 Plateau. From this position the 6th Battalion held off determined enemy attacks on 27-28 April. Daly was wounded on the day of the landing.

On 6 May his unit was shipped from Anzac to Cape Helles and two days later sustained heavy casualties in the battle of Krithia. Daly was promoted major on 16 May and returned with his battalion to Anzac where, throughout June, it was in reserve. On 6 August he took part in the abortive and costly attempt to capture German Officers' Trench at Lone Pine. Afterwards the 6th was sent to Lemnos for a rest but returned in November and remained until the evacuation.

Daly's unit left Egypt for the Western Front early in 1916 and fought in the battles of Pozières and Mouquet Farm before withdrawing to the relative quiet of the Ypres sector. From 22 August to 26 September and for several periods in October-December Daly was the battalion's acting commander. In January 1917 he was awarded the Distinguished Service Order and mentioned in dispatches. Promoted lieut-colonel on 25 February, he was appointed commanding officer of the 6th Battalion — at the age of 26 — and from then until his death also periodically took temporary command of the 2nd Brigade. Though wounded in action at Tremincourt on 26 April, he resumed duty for the 2nd battle of Bullecourt, and for rallying his brigade at Menin Road on 20 September won a second mention in dispatches. He was wounded again at Broodseinde on 4 October.

On 13 April 1918, immediately before the battle of the Lys, Daly checked that his battalion was in position and was riding forward to reconnoitre at La Motte-au-Bois when he was wounded in the abdomen by a shell fragment. He died later that day and was posthumously mentioned in dispatches. Daly Window in Adamson [q.v.7] Hall, Wesley College, is in memory of him. Two of his brothers served in the A.I.F., one in the 12th and the other in the 23rd Battalion. Daly was unmarried.

C. E. W. Bean, *The story of Anzac* (Syd, 1921, 1924); E. Nye (ed), *The history of Wesley College 1865-1919* (Melb, 1921); C. E. W. Bean, *The A.I.F. in France*, 1916-18 (Syd, 1929, 1933, 1937, 1942); G. Blainey et al, *Wesley College. The first hundred years* (Melb, 1967); *Argus*, 4 May 1918

J. WHITELAW

DALY, JOHN JOSEPH (1891-1942), lawyer and politician, was born on 10 November 1891 at Hemington, South Australia, twin son of John Daly, carpenter and unionist, and his wife Margaret, née Hayes. Daly was educated at St John the Baptist School, Thebarton, but left at 13 to serve on a pie and saveloy stall. Encouraged by his father he attended evening classes at Remington Training College, while working there of a day as a rouseabout. Later he became an office-boy in the legal firm of Sir Josiah Symon [q.v.], advancing to the position of conveyancing clerk; in 1912 he became chief conveyancing clerk to W. J. Denny and F. Villeneuve Smith [qq.v.]; he was articled to them in 1914. In April 1919 he was called to the Bar, and did much work for trade unions. It was said he would often take a brief without fee.

Daly was a member of the Australian Workers' Union from 1914 and received life membership of the Tramways Employees' Association for his work during the strike of 1918. He sat on the State (S.A.) executive of the Australian Labor Party in 1918-28 and was president in 1927; he was on the federal executive in 1924-28. National president of the Hibernian Australasian Catholic Benefits Society in 1925-28, he led the South Australian delegation to the 1928 Sydney Eucharistic Congress. He was secretary of the Self-Determination for Ireland League of Australia in 1916 and supported the Irish National Foresters and the Australian Natives' Association. In later life he was an avowed pacifist.

Defeated in the elections for the Legislative Council in 1921 and for the Senate in 1925, he became a senator in 1928. A brilliant speaker, he was soon unanimously elected as leader of the Opposition in the Senate; in 1929, under the Scullin [q.v.] government, he was Senate leader. He was also vice-president of the Executive Council, and minister in charge of development and migration, and of the Council for Scientific and Industrial Research. In 1931 he was minister for defence. During Scullin's absence overseas from August 1930 to January 1931, Daly, acting as attorney-general, reputedly engineered the appointments of H. V. Evatt and E. McTiernan to the High Court: this was against Scullin's expressed wish. Daly also joined with F. G. Anstey [q.v.7] and J. A. Beasley in opposing the deflationary Niemeyer Plan, appearing with J. T. Lang [q.v.] in Queanbeyan. In March 1931 when caucus decided on a cabinet 'spill' Daly, Anstey and Beasley lost their places. By June, however, Daly had changed his views and supported the Premiers' Plan; he was re-elected and remained until January 1932 as minister without portfolio.

Daly's support for the plan induced the South Australian branch to expel him from the party both in 1931 and in 1933, when he pledged his support for any non-Labor candidate who would back Scullin's financial policy. He failed to gain Labor pre-selection in 1934 and after the expiry of his Senate term next year, returned to his law practice. He died on 13 April 1942 at North Adelaide and was buried in the Catholic cemetery, West Terrace. He was survived by his wife Eva, née Bird, whom he had married on 16 October 1918 at St Francis Xavier's Cathedral, Adelaide, and by his five children.

L. F. Crisp, *Ben Chifley* (Melb, 1961); N. Makin, *Federal Labor leaders* (Syd, 1961); I. Young, *Theodore* (Syd, 1971); J. Robertson, *J. H. Scullin* (Perth, 1974); *PD* (Cwlth), 1942, 571-73; *Herald* (Melb), 25 June 1929, 3 Nov 1930, 10, 14 Feb, 15 Apr, 7 June 1933, 14 Aug 1944; *Chronicle* (Adel), 27 June 1929, 16 Apr 1942; *Aust Worker*, 21 Aug, 27 Nov 1929, 15 Apr 1942; *SMH*, 3, 6 Mar, 26 June 1931, 14 Apr 1933, 14 Aug 1934; *South Aust Worker*, 21 Apr 1933, 17 Apr 1942; Supreme Court, No 128 of 1914 (SA).

RAY BROOMHILL

DALYELL, ELSIE JEAN (1881-1948), pathologist, was born on 13 December 1881 at Newtown, Sydney, second daughter of James Melville Dalyell, mining engineer, and his wife Jean, née McGregor. Educated at Sydney Girls' High School under Lucy Garvin [q.v.], she joined the Department of Public Instruction as a pupil-teacher in 1897. Sponsored by the department she completed first year arts and science at the University of Sydney. She suffered a hysterectomy in 1905, and next year resigned as a teacher and transferred to second-year medicine. Entering the Women's College in 1909, she graduated M.B. with first-class honours that year and Ch.M. in 1910. With Mary Burfitt [q.v. Williams], she followed Jessie Aspinall [q.v.7] as a pioneer female resident medical officer at Royal Prince Alfred Hospital. In 1911-12 Elsie Dalyell was the first woman on the full-time medical school staff as demonstrator in pathology, and in December 1912 the first Australian woman elected to a Beit fellowship, which she took up at the Lister Institute of Preventive Medicine, London.

Distracted by the war, she joined Lady Wimborne's Serbian Relief Fund unit which went to Skopje (Uskub) to help with the typhus epidemic in 1915. Rather to her annoyance, she was safe at the Addington Park war hospital, Croydon, when Skopje was overrun by the Bulgarians in October. In 1916 she joined the Scottish Women's Hospitals for Foreign Service unit at Royaumont, France, and afterwards enlisted with the Royal Army Medical Corps, serving in Malta and Salonika, Greece. Early in 1919 she went to Constantinople to deal with cholera, and in June was appointed O.B.E.; she had been twice mentioned in dispatches.

In 1919-22 she worked in Vienna as senior clinician to a research team led by Dr (Dame) Harriette Chick, studying deficiency diseases in children. As part of a re-education programme, Drs Chick and Dalyell presented and published scientific papers in German soon after their arrival. Elsie Dalyell also spoke French. In 1923 the team produced perhaps 'the most complete study' of human rickets prophylaxis ever undertaken.

For family reasons, and in the belief that she had a duty to give Australia the benefit of her experience, she returned in March 1923, travelling via the United States of America for a lecture tour on the Vienna research. The British regretted their loss and the Americans tried to detain her. Ironically, there was no suitable professional opportunity in Sydney. Without capital, her attempt at private practice in Macquarie Street failed. In January 1924 she began duty as assistant microbiologist in the Department of Public Health. There was no prospect of advancement and her life was circumscribed by routine and Wasserman tests for syphilis about which, thanks to her war service, she was an acknowledged expert. Between 1925 and 1935 she was on the committee of the Rachel Forster Hospital for Women and Children and with Dr Maisie Hamilton, was responsible for the venereal diseases clinic which opened there in 1927.

In appearance Elsie Dalyell was of medium height and heavy build with broad forehead, light blue eyes, 'apricot' complexion and 'cream' hair. When in Vienna she adopted a suited mode which, with minor variations according to season, she affected ever after. She read 'omnivorously' and collected etchings and other *objets d'art* with discrimination. All who knew her agreed that she was one of those rare beings whom it was a privilege to know.

She had settled at Seaman Street, Greenwich, soon after her return, sharing her house for some years with the family of her elder sister Lindsay Hazelton. Her sister Elizabeth (Bess) joined her in the mid-1930s. By retirement in 1946, Elsie Dalyell was in bad health with hypertensive arterial disease and a weak heart. She died at home of coronary occlusion on 1 November 1948 and was cremated with Presbyterian forms. Her estate was valued for probate at £7086.

G. E. Hall and A. Cousins (eds), *Book of remembrance of the University of Sydney . . . 1914-1918* (Syd, 1939); *T&CJ*, 25 Dec 1912; *British Medical J*, 21 Dec 1912, 21 Aug 1915, 9 June 1923; *MJA*, 22 Jan 1949; correspondence, Kogarah Public School, 5/16494 (NSWA); The Women's College, *and* Univ records (Univ Syd Archives).

ANN M. MITCHELL

DALZIEL, HENRY (1893-1965), soldier, locomotive fireman and farmer, was born on 18 February 1893 at Irvinebank, Queensland, son of James Dalziel, miner, and his wife Eliza Maggie, née McMillan, both of whom were native-born. He was educated at Irvinebank and became a fireman on the Cairns-Atherton railway.

Dalziel enlisted as a private in the Australian Imperial Force on 16 January 1915 and embarked with reinforcements for the 15th Battalion. Joining his unit at Gallipoli in July, he served in the battle of Sari Bair in August and was eventually evacuated with his battalion to Egypt. On 31 May 1916 he sailed for France, going into the line at Bois Grenier and from July serving on the Somme, at Pozières and Mouquet Farm. In 1917 Dalziel saw action at Gueudecourt, Lagnicourt, Bullecourt and Messines before being wounded by shrapnel at Polygon Wood on 16 October. He resumed duty on 7 June 1918, first as a driver and then as a gunner.

For valour during the battle of Hamel on 4 July Dalziel won the thousandth Victoria Cross awarded. When his battalion's advance met with strong resistance from a heavily armed enemy garrison at Pear Trench, Dalziel as second member of a Lewis-gun team helped his partner to silence machine-gun fire. When fire opened up from another post he dashed forward and, with his revolver, killed or captured the crew and gun, thus allowing the advance to proceed. During this action the tip of his trigger-finger was shot away; he was ordered to the rear, but instead continued to serve his gun in the final storming of Pear Trench. Although again ordered back to the aid-post he began taking ammunition up to the front line, continuing to do so until he was shot in the head.

Dalziel's wound was so severe that his skull was smashed and the brain exposed. He received extensive medical treatment in England before returning to Australia in January 1919. While travelling home by train, he received a hero's welcome at every station from Townsville to Atherton. On 8 April 1920, at the Congregational manse, South Brisbane, he married Ida Maude Ramsay, a nurse who had served with the 17th Australian General Hospital. They took up a soldier-settlement block, which they named Zenith, on the Tolga railway line. As Dalziel was unable to cope with the day-to-day duties of a small mixed farm his wife assumed most of the work-load.

His interest in farming waned after a few years and Dalziel left her to run Zenith and moved south. He worked in a Sydney factory in the late 1920s but by 1933 had settled in Brisbane where he was out of work for some time; he later received a war pension. In the early 1930s he joined the Citizen Military Forces, becoming a sergeant in the 9th/15th Battalion. He developed an interest in songwriting, cultivated at first during long periods of hospitalization; some of his songs, such as *A song of the tableland* and *Love time, merry love time*, were published in England. In 1956 he went to London for the V.C. centenary celebrations.

Dalziel died of a stroke on 24 July 1965 at the Repatriation General Hospital, Greenslopes, Brisbane, and was cremated with military honours.

C. E. W. Bean, *The A.I.F. in France*, 1918 (Syd, 1942); T. P. Chataway, *History of the 15th Battalion A.I.F.* ... (Brisb, 1948); L. Wigmore (ed), *They dared mightily* (Canb, 1963); *London Gazette*, 17 Aug 1918; *Reveille* (Syd), Feb 1929, May 1932, Dec 1964, Sept 1965; *Mufti*, 4 Dec 1965; *Courier Mail*, 21 May 1919, 15-16 Aug 1933, 23 Aug 1956, 26-28 July 1965; *Age*, 26 Apr 1927, 27 July 1965; *Herald* (Melb), 25 Jan 1935; *Sun* (Syd), 10 Jan 1937; *Labor Daily*, 11 Jan 1937; *Tablelands Advertiser*, 25 Apr 1979; information from Mr J. Davey, Townsville, Qld.   H. MAYS

DANEŠ, JIRÍ VÁCLAV (1880-1928), geographer, was born on 23 August 1880 at Nový Dvůr, Bohemia (Czechoslovakia), youngest son of Joseph Daneš (d. 1883), landed proprietor, and his second wife Johana, née Foster. From the age of 10 he was educated at the Prague Gymnasium and in 1898 entered the Czech Charles Ferdinand University (Ph.D., 1902). He also studied at the Humboldt University of Berlin. A bril-

liant linguist, in Prague he was prominent in the Tuesday Society (later chairman) and in the History Club. He was a square-built young man, with 'a black-rimmed *pince-nez* insecurely perched on his finely modelled nose'; essential accessories were 'silk hat, Virginia cigar and cane'.

The possessor of 'a handsome fortune', Daneš travelled widely in south-eastern Europe and the United States of America. His writings on the geomorphological problems of karst (limestone topography) in Bosnia, Hercegovina and in Jamaica won him international repute. Back in Prague in 1907 he became lecturer in geography at the university and also taught at the Technical University of Prague and the Czech Commercial Academy.

In 1909-10, with botanist K. Domin, Daneš made a fifteen-months visit to Java and Australia. He reached Brisbane on 16 December 1910, and explored, often on horseback, almost inaccessible areas, notably round Cairns, the Chillagoe, the Barron River Gorge and the Barkly tableland. He became a corresponding member of the Royal Society of Queensland and the Queensland branch of the Royal Geographical Society of Australasia, and published three papers in their journals in 1910. For literary exercise he translated *Bulletin* verses into Czech and German for publication in Vienna and Prague. From July he briefly visited Sydney, the Jenolan Caves, Melbourne and Adelaide. In Western Australia he went to Yallingup, the goldfields of Coolgardie and Kalgoorlie, and as far north as Leonora.

Daneš returned to Prague in October 1910 and in 1912 became assistant professor at his university. With Domin, he published in two volumes *Dvojím rájem (Through a double paradise)* in 1911-12 and published articles on Australian karst in French, German and English as well as Czech in European journals. He remained in Prague until 1916 when he went to Sarajevo on active service. After the war he returned to the Charles University as professor.

At the end of 1919 Daneš was appointed consul-general for the new republic of Czechoslovakia in Sydney; he and his wife Božena, whom he had married in 1914, arrived in Sydney in August 1920. Successfully stimulating trade relations, in January 1921 he twice addressed meetings of the Australasian Association for the Advancement of Science in Melbourne and later that year visited Tasmania and Papua-New Guinea. In his leisure he concentrated on human geography.

Daneš left Sydney in January 1923 and next year in Prague published his important *Původ a zanikání domorodců v Austrálii a*

Oceánii (Origin and extinction of the Aboriginals in Australia and Oceania). He also wrote an article 'Pleistocene changes of sea-level and the distribution of man' in the *Scottish Geographical Magazine* and one for a Czech journal on the importance of the isolation of Australia. In 1926 his two volume *Tři léta při Tichém océaně (Three years around the Pacific Ocean)* appeared.

Daneš was dean of the faculty of science in 1925-26. He was a member of the Czechoslovak Academy of Sciences, and of many other learned bodies. In December 1927 he began an American lecture tour. On 11 April 1928 he was killed in a car accident at Culver City, Los Angeles, and was cremated; he was survived by his wife. That year the Daneš Foundation was set up by his friends in Prague to promote geographical research. In Australia his penetrating writings on both physical and human geography have largely been ignored by scholars.

J. N. Jennings and G. J. R. Linge, *Of time and place* (Canb, 1980); *Sborník Československé Společnosti Zeměpisné*, 34 (1928), and for publications; *SMH*, 27 Aug 1921, 1 Sep, 20 Dec 1922, 6 Jan 1923, 15 May 1928; *Australasian*, 7 Oct 1922; *Bulletin*, 23 May 1928.   MICHAEL J. CIGLER

DANGLOW, JACOB (1880-1962), rabbi, was born on 28 November 1880 at Wandsworth, Surrey, England, second of nine children of Michael Danglowitz, glazier, originally from Cracow, Galicia, and his wife Jessie, née Loafer. In 1893 Danglow entered Jews' College, London, where he completed his secondary education and was trained to minister to a synagogue in the English-speaking world. From 1899 to 1902 he studied arts at University College, London.

In 1905 Danglow accepted a call to become minister of the St Kilda Hebrew Congregation, and arrived in Victoria on 15 September. He quickly brought his congregation under the jurisdiction of the London-based orthodox chief rabbi of the United Synagogues of Great Britain. In 1911 he was admitted as a full member of the Melbourne Beth Din.

On 24 November 1909 Danglow married May Henrietta Baruch, granddaughter of M. Michaelis [q.v.5], founder of the congregation. He studied arts at the University of Melbourne, graduating B.A. (1908) and M.A. (1911). In 1908 he had been commissioned in the Australian Military Forces and next year was appointed Jewish chaplain. On the outbreak of World War I he served as military censor, and, after repeated requests to his congregation to release him, served overseas in France in 1918 as chaplain to the Australian Imperial Force.

In 1927 the prospering St Kilda Hebrew Congregation dedicated a new synagogue building which now bears the large bronze doors named in Danglow's honour. In 1934 the chief rabbi in London gave permission for Danglow's original title of 'minister' to be changed to 'rabbi', thus according him equality with his colleague at the Melbourne Hebrew Congregation.

Danglow was appointed senior Jewish chaplain to the Australian Army in 1942. He visited New Guinea and the Pacific Islands, and at the request of Army Headquarters, was one of a group investigating the morale of the occupation troops in Japan. As chaplain, he was responsible for the publication of a Passover order of service and a prayer-book designed for Jewish servicemen.

Danglow was an orthodox minister in an Anglo-Australian congregation whose members covered a wide range of religious observance. He parried most attempts to bring about radical change within his community and tried to steer a middle course. For many years he wore the clerical collar usually associated with Anglican clergymen and he was perceived by the non-Jewish community as a very dignified representative of the Jewish faith. His personal sense of loyalty to King and country increasingly placed him in a position of painful conflict with supporters of the Jewish struggle in Palestine for national independence. His stance on Zionism, his apparent lack of sympathy towards Jewish refugees, and the rise of a secular leadership of the post-World War II Melbourne Jewish community tended to restrict his influence in his later years.

A meticulous, well-disciplined man, Danglow inspired great respect. He was an energetic sportsman, enjoying boxing, golf, bowls and billiards; he was a leading Freemason and a well-known after-dinner speaker. He took an active interest in youth work and philanthropy; the 3rd St Kilda Scout Group, founded in 1924, is known as 'Danglow's Own'. The first hospital wing of the Montefiore Home for the Aged is named in his honour.

In 1950 Danglow was appointed O.B.E. and in 1956 C.M.G. He retired officially in 1957 but continued to preach until his successor arrived two years later. His wife died in 1948 and on 7 August 1949 in London he married a widow Diana (Dinah) Rosen, née Hestel. He died at St Kilda on 21 May 1962, leaving two daughters and a son.

N. Rosenthal, *Look back with pride* (Melb, 1971); Aust Jewish Hist Soc, *J*, 4 (1954-58), no 4.
                                                           J. S. LEVI

DANNEVIG, HARALD KRISTIAN (1871-1914), applied scientist, was born on 2

February 1871 on the island of Hisoy, near Arendal, Norway, son of Gunder Mathisen Dannevig, master mariner, and his wife Elise Birgitte, née Smith. His father developed fish hatcheries and came to be regarded as the leading fisheries expert in Europe. From childhood Dannevig was deeply involved in practical fisheries work, netting, steam and sail trawling, and working in his father's hatcheries. He studied at the University of Christiania (Oslo) under Professor G. O. Sars, but in fact his formal educational qualifications were at secondary level. In 1894 Dannevig was selected by the Fishery Board for Scotland to supervise the completion of marine fish hatcheries at Dunbar, and here he met Annie Sanson, daughter of a local draper, and married her on 17 May 1897.

Transferred to the marine station at the Bay of Nigg, near Aberdeen, Dannevig designed new plant and a tidal spawning pond, acted as consultant to the Lancashire Fisheries Committee and in Italy, and spent much time at sea on trawlers. Following agitation about the cost of fish in New South Wales and the under-development of the local fishing industry, Dannevig was chosen by the New South Wales government as the most competent expert available in Europe and was appointed superintendent of fisheries investigations and fish hatcheries in May 1902.

Dannevig reached Sydney in August, in charge of what was said to be the most elaborate attempt to transport live fish ever made: some six hundred plaice, with a number of other species, were landed and placed in holding ponds at Port Hacking, where at Gunnamatta Bay he constructed a hatchery. Within a few weeks of his arrival he was working with D. G. Stead [q.v.] both on land-based experiments and on sea investigations. While his major acclimatization attempts failed, Dannevig and his helpers made headway in establishing the potentiality of fisheries development, and laid the basis for the later (and ill-fated) purchase of State trawlers by the New South Wales government. He was naturalized in 1905.

Dannevig's relations with the chairman of the Board of Fisheries, Frank Farnell [q.v.], were not comfortable, and in July 1908 he became Commonwealth director of fisheries at a salary of £600 a year (reduced to £520 in 1911 for absence without leave and for over-indulgence in alcohol). His work now centred on the Fisheries' investigation ship *Endeavour*, a 331-ton (335 tonnes) trawler especially built for the purpose. Operating out of Melbourne, over the next six years Dannevig identified 6000 square miles (16000 km²) of trawlable fishing grounds

between Port Stephens in New South Wales and the south of Tasmania, and an extra 4000 square miles (10000 km²) of excellent fishing grounds in the Great Australian Bight. He published a series of admirable reports and assiduously collected museum specimens of interest.

On the outbreak of World War I the *Endeavour* was ordered to Macquarie Island to relieve the meteorological station there. Dannevig accompanied the mission out of a sense of duty. The *Endeavour* left Macquarie Island on 3 December 1914 and was never seen again; she was presumed by a marine court of inquiry to have foundered in a heavy gale on 5 December. He was survived by his wife, son and daughter.

Dannevig carried out pioneering work of great scientific importance in a field still neglected in Australia, and long before the establishment of the Commonwealth Council for Scientific and Industrial Research. He was a devoted fieldworker, as well as being an amiable colleague and affectionate family man. Heavy, tall, fresh-faced and good-looking, with steady blue eyes, a large moustache and brown hair brushed up *en brosse*, he wanted to convince Australians that they had rich fisheries resources as yet untouched. He was an expert fly-fisherman' and was interested in photography and yachting. Madame Dannevig, in her youth a singer of some note, was left almost penniless, but developed a career teaching in girls' schools; she died in 1940.

A shell from the Great Australian Bight and an island in the Glennie Group, off Wilson's Promontory, were named after Dannevig, as was a large trawler commissioned in 1946 by the Commonwealth Fisheries' school at Cronulla, Sydney.

Dept of Trade and Customs, *Biological results of the fishing experiments carried on by the F.I.S. 'Endeavour', 1909-1914,* 1-6 (Syd, 1911-1933); *British A'sian,* 4 Mar 1915; naturalization file, A1 05/4620, *and* public service record (IS) SP515 (AAO, Canb); family information.

S. MURRAY-SMITH

D'ARCY, DAME **CONSTANCE ELIZA-BETH** (1879-1950), obstetrician and gynaecologist, was born on 1 June 1879 at Rylstone, New South Wales, fifth daughter of Murty D'Arcy, sergeant of police, and his wife Bridget, née Synnott. She passed the senior public examination in 1894 from Rylstone Public School and, after attending Riviere College, Woollahra, in 1898 she matriculated at the University of Sydney (M.B., Ch.M., 1904). As neither of the Sydney teaching hospitals would accept a woman, she did her residency at the (Royal) Adelaide

Hospital. She became resident medical officer at the Royal Hospital for Women, Paddington, in 1905. She was soon called to give evidence at a coroner's inquiry into a death from septicaemia following induced abortion. Throughout a distinguished career she was concerned to reduce the incidence of maternal death.

D'Arcy opened a practice in Macquarie Street in 1908 and was appointed honorary surgeon at the Royal Hospital for Women. She supported improved standards in nursing and regular antenatal examination and investigated control of sepsis in hospitals. On the executive of the Australian Trained Nurses' Association, she moved the motion in 1923 calling for the formation of the Royal Australian Nursing Federation. She was a member of the Royal College of Obstetricians and Gynaecologists, London, a foundation member of the College of Surgeons of Australasia (Royal Australasian College of Surgeons), and an active member of the Catholic Medical Guild of St Luke. She helped reform the Medical Women's Society of New South Wales, serving as its president from 1933-34. In 1935 she was appointed D.B.E. and invited to deliver the Anne MacKenzie oration to the Australian Institute of Anatomy, Canberra. She spoke on maternal mortality, control of puerperal septicaemia and the rise in deaths from illegal operations. She condemned moves to legalize abortion.

In 1919-49 D'Arcy represented the graduates on the Senate of the University of Sydney, the first woman to be elected. She had been an executive member of the Sydney University Women's Union, the Catholic University Women Graduates' Association and the Sydney University Women Graduates' Association and she remained active in them. While on the senate, she helped to secure recognition of St Vincent's as a teaching hospital and was its honorary gynaecologist in 1923-45. When the National Council of Women, of which she was a member, requested the university in 1922 to establish a chair of obstetrics, D'Arcy steered the proposal through faculty and the senate. Her efforts were supported by public agitation organized by Millicent Preston-Stanley [q.v. Vaughan] calling for 'horses' rights for women'; in 1924 the government made money available. D'Arcy was lecturer in clinical obstetrics 1925-39 at the university, and was associated with later moves to expand staff and to extend laboratory facilities. D'Arcy served on the senate finance committee, the Cancer Research Committee and the conjoint board of Royal Alexandra Hospital for Children and she represented the university on the Australian Council of Hospital Almoners. As deputy

chancellor in 1943-46, the first woman so elected, she took major responsibility in resolving many of the problems associated with the post-war expansion of the university.

In the 1920s D'Arcy helped to organize the sex education work of the National Council of Women. She gave her services also to the Rachel Forster Hospital for Women and Children, founded in 1922 by a group of female doctors who were worried by the difficulties women encountered in securing placements. Aware of prejudice, she established links with other professional women through the Professional Women Workers' Association. Her attempt in 1935 to persuade the university to appoint a woman to its appointment's board revealed her continued concern on this issue. In 1944 she became president of the Business and Professional Women's Club of Sydney.

Renowned for her quick response when called, D'Arcy was chauffeur-driven on her rounds. She was a large woman, heavily built, remembered for her hearty infectious laugh, a gracious manner, and her jewellery — on emergency calls, the first task of the sister on duty was to lock it away. She collected antiques and donated a valuable cabinet to Sancta Sophia College; in 1929 she was a foundation member of its council, which she chaired from 1946. She was honoured by the Pope in 1940 with the Cross Pro Ecclesia et Pontifice.

For many years D'Arcy's two unmarried sisters kept house for her. She died of cerebro-vascular disease in the Sacred Heart Hospice for the Dying, Darlinghurst, on 25 April 1950. After requiem Mass at St Mary's Cathedral, she was buried in Waverley cemetery. To commemorate her service at the Royal Hospital for Women, a ward was named after her.

E. S. Morgan, *A short history of medical women in Australia* (Adel, 1970); National Council of Women (NSW), *Biennial Report*, 1921-34; *MJA*, 30 Mar 1935, 12 Aug 1950, 13 Sept 1958; *Catholic Weekly*, 4 May 1950; *SMH*, 6 June 1935, 26 Apr 1950; Senate minutes, *and* Faculty of Medicine minutes (Univ Syd Archives). HEATHER RADI

DARCY, JAMES LESLIE (1895-1917), boxer and folk hero, was born on 31 October 1895 at Stradbroke, near Maitland, New South Wales, second son of native-born parents Edward Darcy (or Dorsey), labourer and later a share-farmer, and his wife Margaret, née O'Rourke. His grandparents came from Tipperary, Ireland. Leaving Oakhampton Public School in 1907 Les worked as a carter before being apprenticed at 15 to a blacksmith at East Maitland. As his father was at times unemployed, and his elder brother was partly crippled, Les was called upon to help his large family.

Darcy made his first money in the boxing ring at 14. In 1912-13 he won several fights at Newcastle and Maitland. In November 1913 he lost to the Australian welter-weight champion Whitelaw, but his performance attracted the attention of the Sydney promoters. On 18 July 1914 he appeared for the first time at the Sydney Stadium, against the American Fritz Holland. Darcy was already a local hero – his supporters came from Maitland in two special trains. When Holland won on points there was a riot; two months later Darcy lost on a foul to Holland and 'the cognescenti' were ready with elaborate accounts of how Holland had contrived the incident. They need not have worried: Darcy had impressed the promoter R. L. (Snowy) Baker [q.v.7]. He became the stadium's leading drawcard. In January 1915 he fought the American Jeff Smith in a contest billed as a world welter-weight championship. When he lost because his seconds refused to let him continue after being hurt by a foul blow that the referee did not see, the sensation only enhanced his fame. That defeat was his last: until September 1916 he won twenty-two consecutive fights. He was now comparatively well off – when he bought himself out of his indentures in mid-1915 each contest was netting him about £300, and he was also being paid for exhibitions and for acting in a film.

At the end of 1915 Darcy announced his intention to accept an offer of fights in the United States of America but, probably influenced by Baker, he changed his mind. Six months later the political atmosphere had been radically altered by the Easter week rising in Dublin and W. M. Hughes's [q.v.] commitment to conscription; and passports were being refused to men of military age. Darcy began to come under pressure to enlist – partly at least as an example to other young men – and his predicament was aggravated by his Irish-Catholic background. His own attitude was ambivalent, but he was now anxious to go to America. He claimed that he wanted four or five fights there to make his family financially secure, and then he would go to Canada or England to enlist. His decision may have been influenced by E. T. O'Sullivan, an ingratiating adventurer who had made a big impression on the naive boxer. He and O'Sullivan sailed clandestinely from Newcastle on 27 October, the day before the referendum which, had it been carried, would have made him liable to conscription. The patriotic press denounced him as a shirker; so too, with less disinterested motives, did Baker and his connexions.

In New York a major fight was arranged, but it was banned by Governor Whitman, ostensibly because of the manner in which Darcy had left Australia. The decision was disastrous for Darcy: promoters began to lose interest in him. He broke with O'Sullivan, gave some vaudeville exhibitions and on 5 April 1917 took out United States citizenship. A fortnight later, after a bout he had arranged in Louisiana was also banned, he volunteered for the army. Yet another fight was arranged in Memphis, Tennessee, and Darcy's call-up was deferred so that he could train, but on 27 April he collapsed. He was admitted to hospital with septicaemia and endocarditis; his tonsils were removed but he developed pneumonia and died on 24 May; his fiancée Winnie O'Sullivan was at his deathbed. His body was brought back to Australia and, after immense funeral processions in San Francisco and Sydney, was buried in the Catholic section of East Maitland cemetery.

Les Darcy had all the makings of a folk hero. His remarkable ring record – he lost only four professional fights and was never knocked out – was associated with a quite extraordinary physique: a muscular body apparently impervious to the heaviest blows and a reach 7 ins. (18 cm) greater than his height of 5 ft. 7 ins. (170 cm). He neither smoked nor drank, and spent most of his income on his family; he attended Mass most mornings, one of his closest friends being the local priest. His decision to leave Australia secretly, in breach of the War Precautions Act, provided the controversy (and the enemies in high places) without which no hero-figure is complete: his lonely death gave him an aura of martyrdom. So powerful a legend did he become that fifty years after his death flags flew at half-mast, and a memorial at his birthplace was unveiled by Sir William McKell, former governor-general. When he had been dead for two generations, he was still inspiring the pens of Australian nationalist writers.

W. Lawless, *The Darcy story* (Syd, 1919); R. Swanwick, *Les Darcy, Australia's golden boy of boxing* (Syd, 1965); *Sporting Life* (Syd), June 1953; *National Times*, 30 Dec 1978, 6, 13 Jan 1979; document 1698 (pictorial accession 2066, ML); news-cuttings (Newcastle Public Lib, NSW); information from Mr J. Darcy, Adamstown Heights, NSW.

                                    W. G. McMINN

D'ARCY, WILLIAM KNOX (1849-1917), mining entrepreneur, was born on 11 October 1849 at Highweek, Newton Abbot, Devon, England, son of William Francis D'Arcy, solicitor, and his wife Elizabeth Baker, née Bradford. He was a direct descendant of Lord Darcy de Knayth, lord justice and chief governor of Ireland during the fourteenth century and founder of a prominent Anglo-Norman family in Ireland. D'Arcy was educated at Westminster School, London, in 1863-65, then moved with his family in 1866 to Rockhampton, Queensland. He qualified as a solicitor in March 1872, initially working with his father and later in his own practice.

In 1882 D'Arcy began his connexion with mining. In that year the brothers Fred [q.v.5], Edwin and Thomas Morgan pegged out gold claims at Ironstone Mountain (later Mount Morgan), some twenty-four miles (38 km) south of Rockhampton. Unable to raise sufficient funds to exploit their find, they approached T. S. Hall, a bank manager, for capital. On Hall's suggestion, they also approached William Pattison [q.v.5], and D'Arcy. Convinced that the proposition was sound, D'Arcy, Hall and Pattison formed a syndicate. Worried about the initially low rate of recovery, the Morgans sold their interests by October 1883 to the syndicate for approximately £100 000. Though increasingly large profits were soon made, D'Arcy and his partners still had problems. Of particular concern were the claim-jumpers who attempted to move in on parts of the syndicate's area, and D'Arcy's legal training was tested fully in the complicated litigation which resulted. In 1886 the Mount Morgan Gold Mining Co. was established with one million £1 shares. He was one of the eight original shareholders and directors, with 125 000 shares in his own name and 233 000 in trust. As at one stage the shares reached £17 ls. each, he became a millionaire.

Outside his mining interests, he was not a prominent public figure. He lived with his family at Ellen Vanin, a comfortable home in Rockhampton's Wandal district. His main recreations were shooting, racing and rowing. President of a rowing club and on the committee of the Rockhampton Jockey Club, he took no interest in any charitable institutions.

D'Arcy disposed of his legal practice in 1886 and left for England next year, never to return. He remained a director of the Mount Morgan Gold Mining Co. as chairman of its London board. The main reason for his departure was a wish to use his fortune to establish a place in English upper-class society. Despite over twenty years in Australia, he seems to have found that his social ambitions could not be fulfilled there.

He soon put his wealth to work. He purchased Stanmore Hall, an impressive mansion in Middlesex, and a London town house, in both of which he entertained lavishly. In what was commonly seen as a deliberate attempt to emulate the prince of Wales (later King Edward VII), he leased a shooting estate in Norfolk, had a stand at Epsom and went to Marienbad, Germany (Czechoslovakia) for health cures. His growing girth exhibited an inability to resist the attractions of good living. But he was not without financial worries. He and his family lost money through the closure of the Queensland National Bank in 1892 and by the late 1890s the value of his Mount Morgan shares had declined. He also noticed the mounting costs of his extravagant life-style. He was thus prompted to reconsolidate his position through investment in a new mining venture.

The opportunity came in 1900 when Sir Henry Drummond Wolff, a former British minister to Teheran, approached him to invest in Persian oil exploration. Early in 1901 D'Arcy sent to Teheran an emissary who in May obtained a concession to search for oil over 480 000 square miles (1243 000 km^2). D'Arcy agreed to provide all necessary finance for the search. But at the end of 1903 he had spent £150 000 with no result. His financial position was now desperate. He had to mortgage his Mount Morgan shares at a time when they had dropped to £2 10s. each. By May 1905 he had used £225 000 and could spend no more. He began negotiations with the French branch of the Rothschild family for the sale of the concession. But on 20 May the British owned Burmah Oil Co. stepped in with an offer. D'Arcy agreed to it and made over the rights to his concession in return for 170 000 Burmah Oil shares and a payment to cover expenses he had incurred.

On 26 May 1908 Burmah Oil finally found the biggest oilfield yet known in the world in D'Arcy's old concession. This led in 1909 to the formation of a new company, Anglo-Persian Oil, which later became Anglo-Iranian Oil and ultimately British Petroleum. The British government paid £2 million for a controlling interest in the field. D'Arcy was appointed to the board of the new company, where he remained until his death. His wealth was restored: for the second time in his career a gamble had paid off most lucratively.

D'Arcy's character and work still arouse widely varying interpretations. Some observers point to the visionary way in which he established one of Australia's richest gold-mines and secured for Britain the Persian oil concession. Others argue that his achievements are over-rated and that he took credit which should have gone elsewhere. There is some truth in both views. Although he displayed considerable foresight throughout his career, he also owed much to quite extraordinary good luck and the loyalty of associates. He had few, if any, ideals, his main aim being to win and then maintain wealth and social esteem.

He was married twice, first in Sydney on 23 October 1872 at St Patrick's Catholic Church to Elena, daughter of S. B. Birkbeck of Glenmore, near Rockhampton. She died in 1897. His second marriage took place in London on 30 January 1899 to a divorcee, Mrs Ernestine Eliza Effie Nutting, daughter of A. L. Boucicault, a Rockhampton newspaper proprietor. From his first marriage there were two sons and three daughters.

D'Arcy died on 1 May 1917 at Stanmore Hall of broncho-pneumonia, survived by his wife and children. He was buried at Stanmore with Church of England rites. His estate of £984 000 was left almost entirely to his family.

J. G. Pattison, 'Battler's' tales of early Rock-hampton (Melb, 1939); G. Blainey, The rush that never ended (Melb, 1963); Lord Casey, Australian father and son (Lond, 1966); M. R. Kent, Oil and empire (Lond, 1976); A'sian Inst of Mining and Metallurgy, Procs, 115 (1939); Morning Bulletin, 3 Mar 1870, 1 June 1871, 6 Apr 1875, 7 May 1881, 21 Mar 1884, 2 Oct, 2 Dec 1886, 7 Jan, 25 June 1887, 29 May 1900, 12 May 1908, 6 Jan 1939; The Times, 7 May, 17 Sept 1917; G. A. Richard, The great Persian oil fields: how Mt Morgan men held the titles (1934, Oxley Lib, Brisb); Birkbeck – D'Arcy correspondence, 1887-1906 (held by Mr T. Birkbeck, Old Glenmore, near Rockhampton).

DAVID CARMENT

D'ARCY-IRVINE, GERARD ADDINGTON (1862-1932), Anglican bishop, was born on 17 June 1862 at Wandsworth, London, fifth son of Canon Thomas Gorges Henry Mervyn D'Arcy Irvine and his wife Harriet, daughter of General Strover, of the East India Company's army. The family was Anglo-Irish from County Fermanagh and had bred many clergymen. In 1870 his father became headmaster of Napier Grammar School, New Zealand, where Gerard was educated, and moved to Goulburn, New South Wales, in 1879. Completing his schooling there, Gerard became a bank clerk until he entered Moore Theological College, Liverpool, in 1884 (Barker [q.v.3] scholar 1885) to study for the ministry.

D'Arcy-Irvine was made deacon on 27 September 1885 and ordained priest on 19 September 1886 by Bishop Barry [q.v.3]. At Christ Church Cathedral, Newcastle, he married Bessie, daughter of Charles Langley, a civil engineer, on 2 December 1885. His initial curacy was in the railway district of Macdonaldtown, attached to St Stephen's, Newtown (1885-86). After a brief stay at Pitt Town, he served three years at St John's, Parramatta. In both cases, he trained under skilful clergymen, Robert Taylor and W. J.

Günther [qq.v.6,4]. His first parishes were in country towns: at Windsor (1890-93) and Bowral (1893-98). In 1898 he moved to the growing industrial centre of Wollongong, also becoming rural dean and gaol chaplain. He spent nine years on the south coast, developed an affection for its scenery and people and established himself as a notable pastor.

In 1907 D'Arcy-Irvine returned to Sydney, initially to the small inner-city parish of Holy Trinity, Miller's Point, but soon to be archdeacon of Cumberland. His archdeaconry comprised the northern and outer western suburbs, even though in 1912 he moved his own parochial base to the conventional district (later parish) of Rose Bay and Vaucluse. The demands of this rapidly growing middle-class area in the Eastern Suburbs led him to resign some of the administrative posts he had acquired on his elevation, such as honorary secretary of the Church Society for the Diocese of Sydney (Home Mission Society), general secretary of the Centennial Church Extension Fund, and examining chaplain to the archbishop. The addition, in 1915-19, of Watson's Bay to his parochial charge increased his work as a minister while his accession as senior archdeacon in 1917 made him Archbishop Wright's [q.v.] vicar-general and commissary.

In the 1920s Wright suffered ill health while his primatial duties increased, but not until 1926 did he nominate a coadjutor: D'Arcy-Irvine was consecrated on 10 October, and later transferred from Vaucluse to the city parish of St Philip. He was an evident and popular choice: the senior clergyman, an evangelical who conformed to the predominant theological opinion of the diocese, a conservative in matters of constitutional and Prayer Book reform, he was a man of moderate temperament with a reputation as a conciliator. He could be severe on liturgical excesses but he was not a 'party' man. His principal duty was to take over much of the routine work in an expanding diocese. However, he found himself acting for the archbishop, including presiding at several sessions of synod. The Depression added to the problems of the Church, already troubled by controversies over ecclesiastical government and discipline.

D'Arcy-Irvine was not a scholar but he took delight in literature: he was the preacher at Henry Lawson's [q.v.] funeral. In 1899 he published privately a small volume, titled simply Poems: the themes showed his patriotism, his strong moral sense and his love of south coast scenery. In 1905 James Nisbet & Co. of London took over the publication; the sixth edition of 1921 was almost three times the size of the first. D'Arcy-

Irvine's poetic talent did not greatly improve but his range of topics increased as his public horizon grew wider.

On 8 June 1927 D'Arcy-Irvine's wife died; on 20 October 1928 at St Philip's Church he married Florence Gertrude Angus. He died of kidney disease at his home at Double Bay on 18 April 1932 and was buried in South Head cemetery. He was survived by his wife and by two sons and two daughters of his first marriage. Both his sons served overseas in World War I. Memorials to him are at Rose Bay, Wollongong, St Philip's, Sydney, and St Andrew's Cathedral.

His brother Malcolm Mervyn (1870-1937) was educated at St Paul's College, University of Sydney (B.A., 1889; LL.B., 1912), and was admitted as a solicitor in 1892 and to the Bar in 1921. He was a governor of The King's School, Parramatta, a member of the diocesan, provincial and general synods and a member of the convention to frame a constitution for the Church of England in Australia. He had married Effie Jane Mansfield on 15 April 1914. He died in Sydney on 14 September 1937 and was cremated.

Church of England diocese of Sydney, *Votes and Procs of Synod*, 1907-1933; Church of England Hist Soc, *Sydney Journal*, March 1970; *SMH*, 19 Apr 1932; *Aust Church Record*, 5 May 1932; Sydney ordination papers, episcopal registers (Syd Diocesan Registry).   K. J. CABLE

DARLING, HAROLD GORDON (1885-1950), company director, was born on 9 June 1885 in Adelaide, son of John Darling junior [q.v.4] and his wife Jessie, née Dowie. Harold was educated at Prince Alfred College, and in 1903 he entered his father's milling and grain business. On 24 April 1913 in a Presbyterian ceremony at Bundarra, Malvern, Melbourne, he married Dorothy Hazel Heath. On his father's death in March 1914 he became principal of John Darling & Son; the headquarters were moved to Melbourne and Harold made his home there. At the beginning of World War I he volunteered for military service, but agreed to Prime Minister Hughes's [q.v.] request to serve on the advisory council of the Australian Wheat Board.

On 14 April 1914 Darling accepted an invitation to join the board of directors of Broken Hill Proprietary Co. Ltd to fill the vacancy caused by his father's death. Eight years later, on 27 October 1922, he was elected chairman of the board; he was then its youngest member. At his first public address to the shareholders in 1923 he had to announce the first annual loss since 1909 because of a nine-months closure of the steelworks. No dividends were paid between 1921 and 1925 but in those years the company extended its activities into coal-mining, built up a fleet and set up its first subsidiaries. Darling faced what was probably his most difficult meeting with the shareholders in 1930, after a coal stoppage and another year of no dividends, but by 1935 the worst of the company's difficulties were over. Negotiations had begun for the take-over of the local rival Australian Iron & Steel Ltd; two years later B.H.P. was to make its largest profit to that date, passing the £1 million mark.

Darling followed local and international politics with keen interest. Although he believed, in 1934, that Japanese rearmament was defensive, he worried about the defence of Australia and in particular Newcastle. He was friendly with Admiral Hyde [q.v.] and tried to establish closer ties between government and business for the building of ships and aeroplanes. By 1936 B.H.P. had succeeded in putting together a syndicate ready to undertake the manufacture of aircraft; Darling became first chairman of the Commonwealth Aircraft Corporation when it was set up on 17 October. In 1941 he was appointed by the Commonwealth to the Aircraft Advisory Committee, representing the corporation. In 1934 Darling had doubted whether shipbuilding could succeed in Australia as a commercial venture. But his growing conviction of the seriousness of the international situation led him to prepare the company to be ready to accept an official request to begin shipbuilding at Whyalla when it came in 1939.

Censorship prevented Darling from publicly disclosing the extent and nature of some of the company's activities during World War II, and at the same time he found himself defending B.H.P. profits against public and political criticism. In the first years of peace he could outline with pride the company's achievements in war, but shortages in manpower and problems in coal production reached a crisis point. His last meeting with shareholders was in 1949, when the effects of the seven-week general coal strike and a strike in B.H.P.'s iron ore quarries were reflected in a fall of profits. Nevertheless he could look back over a spectacular growth of the company during his chairmanship, from a struggling steelworks at Newcastle to a steel monopoly spanning three States, which marshalled its own mines, transport and fabricating subsidiaries, and made the cheapest steel in the world.

During his years with B.H.P. Darling had worked well with Essington Lewis [q.v.], general manager and later managing director of the company. Darling's grasp of political affairs and technical details, and his financial expertise, allowed him to advise the board on the nature of Lewis's projects and the financing involved; the two men generally agreed beforehand on matters discussed at board meetings. They have been described as a brilliant team, and maintained a close friendship.

In his capacity as chairman of the board of B.H.P., Darling was chairman of Australian Iron & Steel Ltd, Wellington Alluvials Ltd, Stewarts & Lloyds (Aust.) Pty Ltd, Rylands Bros (Aust.) Pty Ltd, and B.H.P. By Products Ltd. As well, he was a director of B.H.P. Collieries Pty Ltd, Tubemakers of Australia Ltd, and British Tube Mills (Aust.) Pty Ltd, Imperial Chemical Industries of Australia and New Zealand Ltd, and the National Bank of Australasia.

By tradition Darling firmly believed that only private enterprise could create prosperity and a stable economy. In the 1930s he was friendly with, though not uncritical of, (Sir) R. G. Menzies. As a private citizen he contributed time, energy and funds to conservative politicians, and in 1942 he was a founder and council-member of the Institute of Public Affairs. At the end of 1944 Darling noted with alarm the Labor government's plan to take over airways, banks and insurance companies, or at least to retain existing wartime controls. He wrote, 'we must . . . face this community with an undivided section of the community that is opposed to socialism and to chaos'.

A serene and cheerful-looking man, Darling enjoyed tennis and golf, but his chief interests were family, politics and the company he headed with such loyalty. Of simple tastes, he dreaded even the restrained entertaining practised by B.H.P. In 1934 he remarked 'Melbourne [is] in the throes of the Duke and centenary. I am very busy dodging almost everything'. His public utterances were confined to shareholders' meetings and company functions. A daughter remembers him as a just, approachable and deeply affectionate father, devoid of personal vanity. A colleague described him as always firm and confident, with great integrity and strength of character. Even when forced publicly to spell gloom he maintained a personal faith in his company and his country.

Darling died on 26 January 1950 of cancer. He was survived by his wife and three children: Elizabeth (married to John Baillieu), Joan (married to Sir Robert Law-Smith) and John. In his lifetime Darling made generous bequests to his home State. In June 1929 he presented the Waite [q.v.6] Agricultural Research Institute with £10000 to extend work on soil conservation. Another donation of £15000 was made to the University of Adelaide for the equipment of a medical school.

In 1951 B.H.P. commissioned a portrait of Darling by William Dargie, and announced the H. G. Darling Memorial Scholarship, tenable at the South Australian School of Mines, for B.H.P. employees and their sons in South Australia.

H. Hughes, *The Australian iron and steel industry, 1848-1962* (Melb, 1964); B.H.P., *Annual Report*, 1922-1950; Board minutes, 1922-1951, *and* correspondence, H. G. Darling and E. Lewis, 1930-1944 (B.H.P. Archives, South Melb); information from Mr C. D. Kemp, Mt. Macedon, Lady Law-Smith, Macedon, Sir Colin Syme, Toorak, Vic.

D. WHEELER

DARLING, JOSEPH (1870-1946), cricketer, pastoralist and politician, was born on 21 November 1870 at Glen Osmond, South Australia, sixth son of John Darling [q.v.4], merchant, and his wife Isabella, née Ferguson. He was educated at Prince Alfred College, Adelaide, where he became devoted to cricket. The day before his fifteenth birthday he set a schoolboy record with 252 runs in a match against the Collegiate School of St Peter. Next year he played cricket for the colony against the Australian XI, and also Australian Rules football for the Adelaide and Suburban Football Association which won the premiership. His father disapproved of this dedication to sport and, after leaving school, Darling spent twelve months at Roseworthy Agricultural College; he worked in a bank and was then appointed manager of one of the family's wheat farms. In 1893 he returned to Adelaide to open a sports depot in Rundle Street and was selected to play for South Australia in intercolonial cricket. On 3 May at Mundoora he married Alice Minna Blanche Francis; they had ten sons and five daughters.

In 1894 Darling played his first Test match against a touring English side. He toured England in 1896, 1899, 1902 and 1905, captaining Australia on the last three trips and against a touring English XI in 1901-02; altogether he played in thirty-one Tests against England and was captain in eighteen, a record unbroken until 1948 by Bradman. Darling was reputed one of the best left-hand batsmen of his day and he headed the Australian batting averages in 1896-99. In 1897-98, playing against A. E. Stoddart's team in Australia, he set a record by making three centuries in five Tests. In scoring his 160 runs in the fifth match in Sydney his century came up in 91 minutes, the fastest made by an Australian in a Test against England. He was also captain in three Test matches against South Africa in 1902. As a leader he inspired his team by his own dogged courage and prowess. Of medium height, thickset and powerful, he was a tremendous hitter and master of the drive, yet able to defend for hours.

In 1900 Darling, retiring from cricket 'in fairness to my wife and children', moved to Stonehenge, a sheep station in the Tasmanian midlands purchased for him by his father. He sold his Adelaide business in 1907. A successful farmer, he pioneered the eradication of the rabbits which overran his and other properties; he took a leading part in the Tasmanian Farmers' Stockowners' and Orchardists' Association and a keen interest in rural industries. He was on the committee of the Royal Hobart Show Council for over 25 years. With South Australian merino rams he built up one of the best half-bred and comeback flocks in the State; his wool topped the Hobart sales on several occasions. In 1920 he introduced subterranean clover to Tasmania. He retained an interest in cricket, playing locally, coaching juniors and writing cricket articles for the *Weekly Courier*. In 1919 he bought a 32-acre (13 ha) property, Claremont House, at Claremont; among the cricket trophies displayed in the main hallway of the homestead were a portrait of his 'white-haired boy' Victor Trumper [q.v.] and the bat used by Trumper in 1899.

An independent member for Cambridge in the Legislative Assembly in 1921-46, Darling was active in the 1922 movement to form a Country Party. In the mid-1930s he obtained an exemption of land tax for the small farmers. He was a member of the Parliamentary Committee on Public Works in 1937-46. In 1945 his charges of maladministration against the Tasmanian Forestry Department led to the appointment of a royal commission whose findings, after Darling's death, proved the minister for forests and two officials guilty of receiving bribes. The last surviving member of the Australian XI which toured England in 1896, Darling, who was appointed C.B.E. in 1938, died after an operation for peritonitis on 2 January 1946 at Hobart. After a Congregational service he was buried in Cornelian Bay cemetery, survived by his wife and twelve of his children.

D. K. Darling, *Test tussles on and off the field* (Hob, 1970); *Weekly Courier* (Launc), 5 Sept 1928, 9 Mar 1933; *SMH*, 9 Feb 1939; *Examiner* (Launc), and *Mercury*, 3 Jan 1946.   D. K. DARLING

DARNELL-SMITH, GEORGE PERCY (1868-1942), biologist, was born on 15 October 1868 at Chipping Norton, Oxfordshire, England, son of William Josiah Smith, surgeon, and his wife Theresa, née Haigh. Educated at University College School, London, he graduated B.Sc. with honours in zoology and botany from University College, University of London, in 1891. He lectured in chemistry and biology at the Merchant Venturers' Technical College, Bristol, from 1893 to 1907, was made a fellow of the (Royal) Institute of Chemistry of Great Britain and Ireland in 1900 and received the B.Sc. *ad eundem* from the University of Bristol in 1910.

In 1907-09 Darnell-Smith was assistant director of technical education in New Zealand and on 19 April 1909 he was appointed assistant microbiologist in the new Bureau of Microbiology in Sydney at a salary of £500. In 1913 when its work was transferred to the Department of Agriculture he became biologist. These were Darnell-Smith's most productive years – he published some eighty articles and notes, mainly in the *Agricultural Gazette of New South Wales*, covering a vast array of topics such as bee diseases; absorption of water by root hairs; flying foxes; diseases of wheat, bananas and pome fruit; fungus diseases of mice; mushrooms; tobacco-curing; and prickly pear. He established the biology branch soundly – he insisted that new staff should have university degrees, supported moves for reasonable salaries and sought funds for overseas training.

By 1915 Darnell-Smith had made his major contribution to world agriculture by developing copper carbonate powder as a fungicide to control bunt, a major disease of wheat that hitherto could only be treated with solutions of bluestone or formalin, thus damaging the seed. Despite conclusive experiments, the importance of his findings was not immediately recognized in Australia; but in the early 1920s Darnell-Smith's dry copper carbonate became the standard treatment for seed wheat in the United States of America. A few years later it was finally adopted in Australia, costing a mere 'tuppence a bushel', and bunt ceased to be a problem.

Through his work and interests Darnell-Smith became closely associated with Professor A. A. Lawson [q.v.] and, inspired by him, graduated D.Sc. at the University of Sydney in 1918; his thesis was published in the *Transactions* of the Royal Society of Edinburgh (1917).

On 1 July 1924 Darnell-Smith also became director of the Botanic Gardens, Sydney, and officer-in-charge of Centennial Park. A keen botanist, he spent most of his time in the gardens. In 1930 he represented the State government at the International Botanical Congress at the University of Cambridge. He resigned as biologist in 1927 and retired as director in 1933. He had been a member of the Linnean Society of New South Wales since 1909.

A most likeable bachelor, Darnell-Smith was an excellent raconteur. He never lost his English reserve yet was approachable. He was very fond of music, practically a chain smoker (rolling his own), somewhat absent-minded, keen on boating and fishing and loved nature – his desk was often adorned with a single perfect flower. He died on 11 April 1942 and was cremated with Presbyterian forms. His estate was sworn for probate at £33 000.

Aust Inst of Agr Science, *J*, 4 (1942); *SMH*, 11 June 1924; Dept of Agriculture records (Syd).
J. KUIPER

DARTNELL, WILLIAM THOMAS (WILBUR TAYLOR) (1885-1915), soldier, actor and clerk, was born on 6 April 1885 at Collingwood, Melbourne, son of English-born Henry Dartnell, fruiterer, and his native-born wife Rose Ann, née Hanley. He was educated in Melbourne and became an actor. On 15 April 1907, at Queen Street, Melbourne, he married Elizabeth Edith Smyth with Presbyterian forms; they settled at Fitzroy.

Dartnell was in South Africa when World War I broke out. He went on to England and on 12 February 1915, using the name Wilbur Taylor Dartnell, joined the 25th (Service) Battalion, Royal Fusiliers (Frontiersmen), as a temporary lieutenant. As the regimental history notes, this battalion 'included men of various ages and with strange experience from all quarters of the globe'. Raised especially for use against German troops in British East Africa, it was the only British unit sent on active service during the war without preliminary training. The Fusiliers reached Mombasa on 6 May and went at once to their military post on the Uganda railway: their main task was to protect the railway from enemy raiding parties and from mid-June they were engaged in raids on Bukoba, the German base for attacks on the Uganda frontier.

In August the battalion established its headquarters at Voi and two of its companies were stationed at Maktau to patrol the frontier. Dartnell, whose rank had been confirmed on 25 July, was assigned on 1 September to a mounted infantry patrol and two days later, near Maktau, his party was ambushed. In the fighting that followed he was wounded in the leg and was being carried away when he realized that the badly wounded could not be removed. 'Knowing that the enemy's black troops murdered the wounded' he 'insisted on being left behind in the hopes of being able to save the lives of the

other wounded men'. Though he was twice asked to leave he ordered his men to abandon him and began firing on the Germans who were within twenty-five yards of his post. When his body was found seven men dead lay around it. He was awarded a posthumous Victoria Cross for giving his own life in a 'gallant attempt to save others'.

Dartnell was buried in Voi cemetery, East Africa. He was survived by his wife and a daughter. At 16 he had served in the South African War with the 5th Victorian (Mounted Rifles) Contingent.

H. C. O'Neill, *The Royal Fusiliers in the great war* (Lond, 1922); L. Wigmore (ed), *They dared mightily* (Canb, 1963); *London Gazette,* 23 Dec 1915; *The Times,* 24 Dec 1915; *Argus,* 6 Jan 1916; *Age,* 24 May 1956.
MERRILYN LINCOLN

DASH, JOHN (1882-1952), trade union official and politician, was born on 31 October 1882 at Blackall, Queensland, son of a German shearer, John Dash, and his Irish wife Margaret, née Mahoney. Educated at the local state school, Jack Dash worked first at Fort Constantine station as a stockman with a reputation for skilled horsemanship. He went to Mount Elliott on the Cloncurry copper-field and was soon involved in unionism. North-western miners' unions merged in 1909 to form the Western Workers' Association with Dash as its secretary. Next year when E. G. Theodore and William McCormack [qq.v.] proposed the amalgamation of non-craft unions throughout North Queensland, Dash extolled its advantages and early in 1911 became northern organizer for the Amalgamated Workers' Association. Miners rarely disputed his authority and judgment which were also greatly respected by management.

Dash moved to Townsville in 1912 as northern district secretary of the Australian Workers' Union, a post he held until elected to the Legislative Assembly in 1920. As an A.W.A. organizer, he had assisted with the 1911 sugar strike and the 1912 general strike in which he had learned to eschew ideology and concentrate on specific claims and grievances. In the Hampden lockout (1913), the railway strike (1917) and the Townsville meatworks strike (1919), he applied the lesson. A pragmatist, keen to avoid militant excesses and a staunch supporter of arbitration, he followed the accepted policy of his union but was criticized as an opportunist and ambitious reactionary by militants and as a direct actionist by non-unionists. An intelligence report on the One Big Union movement at Townsville shrewdly observed that Dash 'sat on the fence as usual though in his heart he is opposed to the scheme seeing by the formation of the One Big Union, his political aspirations also his Industrial career would come to an abrupt end owing to him being of the moderate type and a firm believer in the present form of industrial arbitration'.

On 9 October 1920 Dash won Mundingburra, a safe Labor seat. His parliamentary contributions reflected the same thorough preparation that he had shown in his work as an industrial advocate; however, reticent and retiring, he rarely raised his voice. He maintained strong links with his union and was a regular delegate to its conventions in 1919-36; vice-president for many years, he was president for four months from October 1925. He represented the union on the Queensland central executive of the Australian Labor Party in 1915-16 and 1924-27 before being installed as a convention-selected delegate in 1932-39, and was a delegate to every Labor-in-Politics convention from 1918 to 1932. He was an archetypal 'machine man'.

Dash's career climaxed on 17 June 1932 when he became minister for transport in the first Forgan Smith [q.v.] ministry, but he was never to realize his plans for the transport system. Serious injuries in a rail-motor accident at Thangool on 19 September 1932 permanently affected his health and influenced his eventual retirement to the back-benches on 4 August 1939. In seven years as a minister, Dash was responsible for only three pieces of legislation. The State Transport Act (1932) created a board to co-ordinate activities of the Railway, Main Roads and Police departments; the Railway Superannuation Act (1932) made minor changes; and the Railway Acts Amendment Act (1934) created an employees' appeals board.

In the 1930s Dash dispensed political patronage to unionists and party members in his constituency by placing them in jobs on the northern railways; this helped his re-election in 1941. By 1944 his decreasing mental and physical capacity, attributed to Parkinson's disease, together with the splitting of his local political base over the 'Aid-to-Russia' issue, led to his defeat at the pre-selection ballot. He died on 1 January 1952 after prolonged ill health. He was survived by his wife Violet, née Alone, whom he had married at Selwyn on 13 February 1911, and by three daughters. After a state funeral, he was buried in Nudgee cemetery with Catholic rites.

I. N. Moles, *A majority of one* (St Lucia, 1979); *PD* (Qld), 1932, 1951-52; Australian Labor Party, *Queensland Labor-in-Politics Convention Official Record,* 18 (1944); K. H. Kennedy, 'Theodore, McCormack and the Amalgamated Workers' Association', *Labour Hist,* Nov 1977, no 33; *Worker* (Brisb), 11 Dec 1909, 3 Dec 1925, 7 Jan 1952; *North Qld Register,* 5 Aug 1939, 5 Jan 1952; D. W. Hunt, A history of the labour movement in North Queensland, 1900-1920 (Ph.D. thesis, James Cook Univ, 1974); W. H. Corbould, The life of Alias Jimmy (ML); BP 4/1, 66/5/115 (AAO, Brisb).

K. H. KENNEDY

DASHWOOD, CHARLES JAMES (1842-1919), lawyer, politician, public servant and judge, was born on 17 July 1842 at Dashwood's Gully near Kangarilla, South Australia, second son of George Frederick Dashwood [q.v.1], and his wife Sarah, née Loine. In 1852, after attending the Collegiate School of St Peter, Dashwood went overseas and in 1858 studied civil engineering for a year at the University of Ghent, Belgium. He returned to South Australia and worked on the land and as a clerk of courts from 1865. In 1868 he was articled to (Sir) W. H. Bundey [q.v.3] and was admitted to the Bar in 1873. They were partners until 1884, then Dashwood practised alone till entering into partnership with C. G. Varley in 1890.

In 1887 Dashwood had won the seat of Noarlunga in the House of Assembly with a parochial but fairly progressive programme. He was a fluent and forceful debater, but reluctant to accept party discipline and rather impulsive. In 1892 he was appointed government resident and judge of the Northern Territory. Next year he authorized the public execution of a convicted Aboriginal, Wandy Wandy, at the scene of his crime and ordered that the gallows should remain standing as a warning.

Dashwood later became dubious of the justice of trying blacks in a language and under a system which they did not understand. He grew concerned to curb their ill treatment by Europeans; by 1896 the *Northern Territory Times and Gazette* was describing him as 'the personification of kindness in his dealing with aborigines' and in 1898 it applauded his 'practical commonsense' in this area. However, he was often powerless to punish offences because special protection was not afforded to Aboriginals under the law; he drafted a bill to regulate and supervise their conditions of employment and to prevent the violation of black women. After a first reading in 1899 in Adelaide, the bill was severely criticized by a select committee, before which Dashwood appeared, and it then lapsed. Pastoralists had lobbied against it. Thereafter Dashwood angered landholders by defending Aboriginals' right to retain access to their hunting-grounds and watering-holes. He also alienated 'White Australia' supporters, by advocating limited Asian immigration to the Northern Territory to an 1895 South Australian commission and in a 1902 report on pearl-shelling. The Commonwealth's subsequent policy of allowing the licensed entry of non-European divers stemmed from this report.

In 1904 Dashwood resigned, after a longer administration than any other government resident. Next year he became South Australia's crown solicitor, 'to the surprise and disappointment of the legal profession'. In 1906 on Sir Samuel Way's [q.v.] recommendation he was appointed K.C., which was equally surprising in view of Way's earlier opinion that he was 'scatter-brained'. Dashwood performed creditably until his retirement in 1915.

On 5 February 1916 he married Martha Margarethe Johanna Klevesahl; the marriage was childless. He had earlier fathered an ex-nuptial son who was born in 1892. Dashwood died on 8 July 1919 and was buried in Meadows cemetery. His estate was sworn for probate at £3867. His nature, though satirical, was kindly, but he generally favoured a 'picturesque method of denouncing everything of which he disapproved'.

Observer (Adel), 3 May 1890, 27 July 1895, 12 July 1919; *NT Times and Gazette*, 27 Mar 1896; G. Loughlin, South Australian Queen's Counsel 1865-1972 (B.A. Hons thesis, Univ Adel, 1974); P. Elder, Northern Territory Charlie . . . (B.A. Hons thesis, ANU, 1979).   GRAHAM LOUGHLIN

DATTILO-RUBBO, ANTHONY; *see* RUBBO

DAVEY, ARNOLD EDWIN (1862-1920), flour-miller and grain merchant, was born on 2 March 1862 at Pine Hut, near Truro, South Australia, eldest son of EDWIN DAVEY (1839-1923) and his wife Phillis Vingoe, née Davey, his cousin, whom he had married at Kapunda on 8 March 1860. Edwin, the youngest child of Thomas Davey, farmer and cordwainer, and his wife Margaret, née Lean, was born on 18 July 1839 at Trannack, near Madron, Cornwall, England. He arrived with his family at Port Adelaide in January 1849. They farmed near Salisbury and at Light Pass. In 1851 Edwin went with his brothers to the Victorian gold diggings. He was educated at E. Planta Nesbit's school at Angaston and later studied engineering principles at Nesbit's night school after he began work in his uncle's flour-mill at Daveyston. In 1865 he and his brother James bought the Penrice Steam Flour Mill near Angaston, trading as J. & E. Davey; three years later they were shipping flour in River Murray steamers to the eastern colonies. From 1869 Edwin traded alone, but on turning 21 his sons joined the business; fluent in German, they dealt easily with local German farmers.

Edwin bought his cousin's Daveyston mill in 1875 and, in 1880, built the Excelsior Mill at Eudunda. In 1885 he built the Eureka Roller Mills at Angaston. He leased and operated J. G. Neumann's stone mill at Eudunda in 1880-93 and in 1892 purchased the Salisbury roller mills. In 1901 he acquired the Ultimo Roller Flourmills at Pyrmont, Sydney, doubled their export capacity and took over a Melbourne mill. He developed trade with India, Europe, Egypt, South Africa, America and the Far East; his head office remained in Adelaide. Davey retired in 1906. A Wesleyan Methodist, he had been a preacher and Sunday school superintendent. A handsome, upright man, he lived in Adelaide after 1883 and was a trustee of the Pirie Street Methodist Church and benefactor to the Central Methodist Mission, the Aborigines' Friends' Association and the Young Men's Christian Association. Survived by his wife, two daughters and five sons, he died at Parkside on 8 November 1923 and was buried at Angaston. His estate was valued for probate at £28 892.

Arnold Edwin Davey was educated at Rev. James Leonard's School at Angaston and at Prince Alfred College. In 1883 he entered the Edwin Davey & Sons partnership and successively managed the Eudunda, Penrice and Angaston mills. From 1897 they used the 'Lion' brand trademark still in use in the 1970s. On 20 June 1883 he married Sarah Shannon at Yatara near Kapunda. He was thrice president of the Adelaide Chamber of Commerce, which he represented at overseas congresses, and was also president of the Associated Chambers of Commerce of Australia (1914-15) and of the Millowners' Association of South Australia (1894). He was a Freemason and in 1900 became a justice of the peace. He was a delegate to the Federated Employers' Council of South Australia, was consul for Peru, a director of insurance companies and a member of the Adelaide Voluntary Tribunal of Arbitration in 1896-1920. A well-read man, he took a keen interest in his church. He retired in 1915. While travelling through France, in 1920 he contracted erysipelas and died at Nevers on 8 March, survived by his wife and two sons. His ashes were interred at Payneham cemetery, Adelaide. He had been a popular figure and his untimely death was keenly felt. His estate was valued for probate at £22 016.

W. F. Morrison, *The Aldine history of South Australia*, 2 (Syd, 1890); J. J. Pascoe (ed), *History of Adelaide and vicinity* (Adel, 1901); H. T. Burgess (ed), *Cyclopedia of South Australia*, 1 (Adel, 1907); *Observer* (Adel), 10 May 1902, 16 Sept 1916; *NT Times and Gazette*, 18 Feb 1915; *Advertiser* (Adel), 11 Sept 1916, 18 July 1919, 15 Mar 1920, 9 Nov 1923; *The Times*, 11 Sept 1916; *Register* (Adel), 27 Aug 1919, 15 Mar 1920; *Aust Christian Cwlth*, 26 Mar 1920, 11 Jan 1924; Davey papers *and* MS history, 'For the wind passeth' (held by Mrs J. P. Fielding, Canb).   JEAN P. FIELDING

DAVEY, CONSTANCE MURIEL (1882-1963), psychologist, was born on 4 December 1882 at Nuriootpa, South Australia, daughter of Stephen Henry Davey, bank-manager, and his wife Emily Mary, née Roberts. She was educated at country schools, including Mrs G. L. Barnard's at Clare. An accident, in which she was thrown from a trap and permanently injured her hip and spine, delayed her further education, but in 1908 she began teaching with the Anglican Sisters of the Church, at Port Adelaide. Next year she joined St Peter's Collegiate Girls' School as a mathematics and economics teacher and began studying part time at the University of Adelaide (B.A., 1915; M.A., 1918).

In 1921 'Consie' won the Catherine Helen Spence [q.v.6] scholarship, which she took up next year at University College, University of London, to study psychology (Ph.D., 1924). She observed pioneer work with disturbed children at Leicester and visited the United States of America and Canada to study the teaching of intellectually retarded and delinquent children. In 1924 she became a psychologist in the South Australian Education Department, at a salary of £438. She examined, by testing, and observation of home conditions, all children who were retarded educationally: in 1925 the State's first 'opportunity class' for problem cases and slow learners was established in which twenty children could learn at their own rate, based on Davey's testing of their intelligence. She organized after-care guidance for these pupils to help them find employment after leaving school and provided vocational advice to other school-leavers. In 1931 she introduced a course to train teachers to work with the retarded, modelled on her old course at Birmingham in 1923. It included lectures on the psychology of retardation and behaviour problems, appropriate teaching methods, legal and social implications, remedial physical training and handwork.

Dr Davey was often consulted by other community bodies: she co-operated with the Children's Court and the Children's Welfare Department, ran a clinic at the Adelaide Children's Hospital, and advised Minda Home and other agencies handling problem children. Although she continued with experiments to standardize tests for scholars throughout Australia, Davey always insisted that she was not just an intelligence tester: as a psychologist she handled problems of behaviour. In 1927-50 she lectured in psychology and logic at the university and in 1934 helped establish courses there to train the State's first social workers. She went to England in 1938 and visited child-guidance clinics. On her return she sat on the 1938-39 government committee which made a detailed examination of the State's approach to child delinquency, and recommended important humanitarian reforms based on the idea of 'guardianship'.

In 1942 Davey resigned from the Education Department; there were now 700 children in opportunity classes. The founder of all psychological services to the State's children, in her early years she had been resisted by some colleagues who thought her work a useless frill. But she gradually created a welfare section, and her ability, intelligence and persistence wrought great changes. She introduced teachers to the idea of organizing single classes at different levels to accommodate the varying abilities of their pupils and was concerned for gifted children in a system which emphasized mediocrity. As supervisor in the opportunity classes she was compassionate, unassuming and good humoured: it was her habit to arrive with a box of 'penny sticks' for the children.

Davey belonged to the Women's Non-Party Political Association (League of Women Voters) for thirty years and was its president in 1943-47. The league worked to have women represented on public boards and commissions; it prepared the bill for the Guardianship of Infants Act 1940 which introduced the principle of equal parental guardianship; and brought about reforms in the Children's Court.

From 1945, as a senior research fellow at the university, Davey worked on a historical study of the State's laws relating to children, *Children and their law-makers* (1956). In 1950 she was elected a fellow of the British Psychological Society; in 1940-47 she was president of its South Australian section and in 1947-48 president of the Australian branch. She was appointed O.B.E. in 1955. Dr Davey was a skilful bridge player and loved cricket. The last six years of her life were made difficult by cancer of the thyroid; she died on 4 December 1963 and was cremated. A room in the psychology department at the University of Adelaide is a memorial to her long and useful career.

SA Teachers' J, Feb 1964; *New Horizons in Education*, 51 (1974), p 6; *Advertiser*, 26 Nov 1921, 23 July 1947, 31 Jan 1950, 5 Dec 1963; *Observer*, 18 Oct 1924; *Australasian*, 6 June 1925; *Register*

(Adel), 20 Dec 1927; Jessie Banks, *Personalities remembered*, A.B.C., D5390/60 (SAA); discussion with Mr L. S. Piddington and Miss Mary Smith (tape, held by Mr J. D. C. Robertson, Education Dept, Adel); biog 1047/50, *and* PRG 104 (SAA).

SUZANNE EDGAR

DAVEY, PHILLIP (1896-1953), railwayman and soldier, was born on 10 October 1896 at Unley, South Australia, son of William George Davey, carpenter, and his wife Elizabeth, née O'Neill. Educated at Flinders Street Model School and Goodwood Public School, he worked as a horse-driver at the time of his enlistment in the Australian Imperial Force at Morphettville on 22 December 1914.

Davey embarked on 2 February 1915 at Melbourne with the 10th Battalion's 2nd reinforcements and proceeded to Egypt and Lemnos prior to the attack on Gallipoli on 25 April 1915. He was present at the landing and took part in four days of heavy fighting which followed. He was engaged in the subsequent trench fighting until eventually invalided from the peninsula with enteric fever. After treatment at the 1st Australian General Hospital at Heliopolis, Egypt, he returned to Australia in January 1916. On 27 June Davey re-embarked with the 10th Battalion's 18th reinforcements and proceeded to England. He joined his battalion in France in September just before it moved into the line at Hill 60 in the Ypres sector. He was accidentally wounded on 15 March 1917 and was gassed on 3 October.

At Warneton, Belgium, in the Messines sector on 3 January 1918, Davey gained the Military Medal for crawling into no man's land under heavy fire to rescue a badly wounded comrade. His brother Claude, serving in the same battalion, had received the same award the previous year, only three months before he was killed in action at Bullecourt in 1917. Another brother, Richard, was also awarded it.

Davey was promoted corporal on 24 April 1918. He took part in an attack on enemy positions at Merris, France, on 28 June. His platoon came under heavy fire and the commander was killed. Survivors were forced to shelter in a ditch under almost point-blank fire from a German machine-gun. Davey then made a single-handed attack on the enemy post until forced to return to his own position for more hand-grenades; attacking again, he killed the crew and captured the gun. He then mounted the machine-gun in a new post and efficiently used it during a counter-attack until he was wounded. For his bravery and determination in this action he was awarded the Victoria Cross. Davey's wounds were severe and he was invalided to hospital at Weymouth, England. On 19 October he embarked for return to Australia where he was discharged from the A.I.F. on 24 February next year.

After the war Davey had three separate periods of employment as a labourer and linesman with the South Australian Railways: from 27 April 1926 to 4 October 1938; from 6 March 1939 to 12 February 1942; and from 17 December 1943 to 22 February 1946. He married Eugene Agnes Tomlinson on 25 August 1928, they had no children. He suffered from bronchitis and emphysema for years before his death from a coronary occlusion at the Repatriation General Hospital, Springbank, on 21 December 1953. He was buried with full military honours in the A.I.F. Garden of Memorial cemetery, West Terrace, Adelaide.

(A. Lumb), *History of the 10th Battalion, AIF* (Lond, 1919); C. B. L. Lock, *Fighting 10th . . . A.I.F., 1914-19* (Adel, 1936); L. Wigmore (ed), *They dared mightily* (Canb, 1963); *Western Argus*, 7 Jan 1919.

PETER BURNESS

DAVID, CHARLES ST JOHN (1855?-1924), civil engineer, was born at Chepstow, Monmouthshire, England. He arrived at Moreton Bay, Queensland, aboard the *Ramsay* on 13 January 1880. For three years he worked on railway construction in Queensland, and in 1884-92 was a partner in the Brisbane firm of Brown & David, civil engineers, architects and quantity surveyors. He was also consulting engineer to the Booroodabin suburban municipality and participated in the development of the Brisbane electric tramway.

David was appointed city surveyor in Launceston, Tasmania, on 1 March 1892. His predecessor had presented three proposals for the establishment of a municipal electricity generator to be driven by the South Esk River; David recommended and implemented a scheme which involved driving a tunnel large enough to transfer 62 500 gallons (284 000 L) of water per minute half a mile (800 m) through basalt rock. By late 1895 Launceston's main streets were illuminated by carbon arc lamps energized by Australia's first hydro-electric system. A public electric tramway was advocated and after investigations in 1894 and 1902, and an unsuccessful private venture, a further report in 1909 was adopted. David supervised the design and construction of permanent way, tramsheds and offices for the first tramcar service in 1911. Other achievements included the East Launceston sewerage system and, during the later part of his career, major improvements to the city's waterworks.

Three notable examples of David's ability as engineer, architect and surveyor are prominent in Launceston. In the city centre the southern wing of the town hall, built to a design submitted privately in competition by David in 1904, offers in its plain, neatly proportioned façade a harmonious echo to the classical elegance of the earlier building. Westward of the city, in the savage ravine of the South Esk, David's engineering skill is attested by the sturdy pylons and graceful catenary span of the 1904 Alexandra Suspension Bridge. On the northern verge of Launceston stands Carr Villa cemetery, surveyed, designed and developed from 1902 according to David's directions.

He served in various community organizations. He was a committee-member of the Launceston Mechanics' Institute and Public Library, and in 1907-22 of the Technical School. David advised the Tasmanian Agricultural & Pastoral Society on the construction of Elphin Showground, the Tasmanian Turf Club on alterations to Mowbray Racecourse and acted as honorary consulting engineer to the Northern Tasmanian Fisheries Association. He was a fellow of the Queensland Institute of Architects. Described as 'generous and kindly', and highly valued as a 'general all-round engineer', David died, aged 69, of pneumonia on 17 July 1924 at Wahroonga, New South Wales, while on holiday. His body was returned to Launceston for a civic funeral and burial in a special plot in Carr Villa cemetery. He was survived by an only son in England.

Examiner (Launc), 1 Mar 1892, 11 Dec 1895, 18, 29 July 1924; *Weekly Courier* (Launc), 19 May 1921, 24, 31 July 1924; Immigration records, 1880 (QA).   ALAN JONES

DAVID, SIR TANNATT WILLIAM EDGEWORTH (1858-1934), geologist, was born on 28 January 1858 at the rectory, St Fagans, Glamorganshire, Wales, eldest child of the Rev. William David, sometime fellow of Jesus College, Oxford, and his wife Margaret Harriette, née Thomson, from whose family came the names Tannatt and Edgeworth. At first taught by his father, at 12 David entered Magdalen College School, Oxford, where for some six years he excelled at lessons and games before proceeding to New College in the university as a classical scholar. At moderations in 1878 he gained a first class in classics but a breakdown in health prevented him from reading for final honours. While convalescing he travelled to Canada and then on a round trip to Mel-

bourne in the sailing ship *Yorkshire*. Back at Oxford, David attended Professor Joseph Prestwich's lectures on geology before graduating B.A. in 1881 (M.A. 1926).

Those lectures stimulated David's interest in a science to which he had been introduced by his father, an amateur of fossils as well as antiquities. His original intention to read for Holy Orders faded, to his father's disappointment, as the attractions of geology grew. In 1880, encouraged by a local naturalist, he began to study evidences of glacial action in his native district, work that led next year to his first publication. In 1882 he attended Professor J. W. Judd's course in geology at the Royal College of Science, South Kensington. About the same time, Professor A. Liversidge [q.v.5] was asked by the New South Wales government to find in England a suitable man to fill the post of assistant geological surveyor formerly occupied by Lamont H. Young (1851-1880), who had disappeared in mysterious circumstances while on field-work at Bermagui. Strongly supported by Judd, Prestwich and Professor W. Boyd-Dawkins of Manchester, David was appointed.

He reached Sydney on 27 November 1882 in the steamship *Potosi*. By the end of the year he had prepared a geological sketch map of the Yass district and collected fossils there to replace material lost in the Garden Palace fire. Next March, with his chief C. S. Wilkinson [q.v.6], David examined mining reserves in the New England region and, after Wilkinson's return to Sydney, settled down to a detailed study of the Emmaville district that kept him in the field until August 1884. He published his first monograph in 1887, as *Memoirs*, No.1, of the Geological Survey of New South Wales. Meanwhile, he travelled widely in the colony, reporting on various mineral and water resources.

On 30 July 1885 at St Paul's Church of England, Canterbury, he married Caroline Martha (Cara) Mallett (b. 1856), whom he had met on the voyage to Sydney in 1882. She was travelling to take up her appointment as principal of Hurlstone Training College for female teachers. Much of their early married life was spent in geological field camps and two of their children were born at Maitland. In April 1886 David began a systematic investigation of the lower Hunter River region, that was soon to show publicly the worth of geological surveys. On 3 August he and his assistant G. A. Stonier (d. 1948) discovered at Deep Creek in the Maitland district a seam of coal which by careful mapping they were able to trace in its subsurface distribution. The achievement was no less than the definition of a major new coalfield, the South Maitland, not by accidental prospecting but by the methods of field geology.

The coalfield survey also brought David his first experience as a public lecturer — to an audience of local residents packed into Maitland Town Hall to hear him outline the geology of their district. The success of that occasion was repeated later in Sydney and drew favourable notice from Professors Liversidge and W. J. Stephens [q.v.6]. After some hesitation, David decided to apply for the chair of geology and palaeontology at the University of Sydney, vacant after Stephens's death in 1890; he was selected by the local committee, against the choice of a committee in London appointed by the university to review overseas applicants. In May 1891, David became professor of geology and William Hilton Hovell [q.v.1] lecturer in physical geography. Despite the grand title, his inheritance was a one-man department, miserably equipped and housed in a small cottage. A mining boom in the 1890s, however, helped him press the case for a school of mines within the university. By 1893 he had a new building with lecture theatre and laboratories and his first academic assistant to help cope with growing enrolments. Nevertheless, the distractions of office seem to have had little effect on the flow of his research publications.

Within his first decade as professor he enjoyed world-wide repute, chiefly because of work on a remote coral island in the Pacific. David saw as a challenge the 1896 failure of the party sent by the Royal Society of London to bore a deep section at Funafuti, an atoll in the Ellice Islands. With the help of (Sir) Thomas Anderson Stuart [q.v.], he raised funds for an expedition from Sydney equipped with diamond drills made available by the government. In June 1897 David left for Funafuti accompanied by his wife, a practical engineer and amateur scientist George Sweet, two senior students and a party of workmen. After many difficulties, not all of them mechanical, the drillers had reached a depth of 177 m by the time David went back to Sydney leaving Sweet in charge; he managed to take the work on to 213 m before the workmen refused to continue. Another party sent by David next year finished the job. The remains of shallow-water marine organisms brought from the bottom of the hole, finally 340 m deep, gave striking support for Charles Darwin's [q.v.1] theory that coral atolls had grown progressively on slowly sinking platforms. Although the main technical reports on Funafuti did not appear until 1904, David's part in the venture was recognized by the award of the Bigsby medal by the Geological Society, London, in 1899; next year the Royal Society, London, admitted him a fellow. Mrs

David published an 'unscientific account' of the expedition, *Funafuti: or, three months on a coral island* (1899).

David's earlier interest in glaciation had revived while working in the Hunter River district: in 1885 a colleague from India R. D. Oldham showed him in the field relics of far older glaciation than that of Pleistocene age he knew in Wales. That the Pleistocene Great Ice Age was not a unique event in the earth's history was then a fairly new idea. Prompted by Oldham, David took up the theme with enthusiasm, devoting much time to the study of the late Palaeozoic glacial remains in the Hunter River district and, later, the Pleistocene glaciated country about Mount Kosciusko. By May 1906, when he set out by way of India and Europe for Mexico to attend the tenth International Geological Congress, David had become an authority on past ice ages; they were his theme at the congress. The year 1907 saw completion of part one (the sequel never came!) of *The geology of the Hunter River coal measures* ... promised to the Geological Survey since 1891. With that off his hands, he took a holiday at Kosciusko and learned to ski, a skill soon unexpectedly turned to account.

A few months later Ernest Shackleton invited David to journey south with his expedition and return in the *Nimrod* at the end of the summer. The university granted leave and in December 1907 David, with two former students (Sir) Douglas Mawson and L. A. Cotton [qq.v.] joined Shackleton in New Zealand. Even before his Antarctic landfall, David had decided to stay with the expedition. It meant taking unauthorized leave but the promise of scientific work (and, no doubt, adventure) in such remote parts was tempting beyond refusal. David's fiftieth birthday passed within sight of the active volcano Mount Erebus (3795 m). In March he stood on its summit, leader of the first successful climbing party. Impressed, Shackleton next spring gave him charge of an attempt to reach the south magnetic Pole. The journey of four months during which David, with Mawson and a young Scots doctor Forbes Mackay, dragged laden sledges from sea-level up more than 2200 m to their goal on the ice plateau and back, covering in all some 1250 km, has passed into the annals of polar exploration as an epic of courage and endurance. Captain J. K. Davis [q.v.] of the *Nimrod* praised David highly in his *High latitude* (Melbourne, 1962).

In the general rejoicing at David's return to Sydney late in March 1909, the problem of his absence simply disappeared. Before leaving he had used his influence to secure government grants in aid of the expedition;

now he embarked on a strenuous lecture tour of all the Australian States to raise funds for publication of the scientific results. His flair as a publicist ensured success for the venture just as, later, his whole-hearted support did so much to promote Mawson's Antarctic work. In 1910 David was appointed C.M.G. and that year took his Antarctic lectures to England; during the visit Oxford conferred on him its honorary D.Sc. (1911). He was in England again in 1913 busy with arrangements for the meeting in Australia of the British Association for the Advancement of Science next year. Despite the declaration of war in Europe the conference went ahead. David contributed greatly to its success, not least by the example of his tactful behaviour towards delegates from what had become enemy countries.

The conference over, David involved himself in patriotic efforts and, as president of the Universal Service League, became a leading figure at recruiting rallies. In 1915 he and Professor E. W. Skeats [q.v.] convinced the government that Australia should offer to raise and equip a corps of geologists and miners for service at the front; the offer was accepted by the Imperial government. David, despite his age, managed to enlist in the Australian Imperial Force and was commissioned major in the Mining Battalion on 25 October. He left for France and the Western Front in February 1916 and provided valuable advice on ground water and the siting and design of trenches and tunnels, – valuable pioneering work on military geology. On 6 October he was seriously injured when he fell 24 m when inspecting a well near Vimy Ridge; six weeks later he was back in action but never fully recovered. From June 1917, as chief geologist, he was attached to the inspector of mines at General Headquarters, British Expeditionary Force. Three times mentioned in dispatches, he was awarded the Distinguished Service Order in 1918 and was promoted lieut-colonel. His son served with the British army as regimental medical officer with the 6th Cameron Highlanders, winning the Military Cross, and his daughter Mary served as a motor driver with the Women's Army Auxiliary Corps and Women's Legion.

In 1919 David returned to Australia. He was appointed K.B.E. in 1920 and became known as Sir Edgeworth. He next took up a theme he had long projected, the preparation of a comprehensive account of the geology of Australia. In 1921 and again for 1923-24 he received special leave from the university to travel through the country gathering detail and conferring with colleagues. He resigned his chair in 1924 to devote all his energies to the work but, in

fact, was never to complete it; he visited England in 1925-26. Failing health and a tendency to spread his interests, notably in the case of what he came to believe were ancient arthropod remains found in South Australia, did not help. Nevertheless, by a remarkable effort of will his large-scale *Geological map of the Commonwealth of Australia* and a volume of *Explanatory notes* were finished and published in 1932.

David in his time dominated Australian geological science with a benevolent mastery. International recognition of his work came early. Perhaps not an outstandingly original thinker, his great achievements seem to have derived from a remarkable capacity to recognize opportunities, whether conceptual or more immediately practical, and develop them fruitfully. Close contact with colleagues abroad may have helped him to be innovative in Australia. Yet his was no slavish dependence; he more than any before him conferred on Australian geological science a sense of identity and self-respect. As teacher as well as scientist he made his mark. By all acounts a captivating speaker, David attracted many able students to his subject and, eventually, his profession. He knew his students personally and they, in turn, clearly hero-worshipped the man they called 'The Prof' or 'The Professor' as if there were no other. That one so eminent could be so courteous and considerate enlarged his fame in the university and beyond.

David died of lobar pneumonia on 28 August 1934 in Royal Prince Alfred Hospital, and was accorded a state funeral by the Commonwealth and New South Wales governments; after a service at St Andrew's Anglican Cathedral he was cremated with military honours. He was survived by his wife, son and two daughters. The *Sydney Morning Herald* wrote: 'Never previously in the history of Sydney has there been a more striking manifestation of sorrow, at once sincere and spontaneous, at the passing of a great man, who, by his works, his inspiration, and his quiet charm of personality, had filled a distinctive place, not only in science, but also in the hearts of the community'. After David's death, the State government purchased his manuscript material for the book on the geology of Australia and, repeating David's own instruction, commissioned W. R. Browne to prepare it for publication. Of necessity largely written by Browne though bearing David's name as author, the book appeared in 1950 to complete, in splendid fashion, a record of more than 150 scientific publications and an unknown but considerable number of popular articles in newspapers and magazines.

Scientific honours in abundance had come

to David — honorary doctorates of science were conferred on him by the universities of Manchester, Wales, Cambridge and Sydney, and the LL.D. of St Andrews. Geological and geographical societies across the world honoured him in their several ways; he is still the only Australian resident to have received the senior geological award, the Wollaston medal of the Geological Society of London, given him in 1915. Twice president of the Royal Society of New South Wales (of which he was also (W.B.) Clarke [q.v.3] medallist), of the Australasian Association for the Advancement of Science (recipient of its Mueller [q.v.5] medal) and of the Linnean Society of New South Wales as well as president of the Australian National Research Council (1921-22), David played an active part in the life of these and many other Australian scientific bodies. Memorials to him are too numerous to detail: prizes, appointments, buildings, place-names commemorate him; he has been depicted on two Australian postage stamps. A portrait of David by John Longstaff [q.v.] is held at the University of Sydney and one by Norman Carter [q.v.7] by the Royal Society of New South Wales.

Lady David had a long and distinguished career of service to the community. She was an early president of the Bush Book Club. In World War I she campaigned vigorously and successfully for six o'clock closing of public houses and was president of the Women's National Movement for Social Reform which aimed at the eradication of venereal disease. Her work on behalf of the New South Wales branch of the Girl Guides' Association was outstanding: an original divisional commissioner from 1920, she was State commissioner in 1928-38 and in 1934 was awarded the order of the Silver Fish — the highest honour for officers of the Girl Guide Movement. She died at Hornsby on Christmas Day 1951.

M. E. David, *Professor David* (Lond, 1937) and *Passages of time* (Brisb, 1975); Cardiff Naturalists' Soc, *Trans*, 67 (1934), p 13; Geological Soc of America, *Procs*, 1935, p 215; *Obituary Notices of Fellows of the Roy Soc*, 1 (1935) no 4; Linnean Soc NSW, *Procs*, 61 (1936), p 341; *Sydney Mail*, 4 May 1921; *SMH*, 29, 30, 31 Aug 1934, 2 Jan 1952; David papers (Univ Syd Archives).　　T. G. VALLANCE
D. F. BRANAGAN

DAVIDSON, SIR ALFRED CHARLES (1882-1952), banker, was born on 1 April 1882 in Brisbane, son of James Madgwick Davidson, and his Queensland-born wife Lucy, née Cribb. His father, the second son of Alfred Davidson of Warmley House, Gloucestershire, who brought his family to Queensland in 1863, was manager of the South Brisbane branch of the Bank of New South Wales. Davidson was educated at Brisbane Grammar School, and joined the Bank of New South Wales at the Brisbane office in 1901 after the later stages of his formal education had been interrupted by illness. Early in his career he devoted much of his leisure to private study of banking and finance and to the activities of the South Brisbane Congregational Church.

In 1910 Davidson visited London at his own expense and on his return was appointed to the bank's head office in Sydney. For some years he worked mainly in administration under the watchful eye of the inspector Robert Tate Hilder. On 28 June 1916 at St Peter's Anglican Church, Neutral Bay, he married Dorothea Mary, daughter of Charles L. Tange, solicitor; they had no children. He was transferred to New Zealand in 1922, first as manager of the Gisborne branch and in 1924 as sub-inspector, Wellington. His adaptability and energy won the confidence of his superiors, and he was appointed manager of the Perth branch in 1925.

Developing a lifelong enthusiasm for Western Australia, Davidson plunged quickly into the expansion of business there. He became general manager of the ailing Western Australian Bank in 1926. Finding its condition weaker than expected, with strong support from most of its directors and notably from Hilder among his former colleagues, he negotiated amalgamation with the Bank of New South Wales in March 1927. Appointed inspector in Perth, Davidson was in charge of the amalgamated business in the State. However, he was recalled to Sydney as chief inspector in 1928 and became general manager on 4 January 1929.

His term as general manager of the Bank of New South Wales was one of dynamic leadership of the bank and of controversy on the national stage. Davidson's outstanding position came from a thorough and disciplined practical training, a refusal to be hidebound, a lifetime of self-education in banking and economics, and a receptivity to ideas. Above all, he had drive and self-confidence which harnessed ideas of others into practical and swift decision and action.

Impressed with the necessity for bankers to study the wider aspects and implications of their profession, Davidson became a fellow of the Royal Economic Society in 1925. His interest in economics and finance was influenced and encouraged in Western Australia by his friendship with Professor E. O. G. Shann [q.v.], which brought him into consultation and association with many leading academic economists. With his flair for publicity, he was able to encourage a lively forum for their views which helped to keep the public abreast of current economic controversies. His encouragement of young graduate staff to participate in a wide range of public affairs was later to provide the public service and business with considerable talent. Under Davidson the bank grew and prospered: he negotiated the amalgamation with the Australian Bank of Commerce in 1931; carried out a well-judged building programme and acquired fine city buildings in the low-cost 1930s; increased the number of accounts; carried on highly profitable dealings in foreign exchange; and introduced the travel service which was widely copied by other banks.

Despite the developing balance of payments crisis and growing economic depression, Davidson remained convinced throughout the 1930s that the banks could play a decisive and constructive role under suitable leadership, provided they were not frustrated by political interference. He advocated a central bank and wrote on the subject in 1929, but drew back when E. G. Theodore's [q.v.] bill threatened political control. But the two issues on which he mainly crossed swords with the governor of the Commonwealth Bank of Australia and his fellow bankers were the exchange rate and the interest rate policy. His first show of independence was to increase interest rates in his bank, against the views of the other banks, early in 1930.

Deteriorating gold and foreign exchange reserves called for drastic action to guarantee interest payments on Australia's heavy overseas public debt. Government pressure for exchange control won some sympathy from the banks but, after Theodore proposed a voluntary pooling arrangement, Davidson gained acceptance for the exchange mobilization agreement of 1930, which assured exchange funds to meet all government debt service and other essential requirements; it also left the banks free to use the balance of their exchange earnings in their normal business without loss of independence.

Davidson's battle over the exchange rate was more protracted: preservation of parity with sterling was a sacred cow which growing external weakness made increasingly expensive, perhaps ruinous, to maintain. The Commonwealth Bank and some others thought their defence lay in government control of exports. After bitter arguments with them Davidson acted on his own, obliging the others to follow, to outbid the outside traders, and thus he effectively destroyed the myth of parity with sterling. There was some dispute about the appropriate exchange rate, but Davidson's conviction and initiative late in 1930 and early 1931 gave principle and purpose to the haphazard process of devaluation, and obliged a reluctant Commonwealth Bank to take responsibility for management of the rate. This unpegging of the old parity with sterling was later recognized as one of the most important factors in softening the impact of world depression on Australia and in assisting domestic recovery. In the confusing events surrounding the Premiers' Plan in 1931, Davidson supported the principle of lower interest rates and virtually forced the other bankers to agree, but he was prepared to move only on condition of cuts in government budget deficits and at a pace slower than the government wished. His attitude generally was to co-operate but not to be coerced into precipitate steps. In a practical way he was an early advocate of the new practice of holding treasury bills in his bank's portfolio and of supporting the bond market in conversion operations. He pressed tirelessly colleagues in the business world to keep industry moving and farmers on the land, and in New South Wales he assisted home building. Unfortunately petty wrangling and distrust and suspicion of political motives too often detracted from the efforts of his vigorous personality.

Through the Primary Producers' Advisory Council Davidson was thought to be involved with C.L.A. Abbott and the Old Guard, and he was also suspected in some quarters of association with the New Guard. Nevertheless, as the government's banker he and the bank behaved with circumspection and rectitude in the crisis that led to the sacking of Lang as premier in 1932. In the late 1930s Davidson supported the Heffron group against Lang and involved the bank in the finances of the *Labor Daily*. At the British Commonwealth Relations Conference at Lapstone in 1938, which he enthusiastically supported, he tried to persuade Ernest Bevin to meet Heffron. His excursion into political factionalism helped to strain relations with members of his board.

Deep concern for preserving the banking system from political interference and from the various financial nostrums flourishing in the Depression, caused Davidson to accept the Commonwealth royal commission on the monetary and banking systems in 1935 as a great opportunity: his extensive evidence, thoroughly prepared and impressively presented, was a performance of considerable virtuosity, ranging widely over slightly idealized interpretations of current banking economics and experience. But the Depression had left its mark on public and official thinking. An independent central bank free of political connexion leading a system of banks through discussion and guidance in open-market conditions, which he had advocated from 1929, was no longer a possibility. Indeed, Davidson was hardly the man to play second fiddle to any central bank, however wisely led.

Appointed K.B.E. in 1938, Davidson had passed the peak of his power by 1939. Although he applied himself with customary energy to the defence effort and to problems of wartime banking he was not called on to play a wider role in national affairs. He devoted much effort to a diverse series of welfare organizations and to preparations for post-war conditions, including plans for bank finance of housing. With a wider vision, he returned after a visit to Fiji and New Zealand early in 1944 fired with a sense of the opportunities and responsibilities of Australia and New Zealand in south-east Asia and the Pacific. Preaching that message was his last crusade. He was struck with severe illness on October 1944, and although he hoped to resume duty with the bank, he was persuaded to retire in June 1945.

Sir Alfred spent much time at Leura, where he enjoyed gardening and carpentry. He was president of the Australasian Pioneers' Club, a member of the Union, Australian, University, Royal Automobile and Australian and Leura Golf clubs, the Church of England Sydney Diocesan Synod, and of the Walter and Eliza Hall [qq.v.] and the Long Range Weather Forecasting trusts, and a director of the International Chamber of Commerce. In retirement his main excursion into business life was as chairman of a new, and possibly premature, merchant banking organization in 1950. He died of heart disease in St Luke's Hospital, Darlinghurst, on 18 November 1952 and was cremated after a service at St Andrew's Cathedral; he was survived by his wife. His estate was valued for probate at £36 698.

A dominating figure in the 1930s, Davidson assumed leadership among the banks with ease and confidence. Genial and generous to most people, he was also arrogant and often contemptuous towards his peers, but he won a deep affection from a very wide circle. He used his influence and his own energy to promote and extend the work of many organizations which might otherwise have gone under in the Depression. As a member of the provisional committee he had also helped to establish the Royal Australasian College of Physicians in 1938. To the end he retained a youthful enthusiasm for a diversity of interests, from water divining and organic fertilizers to world politics and philosophy.

Bank of NSW, *Roy Com on monetary and banking systems, 1936* (Syd, 1936); *Roy Com into the monetary and banking systems . . . minutes of evidence*, 1 (Canb, 1936); L. F. Giblin, *The growth of a central bank* (Melb, 1951); R. F. Holder, *Bank of New South Wales: a history* (Syd, 1970); C. B. Schedvin, *Australia and the great depression* (Syd, 1970); *Aust Q*, March 1953, p 42; intelligence reports, SP 1141/1/13, MP 1049/9, file 1887/2/35 (AAO); Bank of NSW Archives (Syd).
R. F. HOLDER

DAVIDSON, SIR COLIN GEORGE WATT (1878-1954), judge, was born on 18 November 1878 at Mudgee, New South Wales, eldest son and second child of native-born parents George Davidson, solicitor, and his wife Jessie, née Watt. He was educated at the Grammar School, Mudgee, and the University of Sydney (B.A., 1899; LL.B., 1901); he helped to support himself by coaching.

Davidson was admitted to the Bar on 24 October 1901, entered Selborne Chambers and read with (Sir) David Ferguson [q.v.]. By 1905 he had joined his lifelong friend John Hammond in Wigram Chambers. Briefs being scarce, they collaborated in writing the *Law of landlord and tenant in New South Wales* (1906, 2nd edition, 1920), for which they received £100 each and much recognition. In 1912-23 he lectured at the university, promoting his view that a law school 'is not a mere factory'. After limiting a wide practice to equity matters, he took silk in 1926.

Three months later Davidson was appointed an acting Supreme Court judge; his appointment was made permanent on 14 February 1927. His fine bearing seemed even more distinguished in his judicial robes but, more than looking the part, he was at home in all jurisdictions and was rarely reversed on appeal. He 'found somewhat irksome at first various traditional restrictions', but increasingly appreciated their advantages. In 1928, as sole royal commissioner, he investigated and found proven allegations of attempted bribery of a minister of the Crown by a member of the Legislative Assembly. In 1930 he heard the long, drawn-out Massy will case: in pronouncing against the validity of the will he castigated the psychiatrist, who had found Massy in full testamentary capacity. In 1940 he became senior puisne judge.

In 1929 Davidson was appointed chairman of the joint Commonwealth and State royal commission into the coal industry. In the comprehensive report he recommended that a board with wide regulatory powers be set up, and warned that half measures would be ineffective. In 1938-39 he chaired the New South Wales royal commission upon the safety and health of workers in coal mines; many of the commission's proposals were incorporated in the Coal Mines Regulation (Further Amendment) Act of 1941. In Feb-

Davidson

ruary that year he became chairman of the Commonwealth Coal Board and in August consultant to the Commonwealth coal commissioner. In January 1945 Davidson was appointed chairman of the Commonwealth royal commission into the industry. He was severely criticized by I. Williams of the Australasian Coal and Shale Employees' (Miners') Federation, but on 4 March 1946 was named sole commissioner. He inspected mines throughout Australia and wrote the exhaustive report himself. Critical of the government's failure to back arbitration decisions and of the miners' lack of discipline, he recommended greater mechanization and a Commonwealth statutory authority to control coal mining. He was made an honorary member of the Australasian Institute of Mining and Metallurgy in 1952.

Davidson was elected to the university senate in 1939 but resigned in 1941 with Sir Percival Halse Rogers, Sir Henry Manning and Sir John Peden [qq.v.], in protest at the senate filling two chairs in the faculty of law, as they believed that permanent appointments should not be made during the war. Soon after the outbreak of World War II Davidson had been appointed chairman of an advisory committee to hear appeals against the exercise of the National Security (General) Regulations and by internees; he was also an official visitor at internment camps at Cowra, Hay, Orange and elsewhere. In 1945-46 he chaired a committee to arrange refresher courses for legal ex-servicemen.

On 17 November 1948 Davidson retired: the chief justice Sir Frederick Jordan [q.v.] praised his 'profoundly judicial mind' and his courtesy. Davidson regretted that the expansion of modern legislation had 'made judicial duties far more arduous', preventing judges from observing 'a former custom of taking a prominent part in cultural and charitable movements in the community'. He was knighted in 1952.

At St James Church, Sydney, on 20 December 1928 Davidson had married Phyllis Hinder, daughter of Dr Richard Theophilus Jones; they lived at Killara and visited Europe in 1934 and the East for three months in 1939. All his life Davidson enjoyed golf and was a member of the Union, Australian and University clubs, Sydney. Sir Colin died in hospital at Chatswood on 8 July 1954 and was cremated with Anglican rites. He was survived by his wife; they were childless. His estate was valued for probate at £9229.

Newspaper Cartoonists' Assn of NSW, *Sydney-ites as we see 'em, 1913-14-15* (Syd, 1915?); T. R Bavin (ed), *The jubilee book of the law school of the University of Sydney* (Syd, 1940); P. H. Davidson,

An outline of the official life of the Hon Sir Colin Davidson ... (Syd, 1964); *NSW State Reports*, 48 (1948); *Aust Law J*, 10 Dec 1948, 22 July 1954; *SMH*, 19 May 1921, 12 Mar, 2 June 1926, 12 Feb 1927, 4 Oct 1930, 27 Sept 1939, 14 Feb, 5, 6 Nov 1941, 23 Mar 1946, 6 Jan 1952, 9, 13 July 1954.
MARTHA RUTLEDGE

DAVIDSON, DANIEL SUTHERLAND (1900-1952), anthropologist, was born on 9 July 1900 at Cohoes, New York, United States of America, son of Matthew Henry Davidson, travelling salesman, and his wife Laura, née Sutherland. After education at the local Egberts High School, from 1920 he attended the University of Pennsylvania, Philadelphia (B.S., 1923; A.M., 1924; Ph.D., 1928). Except for two years in 1932-33 at the University of Buffalo, he was on the staff of the University of Pennsylvania from 1924 to 1946 and associate professor of anthropology there from 1940. He was at the University of Oregon in 1947-48 and was professor of anthropology at the University of Washington, Seattle, in 1949-52.

Though he carried out research on American Indians and wrote a monograph on snowshoes, Davidson's major anthropological work was on Oceania with particular emphasis on Australian Aboriginals. In a number of studies he mapped the geographical distribution of particular cultural traits, interpreting the resulting patterns as largely the result of historical development through innovation and/or diffusion. In 1928 he published his doctoral thesis *The chronological aspects of certain Australian social institutions ...*; it was savagely reviewed by Professor A. R. Radcliffe-Brown [q.v.], who preferred contemporary sociological research of Aboriginal societies to historical reconstruction.

Davidson visited Australia in 1930-31 and 1938-40, examining private and museum collections and carrying out field-work, mainly in northern Australia, where he excavated several prehistoric sites. In 1934 and 1936 he located and edited important, previously unpublished, material by E. Hassell from the 1880s, on Aboriginal life in south-western Australia. His other research resulted in monographs on rock and decorative art, social institutions, tribal distribution and string figures, and in some forty papers on a wide range of subjects, including rafts and canoes, utensils, weapons, stone artefacts, netting and basketry, throwing darts, footwear, mourning caps, fire-making, and the origin of the boomerang. He wrote also on the relationships of the cultures of Australia, Tasmania, Melanesia, Indonesia and Tierra del Fuego, and on trans-Pacific migrations.

Davidson's periods of research in Australia were brief, but so little was then being done in the fields of art and material culture that his perceptive work in these neglected areas was above contemporary Australian standards and has proved of use to later prehistorians. His efforts to delineate tribal groupings and cultural traits across Australia are now dated but were an attempt to provide a comprehensive and developmental view of Aboriginal culture.

Nicknamed 'Sud', Davidson was of medium height and build with dark hair and a trim moustache. The societies to which he belonged included the American Folk-lore Society, of which he was secretary and treasurer in 1942-44. Swimming and mountain climbing were among his favourite recreations. He had married Elma Ely Barber on 21 December 1929; she accompanied him on his visits to Australia. He died of a heart attack at Altamonte Springs, Florida, on 26 December 1952, survived by his wife and daughter.

Oceania, 1 (1930), no 3; *Mankind*, 4 (1953), no 11; *American Anthropologist*, 56 (1954), and for publications; Archives of Universities of Pennsylvania and Oregon; information from Professor J Mulvaney and Dr J. Urry, ANU, Canberra.

F. D. McCARTHY

DAVIDSON, ETHEL SARAH (1872-1939), nurse, was born on 19 June 1872 in Adelaide, daughter of William Davidson, Scottish-born master mariner, and his second wife Elizabeth Jane, née Green. She was orphaned at the age of 5 when her father's brigantine, the *Emily Smith*, was wrecked on Kangaroo Island in May 1877. Her two young brothers and baby sister also drowned. Ethel was the only member of the family not on board the vessel. She was left with three grown half-brothers and three half-sisters from her father's first marriage, all resident in Adelaide.

No details of her education are known but Ethel Davidson trained as a nurse at the Adelaide Hospital, then became district nurse at Prospect. She later engaged in district and private nursing and for some time was on the Central Board of Health. In 1904 she joined the Australian Army Nursing Service. She was working as district nurse at Prospect when on 26 September 1914 she enlisted as a sister in the A.A.N.S., Australian Imperial Force. She left Australia with the first contingent and on reaching Egypt in December was appointed to the Convalescent Depot, Mena; from August 1915 to January 1916 she was acting matron. She was then made temporary matron of the 3rd Australian Auxiliary Hospital at Cairo

and, for distinguished service there, was mentioned in dispatches and awarded the Royal Red Cross, 2nd class. On 24 June she relinquished this position, reverting to the rank of head sister and embarking for London for a six-month appointment in the medical section, A.I.F. Headquarters. She then served briefly at the 2nd A.A.H., Southall, before crossing to France on 28 February 1917 for duty at the 2nd Australian General Hospital, Wimereux. In March she was transferred, as acting matron, to the 2nd Australian Casualty Clearing Station at Trois Arbres, near Steenwerck.

In July Sister Davidson was sent to Italy as temporary matron of the 38th British Stationary Hospital near Genoa; her rank was confirmed in January 1918. During that year, for distinguished service and devotion to duty, she was again mentioned in dispatches and awarded the Royal Red Cross, 1st class. She returned to England in January 1919, serving briefly as matron of the 2nd A.A.H. at Southall. Before embarking for Australia she was appointed C.B.E. in the King's Birthday honours of 3 June.

Matron Davidson was demobilized on 5 December 1919 and that month was appointed matron of the military hospital at Keswick, Adelaide; from 1924 she was also principal matron of the 4th Military District. The hospital was taken over by the Repatriation Commission in 1921 but she remained matron there until she reached retiring age in June 1933. She was president of the Returned Army Nurses' Association of South Australia in 1922-26 and was largely responsible for obtaining the charter which made the association a sub-branch of the Returned Sailors' and Soldiers' Imperial League in 1924.

After a three-month illness Matron Davidson died of cardiovascular and renal disease on 21 April 1939 at her home at Semaphore. The Adelaide *News* reported: 'Her death, almost on the eve of Anzac Day, has cast a gloom over Keswick Hospital. She will be mourned by large numbers of patients and hundreds of returned soldiers with whom she came in contact when on active service and in South Australia'. The *Rising Sun* described her as 'a woman of outstanding character' and 'an exceptionally able leader and organiser'. She was buried in the A.I.F. cemetery, West Terrace, Adelaide.

A. G. Butler (ed), *Official history of the Australian Army Medical Services ... 1914-18*, 1-3 (Melb, 1930, Canb, 1940, 1943); A. G. Price, *Nursing in South Australia ... 1837-1937*, rev edn (Adel, 1939); G. D. Chapman, *Kangaroo Island shipwrecks* (Canb, 1972); *Rising Sun* (Adel), May 1939; *Reveille* (Syd), June 1939; *Advertiser* (Adel), 21-31 May, 2, 8, 14 June 1877, 22 Apr 1939; *News*

(Adel), 21 Apr 1939; S. G. Kenny, *The Australian Army Nursing Service during the great war* (B.A. Hons thesis, Univ Melb, 1975); records (AWM).

JACQUELINE ABBOTT

DAVIDSON, JAMES (1865-1936), shearer, manufacturer and inventor, was born on 18 November 1865 at Barwidgee station, near Stanley, Victoria, son of William Davidson, sawyer, and his wife Eliza, née Ogilvie, both from Aberdeen, Scotland. He began work at 12 'picking up' at Quamby, near Woolsthorpe; at 16 he was shearing and registering a tally of 69; and at 20 had achieved the old allotted tally of 110 a day at Barwidgee and was third best in a team of 28. In 1888 at Dunlop station, Louth, New South Wales, he was one of the forty shearers who – using F. Y. Wolseley's [q.v.6] invention – completed the first entire machine shearing of a flock.

From 1890 Davidson devoted his life to the promotion and improvement of the shearing machine. Employed by Wolseley as a demonstrator at £4 per week and expenses, he toured Victoria, New South Wales and Queensland with John Howard on a sales drive, often in the face of hostility and incipient Luddism from shearers who felt their jobs threatened. In 1892 he became handpiece inspector in Wolseley's Sydney workshop.

The machine made inroads against the blades but the depressed 1890s, general ignorance and the conservatism of graziers resulted in slow sales. In 1900, travelling by bicycle, Davidson toured northern New South Wales and outback Queensland in an unprecedented feat of salesmanship. Carrying seventy pounds (32 kg) of shearing gear (a complete stand) which could be speedily erected and powered by someone pedalling the bicycle, Davidson demonstrated the superiority of the machine over the blades to the unconvinced and often scornful. He showed graziers, in particular, that they were losing about fifteen ounces (425 g) of wool per fleece by adhering to the blades: sales flourished. In 1901 he became second in charge of the Wolseley workshop (from 1893 controlled by Dangar, Gedye & Co.) and personally erected seventy-two stands at F. S. Falkiner's [q.v.4] station, Tuppal, in the Riverina. In 1908 he succeeded Howard as workshop manager. The same year he appeared in *The squatter's daughter* at Sydney's Criterion Theatre, in a scene where he sheared a sheep with the blades.

In 1909 Dangar, Gedye & Co. arranged with the engineering firm R. A. Lister & Co. of Dursley, Gloucestershire, England, to manufacture a new machine. Davidson went to England with a successful design, and so

began his long and fruitful association with the Lister company whose workshop in Sydney he managed for many years. From 1911 until 1936 he patented many improvements to the shearing machine.

Short, stocky, patient, always optimistic and kind to the underdog (he put fifteen fatherless boys through apprenticeships in his workshop), Davidson possessed great mechanical skill and inventiveness; he kept close to the shearers by visiting the sheds from time to time and understood, as only an old blade ringer could, their demands for technical improvements. He won widespread admiration and respect for his great contribution to the wool industry. He died of cancer at his home at Chatswood, Sydney, on 3 October 1936 survived by his wife, Sophia, née Dinger, whom he had married on 5 January 1892 at St Stephen's Presbyterian Church, Bathurst, and by a son and a daughter.

J. G. Smyth, *The man and the industry* (np, 1936?); F. Wheelhouse, *Digging stick to rotary hoe* (Melb, 1966); *SMH*, 6 Oct 1936.   G. P. WALSH

DAVIDSON, JAMES (1885-1945), ecologist, was born on 27 July 1885 at Brimstage, Wirral, Cheshire, England, second son of James Davidson, shepherd and farm bailiff, and his wife Sarah, née Jones. He was educated at Thornton Hough parish school and the University of Liverpool (B.Sc., 1908; M.Sc., 1911; D.Sc., 1915). After graduating he worked with G. H. F. Nuttall at the Cooper Research Laboratories on his pioneering studies on ticks, major vectors of disease in humans and cattle; in 1911 Davidson was awarded the Wolfe-Barry studentship in entomology at the Imperial College of Science and Technology. He later studied briefly in Italy and France.

In World War I he commanded a sanitary section in Sinai, Palestine and on the Somme, where he organized control of flies, mosquitoes and lice. He was promoted captain and mentioned in dispatches. After the war he was sent to Copenhagen to organize the disinfestation of prisoners; he married his beloved Johanne Therese Hornemann there in 1920; they had three sons and a daughter. Davidson then became assistant entomologist at Rothamsted Agricultural Experiment Station, Hertfordshire, England, studying the effects of aphids on plants, and the influence of soil and climate on aphid populations, exerted through the plant.

In 1928 he migrated to Adelaide to take up a departmental headship at the Waite [q.v.6] Agricultural Research Institute in the University of Adelaide. In 1937 he was appointed to the new Waite chair of entomology. In Adelaide Davidson realized that the extremes of climate would have a profound influence on the distribution and numbers of insect species. A leader in the movement to make ecology a quantitive science, he applied rigorous methods to his studies on lucerne fleas, apple thrips, grasshoppers and even the sheep population of South Australia. He developed the concept of 'bio-climatic zones', and mapped Australia into regions where the ratio of rainfall to evaporation determined the limits of distribution of many species. He applied mathematical equations to describe insects' development and the growth of their populations. He set new and exacting standards but was anxious that the man on the land should benefit from research.

Davidson was a humble, gentle, humorous man, with a scientific vision that leapt from painstaking particular observations to the grand generalization. His work contains many detailed studies, always leading towards a general synthesis. His death, on 13 August 1945, following an operation, cut short his major work on the underlying causes of changes in the distribution and abundance of animals. He was buried in the Anglican cemetery at Mitcham. A full bibliography and a more detailed synopsis of his research appeared in the *Transactions* of the Royal Society of South Australia, (1945) of which Davidson had been president in 1937-38.

Advertiser (Adel), 14 Aug 1945.

T. O. BROWNING

DAVIDSON, JAMES EDWARD (1870-1930), journalist and newspaper proprietor, was born on 20 or 21 December 1870 at Pine Hills, Harrow, Victoria, elder son of James Johnstone Davidson, station-hand, and his Scottish-born wife Janet, née Aitchison. After attending Harrow State School, he worked on stations in western New South Wales but in 1887 he became a reporter with the *Port Augusta Dispatch*. From 1893 he worked as a shorthand clerk in the Treasury Department in Perth, then in 1895 became Premier Sir John Forrest's [q.v.] personal assistant. He wrote occasionally for the press, and next year joined the *West Australian* as a reporter. On 5 October 1896 he married Eugenie Louise Jerome Gilbert of Adelaide.

In 1897 Davidson joined the renowned Melbourne *Argus*. His shorthand skill suited him to verbatim political reporting; he became a leading political journalist and covered the Federal conventions. His reputation for fearless investigation grew with his insistent reports of the activities of (Sir)

Thomas Bent [q.v.3], premier from 1904.

From 1905 Davidson edited the *Weekly Times*. To study technical and business aspects of newspaper production he worked on the *Detroit Daily Free Press* in the United States of America in 1906. Returning next year he was promoted to general manager and editor-in-chief of the *Herald*. Before his resignation in 1918, he had established this paper as Australia's leading evening daily and increased its circulation by 80 per cent. Next year Davidson acquired the Port Pirie *Recorder* and the *Barrier Miner* at Broken Hill, where he moved. During the 'Big Strike' of 1919-20 he gained notoriety when he encouraged his reporters to expose the sharp practices of some union organizers.

In 1922 Davidson moved to Adelaide and, in July 1923, began publishing the *News*, a tabloid which, by agreement, replaced the city's two former evening papers. In spite of a doubting market, he floated a public company, News Ltd, with a nominal capital of £250 000, became its managing director, and sold to the new company his two country papers. The presses he purchased from the *Herald*. By 1930 News Ltd was worth £750 000 and owned the weekly *Mail* (Adelaide) and *Daily News* (Perth). It also survived a costly failure to start an evening paper in Hobart in 1924-25.

'J.E.D.' was dark, sturdily built, of medium height. He was said to resemble Dickens's [q.v.4] Boythorn in *Bleak House* – in speech an ogre, in conduct the kindliest of mortals. He had a deserved reputation as an astute businessman and was an honest, dedicated, professional journalist. His writing was concise, direct and morally committed. A socialist in his youth, he fought corruption wherever he found it. He was the first president of the Melbourne Press Bond in 1906 (forerunner of the Australian Journalists' Association) and in 1918 served briefly on the Commonwealth's press censorship advisory board. He was also an able lecturer, a Rotarian, a good amateur boxer and a collector of early Australian literature.

Davidson was a delegate in 1930 to the Imperial Press Conference in London. The day before it opened, on 1 June, he died of pneumonia and alcoholism and was buried beside his brother Alan, explorer and mining engineer, in Putney Vale cemetery. His son Alan had died in an air crash three years earlier. Davidson was survived by his wife, from whom he had separated, and a son Norman, a journalist with the *News*. His estate was sworn for probate at £20 130.

E. Scott, *Australia during the war* (Syd, 1936); Aust Journalists' Assn, *Crusade for journalism*, G. Sparrow ed (Melb, 1960); W. S. Holden, *Australia* goes to press (Melb, 1962); *Bulletin*, 4 May 1905; *Barrier Miner*, 15 Feb 1919, 2 June 1930; *Newspaper News* (Melb), 2 July 1928, 1 Feb, 1 July 1930; *News* (Adel), 2 June 1930, 20-24 July 1973; *Advertiser* (Adel), 3 June 1930; *Argus*, 4, 9 June 1930; *Mail* (Adel), 7 June 1930; B. Hammond, The origins and course of the Broken Hill strike, 1919-20 (B.A. Hons thesis, Univ Melb, 1970); information from Miss M. Howie, Parkside South, Adel.   CARL BRIDGE

DAVIDSON, JOHN EWEN (1840-1923), sugar-planter and miller, was born in London, son of Henry Davidson, merchant and cadet of the Davidsons of Tulloch Castle, Dingwall, Scotland, and his wife Caroline, née Blake. Educated at Harrow and Oxford (B.A., 1862), he visited the West Indies and British Guiana before coming to Australia in 1865. He began as a sugar-planter at Rockingham Bay near Cardwell, Queensland, in 1866; but after his partner's withdrawal and floods in December, he joined T. H. Fitzgerald [q.v.4] at Mackay next year in a sugar and cotton plantation called Alexandria, which was soon devoted to sugar. Building the first iron mill in the district in 1868, they proved sugar commercially viable but, through Davidson's intense conservatism, did not introduce the important vacuum pan process for many years.

Davidson visited most of the world's sugar-producing areas in the next thirty years and became a district leader. His scientific training enabled him to breed new feasible varieties after the disastrous rust epidemic of 1875. Pursuing other interests, he collected Aboriginal artefacts for the British Museum, discovered a new species of plum tree and, with his own telescope, identified the first comet discovered by anyone in Queensland. As chairman of the Pioneer Shire Divisional Board for many years and of the Mackay Planters' Association in 1878-83, he helped improve shipping facilities in the port and river, and eventually became a member of the Mackay Harbour Board. He was also on the committee of the Agricultural Pastoral and Mining Association. From about 1881 he was a partner in the Melbourne firm, W. Sloane & Co. When it became the Melbourne Mackay Sugar Co. in 1882, he managed its six mills and estates, provided with modern and expensive equipment.

Considering Europeans incapable of the heavy work in cane-farming, Davidson was a staunch advocate of coloured labour, arguing that North Queensland would collapse without Pacific islanders. Increasing restrictions forced him eventually to use mainly Asian coolies. When the government threatened to repeal the Indian Immigration Act of 1882, Davidson and a neighbour, Sir

John Lawes, went to London in 1885, seeking the ear of Lord Derby, the colonial secretary. Davidson's letter to Derby, expressing sympathy for the North Queensland separation movement, was sent to Queensland for comment and was published by Premier Sir Samuel Griffith [q.v.] to discredit the coloured-labour lobby by association with the separation movement. Davidson joined the latter but all subsequent efforts by him and others to disentangle the two issues failed.

Testifying in 1888 to the royal commission on the recession in sugar, Davidson reported four of his company's six estates lying idle; he sought protection to counter bounty-fed beet sugar. The approach of Federation, the impending collapse of the coloured-labour system and the introduction of government-sponsored central mills led to the breaking up of sugar estates. The system of which Davidson had been so much a part was dying. About 1900 he retired to England with his family and died at his Oxford home on 2 September 1923.

At St John's Church of England, Darlinghurst, New South Wales, on 1 August 1878, Davidson had married Amy Constance Ashdown; they had two sons and four daughters.

J. L. Parsons, *The sugar industry in the Mackay district* (Adel, 1883); H. L. Roth, *The discovery and settlement of Port Mackay* . . . (Halifax, 1908); C. A. Bernays, *Queensland politics during sixty years* (Brisb, 1919); G. C. Bolton, *A thousand miles away* (Brisb, 1963); E. W. Docker, *The blackbirders* (Syd, 1970); *V&P* (LA Qld), 1885, 1, 377, 1889, 4, 396; *JRHSQ*, 7 (1961-65), no 3; J. E. Davidson diaries, 1865-68 (copy Colonial Sugar Refining Co. Lib, Syd).   J. A. MILLS

DAVIDSON (CHARLES) MARK ANTHONY (1869-1949), politician, was born on 2 May 1869 in Sydney, seventh child of James Davidson, a tailor from Edinburgh, and his Irish wife Margaret, née Moore. He left school at 12 to be apprenticed to a tailor, but joined his married sister at Coonamble. He worked briefly on coastal ships and then tried various occupations, including shearing and tank-sinking in the Monaro and mining in Victoria and at Broken Hill, New South Wales, before joining his carpenter brother at Cobar. After a short time as a builder's labourer, he worked in the Cobar mines, and lost the sight of an eye in an accident about 1903. He opened a hairdresser's and tobacconist's shop and brought a barber from Sydney to teach him the trade. Known to his friends as 'Charlie', he signed the register as Charles when he married Gertrude May Snape at the Presbyterian church on 14 July 1901.

An original member of the Australian Workers' Union, Davidson helped to form the local branch of the Amalgamated Miners' Association. He was also an alderman on the Cobar Municipal Council in· 1913-18 (and promoted railway extension), a member of the District Hospital board, Racing Club, School of Arts and the Eight-Hour Day Sports committees and of the Political Labor League.

Davidson won a Legislative Assembly by-election for Cobar in May 1918; he represented Sturt in 1920-27, Murray in 1927-30 and Cobar again in 1930-47. One of the 'old brigade', he was proud of his bush-worker background, earnest and forthright in debate, and idealistic about social justice for all sections of the community. He tenaciously kept before the House the disadvantages of isolated settlers in the far west and identified himself with the work of Rev. Stanley G. Drummond [q.v.] and the Far West Children's Health Scheme. A critic of the Western Lands Act and its administration, he tried to prevent leases being aggregated into larger holdings. In 1920 he moved for and chaired a select committee on the decline in the metalliferous industry. He pressed for proper control of dust in mines and for the payment of adequate compensation to victims of silicosis and lead poisoning.

Labor whip in 1923-30, Davidson was secretary for public works in Lang's [q.v.] ministry from November 1930 to May 1932. He was expelled from the Labor Party in August 1936 for attending a proscribed Labor Council of New South Wales unions' conference, but was readmitted next year by the State Labor Conference. In 1936-39 he supported R. J. Heffron's attempts to wrest the leadership from Lang; he had written the *Lang plan catechism* (1931?). In September 1939 he was elected secretary of the parliamentary Labor Party.

Often appalled at living conditions in his large electorate, Davidson saved his most trenchant criticism for the treatment of Aboriginals by government agencies. In 1937, against strong opposition, he chaired a select committee on administration of the Aborigines Protection Board. He remained an outspoken advocate of the need for Aboriginal representation on the board.

Davidson died of cancer on 9 January 1949 in Prince Henry Hospital, Sydney; he was survived by his wife and two daughters. His family refused a state funeral and he was buried in the Catholic section of Northern Suburbs cemetery. His estate was valued for probate at £2939.

M. Maclean, *Drummond of the far west* (Syd, 1947); J. T. Lang, *I remember* (Syd, 1956), and *The*

great bust (Syd, 1962); *PP* (LC & LA NSW), 1920, 3, 719; *Labor Daily*, 1 Feb 1924, 2 June 1927; *Cobar Age*, 14 Jan 1949; *Sun* (Syd), 1 Aug 1949; *Sun-Herald*, 28 May 1954; *Daily Telegraph* (Syd), 4 Apr 1954; *Truth* (Syd), 15 Aug 1954.

J. E. GALLAGHER

DAVIDSON, SIR WALTER EDWARD (1859-1923), governor, was born on 20 April 1859 at Valetta, Malta, son of James Davidson of Killyleagh, County Down, Ireland, principal agent in the Peninsular and Oriental Steam Navigation Co., and his wife Sarah, née Humfrey. After education at Magdalen College School, Oxford, he kept three terms at Christ's College, University of Cambridge. In 1880 he entered the Ceylon civil service as a writer. By 1898 he had risen to be chairman of the municipal council and mayor of Colombo, where in 1882 he had married Lillie Harriet Baber. At the Paris exhibition in 1900 he was Ceylon's commissioner and in 1902 was appointed C.B.E. He was colonial secretary in Transvaal, South Africa, in 1902-04, governor of Seychelles Islands in 1904-12, and of Newfoundland in 1913-16. In 1907 he had married Margaret Agnes Fielding in London. His long colonial service was rewarded in 1914 by his appointment as K.C.M.G., and in September 1917 he succeeded Sir Gerald Strickland [q.v.] as governor of New South Wales.

On his arrival in Sydney with his family on 17 February 1918, he was described as over 6 ft. (180 cm) tall, carrying 'an almost pronounced military air'. Despite a reduction by Premier Holman [q.v.] in the governor's allowances, the Davidsons entered enthusiastically into the round of gubernatorial duties, with speeches, official openings and vice-regal functions. For her work with the Red Cross Society, both in Newfoundland and Sydney, Lady Davidson was appointed D.B.E. in 1918. In August 1920 she presided at a meeting to inaugurate the State branch of the Girl Guides' Association. After the war they also had to dedicate numerous war memorials.

In January 1921 Labor premier John Storey [q.v.] sought Davidson's views on the question of additional appointments to the Legislative Council. Though he was then of the opinion that the Upper House ought not to be increased, in August he approved of Storey's nomination of sixteen new members. The refusal by Davidson of a request for a dissolution from Storey's successor James Dooley [q.v.] in December 1921 aroused only token Labor Party objections. On Dooley's advice, Davidson then commissioned Sir George Fuller [q.v.], but the ministry lasted only seven hours. Davidson then refused Fuller's request for a dissolution and re-commissioned Dooley, who subsequently was granted a dissolution. This series of events testified to the governor's impeccable constitutional instinct and political impartiality. Upon Dooley's defeat in the March elections, Davidson wrote to the secretary of state, W. S. Churchill, of his 'Labour friends: they were likeable men, upright and simple, and not ashamed to take advice'. But he liked 'the new lot also: most of them. They are less easily guided'. In September 1922 it was announced that his term of office would be extended until March 1924.

Davidson was influential in organizing the exhibition by Australian artists which was shown at the Royal Academy, Burlington House, London, in October 1923. He was a knight of grace of St John of Jerusalem and a member of the Savile Club, London. He published two books on Ceylon and one on the archives of the Seychelles. While still in office, Davidson died of cardiovascular disease at Government House of 16 September 1923, survived by his wife, one son of his first marriage and two daughters of his second. After a solemn lying-in-state at St Andrew's Anglican Cathedral and an elaborate funeral, he was buried in South Head cemetery, where in 1925 a memorial was erected by public subscription. His portrait was painted by Norman Carter [q.v.7]. Lady Davidson Hospital, Turramurra, commemorates his wife.

SMH, 13 Sept 1917, 16, 18 Feb 1918, 14, 17 Dec 1921, 4 Jan 1922, 17 Sept 1923; *T&CJ*, 19 Sept 1917; *The Times*, 17 Sept 1923; CO 418/168, 208/9818, 5380, 220/27440.   CHRIS CUNNEEN

DAVIDSON, WILLIAM (1844-1920), civil engineer, was born on 6 December 1844 in the village of Moy, County Tyrone, Ireland, son of John Davidson, architect, and his wife Eliza, née McCudden. He was educated at the local National school, which he left when 13: he was described as 'a keen bright boy . . . with a receptive mind, and plenty of push'. After a few months as a clerk in Belfast, he displayed his initiative by working his passage from Liverpool to Melbourne, where he arrived in 1859, walking to Ballarat, and presenting himself to his uncle Robert Davidson, a mining surveyor.

The boy was found work as a 'useful' to a survey party. Before long he was a chainman: when surveying was slack he took to jackerooing or splitting. In 1864 he gained his surveyor's certificate. During the next few years he surveyed underground workings, farming selections, and routes for municipal roads, gaining an intimate knowledge of both north-west Victoria and Gippsland.

In April 1873 the superintending engineer of the Melbourne water supply, Charles Taylor, appointed Davidson as his assistant. When Taylor was dismissed without notice by Graham Berry [q.v.3] in January 1878, Davidson was left in charge. The Melbourne water came from the foothills of the Dividing Range and was carried from the Yan Yean reservoir by aqueduct to a service reservoir at Preston. On 16 March 1878 a major flood destroyed most of the bridge which carried the aqueduct over the Plenty River, and washed out much of the embankment. Davidson saw that the only quick way to restore the supply was to span the gap with a wooden flume on timber supports. Work continued for three days and nights without a halt under his personal supervision, while Melbourne was obliged to cart water from the Yarra. A few weeks later the minister of public works, (Sir) James Patterson [q.v.5] appointed him superintending engineer 'for the outstanding part he had played in expediting repairs and restoring water to Melbourne in three days'.

Demands on the Yan Yean system continued to increase in the 1880s. Davidson extended the catchment in 1883-84 by constructing an aqueduct from Wallaby Creek, in the Goulburn watershed, over a saddle in the Dividing Range, and building the Touroorong Reservoir to regulate the yield. He did the same with Silvery Creek in 1886. The Yan Yean catchment was now fully exploited, and Davidson turned to the Watts River, building a diversion weir and 42 miles (70 km) of aqueduct to Preston. He made sure that all alienated land in the new catchment was resumed and all buildings removed. His forethought extended to planning for a future Maroondah reservoir; and to persuading the government to reserve 115 000 acres (47 000 ha) of the Upper Yarra watershed for Melbourne's future needs. Davidson knew the positions of his mains in Melbourne so intimately that he was sometimes called in to advise the fire brigades where they could obtain the best pressure.

In 1889 Davidson succeeded W. H. Steel as inspector-general of public works and chief engineer of the Melbourne water supply. On 30 June 1891 the latter was transferred to the newly established Melbourne and Metropolitan Board of Works: Davidson perforce severed his long-standing connexion with Yan Yean and Maroondah. He was now in charge of works all over Victoria, including many on the seaboard. During his period of office the Warrnambool breakwater, the Lakes Entrance works and the Portland harbour were built. As the superior officer of

Carlo Catani [q.v.7] he allowed that imaginative man his head. Davidson had much office work to do, but inspected works in the field when he could. 'The weary train journeys do not worry him if there is a good horse to be mounted at his destination'. His influence with the government was seen in 1910 when the O'Shannassy water-supply scheme was approved and the Maroondah reservoir deferred. His last important undertaking was a visit to England to consult Coode [q.v.3] Son & Matthews on plans for Melbourne's harbour: this led to the construction of Station Pier at Port Melbourne.

Davidson was awarded the I.S.O. in 1911 and retired from the public service next year. He continued his ties with the engineering profession: on 4 December 1888 he had been elected to membership of the Institution of Civil Engineers (London), and in 1914-19 was chairman of its Victorian branch. He was lunching with old friends when he collapsed and died of a heart attack on 2 September 1920. He was survived by his wife Elizabeth, née Cherry, whom he had married on 3 January 1874 at St John's Church, Ballarat, and by a son and three daughters.

Davidson was widely and favourably known, a leading member of the Yorick Club, and (rare distinction) an honorary life member of the Victoria Racing Club. He was conscious of his unorthodox route to senior office: 'A man could not do in England what I have done in Victoria. I have learnt my profession by degrees, and I have been paid for learning it'. There can be no doubt of his personal qualities: he was considered 'an ideal public servant, efficient, conscientious and extremely trustworthy'.

Inst of Engineers, Aust, *J,* 6 (1934); *Living City,* 19 (1976); *Australasian,* 28 Feb 1891, 4 Dec 1897; *Punch* (Melb), 1 June 1905; *Age,* and *Argus,* 3 Sept 1920.   RONALD McNICOLL

DAVIDSON, WILLIAM ST JOHN STEVENS (1870-1945), dentist and soldier, was born on 25 June 1870 at Huntly, Victoria, son of William David Baird Davidson, police constable, and his wife Matilda, née Furlonge, both of whom were Mauritian-born. Educated at St Joseph's College, Richmond, he was registered as a dentist on 25 September 1891, and after practising in West Brunswick moved to Warrnambool in the early 1890s. On 4 August 1897 at St Francis Catholic Church, Melbourne, he married Edith Annie Murray Fagan. By 1904 he had established a large practice in Victoria's western district. He was described as 'an ardent supporter of all branches of amateur sport' and a member of the Warr-

nambool hunt, cricket and bowling clubs.

On 1 March 1895 Davidson was commissioned lieutenant in the Victorian Mounted Rifles (the 11th Australian Light Horse from 1903) and in August 1904 he transferred to the Australian Field Artillery. Promoted captain in 1907 and major in 1912, he commanded the Warrnambool battery in 1905-15. He joined the Australian Imperial Force on 20 October 1915 as a major and officer commanding the 10th Battery, 4th A.F.A. Brigade, and on reaching Egypt was also temporary brigade commander for several months. He was promoted lieut-colonel on 1 March 1916 and appointed commanding officer of the 2nd Divisional Ammunition Column. At this time the Australian artillery was being reorganized to provide artillery components for the 4th and 5th Divisions and before leaving for France on 20 March Davidson, from a nucleus of four artillery officers and about ten other ranks, formed a new D.A.C. out of Light Horse details. On 8 April, in France, he commanded the 22nd Howitzer Brigade then, when the howitzer batteries were absorbed into the field artillery brigades, was appointed commander of the 22nd A.F.A. Brigade.

On 4 June Davidson returned to the 2nd D.A.C. as commanding officer, and in July-August served at Poziéres. He commanded the column in operations at Bapaume in March 1917 and was mentioned in dispatches. The divisional artillery served with distinction at Noreuil, left the Somme early in July and was allotted to the Fifth Army's southern division for the Ypres offensive. As C. E. W. Bean [q.v.7] noted, conditions at Ypres strained the endurance of the Australian artillerymen, with the enemy's 'crash' bombardments and shelling with mustard gas causing high casualties. In August-September Davidson's unit was posted to Hill 60. The battery positions suffered severely but in this 'morass of a battlefield' the supply services also bore a heavy share of the strain as they worked day and night bringing ammunition across the mud through 'nightmare barrages'. When the Australian divisional artilleries left his army in September General Gough wrote that they had 'earned the admiration and praise of all'. Later that year Davidson commanded the 2nd D.A.C. at Passchendaele; he was mentioned in dispatches in December and awarded the Distinguished Service Order in January 1918. He retained command of the 2nd D.A.C. until April when he left for Australia.

After the war, Davidson, who had been awarded the Volunteer Officers' Decoration in 1917, served with the Australian Military Forces until 1930, when he was placed on the retired list with the rank of colonel. He had returned to Warrnambool after demobilization and continued in dental practice there until his death on 5 March 1945. He was buried in the local Catholic cemetery.

J. Smith (ed), *Cyclopedia of Victoria*, 2 (Melb, 1904); C. E. W. Bean, *The A.I.F. in France*, 1916-18 (Syd, 1929, 1933, 1937, 1942); *Warrnambool Standard*, 6, 9 Mar 1945; personal records file (AWM).   MERRILYN LINCOLN

DAVIES, DAVID (1864-1939), artist, was born on 21 May 1864 at Ballarat, Victoria, son of Thomas Davies, miner, and his wife Mary, née Harris. His parents were both from South Wales; David was one of six children. As a boy he attended both Redan and Sebastopol state schools and later art classes at the Ballarat School of Mines and Industries. He worked for a short time for a jeweller in Bridge Street, Ballarat, and then in 1887-90 studied at the National Gallery School, Melbourne, under G. F. Folingsby [q.v.4]. In 1885 he became a member of the Buonarotti Club whose members included E. Phillips Fox, Frederick McCubbin and Tom Roberts [qq.v.]. In the late 1880s he and Roberts, Conder [q.v.3], Streeton, Walter Withers [qq.v.] and others frequently painted at Eaglemont, near Heidelberg, at a property owned by Charles Davies, the brother of Davies's future wife. One of his best-known paintings from this period, 'The Burden and Heat of the Day', was subsequently purchased by the Ballarat Fine Art Gallery.

In 1890 Davies left Australia to study in Paris at the Académie Julian under Jean-Paul Laurens. He took a studio flat at 2 Rue d'Odessa and on 18 December 1891 at the British consulate he married fellow student Janet Sophia Davies; Rupert Bunny [q.v.7] and Aby Altson were the witnesses. Soon after their marriage Davies and his wife went to live at St Ives, Cornwall, England, which was already popular with such expatriate Australians as Phillips Fox, Edmund Wyly Grier and the latter's brother Louis. The predominant style at St Ives was that of Whistlerian softness and emphasis on the atmospheric effects of light and mood. It was a style that had enormous appeal for Davies and on his return to Australia in 1893 he began painting romantic impressions of the landscape in the late afternoon and evening light. Davies and his wife settled at Templestowe, Victoria; a daughter was born there, but died a few months later. 'Moonrise', a painting from this period, was purchased by the National Gallery of Victoria; J. S. MacDonald [q.v.] in his small book on Davies described it as 'unique in the beauty of its presentation of all those difficult, elusive components that make up the theme'. Early in 1896, shortly after the birth of a second daughter, the family moved to Cheltenham, Victoria.

In 1897 they returned to England, settling again at St Ives. Next year Davies moved to nearby Lelant Down and over the next few years exhibiting at the New English Art Club, the Royal Academy and the Ridley Art Club. After the birth of a son in January 1900 the family moved along the coast to Carbis Bay, then to Newquay and Tintagel and finally to Wales.

In 1908, probably in an attempt to improve his health, Davies and his family went to live in Dieppe, France, where Janet taught English at a girls' school. At the outbreak of World War I they returned to live in London but afterwards settled again at Dieppe. Davies continued to send paintings to England for exhibition. He left Dieppe from time to time to paint with his friend and sponsor Richard Heyworth in the Cheltenham (England) area and particularly from Heyworth's studio at Sennybridge in the Brecon Beacons in Wales. His paintings from this period were mainly French village scenes and landscapes.

In May 1926 an exhibition of 21 oils and 52 water-colours, mainly French landscapes, was held at the Fine Art Society's galleries, Melbourne. It seems to have been his only one-man exhibition in Australia during his lifetime and was a great success, although he probably never received payment for works sold. In 1932 Davies and his family settled at Looe, Cornwall, and a large exhibition of his work was shown at the Plymouth City Art Gallery.

Davies died at Looe on 26 March 1939 of cardio-vascular degeneration. Five days later his wife Janet died of pneumonia. They were survived by their son and daughter.

J. MacDonald, *The art and life of David Davies* (Melb, 1920); A. A. Cowden, *David Davies, the expatriate period* (Lond, 1978); *Age*, 13 May 1926; *Argus*, 13 May 1926, 10 Aug 1929, camera supp; David Davies papers (LATL).   CANDICE BRUCE

DAVIES, EDWARD HAROLD (1867-1947), musician and music teacher, was born on 18 July 1867 at Oswestry, Shropshire, England, fourth son of John Whitridge Davies, accountant and amateur musician, and his wife Susan, née Gregory. (Sir) H. Walford Davies was his brother. Harold attended Oswestry Grammar School and was then apprenticed in architecture, at the same time studying music with Joseph Bridge at Chester Cathedral. In 1886 he arrived at Kapunda, South Australia, and next year moved to Gawler; he formed musical societies in both towns. He was in England in 1890 where he became an associate of the Royal College of Organists and was organist and choirmaster at the Chapel Royal, Windsor Park. On 26 September 1893 at Gawler he married Ina Jane Deland; they had two daughters and three sons. Davies continued studying at the University of Adelaide (B.Mus., 1896; D.Mus., 1902, the first to be conferred by an Australian university). His examiner found him an enthusiastic musician of the classical school but with broad sympathies in the direction of modern romanticism'.

In 1902 Davies founded, and for twenty years conducted, the Adelaide Bach Society; as organist and choirmaster, he spent twenty years at Kent Town Methodist Church; he taught piano, organ, singing and composition both privately and at the Methodist Ladies College in 1910-19. He promoted music, through the newspapers and later by radio, speaking on such diverse topics as 'Art and materialism', 'Aborigine: a natural musician', and 'System of secondary education – does it produce real culture?'.

Davies was appointed director of the Elder [q.v.4] Conservatorium of Music and Elder professor of music in 1919 and served twenty-eight years as dean of the faculty of music. In 1920 he founded and conducted the South Australian Orchestra and played a major role in both founding and examining for the Australian Music Examinations Board. The fine staff he attracted to the conservatorium established a firm basis for the discipline of music in the State. The faculty of music recorded that he was 'an inspiration and a stimulus to students and professionals alike . . . And above all he . . . exemplified . . . to a high degree the place of music in the art of living'. He was elected a Fellow of the Royal College of Music, London, in 1931.

An interest in Aboriginal music, aroused by T. D. Campbell, led to Davies accompanying members of the university's Board of Anthropological Research on four expeditions to Central and outback South Australia in 1926-30. He was among the pioneering researchers who recorded Aboriginal song (his wax cylinders are in the South Australian Museum). Early publications on this research were 'Palaeolithic music' (*Musical Times* Vol 18, 1927) and an article in the 1927 *Transactions of the Royal Society of South Australia*. The recordings were described by the board as 'probably the most successful attempt so far in this line of research'.

He is remembered as a person deeply interested in aesthetic values and in perfection and use of sound, widely read, sometimes intolerant, and retiring by nature; but once

understood, his colleagues and students found him generous and helpful. He sought to reproduce the English musical scene of his background. Davies was forward looking and ahead of his time in many respects, but some considered that he stayed in the chair too long. He did not retire but died of a heart attack on 1 July 1947, and was cremated.

C. J. Ellis, *Aboriginal music making: a study of Central Australian music* (Adel, 1964); A. M. Moyle, *Handlist of collections of recorded music in Australia and the Torres Strait . . .* (Canb, 1966); V. A. Edgeloe, *University children of the 1880's: law, medicine, music* (Adel, 1978, copy Univ Adel); *Music* (Adel), Jan 1897; *Critic* (Adel), 20 Dec 1902; *Aust Letters,* Mar 1960; *Miscellanea, Musicologica,* 8 (1975); *Mail* (Adel), 23 Aug 1913; *Observer* (Adel), 23 June 1923; *Chronicle* (Adel), 23 July 1931; *Advertiser* (Adel), 2 July 1947.

CATHERINE J. ELLIS

DAVIES, SIR JOHN GEORGE (1846-1913) and his brother CHARLES ELLIS (1847-1921), newspaper proprietors and politicians, were sons of John Davies [q.v.4], founder of the Hobart *Mercury,* and his wife Elizabeth, née Ellis. John George (George) was born on 17 February 1846 at Melbourne, and Charles Ellis on 13 May 1847 at Wellington, New South Wales. George was educated at the Melbourne Church of England Grammar School and The Hutchins and High schools, Hobart, before entering his father's newspaper business as office-boy. He was, however, trained as a journalist and advanced through the ranks to become general manager, though he later relinquished this position in favour of his brother. Charles was also educated at The Hutchins and High schools, graduating associate of Arts in 1865 under the Tasmanian Council of Education's tertiary scheme. He was employed by the Victorian Railways as an engineer in 1866-69 when he too joined the *Mercury* to be trained for management.

The brothers took over the *Mercury* in 1871, eight months before their father died. During their proprietorship the business, which became a limited company in 1895, firmly established itself as the colony's dominant newspaper and printing works. It retained a conservative attitude but its new owners, by continually expanding and modernizing, placed the *Mercury* in an unchallengeable position. The weekly *Tasmanian Mail* was begun during their term of management in 1877.

Charles, as managing director, was effectively in charge of Davies Bros Ltd; George devoted much of his time to public affairs. He was an organizer of the 1883 Juvenile Industrial Exhibition in Hobart and a justice of the peace. Elected an alderman of the Hobart City Council in 1884, he served six terms as mayor before his retirement in 1901. He was in charge of the Tasmanian industrial court at the Melbourne Centennial Exhibition of 1888, and was honorary commissioner for Tasmania at the 1889 Paris Exhibition. Chief magistrate of Hobart in the 1890s, he was appointed first chairman of the Metropolitan Drainage Board in 1899 and was also for many years chairman of the Public Cemetery Trust and of the Hobart Licensing Bench.

Member for Fingal in the House of Assembly from 1884, George Davies was a successful candidate in the newly formed division of Denison in 1909. He had always been politically conservative, having in 1887, for example, opposed changes to the outdated Master and Servant Act (1856). He later joined the Liberal Party, but was never comfortable as a party member. This attitude, strengthened by his newspaper interest and his sensitivity to accusations of bias, caused him to reject the option of entering government. He was, however, chairman of committees from 1892 and Speaker in 1903-13, guiding the assembly through the inevitable dislocation of the new Federal system and of continually fluctuating party alliances. He was appointed C.M.G. in 1901 and was knighted in 1909.

George also had a distinguished career in the local defence forces and as a sportsman. When 17 he joined the Hobart Town Volunteer Rifles; he was made a captain in the Tasmanian Rifle Regiment in 1860 and retired as lieut-colonel in 1891. A fine marksman, captaining the Australian team which won the Kolapore Cup at Bisley, England, in 1902, he was an office-holder in both Tasmanian and national rifle associations during the 1890s and early 1900s. A 'crack bat', he eventually captained Tasmanian cricket teams touring other Australian colonies and New Zealand in 1866-88. He was a founder of the Southern Tasmanian Cricket Association and was largely responsible for the establishment of Tasmania's cricketing headquarters on the Queen's Domain. He wrote cricket articles for the *Tasmanian Mail* under the pseudonym 'Nat Lee'. He was also a football administrator and, as an owner, took a strong interest in horse-racing.

Charles Davies's interests were only slightly less extensive than his brother's. Newspapers, Freemasonry and politics dominated his life — probably in that order — but the theatre (he was co-owner of Hobart's Theatre Royal in the 1890s), agriculture (he helped form the Southern Tasmanian Agricultural and Pastoral Society in 1874 and was its secretary for twenty years),

sport, and horse-ownership and racing administration (he died while travelling to the Launceston Cup in 1921) also attracted his attention. As chief executive of the State's biggest newspaper, he was Tasmanian representative at the Imperial Press Conferences in London (1908) and Ottawa (1920). His twenty-three-year political career began in 1897 with his election to the Legislative Council seat of Cambridge. Strictly independent and, like his brother, refusing to represent any government for fear of conflict with his newspaper proprietorship, he was sometimes called the 'uncrowned King' of Tasmania.

Their Jewish ancestry notwithstanding, both brothers were Freemasons. Their dominance of the Grand Lodge of Tasmania (George, deputy grand master in 1896-1914, was made past grand master in 1910; Charles was grand master in 1896-1914 and 1917-21) was intimately involved with their business and political success and their achievement of a social status sought, but never realized, by their emancipist father. They were both elected members of the Royal Society of Tasmania in 1884.

Both brothers married twice. George, on 27 January 1869 at St John's Church of England, New Town, married Sarah Ann Pearce (d. 1888): they had seven children. His marriage to Constance Charlotte, sister of W. R. Giblin [q.v.4], on 19 November 1891 at New Town produced two sons. Charles married Sophia Margaretta Wilson on 16 March 1870, at the Brunswick Street Wesleyan Church, Fitzroy, Melbourne, and second, on 24 March 1909 with Anglo-Catholic rites, at Evandale, Nellie Grace Collins, by whom he had a son and daughter.

Sir George Davies died of kidney disease on 12 November 1913 at New Town, leaving an estate valued for probate at £23 419. The *Mercury* editorialized: 'He was in no sense a decorative man, but in place of brilliant talents he had solid capacity, the outlook on life of a plain and moderate man, good judgement, and a very genuine desire to give service to his country and his fellow-citizens'. Charles died on 1 February 1921 at Pontville. Both as managing director of the *Mercury* and as a politician he had been conservative and pragmatic, exercising throughout his career, according to his obituary, caution and common sense. His estate was valued for probate at £52 480. The brothers were buried in Cornelian Bay cemetery. Sir George's youngest son from his first marriage, Charles Reginald (1883-1925), having become secretary of Davies Bros Ltd in 1914, took over in 1921 as chairman of directors.

Cyclopedia of Tasmania, 1 (Hob, 1900); *History of*

Freemasonry in Tasmania (Launc, 1935); R. Page, *A history of Tasmanian cricket* (Hob, 1957); P. Bolger, *Hobart Town* (Canb, 1973); *Mercury Centenary Mag*, 5 July 1954; *PTHRA*, Sept 1979, p 85; *Mercury*, 13 Nov 1913, 2 Feb 1921; *Table Talk*, 12 June 1902.
PETER BOYER

DAVIES, WILLIAM (1882?-1956), politician, was born in Abertillery, Wales, son of William Davies, coalminer, and his wife Mary, née Williams. At 12 he was a trapper in coal-mines. From night school he won a miners' scholarship to a summer school at the University of Oxford. He became a Methodist lay preacher, and on 4 August 1903 at the Register Office, Bedwellty, Monmouthshire, he married Edith Hartshorn. They came to New South Wales in 1912 and, after working as a labourer, Davies became a miner in the Wollongong area. He soon became an official for the Illawarra district of the Australasian Coal and Shale Employees' (Miners') Federation.

In the election for the Legislative Assembly on 24 March 1917 he won the seat of Wollongong for the Labor Party, defeating J. B. Nicholson [q.v.], the sitting Nationalist, who had been expelled from the party in 1916 over conscription. Davies was to retain his seat, variously named, for the next thirty-two years, and to dominate Labor politics in the area for nearly forty. In 1920 he told J. L. Campbell [q.v.7], sole royal commissioner into the coal-mining industry and the coal trade, that 'stoppages were rare in individual mines in Wales', and that 'more discipline was exercised there by the unions'.

A loyal supporter of J. T. Lang [q.v.], Davies was minister for public instruction in Lang's second ministry from May to October 1927, and retained the education portfolio in his 1930-32 government; in 1931 he said he preferred economics to Latin in schools. He was careful to maintain good relations with the Teachers' Federation; dismissal of married women teachers on the permanent staff, though mooted, was not carried out, despite the financial difficulties. In local internal Labor political machinations, he was Lang's agent in attempts to dampen criticism by purging the branches of radicals.

In October 1949 Davies resigned his seat in State parliament to contest the Federal elections for the seat of Cunningham, which he held until his death. Survived by his wife, son and daughter, he died on 17 February 1956 and was cremated after a Methodist service. His estate was sworn for probate at £1494. H. V. Evatt remembered him as 'a great orator who had helped to inspire coalminers during industrial troubles'.

B. A. Mitchell, *Teachers, education, and politics* (Brisb, 1975); H. Radi and P. Spearritt (eds), *Jack Lang* (Syd, 1977); *SMH*, 22 Feb 1956.

DAVIS, ARTHUR HOEY (1868-1935), writer, was born on 14 November 1868 at Drayton, Queensland, fifth son and eighth of thirteen children of Thomas Davis, Welsh blacksmith and selector, and his Irish wife Mary, née Green. Leaving the Emu Creek school at 12, Davis began work on local properties and developed his love of horses. He became a clerk in the office of the curator of intestate estates in Brisbane in 1885, and in 1889 was transferred to the sheriff's office in the Supreme Court. In 1893 he was appointed secretary of a treasury committee investigating the Queensland National Bank. During this time he shared lodgings with Cecil Boland, who introduced him to the works of Scott, Thackeray, and Dickens [q.v.4] – later his favourite. On 26 December 1894 Davis married Violet Christina Brodie at Greenmount; they had three sons and a daughter.

Davis had written skits about rowing, which he enjoyed, for the Brisbane *Chronicle* signed 'Steele Rudder' (from essayist Richard Steele and the part of a boat). This was later shortened to 'Steele Rudd'. His first rural sketch, 'Starting the selection', based on his father's experience, appeared in the *Bulletin* on 14 December 1895. Davis became a regular and popular contributor and in 1899 the *Bulletin* published an illustrated collection of the sketches under the title *On our selection*. This was followed by *Our new selection* in 1903. Their success was partly due to the suggestion of A. G. Stephens [q.v.] that the sketches, written originally about different families, be reconstructed as the experiences of the Rudd family.

Promoted to under-sheriff in 1902, Davis had to give the signal at the hanging of Patrick Kenniff [q.v.]; subsequently opposed to capital punishment, he was nervous and irritable for months after the execution, and described the occasion in *The miserable clerk* (1926). In January 1904 Davis lost his post under (Sir Arthur) Morgan's [q.v.] Special Retrenchment Act. Despite convincing official reasons, he believed that his seniors had been jealous of his success ever since the *Bulletin* revealed 'Steele Rudd's' identity in 1897.

Violet Davis, who valued the security of a weekly wage, was aghast when he refused inferior public service employment and formed a company to produce *Steele Rudd's Magazine*; it ran from December 1903 to 1907. Davis began to drink socially to promote circulation and advertising and moved his family to Sydney. Violet's disapproval brought recriminations and discord when the family returned to Brisbane after the magazine collapsed. This marked the start of her serious nervous breakdown.

In 1909 Davis reluctantly bought a farm at Nobby, Queensland, on his wife's insistence. The rights to a stage version of *On our selection* were leased to Bert Bailey [q.v.7]; it was first produced by his company on 4 May 1912 at the Palace Theatre, Sydney. Though it did well in Australia, it failed in London in 1920. Davis remained dissatisfied with Bailey's meagre royalty payments.

Davis became president of the Darling Downs Polo Association in 1913. Chairman of the Cambooya Shire Council in 1914-15, he chaired the local recruiting committee in World War I. The deterioration of his wife's health when their son Gower was wounded on the Somme forced the family to return to Brisbane in 1917 so that she could receive special medical attention. In the same year the play *Grandad Rudd* was produced, and Davis revived his magazine as *Steele Rudd's Annual* (1917-23). By 1919 Violet Davis had broken down completely and was permanently hospitalized. Her affairs were placed in the hands of the public curator and she remained in care until her death at Toowoomba in 1952. The loss of assets made over to her further damaged his finances.

In 1921, Davis became vice-president of the new Queensland Authors' and Artists' Association, and acted as steward in the equestrian section of the Royal National Agricultural and Industrial Association's exhibition in 1920-24. He toured with a print of Raymond Longford's [q.v.] film version of *On our selection* in 1922. Living in a Brisbane hotel in 1923, Davis formed a close friendship with Winifred Cook who had reverted to her maiden name of Hamilton. She became sub-editor of his magazine which, under the name *Steele Rudd's*, was a monthly in 1924-25. With the venture faring badly, Davis moved to Sydney in 1926 to be joined by Winifred Hamilton a few months later. In 1926-27 the magazine became *Steele Rudd's and the Shop Assistants' Magazine*, but Davis continued to live in hardship.

The Depression brought further financial setbacks through the failure of the film version of *The romance of Runnibede* and the bankruptcy of the producer of the stage version of *The Rudd family*. Steele Rudd Productions Pty Ltd, which published the magazine, was in difficulties too. Davis was in dire straits when the *Bulletin* rescued him. A benefit performance on his behalf and a Commonwealth Literary Fund pension from October 1930 also helped.

Winifred Hamilton became engaged to another man in 1932, and Davis took lodgings with Mrs Beatrice Sharp, whom he had met in 1931. In 1933 he was divorced and next year became engaged to Beatrice Sharp, but they never married. Davis was awarded the King's silver jubilee medal in May 1935. He died in the Brisbane General Hospital on 11 October 1935 of cancer, and was buried in Toowong cemetery with Presbyterian forms. His estate was valued for probate at £501.

Davis wrote twenty-four books and six plays and saw three silent and four sound-film adaptations of his work. His early books were his best, providing a wry, sympathetic account of the demanding life of the selector and offering a rounded portrait of Dad Rudd. The work of his middle period was repetitive and stale, with Dad Rudd becoming increasingly farcical. Though Davis was undoubtedly exploiting the character for money by this time, he was also responding to its stage and media metamorphosis. The stage Dad was a less earthy character, and on screen and radio he lost all homespun stolidity and became the grumpy, lovable buffoon of today. At the end of his career, Davis turned to more personal subjects and once more produced work of higher quality. Though he is typically seen as a skilful hack-writer, Davis is better described as a would-be artist who failed. A portrait by Joseph Wolinski is held by the Queensland Art Gallery, and the premier of Queensland unveiled a memorial stone over the grave in 1956.

E. D. Davis, *The life and times of Steele Rudd* (Melb, 1976); A. H. Davis papers, MS 4591 (NL).

VAN IKIN

DAVIS, CHARLES (1824?-1914), businessman, was born in London, son of Thomas Davis, carriage-lamp maker, and his wife Ann, née Young. His name is familiar from the large retail store in Hobart. He showed an early interest in shops by robbing a till in 1840, and on 5 April 1841, at the London Central Criminal Court, he was sentenced to ten years transportation for a second offence, larceny from the person, nominally the theft of a silk handkerchief. Aften ten months in the hulks he sailed for Hobart aboard the *Candahar*, arriving in July 1842. Set to work at Bridgewater and Oyster Cove as a tinsmith, he received his ticket-of-leave in September 1847 and established a small tin and copper-smithing enterprise in a Bathurst Street shed. In October 1848, having 'only three records of a trifling nature . . . made against him', Davis was recommended for the conditional pardon he received in December next year. After a try at Victoria's gold in 1851-52, he returned to his Hobart business.

Davis's rise to prosperity as a hardware merchant was reflected in his private life. The first of his five wives, Emma Hurst, whom he married on 11 September 1848 at St John's Presbyterian Church, was the 16-year-old daughter of a Cambridgeshire horse-stealer. Before her death in 1867 he entered the Memorial Congregation, becoming a respected deacon (1888-91, 1892-95) and representative at Congregational Unions (1894-97). He married Emma Cheshire Bolter, an emancipist's daughter, on 3 April 1868 at the Upper Murray Street Congregationalist Church. Emma died in December that year and on 20 January 1870 Davis married her sister Kezia Cheshire.

Davis flourished in the boom of the 1880s, with the metal-mending and manufacturing workshop becoming augmented by an importing and distributing enterprise. His dissimilar sons, half-brothers Charles junior (b. 1865) and Alfred (b. 1873), entered the business and eventually replaced Davis in responsibility for the running of the two sections. Kezia's death in 1883 brought Davis to wed middle-class, free immigrant, widowed schoolteacher Sarah Anne Blackmore on 31 July 1884. Twelve years later she died and on 28 March 1899 he married Mary Ann Harby, née Morly, widow of a master mariner.

In 1911 Davis's business was floated as a company with Charles junior and Alfred as managers, but the senile Charles senior, small and tattooed, continued to attend the store daily until his death on 21 April 1914. Survived by his fifth wife and his two sons and six daughters, he was buried in Cornelian Bay cemetery after a well-attended funeral at the Holy Trinity Anglican Church. In 1905 Davis had donated the rent of a Murray Street site to the Young Men's Christian Association and gave £1000 to the building fund. But tales of his alms-giving are largely apocryphal: his estate, valued for probate at £69530, was, apart from the Young Men's Christian Association site, divided amongst the clan he had founded.

Cyclopedia of Tasmania 1 (Hob, 1900); P. Bolger, *Hobart Town* (Canb, 1973); *Hobart Town Gazette*, 14 Sept 1847, 3 Dec 1849, 21 Oct 1851; *Mercury*, 11 Dec 1867, 22 Apr 1914; *Daily Post* (Hob), 23, 24 Apr 1914; *Aust Worker*, 30 Apr 1914; Congregational Memorial Church records, NS 477/2-4, 8, 9 (TA).

PETER BOLGER

DAVIS, CHARLES HERBERT (1872-1923), soldier and lawyer, was born on 4 June 1872 at Kilmore, Victoria, third son of William Davis, London-born bank manager, and his wife Ellen Mary Josephine, née Hayes, from Ireland. The family moved to Sandhurst (Bendigo) when Davis was 3 and he was educated at St Andrew's College and Bendigo Grammar School. Articled to a Bendigo lawyer in 1889, he attended the University of Melbourne's articled clerks' course in 1890-92 and was admitted to practice in 1895.

Davis was commissioned in the 4th Battalion of Infantry, Victorian Defence Forces, in 1896, and was promoted captain in 1900. At short notice he commanded the guard of honour at the opening of the first Commonwealth parliament in Melbourne in 1901. In 1904 he was promoted major in the 8th Australian Infantry Regiment which in 1908 formed two battalions; as lieut-colonel in 1910, Davis commanded the 2nd Battalion at Bendigo.

With the reorganization of the forces in 1912 Davis became officer commanding the 67th Infantry, later the 67th (Bendigo) Infantry, until transferred to the unattached list in 1913. On the outbreak of war in 1914 he was appointed senior assistant censor, and then censor (cables) and censor (Melbourne) until transferred to temporary command of the 17th Infantry Brigade in 1915. In February 1916 he joined the Australian Imperial Force and was appointed commanding officer of the 38th Battalion. It arrived in England in August and after training reached France in November, experiencing its first action in the Armentières sector in December. In recognition of his command of large raiding parties, including the most important ever undertaken by Australians on the Western Front — at Houplines on 27 February 1917 — he was awarded the Distinguished Service Order (4 June). His battalion also saw service at Ploegsteert Wood, Messines (June 1917), Ypres and Passchendaele (October), with subsequent holding of the line at the Douve River, Amiens (April 1918) and the Ancre River.

In 1917 and 1918 Davis had temporary command of the 10th Brigade several times before transferring on 18 June as colonel to take charge of the Australian General Base Depot, which was established to facilitate movement of almost 100 000 Australian troops to England for repatriation to Australia. Davis was also commandant of Australian Base Depots, France, until January 1919; he retained command of Australian Base Depots (Le Havre) until July when the depots were closed. He was thrice mentioned in dispatches and was appointed C.B.E. in June 1919. After service in London he returned to Australia in October. His appointment in the A.I.F. was terminated in November although he remained on the reserve of officers.

Described as deliberative, calm and invariably courteous, in civilian life Davis was a leading Bendigo lawyer and citizen. He was secretary of the city's art gallery (1897-1914, 1920), and of the Benevolent Society. Interested in literature and music, he wrote verse, was a talented pianist, and composed for piano and voice.

Davis had married Emily Beatrice Deloitte at St John's Anglican Church, Balmain, Sydney, on 25 April 1907. In 1920 he moved to Sydney where he worked as a representative of a Victorian firm until his sudden death on 11 January 1923 from a perforated ulcer of the bowel. He was buried in the Anglican section of Northern Suburbs cemetery. His wife, two sons and a daughter survived him.

E. Fairey, *The 38th Battalion, A.I.F.* (Bendigo, 1920); Aust Base Depots, Le Havre, *Digger,* 1-2 (1918-19); *Sabretache,* Oct-Dec 1979; *Punch* (Melb), 11 May 1916; *Bendigo Advertiser,* 12 Jan 1923; records (AWM).   J. K. HAKEN

DAVIS, JOHN KING (1884-1967), Antarctic navigator, was born on 19 February 1884 at Kew, Surrey, England, only son of James Green Davis, army coach, and his wife Marion Alice, née King. There were early family connexions with Australia: as a young man his father had taught at Sydney Grammar School for four years, and Henry Edward King [q.v.5], of Queensland, was an uncle.

Davis's formal education, at Colet Court, London, and at Burford Grammar School, Oxfordshire, ended in 1900, when he and his father left London for Cape Town, South Africa. On his own initiative, while his father was absent at Kimberley, he joined the crew of the mail-steamer *Carisbrooke Castle,* as a steward's boy working his passage to England. In that eventful year he signed indentures for four years in the Liverpool full-rigged sailing vessel *Celtic Chief,* and visited Australia for the first time.

Davis completed his apprenticeship as a seaman and passed the Board of Trade examination for the certificate of second mate on 16 July 1905. Between then and June 1906 he served as second mate of the barque *Westland,* trading between England and New Zealand, and in the next year, of the *Port Jackson.* In 1906 in Sydney he gained his first mate's certificate; in New Zealand, in August 1908, his extra master's certificate.

A chance visit to a London exhibition of polar equipment had led to his meeting (Sir) Ernest Shackleton, who had been a member of Scott's National Antarctic Expedition in 1901-04. In July 1907, Davis became chief officer of Shackleton's steam yacht *Nimrod,* sailing for Antarctica on 7 August. For the terminal exploratory voyage in 1909, after Shackleton's highly successful British An-

tarctic Expedition and his relief from the Cape Royds base, Davis commanded the *Nimrod,* sailing via Macquarie Island and Cape Horn. Several doubtful sightings of land in the South Pacific were disproved. Until March 1911, Davis assisted Shackleton in winding up the affairs of the expedition. He was then appointed master of the *Aurora,* and second-in-command of the Australasian Antarctic Expedition of 1911-14, under (Sir) Douglas Mawson [q.v.]; he made five notable cruises, essential in establishing and relieving the wintering bases at Macquarie Island and, on the Antarctic mainland, at Commonwealth Bay and on the Shackleton Ice Shelf.

On the outbreak of World War I, Davis volunteered for active service, and was attached to the military embarkation staff at Sydney. Subsequently he commanded the transport *Boonah* conveying troops and horses to Egypt and England. In October 1916, on behalf of the British, Australian and New Zealand governments, with Shackleton as supernumerary, he commanded the Ross Sea Relief Expedition, mounted to rescue Shackleton's 'shore party' left at McMurdo Sound to support their leader's epic but ill-fated attempt to cross Antarctica from the Weddell Sea. After being marooned for two winters with inadequate supplies and equipment, its members reached New Zealand in the *Aurora* on 9 February 1917.

For twelve months from April 1917, Davis supervised the erection of a mechanical coal-handling plant at Port Pirie, South Australia. Promoted lieut-commander, Royal Australian Naval Reserve, he was then appointed Australian naval transport officer, London, dealing with the repatriation of the Australian Imperial Force. He returned to Australia in October 1919. In 1920 he became Commonwealth director of navigation and next year established a cyclone-warning station on Willis Island in the Coral Sea, occupying the island for six months. He remained director of navigation, not without controversy, until his retirement on 19 February 1949. He took leave to command the *Discovery* during the first voyage (1929-30) of the British, Australian and New Zealand Antarctic Research Expedition under the general leadership of Mawson, returning to his department in July 1930. From 1947 to 1962, Davis was a member of the Australian government's planning committee advising on current Antarctic policy and action. He never lost this deep interest in the Australian National Antarctic Research Expeditions.

For his services to polar exploration Davis was twice invested with the King's Polar Medal, and received clasps to each. The Murchison Award, of the Royal Geographical Society, was bestowed for his navigation and oceanography during the Australian Antarctic Expedition in 1911-14; he became a fellow of the society in 1915. From 1920 Davis was a member of the Royal Society of Victoria, and was its president in 1945 and 1946. In 1965 he was appointed C.B.E. Australia's second station on the Antarctic Continent, established in 1957, was named Davis in his honour. The Davis Sea, west of the Shackleton Ice Shelf, coasting Antarctica between 90° and 95°E, also commemorates the navigator.

Tall, spare, red-headed, with deep-set piercing eyes, Davis (described in 1920) gave a 'general appearance of quiet power'. In all operations for which he was responsible, he revealed courage, judgment and logistic ability. In 1913, Shackleton wrote: 'Captain Davis is the most experienced navigator of Antarctic seas living ... He's an expert on oceanographical work, especially in sounding and dredging in deep waters ... He successfully navigated *Aurora*, landing Dr Mawson at his winter quarters through the stormiest oceans and one of the worst ice seasons ever recorded'. Shackleton's praise of Davis's subsequent landing of Frank Wild's party, 1500 miles (2400 km) to the west, and of completely successful relief expeditions, beset by 'trying and anxious circumstances', is matched by that of Mawson. From his own personal journals, blunt and to the point, one may infer the nature of his trials and dilemmas, and more readily understand why his solutions to them brought such praise. As evident, however, is his impatience with scientists and laymen at sea, his intransigence concerning any factor involving the order and security of his vessel, and his determination, as far as this was concerned, to remain in command.

Davis's contributions to the overall success of Shackleton's and Mawson's expeditions were as unstinted as they were essential; his share of their fame was modest; his loyalty and integrity were absolute. Among the ships' companies, the expedition men, and the supernumeraries alike, he was known for his reserve and sense of responsibility, qualities perhaps inseparable from the loneliness of command at sea. Roald Amundsen had written of one fatal weakness common to many polar expeditions: that the commanders had not always been ships' captains. Once embarked at sea, the expedition had not one leader but two, with incessant friction, divided counsels, and a lowered morale for the subordinate members of the expedition. Davis inserted a lengthy quotation from Amundsen in his diary of the 1929-30 expedition.

When Mawson gained Davis as master of the *Discovery*, they shared a different leadership from that of the 1911-14 expedition, when Mawson was mainly ashore leading sledging parties. These later research expeditions were maritime ventures, investigating and mapping the coast of Antarctica between approximately 140°E and 50°E, anticipating the ceding to Australia of British interests in that large sector, and the eventual proclamation of Australian Antarctic Territory and the Australian Antarctic Acceptance Act of 1933. In the light of both earlier and later expeditions at sea, disagreements between shipmaster and expedition leader appear inevitable. They were, to quote A. Grenfell Price, 'innocent victims of that divided control which ... lessened the value of a number of Antarctic expeditions' though 'neither permitted a temporary quarrel to wreck a life-long friendship'.

The main area of dissension concerned the quantities of coal prudence should reserve for the return passage to Kerguelen. An absolute judgment is impossible. In the event, the *Discovery* reached Kerguelen with ample supplies. A fundamental difference in the attitudes of Mawson and Davis towards the use of aircraft also emerged; the return to Kerguelen earlier than he had expected meant for Mawson the loss of opportunities for mapping from the air, rather than for penetrating the pack ice.

Davis never married; in retirement he lived in Melbourne in a St Kilda Road boarding-house. He died on 8 May 1967 in hospital at Toorak and was buried in Melbourne general cemetery. His estate was valued for probate at $87 407. His publications include *With the 'Aurora' in the Antarctic, 1911-1914* (London, 1919); *Willis Island: a storm warning station in the Coral Sea* (Melbourne, 1923); and *High latitude* (Melbourne, 1962), in collaboration with a close friend, Bedford Osborne. His portrait hangs in the 'gallery of explorers' in the Royal Geographical Society's London headquarters.

E. H. Shackleton, *The heart of the Antarctic* (Lond, 1909); D. Mawson, *The home of the blizzard* (Lond, 1915); R. A. Swan, *Australia in the Antarctic* (Melb, 1961); A. G. Price, *The winning of Australian Antarctica* (Syd, 1962); J. K. Davis papers (LaTL).   JOHN BÉCHERVAISE

DAVIS, JOSEPH (1854-1932), civil engineer, was born on 3 November 1854 at Oldbury, Worcestershire, England, son of Elijah Davis, miner, and his wife Susan, née Clifton. He was educated at Dudley Grammar School and worked in 1872-73 with his father, by then a colliery owner and engineer. In 1874-75 he served his pupillage with

William North & Sons, consulting engineers, and gained experience with several firms before migrating to Australia in 1883, with his wife Carline, née Sheddon, whom he had married at the Register Office, Dudley, on 14 May 1878.

Under a provisional agreement Davis was to have built a railway in Queensland, but with the company's concurrence he joined the New South Wales Department of Public Works on 27 August 1883 as a surveyor and draftsman. Promoted assistant engineer on 1 January 1889 he also became chairman of the Public Service Tender Board. Two years later Davis was appointed supervising engineer to the sewerage construction branch. In 1895 he was in charge of country towns' water-supply and sewerage as principal assistant engineer and in 1897 was also acting government architect. He became engineer-in-chief for sewerage construction in 1896 and was under-secretary of the Department of Public Works from March 1901.

In evidence before the 1896 public works inquiry commission Davis defended serious charges made in parliament against R. R. P. Hickson [q.v.4], engineer-in-chief for sewerage, regarding certain contracts. He became chairman of the Sydney Harbour Bridge Advisory Board on 25 March 1901 and in 1903 recommended that the tender of J. Stewart & Co. for a high level bridge should be accepted. In addition Davis chaired the royal commission on Sydney water-supply and the interstate royal commission on the River Murray in 1902-03. He also served on several committees of inquiry and on the royal commission into the working and administration of the government docks and workshops at Cockatoo Island.

A member of the Institution of Civil Engineers, London, Davis won its Telford premium in 1902 for his paper, 'The sewerage systems of Sydney'. He was also a member of the Institution of Mechanical Engineers, London, and of the Royal Society of New South Wales, and a fellow of the (Royal) Sanitary Institute, London. He sported a neat beard and a luxuriant moustache, and usually wore oval steel-rimmed spectacles.

In March 1907 Davis was transferred to the Agent-General's Office in London as consulting and inspecting engineer. With Joseph Barling [q.v.3] and (Sir) Timothy Coghlan [q.v.] he arranged the New South Wales court at the Franco-British Exhibition in London in 1908. While buying steel for railways he frequently met Krupp in Germany and that year warned Sir J. Hector Carruthers [q.v.7] of the likelihood of war with Germany. On 9 October 1912 he was appointed director-general of public works and returned to Sydney on a salary of £1500. Among his many duties he served on the River Murray commission in 1916 and reported to the Commonwealth government on a sewerage system for Canberra and on the small arms factory at Lithgow. He advocated the North Shore bridge, and was involved in a 'tremendous amount of labour' winding up the affairs of Norton Griffith & Co. when it was unable to fulfil public service contracts during World War I. After Davis retired on 5 March 1917, he settled in London as consulting engineer to the New South Wales government. He was responsible for approving all the steel manufactured in Great Britain for the Sydney Harbour Bridge, as well as electrical equipment and rolling stock for Sydney's suburban railways.

Davis died at Dulwich on 20 January 1932, and was survived by two of his three daughters and by a son James Sheddon, who became a medical practitioner. His estate was valued for probate at £15 155 in New South Wales.

Cyclopedia of N.S.W. (Syd, 1907); *V&P* (LA NSW), 1896, 5, 348, 1899, 1, 847, 1909, 5, 241, 1916 5, 795; Inst of Civil Engineers (Lond), *Minutes of Procs*, Jan 1934, p 542; J. H. Carruthers, Autobiography (NL, Univ Syd Archives); staff records (Dept of Public Works, Syd); Coghlan papers (NL).
                                                    ARTHUR CORBETT

DAVIS, THOMAS MARTIN (1856-1899), trade unionist and politician, was born on 22 January 1856 at Redditch, Worcestershire, England, son of Thomas Davis, fruit merchant, and his wife Ann, née Martin. At 3 he moved to Glasgow with his family. Educated at Glasgow High School and Garnet Bank Academy, at 13 he went to France to learn the language. In 1871-75 he worked at sea, interspersed with some light military experience in South Africa, service as an inspector of the railway line across the Sabi desert in India, and employment as an interpreter in the mines in New Caledonia. About 1876 he settled in Sydney.

Davis continued as a seaman and became a prominent trade unionist. In 1886 he was elected secretary of the Federated Seamen's Union; he was also secretary of its New South Wales branch and was active in the local Maritime Council. That year he was a member of a conference of shipowners and trade unionists which tried, unsuccessfully, to solve growing wages and conditions problems in the industry. In the late 1880s he played an important part in the shipping events that preceded the 1890 maritime strike. During the strike he was on the Labour Defence Committee which controlled the dispute in New South Wales, and on the Intercolonial Labour Conference which tried to control it nation wide; after the strike, he was a member of the royal commission that investigated and reported on it in 1891. His shrewd questioning at the inquiry elucidated many obscure aspects of the strike.

Davis was a foundation member of the West Sydney Labor League in 1891, and was selected as a candidate at the elections that year when Labor won thirty-five seats, including four at West Sydney, an inner-city, waterfront electorate. He was elected the first party whip and, with a clear view of the need for political independence and party solidarity, was one of the few members to remain loyal to conference decisions in 1891-94. He was re-elected in 1894 and 1895 (Sydney-Pyrmont from 1894). On 9 May 1892 at St Barnabas Anglican Church he married Jessie Shaw; they lived at Ashfield.

In parliament he concentrated on shipping problems, primarily to improve working conditions but also to modernize the industry. In evidence in 1897 to the royal commission on the marine board he stressed the need for a fully representative body and said that the Legislative Council had blocked his marine board reconstruction bill. By 1898 Davis, with his weight rapidly increasing, was seriously ill. He did not nominate for the July elections and died of heart valve incompetence on 14 July 1899, survived by his wife and three sons. He was buried in the Anglican section of Waverley cemetery.

Report of the royal commission on strikes (Syd, 1891); B. Nairn, *Civilising capitalism* (Canb, 1973); *V&P* (LA NSW), 1897, 7, 511; *Daily Telegraph* (Syd), 15 June 1894.   BEDE NAIRN

DAVIS, WILLIAM WALTER (1840-1923), pastoralist and politician, was born on 5 July 1840 at Bathurst, New South Wales, son of Ebenezer Davis, plasterer, and his wife Louisa, née Whittaker. At 13 he ran away from home to help to drove a mob of cattle to Burrabogie station, near Hay, where at 16 he was head stockman and developing into a fine horseman. About 1858 he went to the Bourke district as a cattle-dealer and undertook a number of successful pastoral and commercial ventures. At the Sydney Hotel, Rutherglen, Victoria, on 30 August 1861 with the rites of the Independent Church, he married a Catholic dressmaker Anne Heaer. After she died, on 14 November 1870, describing himself as an auctioneer and widower, he married Catharine Maxwell in the Church of England, Bourke.

In 1874 with Alexander Ross & Co. he acquired the 600-square mile (1500 km^2) Kerribree station fifty miles north-west of Bourke. Davis was manager and overlanded large mobs of cattle to Melbourne and Adelaide. The firm became Davis, Dale & Co. and in 1886 purchased from Mary Hannay Foott [q.v.4] and her father Dundoo station, near Eulo, in south-west Queensland. The same year at a cost of £5000 Davis put down the first genuine artesian bore in New South Wales, striking on Kerribree a 15000 gallon (68000 L) flow at a depth of 1200 ft. (360 m). He converted the station to sheep; it sheared up to 130000 annually, all the wool being scoured on the property. He had disposed of his pastoral interests by 1900.

In February 1889 as a 'fairtrader' Davis was returned to the Legislative Assembly for Bourke. Defeated in 1891, and as a protectionist in July 1894 and 1895, he regained Bourke for the National Federal Party, defeating E. D. Millen [q.v.] by nine votes in 1898. He then joined another auctioneer Charles Richard Green, a connexion, in partnership, on 1 August; on 27 August 1900 their firm was sequestrated with debts of £1203. Davis was discharged in April 1903 after an eighteen months suspension for alleged misdemeanours. He resigned from parliament in August 1900 but in September won the by-election and held the seat until July 1904. He was defeated for the Darling in 1907. In August 1900-October 1901 he sat on the royal commission into the condition of Crown tenants [in the] Western Division of New South Wales. By 1905 bad seasons and financial losses had forced him to retire to an orchard at Beecroft near Sydney. In August that year he claimed before the royal commission on the administration of the Lands Department, not without some reason, that he and every other settler in the Western Division had been 'rack rented and plundered' by the land agency boards.

Davis was known as 'Baldy' as one side of his head had been scalded in childhood; he always wore a wig. Henry Lawson [q.v.] in his story 'Baldy Thompson' described him thus: 'Rough squarish face, curly auburn wig, bushy grey eyebrows and moustache, and grizzly stubble – eyes that reminded one of Dampier [q.v.4] the actor.... a squatter of the old order'. He loved an argument, especially about unionism or politics, and was generally voted a hard case. Big-hearted and generous (never refusing a swagman 'tucker') he had a keen sense of humour, a fund of anecdote and was a good story-teller: he himself was the subject of many a camp-fire yarn.

Davis died on 14 September 1923 at his residence, Dutruc Street, Randwick, and was buried with Anglican rites in Randwick cemetery. He was survived by his third wife Florence Jane, née Whittaker, whom he had married on 12 March 1885 at the Church of England, Blayney, and by 16 of his 19 children: 5 sons and 3 daughters of his second and 3 sons and 5 daughters of his third marriage. A number of his sons settled on the land and two saw active service with the first Australian Imperial Force.

PP (LC & LA NSW), 1906, 2, 514, 543, 579; Bourke and District Hist Soc, *Papers on the history of Bourke* . . ., 2 (1967-68); *Pastoral Review*, 16 Oct 1923; *SMH*, 1 Feb 1889, 18 July 1894, 29 July 1898, 15, 18 Sept 1923; *T&CJ*, 20 Apr 1889; Carruthers *and* Parkes correspondence (ML); J. Gormley reminiscences, news-cuttings, vol 3 (ML); Bankruptcy file 14/263 (NSWA).   G. P. WALSH

DAVY, RUBY CLAUDIA EMILY (1883-1949), musician, was born on 22 November 1883 at Salisbury, South Australia, only child of William Charles Davy, shoemaker and brass instrument player, and his wife Louisa Jane, née Litchfield, singer and music teacher. The family's home became a centre of music and drama and Ruby was early encouraged to improvise and compose, to perform on and teach the piano, and to recite. Educated locally, she learned music from her mother and Ernest Mitchell who prepared her for the Elder [q.v.4] Conservatorium of Music (B. Mus., 1907; D. Mus., 1918). She was the first Australian woman to receive a doctorate in music and to become a fellow of Trinity College of Music, London (1921); she also held a diploma in elocution from the London College of Music.

From 1909 Ruby Davy was composing, giving recitals and participating in ensembles. In 1912, as a temporary replacement, she taught theory and counterpoint at the conservatorium. Her parents moved in 1920 to Prospect, where mother and daughter taught music. They worked long hours and many pupils gained high distinctions, but after her parents died in 1929 Dr Davy collapsed and was unable to adjust to life alone. Four years later Pastor John Hewitt of the Apostolic Church persuaded her to return to music.

In 1934 she conducted successful performances of her song, *Australia, fair and free*, in Melbourne and Adelaide; it was later published. That year she began popular lecture recitals on radio and to various associations in Melbourne, where she settled next year: 'Threefold aspect of the beautiful in art' was illustrated with excerpts from the classics, musical monologues, and two of her original compositions for violin. She developed a controversial new topic, 'The evolution of chamber music with special

reference to color', on which she gave three chamber music lectures in 1938. She and Issy Spivakovsky, violinist and cellist, established the Davy Conservatorium of Music at her South Yarra home. Davy's teaching was unconventional: students were encouraged to compose and to break down barriers between the arts.

In 1939 she toured England, Europe and the United States of America. Davy gave three lecture recitals in London with the eminent violinist Albert Sammons, but the critics preferred the sonata duos to the lectures. War curtailed her plans and she returned to Melbourne and teaching. In 1941 she founded and presided over the Society of Women Musicians of Australia, which gave regular monthly musicales in Melbourne. A mastectomy in 1947 affected Davy's playing; she became depressed and died on 12 July 1949. She was buried in West Terrace cemetery, Adelaide.

This frail, eccentric woman, with her expressive, haunting eyes and who dressed unfashionably in long black clothes, is remembered as a teacher rather than a composer. Although the *Australian Musical News* had described her as a 'pianist, musical historian, elocutionist, actress, raconteur, singer, poet and enthusiast', she failed to gain wide recognition; perhaps partly because she was a woman, perhaps because of jealousy of her high academic attainments, perhaps because of her limited experience and naive personality. Relics of her career were placed in Salisbury Institute in 1936. She left £300 to the Elder Conservatorium to found a commemorative prize for the composition of music.

Dr. Ruby Davy biography (Melb, 1936); *Aust Musical News and Musical Digest*, Feb, Mar 1935, Apr 1939; S. O'Toole, A portrait of Dr. Ruby C. E. Davy (B.A. Hons thesis, La Trobe Univ, 1978); R. Davy papers and scrapbook, 1939-40 (Elder Conservatorium collection, Univ Adel).

JOYCE GIBBERD
SILVIA O'TOOLE

DAVY, THOMAS ARTHUR LEWIS (1890-1933), lawyer and politician, was born on 1 May 1890 at Auckland, New Zealand, son of Thomas George Davy, medical practitioner and cultivated linguist and musician, and his wife Emily, née Gates, After eight years in New Zealand the family returned to London in 1894, but migrated to Western Australia next year. The father practised medicine at Coolgardie, Fremantle and West Perth until his death in 1908. Davy was educated at Fremantle and at High School, Perth, and was Rhodes scholar for 1909; he studied jurisprudence at his father's old college, Exeter, at Oxford (B.A., 1913), and was called to the Bar at Gray's Inn, London, that year, and in Western Australia in 1914. He was a partner in the firm of Northmore, Hale & Davy (and later Leake) and became a King's Counsel in 1932.

Davy served with the Royal Field Artillery in France in 1915-16, being wounded in action, and then in India in 1917-19; he reached the rank of acting captain. On 21 December 1915, on leave in London, he married Penelope Ethel, daughter of H. W. Sholl, a Western Australian politician. On his return to Perth Davy served on the State executive of the Returned Sailors' and Soldiers' Imperial League of Australia and was its honorary solicitor from 1923 until his death. From 1920 he sat on the High School's board of governors and was influential, as chairman in 1929, in having the name changed to Hale [q.v.4] School.

In 1924 Davy won the West Perth seat in the Legislative Assembly, despite a dispute over how-to-vote cards with fellow Nationalist and sitting member Edith Cowan [q.v.]. The National Party, led by Sir James Mitchell [q.v.], went into opposition, being known temporarily as the United Party after amalgamation with a breakaway Country Party group. In his first parliamentary session Davy led for the Opposition in debate on important industrial legislation and after the 1927 election was chosen deputy leader of the United Party. Influential in the periodic reorganizations of the party's branch structure before elections, he opposed electoral pacts with the Country Party which limited the National Party's capacity to expand in rural areas. Davy also supported his party's controversial policy of multiple endorsement for parliamentary elections.

In 1930 Davy became attorney-general and in October next year, after (Sir) Norbert Keenan's [q.v.] resignation, also received the education portfolio. In the Depression he worked closely with Mitchell on key legislation and at conferences in the eastern States. Although he went against the majority of his party in opposing secession, he must surely have soon become its leader, but he died suddenly of a heart attack on 18 February 1933, while playing cards with his wife and friends at the Savoy Hotel.

The death of such a talented and personable leader, admired for his sincerity and lack of ostentation, was a great blow to his colleagues. He was buried in the Anglican portion of Karrakatta cemetery, survived by his wife, two daughters and a son.

Rhodes Scholarships, *Records of past scholars elected . . . 1903 and 1927 inclusive* (Oxford, 1931, copy Battye Lib, Perth); G. C. Bolton, *A fine country to starve in* (Perth, 1972); *Western Mail* (Perth), 6 June 1908, 23 Feb 1933; *Listening Post,* 24 Feb 1933; *Aust Law J,* 15 Mar 1933, p 424; *West Australian,* 17-21, 24 Mar 1924, 20 Feb 1933; D. W. Black, The National Party in Western Australia, 1917-1930: its origins and development with an introductory survey of 'Liberal' Party organisation, 1901-1916 (M.A. thesis, Univ WA, 1974); D. H. Rankin, The history and development of the High School Perth, 1858-1925 (1925, held by Battye Lib, Perth).　　　　　　DAVID BLACK

DAWES, NATHANIEL (1843-1910), Anglican bishop, was born on 24 July 1843 at Rye, Sussex, England, son of Edwin Nathaniel Dawes, town clerk of Rye and Winchelsea, and his wife Ann, née Noakes. Educated at the parish school of St Mary the Virgin, Rye, and at a proprietary school in Montpelier, Brighton, Dawes studied mechanics probably at the Free Grammar School, Ashford, became an engineer, and, among other commissions, worked on Blackfriars Bridge. He matriculated in 1868 at Oxford, entered St Alban Hall and graduated in 1872 (M.A. 1875). Made deacon in 1871 and ordained on St Andrew's Day 1872, he served his title as curate of St Peter's, Vauxhall, London, in 1871-77 under Rev. George Herbert; there, he gained a lifelong love of poetry and with J. W. Horsley he published *Practical hints for parochial missions* in 1875. On 11 June 1878 Dawes married Georgina Frances Codd and was inducted vicar of the London slum parish of St Mary's Charterhouse. Persuaded by Bishop Webber [q.v.] to migrate to Queensland, he was inducted as rector of St Andrew's, South Brisbane, in 1886 and collated as archdeacon of Brisbane.

Dawes was consecrated bishop on 1 May 1889 in St Andrew's Cathedral, Sydney, by Archbishop Barry [q.v.3]; he was the first Anglican bishop to be consecrated in Australia. Appointed coadjutor bishop of Brisbane, he was first given pastoral oversight of the Darling downs and later of Rockhampton where he became honorary rector of St Paul's Church. On 12 August 1892 he was elected first bishop of the new diocese of Rockhampton and was enthroned in St Paul's Church which he took for his cathedral.

The diocese, four times the size of England and Wales, had six priests serving in Rockhampton, Gladstone, Mt Morgan, Clermont, Springsure and the far west. Visiting England in 1896 Dawes, with Bishop Westcott and Canon Body of Durham, envisioned a solution to his problem: a community of priests living in a central mission-house under a simple rule to serve the far west. His vision became the 'Bush Brotherhood' when his first recruit, Rev. George Dowglass Halford, arrived at Longreach on 14 September 1897. Dawes attended the Lambeth Conference of 1897 and received an honorary D.D. from Oxford University.

The writings of Dawes on the separate incorporation of his diocese and his charges to synod reveal an incisive mind, a wide and tolerant outlook, good sense and a clear, telling style. In 1903 he declined the vacant see of Brisbane and continued to travel, sometimes more than 5000 miles (8000 km) a year on horseback and buggy on regular visits to every centre of the diocese. Heat and the hazards of bush travel took their toll and he went to England in 1907 for medical treatment. On 27 May 1908, on medical advice, he reluctantly resigned his see and was succeeded by Halford. Dawes died at Malvern, England, on 12 September 1910 of spinal meningitis. He was survived by his wife and their two daughters. Two memorials were raised to him: a fund for training candidates for holy orders, and the stained glass windows in the east end of the sanctuary of St Paul's Cathedral, Rockhampton.

Alcazar Press, *Queensland, 1900* (Brisb, nd); I. Southall, *Parson on the track*, (Melb, 1962); Diocese of Rockhampton, *Yearbook*, 1893-1910.

JOHN BAYTON

DAWSON, ANDREW (ANDERSON) (1863-1910), miner, editor and politician, was born on 16 July 1863 at Rockhampton, Queensland, son of Anderson Dawson, mariner, and his wife Jane, née Smith. He adopted his father's name 'Anderson' before he entered politics. Shortly after his birth, Dawson's parents died and he was placed in a Brisbane orphanage until he was 9. He was then taken by an uncle to Gympie where he attended school until he was 12. He worked at Charters Towers at various occupations including newspaper-running, bullock-driving and mining, becoming head amalgamator of one of the principal gold batteries when only 19. In 1886 he went to the Kimberleys in Western Australia, but failure brought him back to Charters Towers where, on 21 December 1887 according to Presbyterian forms, he married a widow, Caroline Ryan, née Quin.

This was the period of the growth of unionism in Queensland, and Dawson became president of the local Miners' Union. He was Charters Towers chairman of the 1891 strike committee, vice-president of the Queensland Provincial Council of the Australian Labour Federation and helped form the Charters Towers Republican Association. In 1892 he was a member of the Dalrymple Divisional Board. He wrote articles for the *Northern Miner* and, next year, became the first editor of the Charters

Towers *Eagle* which he owned until 1900 with John Dunsford.

In 1893 Dawson and Dunsford were elected to the Legislative Assembly as Labor members for Charters Towers. They were both returned with increasing majorities in 1896 and 1899, when Dawson replaced Thomas Glassey [q.v.] as leader. In parliament Dawson spoke mainly on matters affecting mining and railways; he also objected to Queensland's sending a military contingent to South Africa without parliamentary approval. Outside parliament he became a particular friend of the Liberal barrister T. J. Byrnes [q.v.7], who suggested that he should read for the Bar. Although he began legal studies, ill health (a pulmonary condition contracted as a miner) prevented his continuing. According to C. A. Bernays [q.v.3] Byrnes's death in September 1898 affected Dawson more than any other parliamentarian.

Dawson's friendships generally extended beyond the Labor members and he believed that an alliance with the Liberals would assist Labor into office. Glassey and William Kidston [q.v.] supported this idea. When the government of (Sir) James Dickson [q.v.] resigned on 25 November 1899, Dawson was asked to form a ministry. He expected support from those Liberals and ministerialists who had voted against Dickson, and when this did not eventuate formed a minority Labor government on 1 December 1899 – the famous 'first Labor government in the world'. After the ministerialists elected Robert Philp [q.v.] as leader in place of Dickson, Dawson's government was defeated and resigned on 5 December. The ministry formally ended on 7 December. He had not expected his government to last long but had hoped to demonstrate Labor's desire and willingness to take office.

Continuing ill health forced Dawson to retire as parliamentary leader in August 1900. However, a staunch supporter of Federation, he stood for the Senate in 1901, heading the Queensland poll. He was chairman of the first meeting of the Federal parliamentary Labor Party which elected J. C. Watson [q.v.] as leader. As minister for defence in the Watson government of 1904 he displayed a marked antipathy towards Sir Edward Hutton [q.v.]. Dawson's support for Liberal-Labor alliances and his unwillingness to pay a £50 election levy placed on Queensland Labor senators caused him to lose favour with the extra-parliamentary leaders of the party in Queensland. In the selection of Senate candidates by the central political executive in 1906, he finished fourth and was thus not able to stand for Labor. Reservations expressed in Labor circles, however, resulted in a second meeting when he was placed third on the ticket. Dawson withdrew and then changed his mind, but he was too late. Splitting the Labor vote he ran as an independent, finished last and caused the defeat of Senator W. G. Higgs [q.v.] and the two other Labor candidates.

Dawson retired from politics and died of alcoholism on 20 July 1910 at Brisbane, survived by his wife, two sons and two daughters. He was buried in Toowong cemetery. His contribution to the growth of the Labor Party in Queensland had been significant. He was a reformer, not an ideologue; his later estrangement from the party reflected his unwillingness to oppose judicious alliances with the Liberals. For almost fifty years, however, his name as the 'first Labour premier in the world' was taught to Queensland school children.

Alcazar Press, *Queensland, 1900* (Brisb, nd); C. A. Bernays, *Queensland politics during sixty years* (Brisb, 1919); D. J. Murphy et al (eds), *Prelude to power* (Brisb, 1970); *Labour Hist*, May 1971, no 20, p 1; *Worker* (Brisb), 2 Mar 1901, 28 July 1910; *Table Talk*, 9 May 1901; *Punch* (Melb), 7 July 1904; *Kalgoorlie Miner*, 27 Aug 1904; *Brisbane Courier*, 21 Nov 1906; *Northern Miner*, 21 July 1910.

D. J. MURPHY

DAWSON, PETER SMITH (1882-1961), singer, was born on 31 January 1882 in Adelaide, youngest of nine children of Thomas Dawson, ironworker and plumber, and his wife Alison, née Miller. Peter attended the East Adelaide Primary School and Pulteney Street Grammar School, and was then apprenticed to his father. His parents encouraged his appreciation of music, and when 8 he sang as a boy soprano at a social at the College Park Congregational Church, St Peters, and was later in the St Andrew's Presbyterian Church choir. When 17 he began taking singing lessons from C. J. Stevens and sang at concerts with the Adelaide Grand Orchestra. In 1900 he was a soloist in their performance of Handel's *Messiah*, was successful in several local contests, and won the bass solo section at the South Street Competitions, Ballarat, Victoria. Next year he won an amateur boxing championship.

In 1902, encouraged by Stevens, Dawson went to London and studied with B. L. Bamford, (Sir) Charles Santley, the eminent baritone, and Professor Kantorez. His first engagement was at a church in the East End for a fee of 7s. 6d. He was soon touring in the west of England with the popular concert and opera singer Madame Albani, and singing in London at the Crystal Palace and Queen's Hall promenade concerts. On 20 May 1905 he married Annie Mortimer Noble, a soprano with the stage name of An-

nette George. They had no children and often toured together internationally until a serious car accident ended her public career.

In 1908 Dawson was principal baritone at the Chappell ballad concerts. Next year he sang in *The mastersingers of Nuremberg* at Covent Garden and joined Amy Castles [q.v.7] and her company in touring Australia. Back in London he extended his repertoire from ballads and operatic arias to include German *lieder* and French songs. Leading reviewers of his 1911 concerts agreed that he was the finest English baritone of the day. Dawson was in Australia during World War I; in 1918 he enlisted as a private in the Australian Imperial Force, but did not serve overseas.

For all his success as a concert singer, the gramophone record made Dawson's a household name in many countries; he was one of the first artists to have faith in the process. In 1904 he made a test record for the Edison Bell Phonograph Co., and later in the year began his fifty-year career for His Master's Voice which spanned recording techniques from the two-minute cylinder to the long-playing disc and tape. His early record labels carried such pseudonyms as Frank Danby for light songs, Will Strong for music-hall ditties, and Hector Grant for Scottish songs. For Zonophone he used the names Arthur Walpole, Charles Hardy, Walter Wentworth and Robert Woodville. For some twenty years he was on a substantial annual retainer and did not receive royalties. His eventual total was more than 13 million sales of some 3500 titles. He came to see recording as ' the dominating success of his career'.

Dawson composed many songs under such pseudonyms as J. P. McCall, Evelyn Byrd, Peter Allison, Denton Toms, Charles Weber, Arnold Flint, Gilbert Mundy, Geoffrey Baxter and Alison Miller. He set several of Rudyard Kipling's poems to music: *Boots* and *Route marching* were among the most popular. In 1930-31 he topped the bill in variety at the London Palladium above many famous stars; it was often said that he could have been a professional comedian.

In 1939-47 Dawson lived in Sydney. During the war he sang for the troops and on recruiting drives in Australia and New Zealand. He had plans to retire after the war, but he claimed his tax bills were so crippling that he had to keep singing. His peak earnings between the wars had been about £14 500 a year, but he was a 'hopeless businessman'. On 7 December 1950 he sang the bass solo role in the *Messiah* at the Adelaide Town Hall where he had sung the same part half a century before. In 1951 he published an autobiography *Fifty years of song*. As president of the Australian Songwriters and

Composers' Association in 1953 he pressed for legislation to increase the compulsory radio time for local music. That year his wife 'Nan' died after a long illness. On 29 April 1954 he married her sister Constance Bedford Noble in Sydney. They lived at Dee Why where Dawson enjoyed painting, drawing cartoons and growing roses.

Although Dawson loved the limelight, he remained unspoiled by fame, abhorred 'swank', and was never ashamed of the tattooed wrists that recorded his boyhood 'flames'. Survived by his wife, he died on 27 September 1961 in Sydney; after a funeral at St David's Presbyterian Church, Haberfield, he was buried in Rookwood cemetery. His estate was valued for probate at £1555.

News (Adel), and *Yorkshire Post*, 27 Sept 1961.
JAMES GLENNON

DAY, ERNEST CHARLES (1857-1915), police officer, was born on 30 October 1857 at Sherborne, Dorsetshire, England, son of John Day, surveyor, and his wife Mary Julia, née Bluett. Educated in 1869-71 as a foundationer at Sherborne School, he entered commerce and at 24 was managing a large Southampton brewery owned by his brother. A taste for adventure, titillated by reading tales of Australian bushrangers, decided him to migrate and he sailed for Sydney in the *John Elder*, arriving on 26 May 1883.

Day joined the New South Wales Mounted Police on 11 June, was trained for a few months at the Police Depot in Sydney, and was posted to Gulgong, where he married Nellie Hegarty at St Luke's Anglican Church on 1 May 1884. He was a good horseman and a crack shot with both revolver and rifle. His first promotion, to constable 1st class, came in May 1885 after he and two other policemen showed marked skill and courage in tracking two prisoners, who had been bushranging for over a month after killing a constable and escaping from Coonamble gaol. The pursuit ended in a revolver duel in which the bushrangers were killed. Day next served at Nymagee and Cobar where he helped to break up several gangs of cattle duffers and horse thieves.

By April 1892 Day was stationed at Bourke with the rank of senior sergeant. While there, by disguising himself as a woman, he captured a man known locally as 'Jack the Ripper', who had been molesting girls and women. His most famous case arose from his investigation in 1896 of a murder at Brennan's Bend, on the Darling, which led to the conviction of 'Tommy' Moore, a hawker. Day's prolonged inquiries over a wide area also linked Moore with the unsolved murders of five other men, whose mutilated

bodies had been found over a period of years in western and southern parts of the colony.

Promoted sub-inspector in 1897, Day served at Narrabri and Newcastle where in 1904 he was promoted inspector. In 1907 he was transferred to Sydney, with the rank of superintendent, to take charge of the Police Training Depot and the eastern police district. In March 1910 after further promotion, he was attached to the office of the inspector-general, Thomas Garvin, whom he succeeded on 1 January 1911. As inspector-general, Day was in command of 2600 men. His courteous manners, wide police experience, and the fact that he had risen through the ranks on merit, made 'the General', as they called him, popular with and respected by his men. He was liked too by journalists who found him approachable and informative. He was the first inspector-general to realize how helpful a co-operative press and good public relations could be in police matters.

At Narrabri on 29 November 1899 Day had married Rose Welsh with Catholic rites. Both his wives were Catholics and his children were educated in Catholic schools but he remained an Anglican. Ill health led to his retirement on 9 January 1915 and he died of cirrhosis of the liver at his Moore Park home on 17 January. He was survived by two sons and four daughters of his first marriage and by his second wife and their two sons. After a funeral service at St Matthias's Church of England, Paddington, he was buried in Waverley cemetery. His fellow police officers and men later erected a monument to his memory on his grave. It bears the lines: 'The rank is but the guinea stamp, The man's the gowd for a' that'. Probate was granted on his estate at £3209. His grandson Ernest Robert Day became an inspector in the State Police Force.

A. L. Haydon, *The trooper police of Australia* (Lond, 1911); L. E. Hoban, *A centenary history of the New South Wales police force, 1862-1962* (Syd, 1962); Aust Journalists' Assn, *Copy*, Dec 1913; *Evening News* (Syd), 10 Mar 1910, 2 Dec 1911, 19 Jan 1915; *T&CJ*, 16 Mar 1910, 20 Jan 1915; *Daily Telegraph* (Syd), 24 Dec 1910; *Sun* (Syd), 29 June 1913; *SMH*, 19 Jan 1915; notes on E. C. Day (NSW Police Dept); information from Mr B. C. Day, Paddington, NSW.   HAZEL KING

DAY, ROBERT ALEXANDER (1888-1966), soldier, was born on 29 June 1888 at Rosario, Argentina, son of English-born Robert Day, station-owner, and his second wife Ann, née Allardyce. About 1870 his father had spent some time in New Zealand. In 1911 the family moved to Southernwood, Withersfield, Queensland, where his father took up a sheep and cattle selection, on which Day also worked.

On 2 March 1916 he enlisted in the Australian Imperial Force and embarked from Brisbane with reinforcements for the 15th Battalion in the *Itonus* on 8 August. In January 1917, while with the 4th Training Battalion, he was promoted corporal, and joined the 15th Battalion in France in June, seeing action at Messines and Polygon Wood. In February 1918 he was promoted sergeant and in July, after the battle of Hamel, company sergeant major.

Day distinguished himself in the attack east of Amiens on 8 August, in which the battalion's task was to capture Cérisy. On 3 September he was awarded the Distinguished Conduct Medal 'for conspicuous gallantry and devotion to duty [obtaining] much useful and accurate information by daring patrol work. He also took charge of a bombing party and drove the enemy from a troublesome post'. From 18 to 24 September Day took part in his battalion's last engagement, for the outposts of the Hindenburg line near the village of Jeancourt, and was awarded the Military Medal and Bar. His particular combination of three medals for bravery was rare. Unsuccessful in an attempt to obtain discharge in England, on 8 May 1919 he returned to Australia and on 11 August was demobilized.

Day never returned to Queensland. After sending a telegram to his mother he sailed, via the United States of America, to Argentina, where he took up sheep and cattle raising. In 1924 he married Ana Maria Underwood; they had three children. He died on 1 April 1966 at Trevelin, province of Chubut. The museum there holds a small collection of weapons Day had brought back from the war.

C. E. W. Bean, *The A.I.F. in France*, 1918 (Syd, 1937, 1942); T. P. Chataway, *History of the 15th Battalion A.I.F.*, P. Goldenstedt ed, rev edn (Brisb, 1948); *London Gazette*, 3 Sept 1918, supp, 11 Feb, 17 June 1919; War diary of the 15th Battalion, AIF (AWM); information from E. H. Day, Springsure, Qld, *and* Australian Embassy, Buenos Aires, Argentina.   CHRIS CUNNEEN

DAY, THEODORE ERNEST (1866-1943), surveyor, was born on 7 May 1866 at Forreston near Gumeracha, South Australia, son of Edward Day, storekeeper, and his wife Mary Anne, née Wilkey. Educated at the Grote Street School, at 16 he joined the South Australian Survey Department as a chainman and spent three years on surveys of the west coast.

In 1887 Day became a field cadet; he passed the departmental examinations leading to appointment as a surveyor in 1893

and after the Act of 1896 received a certificate to practise. He ran the west coast survey for the disputed boundary case and was in charge of the vermin destruction branch and vermin-proof fencing. In 1900-10 he lectured at the School of Mines and Industries. He was seconded to Western Australia for three months in 1905 to report on the construction of rabbit-proof barrier fences, and his suggestions were largely implemented in the Vermin Boards Act, 1908. Day also worked with the surveyor-general William Strawbridge on River Murray reclamation and irrigation works. On 7 May 1890 at Manoora he had married Emilie Moore; they had three daughters and two sons.

In 1911 Day joined the Federal Land Tax Office in Adelaide as chief staff valuer, but next year was appointed chief surveyor of the Northern Territory and member of the Northern Territory Land Board at a salary of £650. On 22 March 1915, following the drought of 1914, he set off from Oodnadatta on a nine-month journey to investigate the pastoral possibilities of the country between the overland telegraph line and the Queensland border, and between 21°S and 26°S. The party averaged 16 miles (26 km) per day and by 12 October Day telegraphed that he had mapped 35000 square miles (90000 km^2) of country but that 'this amount of work in such a short period has . . . proved a severe strain on self and party none of whom are now in good health'. In April 1916 he made a second survey of country in the same area, but between the telegraph line and the Western Australian border. On both trips he used camels and Aboriginal guides. Although Day was concerned with the effects of over-stocking in low rainfall areas, and the need for compulsory spelling of the land, he was pleased to report his discovery of much valuable land for pastoral development, 'in areas formerly supposed to consist entirely of sandhills and spinifex'. He described both journeys in a lecture, published by the Royal Geographical Society of Australasia's South Australian branch (1921-22), of which he was a member.

In 1916 Day became head surveyor at Cobdogla for the South Australian Department of Irrigation and Reclamation. In 1919 he was appointed chief surveyor in the Lands and Survey Department and chairman of the Board of Examiners for Surveyors at £450. Two years later this 'highly popular officer' became surveyor-general of the State and chairman of the Pastoral Board. No doubt remembering the isolated settlers that he had met in the Centre, he was a strong advocate for a direct north-south railway link and in 1925 piloted a parliamentary party over possible routes. In

1926-27 he chaired the royal commission on the pastoral industry that recommended reorganization of the board. The commission's recommendations were implemented in the Pastoral Act, 1929. Next year Day resigned as surveyor-general to become the first full-time chairman of the board: over the next five years large areas of land were thrown open for application and leased. Day was also a member of the Town Planning Council and inspector of pastoral lands for soldier settlers. He had been a foundation member of the Commonwealth Institute of Land Valuers and belonged to the South Australian Institute of Surveyors. He was an excellent photographer whose Central Australian lantern lectures were popular.

In 1935 Day retired. He died of chronic myocarditis on 19 August 1943 at Clare survived by his wife and children and was buried in the local cemetery. His estate was sworn for probate at £410. Mount Theo and Mount Day in the Northern Territory are named for him.

Aust Surveyor, May 1928; *Advertiser* (Adel), 10 Mar 1921, 20 Aug 1943; *Observer* (Adel), 27 May 1922, 22 Mar 1926; *Chronicle*, 11 Dec 1930; *Northern Argus* (Clare), 27 Aug 1943; file no 1340 (SAA); A3 items NT 15/5846, 16/1649, 16/1836, 17/77 (AAO); typescript and papers held by Mrs W. Reeves, Beaumont, S.A.   MARLENE MILLAR

DEACON, CLARE (1891-1952), nurse, was born on 13 March 1891 at Pipers River, Tasmania, daughter of William Deacon, farmer, and his wife Ruby Ellen, née Dixon. No details of her early life are known; however, she trained at Hobart Hospital, passing her general nursing examination in 1912.

Clare Deacon enlisted in the Australian Imperial Force on 29 November 1914 as a staff nurse in the Army Nursing Service and was posted to the 2nd Australian General Hospital. She embarked for Egypt on the *Kyarra* with the first contingent and served at Mena throughout the Gallipoli campaign. Promoted to nursing sister in December 1915, she left for France next March and remained with the 2nd A.G.H. in 1916. She was transferred to the 3rd Australian Auxiliary Hospital in February 1917, then in June was temporarily attached to the 2nd Australian Casualty Clearing Station at Trois Arbres near Armentières. On the night of 22 July the station was bombed and Sister Deacon, who was off duty at the time, ran into one of the shattered wards and removed the patients to a place of safety: she was one of four Australian nurses who risked their lives to rescue patients from the burning buildings. For 'coolness and devotion to duty' she, with Sisters Dorothy Cawood [q.v.7] and Alice Ross-King [q.v]

and Staff Nurse Mary Jane Derrer, was awarded the Military Medal, a distinction only awarded for bravery under fire. These were the first Military Medals won by members of the A.A.N.S.

In August Sister Deacon resumed duty with the 2nd A.G.H., remaining with this unit until her return to Australia in April 1918. She was discharged from the A.I.F. in Tasmania in March 1919. A contemporary source described her as 'fresh and girlish-looking', with a charming personality. She married James McGregor, a dentist, on 2 May 1922 at a Melbourne registry office; there were no children of the marriage.

McGregor predeceased her in 1941 and her last years were spent at Crows Nest, Sydney, where she died of meningitis on 7 August 1952.

A. G. Butler (ed), *Official history of the Australian Army Medical Services ... 1914-18*, 3, (Canb, 1943); *London Gazette*, 28 Sept 1917; *A'sian Nurses' J*, 15 Jan 1913, 15 Sept 1917; *Sunday Sun* (Syd), 21 July 1921; *SMH*, 8 Aug 1952; War diary, 2nd Australian Casualty Clearing Station, AIF, July 1917 (AWM).   BARRETT J. CARR

DEAKIN, ALFRED (1856-1919), barrister, journalist and prime minister, was born on 3 August 1856 at Collingwood, Melbourne, younger child of William Deakin of Towcester, Northamptonshire, England, and his wife Sarah, née Bill, of Llanarth, Cardiganshire, Wales. William and Sarah left England in December 1849 in the *Samuel Boddington*, bound for Sydney. In March 1850 they disembarked at Adelaide, where William's married sister lived and where their first child, Catherine Sarah, was born in July. William briefly pursued his former occupations of clerk and shopman before, late in 1851, joining the exodus of men to the goldfields of Victoria. The family soon followed; by 1853 William had abandoned the fields and the Deakins settled in Collingwood (later a part of Fitzroy), where they lived as respectable suburbanites of modest means. William undertook a variety of jobs, storekeeping, water-carting and carrying, before becoming a partner in a coaching business and later manager of Cobb [q.v.3] & Co. in Victoria.

Alfred Deakin began his formal education aged 4 at a boarding-school situated first at Kyneton and later at South Yarra. In 1864 he became a day-boy at the nearby Melbourne Church of England Grammar School. Already Deakin read avidly and day-dreamed habitually, practices which hampered his academic studies. He did not excel at games. Later he looked back upon his schooldays as a time of wasted opportunities. Nonetheless, he won a few subject prizes and survived happily enough to the upper school where he came under the influence of a young master, J. H. Thompson, and the school's renowned headmaster, Dr J. E. Bromby [q.v.3], whose style of oratory, which Deakin's own later closely resembled, fascinated him. At last he was inspired to work seriously. He matriculated in 1871, 'passing' in English and Latin, and 'passing well' in history, algebra and Euclid.

Deakin strayed into the study of law at the University of Melbourne. By evening he attended lectures, by day he earned pocket-money as a schoolteacher and private tutor. He spoke frequently at the University Debating Club, where he met C. H. Pearson [q.v.5]. He gained further skill and experience in the Eclectic Association of Victoria, where members aired current notions on a range of intellectual topics. He was prominent in the spiritualist movement, attending seances, testing phenomena, arranging lectures and conducting the Progressive Lyceum, the spiritualist Sunday school. In 1874 he edited and contributed to the Lyceum Leader and a year later his small volume Quentin Massys; a drama in five acts appeared. In 1877 he published A new pilgrim's progress, a lengthy allegory imbued with the loftiest moral principles, and he became president of the Victorian Association of Spiritualists. He passed in 1877 the final examination for the certificate in law then required for admission to the Victorian Bar. He took chambers in Temple Court, where with little enthusiasm for law and no great expectations he wrote poetry, essays and literary criticism.

An introduction in May 1878 to David Syme [q.v.6] of the Melbourne Age rescued the restless Deakin from his near-briefless career. Syme, who became a close friend, engaged him as a paid contributor of reviews, leaders, sub-leaders and general articles on politics, literature and miscellaneous topics. In 1880 he edited the Leader, the Age's weekly. He excelled at journalism, which became his major occupation for some five years and provided a useful source of income for most of his life. Syme also converted him from free-trade beliefs to protectionist, a change which helped both his journalistic and political ambitions. Deakin's interest in Victorian politics had been aroused by the resignation of the liberal parliamentarian, George Higinbotham [q.v.4] one of his boyhood heroes, the entry into parliament of Pearson, and the constitutional conflict which Deakin described in the memoir (1900) published in 1957 as The crisis in Victorian politics, 1879-1881. With Syme's aid he became the Liberal candidate for West Bourke, a largely rural electorate, which he won narrowly in February 1879.

The young Deakin who entered parliament was an impressive figure. He was six feet (about 183 cm) tall, dark haired and dark eyed, his handsome, alert face fashionably bearded. He spoke rapidly in a rich, baritone voice which, he claimed, bore no trace of 'provincial' accent. In his maiden speech he startled members by announcing his resignation because of doubts about the fairness of the administration of the original poll. He lost the recontested by-election in August and lost again in the general election of February 1880, which also saw the defeat of (Sir) Graham Berry's [q.v.3] government. In July he headed the poll in West Bourke after James Service [q.v.6], 'Conservative' leader, had secured a dissolution of parliament. Despite his youth and inexperience, and in the face of opposition from his own party and the Age, he was prominent in negotiating a compromise between moderates on both sides and helped to secure the Council Reform Act of 1881.

On 3 April 1882 Deakin married 19-year-old Elizabeth Martha Anne ('Pattie'), daughter of wealthy Hugh Junor Browne [q.v.3], a prominent spiritualist. The marriage, disapproved of by the Brownes, brought no material benefit to the Deakins. They lived for a time with Deakin's parents; in 1887 Llanarth, their house in Walsh Street, South Yarra, was completed. For the rest of his active life, Deakin walked, bicycled or took the tram into the city.

From March 1883 to November 1890 Deakin held office in coalition governments. He proved an able administrator, and he practised and polished the art of compromise. He introduced the Factories and Shops Act of 1885, a pioneer social measure based largely on British legislation that had impressed the royal commission of 1884. The Act, though mutilated by the Legislative Council, provided for the regulation and inspection of factories, enforced sanitary regulations, limited the hours of work of females and youths, and compensated workers for injury. He chaired the 1884 royal commission on irrigation, a cause he pressed with fervour. Late in the year he led a small party to California to investigate irrigation and conservation schemes. There he met the Chaffey brothers [qq.v.7] and reported enthusiastically on their experiments. The Chaffeys came to Victoria in 1886 and demonstrated their methods at Mildura. In June Deakin introduced the first legislation in Australia to promote an irrigation system. The bill broke with traditional English riparian law by placing ownership of natural waters under the Crown and provided for the construction of state-aided irrigation works by local trusts. Promise of early success faded because of technical problems, poor choice of associates by the Chaffeys, the depression of the 1890s and one of the worst droughts in Australian history. But in the long run successful irrigation and water schemes became a feature of rural Victoria and Australia.

Late in 1885 Berry and Service retired and were succeeded, as leaders of the coalition, by Deakin and Duncan Gillies [q.v.4]. Deakin, chief secretary, also took the portfolio of water-supply to which was added, in 1890, health and, briefly, solicitor-general. He was Victoria's principal representative at the Colonial Conference of 1887. In London he met and impressed many prominent public figures, politicians, writers and intellectuals and formed lasting friendships. At the conference he played the role of native-born Victorian patriot pressing 'colonial' interests. He argued forcibly for better terms in the naval agreement, under which the colonies paid an annual subsidy towards the cost of an auxiliary squadron for use in Australian waters. With Sir Samuel Griffith [q.v.], Service and Berry he confronted Lord Salisbury [q.v.3, Cecil], prime minister and foreign secretary, over the issue of the New Hebrides. British officials recognized in him the authentic, but not always welcome, voice of colonial nationalism. He returned home to a triumphant welcome.

Melbourne at this time was indeed marvellous and a massive inflow of British capital fuelled the Victorian boom. The coalition won the election of March 1889, but problems over proposed railway construction and use of the militia to protect non-union labour in the maritime strike — an action for which Deakin bore ministerial responsibility — caused the government's defeat in October 1890. By then the land boom was starting to waver and soon the bubble burst. Deakin, like many contemporaries of his social class, speculated heavily in the rush to be rich: he lost his own and his father's savings. Unlike many he repaid his debts. Nonetheless, the picture of him as an innocent intellectual unwittingly caught up in the brutal world of business seems too kind. He was chairman or director of many dubious companies, including those of the notorious boomer James Munro [q.v.5]; Deakin's friend Theodore Fink [q.v.] possibly sometimes persuaded him to lend his name. As joint coalition leader he shared power and responsibility in a government whose own borrowing and investment policies contributed much to the onset of the collapse and the severity of the depression. As an individual investor he sought quick and easy profit with the rest of them.

Outwardly, after the coalition's defeat and financial disaster, Deakin seemed his familiar confident self. Inwardly, as copious note-books and diaries reveal, he was disillusioned. Tortured by self-doubt, he longed to restore his self-respect. He spent the next ten years as an influential back-bencher, the member from 1889 for Essendon and Flemington. Syme urged him to replace Munro as premier, (Sir) George Turner [q.v.] consulted him about the composition of his government in 1894, but he refused all offers of ministerial posts. He returned to the practice of law. He was engaged in several major cases, the most celebrated being as defender without fee in 1892 of the mass murderer F. B. Deeming [q.v.], and as junior to J. L. Purves [q.v.5] in 1893-94 in the lengthy defence of Syme in a libel case. A respectable income at the Bar supplemented his parliamentary salary and helped to support a growing family, which in 1891 had seen the addition of his third and last daughter. In 1893 he published *Irrigated India* and *Temple and tomb in India*, following a short working visit to India and Ceylon (Sri Lanka) financed by Syme. He read everything that came his way in English literature, biography, history and philosophy, French in the original, and German and the classics in translation. He was active in the Theosophical Society until 1896, when he resigned on joining the Australian Church, led by Charles Strong [q.v.6]. He retained a wide interest in public affairs through the Protectionist Association, the National Anti-Sweating League, the Australian Natives' Association, the Imperial Federation League (of which he became president in 1905) and the Federal Council of Australasia. But his main preoccupation in the 1890s was the Federation movement.

Deakin's interest in Federation had been stimulated by Service and heightened by experience at the Colonial Conference of 1887, where colonial division thwarted attempts to overcome Imperial apathy. He attended all the official Federal conferences and conventions. He appears to have helped resolve differences between Gillies and Sir Henry Parkes [q.v.5], who convened the Australasian Federation Conference of 1890. Deakin was the youngest delegate to the National Australasian Convention of 1891 in Sydney, and he polled third in the popular election of ten Victorian delegates to the Australasian Federal Convention of 1897-98: in both he served on the constitutional committee. As a progressive liberal from a large colony he adopted a democratic stance on most issues. He opposed conservative plans for the indirect election of senators and sought a relatively weak 'States House' which he foresaw would be dominated by political parties. On the most vital constitutional issue of all, control of money bills, he tried to limit the Senate's power and make the House of Representatives supreme. He advocated wide taxation powers for the Commonwealth.

Backstage Deakin was the familiar eloquent proposer of compromises, the able conciliator, the tactful smoother of ruffled feathers. Even so, his reputation as an Australian nationalist seeking to overcome colonial parochialism, as a staunch Federationist urging delegates that whenever they detected a Federal interest they should 'provide for it in advance', is not without minor blemish. At the first convention he claimed that special safeguards might need to be made for Victoria's protected factories. He reluctantly approved C. C. Kingston's [q.v.] proposed new Federal arbitration power, and his remarks that it could not possibly become a 'proper subject' for Federal legislation for a very long time and might be exercised 'less satisfactorily' than by individual colonies, did little to advance the idea.

While Deakin played a significant part in making and shaping the Constitution, his contribution to the 'popular' phases of the Federation movement was probably greater. The Constitution bill of 1891 was unpopular, and politicians and public alike lacked enthusiasm. Sir John Robertson's [q.v.6] boast that Federation was as 'dead as Julius Caesar' seemed valid and few but dedicated nationalists mourned its passing. In Victoria, Deakin set out to resurrect the corpse. In March 1893, at the annual conference of the A.N.A., he and Purves urged the association to broaden its appeals and campaigns. Deakin suggested combining with other Federal sympathizers, and (Sir) Edmund Barton [q.v.7] was asked to create a central Federation league in Sydney. Later, Deakin prompted the Prahran branch to propose a Federation league, of which he became foundation executive chairman in 1894.

These efforts, and similar ones of Barton and others in New South Wales, took Federation out of the hands of parliamentarians, and helped to ensure its success. As chairman of the Federation League of Victoria and acknowledged leader and symbol of the cause in the colony, Deakin was the central figure in the referenda campaigns of 1898-99, when the Commonwealth bill was put to the popular test. His celebrated address at the A.N.A. banquet at Bendigo in March 1898 set the tone for the campaign and converted a hostile, but still suspicious, *Age*. A dithering Turner declared for the bill. In 1899 Deakin campaigned in Queensland, which had stood aside until it was clear that Federal union of at least four colonies was about to occur.

London staged the final act of the Feder-

ation movement. In January 1900 Joseph Chamberlain invited the colonies to send delegates for the passing of the Constitution bill through the Imperial parliament. Allan McLean [q.v.], Victorian premier, appointed Deakin, who later in the month sailed for London with his wife, sister and daughters. Barton, Kingston, Sir Philip Fysh [q.v.] of Tasmania and (Sir) James Dickson [q.v.] of Queensland made up the team selected to defend the Constitution to the last comma. In the end differences came down to clause 74, which forbade appeals to the Privy Council in matters affecting the interpretation of the Constitution. At first Chamberlain deleted the whole clause. In this he was fortified by the defection of Dickson, the wavering of some colonial premiers – to whom he had appealed – and the devious conduct of several chief justices, notably Griffith and Sir Samuel Way [q.v.]. Deakin, Barton and Kingston put their case to the British public, at numerous complimentary functions. In the event they compromised: appeals involving constitutional issues required leave of the High Court, otherwise the right of appeal remained unimpaired unless further limited by the parliament of the Commonwealth. The triumphant trio danced 'hand in hand' in jubilation. In July, as he sailed home to a great welcome, an 'Act to constitute the Commonwealth of Australia' received the royal assent.

Deakin made a remarkable decision on his return. In London he had met Lord Glenesk, proprietor, and Nicol Dunn, editor, of the *Morning Post*. In November he accepted an offer to became their 'special' or 'Sydney' correspondent, furnishing weekly letters and occasional cables on Australian politics for £500 a year. In his just completed manuscript (first published in 1944 as *The Federal story*), he recorded an 'inner history' of the Federation movement. An anonymous Deakin was now to write an inner account of Federal politics for a Tory unionist paper even as he was about to become a minister of the Crown, and to remain one for most of the thirteen years of his secret journalism. The money was useful and he persuaded himself that it was his duty to supply an ignorant British public with informed news and views on Australian politics. Later, in 1904-05, he was to write unsigned articles for the London *National Review*. The letters and articles were to prove vivid in style, intelligent in comment, relatively free from bias and mildly critical of himself on occasions. By any standards it was extraordinary.

The turn of the century was a momentous time in the history of Australia and the Empire. Queen Victoria died and the South African War was being fought. Australians looked to the coming of the Commonwealth, and aspiring Federal politicians looked forward to the general election in March 1901. Deakin formed the National Liberal Organization, which united wings of the Liberal Party in Victoria, and as founder-president he espoused progressive liberal policies and selected candidates. He exchanged letters with Barton and Kingston, discussing platforms and tactics. The earl of Hopetoun [q.v.], governor-general, blundered in asking Sir William Lyne [q.v.], premier of New South Wales but an anti-Federationist in the referenda, to form a caretaker cabinet. Deakin's refusal to serve under Lyne proved decisive, and Hopetoun called upon Barton.

Deakin helped to select the 'shadow cabinet' and advised on the number and nature of departments and the distribution of portfolios. He himself was sworn in as attorney-general: the youngest member of cabinet. With fellow members he devised the Protectionist policy speech, delivered by Barton at Maitland on 17 January 1901.

The first Federal election resulted in a narrow majority for the Protectionists over Free Traders. Labor came in third and declared its tactics of support-in-return-for-concessions, which in practice meant giving general support to the Barton government. Free Traders outnumbered Protectionists in the Senate, and Labor surprised even itself by winning the balance of nearly a quarter of the seats. Deakin won handsomely in Ballarat, which he held until he retired in 1913.

Federal parliament opened in May and the Barton ministry in general, and Deakin in particular, faced daunting tasks. As leader of the House Deakin was frequently in charge of parliamentary business, and as attorney-general he headed a department which drafted bills for foundation machinery and policies, and provided advice and opinions on points of law for other ministers. While (Sir) R. R. Garran [q.v.], his energetic departmental secretary, was indispensable, Deakin was an active attorney-general, especially in preparing opinions and drafting bills for the public service, arbitration and the High Court. On the immigration restriction bill he supported Barton against Labor, who wanted more direct methods of exclusion than the dictation test. His famous second reading speech on the bill lacked the vicious racism of many others, but his claim that Japanese must be kept out because of their good qualities, not their bad, neither pleased nor placated them. He took no part in interminable debates on the tariff, but his diplomacy in September 1902 averted possible deadlock between the Senate and House, and secured the measure which set the Commonwealth on the path to financial independence. By this time he was acting prime minister, a post he filled for six months while Barton attended the coronation and the Colonial Conference.

White Australia legislation was never in real danger and a uniform tariff had to be passed, but the Judiciary Act of 1903 needed all Deakin's negotiating skills. The Constitution provided for a High Court, but it set down no mandatory timetable for its creation and the bill met unexpected hostility. Inside Federal parliament (Sir) George Reid [q.v.], Opposition leader, played politics, blaming the government both for undue haste and improper delay. Many Protectionists were uneasy. Outside, State politicians, newspapers and the public condemned the proposal on State-rights grounds and with telling charges of Federal extravagance. Deakin's masterful second reading speech in March 1902 was widely regarded as a supreme example of parliamentary advocacy. In the end, passage of the bill probably owed less to the speech than to personal loyalty to 'affable Alfred' and hints of his possible resignation. While the bill to found the High Court was Deakin's most 'cherished' measure, according to the anonymous correspondent, the conciliation and arbitration bill was Kingston's. Kingston, pioneer of compulsory arbitration, became its first Federal casualty when, in July 1903, he resigned over cabinet's refusal to extend the bill's scope to all seamen engaged in coastal trade. Deakin took charge of the measure. Most members agreed with the principle of arbitration, but disagreement arose on detail. Labor's Andrew Fisher [q.v.], assisted by the Opposition, amended the bill to include State railway-workers. Deakin abandoned the bill for the time being.

When Barton retired to the High Court in September Deakin succeeded him as prime minister and minister of external affairs. He made several ministerial changes, bringing in Thomas Playford [q.v.] and (Sir) Austin Chapman [q.v.7]. Deakin retained office in the December election, which produced three almost equal parties in the House, with informal Labor support. His government was short lived. He reintroduced the arbitration bill in March 1904, but Labor amended the bill to apply it to State public servants, a move he believed unconstitutional. He treated the defeat as a matter of no confidence and advised Lord Northcote [q.v.], governor-general, to send for J. C. Watson [q.v.], Labor leader. Watson had less chance of keeping office than Deakin, who promised him 'fair play' provided he acquired a 'constitutional' majority. Labor, however, took office in April without making overtures to radical Protectionists such as Lyne and (Sir) Isaac Isaacs [q.v.].

In May Deakin urged his party to accept Reid's terms for a working alliance though he himself would not serve in any coalition with Reid, whom he disliked and mistrusted. A divided Protectionist Party refused the offer and Watson's belated overtures. Labor pressed on with the arbitration bill until halted by (Sir) J. W. McCay [q.v.] who, with Deakin's concurrence, later moved against its recommittal. Watson resigned in August after two days of bitter debate. Deakin's role in the affair marred his reputation and he lost much goodwill in parliament. Nevertheless, his own unexpected resignation, which forced Labor to accept responsibility for its actions, was a shrewd tactic. Labor's short, barren period of government curbed its irresponsible conduct and made it wary of taking office.

Deakin declined to join the Reid-McLean coalition of conservative Free Traders and Protectionists, but an opportunity for a return to office arose during the long parliamentary recess. The campaigns in New South Wales of anti-socialist leagues, which seemed much like old free-trade bodies under new guise, and ideas of forming similar ones in Victoria, made Protectionists suspicious of Reid's motives. Multitarious pressure mounted to depose Reid before he called a premature election designed, the argument ran, to advantage Free Traders by prolonging the fiscal truce. Deakin warned that the anticipated reports of the tariff commission, appointed in December 1904, would inevitably disturb the truce. His speech at Ballarat in June just before parliament reassembled was regarded as a 'Notice to Quit'. Northcote's speech mentioned only one bill, and Deakin carried an amendment to the address-in-reply. Northcote refused a dissolution and called upon Deakin, who had Watson's assurance of 'cordial and generous support' for the remainder of the parliament. Reid's charges of treachery were to be expected, but Deakin's seemingly shabby treatment of the four Protectionists in the coalition, especially of Turner, lost him further goodwill and respect.

The second Deakin ministry, July 1905-November 1908, was remarkably productive. Many national policies and much practical legislation were placed on the statute books or would soon become law after the government's fall. Measures fixed the capital site, authorized the survey of a trans-continental railway-route, and provided for Australian statistics, meteorology, wireless telegraphy and copyright. The Contract Immigrants Act of 1905 established stringent procedures and safeguards for admitting contract labour, and the Commonwealth assumed full control of the former British New Guinea. The first protective Federal tariff was passed. 'New Protection' tried in devious ways to link the Commonwealth's exclusive control of the tariff with the State's power over wages and prices. The Commonwealth Literary Fund came into being and Australia involved itself in Antarctica. The Surplus Revenue Act of 1908 set the Commonwealth on the path to financial independence and dominance. Naval and military defence innovations were under way. Old-age pensions were introduced.

Most of these measures were the responsibility of Deakin's ministerial colleagues such as Lyne, Isaacs, Sir John Forrest, (Sir) Littleton Groom and Sir Thomas Ewing [qq.v.], and they were not his in any personal sense. But Deakin selected his colleagues and he led and kept in office a cabinet wherein he was manifestly not merely first among equals. Many were consensus policies favoured by members of all parties. Old-age pensions, for example, was a common cause. New Protection was neither a subtle scheme devised by Deakin to convert Labor to protection nor a Labor concession forced from Deakin, but an evolutionary policy sought by Free Traders, Protectionists and Laborites alike: none were more determined than Free Traders that if there was to be a system of protection it must take the new form. Conservative opponents of Deakin and some Labor politicians claimed that he was under Labor's thumb, the one to deny him credit, the other to claim it for themselves. Labor, however, was in a weak tactical position. Watson could not bargain or negotiate with Reid, now anti-socialist leader, and play him off against Deakin, and Labor's own brief spell of office in 1904 showed it was unlikely to govern effectively on its own.

Labor support for Deakin was vital, but it is doubtful if he conceded much in return. Though the platforms of the two parties had much in common, some policies were peculiarly Labor. None of them were implemented by Deakin, or Barton. The Immigration Restriction Act retained its indirect method of exclusion, and Deakin refused preference to unionists in his arbitration bill; there was no referendum on the tariff as favoured by Labor, no land tax or nationalization of monopolies. If anyone held the balance in parliament it was Deakin, between Labor and 'socialism' on the left and free trade or anti-socialism on the right. His negotiating skills, personal qualities and good relations with Watson enabled the Protectionist Party to retain office even after it emerged from the election of 1906 as the smallest of the three elevens. He provided stability of government enabling the passing of constructive legislation, and at the time only he seemed able to do that.

Deakin, by inclination and by virtue of his position as prime minister and minister of external affairs, was closely concerned with the related fields of 'foreign' policy, Imperial relations and defence. He took direct interest in Papua, where a faction-ridden administration limped on. In August 1906 he appointed a royal commission, which recommended the removal of the administrator, Captain F. R. Barton, and the sacking of some principal officers. In November 1908 he named (Sir) Hubert Murray [q.v.], then chief judicial officer and acting administrator, as lieut-governor, an appointment Labor confirmed, and the thirty-year reign of the benevolent paternalist began. Deakin resumed old battles with the Imperial government over the future of the New Hebrides, urging that France be induced to accept British annexation. Apparent British ineptitude and the secretive nature of Anglo-French negotiations confirmed his low opinion of the Colonial Office. In the end, fearful of German activity in the islands, he perforce pressed for the immediate proclamation of the joint protectorate.

In March 1907 Deakin left for the Imperial Conference in London with three main aims: to reform Imperial organization, to advance the cause of Imperial preference and to revise the naval agreement. He was the most active and outspoken colonial premier on the theme that the Empire must draw closer together lest it fall apart. His proposal for a permanent Imperial secretariat to give self-governing dominions an effective voice in foreign policy, defence and economic co-operation, received a cold reception. The Colonial Office saw it as an attempt to undermine its authority, doubts about ministerial control arose and the idea lacked definition and practicality. Lord Elgin's creation of a dominions division of the Colonial Office was not much more than a change of name.

Deakin's pleas for Imperial preference as a means of strengthening the Empire politically and economically met with little support from colonial premiers and outright opposition from the British government. Sir Wilfred Laurier, Canada, was prepared to accept it if it was offered, Louis Botha, South Africa, spoke negatively. Neither, for domestic reasons, wanted further Imperial entanglements. Deakin's public campaign on the question touched sensitive issues in British politics. To conservative newspapers and Tories he was a hero, to their liberal counterparts a villain. Asquith and Lloyd George remained implacably opposed. The Admiralty was more sympathetic to the notion of an Australian naval force, but differences on the naval agreement were not resolved.

Deakin had disliked the naval agreement since its inception in 1902, and his sustained efforts to implement Australian naval aspirations began several years before the Imperial Conference. He had also long believed in the virtues of universal military service; by December 1907, when he introduced the first bill to embrace such a scheme, Labor was about to adopt the idea and parliamentarians and the public at large had already been converted. Naval affairs, a more complex issue, inevitably involved the British government, the Admiralty, naval tactics and grand strategy, and from mid-1905 to early 1910 the subject absorbed him. He attacked the agreement and the Admiralty, and the rebuffs and insensitive denials of Australian naval ambitions merely spurred him on. Late in 1906 he announced an intended purchase of destroyers, but at the Imperial Conference the first lord, Tweedmouth, recommended submarines.

In 1908 Deakin placed further pressure on the Colonial Office and the Admiralty with his timely invitation to the American 'Great White Fleet' to visit Australian ports. By the time he resigned in November no vessels had been ordered but the Surplus Revenue Act of 1908 provided £250 000 for naval expenditure, a sum Labor used later. Eventually, after the naval scare of 1909, when Deakin played the opportunist by joining the cry for the gift of a dreadnought to Britain, the Admiralty suggested a powerful Australian fleet unit. For Deakin, the type of vessels and strategic questions such as those arising from the Russo-Japanese War of 1904-05 were secondary issues. The Commonwealth's defence power provided him with a means to two related ends, one external the other internal. An Australia prepared to share Britain's defence burden by being more self-reliant, particularly in naval defence, would earn a voice in Imperial policy. Service for the Commonwealth, especially military training for youths, would instil the 'maximum of good citizenship' and foster a 'sense of national unity' and a 'national spirit'. For Deakin acquisition of a navy and introduction of compulsory military service were essential steps in the evolution from colony to nation within the British Empire.

On returning from the Imperial Conference Deakin faced acute health and political problems. He travelled badly, slept fitfully and had frequent attacks of giddiness and exhaustion. His memory and speech faltered and he suffered a breakdown. Forrest, an old colleague, resigned in July 1907 over the Liberal-Labor relationship, which became more difficult after Watson resigned the leadership in October. Labor withdrew its support in November 1908 and the earl of Dudley [q.v.], governor-general, sent for Fisher. Deakin came under pressure to form a united front against Labor, whose militant 'machine' and electoral activities he feared increasingly. As Labor ranks had swelled at successive elections so Liberal-Protectionist numbers dwindled until the party was the smallest in the House, and its future looked bleak. Labor radicalism had outflanked and outpaced Deakinite liberalism. Neither (Sir) Joseph Cook [q.v.], who had succeeded Reid, nor Forrest would serve under one another. Deakin, waiting in the wings, convinced himself that he could liberalize the conservatives and preserve radical liberalism. In May 1909 he agreed to the fusion of anti-socialists, Liberal-Protectionists and Forrest's 'corner' group. A bewildered Fisher was curtly dismissed. Close friends still believed in Deakin's integrity, but to many others his actions seemed nothing but a naked grab for power, a base move to regain office at any price by a man who thought he was indispensable. The political confusion produced some of the most dramatic scenes in Federal parliamentary history. Lyne – never a friend of Deakin and now a foe – denounced his former leader as a 'Judas', a charge which the vindictive W. M. Hughes [q.v.] believed slandered the disciple.

Deakin was sworn in for the third and last time as prime minister on 2 June 1909. The Fusion government, given its short span of life and the few points of agreement between the uniting parties, was remarkably active. Deakin ordered the *Australia,* the nation's own dreadnought battle cruiser and pride of the fleet unit. He invited the legendary Lord Kitchener to visit Australia to advise on military defence: later Labor largely implemented suggested changes in organization and creation of a military staff college. Bills were introduced to transfer the Northern Territory to the Commonwealth and to set up the Inter-State Commission, and one was passed to establish the high commission in London. Negotiations between Deakin, Forrest and State premiers produced the financial agreement of 1909, which gave the States *per capita* grants of 25s. annually: Deakin's attempted constitutional amendment failed in 1910, but in practice the agreement determined Commonwealth-State financial arrangements until 1927.

The Fusion government entered the election of April 1910 confident of victory, but in the event it was routed. In a heavy poll Labor gained absolute majorities in both the House and Senate. Deakin, who campaigned on a mainly negative anti-Labor platform, barely escaped defeat in Ballarat. Only a handful of his personal followers survived. He was ill-suited to the negative role of Opposition leader, especially as Labor was advancing many of his own, unfinished measures. His extensive campaign in 1911 against Labor proposals to amend the Constitution carried more conviction, but he retired in January 1913, a spent force. His last act as a politician was to support Cook against Forrest in the leadership contest.

In May 1913 Deakin emerged from retirement at Ballara, his hideaway at Point Lonsdale, to campaign against Labor's resubmitted referenda proposals. Later he declined Cook's offer of the first chairmanship of the Inter-State Commission. In August 1914 he became chairman of the royal commission to investigate wartime food supplies and prices and his colleagues carried him. As president of an Australian commission for the international exhibition at San Francisco he toured California in April 1915 with Pattie, but resigned after a renewed dispute with Hugh Mahon [q.v.], Labor minister of external affairs. His health deteriorated and he visited specialists in London and New York in 1916-17. In retirement and in decline his increasingly introspective notebooks reflected his despairing sense of the emptiness of existence, the loneliness of a man spiritually and intellectually isolated for most of his life. Like many affable people he had few intimate friends, and apparently none knew the inner Deakin. After 1916 he lived as a recluse, his memory decayed, the famed silver tongue stilled. He died of meningo-encephalitis on 7 October 1919, survived by his wife and daughters. As befitted this independent Australian Briton he was given a state funeral, his coffin draped with the Union Jack. He was buried in St Kilda cemetery.

His wife Pattie, who died on 30 December 1934, was well known for her work for children's welfare, particularly the kindergarten, crèche and playgrounds movements, and for servicemen during World War I. Ivy, the eldest daughter, married Herbert Brookes [q.v.7], Stella married (Sir) David Rivett [q.v.] and Vera (Sir) Thomas Walter White. Deakin's sister Kate (or Katie) died unmarried in 1937; a talented pianist, she shared and encouraged her brother's interest in literature and remained his lifelong mentor and confidante.

Alfred Deakin, dominant figure of the first decade of Federation, was a complex character, the outer man the generally charming, confident, intelligent politician, the inner man the often morose, insecure, frustrated intellectual. The young man attracted to spiritualism and theosophy wanted to be a philosopher, poet, dramatist: instead he merely became a statesman. He was a gifted politician in an era that lent itself to his natural talents of compromise and persuasion. He had integrity, though he could play the opportunist when the need arose and the Fusion sullied his reputation for some. He was unusually modest and circumspect, declining all British offers of titles and distinctions in the belief that he had not earned them and that his independence might be compromised. In the late nineteenth century and early twentieth century he epitomized Victorian liberalism. His services to the Federation movement and the new nation were immense. The Commonwealth briefly gained recognition as a national laboratory for social experimentation and positive liberalism, and Deakin more than anyone brought that about. He was the embodiment of dual nationalism: pride in Australia went hand in hand with pride in Empire, membership of the A.N.A. with membership of the Imperial Federation League. He had a mystical faith in the virtues of the British race and his vision was of a great white Australia living at one with and within a greater white Empire. The tragedy was that he became an anachronism. Liberalism blossomed and withered in his own time, and the middle ground disappeared beneath his feet. The sun was already setting on the Empire he envisaged.

National A'sian Convention, Syd, *Official record of the proceedings and debates* (Syd, 1891); A'sian Federal Convention, *Official report of debates* (Adel, 1897), and . . . *record of debates* (Melb, 1898); H. G. Turner, *The first decade of the Australian Commonwealth* (Melb, 1911); W. Murdoch, *Alfred Deakin* (Lond, 1923); A. Deakin, *The federal story*, J. A. La Nauze ed (Melb, 1963); J. A. La Nauze, *Alfred Deakin* (Melb, 1965); A. Deakin, *Federated Australia*, J. A. La Nauze ed (Melb, 1968); G. Serle, *The rush to be rich* (Melb, 1971); J. A. La Nauze, *The making of the Australian constitution* (Melb, 1972); R. Norris, *The emergent Commonwealth* (Melb, 1975); P. Loveday, et al (eds), *The emergence of the Australian party system* (Syd, 1977); *Hist Studies*, no 55, Oct 1970, p 376; L. D. Atkinson, Australian defence policy: a study of empire and nation (Ph.D. thesis, ANU, 1964); E. Barton papers, *and* Deakin papers (NL).   R. NORRIS

DEAMER, MARY ELIZABETH KATH-LEEN DULCIE (1890-1972), writer and Bohemian, was born on 13 December 1890 at Christchurch, New Zealand, daughter of George Edwin Deamer, a physician from Lincolnshire, and his New Zealand-born wife Mable, née Reader. She was taught at home by her mother, who had been a governess. At 9 Dulcie appeared on the stage as a child with R. Brough's [q.v.3] Comedy Company.

About 1902 the family moved to Featherston in the North Island. Later she was sent to friends in Wellington for elocution and ballet lessons as stage-training.

In 1906 Dulcie won first prize in a *Lone Hand* competition with a 'highly imaginative' Stone Age story: Norman Lindsay's [q.v.] illustrations shocked her family. Later Dulcie admitted: 'Even at that tender age I loved blood, murder and violence'. Next year she joined a touring theatrical company and met 32-year-old Albert Goldberg (d. 1934), known as Goldie, who was working for J. C. Williamson [q.v.6]. In the Roman Catholic Cathedral, Perth, she married him on 8 August 1907. They left at once for a tour of the Far East with Hugh Ward's [q.v.] company. She played small parts and sought copy for *Lone Hand*. In Sydney in December 1910 she reported the Billy Papke-Dave Smith fight for its promoter H. D. Macintosh [q.v.].

In the crowded years 1908-1924 Dulcie bore six children (two sons died in infancy), travelled overseas in 1912, 1913-14, 1916-19 and 1921 and published a collection of short stories and four novels — *The suttee of Safa* (New York, 1913) 'a hot and strong love story about Akbar the Great'; *Revelation* (London, 1921) and *The street of the gazelle* (London, 1922), set in Jerusalem at the time of Christ; and *The devil's saint* (London, 1924). Three were syndicated in Randolph Hearst's newspapers in the United States of America. Her themes, including witchcraft, gave 'free play to the lavish style of her writing, displaying opulence and sensuality or squalor of traditional scenes'.

Her parents had moved to Sydney and Dulcie left her children with her mother to bring up. After she and her husband had separated in 1922 she lived at Kings Cross. As a freelance journalist she contributed stories, articles and verse to the *Australian Woman's Mirror*, other journals and newspapers, such as the *Bulletin* and the *Sydney Morning Herald*, often using pseudonyms. She was a founder in 1929 and committee-member of the Fellowship of Australian Writers. From 1930 she received a £52 pension from the Commonwealth Literary Fund.

Dulcie Deamer mixed with the 'starving artists, poor musicians, writers scratching for a living, bit actors, and people with all sorts of strange jobs', who met at Sam Rosa's [q.v.] restaurant and 'Theo's Club' where they crowned her 'Queen of Bohemia' on 13 July 1925. She often appeared in her famous leopard skin which she had first worn at the Artists' Ball on 27 September 1923. With a dash of Spanish blood, she was small and slight with 'jewel-bright' dark eyes and long flowing black hair. Zora Cross [q.v.] described her in 1928 as 'Speedy as a swallow in movement, quick as sunlight in speech . . . [and] restless as the sea'. Full of *joie de vivre*, she enlivened many a party by doing the splits and dancing the hula-hula.

In the 1930s Dulcie Deamer wrote plays; several were produced at the Tom Thumb Theatre, and *That by which men live* (1936) and *Victory* (1938) at Beryl Bryant's Playhouse. The *Sydney Morning Herald* theatre critic found her a 'playwright of powerful imagination'. She also published another novel, *Holiday*, dealing with the persecution of early Christians, in 1940, and two volumes of mystical poetry, *Messalina* (1932) and *The silver branch* (1948).

For Dulcie Deamer and her friends, 'the Cross' was never the same after the influx of American servicemen in World War II and the burgeoning of shops, cafés and neon lights. In the 1960s she wrote her autobiography, 'The golden decade', but it was never published. On 16 August 1972 she died in the Little Sisters of the Poor home, Randwick, and was buried in the Catholic section of Botany cemetery. She was survived by a son and daughter; her son Christopher was drowned when H.M.A.S. *Parramatta* was torpedoed off Tobruk in November 1941. Her portrait was painted in London about 1921 by Helen Donald-Smith.

Theatre (Syd & Melb), 1 Mar 1912, 1 Oct 1919; *Aust Woman's Mirror*, 14 Aug 1928; *Wentworth Mag*, Dec 1929; *All About Books*, 13 Nov 1933, 14 Nov 1935, 12 May 1936; *People*, 26 Apr 1950; *Australasian*, 6 Oct 1923; *SMH*, 26 Sept 1938, 15 Aug 1972; *Bulletin*, 12 Jan 1949; *Sun-Herald*, 2 Oct 1955; *Daily Mirror*, 20 Sept 1972; Brady papers (Oxley Lib, Brisb); D. Deamer papers *and* autobiography, *and* K. I. MacKenzie, Correspondence, vol 7 (ML).   MARTHA RUTLEDGE

DEAN, GEORGE (1867-1933), ferry-boat master and poisoner, was born on 14 November 1867 at Albury, New South Wales, son of Irish parents George Deane, miner, and his wife Annie, née Byrne. His mother later lived with a man named Finch. At Narrandera, as George Finch, Dean, aged 12, was convicted of using a horse illegally on 28 November 1879; he spent three months in Wagga Wagga gaol as he could not pay the £5 fine.

Taken to Sydney by his 'foster-father', Dean worked for a blacksmith, and about 1884 began working for the North Shore Steam Ferry Co. On 10 July 1888 he was issued with his master's certificate, and from 1890 was master of the *Possum*, running between Circular Quay and Milsons Point at night. Dean, who was handsome with a trim moustache and a reputation for bravery, was popular with his passengers. On 8 March

1894 at St David's Anglican Church, Surry Hills, he married Sarah Annie Gaynor; she was known as Mary Seymour and was the daughter of Caroline (Catherine) Asbury, late Adams, alias Seymour, who had been transported to Van Diemen's Land in 1852 for pick-pocketing; her father was an ex-convict, Denis Gaynor. The Deans' marriage was soon a failure, with much mother-in-law trouble; however, Mary gave birth to a daughter on 26 December.

On 8 March 1895 Dean was arrested and charged with having poisoned his wife with intent to murder. Defended by R. D. Meagher [q.v.], he was tried before (Sir) William Windeyer [q.v.6], and convicted and sentenced to death on 6 April; the sentence was commuted to life imprisonment. The 'lemon-syrup case' created a sensation – there was a public outcry that Dean had not had a fair trial and was innocent; the Central and North Shore Defence committees were set up and public meetings held. Meagher and his partner W. P. Crick [q.v.], in parliament, mounted an attack on Windeyer, accused Mary Dean and Mrs Seymour of conspiracy and agitated for an inquiry.

On 7 May F. E. Rogers, Q.C. [q.v.], and two physicians P. Sydney Jones and F. N. Manning [qq.v.4, 5] were appointed to a royal commission. Among others Captain Thomas Summerbell, his employer, testified that Dean was 'trust-worthy, honest, courteous to his passengers'. Copious evidence showed that Mary Dean's mother was a woman of ill repute and an associate of criminals. The two doctors recommended release; but Rogers, the chairman, although acknowledging the many problems in the case, dissented. Dean was granted a free pardon on 28 June. He returned to his job and became master of a larger ferry, the *Wallaby*.

On 18 July Meagher, who was running for parliament, consulted Sir Julian Salomons, Q.C. [q.v.6], about taking action against the *Daily Telegraph* for criticizing his handling of the case, and boasted that on 9 April he had tricked Dean into admitting his guilt. Salomons, in a professional dilemma, consulted the attorney-general J. H. Want [q.v.]. Rumours began to circulate and questions were asked in parliament. On 24 September Dean petitioned parliament and soon followed it with an affirmation of his innocence. Salomons made a dramatic revelation in the Legislative Council and was savaged by Crick; on 4 October R. B. Smith, the chemist who had supplied Dean with poison, came forward. Dean was again arrested, confessed in writing on 9 October, and was sentenced to fourteen years imprisonment for perjury on 24 October. In December Meagher, Crick,

Dean, Daniel Green [q.v.] and Jane Reynolds were tried for conspiracy to 'pervert the course of justice'; Dean and Meagher were convicted, but the conviction was quashed on appeal. Two appeals by Dean against his perjury conviction failed.

Mary Dean divorced her husband on 1 September 1896 and in 1900 married Benjamin William Bridge. Dean was released from Goulburn gaol on 8 December 1904 with remissions for good conduct and resumed his old position. By 1913 he had returned to the Riverina and worked as an engineer on Canoon station, Hay, until about 1930. He died of endocarditis in hospital on 7 May 1933 and was buried in the Anglican section of Hay cemetery. He was survived by his daughter.

The lawyers involved had little doubt of Dean's guilt but his motive remains obscure.

C. K. Allen, *Aspects of justice* (Lond, 1958); C. Pearl, *Wild men of Sydney* (Lond, 1958); L. Blackwell, *Death cell at Darlinghurst* (Lond, 1970); Roy Com . . . into case of George Dean, Report, *PP* (NSW), 1894-95, 3, 707; *PD* (NSW), 1894-95, p 5340, 1895, p 1082, 1235, 1242, 1286, 1482, 1522, 3538; *V&P* (LA NSW), 1895, 3, 175; *NSW Law Reports*, 17 (1896), p 35, 132, 224; *Bulletin*, 16 June 1900, 15 Dec 1904, 19 Jan 1905; *SMH*, 20, 22, 23, 25 Mar, 5, 6, 8 Apr 1895, 10 May 1933; *Sydney Mail*, 19 Oct 1895; *Daily Telegraph* (Syd), 16 July 1895; J. H. Carruthers, Autobiography (NL); Attorney-General and Justice Dept, special bundle 5/7744 (NSWA).   MARTHA RUTLEDGE

DEAN, GEORGE HENRY (1859-1953), soldier, stock and station agent and grazier, was born on 29 June 1859 at Campbelltown, South Australia, son of English-born William Dean, stock and station agent and pastoralist, and his wife Esther, née Gardner. He attended the Collegiate School of St Peter, Adelaide, from 1867 and at 18 joined his father's agency which was then known as Dean & Laughton.

On 10 June 1877 Dean enlisted as a private in the South Australian Mounted Rifles (Militia). He was commissioned lieutenant in 1880 and soon afterwards went to India as secretary to Colonel J. A. Fergusson, assistant adjutant general in South Australia, whose mission was to arrange the indenture of coolie labour for the Northern Territory. On 14 December 1882, at Clayton Congregational Church, Kensington, Dean married Florence Ida, daughter of (Sir) Edwin Smith [q.v.6], and next year went into partnership with his father, their firm becoming known as William Dean & Son. After his father's death in 1896 he managed the stock and station agency alone. He kept up his military associations and was promoted captain (S.A.M.R.) in 1885, major

in 1895 and lieut-colonel in 1900. Next year he was awarded the Volunteer Officers' Decoration. In 1903-09 he was officer commanding the 16th Light Horse Regiment, Australian Military Forces, and was promoted colonel in April 1909. In July 1912 he was appointed to command the 8th Light Horse Brigade.

Soon after the outbreak of World War I Dean became chairman of a 4th Military District committee charged with selection of officers for the Australian Imperial Force. He was appointed to the A.I.F. on 11 March 1915 as a lieut-colonel and from 4 May commanded the 13th Light Horse Regiment which served, unmounted, at Gallipoli from early September. Next month Dean, ill with typhoid and enteric fever, was evacuated to Malta and then to England. He was discharged from the A.I.F. in July 1916, though in 1916-18 he held several temporary appointments as officer commanding troops on transports. Four of his five sons served overseas in 1914-18; the fifth, medically unfit for active service, was placed in charge of a recruiting depot.

Dean had held the rank of colonel in the Australian Military Forces from October 1916 and in 1920, after forty-three years of service, was placed on the reserve of officers with the honorary rank of brigadier general. Before embarking for active service he had sold his stock and station agency and after the war he invested in a grazing property. He also devoted much of his time to the formation of the Returned Sailors' and Soldiers' Imperial League of Australia, was an active Freemason and kept up a lifelong interest in sport, especially rifle-shooting. In 1888 he had been responsible for the formation of a controlling body of rifle clubs, later to be known as the Commonwealth Council of Rifle Associations, and was its chairman in 1903-21. In 1913 he took the Australian rifle team to Bisley, England, and in 1932 was appointed C.B.E. in recognition of his contribution to rifle-shooting. In 1948 the Port Adelaide rifle range was renamed the Dean Range in his honour.

Survived by his only daughter and five sons, he died at his Gilberton home on 12 February 1953 and was buried with full military honours in Mitcham cemetery.

Dean's son, EDWIN THEYER (1884-1970), was born on 11 December 1884 in Adelaide. After attending the Collegiate School of St Peter he joined his family's stock and station agency. Keenly interested in military affairs, he was commissioned second lieutenant in the Australian Field Artillery, Australian Military Forces, in 1905 and was promoted lieutenant in 1907 and captain in 1908. He served with the 34th Battery in 1909-12 and was then transferred to the unattached list. He married Gladys Jean Grieve at Stow Memorial (Congregational) Church, Adelaide, on 3 December 1912.

Just before World War I Dean resumed duty with the A.F.A. By July 1915 the 2nd Division, A.I.F., was being formed in Egypt and required an artillery component. A battery, to be known as the 18th Battery, 6th Field Artillery Brigade, was raised in South Australia, and on 20 October Dean, as its commanding officer, was appointed to the A.I.F. as a major. He embarked in November on the *Botanist* and in 1916-17 commanded the battery in Flanders and on the Somme. In January 1917 he held temporary command of the 6th Field Artillery Brigade. He was gassed on 4 June but resumed duty on 27 September. In August he was awarded the Distinguished Service Order, the citation stating that he had 'displayed the greatest fearlessness and gallantry in personally extinguishing three serious fires amongst his gun pits and ammunition, working at the imminent risk of his own life'.

On 4 October Dean was transferred to the 1st Field Artillery Brigade as commanding officer and was promoted lieut-colonel on 1 November. His unit was then serving in the Ypres sector and he retained command until the end of the war except for brief periods when he held temporary commands in the Royal Artillery. He was mentioned in dispatches four times in 1917-18 and awarded the Légion d'honneur in 1919. Discharged from the A.I.F. in June 1919, he was placed on the reserve of officers in August 1920 in the rank of lieut-colonel; he later edited a book, published in Adelaide, on the war service of the 1st Australian Field Artillery Brigade. After demobilization he settled on a grazing property, Karinya station, at Moculta near Angaston. He was awarded the Volunteer Officers' Decoration in 1926.

In World War II Dean was commandant of the Loveday Internment Group near Barmera and for his services was appointed M.B.E. The complex was disbanded in 1946 and that year he published a booklet on the history of internment in South Australia in 1940-46. In 1947 he was placed on the retired list with the honorary rank of colonel. He then resumed his pastoral activities at Angaston where, survived by a son and two daughters, he died on 3 June 1970. He was buried in the local cemetery.

H. T. Burgess (ed), *Cyclopedia of South Australia*, 1, (Adel, 1907); J. Dyer, *The story of the 18th Battery, 6th Brigade Field Artillery, 1st AIF, 1915-19* (Tusmore, SA, 1965); *London Gazette*, 2 Jan, 1 June, 16 Aug, 28 Dec 1917, 31 Dec 1918; *Anzac Bulletin*, 22 Aug 1917; *Register* (Adel), 11 Aug 1920, 18 May 1921; *Advertiser* (Adel), 18 June 1932, 29 June 1949, 13 Feb 1953, 6 June 1970; *Leader* (Angaston), 11 June 1970; A.B.C., Personalities remembered (copy, SAA).

H. J. ZWILLENBERG

DEANE, HENRY (1847-1924), engineer and scientist, was born on 26 March 1847 at Clapham Common, London, son of Henry Deane, chemist and fellow of the Linnean Society, and his wife Jemima, née Elliott. After schooling in England, he was educated in Ireland at Queen's College, Galway, (B.A., 1865; M.A., 1882), and completed his training at King's College, London, as an occasional student. He served his pupillage in the office of Sir John Fowler, from 1869 worked for Waring Bros on the construction of the East Hungarian railways, and from 1871 in the shipbuilding yards of the Danube Steam Navigation Co. at Altogen. On 19 October 1873 at Budapest he married a Hungarian, Anna Mathilde Schramb. In 1875 he joined (Sir) Benjamin Baker in England and in 1877 he helped to build sugarworks in the Philippines.

In January 1880 Deane arrived in Sydney in the *Kent* and on 20 February was appointed a railway surveyor under John Whitton [q.v.6]. From 1881 he was district engineer, working on the Gunnedah-Narrabri extension, then on the construction of the Homebush to Hawkesbury River railway. Inspecting engineer from 1886, he was confirmed as engineer-in-chief for railway construction on 1 July 1891 after acting since Whitton's retirement. He was also responsible for the tramways from 1899. After consultations with E. M. G. Eddy [q.v.], chief railway commissioner, he supervised improvements to the gradients and curves, and began to abolish zig-zags on the western line. In 1894 and in 1904-05, after the abolition of the railway construction branch, he visited the United States of America and Europe on behalf of the government. He retired in May 1906.

Deane set up in private practice in Sydney and became consultant to the Commonwealth Oil Corporation Ltd and was responsible for the construction of its railway from Newnes to Clarence. In 1908 he was appointed consulting engineer for the survey of the transcontinental railway between Port Augusta and Kalgoorlie; in 1911 he reported to parliament on the proposed line, and in 1912 became engineer-in-chief for the new Commonwealth railways construction branch. He met many difficulties in building about 1100 miles (1800 km) of line through a desert region, advocating Paragon diesel-electric locomotives; he was troubled by the insubordinate Henry Chinn [q.v.7]. In 1914 he resigned and practised as a consulting engineer in Melbourne. He had been a member of the Institution of Civil Engineers, London, from 1886 and Australasian member of its council, president of the Institution of Surveyors, New South Wales, in 1894-95, and a member of the Sydney University Engineering Society; in 1920 he was a founding associate member of the Institution of Engineers, Australia. In 1912 he was commissioned colonel in the Engineer and Railway Staff Corps in the Commonwealth Military Forces.

'An accomplished botanist', Deane carried out much work on the tertiary fossil flora of eastern Australia. He was in close touch with such notable scientists as R. D. Fitzgerald, F. von Mueller, Dr W. Woolls [qq.v.4,5,6] and (Sir) Baldwin Spencer [q.v.]. He published many papers, often with J. H. Maiden [q.v.], on botany and paleontology and made a special study of Australian timbers (*Eucalyptus deanei* was named after him). He was president of the Linnean Society of New South Wales in 1895-96 and 1896-97, and of the local Royal Society in 1897 and 1907, and a fellow of the Linnean, (Royal) Meteorological and Royal Horticultural societies, London. In Melbourne he was a member of the Royal Society of Victoria and was a council-member of the Australian Forest League. By 1909 he was balding, with an impressive white beard, moustache and side-whiskers.

On 12 March 1924 Deane died suddenly while working in his garden at Malvern and was buried with Anglican rites in Brighton cemetery. He was survived by one son and two daughters of his first marriage, and by his second wife Mary Lillias, née Lumsdaine, whom he had married in Sydney on 5 February 1890, and by their two sons and a daughter. His eldest son Henry James was a distinguished civil engineer and his younger sons served overseas with the first Australian Imperial Force.

Cyclopedia of N.S.W. (Syd, 1907); J. Marshall, *A biographical dictionary of railway engineers* (Newton Abbot, 1978); *Industrial Aust and Mining Standard,* 14 Feb 1914; Linnean Soc NSW, *Procs,* 49 (1924), p iv; Roy Soc NSW, *J,* 58 (1924), p 5; *SMH,* 13 Mar 1924; H. Deane, Correspondence and papers (NL); ML printed cat and for publications.

J. D. WALKER

DEANE, JOHN HORACE (1842-1913), miner, pastoralist and politician, was born on 24 January 1842 at Cootehill, County Cavan, Ireland, son of George Deane, farmer, and his wife Elizabeth, née Mahood. Educated at the local school, he worked in farming and building until his migration to Queensland. Landing from the *Beejapore* at Rockhampton in June 1863, Deane went to the Peak Downs diggings near Clermont

and, after failing as a prospector, became a storekeeper and carter at Lilydale. In 1866 he overlanded with his team to the New Cape River rush; once again he was a storekeeper and carter. As Cape River declined, he moved east to Townsville where for several years he was a successful publican and butcher.

Moving to the Ravenswood goldfield in 1868, Deane erected one of the first North Queensland batteries on the Broughton River. For a time his Defiance Mill was the main crushing centre for the Ravenswood-Charters Towers region. He soon moved his mill to Charters Towers and settled there. Before the advent of the large mining companies, his financing of small prospecting syndicates gave him interests in valuable properties including the Alabama, the St Patrick's, the Black Jack and the Papuan. He continued carting but in 1875 also established a foundry and, following experiments, became one of the founders of the Charters Towers Pyrites Co. which treated tailings until the process was superseded by the cyanide process.

As the big mining companies began to dominate Charters Towers in the 1880s, Deane moved into the pastoral industry in spite of a growing marketing crisis in beef. He was among the foundation directors of the Alligator Creek Meat Export Co. at Townsville in 1890 and a shareholder in the Ross River plant. In partnership with fellow Irishman Joseph Woodburn, he also purchased the Bluff station, twenty miles (32 km) south of Charters Towers, and in 1893 Woodburn, Deane and F. Hamilton founded the Burdekin Meat Export Co. at Sellheim on the Burdekin River west of Townsville. A partner for seventeen years, Deane was resident manager until his retirement in 1912. Initially the Burdekin works functioned as a boiling-down plant. Experiments in meat canning failed and the production of meat extract had limited success. From the early 1900s, however, its export of frozen carcasses brought some security to the beef industry in the region.

Deane won the Legislative Assembly seat of Townsville in November 1878 as a member of the McIlwraith [q.v.5] faction, but resigned in favour of John Murtagh Macrossan [q.v.5] in February 1879. Appointed to the Legislative Council in July 1889, he was an undistinguished member, often absent from sittings, but he was a strong advocate of both northern separation and Federation. He served on the Dalrymple Divisional Board and Shire Council in 1879-1912 and chaired it several times including the inaugural term. A member of the Thuringowa Divisional Board from 1893 to 1899, he was government representative on the Townsville Harbour Board from August 1899 to October 1913 and chairman of its works committee in 1904-11. At Charters Towers he had served on the hospital committee and been a member of the Towers Jockey Club. Deane Street was named after him.

In 1912 Deane retired to Townsville where his property included several shops in Flinders Street. He moved from his home Rossleigh on Ross River to Crows Nest on Melton Hill. He died there on 27 October 1913 and was buried in the old West End cemetery, with Church of England rites. His estate, valued for probate at £17 091, was left to his widow Mary Ann, née Gologly, whom he had married at Rockhampton on 10 December 1864, and to their surviving three daughters and son.

John Deane was respected for his public service, his administrative ability and his business acumen. He had a predilection for pyjamas instead of a business suit, and his twenty-two stone (140 kg) figure led one historian to describe him as 'Falstaffian'. To an old political acquaintance however, he was 'altogether a very fine specimen of a pioneer'.

J. Black (ed), *Queensland pioneer book* (Charters Towers, 1931); *PD* (Qld), 1913, p 2222; *Cummins & Campbell's Mthly Mag,* June 1936; *Townsville Evening Star,* 27 Oct 1913; *Northern Miner,* 28 Oct 1913; *North Qld Register,* 3 Nov 1913; *Queenslander,* 11 Nov 1913; minutes, 8 Mar 1893-22 Sept 1897 (Thuringowa Divisional Bd, held by QA), *and* 10 Aug 1899-13 Nov 1913 (Townsville Harbour Bd), *and* 14 Jan 1902-9 Jan 1912 (Dalrymple Divisional Bd, and Shire Council, Charters Towers).   ANNE ALLINGHAM

DEANE, PERCIVAL EDGAR (1890-1946), public servant, was born on 10 August 1890 at Port Melbourne, fourth child and third son of the eight children of John Henry Deane, carpenter, later master builder, and his wife Elizabeth Mary, née Maltravers, both Victorian-born. Deane won a scholarship from state school to University High School, a private institution. Precociously interested in 'merchanting his intelligence', and named after Rev. A. R. Edgar [q.v.] of Wesley Church, Melbourne, he became a Methodist lay preacher (he was a dedicated agnostic in later life), peddled typewriters, became an expert shorthand-writer, was employed by James Service [q.v.6] & Co., and worked as a clerk with the University of Melbourne, where he came under the notice of (Sir) James Barrett [q.v.7]. Between 18 and 23 he worked with trade and business magazines, becoming part-owner of two

companies and the founder and editor of the *Australian Golfer;* he was himself an outstanding player.

Enlisting as a private in the Australian Imperial Force in September 1914, Deane was posted to the 1st Australian General Hospital in Egypt, where Barrett was registrar, and was soon promoted lieutenant with the position of quartermaster. In the internecine struggles which marked the affairs of this unit in 1915, Deane allied himself firmly with Barrett; when, suffering from overstrain, he was invalided back to Australia in April 1916, he regularly informed Barrett both on politics generally and on the ramifications of the 'Barrett case' in Australia; he published *The Australian Army Medical Corps in Egypt* (1918) with him.

The turning-point in Deane's life came with his appointment in November 1916, after his discharge, to be private secretary to the prime minister, W. M. Hughes [q.v.], at a salary of £408. It was said that Deane came to live 'inside the Prime Minister's brain', and Hughes, at first irritated by Deane's 'smooth pink complexion, orderly hair and ivory smile' soon found irresistible his audacious humour, immense capacity for long hours and skilful organizing, and ability to project and develop Hughes's own ideas. Shortly after taking up his post Deane fell in love with Hughes's typist, Ruth Marjorie Manning; they were married at St Peter's Church, Melbourne, on 6 October 1917.

Deane attended Imperial conferences in Britain with Hughes in 1918 and 1921 (and with (Viscount) S. M. Bruce [q.v.7] in 1926). He proved invaluable as a member of and secretary to the Australian delegation to the Versailles Peace Conference and walked, if not with kings, at least with presidents and prime ministers. Deane was rewarded for his services with the C.M.G. and in February 1921 with the secretaryship of the Prime Minister's Department, at £1250 a year. He now became 'unquestionably the most discussed of Federal Government officials', his 'impenetrable nonchalance' and status as Hughes's *alter ego* making him 'the one everyone wanted to know'.

Deane guided Hughes's diatribes against Bolshevism, the Country Party and liberalism, soothing the prime minister in agitated moments, and being 'masterful in a cozening sort of way'. The relationship, which aroused much jealousy, reached almost filial levels. After Deane's death his wife wrote to Hughes that all his life Percy held to the view that his association with Hughes was 'the greatest and most satisfying thing that ever happened to him', while Hughes publicly declared that Deane's intellect and character were the finest he had known.

Deane's star first began to dim with the defeat of Hughes in 1923, which coincided with a royal commission into government sugar purchases; he asked to be relieved of his duties while a charge that he had received a gift of £1000 was investigated. Deane was unreservedly cleared of financial implication. The new prime minister, Bruce, recognized and for many years utilized Deane's capacities, but he did not appreciate his style and suspected his close relationship with Hughes.

Soon after taking office Bruce reduced the Prime Minister's Department; despite strong rumours that Deane was to accept an appointment with private industry, he stayed. The move to Canberra in 1927, however, put a further strain on Deane. A man of creative and Bohemian tastes – he was a clever sketcher, an exuberant versifier, a public speaker much in demand and a book-collector with a liking for unexpurgated editions – he had little desire to lead a public service life in a small town. He took to drink and dalliance, as later in life to gambling; nor, in strait-laced Canberra, was he popular for his quips. With the increasing Hughes attacks on the coalition government, and the leakage of material from the Prime Minister's Department, Bruce appointed Deane secretary of the Department of Home Affairs from the beginning of 1929. Of the ensuing public service and newspaper furore Deane said: 'It is the fierce light that beats upon the thrown'.

In 1932 the Department of Home Affairs was abolished, and Deane became a member of the War Pensions Entitlement Appeals Tribunal. From this position he retired to Melbourne in 1936, with a medical certificate specifying 'myocarditis' and a pension of £416. It had been, says his daughter and only child, a 'meteoric fall', and Deane was still only 47: 'The gardeners and chauffeurs dropped away'.

Deane deteriorated rapidly after his retirement, breaking his hip in a street fall and eventually becoming bedridden. A 'wasted life', many said, but his daughter speaks of a man who was 'wise and kind and witty all his life', and not least when he was down: a humorous observer of the twists of fate, active with his pen and whittling knife, and a great spinner of stories to children around his bed. He died of cancer at Caulfield on 17 August 1946. His wife died in 1977.

Contemporary evidence is unanimous as to Deane's 'amazing reserves of amiability' and to his 'indefinable air of smiling wisdom'. Among many friends were E. J. Brady [q.v.7], Norman Lindsay, Harold Herbert [qq.v.] and a number of the prominent car-

toonists of the day, whose work he collected. And he was a deeply affectionate father. He reached the top early, responded to the excitements of power, then glimpsed the hollowness of his achievements. A lesser man would not have looked back, but Percy Deane loved life more than legislation.

J. W. Barrett papers (AWM); CP 268/1, item 1/35, CRS A2, item 1916/2232, A220, item S29/1 (AAO); family papers; information from Ms Shirley Deane, Cameroon, Africa, *and* Mr B. M. Deane, Mont Albert, Melbourne.   S. MURRAY-SMITH

DE BAVAY, AUGUSTE JOSEPH FRANCOIS (1856-1944), brewer, chemist, bacteriologist and metallurgist, was born on 9 June 1856 at Vilvoorde, Belgium, son of Xavier de Bavay, whose family can be traced to at least 1193, and his wife Marie Thérèse née de Bontridder. Auguste was educated at college in Namur, graduating as a surveyor in 1873. After further education at Gembloux, he worked as a brewer and chemist, establishing links with Louis Pasteur and others active in research in France and Belgium. Opportunities in Europe did not offer de Bavay the recognition and remuneration he required; in the late 1870s he left Belgium to become a plantation manager in Ceylon.

In March 1884 de Bavay arrived in Melbourne to take up the position of brewer with T. and A. Aitken's Victoria Parade brewery and distillery; his salary was £6 a week with a commission of 1s. on every hogshead of good beer. On 21 March 1885 at St Patrick's Cathedral, he married Anna Heinzle, German-born daughter of a furniture warehouseman.

In the 1880s, the top fermentation process was the only one available to colonial brewers. De Bavay, well aware of the importance of yeast in the process, began searching for a way of avoiding wild yeasts which caused unwanted secondary and tertiary fermentations. His first breakthrough came late in 1884. In that year the Dane, E. C. Hansen, published evidence showing that only the use of pure cultures would guarantee success. De Bavay now attempted to grow pure yeast cultures. C. W. Chateau Müller of Terry's West End brewery was also using Hansen's researches and by 1887-88 both chemists reported considerable success. De Bavay, however, soon became the Australian expert on yeasts, receiving Hansen's congratulations for his discovery of an Australian wild yeast, which the Dane named *S. de Bavii* in his honour. Then in 1888 de Bavay developed 'Australian No. 2', the first pure yeast used commercially in Australia and possibly the world's first pure culture ever used in top fermentation brewing. He followed this in 1889 with 'Melbourne No. 1', which became the basis of colonial and Australian brewing: de Bavay had succeeded in producing a peculiarly Australian beer, establishing Melbourne at the forefront of brewing technology. He was now in demand as a teacher, his most famous pupil probably being John Breheny.

The problems of top fermentation brewing encouraged de Bavay to explore the possibilities of lager-brewing. It was not until the late 1880s that inventions in ice-making technology encouraged entrepreneurs to enter the lucrative Melbourne market. The most successful were W. M. and R. Foster from New York, who built a large brewery in Collingwood in 1888. De Bavay's reputation and his interest in lager were known to Montague Cohen [q.v.], a director of Fosters, who in 1894 persuaded de Bavay to join the company as chief brewer. It was a shrewd move. By 1895 de Bavay had greatly increased production and had also developed a trade in draught beer which gave Fosters over forty outlets in Melbourne's city and suburbs.

By the late 1890s de Bavay had been converted away from the traditional Australian ale he had helped to create and in 1898 he engaged in a bitter newspaper dispute with Emil Resch [q.v.] in which he defended the superiority of 'malt and hops' beer over 'sugar' beer. It was a surprising volte-face for the man who had so proudly sent three hogsheads of his running ales to the London brewers' annual exhibition in 1889. He also turned his attention to wine, establishing a vineyard at Woori Yallock in 1897 in partnership with Cohen.

De Bavay regarded himself as primarily a bacteriologist. In 1889 his charge that the city's fire-plugs admitted sewerage and typhoid germs to the domestic water-supply resulted in a royal commission and the eventual removal of the devices; the purity of the city's drinking water improved markedly and de Bavay was a popular hero. He believed that he had discovered a cure for typhoid and diphtheria and in 1891 presented a paper on the subject to the Victorian branch of the British Medical Association. Later that year while on a six-month sabbatical he visited Pasteur's laboratories in France and was presented with a bottle of the first anti-toxin against diphtheria, which he donated to the Melbourne Hospital. He had cultivated strong links with Victorian hospitals and the University of Melbourne, and acted as bacteriologist for the university until Thomas Cherry's [q.v.7] appointment as lecturer in 1900.

De Bavay turned his attention to the technological problems of mining at Broken Hill, especially the difficulties of ore extraction. In his search for a new method to recover zinc blende, he became involved in the bitter struggle between C. V. Potter and G. Delprat [qq.v.] but by July 1904 he had evolved his own process. Working in his laboratory at Fosters, and with the encouragement of Cohen and W. L. Baillieu [q.v.7], de Bavay discovered the skin or film flotation process; its major difficulty was that a huge surface of water was required to ensure a large output.

In 1904, in partnership with Cohen and Baillieu, he formed de Bavay's Sulphide Process Co. Ltd; in September 1905 a new company was formed, de Bavay's Treatment Co. Ltd; in October 1908 he was paid £6583 in cash and shares for his five patents dealing with extraction of zinc blende; and in 1909 Amalgamated Zinc (de Bavay's) Ltd was established to exploit the process. He was the inventor but Baillieu was the entrepreneur who made a fortune; in his hands the company prospered.

In 1900 de Bavay had signed a long-term contract with Fosters, but he also acted as consultant for the Swan Brewery in Western Australia, the Cascade Brewery in Tasmania and after 1907, Carlton and United Breweries – all Cohen and Baillieu interests. At the outbreak of World War I de Bavay was asked by Senator Pearce [q.v.], minister of defence, to investigate the possibility of manufacturing acetone for use in producing cordite. Within two weeks he had developed a process based on the fermentation and distillation of molasses, and as a result was asked to design and build the Commonwealth Acetate of Lime Factory on the Brisbane River. His son John Francis Xavier assisted him in this task. De Bavay made no money from his invention; it was, he claimed, his gift to the Commonwealth.

After the war de Bavay continued to act as a consulting brewer. He maintained his experiments in bacteriology and pursued metallurgical studies and research into the wine industry. He had also been involved from 1904 in the foundation of an Australian paper industry.

De Bavay had a lifelong passion for the genealogy of his family. He enjoyed tennis and shooting and one of his great pleasures in life was cigar-smoking. His wife died on 29 October 1933. De Bavay died at his home in Studley Park Road, Kew, on 16 November 1944 and was buried in Melbourne general cemetery. He was survived by two sons, both of whom worked in the brewing industry, and by two daughters.

De Bavay was naturalized in November 1902. He was appointed O.B.E. in 1918 and also won Papal and Belgian honours. His contribution to Australian life was great, yet he was never well known. His reputation as a scientist and the esteem of his colleagues concerned him more than the pursuit of fame or material possessions.

J. S. Lyng, *Non-Britishers in Australia* (Melb, 1927); G. Blainey, *The rush that never ended* (Melb, 1963); W. S. Robinson, *If I remember rightly*, G. Blainey ed (Melb, 1967).   GEORGE PARSONS

DE BERNALES, CLAUDE ALBO (1876-1963), mining promoter and investor, was born on 31 May 1876 in London, only son of Major Manuel Edgar Albo de Bernales, and his wife Emma Jane, née Belden. His mother was American and his father Basque. Educated at the Free Grammar School, Uppingham, Rutland, in 1891, in Paris where his parents lived, and at the University of Heidelberg, he did not graduate, but migrated to the Western Australian goldfields in 1897.

Arriving at Coolgardie with £5, he borrowed £50, moved to Kalgoorlie and sold machinery. Handsome, tall (approximately 185 cm), alert, proud of his origins and always expensively dressed, he dominated any assembly of men, free and easy miners or conservative bankers. His appearance was a major asset. Even on the dusty goldfields, cycling from mine to mine, he always carried a clean collar and shirt and changed before calling on the managers.

On 19 May 1903 at Kalgoorlie, de Bernales married Bessie Picken Berry (d. 1927). His salesmanship and charm soon brought modest wealth and in 1909 he became managing director of the Kalgoorlie Foundry, a major supplier of mining plant. He became a director of Hoskins Foundry, Perth, in 1912 and settled there in 1915, becoming a lavish spender with an elegance to which most West Australians were unused. It was around this time that he began to sign with surname only. His rapid rise demonstrated his ability to find and use the best talents available. Premier Philip Collier [q.v.] reportedly said that if he saw de Bernales alone, the latter would emerge with all the State's assets at his disposal.

As a member of the Kalgoorlie Chamber of Mines in 1911-13, de Bernales began his career as a mining promoter. With mining engineer Henry Urquhart, he acquired a number of leases at Wiluna, 300 miles (480 km) north of Kalgoorlie. The ore was impregnated with arsenical pyrites, but a successful flotation treatment was devised. De Bernales went to London in 1926 and raised £1 million to work Wiluna mines. A later issue of promissory notes for £300 000 was backed by the State government. When the mine opened in 1931 it created a new community of 10 000 and within four years produced gold worth £3 million. Serving as a spur for the revival of other gold mines, Wiluna eventually earned £12 million.

As the Depression deepened, de Bernales launched his gold bonus campaign, which eventually won a Federal bounty of £1 an ounce on gold produced in excess of the 1928-30 average. By the time that the Gold Bounty Acts became law in 1930 and 1931, the collapse of the exchange rate had raised gold well beyond the rate of bounty paid. The campaign showed de Bernales as an organizing genius: there were few prominent people in all sections of the industry who did not endorse it.

To provide the base for his plans, de Bernales next induced the government to reserve huge auriferous areas. In 1932 he went to London, which he made his base, formed twelve new companies and sold gold leases to each in return for shares with a face value of £1 261 000 issued to his family and friends. These transactions convinced investors that the companies were busily opening new mines. In 1933-35, he floated eight further companies with a nominal capital of £6 110 000 – a major factor in the inflow of overseas capital for Australian mining. His most prestigious *coup* came in 1936 when he won control of Great Boulder Proprietary Gold Mine, one of the oldest and richest mines of the 'Golden Mile'. A few of his companies or their subsidiaries were also able to participate in new gold fields at Yellowdine and Marble Bar.

De Bernales's mining empire was one vast interlocking organization. Some of the companies failed but his proportion of successes was better than average for the industry. He received £1 million from his London flotations, a fourth in cash, the rest in shares. He had visited Western Australia in 1935-36 with ex-governor Sir William Campion [q.v.7], and a co-director, and was hailed as the State's greatest ambassador. While there he acquired properties in Melbourne and Perth and launched his flamboyant mock-Tudor shopping arcade, London Court, which is still a feature of Perth. His personal office in London House, Murray Street, was decorated sumptuously, as was his mansion in Roehampton, Surrey, England.

The empire began to crumble early in 1939; underground opposition from powerful financial institutions was a factor. Some shareholders in Great Boulder Proprietary Gold Mine accused de Bernales of mismanagement. Though the Beaverbrook press attacked him, he was supported by leading mining men and most newspapers. In July, however, the London Stock Exchange suspended trading in seven of his companies without giving reasons. This action, the war and the antagonism of financiers forced his companies into liquidation. Then a body of shareholders in Great Boulder Mining and Finance Ltd sought to recover their investment. The case dragged on for ten years and was finally settled for £125000. In 1947, he was found liable for British income tax on a profit of £1382000 from share dealings. In 1945-48 his affairs were investigated by detectives for the senior official receiver. Despite the attorney-general's decision that there was a prima facie case that an offence had been committed, action against him was deferred because of his weak heart. He became a recluse in his house at Selsey Hill and died on 9 December 1963. He was survived by his second wife Helen Florence Berry, née Alger, a widow, whom he had married at St Phillip's Church of England, Cottesloe, Perth, on 5 February 1930 and by two daughters of his first marriage.

De Bernales was a legend, larger than life: by personal magnetism and financial acumen he won concessions and became wealthy. His ability to attract new capital and his self-confidence transformed the Western Australian mining industry in the 1930s. In his ten most successful years gold production in the State increased from £1600000 to £11800000 and employment in the industry quadrupled. It was not for nothing that he was known as 'the man with the Midas touch'.

G. Blainey, *The rush that never ended* (Melb, 1969); G. D. Snooks, *Depression and recovery in Western Australia, 1928/29-1938/39* (Nedlands, 1974); *West Aust Mining and Commercial Review*, 3 Aug, p 17, 21 Dec, p 14, 1935, July 1936, p 152; *Golden West*, 1937-38, p 25, *Western Argus*, 1 Mar 1921; *The Times*, 29 Apr, 23 May 1952, 13 Dec 1963; *Daily News* (Perth), 25 May, 26 Oct 1935, 29 Aug, 21, 23 Sept, 12 Nov, 28 Dec 1940; *West Australian*, 10 Dec 1963; *SMH*, 18 Jan 1949.

JOHN H. LAURENCE

DE BEUZEVILLE, WILFRED ALEXANDER WATT (1884-1954), forester, was born at Aston station, Bombala, New South Wales, on 13 February 1884, son of James Paroissien Beuzeville, station manager, and his wife Hannah Ann, née Watt, and grandson of James Beuzeville [q.v.3]. He was educated at a private school at Bombala and at Tumut Superior Public School, passing the junior public examination in 1899, then worked on the land. He was a grazier at Tumut when he married Frances Helena Ratliff on 9 January 1907 with Anglican rites.

De Beuzeville joined the Department of Forestry (Forestry Commission from 1916) on 26 March 1912, and was stationed at Warialda. As a forest assessor from November 1915, he surveyed the resources of the Pilliga scrub, south-west of Narrabri, and worked directly under E. H. F. Swain [q.v.]. In 1920 he became assistant forester at Tumbarumba and in 1925 was promoted senior forester. At Tumut from September 1925 until 1928 he supervised the establishment of the conifer plantations. With the local headmaster C. A. Teasdale he helped to establish the Tumut School Forest, which interested children in forestry, and became a source of revenue for the school. From 1928 he was stationed in the metropolitan district, Sydney.

De Beuzeville showed great interest in the native forest flora, particularly the eucalypts, which he studied avidly. While in the Tumut district he found and collected specimens of the snow gum that was named *Eucalyptus debeuzevillei* (now E. *pauciflora* ssp. *debeuzevillei*) after him. He corresponded with J. H. Maiden [q.v.] and contributed to his *A critical revision of the genus eucalyptus* (1903-33). De Beuzeville made extensive collections of specimens for the National Herbarium of New South Wales. In 1930-35 he obtained numerous botanical and timber samples for the forest products division of the Commonwealth Council for Scientific and Industrial Research, Canberra.

Supported and guided by Swain, who became commissioner of forestry in 1935, de Beuzeville travelled widely into many of the previously little-known forested areas along the eastern escarpment zone, reporting on their timber resources and paving the way for their later development. He selected and arranged the purchase of the land for the Cumberland State Forest at West Pennant Hills, overseeing its development as one of the finest arboreta in Australia; expanded the Forestry Commission's nurseries that supplied seedlings for use on farms; and promoted the wider use of native plants. In 1938 he became a divisional officer and from 1947 headed the new forest ecology branch. He refined Swain's climatological classification and tried to apply it on the basis of inadequate weather information to the State. He published the *Climatological basis of forestry* (1943) and *Australian trees for Australian planting* (1947).

After he retired in 1948 de Beuzeville worked in Australia for the Food and Agriculture Organization of the United Nations on the selection of eucalypts suitable for planting in Ethiopia. In 1949-50 he visited Britain and Europe. He was a fellow of the Royal and Linnean societies of New South Wales and was a member of the Empire Forestry Association, England, from

1924 and of the Institute of Foresters of Australia from 1939.

Survived by a son and daughter, de Beuzeville died of coronary-vascular disease in hospital at Kiama on 28 March 1954 and was cremated.

Linnean Soc NSW, Procs, 80 (1955); de Beuzeville papers (ML); information from family, *and* NSW Forestry Commission (Syd).

L. T. CARRON

DE BURGH, ERNEST MACARTNEY (1863-1929), civil engineer, was born on 18 January 1863 at Sandymount, Dublin, Ireland, youngest son of Rev. William de Burgh, and his wife Janette, née Macartney. He was educated at Rathmines School and the Royal College of Science for Ireland, and for a time was engaged on railway construction in Ireland.

On 21 March 1885 de Burgh arrived in Melbourne in the *Orient* and on 30 April joined the New South Wales Department of Public Works. He was engaged for two years on survey work for Sydney's southern outfall sewer and in 1887 was sent to construct bridges over the Murrumbidgee and Snowy rivers. In 1891 he became supervising bridge engineer and in 1901-03 engineer for bridges; he superintended the construction of those over the Darling at Wilcannia and Wentworth, the Murray at Albury, Corowa, Mulwala, and Koondrook and Swan Hill, Victoria, the Murrumbidgee at Wagga Wagga and Darlington Point, the Hunter at Singleton and Morpeth, the Macleay at Kempsey, and the Tweed at Murwillumbah. In his spare time he enjoyed golf and photography.

On 1 July 1903 de Burgh became acting principal assistant engineer for rivers, water-supply and drainage and was a member of the Sydney Harbour Bridge Advisory Board. Confirmed in his position next year, he was sent to England and France to study dam construction and water-supply. On his return he was given special responsibility for the construction of Cataract Dam for the Sydney water-supply and served on the royal commission to report upon the project. In 1910-13 he represented the State government at engineers' conferences leading to the River Murray Waters Act. He was associated with L. A. B. Wade in the design and construction of Burrinjuck Dam and the Murrumbidgee Irrigation Scheme.

On 16 April 1909 de Burgh became chief engineer for harbours and water-supply, and in 1911-13 was also a member of the committee of management of Cockatoo Island Dockyard. On 26 February 1913 he was appointed chief engineer for water-supply and

sewerage, and was responsible for the design and construction of the Cordeaux, Avon and Nepean dams (Sydney water-supply), the Chichester scheme for Newcastle and the Umberumberka scheme for Broken Hill. In 1921-25 he was a member of the Federal Capital Advisory Committee and prepared the original plans for Canberra's water-supply. C. S. Daley [q.v.] recalled that although he was often 'a drastic critic in expression, at the same time he possessed that characteristic Irish wit and humour that removed the sting but left the logic. He was adept at dealing with politicians, and it was a delight to hear him giving advice, in a racy manner, to the ministers'.

De Burgh was a member of the Institution of Civil Engineers, London, and twice won the Telford premium. He was regarded as one of the ablest civil engineers in Australia when he retired on 22 November 1927. His last year in office had been marred by illness, and he died of tuberculosis at his home at Vaucluse on 4 April 1929 and was cremated with Anglican rites. He was survived by his wife Constance Mary, née Yeo, whom he married at All Saints Church, Woollahra, on 20 March 1888, and by two sons and a daughter. De Burgh's Bridge over the Lane Cove River, Sydney, is named after him.

T&CJ, 25 Sept 1907; *SMH*, 16 July, 14 Sept 1927, 5, 6, 11 Apr 1929; *Canb Times*, 19 June 1965; Public Works Dept, Records, *and* Annual Report, 1919-26 (NSWA).

J. M. ANTILL

DECHAINEUX, FLORENT VINCENT EMILE LUCIEN (1869-1957), art educationist, was born on 15 July 1869 at Liège, Belgium, son of François Prosper Dechaineux and his wife Josephine Leopold Leontine, née Houet. He came to Australia in 1884 with his parents who had invested in a worthless citrus orchard and a salted goldmine. In 1885-88 Dechaineux studied art at Sydney Technical College as an evening student under Lucien Henry [q.v.4], working as a house-painter by day. He then studied with Julian Ashton [q.v.7] at the Art Society of New South Wales while he practised architecture, architectural sculpture and decoration, finally succeeding Henry as lecturer in design at Sydney's Technical College. On 23 December 1891 at St John's Church of England, Darlinghurst, he married a Tasmanian, Isabella (Ella) Jane Briant (d. 1908), and in 1895 was appointed instructor in technical art at Launceston Technical School, Tasmania. He became art master of the Education Department of Tasmania and in 1907 principal and lecturer in art at Hobart Technical School.

For the next thirty-three years Dechaineux continued in his dual capacity at the school, which when he retired in December 1939 had more than 1000 students. He also sat on the Architects' Registration Board and acted as examiner in drawing for the University of Tasmania. Dechaineux came to Tasmania at a time when interest in cultural matters was growing. The arrival of a dedicated artist with enthusiasm for instructing others could not fail to have major impact on art and culture generally. It was said that with him 'every day . . . was an inspiration; he was not an easy taskmaster; nothing second-rate was good enough; his credo was "always aim at the highest"'.

Dechaineux's principal interest was in water-colours but he was also a sculptor and etcher and was proficient in oils, a talent shared with his second wife Mary, née Giblin, whom he married on 21 December 1909 at Hobart, according to Baptist forms. He designed the stained-glass war memorial window in Holy Trinity Church, Hobart, the Town Hall great honour-roll carved by Ellen Nora Payne [q.v.] and, with his partner, the western extension of The Hutchins School. He and his wife were keen bushwalkers and organized large summer camping-parties for artists on the east coast; they also formed a book club for debating and reading. On his retirement he rented a large room in Collins Street where friends and young artists came to talk and pursue their work under his tutelage. He had been a member of the Royal Society of Tasmania from 1908.

Dechaineux died on 4 April 1957 at Hobart, survived by his wife, their son and daughter, and by a daughter of his previous marriage. He was buried in Cornelian Bay cemetery. Three of his paintings, including a portrait of his son Emile (1902-44) who, in command of H.M.A.S. *Australia*, was killed in action, hang in the Tasmanian Art Gallery. A portrait of Dechaineux by Jack Carington Smith, paid for by public subscription, also hangs in the gallery, and another by the same artist is in the Adelaide Art Gallery. The 1956 extension to the Hobart Technical College is named in Dechaineux's honour.

F. Bowden and M. Crawford (eds), *The story of Trinity* (Hob, 1933); J. Cato, *I can take it* (Melb, 1947); *Examiner* (Launc), 30 Oct, 16 Dec 1939; *Mercury*, 5 Apr 1957. A. E. HALLER-GRIFFITS

DE CHAIR, SIR DUDLEY RAWSON STRATFORD (1864-1958), governor, was born on 30 August 1864 at Lennoxville, Quebec, Canada, son of Dudley Raikes de Chair and his wife Frances Emily, sister of Admiral (Sir) Harry Rawson [q.v.]. The family returned to England in 1870. In 1878

de Chair joined the Royal Navy's H.M.S. *Britannia*; passing out as midshipman in 1880, he joined the *Alexandra*, flagship in the Mediterranean. In 1882 his six-week captivity by Arabi Pasha brought headlines in England. He was promoted commander in 1897, captain in 1902. At Torwood, Devon, on 21 April 1903 he married Enid Struben.

The highlight of de Chair's naval career came in 1915-16 when, as rear admiral commanding the tenth cruiser squadron, he was responsible for the effective North Sea blockade of Germany. Appointed K.B.E. in 1916, in September next year he took over the third battle squadron and was promoted vice admiral. He was relieved of his command and placed on half pay, after refusing a post on the Board of Admiralty and criticizing the treatment of Lord Jellicoe. In July 1918 de Chair took command of coast-guard and reserves and in 1920 was promoted admiral. He was president of the inter-allied commission on enemy warships in 1921-23.

De Chair became governor of New South Wales in October 1923, arriving in Sydney with his wife on 28 February 1924. He quickly formed a close friendship with Nationalist premier Sir George Fuller [q.v.]. The May 1925 election brought to office a Labor government, determined, in the governor's view, on 'radical and far-reaching legislation, which had not been foreshadowed in their election speeches'. He decided 'to aim at a policy of reasonable moderation, but also of caution, before granting really extreme or dangerous demands'.

In September J. T. Lang [q.v.] asked de Chair to appoint twenty-five new members to the Legislative Council. Initially agreeing only to fifteen, in December the governor capitulated, on condition that the appointments should not be used to abolish the council. Describing his first clash with a governor as 'a most courteous affair', Lang claimed he 'flatly refused to give the undertaking'. By insisting that their correspondence be published de Chair revealed his extensive resistance, thereby entering clearly into the political arena. To the governor's delight the abolition attempt failed. When Lang requested still more appointments, including women, de Chair refused: 'I told him what I thought of him, and the way in which he had deceived me'. Despite a special mission to England by the attorney-general, de Chair remained firm, believing that 'foreign elements were behind the movement to recall the Governor, and wreck the Constitution, and to establish a Communist Government'.

In May 1927, wishing without his cabinet's agreement to call an early election,

De Chair

Lang resigned, was reappointed, selected a new ministry and then obtained a dissolution for an October election. During these events de Chair was secretly advised by Chief Justice Sir Philip Street [q.v.]. (Sir) Thomas Bavin's [q.v.7] subsequent victory ended for de Chair 'two years of most difficult and unpleasant political strife. In getting the Premier to the point of dissolution, I knew I had been skating on very thin ice.'

Invited by Bavin to remain beyond his term of office, de Chair obtained a year's extension from a reluctant Dominions Office. He retired on 8 April 1930 and thereafter lived mainly in London. He was appointed K.C.M.G. in 1933. Survived by his wife, two sons and daughter, he died at Brighton on 17 August 1958, leaving an estate valued for probate at £1295. His ashes were scattered in the English Channel. His autobiography, *The sea is strong*, was published posthumously in 1961.

DNB, 1951-60; J. T. Lang, *I remember* (Syd, 1956); H. V. Evatt, *The king and his dominion governors* (Lond, 1967); *PP* (LC & LA NSW), 1925-26, 1, 343; *SMH*, 2 Jan, 28 Feb 1924, 21, 22, 24 Dec 1925, 1, 7 Apr 1926; de Chair, unpublished memoirs (Imperial War Museum, Lond); DO 35/2, 22, 45, 66.   CHRIS CUNNEEN

DE CRESPIGNY; *see* CHAMPION DE CRESPIGNY

DEEMING, FREDERICK (BAILEY) (1853-1892), murderer, was born on 30 July 1853 at Ashby de la Zouch, Leicestershire, England, son of Thomas Deeming, brazier, and his wife Ann, née Bailey. Little is known of his early life but Deeming asserted that he had spent years in asylums (as had both parents) and that he was epileptic from the age of 18. (His brother Albert denied these claims.) He ran off to sea at about 16.

On 28 February 1881 at Tranmore, Cheshire, he married Marie James. In August he deserted the *Vereus* in Sydney, worked there as a plumber and gas-fitter and in April 1882 was sentenced to six weeks gaol for the larceny of eight gas-burners. Marie joined him in Sydney on 1 July: they had three girls, of whom two were born in Sydney, and a boy. After working as a gas-fitter in Melbourne and at Rockhampton, Queensland, he returned to Sydney in 1884 where he prospered briefly in business on his own account, but in December 1887 he was declared bankrupt and received fourteen days gaol for perjury. By January 1888 he was in Cape Town, using the name Harry Lawson, and was involved in successful frauds and theft in Klerksdorp and Johannesburg.

In England on 18 February 1890 he went through a form of marriage at Beverley, Yorkshire, with Helen Matheson, posing as Lawson, an Australian sheep-farmer. He paid for the wedding with the proceeds of fraud, then hurriedly left England alone in the *Coleridge*. Arrested at Montevideo, Uruguay, he was extradited and spent nine months in gaol at Hull for fraud, but was not prosecuted for bigamy. After his release in July 1891, he rented Dinham Villa, at Rainhill, Lancashire, under the name of Albert Oliver Williams, and was briefly reunited with his wife Marie and children.

On 22 September at St Anne's, Rainhill, as Williams, 'army inspector', Deeming married Emily Lydia Mather and the wedding was followed by a lavish banquet. The couple left England, arriving in Melbourne in the *Kaiser Wilhelm II* on 15 December. Under the name of Druin he rented a brick cottage, which still stands, at 57 Andrew Street, Windsor, and there on or about Christmas Day he battered his wife round the head, cut her throat and buried her under the second bedroom hearthstone, cementing her body in with materials he had bought a week earlier. During January 1892, as Dawson, he auctioned his African effects and Emily Mather's clothes, defrauded a jeweller, wrote to a matrimonial agency (as Duncan) seeking a wife, sailed to Sydney, and became engaged to Kate Rounsefell at Bathurst. He then departed to Western Australia, and, as Baron Swanston, sought work as a mining engineer.

On 3 March a disagreeable smell at 57 Andrew Street led to the discovery of Emily Mather's body. A banquet invitation from Rainhill in the name of A. O. Williams was also found in the house. On 11 March Deeming was arrested at Southern Cross, Western Australia. Investigations of his Rainhill activities were begun, and on 16 March the recently cemented floor of the Dinham Villa kitchen was dug up and the bodies of Marie (née James) and their four children were found.

Deeming was returned to Melbourne by 1 April and, after a two-day inquest on Emily Mather, Dr J. E. Neild [q.v.5], acting coroner, committed him for trial. He was subject to enormous, even frenzied, vilification, and all Australia was affected by the mass hysteria of 'Deemania'. His counsel, William Forlonge and Alfred Deakin [q.v.], sought a month's adjournment to enable evidence of Deeming's psychiatric history to be secured and to allow the hysteria to abate. (Sir) Henry Hodges [q.v.] granted one week. The trial took place on 28-30 April and 2 May. Deeming, who was tried under the name of Williams, relied on a defence of insanity but the psychiatric evidence by doctors J. W.

Springthorpe and J. Y. Fishbourne [qq.v.] was inadequately presented, although it seems clear that he was epileptic. The jury speedily convicted Deeming and he was sentenced to death. On 9 May the Executive Council confirmed the death sentence, on 19th the judicial committee of the Privy Council refused leave to appeal, and on 23rd Deeming was hanged. He wrote an autobiography in gaol which was destroyed.

Melbourne's newspapers proclaimed Deeming guilty before his trial, describing him as 'the criminal of the century' and 'a human tiger'. A play, *Wilful murder,* based on the Windsor murder, was performed in March and April. Some writers accused him of being 'Jack the Ripper'. Certainly his right to trial before an unprejudiced jury was destroyed. A few newspapers described his appearance as 'ape-like', and years later Sir Colin Mackenzie [q.v.] said that his skull resembled that of a gorilla. Contemporary photographs do not suggest any physical abnormality and there were many, including his victims, who must have considered him charming and personable.

The Windsor and Rainhill murders (Melb, 1892); J. A. La Nauze, *Alfred Deakin* (Melb, 1965); J. S. O'Sullivan, *A most unique ruffian* (Melb, 1968); *Ex parte Deeming, Law Reports, Appeal Cases* (HL and PC), 1892, p 422.

BARRY O. JONES

DE GARIS, CLEMENT JOHN (1884-1926), financier, was born on 22 November 1884 at North Melbourne, eldest son of Elisha Clement De Garis [q.v.] and his wife Elizabeth, née Buncle. 'Jack' De Garis grew up in the struggling early days of his father's business at Mildura and when 9 had to leave school with an exemption certificate to work for his father. By 14 he had saved enough from his wages to pay his own fees for two years at Wesley College, Melbourne.

At 17 Jack returned to Mildura to manage part of the family business. Shown the sales figures he was expected to maintain, he resolved to double them. In fact he tripled them in eighteen months and at 21 was left in sole charge of the Mildura enterprises. Short and compactly built, he was a man of effervescent charm and superhuman energy – a 'prince of ballyhoo' as the theatrical entrepreneur Claude Kingston later described him. On 26 September 1907 at the Methodist Church, Mildura, he married Rene Vera Corbould; they had three daughters.

De Garis's confidence in the dried-fruits industry exceeded even that of his father. In 1910 he made his first venture alone and borrowed £15 000 to build a modern packing-shed, Sarnia Packing Pty Ltd. Three years later, ambitious to father a settlement,

he raised £22 000 to buy 10 000 acres (4050 ha) of the old Pyap Village Estate where the South Australian government had already buried £25 000 and a Melbourne syndicate had failed. He installed overhead irrigation and moved eighty employees into stone cottages. A school, library, billiard-table and a baby bonus that anticipated Andrew Fisher's [q.v.] child endowment – all testified to his thoroughness and paternalism. The community survived a savage drought in 1914 and gradually prospered.

In 1919 a shortage of shipping space for sixteen weeks exposed the dried-fruits industry's excessive dependence on the British market. De Garis persuaded the Australian Dried Fruits Association to vote him £20 000 to mount a nation-wide publicity campaign to expand the home market. Using new American gimmicks the campaign comprised competitions, recipe books, children's books, cartoons and pamphlets. Australians danced to the 'Sun-Raysed Waltz' and the town halls of the capitals hosted free screenings of a film about Mildura. Even the influenza epidemic of 1919 was exploited:

I fear no more the dreaded 'flu,

For Sunraysed fruits will pull me through.

De Garis's ambitions took on a manic quality and he began to see himself as all things to all men. A self-constituted patron of the arts, he launched a Great Australian Novel Competition, won by Frank A. Russell with *Ashes of achievement.* De Garis himself had artistic aspirations: infatuated with the theatre, he wrote a musical comedy, *F.F.F.* He timed the première in Perth to coincide with an advertising campaign for Sunraysed fruits and brochures were posted to all listed in the Perth telephone directory. Theatre-goers suspected *F.F.F.* to be yet another stunt for dried fruits and the show was a box-office disaster. De Garis published numerous short stories, a war drama *Ambition run mad* (1914) and a novel, largely autobiographical, *Victories of failure* (1925). His *Sunraysia Daily* attained a high standard with a staff of nearly a hundred based in Mildura.

During the influenza epidemic De Garis clashed in Mildura with the swindler and journalist G. H. Cochrane, better known as Grant Hervey [q.v.]. Masquerading as an American, a giant swathed in an astrakhan coat, Hervey called on the people of Mildura to secede from the State of Victoria under his leadership. Within a week subscriptions of £5 a head were being raised to pay his fare to London. But Hervey had not reckoned on De Garis who swiftly exposed him as a fraud.

De Garis's restless nature now sought another challenge – aviation. Not content with pioneering the use of private aircraft to conduct business, he established several interstate flying records. During a flight to Perth in 1920 he conceived another scheme – a new settlement on 50 000 acres (20 000 ha) at Kendenup, formerly the home of the Hassell [q.v.4] family. He made his home there in December 1921 and 350 settlers were installed to grow apples, potatoes and farm produce. The land held greater promise than Pyap, but De Garis, in haste, raised finance on too insecure a base for safety. Grant Hervey now reappeared in Mildura seeking revenge and alleged that De Garis was on the point of bankruptcy. A 'Citizens' Vigilance Committee' was formed to defend his honour and Hervey was tarred and feathered.

Suddenly, despite frantic juggling, the Kendenup finances failed and De Garis went to the United States of America to raise new capital. A quarter of a million dollars were promised but never eventuated. He was later exonerated of charges of fraud by a royal commission, but suggestions of dishonesty hurt him deeply. He had been extravagant and absurdly sanguine but he prided himself on his commercial integrity. Other investments failed and he plunged into desperate schemes to raise finance through real estate and drilling for oil on the Mornington Peninsula in Victoria. By 5 January 1925 he had lost touch with reality and he faked suicide by drowning in Port Phillip Bay, having that afternoon written almost seventy farewell letters. A week later he was apprehended on a boat bound for New Zealand and it is said that his persuasiveness was such that he sold land to one of the detectives who extradited him. Acquitted in October of a charge of passing a valueless cheque, he returned to retrieving his financial position. But the strain was too much. On 17 August 1926, after waking 'believing I had the greatest day's work of my life to accomplish and the certainty of all the debts paid', he suffered another disappointment and gassed himself at his Mornington home. He died apparently believing he was worth £1 million.

De Garis had divorced his first wife in May 1923 and on 27 June that year married his former private secretary, Violet May Austin, who bore him a daughter. He was buried in Brighton cemetery.

E. Hill, *Water into gold* (Melb, 1937); C. Kingston, *It don't seem a day too much* (Adel, 1971); K. Dunstan, *Ratbags* (Melb, 1980); A. T. Stirling, *Gang forward* (Melb, 1972); *Punch* (Melb), 15 Jan 1925; *Age*, 18, 19 Aug 1926. JANET McCALMAN

DE GARIS, ELISHA (ELIZEE) CLEMENT (1851-1948), irrigationist, was born on 17 September 1851 at St Martin, Guernsey, Channel Islands, first child of Elisha (Elizée) De Garis, carpenter, and his wife Mary, née Roberts. The family came to Australia in 1854 and settled in Adelaide and later Naracoorte where Elisha senior flourished as a builder. Elisha junior was educated at the Collegiate School of St Peter, Adelaide, then in 1872 went to Melbourne to study architecture with the firm of Crouch and Wilson. In 1876 he joined the Wesleyan Methodist Church as a home missionary and was ordained four years later. At the time of his marriage on 2 February 1881 to Elizabeth, daughter of John Buncle [q.v.3], he was serving at Charlton; in 1882 he was ordained as the minister at Durham Ox and Kerang.

The plight of the drought-stricken farmers in his circuit moved De Garis to advocate the irrigation schemes of Hugh McColl [q.v.5]. With his architectural training, flair for journalism and implacable determination he emerged as a formidable yet disinterested leader of the irrigationists. As irrigation correspondent for the Melbourne *Daily Telegraph* he helped to persuade Alfred Deakin [q.v.] to see the Chaffey brothers [qq.v.7] in the United States of America. De Garis was founding chairman of the Tragowel Plains Irrigation and Water Supply Trust, the first set up under the 1886 Act, and next year established the Central Irrigation League, serving it as chairman for four years. He edited his own newspaper the *Australian Irrigationist* for two years before it merged with the *Weekly Times*. Fired with ideals of self-help he created the Associated Australian Yeomanry, a farmers' distribution co-operative.

A commissioner of the Melbourne Centennial International Exhibition, by 1888 De Garis had emerged as a lobbyist and publicist of singular flair, his talents overflowing the constraints of the ministry. In 1886 the Wesleyan United Conference had voted him a probationer to free him from his pastoral duties, but by 1887 he could no longer resist the lure of the temporal world and renounced the cloth. He served as a lay preacher for the rest of his life and was a member of Methodist conferences until his ninety-fifth year.

De Garis joined George Chaffey in his market garden irrigation venture at Werribee for three years before moving at the end of 1891 to Mildura, where he built up varied businesses as an auctioneer and real estate agent, dried-fruits broker and financier. One of the foundation members of the Australian Dried Fruits Association, he threw himself into community life and politics, serving on the infant Mildura Shire Council and as president in 1907-08. In 1908 he left his Mildura affairs in the hands of his precocious son, C. J. (Jack) De Garis [q.v.] and moved to Melbourne to establish a dried-fruit agency.

De Garis bought a mansion at Sandringham and entertained lavishly. He soon revealed his political ambitions and in 1909 was elected to the Moorabbin Shire Council as a representative of the Sandringham separatists. He failed to win the State seat of Brighton on the death of Sir Thomas Bent [q.v.3], then in 1910 suffered an ignominious defeat by Frank Tudor [q.v.] in the Federal seat of Yarra, where rough treatment by the Richmond Laborites doused his political hopes.

In 1916 De Garis returned for three years to Guernsey from where he supervised the London sales of dried fruits. With characteristic egotism he collected during the war a 'family' of 400 Australian servicemen with whom he corresponded by circular letters full of personal news and spiritual solace. In 1918 his first wife died; on 23 April 1919 at Auburn, Melbourne, he married Mary Evaleen (1858-1927), daughter of Rev. J. S. Waugh [q.v.6].

Still active in business and the church until his mid-nineties, De Garis became a daunting patriarch. He died at Geelong on 2 July 1948 and was buried in Brighton cemetery. He was survived by three of his eight children, of whom MARY CLEMENTINA (1881-1963), born on 16 December 1881, elder of twin girls, achieved distinction. Her father's Mildura business prospered just in time to pay for a final year's schooling for 'Clemmie' at the Methodist Ladies' College in Melbourne, where she was dux in 1898. She matriculated with exhibitions in English and history, then graduated with high honours in medicine from the University of Melbourne. In 1907 she became the second woman in Victoria to take out an M.D. On the death of her fiancé in World War I, she served for fifteen months as head of the Scottish Women's Hospitals for Foreign Service attached to the Serbian Army and was decorated by the Serbian government. After post-graduate study overseas, she practised with distinction as an obstetrician in Geelong and was a pioneer in the feeding of high protein diets to pregnant women. Her publications include *Clinical notes and deductions of a peripatetic* (London, 1926). She died at Geelong on 18 November 1963.

J. Smith (ed), *Cyclopedia of Victoria*, 3 (Melb, 1905); M. S. Sharland, *These verdant plains* (Melb, 1971); *Aqua*, Sept 1956; *Univ Melb Gazette*, 21 Feb 1964; E. C. de Garis papers (LaTL); information from Mr C. de Garis, Brighton, Vic.

JANET MCCALMAN

DE HAMEL, LANCEL VICTOR (1849-1894), solicitor and politician, was born on 16 September 1849 at Stoke Newington, London, son of Felix John de Hamel, solicitor, and his wife Eliza, née Bond. The family had fled from France to England about 1792. De Hamel trained in law and in 1874-86 was solicitor to the Board of Trade, at Newcastle upon Tyne. His work mainly involved wreck inquiries and shipping cases. He was an active member of the Conservative Party, a founder of the Newcastle Conservative Club, and captain of the 3rd Volunteer Battalion of the Northumberland Fusiliers. In the early 1880s he initiated and went on an unsuccessful expedition to search for buried treasure on a Pacific island.

Small, weak and delicate, he was yet full of nervous energy and inclined to overwork. De Hamel migrated to Albany, Western Australia, for his health's sake in 1886, a year after his father's death. Although wealthy, he was too energetic to remain inactive and soon became embroiled in local politics. An excellent orator, persuasive and something of a demagogue, he rose rapidly to prominence using local resentment of the Perth-centred colonial government to good effect. One opponent conceded that he thawed out iciness, destroyed apathy and quickened local patriotism. In May 1888 he established the *Australian Advertiser* (later *Albany Advertiser*) and, with its assistance, was elected mayor in November 1888 and next year defeated Sir Thomas Cockburn-Campbell [q.v.3] for the Albany seat in the Legislative Council. In December 1890 he won the same seat in the new Legislative Assembly. About 1892 he established a legal firm with J. M. Speed.

De Hamel was seen as an agitator and trouble-maker by the Perth establishment, newspapers and Governor Broome [q.v.3]. An attempt in 1889-90 to have the south-west remain a Crown colony when Western Australia achieved its independence, reinforced this view. De Hamel's abilities, however, soon won him repute, if not popularity. A constant thorn in the side of Sir John Forrest [q.v.], De Hamel rose by 1893 to be leader of the few diverse elements in opposition to Forrest's government. He displayed a strange mixture of liberalism and toryism in parliament, especially over franchise reform, but was credited with having been a major factor in forcing Forrest to widen electoral suffrage.

De Hamel drifted away from the parochial issues of his Albany electorate, especially after his wife Marion Eugenie, née Hammond, whom he had married in 1877, and one of their twin infants, died there in 1891, leaving him with three young children. In the July 1894 elections he stood unsuccessfully for the goldfields seat of Yilgarn. A few weeks later he contracted typhoid and, sapped by his electoral defeat and failed mining speculations, died intestate at Coolgardie on 25 November.

D. S. Garden, *Albany* (Melb, 1977); *Albany Mail,* 19 Nov 1887, 31 Mar 1888, 2 Feb 1889; *Daily News* (Perth), 24 Jan 1889; *Aust Advertiser,* 17 June 1889, 2 Dec 1891, 28 Nov 1894; *West Australian,* 27 Nov 1894; *Geraldton Express,* 30 Nov 1894; *British A'sian,* 3 Jan 1895.   DONALD S. GARDEN

DELANY, PATRICK (1853-1926), archbishop, was born on 1 February 1853 at Tonacor, parish of Killian, County Galway, Ireland, son of John Delany and his wife Margaret, née Mannion. Despite his father's death in 1860 and the general poverty of the district, Patrick's scholastic promise at the Franciscan Brothers' school in nearby Mountbellew ensured his further education at the Jesuits' St Ignatius College, Galway. He then entered their novitiate at Milltown Park near Dublin, but in September 1874 was accepted at All Hallows College. Ordained on 9 November 1879, he was released from a commitment to St Paul's, Minnesota, United States of America, and undertook further study at the Institut Catholique, Paris, gaining the degree of Bachelor of Sacred Theology; he returned to All Hallows as lecturer in history and canon law.

In 1885 he was sent to Australia to raise money for the college and stayed as private secretary to Bishop James Moore [q.v.5] of Ballarat. He accompanied Moore to Rome in 1887 and received the degree of D.D. from Pope Leo XIII. Diocesan consultor and examiner in synod in 1890 he was a regular contributor to *Austral Light,* espousing 'liberal, even radical views'. Despite his expressed reluctance he was appointed coadjutor bishop of Hobart and was consecrated titular bishop of Laranda on 10 December 1893. Over the next fourteen years he assisted Archbishop Daniel Murphy [q.v.5], contributed to the *Australasian Catholic Record,* attended interstate church conferences and synods and in 1904 formed the ecclesiastical fund for the education of priests. With special approval from Rome for retention of the title of archbishop, Delany succeeded Murphy on 29 December 1907. Next March he sailed for Ireland where he arranged for the Christian Brothers to take over the partly built St Virgil's College in Hobart. At All Hallows he ensured a continuing supply of priests for Tasmania. He also made provision for priests to undertake additional studies at European universities and advertised Tasmania extensively as a home for immigrants with

moderate capital. He returned to Hobart in February 1909.

Delany's special work in the archdiocese was in education. He personally examined in the schools and insisted on regular attendance as the basis for improved standards. An admirer of W. L. Neale [q.v.], he arranged for government inspection of Catholic primary schools and the training of teachers at mainland colleges; he regularly lectured to teachers, especially on psychology. The many schools opened during his episcopate included St Virgil's College and St Patrick's College, Launceston. He encouraged the formation of clubs and societies for the laity and on his frequent parish visitations urged the benefits of Catholic newspapers and libraries. After a visit to New Zealand in 1909 he praised its type of socialism and advocated closer settlement and increased workers' rights in Tasmania. In World War I he favoured conscription and forbade priests to engage in newspaper controversy during the 1916-17 campaigns. A scholar, writer and proficient linguist, possessed of personal charm, he was a modest and retiring man in private life. With failing health from 1918, Delany died on 7 May 1926 at Hobart and was buried in St Mary's Cathedral. In 1928 a statue to his memory was erected by the priests of the archdiocese at Mount St Canice Convent, Sandy Bay.

Catholic Mag, Jan, Sept-Nov 1916, Aug 1918; *Morning Star* (Launc), 29 July, 4 Nov, 9, 16 Dec 1893; *Catholic Standard,* Aug-Dec 1893, Jan, Mar 1894, 13 May 1926, 22 Mar 1928; *Monitor* (Launc), 8 Sept, 6 Oct 1894, 21 Aug, 27 Nov 1896, 29 Jan, 12, 19 Feb 1909, 4 Nov 1910, 29 May 1914, 5 Feb 1915; *Mercury,* 8 May 1926; *Weekly Courier* (Launc), 13 May,1926; Delany papers, diocesan archives (Univ Tas); MDHC Archives (Fitzroy, Vic).   MARY NICHOLLS

DE LARGIE, HUGH (1859-1947), miner, trade unionist and politician, was born on 24 March 1859 at Airdrie, Scotland, son of Archibald Hamilton de Largie, coalminer, and his wife Mary, née McLaren, both of whom died while he was very young. De Largie received primary education at St Margaret's School and from 10 worked in the Lanarkshire mines. He became active in the local miners' union and the Scottish political labour movement. At 25 he married Mary McGregor at Glasgow. Hugh and Mary, devout Roman Catholics, migrated in 1887 to Queensland, where de Largie helped return Thomas Glassey [q.v.] to parliament. Next year they moved to the Illawarra district in New South Wales and, during the 1890 maritime strike, he acted as delegate for the Mount Kembla miners. Later, in the Newcastle mining district of Wallsend, he worked as mines' delegate and secretary to both the local branch of the Australian Socialist League and the Labor Electoral League.

Because his politics barred him from working as a miner in Newcastle, in 1895 the family moved to the Western Australian goldfields. De Largie rose to prominence in the Amalgamated Workers' Association, established in January 1897, a union of industrial workers favouring 'one big union' and opposed to craft unions. The first Western Australian Trades' Union and Labour Congress, which was called by the A.W.A., was held at Coolgardie in April 1899; he was elected president of the goldfields division of the joint Labor parliamentary committee. He and (Sir) G. F. Pearce [q.v.] were the two Labor candidates for the Senate in the first Federal elections; both were elected.

An equable, humourless person, de Largie spoke in a 'plain and fearless fashion' with a pronounced Scots accent. In the Senate he advocated the White Australia policy and favoured protection over free trade. In 1908 he presided over a conciliation board to settle a mining dispute at Airlie, New South Wales. He sat on royal commissions on navigation (1906), postal services (1908-10), and the pearl-shell industry (1916). He chaired parliamentary select committees on the case of H. Chinn [q.v.7] in 1913, and in 1920-21 on Senate officials. He was Labor whip in the Senate in 1907-14 and ministerial whip in 1910-13 and 1917-22. In the latter term, it was as a Nationalist senator, having followed W. M. Hughes [q.v.] out of the Australian Labor Party in the conscription split of 1916. This stand reflected the overwhelming vote for conscription in his own State and on the goldfields. In 1916 he visited England in connexion with the Imperial Parliamentary Association. He lost his Senate seat in 1922.

De Largie toured Europe and Britain again in 1928, looking into the coal trade. In retirement he retained an interest in conciliation and arbitration matters and helped set up the Association of Members of the First Federal Parliament. He lived at St Kilda, Melbourne, before moving to Sydney in 1940; his last visit to Western Australia had been in 1937. On 8 January 1946, following the death of his first wife, he married Elizabeth Jeannie Marie Renoua Renouard at Darlinghurst, New South Wales. She and the four children of his earlier marriage survived him when he died at Randwick on 9 May 1947. He was buried in Rookwood cemetery.

J. S. Battye (ed), *Cyclopedia of Western Australia*, 1 (Adel, 1912); *Kondinin: then and now* (Perth, 1961?,copy Battye Lib); D. J. Murphy (ed), *Labor in politics* (Brisb, 1975); *Westralian Worker*, 11, 25 Jan, 8 Feb, 6 Dec 1901; *SMH*, 12 May 1947; *West Australian*, 13 May 1947; H. J. Gibbney, Working class organization in West Australia from 1880 to 1902 (B.A. Hons thesis, Univ WA, 1949); An economic history of Western Australia . . ., *and* interview with Tom Bath, 1953, Somerville papers, *also* biog note RM 305 (Battye Lib, Perth); information from Mrs B. McDermott, East St Kilda, Melb, *and* Mr D. H. de Largie, Salter Point, Perth.   HOWARD J. SMITH

DE LISSA, LILLIAN DAPHNE (1885-1967), educator, was born on 25 October 1885 at Darlinghurst, Sydney, daughter of Montague de Lissa, merchant, and his wife Julia, née Joseph; they were Jewish. She was educated at Riviere College, Woollahra. Musically gifted, she became an accomplished pianist but, on seeing the transformation of slum children by the Woolloomooloo free kindergarten, she dedicated herself to the education of young children. In 1902 she entered the Kindergarten College, Sydney, and was influenced by the principal Frances Newton who had trained in Chicago. De Lissa graduated brilliantly and in 1904-05 was a kindergarten director; she then took a course in training teachers. In 1905 she accompanied Newton to Adelaide at the expense of Rev. Bertram Hawker, a philanthropist, to demonstrate kindergarten methods; their work led to the formation of the Kindergarten Union of South Australia.

Next year de Lissa became director of the first Adelaide free kindergarten, Franklin Street, in a cottage in the city's slums, where she was assisted by young women voluntary helpers. She used Froebelian methods and continually related theory to practice, regarding improved child welfare and education as the basis of social reform. She was not a practising Jew but applied general biblical moral precepts in teaching and encouraged the children to celebrate the major Christian festivals. She held extra classes for older children, arranged mothers' meetings and made home visits where she gave informal instruction in hygiene and child care. Her compassion was tempered by a sharp intellect, while her personality, beauty, and logical claims for kindergarten principles attracted support for the Kindergarten Union. She persuaded it to establish the Adelaide Kindergarten Training College for teachers which opened in 1907 with eleven students; she was principal and also director of the union.

Modelling the two-year course on the Sydney curriculum, de Lissa taught the professional subjects; specialist lecturers included Professor William Mitchell, Dr Helen Mayo and Mrs Lucy Morice [qq.v.], secretary of the union and her close friend.

The college flourished in spite of lack of funds and makeshift accommodation; in 1915 Robert Barr Smith [q.v.6] donated a substantial house. From 1908 more kindergartens had opened, mainly in poor areas, using de Lissa's advice. Her visit to Perth in 1911 resulted in the establishment of the Kindergarten Union of Western Australia. In 1913 she began a successful evening course for Sunday school teachers.

In 1909 de Lissa was a foundation member and briefly a councillor, of the Women's Political Association, and a member of the first committee of the School for Mothers which met in the Franklin Street Kindergarten; next year she successfully led a crusade against a proposal to absorb the Kindergarten Training College into the University Training College, with herself as lecturer. The victory was confirmed by her evidence to a 1912 royal commission into education which resulted in continued government financial support for the union and consequent independence for the college.

At Hawker's expense and suggestion, de Lissa went abroad in December 1913 primarily to study Maria Montessori's methods in Rome. She gained the Montessori diploma and travelled widely to compile her report for the South Australian government, 'Education in certain European countries' (1915). At the first Montessori conference, organized by Hawker at East Runton, Norfolk, England, she was opening speaker. A group of 'New Educationists' invited her to open an English college for teachers of young children, but she returned to Adelaide in 1915, introducing some Montessori methods to the college and kindergartens, and instructing her successors. In 1917 she went to England and became foundation principal of Gipsy Hill College, Surrey, where she attracted English and overseas students.

In 1918 de Lissa married businessman Harold Turner-Thompson; by 1930 they were divorced. In 1923 she helped found the Nursery School Association of Great Britain and Northern Ireland, becoming first vice-president, then chairman of the executive in 1929-38; she stimulated the establishment of branches. She published *Life in the nursery school* (London, 1939); the second edition was *Life in the nursery school and in early babyhood* (London, 1949). She contributed to several books, published articles, spoke at conferences, arranged exhibitions and guided Gipsy Hill College through wartime difficulties and moves. In 1943 she lectured for six months in the United States of America, under the auspices of the British Ministry of Information and the Child Study Association of America, extending her tour in response to capacity audiences. She influenced the decision to have nursery schools included in the 1944 British Education Act.

Adaptable and farsighted, de Lissa continued to advise on early childhood issues after retiring in 1946 to her cottage and garden in Oxshott, Surrey. She was chairman of the Consultative Committee on Nursery-Infant Education in 1946-49. In 1955 she returned to Adelaide for the golden jubilee of the Kindergarten Union, addressing meetings and visiting kindergartens.

De Lissa died at Dorking, Surrey, on 16 October 1967. Her portrait (1953) hangs at Gipsy Hill and a major building, de Lissa Hall, was completed there in 1972. In 1971 the Lillian de Lissa Nursery School opened in Birmingham, established through an appeal in her memory. In 1979 the former Adelaide Kindergarten Training College became the de Lissa Institute of Early Childhood Studies within Hartley College of Advanced Education. A hall in the Hartley College is also named after her.

Gipsy Hill Training College for Teachers of Young Children, *Prospectus* (np, 1917?); H. Jones, 'The acceptable crusader . . .', *Melbourne studies in education, 1975*, S. Murray-Smith ed (Melb, 1975); *PP* (SA), 1913, 3 (75); Kindergarten Union of SA, *Annual Report*, 1906-17; Nursery School Assn of Great Britain and Northern Ireland, *News Sheet*, no 11, Nov 1967; L. de Lissa papers (SAA); Kindergarten Union of SA, Executive Cttee minute-book, 1908-23 (SAA); Adel Kindergarten Training College, Council minute-book, 1909-38 (SAA); family and other information.   HELEN JONES

DELPRAT, GUILLAUME DANIEL (1856-1937), engineer, metallurgist, and pioneer industrialist, was born on 1 September 1856 at Delft, Holland, son of Major General Felix Albert Theodore Delprat (1812-1888), sometime minister of war, and his wife Elisabeth Francina, née van Santen Kolff. The family moved to Amsterdam in 1865 where he attended a local high school. From 1873 to 1877 he served an engineering apprenticeship on the ill-fated Tay Bridge in Scotland – when he attended science and physics classes at Newport, learned differential and integral calculus from his father by post, and added Italian to his command of French, English and German. On his return to Holland he is said to have acted as assistant to J. van der Waals, professor of physics at the University of Amsterdam. On 4 September 1879 in Holland he married Henrietta Maria Wilhelmina Sophia Jas.

In 1879 Delprat began a mining career in Spain at the Tharsis Sulphur and Copper

Mines. Three years later he switched to the Bede Metal Co., becoming general manager of its Spanish concerns at a salary of £700. Energetic and resourceful, he won much renown for his location and working of forgotten Roman silver mines. From 1891 for a time he was based in London where he became a Freemason. In February 1892 he published in *Transactions of the American Institute of Mining Engineers* an article, 'Extraction of ore from wide veins or masses', which first alerted Broken Hill Proprietary Co. Ltd to his potential. Though he continued to work for Bede's he also took up consulting engineering partnerships. By the mid-1890s he was a well-known mining authority as a result of the expansion of his work to Mexico and North America.

In June 1898 Delprat accepted an offer to become assistant general manager of B.H.P. On 3 September he arrived in Adelaide where he was met by the general manager (Sir) Alexander Stewart [q.v.], whom he succeeded next year. Delprat's wife and five of their seven children arrived in January 1899 and, after a period in Broken Hill, settled in Adelaide from 1904 where they remained until moving to Melbourne in 1913. Delprat himself spent many of these years at Broken Hill. In 1904 he was naturalized.

In the early 1900s depressed prices and wasteful ore extraction methods limited profits. Delprat played an important part in the perfecting of a technique that came to be known as the [C.V.] Potter [q.v.]-Delprat flotation process; it revolutionized sulphide ore treatment and brought enormous profits from the metal content of millions of tons [tonnes] of formerly useless tailings. He received from B.H.P. £1000 for his patents and from January 1903 his salary was raised from £3000 to £4000. Delprat secured B.H.P.'s profitability through a switch of emphasis from silver-lead to zinc and sulphur, a detailed survey of ore reserves, the sinking of another shaft, and the addition of another mill, thereby more than doubling the output of sulphide ore. Perhaps his major contribution, however, was to foresee the exhaustion of the Broken Hill mine and to push for the removal of the company's smelters to Port Pirie and for the construction of its Iron Knob railways, in preparation for the exploitation of its ore resources there. The diversion of the company's interests from those of Broken Hill, was underlined both by Delprat's quitting the Mine Managers' Association presidency during the 1908-09 industrial dispute, and by the company's abrasive industrial relations during that dispute. His actions attracted the criticism of some of Broken Hill's other managers, notably W. S. Robinson [q.v.]

who, in his memoirs, accused Delprat of sharp practice.

In 1911 Delprat, with the help of John Darling [q.v.4, J. Darling], persuaded B.H.P.'s board to consider establishing a steelworks utilizing the Iron Knob deposit. Delprat had visited Europe and America in 1907 to assess overseas developments. On six months leave from July 1911, he visited America, Britain and Europe to investigate their steel industries. His report was accepted by B.H.P.'s board, as was his suggestion to employ an American steel expert, David Baker, as manager. Delprat was prominent and effective in the complex negotiations with the Commonwealth and New South Wales governments which led to the signing of a contract on 24 September 1912 for the erection of the B.H.P. steelworks at Newcastle. The works were opened on 2 June 1915 by the governor-general, Sir Ronald Munro Ferguson [q.v.], with whom Delprat forged a close relationship.

The establishment of the Newcastle works represented Delprat's crowning achievement. His vision, judgment and timing were vindicated not only by their opening in the early months of World War I, but also by his choice of American rather than the cheaper, but strategically vulnerable, German steel-making plant. His achievement was recognized officially in 1918 when he was appointed C.B.E. His only failure in connexion with the Newcastle works was the abandonment of his shipbuilding plans, in deference to Prime Minister Hughes's [q.v.] proposals for government enterprise.

During World War I Delprat was on the original sub-committee which established the Commonwealth Bureau of Science and Industry and on its advisory council. He was also on the defence Board for Construction of Aeroplanes and the Arsenal Construction Committee. In 1919 Delprat again made a working visit to America, Britain and Europe. In March 1921, after some of his decisions had been criticized by his heir apparent, Essington Lewis [q.v.], and then overturned by the B.H.P. board, Delprat resigned as general manager, but continued as consultant engineer for two years at the same salary.

In a speech in 1920 Delprat denied being the initiator of the Australian steel industry. However he believed that the great wealth taken from Broken Hill had imposed upon B.H.P. a responsibility to reinvest at least a portion in Australia's future; and it was his suggestion to make that investment in steel. He had sought to avoid ancillary ventures to permit concentration on making as much high quality steel as possible; so he had encouraged B.H.P.'s biggest customers to settle near the Newcastle works. Baker had persuaded him to this policy, but it did not long survive Delprat's retirement — yet it laid the foundations of B.H.P.'s future dominance of Australian industry.

In retirement, with H. V. McKay [q.v.] and others, Delprat was a founder and tireless worker for the Single Purpose League which from 1922 to 1924 devoted itself to ending compulsory arbitration. He became chairman of Rylands Bros Ltd in 1921. Until 1928 he was an active council-member (and sometime president) of the Australasian Institute of Mining and Metallurgy which in 1935 awarded him a medal and life membership. He was also made a life member of the (Royal) Melbourne Hospital on whose board he had served for many years. In 1918 he had been admitted as an associate member of the Australian Chemical Institute; in 1920 he was elected fellow of the Royal Society for the Encouragement of Arts, Manufactures and Commerce, London; in 1935 he was elected to honorary membership of the American Institute of Mining and Metallurgical Engineers in recognition of his contribution to the development of the flotation process and his pioneering work in Australia's iron and steel industry. In the later 1920s he began to spend more time at his Healesville property and at wireless and sculpture; his bust of Braille won him the award of a silver medal by the French government in 1929.

Delprat made his last visit to Newcastle in September 1935. On 15 March 1937 he died in Melbourne after a short illness and was cremated. To his wife, who died on 5 December in the same year, and to his two sons and five daughters, one of whom married (Sir) Douglas Mawson [q.v.], he left an estate valued for probate in Victoria at £53 005, at £5687 in New South Wales and at £900 in South Australia.

B.H.P., *Iron and steel industry* (Melb, 1914); R. Bridges, *From silver to steel* (Melb, 1920); F. A. Mawson, *A vision of steel* (Melb, 1958); G. Blainey, *The rush that never ended* (Melb, 1963); H. Hughes, *The Australian iron and steel industry, 1848-1962* (Melb, 1964); G. Blainey, *The steel master* (Melb, 1971); A. Trengove, *'What's good for Australia...!'* (Syd, 1975); B. Kennedy, *Silver, sin, and sixpenny ale* (Melb, 1978); Sel Cttee, Newcastle Iron and Steel Works bill, *V&P* (NSW LA) 1912, 3, 443; Broken Hill Associated Smelters ... collection (Univ Melb Archives); H. B. Higgins papers (NL).

GRAEME OSBORNE

DEMAINE, WILLIAM HALLIWELL (1859-1939), printer, newspaper proprietor and politician, was born on 25 February 1859 at Bradford, Yorkshire, England, son of Joseph Demaine, cabinetmaker, and his wife Elizabeth, née Halliwell. Apprenticed to a lithographic printer, he went with his family to Uruguay and Argentina about 1874. Returning in 1879, he married Mary Susannah Preston at Bradford on 10 January 1880. She objected to settling in South America, so they migrated to Queensland, landing at Maryborough in March; they were to have nine children.

Demaine worked as a joiner for Fairlie & Sons, formed an Eight Hour Association in 1882, and participated in a campaign to remove black labour from the sugar industry. In 1890 he left Fairlie's and formed the General Labourers' Union, absorbed later by the Australian Workers' Union. Secretary of the Wide Bay and Burnett Branch of the Australian Labor Federation, he organized support for the shearers in the 1891 pastoral strike, represented the Maryborough Workers' Political Organization at the first Labor-in-Politics convention of 1892, and was elected to the central political executive in 1892-94. Though William Lane [q.v.] went to Paraguay on his advice, Demaine considered his own family and stayed behind.

He earned a precarious living through the 1890s, in business as a cabinetmaker in 1892 and as a casual workman and part-time union secretary. In 1898, with Charles McGhie, he founded the weekly newspaper *Alert* which he edited until his death. It, too, had a precarious existence over forty years.

In 1901 Demaine again attended the Labor-in-Politics convention. Elected to the central political executive, he attended every convention and remained a member of the executive until 1938. He won the presidency by one vote from T. J. Ryan [q.v.] in 1916 and held it unopposed for twenty-two years. Gradually, as real power shifted to the State secretary of the Australian Workers' Union, he was left as a figure-head. Although he was effective and impartial at the small central executive meetings, he was not strong enough to control the unwieldy convention satisfactorily and was elected chairman only in 1923. His continued presidency was a measure of his general respect in the labour movement.

Demaine was a fierce opponent of conscription and corresponded at length on the subject with Andrew Fisher [q.v.] in London. Appointed to the Legislative Council in October 1917, he voted for its abolition in 1922. In the party he supported a minority urging education as an instrument of reform. Under Labor governments his radicalism was tempered; he blamed the loss of office in 1929 on the impatience of militant industrialists and firmly supported the moderate reform programme of the Forgan Smith [q.v.] government.

Entering local politics briefly in 1895 on the municipal council and the fire brigade board, Demaine rejoined the council in April 1924 and became mayor in March 1933. Willing to use political friends for the benefit of his town, he was able to keep Walker's Union Foundry, the biggest local employer, provided with government contracts through hard times. Despite rejection of a sewerage scheme at a civic plebiscite, he secured a government loan, did the work by day labour, added repayments to the rates and thus made Maryborough one of the first sewered cities in Queensland. His nomination for mayor in 1937 was signed by all aldermen, irrespective of party. In 1925-30 and 1931-39 Demaine was government nominee and chairman of the Maryborough Hospital board. He was also at various times chairman of the fire brigade board, trustee of the Trades Hall and government nominee on the boards of the Maryborough grammar schools. Foundation secretary of the Workers' Political Organization in 1890, he remained secretary of the Maryborough branch of the Australian Labor Party in 1939. By winning the Maryborough seat without opposition at a Legislative Assembly by-election in February 1937, he became the oldest person to enter the Queensland parliament; he did not stand in 1938.

Demaine died at Maryborough on 18 August 1939 and was buried in the local cemetery after a state funeral. He had been an enthusiastic Bible-reader but a convinced agnostic. His old friend J. S. Collings [q.v.] honoured a long-standing pact by delivering a panegyric at the grave.

Nurtured on the rhetorical radicalism of the 1880s and 1890s, Demaine became a supporter of Labor's substantial practical reforms. He retained the regard of radicals because of past struggles, while becoming a confidant of the real leaders of the Labor Party. Always immaculate, he neither smoked nor drank. He was commemorated by a Demaine wing for the Maryborough Base Hospital, a medal for schoolchildren and the Demaine building housing the State Government Insurance Office at Maryborough.

D. J. Murphy, R. B. Joyce and C. A. Hughes (eds), *Labor in power . . . Queensland 1915-1957* (Brisb, 1979); *Maryborough Chronicle*, 19 Aug 1939; *Aust Worker*, 23 Aug 1939; Fisher papers (NL).

D. J. MURPHY

DE MAISTRE, LeROY LEVESON LAURENT JOSEPH (1894-1968), painter, was born LeRoi Levistan de Mestre on 27 March 1894 at Maryvale, Bowral, New South Wales, son of Etienne Livingstone de Mestre [q.v.4], gentleman, and his wife Clara Eliza, née Rowe, and grandson of Prosper de Mestre [q.v.1]. From 1898 the family lived at Mount Valdemar, Sutton Forest, where he was educated by tutors and governesses. In 1913 Roi went to Sydney to study the violin and viola at the New South Wales State Conservatorium of Music, and painting at the Royal Art Society of New South Wales, under Norman Carter [q.v.7] and Dattilo Rubbo [q.v.], who encouraged interest in Post-Impressionism. He also studied at Julian Ashton's [q.v.7] Sydney Art School.

In 1916, as Roi Livingstone de Mestre, he tried to enlist in the Australian Imperial Force; he was accepted for home service, as his chest measurement was not up to standard. Discharged in 1917 with general debility, he became interested in the treatment of shell-shock patients by putting them in rooms painted in soothing colour combinations. In November 1916, as Roi de Mestre, he had first exhibited. That year's paintings were Impressionist interiors and landscapes, impasted and concerned with the effects of light. With the Conservatorium director's son, Adrien Verbrugghen, he theorized about the relationship between painting, music and colour.

Influenced by recent American books, de Mestre and Roland Wakelin [q.v.] in August 1919 shared an exhibition of vivid flat-pattern landscape paintings: titles like 'Synchromy in Orange Red' were used, and interior decoration schemes by de Mestre showed a room in 'Blue Green Major' leading into another in 'Yellow Green Minor'. This 'colour-music' exhibition became part of Australia's art-folklore as 'pictures you could whistle'. Later in 1919 they painted, but did not publicly exhibit, some of Australia's first abstract paintings. After 1919 de Mestre virtually abandoned colour-music and abstraction, though in London in 1934 he reworked some ideas. Instead his paintings of 1921-22 are experiments in Max Meldrum's [q.v.] opposite theory of impersonal, unemotional tonalism.

In 1923 de Mestre was awarded a travelling scholarship by the Society of Artists, Sydney. He spent three years abroad, first in London, then in France in Paris and St Jean de Luz. On returning to Sydney he held one-man shows in 1926 and 1928; contributed to annual exhibitions including the new Contemporary Group formed in 1926 by George Lambert and Thea Proctor [qq.v.]; conducted classes in modern art in his studio in Burdekin House, Macquarie Street; and in 1929 organized the Burdekin House Exhibition of interior design, mostly antiques — but de Mestre designed one of six sensational modern rooms. From his family's position in society he helped to make modern art fashionable in Sydney in the late 1920s, even in Government House circles, but his paintings became tame exercises in Fauvism and Post-Impressionism.

In March 1930 he left Australia permanently. Henceforth he called himself Roy de Maistre, believing the modern spelling suited a modern painter. By the 1950s he had added the name Laurent, mistakenly believing in his own royal blood via Madame de St Laurent, mistress of Edward, duke of Kent, Queen Victoria's father; eventually he also added the name Joseph, in acknowledgment of a connexion with the philosopher, Joseph de Maistre, and changed the spelling of Levistan to Leveson.

From 1930 de Maistre is best considered a British artist. He held one-man shows at the Beaux-Arts Gallery, London, (1930), in the studio of his colleague Francis Bacon later that year; at Bernheim Jeune, Paris, (1932), Mayor Gallery, London, (1934) and at Calmann Gallery, London, (1938). His work was illustrated in several editions of Herbert Read's influential book *Art Now*. In 1934 he conducted a painting school with Martin Block. From 1936 his home and studio was at 13 Eccleston Street, Westminster. Patrick White, who for ten years rented a flat upstairs, collected his paintings, dedicated his first novel to de Maistre and acknowledged his influence on his writing.

De Maistre's paintings from the 1930s onwards are generally Cubist in style. Academic society portraits occur at all times. Occasionally biomorphic, Surrealist forms occur in 1930s paintings, and ambiguous content; so do variations on other masters, Mantegna, Piero, Courbet, or on newspaper photographs of royalty. Religious subjects begin later with his conversion to Roman Catholicism. Systematic variations on his own compositions became numerous. His webs of angled Cubist interlace and pattern are perfect forms for his obsessive ideas about the web of ancestry, family, friendship.

While working for the British Red Cross Society in 1938-43 de Maistre scarcely painted, but thenceforth he was an establishment artist. In 1962 he was appointed C.B.E. He exhibited with the Royal Academy of Arts from 1951 and was represented in Arts Council of Great Britain exhibitions; his work was bought for the Tate Gallery and other art museums, and was frequently discussed in the writings of Sir John Rothenstein. His modern religious pictures were sought for public collections and exhibitions; he painted a series of Stations of the Cross for Westminster Cathedral and two triptychs for St Aidan's Church, East Acton. Besides religion his late paintings often dwelt on interior intimacies of his

studio home and its artfully cluttered bric-à-brac. These included his finest works.

De Maistre died at his Eccleston Street home on 1 March 1968 and was cremated after a service at the Brompton Oratory. In 1974 Patrick White gave all his paintings by de Maistre to the Art Gallery of New South Wales, which in 1976 exhibited its complete holding of his works.

J. K. M. Rothenstein, *Modern English painters* (Lond, 1956); *Roy de Maistre*, exhibition cat, Whitechapel Art Gallery (Lond, 1960); M. Gillen, *The prince and his lady* (Lond, 1970); *Roy de Maistre*, exhibition cat, Art Gallery of NSW (Syd, 1976); de Maistre papers (Art Gallery of NSW Lib).

DANIEL THOMAS

DE MOLE, LANCELOT ELDIN (1880-1950), engineer and inventor, was born on 13 March 1880 in Adelaide, son of William Frederick de Mole, architect and surveyor, and his wife Emily, née Moulden. He was reputedly a great-grandson of Henry Maudslay (1771-1831), the noted British engineer and inventor. When he was 7 the family moved to Victoria where Lancelot attended Melbourne Church of England Grammar School until 1891 and completed his education at Berwick Grammar School. He became a draftsman and before World War I worked on mining, surveying and engineering projects in several States. His early inventions were claimed to include an automatic telephone, designed three years before a similar type was introduced into the United States of America, which the Australian Postal Department declined to test.

While surveying in difficult country near Geraldton, Western Australia, in 1911, de Mole hit upon an idea for a tracked armoured vehicle and next year sent sketches of his design to the British War Office. He described the principle of his vehicle as follows:

> It can be steered to the right or left, when proceeding forwards, by altering the direction that the chain-rail is laid in by screwing the front portions to one side or the other . . .; or steered, when proceeding backwards, by pressing the bogie nearest the rear end of the tank to one side by means of the screw gear . . . or a hydraulic ram controlled by the steersman, thereby causing the body of the vehicle to be thrown to the right or left as required so that, as the vehicle proceeds, the links of the chain will be laid to the right or left of the line that the vehicle has been proceeding on and so form a curve, which as the vehicle proceeds will alter the direction of travel.

He was notified in June 1913 that his idea had been rejected, though only some of his drawings were returned. He resisted urging from friends to sell the design to the German consul in Perth.

On 21 July 1915, at St Matthew's Church, Kensington, Adelaide, de Mole married Harriett Josephine Walter; at the time he was employed as a draftsman in the Engineering Department of the South Australian Public Service. That year he resubmitted drawings of his design to the War Office but was told that a working model must be provided before the invention could be considered. He then attempted to interest the Australian Inventions Board, but failed. He had a model constructed and, being without means to travel to England, tried to enlist in the Australian Imperial Force but was rejected as medically unfit. When the first crude British tanks took the field in 1916, de Mole realized that his idea had been ignored and held that his design was superior. With the encouragement and assistance of (Sir) Harold Leslie Boyce [q.v.7], then a lieutenant in the 10th Battalion, he was accepted for active service on 26 September 1917. He embarked for England, taking his model with him, and was able to demonstrate it to the British Inventions Committee, which recommended it to the Tank Board. However, it was misplaced for six weeks, and before it could be demonstrated to the board Private de Mole was sent to France in March 1918 with reinforcements for the 10th Battalion. In January 1919 he was attached, as a temporary corporal, to the ammunition workers' depot at A.I.F. Headquarters, London.

In 1919 de Mole lodged claims with the British royal commission on awards to inventors, but the judgment handed down in November was unfavourable. The credit of designing the tanks actually used was attributed to two British inventors and while the commission noted that de Mole 'had made and reduced to practical shape, as far back as the year 1912, a brilliant invention which anticipated, and in some respects surpassed, that actually put into use in the year 1916' it found that 'a claimant must show a causal connection between the making of his invention and the user of any similar invention by the Government'. The commission considered that the designs which the War Office had kept since 1912 had in no way been employed. De Mole was, however, awarded £965 for expenses and made an honorary corporal; in 1920 he was appointed C.B.E.

De Mole returned to Australia in February 1920 and it is claimed that he later patented throughout the world a new style of motor-lorry chassis especially designed for heavy work. Records show only that he had made application for patents for several devices in the years before World War I, and that neither this nor his telephone was among them. The applications he did make – for improvements on chain-rail vehicles (1912), an apparatus for destroying prickly pear (1913), and improvements on rotary engines (1913-14) – were never seen through to acceptance; the prickly pear device was simply permitted to lapse, and only provisional specifications had been submitted for the others and completed designs were never presented.

After the war de Mole became an engineer in the design branch of the Sydney Water Board. In June 1940 he suggested to defence authorities a shell which would erect a fence or screen of suspended wires as a defence against enemy aircraft. The shell, which could be fired from the ground or from an aircraft, would release an encased charge on a steel wire 500-1000 ft. (150-300 m) long attached to a parachute to slow its descent. The Army Headquarters Invention Board decided that the design had 'possibilities' and de Mole obtained a favourable hearing from Prime Minister (Sir) Robert Menzies for his device, but when relayed to London the British authorities responded that similar suggestions had already been examined and found 'impracticable'.

De Mole died, after a long illness, at the Liverpool State Hospital, Sydney, on 6 May 1950. He was cremated with Presbyterian forms. A model of his tank is on display at the Australian War Memorial, Canberra.

E. Scott, *Australia during the war* (Syd, 1936); Melb C. of E. Grammar School, *Liber Melburniensis* (Melb, 1937); A. H. Corbett, *The Institution of Engineers, Australia* (Syd, 1973); *Lone Hand*, Apr 1920; *Army J*, Aug 1970; *Sabretache*, Mar-June 1979; *Argus*, 6 Nov, 2 Dec 1919; *Western Argus*, 3 May 1921; *Daily News* (Perth), 31 Oct 1936; *Advertiser* (Adel), 13 May 1950, 11 Nov 1964; *SMH*, 11 Jan 1969; De Mole papers (AWM).

C. D. COULTHARD-CLARK

DENDY, ARTHUR (1865-1925), zoologist, was born on 20 January 1865 at Patricroft, Manchester, England, eighth child of John Dendy, silk manufacturer, and his wife Sarah, née Beard. After graduating in 1885 with an honours degree in zoology from Owens College, Victoria University, Manchester (M.Sc., 1887; D.Sc., 1891), Dendy joined the editorial staff compiling the reports of the *Challenger* including that on monaxonid sponges. He was then appointed to the staff of the British Museum, Natural History, to continue his work on sponges, including a collection from J. Bracebridge Wilson [q.v.6] from Port Phillip Bay, Victoria. In 1888, on the recommendation of Professor Baldwin Spencer [q.v.], he was appointed demonstrator and assistant lecturer in biology at the University of Melbourne. On 5 December 1888 he married

Ada Margaret Courtauld, who had followed him out from England; the ceremony was conducted by Rev. E. H. Sugden [q.v.] at Spencer's St Kilda home. The Dendys were to have three daughters and a son.

On arrival in Melbourne Dendy had joined the Royal Society of Victoria and the Field Naturalists' Club of Victoria. He also joined the Australasian Association for the Advancement of Science, being secretary of Section D Biology for the Melbourne meeting in 1891, and section-president at Brisbane in 1895.

Dendy undertook the identification and description of the 'nearly two thousand specimens' of sponges dredged from around Port Phillip Heads by Bracebridge Wilson, as part of the Port Phillip Biological Survey begun by the Royal Society of Victoria in 1887. This work resulted in ten major papers on the anatomy and systematics of southern Australian sponges, in which he described eighty-seven new species. It laid the groundwork for his complete revision of the phylum Porifera, on which he became a world authority.

Dendy was the first scientist to carry out systematic research on the cryptic terrestrial invertebrate fauna of Victoria. The term cryptozoa was coined by him to describe the light-abhorring animals found under logs or stones in damp, dark situations. He described new taxa, and recorded new observations on *Peripatus*, land planarians and land nemerteans. Many of his papers are still standard works; this is especially true of his work on land planarians, on which he published sixteen papers and of which he erected seventy-nine new taxa.

In 1893 Dendy was appointed professor of biology at Canterbury College, University of New Zealand, in 1903 professor of biology at the University of Cape Town, South Africa, and in 1905 professor of zoology at King's College, London. He visited Melbourne again for the 1914 meeting of the British Association for the Advancement of Science.

Following an operation for chronic appendicitis, Dendy died on 24 March 1925 at King's College Hospital. Although he had spent only six years in Australia, during that time he had made significant contributions to the knowledge of Australian fauna. On that groundwork Dendy built his major contributions to zoological science.

H. McLachlan, *Records of a family 1800-1933* (Manchester, 1935); *Nature* (Lond), 115 (1925); Quekett Microscopical Club, *J*, Nov 1925; *Victorian Naturalist*, 42 (1925-26); Linnean Soc NSW, *Procs*, 51 (1926), viii.   BRIAN J. SMITH

DENEHY, CHARLES ALOYSIUS (1879-1968), soldier and schoolteacher, was born on 15 October 1879 at Carlton, Melbourne, son of Irish-born Daniel Francis Denehy, journalist, and his wife Maria Teresa, née Cleary. He matriculated from St Patrick's College, East Melbourne, where he was dux, and joined the Victorian Education Department. From 1902 he taught in little bush schools such as Delegate River, Tallageira, Upper Gundowring and Kevington, and at Rutherglen in 1911-14. From 1912 Denehy served in the militia as a second lieutenant in the 60th and 58th Battalions.

He enlisted in the Australian Imperial Force on 15 August 1914 and was commissioned second lieutenant in the 7th Battalion. After training in Egypt the battalion took part in the landing at Anzac Cove on 25 April 1915. Denehy, now a lieutenant, was wounded during the landing and evacuated via Egypt to England. He rejoined his unit in September, was promoted captain in October, and was in charge of the last elements from the 7th during the successful evacuation from Gallipoli.

He arrived in France with the recently formed 57th Battalion in June 1916 but next month was transferred to temporary command of the 58th, just in time to take part in the battle of Fromelles in which the unit suffered heavy casualties. Denehy's accurate reports were among the first indications that the attack had totally failed, and later he was prominent in restoring the defence. On 27 August he was confirmed as commanding officer of the 58th Battalion and promoted lieut-colonel.

Denehy commanded this battalion throughout 1917. Following the heavy fighting at Bullecourt in May he was awarded the Distinguished Service Order for 'conspicuous gallantry and ability'. He was gassed near Ypres in October and was invalided for one month. In March 1918 the battalion was one of those rushed south from Flanders to the Somme to help stem the great German offensive threatening Amiens. On 22 April Denehy requested a transfer to his old battalion, the 57th. No sooner had this been effected than he had to return to the 58th because of the German capture of Villers-Bretonneux. In the remarkable night counter-attack on 25 April, the 58th Battalion played only a minor part, being held in reserve.

On 1 May Denehy's transfer to the 57th was confirmed. He led this unit during the offensives of August-October. He particularly distinguished himself in the fighting around Bellicourt during the breaching of the Hindenburg line. The 57th Battalion were to pass through American troops who had carried out the initial assaults. Discovering that the Americans were disorganized and had failed to secure their objectives, Denehy collected them together and restored the situation. Later in the day he led his battalion further forward and consolidated on the Le Catelet line despite absence of artillery and tank support. For his gallantry and leadership he was awarded a Bar to his D.S.O.

Denehy was one of the first commanders to master the tactics of infantry-tank cooperation, and was employed to instruct Australian and other troops on the use of tanks; for this he was awarded the Belgian Croix de Guerre. He was three times mentioned in dispatches. After the Armistice he studied at the Sorbonne and developed a lifelong interest in the French language. He returned to Australia in January 1920.

Denehy went back to schoolteaching in Victoria. He was head-teacher at Rutherglen in 1926-34 and Westgarth Central in 1935-45. Although he had reached retirement age in 1944 he continued at Middle Park Central until 1956. He specialized in the teaching of French and Latin. After World War II he attended the University of Melbourne, graduating B.A. in 1949 when nearly 70. He had retained his interest in the army and commanded the 57th and 60th Battalions, Australian Military Forces, in 1920-26, and the 2nd Victorian Battalion of the Volunteer Defence Corps in 1942-45. When 82 he had the honour of leading the 1962 Anzac Day march in Melbourne.

Denehy married Margaret Burnett Douglas (d. 1936) in Melbourne on 6 April 1904; they had one son and two daughters. In December 1950 he married Madge Elizabeth Tilley who survived him. Denehy is described as a quiet, scholarly man of generally conservative views, fond of reading and music. He trained successful school and church choirs wherever he was living. After his final retirement he moved to Kyneton. He died there on 22 April 1968 and was buried in the Catholic section of Box Hill cemetery.

C. E. W. Bean, *The A.I.F. in France,* 1916-18 (Syd, 1929, 1933, 1937, 1942); *London Gazette,* 2 Jan, 17 July, 25 Dec 1917, 8 Mar, 5 Apr, 8 July 1919; *Sun-News Pictorial,* 25 Apr 1962; records (AWM); register of careers (history section, Education Dept, Melb); Denehy diary, 1914-19 (held by Mrs M Denehy, Warragul, Vic); information from Mrs J. F. Timberlake, Geelong.　　E. J. O'DONNELL

DENHAM, DIGBY FRANK (1859-1944), produce merchant, businessman and politician, was born on 25 January 1859 at Langport, Somerset, England, son of William Denham, baker, and his wife Edna Grace, née Cooke. In July 1873 after educa-

tion at Langport Grammar School he was indentured to a drapery firm. In 1881 Denham migrated to South Australia where he formed a business partnership in Mallala with George Cable Knight, a commercial traveller. He married Knight's sister Alice Maud at North Adelaide on 16 April 1884: they had two daughters and a son Harold, who was awarded a Rhodes scholarship in 1911.

The Mallala partnership was dissolved in 1885 when Denham followed his brother to Sydney and to a partnership in John Melliday & Co. He opened a branch of that firm in Brisbane in 1886. In 1890 the Denhams bought out Melliday and changed the company's name to Denham Bros, produce and grain merchants. Eventually the Brisbane and Sydney establishments became separate companies, and Denham began new businesses at Warwick, Clifton and Rockhampton. In 1893, against the advice of his brother, he opened the Silverwood Butter Factory at Warwick in partnership with John Reid [q.v.]; he and Reid later opened a cheese factory at Yangen. Denham became associated with several other companies: in the early 1900s he was chairman of directors of the New Swanbank Colliery Co. and one of the leading businessmen in Brisbane.

In 1893 Denham entered local government as a member of the Stephens Divisional Board where he served for nine years, four as chairman. In June 1902 he was elected to the Legislative Assembly for Oxley. His decision to enter parliament reflected his ambition, but he also desired to inject more business influence into politics and to oppose a State income tax which Robert Philp's [q.v.] government proposed. Denham joined a group of Brisbane businessmen who in 1902-15 enjoyed their last period of political influence in a State dominated by rural interests. Changing his views on the income tax, after he became premier in 1911 Denham remarked that it was not high enough.

In September 1903 Philp's government had resigned when its income tax measures were narrowly passed with three supporters, including Denham, crossing the floor. A Liberal-Labor coalition government headed by (Sir) Arthur Morgan [q.v.] was formed and Denham, after some hesitation, accepted the home secretary and agriculture portfolios. In April 1904, Denham became minister for agriculture and for public works. When William Kidston [q.v.], Morgan's successor as premier, retained office in January 1906 in a minority government, Denham's ambition kept him in the coalition, as secretary for agriculture and railways; but he was uneasy at having his true political allies opposed to him. In February 1907, sensing that a new anti-

Labor coalition could be formed, he resigned his portfolios. Kidston was forced out of office and Philp headed a new conservative ministry in November. Denham, home secretary, became the second ranking minister. Philp lost office in the February 1908 election, but when Kidston amalgamated his own and Philp's party that year, Denham returned to the ministry as secretary for public lands. In February 1911 he succeeded Kidston as premier. Denham refused a knighthood in 1913.

As an administrator he had a reputation for efficiency, but as home secretary he produced few reforms. His period in agriculture saw a return to good seasons and increased production without much need for innovation. Denham's major contribution was the 1910 Land Act, which consolidated the Acts and amendments of the previous fifty years and removed much confusion. He was widely praised for his grasp of the legislation.

During his period as premier Denham saw the emergence within his own party of a farmers' parliamentary group, a reaction against his legislation which farmers regarded as benefiting urban produce merchants and companies like the Colonial Sugar Refining Co. Denham had further problems at the end of 1911 over a liquor bill, which the Legislative Council refused to pass. A major constitutional crisis which threatened to split the Liberal Party was averted only when the tramway and general strike erupted in Brisbane on 18 January 1912. The *Courier* called the strike a 'godsend to the government'.

During the strike Denham received many telegrams praising his efforts to maintain law and order; but he was widely criticized for the violence of the police and special constables towards the strikers. It is apparent that he genuinely feared a revolution. When the Commonwealth rejected his request to supply troops to put down the strike, Denham discussed with the governor, Sir William MacGregor [q.v.5], the landing of troops from a German warship then off the Queensland coast, to assist in maintaining law and order. Having the full support of MacGregor, Denham called an immediate election; he lost seats in Brisbane, but won others in rural areas and retained office.

After the election Denham carried the Industrial Peace Act (1912) which established an Industrial Court that did not recognize trade unions. By 1913 he was running into increasing problems with the farmers' representatives in his party. At the end of that year, prior to his visit to Britain, Denham exacerbated his problems by holding a plebiscite among his parliamentary colleagues on the acting premiership rather than making the customary nomination. At the outbreak of war, however, he exhibited firmness in introducing legislation to deal with meat companies and other businesses which had tried to exploit the confusion. At the election in May 1915, the Liberals were defeated and Denham lost his own seat.

Following his defeat, he refused all requests to re-enter politics, and returned to his business, having spent almost twelve years as a cabinet minister during one of the most turbulent periods of Queensland politics. Denham's political career had coincided with the emergence of Labor as the then most efficient party in Queensland, and with the division of the non-Labor forces into rural and urban parties. He remained essentially a nineteenth-century liberal. Business, not politics, was his primary interest and, as premier, he did not devote his time wholly to the latter. Nevertheless Bernays [q.v.3] described him as 'among the best of our public men'.

In the late 1920s he established a branch of Denham Bros at Maryborough and became a director of the Australian Mutual Provident Society, Queensland Trustees Ltd, and Walker's Ltd in Maryborough. His produce businesses again prospered and his employees were made shareholders. A strongly religious man who, after his arrival in Brisbane, changed from an Anglican to a Baptist, Denham was a deacon at the City Tabernacle; the pulpit there was donated by his daughter Winnifred in his and his wife's honour. He keenly supported the establishment of the University of Queensland and the building of its Women's College. He also worked hard in support of a Queensland ambulance service.

Denham died on 10 May 1944 at Annerley, survived by his wife and children. His family declined a state funeral. Denhams in Brisbane went into voluntary liquidation but the companies in Maryborough and Rockhampton continued. Denham's estate was valued for probate at £44 085.

D. J. Murphy, *T. J. Ryan* (Brisb, 1975); *Brisbane Courier*, 17 Sept 1903, 13 Mar 1907; Denham papers (Oxley Lib, Brisb).   D. J. MURPHY

DENHAM, HOWARD KYNASTON (1883-1972), soldier and medical practitioner, was born on 14 February 1883 at Glebe Point, Sydney, son of Edward William Richard Denham, merchant, and his wife Julia Frances, née Knight, both from Somerset, England. He was a nephew of Digby Frank Denham [q.v.].

Because of poor health, Denham was tutored privately before attending Ashfield Grammar School and the University of Sydney (B.A., 1903; LL.B., 1906). He was admitted to the New South Wales Bar in 1907 and practised in Phillip Street, Sydney. Family pressure had influenced him to study law, and as he was not happy as a barrister he returned to the university in 1911 to study medicine, his original choice of career.

Denham had joined the University Volunteer Rifle Corps in 1901 (renamed the Sydney University Scouts in 1903) and was commissioned second lieutenant in 1905. He gained the university's Diploma in Military Science in 1908, and in 1913 reached the rank of major. After graduating M.B., Ch. M., in 1915, he enlisted in the Australian Imperial Force on 5 August as a combatant officer, and was posted to the 30th Battalion as major and company commander. On 6 October he married Gertrude Rosina Silburn Jenkins at the Congregational Church, Pitt Street. A month later he embarked for Egypt where he served in the Suez Canal Zone. He was transferred to the 46th Battalion as second-in-command in March 1916 and saw further service in Egypt before the unit left for France in June.

Denham first saw action on the Western Front in July. He fought at Pozières in August and served in the Somme trenches during the following winter. In December he was appointed lieut-colonel and battalion commander, and in January 1917 was mentioned in dispatches. On 11 April his battalion led the 12th Brigade's attack at Bullecourt. The official historian recorded that Denham 'despite long experience and militia training and fine qualities of brain and character, was not apt in handling men' and that his orders for Bullecourt did not follow the final instructions from the higher staffs, apparently because of some ambiguity in directions given at brigade headquarters. The resulting confusion delayed the brigade's advance, although it seized part of the enemy's trenches until obliged to fall back. Nevertheless, in June Denham received the Distinguished Service Order 'for distinguished service in the field' and was again mentioned in dispatches. His own account of the events of 11 April was later published in Reveille (April, 1933). In June 1917 he took part in the battle of Messines; his last major action was at Passchendaele, in October.

Relinquishing his command in December because of sickness, by February 1918 Denham had recovered sufficiently to take command of the 12th Training Battalion in England but further illness caused his return to Australia in May. He was demobilized in December and returned to the Sydney University Scouts, commanding the unit until March 1921. He later received the Volunteer Officers' Decoration.

In 1919 Denham had entered private medical practice at Randwick, and in 1921 he moved to a practice at Coonabarabran. He joined the New South Wales Department of Public Health in 1924 as senior medical officer at Waterfall Sanitarium and became, in 1929, director of the tuberculosis division, and thereby a member of the Board of Control of the Campaign against Tuberculosis. In 1931 he also became medical superintendent at Newington State Hospital and Home for Women, filling both posts until his appointment in the tuberculosis division ended in 1934. In 1930-37 he was honorary chairman of examination committees, on the New South Wales Nurses' Registration Board. He left Newington in 1937 to join the New South Wales Workers' Compensation Commission as chief medical referee, and after retiring from full-time service in 1947 continued with the commission as a part-time medical referee until 1968.

Denham was a Freemason from 1911 to 1930 and for a time was worshipful master of Ionic Lodge, Sydney. He was rather reserved in his later years, his recreational interests reflecting his private nature: tapestry and woodcarving — originally taken up as therapy after his war service — and collecting coins, stamps, antique porcelain, clocks and furniture. He had a great love of domestic animals, read widely — particularly English history — and researched his family's genealogy.

Denham died at Cremorne on 21 October 1972 and was cremated with Anglican rites. His wife and two daughters had predeceased him. His estate was sworn for probate at $102 400.

C. E. W. Bean, The A.I.F. in France, 1917 (Syd, 1933); H. Sloan (ed), The purple and gold ... 30th Battalion, A.I.F. (Syd, 1938); University of Sydney, book of remembrance, 1914-18 (Syd, 1939); A. B. Lilley, Sydney University Regiment (Canb, 1974); London Gazette, 2 Jan, 1, 4 June 1917; Dept of Public Health, Records, (NSWA); War diaries, 30th, and 46th battalions, AIF (AWM);Univ Syd Archives; information from Mrs J Hutchins, North Sydney, NSW.   J. B. HOPLEY

DENISON, SIR HUGH ROBERT (1865-1940), tobacco manufacturer, newspaper proprietor, and philanthropist, was born on 11 November 1865 at South Lead, near Forbes, New South Wales, eldest son of Robert Dixson (d. 1891), tobacco manufacturer in Melbourne and Adelaide, and his wife Ruth, née Whingates, and grandson of Hugh Dixson [q.v.4]. On 28 March 1907 he changed his name by deed poll to Denison to avoid confusion with his uncle (Sir) Hugh Dixson [q.v.]. He was educated at Scotch College, Melbourne, Prince Alfred College, Adelaide, and in 1881-83 at University College School, London. In 1884 he worked for J. W. Wright & Co. on the transcontinental railway in Western Australia, but next year returned to Adelaide to work for his father in Robert Dixson & Co.

Dixson represented Gawler Ward in 1888-89 on the Adelaide City Council then went to Perth to establish a tobacco factory. At St John's Anglican Church, Fremantle, he married Sara Rachel Forster Fothergill on 26 April 1893. That year he bought the Adelaide business and the Western Australian branch from his father's estate and soon returned to Adelaide to live. In 1901 he won a House of Assembly by-election for North Adelaide and next year was elected for Adelaide. In July 1904 he supported J. G. Jenkins's [q.v.] ministry, fearing that a Labor government would lead to socialism.

In 1902 the family's separate tobacco interests were merged in the Dixson Tobacco Co. which next year joined William Cameron Bros & Co. Pty, Melbourne, to form the British-Australasian Tobacco Co. Ltd; Dixson became a director. Early in 1905 he moved to Sydney. Later he also became a director of several newsprint companies.

Denison formed Sun Newspaper Ltd in 1910 to take over the publication of the *Sunday Sun* and *Australian Star* (renamed the *Sun*). He remained chairman until 1940. The *Sun* was the first Australian daily to carry news on its front page. He managed to break through the cable combine, with the unintentional help of the Fisher [q.v.] Labor government, which subsidized an independent service.

In the bitter press war of the 1920s, Denison invaded Melbourne in 1922 with the *Sun-News Pictorial* and later the *Evening Sun*, but in 1925 had to withdraw. In an effort to halt the crippling pace, in 1929 he formed Associated Newspapers Ltd, with S. Bennett [q.v.3] Ltd and Sun Newspapers and Daily Telegraph Pictorial Ltd, which he had acquired in December 1927 as subsidiaries. Associated Newspapers also bought the *Sunday Guardian* and *Daily Guardian* from (Sir) Joynton Smith [q.v.]. Denison now controlled two morning, two evening and four Sunday papers in Sydney but by late 1931 these had been reduced to one of each. In 1930-31 the value of the shares fell but he survived an attempt to remove him as chairman. He was a delegate to the Imperial Press Conference in Ottawa in 1920, Sydney in 1925 and London in 1930. In 1933 he sued "Truth" and "Sportsman" Ltd for libel and, after much publicity, won a farthing damages.

Denison took a keen interest in wireless: in 1910 he was a director of the Australasian Wireless Co. Ltd, which in 1913 was taken over by Amalgamated Wireless (Australasia) Ltd; Denison was managing director until 1917 when (Sir) Ernest Fisk [q.v.] took over. In 1938 he founded and was chairman of Macquarie Broadcasting Services Pty Ltd, which controlled fifteen radio stations in Australia including 2GB, 2CA and 2HR.

A strong believer in the British Empire, Denison gave £10 000 to the Dreadnought Fund in 1910 and largely financed (Sir) Douglas Mawson's [q.v.] Antarctic expedition. In World War I he helped to found the Citizens' War Chest Fund and subscribed generously to government war loans and the Australian Red Cross Society. In 1919 he gave £25 000 to the jubilee building fund of the Royal Colonial Institute (from 1927 the Royal Empire Society), London. He helped to found the New South Wales branch and was president in 1921-26, 1932-38 and 1939-40. In 1921 he gave the society a building in Bligh Street as its Sydney headquarters and paid for its furnishing. He was a 'staunch friend' to the Returned Sailors' and Soldiers' Imperial League of Australia and helped to finance *Reveille*.

Appointed K.B.E. in 1923, Sir Hugh represented New South Wales at the British Empire Exhibition, London, in 1924-25. In 1926-28 he was commissioner for Australia in the United States of America. Based in New York, he was hampered in trade relations by America's protective tariff, and generally by lack of diplomatic status. He strongly urged (Viscount) S. M. Bruce [q.v.7] to establish an Australian legation in Washington.

Distinguished-looking, with a neat moustache, Denison was a gifted public speaker, and an approachable and courteous man; he was a member of the Union Club. With a resonant baritone voice, he had sung in the choir of St Peter's Cathedral, Adelaide, and performed solos in oratorios. He was a keen sportsman, interested in rowing, cricket, football and bowls, and often played at Royal Sydney Golf Club. In 1905 he bought the yearling Poseidon for 500 guineas and in 1906-07 won the Australian Jockey Club Derby and St Leger, the Victoria Derby and St Leger, the Melbourne Cup and the Caulfield Cup twice. Poseidon won over £20 000 in prize money. In 1908 he bought Guntawang, near Gulgong, from the estate of Richard Rouse [q.v.6], renamed it Eumaralla Estate, and bred thoroughbred horses and Dorset Horn sheep. He remained interested in racing and won the Moonee Valley Cup with Dark Chief in 1936.

On a visit to Melbourne, Denison died of

cancer on 23 November 1940 and was cremated; a memorial service was held at St Andrew's Anglican Cathedral, Sydney. He was survived by his wife and three sons. After providing for his family, he left part of his estate, valued for probate at £203 602, to the Sir Hugh Denison Foundation and St Paul's College in the University of Sydney, and to the Church of England Homes at Carlingford.

Pastoralists' Review Pty Ltd, *Pastoral homes of Australia*, New South Wales (Melb, 1910); D. M. Barrie, *Turf cavalcade* (Syd, 1960); *Aust Tobacco J*, 23 June 1904, 27 Jan 1905, 15 Apr 1907; Roy Cwlth Soc, Lond, *United Empire*, 12 (1921), 31 (1940); *Rydge's Business J*, 1 Sept 1929; *Observer* (Adel), 8 June 1901; *Sun* (Syd), 2 June 1923, 23, 25 Nov 1940; *SMH*, 18 May 1926, 3, 5 Dec 1927, 12 Jan 1928, 7, 15 Dec 1933; *Argus* and *The Times*, 25 Nov 1940; CRS A461/B348/1/13 (AAO, Canb); information from Mr J. L. Denison, Roy Cwlth Soc (NSW), and Associated Newspapers Ltd, Syd.

R. B. WALKER

DENMAN, THOMAS, 3RD BARON (1874-1954), governor-general, was born on 16 November 1874 in London, son of Richard Denman, assistant clerk of assize, and his wife Helen Mary, née McMicking. Educated at the Royal Military College, Sandhurst, he succeeded his great uncle as baron in 1894. A lieutenant in the Royal Scots, he served in the South African War in 1901 in the Middlesex Squadron of the Imperial Yeomanry, and was wounded. On 26 November 1903 in London he married GERTRUDE MARY (born 7 November 1884), daughter of Sir Weetman Pearson (1st Viscount Cowdray). A Liberal, Denman was chief government whip in the House of Lords in 1907-11. His appointment as governor-general of Australia was announced in March 1911 and he was appointed G.C.M.G.

The youthful Denmans arrived in Melbourne on 31 July. 'The people I like best are the Labour people', wrote Lady Denman to her brother, and, unlike his predecessor, Lord Dudley [q.v.], Denman maintained very cordial relations with the Labor government of Andrew Fisher [q.v.]. Guaranteed financial support by Lord Cowdray, the Denmans spent generously, but were not ostentatious, attempting to introduce a more relaxed atmosphere to Government House. Lady Denman was also especially interested in the Melbourne Repertory Theatre Club and made a close friend of Melba [q.v.] whom she thought 'much more human than most people'. In spite of constant poor health — Australia's wattle gave him asthma and he suffered from chronic bronchitis — Denman carried out his official duties conscientiously, especially at sporting functions; he had been a champion horseman. The principal ceremonial occasion during his term was the inauguration of the Federal capital on 12 March 1913, when Lady Denman, tall, slim with an aquiline nose and red hair, wearing an extravagantly feathered hat, outshone her husband, his own plumes notwithstanding.

In 1913 the Colonial Office was vexed by Denman's assertion of Australia's right to 'complete control of her own fleet unit'. London's dissatisfaction was heightened by the action of James McGowen's [q.v.] New South Wales government in terminating the use of Government House, Sydney, as official residence of the governor-general. The farewell levée there was held in October 1912. Denman believed that 'the eviction' 'tended seriously to impair the prestige and position of the Governor-General'. Lack of sympathy with (Sir) Joseph Cook's [q.v.] government, leading to a dispute with E. D. Millen [q.v.], minister for defence, over Denman's literal interpretation of his role as commander-in-chief, further weakened his position.

He informed the secretary of state for colonies in November 1913 that, for private reasons, he must resign. Strains in his marriage, Lady Denman's dislike of vice-regal life in Australia, as well as ill health (the place of governor-general was 'a position not to be sneezed at', quipped one newspaper), had contributed to the decision to end his term prematurely. Again displeased, the Colonial Office refused his request to be allowed to stay to July 1914. He left Australia on 18 May. Though criticized in the English press, he was praised in Australia, even by the *Bulletin*.

Denman was a lieut-colonel commanding a Yeomanry regiment in 1914-15. After the war he took part regularly in Lords debates, often presenting Australia's point of view; in 1919-24 he was Liberal chief whip. Billiards and golf were his recreations, Brooks's and the Batchelors' his clubs. Lady Denman was chairman of the National Federation of Women's Institutes in 1917-46 and of the National Birth Control (Family Planning) Association in 1930-54. In 1939-45 she was director of the Women's Land Army. She was appointed C.B.E. in 1920, D.B.E. in 1933 and G.B.E. in 1951. Her death on 2 June 1954 was followed on 24 June, at Hove, Sussex, by Lord Denman's. He was survived by a son and daughter. A portrait by Max Meldrum [q.v.] is in Parliament House, Canberra.

DNB, 1951-60; G. Huxley, *Lady Denman, G.B.E. . . .* (Lond, 1961); *Australasian*, 15 Mar 1913; *The Times*, 3, 25 June 1954; C. Cunneen, The role of the governor-general in Australia 1901-1927 (Ph.D. thesis, ANU, 1973).   CHRIS CUNNEEN

DENNIS, CLARENCE MICHAEL JAMES (1876-1938), poet, was born on 7 September 1876 at Auburn, South Australia, first of three sons of James Dennis and his second wife Katherine (Kate) Frances, née Tobin, who was born in 1851 at Killaloe, Ireland. James Dennis, born in 1828 in County Cork, Ireland, had arrived in South Australia in the early 1860s, becoming the licensee of the District (later Auburn) Hotel. In 1880 he took over a Gladstone hotel, and in August 1889 the Beetaloo Hotel at Laura. C. J. Dennis began his education in September 1881 at Gladstone Primary School, where he edited the three issues of the *Weary Weekly*; he then attended St Aloysius' College, Sevenhill, and Christian Brothers' College, Adelaide, where he contributed to *Interesting Scraps*.

Kate Dennis died on 16 August 1890, and her two sisters cared for the children. C. J. Dennis left school at 17, becoming a junior clerk at an Adelaide stock and station agency and wool-buying firm, but was discharged for reading Rider Haggard during working hours. He then worked as junior law clerk with Jack Stockdale, a Laura solicitor. At 19 he published his first verse in the *Laura Standard*, and other early verse, including 'Snakes', appeared in the *Register* and the *Evening Journal*, Adelaide. He joined the *Critic* staff in 1898 for a year, but returned to act as barman at the Beetaloo Hotel. Following a disagreement with his father, he worked for eighteen months in various occupations at Broken Hill, New South Wales. His health failed and he returned to his aunts in Adelaide, where in 1901 he rejoined the *Critic* staff. His first contribution published by the Sydney *Bulletin* was "Urry" on 19 November 1903.

Dennis joined with A. E. Martin in launching the *Gadfly* on 14 February 1906; under various pseudonyms he contributed over 200 items of verse and prose until his departure for Melbourne in November 1907. His style and pungent wit, with verse often prefaced by classical or topical quotations, reminded readers of Thomas Hood and the American, Wallace Irwin. Other contemporary writers of similar verse were E. G. Murphy, W. T. Goodge and Louis Esson [qq.v.].

Dennis was a freelance journalist during 1908 but in meeting with writers, poets and artists 'he expended his slight funds and slight physique much too carelessly, and in time his appearance fell far below the dapper standard of *Gadfly* days'. Bouts of intemperance were to recur occasionally in later years. Late in 1908 he camped with artist Hal Waugh at Toolangi, in the hills forty-five miles (72 km) north-east of Melbourne; this area was to be home for most of the remainder of his life. When he moved from the tent to a timber-getter's house nearby he met R. H. Croll [q.v.], who in turn introduced him in October 1913 to J. G. (Garry) Roberts [q.v.] and his wife. Roberts, who had a wide circle of literary friends, invited Dennis to camp in an old tramway bus at Kallista, and became his confidant and friend. 'Den' wrote much of *The songs of a sentimental bloke* at Kallista and dedicated the book to Roberts and his wife.

Backblock ballads and other verses had been published in 1913 by E. W. Cole [q.v.3] but was not a financial success. The front cover was illustrated by David Low who shared a studio with Hal Gye [qq.v.]. The book contained a 'Glossary: for the use of the thoroughly genteel' – the forerunner of similar glossaries in four later works. Also included were four sections of *The sentimental bloke*, first published in the *Bulletin*, and 'The Austral-aise'. This too had been published in the *Bulletin*, in 1908, winning a special prize in a national song competition; in 1915 it was reprinted with alterations, dedicated to the Australian Imperial Force.

After writing feature articles for the *Herald* and *Weekly Times*, Dennis worked in Sydney in 1914 on the *Australian Worker* and the *Call*. Following the declaration of war in August 1914, he was employed at the Navy Office and then became secretary to the Federal attorney-general, Senator E. J. Russell [q.v.]. In David Low's studio he met Olive Harriet, daughter of John Herron, and they were married on 28 June 1917. She was the author under the pseudonym 'Margaret Herron' of *My dear* (1928), *Seed and stubble* (1936) and the biographical *Down the years* (1953), and died in 1968.

The songs of a sentimental bloke was published in October 1915; twelve of the fourteen poems had appeared in the *Bulletin* since 1909. It was an immediate success, requiring three editions in 1915, nine in 1916, and three in 1917; by 1976 fifty-seven editions had been published in Australia, England, the United States of America and Canada, covering 285 000 copies. A very human story, it was simply and humorously told in dialect verse which could be as easily spoken as read. Dennis said of this verse 'that slang is the illegitimate sister of poetry, and if an illegitimate relationship is the nearest I can get I am content'. He had 'tried to tell a common but very beautiful story in coarse language, to prove – amongst other things – that life and love can be just as real and splendid to the "common" bloke as to the "cultured"'. Well produced by Angus [q.v.7] and Robertson [q.v.], the book had a foreword by Henry Lawson [q.v.] and appealing illustrations by Hal Gye, who was to collaborate on most of Dennis's future works. Just as important was the timing of the publication; it reached a public depressed by enormous war casualties. Thousands of copies of the 'trench' pocket edition were sent to overseas troops. The work was widely recited, produced as silent (1918) and sound (1932) films, a stage play (1922), a musical (1961), and many gramophone recordings and radio and television programmes.

The moods of Ginger Mick, a sequel to *The sentimental bloke*, was published in October 1916 in an unprecedented first run for verse of 39 324 copies. 'The battle of the Wazzir' was deleted from this work by the censor. Dennis was described at this time as having 'the nervous and imaginative temperament, infused with a sense of humour, that comes of his Irish-Australian breeding. He is tall enough to look a small man straight in the eyes. He is of slight but enduring physique, and the lines about his clean-shaven mouth prove that he has learned patience and does not despair of learning wisdom. An aquiline nose and slate grey eyes give his face the quaint suggestion of a philosophic diagram, while a half-hidden twinkle suggests that it may have a humorous footnote. Dark hair is brushed straight back'.

Dennis considered that one of his best works was *The Glugs of Gosh* (1917). However the veiled political and economic satirical verse was lost on the public. A small Christmas 1917 booklet on *Doreen* proved popular but the prepared 'Limpy Ben' booklet for 1918 was not published. *Digger Smith* (1918) and *Jim of the hills* (1919) followed. *A book for kids*, written and illustrated by Dennis, was published in 1921 and went to several editions.

Dennis had a flair for journalism and turned to the Melbourne *Herald* in May 1922 when he found that he could no longer live on income from his works. He contributed over 3000 times to a daily column during the next sixteen years. He also concentrated on various series, commencing with 'The mooch of life' and ending with 'Ditties of debunk'. His series using Ben Bowyang in 'Letters from the bush' was also popular. The need to write topical verse within a limited time-span affected the quality of his work and the output of other material.

Rose of Spadgers was published in 1924 as a sequel to *Ginger Mick. The singing garden* (1935) was written around Arden, the house that Dennis had built at Toolangi after his marriage, and is the poet at his serious best. Arden was destroyed by fire in February 1965, but is commemorated by cairns and plaques in the still-existing garden.

Dennis had suffered from asthma for several years and died in a private hospital in Melbourne on 22 June 1938 of cardio-respi-

ratory failure. His grave at Box Hill bears an extract from *The singing garden*:

Now is the healing, quiet hour that fills
This gay, green world with peace and grateful rest.

Memorials have been raised in Melbourne, and Auburn, South Australia, and the centenary of his birth was celebrated in 1976 by various competitions, books, articles, readings and exhibitions.

Dennis was an outstanding popular poet. His reputation was built largely around *The sentimental bloke* which had a phenomenal success because of the wide appeal of the sentiment and humour in its simple love story. It was maintained by his other works and his contributions over many years to the Melbourne *Herald*.

A. H. Chisholm, *The making of a sentimental bloke* (Melb, 1946?); C. J. Dennis, *Selected verse . . .* chosen by A. H. Chisholm (Syd 1950?); I. F. McLaren, *C. J. Dennis* (Melb, 1961), and *C. J. Dennis: a chronological checklist* (Adel, 1976); G. W. Hutton, *C. J. Dennis, the sentimental bloke* (Melb, 1976); B. Watts (ed), *The world of the sentimental bloke* (Syd, 1976); I. F. McLaren, *C. J. Dennis, a comprehensive bibliography* (Adel, 1979); G. Innes, *C. J. Dennis: a personal sketch* (Angus & Robertson papers, ML).   IAN F. McLAREN

DENNY, WILLIAM JOSEPH (1872-1946), solicitor, politician and soldier, was born on 6 December 1872 in Adelaide, son of Thomas Denny, publican, and his wife Annie, née Dwyer. Educated at the Christian Brothers' College, he was a clerk until 1896 when he became editor of the Catholic *Southern Cross*. On the Adelaide City Council from 1898, in 1899 he failed to win the West Adelaide seat in the House of Assembly. But he won it in 1900 and held it until 1933 (Adelaide from 1902).

Denny studied law from 1903 and was admitted to the Supreme Court in 1908. Before the 1905 election he had joined the United Labor Party and retained Adelaide for that party. As attorney-general and minister for the Northern Territory in the Verran [q.v.] government of 1910-12, he negotiated the transfer of the Territory to Commonwealth control. He secured important reforms. His 1911 Women Lawyers Act enabled women to practise law.

On 17 August 1915 Denny enlisted in the Australian Imperial Force as a trooper and in January 1916 was commissioned as a second lieutenant in the 9th Light Horse Regiment. In Egypt he transferred to the 5th Divisional Artillery and was promoted lieutenant in June. In France he served with the 5th Divisional Ammunition Column and, from mid-1917, with the 1st Divisional Artillery. He was severely wounded at Ypres on

15 September while leading a convoy of bombs and ammunition into the forward area and was awarded the Military Cross. From January 1918 he was attached to the repatriation section at A.I.F. Administrative Headquarters, London, and was promoted captain in September. He resigned his commission in 1919 and published *The diggers*.

On 15 January 1920 Denny married Winertide Mary Leahy, a pianist and singer, in Adelaide. He resumed his legal and parliamentary work: in 1924-27 he was attorney-general and minister for housing, irrigation and repatriation in the Gunn-Hill [qq.v.] government, and carried several major legal reforms. He was attorney-general and minister for local government and railways in the Hill government of 1930-33 and in 1931, with the rest of that ministry, was expelled from the Labor Party for supporting the Premiers' Plan. The group formed the Parliamentary Labor Party but at the 1933 elections Denny lost his seat to a Lang [q.v.] Labor Party candidate. Despite rheumatoid arthritis, he practised law until his death, and wrote an autobiography, *A digger at home and abroad* (1942). Survived by his wife, one son and three daughters, he died on 2 May 1946 and was buried in West Terrace cemetery after a state funeral.

Tall, with long spindly legs, Denny was a cartoonist's delight and was nicknamed 'Walking Willie'. His preferred reading was Shakespeare and the Bible and he quoted liberally from both. His integrity, versatility and wide knowledge were unquestioned, and he was proud of the democratic legislation he had sponsored.

H. T. Burgess (ed), *Cyclopedia of South Australia* 1 (Adel, 1907); T. H. Smeaton, *The people in politics* (Adel, 1914); Universal Publicity Co., *The official civic record of South Australia* (Adel, 1936); *PP* (SA), 1940 (74); *Observer* (Adel), 4 Feb 1889; *Chronicle* (Adel), 11 Dec 1930; *Advertiser* (Adel), 28-31 Mar, 13 Apr 1933, 3 May 1946; information from Mrs M. A. Kenihan, Toorak Gardens, SA.

MERRILYN LINCOLN

DENTON, JAMES SAMUEL (1875-1963), civil servant, soldier, politician and farmer, was born on 11 December 1875 in Adelaide, son of Cincinnatus Denton, shipwright, and his wife Margaret, née Smith. In 1887 the family moved to Melbourne, where he was educated. He joined the Western Australian Department of Mines and Railways as a clerk on 18 November 1896 and eventually became second in charge of the ways and works workshop, West Midland. On 5 July 1899, at St Paul's Anglican Church, Perth, he married Eleanor Annie Hembry.

Denton was commissioned second lieutenant in the 11th Australian Infantry Regiment (militia) on 22 November 1899 and was promoted lieutenant in 1902 and captain in 1907. In 1912 he transferred to the 88th (Perth) Infantry, and became a major on 3 August 1914. Five days later, he joined the Australian Imperial Force as a captain and was appointed officer commanding 'D' Company, 11th Battalion, which embarked for Egypt in November. He was promoted major on 1 January 1915.

The 11th Battalion took part in the landing at Gallipoli on 25 April and, although immediately wounded in the leg, Denton remained on duty, distinguishing himself by obtaining and transmitting information to ships' guns and field and mountain batteries. Later he and twenty men held a trench for over six days, during which time they repulsed several determined attacks. Only after these feats, for which he was mentioned in dispatches, was Denton evacuated for treatment of his wound. He returned to duty on 12 May and when, in June, he was awarded the Distinguished Service Order for 'gallantry and devotion to duty', he became the first officer of both the 11th Battalion and the 3rd Brigade to win that honour.

On 18 July Denton was again evacuated and hospitalized at Malta. He rejoined his unit in Egypt in January 1916 as second-in-command and, after training and garrison duties in the Canal Zone, embarked for France on 30 March. The 11th moved into the line at Fleurbaix on 20 May and, in the savage fighting at Pozières in July and August, sustained heavy casualties. At Ypres on 22 September Denton was made temporary lieut-colonel and, except for leading the 10th Battalion on 27-30 September at Hill 60, held temporary command of the 11th until 3 October. He was then granted three months home leave, as his wife was mortally ill.

After resuming duty Denton briefly commanded the 70th Battalion in England, then on 20 March 1917 was appointed commanding officer of the 49th. He crossed to France on 10 September and though wounded on 26 September remained on duty; his rank was confirmed next day. He commanded the battalion in several major operations, including the battle of Dernancourt, until he was wounded again on 22 May 1918 and evacuated to England. On 3 June he was made commander of the 3rd Training Brigade, a post which he held until January 1919. His A.I.F. appointment ended in August, and in 1920 he was placed on the reserve of officers, Australian Military Forces, in the rank of lieut-colonel.

After demobilization Denton took up

farming in the Berkshire valley, Western Australia. He married Alice Marguerite Donovan at St Thomas Catholic Church, Claremont, on 22 February 1922. The year before he had entered politics (as member of the Legislative Assembly for Moore) because he believed that returned soldiers would not receive adequate rehabilitation benefits unless they had political representation. Although originally elected on the Country Party ticket, he joined the Nationalists in 1923. Having lost his seat in 1927, he retired from politics in 1929 after failing to win Irwin. In 1935-40 he was State general secretary of the New Settlers' League of Australia, an organization with which he had been associated since the war. While in parliament he had criticized the criteria used for selecting migrants to take up farming in Western Australia: he had advocated selection only of rural workers, that they should be medically examined to determine their fitness to go on the land, and that preference should be given to ex-servicemen from the eastern States.

A progressive man, Denton eschewed the conservative or traditionalist approach. He once showed his disregard for convention by inviting his wife into the chamber of the Legislative Assembly during prayers, an act which earned him the displeasure of the House.

Denton's second wife predeceased him and, survived by their son, he died on 3 June 1963 at Nedlands, Perth. He was buried in Karrakatta cemetery with Catholic rites. Despite his distinguished war record he was, in his own words, 'a man of peace and not a militarist'.

History of the 10th Battalion, A.I.F. (Lond, 1919); C. B. L. Lock, *Fighting 10th . . . A.I.F., 1914-19* (Adel, 1936); W. C. Belford, *Legs-eleven . . . the 11th Battalion A.I.F.* (Perth, 1940); *London Gazette*, 3 June, 5 Aug 1915.   R. D. MANLEY

DERHAM, ENID (1882-1941), university lecturer and poet, was born on 24 March 1882 at Hawthorn, Melbourne, eldest daughter of Thomas Plumley Derham, Bristol-born solicitor, and his wife Ellen Hyde, née Hodgson, of Melbourne. Enid was educated first at Hessle College, Camberwell, then at the Presbyterian Ladies' College. Hers was the last generation of P.L.C. girls to be educated in the strictly classical tradition. Having won a non-resident exhibition to Ormond College, she entered the University of Melbourne in 1900. She completed a B.A. degree under Professor T. G. Tucker [q.v.] in classical philology in 1903, with first place and first-class honours, and

was awarded a scholarship to complete her M.A. In December 1904 she won the Shakespeare scholarship, and in 1905 gained first-class honours (and second place) in modern languages and literature.

For some years she tutored in English at Trinity and Ormond colleges, as well as lecturing for the University Extension Board and the Workers' Educational Association. In 1912 she became a foundation member of both the Lyceum Club and the Classical Association of Victoria. Shortly before World War I, she spent six months at Oxford, studying Anglo-Saxon and Old English, then returned to Melbourne and resumed tutoring in the colleges.

In 1921 Miss Derham accepted a temporary appointment as lecturer in English at the University of Western Australia, and the next year was appointed lecturer in English at the University of Melbourne, being the first woman to hold an appointment in that department. Her commencing salary of £400 rose to £450 in 1924, by which time she was senior lecturer. When she was granted twelve months leave from February 1927, to enable her to work at Oxford, a large part of her salary (then £525) was reserved to meet the cost of her replacement, but £200 was paid to her during her absence.

Her academic career, which began brilliantly, was full but unremarkable, except for a brief term as acting professor in 1938. Professor Cowling described her as 'one of Tucker's best pupils', but there is no evidence that the early promise was fulfilled. Her scholarly output was slight and her effectiveness as a teacher was marred by poor technique. Yet she clearly enjoyed her work. Former colleagues describe her as warm hearted and gracious, always pleasant and always busy.

Enid Derham is remembered mainly as a minor lyric poet, who first captured the attention of literary critics with the publication of a slender volume entitled *The mountain road and other verses*. Over the years she contributed irregularly to literary periodicals, but it was only in 1958, with the posthumous publication of a selection of her best poems, some previously unknown, that her reputation was established. The later poems, especially, reveal an intensity of emotion, even passion, quite unsuspected by those who knew her well. She died suddenly of cerebral haemorrhage at her home at Kew on 13 November 1941, and was cremated.

Z. Cross, *An introduction to the study of Australian literature* (Syd, 1922); M. O. Reid, *The ladies came to stay* (Melb, 1960); *Punch* (Melb), 13 Apr 1922; *Argus*, 15 Nov 1941; ML printed cat for publications.   IMELDA PALMER

DE ROUGEMONT, LOUIS (1847-1921), hoaxer, was born Henri Louis Grin on 12 November 1847 at Gressy, Vaud canton, Switzerland, son of Antoine Samuel Emanuel Grin, farmer, and his wife Jeanne, née Perret. Educated at a local primary school, he moved with his family to Yverdon, where he worked in his father's wagon business. At about 16 he became a footman to the actress Fanny Kemble, touring extensively and learning fluent English. In 1870-74 he was a valet in London, and in 1875 came to Australia as a butler with the new governor of Western Australia, Sir William Robinson [q.v.6]; to Lady Robinson he was insolent and ambitious, and left after five months.

In June Grin become master and owner of the pearling cutter *Ada*, which was posted missing in February 1877 some months before it was found wrecked near Cooktown, Queensland; Grin claimed to have sailed the 3000 miles (4800 km) from Fremantle and to have been the sole survivor of an attack by Aboriginals at Lacrosse Island. By May 1880 he had arrived in Sydney. He worked as a dishwasher, waiter and seller of real estate and mining shares, but mainly as a photographer. On 3 April 1882, as Henri Louis Grien, he married Eliza Jane Ravenscroft at the Presbyterian manse, Newtown; they had seven children. He was also known as 'Green' and 'Grein'.

Early in 1897 Grin deserted Eliza and fled Sydney taking a copy of the diary of a bushman, Harry Stockdale. He surfaced in New Zealand as a spiritualist and then worked his way to England, arriving in March 1898. As Louis de Rougemont he called on (Sir) J. Henniker Heaton [q.v.4], who gave him a letter of introduction to the editor of the new *Wide World Magazine*. From August 1898 to May 1899 it serialized 'The adventures of Louis de Rougemont', which focused fancifully on the astounding experiences he had had while allegedly spending thirty odd years as a castaway among the Aboriginals of North-West and Central Australia. The articles were republished as *The adventures of Louis de Rougemont, as told by himself* (1899); they were fluently and cleverly written, but essentially the plausible concoction of a colonial Munchausen.

In the furore that erupted de Rougemont was supported by his publishers and by John Moresby [q.v.5]; he lectured in September 1898 to the geography and anthropology sections of the Bristol meeting of the British Association for the Advancement of Science. But his claims were doubted by Louis Becke [q.v.7] and strongly disputed by D. W. Carnegie [q.v.7] in the London *Daily Chronicle*. Assisted by revelations in the Sydney *Evening News* and *Daily Telegraph*, the London paper established that the hoaxer had been identified by Eliza from a copy of *Wide World*; the *Chronicle*'s articles, republished as *Grien on Rougemont; or, the story of a modern Robinson Crusoe* (London, 1898), provide the information on Grin's Life from which most subsequent accounts derived.

At the time of the controversy de Rougemont was described as tall and lightly built with a thin, seamed face, full eyes, heavy lids, bristly hair, pointed beard and cultured voice; as caricatured by Phil May [q.v.5] he looked remarkably like May's *Bulletin* companion of the 1880's, Livingston Hopkins [q.v.4]. In 1899 he was a music-hall attraction in South Africa as 'The greatest liar on earth'; on a similar tour of Australia in 1901 he was booed from the stage. As 'Louis Redman', handyman, he died in London on 9 June 1921, and was buried in Kensal Green cemetery with Roman Catholic rites. He was survived by his second wife Thirza Ann Wolf, née Ellis, divorcee, whom, as Louis de Rougemont, he had married on 28 July 1915. She had his death certificate amended in 1929.

F. A. Kemble, *Further records, 1848-1883* (Lond, 1890); N. Gould, *The magic of sport* (Lond, 1909); J. W. Kirwan, *An empty land* (Lond, 1934); F. Clune, *The greatest liar on earth* (Melb, 1945); A. Sykes, *Five plays for radio* (Syd, 1975); G. J. Maslen, *The most amazing story a man ever lived to tell* (Syd, 1977), and for bibliog; *Daily Telegraph* (Syd), 14, 16, 21 Sept, 3, 28 Oct 1898; *Evening News* (Syd), 20, 21 Sept 1898; *Arrow* (Syd), 26 Nov 1898-14 Jan 1899; *The Times*, 11, 13, 15 June 1921.

B. G. ANDREWS

DESBROWE-ANNEAR; *see* ANNEAR

DESMOND, ANNA MARIA (1839-1921), best known as Mother Benigna, nun and teacher, was born on 6 December 1839 at Bantry, County Cork, Ireland, daughter of Patrick Desmond, lawyer, and his English wife Esther, née Jagoe. Educated at home in singing, instrumental music, dancing and languages, she helped in the relief of the poor, admired her father's fight against injustice and acquired the Christian vision which governed her life. In 1862 her application to enter the Convent of Mercy of Cappoquin was granted and she was given the name of Sister Francis Xavier. She took her final vows on 26 November 1865.

In 1871 Mother Vincent Whitty [q.v.6] returned to Ireland seeking recruits and Sister Francis Xavier volunteered. As there was a nun of the same name aboard the *Silver Eagle* on which she travelled to Australia, she took the new name Sister Benigna. She landed in Brisbane on 24 May 1872.

Helping to establish a convent at Rockhampton in 1873, next year she returned to Brisbane where she taught music and carried out charitable work until 1878. When the Sisters of St Joseph were recalled from his area, Father W. M. Walsh of Townsville invited the Sisters of Mercy to provide religious education. They arrived on 13 November 1878 and prepared to reopen St Joseph's School for the 1879 school year. Sister Benigna took charge of the community in January.

The Sisters had to support themselves and pay their lay teachers without a government subsidy. Under Sister Benigna's leadership some members of the community taught music and this, with the assistance and generosity of friends, kept the school and convent going. The Sisters also did much charitable work and soon saw the need for and established a boarding school for country girls. Their courage and hard work helped them to recover from a great set-back in 1892 when the church, and even the ground on which it stood, were washed away by torrential flooding.

On 11 February 1902 Bishop Joseph Higgins [q.v.] appointed Sister Benigna as Mother Superior of an autonomous St Patrick's Convent at Townsville which became the mother house for branches at Ravenswood and Bowen. In 1903 Mother Benigna and Mother Bernardine visited Ireland. They brought back ten recruits who were sent to staff various already established schools. Mother Benigna also did much to pave the way for the establishment of the Christian Brothers School at Townsville. In 1905 a delegation of businessmen asked her to found a girls' secondary school at Townsville and St Patrick's High School was opened with forty students. For many years the school was a centre of culture in Townsville and its ecumenism and high standard of education did much to break down bigotry.

Mother Benigna's golden jubilee in 1915 was celebrated by all classes and creeds in the city. Her humble honest faith, her gentle disposition and her hard work and charity within the district had won her many friends and admirers, both within and without the Church. Mother Benigna died on 24 November 1921 and was buried in Townsville cemetery after a requiem Mass in her beloved church, St Joseph's, The Strand.

M. X. O'Donoghue, *Beyond our dreams* (Brisb, 1961); *St Joseph's School Centenary Mag* (Townsville), 1977; *Townsville Daily Bulletin*, 26, 29 Nov 1915, 25 Nov 1921; *Catholic Advocate*, 8 Dec 1921; Sisters of Mercy Archives (Brisb, Rockhampton, Townsville), including C. Clamp, Biography of Mother Benigna Desmond (Townsville).
A. J. McELLIGOTT

DESMOND, ARTHUR (c. 1859-1926?), agitator and author, was born probably in New Zealand, son of an Irish father and an English mother. Desmond may not have been his correct name. For a time he was sailor, shepherd, drover and musterer. In July 1884 and September 1887 he was an unsuccessful radical candidate for Hawke's Bay, against the squatters' man Captain (Sir) William Russell. Desmond proclaimed himself a follower of Henry George [q.v.4], demanding land nationalization and the establishment of a state bank. In February 1889 he appeared at Gisborne, where he took the platform in support of the Maori leader Te Kooti; the Sydney *Bulletin* in March published Desmond's poem, 'The song of Te Kooti', and other verses in the next two years.

By January 1890 Desmond was at Auckland, where, after a brief association with Henry George followers, he organized trade unions, being active in the Timber Workers' Union. In October 1890 he began a radical newspaper, the *Tribune*, which closed after eight issues. A pamphlet of his, *Christ as a social reformer* (1890), was later shown to be plagiarized from an American magazine. By December he was in Wellington, where it was his practice to address workers on Sunday afternoons at the wharf gates.

About November 1892 Desmond came to Sydney, and soon gravitated to W. H. MacNamara's [q.v.] bookshop where socialism was a staple. With his flamboyant style and striking appearance (red-bearded and red-headed) Desmond became a leading figure. He acquired a reputation in his group as a banking expert; in May 1893 there appeared the first issue of *Hard Cash*, which he is said to have edited. It attacked banks and exposed the self-interest of capitalists and clergymen. Although MacNamara and S. A. Rosa [q.v.] were gaoled for publishing it, Desmond eluded the police; but he was fined for posting a notice 'gone bung' on a Sydney bank. From November 1893 to January 1894 he printed and published the iconoclastic *Standard Bearer*, edited by 'Hard Kash'.

In late 1893 the depression in Sydney had begun to bite and Desmond was prominent in the Active Service Brigade, an organization of radicals including Tommy Dodd and John Dwyer which aimed to disrupt meetings of conservative politicians. The brigade obtained premises in Castlereagh Street, where beds were provided for the homeless and workless for 3d. per night.

By the end of 1893 Desmond had left the

Active Service Brigade and joined the Labor Party. At the unity conference in November, Desmond was one of those credited with authorship of the phrase 'undying hostility' in a resolution expelling four Labor parliamentarians. In June next year he was proposed as a Labor candidate for Durham in the general election but he declined to stand. Instead he helped to organize the campaign which secured the election of J. C. Watson [q.v.] for Young. He wrote poetry regularly in 1894 for the socialist magazine, *New Order*.

About 1895 Desmond left Australia, apparently for the United States of America. Reputedly he took a manuscript, which was published under the pseudonym 'Ragnar Redbeard' in Chicago in 1896 as the *Survival of the fittest*, later retitled *Might is right*. Denouncing women and Christianity, this was a vitriolic, racist hymn to the doctrine of force, apparently based on the ideas of Nietzsche and Stirner.

Desmond's subsequent movements are obscure. Reports claim he visited Britain, South Africa and even Manchuria before 1902. His death is reported to have occurred in Palestine in 1926, although other reports that year claimed that he was 'still alive and living in Chicago', conducting a bookstore. Probably his greatest significance in Australia was as an influence on Henry Lawson, W. M. Hughes and on J. T. Lang's [qq.v.] concept of 'money power'.

Aust Journalists' Assn, *Copy*, 1 Dec 1913; *Ross's Mthly*, 17 Apr 1920; *NZ Mthly Review*, Aug 1960; *Overland*, 38, Mar 1968; *Tocsin*, 17, 24 May, 21 June 1900; *Bulletin*, 12 June, 10 July 1919, 5 July 1923, 14 Aug 1924, 30 Dec 1926; *Aust Worker*, 14 Apr 1926, 16 Mar, 11 May, 22 June 1927; *Windsor and Richmond Gazette*, 8 Oct, 26 Nov 1926; information from Mr H. O. Roth, Auckland, NZ, *and* Mr R. N. James, Canb.   CHRIS CUNNEEN

DESPEISSIS, JEAN MARIE ADRIAN (1860-1927), agricultural expert, was born on 28 December 1860 on the estate of his French sugar-planter family at Mapou, Mauritius, son of Marie Augustin Despeissis and his wife Jeanne Marie Emilie, née Daunty. He studied medicine at the Royal College at Port-Louis, but left without qualifying when sent to India by the government to investigate methods by which beet-sugar importers from Germany were competing for the local market against Mauritian cane-sugar.

On his return in 1886 Despeissis became the island's executive commissioner at the Colonial and Indian Exhibition, London. He then studied for three years at the Royal Agricultural College, Cirencester. He graduated with honours and became a member of the Royal Agricultural Society of England (1889). Despeissis next trained at the Institut National Agronomique and the Institut Pasteur in Paris; at the latter he carried out research on experimental fermentation. He furthered his practical experience in vine-growing and wine-making at W. & A. Gilbey's Medoc vineyards and at Montpellier.

Adrian's father was now an adviser on refining processes to the Colonial Sugar Refining Co. in Sydney. In 1890 Adrian Despeissis became consulting viticulturist and inspector of agriculture for the government of New South Wales. In 1894 he went to Western Australia for nine months to help establish the Bureau of Agriculture, which he joined that year as a viticultural and horticultural expert and inspector. He was an early advocate of cotton-growing in the north and the first to warn of soil erosion on the Kimberley river-frontages (1905-08). He travelled extensively within the State and in 1906 was sent to Algeria, Spain and Portugal to study viticulture. On returning next year he became under-secretary and acting director of agriculture and in 1910 investigated tropical agriculture in Queensland, Malaya, Singapore and Java. After being commissioner of tropical agriculture for the North-West of Western Australia in 1910-12, he retired.

Despeissis established the Santa Rosa Wine & Distilleries Ltd at Guildford with J. L. Nanson [q.v.] and L. Lindley-Cowen, and managed it. From 1923 he served a term as director of agriculture in Fiji, then retired again to Guildford. (Sir) John Northmore [q.v.] bought his share in Santa Rosa and the name was changed to Valencia Vineyards Ltd. In 1927 Despeissis briefly advised the State government on the establishment of introduced pastures and fodder plants around Wyndham. While in the area preparing for this work he caught pneumonia and died in the town on 2 May. On 20 April 1901 at Claremont, he had married Laetitia Ellen Wyndham, granddaughter of George Wyndham [q.v.2]; she and their only child, a son, survived him. He was buried in the local cemetery.

An intrepid traveller, regarded as an official of 'unfailing integrity and courtesy', Despeissis wrote extensively in scientific journals. His major work was the *Handbook of horticulture & viticulture of Western Australia* (1895). He was sometime chairman of the Soldier Settlement Scheme and a member of the Railway Advisory Board and the Land Purchase Board.

J. S. Battye (ed), *Cyclopedia of Western Australia*, 1 (Adel, 1912); *Western Mail* (Perth), 22 Apr 1911, 9 Mar 1912; *West Australian*, 7 May 1927; information from Mr J. L. d'Espeissis, Peppermint Grove, WA.   P. E. MASKELL

DETHRIDGE, GEORGE JAMES (1863-1938), judge, was born on 2 November 1863 at Sandhurst (Bendigo), Victoria, son of James Dethridge, postal clerk, and his wife Mary, née Kipling. His younger brother was John Stewart [q.v.]. The family settled in the Melbourne suburb of Richmond when he was quite young. After education at St Stephen's Church School, Richmond, and Brunswick College, he was apprenticed to a jeweller before turning to legal studies. He was resident at Trinity College, University of Melbourne, and graduated B.A., 1890; LL.B., 1893; and LL.M., 1897.

In 1893 Dethridge was called to the Victorian Bar, at a time of economic recession when briefs for unknown juniors were neither common nor highly marked. Taking whatever came his way, by the turn of the century he slowly began to establish a sound common law practice. On 29 June 1907, in a ceremony conducted by Charles Strong [q.v.6] at the Australian Church he married 29-year-old Rosina Hughes; they had two sons and two daughters.

An extrovert by nature, a good conversationalist who was willing to listen, Dethridge was popular with his fellow barristers. His capacity to avoid rubbing people up the wrong way even in situations of opposition, and his scrupulous attention to detail, led to his being used on several occasions as an arbitrator.

In 1919 Dethridge was appointed to a royal commission to inquire into conditions of wharf labourers at Port Melbourne. His success in handling the assignment led to his appointment next year as a County Court judge. Sir Robert Menzies later described him as of middle height and of medium build, with 'a sort of barking and emphatic manner of speech which . . . concealed beneath it a quick mind and a somewhat Rabelaisian humour'. In 1926 when a separate Commonwealth Court of Conciliation and Arbitration was set up, Dethridge was appointed first chief judge on 20 July with fellow-judges Lukin [q.v.] and Beeby [q.v.7]. His reputation for getting on with people, perhaps more than legal erudition or experience, had determined his selection over more senior men.

If any single feature stands most to his credit it must be his handling of his court through very difficult times of intense political and economic activity. His first sitting was in August, and in September the Federal government sought to secure by referendum greater industrial powers in order to remove the dual exercise of conciliation and arbitration by the Commonwealth and the States. However, attempts over the next three years to alter the Conciliation and Arbitration Act were overshadowed by the onslaught of the Depression, and the court became the arena of the fight by trade unions to preserve existing standards. Dethridge, as chief judge, was responsible for first listing and then presiding over a general hearing of these matters in 1931. The court refused to depart from the existing method of calculating the basic wage but awarded a measure of immediate relief to employers by reducing all rates under its awards by 10 per cent. He presided over subsequent major inquiries into general wage rates, mostly arising from applications to restore this cut, in 1934 and 1937.

As an arbitration judge, Dethridge can be summed up as a cautious but flexible conservative. He was meticulous, sometimes to the point of being tedious. Though not by nature a social reformer of the school of Higgins [q.v.], he, more than his colleagues, made the effort to keep abreast of social and economic writings. His interest in current theories led to his tendency to ruminate from the bench and he was regarded professionally as something of a talker. On the other hand the respect and indeed affection that he acquired from the trade union movement stemmed from his willingness to listen to any proposition with patience. He was regarded as a considerate judge, willing 'to give the unions a go'. Perhaps his rapport was assisted by his early experience in the jewellery trade. He is remembered as carrying stubs of pencil and worn pieces of rubber in his pocket, which he needed because he never crossed out in drafts but erased and rewrote in careful, legible script.

In 1929 Dethridge was appointed to inquire into allegations affecting members of the Parliamentary Joint Committee of Public Accounts in connexion with claims made by broadcasting companies against the Commonwealth government. In 1938 he chaired a royal commission on doctors' remuneration for national insurance service and other contract practice. However, the report was never written and the inquiry lapsed, for on 29 December 1938 Dethridge died in hospital in Melbourne. He was survived by his wife and children and was cremated.

R. G. Menzies, *The measure of the years* (Melb, 1970); *Aust Law J*, 20 Jan 1939, p 362; *Argus*, and *SMH*, 30 Dec 1938.   IAN G. SHARP

DETHRIDGE, JOHN STEWART (1865-1926), civil engineer, was born on 25 June 1865 at South Yarra, Melbourne, son of

James Dethridge, a clerk in the Department of Posts and Telegraphs, and his wife Mary, née Kipling. His elder brother was Judge George James Dethridge [q.v.]. John left school early and entered the building trade. In April 1888 he joined the Department of Public Works as an inspector of works, and five years later he was promoted to the Mines and Water Supply Department as inspector-in-charge of the Coliban water-supply and irrigation system.

In 1897 Dethridge passed his water-supply examinations, which qualified him for the professional division, and in 1899 he resigned his permanent appointment in the general division to accept a temporary appointment as assistant engineer. He became a permanent professional officer in 1902. At this time he was overseeing the works being executed by the Mildura Irrigation Trust.

In 1903 Dethridge was appointed executive engineer for the Goulburn River works, which included the Nagambie Weir and the Waranga Basin. He was responsible for the raising of the Waranga embankment and for the design of the Sugarloaf Weir. During his years of close association with the Goulburn irrigation system he developed his direct measuring water-meter for use in flood irrigation, a simple, robust and inexpensive device which he refused to patent. It became standard throughout the Victorian irrigation areas, and has been widely adopted overseas.

In April 1907 Dethridge was promoted to engineer and given charge of the Carrum as well as the Goulburn-Waranga works. Next year he became deputy chief engineer of the department, the senior professional officer concerned with irrigation. In 1911 he was appointed to a vacancy as one of the three commissioners of the recently formed State Rivers and Water Supply Commission. For four years he served under the chairmanship of Elwood Mead [q.v.], an eminent engineer. But in 1915, when W. Cattanach [q.v.7] took over as chief commissioner, Dethridge became the senior engineer in the commission. His engineering ability was of special significance to Victoria during the next eleven years, which saw the doubling of the water storage of the State.

Dethridge was the Victorian representative at the Interstate Conference of Engineers (1913) which formulated the River Murray Agreement. When the River Murray Commission was set up on 1 February 1917 Dethridge acted for his State. In the next few years the Murray was regulated by a series of locked weirs, of which Dethridge designed two, those at Torumbarry, below Echuca, and at Mildura. These were novel structures. Each consisted of a row of steel trestles mounted on wheels so that they could be rolled completely out of the river in time of flood.

Dethridge was also associated with the first Eildon Reservoir and the Pyke's Creek and Melton reservoirs on the Werribee River. He was an active member of the Institution of Civil Engineers (London), to which he had been elected in 1909, and was chairman of the local association of the institution in 1923-24.

Dethridge had not yet yet retired when he died on 15 May 1926 at his house at Brighton Beach, after an illness of some months. He was survived by his wife, the former Margaret Robinson of Horsham, whom he had married on 30 October 1895, and by nine of his eleven children.

John Dethridge's all-round ability is shown by his rise to professional status from his early occupation as a building worker, and by his advancement from assistant engineer to commissioner in only twelve years. He was admired and liked even by the most junior members of his staff — which was a rarity in those days. His Eildon Weir has been submerged by the much larger Eildon Dam, but most of his works survive as his monuments, as do the ubiquitous Dethridge water-meters; and his ingenious weirs on the Murray are in full use after many decades.

Aqua, March 1958; *Age*, and *Argus*, 17 May 1926.   RONALD McNICOLL

DE TOURCEY; *see* COLLINGRIDGE DE TOURCEY

DETTMANN, HERBERT STANLEY (1875-1940), headmaster, was born on 25 October 1875 at Bathurst, New South Wales, eldest son of John Dettmann, native-born schoolteacher, and his English wife Elizabeth Love, née Catt. He was dux of Fort Street Public School at 13 and later of Sydney Boys' High School, and won a scholarship to the University of Sydney. As an undergraduate he won Professor (Sir) Mungo MacCallum's [q.v.] English prize three times and the (W. C.) Wentworth [q.v.2] medal. He created a record by graduating B.A. in 1897 with first-class honours in four subjects — English, German, Latin and Greek — and as a graduate won the Wentworth medal twice.

Awarded the Woolley [q.v.6] scholarship for travelling in 1899, Dettmann entered Balliol College, Oxford (B.A., 1902; B.C.L. and M.A., 1906). He made lifelong friendships (maintained by correspondence) with A. D. Lindsay, master of Balliol, and F. M. Powicke, the medieval historian. His father's fatal illness caused him to abandon hopes of a fellowship and to return to Australia in 1903. In 1903-08 he taught English at Sydney Grammar School under A. B. Weigall [q.v.6]. He acted as professor of classics at the University of Adelaide and was awarded an honorary M.A. in 1906.

On 1 June 1908 at Balmain, Sydney, Dettmann married Nell Lodder with Presbyterian forms, and that year went to New Zealand as professor of classics at Auckland University College. He was chairman of the professorial board and a fellow of the Senate of the University of New Zealand and captained the university cricket team. He was also chairman of the Auckland Cricket Association and of the board of governors of King's College, Auckland.

In 1923 Dettmann became the first Australian-born headmaster of Sydney Grammar School. In response to requests from old Sydneians a boarding-house run by the school was opened at Randwick with twenty-seven boys, including his two sons. Although the 1854 Act of parliament setting up the school explicitly stated its non-denominational character, Dettmann decided in 1927 to hold a religious assembly twice a term and set aside time for the study of the Bible as literature. In the early 1930s he had to contend with the effects of the Depression: the decline in enrolments from nearly 700 in 1930 to 511 in 1933 seriously affected the school's finances, expecially as he was unwilling to retrench masters and thought it impossible to raise fees. Stringent economies had to be made and he kept Greek going by teaching boys himself. Enrolments gradually rose to 705 in 1940.

Dettmann taught by example. A distinguished scholar, he was noted for his unusual approach and ideas, common sense, moderation and, above all, his sense of humour. He was never too busy to talk to boys individually or to help or coach them. He believed in the benefit of sport and physical education and was a loyal supporter of the Athletic Association of the Great Public Schools of New South Wales. In 1936 he introduced a compulsory school uniform. A witty speaker, he made assemblies and speech days entertaining occasions.

Occasionally Dettmann wrote articles for the *Sydney Morning Herald*. He was a member of the Union and Old Sydneians clubs and enjoyed playing tennis and bridge, and reading 'detective yarns'. He died suddenly with coronary occlusion at his home at Gordon on 1 January 1940 and was cremated. He was survived by his wife, two sons and two daughters.

W. F. Richardson, Fifty years of classics (Auckland, 1966); *Sydneian*, 1957, centenary no; *SMH*, 16 Aug 1923, 22 Jan 1940; Sydney Grammar School Archives; family papers (held by D. Kacfas, *and* H. K. S. Dettmann, Wahroonga, Sydney).

A. M. MACKERRAS

DEVANNY, JANE (1894-1962), writer, known as Jean, was born on 7 January 1894 at Ferntown, Collingwood, New Zealand, eighth of ten children of William Crook, boilermaker and miner, and his wife Jane, née Appleyard. She left school at 13 but read voraciously, observed constantly and was profoundly influenced by the premature death of her father and by trade union militancy. When barely 17 she met the militant Francis Harold (Hal) Devanny (1888-1966); they married in 1911 at Palmerston and soon had a son and two daughters. Jean became active in the labour movement, early contact with Marxist and other theories of socialism leading to the public speaking that filled much of her life. 'Spiritually committed to writing' by about 1923, her first novel, *The butcher shop* (1926), was a *succès de scandale* for its explicit condemnation of sexual oppression in marriage. Over the next three decades she published twenty books and many short stories and articles in Australia, England, United States of America, Germany and Russia.

The Devannys moved to Sydney in 1929, hoping to improve the health of their son who died in 1934. Jean was employed as a domestic in western New South Wales, then joined the Australian Communist Party in late 1930 or early 1931, was appointed national secretary of Workers' International Relief and in 1931 attended its Berlin conference. Despite an eight months organizing tour on behalf of the party in Queensland in 1935, she faced increasing official dissatisfaction which resulted in 1940 in her expulsion. Although she rejoined the party in 1944, she had lost many illusions and left it in 1949.

Jean Devanny played an active role in literary organizations. She helped to found the Writers League with Katharine Susannah Prichard [q.v.] and Egon Kisch, and was its first president in 1935; in 1937 it was converted into the Writers Association. By 1945 she was a leading light in the presentation by the Fellowship of Australian Writers of a submission to the Tariff Board seeking literary protection. The last two decades of her life were spent in North Queensland. During this period, she documented much of the area in very readable 'walkabout' books and articles. She died with chronic leukaemia at Townsville on 8 March 1962 and was cremated at Rockhampton.

Jean Devanny had close friendships with Miles Franklin [q.v.], Marjorie Barnard and Winifred Hamilton, but her literary contemporaries found her intensity disturbing. To Miles Franklin she was 'vivid, valiant, temerarious', a person of extraordinary energy. Nettie Palmer [q.v.] respected her courage, admired her generosity and friendliness but 'resented her general cocksureness'. Hugh McCrae [q.v.] spoke of 'a tongue like an axe in a wood-chopping contest'. For her the novel was an instrument for propaganda, written often in a 'fiery agitational style'. Well aware of her own literary defects, Devanny feared she had wasted her life: 'I realise now that I have not exploited the small measure of ability for writing I possess one whit. I never really got down to it and THOUGHT. Thought was reserved for politics'.

Aust Academic and Research Libraries, 1 (1970), p 66; *North Qld Register*, 17 Mar 1962; J. Devanny papers, and autobiography, The river flows on (James Cook Univ Lib, Townsville); information from Mrs P. Hurd, Townsville, Qld.

RON STORE

DEVENISH-MEARES; *see* MEARES

DEVINE, SIR HUGH BERCHMANS (1878-1959), surgeon, was born on 13 May 1878 at Little River, Victoria, eldest son of John Devine, farmer, and his wife Mary Anne, née Gleeson, both born in Geelong. His family was Catholic and he was educated at St Patrick's College, Ballarat. After matriculation in 1894 he studied pharmacy and was employed by Henry Francis of Bourke Street, Melbourne; he was registered as a pharmacist on 10 January 1900.

In 1902 Devine began his medical studies and was resident at Queen's College, University of Melbourne. After a brilliant course he graduated in 1906, gaining the Beaney [q.v.3] scholarship in surgery. He was resident medical officer at the (Royal) Melbourne Hospital and then acting superintendent. Influenced at this time by (Sir) Thomas Dunhill [q.v.], whose brother he had known well, he joined the staff of the young St Vincent's Hospital. The high quality of work of Devine, Dunhill and their colleagues gave impetus to the hospital's growth and gained for it added status when it became affiliated with the University of Melbourne as a clinical school. Devine himself made important contributions to the development of St Vincent's both as a hospital and as a teaching school. He was for a time dean of the clinical school and eventually honorary consulting surgeon to the hospital.

On 26 July 1911 at St Patrick's Cathedral, Devine married Mary Josephine O'Donnell. Later that year he went abroad to study at the renowned Allgemeines Krankenhaus, Vienna. At this time the use of X-rays in clinical medicine was in its infancy and its development was a feature of the Viennese School. Devine was quick to realize its potential in the early accurate pre-operative diagnosis of disorders of the stomach and colon and this was a factor in directing his interest to surgery of these parts.

After further study in Britain and the United States of America Devine returned to Melbourne. In 1914 he obtained the degree of master of surgery of the University of Melbourne and quickly became involved in a rapidly growing private practice. Surgical distinction came to him soon and he was recognized by his colleagues as in the forefront of his specialty.

Devine was one of the original advocates for the formation of a surgical college and played a decisive role in the development from 1928 of the Royal Australasian College of Surgeons (originally the College of Surgeons of Australasia). He was founder, a foundation fellow, a member of council, and president in 1939-41. He was largely responsible for the newly formed college gaining from the Hogan [q.v.] government tenancy of the island of land in Spring Street on which its building stands. In 1928 he edited the first number of the journal of the college, the *Australian and New Zealand Journal of Surgery.* He continued as editor for eighteen months and then for the next twenty years chaired the editorial committee.

For ten years from 1936 Devine was first chairman of the executive committee of the Anti-Cancer Council of Victoria. He was knighted in 1936 and in 1945 was made an honorary fellow of the Royal College of Surgeons of England. Other honorary fellowships were bestowed upon him by the Association of Surgeons of Great Britain and Ireland, the Royal Society of Medicine and its proctological section, the American College of Surgeons, the International College of Surgeons and the Greek Surgical Society.

His surgical repertoire included all the routine operations of the abdomen, neck and limbs, but he was at his best when operating in the confined space of the abdomen, especially the upper abdomen. His *Surgery of the alimentary tract* (1940) is a lasting record of his pre-eminence in this field. It contains almost 700 illustrations and, drawing as it did on his own surgical experience, is rich in original thought and method. *The surgery of the colon and rectum,* which he wrote in collaboration with his son, was published in 1948. Throughout his career he contributed regularly to surgical periodicals, yet his ability to write in a more popular vein is shown by newspaper articles such as 'Good doctoring for the people' (1945) and 'The tragedy and challenge of national health' (1951).

In 1952 Devine became chairman of a committee to administer a sum of money left by Michael ('Jack') Holt [q.v.] of Mordialloc to St Vincent's Hospital for purposes of research. His part in the formation of the St Vincent's School of Medical Research and his choice of its founding director, Dr Pehr Edman, may yet be considered his most lasting memorial.

Vigorous, energetic and robust, Devine enjoyed many outdoor sports, particularly tennis, golf, shooting, fishing, and sailing his ocean-going yacht. He spent at least six weeks of the year at his seaside home at Flinders, where he also prepared and wrote his books. The death in 1955 of his son John, a prominent surgeon and author of *The Rats of Tobruk*, was a heavy blow. Sir Hugh Devine died on 18 July 1959 and was buried in Melbourne general cemetery. He was survived by his two daughters.

In 1965 the Hugh Devine chair of surgery was established in the University of Melbourne to commemorate his services as a distinguished surgeon at St Vincent's Hospital, where the professorial unit is located. In 1972 the council of the Royal Australasian College of Surgeons approved a medal to be struck to honour and perpetuate his name, to signify the highest honour the college can bestow upon a fellow during his lifetime.

A portrait by W. B. McInnes [q.v.] hangs in the College of Surgeons, Spring Street.

Aust and NZ J of Surgery, Aug 1959, p 1, 4; *MJA*, 21 Nov 1959, p 777; *Age*, 10, 12, 13 Mar 1945, 20 July 1959; Roy A'sian College of Surgeons Archives (Melb); St Vincent's Hospital Archives (Melb); family papers (held by Mrs F. J. Bryan, Hawthorn, and Mrs E. F. Gleeson, Toorak, Vic).

JOHN HORAN

DEVINE, MATILDA (MARY) (1900-1970), madam, was born on 8 September 1900 at Camberwell, London, daughter of Edward Twiss, bricklayer, and his wife Alice, née Tubb(s). On 12 August 1917 at the Church of the Sacred Heart of Jesus, Camberwell, she married James Edward Joseph Devine, an Australian digger and ex-shearer. He returned to Australia in 1919; Tilly followed in the 'bride' ship, *Waimana*, reaching Sydney on 13 January 1920.

Jim Devine became a hire-car proprietor in Sydney and acted as protector, chauffeur and 'get-away' man when Tilly began to work as a prostitute, enabling her to operate independently of both the police and the underworld – at the cost of frequent arrests. From 18 June 1921 she had seventy-nine convictions on prostitution-related charges, such as offensive behaviour and indecent language, until May 1925, when she was imprisoned for two years for malicious wounding; she had walked into a barber's shop and slashed a man with a razor. She was referred to by the press as the 'Worst Woman in Sydney' and 'The Queen of the Night'. Colourful reports appeared about her court-room performances which were always witnessed by a packed gallery.

In the late 1920s Jim Devine became more deeply involved in underworld activity, then dominated by cocaine and 'sly grog' traffic and competing razor gangs, while Tilly emerged as a 'chaperone of magdalenes'. The base of their combined operations was their house at Maroubra.

Tilly's arrests in the 1930s were fewer, but were usually for the more serious charge of consorting with known prostitutes, and resulted in a years 'voluntary absence' in England and several short prison sentences.

By the beginning of World War II Tilly Devine had a well-established business, comprising properties in Palmer Street, Woolloomooloo, and a staff which included 'bouncers' and bodyguards: she was excellently placed with her rival Kate Leigh [q.v.] to capitalize on the demand in wartime Sydney for brothel services. Now affectionately known as the 'Queen of the 'Loo' she held lavish parties, contributed generously to the war effort, dressed opulently, and became notorious for her array of diamond rings. No longer needing her husband's protection, and hindered by his increasing violence towards her, she divorced him in August 1943 on the grounds of cruelty. On 19 May 1945 at her home, 191 Palmer Street, she married, with Presbyterian forms, Eric Parsons, a seaman. In 1953 she visited London to see the Coronation procession. Nevertheless, during the war and post-war years she appeared in court periodically on assault and similar charges.

Tilly Devine continued to operate her Palmer Street brothel until 1968. However, in the 1950s and 1960s, the scale and prominence of her operations lessened. In 1955 she had to pay more than £20 000 in income tax and fines.

She had suffered from chronic bronchitis for twenty years when she died in Concord Repatriation General Hospital, Sydney, on 24 November 1970; she was cremated with Catholic rites. Her estate was valued for probate at $11 007. One of the beneficiaries was the son adopted during her second marriage. The two children of her first marriage had predeceased her. Since her death, Tilly Devine has attained almost legendary stature – incidents in her life inspired Peter Kenna's play, *The slaughter of St. Teresa's Day* (1973), and her exploits are often referred to and recounted in the communities in which she operated.

V. Kelly, *Rugged angel* (Syd, 1961); *Daily Mirror* (Syd), 24 Nov 1970; *Daily Telegraph* (Syd), 25 Nov 1970; Syd Quarter Sessions – Clerk of the Peace, Depositions and papers, 1 May 1925, 19/7289 (NSWA).   JUDITH ALLEN
                                                     BAIBA IRVING

DEVINE, WILLIAM (1887-1959), Catholic priest and military chaplain, was born on 5 October 1887 at Castlederg, County Tyrone, Ireland, son of George Devine, draper, and his wife Catherine, née McGlinchey. He was educated at Drumnabey National School, St Columb's College, Derry, and St Patrick's College, Maynooth, and was ordained priest for the diocese of Derry in 1912. As a student at Maynooth he was strongly influenced by the president, Daniel Mannix [q.v.], and followed him to Melbourne in 1913 where he was appointed to the South Yarra parish and then to Coburg in 1914.

Devine enlisted in the Australian Imperial Force on 1 July 1915 as a chaplain 4th class (captain) and joined the 48th Battalion when it was formed at Tel-el-Kebir, Egypt, in March 1916. After it was transferred to France in June, he saw much of the fighting around Pozières, Mouquet Farm, Flers, Gueudecourt and Ypres. Uninjured, he succumbed to the harsh winter of 1916-17 and was invalided to Ireland, resuming duty late in February. He served with the battalion throughout 1917, returning to Melbourne briefly in 1918 as a transport chaplain, but was back at the front in May, remaining with the A.I.F. until 8 September 1919.

It was rare for a chaplain to remain for so long on continuous service and rarer still to spend such a long time with one battalion. Such devotion to his men at least partially accounts for Devine's popularity. On 1 May 1917 he was awarded the French Croix de Guerre for 'conspicuous services', and next year he won the Military Cross for 'conspicuous gallantry and devotion to duty' east of Hamel on 8 August; following the advance closely, he remained with the troops under heavy artillery fire and assisting the wounded. The battalion was 'overjoyed at the news' of the honour, according to the compiler of the war diary.

In *The story of a battalion* (Melbourne, 1919) Devine gave an excellent portrait of the 48th; unlike most unit historians he refrains from providing a catalogue of names and exploits, but seeks instead to depict the spirit of the battalion as a whole, almost as if it had a life of its own. From his book it would seem that Devine succeeded as a chaplain and enjoyed his work; it demonstrates love for his men, sympathy and concern for their welfare, ability to share their life and acceptance of their ways. He was also critical of the overall conduct of the war and the apparent carelessness of the higher command for the lives of common soldiers.

Returning to Melbourne in 1919, he was stationed at Lancefield as a curate and, still devoted to Mannix, now archbishop of Melbourne, he brought together thirteen Victoria Cross winners to act as his guard of honour in the 1920 St Patrick's Day procession. This was a considerable coup, demonstrating graphically the extent of Australian Catholic loyalty and heroism, qualities under challenge from the Protestant majority in the heightened sectarian turmoil of the time.

Devine returned to Ireland and the diocese of Derry before joining the Maynooth Mission to China (the Columban Fathers) in 1927 and lecturing in history at the Tientsin University in Hankow. In 1930 he returned to Derry as curate of Dungiven and Sion Mills. During World War II he served as a chaplain with the Royal Navy, first on an unofficial basis at Derry, whence he often sailed with convoys in the North Atlantic, and then officially at Taranto, Italy. In 1944 the Vatican sent him on a mission to Yugoslavia which he believed compromised his position as a chaplain.

Devine returned to Derry in 1946 and was appointed parish priest of Clonmany in County Donegal in 1947; he worked there continuously for ten years, except for a brief visit to Melbourne in the 1950s. He died in a Dublin hospital on 19 October 1959.

C. E. W. Bean, *The A.I.F. in France*, 1916 (Syd, 1929); *London Gazette*, 1 May 1917, 7 Nov 1918; *Advocate* (Melb), 15 Feb 1913, 28 Feb 1914, 3 July 1915, 17 June 1916, 12, 19 May 1917, 6 Apr 1918; *Argus*, 22 Mar 1920; information from Rev. T. P. Donnelly, Castlederg, Ireland; War Diary, 48th Battalion, AIF (AWM).   MICHAEL MCKERNAN

DEXTER, WALTER ERNEST (1873-1950), master mariner, Anglican minister and military chaplain, was born on 31 August 1873 at Birkenhead, Cheshire, England, youngest son of Thomas Dexter, shipwright, and his wife Martha, née Grundy. Educated at St Catherine's School, Higher Tranmere, he was indentured at 14 for five years at wages of 'nothing plus twelve shillings for washing' on the barque *Buckingham*. At the end of his first voyage he ran away in Calcutta, stowed away to New York where he worked in a biscuit factory and as a lift attendant, and returned to the sea in 1890 aboard the *Pythomene* of which his eldest brother was master.

Records survive of thirty-seven voyages to world ports – including Melbourne in 1893 – in sail and steam from 1888 to 1900, as Dexter progressed from 'boy', through lamp-trimmer, able seaman, and the grades of mate. In March 1899 he passed the examination for his master's certificate. By February 1900 he was first mate of the *Akbar* based at Mauritius. Between February 1900 and January 1901 he fought in the South African War as a trooper in Lumsden's Horse, a unit of mounted volunteers recruited in India; he won the Distinguished Conduct Medal – followed after discharge by an award from the Royal Humane Society for gallantry at the wreck of the *Taher* off Mauritius in March 1901. Returning to the sea, he became master of the *Afghan* carrying Moslem pilgrims – whose piety impressed him – to Mecca, then traded in the off-season. On 16 September 1902 in Mauritius he married Frances Louisa Carroll, née Rohan, who died one year later. He joined the Freemasons and began also to feel 'a driving force ... certainly not myself'. After studying at sea (Latin, Greek, Hebrew), he entered Durham University in 1906 with the intention of joining the Anglican ministry. Graduating M.A. and L.Th. in 1908, he was ordained and appointed curate at Walbone, Newcastle upon Tyne, until 1910 when he was sent to the new coal-mining town of Wonthaggi in Victoria. For two years his tent was his vicarage before he was transferred to South Melbourne. On 8 April 1913 he married Dora Stirling Roadknight at Christ Church, Ormond.

Enlisting in the Australian Imperial Force on the outbreak of World War I, Dexter was one of twelve chaplains whose appointments dated from 8 September 1914. He sailed with the first convoy and served in Egypt and on the Suez Canal; he then tended the Anzac wounded on a hospital ship and joined the troops on Gallipoli. First with the 5th Battalion, then the 2nd Brigade, and finally as an acting senior chaplain, he shared the lives and dangers of the men, helping them practically and spiritually, and using effectively his long experience of acquiring things – as a piece of A.I.F. doggerel 'The pinching padre' attests. 'He was as good as a doctor', wrote a sergeant. He was entrusted with the task of carefully surveying the cemeteries before leaving Gallipoli on 17 December 1915, and was one of two chaplains awarded the Distinguished Service Order.

After a brief stay in Egypt and Sinai, he went to France in April 1916. From Pozières in July to the A.I.F.'s battles in August 1918, with a short period at A.I.F. Headquarters in London, he tended the troops' welfare as a senior chaplain and as a compassionate 'handyman'. One example is given by the official war historian: 'Chaplain Dexter, with support from the Australian Comforts Fund, established at the corner of Bécourt Wood a coffee stall which henceforth became a cherished institution on the edge of every Australian battlefield'. In 1918 he was awarded the Military Cross, becoming the most decorated chaplain in the A.I.F.

Returning to Melbourne in 1920 after serving on the demobilization staff in London, he had doubts about resuming parish work 'after all this amongst men', and tried a soldier-settler's block at Kilsyth. The venture failed and he returned to the Church: at Romsey parish in 1924-27, Lara in 1927-40, and West Footscray in 1940-47. Pastoral duties, civic affairs, education (Dip. Ed., Melbourne), teaching, writing and war commemoration services occupied his time. At the Lara church Armistice Day service in November 1934 the poet laureate John Masefield read for the first time his poem 'For the dead at Gallipoli'. Masefield also assisted towards the publication in 1938 of Dexter's sea-book *Rope-yarns, marline-spikes and tar.*

He died on 31 August 1950 at his East Malvern home, survived by his wife, five sons (all of whom served in World War II) and one daughter. 'The press has told us of his amazing career, his distinctions, his activities and his varied ministry', wrote a wartime colleague, then archbishop of Melbourne; 'he was a man of great gifts'.

C. E. W. Bean, *The A.I.F. in France*, 1916 (Syd, 1929), and *Gallipoli mission* (Canb, 1948); *Church of England Messenger* (Vic), 26 Feb, 7 May 1915, 28 Jan 1916, 8 Sept 1950; *Reveille* (Syd), Sept 1931; *JRAHS*, 64 (1978), pt 3, 145; *Church Standard*, 2 July 1915, 22 Sept 1950; *Geelong Advertiser*, 4 Nov 1950; W. E. Dexter, personal papers, war diaries *and* MSS (held by D. Dexter, Turner, ACT); file MP473/5/805 (AAO, Melb).   DAVID DEXTER

D'HAGE, LUDWIG (1863-1960), musician, was born on 7 May 1863 at Schluckenau, Bohemia, son of Ludwig D'Hage, a Pole 'of independent means', and his Bohemian wife Helena, née Sedlicz. Educated in Vienna, he studied violin and piano at the conservatorium of the Gesellschaft der Musikfreunde in Wien in 1877-80, but left suddenly in March 1880 without taking a degree, probably because of family quarrels. He arrived in Melbourne in October as a member of Wildner's Strauss Austrian Band, imported for the International Exhibition.

When the band broke up in Sydney, he worked there for a time, then went to Rockhampton, Queensland, in 1885 to teach music under the name Louis D. Hage.

In February 1887 D'Hage made his debut as conductor of the Rockhampton Philharmonic Society and next year took over the Orpheus Club Orchestra. In twenty-five years he made it Queensland's best orchestra though he never had more than twenty-two players. They included his pupils Ernest N. Symons, a flautist acclaimed by John Lemmone [q.v.], and the pianist Molly Hourigan who later distinguished herself at the Brussels Conservatoire. D'Hage's pupils won outstanding results in Royal Academy examinations and sometimes surpassed the honours won in Brisbane. Alma Moodie, a child prodigy from Mount Morgan, was discovered by him and kept in touch with him after she had won success in Europe.

When in 1910 several members of the Orpheus Club Orchestra took professional theatre engagements, D'Hage refused to conduct the remnant. He moved to Sydney in 1912˙ and began taking work in various professional groups, including Cyril Monk's [q.v.] Austral String Quartet and the new Conservatorium Orchestra. During World War I, he was deemed an enemy alien and his plans to go to the United States of America were thwarted. He applied for naturalization in 1916 but was refused. A second application in 1920 was deferred despite support from T. J. Ryan and G. S. Curtis [qq.v.]. He was finally naturalized in January 1922.

In Rockhampton in 1921 D'Hage gave a second farewell concert, a performance of six violin sonatas which packed the 1500 seats of the Theatre Royal. He failed to find an appropriate place in the Sydney musical establishment and made his living entirely by private teaching. D'Hage had married Isabella Redmond in Sydney about 1883. They had two sons, both of whom died, and the marriage broke down. On 9 February 1918 at Mosman Registry office, he married Mary Eleanor Humble; they had four children. After breaking his leg in an accident when he was 96, he died on 22 April 1960 and was cremated.

B. and F. Mackenzie, *Singers of Australia* (Melb, 1967); *Australasian*, 9 Oct 1880; *Sydney Mail*, 29 Jan, 9, 16 Apr 1881; *Morning Bulletin*, 5 Feb 1887, 6, 14 Oct 1897, 26 June 1907, 10 Aug 1908, 17 Mar, 8 Aug 1910, 6 Sept 1918, 6 Aug 1920, 27 July 1921, 13 Mar 1929, 26 Aug 1955, 29 Apr 1960; Ballard collection of Rockhampton theatre programmes (Rockhampton and District Hist Soc); A1 20/6178, 21/21390 (AAO, Canb).   Lorna L. McDonald

DIBDIN, EDWARD JOHN (1886-1963), soldier and accountant, was born on 4 Jan-uary 1886 at Rockhampton, Queensland, ninth surviving child of Robert Lowes Dibdin, auctioneer and later accountant, and his wife Emma, née Horler, both London-born. Educated at Rockhampton state and grammar schools, he became an accountant and joined the Mount Morgan Mining Co. On 6 October 1909 at St Paul's Anglican Cathedral, Rockhampton, he married Amelia Lucy McMaster.

Dibdin had long been attracted to soldiering, having entered the senior cadets in 1901 and attained the rank of sergeant. In 1904 he joined the 15th Australian Light Horse Regiment as a trooper and rose through the ranks to be commissioned as second lieutenant in 1908. Two years later he took up soldiering as a profession when appointed temporary area officer at Mount Morgan. In July 1912 he became second lieutenant in the 1st Australian Light Horse Regiment (Central Queensland Light Horse) and area officer for Rockhampton, an appointment he held when war began. In March 1915 he took on temporary duties for the Administrative and Instructional Staff and in July was promoted lieutenant.

Dibdin joined the Australian Imperial Force as a lieutenant on 1 April 1916 and on 1 May was promoted captain and appointed adjutant of the 42nd Battalion, embarking from Sydney on 5 June. Following training in England and service in the trenches at Armentières and Ploegsteert, France, until April 1917, he had two months in hospital, missing the battle of Messines. He returned as adjutant of the 42nd and served through the 3rd battle of Ypres. Early in 1918 he took part in operations on the Somme at Sailly-Le-Sec, Morlancourt, Villers-Bretonneux and Hamel, and was promoted major on 10 May. His administrative ability showed out during reorganization of the 11th Brigade in late June-early July. On 4 July he commanded the 42nd 'with great skill and initiative' during the battle of Hamel and later in life remembered this offensive as his most dramatic wartime experience.

In the battle of 8 August the 42nd was left flank battalion of the Australian Corps; following tanks it achieved all its objectives and also captured over 300 prisoners, machine-guns and trench-mortars, while suffering few losses. Casualties were severe in the attack on German positions at St Germain's Wood four days later, mainly because this operation was carried out in daylight and without artillery support. Under Dibdin's skilful leadership the enemy post was captured and held in spite of heavy shelling with mustard gas and high explosives. From late August to 9 September he successfully led the 41st Battalion in the advance from Mont St Quentin to Roisel. He was mentioned in dispatches in November and awarded the Distinguished Service Order in the 1919 New Year honours for distinguished service from February to September 1918.

Back in Australia by mid-1919, Dibdin resumed militia service with the 5th Light Horse and in 1921-24 served as captain, major and commanding officer of the 49th Battalion. Having in 1920 become honorary secretary of the Queensland branch of the Returned Sailors' and Soldiers' Imperial League of Australia, in 1924 he took up the paid position of federal secretary for the league in Melbourne. Working closely with the president, (Sir) Gilbert Dyett [q.v.], he campaigned for preference in employment for returned soldiers and easier financial terms for soldier-settlers, and was adept in lobbying governments. In 1929 he became the league's representative on the Commonwealth War Pensions Entitlement Appeal Tribunal, a position he held until retirement in 1949.

Meanwhile, apart from Masonic activities, Dibdin had regarded soldiering as his recreation. For five years to 1930 he commanded the 32nd (Footscray) Regiment in Melbourne, retiring as its honorary colonel. His reputation for sound administration, courageous soldiering and especially for humane leadership endeared him to the 42nd Association which he helped found and which elected him president in the immediate post-war years. He helped compile the battalion history and, assisted by his wife's hospitality, maintained his wartime friendships. Predeceased by her, he died at Windsor, Melbourne, on 19 August 1963, survived by a son and a daughter. He was cremated.

C. E.W. Bean, *The A.I.F. in France*, 1918 (Syd, 1937); V. Brahms (ed), *The spirit of the Forty-Second* (Brisb, 1938); G. L. Kristianson, *The politics of patriotism* (Canb, 1966); *London Gazette*, 31 Dec 1918, 1 Jan 1919; Dibdin file, war records section (AWM).   MARGOT Z. SIMINGTON

DICK, JAMES ADAM (1866-1942), physician and army officer was born on 28 January 1866 at Windsor, New South Wales, eldest son of James Adam Dick, postmaster, and his wife Jean, née Benson. He was educated at Windsor public and grammar schools, at the universities of Sydney (B.A., 1886) and Edinburgh (M.B., C.M., 1891; M.D., 1892; F.R.C.S.E., 1901) and the Rotunda Hospital, Dublin (L.M., 1891). In religion he was Presbyterian.

In 1893 Dick settled at Randwick, Sydney, where he developed a huge practice and a high reputation as doctor and citizen. In 1894

he was appointed honorary medical officer to the Home for the Aged and Infirm, Randwick, and the Asylum for Children. On 25 April 1911, at St Jude's Church of England, Randwick, he married Lillian Louise Wall. It was a grand function, complete with military ceremonial, and attracted several thousand spectators. The couple lived in formal style at Catfoss, Belmore Road, a two-storied sandstone mansion.

A strong sense of duty and good organizing ability found expression in serving professional and community organizations long and well. Dick was particularly active in the British Medical Association, being State president in 1910-11 and a federal councillor in 1932-36. For many years he was also a member of the Medical Board of New South Wales and a councillor of St Andrew's College, University of Sydney. A regular attender at medical congresses, he contributed a notable paper on bubonic plague, jointly with Dr F. Tidswell, to the Intercolonial Medical Congress, 1899. Bubonic plague hit Sydney in 1900, recurring sporadically for a decade. A brother, Dr Robert Dick (1869-1943), worked in a team under Dr J. Ashburton Thompson [q.v.], which demonstrated to the world how this scourge could be beaten. Robert Dick became director-general of public health for New South Wales in 1924-34. After service with the British Army in World War I, he had retired from the Australian Military Forces as colonel in 1925.

Like his father and brother, James Adam Dick had an enthusiasm for military pursuits. During the South African War he enlisted with the second contingent of the New South Wales Army Medical Corps which embarked in January 1900. With the first contingent, this formed a well-trained, well-equipped and impressively mobile medical corps, which drew special praise from Lord Roberts. Lieutenant Dick served at Paardeburg, Poplar Grove, Driefontein, Vet River, Zand River, Johannesburg, Pretoria, Diamond Hill and east of Pretoria. He was mentioned in dispatches and awarded the Queen's medal with six clasps.

Dick joined the Australian Imperial Force in May 1915 as lieut-colonel. He was second-in-command, 3rd Australian General Hospital, Lemnos, until transferred in January 1916 to the 2nd A.G.H., Cairo, crossing with it to Wimereux, France, in March. In October he took command of No. 1 Casualty Clearing Station. As colonel he was sent in October 1917 to command the 1st A.G.H. at Rouen, removing with it to England after the Armistice. He returned to Australia in 1919. He was twice mentioned in dispatches and was appointed C.M.G. in 1919.

A medical colleague described Dick as

'a sturdy, industrious fellow, of high principle – a first class doctor, who made it his business to learn drill and much else . . . He had a huge kit and was something of a high class old maid in his habits, but I am glad to be able to add, an eminently virtuous one . . . I take off my hat to him'. He died on 23 December 1942 at his Randwick home and was buried in the Presbyterian section of Randwick cemetery. His wife survived him. They had no children.

R. Scot Skirving, *Our army in South Africa* (Syd, 1901); Aust Defence Dept, *Official records of the Australian military contingents to the war in South Africa*, P. L. Murray ed (Melb, 1911); A. G. Butler (ed), *Official history of the Australian Army Medical Services . . . 1914-18*, 1-3 (Melb, 1930, Canb, 1940, 1943); *University of Sydney, book of remembrance, 1914-18* (Syd, 1939); L. M. Field, *The forgotten war* (Melb, 1979); Roy Soc NSW, *J*, 77 (1943), p 173; *MJA*, 27 Mar 1943; *SMH*, 29 Apr 1911; R. Scot Skirving, Memoirs, vol 3 (Basser Lib, Canb); records (AWM); information from Dr J. C. Dick, Ballarat, Vic.   PATRICIA MORISON

DICKINSON, EDWARD ALEXANDER (1903-1937), newspaper editor and political activist, was born on 21 April 1903 at Grimsby, England, son of Edward Dickinson, fish merchant, and his wife Mary Cormack, née Ross. Ted came to Melbourne with his family as a small child. His father was killed soon after and his mother remarried and moved to New South Wales. In 1923 he returned to Melbourne, studied with the Workers' Educational Association and became friends with Charlie Reeves, one of the Industrial Workers of the World leaders who had been gaoled in 1917. Dickinson became a leading figure in the I.W.W. in Melbourne and later in Sydney, where he became known as a Domain orator: he was a stirring, enthusiastic and fiery speaker.

In 1928-29 Dickinson was in Adelaide to revive the I.W.W. newspaper *Direct Action*. He was extensively involved in political activity with those out of work. Especially concerned with attempted evictions, he tried to organize unemployed workers who gathered daily at the Adelaide Labor Exchange. During the 1928 waterfront strike Dickinson was active both in Adelaide and the Port. On 1 October 1928 he was arrested as 'one of the leaders' of a 'riot' which had occurred on 27 September when 5000 unionists drove scabs off the ships at the Port. Dickinson was charged with 'unlawfully taking part in a riot' and 'seditious libel' for several articles in *Direct Action*. He received six months imprisonment for sedition and three months for riot and was fined £50.

On 19 October 1929 at Holy Trinity Church, Adelaide, Dickinson married Myrtle Ellen Ankers, tailoress. At the end of that year he was employed as the representative of an oil company which sent him to England. There, again unemployed, he set up a fish stall at Battersea markets and survived the Depression. Politically active, he went on hunger marches and spoke regularly in Hyde Park. He helped form a broad organization to oppose Sir Oswald Mosley's Fascists and the Chamberlain government's appeasement policies. In 1935 when the Labor Party leader Clement Attlee condemned the Italian invasion of Abyssinia, Italy's foreign minister challenged him to a duel. Shortly after, speaking at Hyde Park, Dickinson accepted the challenge on behalf of the peace movement; he added that he had spent many years in the Australian bush and was familiar with firearms though he preferred boxing gloves.

At the end of 1936 Dickinson went to Spain to fight with the International Brigade against Franco. He became a lieutenant, second in charge of a machine-gun company of the British Battalion. Reports emphasized his abilities as a 'born leader' and organizer. His commanding officer described him as 'a brilliant man with a dynamic personality'.

Dickinson was captured by the Fascist forces on 12 February 1937; after two comrades were shot, he is reputed to have said: 'If I had a bunch of Australian bushmen here we'd have pushed you bastards into the sea long ago'. He was immediately taken aside and shot. As the order to fire was given, he called to the other prisoners: 'Keep your chins up, boys. Salud!'.

T. Wintringham, *English captain* (Lond, 1939); N. Palmer et al, *Australians in Spain* (Syd, 1948); L. Fox (ed), *Depression down under* (Syd, 1977); *Direct Action* (Adel), 5 May, 20 Oct, 17 Nov 1928, 9 Feb 1929; *Mail* (Adel), 11 Feb 1939; R. N. Wait, Reactions to demonstrations and riots in Adelaide, 1928 to 1932 (M.A. thesis, Univ Adel, 1973); information from Mr R. Dickinson, Syd.

RAY BROOMHILL

DICKINSON, SIDNEY (1851-1919), art critic and journalist, was born on 27 March 1851 at West Springfield, Massachusetts, United States of America, son of Henry H. W. Dickinson, paper manufacturer, and his wife Angeline, née Dunham. Well-educated, he held a Master of Arts degree. In the 1880s Dickinson became known in America as a lecturer and writer on art. On 28 June 1888 in the *Almeda* he arrived in Sydney with his wife. He described himself as Australian correspondent for the *New York Herald*, and claimed to have lived in Hawaii for five years. During the following months he delivered a series of lectures in Sydney, including a course at the National Art Gallery of New South Wales. After a month in Melbourne, the Dickinsons returned to Sydney then toured New Zealand before visiting London and the Paris Universal Exhibition of 1889. By January next year they were back in Melbourne where, with their wide knowledge of the world, they soon became ornaments in the cultural life. In 1890 Mrs Dickinson was first executive vice-president of the Austral Salon, to which in October she read a paper on Hindu philosophy.

From 1890 Dickinson was honorary secretary to the Victorian Artists' Society; in 'What should Australians paint?', in the *Australasian Critic* in October, he encouraged the Heidelberg school of Tom Roberts and Frederick McCubbin [qq.v.], urging that 'It should be the ambition of our artists to present on canvas the earnestness, rigour, pathos and heroism of the life that is about them'. In April 1891 he requested permission from Henry Parkes [q.v.5] to 'travel in a visiting man-of-war to Solomon Islands to get material for articles for Scribner's Magazine'. He explained that he was acting as special correspondent in Australia for the *New York Times* and the *Boston Morning Journal*.

Among many important articles Dickinson published in the *Australasian Critic* in 1889-91 was 'Wanted: a standard in art criticism' in June 1891. In this he observed that, in Australia, painting was regarded as 'a light and graceful recreation which, when cultivated in a spirit of dilettantism, may evoke a languid interest and give to ladies an opportunity to enjoy afternoon tea amongst attractive surroundings. "Art for art's sake" is an idea that finds little occasion for lodgment in the chinks of our busy day of money-getting'. He also contributed accounts of Australian subjects to *Scribner's Magazine* and the *Scientific American*.

It is not known when the Dickinsons returned to America, but he continued to work as a journalist and lecturer. On 7 February 1919 Sidney died at Oberlin, Ohio, after being accidentally struck by a street-car. Predeceased by his wife, he was survived by at least one son.

Bernard Smith, *Place, taste and tradition* (Syd, 1945), and *Documents on art and taste in Australia* (Melb, 1975); *Critic* (Adel), 1 Oct 1890, 1 June 1891.

BERNARD SMITH

DICKSON, JAMES (1859-1949), merchant and draper, was born on 23 September 1859 at Warrnambool, Victoria, son of James Dickson, merchant and draper, and his wife Susan Murray, née Ritchie, both from Scotland. In 1870 Dickson's father travelled to London with his family to manage the branch of the business there, and did not return until 1880. During this period young James was educated at Park School, Glasgow, Scotland.

Dickson's father, together with John Glass Cramond, had laid the foundation for a general store in Warrnambool on 20 August 1855. Cramond & Dickson's came to concentrate on drapery, which was bought in London and exported directly to Warrnambool. Before its closure in 1974 it reputedly held the Victorian record for the oldest continuing business firm operating under the original name. James Dickson junior spent his working life within the firm. When his father departed for the London branch for a further term in 1887, he became manager of the Warrnambool business; he was eventually senior partner. His capacity for business was undoubted and the firm seems to have won the loyalty of its staff. Outgoing and affable, he was popular with his employees.

Dickson was one of those leading citizens whose activities contributed to the growth of the commercial heart of the city of Warrnambool, in particular of the large firms on which residents relied heavily for employment. He was a member of the original directorate of the Warrnambool Woollen Mill (registered as a company in October 1909), and an original guarantor and director of the Warrnambool Butter and Cheese Factory Co. Ltd formed in May 1888. He also served on the committee of management of the Warrnambool and District Base Hospital for nearly fifty years. Despite his wide-ranging public activities, he had little active interest in politics, though he was on the town council in 1891-94: his election at his first attempt, as a young man, with a comfortable majority over the sitting representative, reflected his standing in the community. He was a keen sportsman who raced horses which won both in the Western district and in Melbourne. He had a lifetime involvement in the Warrnambool Racing and the Warrnambool Amateur Turf clubs, serving as president of both organizations.

On 11 September 1888, at the Presbyterian Church, South Yarra, Dickson married Mary Glass Cramond, daughter of the co-founder of the family business; she also had been born in Warrnambool. Of their eight children, John Russell was killed in action in France during World War I, while David succeeded his father as senior partner in Cramond & Dickson's. Dickson died on 2 February 1949 in hospital at Warrnambool and was buried in the town cemetery after a Presbyterian service. He was survived by his wife, three daughters and three sons. His estate was valued for probate at £28658.

C. E. Sayers, *By these we flourish* (Melb, 1969); *Warrnambool Standard*, 2 Feb 1949, 27 July 1974; family scrapbook (held by Mr D. Dickson, Merri St, Warrnambool).   JOHN WARHURST

DICKSON, SIR JAMES ROBERT (1832-1901), businessman and premier, was born on 30 November 1832 at Plymouth, Devon, England, only son of James Dickson and his wife Mary Maria, née Palmer. He was educated at Glasgow High School, and served as a junior clerk in the City of Glasgow Bank before migrating to Victoria in 1854. He worked first in the Bank of Australasia and then in his merchant cousin's firm, Rae, Dickson & Co. In 1862 he moved to Queensland, taking a position with the estate agent Arthur Martin until establishing his own business in the early 1870s. As an auctioneer and estate agent he acquired wealth and built Toorak House on a magnificent site near the Brisbane River, where he enjoyed what the family firm, in characteristic style, described as 'views marvellous in their magnificence' and 'a varied panorama of ineffable loveliness and grandeur'. Despite these distractions he remained assiduous in his attentions to business and was chairman of the Brisbane Permanent Building and Banking Co. from 1876, foundation chairman of the Queensland Trustees from 1883, and chairman of the Royal Bank of Queensland in the crisis year of 1893.

In 1873 Dickson won the Enoggera seat in the Legislative Assembly. Ministerial office followed rapidly; he was secretary for public works and mines in May-June 1876, and colonial treasurer from June 1876 to January 1879 and from December 1883 to August 1887. In this era of optimism and lavish borrowing he showed his expertise by handling the £10 million loan of 1884. He resigned in August 1887 after disagreement with more radical colleagues over their proposals for a land tax and with the ringing pronouncement that he had yet to learn why it should be 'a crime to be a freeholder'. His constituents seem to have approved the resignation, for his vacation of his assembly seat, to test their judgment, was followed by overwhelming victory in a keenly contested by-election in September. But his seat was less secure than this win suggested: after a redistribution of constituencies and the intervention of a rival Liberal candidate he was defeated in the Toombul portion of his old electorate in the 1888 general election.

Next year Dickson retired from his auctioneering business and travelled widely in Europe. Soon after his return, at a by-election in April 1892, he won the Bulimba seat by supporting Sir Samuel Griffith [q.v.] on the need to resume the importation of South Sea islanders for labour in the Queensland tropics. However, he had to wait for ministerial office until February 1897 when he was appointed to the minor role of secretary for railways in the Nelson [q.v.] government. Thereafter, Dickson's rise was rapid; he became postmaster-general in March, home secretary in March 1898, retaining this place in the Byrnes [q.v.7] ministry, and premier, however stopgap, in October after Byrnes died suddenly and (Sir) Robert Philp [q.v.] was reluctant to accept the office. Alfred Deakin [q.v.] later maintained that Philp, favoured for the premiership by the Liberal caucus, withheld his candidature on the understanding that Dickson, who, as Queensland's representative in the Federal councils of 1886 and 1888 had opposed the colony's participation in the Convention movement, should now fight the Brisbane commercial-oriented opposition to Federation and rally support for the cause. Whatever the truth of this contention, or of Sir Thomas McIlwraith's [q.v.5] less-charitable observation that Dickson supported Federation primarily to promote his own self-esteem, the ministry was chiefly notable for its successful conduct of the Queensland referendum on the Commonwealth bill, on 2 September 1899. Deakin was to acknowledge Dickson's 'invaluable assistance' in the contest, noting that 'his government was by no means unanimous for federation, Parliament distinctly critical, the Assembly about equally divided, the Council emphatically hostile', and the metropolis opposed to a measure which seemed to threaten Brisbane's trade.

Prudently Dickson had introduced a provision whereby Queensland might be divided for the purpose of electing members of the Senate, and this prospect, naturally attractive to the sparsely inhabited north, was a factor, if only minor, in solidifying North Queensland's overwhelming and decisive vote for Federation.

The Dickson ministry did not long survive the referendum, but its successor, the Anderson Dawson [q.v.] Labor ministry was promptly rejected by the assembly, and Dickson returned to office as chief secretary in Philp's administration. He thus became a member of the Australian delegation to England in connexion with the passage of the Commonwealth bill through the Imperial parliament. In England he sided with Joseph Chamberlain in opposing the proposed abolition of the right of appeal from the High Court of Australia to the Privy Council. Dickson's stand symbolized the man: the enthusiastic Imperialist, whose ministry had seen that Queensland was the first colony to offer troops to vindicate the

Imperial cause against the Transvaal, and who disapproved of colonial separatism; and the 'commercial man' who welcomed the British House of Lords as a security for property and business interests in a Federation which might move in a radical direction. It also reflected, according to Deakin, the continuing influence of Griffith, still manipulating the affairs of Queensland from the Queensland bench. In the event Chamberlain, Griffith and Dickson secured only a severely qualified success.

The final stage of Dickson's career was tragic, dramatic and brief. Appointed K.C.M.G. in January 1901 and minister of defence in the first Federal administration, he was taken ill at the Commonwealth's inaugural ceremonies in Sydney, and died there on 10 January after one week in office – he had been a diabetic for about eighteen years. Queensland provided a state funeral for the businessman-politician who somewhat accidentally had become one of its leading Federal spokesmen. He was buried in Nundah cemetery.

Dickson was for many years a prominent layman in the Church of England, particularly as financial adviser to the diocese of Brisbane. He was a justice of the peace and a fellow of the Royal Geographical Society of Great Britain and of the Royal Colonial and Imperial Institute. He married first Annie Ely (1838-1880) on 8 November 1855 at Collingwood, Victoria, and second, on 5 January 1882 at Carcoar, New South Wales, Mary MacKinlay (1841-1902) who became the first headmistress of the Brisbane Girls' Grammar School. He was survived by six sons and seven daughters of the first marriage. His second son, Frederick (1859-1928), became Crown prosecutor in Brisbane and as acting judge of the Arbitration Court handed down the Dickson award for the sugar industry in 1916. Portraits are in Parliament House, Canberra, and in the board room of the Brisbane Permanent Building & Banking Co.

Alcazar Press, *Queensland, 1900* (Brisb, nd); C. A. Bernays, *Queensland politics during sixty years* (Brisb, 1919); A. Deakin, *The federal story*, J. A. La Nauze ed (Melb, 1963); *Brisbane Courier*, 10, 14 Jan 1901; family information.   D. D. CUTHBERT

DILL MACKY, WILLIAM MARCUS (1849-1913), Presbyterian minister, was born on 8 June 1849 at Lisfannan, County Donegal, Ireland, one of five children of William Macky, farmer, and his wife Susannah, née Dill, both descendants of seventeenth-century colonists and clerics. In the early 1850s his father disappeared on the Victorian goldfields. Dill Macky was educated in the classics at S. McQuilkin's school, Londonderry, and studied arts and theology at Magee Presbyterian College, Londonderry, in 1866-67 and 1868-73. Licensed by the Derry Presbytery in May 1876, he was ordained by the Presbytery of Magherafelt in November, after being called to Draperstown church. On 24 May 1881 he married Ellen Elizabeth Morwood, daughter of a medical practitioner.

Dill Macky's Protestant leanings were reinforced by membership of one of the clubs of Apprentice Boys of Derry. He alone of his Magherafelt Presbytery opposed Home Rule as 'Rome Rule', and his conservative political activities in Derry caused such reactions that he armed himself with a six-shooter. In 1886 he migrated to New South Wales with his family, reaching Sydney on 26 December in the *Austral*. On 17 May he was inducted to the Scots Church where he remained until 1913. He was a prominent Freemason and within a year of his arrival had joined the Loyal Orange Institution of New South Wales, and was grand chaplain.

Dill Macky lectured in systematic and biblical theology at St Andrew's College, University of Sydney; he was senior Presbyterian chaplain to the military forces in 1892-1904; a founder with A. A. Aspinall [q.v.7] and a council-member of Scots College, Sydney, in the early 1890s; moderator of the General Assembly of the Presbyterian Church of New South Wales; president of the Young People's Society of Christian Endeavour in 1898 and editor of its journal, the *Roll Call*; president of the Evangelical Council of New South Wales in 1900; and an executive member of the New South Wales Alliance for the Suppression of Intemperance, five mission boards and several refuges.

The prominence Dill Macky attained as a cleric could have rested on his energetic pastoral work alone (although in his latter years the Scots Church was in decline). His preaching was of a high calibre – both impassioned and quietly sensitive, powerful yet humble – and left a marked impression on his listeners. However, he was also a controversial and militant Protestant, with an impeccable Irish Protestant lineage. Within five years of his arrival in Sydney he had become a publicist and by 1900 was the acknowledged Protestant champion. That year he gained notoriety for supporting Arthur Coningham [q.v.] in his attempt to divorce his wife for alleged adultery with Dean Denis O'Haran [q.v.], administrator of St Mary's Cathedral.

In response to this and other sectarian explosions, in June 1901 Dill Macky formed and was first president of the Australian Protestant Defence Association, which reached a membership of 22 000 with 135 branches by 1904. In 1902-04 he edited the *Watchman*, which, filled with anti-Catholic fanaticism, sold 20 000 copies a week. In 1902-03 Dill Macky attacked the prime minister Sir Edmund Barton [q.v.7] for visiting the Pope and organized a petition to the Federal parliament with over 30 000 signatures. While stumping the country that year he was shot at and stoned at Wyalong and Temora where the Riot Act was read. The sectarian animosity culminated in the 1904 State elections, narrowly won by (Sir) Joseph Hector Carruthers [q.v.7] with the help of the Protestant vote; thereafter it subsided much to the chagrin of Dill Macky and militants on both sides.

Strongly conservative and evangelical in his theology, he fervently believed in the imminence of the millennium. Dill Macky's refusal to consider the higher criticism of the Bible led the students at St Andrew's College in 1907 to decline to be taught by him; they claimed his lectures did not enable them to cope with modern biblical scholarship. Dill Macky resigned, typically declaring there was 'a flood of rationalism that is sweeping into our church'. His Irish heritage encouraged him to see conspiracies everywhere.

In 1901 Dill Macky had been awarded an honorary doctorate of divinity by the Presbyterian Theological Faculty, Ireland. During his life he received at least six testimonials, including one in 1909 when he was presented with a purse of over £1000 on the eve of a visit to Europe. He evoked strong feelings: to Catholics and some Protestants he was a fiery bigot, but most Protestants, at a time when sectarianism was fashionable, respected his anti-Catholicism. To his friends he was warm, gentle and sincere. He always claimed to have Catholic friends, yet carried a revolver most of his life.

Dill Macky died of cancer at his daughter's home at Neutral Bay on 15 November 1913 and was buried in Rookwood cemetery with Orange and Masonic rites. He was survived by his wife, three sons and five daughters.

P. Ford, *Cardinal Moran and the A.L.P.* (Melb, 1966); *Messenger* (Presbyterian, NSW), 16 Aug 1907, 5 June 1908, 24 Oct 1913; *Aust Baptist*, 21 Oct 1913; *Aust Christian World*, 19 Apr, 6 Sept 1901, 15 Jan 1909, 9 Sept 1910, 24 Oct, 7 Nov 1913; *SMH*, 22 June 1901, 28, 30 Mar 1903, 9-30 May, 12 June 1907, 16, 18 Oct 1913; *Methodist* (Syd), 18 Oct 1913; R. L. Broome, Protestantism in New South Wales society 1900-1914 (Ph.D. thesis, Univ Syd, 1974); Susannah D. Stevenson family papers (ML).

RICHARD BROOME

DIXON, GRAHAM PATRICK (1873-1947), soldier and surgeon, was born on 16 May 1873 in Brisbane, son of Joseph Black Dixon, bank-manager, and his wife Louisa Jane, née Sloan, both native-born. An outstanding scholar, he was educated at Brisbane Grammar School and the University of Sydney (Queensland exhibitioner 1891, Renwick and Harris scholar). He graduated in 1896 (M.B., Ch.M.), a university medallist and prizeman in surgery, anatomy and physiology.

Dixon's long association with the Children's Hospital, Brisbane, began in 1897 when he was appointed as a medical officer; from 1900 he was to act as honorary surgeon for long periods. In 1899 he set up what was to become a busy general practice at Maryborough where his alertness helped to arrest a plague epidemic in 1905. During 1910 he studied in England, Scotland, France and Switzerland, returning to Brisbane to practise as a consulting surgeon in Wickham Terrace.

Since 1900 Dixon had been a captain in the Australian Army Medical Corps (militia), and in August 1914 he joined the 3rd Field Ambulance, Australian Imperial Force. He sailed for Egypt with the first contingent in September and was promoted major in October. He was one of the first medical officers ashore at Gallipoli where he served until the evacuation. In January 1916 he was appointed lieut-colonel and commander of the 1st Light Horse Field Ambulance at Heliopolis. After refitting, the field ambulance established Bir Salmana camp and Dixon commanded his unit with distinction and selflessness through the battles of Minia, Romani and El Arish in the extraordinary conditions of the Sinai campaign. He assumed duty as assistant director of medical services, Anzac Mounted Division, in July 1917 as a temporary colonel, and for the next year followed the Palestine campaign. In April 1918 his rank was confirmed but soon afterwards he was invalided to Australia. During his four years continuous service in the field he had been conspicuous for efficient administration and wise surgery. He was twice mentioned in dispatches and in 1919 was appointed C.B.E.

In December 1918 Dixon was employed at the 6th Australian General Hospital at Kangaroo Point in Queensland. He also became surgeon at the Repatriation Hospital, Rosemount, where 'Dr Pat's' genial nature and compassionate care endeared him to the ex-servicemen he was to attend for twenty-seven years.

After the war Dixon returned to his practice as one of the leading surgeons of Brisbane and to the Children's Hospital. Of unassuming nature, he enjoyed the deep respect of his colleagues. He was a foundation fellow of the College of Surgeons of

Australasia, and for many years was a councillor of the Queensland branch of the British Medical Association; he was president in 1922. He was a councillor of the Medical Defence Society and its president in 1945-47. From his student days he was an active sportsman and held trophies for horsemanship. He died, unmarried, on 7 August 1947 in Brisbane and was cremated with Anglican rites.

University of Sydney, book of remembrance, 1914-18 (Syd, 1939); *London Gazette,* 13 Dec 1916, 1, 22 Jan 1919; *MJA,* 25 Oct 1947, 12 Mar 1966; *Courier Mail,* 9 Aug 1947; War diaries, 3rd Field Ambulance, *and* 1st Light Horse Field Ambulance, *and* Anzac Mounted Division, AIF (AWM).

M. J. E. STEVEN
BRYAN GANDEVIA

DIXON, HORACE HENRY (1869-1964), schoolmaster and bishop, was born on 1 August 1869 at Cambridge, England, one of eleven children of Thomas Dixon, bookseller, and his wife Lucy Ellen, née Eastgate. Starting his career as a teacher, he worked for three years as a housemaster at Warkworth House, Cambridge, before graduating through Fitzwilliam Hall (for non-collegiate students), Cambridge (B.A., 1892; M.A., 1908). Ordained in St Alban's Abbey (deacon 1893, priest 1894) he served in the parishes of Epping in 1893-94, St Michael and All Angels, Walthamstow, in 1894-97 and St Matthew's, Burnley, in 1898-99, and worked briefly in the East End of London. On 23 November 1897 at Margate, Kent, he married Florence Marie Godbold (d. 1932).

Bishop W. T. Webber [q.v.] recruited Dixon for Queensland. Arriving in Brisbane in 1899, he was assigned to Southport, an immense parish covering more than 2000 square miles (5000 km²) from Beenleigh to the New South Wales border; he had to cover it all on horseback. He was constantly reminded that Southport was the main seaside resort of southern Queensland, and it occurred to him that the town was the natural centre for a school. He discussed the idea in 1901 with two men who knew the district well, E. J. Stevens, M.L.A., and Dr R. S. Berry, who practised in Southport. Both promised support. A group of buildings on the Nerang River, known as 'Government House and Estate' had been used as a summer residence by governors of Queensland but was no longer required. Dixon secured a one-year lease of the property rent free if he paid for repairs, with an option to purchase after three years for £1000. Webber was sympathetic but the diocese was unable to finance the scheme and it was eventually arranged that Dixon would accept personal responsibility. If the school proved successful, the Church would take it over as soon as possible as a diocesan school for boys.

Financed by a loan from his sponsors, the repairs were undertaken by Dixon and helpers. Two boarders entered the school in September 1901. There were six boarders and 1 or 2 day-boys at the beginning of 1902, about 35 boys at the end of 1903 and 45 at the end of 1904. That year the number of applications encouraged him to proceed with purchase of the buildings and four acres (1.6 ha) of land as soon as the lease expired. He relinquished his incumbency of St Peter's parish, Southport, in 1905. Help was difficult to obtain and he found his spare time occupied with carpentering, woodcutting, clearing, road-mending or repairing machinery; electric light did not reach the school till 1920 and town water about 1930.

Energetic and a visionary, Dixon stamped himself as a colourful schoolmaster. He aimed at 'the highest possible moral and physical attainment'. By a combination of showmanship and bluff and intimate knowledge of his pupils, he earned great popularity with them. Sometimes stern and hard, he was often witty and full of fun, enjoyed a practical joke, and respected those who could take it and look after themselves. He had a most impressive sonorous voice and manner so that congregations listened to him almost with awe. About 1903 the boys nicknamed him 'Jimmy', and his assistant master 'Joey', after the Aboriginals Jimmy Governor [q.v.] and his brother Joe, outlawed in New South Wales. The name stuck to Dixon all his life.

The school became recognized in 1907 as the diocesan school for boys and in 1913 it was taken over by the diocese and renamed the Southport School. Dixon carried on, participating keenly and successfully in football, cricket, tennis, shooting, rowing and cadets, besides teaching in class and acting as chaplain. He retired in December 1929, leaving one of the best-known and largest boarding-schools in Queensland with over two hundred boarders.

Dixon had been a controversial figure who was not always appreciated. He was a strong man who rarely failed to get his own way, but the academic standards of the school and its emphasis on sport were criticized. Few of the sons of graziers who made up the great majority of the boys were interested in proceeding to higher education; but in the late 1920s standards did improve markedly.

An honorary canon since 1919, Dixon was appointed in 1930 canon residentiary at St John's Cathedral and archdeacon of Brisbane; he became dean of Brisbane in 1931, and was consecrated bishop coadjutor in 1932, receiving an honorary doctorate from the Australian College of Theology. He was disappointed not to be elected archbishop in 1934 and did not get on well with Archbishop J. W. C. Wand [q.v.]. As an administrator Dixon had some reputation for treating junior clergy like schoolboys. Much of his work came to be concentrated on directing the Queensland Social Service League. He was on friendly terms with Wand's successor, Archbishop R. C. Halse. Said to be the world's oldest active Anglican prelate, Dixon was appointed C.B.E. in 1960 and retired next year. In his latter years, groups of Southport old boys made a practice of visiting him on his birthday. He died on 8 November 1964 at St Martin's Private Hospital and was buried in Lutwyche cemetery. He was survived by his wife Enid Rose, née Morgan-Jones, whom he had married on 15 August 1936, and by the two sons of his first marriage.

C. E. W. Bean, *Here, my son* (Syd, 1950); R. Goodman, *Secondary education in Queensland 1860-1960* (Canb, 1968); H. H. Power, *Bush doctor* (Adel, 1970); Church of England, Diocese of Brisb, *Church Chronicle*, 1 Dec 1964; *Queenslander*, 14 Sept 1918, 3 Oct 1929, 19 Mar, 31 Dec 1931, 7 Jan 1932; *Courier Mail*, 20 Feb 1961, 9 Nov 1964; *RHSQJ*, 10 (1975), no 1, and for bibliog; K. Rayner, The history of the Church of England in Queensland (Ph.D. thesis, Univ Qld, 1962); Diocesan council Cttee on The Southport School, Report 1909 (C. of E. Diocesan Archives, Brisb).

C. G. PEARCE

DIXSON, SIR HUGH (1841-1926), tobacco manufacturer and philanthropist, and THOMAS STORIE (1854-1932), medical practitioner, were born on 29 January 1841 and 10 April 1854 in Sydney, sons of Hugh Dixson [q.v.4], tobacco manufacturer, and his wife Helen, née Craig. Hugh was educated at W. T. Cape's [q.v.1] Elfred House Private School then worked for Phillip McMahon, a timber-merchant. In 1856 he entered his father's firm and, with his brother Robert, became a partner in 1864. On 3 July 1866 at Raymond Terrace he married EMMA ELIZABETH (1844-1922), daughter of William Edward Shaw; her sister Alice married Thomas Baker [q.v.7].

The firm prospered, partly due to the impetus of the American Civil War, and expanded to Melbourne and Adelaide, where it became Robert Dixson & Co. On the death of his father in 1880 Dixson became head of Dixson & Sons Ltd and in 1883 built a massive warehouse and factory on the corner of Elizabeth and Park streets. In the late 1880s he introduced a profit-sharing scheme with employees. In 1903 he and his nephew (Sir) Hugh Denison [q.v.] organized the merger of the family companies with William Camer-

on Bros & Co. Pty, Melbourne; Dixson was chairman of the new British-Australasian Tobacco Co. Ltd. He was also chairman of the City Bank of Sydney, and the Strand Electric Lighting Co. Ltd, proprietor of the Strand Arcade and, in 1897-98, president of the Chamber of Manufactures of New South Wales. In 1904 he set up and became chairman of the Dixson Trust Ltd.

Staunch Baptists, Dixson and his wife originated many trust funds for the Church, including £10 000 for aged and infirm ministers. He was president of the Baptist Union of New South Wales in 1895-96, the Baptist Home Mission Society until 1926 and of the Young Men's Christian Association in 1900-02 and in 1909, and a director of Royal Prince Alfred Hospital. Lady Dixson was a life governor of the Queen Victoria Homes for Consumptives, the Women's Hospital, Crown Street, Royal Prince Alfred Hospital and of the Infants' Home, Ashfield, a life vice-president of the British Empire League in Australia, the National Council of Women of New South Wales, and the Victoria League; president of the women's auxiliary of the Sydney City Mission and the Veterans' Home of New South Wales and vice-president of the New South Wales Home for Incurables, Ryde (to which they gave £20 000), and the Fresh Air League; she also founded the Sydney Medical Mission. Among Dixson's many benefactions were £5000 each to the Dreadnought Fund, the Chamber of Commerce War Food fund and the Y.M.C.A.'s building fund; and £7500 to the University of Sydney to buy a collection of minerals from the Barrier district; he and his wife were as charitable privately as publicly.

Dixson was a noted horticulturist and became a member of the Linnean Society of New South Wales in 1887 and the Australasian Association for the Advancement of Science in 1898. At his home, Abergeldie, Summer Hill, his garden contained many exotic and rare plants; he contributed articles to such journals as the *Agricultural Gazette of New South Wales*. Bespectacled and bearded with curling side-whiskers, he was knighted in 1921. Lady Dixson enthusiastically collected rare china and owned a tea-service that had belonged to Marie Antoinette.

She died in Sydney on 12 April 1922 and Sir Hugh at Colombo on 11 May 1926; they were survived by two of their six sons and by four daughters; one son Lieutenant Thomas Storie Dixson, Coldstream Guards, was killed on active service in France in World War I. Sir Hugh left his estate, valued for probate at £143 194, to his children and grandchildren.

Thomas was educated at Sydney Grammar School and privately by Rev. Barzillai

Quaife [q.v.2]. At 18 he went to the University of Edinburgh (M.B., C.M., 1877), where he was influenced by Lister. He studied in Dublin, Berlin and Vienna before returning to Sydney, where he was appointed lecturer in materia medica and therapeutics at the University of Sydney in 1883-1917. He spent two years leave at the University of Strassburg (Strasbourg), Germany, where he isolated the poisonous principle of the castor oil bean and translated O. Schmiedeberg's *Elements of pharmacology* (Edinburgh, 1887) under the author's supervision, to meet the need for a text-book in English-speaking universities. On 11 October 1887 at Inch, Aberdeenshire, Scotland, he married his first cousin Janet Maria Holdway Storie, and added Storie to his name.

On his return to Sydney Dixson was honorary physician in 1889-1914, honorary consulting physician in 1914-21 and director of the department of special therapeutics in 1909-21 at Sydney Hospital. He helped to found the Renwick Hospital for Infants, was associated with the Greycliffe (Lady Edeline) Hospital for Babies, and the Sydney Medical Mission, and was president of the New South Wales Institution for the Deaf and Dumb and the Blind. Dixson was active on the New South Wales branch of the British Medical Association and was president of the Medical Board of New South Wales in 1919-32. He did devoted work for the St John Ambulance Brigade, published a pamphlet on its history in New South Wales in 1918, was appointed a knight of St John of Jerusalem in 1919 and was chief commissioner of the Commonwealth of Australia (Western Australia excepted) in 1923-32. He contributed several articles to the *Australian Medical Journal*.

Interested in science from his university days, Dixson was a councillor of the Linnean Society of New South Wales for fifty years (1882-1932) and its president in 1903-05. In 1898 he became a trustee of the Australian Museum, Sydney, and was president in 1918-25; there he helped to organize popular lectures and planned a children's museum. He also contributed valuable information on the preservation and display of specimens. A member for forty-four years, he was an honorary vice-president of the Highland Society of New South Wales and a member of the Geographical Society.

Dixson had suffered from diabetes for twenty years when he died on 9 December 1932 at his home, Edgewater, Cremorne; he was cremated with Presbyterian forms. He was survived by his wife and by three daughters; his estate was valued for probate at £7836.

Sir Hugh Dixson's eldest surviving son SIR WILLIAM (1870-1952), businessman and collector of Australiana, was born on 18 April 1870 in Sydney. Educated at All Saints College, Bathurst, he qualified as an engineer in Scotland in 1889-96. On his return to Sydney he worked for several years for Norman Selfe [q.v.6]. He was a director of Dixson & Sons Ltd in 1899-1903, the British-Australasian Tobacco Co. Ltd in 1903-08, the City Bank of Sydney (1909-17) and of the Dixson Trust Ltd 1909-52 and Timbrol Ltd until 1952. William began collecting rare books and manuscripts for use in his 'own historical researches' but when he learned that the income from David Scott Mitchell's [q.v.5] bequest to the Public Library of New South Wales could not be spent on pictures, he 'decided to give special attention to them'.

Dixson first offered his pictures to the State in 1919 and again in 1924, adding that he would bequeath the remainder of his pictures and collections of Australiana, including manuscripts, books, coins and stamps, to the library on similar conditions to Mitchell's bequest: the Dixson Gallery was opened in October 1929. He later gave to the library other pictures, including a number by artists who accompanied Captain Cook [q.v.1], its great bronze entrance doors, three stained-glass windows in the main reading room, and £15 000, the income of which is used to buy historical pictures.

In 1937-39 Dixson gave a total of £5000 to assist in establishing a library at the New England University College, Armidale, which is named in his honour; he also presented some 1500 anthropological specimens from Australasia, New Guinea and the Bismarck Archipelago to the Australian Museum. He was a benefactor and fellow of the Royal Australian Historical Society, contributing many articles to its *Journal*, and a member of the Geographical, Royal and Linnean societies of New South Wales. Like his parents, he aided hospitals and institutions and was treasurer and president of the Queen Victoria Homes. He was knighted in 1939. Although 'reserved and retiring', he was a 'very kindly gentleman', with neatly brushed hair and a trim beard and moustache. He was a member of Killara Golf Club, and was an excellent photographer.

Sir William, a bachelor, died in hospital at Chatswood on 17 August 1952 and was cremated with Anglican rites. His estate was valued for probate at £429 132; in addition to his promised bequests, he left all his shares in the British Tobacco Co. (Australia) Ltd (about £114 000) to the trustee of the Public Library to set up the William Dixson Foundation to benefit students by reproducing, with 'no editing whatsoever', manuscripts relating to Australasia and the Pacific, reprinting rare books and translating manuscripts into English. The Dixson Library, housing his great collections, was opened in 1959.

A portrait of Sir William by Norman Carter [q.v.7] is held by the University of New England and Lionel Lindsay [q.v.] did a portrait etching.

Cyclopedia of N.S.W. (Syd, 1907); D. H. Drummond, *A university is born* (Syd, 1959); A. C. Prior, *Some fell on good ground* (Syd, 1966); Linnean Soc NSW, *Procs*, 58 (1933); *Aust Museum mag*, 5 (1933), no 1, 10 (1952), no 9; *JRAHS*, 38 (1952) pt 6; *Aust Manufactures' J*, 16 May 1910; *Banking and Insurance Review*, 28 Aug 1916; *Daily Telegraph* (Syd), 17 Mar 1915; *SMH*, 13 Apr 1922, 13 May 1926, 10 Dec 1932, 2 Jan 1939; ML printed cat; Dixson correspondence and papers, *and* Dixson family biog file (Dixson Lib, Syd).   B. COOK

DIXSON, HUGH ROBERT: *see* DENISON

DOBBIE, EDWARD DAVID (1857-1915), judge, was born on 22 February 1857 in Dublin, son of Richard Dobbie, upholsterer, and his wife Jane, née Gill. Migrating to Tasmania with his parents about 1858, he was educated at both state and private schools entering The Hutchins School, Hobart, in 1869. Articled to Charles Ball of the firm Gill & Ball, Dobbie was admitted to the Supreme Court of Tasmania in July 1882 and began his public service career as a parliamentary draftsman the following March. On 10 December 1887 at St Andrew's Presbyterian Church he married Alice Anne MacMillan; they had four daughters and two sons.

Dobbie had been appointed crown solicitor and clerk of the peace in March; he relinquished the former office in January 1895 when he became secretary to the Law Department. During this period he was also registrar of building societies. He held these places until his appointment as recorder and commissioner in bankruptcy, Launceston, and commissioner of the Court of Requests in January 1889. He became solicitor-general in April 1902.

Dobbie's career as solicitor-general was relatively undistinguished. Nevertheless he was involved in a number of cases which, if not of great legal import, did arouse considerable local interest. One macabre case concerned the closing down of the Queenborough cemetery when, after a series of heavy rains, corpses were washed out of the graves and it was discovered that as many as six bodies had been interred in a single plot. A highlight of his career as solicitor-general was his visit to the United Kingdom in 1904 as a result of an appeal to the Privy Council

by the Van Diemen's Land Co., following a decision of the Supreme Court against the Marine Board of Table Cape. Dobbie presented the case on behalf of the Marine Board and the State government; the case went against him. During this period his many letters to his wife provide interesting comment on the social and political life of London.

Dobbie continued to read up constitutional law, and after 1901 became, with Herbert Nicholls [q.v.], one of Tasmania's foremost exponents of Federation. He was a member of the royal commission on the charitable institutions of Tasmania (1888) and also of the controversial royal commission into the system of state school education (1907).

On 1 September 1913 Dobbie was appointed an acting puisne judge of the Supreme Court and was confirmed in the position on 1 January next year. His brief career as a judge (the shortest on record in Tasmania) ended with his death of heart disease on 23 August 1915 at Sandy Bay. He was buried in the Congregationalist section of Cornelian Bay cemetery. He probably never reached the pinnacle of his legal career. His judgments, although generally sound, lack the depth of experience which he might have acquired later. On the other hand his work as a parliamentary draftsman during his early years undoubtedly benefited him; a sincere, unostentatious man, he showed a thorough concern with detail as much as with broad principles. His estate was valued for probate at £1640.

Cyclopedia of Tasmania, 1 (Hob, 1900); J. N. D. Harrison, *Court in the colony* (Hob, 1974); *Argus*, 24 Aug 1915; *Mercury*, 24, 25 Aug 1915; information from Mrs H. R. Dobbie, Moonah, Tas.

DAVID L. MULCAHY

DOBSON, EMILY (1842-1934), philanthropist, was born on 10 October 1842 at Port Arthur, Van Diemen's Land, daughter of Thomas James Lempriere [q.v.2] and his wife Charlotte, née Smith. Emily had no formal schooling but was educated by her father whose wide interests and social conscience she made her own. On 4 February 1868 at the Bothwell Church of England she married Henry Dobson [q.v.], a lawyer and later Tasmanian premier who shared her philanthropic ideas; they had two sons and three daughters.

Emily's prominence in public welfare coincided with her husband's early parliamentary career. In September 1891 she became secretary of the Women's Sanitary Association (later the Women's Health Association, of which she was vice-president), founded to combat the typhoid then raging in Hobart. Undaunted by the *Mercury*'s occasional ridicule, the women regularly petitioned the local council and, with the men's Sanitary and General Improvement Association, ran candidates in the municipal election of 1892. In June 1893 Mrs Dobson's Relief Restaurant Committee began a soup kitchen in Hobart; later that year, with the unemployment crisis lessening, it initiated the Association for Improvement of Dwellings of the Working Classes. In November, however, the committee's imagination was captured by Henry Dobson's exposition of the Southport village settlement scheme and its funds and energies were diverted to it. Next year Emily, as president and managing secretary of the Village Settlement Committee, spent some days under canvas with the pioneers; the settlement received her backing until its failure in 1898.

Emily was also founding president of the Ministering Children's League in 1892, the ladies' committee of the Blind, Deaf and Dumb Institution in 1898 and was for many years president of the committee of management of the Victoria Convalescent Home at Lindisfarne. An early supporter of the Amateur Nursing Band, she began with others the New Town Consumptives' Sanatorium in 1905, was later a life patroness of the Tasmanian Bush Nursing Association and a first vice-president in 1918 of the Child Welfare Association. Like her husband she encouraged temperance (she was a long-term vice-president of the Women's Christian Temperance Union of Tasmania) and worked for educational reform, partnering Dobson in the establishment of the Free Kindergarten Association in 1911.

After a meeting with Miss Baden-Powell in England that year she established the Girl Guides' Association of Tasmania and assumed the position of State commissioner; she was awarded a medal from the London Girl Guide headquarters in 1931. A vice-president of the Tasmanian branch of the League of Nations Union and of the Victoria League of Tasmania, she was a founder in 1901 and sometime president of the Tasmanian branch of the Alliance Française. During World War I she taught colloquial French to soldiers at Claremont camp and in December 1930 received the insignia of the Order of Officier d'Instruction Publique.

Throughout her life Emily championed the cause of women. She founded the Tasmanian Lyceum Club and worked for the Women's Non-Party League of Hobart. A vice-president of the newly formed Tasmanian section of the National Council of Women in 1899 she was president of the federal body in 1906-21. She attended the first meeting of the International Council of Women in London in 1899 and almost every following executive meeting and quinquennial conference until 1932 when she made her thirty-third visit overseas: she was made an honorary vice-president of the International Council in 1925 and was later a patroness. She represented the Tasmanian government at the 1907 Women's Work Exhibition in Melbourne. In Tasmania the National Council of Women commemorated her outstanding public service by the establishment in 1919 of the Emily Dobson Philanthropic Prize Competition for welfare organizations. Affectionately known as the 'Grand Old Lady' she died on 5 June 1934 in Hobart and was buried in Queenborough cemetery.

History of National Councils of Women in Tasmania 1899-1968 (Hob, nd, copy SLT); B. Teniswood, *Guiding in Tasmania, 1911-1973* (Hob, 1974); P. F. Bolger, 'The Southport settlement', *PTHRA*, 12 (1965), no 4; *Mercury*, 8-12 Sept, 24 Oct 1891, 30 Aug, 10 Dec 1892, 3-19 June, 24 July, 25, 26 Sept, 6, 11 Nov 1893, 6 June 1934; *Tas Mail*, 19 May 1921; *Weekly Courier* (Launc), 3 Oct 1928, 24 Dec 1930, 7 June 1934.   I. A. REYNOLDS

DOBSON, HENRY (1841-1918), lawyer and politician, was born on 24 December 1841 in Hobart, son of John Dobson, solicitor, and his second wife Kate, née Willis. Like his brother Alfred and his half-brothers William Lambert and Frank [qq.v.4] he was educated at The Hutchins School. After some time in a merchant's office he commenced legal training with Allport, Roberts and Allport, and was called to the Tasmanian Bar on 30 December 1864. As the partner of W. R. Giblin [q.v.4] in 1865-70 and from 1887 as senior partner in the firm of Dobson, Mitchell and Allport he became one of the most trusted family lawyers in the colony.

Elected for Brighton to the House of Assembly in 1891 he was soon chosen as leader of the Opposition, probably because of his family connexions and his wealth at a time when many other prominent politicians were embarrassed by the economic depression. After the Fysh [q.v.] ministry was defeated Dobson became premier on 17 August 1892. His period in office, following the over-spending of previous administrations, was a disastrous one. His policy of drastic retrenchment was rejected, and he obtained a dissolution. With the situation unchanged after the election he resigned on 14 April 1894; he held his seat until 1899. An ardent Federalist, he was a member of the Federal Council of Australasia from 1893 and represented Tasmania at the 1897-98 convention. Elected to the Senate in 1901 he was temporary chairman of committees in 1904-08 and chairman in 1908-09. After his defeat in 1910 he retired from politics.

With Giblin, J. B. Walker [q.v.6] and others Dobson was a founder in 1864 of the Working Men's Club. In an attempt to relieve the unemployment of the 1890s he gave much personal support to the establishment in 1894 of a partially self-supporting, though finally unsuccessful, village settlement at Southport; his enthusiasm was surpassed only by that of his wife Emily Lempriere [q.v. Dobson] whom he had married on 4 February 1868 in the Bothwell Church of England. Keenly interested in education, he earned the hostility of many employers in 1898 by implementing the amendment to the Education Act (1885) which made attendance at school compulsory for five days a week. He also sponsored the introduction of kindergartens. Paramount among his public works was his advocacy of Tasmania as a tourist resort. Founder and president in 1895-1914 of the Tasmanian Tourist Association he worked for the establishment of the official Tourist and Information Bureau and of the Scenery Preservation Board in 1915. He was chairman of the National Park Board in 1917-18. He also appointed the developing fruit-growing industry.

A highly cultivated man with a love of good music, literature and sport, Dobson belonged to the Royal Society of Tasmania from 1861, and the Tasmanian Club from 1866, and was president of the Athenaeum Club in 1895-1906. He held tenaciously to views many of which, while not immediately popular, subsequently proved sound. He died on 10 October 1918 at Hobart survived by his wife, four daughters and the elder of two sons, and was buried in Queenborough cemetery.

Cyclopedia of Tasmania (Hob, 1900); W. R. Barrett, *History of the Church of England in Tasmania* (Hob, 1942); F. C. Green (ed), *A century of responsible government 1856-1956* (Hob, 1956); Roy Soc Tas, *Procs*, 1918; P. F. Bolger, 'The Southport settlement', *PTHRA*, 12 (1965), pt 4; *Table Talk*, 25 Apr 1901; *Punch* (Melb), 7 Dec 1905; *Mercury*, 11 Oct 1918.   E. M. DOLLERY*

DOCKER, ERNEST BROUGHAM (1842-1923), judge and photographer, was born on 1 April 1842 at Thornwaite, near Scone, New South Wales, the eldest son of Joseph Docker [q.v.4] and his second wife Matilda, née Brougham. Educated at the Collegiate School, Cook's River, in 1860 he won the [Sir William] Denison [q.v.4] scholarship to enter St Paul's College, University of Sydney, where he lived up to his early promise,

winning the University Medal for English verse in 1861 and the Wentworth medal for an English essay in 1862. He graduated B.A. in 1863 and M.A. in 1865, then turned his attention to the law.

Admitted to the colonial Bar on 28 June 1867, Docker advanced steadily in his profession, becoming crown prosecutor for the northern district in 1875, the south-western district in 1878, and judge of the District Court and chairman of Quarter Sessions for the north-western district in 1881. In 1884-1912 he was in the western district. He was conscientious on the bench, working long hours, arranging his sittings conveniently for suitors, and taking additional courts, often without remuneration. His legal knowledge was sound but his forthright manner, cutting wit and severe sentences upon hardened criminals drew criticism. He was concerned, however, that justice should always be done. He opposed shorthand writers in the court but urged the adoption of English criminal law reforms, changes in the perjury law, and an end to restrictions upon the competency of witnesses to give evidence; he also wanted public prosecutors instead of the police for Crown cases in the lower courts. In 1894 he was appointed to hold a murder trial on Norfolk Island and in 1912 he transferred to the metropolitan District Court. He retired in 1918 after the passage of the Judges Retirement Act.

Docker was a notable amateur photographer. He took lessons from William Hetzer and in 1858, with his father, began experiments with a wet-plate process. Between 1860 and 1868 Docker was sensitizing his own dry plates by the tannin-collodion-albumen process, although dry plates were not widely used until the early 1880s. Joining the Royal Society of New South Wales in 1876, he used his own extensive collection of photographs for many illustrated addresses before it. He did much to promote photography through his articles in overseas and Australian journals, particularly in the *British Journal of Photography*, and as president of the Photographic Society of New South Wales in 1894-1907.

Docker also devoted much time to the Church of England and was a synodsman for the Sydney and Bathurst dioceses. He was a council-member of The King's School, Parramatta, and a member of the Royal Australian Historical Society. Attracted to literature, he published several volumes of sacred hymns and poems; Henry Kendall [q.v.5] praised them and valued Docker's opinions of his own work and the judge's faith in his 'attempts to initiate a purely Australian literature'. A keen sportsman, Docker enjoyed cricket, tennis and duck-shooting and whist or bridge in the evenings. On 25 June 1873 at Wangaratta, Victoria, he had married Clarissa Mary, daughter of Archdeacon J. K. Tucker. She died on 3 June 1918, the judge at his waterfront home, Mostyn, Elizabeth Bay, on 12 August 1923. He was survived by seven daughters and two sons; the younger son Ernest won the Military Cross in World War I.

Cyclopedia of N.S.W. (Syd, 1907); J. Cato, *The story of the camera in Australia* (Melb, 1955); H. T. E. Holt, *A court rises* (Syd, 1976); *V&P* (LA NSW), 1883, 1, 477-97, 599; *Law Chronicle*, 30 June 1897; *SMH*, 15 Nov 1895, 1 Aug 1916, 9 Apr, 30 Nov, 21 Dec 1918, 13, 14 Aug 1923; *T&CJ*, 12 June 1918; H. C. Kendall-Docker letters 1865-81, AK 39/12 (ML); G. Lissant, Notes on the Docker family of Westmorland (ML).   STEWART WOODMAN

DODD, ARTHUR WILLIAM (1894-1961), soldier, station-manager and pastoral adviser, was born on 12 August 1894 at Kew, Melbourne, only son of Henry Alexander Dodd, merchant and later sharebroker, and his wife Mary Alexander, née King, both Melbourne born. He attended Trinity Grammar School, Kew, in 1904-10, represented the school at cricket, football, tennis and athletics, and was a member of the cadets. He became a clerk with the Royal Bank of Australasia, served in the peacetime forces as gunner and bombardier in the 9th Battery, Australian Field Artillery, and was commissioned second lieutenant in September 1913.

Dodd enlisted in the Australian Imperial Force and was posted to the 6th Battery, 2nd Field Artillery Brigade, on 18 August 1914 with the rank of second lieutenant. He embarked for Egypt in October and next February was promoted lieutenant. His unit landed at Cape Helles in April 1915 with the British 29th Division and took part in operations at Krithia in May-June; in August it was moved to Anzac Cove where Dodd was wounded on 12 November but remained on duty. The 6th Battery served at Gallipoli until the evacuation, then returned to Egypt. Promoted captain on 12 March 1916, Dodd was given command of the newly formed 23rd Battery, but a week later returned to command the 6th, an appointment he was to hold until the end of the war.

Dodd reached France in April and his battery went into action at Hazebrouck; in July he took part in operations at Pozières and then followed the German retreat to the Hindenburg line. He was awarded the Military Cross for meritorious service throughout this period, especially during the capture of Pozières. In January 1917 he was promoted major and next month received the Order of the White Eagle of Serbia. He

fought at Lagnicourt in April and in the 3rd battle of Ypres in July; here the Australian artillery suffered crippling losses and Dodd was wounded and evacuated, resuming command in October for the 2nd battle of Passchendaele. His battery was put out of action by enemy gas on 29 October and he was gassed and hospitalized for three months. He was wounded again on 1 March 1918 but remained on duty.

In April-June Dodd served at Hazebrouck and Merris and took temporary command of the 2nd Field Artillery Brigade at Villers-Bretonneux in the battle on 8 August. His final service was on 2-3 October in operations at Nauroy and Bellicourt. He was wounded for the fifth time when, after four hours of intense enemy bombardment, a gas-shell struck the side of his dug-out, immersing him in a thick cloud of gas. Though suffering severely he completed his orders for an attack on Beaurevoir. For showing 'courage and determination of a high order' he was awarded the Distinguished Service Order; he was also twice mentioned in dispatches during the war.

Dodd was demobilized in November 1919. Next year he bought a property near Liverpool, New South Wales, in partnership with a wartime friend and when this venture failed moved north where he worked as a jackeroo on Eversham station, Longreach, Queensland, and then as a head-stockman and sub-manager on Lake Nash station, Northern Territory. In 1926 he was made overseer of Winslade station, near Cloncurry, Queensland, and in 1928 became its manager. The year before, on 22 November, he had married Muriel Mabel Maud Simmonds at St Patrick's Cathedral, Melbourne. He remained at Winslade until 1940 when he became a pastoral inspector with Goldsbrough [q.v.4] Mort [q.v.5] & Co.; in 1943-49 he was a supervisor of company properties and in 1949-52 managed the firm's Brisbane office. He remained with Goldsbrough Mort as a pastoral adviser until 1955.

In retirement Dodd began a history of the 6th Battery in World War I; though incomplete it contains several graphic accounts of actions in which his unit participated, as well as personal anecdotes and asides. Survived by his wife and three daughters, he died of cerebro-vascular disease on 12 December 1961 at Hamilton and was cremated.

C. E. W. Bean, *The story of Anzac* (Syd, 1921, 1924), and *The A.I.F. in France, 1917-18* (Syd, 1933, 1937, 1942); *London Gazette*, 1 Jan, 15 Feb 1917, 27 Dec 1918, 11 July, 4 Oct 1919; Goldsbrough Mort & Co. records (ANU Archives); records (AWM); information from Mrs M. Dodd, Clayfield, Qld, *and* Trinity Grammar School, Kew, Vic., *and* Mr S. Wharton, Banora Point, *and* Mr J. Sutherland, Beecroft, NSW.   M. FREIBERG

DODD, JOSIAH EUSTACE (1856-1952), organbuilder, was born on 16 August 1856 at Richmond, Melbourne, son of Ebenezer Daniel Dodd, London-born clerk, and his wife Johanna, née Moloney, from Tipperary, Ireland. After education at St Stephen's Church Schools, Richmond, he was apprenticed to the firm of George Fincham [q.v.4], organbuilder. On 10 April 1879 at Richmond, Dodd married, with Baptist forms, Jessie Lovat Fraser, from Inverness, Scotland; they had two sons and a daughter.

In 1881 the firm opened a branch in Adelaide with Dodd as co-manager and, from 1888, manager. In 1894 he purchased the Adelaide business and began many notable instruments, the three most significant in Adelaide being those for Clayton Congregational Church, Norwood (1897), the Methodist Church, Kent Town (1898), and the Elder Hall, University of Adelaide (1901), now in St Mark's Roman Catholic Cathedral, Port Pirie. Dodd had almost a complete monopoly on organ-building in South Australia. He set out to discourage Church authorities from importing English organs, and there was virtually no competition from local builders because of his immense technical ability and business acumen. He expanded the activity to include pianoforte renovation and, from 1918, theatre organs, employing twenty hands. In 1903 the firm established a branch in Western Australia managed by Dodd's eldest son Ebenezer, and the organ of St George's Cathedral, Perth, was rebuilt and enlarged. In 1918 a branch was opened in Melbourne under the aegis of the second son Eustace (D. E. Dodd).

The firm built over eighty new instruments and rebuilt and renovated countless others in all States except Queensland. The organs at St Mary's Cathedral, Perth (1910), St John's Cathedral, Napier, New Zealand (1910), Patterson Street Methodist Church, Launceston, Tasmania (1912), St Carthage's Cathedral, Lismore, New South Wales (1912) and St Joseph's Church, Malvern, Victoria (1917) were good examples of his larger instruments.

Dodd's contribution to the art of organbuilding was a conception of the romantic-symphonic organ and provision of considerable mechanical aids to give flexibility to the player. He had great ability in the romantic style as a tonal voicer. However, by 1935 he was rather set in his ways. Some members of his firm broke away to form the Gunstar Organ Works, building extension organs with electro-pneumatic action. When during World War II trade declined and parts were virtually unobtainable, the two firms merged to become 'J. E. Dodd & Sons, Gunstar Organ Works', which still operates.

Dodd was a prodigious worker and on one occasion in his old age (he worked until two days before his death), he collapsed and was unconscious for three minutes. When he came to, he pointed to a workman and, typically, said 'That's not the way to hammer that!' He was a Freemason and a member of Clayton Congregational Church and later Trinity Methodist Church, Glenelg. He died of a coronary occlusion at his home at Glenelg on 30 January 1952 and was buried in St Jude's cemetery, Brighton.

H. T. Burgess (ed), *Cyclopedia of South Australia*, 2 (Adel, 1909); B. A. Naylor, Organ building in South Australia (M. Mus. thesis, Univ Adel, 1973); J. E. Dodd & Sons, Manufacturing catalogues, letter and day-books (Gunstar Organ Works, Plympton, SA).   BRUCE NAYLOR

DODDS, THOMAS HENRY (1873-1943), soldier, was born on 11 November 1873 at Gateshead, County Durham, England, son of Thomas Dodds, manager of the *British Workman*, and his wife Jane, née Smith. The family migrated to Australia in 1883, settling in Brisbane where Dodds attended the Fortitude Valley State School and the Brisbane Normal School. He entered the Queensland Department of Public Instruction as a teacher in 1888. Attracted by the volunteer movement he enlisted in 1892 and was commissioned in the Queensland Teachers' Corps in 1899.

Dodds served in the South African War as adjutant of the 5th (Queensland Imperial Bushmen) Contingent in 1901-02. When the Bushmen and other units were attacked and almost overwhelmed by a superior force of Boers at Onverwacht, he rallied the surviving Queenslanders and held on to a ridge until help arrived. For this and other spirited actions he was mentioned in dispatches and awarded the Distinguished Service Order. He was also promoted honorary captain. He returned from South Africa in May 1902 and on 29 December, at the Baptist Church, Fortitude Valley, he married Elizabeth Jane Hancock.

In July 1906 Dodds exchanged teaching for a regular commission in the Administrative and Instructional Staff. Although he was again a lieutenant and did not become a captain until 1910 his rise was to be unusually rapid. His chance came in 1911 when he was moved from Brisbane to Army Headquarters in Melbourne. There he quickly came under the eye of Lieut-Colonel J. G. Legge [q.v.] who was responsible for the planning and organization of the new compulsory training scheme. Dodds's capacity as an administrative staff officer was soon demonstrated. He was made secretary of the War Railway Council and in July 1911 was appointed director of personnel although still a captain. In 1913 he was promoted major.

When war broke out in August 1914, Dodds was assistant adjutant general and director of personnel so that when the adjutant general, Lieut-Colonel V. C. M. Sellheim [q.v.], was transferred to the Australian Imperial Force, Dodds moved easily into his appointment, was promoted lieutcolonel, and became a temporary member of the Military Board. However, like a number of other officers, his very ability kept him in Australia while most of his friends were at the front; the dispatch of the 1st Division and the 1st Light Horse Brigade and their successors left the army in Australia dangerously short of useful officers. Dodds's requests for employment with the A.I.F. were twice refused as was the request of Major General Legge who wanted him as senior administrative staff officer in the 2nd Division.

Even before he became adjutant general, Dodds had become known as a bluff, outspoken and formidable officer. Given the range of his responsibilities for the personnel of the army, including the recruitment of the A.I.F. until 1916, it was fortunate that a man of such strength of character and energy was available. Dodds was not content to limit his interests to the army in Australia. He was one of the earliest and strongest proponents of the 'Australianisation' of the commands and staffs of the A.I.F., strongly pressing this policy on the minister for defence, Senator G. F. Pearce [q.v.]. In the opinion of one of the closest observers of the wartime government, Governor-General Sir Ronald Munro Ferguson [q.v.], Dodds was the strongest member of the Military Board and exerted too much influence over the minister; Munro Ferguson described Dodds as one 'of the rough and ready school ... hard working and capable but ill-mannered, violent and prejudiced ... tho' to me personally his demeanour is irreproachable and he is helpful'. In a less exalted position, C. E. W. Bean's [q.v.7] assistant, A. W. Bazley, confessed that he was always rather afraid when he had to approach Dodds but he, too, found him helpful in relation to the war history.

Release came for Dodds early in 1917 when he was appointed to the staff of Lieut-General Sir William Birdwood [q.v.7] as deputy adjutant general, A.I.F. At headquarters of 1st Anzac Corps (later the Australian Corps) Dodds soon won Birdwood's approval. He stood up to the prime minister, W. M. Hughes [q.v.], who made an angry scene when Dodds refused to issue certain orders without Birdwood's approval; 'I have complete confidence in his work and loyalty' wrote the latter to the governor-general. When Birdwood went to command the Fifth Army, Dodds accompanied him to handle Australian personnel matters.

In October 1918 Dodds, now brigadier general, succeeded Brigadier General T. Griffiths [q.v.] as commandant of A.I.F. Administrative Headquarters in London. He returned to Melbourne in May 1919. For his services he was twice mentioned in dispatches and was appointed C.M.G. In the early post-war years he became interested in the work of the Returned Sailors' and Soldiers' Imperial League of Australia, joining the Hawthorn sub-branch.

When the prince of Wales toured Australia in 1920, Dodds was deputy directorgeneral of the royal visit. For this work he was appointed C.V.O. However, it was a brief interlude in his work as military secretary at A.H.Q., 1920-22, and colonel, administrative staff in the Adjutant General's Branch, 1922-24. The chief of the General Staff, his old friend Sir Harry Chauvel [q.v.7], sent him to London as colonel, General Staff, at the Australian High Commission and Australian representative at the War Office, from January 1925. After this well-earned change of duties, Chauvel brought him back in 1927 to command the 2nd District Base in Sydney and the 1st Division. In 1929 Dodds returned to the Military Board as adjutant general to face the heavy tasks of holding the army together during the Depression, with all its consequent retrenchments, and the replacement of the compulsory system which he had helped to create by a volunteer militia. He was promoted major general in 1930. When he retired in 1934 the volunteer force was in being, although short of men.

In 1931-41 Dodds held the post of honorary federal treasurer of the R.S.L. For a time he was active in local government, having been elected to the Hawthorn City Council in 1935. He was a regular worshipper at St Mark's Church of England, Camberwell, and served on the parish council.

Dodds died suddenly on 15 October 1943 of a heart attack, and was accorded full military honours at his funeral. He was survived by his wife and two daughters, his son Lieut-Colonel N. G. Dodds, also an able administrator, having died on active service with the A.I.F. in 1942. Dodds's portrait by James Quinn [q.v.] is in the Australian War Memorial.

Aust Defence Dept, *Official records of the military contingents to the war in South Africa*, P. L. Murray ed (Melb, 1911); C. E. W. Bean, *The story of Anzac* (Syd, 1924), and *The A.I.F. in France*, 1916-18 (Syd, 1929, 1933, 1937, 1942); *London Gazette*, 29 July, 31 Oct 1902, 28 Dec 1917, 28 May,

3 June 1918, 18 Aug 1920; *Punch* (Melb), 15 Apr 1915, 8 Feb 1917; *Qld Digger*, 1 Mar 1933; Birdwood papers (AWM); Novar papers (NL).

                                                    A. J. HILL

DODS, ROBERT SMITH (ROBIN) (1868-1920), architect, was born on 9 June 1868 at Dunedin, New Zealand, eldest of three sons of Robert Smith Dods, wholesale grocer, and his wife Elizabeth Gray, née Stodart, both Edinburgh Scots. He came to be known as Robin. The family returned to Britain in the early 1870s and the father died in Edinburgh in 1876. Elizabeth and her children left Scotland for Brisbane to join her mother and in 1880 she married the ship's surgeon, Charles F. Marks [q.v.], whom she had met on the voyage; they had four children. He eventually settled into a practice in Wickham Terrace, Brisbane.

Robin was educated at the Brisbane Boys' Grammar School and in 1886 was sent to Edinburgh to serve articles with Hay & Henderson, architects. He also attended evening classes at the Edinburgh Architectural Association until 1890 and formed there a lasting friendship with (Sir) Robert Lorimer (1864-1929). In 1890 Dods moved to London, where he worked with the fortifications branch of the War Office and in the office of (Sir) Aston Webb. In 1891 he was admitted to the Royal Institute of British Architects and travelled in Italy. There he first met Mary Marian King, daughter of an American clergyman, whom he married at Woollahra, Sydney, on 21 March 1899.

In London Dods contributed measured drawings to the Architectural Association's *A.A. Sketchbook* and in 1893 won a special award in the Tite prize competition. Next year he was runner-up for the more valuable Soane medallion, and was employed by Webb to prepare the drawings for his successful entry in a competition for Christ's Hospital schools at Horsham, Sussex.

Dods visited his mother in Brisbane in 1894 and while there completed designs which subsequently won a competition for a nurses' home at Brisbane Hospital. He was offered a partnership with John Hall & Son and, returning to Brisbane in 1896, started practice with Hall's son Francis as Hall & Dods. The hospital proved a valuable client over the next decade.

By 1900 Dods had designed a handful of houses, including his own at New Farm (demolished), and several small commercial buildings in the city. His domestic work adopted many local techniques in wood but had a sophisticated discipline and a common-sense response to climate which were radically new. Influenced by C. F. A. Voysey, and like contemporaries in Britain including Lorimer and Lutyens, his early work was full of the romance of an arts and crafts philosophy which he never completely lost. Dods entered another competition for the new Brisbane Post Office in 1900. After inspecting the main southern post offices, he produced a design in the style of freely interpreted 'William and Mary' which won second place and a premium but failed to secure the commission.

The turning-point came in 1904 when, as architect for the Brisbane diocese of the Church of England, he accepted responsibility for building the last and possibly the finest design of the English architect J. L. Pearson. When the ambitious cathedral church of St John was opened in 1910, the east end, transepts and two bays of the nave had been completed under Dods's direction. He designed other buildings in the cathedral group, including the schools in 1904 and the church offices in 1910.

After twelve years in practice, Hall & Dods had secured some substantial clients. The Catholic Church had commissioned a new hospital, the Mater Misericordiae in South Brisbane. They had worked also for the New Zealand Insurance Co., the Australian Mutual Provident Society and the Bank of New South Wales. Although the partnership inherited the reputation of Hall senior, its success was due more to Dods's ability and to the influence of his family. To his mother's financial acumen was added the standing, as members of parliament, of both his stepfather and his uncle James Stodart [q.v.].

Dods himself combined immense charm, wit, and natural ability with discriminating and impeccable taste. He was passionate about his work and derived great pleasure from it, seeking, in both his buildings and writing, an appropriate Australian architecture. He contributed several times to the premier English journal the *Builder*. He was interested in politics, literature and the arts generally; he read essays and especially Robert Louis Stevenson. He encouraged then unknown figures, such as Dorothea Mackellar, J. J. Hilder and Hardy Wilson [qq.v.].

His mother's death in 1908 devastated Dods; soon after, the firm was supplanted as architects for the Brisbane Town Hall, and the pressure affected his health. In 1909 he ceased practice for almost a year and travelled in North America and Europe, calling on professional associates and examining architectural treasures. With Lorimer he travelled in Italy, until influenza brought him down. The damaging effect of the northern winters on his health probably dissuaded him from staying permanently in Britain.

Back in Brisbane Dods entered competitions for the completion of St Stephen's Catholic Cathedral, and for the Geelong Church of England Grammar School, but neither yielded a commission. Late in 1913 he moved to Sydney but not before completing some of his best work, including the chapel for the archbishop of Brisbane at Milton, the Australian Mercantile Land & Finance Co.'s offices and, perhaps his finest work, St Brigid's Catholic Church at Red Hill.

The move to Sydney was prompted by an invitation from the Bank of New South Wales to design its Royal Exchange branch, and he was able to secure a partnership in Spain & Cosh, for whom he had prepared a design for the *Daily Telegraph* building in Castlereagh Street in 1912. With the outbreak of war, investment was curtailed, building of the bank was abandoned, and the practice was fortunate in having a small continuity of work. Dods devoted himself to the affairs of the local institute of architects, the Arts and Crafts Society and writing. With a kidney disease which affected his eye-sight, he knew that he had not long to live.

Confidence returned with the armistice and Dods was engaged on the South British Insurance Co. building in Hunter Street (demolished) and the Newcastle Club; he did not live to see either completed. In 1919, collaborating with other prominent architects in writing *Domestic architecture in Australia*, he confirmed a national debt to Francis Greenway [q.v.1] and looked hopefully toward America, not to Frank Lloyd Wright or Walter Burley Griffin [q.v.] but to a more conservative movement based on the European tradition. He moved into a new home at Edgecliff and died there soon after of 'subacute nephritis' on 23 July 1920. He was buried in the Church of England section of South Head cemetery. His estate, valued for probate at £10 752, was left to his wife and two children. His son, (Sir) Lorimer Fenton, became prominent in medical research.

Dods drew from many sources, fully exploiting what he saw as the regional tradition and sensible climatic controls. Within a confident vocabulary of style he emphasized certain elements to achieve proportions of rare quality and an architecture of distinction.

R. Boyd, *Australia's home* (Melb, 1952); P. Cox and H. Tanner (eds), *Twelve Australian architects* (Syd, 1979); *JRHSQ*, 8 (1968-69), no 4, p 649; J. S. Egan, The work of Robin Dods . . . (B. Arch thesis, Univ Syd); R. J. Riddel, R. S. Dods in Sydney, 1913-20 (conference paper, Art Assn of Aust, 1979); R. S. Lorimer, Letters to R. S. Dods, 1896-1920 (Univ Edinb); R. S. Dods, Diary 1909 (held by Mrs E. Farfan, Brisb); J. Hall & Son, Tender-book, 2 (1859-1912) (copy Oxley Lib, Brisb); correspondence, Hall & Dods *and* Spain, Cosh & Dods (Bank of NSW Archives, Syd).   R. J. RIDDEL

DONALD, WILLIAM HENRY (1875-1946), journalist, foreign correspondent and adviser, was born on 22 June 1875 at Lithgow, New South Wales, second surviving son of George McGarvie Donald (1846-1930), a native-born mason, and his English wife Mary Ann (Marion), née Wiles. George became a building contractor, was first mayor of Lithgow in 1889 and in 1891-94 represented Hartley in the Legislative Assembly as a free trader. William was educated at Lithgow Public School and Cooerwull Academy, Bowenfels. Prevented from following his father's trade by an injury, he became a printer and a journalist. He worked on the Bathurst *National Advocate*, the Sydney *Daily Telegraph* and the Melbourne *Argus*.

In 1903 Donald accepted a position with the Hong Kong *China Mail*. On 17 September 1904 at the Wesleyan Methodist Church, Wanchai, Hong Kong, he married Mary Wall (d. 1972), English-born daughter of a Sydney contractor. He became managing director of the *China Mail* but in 1908 resigned, having been appointed South China representative of the *New York Herald* in 1905; he covered the 1911 revolution, during which he 'advised' the short-lived government of Sun Yat-sen in its negotiations with foreign powers. He remained in Hong Kong until 1911 when he moved to Shanghai and in 1913 to Peking.

From 1912 he edited the *Far Eastern Review*, but resigned in 1920 because of a clash with its owner George Bronson Rea over Japan's role in China. Although initially an admirer of Japan – in 1908 he had received a minor Japanese decoration for his coverage of the Russo-Japanese War (1904-05) – by 1915 he had become an extremely vocal critic of Japanese imperialism.

Donald's next position as director of the Bureau of Economic Information in Peking was a continuation of his work with the *Far Eastern Review*. While living in Peking he pursued active journalistic work, often deputizing for David Fraser, the London *Times* correspondent, and serving as correspondent for the *Manchester Guardian*. In 1928, as a result of financial pressure exerted on the bureau by the newly established Nationalist government, he resigned and went north to Manchuria where he was appointed adviser to the 'Young Marshal', Chang Hsueh-liang; this move began the most important and most baffling chapter of Donald's career.

There seems little doubt that he displayed a paternal interest in Chang Hsueh-liang, and played a key role in his rehabilitation after defeats in Manchuria and Jehol at the hands of Japan (1931-32). In 1933 he persuaded Chang to undergo a cure for opium addiction and that year accompanied him on a European tour. Upon their return to China, Donald remained with Chang until 1935, when he gravitated towards the Generalissimo and Madam Chiang Kai-shek.

The extent of Donald's influence in 1935-40 is very difficult to fathom — some argue that he was no more than a glorified public relations officer, others that he played a significant role in policy formulation. But there can be no doubt that his mediation during the Sian *coup d'état* in December 1936, when Chang Hsueh-liang's disaffected subordinates detained Chiang Kai-shek, represented the high point of his career in China.

When Donald left Chungking in May 1940, after a disagreement with Chiang Kai-shek over Chinese policy towards Germany, the British minister at the time described him as a 'garrulous old man'. However it was at Madam Chiang's request that he was returning to China, after touring the Pacific in 1940-41, when he was captured in Manila in January 1942. Throughout his captivity, first in the University of Santo Tomas Camp then in Los Banos, he managed to conceal his identity.

Liberated in February 1945, Donald chose repatriation to the United States of America, but failing to regain his health, he went to Tahiti to recuperate. Falling ill there, he was flown to Honolulu, thence Shanghai, where he died on 9 November 1946. He was survived by his wife, from whom he had separated about 1920, and by his daughter, Muriel Mary, born at Hong Kong on 22 July 1909 who died on 21 April 1973 in California, where they were living.

E. A. Selle, *Donald of China* (Syd, 1948); *Daily Telegraph* (Syd), 30 June 1891; *SMH*, 10 July 1930; Harold K. Hochschild papers (New York); N. T. Johnson papers (Lib Congress); J. M. McHugh papers (Cornell Univ, New York); G. E. Morrison papers (ML); FO 371 800 (PRO, Lond).

                                    WINSTON G. LEWIS

DONALDSON, JOHN (1886-1933), athlete, was born on 16 March 1886 at Raywood, Victoria, eldest child of John Donaldson and his wife Martha née Smith, both Victorian-born. Donaldson senior, a well-known sportsman in northern Victoria, was successively hairdresser, storekeeper, farmer and publican, becoming licensee of the Royal Hotel, Kerang, about 1900.

Educated at local state schools, young Jack Donaldson worked at a Kerang store and flour-mill, and trained and rode his father's trotters before devoting himself to professional running. After some success as a schoolboy athlete Donaldson first became widely known in 1906 when he ran second in the Stawell Gift, travelled overnight to Bendigo, and won both the 130 and 220 yards there. Over the next two years he had numerous victories at meetings in eastern Australia in spite of his rapidly increased handicap.

With his manager, E. R. ('Mick') Terry, Donaldson sailed for South Africa in 1909. A 'cocky youngster in those days', he was ready to challenge the world's best. Competing against Charles Holway of America and Arthur Postle [q.v.] of Australia at meetings organized by Rufe Naylor [q.v.], Donaldson broke several world records, but failed to demonstrate that he was the world's fastest sprinter when he went on to England in 1910. He broke his return voyage to beat R. E. Walker, the 1908 Olympic winner, in a challenge for £100 over 100 yards at Johannesburg. Back in Australia in 1911 he again ran in a series of well-promoted match races against Holway and Postle. In September a crowd of 6000 at the Sydney Sports Ground 'howled with delight' when Donaldson ended weeks of dispute by beating Holway over 130 yards. Returning to England in 1912 Donaldson confirmed his pre-eminence in professional running. At meetings usually held in the north of England, Wales and Scotland, he ran for appearance money, prizes and bets.

'With matches as scarce as hens' teeth and handicaps almost hopeless', Donaldson turned to track management. Although he argued that as an Australian he could not be conscripted, in 1916 he was charged with being an absentee from service and ordered to join the British Army. After seeing 'something of the real war game' with the 7th Manchesters at Arras Donaldson became a physical education instructor. He made a brief return to professional running in Britain before going to the United States of America in 1919. Declining chances to coach, Donaldson worked for Wanamakers, a New York retailer. He died by gassing himself in his apartment in the Bronx on 1 September 1933. In a note he said that a 'nervous disorder' had driven him to suicide. Survived by his wife Ethel, née Auer, and two daughters, he was buried in Galilee cemetery, Pennsylvania.

Only 5 ft. 8 in. (173 cm) tall and 10 st. 4 lbs. (65 kg) in weight, but broad shouldered, Donaldson ran with a long, gliding stride and high arm action. His title, 'Blue Streak', derived from his well-known blue singlet marked with a large white 'A'. Among many world records, Donaldson's most enduring feats were 9.375 seconds for 100 yards run in Johannesburg, 1910; and 12 seconds for 130 yards run in Sydney, 1911. His 100 yard time was not beaten by an amateur or a professional until 1948 and the 130 yard record stood until 1951. The fact that his records survived into an era of better coaching, tracks and equipment (including starting blocks) is evidence of his exceptional talent. A drinking fountain in his memory was unveiled at Stawell in April 1939.

J. Pollard, *The Ampol book of Australian sporting records* (Syd, 1968); K. Dunstan, *Sports* (Melb, 1973); *VHM*, 32 (1961), no 125, p 32; *Argus*, 15 Feb 1910, 13 Apr, 9 May, 25 Sept 1911, 14 Sept 1916; *Bulletin*, 28 Sept 1911; *Sporting Globe*, 13 Jan-17 Feb 1932; *New York Times*, 3 Sept 1933; *Inglewood Advertiser*, 8 Sept 1933; *Canb Times*, 14 Mar 1970.

H. N. NELSON

DONALDSON, ROBERT THOMAS (1851-1936), politician and inspector of Aborigines, was born in January 1851 in County Westmeath, Ireland, son of Thomas Willett Donaldson, farmer, and his wife Barbara, née Shafgotch. Brought to Australia by his family about 1863, in the 1860s and 1870s he worked on stations, and prospected and explored in northern and central Queensland. He visited Britain in 1878 and on returning to Queensland became an inspector of railway construction. On 25 July 1882 at St Patrick's Catholic Church, Sydney, he married Edith Meek.

Moving to New South Wales, Donaldson became contractor's manager for McSharry & Co. for the construction of the Cootamundra-Gundagai railway line in 1883. He settled in Tumut where he bought a butcher's business. An alderman on the Tumut Municipal Council, he was mayor in 1897 and 1898.

As an independent, Donaldson was elected to the Legislative Assembly for Tumut in July 1898. Re-elected as a Progressive in 1901, he represented Wynyard from 1904, as an independent Liberal from 1907. He lost his seat in 1913 after a redistribution. In parliament Donaldson spoke on a narrow range of issues – railways, roads, sheepstealing, travelling stock, country schools and land settlement. He often pressed country interests against the city, and opposed the enfranchisement of women. He also expressed racist views about Chinese and Indian itinerant hawkers and about Aboriginals. On several occasions he vigorously defended some person or official whom he felt had suffered an injustice: in September 1912 he introduced a controver-

sial private member's bill to force the readmission of R. D. Meagher [q.v.] as a solicitor. He was a member of the Parliamentary Standing Committee on Public Works and from 1906 a member of the Board of Fisheries.

Interested in Aboriginals from his Queensland experiences, Donaldson devoted much energy to the Board for the Protection of Aborigines, to which he had been appointed on 14 December 1904. He helped the board to draft a bill increasing its powers in the control of Aboriginals, which was finally enacted in 1909. In its reports the board expressed concern about the rapidly increasing numbers of part-Aboriginals living on its reserves, whom it described as idle and 'a positive menace to the State'. It aimed to remove young Aboriginals from their kin on reserves to be trained at special, segregated children's homes, and boarded out or placed in 'apprenticeships' as farm labourers or in domestic service.

Donaldson resigned from the board when he was appointed on 1 October 1915, in controversial circumstances, to its staff as one of the first inspectors of Aboriginals. He travelled throughout the State, inspecting all Aboriginal stations and reserves; he reported on local management and attended to such technical and maintenance matters as windmills, engines and water supplies. Sincerely believing in the policy, he was responsible for implementing the programme of removing 'orphan and neglected' children from their Aboriginal families for training and apprenticeships. As the board's agent with absolute power to inspect Aboriginal homes and remove children, he was feared and hated by two generations of Aboriginals throughout New South Wales. In particular he was never forgiven for the raid on Cumeroogunga Aboriginal station in 1919. In his sixties he 'was a big man, powerfully built, six feet tall, with broad shoulders and barrel chest supporting his short thick neck, ... and a large jaw, thick and round as a Soccer ball'.

Donaldson retired on 31 May 1929; he died at his home at Randwick, Sydney, on 5 August 1936 and was cremated with Anglican rites. He was survived by his wife, four sons and a daughter.

J. Horner, *Vote Ferguson for Aboriginal freedom* (Syd, 1974); *SMH*, 8 Aug 1936.

PHILIP FELTON

DONALDSON, ST CLAIR GEORGE ALFRED (1863-1935), Anglican archbishop, was born on 11 February 1863 in London, third son of Sir Stuart Alexander Donaldson [q.v.4] and his wife Amelia, née Cowper. He

attended Eton and was foundation scholar
at Trinity College, Cambridge, where he
graduated B.A. in 1885 with a first-class in
classics; in 1887 he gained a first in theology.
After training for the ministry at Wells
Theological College, he was ordained deacon in 1888 and priest in 1889, was briefly
curate at Bethnal Green, resident chaplain
to the archbishop of Canterbury, E. W.
Benson, in 1888-91, and headed the Eton
Mission at Hackney Wick in 1891-1900.
President of the London Junior Missionary
Association, he then travelled in South
Africa, India and Ceylon, and was rural dean
of Hornsey in 1902-04. Chosen by the archbishop of Canterbury, R. T. Davidson, to
succeed W. T. T. Webber [q.v.] as bishop of
Brisbane, and enthroned there in December
1904, he became the first archbishop of
Brisbane next year when the dioceses in
Queensland and New Guinea were formed
into a province. He held this office until 1921,
his stature and influence helping to make his
province the most cohesive in Australia.

Donaldson's eminence was as a farsighted
all-round churchman. Aiming at making
Brisbane 'the Antioch of Australia', the
jumping-off ground for missionary endeavours, he extended the Bush Brotherhood scheme, reorganized the church missionary societies, and showed particular
solicitude for Aboriginals. Yarrabah Aboriginal Mission was one of many institutions
to benefit from his private generosity (£3000
in 1918). He gave impetus to the building of
St John's Cathedral in Brisbane, and to the
crusade (successful in the 1910 referendum)
for religious teaching in state schools. He
was a member of the Senate of the University of Queensland in 1916-21 and was largely responsible for establishing St John's
College. Nundah Theological College (later
St Francis) began in 1907 and by 1921 over
two-thirds of Brisbane's clergy were Aus-
tralian-trained. He was a strong advocate of
autonomy for the Australian Church.

The Church's impact he believed should
be widespread: 'Go for the enemy's stronghold. The Queensland Club: the Trades Hall:
the Race-course'. He directed attention to
the underlying moral causes of industrial
unrest and the 'inward spiritual significance
of the Labour movement', and offered to
mediate in the 1912 Brisbane strike. He improved inter-church relations, especially
with the Greek Orthodox Church, but in
February 1917, contrary to his usual detachment from sectarianism, he responded
when challenged by Archbishop Duhig
[q.v.] and gave examples of Roman Catholic
actions he considered detrimental to national unity. Emphasizing that Christian
patriotism demanded sacrifice, and that the
financial burden of the war was falling on the

wealthy while the workers were getting
richer, he supported conscription. He sponsored the building of St Martin's Hospital as
a war memorial and promoted the League of
Nations, criticizing Hughes's [q.v.] scep-
ticism towards it.

Donaldson's intensely religious personal
life was marked by evangelical simplicity,
but his essential catholicism told against
him in elections for the Australian primacy
(1909) and the archbishopric of Melbourne
(1921). Although not a quick thinker he
could be a powerful preacher. Perhaps the
bulk of the laity 'were slow to catch fire from
his own burning zeal', as the archbishop of
Canterbury, C. G. Lang, wrote of him later,
but Donaldson exerted a lasting influence on
many of his clergy, particularly those on
whom he most relied such as de Witt Batty
[q.v.7] and H. F. Le Fanu [q.v.]. A bachelor of
striking presence, considerable charm and
humour, he inspired deep affection in those
who knew him well, but his fundamental
reserve occasionally made him seem aloof
and he was most at ease in the upper strata of
society. Lord Chelmsford [q.v.7], with whom
he shared a love of music, was a close friend.
He returned several times to England and
received the honorary degrees of D.D. from
Cambridge in 1904 and Oxford in 1920, and
of D.C.L. from Durham in 1908.

From 1921 until his death there on 7
December 1935 Donaldson was bishop of
Salisbury, England, where an original feature of his episcopate was the attention paid
to educated people detached from the
Church. He was appointed prelate of the
Order of St Michael and St George in 1933.
Again much of his effort was concentrated
on missionary work; he was chairman of the
Missionary Council in 1921-33. Donaldson
retained Australian friendships and interests, and helped in the choice of J. W. C.
Wand [q.v.] as archbishop of Brisbane. His
estate of £48544, left mainly to relatives,
included bequests of £4000 to endowment
funds in Brisbane. The notes he left of his
daily thoughts and prayers were posthumously published as *A meditation on the Acts
of the Apostles* (London, 1937).

C. T. Dimont and F. de Witt Batty, *St. Clair
Donaldson* (Lond, 1939); *PD* (Qld), 1912, p 263;
British A'sian, 27 July 1916; *Worker* (Brisb), 2 Mar
1912; *Daily Mail* (Brisb), 27 Feb 1917; *SMH*, 13 Oct
1921, 29 Jan 1923, 13 Dec 1935; *Queenslander*, 25
June, 23 Aug 1934; *Courier Mail*, 9 Dec 1935; *The
Times*, 9, 11, 12 Dec 1935; K. Rayner, The history
of the Church of England in Queensland (Ph.D.
thesis, Univ Qld, 1962).   BETTY CROUCHLEY

DONNELLY, JOHN FRANCIS (1885-
1962), soldier, grazier and auctioneer, was
born on 28 June 1885 at Bywong station,

Gundaroo, New South Wales, son of Patrick Joseph Bede Donnelly, grazier, and his wife Aimée Stewart, née Massey. He was educated at St Patrick's College, Goulburn, and returned to the family property. At 19 he enlisted in the local militia, the 3rd Light Horse Regiment, and in November 1905 was commissioned second lieutenant in the unit (now the 7th Light Horse). Promoted lieutenant in 1908, he resigned two years later to join the permanent staff of the Australian Military Forces as a staff sergeant major. He served as an instructor in Eastern Command (New South Wales) until World War I.

On 1 September 1914 Donnelly was appointed to the Australian Imperial Force as a regimental quartermaster sergeant with 1st Division headquarters. He embarked for Egypt that month and reached Gallipoli on 28 June 1915 but within a week was slightly wounded and evacuated. He returned to Anzac and was commissioned as a second lieutenant in the 9th Battalion on 4 August. Because of his administrative ability he remained a platoon commander for only two months, and in October was promoted lieutenant and posted to 2nd Division headquarters as an aide-de camp and camp commandant. After the evacuation from Gallipoli he filled several staff appointments until 14 March 1916, when he was promoted captain and transferred to the 2nd Pioneer Battalion as adjutant. He embarked for France that month and until the Armistice remained with the 2nd Pioneers; he became a company commander in February 1917 and was promoted major in March. His unit was frequently in the firing line, either building defence works or taking part in offensives. On 3 May 1917, during the 2nd battle of Bullecourt, he commanded several of the battalion's companies while they dug a 1150 yard (1050 m) communication trench from the railway near Bullecourt to the Hindenburg line. Working under heavy shell-fire and continuously hampered by carrying parties using the half-dug trench, they completed the task in seven hours. C. E. W. Bean [q.v.7] considered this 'one of the finest achievements of the Australian pioneers'. Donnelly was wounded next day but remained on duty; he was awarded the Distinguished Service Order in the King's Birthday honours in June and was also mentioned in dispatches three times during the war.

On 17 February 1919 he was promoted lieut-colonel and commanded the 1st Pioneer Battalion from then until its disbandment. Donnelly returned to Australia in July and his A.I.F. appointment ended in November when he also took his discharge from the A.M.F. in the rank of warrant officer. He returned to Bungendore, New

South Wales, and became an auctioneer. In 1923 he married Ellen Margaret Cranney at Queanbeyan. Having rejoined the militia as a major in the 7th Light Horse Regiment, he commanded the unit in 1922-28. He was awarded the Volunteer Officers' Decoration in 1931, and was placed on the retired list with the honorary rank of colonel in 1941. In the late 1950s he moved to Canberra where, survived by his wife, a son and two daughters, he died of cancer on 18 September 1962 and was buried in Canberra cemetery with Catholic rites.

C. E. W. Bean, *The A.I.F. in France*, 1917 (Syd, 1933); *London Gazette*, 2 Jan, 4 June, 23 July 1917, 11 July 1919; *Pastoral Review*, 16 Aug 1918; records (AWM).   K. R. WHITE

DONOHOE, JAMES JOSEPH (c. 1860-1925), horse-trainer, was born in Cavan, Ireland, son of Patrick Donohoe, farmer, and his wife Mary, née Smith. About 1870, probably with a brother, he came to South Australia. For a time he was in Melbourne, but by 1885 was a coach and cab proprietor in Sydney. On 15 February 1887 at St Francis Xavier Catholic Church, Wollongong, he married Catherine McDonough, Australian-born of Irish parents. After moving around the city and Redfern areas, by 1894 the Donohoes were in Kensington, heartland of Sydney's horse-racing, living for many years near a side-entrance to Randwick racecourse. Racing was decidedly their game.

Jim Donohoe's stamping-grounds were not the upper echelons of the sport, however, but the pony tracks, where he was closely associated with John Wren and (Sir) James Joynton Smith [qq.v.]. Also connected with trotting, he had been prominent in the Sydney Driving Park. When Joynton Smith set out to establish a new racecourse at Zetland, he choose Donohoe, 'as loyal a soul as ever lived', to supervise its building, and thereafter to be its manager. Victoria Park opened on 15 January 1908, the most modern of the pony tracks.

A big man, with a genial Irish nature, Donohoe was a popular figure on racecourses in Sydney, and also in Melbourne where he was a frequent visitor for important meetings. Barely literate, but no prodigal, he was a shrewd gambler, and his wife invested windfalls in semi-detached cottages. Survived by her and by five sons, John Aloysius (1888-1967), James (1891-1959), William Patrick (1894-1954), Francis Patrick (1898-1973) and Charles Joseph (1902-1973), Donohoe died of cancer at his home in Doncaster Avenue on 19 February 1925, and was buried in Waverley cemetery after a requiem Mass. Among the mourners were Wren, who had come especially from Melbourne, and Joynton Smith.

WILLIAM PATRICK was born on 26 March 1894 at Surry Hills. Educated at the convent school, Kensington, he began work in 1908 at Joynton Smith's Arcadia Hotel. In 1910 he became a clerk at Victoria Park. John, like his father a trainer, won the Chelmsford [q.v.7] Stakes in 1915 with Garlin, owned by Wren. James junior, later chairman of stewards for the Australian Jockey Club, became stipendiary steward at Victoria Park, where, in January 1923, Bill was appointed secretary. The two youngest brothers received the better education, at Christian Brothers' College, Waverley. Frank served articles and was admitted as a solicitor on 30 October 1930. Charles, a leading tennis-player, became a caterer. Meanwhile, Bill had become a director of Stadiums Ltd in 1928 and manager of Canterbury velodrome in 1929. In 1933 he was managing director of the former, and brought such boxers as Archie Moore to Sydney. Bill was also managing director of Victoria Park (until it was sold for a motor vehicle factory) and of the Arcadia and Carrington hotel companies. In 1950 he was a director of "Truth" and "Sportsman" Ltd. Frank, Wren's friend and legal representative in Sydney, was a director of Stadiums Ltd, Smiths Newspapers Ltd and Australian Cyanamid, chairman of Comeng Holdings Ltd, and, with Bill, a trustee of Joynton Smith's will.

In 1952 the Donohoes pulled off a spectacular and profitable *coup*, when Prelate, part-owned by Frank and trained by John, won four races in a row, culminating in the Doncaster. Survived by two daughters of his marriage on 6 March 1926 to Elizabeth Josephine Dwyer, Bill died at Kensington of heart disease on 6 August 1954. One of Frank's sons was mayor of Woollahra in 1980. In three generations the Donohoes had progressed, via the race track and the boxing ring, from battling Irish migrants to wealthy respectability. They were those rarest of mortals — racehorse fanciers who won.

J. Joynton Smith, *My life story* (Syd, 1927); *PP* (NSW), 1923, 3, p 1333; *Referee*, 22 Jan 1908, 3 Jan 1923, 25 Feb 1925; *SMH*, 22 Feb 1925, 7 Aug 1954; information from Mr F. P. and Miss K. Donohoe, Vaucluse, Sydney.   CHRIS CUNNEEN

DONOVAN, THOMAS JOSEPH (1843-1929), benefactor, was born on 26 April 1843 in Sydney, son of Jeremiah Donovan, merchant, and his wife Mary, née Dolan. Educated at St Mary's Seminary, at W. T.

Cape's [q.v.1] school, and at Sydney Grammar School, Donovan worked for the Bank of Australasia until 1872. After a short and successful period as a vigneron at Albury he settled in Europe, where for twenty-five years he wintered in the Mediterranean and spent the summer months in England. He studied law but, although admitted in 1884 to the Middle Temple in London and to the New South Wales Bar, never seems to have practised. He also commenced the study of Elizabethan drama which led him to edit *English historical plays* (2v. 1896) and *The Falstaff plays of William Shakespeare* (1925); to write *The true text of Shakespeare and his fellow playwrights* (1923); and to collect the fine library centred on Shakespeare and his contemporaries which was presented to the University of Sydney in 1926. As an editor Donovan conformed to a nineteenth-century tradition which permitted the bowdlerization of the text.

Around 1900 Donovan retired to New South Wales and lived as a gentleman at Darling Point. Little is known of him until 1914, when an endowment of £30 000 to St John's College, University of Sydney, was announced; the money went instead in 1915 towards the foundation of Newman College at the University of Melbourne, in the form of bursaries there for the children of members of the Australian Imperial Force. Among other benefactions were the erection of a chapel for the Marist Brothers at Mount St Gregory near Campbelltown, the gift of land for a farm school for boys in the same area, and in 1923 the establishment of the Donovan Trust for the promotion of astronomical education in Australia. The trust has operated since 1925, providing funds for lectures, medals, bursaries and prizes.

A bachelor, Donovan died at Darling Point on 12 January 1929 and was buried in the Catholic section of Waverley cemetery; he was survived by a sister and a brother. His estate was sworn for probate at £30 854; under the terms of his will, it was to be invested in Commonwealth government stock for eight years and then offered to the Abbot of Downside, Bath, England, for the establishment of a Benedictine school for boys in New South Wales or the Federal Capital Territory. The offer was declined, and the bequest passed instead to the Sisters of Mercy at Goulburn for the establishment of a hospital for women and children at Cootamundra.

British Astronomical Assn (NSW branch), *Bulletin*, 1932, no 113; Univ Melb, *Calendar*, 1980; *T&CJ*, 20 May 1914; *Argus*, 6 Jan 1916; *SMH*, 2, 3 Nov 1923, 5 June, 25 Sept 1926, 2 July 1927, 15 Jan, 11 July, 12 Sept 1929; information from Assoc Prof A. G. Little, Univ Syd.   B. G. ANDREWS

DOOLETTE, SIR GEORGE PHILIP (1840-1924) and his son DORHAM LONGFORD (1872-1925), were mining entrepreneurs. George was born on 24 January 1840 at Sandford, near Dublin, son of George Dorham Doolette and his wife Eliza, née Raynard. The family migrated to South Australia in 1855 in the *Nashwauk*. Doolette, with some experience in the softgoods trade in Ireland, eventually joined the firm of A. Macgeorge & Co., Adelaide, later becoming sole proprietor. He was a foundation member of the South Australian Chamber of Manufactures in 1869 and from 1874 owner of a tailoring and outfitting business, briefly at Moonta, and then in King William Street, Adelaide.

Like other Adelaide businessmen, Doolette speculated in the 1880s in Broken Hill and other mining ventures. He also had interests in pastoral properties, establishing a partnership with Philip Charley. In 1893, with (Sir) George Brookman [q.v.7] and others, he formed the Adelaide Prospecting Party, which dispatched W. G. Brookman [q.v.7] and S. W. Pearce [q.v.] to Western Australia – their mineral claims were at the heart of the later Golden Mile at Kalgoorlie. The syndicate was reconstructed as the Coolgardie Gold Mining and Prospecting Co. (W.A.) Ltd, but a desperate need for finance forced it to send Doolette, a director, to London. Arriving in March 1894 during a temporary investing slump, he needed the help of the financier John Waddington to float off the Great Boulder and other claims. Doolette remained in London as mining promoter and administrator though his role was not without question in Australia. Chairman of the Western Australian Mineowners' Association and of several companies, including the Great Boulder Proprietary Gold Mines Ltd and Oroya Brown Hill Co. Ltd, and director of the Sons of Gwalia Ltd, he dined regularly at the City Liberal Club with Lionel and W. S. Robinson [qq.v.] and William Clark, the great promoters of Australian mines. He also financed various of his son's explorations. Doolette was received with acclaim in Kalgoorlie in 1907 but thereafter his contacts with Australia were less direct. During World War I he took an active interest in the Australian Red Cross Society and in hospital facilities for Australian soldiers, and was knighted in 1916.

In South Australia, Doolette had been a supporter of philanthropic causes. A justice of the peace from 1887, he was vice-president of the Young Men's Christian Association in 1884-85, treasurer of the London Missionary Society and in 1885-86 president of the Congregational Union. In England he became a fellow of the Royal Colonial Institute (1894) and of the Royal Geographical Society (1907). He owned a fine estate at Caterham, Surrey, where he was keenly interested in flower-growing. His first wife Mary Bartlett McEwin, whom he had married on 9 November 1865 with Presbyterian forms at Glen Ewin, Highercombe, South Australia, had died in 1890; she was survived by her son Dorham and a daughter. On 25 September 1895 in Birmingham Doolette married Fanny Lillie Robinson (d. 1916), daughter of the noted Congregational clergyman R. W. Dale [q.v.4]. Doolette died on 19 January 1924 at Caterham, leaving an estate valued for probate at £10 186. His ashes were taken to Adelaide for interment in North Road cemetery.

Dorham Doolette, born on 20 May 1872 in Adelaide, was an able student at Whinham College and at the University of Adelaide where in 1888 he began an arts and in 1893 a medical course. He abandoned his studies to follow the gold rush to Western Australia. As a working prospector 'Dorrie' became a fine bushman and gained extensive knowledge of practical gold-mining. He joined the disastrous Siberia and Kurnalpi rushes and several times saw friends die of typhoid. As a pioneer of Kalgoorlie he pegged out the rich Golden Horseshoe, Golden Link, Boulder Central and Chaffer's mines for the Adelaide syndicate. In 1895, prospecting with Charles Northmore in the Niagara district, he discovered the Challenge and Golden Monarch mines; the proceeds of their sale provided him with a trip to England.

On his return Doolette traversed the North Coolgardie field and the Collie coalfield; he made no important finds and in December 1897 was declared bankrupt. Next year he visited the Northern Territory Arltunga field but again returned to Western Australia where, for several years, he was field examiner for Great Boulder No.1 Ltd. In 1905 he became manager of the Never Never mine at Southern Cross and in 1908 manager of Great Boulder's St George Mine at Mount Magnet. He continued to finance prospectors to look for gold for him and in April 1910 one of them, Charles Jones, reported a promising find in the Yilgarn district, about 22 miles (35 km) from Southern Cross. The first crushing yielded 5½ ounces to the ton; three months later this had doubled and by November had reached 21 ounces to the ton. Doolette, owner with Vincent Shallcross, floated the mine in London as the Bullfinch Proprietary (W.A.) Ltd, with G. P. Doolette as chairman.

Now a rich man, Dorham Doolette enjoyed his wealth. He bought a string of racehorses for his stud at Broadford, Victoria. He was generous and gregarious and his friends appreciated his sense of humour. In England in 1911 to promote the Bullfinch he was welcomed as a man of charm and culture; his bush ballads had been published in the *Bulletin* and the Kalgoorlie *Sun* under the pen-name of 'The Prodigal'. But the Bullfinch, rich on the surface, failed to fulfil its early promise, and his prosperity began to decline. He also suffered a personal tragedy when his wife, Adeline Navera, née Weeks, whom he had married on 18 May 1910 at All Saints Church of England, Mount Magnet, Western Australia, died in 1917 aged 31. On 8 May 1920 at Claremont he married her sister, Edna Isabelle.

Doolette died of chronic renal disease on 1 December 1925 in Perth, survived by his wife and their son and by a son and daughter of the first marriage to whom he had been an excellent father. In an obituary the *Bulletin* described him as the promoter of the 'outrageously over-capitalized' Bullfinch; but a better measure of his influence may be gained from the claim of the Melbourne *Argus* that he had 'formed more prospecting syndicates than any other man' in the history of Western Australia.

W. B. Kimberly (ed), *History of West Australia* (Melb, 1897); J. J. Pascoe (ed), *History of Adelaide and vicinity* (Adel, 1901); J. S. Battye (ed), *Cyclopedia of Western Australia*, 2 (Adel, 1913); *British A'sian*, 3 Nov 1910, 12 Jan, 9 Feb, 2 Mar 1911; *Western Mail* (Perth), 5, 19 Nov 1910, 9 Dec 1911, 30 Mar 1912, 24 Jan 1924; *Advertiser* (Adel), 29 Feb 1896, 22 Jan 1924; *Observer* (Adel), 28 Aug 1897, 5 Dec 1925; *Register* (Adel), 2 Sept 1899, 21, 22 Jan 1924; *Western Argus*, 24 May 1900, 22 Jan, 5 Feb 1907, 5 Feb 1924; *The Times*, and *West Australian*, 21 Jan 1924; *Argus*, 3 Dec 1925; *Bulletin*, 10 Dec 1925; *Countryman* (Perth), 13 May 1965.

R. M. GIBBS
A. McLEARY

DOOLEY, JAMES THOMAS (1877-1950), politician, was born on 26 April 1877 at Carrick Crean, Longford, Ireland, fourth son of Thomas Dooley, farmer and gardener, and his wife Elizabeth, née O'Connor. On 1 August 1885, in the *Dorunda*, the family arrived in Brisbane, where, after attending a state school, at 12 Jim began work as a draper's assistant; later he was apprenticed to a tailor and attended technical college evening classes, joining the college literary and debating society, to which his future wife, a millinery instructor, also belonged, and the Labor Party. About 1901 he came to New South Wales and worked at Cobar and other outback towns including Lithgow, where he set up as a tailor. On 21 February 1905 at Paddington registry office he married Kate Rodé Trundle.

His business flourishing, Dooley became president of the Lithgow branch of the Labor Party, and in September 1907 narrowly defeated the sitting Liberal for the State seat of Hartley; he became the youngest member of the assembly — a 10-stone (63 kg) stripling. Subsequently his majorities, and his girth, increased: by 1921 he was 16 stone (101 kg). From 1920 he represented Bathurst. A keen amateur Shakespearian actor and performer of comic songs, he was an eloquent platform speaker and an effective debater in the assembly, 'bubbling over with good humour'. He belonged to the Federated Clothing Trades. During World War I he opposed conscription, and in October 1916 was one of the twenty party members who remained in the party when W. A. Holman [q.v.] and others were expelled. Next month caucus elected Dooley as deputy-leader to Ernest Durack [q.v.] and on the latter's resignation in February 1917, as deputy to John Storey [q.v.]. It was later asserted that Dooley had been elected leader in 1917 but unselfishly stood down in favour of Storey, who, seeking unanimous support, would not submit to a contest. At his own expense Dooley visited the United States of America in 1919 with his friend T. D. Mutch [q.v.] to study state industrial undertakings and labour conditions.

In April 1920 Labor narrowly won office and Dooley became chief secretary and minister for housing; he was responsible for State enterprises, including brickworks and fishing trawlers, as well as the police force. In November internal party strains became public, particularly involving Dooley on one side and Jack Bailey [q.v.7] and J. J. G. McGirr [q.v.] on the other. Bribery allegations against Dooley, instigated by Bailey, were rejected by R. D. Pring's [q.v.] royal commission. During Storey's absences, on a visit to England in January to July 1921, and during his recurrent bouts of illness, Dooley acted as premier. On Storey's death Dooley took over on 8 October 1921, defeating McGirr, who became deputy-leader. Even the *Sydney Morning Herald* regarded the new premier's conscientiousness and industry as unquestionable.

The government was defeated on 13 December after Speaker (Sir) Daniel Levy [q.v.] stood down. Refused a dissolution by Governor Davidson [q.v.] Dooley resigned, but the Fuller [q.v.] ministry of 21 December lasted only 7 hours and Davidson recommissioned Dooley. A dispute between the premier and McGirr, with the latter publicly attacking 'Dooleyism', chiefly over an early election, added to the government's factional troubles. After a bitter campaign, shadowed by the Sister Ligouri [q.v. Bridget Partridge] affair, with Labor categorized as

'Rome-ridden from A to Z', Fuller won the March 1922 election.

Moderate and honest, the Storey-Dooley government had seen the motherhood endowment bill stalled in the Legislative Council during its last confused months of office. But it had enacted important legislation on arbitration, profiteering and price control, had appointed (Sir) George Beeby [q.v.7] as a judge of the industrial court and had inaugurated the Rural Bank department of the Government Savings Bank. It had also provided financial assistance to Henry Lawson [q.v.]. Dooley had been a driving but moderating force, earning some dissatisfaction for an apparent toleration of a high rate of unemployment and a refusal to go beyond W. Edmunds's [q.v.] recommendations regarding employment for the 1917 strikers. The ministry's defeat through sectarian political expediency reflected against its opponents rather than itself; as the governor discerned, 'it left office with untarnished honour and with the respect of the community'.

Political defeat was followed by a struggle for power within the New South Wales Labor Party. In December, with Matt Charlton [q.v.7] and Albert Gardiner [q.v.], Dooley circularized to Labour Leagues and unions a proposal to reform the party's State organization. Summoned by the Australian Workers' Union-dominated executive, Dooley denied that he had imputed any corruption. But the power-struggle continued and in February 1923 the executive censured Dooley for the appointment (eighteen months earlier) of J. B. Suttor to the Legislative Council. Dooley reacted by alleging that the executive was dominated by 'a gang of uncouth crooks' and was expelled; the executive then elected McGirr leader of the State Labor caucus. But a majority of caucus pledged support for Dooley. The Federal executive intervened and appointed W. F. Dunn [q.v.] as temporary leader, but at the State conference in June, when Bailey was himself expelled, Dooley was reinstated. His effectiveness during this turmoil was hampered by a severe ankle injury, involving periods of hospitalization. During the negotiations J. T Lang [q.v.] acted as his organizer.

On 1 August, dispirited by internal disloyalty and without any real power base in the new executive, now dominated by A. C. Willis [q.v.], Dooley resigned as leader and was replaced by Lang. When Labor returned to power in June 1925, Dooley was elected Speaker; he extended the rights of private members, but an attempt to safeguard salaries of parliamentary officers was blocked by Lang. In 1927 Dooley lost preselection for Hartley to a miners' nominee,

possibly through Lang's influence. But he had long lived outside his mining electorate, at Bronte, and always lacked significant union support. He tried his hand at hotel-broking and management at Leura and Lithgow, but was not successful. As an independent Labor candidate he failed for the Senate in 1931 and next year for the State seat of Hartley. He was for a time in Brisbane, but by June 1940, back in Sydney, was reduced to accepting a £4 per week allowance from the Mair [q.v.] government. In September he opposed W. M. Hughes [q.v.] for North Sydney, and again lost.

'Genial, generous, Pickwickian in appearance', in his youth Dooley had enjoyed surfing and bush-walking, particularly in the Blue Mountains. But he was not a patron of sport. In the 'twenties he took to dancing and 'acquired some note as a jazzer'. His wife had died in 1936, and on 16 March 1946 at St Pius Catholic Church, Enmore, he married Irene Mary Kenney, a dressmaker. After a stroke he was admitted to the State hospital, Liverpool, in October 1948. Survived by his wife and by the son and daughter of his first marriage, Dooley died on 2 January 1950 and was buried in the Catholic section of Botany cemetery.

J. T. Lang, *I remember* (Syd, 1956); G. N. Hawker, *The parliament of New South Wales 1856-1965* (Syd, 1971); V. G. Kelly, *A man of the people* (Syd, 1971); H. Radi and P. Spearritt (eds) *J. T. Lang* (Syd, 1977); *SMH*, 12 Apr, 15, 17, 18 Nov, 25 Dec 1920, 10 Oct, 17 Dec 1921, 18 Jan, 30 Dec 1922, 24, 26 Feb, 2, 10, 14, 16, 23 Mar, 28 June, 1 Aug 1923; *Aust Worker*, 15 Apr 1920, 13 June 1923; *Freeman's J*, 15 Apr 1920; *Daily Telegraph* (Syd), 10 Oct 1921; CO 418/220.25199 folio 40-42.

CHRIS CUNNEEN

DOOLEY, JOHN BRAIDWOOD (1883-1961), trade union organizer and senator, was born on 11 November 1883 at Tumbarumba, New South Wales, son of John Dooley, labourer and unionist, and his wife Sarah Anne, née Harvey. Educated at Wagga Wagga Superior Public School and at Courabyra, Dooley worked at an early age as a shearer and miner. In 1898 he supported the fight against wage reductions at the Adelong Gibraltar gold mine and in 1901-04, as an organizer of the Rural Workers' Union, was involved in shearing disputes. He became converted to the conciliation and arbitration system.

In 1910 Dooley, then a labourer on the Sydney railways, organized the tramway permanent way employees into the Railway Workers' and General Labourers' Association. He was honorary secretary of the Tramway Permanent Way section of the union for three years and an assessor on the

Tramway (Permanent Way) Wages Board. He aided the entry of the association into the Australian Workers' Union in 1916 as the Railway Workers' Industry branch, and that year was elected its Newcastle district organizer. He became president of the Lambton No-Conscription Council and for two years was a member of the New South Wales central executive of the Australian Labor Party. President of the Railway Workers' Industry branch in 1919 and 1920, Dooley was an organizer in 1918-20 and a delegate to several Australian Labor Party conferences, Australian Workers' Union conventions and the 1921 All-Australian Trade Union Congress in Melbourne. However, he lost his bids to become secretary in 1921 and 1922 and to regain his presidency in 1923.

Failing to establish a business of his own, Dooley continued as a labourer until he became works foreman for the New South Wales Water Conservation and Irrigation Commission in the Murrumbidgee Irrigation Area. While in charge of concreting work on the Burrinjuck Dam he formed the Burrinjuck branch of the Labor Party and was its president until 1925, when he was defeated in the Senate elections. Dooley then returned to Sydney where he was a successful A.W.U.-sponsored Senate candidate in 1928.

In parliament he spoke in favour of arbitration and the White Australia policy, and against the Transport Workers' Act (1928). He served on many parliamentary committees including the Joint Committee on Public Works. Deputy leader of the Senate in August-October 1929 and February-August 1932 he was assistant minister for works and railways from March 1931, aligning himself with the Scullin-Theodore [qq.v.] section of the party against the Lang [q.v.] faction. Towards the end of 1931 he administered the Department of Home Affairs. Defeated in the September 1934 elections, when the A.W.U. gave its support to the Lang group, Dooley retired from public life to earn his living as a works supervisor. He died on 2 August 1961 at St George Hospital, Kogarah, where he had been ill for some time. Survived by his wife Julia May Bourgoir, whom he had married on 11 January 1909 at the Tumut Roman Catholic Church, and by his six daughters and two of his three sons, Dooley was cremated after a state funeral. His estate was valued for probate at £2628.

Labor Daily, 26 Nov 1924, 10 Oct, 13 Nov 1928; *SMH*, 23 Mar, 1 Apr 1925, 6 Dec 1928, 4 Feb 1930, 3 Mar, 11 Sept 1931, 4 Aug 1961; *Aust Worker*, 12 Oct 1916, 1 Feb 1917, 30 Jan 1919, 29 Jan 1920, 20 Jan 1921, 2 Feb 1922, 24 Jan 1923, 14 Oct 1925, 11 Dec 1929.   ROBIN GOLLAN
                                                          MOIRA SCOLLAY

DOORLY, JAMES GERALD STOKELY (1880-1956), master mariner and author, was born on 4 June 1880 at Port of Spain, Trinidad, son of Rev. Wiltshire Stokely Doorly, later archdeacon of Trinidad, and his wife Jane Cumming, née Driggs. Gerald was educated at Queen's Royal College, Trinidad, and from 1894 in the Thames Nautical Training College, H.M.S. *Worcester*, for the mercantile marine. A fellow cadet and friend was E. R. G. R. Evans (later Admiral Lord Mountevans). Doorly graduated Queen's gold medallist in 1897, served his apprenticeship in sail and in 1901-02 did troop- and hospital-ship work with the Peninsular and Oriental Steam Navigation Co. in the South African War.

In 1902-04 Doorly and Evans served together as junior officers in the S.Y. *Morning*, the supply ship to Captain R. F. Scott's *Discovery* of the National Antarctic Expedition. Doorly was awarded the Polar Service medal for his work in the *Morning*, which freed the *Discovery* from her icebound anchorage.

Doorly had gained his mate's certificate in Hobart in December 1903 and his master's certificate in London a year later. After a few months with the West India Mail Service, in 1905 he joined the Union Steam Ship Co. of New Zealand; on 18 November 1908 at Knox Church, Dunedin, he married Forrestina (Ina) Muriel Whitson, daughter of the secretary of the company. Excellent seamanship and good management of men brought him command of the *Komata* in July 1911 and thereafter some twenty-three of the fleet's ships plying between Australian and New Zealand ports. During World War I he commanded New Zealand troop transports and Admiralty colliers, and in November 1917 survived the loss of his ship *Aparimo* by torpedo in the English Channel.

In November 1922 and January 1925 Doorly was involved in separate court cases settling union disputes arising from his shipping company's refusal to pay Australian award rates to men shipped in Australian ports. In June 1925 he left the company and went to Melbourne to join the Port Phillip Sea Pilots' Service. During World War II he brought troops and merchant convoys through the Rip. He retired in 1945.

Doorly's admission to the élite pilots' service is evidence of his outstanding ability as a master mariner. He was also gifted as a musician, singer and light composer: Evans testified that without Doorly, the men of the *Morning* and *Discovery* would have been hard-pushed to survive the disappointments and long voyages of the Antarctic expedition. In 1943 Doorly published in Melbourne his *Songs of the 'Morning'*, with words by J. P. Morrison set to Doorly's music.

Doorly also published an account of the 1902-04 expedition to show that Scott's life was as worthy of fame as his heroic death. In *The handmaiden of the navy* (1919) and *In the wake* (1937) he publicized the important work done by the merchant navy, particularly its war-time contribution. He also wrote short stories and articles for *Blackwood's Magazine*, the Sydney *Bulletin* and the Melbourne *Argus* and *Herald*. Doorly was a member of the International P.E.N. Club (Melbourne) and the Bread and Cheese Club (1938-56), and in 1945-46 edited the (*Annual*) *Dog Watch*, the journal of the Shiplovers' Society. He was also in demand as a lecturer to community groups in Melbourne.

Doorly's first wife died in August 1933; on 29 December 1934 in Melbourne he married a divorcee, Bertha Lutzia Wildman, née Webber. About 1951 he moved to New Zealand; he died in Wellington on 3 November 1956, survived by his second wife and two daughters of his first marriage.

H. W. Malloch, *Fellows all* (Melb, 1943); Shiplovers' Soc of Vic, *Annual Dog Watch*, 1945, 1946, 1948; *Bohemia*, 12 (1957), no 7; R. H. Croll papers (LaTL); MSS cats, *and* uncat MSS 1858 (ML).

JILL EASTWOOD

DORRINGTON, ALBERT (1874?-1953), author and journalist, was born probably on 27 September 1874 at Fulham, London, son of William Dorrington, policeman, and his wife Hannah, née Byford. He was educated at King Edward's School, Birmingham. When he was about 16 he 'drifted' to Australia where, after brief stays in Melbourne and Adelaide, he travelled through the German settlements in South Australia; in Queensland, the Torres Strait, and Palmerston (Darwin); and in outlying western New South Wales, supporting himself through canvassing and other jobs. Germans, Chinese, Kanakas, Afghans and Japanese, often unpleasantly perceived, populate much of his fiction. In 1899 Dorrington settled at Waitara, Sydney, where he lived with Leonora Anderson, who bore him several daughters. For seven years he replated silverware for a Pitt Street company.

Dorrington started writing for the *Bulletin* in the late 1890s, often as 'A.D.' or 'Alba Dorian'. After 1900 he also contributed to such publications as the *Freeman's Journal*, the *Australian Worker*, *Steele Rudd's Magazine* and the *Bookfellow*. Among his close friends were James Dwyer and Victor Daley [qq.v.]; he perceived, ahead of his time, the literary sophistication of Joseph Furphy [q.v.]. A. G. Stephens [q.v.] promoted

Dorrington's early fiction, publishing *Castro's last sacrament, and other stories* (1900), and collaborating to write a romantic novel, *The lady Calphurnia royal*, serialized in the *Bookfellow* in 1907, and published in London in 1909. The two quarrelled bitterly for decades, first in Australia over personal matters, and later concerning arrangements for the novel's publication in Britain and the United States of America. Dorrington had left Australia in 1907, arguing that local conditions provided 'no opening'; that Australian critics neglected promising writers other than those of assured position; and that cheap English periodical literature had swamped the local market.

After visiting Ceylon, Dorrington settled near London, and published a misleading account of allegedly exotic colonial hardships as an orchardist, which Stephens in Australia exposed and derided. Later Stephens, Louis Becke and Randolph Bedford [qq.v.7] accused Dorrington of plagiarism; but in London he gained recognition for newspaper serials, in the *Daily Telegraph* and elsewhere, and for stories for the *Pall Mall Magazine* and other magazines. He remained a Fleet Street journalist, and published thirteen more volumes of fiction, including eight novels which were translated into five languages. In London he was acquainted with Joseph Conrad. Brought up a Roman Catholic, he became an atheist. He lived quietly, in his later years receiving little recognition, at Ruislip, Middlesex, England, where he died on 9 April 1953. He was survived by at least one daughter, but left his estate to Vera Maude Beasley in recognition of the 'generous way in which she rebuilt my house at Ickenham Road and installed every modern convenience at her own expense'.

An adventurous literary survivor, in whom financial need fostered a certain professional opportunism, Dorrington was at times unreliable and inaccurate as journalist and commentator; and in Britain he successfully tailored a substantial artistic talent to fit his pocket. In his best Australian stories, restraint and realism alleviate the artificiality of his plots. His depiction of bush life, which he saw as 'a joke flung against a tragedy', drew critical acclaim; 'A bush tanqueray', probably his most frequently anthologized story, was reprinted in the *Bulletin* centenary issue (1980). *Children of the cloven hoof* (London, 1911), one of his more serious novels, interestingly studies interactions amongst squatters, selectors and other representatives of pastoral life. His later popular fiction, much of which is set in or near Australia, relies heavily on sensationalism, mystery, romance and exotic settings.

Steele Rudd's Mag, Jan 1907; *Bookfellow*, 4 July, 15 Aug 1907, 1 Nov 1912; *Contemporary Review* (Lond), Aug 1912; *Bulletin*, 3 Nov 1900, 4 June 1930; A. G. Stephens papers, vol 3, *and* news-cuttings (ML).   KEN STEWART

DOUGLAS, ROGER (1894-1919), printer, soldier and aviator, was born on 5 June 1894 at Charters Towers, Queensland, son of Walter Douglas, miner, and his wife Alice, née Grattan. He was educated at a state school before commencing work on the *Northern Miner*, Charters Towers. Later he joined the *Townsville Daily Bulletin* as a linotype operator. A keen boxer, Douglas had been the lightweight and welterweight champion of Queensland. His mates acknowledged his prowess by nicknaming him 'Dodger'.

Before World War I Douglas served as a citizen soldier in the 1st Australian Garrison Artillery, then, after war broke out, spent six months on garrison duty at Thursday Island. On 11 May 1915 he enlisted in Brisbane as a private in the Australian Imperial Force, embarking late in June as a machine-gunner in the 25th Battalion. The 25th saw action on Gallipoli from 11 July 1915 until the evacuation; Douglas was promoted corporal, then sergeant in October.

In March 1916 the battalion was shipped to France and Douglas transferred to the 7th Machine-Gun Company. In an action at Pozières in early August, he 'rallied part of the infantry and guided them over the captured positions under heavy fire when they were without leaders and disorganized. He [then] helped materially to repel counterattacks'. His bravery was rewarded with a second lieutenant's commission and a Distinguished Conduct Medal. On 25 November he was promoted lieutenant.

On 28 December 1917 Douglas was awarded the Military Cross in recognition of his gallantry at Polygon Wood in September. He had left the Machine-Gun Company on 26 November to join the Australian Flying Corps. He began his training at Reading, England, in March 1918 and graduated as a pilot on 5 May. He never flew in combat but was appointed an instructor with the 5th Australian Training Squadron in England.

Douglas was still in England when the Australian government' announced in March 1919 that it would award a £10000 prize to the first Australian aviator to fly from Britain to Australia. He resolved to enter the contest. Lieutenant J. S. L. Ross from Moruya, New South Wales, was to be navigator and co-pilot of their 450 h.p. Alliance aircraft named 'Endeavour'. On 30 October, the day they hoped to set off, the plane suffered a minor crash which necessitated repairs to the chassis and body. That day Douglas had been cautious but confident about the flight when he stated that 'only a mishap ... will prevent us landing in Australia'. They finally took off from Hounslow near London, at 11.30 a.m. on 13 November after bad weather had delayed the departure. The plane had flown only six miles when it appeared to fall out of a cloud over Surbiton, enter a spin, then crash into an orchard and explode. Both men were killed. A verdict of accidental death was returned; the coroner refused to consider claims by Douglas's fiancée Mabel Woolley that the aircraft was not fully repaired until the night before departure, thus restricting Douglas's test-flying in the rebuilt machine to a mere five minutes. Douglas and Ross were buried with full military honours in Brookwood cemetery.

F. M. Cutlack, *The Australian Flying Corps* . . . *1914-18* (Syd, 1923); W. A. Carne, *In good company: 6th Australian Machine-Gun Company* . . . *1915-19* (Melb, 1937); *London Gazette*, 28 Dec 1917, 1 Jan 1918 (supp); *Sea, Land and Air*, Dec 1919; *Reveille* (Syd), May 1931; *Argus*, 11 Oct, 3, 15, 17, 21 Nov 1919; *The Times*, 17 Oct, 14, 18 Nov 1919; *SMH*, 1, 15, 21, 22 Nov 1919, 1 Jan, 13 Mar 1920; *Sun* (Syd), 14, 16 Nov 1919; *North Queensland Register*, 17 Nov 1919; file 12/11/4085 (AWM).

KEVIN J. FEWSTER

DOVE, FREDERICK ALLAN (1867-1913), soldier and teacher, was born on 21 December 1867 in Sydney, son of Daniel Dove, contractor, and Annie Bell. He became a pupil-teacher at Newtown Public School in 1883 and after graduating from Fort Street Training School in 1888 taught for the next eleven years at several Sydney primary schools, including Fort Street, Crown Street and Camperdown. His soldiering began in 1897 when he was commissioned second lieutenant in the 5th Infantry Regiment (Volunteers); he was promoted lieutenant in 1898 and captain in 1899.

After the South African War broke out Dove joined the New South Wales Infantry, the only infantry contingent recruited in the colony, as a lieutenant. His company joined the 1st Australian Regiment at Cape Town in December 1899 and for two months served with the Kimberley Relief Force. In February 1900 the company was converted to 'E' Squadron, New South Wales Mounted Rifles, and, commanded by Captain J. G. Legge [q.v.], accompanied Major General R. A. P. Clement's column via Colesberg to Norval's Pont, Orange River, and to Bloemfontein. Legge reported that on 22 February 'Lieutenant Dove did an excellent piece of scouting . . . with his division, and drove off the Boer patrols, thus rendering the advance of the guns possible'. Four days later Dove was slightly wounded at Maeder's Farm. Under Captain W. Holmes [q.v.] his unit then joined General (Sir) Ian Hamilton's column for operations at Pretoria and Diamond Hill.

In April, during the advance on Houtnek, Dove's successful reconnaissance of enemy positions and his command of a detachment which held an advanced post for a whole day earned Hamilton's praise. When Holmes was wounded at Diamond Hill on 12 June Dove was promoted captain and led 'E' Squadron in operations against De Wet and De La Rey in the Transvaal and northern Orange River Colony. For meritorious service in South Africa he was mentioned in dispatches and awarded the Distinguished Service Order. Lieut-Colonel De Lisle commented: 'On numerous occasions he has volunteered for dangerous undertakings at night. He is a wonderful scout, and on no single occasion has he failed to accomplish his objective, nor has he lost a man accompanying him'.

Dove returned with his unit to Sydney in January 1901. He resumed teaching at Barmedman, New South Wales, but enlisted again next year as captain and adjutant of the 3rd Battalion, Australian Commonwealth Horse. The battalion embarked on 2 April. Peace was only two months off, however, so by August, after brief service as a staff officer of the Australian Brigade at Newcastle, Natal, Dove was back in Sydney. After serving as a brevet major in the New South Wales Scottish Rifles he was made a captain on the reserve of officers in 1904. That year, on 27 December, at the Presbyterian church, Hill End, he married Adelaide Bryant; the marriage was dissolved on 21 April 1910 with Dove as petitioner and on 11 May he married Margaret Morrison Myles at the Presbyterian manse, Waverley.

In May 1906 Dove had joined the Permanent Forces as a captain on the Administrative and Instructional Staff; he became director of equipment at Army Headquarters, Melbourne, in August 1911 and in October was promoted major. Next January he was appointed president of the examination board for first appointment and transfer of Administrative and Instructional Staff, but illness prevented him from performing his duties after April 1912. Much respected, he died in Sydney Hospital on 9 December 1913 of paraplegia from hydatids of the spine. He was buried with Anglican rites in Waverley cemetery and was survived by his wife, a seven-year-old son from his first marriage and a two-year-old daughter.

Aust Defence Dept, *Official records of the Australian military contingents to the war in South Africa*, P. L. Murray ed (Melb, 1911); R. L. Wallace, *The Australians at the Boer War* (Canb, 1976); *London Gazette*, 16, 19 Apr 1901; *T&CJ*, 10, 17 Dec 1913; register of careers (history section, Education Dept, Syd).   Margot Z. Simington

DOWLING, EDWARD (1843-1912), public servant and Federationist, was born on 16 June 1843 in Sydney, son of Edward Dowling, painter, and his wife Jane, née Ruttle. After elementary education, in 1853 he entered the office of a Sydney merchant, transferring on 4 August 1856 to the Government Printing Office where he worked as office boy and compositor. From November 1872 he was reviser and from March 1882 accountant, compiling several statistical and descriptive publications.

Dowling was an early advocate of education for working-men: in 1861 he became honorary secretary of Sydney's first 'mutual improvement' group, which was associated with the Pitt Street Congregational Church. A vice-president of the Sydney Mechanics' School of Arts in 1869-83, he was mainly responsible for starting science classes there. In 1873 he moved for the establishment of a working-men's college and was chairman of its committee until 1883. He impressed the delegates with a paper on technical education at the first Inter-Colonial Trades' Union Congress, Sydney, in 1879. When the Board of Technical Education was set up in 1883 he became its full-time secretary and did most of the executive work involved in establishing the Sydney Technical College and its early branches. In 1887 Dowling's health broke down. While convalescing he visited England to inspect technical colleges; on his return he recommended starting day-time courses. He also tried to persuade the government to establish a technical university. When in 1889 the board was abolished and technical education made the direct responsibility of a cabinet minister, Dowling was allowed to retire from the public service on grounds of ill health.

At the time of his retirement Dowling was secretary of the New South Wales branch of the Australian Natives' Association; he now became a leader in its campaign for the Federation of the colonies. In January 1890 as a New South Wales delegate he attended the association's conference in Melbourne, and was then sent to North America to inquire into the working of federal institutions in the United States of America and Canada. He published *Australia and America in 1892: a contrast* (1893) and in 1896 a pamphlet, *Federation*.

When (Sir) Edmund Barton [q.v.7]

launched the Central Federation League in Sydney in June 1893 Dowling became joint secretary-treasurer with A. P. Canaway. After Canaway's resignation over policy differences in 1897 he became sole honorary secretary, and was secretary of the Australasian Federation League of New South Wales until it was dissolved in 1909. Despite his indifferent health he seldom missed a meeting and was an energetic and competent executive officer. In 1899 he was largely responsible for the financial management of the United Federal Executive, organized by Barton to mount a massive campaign for 'yes' in the referendum in New South Wales. The rules of the Australasian Federation League provided that it defend 'the Federal Union of Australia' after its attainment: Dowling took a particular interest in resisting attempts to have the Federal capital provisions of the Constitution abrogated.

From 1910 Dowling's principal interests were his membership of the Aborigines Protection Board and his occasional sittings on the Burwood bench of magistrates. He was, in the best sense of the term, a self-made man, one who by practising his belief in the virtues of self-help and study raised himself into the ranks of the middle classes without losing contact with his working-class origins. As the kind of man who makes a vocation of working for good causes, he was a lifelong supporter of such bodies as the Young Men's Christian Association and the Bands of Hope. He was a teetotaller. He helped to establish several Congregational churches and the (Royal) Australian Historical Society. In none of the bodies for which he worked was he the most prominent leader: in all of them he was a hard-working, unobtrusive executive.

Dowling died of heart disease at his Mosman home on 16 October 1912 and was buried in the Methodist section of Rookwood cemetery. He was survived by his wife Hannah, née Luton, a mantlemaker, whom he had married in Sydney with Congregational forms on 25 January 1868, and by two sons and three daughters.

Cyclopedia of N.S.W. (Syd, 1907); *SMH*, 18 Oct 1912; A'sian Federation League, *Commonwealth*, Oct 1894; A'sian Federation League (Dowling) papers (NL).   W. G. McMINN

DOWNER, SIR JOHN WILLIAM (1843-1915), lawyer and politician, was born on 6 July 1843 in Adelaide, son of Henry Downer, a tailor who had migrated to South Australia from England in 1838, and his wife Jane, née Field. He won a scholarship to the Collegiate School of St Peter, Adelaide, where he proved brilliant. He was articled to his brother Henry Edward and (Sir) James Penn Boucaut [q.v.3], and admitted to the Bar on 23 March 1867. He soon became a prominent barrister and, with his brother George, founded a leading legal firm, J. & G. Downer. In 1878 he became a Q.C. and in the same year entered the House of Assembly as a member for Barossa, which he represented until 1901.

His talents were soon recognized and he was attorney-general in (Sir) J. C. Bray's [q.v.3] ministry in 1881-84. Downer's concern for legal reform was a feature of this period: in 1882 he carried a bill which allowed persons charged with criminal offences to give evidence under oath, and he amended the Insolvency and Marriage Acts. He devoted his greatest effort to the Married Women's Property Act, which was finally passed in 1883. An early supporter of women's suffrage, when the legislation was introduced, he opposed the inclusion of a property qualification clause. Although he believed that women had 'purer and higher notions' than men, he could not concede them the right to become members of parliament.

Downer was seen as the Bray ministry's strongest member and was the obvious choice to lead the Opposition during Bray's absence in Europe in 1885. Before Bray's return Downer successfully carried a motion of no confidence in the (Sir) John Colton [q.v.3] ministry and assumed office as premier and attorney-general on 16 June 1885. Faced with economic depression in South Australia, he attempted to reduce the deficit by cutting government expenditure while increasing revenue by a protective tariff. Measures were taken however to find jobs for the unemployed on public works. Next year he opened negotiations with the Chaffey brothers [q.v.7] for their carrying out an extensive irrigation scheme at Renmark. His interest in Federation led him to introduce a bill to bring into operation in South Australia the Act of the Imperial Parliament which had constituted a Federal Council of Australasia, but it had to be withdrawn. In other matters he usually dominated the House, so much so that the Adelaide *Observer* spoke of him as self-opinionated, 'a second Bismarck, with a too yielding Reichstag'. Perhaps for this reason he felt it safe in 1887 to attend the Imperial Conference in London on the eve of an election, and in the face of disapproval throughout the colony.

At the conference Downer shone as one of the Australian colonies' leading political and legal figures: on behalf of the English Marriage Law Reform Association, he tried to persuade the British government to bring the English law relating to marriage with a deceased wife's sister into line with the more liberal colonial legislation. More importantly, he argued the need for a bill in the Imperial Parliament to make colonial judgments enforceable in the United Kingdom as a practical step towards Imperial Federation. He also argued for a uniform law for the Empire in relation to the winding up of estates in bankruptcy, but the British politely refused to endorse any such enthusiastic schemes. Before the conference he learnt that he was to be personally knighted by Queen Victoria. This pleasure and the recognition he received in London was only equalled by his disappointment on returning to Australia, when he discovered at Albany that his government had fallen. In the elections he had lost many supporters, particularly in Adelaide, to trade union candidates.

Downer was not to return to office until October 1892 and this ministry, in which he was premier and successively chief secretary and treasurer, lasted for only eight months. He was forced to resign when, after an election, C. C. Kingston [q.v.], who had voted with Downer to defeat the previous ministry, was able to put together a coalition supported by the newly formed United Labor Party. Downer remarked of this party: 'They are very clever fellows. I have great respect for . . . the way they use either side for their purposes with absolute impartiality'. For most of the period until 1899 Downer led the Opposition.

As a delegate to the Intercolonial Convention of 1883 and as a member of the Federal Council of Australasia in 1889, he had played a minor role, but by the Sydney Convention of 1891 he was one of the leading conservative spokesmen. His great interest was the future Upper House's role as a States' house: Downer supported those who wanted a powerful Senate similar to that of the United States of America. The principle of responsible government was not to overrule States' rights. He opposed viewing the Senate as being like existing Legislative Councils or the House of Lords, and was concerned that it would be powerful enough to attract the best intellects, by offering its members a sense of authority and power.

At the Australasian Federal Convention of 1897 in Adelaide Downer was a member of the constitutional and drafting committees, some of the work of which was done in his house where (Sir) Edmund Barton [q.v.7] was a guest. Downer wished to preserve the clauses of the 1891 bill relating to appeals to the Privy Council. He forcibly argued that the constitution should let the new nation manage its own judicial affairs. When these clauses were whittled away, he questioned whether the delegates 'would ever get out of

swaddling clothes'. On (Sir) Simon Fraser's [q.v.4] interjection that they were not here to 'cut the painter' with Great Britain, Downer replied: 'We have come to the conclusion that we may cease to be provincial, and form the foundation of a nation. We do not propose in any way to separate from the British Crown, in fact we look to it with reverence. We consider ourselves the same people, but the very essence of the difference is that we think that we can make laws which will suffice us; in other words, to put it colloquially, we think we can manage our own affairs'.

In the elections for the first Commonwealth parliament Downer was returned as one of the six South Australian senators. He was so interested in the constitutional position of the Senate, that one colleague remarked that Downer reminded him of the gentleman who under all circumstances would drag King Charles's head into the discussion. While Downer doggedly defended the Senate's constitutional rights – and he believed those rights extended to the removal of governments – he was also a firm believer in the importance of convention. He fought a move in the Senate to delay passage of a supply bill: 'In every constitutionally governed state the practice has been to pass Supply Bills practically as a matter of course', and during the controversy over Lord Hopetoun's [q.v.] resignation he again cited convention when he pleaded that 'It is a well understood principle of constitutional government that it is undesirable for the Governor General to take an active part in debatable politics'.

In this first parliament Downer supported Barton's ministry although at times he was unenthusiastic about its legislation. He believed the Immigration Restriction Act did not deserve high priority and objected to what he described as 'this general running amok with the name of white Australia'. Nor did he bear kindly with cant about the white man's civilizing mission; 'When the British came here the population was black. Through the ennobling influences of the civilised whites, the blacks are nearly all dead'. The legislation that he thought deserved greater priority was that which would establish the High Court of Australia, the body which he saw as the final arbiter between the two parliamentary Houses. Privately, he hoped that with his long service to the Federal cause, his acknowledged position as one of the leading constitutional lawyers of the day, and his friendship with Barton, he would be assured of one of the seats. Despite Barton's support, his appointment was opposed in cabinet by certain members who disapproved of what they considered were his rather self-indulgent habits. His failure to be appointed when the court was announced in 1903 was the great disappointment of his life.

Before the announcement of the High Court, he had decided to retire from the Senate. He had never been wealthy and had relied upon work at the Bar to earn a living. While a member of the South Australian parliament he had combined both careers, but the need to spend so much time in Melbourne had interfered with his practice. In 1905, however, he was elected to the South Australian Legislative Council as a representative of the Southern Districts. He remained a member until his death at his home in North Adelaide from cancer on 2 August 1915. His estate was valued for probate at £14 190.

Downer was a politician of strange contrasts. He often took up positions which, at least for a self-styled nineteenth-century conservative, did not quite fit this image: witness his promoting women's rights and his opposition to appeals to the Privy Council. His abhorrence of jingoistic racism was a rare virtue in the first Commonwealth parliament. Despite his affectionate loyalty to the British Crown and England, he devoted much time to creating an independent Australia. Sir John Cockburn [q.v.] wrote of him in the 1920s: 'Of all the leaders I have been associated with Sir John Downer stands out as a chivalrous, honorable, and straight forward man'. Alfred Deakin [q.v.] described him as 'bull-headed, and rather thick-necked, . . . with the dogged set of the mouth of a prize fighter' and 'smallish eyes'. Deakin found him to be suave, clear and effective and believed that only reserve and indolence had prevented him from playing a far greater part in the Federal movement.

He was married twice: first to Elizabeth Henderson (d. 1896); and second, on 29 November 1899, in Sydney, to Una Stella Haslingden Russell, artist. He was survived by a son from each marriage (Sir Alexander Downer being his son by the second marriage); two sons had predeceased him. Besides his elder brother and legal partner George, who was a noted pastoralist, his other brother Henry was a member of the House of Assembly in 1881-96 and in 1890 served briefly in Cockburn's ministry as attorney-general. All were Anglicans.

In Canberra the suburb of Downer and a sculptured fountain commemorate Sir John.

PD (SA), 1883-84, 2031; Intercolonial Convention 1883, *Report of the proceedings. . . Syd. . .* (Syd, 1883); Colonial Conference 1887, *Proceedings* (Lond, 1887); National A'sian Conventions, 1891 to 1898, *Proceedings . . .* (Syd, 1891, *and* Adel, 1897, *and* Syd, 1898, *and* Melb, 1898); *British A'sian*, 17 June 1887; E. Barton, *and* Deakin papers, *and* P. M. Glynn, Diaries, 1880-1918 (NL). PETER BARTLETT

DOWNES, RUPERT MAJOR (1885-1945), surgeon and soldier, was born on 10 February 1885 at Mitcham, Adelaide, youngest child of Major General Major Francis Downes [q.v.4] and his wife Helen Maria, née Chamberlin. Rupert was educated at Haileybury College, Melbourne, and at Ormond College, University of Melbourne (M.B., Ch.B., 1907; M.D., 1911; M.S., 1912). When still at school, he had joined the Victorian Horse Artillery (Rupertswood Battery) as a trumpeter and he had served in the Melbourne University Rifles. In July 1908 he was commissioned as a captain in the Australian Army Medical Corps.

The first six years of his career were fruitful and happy ones. Downes was a demonstrator in anatomy at the university and a tutor at Ormond, and worked as a clinical surgical assistant at the Melbourne and Children's hospitals. At the same time he threw himself into the work of the A.A.M.C., being promoted major in 1913. On 20 November he married Doris Mary Robb at St John's Church, Toorak.

When the Australian Imperial Force was raised in 1914, Downes was given command of the 2nd Light Horse Field Ambulance and promoted lieut-colonel, the youngest in the A.I.F. Before sailing for Egypt he was transferred to the 3rd L.H.F.A. which he led on Gallipoli where he won a name as an outstanding commander. On the formation of the Anzac Mounted Division in March 1916, Downes became its assistant director of medical services (senior medical officer) with the rank of colonel. He was also appointed A.D.M.S. of the Australian base in Egypt, and successfully combined the two roles for the remainder of the war.

Downes was remarkable as innovator and organizer. He introduced a sledge for moving casualties over sand. As casualty clearing stations were immobile, he divided his field ambulances so that the mobile sections moved close to the battle while the stationary tented sections, some miles back, provided more extensive treatment in safer conditions. Downes also created a mobile surgical unit. His reputation was such that when the Desert Mounted Corps was organized in August 1917, he was appointed its deputy director of medical services.

In the Jordan Valley in 1918, Downes's anti-malarial measures kept sickness at acceptable levels; he had been greatly assisted by the Anzac Field Laboratory which he had raised in 1916. During the battle for Es Salt in May, he delivered medical supplies by dropping them from aircraft. In the advance to Damascus in September his medical arrangements were stretched to the limit. Then in Damascus, came the 'blizzard' of malaria, as he described it, when the weary troops went sick by the thousand. Downes and his medical units had to cope also with the great epidemic of influenza and with thousands of sick and wounded prisoners. Written from his diaries, his subsequent account of this situation and its gradual transformation, disposes completely of the romantic story in T. E. Lawrence's *Seven pillars of wisdom*. Almost all of the medical officers, including Downes, were stricken with malaria; he stayed at his post and, with immense determination, saw his unit through their bitterest trial.

Downes was appointed C.M.G. in January 1918 and mentioned in dispatches six times. His wife was appointed O.B.E. for work among soldiers' families. It was fitting that he was invited to write the section on the Sinai and Palestine campaign in Volume I of the *Official history of the Australian Army Medical Services*; and he was engaged in this work while rebuilding his surgical practice in Melbourne. Downes became an honorary consulting surgeon at the Children's and Victorian Eye and Ear hospitals, honorary surgeon at Prince Henry Hospital, and in 1927 a foundation fellow of the College of Surgeons of Australasia. He was president of the Victorian branch of the British Medical Association in 1935 and lectured on medical ethics and professional conduct at the University of Melbourne. He was chairman of the Masseurs' Registration Board, a councillor of the Victorian division of the Australian Red Cross, and chairman of the Red Cross National Council in 1939. He became commissioner of the St John Ambulance Brigade and was president of the St John Ambulance Association for eight years. In 1929 he was appointed a commander of the Order of St John of Jerusalem and a knight of grace in 1937.

Downes's passion for military medicine had taken him back to the army in 1919 as an area medical officer. In 1921 he was a member of the committee charged with planning the reorganization of the Army Medical Service and the employment of the profession during an emergency. He was also appointed D.D.M.S., 3rd Military District (Victoria). His enthusiasm inspired some doctors to join and others to return to the Medical Corps. Using his great experience of mobile warfare, he held tactical exercises which stimulated the keenness of the young medical officers. According to Major General Sir Samuel Burston 'He was never a talker and more by example than by precept he indicated clearly what was expected of an officer of the Army Medical Corps . . . The officers trained by him during this period were to be amongst the most valued of the senior officers of the corps in World War II'.

In 1928 Downes joined a committee appointed to examine the mobilization of Australian medical resources for war. He vigorously opposed the concept, already accepted by some, of conscription of doctors and medical students under the direction of the minister of health. He went to Britain and Europe in 1933 to study army medical problems and developments in surgery of the brain and the central nervous system.

In August 1934 Downes was appointed director general of medical services and was promoted major general next year. Thus his earliest ambition of being a regular soldier was at last attained, although at the cost of relinquishing his surgical practice. He began work under the shadow of the death of his only son and when the army was starved of men, money and equipment. All his training, experience and interests combined to fit him for his new post at a time when war seemed imminent. 'Both by training, and by temperament Downes was a soldier to his finger tips', as Colonel A. G. Butler [q.v.7] has written, but he was also one of the leaders of his profession, widely read and of limitless physical energy. He was soon to show that he was also a man of vision.

In the five years to the outbreak of war in 1939, Downes selected and trained many leaders of the A.A.M.C., foresaw civil as well as military medical problems, planned their solution and pioneered major developments in the medical side of recruitment. Urgent as these preparations were he never lost sight of the medical needs of the Australian people.

He had the help initially of only two regular staff officers and he co-operated with Dr J. H. L. Cumpston [q.v.], Commonwealth director of health. Downes was chairman of the board which in 1935 reorganized army medical equipment and examined the possibility of its local manufacture. His report foreshadowed the wartime control later effected through the Medical Equipment Control Committee. In 1937-38 he led in establishing the Central Medical Co-ordination Committee 'to co-ordinate arrangements for provision of medical men, material and hospital accommodation' and he chaired its sub-committee on supply of equipment. On Downes's initiative funds were provided in 1939 in time to import large quantities of drugs and equipment before war began; the M.E.C.C. with its parent committee efficiently allocated medical resources during World War II.

Downes's interest in training was felt throughout the Medical Corps. In 1936 in the first major tactical exercise for medical officers, for five days the medical problems of a Japanese invasion were studied on the ground between Goulburn and Wollongong.

He also looked into the future when, in 1937, he called for a report on the medical and hygienic aspects of the Territory of New Guinea. He also fostered the development of women's services such as the Voluntary Aid Detachments.

In March 1939 Downes began a tour of military and other medical centres in India, the Middle East and Britain, returning in October. While in London, he took steps to obtain the services as consultants of two eminent Australians, the surgeon Sir Thomas Dunhill [q.v.] and (Sir) Neil Fairley, an expert in tropical diseases. Foreseeing the scale of the war, Downes began to press for the building of major military hospitals in the capital cities. He argued that after the war they should be handed over to the Repatriation Commission for the care of sick and disabled ex-service people. Despite strong opposition, especially on the grounds of cost, Downes persisted in his advocacy until in October 1940 he won his case. Time vindicated his judgment: the great hospitals such as Concord and Heidelberg are Rupert Downes's memorial.

He revolutionized the medical side of recruiting for the A.I.F. Radiography of the chest by means of miniature fluorography was introduced; every soldier's blood group was determined and recorded on his identity discs and all were inoculated against tetanus, smallpox, typhoid and paratyphoid fevers. Downes was also concerned that volunteers should be medically examined under proper conditions. He had to cope with 'the reluctance of some staff officers to regard the D.G.M.S. as the responsible technical adviser on medical affairs' and there were difficulties with the adjutant general to whom he was responsible. It must have been a solace when Burston wrote from the Middle East: 'I think it is safe to say that there has probably never been a force sent overseas from any country better equipped on the medical side'.

In November 1940 Downes had been appointed director of medical services, A.I.F. (Middle East), but General Sir Thomas Blamey had already appointed Burston to that post. There the matter rested until March 1941 when Downes was made inspector general of medical services by the minister of the army, (Sir) Percy Spender, without reference to the Military Board. While the growth of the army in Australia and of the A.I.F. overseas may well have justified such an appointment, its manner appears to have been highly irregular. Nevertheless, Downes welcomed the opportunity, implicit in the appointment, to visit operational areas. After inspecting major Australian centres, he went to the Dutch East Indies and Malaya, then on to Egypt, Palestine and Syria and home through India and Ceylon. Early in 1942 he inspected medical units at Port Moresby. When Blamey reorganized the army in March 1942, he made Burston D.G.M.S. Downes went to the Second Army as D.M.S. so that he now found himself serving under his recent subordinate and friend of long standing. Though he was in a backwater of the war, his responsibilities extended from the Queensland border to Hobart and Adelaide.

As Downes was almost 60 he had soon to retire, but as this day approached he was invited to write the medical history of Australia in the war. He accepted enthusiastically and began work with characteristic vigour. He was engaged on his new task when he decided to accompany Major General G. A. Vasey to New Guinea; on 5 March 1945 their aircraft crashed in the sea off Cairns with the loss of all on board. Downes was buried in Cairns War Cemetery with military honours. He was survived by his wife and two daughters.

In his dedicated career, Downes won the admiration of the medical profession in peace and war. Whatever his role, whether surgeon, medical historian or commander, he impressed men by his intelligence, his selflessness and his drive. 'His directness, his robustness, his disdain of intrigue in any form, were his inspirational qualities to a rare degree and the success of the Medical Service in this war must be credited to Rupert Downes'. In these words the council of the B.M.A. in Victoria recognized his quality and his contribution to the well-being of Australian soldiers and thus to their success in war. The Royal Australasian College of Surgeons established the Rupert Downes Memorial Lecture in his honour. To the amazement and dismay of his colleagues, his services from 1919 until his death were accepted by both the army and successive governments without any mark of distinction being bestowed upon him.

A. G. Butler (ed), *Official history of the Australian Army Medical Services . . . 1914-18*, 1 (Melb, 1930); A. S. Walker, *Middle East and Far East* (Canb, 1953), and *The island campaigns* (Canb, 1957); A. J. Hill, *Chauvel of the Light Horse* (Melb, 1978); *London Gazette*, 13 Oct 1916, 28 June 1917, 1, 12 Jan 1918, 22 Jan, 5 June 1919; *MJA*, 28 Apr 1945, 24 Feb 1951, 17 July 1954, 21 Dec 1957, 20 Jan 1962; R. M. Downes, Diary 1915-19 (AWM).

A. J. HILL

DOWNEY, MICHAEL HENRY (1877-1933), psychiatrist and army medical officer, was born on 20 October 1877 at Toolleen, Victoria, son of Irish-born William Downey, farmer, and his wife Ann, née Lynch. He was educated at Echuca Grammar School and in 1895 joined the Victorian Rangers. He began medicine at the University of Melbourne in 1896 and joined the University Officers' Corps in 1898, but moved to the University of Edinburgh (L.R.C.P., L.R.C.S., 1901). After service in the South African War in Cape Colony and western Transvaal as surgeon to the Royal Army Medical Corps, Downey returned to the University of Melbourne (M.B., B.S., 1904).

He had studied mental diseases with Sir Thomas Clouston at Edinburgh and W. Beattie Smith [q.v.] at Melbourne, and on 15 June 1905 was appointed assistant resident medical officer at Parkside Mental Asylum, Adelaide; from 1 January 1916 he was superintendent. From 1912 he lectured in psychological medicine at the University of Adelaide and about this time began negotiations for lunacy reform with the chief secretary. He recommended that Parkside asylum be renamed, that a filter in the form of a receiving house should be established between the patient's home and the asylum, and that private hospitals should be set up for patients, whose relatives objected to sending them to official mental institutions. All three proposals were eventually adopted.

In April 1909 Downey had been commissioned as a captain in the Australian Army Medical Corps and was promoted major in 1912 and lieut-colonel in 1915. On 10 February 1916 he joined the Australian Imperial Force in command of the 11th Australian Field Ambulance which, after training on Salisbury plain, England, took over the Divisional Rest Station at Steenwerck, France, on 30 November. Downey showed conspicuous ability as a leader and organizer. During the battle of Messines on 7 June 1917 he won the Distinguished Service Order for his part in the evacuation of wounded from the Advanced Dressing Station at Kandahar Farm; his devotion to duty and untiring energy inspired all under him, and the removal of 3000 wounded in seven days 'went without a hitch'. During the 3rd battle of Ypres Downey commanded II Anzac Corps Main Dressing Station and on 20 October he was promoted temporary colonel and assistant director of medical services, 5th Division; his rank was confirmed on 26 April 1918. He served throughout that year with the 5th Division. In January 1919 he was admitted to hospital; he returned to Australia and left the A.I.F. on 27 June. He had been mentioned in dispatches three times.

Downey commanded the 6th Cavalry Field Ambulance from 1920 to 1926 when he retired from the A.A.M.C. He had returned to his position as superintendent at Parkside, the only mental hospital in South Australia until Northfield opened in 1929, and in 1920-33 also lectured in psychological medicine at the University of Adelaide. In 1929 he presented a paper to the Australasian Medical Congress on the use of malaria in the treatment of general paralysis of the insane.

He died suddenly of heart disease at Calvary Hospital, North Adelaide, on 17 April 1933, and was buried in the Catholic section of West Terrace cemetery. He was survived by his wife Eva Agnes, née O'Brien, whom he had married at St Patrick's Cathedral, Melbourne, on 23 May 1906, and by their son. The Downey Receiving House, Glenside, honours his name.

Univ Melb, *Record of active service* (Melb, 1926); C. E. W. Bean, *The A.I.F. in France*, 1917-18 (Syd, 1933, 1937, 1942); A. G. Price, *Nursing in South Australia... 1837-1937*, rev edn (Adel, 1939); A. G. Butler (ed), *Official history of the Australian Army Medical Services... 1914-18*, 3 (Canb, 1943); H. T. Kay, ... *the centenary of Glenside Hospital* (Adel, 1970); *Weekly Times* (Melb), 4 Feb 1905; *Advertiser* (Adel), 18-19 Apr 1933; *Chronicle* (Adel), 20 Apr 1933; Downey file, war records section (AWM).

JEAN P. FIELDING

DOWSE, RICHARD (1866-1955), soldier and public servant, was born on 29 June 1866 at Portsea, Hampshire, England, son of Henry James Dowse, civil servant, and his wife Rosa, née Stevens. He attended a private school and the Surrey County School and in 1883 joined the 3rd Volunteer Battalion, Hampshire Regiment, as a private, serving until May 1885. Later that year he migrated to Queensland and in September enlisted in the Queensland Volunteer Rifles; after serving in all ranks up to colour sergeant he was commissioned second lieutenant in October 1889 and promoted lieutenant in December. Next year, on 12 May, he married Sophia Mary Kate Austin at St Mary's Anglican Church, Kangaroo Point; at the time he was working as a clerk with the Australian Joint Stock Bank, Brisbane.

Dowse was made a captain in the Volunteer Forces in March 1892 and four years later he was appointed adjutant of the 1st Battalion, Queensland Mounted Infantry. In November 1899 he embarked as a lieutenant with the 1st Queensland Mounted Infantry Contingent for South Africa, remaining on active service until December 1900. He saw action at the relief of Kimberley and in operations in the Orange Free State, Cape Colony and Transvaal, including significant engagements at Paardeberg, Poplar Grove, Driefontein, Vet River, Johannesburg and Pretoria. After returning home he joined the Permanent Military Forces as a lieutenant and was appointed a captain on the Administrative and Instructional Staff in July 1901. In 1902-11 he served as a staff officer in Queensland and Victoria and was promoted major in 1909.

In October 1911 Dowse was appointed deputy assistant quartermaster general for the 3rd Military District and in 1913 became A.Q.M.G. From the beginning of World War I he was engaged in the equipping and dispatch of units for overseas service; then, in February 1916, he was appointed to the Australian Imperial Force as a lieut-colonel and commanding officer of the 3rd Divisional Train. He embarked in June and after training in England served in the Armentières sector from November. In March 1917 he was appointed deputy assistant adjutant general of the 4th Division and held this post during operations at Bullecourt and Messines. An appointment as the division's assistant adjutant and quartermaster general in July enabled him to contribute to preparations for the battles of Ypres and Passchendaele, and in 1918 Villers-Bretonneux and the advance to the Hindenburg line. For outstanding service during the war he was awarded the Distinguished Service Order in the New Year honours of 1918 and was twice mentioned in dispatches.

Dowse returned to Australia in February 1920 and served as a brevet colonel in the Staff Corps, Australian Military Forces, until 1922 when he retired from the army. In 1923-30 he was marshal to the chief justice of the High Court of Australia. On 27 December 1933, at St Canice's Catholic Church, Elizabeth Bay, Sydney, he married a widow, Alice Nicolson. During World War II he served as manpower officer for the 2nd Military District. 'Dickie' Dowse was 'the perfect English gentleman, considerate and courteous in all circumstances, the complete host and charming friend'. He was an active member of Legacy from 1930 until his death. Retired without a service pension, he found life hard until he was granted a totally and permanently incapacitated pension in his later years. Survived by his wife and three children from his first marriage, he died at the War Veterans' Home, Narrabeen, on 24 May 1955 and was cremated with Anglican rites.

Aust Defence Dept, *Official records of the Australian military contingents to the war in South Africa*, P. L. Murray ed (Melb, 1911); *London Gazette*, 28 Dec 1917, 1 Jan, 20 Dec 1918; *Bulletin*, 4 Aug 1954; *Sydney Legacy Bulletin*, 2 June 1955; Dowse file, war records section (AWM).

C. C. FALK

DOYLE, JEREMIAH JOSEPH (1849-1909), Catholic bishop, was born on 5 December 1849 at Kilmurry, County Cork, Ireland, son of Daniel Doyle, farmer, and his wife Ellen, née Murphy. He was educated in classics at Mount Melleray College, Waterford, and the Catholic Missionary College of All Hallows, Dublin. Ordained on 24 June 1874 for the diocese of Armidale, New South Wales, he then set out for Australia; after being shipwrecked in the Bay of Biscay he arrived in Sydney in the *Lincolnshire* in November 1874.

At Armidale Doyle's zeal for education and loyalty in the troubled days of Bishop O'Mahony's [q.v.5] administration impressed his superiors; for a time he was in charge of the Armidale church. In 1878 he was transferred to Casino with general responsibility for the north coast. Appointed dean in 1886, Doyle was consecrated first bishop of Grafton by Cardinal Moran [q.v.] in St Mary's Cathedral, Sydney, on 28 August 1887. He spent six months in Grafton before returning to Lismore, which had better communications, more Catholics and, he believed, a better future.

His involvement in the civil and religious life of the undeveloped district won him great respect. At Lismore in 1880 in a typhoid epidemic Doyle had regularly visited the homes of the sick of all denominations. He was sometime president of the Lismore School of Arts, the Lismore Agricultural and Industrial Society and the hospital board. His organizing capacity was his 'strongest characteristic', and his wit often rendered discussions 'less acrimonious'. He gave evidence three times to the Parliamentary Standing Committee on Public Works, strenuously advocating the northern extension of the railway and a breakwater at Byron Bay. He also promoted the development of a water and gas supply for Lismore and claimed to be responsible for the installation of the telephone.

Doyle showed a continuing interest in education: the number of schools in his 11 000-square mile (28 000 km^2) diocese had increased from nine to twenty-three by 1909. The Sisters of Mercy had come to Grafton to teach in 1883 and by 1907 had seven establishments. In 1886 Doyle brought the Presentation Sisters to Lismore; later they were joined by the Sisters of the Sacred Heart and the Josephite Sisters. But their male counterparts, scarce throughout the country, were not represented. In 1890 Doyle was appointed to a committee established by the Australian hierarchy to set up standards of proficiency for Catholic schools.

In 1891 and 1900 Doyle went to Rome; on his second visit he succeeded in getting the name and seat of his diocese changed to Lismore. In 1892 the foundation stone of St Carthage's Cathedral, Lismore, had been laid, but building did not continue till 1904; the partially built stone cathedral was burnt down and restarted in 1905: it was dedicated in 1907. Doyle inherited from Bishop Torreggiani [q.v.6] a legal wrangle over property with a bucolic Grafton priest Dean O'Sullivan, who was successfully sued by the Australian Joint Stock Bank for debts incurred before the diocese was created. These debts made it impossible for Doyle to maintain students at St Patrick's College, Manly, without help from Moran. The Roman Catholic Diocese of Lismore Church Lands Act of 1908 helped to clarify this situation.

Doyle died of cerebral haemorrhage in his house at Lismore on 4 June 1909 and was buried in St Carthage's Cathedral.

R. Fogarty, *Catholic education in Australia 1806-1950* (Melb, 1959); K. T. Livingston, *The emergence of an Australian Catholic priesthood, 1835-1915* (Syd, 1977); *V&P* (LA NSW), 1890, 6, 63, 1892-93, 6, 79, 1901, 6, 35, 46; *Northern Star* (Lismore), 7 June 1909; *T&CJ*, 9 June 1909; *Catholic Press*, 10 June 1909; Diocesan Archives (St Mary's Cathedral, Syd).   GREGORY HAINES

DOYLE, STUART FRANK (1887-1945), film and radio entrepreneur, was born on 1 December 1887 at Leichhardt, Sydney, second son of English parents Frank Doyle, draper's assistant, and his wife Jane Grinsell, née Robinson. Brought up and educated at Blackheath, he became assistant librarian at the Law Institute of New South Wales in 1903 and next year joined Norton [q.v.5] Smith & Co. At 19, as 'Frank Stuart', he toured the State as a one-man entertainer and from 1909 worked for the (Greater) J. D. Williams Amusement Co. Ltd in Queensland then Sydney. It amalgamated in 1913 with four companies into Union Theatres Ltd (exhibition) and Australasian Films Ltd (distribution). Doyle's progress became rapid: business manager, a joint managing director, and by 1929 managing director of Australasian Films and a director of at least eight associated companies. On 4 May 1912 at Petersham he had married Louise Marie Wilhelmina Fredericke Reinke, daughter of a grazier.

Becoming the most powerful and flamboyant of early Australian film men, Doyle exercised his talent for publicity wherever possible. In 1929 he contributed to the fall of the Bruce [q.v.7]-Page [q.v.] government by prompting a massive campaign against the Federal amusement tax.

In 1921 Doyle had launched Union Theatres on large-scale modernization of old cinemas, pioneering new standards of comfort. In 1927 he opened Australia's first 'atmospheric' theatre in Sydney, the Capitol, based on an American design, and in 1929 the elaborate State Theatre, followed by the 3000-seat State Theatre, Melbourne. His ambition was partly fired by a desire to outclass his rival F. W. Thring [q.v.].

With Frank Albert [q.v.7] and Sir Benjamin Fuller [q.v.], in 1929 Doyle founded the Australian Broadcasting Co. to provide a national wireless service. When it was taken over by the Federal government in 1932 and converted into the Australian Broadcasting Commission, they set up the Commonwealth Broadcasting Corporation Ltd (with Doyle as chairman), which acquired station 2UW, Sydney, and rapidly expanded. The financial failure of the new picture palaces in the Depression forced the liquidation of Union Theatres in 1931. Doyle set up a new company, Greater Union Theatres Ltd, to buy its assets for some £400 000, the amount of its overdraft. The new overdraft lasted until 1942.

Nevertheless Doyle went ahead in 1932 and became managing director of a new company, Cinesound Productions Ltd, which began a film-making programme with *On our selection* (1932) starring Bert Bailey [q.v.7]. Sound news-reels and the success of sixteen more features justified Doyle's gamble. Under immense pressure by the Greater Union's board and the English, Scottish and Australian Bank, Doyle travelled overseas in 1936, seeking capital. By his return in September, N. B. Rydge had become chairman. In June 1937 Doyle was persuaded to resign from all the associated companies, partly solaced by the gift of Greater Union's interest in the Commonwealth Broadcasting Co.

While announcing elaborate plans, Doyle was shaken by his abrupt severance from film business. He became chairman and managing director of the Aircraft Development Co. and during World War II was contracted to make aircraft self-sealing petrol tanks. A lover of boating, he was a member of the Royal Prince Alfred Yacht Club and commodore of the Royal Motor Yacht Club of New South Wales: his luxurious motor yacht *Miramar* was taken over by the Royal Australian Navy during the war.

Doyle died suddenly with cardio-vascular disease at his home at Wahroonga on 20 October 1945 and was buried in the Anglican section of South Head cemetery. Survived by his wife and daughter, he left an estate valued for probate at £69 002. Doyle was a visionary, innovator and gambler; at first, his qualities combined with, but later outweighed, his business ability. He became an international figure through his dominance in Australia of film exhibition, distribution and production.

A. Wildavsky and D. Carboch, *Studies in Australian politics* (Melb, 1958); K. G. Hall, *Directed by Ken G. Hall* (Melb, 1977); *A'sian Picture Mag*, 1 July 1920; *Everyone's*, 17 Mar, 19 May, 2, 30 June 1937; *Film Weekly*, 25 Oct 1945; *Smith's Weekly* (Syd), 2 July 1925, 4 Dec 1926; *SMH*, 22 Oct 1945; A. F. Pike, The history of an Australian film production company: Cinesound, 1932-1970 (M.A thesis, ANU, 1972).   GRAHAM SHIRLEY

DRAKE, JAMES GEORGE (1850-1941), journalist, lawyer and politician, was born on 26 April 1850 in London, son of Edward Drake, licensed victualler, and his wife Ann Fanny, née Hyde. Educated mainly at King's College School, he worked for several years for merchants Samuel Hanson, Son, Evison & Barter. On 14 January 1874 he arrived at Brisbane in the *Abbey Holme*; seeking work he went to Stanthorpe but eventually found a place in a Toowoomba store. Returning to Brisbane, he worked as clerk for ten months until June 1875 with Brabant & Co., merchants, then as a journalist with the *Bundaberg Star*.

In two years Drake worked for the *Daily Northern Argus* (Rockhampton), the *Telegraph* (Brisbane), the *Brisbane Courier* and, briefly, the Melbourne *Argus*. He also spent a short period at Barcoo as a jackaroo. A competent shorthand writer, later president of the Queensland Shorthand Writers' Association, Drake joined the parliamentary reporting staff in 1876 and stayed there for six years. From May 1881 he read for the Bar entrance examination with Granville Miller, later a judge, and was admitted on 6 June 1882. In partnership with Magnus Jensen, he established a flourishing practice and, objecting to the division of the profession, insisted on being known as a legal practitioner.

Long a radical, Drake's objection to Asian immigration into Queensland led him into association with William Lane [q.v.]; he became a shareholder, writer and joint editor of Lane's *Boomerang* in 1887 and was prominent in its reconstruction under Gresley Lukin [q.v.5] in 1890. He stood unsuccessfully for the Legislative Assembly seat of Enoggera against (Sir) James Dickson [q.v.] in 1887; at the general election of March 1888 which followed the resignation of Sir Samuel Griffith's [q.v.] government he won the seat. He was a personal follower of Griffith until the latter's elevation to the bench, then followed an independent line. Despite his radical ideas, he refused to join the Labor Party and in 1896 became leader of a small group called the Independent Opposition. He was vice-president of the Progressive League in February 1899, but at the end of the year accepted appointment as government leader in the Legislative Council and as postmaster-general and secretary for public instruction in the ministry of (Sir) Robert Philp [q.v.]. He was assiduous in enforcing the compulsory clauses of the Education Act.

A Federation enthusiast from the 1880s, Drake was one of the principal publicists of the movement in Queensland. He wrote frequently in newspapers, published the pamphlet *Federation, Imperial or democratic* in 1896 and in February 1899-January 1901 ran his own fortnightly paper *Progress* for the cause. Winning election to the first Senate as a Protectionist, he was chosen when Dickson died to be postmaster-general in Barton's [q.v.7] first ministry (1901-03). He was probably also party whip. Melbourne *Punch* described him as stolid, 'a plodder — thorough rather than brilliant', a 'slow, deliberate, grave speaker' yet with 'a sense of humour, a gift of portraiture, a good memory and a thorough knowledge of English literature'.

A lieutenant in the 1st (Moreton) Regiment of the Queensland Defence Force in 1886, Drake was a major by 1901. He had been vice-president of the Queensland United Service Institution. His brief period as minister for defence in August-September 1903 was terminated, however, by the reconstruction of the ministry after Barton's resignation. He became attorney-general in the succeeding Deakin [q.v.] ministry but his term was again cut short when the government resigned in April 1904. Vice-president of the Executive Council in the Reid-McLean [qq.v.] ministry of 1904-05, he was not included in the next Deakin government. In January-June 1906 Drake ran a newspaper, *Commonwealth*, in Brisbane to counteract State hostility to the Commonwealth, but did not nominate for re-election in December and returned to the law in Brisbane. In the Queensland general election of 1907 he stood against E.B. Forrest [q.v.] at North Brisbane as an Independent Liberal but received only 137 votes.

Drake was crown prosecutor in 1910-20 with right of private practice and served occasionally as a deputy judge in district courts. After 1920 he appeared in public life only as a councillor of the Brisbane branch of the Royal Society of St George and as chairman of the local committee for Trinity College of Music, London. He died at Brisbane Hospital on 1 August 1941 and was buried in Toowong cemetery. On 25 June 1897 in a private house in Quay Street, Brisbane, he had married Mary Street with Baptist forms. Four children survived him.

Alcazar Press, *Queensland, 1900* (Brisb, nd); R. Johnston, *History of the Queensland Bar* (Brisb, 1979); *Brisbane Courier*, 23 Mar 1888, 18 June

1894, 24 Aug 1898; *Boomerang* (Brisb), 12 May 1888; *Table Talk*, 7 Feb 1901, 10 Apr 1902; *Punch* (Melb), 30 Mar 1905; *Commonwealth* (Brisb), 30 June 1906; Barton, *and* Deakin papers (NL); Drake papers (Fryer Lib, Univ Qld, *and* NL), and reminiscences (typescript, nd, Oxley Lib, Brisb).

H. J. GIBBNEY

DRAKE-BROCKMAN, EDMUND ALFRED (1884-1949), judge, soldier and politician, was born on 21 February 1884 at Busselton, Western Australia, son of Frederick Slade Drake-Brockman [q.v.], and his wife Grace Vernon, née Bussell. Educated at the Anglican Guildford Grammar School, Drake-Brockman was influenced by the school's strong tradition of military training and in 1903 joined the Citizen Military Forces. In 1908-09 he attended a special course of training with the Imperial Forces at the Staff College, Quetta, India, and by 1911 was a major. He had served his articles with the firm of James [Sir Walter, q.v.] and Derbyshire, Perth solicitors, and was admitted to practice in 1909. On 9 April 1912 at Hawthorn, Melbourne, he married Constance Andrews.

On 25 August 1914 Drake-Brockman joined the Australian Imperial Force as a major in the 11th Battalion, which he commanded during the landing at Gallipoli on 25 April 1915. After several narrow escapes he was wounded on 15 July and was evacuated to Malta and England before being invalided to Australia in October. He was appointed C.M.G. for his work on Gallipoli. He returned to Egypt in April 1916 and, as lieut-colonel, took command of the 16th Battalion on 11 May. In the operations in France at Pozières and Mouquet Farm, and at Bullecourt in 1917, the battalion suffered very heavy casualties. Drake-Brockman commanded the 4th Training Battalion on Salisbury plain, England, from October 1917 to February 1918 when he returned to the 16th Battalion, which then served at Hébuterne, Villers-Bretonneux, Hamel and in the offensive from 8 August. That month he took command of the 4th Brigade and in October was promoted colonel and temporary brigadier general. Drake-Brockman had taken part in nearly all the major actions of the A.I.F. with great distinction. He was awarded the Distinguished Service Order in December 1917 and the Montenegrin Order of Danilo (fourth class), was appointed C.B. in June 1919 and was mentioned in dispatches six times. He remained on the active list; promoted major general in 1937, during World War II he commanded the 3rd (Militia) Division until 1942.

After World War I Drake-Brockman returned to legal work in Perth and politics. He was elected as a Nationalist senator for his State in 1919 and admitted to the Victorian Bar next year. In 1924 he became president of the Australian Employers' Federation, and next year represented Australia at the League of Nations Assembly, Geneva. Drake-Brockman was a reliable party man, and in 1923-26 was government whip; but he retired from parliament in 1926 to facilitate his party's arrangements with the Country Party. Next April he joined (Sir) G. S. Beeby [q.v.7], G. J. Dethridge and L. O. Lukin [qq.v.] as a judge of the recently reconstituted Commonwealth Court of Conciliation and Arbitration. His appointment was bitterly criticized because of his political and economic affiliations, but he lived down this hostility; the Australian Council of Trade Unions came to appreciate his 'common-sense and at times unorthodox methods'. During the early difficult years of the court Drake-Brockman made awards in some major industries, particularly the railways – after seven years and four million words in transcript. In the 1934 basic wage inquiry, with the chief judge, he provided the majority decision calling for 'some system of family or child endowment'.

By World War II Drake-Brockman had become the senior and most experienced judge. In 1939-40 he made awards in the coal-mining industry, previously governed by State awards. It has been claimed that 'the changes were the greatest ever made to the advantage of the workers in the mining or any other industry'. They included the 40-hour week for underground workers and paid annual leave. In his survey of the industry Drake-Brockman stated that the 'history of the coal-mining industry in Australia ... may be described as an unbridled and unregulated contest between employers and employees ... and actuated only by the rules of the jungle'. A system of local reference boards and a central reference board under his chairmanship was created, but in 1943 the dissatisfaction of the Miners' Federation led to his replacement.

Throughout the pre-war and early war years, 'the Drake', as he was usually known, was regarded as a conservative judge who adhered rigidly to the orthodox principle of capacity to pay. However, with increasing confidence, a pragmatic strain emerged: in 1943 he varied the clothing trades award to lift the minimum wage for journeywomen to 75 per cent of the male needs basic wage and extended it to the rubber industry. These were seen as attraction wages, a principle strongly rejected by Chief Judge Piper [q.v.] and judges O'Mara and Kelly. Drake-Brockman's action was mainly dictated by wartime competition for female labour. That he did not see it as a bold social step in women's wage fixation was clear from his cautious reference to departing, 'to some extent', from the 'sound economic basis of wage fixation which has always guided the Court when making awards for this industry'. He stressed that his orders in the clothing and rubber industries were to have wartime operation only. Nevertheless in the 1945 female minimum rates case, judges Drake-Brockman and A. W. Foster [q.v.] provided the minority judgment in favour of a general prescription of 75 per cent. (It was not until 1950 that this minority view was adopted by the court.)

Increasingly over the later war years and into the post-war period, he became the *de facto* head of the arbitration court. Partly this was because Chief Judge Piper was failing, but it also reflected Drake-Brockman's longer experience and his ability to work with others with that unquestioned confidence of right to rule, which had marked him out as commanding officer and parliamentary whip. For example, it was the senior, and not the chief judge, who presided over the politically sensitive series of hearings on standard hours of work and the basic wage which began in October 1945. Hours per week were reduced from forty-four to forty as from the beginning of 1948, and a 7s. per week increase in the needs basic wage was awarded, as an interim measure, pending full inquiry into the proper post-war level of that wage. It was no surprise that he was appointed by the Chifley Labor government as chief judge in June 1947. But Drake-Brockman suffered for most of the next two years from arteriosclerosis, which he believed to have been caused by the strain of the protracted 40-hour case and which necessitated his carrying out most of his duties from his sick bed.

His strengths had been those of personality rather than intellect. He was an effective negotiator and arbitrated easily and confidently. Moreover his practical, humane approach to problems, allied to his political sensing of current needs, attuned him to the Labor government's concern for full employment and the avoidance of situations which might jeopardize the employment of demobilized soldiers. For the two years of his appointment there was respect and easy understanding between the prime minister and the chief judge, and union leaders felt that he appreciated their point of view at times when others had accused them of being recalcitrant and illogical. Edmund Drake-Brockman was not a lawyer's judge like his successor Kelly. Nor was he a social innovator in the mould of H. B. Higgins [q.v.]. His contribution to history was that his mixture of conservatism and pragmatism, expressed by a reliable personality, carried the institution of industrial arbitration through what could have been stormy times of transition from war to peacetime activity.

Predeceased by his wife, he died on 1 June 1949 at Tarnook, Victoria, and was cremated. Two daughters and a son survived him.

C. E. W. Bean, *The story of Anzac* (Syd, 1921, 1924), and *The A.I.F. in France*, 1916-18 (Syd, 1929, 1933, 1937, 1942); R. Gollan, *The coalminers of New South Wales* (Melb, 1963); E. Ross, *A history of the Miners' Federation of Australia* (Syd, 1970); *PD* (Cwlth), 1926 p 3269; *Reveille* (Syd), Nov 1935; *Aust Law J*, 23 (1949-50), p 90; *Herald* (Melb), 22 July 1947, 2 June 1949; *West Australian*, 3 June 1949; A2153 (AAO).   IAN G. SHARP

DRAKE-BROCKMAN,   FREDERICK SLADE (1857-1917), surveyor and explorer, was born on 9 July 1857 at Seabrook, near Northam, Western Australia, son of Edmund Ralph Brockman, gentleman-farmer, and his wife Elizabeth Deborah, née Slade. Although properly a member of the Drake-Brockman family, he styled himself Brockman; his descendants, however, reverted to the ancestral name. The combined form originated in 1768 when the surnames of Ralph Drake and his wife Caroline were combined by Act of parliament. He was educated at Bishop Hale's [q.v.4] school and articled in 1878 to surveyor J. S. Brooking. While stationed at the Preston River he married Grace Vernon, daughter of Alfred Pickmore Bussell [q.v.3], on 20 February 1882 at St Mary's Church, Busselton. She was the heroine of the *Georgette* disaster (1875) when she helped to save some fifty lives.

Drake-Brockman joined the Department of Public Works and Railways in 1886 and was surveyor-in-charge of road and telegraph routes from Wyndham to Hall's Creek; his last campsite being known as 'the Brockman'. In May 1891 he transferred to Lands and Surveys, becoming chief inspecting surveyor in 1894. As staff surveyor he oversaw the drainage of the Harvey and Stirling estates and marked out the second line of the rabbit-proof fence from the Murchison to the Eucla. After the department's decentralization in 1910, Drake-Brockman served as district surveyor for Nelson until appointed surveyor-general in June 1915.

An impressive explorer, Drake-Brockman was accompanied by eleven men when in 1901 he penetrated previously uncharted territory in the Kimberley, north of latitude 17°. His senior officers, Charles Crossland, second-in-command, Dr F. M. House, botanist, and A. Gibb Maitland [q.v.], the government geologist, explored areas at right angles to the main route, thus reducing the exploration time schedule to six months and eighteen days. Leaving Wyndham on 9 May, the explorers followed the Pentecost River then pushed north-west through the Leopold Range to Walcott Inlet and returned along the Drysdale River on the 15th parallel to reach their depot on 26 November, having passed many Aboriginals *en route*. Discarding a faulty chronometer, Drake-Brockman checked his course by a system of rough triangulation between prominent landmarks and measured distance by astronomical bearings.

By identifying topographical features mentioned by Sir George Grey [q.v.1], T. C. Sholl and F. H. Hann [q.v.4] and naming others including the Princess May Ranges and the Calder and King Edward rivers, Drake-Brockman succeeded in reconciling existing discrepancies and so completed reliable plans. His party also gathered geographical, geological and botanical information, and Aboriginal artefacts and ornithological specimens for the Western Australian Museum; the black grass wren *Amytis (Amytornis) Housei* was new to science. Because of tick infestation near North Mount Cockburn, Drake-Brockman advised against a stockroute to Wyndham, instead recommending Napier, Broome Bay, as an outlet for pastures on the Synott tableland and north of the Leopold Range. His report of the exploration was published in Parliamentary Papers next year.

In the south-west, Drake-Brockman's 1904 report and classification of land for stock, dairying, fruit and potato growing between the Vasse and Shannon rivers, was a precursor to development. He declared in 1913 the resultant subdivision to be 'probably the finest cadastral survey that has been effected in Australia'. During his career he was chairman of the land section of the Repatriation Board, the Wodgil Board, the Town Planning Association and the Licensed Surveyors Advisory Board, and a member of the Railway Advisory Board. In England in 1905 he actively promoted migration to Western Australia.

Tall and straight as a ramrod, with a long gingerish moustache and penetrating blue eyes, Drake-Brockman was very much a family man, whose colourful yarns were spiked with humour. He died of pneumonia on 11 September 1917, survived by his wife, three daughters and four sons, most of whom had distinguished careers: Geoffrey (1885-1977) was engineer for the north-west in 1927-41 and director, engineering services, Army Headquarters, in 1941-43; Karl Edgar (b. 1891) was a Rhodes Scholar (1910), a member of the 5th Royal Fusiliers in 1915-18

and a puisne judge in New Guinea in 1921. E. A. Drake-Brockman and Deborah V. Hackett [qq.v.] were also his children. His estate was declared for probate at £1018 and he was buried in the Anglican section at Karrakatta cemetery.

D. H. Drake-Brockman, *Record of the Brockman and Drake-Brockman family* (priv print, Sussex, 1936); G. Drake-Brockman, *The turning wheel* (Perth, 1960); *Western Mail* (Perth), 14 Sept 1917; *Survey J of WA*, Feb 1918.   WENDY BIRMAN

DRAPER, ALEXANDER FREDERICK JOHN (1863-1928), businessman and politician, was born on 5 April 1863 at Williamstown, Victoria, eldest of seventeen children of Henry John Mollett Draper, pilot, and his wife Eileen, née Young. At 16 he entered the Bank of Australasia and served in country towns of New South Wales and Victoria. He was transferred in 1884 to Townsville, Queensland, then to Charters Towers. When he settled at Cairns as manager, his ability, energy and interest in local affairs soon became apparent in the railway league, hospital committee, fire brigade, whose board he frequently chaired, progress association and sporting bodies. He was also a captain of volunteers. He married Georgina Mary Capron at Williamstown on 9 April 1885.

Recognizing the agricultural and mineral potential of the Cairns district, Queensland, Draper left the bank that year. In 1884 he became one of the first shippers of bananas, which were grown by immigrant Chinese, and which during the 1890s were the economic mainstay of Cairns. More than any other European, he maintained close connexions with the industry until its virtual demise about 1913. With W. D. Hobson and others, he bought the ill-fated Hop Wah sugar plantation in 1886. The partnership was dissolved when the plantation continued to fail and Draper set up on his own as an auctioneer and commission agent. A. J. Draper & Co. financed many local farmers.

He supported the conservative candidate R. A. Kingsford [q.v.5] at both the divisional board elections of 1885 and the Legislative Assembly elections of 1888. Elected next year to the Cairns Town Council, he rapidly became prominent, served as mayor in 1892-93, 1896-97, 1902, 1918, and 1924-27, and resigned from the council only when defeated for the mayoralty in April 1927. His insistence on economy in the 1890s was not entirely popular; his outspokenness made political enemies, and because of close Chinese friendships he was often labelled pro-Chinese. Secretary also of the Barron Divisional Board in 1893-1919, he helped to found the Cairns Stock Exchange and chaired both the board of enquiry into hydro-electricity and the Patriotic League.

Though urged to enter Federal politics, Draper stayed in Cairns because he believed in the importance of local issues and because of his extensive business interests. In January 1885 he and Hobson had founded the *Cairns Chronicle* supporting Sir Thomas McIlwraith [q.v.5]. Draper's brother Edwin (d. 1901) was involved, as editor, in a horsewhipping, a libel action and much besides. In 1893, partly as a result of the depression, Draper was briefly in voluntary liquidation and lost control of the *Chronicle*, but he recovered rapidly and never again looked back. By the turn of the century, he had interests in mining and an increasing involvement in the sugar industry.

The Mulgrave mill was the first central sugar-mill established in the district under the Sugar Works Guarantee Act of 1893. In 1897 Draper was appointed chairman of directors and was largely responsible for heavy borrowing to extend the mill's facilities. When loan interest payments proved burdensome, the shareholders threatened revolt but good results in 1899 restored Draper's reputation and he remained a director until his death. He himself grew cane at Babinda, encouraged others and actively campaigned for a mill which was established there in 1911.

Threats to the future of Pacific island labour at the turn of the century caused widespread apprehension among sugar-planters and Draper was among those urging its continuation. He admitted later that his fears had not been realized. Nevertheless, the first twenty years of the century were an uneasy period for planters. Draper was foundation chairman of both the Queensland Sugar Producers' Association (1907) and the Cairns Cane Growers' Association (1911), formed to combat labour problems. The latter was partly a response to increasing strength and militancy of the unions; consistently an anti-unionist, Draper was anathema to the labour movement. His interest in the *Cairns Post*, revived by E. Draper & Co. in 1895, led to the establishment about 1900 of the Labour-oriented *Cairns Times*, eventually taken over directly by the unions. During the strike of 1925 he was a member of a committee to organize the loading of sugar by farmers in defiance of striking wharflabourers, and headed the procession of farmers through Cairns to the wharf; the incident possibly helped to lose him the mayoralty.

Thereafter, Draper abandoned politics but remained active in the sugar industry. During a trip to Brisbane to attend meetings of the Australian Sugar Producers' As-

sociation and the Cane Growers' Council, he died of vascular disease on 21 March 1928, survived by his wife and six daughters. He was buried at Cairns and left an estate valued for probate at £49 989.

Cairns Post Pty Ltd, *The life of A. J. Draper* (Cairns, 1931); D. Jones, *Trinity Phoenix* (Cairns, 1976); *Aust Sugar J*, July 1976, p 196; liquidation files, SCT/11/W8/1893 (QA). CATHERINE MAY

DRAPER, THOMAS PERCY (1864-1946), politician and judge, was born on 29 December 1864 at Warrington, Lancashire, England, son of Thomas Draper, tanner, and his wife Annie, née Webster. He was educated at Tonbridge School, 1880-83, and Clare College, Cambridge, 1883-86, taking first-class honours in classics. Called to the Bar at the Inner Temple in January 1891, he migrated that year to Western Australia, where he taught for a term at the High School, Perth, and practised law on the goldfields. Possibly through his prowess as a cricketer he soon attracted attention and advanced rapidly from associate to Mr Justice Hensman [q.v.4] in 1892, to secretary of the Crown Law Department (1893); in private practice in 1894-96, he practised in Coolgardie in 1896-97 and became a partner in Parker & Parker in 1901. In 1898 he narrowly defeated Frank Wilson [q.v.] for an East Ward seat on the Perth City Council. He served on the works, health, and finance committees, and was interested in town planning until his resignation in 1901.

Draper was described in 1905 as having 'a saintly ascetic expression'. In spite of a diffident manner and squeaky treble voice, he succeeded in entering the Legislative Assembly at a by-election for West Perth in September 1907. A developer himself and a nominee of the (Liberal) National Political League, he campaigned in opposition to the land tax proposals of (Sir) Newton Moore's [q.v.] ministry, which were thought disadvantageous to urban landowners. His victory encouraged the Legislative Council to reject the bill and provoked a constitutional crisis. Draper remained on the Liberal back-benches, an occasional critic of government expenditure until, having become a King's Counsel in 1910, he retired next year to practise law.

In World War I Draper was chairman of the Red Cross in Western Australia and was appointed C.B.E. in 1918 for his work. He also served on the Senate of the University of Western Australia in 1914-1920. Returning to politics in 1917 as a Nationalist, he regained the West Perth seat and in May 1919 became attorney-general in (Sir) James Mitchell's [q.v.] first ministry. During his term the matrimonial laws were amended to recognize five years desertion as grounds for divorce. He introduced a number of changes to the Electoral Act, notably allowing women to run for parliament. His constituency included a high proportion of women and at the 1921 elections Draper lost the seat to Edith Cowan [q.v.].

That year he was appointed a judge of the Supreme Court of Western Australia. Until the appointment of (Sir) Walter Dwyer [q.v.] in 1925, Draper presided over much arbitration work; he was also judge in many important criminal trials. In 1939 he retired. His recreations at this time were golf, walking and bird-watching. On 15 July 1894, he had married Mabel Constance, daughter of (Sir Stephen) Henry Parker [q.v.],senior partner in his firm. They had four sons and two daughters. She died in 1930 and on 9 April 1931 he married Bessie Melrose Barker, a widow. Draper died at West Perth on 11 July 1946 and was buried in the Anglican section of Karrakatta cemetery. His estate was sworn for probate at £938.

Truthful Thomas, *Through the spy-glass* (Perth, 1905); C.T. Stannage, *The people of Perth* (Perth, 1979); *Western Mail* (Perth), 5 Oct 1917; *Aust Law J*, 12 (1938-39); *West Australian*, 22 Dec 1938, 12 July 1946.   G. C. BOLTON
                                          PAT SIMPSON

DREW, JOHN MICHAEL (1865-1947), journalist and politician, was born on 17 October 1865 at Wanerenooka near Northampton, Western Australia, eldest son of Cornelius Drew, farmer, and his wife Mary, née Gavin. Drew left school at 15 and worked as a telegraphist for two years, then for Gale, Monger & Co. at Geraldton before teaching for two years at the Northampton Assisted School. He began contributing regularly to the Catholic *Record*, whose editor, Rev. John O'Reily [q.v.], persuaded him in 1885 to learn journalism with him at Fremantle. This led to a sub-editorship with the paper.

In 1890 Drew resigned, returned to Northampton and planted a successful orchard and vineyard. That year he became secretary and manager of the company which produced the *Victorian Express* and in 1892 became editor. Two years later the paper's name was changed to the *Geraldton Express*; it grew to achieve the largest circulation of any provincial paper in the colony. In 1912 Drew bought it. As editor he was scrupulous, honest and unbiased: that year he spent fourteen days in gaol for refusing to name a correspondent to the paper who had criticized the local government hospital's doctor. He proudly described his paper, which voiced hostility to Sir John

Forrest's [q.v.] government, as 'a scourge of injustice, the scourge of inhumanity, the scourge of the oppressors of the poor and of public robbers'. On 19 February 1895 at Geraldton he married Mary Frances Commerford.

Sympathetic to the newly formed Political Labor Party, Drew championed the underprivileged and argued for a more equitable society. He strongly advocated the rights of the town and district of Geraldton, and although he criticized insular attitudes, he always sympathized with isolated people deprived of urban comforts. The paper was a vociferous opponent of Federation and in 1899 Drew appeared before a joint select committee to give his arguments, at great length, against the draft bill to set up the Commonwealth; he considered that though the constitution was democratic in theory, it would prove very conservative in practice. Next year he was elected as an independent member for the Central Province of the Legislative Council. In 1904 when the Labor Party first came to power under Henry Daglish [q.v.] it lacked representation in the Legislative Council. Drew and three other independents promised their support and he became minister for lands (August 1904-June 1905) and, in 1905, minister for agriculture, colonial secretary and leader in the council.

At a Geraldton policy speech for the ministerial elections in August, he announced that he would not join the party or support abolition of the council. He favoured old-age pensions (and a state lottery to finance them), payment of members and the breaking up and repurchase of large landed estates. Drew wanted closer settlement of the land for the small man, preferably on a leasehold basis, and agreed with the P.L.P. plank advocating taxation of all land not profitably used. He also favoured liberal exemption from taxation for those using land to the advantage of the state and for selectors during the first three years of their tenure. He opposed the P.L.P. planks which wanted to stop further alienation of crown land, and to redistribute seats on a population basis and he was also against extending universal suffrage to the Legislative Council. The ministry fell next year and was defeated at the October elections, but Drew retained his seat as an independent. In 1905 he relinquished the editorship of the *Express*. At this time he was described by a pamphleteer as having a small face with a big forehead; sharp-featured, he had a fair, ruddy complexion and ginger hair turning grey.

At the P.L.P.'s 1910 congress it was determined that future ministries would be elected by caucus. Drew's subsequent admission to caucus sittings brought strong criticism. But the party's State executive was assured of his loyalty and it was made clear to the parliamentary party that six months membership would be necessary for future admission to cabinet. Drew then became a financial member of the party. In 1911 when Labor again won office under John Scaddan [q.v.], Drew and W. C. Angwin [q.v.7] were the only coastal members re-elected and, with Jabez Dodd, were known as men of strong principle. Drew again became colonial secretary.

The P.L.P. now embarked on a policy of socialism: plans were set in motion for workers' homes, a state shipping service, a dairy and sawmills, purchase of the metropolitan tramways and establishment of a state-owned meat industry. The government obtained a metropolitan electricity plant, bought the river ferry and set up a co-ordinated fishing industry. At the party's 1916 Kalgoorlie congress, Drew backed conscription, but this issue, coupled with what was seen as ministerial inexperience, led to their losing the 1918 election. Drew suffered his only political defeat.

He regained office with the party in 1924 and, under Philip Collier [q.v.], administered the portfolios of education, health and the North-West as well as being chief secretary. He continued to do so until 1930 when Collier's government resigned; in 1933 he again became chief secretary but on 27 August 1936 retired to private membership. Drew had been liked for his unassuming manner during his long term as a member: he came to be seen as an elder of parliament, respected by all parties. As a journalist he had taken pride in his 'unswerving independence' and he tried to maintain that approach in politics; but years of fighting Labor's battles in a hostile Upper House blunted his force. Although he was a moderate and, perhaps an unimaginative administrator, he successfully fought for preservation of the State's history and for prison reform, on which he published two pamphlets. He contributed regularly to the Sydney *Bulletin* and was a member of the Senate of the University of Western Australia from 1925.

Predeceased by his wife, Drew died of cancer on 17 July 1947 at Perth and was buried in the Catholic section of Karrakatta cemetery. He was survived by a daughter and a son.

Truthful Thomas, *Through the spy-glass* (Perth, 1905); C. T. Stannage, *The people of Perth* (Perth, 1979); *V&P* (LA WA), 1899 (A10); *Labour Hist*, May 1962, no 2, p 48; *Univ Studies in History* (WA), Oct 1959, p 58; *Western Argus*, 24 May 1900; *West Australian*, 22 Aug 1904, 18 July 1947; *Westralian Worker*, 29 Sept 1905; *Geraldton Express*, nd, c.1897, Murchison goldfields supp; H. J. Gibbney,

Working class organization in West Australia from 1880 to 1902 (B.A. Hons thesis, Univ WA, 1949); A. H. Panton, *Political history of the ALP in Western Australia* (Battye Lib, Perth).

MARY ALBERTUS BAIN

DRUMMOND, DAVID HENRY (1890-1965), farmer and politician, was born on 11 February 1890 at Lewisham, Sydney, fourth son of Scottish parents Morris Cook Drummond (d. 1896), stonemason, and his wife Catherine (d. 1892), née McMillan. He was educated at public schools and, in 1901, at Scots College until financial problems forced him to leave in May 1902 to begin work. In October he came into the custody of the New South Wales State Children's Relief Board as a ward of the state.

In 1907 Drummond went to Armidale as a farm-hand and in 1911 moved to Inverell as a share-farmer and manager of Oakwood, a wheat-property. On 11 March 1913 at Uralla he married Pearl Hilda Victoria Goode, daughter of a grazier. A childhood infection had left him deaf and in 1915 he was rejected for war service. He was active in the Farmers and Settlers' Association, and in 1919 became an organizer for the new Progressive Party, formed by the F.S.A. and the Graziers' Association of New South Wales. In the elections of 1920 he and (Sir) Michael Bruxner [q.v.7] won seats in the Legislative Assembly. Drummond retained his place in 1922 and 1925, and on the return to single-member seats in 1927 he won Armidale, keeping it until 1949.

In 1921 Drummond was one of the 'True Blues' who stood out against a coalition with (Sir) George Fuller [q.v.], and later described themselves as the Country Party. He was on the Parliamentary Standing Committee on Public Works in 1922-25 and deputy chairman of committees from 1922 to 1927. From 1925 he was on the executive of the F.S.A. and was its president in 1927-28. He was a foundation executive-member of the Northern New State Movement.

Drummond was minister for education in the Bavin [q.v.7] ministry in 1927-30, and again in the Stevens-Bruxner and Mair-Bruxner [qq.v.] coalitions from 1932 to 1941. He proved an energetic and authoritative minister. At first he concentrated on rural education: the junior farmers' movement, Australia's first country teachers' college (at Armidale), and increased construction of small rural schools.

During his long second term he widened his perspectives. Aware of the importance of technical education, he established in 1936 the Council of State Education Ministers to seek Commonwealth assistance for it. He desired to 'develop local participation in education', and his Technical Education Act of 1940 shared the control of technical colleges with various local authorities. He also promoted the University of New England, established as a college of the University of Sydney in 1937. Drummond was a member of its council from 1954 and was given an honorary D. Litt. in 1957. His account of the foundation of the university was published in 1959 as *A university is born*.

Drummond had ministerial responsibility also for the New South Wales Child Welfare Department, which had replaced the State Children's Relief Board in 1923. His Child Welfare Act of 1939 provided the legislative framework for children's welfare for the next forty years. Widely read and well-known for his love of literature, he also carried through the Library Act which established the State system of public libraries. The same year he was made an honorary fellow of the Royal Australian Historical Society.

Throughout his career Drummond was interested in constitutional issues. He played an important part in the reconstruction of the Legislative Council in 1933, and published three books and several articles on constitutional topics. In 1931 he was prominent in the merger of the new State movements with the Country Party to form the United Country Movement. As deputy leader of the parliamentary party in 1939-49, he helped to reorganize the party after its 1941 election disaster, and to write its new constitution of 1946.

Drummond resigned his seat in 1949 and won New England in the Federal elections. He became an influential back-bencher, heading discussions which lead to the formation of the Parliamentary Joint Committee of Constitutional Review in 1956; its report in 1959 recommended an easier passage for proposals to create new States, a matter favoured by Drummond for forty years. He was also a member of the Joint Parliamentary Committee on Foreign Affairs from 1952 to 1961, and attended the Inter-Parliamentary Union Conference of 1956 in Bangkok. He retired from parliament in 1963.

In Armidale, Drummond was a leading citizen, and a director of the Armidale Newspaper Co. Ltd, Northern Newspapers Pty Ltd, and Television New England Ltd. The *Armidale Express* faithfully echoed his ideas and publicized his achievements. He was a regular churchgoer and a committed Christian, while his family background gave him a continuing concern for the underdog. He was a big man, with a sonorous voice and a certain presence. He enjoyed tennis and fishing, was a foundation member of the Australian Geographical Society in 1943, and belonged to the University and Great Public Schools clubs.

Drummond was seriously injured and his wife killed in a car crash in 1958; on 21 December 1959 at St Stephen's Presbyterian Church, Sydney, he married Amy Laing. He died in hospital at Armidale on 13 June 1965 and was buried in the Methodist section of Armidale cemetery after a service in the Presbyterian church. He was survived by his second wife and four of six daughters of his first marriage. Portraits by Norman Carter [q.v.7] are held by the University of New England and the Armidale College of Advanced Education, and one by Judy Cassab is in the university's Drummond College. In Armidale a school and park were also named after him, and a memorial has been built overlooking the city.

U. R. Ellis, *New Australian states* (Syd, 1933), and *The Country Party* (Melb, 1958); D. Aitkin, *The colonel* (Canb, 1969), and *The Country Party in New South Wales* (Canb, 1972); C. B. Newling, *The long day wanes* (Syd, 1973); B. A. Mitchell, *Teachers, education, and politics* (Brisb, 1975); B. Bessant and A. Spaull, *Politics and schooling* (Melb, 1976); Armidale Hist Soc, *J and Procs,* Mar 1979.

                                              JIM BELSHAW

DRUMMOND, STANLEY GILLICK (1884-1943), Methodist minister and founder of the Far West Children's Health Scheme, was born on 22 May 1884 at Attunga, New South Wales, elder son of James Drummond and his native-born wife Mary Jane, née Richardson. His father was born at Beechworth, Victoria, and was a saddler by trade; he and his wife taught in New South Wales public schools. Stanley was educated at various schools where his father taught, but was not a keen student and on leaving school became a junior clerk in the Department of Lands at Queanbeyan. After contracting pneumonia he followed medical advice and took up outdoor work as a carpenter's assistant.

Drummond suddenly decided to enter the Methodist ministry, studied at the Sydney Central Methodist Mission, and in late 1909 took charge of the Home Mission station at Bulahdelah. In his first year he was thrown from a sulky on to his hip and spent eighteen months in pain in an iron splint, moving with the aid of crutches. He eventually recovered but retained a slight limp. At Bowral on 13 November 1911, describing himself as an artist, he married 35-year-old Lucy Doust, who had been a mission sister at the Central Methodist Mission.

Admitted to the ministry, Drummond was in charge of the Rylstone circuit (1914-18), Canowindra (1919-22) and Yass (1923). In April next year he became superintendent of the Far West Mission based at Cobar and travelled extensively with his wife in the heat and dust of the area. Recuperating on Manly Beach from the removal of his gall bladder, he had on 6 December what he described as an inspiration: 'to bring from the Far West to the seaside, children of the kind who would otherwise never see the sea during their childhood'. The Drummonds returned to Cobar, and in January 1925 brought to Sydney a party of 58 children and 6 mothers, whereupon Drummond returned to organize a second group of 128. The speed and enthusiasm with which he acted were typical — details were left to others with resulting financial troubles and chaotic arrangements. Drummond also learned that many children needed not so much a seaside holiday as medical, surgical and dental attention, and the original idea was changed to become the Far West Children's Health Scheme.

In 1926 he enlisted the co-operation of teachers, clergy and police to select children for the health scheme, and also secured the enthusiastic help of the member for Bourke, M. A. Davidson [q.v.]. In 1927 Drummond's health deteriorated and he chose to abandon his Church position and risk financial insecurity, which was partly relieved by £250 damages he received for being hit by a car in 1928. The scheme expanded after 1930; trains and planes were used by travelling clinics and sisters in the west. In 1933 he was appointed M.B.E., and in July published in *Health* his account of the inspiration and innovations of the operation. With the addition of public funds the Drummond Far West Home was opened at Manly in 1935. In 1936 Drummond suffered a severe heart attack and increasing deafness. He died of cancer on 24 April 1943 and was cremated with Methodist forms; his wife had died on 18 December 1942.

Drummond was an inspired man from that moment on Manly Beach in 1924 and he did not spare himself, his devoted wife or other supporters in pursuing the dream of helping far west children. He was a sincere idealist whose ideas captured the enthusiasm of others; leading figures in education, the railways, and the medical profession co-operated willingly; valuable publicity and other help was obtained from Drummond's contacts with the *Sydney Morning Herald* and such leading citizens as the governor Sir Philip Game [q.v.] and his wife. Drummond's inspiration seemed to have had little of a directly religious nature in it — he rarely talked of religion and insisted that the scheme was non-sectarian. He was spurred by his own pain from the hip injury, his love of children combined with disappointment at having none of his own, and his

acquaintance with difficulties of life in the outback.

M. Maclean, *Drummond of the far west* (Syd, 1947); P. Wearn, *The magic shoulder* (Syd, 1966); Far West Children's Health Scheme (Syd), *Annual Report*, 1936-40; information from Mr N. W. Drummond, Royal Far West Children's Health Scheme, Manly.   BRUCE MITCHELL

DRYER, ALBERT THOMAS (1888-1963), medical practitioner and Irish republican, was born on 1 March 1888 at Balmain, Sydney, son of Albert James Dryer, a Sydney-born clerk, and his Irish wife Mary Ann, née Cusick. He was educated in various primary schools at Singleton and Sydney in 1896-1904, then at night schools. In 1911 he matriculated at the University of Sydney (B.A., 1914).

Dryer began his working life in Melbourne in 1905, with several short-term jobs. He entered the Victorian Public Service in 1907, and in 1908 the Commonwealth Customs Department as a clerk in Melbourne, being transferred to Sydney in 1909. In 1914 he read Alice Stopford Green's *Irish Nationality* (1911) which converted him to passionate interest in the cause of Irish independence. With that objective, he founded the Irish National Association of New South Wales in Sydney on 21 July 1915. Following the 1916 Easter Rebellion in Dublin, this small but militant association, which had spread to Melbourne and Brisbane, came under increasing government suspicion as disloyal and revolutionary. In June 1918 seven of its members, including Dryer, were interned in Darlinghurst gaol as suspected members of the proscribed, secret Irish Republican Brotherhood; an inquiry was conducted by (Sir) John Harvey [q.v.] in August. Dryer was released in February 1919 but, dismissed from the Department of Customs, he opened a short-lived Irish book depot.

After failing in such ventures as bookkeeping, coaching and shopkeeping, including his own Academic Coaching College, he attended Sydney Technical College (associate in science and biology 1926) and in 1929 passed first-year medicine at the university without attending lectures. In 1932 he borrowed money to enter medical school full-time and graduated M.B., B.S. in 1938. After a series of locum tenens appointments, he set up practice at Fairfield in 1940, moving to Singleton after World War II. Until 1963 Dryer remained a central figure in the Irish National Association, and did much to secure the building of its present premises in Devonshire Street, Sydney; its library is named as his memorial. He organized the Sydney visit of Eamon de Valera in 1948, when he also founded the Australian League for an Undivided Ireland, which existed until 1954.

Dryer never visited Ireland, but his devotion to the cause of Irish independence, and particularly the party of de Valera was constant, selfless and total. With great ability and remarkable strength of character and purpose, he was essentially a romantic idealist to whom Ireland represented all that was noble in human affairs. His high intelligence and gentlemanly disposition stopped him well short of any fanaticism, but the realities of indifference and in-fighting which afflicted the Irish cause in Australia were a source of deep disappointment and frustration to him.

At St Mary's Cathedral, Sydney, Dryer had married Elizabeth Ellen Haynes, on 29 April 1933: they had been engaged since 1915 because of the insecurity of his employment. Their only child Albert Benjamin was born in 1934. Dryer died of cancer in Lewisham Hospital, Sydney, on 11 April 1963, survived by his wife and son. A devout Roman Catholic, he was buried at Singleton.

PTHRA, 21 (1974), no 4; P. O'Farrell, The formation of the Irish National Association of New South Wales, Sydney: July 1915-April 1916 (copy held by author); Dryer family papers, (notes held by P. O'Farrell, Univ NSW).

PATRICK O'FARRELL

DUCKWORTH, ARTHUR (1861-1943), accountant and economist, was born on 11 February 1861, at Tollington, near Bury, Lancashire, England, son of Zaccheus Duckworth, a cotton-mill manager, and his wife Jane, née Hamer. At 11 he began work in the Manchester office of a Scottish insurance company but in early 1875 he migrated to Victoria with his family. In February Duckworth became a clerk in the Melbourne branch of the Australian Mutual Provident Society and in 1882 was transferred to Sydney. On 9 July 1888 at Richmond, Melbourne, he married Matilda Crowther with Wesleyan forms.

An enthusiastic and energetic amateur economist, Duckworth was a stalwart of the Australian Economic Association, which operated in Sydney in 1887-98, serving briefly as secretary then as editor of its periodical the *Australian Economist*. His vigour and business experience help to explain the success and longevity of the journal, one of the first of its kind in the English-speaking world. Like others in the association Duckworth was intellectually eclectic. He could defend tariff protection with arguments from German as well as Anglo-Saxon authorities, and he was a convinced bimetallist. But he was sceptical of land reform, especially along lines proposed by Henry George [q.v.4].

At a time when the rest of the world was watching Australian experiments, at least as much as Australia was looking abroad, Duckworth was an effective communicator in both directions. He regularly commented on Australian affairs for the Royal Economic Society's *Economic Journal*, which began publication in London in 1890. Appointed correspondent for New South Wales in 1891, he wrote on such subjects of wide interest as labour disputes, changes in the price level, and the growth of protection. His work on Australian demographic change, where his actuarial experience stood him in good stead, attracted the attention of Professor F. Y. Edgeworth of Oxford.

Duckworth was also an active organizer of and contributor to the economic science section of the Royal Society of New South Wales, the social and statistical science section of the Australasian Association for the Advancement of Science, and the Actuarial Society of New South Wales. He was one of the two Australians who addressed the economic science section of the British Association for the Advancement of Science when it met in Australia in 1914. Professor S. J. Butlin believed that the strength of Duckworth's writings lay 'in the systematic collection and presentation of data rather than in any profundity of thought'.

After rising to become chief accountant, Duckworth retired in 1925 after fifty years service with the A.M.P. In retirement at Malabar, a seaside suburb of Sydney, he devoted himself to his garden and library, turning towards theology and economic history. Survived by three of his four sons, he died at his home on 22 September 1943 and was buried in Waverley cemetery with Anglican rites. His estate was valued for probate at £20 954.

His combination of a business career with a central place in the early days of economic science in Australia was made possible by the slow professionalization of the subject. The exceptional contributions of a person like Duckworth indicate what may have been lost in this development.

J. A La Nauze, *Political economy in Australia* (Melb, 1949); C. D. W. Goodwin, *Economic enquiry in Australia*, and *The image of Australia* (Durham, N.C., 1966, *and* 1974); Roy Economic Soc, *Economic J*, 54 (1944); *Economic Record*, 23 (1947); *SMH*, 24 Sept 1943.

CRAUFURD D. W. GOODWIN

DUDLEY, WILLIAM HUMBLE WARD, 2ND EARL (1867-1932), governor-general,

was born on 25 May 1867 in London, son of
William Ward, 1st earl, and his second wife
Georgiana Elizabeth, née Moncreiffe. His
mother, one of the beauties of her generation, was a favourite of the prince of Wales.
Educated at Eton, Dudley came into great
wealth when he succeeded his father in 1885,
and on a yachting cruise visited Australia in
1886-87. Tall and handsome, he was slightly
lame from a childhood accident. On 14
September 1891 at Chelsea he married
RACHEL (b. 1867), daughter of Charles Gur-
ney. Intelligent and forceful, though with 'a
reserved even absent manner', she was described by Ada Holman [q.v.] as 'beautiful
as a marble statue . . . a carved lily'. A
Conservative, Dudley was parliamentary
secretary to the Board of Trade in 1895-
1902, and in 1902-05 an extravagant and
controversial lord lieutenant of Ireland. In
1899 he had served briefly in the South
African war. In March 1908, partly at the
urging of King Edward VII, Dudley was
appointed governor-general of Australia, a
post which the Liberals had found difficult to
fill because of their weakness in the House of
Lords and Australia's apparent preference
for a rich peer.

Sworn in at Sydney on 8 September,
Dudley proceeded to Melbourne to a ceremonial welcome which prompted the
Worker to complain of 'a sham Australian
court of St James'. In less than a year, on 27
May 1909, the defeat of Andrew Fisher's
[q.v.] Labor government, and Fisher's
request for a dissolution, brought into
operation the constitutional functions of the
office. After obtaining advice secretly from
Chief Justice Griffith [q.v.], Dudley refused
the request, and on 2 June Alfred Deakin
[q.v.] formed his third ministry. During her
husband's governor-generalship Lady Dudley also asserted herself in the public arena:
in August 1909 she launched what became
Lady Dudley's Bush Nursing Scheme, but
the project faltered through lack of funds.

By October 1910 the Dudleys' estrangement (they separated in 1912) had virtually become common knowledge; John
Norton's [q.v.] *Truth* charged the earl with
'concupiscent capers'. Other newspapers
reported that relations between Dudley and
the second Fisher cabinet, which had taken
office in April 1910, were strained. Partly
this resulted from Labor discontent with the
increasing vice-regal allowance. In March
1911, after months of rumours of impending
retirement, it was announced that, for personal reasons, Dudley was returning to
England. On 31 July he relinquished office.
Deakin wrote of him:'His ambition was high
but his interests were short-lived . . . He did
nothing really important, nothing thoroughly, nothing consistently . . . He re-

mained . . . a very ineffective and not very
popular figurehead'.

During World War I Dudley commanded
a Yeomanry unit in Egypt and Gallipoli.
Lady Dudley also served, setting up a hospital for Australians, and clubs for officers in
northern France. In 1918 she was appointed
C.B.E. and was awarded the Royal Red
Cross. She drowned on 26 June 1920 while
sea-bathing in Ireland. In 1924 Lord Dudley
married Gertie Millar, musical comedy actress (the original 'Our Miss Gibbs') and
widow of Lionel Monckton. Survived by the
four sons and three daughters of his first
marriage, Dudley died of cancer in London
on 29 June 1932. A portrait by John Longstaff
[q.v.] is in Parliament House, Canberra.

D.N.B., 1931-40; *The Times*, 7 Nov 1918, 28 June
1920, 30 June 1932; C. Cunneen, The role of the
governor-general in Australia 1901-1927 (Ph.D.
thesis, ANU, 1973); Deakin papers, MS 1540/
19/275 (NL).   CHRIS CUNNEEN

DUESBURY, FRANK WENTWORTH
(1889-1960), chartered accountant and businessman, was born on 11 February 1889 at
Petersham, Sydney, elder son of John William Duesbury, an accountant from Derbyshire, and his native-born wife Mary, née
Biggs. His father, whose ancestor had
founded the manufacture of Royal Crown
Derby porcelain in 1750, migrated to Sydney
as a child in 1863 and became well known as
a public accountant, business entrepreneur
and innovator. Frank was educated at the
Grammar School, Mudgee, then worked in a
bank at Newcastle. He was practising as an
accountant in Sydney when he married
Nellie Madge, daughter of Captain Fergus
Cumming, on 19 September 1914 at Christ
Church Cathedral, Newcastle.

In 1921 Duesbury was a fellow of the
Institute of Incorporated Accountants of
New South Wales, of which body he was a
councillor and vice-president of its Students'
Society. When the institute was absorbed
into the Commonwealth Institute of Accountants in 1930, Duesbury was admitted
as a fellow. He was also an original fellow of
the Institute of Chartered Accountants in
Australia in 1928 and thereafter practised as
a chartered accountant, having founded the
firm of F. W. Duesbury & Co. in 1927.

As a professional accountant Frank
Duesbury's services were much sought after
– he became chairman of the P. & M. Co.
(Aust.) Ltd, Smith Sons & Rees Ltd, and
Brico (Aust.) Pty Ltd, and was a director of
such companies as Goodlet [q.v.4] & Smith
Ltd, W. H. Paling [q.v.5] & Co. Ltd, R. Fowler
[q.v.4] Ltd, Sargents Ltd, Music Houses of
Australia Ltd, Federal Mutual Insurance of

Australia Ltd and Newbold General Refractories Ltd. In 1959 he was voted out of the chair of Smith Sons & Rees Ltd when three directors reneged on accepting a take-over offer by Repco Ltd that he had negotiated; he resigned from the board and the offer lapsed.

Duesbury was interested in horse-breeding and racing administration. Already a committee-member of the Rosehill Racing Club, he was elected to the committee of the Australian Jockey Club in June 1942. He first leased Yarraman Park, Scone, and then bought successively Minnaville, Castlereagh (from which he derived an income of £600 a month from its river-gravel deposits), and Hobartville, Richmond. He looked after the financial affairs of A. W. (Frank) Thompson, owner of Widden Stud, Denman, whom he partnered in several breeding and racing ventures: little prize-money was won but many famous brood mares were bred. He was part-owner of Escutcheon, Hesione and Minnamurra, the dam of Achilles.

Survived by his wife and two daughters, Duesbury died in St Luke's Hospital, Darlinghurst, on 11 July 1960 and was cremated with Anglican rites. His estate was valued for probate at £128294.

B. Dalhunty, *The Dalhunty papers* (Syd, 1959); Inst of Incorporated Accountants of NSW, *Thirteenth Annual Report*, 1921; Cwlth Inst of Accountants, *Year Book*, 1937; *SMH*, 28 Aug 1959, 12 July 1960; Aust Jockey Club, Records (Randwick, NSW); Sydney Stock Exchange, Company records; family information.   R. G. DRYEN

DU FAUR, EMMELINE FREDA (1882-1935), mountaineer, was born on 16 September 1882 at Croydon, Sydney, daughter of Frederick Eccleston Du Faur [q.v.4] and his second wife Blanche Elizabeth Mary, daughter of Professor Woolley [q.v.6]. Educated at Sydney Church of England Grammar School for Girls under Edith Badham [q.v.7], Freda spent much of her leisure scrambling, with only a dog for company, in the gullies of the new national park at Ku-ring-gai Chase. She became a confident rock climber with a love for exploring. Although she began training as a nurse, she failed to complete the course because of her 'sensitive, highly strung nature'.

In 1906 Freda Du Faur went to New Zealand to see the Christchurch exhibition. She visited Mount Cook and was immediately captivated by the mountains and snow. At the end of 1908, after she had spent another two weeks in the Mount Cook area, Peter Graham, a New Zealand guide, agreed to teach her snow and ice craft. Back in New Zealand in December 1909, she undertook a series of increasingly difficult climbs. Her proposal to climb and bivouac in the sole company of Graham, although a man of acknowledged propriety, caused a flutter: to preserve her reputation she was compelled to take a third person to act as porter. Not until her fame as a mountaineer was established was she able to dispense with a chaperon. She always wore a skirt while climbing despite objections.

After three months training under the care of her greatest friend Muriel Cadogan at the Dupain Institute of Physical Education in Sydney, she returned to New Zealand in November 1910. On 3 December, guided by Peter and Alex Graham, Freda Du Faur became the first woman to climb Mount Cook (3760 m), New Zealand's highest peak, in the then record time of six hours. 'I gained the summit . . . feeling very little, very lonely and much inclined to cry'. In the same season she climbed Mounts De la Beche (2979 m), Green (2828 m) and Chudleigh (2944 m, a first ascent). Although climbing late in the season next year, she conquered a virgin peak now named Mount Du Faur (2389 m), Mount Nazomi (2953 m, also a first ascent), Mount Tasman (3497 m, second ascent), Mount Dampier (3430 m, first ascent), and Mount Lendenfeld (3192 m, second ascent). In her final season she made first ascents of Mount Pibrac (2567 m) and Mount Cadogan (2398 m), both of which she named. On 4 January 1913 she accomplished the feat with which her name will always be associated – the first grand traverse of the three peaks of Mount Cook, with guides Peter Graham and David Thomson. The grand traverse is still regarded as the classic climb of the New Zealand Alps. On 10 February the same party made the first traverse of Mount Sefton (3149 m).

From 1914 Freda Du Faur lived in England, drawn there by Muriel Cadogan; they lived for some time at Bournemouth. In 1915 she published *The conquest of Mount Cook and other climbs* in London (a reprint appeared in Sydney in 1936). Saddened by the death of her great friend in June 1929, she returned to Australia to live at Dee Why, initially with her brother's family and then in a cottage of her own. Her main interest was walking in the bush behind Dee Why and Collaroy; she was noticeably withdrawn and lonely. She died of self-inflicted carbon monoxide poisoning on or about 11 September 1935 and was buried in the Church of England cemetery at Manly. She never married.

Freda Du Faur's record of first ascents and difficult climbs made her pre-eminent among mountaineers of her time in New Zealand. She enjoyed the fame which followed her successes on Mount Cook, and was

Du Faur

feminine enough to take trouble with her appearance after the most arduous ascents. She was an agile climber, especially on rock, with great endurance.

J. G. Wilson, *Aorangi* (Christchurch, 1968); *NZ Alpine J*, 1936, p 388; information from Mr J. G. Du Faur, Seaforth, NSW.   E. J. O'DONNELL

DUFF, SIR ROBERT WILLIAM (1835-1895), governor, was born on 8 May 1835 at Fetteresso, Kincardineshire, Scotland, only son of Arthur Duff Abercromby, of Glassaugh, Banffshire, and his wife Elizabeth, née Innes. His father had assumed the surname Abercromby on inheriting his mother's estates. Robert was educated at Blackheath School, London, and in 1848 joined the Royal Navy. He was promoted sub-lieutenant in 1854 and lieutenant in 1856, retiring with the rank of commander in 1870. On succeeding to the extensive estates of his uncle, including Fetteresso Castle, he assumed the surname Duff early in 1862. He was a keen sportsman and good shot, and was a member of Brooks's, the Devonshire and the Turf clubs. On 21 January 1871 in London he married Louisa, daughter of Sir William Scott, baronet.

From May 1861 until March 1893 he sat in the House of Commons for Banffshire and, one of the 'Adullamites', followed Robert Lowe [q.v.2] in opposing Lord Russell's 1866 reform bill. Later a Gladstonian Liberal, Duff was a junior lord of the treasury in 1882-85, and a civil lord of the Admiralty in 1886; he became a privy councillor in 1892.

On the resignation of Lord Jersey [q.v.] as governor of New South Wales, Gladstone, opposed to the tradition of appointing a peer, wrote to Lord Ripon, secretary of state for the colonies: 'We of the H. of C. should like to see (Rt.Hon.) R. Duff. He would we believe do it well and other considerations recommend him'. Duff was appointed in March 1893 and arrived in Sydney with his family in the *Parramatta* on 29 May. Before leaving England he had been appointed G.C.M.G. Duff's first year was troubled. While on a cruise in H.M.S. *Orlando* he was asked by the premier Sir George Dibbs [q.v.4] to telegraph his assent to a proclamation abolishing the old electoral rolls and constituencies, and did so on 5 October. Ripon thought Dibbs's proceedings 'partook of the nature of sharp practice'.

In December Duff found himself in a dilemma when a motion of no confidence was carried against (Sir) Edmund Barton [q.v.7], attorney-general, and R. E. O'Connor [q.v.], minister for justice, for holding briefs against the Crown. If he had forced the

reluctant Dibbs to resign by refusing his advice to prorogue parliament on 8 December, the dismantled electoral machinery would have precluded the new ministers from standing for ministerial re-election; and they would have been unlikely to get supply. Duff was accused of partisanship by Sir Henry Parkes [q.v.5] and other free traders, and criticized in the press, but he believed his decision had been justified. He privately disapproved of Dibbs's action and his own Liberal background made him unsympathetic to the protectionist leader.

After losing the July 1894 elections, Dibbs asked the governor to nominate ten new members to the Legislative Council. Duff offered to make three appointments, but Dibbs resigned. The governor 'was sorry to have to report [to Ripon] Dibbs conduct in attempting to intimidate me by writing a memo full of false statements censuring my conduct, & then offering to withdraw it, if I would accede to his request'. He got on more comfortably with the new premier (Sir) George Reid [q.v.].

On the Imperial level Duff was involved in the protracted negotiations for compensation for the seizure of the *Costa Rica Packet* in the Dutch East Indies. When the Sino-Japanese war broke out he warned the New South Wales government of the dangers to neutral ships trading in coal with the belligerents and told the Colonial Office 'I do not want another "Costa Rica" case'. Handsome, bearded, with a luxuriantly curling moustache and high forehead, Duff carried out his duties with dignity. A prominent Freemason in Scotland, he was installed by Lord Kintore [q.v.5] as grand master of the United Grand Lodge of New South Wales soon after his arrival.

In February 1895 Duff visited Hobart; he became ill and on 9 March his medical attendant Dr Thomas Fiaschi [q.v.] was summoned. The governor returned to Sydney where he died at Government House with multiple hepatic abscesses and septicaemia on 15 March. The first New South Wales governor to die in office, he was buried in Waverley cemetery with Anglican and Masonic rites, in an impressive military ceremony; his funeral hatchment is in the Church of St James, Sydney. He was survived by his wife, three sons and four daughters.

DNB, to 1900, supp (vol 20); H. Stenton, *Who's who of British members of parliament* . . . 1, 2 (Lond, 1976); British A'sian, 16 Mar 1895; *JRAHS*, 56 (1970), pt 4, p 296; *Australasian*, and *Sydney Mail*, 4 Mar 1893; *SMH*, 11, 12 Dec 1893, 16, 18 Mar 1895; *The Times*, 16 Mar 1895; Lord Ripon papers (British Lib); CO 201/614-15.

MARTHA RUTLEDGE

DUFFIELD, WALTER GEOFFREY (1879-1929), astronomer, was born on 12 August 1879 at Gawler, South Australia, son of David Walter Duffield, merchant, and his wife Florence Evangeline, née Kirkpatrick, and grandson of Walter Duffield [q.v.4]. He attended Queen's School and the Collegiate School of St Peter, Adelaide. After graduating B.Sc. from the University of Adelaide in 1900 he won the Angas [q.v.3] engineering scholarship and entered Trinity College, Cambridge, England, where he obtained his B.A. after two years. He spent 1903 at the National Physical Laboratory on a Nobel research studentship.

Duffield then began research at the Victoria University of Manchester on the effects of pressure on arc spectra. His work, facilitated by a Royal Society Mackinnon studentship in 1906 and 1907, led to a D.Sc. (1908) and was described in four memoirs of the *Philosophical Transactions of the Royal Society* between 1907 and 1910. In 1910-23 Duffield was professor of physics at University College, Reading. He investigated the measurement of gravity at sea, undertaking experimental work during voyages to Australia in 1914 and 1923. He served in the Royal Flying Corps and Air Force in 1914-19.

In 1905 at Oxford and 1907 in Paris, Duffield attended meetings of the International Union for Solar Research, and assisted in editing the proceedings. Noting the lack of solar observatories near the longitude of eastern Australia he promoted the idea of an Australian establishment. In 1908 he became secretary of a committee appointed by the British Association for the Advancement of Science to forward the scheme, and next year visited Australia to pursue contacts with scientists and government. By 1910-11 a site on Mount Stromlo, Australian Capital Territory, had been chosen and a telescope erected for testing local conditions. Duffield inspected the site in 1914 but the war prevented any development. The final decision to proceed was taken in 1923 and Duffield was appointed first director of the Commonwealth Solar Observatory in January 1924.

Duffield intended the work of the observatory to embrace studies of the sun and its variations, geophysics that might be influenced by the sun, spectroscopy of the sun and relevant laboratory sources, and southern sky astronomy. A chronic asthmatic, he died of pneumonia on 1 August 1929 at Mount Stromlo while work was still in the preliminary stages. However, he had been able to supervise the completion of the buildings, the installation of equipment, the initial laboratory experimentation, and the photographing of stellar spectra. He wrote 'The luminosity of the night sky', which

appeared in the *Memoirs of the Commonwealth Solar Observatory* in 1928.

Duffield was a fellow of the Royal Astronomical Society from 1908, and helped to form the Canberra University College. Remembered as sympathetic and kindly, he was a foundation member of the Canberra Rotary Club and a double-bass player in the Stromberra Quintet. He was survived by his wife Doris Tennant Boult whom he had married on 9 June 1909 at St Peter's Anglican Church, Glenelg, South Australia, and by three children. His estate was valued for probate at £70 096. His grave lies on a western slope of Mount Stromlo, commanding a view of the observatory, and there is a commemorative plaque in St John's Church, Canberra.

E. H. Coombe (ed), *History of Gawler 1837 to 1908* (Adel, 1910); Roy Astronomical Soc, *Monthly Notices*, 90 (1930), no 4; *SMH*, 23 July, 8 Sept 1923, 2 Aug 1929; *Observer* (Adel), 24 Nov 1923, 21 Feb 1925; *Chronicle* (Adel), 8 Aug 1929; biog file (NL).

C. W. ALLEN

DUFFY, SIR CHARLES LEONARD GAVAN (1882-1961), judge, was born on 15 June 1882 at Caulfield, Melbourne, eldest son of (Sir) Frank Gavan Duffy [q.v.] and his wife Ellen Mary, née Torr. Duffy was educated at St Ignatius College, Riverview, Sydney, and at Xavier College, Melbourne, and entered Trinity College, University of Melbourne, where he studied law. He was then articled to C. J. Ahern at Wangaratta and on 1 December 1908 was admitted to the Bar, reading in the chambers of his relation (Sir) Hayden Starke [q.v.]. His urbane temperament and personal charm coupled with sound legal knowledge and considerable capacity as an advocate soon enabled him to gain a secure foothold at the Victorian Bar.

In 1908 Duffy joined the Australian Field Artillery as a second lieutenant, resigning in 1910. In April 1915 he enlisted in the Australian Imperial Force and in June went abroad as a second lieutenant in the A.F.A. Serving on Gallipoli and in France, he was promoted captain in January 1917, and temporary major in August commanding the 4th Field Battery, but was gassed in November. Rejoining his unit next May, he was wounded in September 1918 while in command of the battery. He was mentioned in dispatches, returning to Australia as a substantive major in August 1919. On 29 December at St Stanislaus Church, Toorak, he married Mary Marjorie Alexa Back (d.1959). Their only children, twin boys, died at birth.

On 30 May 1933, following the death of Sir Leo Cussen [q.v.], Duffy was appointed a justice of the Supreme Court of Victoria. The choice was popular and he proved a competent judge, gifted with keen memory and complete independence of mind and conducting his court admirably. At all times Duffy was courteous, considerate, and whimsically good humoured, but nevertheless dispatched business with firmness. His judgments, though not perhaps as deeply learned as some of his colleagues', displayed unerring instinct for legal principles and were sound and practical. On 1 January 1952 he was knighted for his services to the law.

In his early days Duffy enjoyed horse-riding and later was a modest but enthusiastic golfer. He was also extremely well read and enjoyed reciting poetry, especially Australian verse, but otherwise had few interests outside the law. Warm-hearted and kindly, he enjoyed a wide circle of friends. For many years he was a member of the Melbourne Club and in 1944 was elected its president.

Duffy's last years were burdened by physical disability but as one of the last Victorian judges not subject to compulsory retirement he continued to sit on the bench until a few days before his death, in so doing demonstrating considerable personal courage. He died on 12 August 1961 at East Melbourne and was buried in Boroondara cemetery, Kew. A handsome tribute to him as 'a great citizen and a distinguished judge' was paid in the Victorian Supreme Court by Chief Justice Sir Edmund Herring.

Aust Law J, 15 June 1933, p227; *Univ of Melb Gazette,* Dec 1961; *Victorian Reports,* 1961; *Argus,* 31 May 1933; *Age,* 14 Aug 1961; National Memorials Cttee notes (Duffy biog file, NL).

CHARLES FRANCIS

DUFFY, SIR FRANK GAVAN (1852-1936), chief justice, and CHARLES GAVAN (1855-1932), public servant, were born on 29 February 1852 and 27 August 1855 in Dublin, first and second sons of (Sir) Charles Gavan Duffy [q.v.4] and his second wife Susan, née Hughes. They came to Victoria with their parents in 1856. Frank was sent to England to attend Stonyhurst College, Lancashire, from 1865 to 1869. His education continued at the University of Melbourne, where he graduated B.A. in 1872 and obtained both his M.A. and LL.B. in 1882, having won the Bowen [q.v.3] prize in 1874. While studying he worked for a time as a clerk in the public service. On 3 April 1880 at St Mary's Catholic Church, St Kilda, he married Ellen Mary Torr.

In 1874 Duffy was admitted to the Bar. After four briefless years he gradually began to make a name for himself, first in the County Court and later in the Supreme Court. He often appeared with, or against, the redoubtable J. L. Purves [q.v.5]; they were regarded as the best trial lawyers of their time. Duffy took silk in 1901 and after Purves died in 1910 was the only K.C. in Melbourne.

Duffy was considered a sound lawyer, but his outstanding gift was as an advocate. It was said of him by Sir Owen Dixon, that he practised advocacy with extraordinary success and could make bricks without straw in open court. The other attributes for which he was renowned were a sharp wit and a keen sense of humour. He practised these gifts with much charm, aided by an easy eloquence and brilliant reasoning, which were conveyed forcefully and with speed. He was a formidable protagonist in court and a powerful cross-examiner. Yet he was never unfair to witnesses or parties. These qualities no doubt contributed to his wide popularity among his colleagues in the legal profession.

Among the noteworthy cases in which Duffy appeared was his defence in 1892 of the land speculator, Sir Matthew Davies [q.v.4]. (Duffy, himself involved in the crash following the land boom, paid his creditors 3d. in the £ at the time and gained a clear discharge; years later he was able to pay these debts in full.) In 1893 he appeared for Richard Speight [q.v.6], commissioner for railways, in a libel action against David Syme [q.v.6] of the *Age,* which went for eighty days and involved a claim for £25 000. After Federation he often appeared on behalf of the Commonwealth in constitutional cases in the High Court of Australia.

Duffy's busy practice did not prevent him from lecturing in contract and property at the university. He was also the author of a number of legal textbooks. In 1879 he founded the *Australian Law Times,* and in 1907 became the editor of the *Victorian Law Reports.*

In February 1913 Duffy was appointed to the vacancy on the High Court caused by the death of Mr Justice R. E. O'Connor [q.v.]. His appointment was followed by the creation of two new judges, (Sir) Charles Powers and (Sir) George Rich [qq.v.]. These three appointments initiated a new phase in constitutional interpretation. The two surviving original members of the court, Chief Justice Sir Samuel Griffith [q.v.] and Sir Edmund Barton [q.v.7] now consistently found themselves in a minority. The new appointees tended to support (Sir) Isaac Isaacs and H. B. Higgins [qq.v.] in applying common law principles of statutory construction to the Constitution, rather than relying on preconceptions based on participation in the Federal Convention debates. As time went on, however, Duffy's views showed an increasing State-rights orientation, as is shown by his dissents in leading constitutional cases, most notably in the seminal *Amalgamated Society of Engineers* v. *Adelaide Steamship Co. Ltd* (Engineers') case (1920) which cleared the way to an expansionist view of Federal powers.

On the swearing-in of Sir Isaac Isaacs as governor-general on 22 January 1931 Duffy, now 78, was appointed chief justice, in which office he was to continue for nearly five years. There had been some speculation that the Labor government would appoint Mr Justice Evatt who had not long been on the bench. Duffy's appointment was seen as a rebuff to the militant section of caucus. In 1929 he was appointed K.C.M.G. and in 1932 a Privy Councillor. He retired in October 1935 and died on 29 July 1936, survived by his wife and three sons, of whom the eldest was (Sir) Charles Leonard [q.v.]; a daughter and three sons predeceased him. Shortly before his death he accepted an invitation to take part in the tercentenary celebrations of Harvard University, but did not live to do so. His portrait, by W. B. McInnes [q.v.], hangs in the High Court building in Canberra. Another, by P. I. White, is in the possession of the Victorian Bar.

Duffy, by inclination a liberal but never active in politics, refused Senate nomination when it was offered to him. Among his outstanding qualities were his great kindness, as well as his extensive learning. He was said to have enjoyed hunting and to have been a crack shot in younger years. He was fluent in French and Italian. His poem 'A dream of fair judges', a parody of Tennyson's 'A dream of fair women' which he published, under the pseudonym 'Vie Manquée', in June 1892 in the *Summons*, the journal of the Melbourne Articled Law Clerks' Society, caused a considerable stir in legal circles and was remembered for many years.

His brother Charles Gavan attended St Patrick's College, Melbourne, and Stonyhurst College. He studied law at the University of Melbourne, graduating LL.B. in 1880, and was admitted to the Victorian Bar in the same year, but never practised. In 1871 he joined the staff of the Victorian Chief Secretary's Office and acted as private secretary to his father who was then premier. In 1878 he transferred to the Legislative Assembly as assistant clerk of committees and private secretary to several successive Speakers, being appointed clerk assistant of the Legislative Assembly in 1891. He acted as assistant secretary to the Australasian Federal Convention of 1897 and assisted (Sir) Robert Garran [q.v.] in putting the final corrections to the Commonwealth Constitution. For his part in this

work he was appointed C.M.G. in 1904.

After Federation Duffy moved to the Commonwealth Public Service and in May 1901 became clerk assistant in the Senate, and in July clerk of the House of Representatives. He served as secretary to the Federal War Committee in 1915-16 and was clerk of the Senate from 1917 to 1920, when he retired. Duffy married Ella, daughter of Allan McLean [q.v.], later premier of Victoria, on 18 April 1893, and had one son. Duffy died on 23 February 1932, and was buried in Boroondara cemetery.

Charles Gavan Duffy was well known for his exceptional knowledge of parliamentary procedure. He was the author of *Speakers' rulings 1856-7 to 1893* and of *Index to resolutions passed in the Legislative Assembly of Victoria*.

G. Sawer, *Australian Federal politics and law 1901-1929* (Melb, 1956); O. Dixon, *Jesting pilate* (Syd, 1965); A. Dean, *A multitude of counsellors* (Melb, 1968); G. Sawer, *Australian federalism in the courts* (Melb, 1968); R. G. Menzies, *The measure of the years* (Melb, 1970); *Aust Law J*, 9 (1935), p 239, 9 (1936), p 336, 10 (1936), p 158; *Australasian*, 29 Apr 1893; *Table Talk*, 11 July 1901; *Punch* (Melb), 5 Dec 1912, 5 Feb 1917; *Daily Standard*, 1 Jan, 7 Feb 1913; *SMH*, 23 Jan 1917; *Chronicle* (Adel), 9 Mar 1929, 29 Jan 1931; *Argus*, 24 Jan 1931, 24 Feb 1932, 30 July 1936; *Age*, 24 Feb 1932, 30 July 1936; *Queenslander*, 3 Mar 1932.

H. A. FINLAY

DUFFY, MAURICE BOYCE (1886-1957), accountant and union official, was born on 17 November 1886 at Iron Bark, Sandhurst (Bendigo), Victoria, second son of Richard Duffy, baker, and his wife Elizabeth Ann, née Boyce, both born at Castlemaine. After education by the Marist Brothers at Bendigo, and at Xavier College, Melbourne, 'Morrie' Duffy became assistant secretary of Strathfieldsaye Shire and then principal of a business college at Bendigo. On 10 January 1912 at Sacred Heart Cathedral he married 34-year-old Mary Theresa Henke, daughter of a miner; they had two sons and two daughters.

After World War I, when he handled contracts for army supplies, Duffy came to prominence in the labour movement in Melbourne. Beginning as a clerk in the Trades Hall office and as a Clerks' Union delegate, he moved up through the Trades Hall Council. In 1921-22 he was president, and thereafter a member of key committees; in 1923 he was placed in charge of its Research and Information Bureau (at £7 a week); from August 1924 he was assistant secretary (at about £9) and from October 1929 to the end of 1930, secretary of the T.H.C. From 1918 to 1929, with a couple of breaks, he was on the central executive of the Victorian branch of the Australian Labor Party, and was its president in 1924-25 and a delegate to federal conference in 1924.

Meanwhile, Duffy had been member of three Commonwealth royal commissions: on taxation (appointed 1920), on Crown lease-holds (1924) and on the Constitution (1927); with T. R. Ashworth [q.v.7] and D. L. McNamara [q.v.] he reported strongly in favour of increased Federal powers. Duffy took an interest in education: he was appointed to the Council of Public Education representing industrial interests in 1927; in 1931 he was made a councillor of the Working Men's College, and that year was appointed to the Apprenticeship Commission and to the board of inquiry into the Victorian Education Department.

Reserved, well-dressed and an incessant cigar smoker, Duffy held very moderate views. He was an administrator rather than an activist, and was regarded as an expert on finance. With the onset of the Depression he protested against attacks on living standards and was critical of private banks and interest rates; but he was to defend the Labor governments' acceptance of the Premiers' Plan.

In 1930, to the dismay of the labour movement, the Federal Labor cabinet reappointed Sir Robert Gibson [q.v.] as chairman of the Commonwealth Bank Board; at the same time, however, Duffy was appointed to the board for seven years at £600. He was reappointed in 1937 and 1944. His colleague L. F. Giblin [q.v.] considered he 'brought a new outlook and a sturdily independent mind to banking problems'. In 1945, when the board was abolished, Duffy was appointed chairman of the Commonwealth Bank Promotions Appeal Board for six years. During World War II he had also been deputy chief inspector, stores and clothing, Department of the Army.

In 1932, despite T.H.C. objections, Duffy had attended the Ottawa Imperial Economic Conference as workers' consultant to the Australian delegation, and on his return insisted that the Ottawa Agreement be given a fair trial, though it was condemned by the labour movement.

Duffy was secretary, until his death, of the Industrial Printing and Publicity Co. and from association with its radio station 3KZ, he contributed to the development of broadcasting. He was first president of the Australian Federation of Commercial Broadcasting Stations in 1930-34 and for some years its secretary-general. In 1939 he helped to establish 3CS (Colac Broadcasting Co. Pty Ltd) of which he was initially a director, general manager and secretary, and later chairman of directors.

For many years Duffy lived at Windsor. He died after a fall on 30 October 1957, survived by his wife and children, and was buried in St Kilda cemetery. His estate was valued for probate at £5168.

L. F. Giblin, *The growth of a central bank* (Melb, 1951); L. J. Louis, *Trade unions and the depression* (Canb, 1968); *Punch* (Melb), 6 Nov 1924; *Argus*, 2, 8, 9, 26 Sept 1930, 19, 22 Apr, 6 Aug, 6 Dec 1932; *Labor Call*, 11, 18 Sept, 16 Oct 1930; *Bulletin*, 17 Sept 1930; *Aust Worker*, 8 Oct 1930; *SMH*, 17 Jan 1934, 28 Aug 1945; *Herald* (Melb), 31 Oct, 1 Nov 1957; Trades Hall Council (Melb), Minute-books (ANU Archives).   L. J. LOUIS

DUGGAN, BERNARD OSCAR CHARLES (1887-1963), soldier and farmer, was born on 12 January 1887 at Sutherlands Plains, near St Arnaud, Victoria, son of John Duggan, farmer, and his wife Sarah Frances, née Olarenshaw, both native-born. He was educated at the Sutherland and Swanwater state schools and the St Arnaud School of Mines, then became a farmer. Developing an early interest in military affairs, he joined the Victorian Rangers (militia) as a private in 1907; he was commissioned second lieutenant in 1910 and promoted lieutenant three years later. By 1914 he was in charge of home defence training in the St Arnaud district; he was also a prominent sportsman, excelling at football and tennis, and a competent violinist, much in demand at social gatherings.

In November 1914 Duggan was assigned to the Broadmeadows officers' school and for a short time served as second-in-command of the infantry garrison at Queenscliff. In April 1915 he joined the Australian Imperial Force as a lieutenant in the 21st Battalion. Promoted captain on 1 May, he sailed from Melbourne a week later as officer commanding 'D' Company and, after a period of training in Egypt, reached Gallipoli on 7 September. He commanded parts of the defences at Courtney's Post and Lone Pine and, during the evacuation, was in the rear party. An elaborate system of self-firing rifles had been devised along the trenches to prevent the Turks from suspecting an allied withdrawal and it was Duggan who in his area, late on 19 December, discovered that the fuses were wet with dew and in danger of not firing. He experimented with fuses of tow, which worked well, and the ghostly rifles continued to fire at random intervals until morning. He was one of the last to leave Anzac Cove.

Duggan's battalion was rested and reorganized in Egypt and in March 1916 he was promoted major and sent to France. He fought first on the Somme, at Pozières and Mouquet Farm, serving as second-in-command. From September 1916 to January 1917 he was in the Ypres, Flers and Gueudecourt sectors and several times was acting commander. On 31 January he was transferred to the 23rd Battalion as commanding officer but relinquished this appointment on 27 February when he was evacuated with trench fever. Promoted temporary lieut-colonel in June, he rejoined the 21st Battalion as commanding officer and served in the 3rd battle of Ypres late that year and at Warneton and Ploegsteert early in 1918. He was awarded the Distinguished Service Order in the 1918 New Year honours. From then until the Armistice he commanded the 21st in all its operations, except at Hamel when he was again evacuated with trench fever, serving in the capture of Ville-sur-Ancre, Frise, Mont St Quentin and Montbrehain. He won a Bar to his D.S.O. for exemplary zeal and energy at Montbrehain on 5 October; he and his shrunken battalion were then withdrawn from the line. In addition to his D.S.O. and Bar he was mentioned in dispatches three times during the war.

Bernie Duggan returned to Australia on 10 May 1919, exactly four years after his departure. He received a rousing public welcome at St Arnaud where he was described by the men of his battalion as well liked and highly respected, an officer who had 'won his laurels through stepping from shell hole to shell hole, and not in the security of a dug out'. On 17 November 1920 he married Annie Jackson, an army nurse, at St Mary's Catholic Church, East St Kilda; they had no children. He was placed on the reserve of officers in 1921 and returned to the family farm at Sutherland. In World War II he acted as lieut-colonel in charge of the 2nd/23rd Training Battalion and as commander at the Ballarat training camp. In retirement he lived at Geelong and Ballarat where, survived by his wife, he died of a cerebral haemorrhage on 27 December 1963. He was buried in the Catholic section of St Arnaud cemetery.

C. E. W. Bean, *The story of Anzac* (Syd, 1921, 1924), and *The A.I.F. in France*, 1916-18 (Syd, 1929, 1933, 1937, 1942); *London Gazette*, 28 Dec 1917, 1 Jan, 31 Dec 1918, 2 Apr, 11 July 1919; *St Arnaud Mercury*, 5 Jan 1918, 24, 28 May, 4 June 1919, 28 Dec 1963; Duggan file, war records section (AWM).   ANNE BEGGS SUNTER

DUGGAN, EDMUND (1862?-1938), actor and playwright, was born at Lismore, County Waterford, Ireland, son of Dennis Duggan, farmer, and his wife Mary Ann, née Walsh. He came to Victoria with his parents at the age of 9. After education at St Patrick's College, East Melbourne, he worked in a Flinders Lane warehouse.

Duggan's great love was Shakespeare. With his brother Patrick (P.J.) he helped to found the Roscians, a club whose members met to study Shakespeare, occasionally performing for charity; Edmund played Horatio to P.J.'s Hamlet on 19 August 1879. When 22 he decided to try his luck as a professional actor. His early experience was with George Titheradge's [q.v.6] company, and at the Gaiety Theatre, Sydney. In September 1890 he helped to manage his sister Eugenie's début as Juliet at the Theatre Royal, Melbourne, P.J. playing Mercutio. Soon afterwards P.J. left for the United States of America, where he made his career until his death in 1910. Another sister, Kathleen, also went on the stage.

In the 1890s Duggan had his own country touring company, performed with Alfred Dampier [q.v.4], and was actor and stage-manager with stars such as Myra Kemble [q.v.5] and the Charles Holloway-William Anderson [q.v.7] company. In 1900 Anderson (who had married Eugenie) 'inherited' the Duggans from Holloway as leading members of his 'Famous Dramatic Organisation'.

Duggan was noted for his comic Irish roles, but is remembered today as co-author of several melodramas characterized by their natural depiction of bush life. In 1891 in Sydney, he had staged his melodrama *The democrat*, revived as *Eureka stockade* in Adelaide in 1897, together with his dramatization of *For the term of his natural life*. In 1906 Anderson produced Duggan's version of *Lady Audley's secret*. In 1907 *The squatter's daughter*, written by Duggan and Bert Bailey [q.v.7] or 'Albert Edmunds', was performed in Melbourne; it had a near-record run, and was filmed with the original cast in 1910. In 1909 Duggan and Bailey's play *The man from outback* was staged, and in 1911 Duggan's own play, *My mate*, was produced at the King's, Melbourne, featuring readings from Adam Lindsay Gordon [q.v.4] — Duggan was vice-president of a Gordon memorial society. In September 1912 Anderson handed over the King's theatre to Bailey with Julius Grant as managing director and Duggan as acting manager, opening with the famous dramatization of *On our selection*, advertised as by 'Albert Edmunds and B. Smith', and with Duggan playing the Irishman, Maloney. Another 'Albert Edmunds' play, *The native born*, followed in 1913.

Duggan remained with the Bailey-Grant management at the King's, touring Australia and New Zealand in his own and other melodramas, and producing a revival of *On our selection* in Melbourne in 1920. He persuaded 'Steele Rudd' [q.v. A. H. Davis] to write *The Rudd family* which he produced in 1928, starring as 'Dad'.

A genial personality, Duggan was well known as a rower with the Yarra Yarra club. On 7 October 1899 in Sydney, he had married Beatrice Hamea. Duggan died of heart failure in Melbourne on 2 August 1938, survived by his two daughters, and was buried in Boroondara cemetery. His estate was valued for probate at £75.

E. D. Davis, *The life and times of Steele Rudd* (Melb, 1976); *Theatre Mag* (Syd, Melb), 1 July 1912, 1 May, 1 Sept 1913; *Quadrant*, Jan 1976, p 19; *Australasian*, 23 Aug 1879, 22 Aug 1908; *Table Talk*, 11 Jan 1900.   MARGARET WILLIAMS

DUGGAN, WILLIAM JOSEPH (1884-1934), trade union official, was born on 31 January 1884 at 23 Spencer Street, (West) Melbourne, son of William Duggan, ironmoulder, and his wife Elizabeth Margaret, née Whitmore, both Melbourne-born. After education at West Melbourne State School, Duggan worked for an estate agent, but soon left to qualify as a plumber. After six years he joined the navy and in the next five years his knowledge of the world was expanded by extensive travel and by avid reading, the start of a sustained process of self-education. He also became champion boxer of the squadron.

On leaving the navy, Billy Duggan resumed work as a plumber and on 12 March 1910 at St James Old Cathedral, Melbourne, married Frances Annie Barratt. At this time he advocated military training, maintaining that any citizen force should be officered by working men's sons: he joined the Commonwealth Military Cadet Corps and in March 1912 was commissioned provisionally as lieutenant but resigned next year. In 1916-17 he was to oppose conscription.

On 11 October 1910 Duggan was admitted to membership of the United Operative Plumbers and Gasfitters' Society of Victoria (from April 1912 the Australian Plumbers and Gasfitters Employees' Union). By August 1911 he was vice-president, and in January 1912 was elected first organizer. His salary of £3.6s. a week was raised in December 1913 to £3.15s. and there were further increases in 1916 and 1924. Duggan was also on the federal body of his union, and was active on the United Building Trades Council which in 1914 became the Building Trades Federation with Duggan as its first secretary. In 1917, as an employees' representative, he contributed substantially to a Federal government shipbuilding scheme, and in March 1918 was appointed to the Shipbuilding Tribunal.

In the 1920s Duggan rose to prominence in the labour movement. A delegate from the Plumbers' Union from 1916, he came to play a leading role on the Trades Hall Council. He was president in 1926-27, thereafter sitting on the executive and disputes committees, and was secretary from the end of 1930. In May 1927 he was chairman of the Third All-Australian Trade Union Congress which set up the Australasian Council of Trade Unions; he was elected president unopposed and held the position until 1934. With C. A. Crofts [q.v.] he did much to establish the authority of the A.C.T.U.

Meanwhile, Duggan had assumed important positions in the Australian Labor Party. He was first president of the Metropolitan Council in 1926 and Victorian president in 1928-29. A delegate to federal conference from the late 1920s, he was a member of the federal executive from 1929 until March 1931 and again in June 1932, and a vice-president from 1929 until February 1931. He unsuccessfully contested a selection ballot for the Federal seat of Bendigo in 1928, but came close to winning Henty for Labor in 1929. From August 1924 until defeated in August 1930, he was a Coburg councillor, and was mayor in 1928-29. He was also a justice of the peace.

Duggan was an effective chairman and an astute negotiator who sought conciliation rather than industrial conflict. He was regarded as one of Labor's best speakers, who displayed tact, logic and forbearance. A typical reformist official, he advocated political action, but with the Depression came into conflict with Labor governments over workers' living standards.

Duggan suffered for some six years from a duodenal ulcer before his death on 4 July 1934 at his home at Moreland. He was buried in Melbourne general cemetery after services conducted by Dr Strong [q.v.6] at the Trades Hall and by Presbyterian and Methodist ministers, J. T. Lawton [q.v.] and J. H. Cain, at the graveside. He was survived by his wife and two daughters.

L. J. Louis, *Trade unions and the depression* (Canb, 1968); *Labor Call*, 12 May 1927, 13 Nov 1930, 5, 12 July 1934; *Table Talk*, 3 Jan 1929; *Aust Worker*, 11 July 1934; *Argus*, 5, 6 July 1934; G. Dunkley, The ACTU 1927-1950: politics, organization and economic policy (Ph.D. thesis, Monash Univ, 1974); Aust Plumbers and Gasfitters Employees' Union (Melb), *and* Trades Hall Council (Melb), Minute-books (ANU Archives).
L. J. LOUIS

DUHIG, SIR JAMES (1871-1965), Catholic archbishop, was born on 2 September 1871 at Killila near Broadford, Limerick, Ireland, youngest son and one of seven children of

John Duhig, cottier and rural tradesman, and his wife Margaret, née Barry. On John Duhig's early death the family moved to Middlesbrough, Yorkshire, England, where the elder sons worked in the iron-foundries. When a depression sent the family temporarily back to Ireland, they were evicted from their holding. They joined the continuing Irish migration, the eldest son going to Chicago, United States of America, and the rest of the family to Brisbane. James arrived with his mother and two other children on 8 April 1885 aboard the *Mackara*, the three older children having preceded them to establish a home. The youngest child Ellen (1874-1960) subsequently entered the Good Samaritan Order. Duhig's nephew James Vincent [q.v.] became a prominent pathologist.

James was educated in village schools in Limerick and a Catholic school at Middlesbrough. In Brisbane he attended the Irish Christian Brothers' College of St Joseph's, Gregory Terrace. He did clerical work for a city firm and engaged in youth and catechetical work for his home parish of Wooloowin. In this latter he caught the attention of the archbishop of Brisbane, Robert Dunne, who sent him back to Gregory Terrace to complete his secondary studies and to perfect his Latin. In 1891 he enrolled in the Irish College, Rome, and studied for the priesthood at the Urban University of Propaganda Fide. There he cultivated a love of art and literature and developed his own lucid and eloquent eighteenth-century prose style. He also caught a notion of the official Church's role in society that went back to the exuberant counter-reform. Ordained priest on 19 September 1896, he returned to Brisbane next year with a vision beyond the colonial horizon.

Duhig worked as curate in the industrial town of Ipswich, with special responsibility for country districts around it. Circumstances forced on him early experience of administration and building, which became his characteristic, absorbing passion. Success brought him to Brisbane as administrator of St Stephen's Cathedral in March 1905 and in December to the see of Rockhampton, where he was consecrated by his former mentor in Rome, Michael Kelly [q.v.], now archbishop of Sydney. On 26 February 1912 he was back in Brisbane as titular archbishop of Amida and coadjutor to Dunne, whom he succeeded as archbishop in 1917.

The archdiocese of Rockhampton covered 360 000 square miles (932 000 km²), that of Brisbane 200 000 (518 000 km²); Duhig travelled constantly, being one of the earliest passengers of Qantas and other nascent airlines in the north-west. His driving energy and lively community interests brought him an intimate knowledge of the religious and socio-economic problems of all but the far north of Queensland. Continuing to interpret his role as one of service to the community, he saw his unusually wide acquaintance with the State as giving him the opportunity to act as a guiding voice in its proper development. Concerned with the spread of justice to all, he was heard for decades on such topics as urban development, artistic opportunity, land settlement and higher education. His socially conservative pastoral letters stressed the need to maintain the sanctity of the home; he blamed the cinema for lack of cohesion in family life and for the 'perversion of the young'. A volume of his selected public addresses was published in 1934. His autobiography, *Crowded years* (Sydney), full of anecdotes about his journeys in the outback, followed in 1947.

His pastoral practice differed from that of his predecessor and of the Moran [q.v.] hierarchy of Australia. Duhig believed in small units, based on closeness of contact between clergy and people and easy access to church, school and charitable institutions. This meant creating many new parishes (he opened his fiftieth in 1955) and the introduction of many new religious communities. Previously two religious orders, the Irish Christian Brothers and the Sisters of Mercy, monopolized the schools and institutions of Queensland. Without discouraging their further expansion, he introduced twenty more orders of brothers and sisters. He also attracted fifteen orders of priests, many of them in the first ten years of his long episcopate.

This all gave scope for Duhig's absorbing interest in the acquisition of properties and in building. The physical structure of Brisbane, with its multitude of steep hills, allowed him to create a highly visible Church and offer the city an architectural gift of, and stimulus to, style. In fifty years he added over 400 major buildings (religious, educational and charitable institutions, and hospitals) to his diocese and spent £3 million. Since in 1929 much of the rural area was cut off in the new diocese of Toowoomba, most of this was in Brisbane.

The apex of the design was to have been a new Cathedral of the Holy Name in the Valley sector of the city, which Duhig, with many others, saw as the proper heart of a new and grander Brisbane. The cathedral was planned as the largest to be built anywhere in the world since the seventeenth century. It was a work not only of ecclesiastical purpose but of civic pride and State development; for Duhig proposed to pay for it with dividends from his investments in

Roma oil-wells. The spectacular foundation ceremony, in the presence of a papal legate in 1928, was followed by a more spectacular collapse in the Depression. The oil-wells and the cathedral were both casualties. A court action was brought by the Sydney architect Jack Francis Hennessy against Duhig in 1949 for non-payment of fees for the cathedral plans and specifications; Hennessy was awarded £25 750.

The thirty-five years of episcopate left to Duhig after the cathedral failure were given to energetic but less innovative leadership in church and state. Education was always a principal concern. Committed to the separate education of all Catholic children, he provided for a primary school, run by nuns, in each parish. Intent on the social mobility of Irish Catholics, he encouraged parents to give their children secondary education and he fostered thirty new high schools for this purpose. An early advocate and benefactor of the University of Queensland, he provided two university colleges at St Lucia. Before his death in 1965 it was already evident that in the post-war expansion it was not possible to maintain the total alternative system, and government assistance had begun; but his achievement was probably the most complete embodiment of the century-old Catholic policy on education.

His stance within the Church was not deeply theological. An eloquent preacher, he lauded and encouraged, rather than expounded, a traditional faith. Yet his basic attitudes proved to be compatible with the renewal of the Church at the Second Vatican Council. He took no active part in the council, but he had always been open to lay activity, and he was tolerant and – perhaps uncritically – encouraging to all initiative. In his earliest years he had belonged to the Catholic Literary and Debating Society and he then founded the Catholic Young Men's Society, in which many future leaders in church and state in Queensland were stimulated to develop their talents. This gave way in the 1930s and 1940s to the varied forms of Catholic Action, which flourished in Queensland only slightly less than in Victoria. Like Daniel Mannix [q.v.], he preceded and outlasted the highly centralized and clericalized style of Church administration which came into full development at the end of World War I with the publication of the Code of Canon Law. He did not favour the style and saw it reversed by the Second Vatican Council.

Duhig differed from Mannix in his view of how Church leadership should be exercised in the community. In contentious times he advocated reconciliation and friendly relations with other Christian Churches. He fostered ecumenism for common-sense reasons long before it was popular on theological grounds. Never a great wit like Mannix, he saw early that such sharpness left wounds that entrenched rather than removed animosity. As well, he believed that the Churches had the duty to show harmony to the community, another instinctive assumption of an attitude that became characteristic of conciliar theology.

Duhig was politically neutral in party strife. Firmly opposed to socialism in its more dogmatic forms, he spoke against the Labor policy in the controversy over the Chifley bank nationalization in 1947. During the 1951 referendum on the banning of the Communist Party he openly advocated a 'yes' vote. Yet he was not a party man. His politics, like his prose, were eighteenth century. He followed persons with flair and ideals like his own – in later years, (Sir) Robert Menzies, another of the Queen's men; but earlier, Labor men like Ned Hanlon. In the 1957 Labor split he remained aloof, occupying a position mid-way between those of Mannix and Cardinal Gilroy.

His Irish attitudes were markedly different from those of Mannix. His Ireland was the subject of the British Crown, if not of the parliament of Westminster. During the crises of the Easter rising in Dublin and the Australian conscription referenda of World War I, he strove to maintain both an Irish and a British attitude. He condemned the rebellion, while bitterly denouncing the repression. Neither event interfered with his commitment to recruitment of forces for the war. From 16 May 1914 he was a senior army chaplain in Queensland. In Dublin during the Irish Civil War in 1922 he strongly condemned de Valera's refusal to accept the treaty – significantly, in the company of the Anglo-Irish Bernard Shaw, Sir John Lavery and Oliver St John Gogarty. Appointed C.M.G. in 1954, he willingly became, in 1959, the first Roman Catholic archbishop in Australia to accept a knighthood (K.C.M.G.). Moreover, Duhig's experience was more continental than that of Mannix. During the 1930s and 1940s he was the champion of Italian migration, and he provided for the religious care and assimilation into the community of the great post-war migrant flood.

Duhig's kindness and gentleness, his fondness for children, and his compassion, were well known. Prelates from all over Australia joined in the Brisbane celebrations of his silver jubilee in 1930, his golden jubilee as a priest in 1946, and his episcopal golden jubilee in 1955. His several trips to Europe and America culminated in his leading the Australian pilgrimage to Rome in 1950. President of the Brisbane branch of the

Royal Geographical Society of Australasia in 1926-38, he was awarded the Thomson Foundation gold medal in 1941. He was a member of the Senate of the University of Queensland in 1917-65 and received honorary doctorates of laws from the universities of Queensland (1947) and Ottawa (1947), and from the National University of Ireland (1955). He was also a substantial art patron and the walls of his home at New Farm were covered with paintings. He died there on 10 April 1965 and was buried in the vault of St Stephen's Cathedral. Most of his estate, valued for probate at £8052, was left to the Church. Of many portraits, one by Alexander Colquhoun [q.v.] hangs at the University of Queensland and another by William Dargie is held at the Pius XII Seminary, Banyo, Brisbane.

When he was nominated to Rockhampton in 1905 by Pius X, Duhig was the youngest Roman Catholic bishop in the world. When he died, under Paul VI, he had been the longest in office — just a few months short of sixty years. To have led his Church for so long, and been a leader in his State, made him one of the shaping influences on his community.

V. L. Gray, *Catholicism in Queensland* (Brisb, 1910); P. J. O'Farrell, *The Catholic Church and the community in Australia: a history* (Melb, 1977); *Daily Standard*, 1 Oct 1917; *Catholic Weekly* (Syd), 10 Nov 1955; *Catholic Leader*, 30 July 1964-14 Jan 1965; *Bulletin*, 9 Nov 1963; *SMH*, 12 Apr 1965; Diocesan Archives (Brisb).   T. P. BOLAND

DUHIG, JAMES VINCENT (1889-1963), medical practitioner, was born on 22 November 1889 in Brisbane, son of Thaddeus Duhig, carpenter, and his wife Ellen, née Shine, both Irish-born. Educated at Holy Cross Convent School, Wooloowin, the Eagle Junction State School and St Joseph's College, Nudgee, he distinguished himself in the 1907 leaving certificate examination by taking first place in five subjects and winning the Queensland exhibition; next year he entered the University of Sydney as a language student, but in 1909 he changed to medicine (M.B., Ch.M., 1914).

On 3 January 1917 in Sydney, Duhig married Kathleen Mary Taylor and in June he left for Europe as a medical officer in the Australian Imperial Force. After service mainly in field ambulances and general hospitals, he was demobilized as a major in 1919 and undertook postgraduate work in pathology at King's College Hospital, London, from April to July. On his return, he established pathology laboratories at the Mater Misericordiae Hospital in 1920 and the Brisbane General Hospital in 1924. From 1920 he practised as a pathologist in Wickham Terrace. He became Australian president of the Association of Clinical Pathologists and urged the establishment of the College of Pathologists of Australia of which he was later an honorary member. A militant campaigner for the establishment of a medical school in Queensland, he was first professor of pathology at the University of Queensland in 1938-47. He founded the Red Cross Blood Bank in Queensland.

A man of brilliant intellect, Duhig was not restricted by his profession. He investigated the venomous fish of Queensland and contributed dissections of the stone-fish venom apparatus to the Queensland Museum. President of the Royal Queensland Art Society for ten years, he left much of his personal art collection to the university. Co-founder of the Brisbane Repertory Theatre Society, he won the Laura Bogue Luffman [q.v.] prize with his one-act play, *The ruling passion*, published in 1935. In 1942-43 he had some association with C. B. Christesen and *Meanjin Papers*.

Often controversial but never dull, Duhig was especially noted for his vigorous, outspoken opposition to all forms of hypocrisy. A nephew of Brisbane's Archbishop James Duhig [q.v.], he was brought up as a Catholic but became a president and patron of the Queensland Rationalist Society. He took an impish delight in publicly baiting his distinguished relative, announcing that religious beliefs frustrated honest thinking. He was a vigorous opponent throughout his life of book censorship and was president of the Book Censorship Abolition League of Queensland in 1935. At the same time he advocated the prohibition of alcohol and in 1946 was president of Queensland Co-operative Hotels Ltd, an offshoot of the Liquor Reform Society. Reform of military drinking, he believed, should begin in officers' messes.

Small, slight but furiously energetic, Duhig allied himself during the Depression with radical causes and led deputations demanding help for the unemployed. Because of these activities, the fact that he had visited Russia and his medical aid to Russia's campaign in World War II, he was branded as a fellow-traveller by many. They failed to realise that he could never have espoused communism because he was always a champion of free speech and free thought.

Duhig died in St Andrew's Hospital, Brisbane, on 14 April 1963, following a myocardial infarct. He was survived by his wife, two daughters and two sons, both pathologists. His ashes were transferred to the grave of his wife at Nudgee cemetery after her death. A portrait by Roy Dalgarno is in the University of Queensland; another by Sylvia Harris is held in the family.

Rationalist, Feb 1946, p 360, Mar 1947, p 15; *MJA*, 17, 24 Aug 1963, p 269, 336; *Courier Mail*, 15 Apr 1963.   C. A. C. LEGGETT

DUIGAN, JOHN ROBERTSON (1882-1951), pioneer aviator and electrical engineer, was born on 31 May 1882 at Terang, Victoria, elder son of John Charles Duigan, bank manager and grazier, and his wife, Jane, née Robertson, both native-born. He was educated at Brighton Grammar School and matriculated in 1899. In 1902 he went to England, enrolling in the City and Guilds of London Technical College, Finsbury, and obtaining a certificate in electrical engineering in 1904. Next year he qualified in motor engineering and driving at Battersea Polytechnical College and then worked for the Wakefield and District Light Railway, Yorkshire. Returning to Melbourne in 1908, he worked with G. Weymouth Pty Ltd, electrical engineers, but later that year went to live on a family property, Spring Plains station, Mia Mia.

Duigan's experiments in aviation dated from 1908 when he constructed an unsuccessful kite and then began building a Wright-type glider that was completed and flown on a tether wire in 1909. It was capable of lifting two people off the ground. Before September 1909 he began construction of a powered aircraft of his own design. Apart from the engine, which was built by J. E. Tilly in Melbourne, the whole of the aircraft was made by Duigan at Spring Plains. His younger brother Reginald helped to assemble the aircraft and John first 'flew' in it hopping about twenty feet (6 m) on 16 July 1910. But by early October he was flying nearly 200 yards (183 m). These were the first flights in Australia of a locally designed and built aircraft.

In 1909 the Commonwealth government had offered a £5000 prize to the inventor or designer of a flying machine suitable for military purposes. Believing his machine to be ineligible for entry because it was not capable of 'poising', Duigan did not submit an entry by the due date of March 1910. Later he found that 'poising' had been defined simply as the capability of turning within a half-mile circle and he submitted a late entry in August. The Commonwealth refused to accept this entry although the Defence Department requested a demonstration of the machine which took place in May 1911. The aircraft was never flown again and was presented to the Science Museum of Victoria by Duigan in 1920.

Duigan returned to England in 1911 and obtained a flying licence from the International Aeronautical Federation in April 1912. He bought an Avro aeroplane and spent some months in developmental work on it at the A. V. Roe works in Huntingdon before selling it. Reginald joined him in England and before returning to Australia they bought an engine, which was used in an aircraft they built at their father's Ivanhoe home. It was flown at Keilor in February 1913 and was extensively damaged in a crash; though later repaired it was not flown again. Duigan's offer to sell it to the Commonwealth government in February 1915 for use at the Central Flying School at Point Cook was not accepted. Its ultimate fate is not known. On 26 November 1913 Duigan married Kathleen Rebecca Corney, a nursing sister, at St Paul's Anglican Church, Caulfield.

On 14 March 1916 he was commissioned as a lieutenant in No. 2 Squadron, Australian Flying Corps, and was appointed to command the squadron's 2nd Flight in August. He embarked in October and, after training in England, was promoted captain and confirmed as a flight commander in August 1917. Proceeding to France, Duigan went into action with No. 3 Squadron. He was awarded the Military Cross for gallantry in action on 9 May 1918 when his aircraft was attacked by four German planes over Villers-Bretonneux: although severely wounded he shot down one of the enemy and landed safely. His appointment with the A.F.C. ended on 15 July 1919 and he resumed work in Melbourne as an electrical engineer. In 1928 he moved to Yarrawonga where he conducted a motor engineering business until 1941. He returned to Melbourne that year and for the rest of World War II was employed in the quality control branch of the Royal Australian Air Force. He then lived in retirement at Ringwood where, survived by his wife, he died of cancer on 11 June 1951. He was cremated with Presbyterian forms.

Duigan occupies a special place in Australia's aviation history as he was the first Australian to design, build and fly an aeroplane in Australia but he appears not to have been involved in the development of aviation in a policy or technical sense. A memorial to him was unveiled on the Mia Mia-Lancefield road, near the site of the first flight, on 28 May 1960.

London Gazette, 13 Sept 1918; *Aero* (Lond), 3 Aug 1910, 8 Mar 1911; *Flight* (Lond), 10 June 1911, 6 Apr 1912; *Aircraft* (Melb), Oct 1960; *VHM*, 45 (1974); *Australasian*, 15 Oct 1910, 6 May 1911, 18 May 1912, 22 Feb 1913; *Argus*, 28 Jan, 1 June 1911, 19 Feb 1912; *Colac Herald*, 6 May 1960; *Age*, 30

May 1960; Science Museum of Vic, official files (Melb); Hargrave memorial lecture, 1962 (Roy Aeronautical Soc, Vic Branch); War diary, No. 3 Squadron, A.F.C. (AWM).   F. J. KENDALL

DUMARESQ, JOHN SAUMAREZ (1873-1922), rear admiral, was born on 26 October 1873 at Tivoli House, Rose Bay, Sydney, son of William Alexander Dumaresq, pastoralist, of Furracabad station, Glen Innes, New South Wales, and his English-born wife Edith Helen, née Gladstone. Though Dumaresq was brought up in England from the age of 2, his family ties with Australia dated from 1825 when his grandfather, William John Dumaresq [q.v.1] had come to New South Wales with his brother-in-law Governor Darling [q.v.1], and established an estate near Scone and large pastoral runs in the New England district.

On 15 July 1886 Dumaresq entered the Royal Navy as a cadet in H.M.S. Britannia; he was commissioned lieutenant on 28 August 1894 and after a period at sea with the Channel Fleet began to specialize in torpedo work. Promoted commander in 1904, he was attached to the Admiralty to supervise the equipment of torpedo vessels. By then he was recognized as one of the navy's most innovative officers and he devoted much of his time to the science of naval warfare. Switching his experiments from torpedoes to gun-room control, he invented a calculating instrument by which the rate of movement of enemy warships could be determined within seconds; this range-finder, named the Dumaresq by a grateful Admiralty, gave naval gunnery an unprecedented accuracy. On 18 September 1907 he married Christian Elizabeth Louisa, daughter of Sir Charles Dalrymple, baronet. Next year he commanded the torpedo flotilla which escorted King Edward VII on his visit to the Tsar of Russia and for his services was appointed M.V.O. and awarded the Order of St Catherine of Russia. He was then appointed Commander of the Swift and the Nith, torpedo-boat destroyers of the Home Fleet.

A captain from 30 June 1910, Dumaresq studied at the Royal Naval War College, Portsmouth, and invented several fire-control devices which were used in World War I. From December 1913 he commanded the Shannon, 2nd Light Cruiser Squadron. The Shannon led the squadron into action when Admiral Jellicoe's Grand Fleet intercepted the German High Sea Fleet at the battle of Jutland; Dumaresq's squadron was used to screen Jellicoe's six lines of battleships. For outstanding service in this action he was created C.B. At Jutland he first conceived the idea of launching aircraft from the decks of cruisers rather than lowering them into the sea. On 5 February 1917 he was transferred on loan to the Royal Australian Navy as captain of H.M.A.S. Sydney and the R.A.N.'s second senior officer. The Sydney at that time was with the 2nd Light Cruiser Squadron, Grand Fleet, and Dumaresq was the squadron's second-in-command. In May he took part in an action with a Zeppelin in the North Sea; with her six-inch (152 mm) guns the Sydney forced the airship up out of range but it then stalked the vessel, dropping bombs around it. With his back against the bridge-screen and his feet against the base of the compass Dumaresq became probably the first naval officer to develop the zig-zag system of bomb avoidance. For almost two hours he weaved in evasive action until the Zeppelin ran out of bombs. In November, while the Sydney was being refitted, he commanded H.M.S. Repulse in the battle of Heligoland: in a clash with the German flagship, Königsberg, the Repulse smashed her funnel and set her on fire.

The Sydney rejoined the squadron on 1 December 1917. The R.A.N.'s official war historian, A. W. Jose [q.v.], wrote that, at this time, Dumaresq 'was a man of exceptional ability and vivid imagination – an originator, both of novel devices and of tactical ideas. When he joined the Sydney he was in the thick of a campaign for inducing the Admiralty to use light cruisers against the Zeppelins which were at the time infesting the North Sea area – a scheme which in the end involved the installation of launching-platforms for aeroplanes on the cruisers'. Dumaresq was jubilant when, during the refitting of the Sydney, the Admiralty authorized installation of the first launching-platform to be fitted to a ship; one was later added to H.M.A.S. Melbourne. The first flight was successfully accomplished off the Sydney's platform on 8 December 1917 and the plane soon proved its value by driving off Zeppelins before they could get within bombing range of the ship. Dumaresq's planes again proved their worth when Admiral Beatty launched a raid on enemy minesweepers in Heligoland Bight in June 1918: two land-based enemy reconnaissance planes were flying towards the British ships when Dumaresq's pilots chased one off and shot the other down. He continued to command the Sydney until 28 February 1919 and for the next month was based in London.

On 22 March Dumaresq was appointed commodore commanding the Australian Fleet, a post which brought fresh challenges. In June, when he was bringing H.M.A.S. Australia back from London to Sydney, the vessel stopped at Fremantle and about a hundred of the ship's company asked that her departure be delayed for one day. Captain C. L. Cumberlege [q.v.], supported by Dumaresq, refused the request and later seven men were summarily sentenced to imprisonment and five court-martialled for mutiny and sentenced to longer terms. Dumaresq regarded the matter as one purely involving naval discipline and when the five men were eventually released through political pressure both he and Rear Admiral Edmund Grant, first member of the Australian Naval Board, tendered their resignations. These were later withdrawn.

Dumaresq was appointed C.V.O. in 1920. He was promoted rear admiral in June 1921, becoming the first Australian-born officer to hold that rank and to command the R.A.N. He brought to the small but professional Australian navy very high standards of discipline and competence. The measure of his success was the long succession of distinctions gained by R.A.N. officers attending Royal Navy training establishments and, ultimately, the high standard of leadership in the R.A.N. in World War II. The stringent financial restrictions imposed on the Australian Fleet from 1920 brought Dumaresq into constant conflict with the Australian government as he sought to protect the navy's interests. His service with the R.A.N. ended on 29 April 1922 when he reverted to the Royal Navy. Speaking on his flagship before leaving Sydney, he strongly criticised the attitudes and apathy of the nation towards defence expenditure. He left for England on the Japanese liner, *Tango Maru*, but on nearing the Philippines, fell ill with pneumonia and died at the American Military Hospital, Manila, on 22 July. In a ceremony attended by 1200 United States troops, he was buried in San Pedro Macati cemetery with full military honours. He was survived by his wife, two sons and two daughters.

Although a strict disciplinarian 'D.Q.', as he was known in Australia, was popular with all ranks and gave the navy a spirit it had never possessed. Of a cheerful disposition, he soon had the whole fleet involved in off-duty sports while he himself regularly took part in yachting events on Sydney Harbour. He detested personal publicity. His contribution to the R.A.N. had been considerable. He had brought the fleet to a high standard of efficiency despite the severe restrictions of the period and had welded it into a highly proficient force after its dispersal during the war years.

A. W. Jose, *The Royal Australian Navy 1914-1918* (Syd, 1928); *Royal Australian Navy, jubilee souvenir* (Canb, 1961); *Sea, Land, and Air*, Aug 1922; *Parade*, July 1959; *Public Administration* (Syd), 29 (1970), no 3; *Naval Hist Review*, Summer 1972, no 1; *SMH*, 14, 24, 26 July 1922; *Daily Mirror* (Syd), 29 Oct 1973.   PETER FIRKINS

DUMOLO, HARRIET ALICE (1875-1944), kindergarten teacher, and NONA (1877-1966), headmistress, were born on 17 September 1875 at Ladybank, Tamworth, Warwickshire, England, and on 14 June 1877 at Glascote, near Tamworth, the elder daughters of John Thomas Dumolo, colliery proprietor, and his wife Alice (d. 1944), née Hodgkinson. On 21 November 1881 John Dumolo arrived in Sydney in the *Cuzco* with his family, including his third daughter Elsie, and set up as a chemist and druggist, first at Waterloo, then at St Leonards. The three girls were educated at the Misses Lygons and at Arnold's College for Girls (later Redlands School) at Fitzroy Street, North Sydney, where they passed the junior public examination.

In 1897 Harriet, known to her family as Haddie, was one of the first five students to be awarded a kindergarten teacher's certificate by the Teachers' Association of New South Wales. In 1903 she was headmistress of St Philip's kindergarten, then entered the Kindergarten College, graduating in 1905. In 1907 she became director of three kindergartens at Newcastle and was in charge of training student teachers until 1909 when she joined the staff of the college. Next year she visited England and Europe. In 1912 she was appointed acting principal of the college, becoming principal next year.

A spirit of inquiry and experiment, linked to the ideals of community service and personal development were the outstanding features of Miss Dumolo's leadership. In training students she emphasized 'Froebelian theory and practice and John Dewey's interpretation of it'. Believing the community would benefit by spreading the principles of Froebel beyond the kindergarten, she offered special courses and training classes for Sunday school teachers of all denominations. In 1925 the college moved to its present site at Henrietta Street, Waverley, and was renamed the Sydney Kindergarten Training College. In Froebel House, for resident students, Miss Dumolo was able to express her gift for home-making and her belief that beauty was an influence for good. Zoe Benjamin [q.v.7] admired her 'gracious and serene personality' and 'calm wisdom'. Following a visit to England and the United States of America in 1927, she incorporated new knowledge of child growth and development, making kindergarten programmes less formal.

Harriet Dumolo retired in 1932 and in 1935 was awarded King George V's silver jubilee medal. She had been a founder of the Parks and Playgrounds Movement of New South Wales, served on the council of Abbotsleigh Church of England School for

Girls for eight years, and with her former students founded the Frances Newton Kindergarten. She died of cerebral haemorrhage on 3 February 1944 at the family home at Beaconsfield Parade, Lindfield and was cremated. In 1951 the Harriet Dumolo Memorial Room was opened at the Kindergarten College.

Nona, who suffered all her life from a double curvature of the spine, attended the University of Sydney (B.A., 1898). Her first post was as afternoon-governess to the daughters of the governor-general, Lord Dudley [q.v.]. She then joined Edith Badham's [q.v.7] staff at the Sydney Church of England Girls' Grammar School and in 1911 became headmistress of its North Sydney day-school which opened in the parish hall of Christ Church, Lavender Bay. In 1916 it moved to new premises, Toongarrah, Bay Road. Known to her pupils as 'Dum' or 'Dummie', she believed in discipline but was never harsh. She was an excellent teacher of French and Latin. She resigned in 1923 and next year studied at the Sorbonne (Université de Paris), gaining its diploma.

In 1925 Nona was appointed headmistress of the New England Girls' School, at Armidale. In running a boarding school she made an indelible impression on the girls and staff and expected a very high standard. She effected several outstanding and modern staff appointments. Both art and music had a prominent place in the curriculum.

Tall (about 177 cm) 'with fair, wavy hair, rather spare frame and broadshouldered', Nona Dumolo had a well-modulated and resonant voice and 'a glorious sort of deadpan humour'; she nearly always wore tweed skirts, well-cut silk blouses, and brown-calf laced boots. After her retirement at Easter 1939, she took scripture classes at Lindfield Public School, ran a training class for Sunday school teachers and during World War II organized the Lindfield Welfare Workers to sew and knit. She died at her home there on 4 May 1966 and was cremated. Her estate was valued for probate at £47069.

Their younger sister ELSIE (1879-1963) was born on 19 November 1879 at Glascote. She studied elocution with Rose Seton in Sydney and later with Elsie Fogarty in London. A very handsome, dark woman, she taught speech and drama in many leading schools in Sydney including the Kindergarten College and S.C.E.G.G.S., North Sydney. Every year she visited N.E.G.S. to produce the school plays which were performed in the Armidale Town Hall. She died at the family home at Lindfield on 18 February 1963 and was cremated.

All three sisters were active parish workers for St Alban's Anglican Church, Lindfield. Harriet was treasurer of its Women's Guild. Memorials to Elsie and Nona are in the church.

Aust Kindergarten Mag, 1910-15; *SMH*, 26 Mar 1924, 5 Nov 1932, 11 May 1944; Annual Reports, 1912-34 (Kindergarten Union of NSW, Syd); Froebel House papers, 1913-32 (Syd Kindergarten Teacher's College Archives); information from Dr Kelvin Grose (Univ of New England, NSW).

MARY WALKER

DUN, PERCY MUIR (1894-1971), soldier, sawmill-manager and grazier, was born on 9 October 1894 at Yawkecarba, Stroud, New South Wales, ninth surviving child of Thomas Dun, grazier, and his wife Elizabeth, née Miles, both native-born. He was educated at home and later worked as a storekeeper.

Dun enlisted as a private in the Australian Imperial Force on 7 February 1916 and was allotted to the first reinforcements for the 35th Battalion; in May he embarked for training in England. Promoted lance corporal in September, he was posted to France in November and was made a corporal that month. The 35th Battalion went into the Armentières sector and, in the winter of 1916-17, gained valuable experience in raiding and patrolling. Dun's first major action was the battle of Messines in June 1917; badly wounded, he did not resume duty until 30 September and for gallantry at Messines was awarded the Military Medal and promoted sergeant in October. He was again wounded on 12 October in the 2nd battle of Passchendaele.

After resuming duty on 8 November Dun was commissioned second lieutenant and transferred to the 38th Battalion; he was serving with this unit when he won the Military Cross for gallantry in a raid on enemy trenches. The citation stated that he had 'led his men with great dash and determination, killing the crew of a machine gun and capturing the gun'. On 2 April 1918 he was promoted lieutenant and transferred back to the 35th Battalion. He served at Villers-Bretonneux in April, at Morlancourt in May and in the battle of Amiens in August. Though wounded on 8 August he remained on duty. Three weeks later, during the Battalion's attack on Curlu, he 'led his men splendidly through dense fog and on two occasions headed a charge against machine guns, capturing the guns and some forty prisoners'. His 'determined courage cheered his men and was largely instrumental in getting them forward'. Of this action a battalion sergeant stated: 'Lieutenant Dun really deserved the V.C.; his men would follow him anywhere'. He was awarded a Bar to his Military Cross but he had been wounded, for the fourth time, at

Curlu and saw no further active service. In addition to his three decorations he was mentioned in dispatches.

Dun returned to Australia in June 1919 and his A.I.F. appointment ended on 28 July. After demobilization he worked in a sawmill at Glenreagh, New South Wales, and, by the time of his marriage to Violet Rachel Andrews on 22 April 1933, was the mill's accountant. He ultimately became manager, and retired in 1960. While employed at the sawmill he built up a grazing property in the district and continued to work it until his death. Survived by his wife, a son and a daughter, he died at Grafton of heart disease on 12 October 1971 and was buried in Clarence lawn cemetery, South Grafton.

M. E. Lyne, *Newcastle's own: the story of the 35th Battalion, A.I.F.* (Newcastle, nd); E. Fairey, *The 38th Battalion, A.I.F.* (Bendigo, 1929); C. E. W. Bean, *The A.I.F. in France*, 1917-18 (Syd, 1933, 1937, 1942); *London Gazette*, 14 Aug 1917, 13 May, 7 Nov 1918; information from A. W. Dun, Glenreagh, N.S.W.
K. R. WHITE

DUN, WILLIAM SUTHERLAND (1868-1934), palaeontologist, was born on 1 July 1868 at Cleveland House, Cheltenham, Gloucestershire, England, son of Major Percy Henderson Dun, formerly of the East India Co.'s army, and his wife Catherine Eliza Jane, née Duncan. About a year later the family settled in Sydney, where William was educated at Newington College.

On 8 April 1890 Dun became a probationer in the Geological Survey of New South Wales; from time to time he assisted (Sir) Edgeworth David [q.v.] in his study of the Hunter River coalfield and took charge of departmental exhibits at country and intercolonial centres. By 1891, then an assistant, he had begun a fruitful association with Robert Etheridge junior [q.v.]. Next year Dun published his first scientific paper and at the end of 1892, as an irregular student at the University of Sydney, passed the final examinations in geology and palaeontology with the rank of first-class honours. When Etheridge was seconded to the Australian Museum, Sydney, in 1893, Dun took charge of the survey's palaeontological work and its library. On 6 October 1896 in Sydney he married Jennie McKay.

In 1899 Dun became palaeontologist and librarian, holding the dual appointment until he retired on 30 June 1933. During David's absence overseas in 1897 he lectured at the university and from 1902 was lecturer in palaeontology, a special part-time post that was renewed triennially until 1934. He was also honorary palaeontologist to the Australian Museum.

Dun's publications cover virtually the whole range of palaeobotany and palaeozoology, but his special interests lay with brachiopods and molluscs, particularly late palaeozoic forms. Although of necessity he dealt chiefly with New South Wales fossils, he also investigated collections submitted to him from other parts of Australia. His summary papers on Australian palaeontology, published in 1914 and 1926, reveal his all-round grasp, while his wide acquaintance with geological literature as well as his bibliographical abilities are evident in a series of catalogues on subjects including mining and underground water.

Well-known as a genial character, Dun was respected for his tact, sound judgment, careful work and readiness to co-operate; he had a wide circle of professional friends. A councillor for many years, he was president of the Linnean Society of New South Wales in 1913-15 and of the local Royal Society in 1918. He contributed greatly to the success of the geological programme of the British Association for the Advancement of Science when it met in Australia in 1914, and was a valued associate member of the Australian National Research Council in 1922-34. Directly and indirectly he had an important influence on Australian geology and in 1932 was honoured by a corresponding membership of the Linnean Society of New South Wales.

After a long illness, Dun died of cancer at his Mosman home on 7 October 1934 and was cremated with Anglican rites. He was survived by a son and daughter of his first marriage, and by his second wife Mabel, née Edgar, whom he had married at Forbes on 2 December 1909, and by their son and daughter.

Linnean Soc NSW, *Procs*, 60 (1935); Roy Soc NSW, *J*, 69 (1935); Aust National Research Council, *Annual Report*, 1935; *SMH*, 9 Oct 1934.
D. F. BRANAGAN
T. G. VALLANCE

DUNBABIN, ROBERT LESLIE (1869-1949), classical scholar, was born on 16 July 1869 at Cambridge, Tasmania, son of John Dunbabin, farmer, and his wife Mary, née Murdoch. He was a cousin of T. C. Dunbabin [q.v.]. Educated at The Hutchins School, Hobart, in 1886-88, he won a Tasmanian government scholarship to Corpus Christi College, Oxford, England, where he studied classics, graduating B.A. in 1892. In 1894-95 he taught at Melbourne Church of England Grammar School, then at The Hutchins School in 1897-1901 before accepting a lectureship in mental and moral science at the University of Tasmania. He was temporary associate professor of classics at the University of Adelaide in 1905; he returned to Hobart next year as lecturer in classics and modern history in addition to mental and moral science. Promoted assistant professor in 1914 he was appointed to the chair when the classics and English departments were separated in 1917. On his retirement in 1940 he was made emeritus professor.

Dunbabin was highly regarded as a scholar. A typical philologist of the old school he nevertheless displayed a wide range of interests outside the classical languages, with a passion for accuracy in detail. He contributed many short notes to the *Classical Review* and *Classical Quarterly* on small but often important points of etymology, paleography and lexicography as well as geographical, zoological and even mechanical matters. In correspondence he offered many items for the revision of H. G. Liddell and R. Scott's *Greek-English lexicon*. But he never discussed the literary qualities of classical texts or general interpretations of ancient history despite his close knowledge. He published no monographs. Former pupils recall his demanding standards of accuracy. He was equally critical of fellow classicists, writing disparagingly of A. E. Housman's appointment as Regius Professor at Cambridge and of Jack Lindsay's translation of the poetry of Gaius Catullus (1929). The same concern for meticulous scholarship motivated his bitter opposition to courses in 'classical civilization' or 'classics in translation'. This rigidity may well have made him unsuitable as a vice-chancellor, which position, attained in 1933, he soon relinquished 'on medical advice'. However, he took a leading part in university administration as a member of the professorial board (1914-39), the Rhodes scholarship committee (1922-47) and the university council (1921-26 and 1933).

Dunbabin wrote everything down. Communications on small matters with local colleagues became formal letters. Diaries contain detail about garden-planting, phone-calls, tram-fares or expenses on occasional outings with ladies. Unmarried, and adhering to no religious faith, he died on 15 October 1949 leaving an estate valued for probate at £7709; he was buried at Bream Creek, the home of his parents for many years. His library, which included the complete works of P. G. Wodehouse, was left to the university with the proviso that the books were only to be used by the professor of classics. A classical scholarship for which he provided £5000 had conditions so stringent they had to be legally amended before any candidate could appear.

Mercury, 17 Oct 1949; Dunbabin papers (Univ

Tas); family papers (held by Mr T. Dunbabin, Bangor, Dunalley, Tas).   K. H. WATERS

DUNBABIN, THOMAS CHARLES (1883-1973), journalist, was born on 6 July 1883 at Bream Creek, Tasmania, son of Thomas Dunbabin, farmer, and his wife Sarah Ada, née Murdoch. He was first cousin to Robert Leslie Dunbabin [q.v.]. Educated privately, then at Officer College, Hobart, he graduated from the University of Tasmania (B.A., 1905; M.A., 1910), winning a Rhodes scholarship and going up to Corpus Christi College, Oxford, in 1906. Graduating B.A. in 1908 he became geography scholar, gained the geography diploma in 1909 and returned to Hobart where he began a journalistic career on the *Mercury*, reputedly as the result of a bet with the owner, Charles Davies [q.v.]. On 29 December 1909 Dunbabin married Beatrice Isabel Needham with Congregational forms.

After a period on the Melbourne *Argus* about 1920, he moved to Sydney, becoming news-editor of the *Sun* in 1926, then working as editor of the *Daily Telegraph* in 1931-34 and of the *Sun* in 1934-36. Dunbabin spent 1929-31 and 1936-38 in London as manager of the Australian Newspapers Cable Service. Early in World War II he became a press censorship liaison officer with Eastern Command, while continuing to contribute special articles to the *Telegraph*. In 1944 he went to Ottawa as press attaché to the Australian legation. Briefly director of the Australian News and Information Bureau in London (1945-47) and New York (1947-48), he also worked in the Sydney office of the bureau after his Ottawa post was abolished in 1950. He then returned to Canada where he remained representative for Consolidated Press (Sydney) until 1955.

Dunbabin's journalistic writings, mainly on historical and geographical topics are ephemeral; he had no well-defined ideology, but was highly patriotic, with particular interest in whalers and men of the sea. A predilection for curious detail is exemplified by his column in the *Sun*, 'Does Ripley know this?', and in his serious writings by a leaning to the anecdotal and picturesque rather than analysis and interpretation. In 1912 he succeeded in interviewing Roald Amundsen on his return from the South Pole, but failed to obtain confirmation of his success. Dunbabin's first monograph *The making of Australasia* (London, 1922) was for some time popular in the schools. He also wrote *Sailing the world's edge: sea stories from old Sydney* (London, 1931) and *Slavers of the South Seas* (Sydney, 1935). In 1954 he printed privately in Hobart *A farm at the world's end*, a history of the Dunbabin family.

An omnivorous reader with a highly retentive memory, Dunbabin also enjoyed sport, particularly rowing and cross-country running. An interest in fish and birds led to membership of the Royal Zoological Society of New South Wales. He was a teetotaller. A solid, powerful-looking man with many friends in all professions, he was remembered for 'his wit, bluntness, occasional impetuous lack of tact, absent-mindedness and his extraordinary disregard for many of the small conventions'; he commonly addressed his fellows as 'old fish'. Dunbabin died on 2 October 1973 at Ottawa, survived by his wife and daughter. His son, Thomas James (1911-55), was a distinguished classicist and archaeologist who, as a member of the British Intelligence Corps during World War II, became a leader of the resistance in Crete.

Aust Information Service Weekly Newsletter, 5 Oct 1973; Roy Zoological Soc NSW, *Koolewong*, Mar 1974; *People* (Syd), 31 Jan 1951; *SMH*, 6 Oct 1973; *Mercury*, 18 Oct 1973.   K. H. WATERS

DUNCAN, ANNIE JANE (1858-1943), factory inspector, was born on 25 September 1858 at Port Adelaide, South Australia, elder daughter of Handasyde Duncan [q.v.1], physician, and his second wife Anne (d. 1861), née Williams. After the death of her mother and stepmother, Annie and her sister Mary were brought up and educated by female servants and relatives.

From 16 Annie kept house for her father; he died in 1878 and left her a small annuity. She went to live with an aunt at Dashwood Gully and shared the fashionable activities of girls of her class: singing and dancing lessons, archery, spending her dress allowance, and amateur theatricals, but did not take her admirers 'very seriously'. On 27 December 1884 Mary married Arthur Hammerton Champion, soon to become headmaster of Launceston Church Grammar School, Tasmania. When her sister became a semi-invalid, Annie joined their household and took charge of the kitchen and mending.

The depression of the early 1890s changed Annie Duncan's life-style, and in 1893 she travelled abroad: in London she realized that she would have to seek work or return home. Through an introduction to Lucy Deane, one of the first female inspectors of workshops in England, she took courses with the National Health Society and the (Royal) Sanitary Institute. In April 1894 she passed the examination for inspector of nuisances and was appointed to the South Kensington district. She found her new life 'in the ranks of workers' enthralling and that 'a sisterhood' opened up to her. She mixed with

women in similar occupations such as Rose Squire and Adelaide Anderson and met Beatrice and Sidney Webb. When her appointment was not renewed she travelled in Europe then returned to Australia.

On 8 February 1897 Duncan was appointed factory inspector in the labour and industry branch of the New South Wales Department of Public Instruction under the Factories and Shops Act of 1896; she was promoted senior inspector in 1912. Her ability to create in a few words a sense of the plight of individual women in factories, laundries and workrooms, or to express the misery of homeworkers in the clothing trade made her reports a striking record of contemporary social conditions. In 1904 she contributed an article, 'Women's place in the industrial world', to the *Public Service Journal*.

Unequivocally condemning filthy and overcrowded working conditions, Duncan argued that an appointment of a female doctor to the factory department would be 'invaluable not only in eliminating work which is absolutely poisonous or dangerous, but also in eliminating all conditions which are unfavourable to health'. In politics she was conservative and was particularly unsympathetic to the industrial policies of the State Labor government. She increasingly believed that her position in the Department of Labour and Industry was undermined by her lack of enthusiasm for the Labor Party. She retired in 1918.

Duncan was a practising Anglican and a member of the Women's Auxiliary of the Australian Board of Missions and the Girls' Friendly Society. In the early 1900s she was involved in the National Council of Women of New South Wales, enlisting its support in her fight against industrial disease, and was a founder of the Business and Professional Women's Club of Sydney and a member of the Women's Club. In the 1920s she travelled in Australia and overseas. On her return in 1930 she lived in Adelaide where she was a member of the Adelaide Music Salon, the Alliance Française, the Victoria League and the Lyceum Club. In 1937-40 she lived in a boarding house at Kings Cross, Sydney, a way of life she found congenial, but returned to North Adelaide in 1940.

Annie Duncan died in hospital at College Park on 13 September 1943. She had seen herself both as a precursor in her profession in England and Australia, and a pioneer career woman among those of her social standing in New South Wales. Her estate was valued there for probate at £2565, and £169 in South Australia.

E. Ryan and A. Conlon, *Gentle invaders* (Syd, 1975); K. Daniels et al (eds), *Women in Australia*

(Canb, 1977); *Lone Hand*, 2 Dec 1912; *SMH*, 11 Feb 1914; *Sun* (Syd), 17 Mar 1918; A.J. Duncan papers (SAA).
KAY DANIELS

DUNCAN, WALTER JOHN CLARE (1894-1939), bank officer and soldier, was born on 27 January 1894 at Inverell, New South Wales, eldest son of Walter Sydney Duncan, bank clerk and station-manager, and his wife Margaret McIntyre, née McGregor. Educated at Inverell Grammar School, he joined the Bank of New South Wales at Barraba in 1910 and was transferred to Narrabri in 1911, Coonabarabran in 1915 and Sydney in 1916. He served for four years in the militia with the 5th Australian Light Horse (New England) Regiment before World War I. His paternal grandfather and two uncles had reached general rank in the British and Indian armies.

On 6 August 1914 Duncan had tried to enlist in the Australian Imperial Force but was rejected because of insufficient chest measurement. Undeterred, he developed his physique and by March 1915 was a sergeant in the light horse. That month he gained a militia commission in the 13th Infantry Battalion and in December rejoined the 5th Light Horse. He was accepted for the A.I.F. on 7 March 1916 as a lieutenant in the newly formed 33rd Battalion and on reaching France in November went into the line at Armentières. His first major action was the battle of Messines where he won the Military Cross. His conspicuous gallantry in assault and his daring leadership inspired his men until he was severely wounded on 10 June. On rejoining his unit he was promoted captain in November and for the next two months was attached, for a liaison course, to the Australian Flying Corps.

When a company commander in 1918 at Villers-Bretonneux, Duncan received the Distinguished Service Order. His 150 men, with seven Lewis-guns, gained an excellent defensive position on 4 April and inflicted heavy casualties. Next day he led an advance and throughout the action provided valuable information to headquarters. The citation praised his 'sound judgement and initiative' and his 'gallant, fearless and cheerful bearing'. He was gassed on 17 April and was out of the line until 8 August. He was awarded a Bar to his D.S.O. for gallantry in operations near Bouchavesnes on 31 August in the struggle for Mont St Quentin: with magnificent dash and daring he led the 33rd's left assaulting company in a series of formidable engagements at Marrières Wood and on the Bapaume-Péronne road. He was twice mentioned in dispatches in 1918-19. His brother, Private William Duncan, was killed in action at Pozières.

Duncan's A.I.F. appointment ended in England on 17 December 1918 after he had received a probationary lieutenancy in the 1st Battalion, Queen Victoria's Own Guides, Indian Army. He reached India in January. When the army was reorganized in 1922 the Guides Infantry was incorporated into the Frontier Force Regiment as its 5th Battalion. Except for short periods Duncan served with the guides and other battalions of the F.F.R. until his death, seeing active service on the Frontier in 1919, 1930 and 1935; he was promoted major in 1934. He had married Jean Gordon on 10 January 1931 at Kohat. Duncan died of an aortic aneurysm on 19 October 1939 at Peshawar and was buried at Mardan with full military honours.

Bank of New South Wales roll of honour (Syd, 1921); C.E.W. Bean, *The A.I.F. in France, 1918* (Syd, 1937, 1942); W. E. H. Condon, *The Frontier Force Regiment* (Aldershot, 1962); *London Gazette*, 25 Aug 1917, 26 July, 3 Dec 1918, 1 Jan, 11 July 1919; *Reveille* (Syd), July 1935; *Inverell Times*, 20 Oct 1939, 26 Apr 1977; *SMH* 23 Oct 1939; information from Mrs C. Hocking, Lindfield, *and* Mrs C. Vyner, *and* Avern McIntyre & Co, Inverell, NSW, *and* the Australian Embassy, Islamabad.
JOHN ATCHISON

DUNCAN, WALTER LESLIE (1883-1947), politician, was born on 14 March 1883 at Armidale, New South Wales, son of John Mackie Duncan, miller, and his wife Margaret, née McDowell. He was educated at Armidale Superior Public School, worked as a clerk and became president of the United Clerks' Union of New South Wales and of the Labor Council in 1911. In 1914-16 he was on the executive of the Coke Workers' Association of New South Wales. He contested the Legislative Assembly seats of Granville in 1907 and Waverley in 1910 as a Labor candidate, but, a devoted follower of W. M. Hughes [q.v.], left the Labor Party over conscription and stood for Granville in 1917 as a Nationalist.

After serving in the Australian Imperial Force in 1917-19 Duncan was elected to the Senate in 1919, his pre-war industrial and political experience standing him in good stead. Strongly protectionist, he remained over the next decade a representative of the ex-Labor element of the disparate National Party, and an ally of Hughes's in his occasional battles with the Liberal elements among the Nationalists. Duncan encouraged the idea of a progressive centre party. He served on the royal commissions on the Navigation Act (1923-25) and on the moving-picture industry (1927-28) and was briefly acting government whip (1924) and temporary chairman of committees (1924-25). He was a vice-president of the National

Association of New South Wales in 1924-25 and 1926-27.

Duncan, as a senator, did not take part directly in the fall of the Bruce-Page [q.v.7, q.v.] government in 1929, but his support for Commonwealth arbitration and protection, and his opposition to the entertainment tax paralleled the views of some of the House of Representatives dissidents. He was close to W. M. Marks [q.v.], a key rebel, as well as to Hughes. Excluded from the National Party after the election, he helped Hughes to establish the Australian Party and became a vice-president and a parliamentary representative until the party's demise in 1930. After his attempt to gain selection for the new United Australia Party in 1931 had been vetoed by its Country Party allies, he stood unsuccessfully for the All-For-Australia League in Warringah. In 1935, however, he contested Illawarra in the New South Wales Legislative Assembly elections for the United Australia and Country Party coalition, and in 1940 he stood for the House of Representatives in Werriwa as a United Australia Party candidate; he was defeated both times.

Duncan married three times: to Ellen Cousins Riley on 31 December 1910 at New Town, to Kathleen Annie Flemming on 6 June 1923 in Canberra, and to Eileen Eliza Coutman on 18 April 1946 at Tamworth, New South Wales. His first wife was the sister of Labor politician E. C. Riley [q.v.]. Duncan, a Presbyterian, died of pneumonia and nephritis on 28 May 1947 at West Tamworth, leaving three sons from his first marriage and a daughter from his second. His estate was valued for probate at £1376.

A. Wildavsky and D. Carboch, *Studies in Australian politics* (Melb, 1958); T. Matthews, 'The All for Australia League', in 'The great Depression in Australia', *Labor Hist*, 1970, no 17; Labor Council of NSW, *Report*, 1908-16 (copy, NL); *Fighting Line*, 27 Nov 1919; *Bulletin*, and *SMH*, 2 Dec 1931.

DAVID STEPHENS

DUNHILL, SIR THOMAS PEEL (1876-1957), surgeon, was born on 3 December 1876 at Tragowel, a grazing property near Kerang, Victoria, son of John Webster Dunhill, station-manager from Yorkshire, England, and his wife Mary Elizabeth, née Peel. His father died of typhoid fever in 1878; his mother then returned to her birthplace, Inverleigh, near Geelong. She later married a miner, William Lawry, and the family moved to Daylesford, where Tom attended the local grammar school. After matriculating at the University of Melbourne, he studied pharmacy and was registered in June 1898, but he never practised. Instead, in 1899 he began to study medicine.

Dunhill's undergraduate career was brilliant. He graduated in 1903 with three first-class honours and exhibitions in medicine and in obstetrics and gynaecology. The tragic death of his younger brother John, a doctor of exceptional ability who died from septic complications while trying to save a patient, spurred him to a single-minded application of his studies, further accentuating a certain reserve in his make-up. He joined the resident staff at the (Royal) Melbourne Hospital, and here he began his lifelong interest in the thyroid gland and in particular exophthalmic goitre. He practised removal of the thyroid gland in goats and then fed the goat milk to patients suffering from thyrotoxicosis, as was the custom at that time.

Although Dunhill was showing outstanding qualities, his career prospects at the Melbourne Hospital were dim. He came from the country and had little money and no connexions. However, his talents came to the notice of Mother Berchmans Daly [q.v.], and in 1905 at her invitation, he joined the staff at St Vincent's Hospital as physician to the out-patients department. In 1906 he was awarded a doctorate in medicine from the University of Melbourne and, deciding on a surgical career, was immediately appointed surgeon to out-patients at St Vincent's.

By this time Dunhill had become disenchanted with the medical treatment of exophthalmic goitre and in 1907, against all prevailing opinion, he decided to carry out removal of the thyroid gland as the definitive cure for the condition. More important, he carried out thyroidectomy in patients who were suffering from cardiac failure as a result of the over-active thyroid gland. He was spectacularly successful and by 1910 had performed 312 operations on the thyroid with a mortality rate of 1 per cent; at that time the mortality of thyroidectomy in the great London hospitals was over 30 per cent. Dunhill pioneered the bilateral resection operation on the thyroid and was the first surgeon to advocate and carry out surgery successfully in the thyrocardiac. By 1911 he was the leading surgeon in his field in Australasia and in that year visited surgical centres in England and the United States of America. His paper delivered to the Royal Society of Medicine in London in 1912, describing his results in the surgical treatment of exophthalmic goitre, produced a sensation.

On returning to Australia in 1912 Dunhill was made surgeon to in-patients at St Vincent's Hospital and chairman of the medical staff. On 12 February 1914 he married a widow, Edith Florence McKellar, née Affleck. He acquired a wine-cellar and his somewhat 'straight laced' outlook on life mellowed a little.

In January 1906 Dunhill had been commissioned a captain in the Australian Army Medical Corps. On the outbreak of World War I he enlisted in the Australian Imperial Force as a major and was allotted to the 1st Australian General Hospital. In July 1918 he was appointed consulting surgeon to the Rouen area in France, and there he met and impressed many leading English surgeons, particularly George Gask. Dunhill was mentioned in dispatches three times and was appointed C.V.O and C.M.G. in 1919. During the war he was asked to operate on a number of desperately ill thyroid patients in London (the English surgeons had refused to do so) and all recovered. The foundations were thereby laid for his future successes in England.

Dunhill returned to Australia in 1919 with the rank of colonel and rejoined the staff of St Vincent's. A brilliant and lucrative surgical career in Australia lay before him. In 1920, however, he accepted an invitation from Gask to join the professional surgical unit at St Bartholomew's Hospital, London. Within a few years he had established himself as the leading thyroid surgeon in England and the best general surgeon at St Bartholomew's. Eminent overseas surgeons flocked to his operating theatre to witness his technique. His greatest triumph, however, was in medical education. By patient and persistent application he convinced the physicians to refer thyrotoxic patients for surgery before they became desperately ill. In this he was aided by such outstanding English physicians as Dr John Parkinson, Lord Dawson and Sir Thomas (Lord) Horder. Dunhill was appointed surgeon to George V in 1928 and then successively to Edward VIII, George VI (becoming sergeant surgeon in 1949) and finally extra surgeon to Elizabeth II.

Many honours were showered on the expatriate Australian. In 1930 the fellowship of the (Royal) College of Surgeons of Australasia was bestowed on him and he was appointed K.C.V.O. in 1933 and G.C.V.O in 1949. In 1939 the Royal College of Surgeons of England conferred on him an honorary fellowship, the first to a surgeon still in active surgical practice in England. During World War II Dunhill was appointed consulting surgeon to the A.I.F. with the rank of brigadier. Although he had retired from active hospital work at St Bartholomew's he participated in the emergency wartime medical services.

Dunhill taught and influenced succeeding generations of surgeons by example and by practice: lecturing and writing did not come easily to him. The pragmatic streak was evident in his younger days for he was a keen exponent of the outdoor life. Although short and rather frail-looking, he was physically tough: a capable canoeist, a mountaineer and an enthusiast for snow-sports. Before 1913 he often fished on the Snowy River; later he spent weeks on the west coast of Norway. He was an expert gardener and collected antique furniture.

Dunhill's wife died in 1942. His last years were marked by increasing ill health and he was plagued by the insomnia which had worried him all his life. He died a somewhat lonely man at his home Tragowel, Hampstead, on 22 December 1957. He left an estate valued for probate at £138 461. His portrait by James Gunn hangs in the College of Surgeons, Spring Street, Melbourne.

Archibald Watson memorial lecture (Melb, priv print, 1967, copy RACS); St Vincent's Hospital (Melb), *Annual Report,* 1905-20; *British Medical J,* 4 Jan 1958, p 43; *MJA*, 22 Mar 1958, p 404; *Medical History,* Jan 1974, p 22.   IVO D. VELLAR

DUNKLEY, LOUISA MARGARET (1866-1927), union leader and feminist, was born on 28 May 1866 at Richmond, Melbourne, daughter of William James Dunkley, boot-importer, and his wife Mary Ann, née Regan, both from London. After education at suburban Catholic girls' schools, Louisa Dunkley entered the Postmaster-General's Department in 1882 as a junior assistant. She studied telegraphy and in 1888 qualified as an operator, working in Melbourne metropolitan post and telegraph offices until 1890. She was then transferred to the Chief Telegraph Office and, after passing the necessary proficiency tests, was appointed as a telegraphist.

Miss Dunkley became interested in unionism in the early 1890s from her experience of the unfair conditions in pay and status of women workers in the Victorian public service. Encouraged by the first advances towards equal pay and status in 1895 by women telegraphists in the colony of New South Wales, Louisa Dunkley and a committee of Victorian women telegraphists and postmistresses decided to present a case for equal pay for their colleagues in the Post and Telegraph Department of Victoria. Her brilliant advocacy won widespread praise. In the outcome she and her colleagues received large increases in salary, though not equality with men telegraphists, whose salaries were reduced in the public service retrenchments and general salary reductions at the time.

In the next three years the Melbourne telegraph administration subjected Miss Dunkley and other women telegraphists to many indignities. She and others sparked off a controversy in the Victorian press and parliament. An inquiry found many deplorable actions and had them remedied, but Miss Dunkley was transferred to a suburban post office where she could make contact with her supporters only over the telegraph lines.

Determined still to secure equal pay and status for women, early in 1900 Miss Dunkley and her colleagues established the Victorian Women's Post and Telegraph Association. As they would come under the new Commonwealth Public Service, she convinced the new women's association that it should take its programme to the all-colonies conference of telegraphists to be held in Sydney in October. She was elected a delegate and at the conference her advocacy of equal pay and status under new Commonwealth conditions was endorsed.

At the close of the conference, R. J. Meagher [q.v.], a Tasmanian delegate, gave notice that he opposed the policy and would have it reversed. As Louisa Dunkley and her supporters developed a vigorous campaign of letter-writing, public meetings, interviews and lobbying of Federal politicians, Meagher began his attacks on equal pay in the New South Wales and Federal associations' journal, the *Transmitter*. Miss Dunkley answered every attack forcefully and, at the same time, she and her colleagues in the newly established Victorian Women's Post and Telegraph Association won majority support in parliament for an equal pay provision for telegraphists and postmistresses in the Commonwealth Public Service Act of 1902 — this has applied generally ever since.

At the Sydney conference in 1900 Louisa Dunkley had met Edward Charles Kraegen [q.v.]. On their marriage to him on 22 December 1903 at St Alipius Church, Oakleigh, Melbourne, she resigned from the Postmaster-General's Department. A daughter was born in 1904 and a son in 1906. She died of cancer on 10 March 1927 at Longueville, Sydney, and was buried in Northern Suburbs cemetery. Her husband and children survived her.

Louisa Dunkley is remembered for her unique work in establishing the first separate union for women for the express purpose of securing and then maintaining equal pay and status. Her polemic on equal pay with Meagher is outstanding in Australian industrial history. In her letters she displayed an understanding of male to female and unionist to non-unionist relationships that remains relevant in industrial relations.

J. S. Baker, *Communicators and their first trade unions* (Syd, 1980); Men, machines, history: the history of the early telegraph and post office associations of Australia (ML).   JOHN S. BAKER

DUNLOP, JAMES MATTHEW (1867-1949), and **WILLIAM PHILIP** (1877-1954), merchants, were born on 15 April 1867 and 23 October 1877, in Edinburgh, Scotland, eldest and second sons of John Sym Dunlop (1844-1912) and his wife Margaret, née Munro (d. 1931). Their uncle William Philip senior (d. 1906) came to Australia from Scotland in 1861 and was salesman in the paper firm of Alexander Cowan & Co. Ltd. About 1867 he returned to Edinburgh and took George Murray as partner: the firm traded in Sydney as Murray, Dunlop & Co. About 1873 he and Frederick Lewis Edwards (1828-1906), law stationer and bookseller, founded Edwards, Dunlop & Co. Ltd, paper merchants and wholesale stationers, of Sydney and London.

After attending George Watson's College, Edinburgh, James Matthew arrived in New South Wales with his family in 1879 and, on completing his education at the Cooerwull Academy, Bowenfels, joined the firm. In May 1886 it became a public company: the consideration paid being £107 000 in fully paid £1 shares. Edwards managed the London buying office while William senior and John took care of the Sydney distributing side. On his father's death in 1912 James became chairman and managing director of the Australian operations. A branch had been opened in Brisbane in the 1880s and through careful and conservative management the firm survived the depression, a disastrous fire in 1906 and paper supply and shipping shortages in World War I. Operations were extended to Melbourne in 1920 and to Perth in 1937–38.

James was president of the Sydney Chamber of Commerce in 1924-27 and of the Associated Chambers of Commerce of Australia in 1926–27. He was also chairman of Paget Manufacturing Co. Ltd and a director of the Bank of New South Wales in 1927-30. A staunch Presbyterian, like his father, he was a director of the Burnside Presbyterian Orphan Homes for many years and generously supported the Salvation Army. Of a somewhat devout and retiring disposition, he spent his spare time mainly in farming pursuits. He died unmarried on 21 August 1949 at his home Munro Park, Sutton Forest, and was cremated. His estate was valued for probate at £191 433.

William Philip, junior, was educated at Sydney Boys' High School and at 16 joined the company; appointed a director in 1903, he was vice-chairman for thirty-seven years until 1949 when he became chairman and managing director. He was the driving force behind the growth of the firm which until 1944 concentrated on wholesale merchandising. He was fond of saying that 'Not a wheel turns inside these doors', but that year the firm bought Galwey & Co. Pty Ltd, a manufacturing stationer. Since 1959 the firm has expanded vigorously throughout Australia, New Zealand and Papua New Guinea and has played a leading role in the development of the newspaper and printing trades; among its agencies for newsprint and others papers is Stora Kopparbergs of Sweden, the oldest known company in the world.

Dunlop was very good natured and generous, with a sense of humour; he was fond of travel, cards, reading and the theatre. He enjoyed gambling on a modest budget at Monte Carlo. Very active in tennis affairs, he was president of the New South Wales Lawn Tennis Association in 1909-10 and 1914 and was senior vice-president of the Lawn Tennis Association of Australia in 1926. He later enjoyed golf and, with his brother, was a member of the Australian Club. He was honorary treasurer of the Citizens Reform Association and in 1924-50 of the Royal Alexandra Hospital for Children. He died on 2 August 1954 at his home at Edgecliff, Sydney, and was cremated with Presbyterian forms. He was survived by his wife Mary Josephine, née Smith, whom he had married on 20 February 1908 at the Scots Church, Sydney, and by a daughter and son (Sir) John Dunlop. His estate was valued for probate at £117 938.

Daily Telegraph (Syd), 31 Mar, 4 Sep 1906, 16 May 1912; *Sunday Times* (Syd), 1 Apr 1906; *SMH* 24 July, 2 Sept 1906, 8 Dec 1922, 7 Dec 1923, 21 May 1926, 30 Mar 1935, 22 Aug 1949, 3 Aug 1954; *T&CJ*, 18 Jan 1911, 20 May 1912; *Bulletin*, 23 May 1912, 1 Sep 1928; *Smith's Weekly* (Syd), 11 Aug 1923; *Labor Daily*, 17 July 1925; *Manning River Times*, 21 May 1949; Edwards Dunlop & Co. Ltd, Records (Syd).   G. P. WALSH

DUNN, ANDREW (1854-1934), ANDREW (1880-1956) and WILLIAM HERBERT ALAN (1883-1961) were father and sons, and founders of a newspaper empire in central Queensland. Andrew senior was born on 24 May 1854 at Greenock, Scotland, son of Andrew Dunn, merchant, and his wife Ann, née Anderson. Educated at Greenock, he went to sea and worked for a Calcutta tea merchant before returning to become a cadet architectural draughtsman. On 4 November 1879, at Greenock, he married Katharine McIntyre; of their five sons, one died in infancy. The couple migrated to Queensland in 1880 so that Kate could accept a teaching appointment with the Department of Public Instruction. She became head of the Girls' South State School at Toowoomba while Andrew took on building. In 1885 they moved to Maryborough when she took over its Central Girls'

School; she died there on 5 July 1889.

Dunn, at first a plumber, had become business-manager of the daily *Maryborough Chronicle* before August 1888 when the directors gave him a bonus for efficiency. Within six months he had bought twenty-four shares and had become a director. By 1891 he was chairman at a time when the paper was in difficulties. On 18 November he married another teacher, Jane, daughter of James Cran [q.v.] of Yengarie. She bore him two sons and two daughters and was said to have been an astute business adviser.

As the *Chronicle* struggled out of its difficulties in the late 1890s, Dunn entered Maryborough local politics and served as mayor in 1903 and 1914; he was an alderman in 1904-13 and again in 1915. Appointed as a Liberal, he sat in the Legislative Council in 1914-22. Inspired by the examples of the Buzacott [q.v.3], Groom [q.v.4] and (James) Morgan [q.v.5] families, Dunn planned to have several sons trained in various departments of newspaper work and for others to be available if required. When the daily *Chronicle* and weekly *Colonist* showed a first substantial profit in 1911, the family bought a controlling interest in the Rockhampton *Morning Bulletin*, installing Andrew junior as editor and his brother W. H. A. (Herbert) as chief of staff. Other brothers joined the paper later. In 1914 they bought the *Warwick Argus* and Herbert became its managing editor.

Deciding that the small independent newspaper could not survive in towns within easy reach of the metropolitan press, the family undertook an amalgamation programme. In February 1919 they merged the *Warwick Argus* with the Irwin family's *Warwick Examiner and Times* to form the *Warwick Daily News* with Herbert as managing editor. About the same time they took over the *Wide Bay and Burnett News* and combined it with the *Maryborough Chronicle*. After buying the Groom interest in the *Toowoomba Chronicle* they merged it with the competing daily *Darling Downs Gazette* on 2 October 1922. As Rockhampton seemed beyond the range of the metropolitan press the *Morning Bulletin* continued unchanged in association with the *Evening News*, bought from the Purcell Trust in 1929.

Andrew senior was a founder of the Queensland Country Press Association in 1907, a committee-member till his death, president several times, and chairman of directors of the association's business subsidiary, Queensland Country Press Ltd, in 1931-34. He was involved with the local chamber of commerce, harbour board, school of arts and technical college, and was an elder of St Stephen's Presbyterian Church, Maryborough, for many years.

The family enterprise began keeping minutes of its business meetings in 1929. Although there was a semi-autonomous board in each town, Andrew senior co-ordinated them all. Family meetings discussed such matters as capital expenditure and the appointment of senior staff. Wills were written to ensure that shares stayed in the family. A family bank account was opened in 1930 but it was only in 1957 that a family holding company was incorporated.

Jane Dunn died in August 1930 and Andrew senior married Marcella Heller Foote in Sydney on 23 February 1932; she bore him no children. He died in Brisbane on 29 April 1934 and was buried in Maryborough cemetery. His estate, valued for probate at £36 286, was left to a family trust.

Andrew junior was born at Toowoomba on 7 May 1880 and was educated in Maryborough at the Christian Brothers' College and the grammar school. Apprenticed as a printer to the *Maryborough Chronicle*, he was transferred to the literary staff as a cadet when he showed writing ability. Joining the new Brisbane *Daily Mail* about 1904, he won praise as a reporter and writer of news commentaries, then moved to the Rockhampton *Morning Bulletin* in 1905. When the family bought a controlling interest from the McIlwraith-Blair [qq.v.5, 7] partnership in 1911, he was senior enough to become editor, which he remained for forty-three years. In 1934 he succeeded his father as chairman of the Rockhampton, Maryborough and Toowoomba newspaper companies and on the board of Queensland Country Press Ltd. A 'clear and forceful writer with a scrupulous sense of fairness and tolerance', he wrote a weekly column under the pen-name 'Lictor' and was a competent dramatic critic. He believed that 'Our function is to produce a good newspaper. If you produce a good newspaper, you deserve some reward . . . Don't slant; don't sensationalise; reserve comment for editorials; don't blow a story up'. He had married Ivy Adeline Mary Lucas at North Rockhampton on 16 June 1909; they had seven children. He died at Maryborough on 31 January 1956 and was cremated in Rockhampton.

Herbert was born at Toowoomba on 11 September 1883 and educated at the Maryborough Grammar School. He joined the literary staff of the *Maryborough Chronicle* in 1901 and later worked on the *Brisbane Courier* and the *Bundaberg Mail*. After his Rockhampton and Warwick positions, he was managing editor of the *Toowoomba Chronicle and Darling Downs Gazette* till 1922 when he became chairman of the Toowoomba Newspaper Co. Pty. Ltd. After visiting England in the late 1920s, he in-

stalled dictaphones to take copy by telephone from the Country Press Association's news service in Brisbane, and later advocated the use of teleprinters. He was said to be a shorthand and typing expert, a witty paragraphist, a capable sub-editor and an editor who set high standards of writing, accuracy and fairness. He died at Sandgate on 4 April 1961, survived by his wife Agnes Jessie, née Hill, whom he had married at Bundaberg on 5 September 1908, and their three children. He left his estate, valued for probate at £98 133, to his family.

Newspaper News, 2 Sept 1929; *Maryborough Chronicle*, 6 July 1889, 15 Aug 1930; *Morning Bulletin*, 8 July 1961, centenary issue; *Toowoomba Chronicle*, 30 Apr 1934, 15 July 1961, centenary supp; minute-books, Maryborough Newspaper Co, held by Provincial Newspapers (Qld) Ltd, Brisb, *and* Qld Country Press, held by Regional Dailies of Aust Ltd (Qld Division), Brisb; information from Mr L. S. Dunn, Provincial Newspapers (Qld) Ltd, Brisb, *and* Mr A. Dunn, Caloundra, Qld.

ROD KIRKPATRICK

DUNN, EDWARD JOHN (1844-1937), geologist, was born on 1 November 1844 at Bedminster near Bristol, England, son of Edward Herbert Dunn, printer, of Cheltenham, and his wife Betsy, née Robinson. He migrated to New South Wales with his parents in 1849. At first they lived near Goulburn, but in 1856 moved to Beechworth in Victoria. Dunn was educated privately and at Beechworth Church of England Grammar School. From boyhood he was an ardent collector of minerals and rocks. In 1860 he joined the staff of the local Lands Survey Office, and four years later transferred to the Geological Survey of the Mines Department where he trained under A. R. C. Selwyn and G. H. F. Ulrich [qq.v.6]. He discovered curious specimens of chalcedony containing fluid near Beechworth; these specimens formed the subject of his first published scientific article. In 1869 he qualified as a mining surveyor.

In 1871 Dunn left Australia for South Africa, where he was appointed government geologist for Cape Colony. His pioneer geological work there included a part in the discovery of diamonds and the opening of the Kimberley diamond mines, and investigations of the goldfields of Transvaal and the coal deposits of Cape Colony. He became interested in anthropology and made extensive collections of the weapons and implements used by the tribes including those of the south-west African Bushman which he later donated to the Pitt-Rivers Museum, Oxford. He also built up a valuable private collection of geological specimens, including gold and diamonds. Dunn had returned to England to study in 1873, and again in 1875, when on 7 July at St Helier, Jersey, Channel Islands, he married Elizabeth Julia Perchard.

Dunn returned to Australia in 1886 and, with Melbourne as his base, worked as a consulting geologist throughout Australasia and in New Caledonia. In 1886 near Heathcote he discovered and mapped the first rocks of Cambrian age to be found in Victoria. He also discovered very old (Permian) rocks of glacial origin and published the first of several scientific articles on them in 1888. Between 1889 and 1894 he carried out perhaps his best geological work in demonstrating the essential structures of the Bendigo goldfield.

In September 1904 Dunn was appointed director of the Geological Survey in the Victorian Department of Mines and Water Supply. He was closely connected with the discovery of black coal deposits in Gippsland, which led to the development of the State Coal Mine at Wonthaggi in 1909. He studied the geology and physiography of Mount Buffalo and helped to make it popular as a tourist resort; Mount Dunn is named after him. In 1911 his book, *Pebbles*, was published in Melbourne. Dunn's work in the Geological Survey was concerned mainly with economic geology, but other tasks included a study of australites; he donated his private collection of 120 of these to the British Museum.

After his retirement in 1912 from the Geological Survey Dunn worked for many years as a consulting geologist. His books, *Geology of gold* and *The Bushman*, were published in London in 1929 and 1931. In 1884 he was elected a fellow of the Geological Society of London, which in 1905 awarded him its Murchison medal for his geological work in Australia and South Africa. Dunn was an excellent field geologist and administrator. He was a skilful and discerning collector and was meticulous as a curator. Most of the large private collections of minerals, rocks and ethnological artefacts that he had not disposed of during his lifetime are now in the National Museum of Victoria. He died at his home in Kew, Melbourne, on 20 April 1937 and was survived by his wife, one son and two daughters. He was buried in Kew cemetery.

J. V. Zelizko, *In memory of Edward John Dunn, geologist* (Melb, 1937); *Industrial Aust and Mining Standard*, 16 May 1912, p 448, 30 Oct 1924, p 634, 1 May 1937, p 114; *Vic Naturalist*, 54 (1937-38), p 20.   A. W. BEASLEY

DUNN, JAMES PATRICK DIGGER (1887-1945), politician, was born on 20 August 1887 at Kirkdale, Liverpool, Lancashire, England, son of Thomas Dunn, marine officer, and his wife Margaret, née Kavanagh. He went to sea aged 16 but jumped ship in South Africa, where he became an apprentice engineer at Simonstown. After the South African War he worked in Sydney for the Glencairn Glass Co. and then in New Zealand as miner, timber-trucker and wharflabourer. He became vice-president of the Westland Trades and Labour Council, founding president of the Greymouth Drivers' Union and was defeated as the Waterside Workers' Union candidate for the Greymouth Borough Council elections in April 1909. After his involvement in the Blackball miners' coal strike he moved to Queensland.

A member of the Australian Workers' Union Dunn was active in the 1911 sugar strike. In 1912 he worked as an engine driver at the Cockatoo Island dockyard, Sydney; he joined the Federated Ironworkers of Australia in September 1913, and in January-June 1914 was delegate to the Trades and Labor Council and the Iron Trades Federation, although he attended meetings infrequently. He then served with the Australian Naval and Military Force in New Guinea and in November 1915 enlisted with the Australian Imperial Force. He was gassed in France in 1918.

On his return to Australia in 1919, Dunn ran unsuccessfully as a Labor candidate for Wentworth in the Federal elections. A member of the central executive of the New South Wales branch of the Australian Labor Party in 1921, he was defeated as Senate candidate several times before his election in 1928; in the Senate he joined the J. A. Beasley group of J. T. Lang [q.v.] supporters. He was party, then government whip until March 1931 when he formally defected with Beasley. Dunn remained leader of the Lang Senate group of two until his defeat in 1934. From June 1935 he worked as tariff consultant, manufacturer and advertising agent.

Dunn's limited importance derived from Lang's need for Federal contacts. In 1931 he had helped to defeat Scullin's [q.v.] Federal Labor government in a way typical of his role as go-between. Information given to Dunn that E. G. Theodore [q.v.] had corruptly distributed unemployment relief work was used by Beasley in November for a censure in the Lower House; the timing stemmed from Sir Hal Colebatch's [q.v.] advice to Dunn that some of the Beasley group might soon return to Federal Labor. Dunn, through Colebatch, ensured that all Opposition Nationalists were present for the crucial vote. Generally Dunn's flamboyance helped compensate for the lack of numbers of the Lang group. He described Theodore as a 'political turkeycock'; Sir George Pearce [q.v.], he said, possessed 'a mind as dirty and filthy as a sewer'; he raged against 'the rich man's gold'.

Adopting the name 'Digger', Dunn showed concern for ex-servicemen in his parliamentary speeches and questions. In 1945 he vainly opposed the appointment of a non-returned man to the Australian Broadcasting Commission. His loyalty to ex-servicemen finally led to his second break with Labor. After failing at Leichhardt in the 1938 State elections and at Manly in 1941 and 1944, he was not pre-selected for the Manly by-election in September 1945; complaining that the selected candidate was not a returned soldier, he resigned from the party to stand on behalf of the Soldiers' Party. His preferences assisted the Liberal candidate to win and his 'scurrilous campaign' against Labor precipitated his expulsion. He died of cardiac disease on 21 November 1945 at Dee Why and was buried in the Roman Catholic cemetery at Frenchs Forest, survived by two sons and a daughter. Dunn had married Alice Mary Hynes on 2 February 1924 at Paddington. After much personal and financial stress, he divorced his wife in 1933.

J. Robertson, *J. H. Scullin* (Perth, 1974); *PD* (Cwlth), 1929, p 65, 301, 1931, p 1810, 1935, p 397; *Grey River Argus* (NZ), 19 Mar, 28 Apr, 13 May 1909, 14 Jan 1910; *Aust Worker*, 20 Nov 1919, 27 Nov 1929; *SMH*, 1 Apr 1925, 18 Feb, 7 Sept 1932, 17 Mar, 28 June 1933, 5 July 1935, 18 Feb 1937, 10, 11, 17, 24 Apr, 25 Aug, 29 Sept, 30 Oct, 22 Nov 1945; Federated Ironworkers of Aust (Sydney), Minutes 1913-14, E102/31 (ANU Archives).

DAVID STEPHENS

DUNN, WILLIAM FRASER (1877-1951), politician, was born on 2 February 1877 at McLachlan Creek, Gundaroo, New South Wales, twin son of Francis Dunn, Yorkshire-born farmer, and his native-born wife, Emily, née Fraser. Educated at Sutton and Queanbeyan public schools, at 15 he worked on his father's farm; later in the 1890s he acquired his own property in the district. He joined the local Labor League and in 1899, following a football accident, became a schoolteacher, later serving in several country towns.

At the State general election in 1910, Dunn was one of several professional people nominated by Labor. He won Mudgee and the party narrowly formed its first government. His background reinforced Labor's strong rural link and predisposed him to favour freehold against leasehold; when the latter seemed about to prevail, he resigned his seat in July 1911 but was reassured, and regained it at the by-election in August.

Dunn joined the Army Service Corps, Australian Imperial Force, in December 1915. In March next year he became a second lieutenant and on 28 April at St Michael's Anglican Church, Surry Hills, married Minnie Jane Elizabeth Durrington. In May he was promoted lieutenant, appointed quartermaster of the 35th Battalion and left Sydney. Attached to the British Expeditionary Force in November, he was quartermaster and honorary captain in the A.I.F. in March 1917, when he went on sick leave. He returned to Australia in July and was discharged in March 1918.

In 1916 Dunn had chaired the royal commission into rural, pastoral, agricultural and dairying interests. Resuming his parliamentary career in 1918, he became minister for agriculture in J. Storey's and J. Dooley's [qq.v.] cabinets from April 1920 to April 1922. He deprecated city-country rivalry and consolidated Labor's rural support by energetic and perceptive administration of his sensitive portfolio. He was also chairman of the New South Wales Wheat Board and a member of the Australian Wheat Board; a council-member of the Royal Agricultural Society, he was chairman of the Water Conservation and Irrigation Commission. He stressed the government's role in organized marketing, encouraged rural co-operatives and in 1920 set up the Rural Bank Department (Rural Bank of New South Wales) of the Government Savings Bank.

Dunn had no power base in the Labor Party, but his repute and geniality secured him a following. Although apparently timorous and wary of 'the numbers game', he played it with skill. He was deputy leader of the party in 1922-23; in factional manoeuvrings in March-May 1923, related to the expulsion of Dooley and the appointment by the State executive of J. J. G. McGirr [q.v.] in his place, Dunn was made stopgap leader by the Federal executive until the State annual conference in June. J. T. Lang [q.v.] defeated him for the leadership in August.

Dunn was again minister for agriculture in Lang's cabinet from 17 June 1925 to 26 May 1927, and also assistant minister for lands and minister for forests from 25 November 1926 to 26 May 1927. In 1925 he increased the employment of various agricultural experts. After charges were made about the purchase and resale of cornsacks, he was exonerated by a royal commission. He visited Europe and the United States of America in 1926 to inquire into marketing and irrigation. Next year he joined in the caucus revolt against Lang's leadership; quitting the cabinet on 26 May he became deputy leader of the anti-Lang group. By 1930 unity was restored, and

Dunn became minister for agriculture and for forests until 13 May 1932, when the premier was dismissed by Governor Sir Phillip Game [q.v.]. That year Dunn lost his only election but won again in 1935.

Dunn was in (Sir) William McKell and James McGirr's cabinets of 1941-47 — as minister of agriculture and forests, 1941-44, of conservation, 1944-46, and lands, 1946-47. He failed to be elected to McGirr's second 1947 ministry and retired from parliament in 1950. Childless, and survived by his wife, he died at a hospital at Moore Park on 10 July 1951 and was cremated. His estate was sworn for probate at £30 094.

H. V. Evatt, *Australian Labour leader* . . . *W. A. Holman* (Syd, 1942); *PP* (LC & LA, NSW), 1917-18, 1, 157, 1925-26, 1, 55; *PD* (NSW) 1951, p 196, 2942; *SMH*, 18 Oct 1910, 12 Apr, 4 Dec 1920, 17 Feb, 11 Oct 1921, 25 Apr 1922, 27 Apr 1923, 16 Oct 1925, 6 Sept 1926, 15 Apr, 10 June 1927, 13 Mar, 18 Aug 1931, 9 Sept 1936, 28 May 1942, 12 Apr 1944, 22 Mar 1945, 22 Apr 1946, 5 Feb, 16 May 1947, 11 July 1951; *Mudgee Guardian*, 25 May 1950.

BEDE NAIRN

DUNNE, JOHN (1845-1919), Roman Catholic bishop, was born on 8 June 1845 at Tooreigh, Mitchelstown, County Cork, Ireland, son of Michael Dunne, farmer, and his wife Mary, née Hennessy. He was educated by the Christian Brothers at Mitchelstown, and Mount Melleray College, and studied for the priesthood at the Catholic Missionary College of All Hallows, Drumcondra (Dublin), where he was ordained priest on 24 June 1870.

Dunne reached Sydney in 1871, probably in the *Glendower*, on 2 February, and was sent to the Bathurst diocese. He served in the wild Fish River district, at Mudgee and at Wentworth on the Darling. In 1875 he became parish priest at Dubbo and lived in a tent until he had built a brick church and the Convent of Mercy, which had day and boarding schools by 1885. That year he was called to Bathurst by Bishop Byrne [q.v.3] and administered the cathedral parish. Under his supervision the Patrician Brothers' monastery was built and the cathedral enlarged. At his own request he returned to Dubbo in 1896 and raised over £4000 to liquidate the debt on the church. He was recalled to Bathurst as vicar-general in August 1900.

Following Byrne's death, Dunne was elected bishop of Bathurst on 12 January 1901 and was consecrated by Cardinal Moran [q.v.] on 8 September. As a pioneering priest and as bishop, Dunne was laborious, much enduring and resourceful. He travelled throughout his diocese, and was ready to stand in for the youngest curate. He had an easy, sympathetic and unaffected relationship with his clergy and a sound knowledge of people. Widely known as the 'Builder Bishop', he ensured that every parish had a church, school, presbytery and convent. In Bathurst he raised the money to build St Joseph's Mount and Orphanage, St Philomena's School and the stately Bishop's House. Keenly interested in St Stanislaus' College, he gave generously to finance its 1907 additions. Throughout his life Dunne promoted Catholic education. As a prudent and skilful administrator and a near-genius at raising money, he made the 'voluntary system' work in his diocese. Before he visited Europe in 1906, he was presented with a purse containing £1000, most of which he characteristically saved during his year's absence, and presented the remainder to St Stanislaus College.

Dunne had a masculine, forthright figure, with clear-cut features and a gentle countenance. Greatly beloved by his parishioners, he died of cancer at Bishop's House on 22 August 1919 and was buried in the Catholic section of Bathurst cemetery.

National Advocate, 23, 25, 27 Aug 1919, 13 Nov 1922, St Vincent's Hospital souvenir supp; *Echoes from St Stanislaus*, June 1921, p 8; *Freeman's J* (Syd), 28 August 1919.   K. M. MANNING

DUNNINGHAM, SIR JOHN MONTGOMERY (1884-1938), bookmaker and politician, was born on 21 January 1884 in Sydney, son of English parents John Dunningham, labourer, and his wife Annie, née Fowler. He was educated at Forest Lodge Public School and St James College, Sydney. After working as an assistant at the library of the Sydney Mechanics' School of Arts, he took positions at Alex Cowan & Sons Ltd, paper merchants, and the Australian Gas Light Co. Displaying early ability as an organizer, he became secretary of the fitters' section of the New South Wales branch of the Federated Gas Employees' Industrial Union.

By 1911 Dunningham had established a hatter and mercer's shop in the Imperial Arcade, between Pitt and Castlereagh streets. On 22 February 1913 he married a widow Mary Agnes Britnall, née Hossack. Dunningham persevered with his shop until 1917, when he set up as a bookmaker; he graduated through the Flat, the St Leger and the Paddock, and respectability was conferred with committee membership of Tattersall's Club; he served as treasurer in 1928-31.

Dunningham was an alderman on Randwick Municipal Council in 1917-31 and was mayor in 1927-28. Local government provided the springboard to politics. He won the Legislative Assembly seat of Coogee for the Nationalists at a by-election in September 1928 and held it until 1938. He was whip for the Nationalists while in Opposition from 1930, remaining a bookmaker until 1932. Named minister for labour and industry in May 1932, he was one of (Sir) Bertram Stevens's [q.v.] more popular appointments as his bookmaking background gave him the appearance of being 'one of the boys'; many Labor members made a point of calling him 'Jack'. Yet that year he proposed amendments to the Industrial Arbitration Act which would have severely curtailed union power had they been adopted. The Communist *Worker's Weekly* later nicknamed him 'Slave Camp Dunningham' because of his allegedly harsh treatment of the unemployed. In 1935 he visited England, Europe and the Soviet Union and was appalled at the poor standard of living in the latter. On his return he wrote a short report, *British unemployment insurance law* (1936).

In 1936 Dunningham was appointed minister in charge of preparations for Australia's 150th Anniversary celebrations and of those for the coronation in 1937. He was ideal for the job given his positions on sporting and other bodies — past president of the New South Wales Amateur Athletic Association, vice-president of the Royal Life Saving Society and of the New South Wales Rugby Union, and council-member of the National Roads and Motorist's Association and of the Royal Agricultural Society of New South Wales, and an office-bearer in local football, cricket, swimming and tennis clubs. He was also an active Anglican, excellent after-dinner speaker and sometime church organist. His organizing abilities were shown to good effect in these celebrations, the most elaborate ever held in Australia. However his desire to exclude the convict heritage, bushranging and Aboriginals roused some adverse criticism. The Aboriginals' day of mourning for the white man's seizure of their country held in Sydney on Australia Day 1938 was not part of his programme.

On 26 May 1938 Dunningham collapsed and died with heart disease in his office; he was buried with Anglican rites in Waverley cemetery after a service in St Andrew's Cathedral. Survived by his wife and son, he left an estate valued for probate at £17 287, almost half in realty. He was posthumously appointed K.B.E. in June; later a park at North Cronulla and a wing of Eastern Suburbs Hospital were named after him.

W. B. Lynch and F. A. Larcombe, *Randwick, 1859-1959* (Syd, 1959); *PD*(NSW), 1938, p 2; *SMH,* 24 Sept 1928, 27, 28 May, 2 July 1938; *Aust National Review,* 28 June 1932; *Bulletin,* 19 Oct 1932; *Worker's Weekly,* 24 Dec 1937; *Referee,* 26 May 1938; J. M. McCarthy, The Stevens-Bruxner government, 1932-1939 (M.A. thesis, Univ NSW, 1967); information from Aust Jockey Club, Syd.

PETER SPEARRITT

DUNSTAN, SIR ALBERT ARTHUR (1882-1950), premier, was born on 26 July 1882 at Donald East, Victoria, tenth son and thirteenth child of Thomas Dunstan, a selector who had migrated in the gold rushes from Cornwall, England, and his wife Sarah, née Briggs, from Norfolk. After education at the local state school Dunstan took up wheat-growing. In 1907 he left the family farm at Cope Cope to open a pioneer block at Jondaryan, Queensland — living in a tent, because there was neither time nor money to build a shack. He returned to Victoria in 1909 to farm at Goschen, near Swan Hill, where on 6 April 1911 with Presbyterian forms, he married Jessie Gerard Chisholm; they had four daughters and two sons. Dunstan maintained a farm at Kaneira (Culgoa), though living at Fern Tree Gully in 1916 and Melbourne in 1917, before selling up and moving to the Bendigo district early in 1918. He ran sheep on a freehold property at Kamarooka from the early 1920s until 1933, employing a manager; the family lived at Bendigo until 1943, when Dunstan made his home in Melbourne.

In 1916 he had joined the Kaneira branch of the newly formed Victorian Farmers' Union. On moving to Bendigo he became active in the local branch and was endorsed as the party's candidate for the Legislative Assembly seat of Eaglehawk in the 1920 election. He narrowly won on National Party preferences from Labor's Thomas Tunnecliffe [q.v.], holding the seat (renamed Korong-Eaglehawk in 1926 and Korong in 1944) for the next thirty years. A short, stocky man, with shrewd blue eyes and a 'curiously frog-like mouth', Dunstan was a forthright and effective speaker. He was to become known as an unruffled political fighter and for his ability to make lightning assessments of the practical possibilities of any situation.

He was one of thirteen V.F.U members led by John Allan [q.v.7] who held the balance of power in the Legislative Assembly. Despite its electoral success, the party lacked cohesion and Dunstan was the principal spokesman for the more radical rural voters; in a split in September 1921 he voted with Labor while Allan led most of the party in voting to save the Nationalist government. He sought to undermine Allan by appealing for the V.F.U. council's support in censuring him for keeping the Nationalists in power. Dunstan, who was excluded from office in the subsequent Lawson [q.v.]-Allan and Allan-Peacock [q.v.] ministries, led a faction which quarrelled with the majority of parliamentary party members on the issues of composite ministries, redistribution and the compulsory wheat pool. In April 1926 they formed a separate party which adopted the name Country Progressive Party. Dunstan, at first its sole assembly member, became the acknowledged leader of a bloc of four (and one legislative councillor) after the 1927 election. In September 1930 the C.P.P. merged with the Victorian Country Party (as the V.F.U. was now named) to become the United Country Party with Allan as parliamentary leader; in a gesture of unity, Dunstan was accepted as deputy leader.

Until the 1935 election, he seemed to react more passively to events. In the May 1932 elections the United Australia Party led by Sir Stanley Argyle [q.v.7] made significant gains and a composite ministry was formed with the Country Party. Dunstan served as commissioner of Crown lands and survey, minister of forests, and president of the Board of Land and Works until 20 March 1935.

However, throughout this term a determination to end the Country Party's association with the U.A.P. developed within the organization, with A. E. Hocking as principal spokesman on the party's executive. All efforts to force the withdrawal of the Country Party ministers had failed but soon after the March 1935 election Tunnecliffe, now the Labor leader, proposed that the Country Party turn out the Argyle ministry with Labor's assistance and govern with its support. (A. A. Calwell later claimed that this proposal was inspired by him and that John Wren's [q.v.] influence over his 'close friend' Dunstan had much to do with bringing it about.) Dunstan played along with both Hocking and Argyle pending a final decision; he received crucial support from Hocking in wresting the parliamentary leadership from (Sir) Murray Bourchier [q.v.7], who had succeeded Allan in 1933, and then accepted the deputy premiership from Argyle. The Country Party's withdrawal from the ministry was secured on 19 March by a motion carried by a joint meeting of the party executive and the parliamentary party. Without advising the meeting for or against withdrawal, Dunstan had 'urged members to take a definite line of action and not sidetrack the issue', and promised to abide loyally by its decision. On 28 March the Country Party joined with the Labor Party in the Legislative Assembly to carry a motion of no confidence in the reconstructed Argyle ministry.

Dunstan's cabinet composed entirely of Country Party members lasted from 2 April 1935 until 14 September 1943. It relied on Labor support until the beginning of the 1942 session, and then continued in office with U.A.P. support until after the 1943 elections. Defeated on the issue of electoral redistribution in the Legislative Assembly on 9 September 1943, Dunstan resigned. A minority Labor government led by John Cain was sworn in but governed for only five days. Defeated in the assembly, Cain was refused a dissolution and thereupon resigned. Dunstan was then commissioned and formed a composite ministry without any consultation with the party executive. The Country Party elected its ministers and the U.A.P. leader, Tom Hollway, selected an equal number of U.A.P. ministers; Dunstan allocated the portfolios. As well as being premier from 2 April 1935 until 14 September 1943, Dunstan was also treasurer, and solicitor-general from 22 April 1938 and minister of decentralization from 1 March 1943. From 18 September 1943 to 2 October 1945 he was premier, treasurer and minister of decentralization.

The factors responsible for projecting the Country Party into office in its own right in 1935 were, on the face of it, so fortuitous that the new government had difficulty in broadening the scope of Bourchier's somewhat negative statement of policy into a programme which would not seem to rely too much on commitments to the Labor Party. To the rescue came E. J. Hogan [q.v.], a former Labor premier turned independent, who had switched to the Country Party when Dunstan offered him the agriculture portfolio. He was able to resuscitate a marketing bill almost identical to the one introduced in 1930 by his own government with C.P.P. support – in 1935 the legislation emerged from the Victorian parliament bearing the imprint of all parties and especially that of the Legislative Council. At the same time the Dunstan government passed measures for rural rehabilitation through debt adjustment, something to which the Argyle ministry had been broadly committed before the 1935 election because the Commonwealth government was providing finance. The form the legislation took, however, owed its inspiration to a programme advocated by a non-party organization, the Primary Producers' Restoration League, which Dunstan had done his best to discredit. Yet he was to claim repeatedly that these laws were the outstanding achievement of his government.

Labor's influence was to be seen in legislation for workers' compensation, hire purchase, factory Acts, the establishment of the Housing Commission of Victoria, and in

Dunstan's subsequent attempts to reform the Legislative Council. His less than wholehearted efforts to reform the Upper House dragged on for more than a year with an assembly election interrupting them. The result was the institution of a double dissolution procedure to break deadlocks; it has never been used and it could not have prevented two successful attempts by the council in 1947 and 1952 to force a government to the polls through the refusal of supply. This prolonged endeavour at constitutional reform served to keep the Labor Party happy, conscious as its members were of the obstacles an unreformed Upper House would pose to any future Labor government.

Other actions of the Dunstan government, legislative and otherwise, which were intended to mollify the Labor Party were perhaps not for the squeamish. Some adroit footwork on Dunstan's part resulted in a royal commission report into allegations of bribery against certain Labor members (in the interests of defeating a government-inspired bill) which did not affect them as adversely as might have been the case if Dunstan, although blameless himself, had divulged all he knew. This intricate exercise in obfuscation enabled him to move against Hocking, who by now was something of an irritant, and repay one or two old scores. When threatened with a hostile party conference in 1940 as a result of his vindictive conduct towards Hocking, Dunstan called a snap election which, thanks to Labor's continued support, left his government's situation unchanged. Despite the overwhelming support of the party organization, Hocking backed down when Dunstan intimated that a hostile conference vote would result in the cabinet walking out. By now Hocking's work in devising organizational machinery to control parliamentary members lay in ruins. Labor support was also not wanting when another royal commission, this time to enquire into the causes of the 1939 bushfires, pointedly implied that there had been serious instances of ministerial incompetence.

Two important acts of the Dunstan government which were unrelated to Country Party policy were the removal of the Royal Melbourne Hospital to a new site in Parkville and the sale of Crown land at Fishermen's Bend to General Motors-Holden [q.v.] Ltd. In the latter case, the responsibility of the final decision must be accounted Dunstan's own.

In 1936 he brought down what was generally acclaimed as the 'Recovery Budget'. Provision for reduction in taxation earned him commendation in some metropolitan circles; but, with his eye always on rural areas, he provided for a continuance of direct concessions to primary producers in respect of payments for losses on soldier and closer settlement, reduction of railway freight charges on certain primary products and alleviation of costs and expenses connected with the destruction of vermin and noxious weeds; in addition other grants and advances were made under the general heading of rural relief. Crown employees' salaries and State pensions (which had been reduced as a Depression measure) were fully restored and increased provision was made for education. (These last items of expenditure were not lavishly funded in the later years of the Dunstan administration).

But for the five-day Labor interlude, his term of office as premier took in the whole period of World War II. Such reformist enthusiasm as had been kindled in Dunstan by his reliance on Labor support was dampened by wartime conditions when he specifically repudiated any espousal of 'contentious legislation', a very comprehensive category as it turned out. This deliberate *immobilisme* only served to encourage those within the Labor party hostile to continuing their party's support for him.

The Dunstan-Hollway composite government of September 1943 to October 1945 was a most unhappy marriage of convenience. The State parliamentary U.A.P., which changed its name to Liberal in March 1945, was determined to get some form of redistribution of electorates. Dunstan was determined to stay in office and play for time, but the results of his idiosyncratic administration over the years brought an outcrop of troubles and unprecedented criticism. Discontent among teachers and public servants over salaries and working conditions brought much opprobrium upon his head. Ultimately a redistribution was passed but gradually the tensions in the coalition parties became intolerable, and defectors from both parties combined with Labor and some Independents to defeat the government in the assembly late in 1945 on an appropriation bill. A minority government, made up of non-Labor dissidents led by Ian Macfarlan, was able to pass supply with Labor support. The resulting election brought Labor to office. After the 1945 election, Dunstan wisely declined to nominate for his party's leadership which passed to (Sir) John McDonald.

In 1947 Dunstan entered a Liberal-Country Party composite ministry (the Hollway-McDonald government) as minister of health, his very presence at McDonald's insistence being at first strongly resisted by Hollway and then suffered with loathing. Within a year this ministry fell apart. In November 1948 a rift appeared in the coalition over settlement of the essential services legislation and Hollway, claiming that Dunstan's incorrigible urge to intrigue left him with no choice, demanded his resignation. He was then given authority by the Liberal Party to select a new cabinet excluding Country Party members. (Ironically in June 1948 Dunstan had been appointed K.C.M.G. on a recommendation which must at some stage have been approved by Hollway).

Sir Albert Dunstan spent the last two years of his life as a private member. He had just returned from a three-day tour of his electorate when he collapsed and died of coronary vascular disease at his Camberwell home on 14 April 1950. He was survived by his wife and children and was cremated after a state funeral. A keen follower of the share market, and successful as a small investor, Dunstan left an estate valued for probate at £17 370.

Whether he was in the leadership of the Country Party or out of it Dunstan seemed to hold the key to its fortunes. Moreover, he seems to have been pivotal to the chances and changes of Victorian politics over thirty years. He might well be judged to have lacked statesmanship, but statesmanship was not the key to survival in Victorian politics, and Dunstan was without peer in his ability to survive.

B. D. Graham, *The formation of the Australian Country Parties* (Canb, 1966); A. A. Calwell, *Be just and fear not* (Melb, 1972); F. Howard, *Kent Hughes* (Melb, 1972); *Bendigo Advertiser*, 27, 30 Oct 1920, 15 Apr 1950; *Table Talk*, 13 Sept 1928; *Sunraysia Daily*, 19 Jan 1940; *St Arnaud Mercury*, 13 Mar 1940; *Age*, and *Argus*, and *Herald* (Melb), 15 April 1950; F. W. Eggleston, Confidential notes: the Victorian parliament as I knew it (Menzies Lib, ANU); J. B. Paul, The premiership of Sir Albert Dunstan (M.A. thesis, Univ NSW, 1960); family information.   J. B. PAUL

DUNSTAN, BENJAMIN (1864-1933), geologist and public servant, was born on 8 July 1864 at Vaughan, Victoria, son of Benjamin Dunstan, a Cornish miner, and his wife Hannah, née Phillips. He is supposed to have shown an early interest in geology at the age of 9 by collecting sand samples from Brighton beach and taking them to the University of Melbourne. Believed to have attended the Bendigo School of Mines, he was later an evening student at Sydney Technical College, graduating in 1887 with honours in geology, mineralogy and mining. After graduation, he was employed by Cox & Seaver, consulting civil and mining engineers of Sydney, as assayer and draughtsman. On 27 December 1893 at St Paul's Anglican Church he married Ada May Wright.

Dunstan succeeded S. H. Cox as lecturer in geology, mineralogy and mining at Sydney Technical College, probably in 1891; he also acted as consulting geologist to the Australian Agricultural Co., Newcastle. He resigned in 1897 to join the Geological Survey of Queensland as assistant geologist, under R. L. Jack [q.v.4]. Appointed acting government geologist on 1 July 1902, on the retrenchment of Jack's successor W. H. Rands, he was not confirmed in the position until 1908; his title was altered to chief government geologist in 1915.

The range of Dunstan's geological interests was very broad. While a lecturer he investigated and made considerable collections of fossils from the Mesozoic rocks of the Sydney area. In Queensland he investigated the geology of central and northern Queensland, the coal deposits of the Dawson, Bowen, Styx and Burrum areas, the Anakie sapphire field and the Clermont and Croydon mineral fields. He prepared detailed geological maps of the Gympie goldfield and three editions of the geological map of Queensland; he provided geological information for palaeobotanical reports published by the Survey, by A. B. Walkom on the Mesozoic flora of Queensland (1915-19) and by B. Sahni on Mesozoic and Tertiary plant fossils (1920), and for studies by R. J. Tillyard [q.v.] on Mesozoic and Tertiary insects of Queensland and New South Wales (1916 and 1923).

Dunstan both wrote and illustrated the section on Coleoptera in Tillyard's paper of 1923; he was also the author of an important series of articles on Queensland's industrial minerals (1920-21). Undoubtedly his best known work was the compilation of the monumental *Queensland mineral index* (Brisbane, 1913). Begun unofficially in 1901 as a card index, the completed work of 18 000 entries included details of mineral fields with references to geological reports, coloured geological maps, mineral production statistics, bore details and coal analyses.

The amount and diversity of Dunstan's work are the more remarkable when his administrative duties are considered. He initiated many changes within the Survey to improve efficiency, established a proper reference library and reorganized the format of official publications. He worked tirelessly to build up the Survey despite being hampered by lack of staff. After 1908 numbers improved, until by 1914, the 'heyday of Dunstan's rule', the Survey promised to be an outstanding institution. World War I, however, brought about a disheartening fragmentation and he never seemed to recover his earlier enthusiasm.

Dunstan believed strongly in the administration of technical departments by technical persons and advocated the establishment of a geological and mining museum.

Involved with many official organizations and conferences on geology, geophysics, artesian water and technical education, he was responsible for what may have been the first use of aerial photography for geological purposes in Australia, photographing, and producing a photographic mosaic of six square miles of the newly discovered Mount Isa mineral field in 1924. His strongly worded recommendations played a significant part in the decision to build the strategic railway line from Duchess to Mount Isa.

In the late 1920s Dunstan became convinced of the value of geophysical methods in mineral exploration; in 1928-29 he went to Germany to investigate methods used by the Elbof Geophysical Co. and also visited Poland, Romania, Britain and the United States of America. Unfortunately, his compulsory retirement from the Public Service on 31 January 1931 prevented any real implementation of his findings. He then became a consultant for the Commonwealth government in New Guinea and for private companies.

A small man, with great personal charm, Dunstan was a fellow of Sydney Technical College and of the Geological Society of London. He was a connoisseur of gemstones, a photographer and water-colour artist and was interested in music. He died of cancer on 2 September 1933 at Toowong, survived by his wife and by one son and three daughters. He was buried in Toowong cemetery.

Geological Survey of Qld, Dept of Mines, *Annual Report*, 1897-1933; Roy Soc Qld, *Procs*, 68 (1956), no 10, p 51; *Queenslander*, 1 Jan 1931; information from Miss B. C. Dunstan, Hornsby, NSW.

I. G. SANKER

DUNSTAN, EDWARD TREMAYNE (1861-1913), Congregational minister, was born on 10 January 1861 at Kirkhampton, Cornwall, England, son of John Francis Dunstan, schoolmaster, and his wife Eliza, née Davies. Educated at the Wesleyan Theological Institute on Richmond Hill, in 1879 he entered the Methodist ministry and became a missionary in South Africa, but resigned to take charge of a union church there. He later claimed to have entered the Congregational ministry in 1881. About 1885 he returned to England and was sometime assistant to the celebrated Baptist preacher, John Clifford, of Westbourne Park Chapel. He claimed to be a Baptist minister when he married Jane Louisa Caroline Smith on 13 April 1886 at the Poplar Wesleyan Chapel, London. Assisted by the Colonial Missionary Society, he arrived in Perth in 1888 as minister of the Trinity Congregational Church. His preaching was so popular that he was able to rebuild the church; he also established a school and a journal, the *Sentinel*, but both failed in 1891.

Dunstan was an impassioned preacher, 'rather in the habit of wearing my heart upon my sleeve'. Invited in 1894 to the Pitt Street Congregational Church, Sydney, in January next year he was confirmed as its permanent pastor. In 1895-1902 he edited the *Watchman*, in which he attacked Roman and Anglo-Catholicism and the Political Labor League. In 1896-97 he was chairman of the Congregational Union of New South Wales; until 1902 he sat on its standing committee and was their delegate on the *Australasian Independent*. He preached from Congregational pulpits in many Australasian capitals, and in 1895-99 published collections of his sermons and his controversies with Cardinal Moran [q.v.]. He conducted frequent lecture tours, sometimes on behalf of the Young Men's Christian Association and the Independent Order of Oddfellows.

Negligent with money, Dunstan was continually borrowing. On 14 July 1902 as 'T. Duncan', he suddenly left for Brisbane, and soon sailed for Vancouver. He tried to raise funds in the United States of America but was refused pastorates after the Congregational Union of New South Wales had declared his pulpit vacant and condemned his flight. He appealed to the Congregational Union in England, which paid for him to return to Sydney in December 1902. Next February he was declared bankrupt, with unsecured debts of £3106. Although he alleged persecution by the petitioning creditor T. E. Rofe, the official assignee declared his conduct 'highly reprehensible, immoral and dishonourable'.

In January 1903 Dunstan formed his own congregation, preponderantly of females and proselytes from the Pitt Street Congregational Church. Known as the Whitefield Church, it held services at the Protestant Hall in Castlereagh Street where Dunstan printed, published and edited the *Whitefield Press* (1903-07). He also conducted elocution classes, established an institute, a Sunday school and a literary and debating society, at which he gave recitals from Tennyson. In April 1904 he established an affiliated congregation at Glebe. In mid-1909 he hastily left Sydney, again owing money, and in October the Whitefield Church applied to re-enter the Congregational Union.

By April 1910 Dunstan was preaching in Seattle, U.S.A., and later became minister of the Congregational Church, West Seattle, where he died of coronary vascular disease on 18 February 1913. He was survived by his wife and seven children.

A'sian Independent, 15 Mar 1902, 16 Feb 1903; *Congregationalist* (Syd), 1 Nov 1909, 10 Mar 1913; *Aust Christian World,* 28 Feb 1913; Bankruptcy file 15454 *(NSWA).*   RUTH TEALE

DUNSTAN, THOMAS (1873-1954), newspaper proprietor and politician, was born on 20 April 1873 at Waiokaraka, Thames, New Zealand, eldest son of Nicholas John Dunstan, miner, and his wife Esther Mary Ann, née Connon. In the early 1880s the family ventured to Gympie, Queensland, and Thomas was apprenticed to the *Gympie Times;* later he sailed to Sydney to work as a compositor. He returned to Gympie in the mid-1890s and after a short time as compositor on the *Gympie Miner* joined the Labor *Gympie Truth* as reporter, secretary and canvasser at the request of Andrew Fisher [q.v.], a director of the paper. The following period of financial hardship and political ostracism taught Dunstan the necessity for strict party solidarity. Modest and unassuming, he received much encouragement from Fisher with whom he shared lodgings and, for a time, a tent. In 1901 Henry Boote [q.v.7] left the *Truth* and Dunstan became editor-manager. With Jack Priddy he purchased the newspaper and eventually, with Fisher as guarantor, became sole owner. He ran the paper, with the assistance of his sons, until publication ceased in 1942.

Dunstan was the Legislative Assembly member for Gympie (later renamed Nash) from 22 May 1915 to 11 May 1929. Unsuccessful in 1932, he was again returned on 11 May 1935 and held the seat until at 80, the oldest member of the House, he retired on 6 March 1953. In what had become a rural electorate, Dunstan used the two themes behind Labor's establishment of state enterprises — the lowering of prices and the attack on monopolies — particularly well, constantly arguing that these were the basis of a close identity between workers and primary producers. As the local member he 'always had an ear for the requirements of the district and the difficulties of his people'. Pragmatic in approach, he believed in an evolutionary development of a new order — 'We do not propose as a party to pull down the social edifice, in order to build a new one, and meanwhile ask the people to sleep beneath the trees'. But after Labor's first years in power he felt that the workers had not fully seized the opportunities with which the government had presented them. Dunstan was minister without portfolio under W. N. Gillies [q.v.] from 26 February to 22 October 1925 and then secretary for public lands from 22 October 1925 to 21 May 1929 in the W. McCormack [q.v.] government. While he did not make great initiatives, he gained a reputation as a sympathetic administrator. It was said that many soldier settlers had reason to thank him for his kindly support. In 1920-24 and 1939-49 as temporary chairman of committees, he did much to make the parliamentary library an excellent collection. A strong democrat with a firm belief in the dignity and importance of the assembly, Dunstan was also noted as a keen artist who would busily sketch 'the features and gestures of some member who was haranguing Mr Speaker and a bored house'.

On 27 February 1901 at St Andrew's Church of England, One Mile, Gympie, he had married Mary Lydamont, by whom he had five sons and two daughters. On 19 June 1954, two years after her death, he died in the Dunstan ward of the Gympie General Hospital and after a state funeral was buried in Gympie cemetery.

C. L. Lack (ed), *Three decades of Queensland political history, 1929-1960* (Brisb, 1962); *PD* (Qld), 1954-55, 8; *Daily Standard,* 11 May 1915; *Gympie Times,* 22 June 1954; Fisher papers (NL).

I. G. CARNELL

DUNSTAN, WILLIAM (1895-1957), soldier and newspaper manager, was born on 8 March 1895 at Ballarat East, Victoria, fourth child and third son of William John Dunstan, bootmaker, and his wife Henrietta, née Mitchell. At Golden Point State School he was a very bright pupil. He left school at 15 to join the clerical staff of Snows [q.v.], drapers at Ballarat. He served under the compulsory training scheme as a cadet gaining the cadet rank of captain, Australian Military Forces, and in July 1914 was commissioned lieutenant in the militia with the 70th Infantry (Ballarat Regiment).

On 2 June 1915 Dunstan enlisted in the Australian Imperial Force as a private and a fortnight later embarked for Egypt as an acting sergeant of the 6th Reinforcements of the 7th Battalion. From 5 August he was an acting corporal with the 7th on Gallipoli where four days later he won the Victoria Cross for conspicuous bravery at Lone Pine. Early on 9 August the Turks made a determined counter-attack on a newly captured trench held by Lieutenant F. H. Tubb [q.v.] and ten men. Two men were told to remain on the floor of the trench to catch and throw back enemy bombs or to smother their explosions with overcoats; both were soon mutilated. Tubb, with Corporal Dunstan, Corporal A. S. Burton [q.v.7] and six others, kept firing over the parapet. Several bombs burst simultaneously in the trench killing or wounding five men. Tubb continued to fight, supported only by Dunstan and Burton until a violent explosion blew down the barricade. Tubb drove the Turks off and Dunstan and Burton were rebuilding it when a bomb burst between them, killing Burton and temporarily blinding Dunstan. He was invalided to Australia and discharged on 1 February 1916 having been twice mentioned in dispatches. He then rejoined the Citizen Forces, serving in the rank of lieutenant as area officer, Ballarat, and acting brigade major, 18th Infantry Brigade. His army career concluded when he transferred to the 6th Infantry Battalion in Melbourne in 1921, the unattached list in 1923 and the reserve of officers in 1928, retiring as lieutenant.

On 10 June 1916 he was presented with the V.C. by the governor-general on the steps of Parliament House, Melbourne. This was the occasion for an outburst of exceptional public fervour. 'A reserved man disliking fuss', Dunstan found it a great ordeal.

On 9 November 1918 he married a Ballarat girl, Marjorie Lillian Stewart Carnell, at St. Paul's Church of England, Ballarat East. Two sons and a daughter, all of whom served in World War II, were born of this marriage. Dunstan moved to Melbourne to take a position in the Repatriation Department and in 1921 joined the staff of the Herald and Weekly Times Ltd as an accountant under (Sir) Keith Murdoch. He gradually took over the administration of the *Herald* group as chief accountant, company secretary, and general manager from 1934.

He was a considerate staff manager, conscientious and upright, with a gift for readily making friends in all walks of life. He was allowed a great deal of freedom in the administration of the *Herald* and was highly regarded in business, judicial and parliamentary circles. He had a particular interest in Australian Newsprint Mills Ltd, the consortium which established Australia's first plant to make newsprint from hardwood at New Norfolk, Tasmania, and was well known to businessmen in England, the United States of America and Canada for his work in the industry.

In 1953 the effect of his war wounds forced his resignation as general manager and he then became a director of the *Herald* and several other companies. He was a member of the Naval and Military, Australian, Athenaeum, the Royal Melbourne and Metropolitan golf, and the main racing clubs.

Survived by his wife and children, Dunstan died suddenly of coronary vascular disease on 2 March 1957 and was cremated after a funeral service at Christ Church, South Yarra, attended by over 800 people including seven V.C. winners.

C. E. W. Bean, *The story of Anzac*, 2 (Syd, 1924); A. Dean and E. W. Gutteridge, *The Seventh Battalion, A.I.F.* (Melb, 1933); L. Wigmore (ed), *They dared mightily* (Canb, 1963); *London Gazette*, 15 Oct 1915, 28 Jan, 24 Mar 1916; *SMH*, 23 Oct 1915; *Mufti*, Oct 1935; *Herald* (Melb), 3 Jan 1948, 18 Jan 1951, 9 Dec 1953, 13 Aug 1956, 4, 5 Mar 1957; *Reveille* (Syd), Apr 1957.   R. P. SERLE

DUNSTAN, WILLIAM JOHN (1873-1930), trade union official and public servant, was born on 13 October 1873 at Eldorado, near Beechworth, Victoria, son of Ralph Henry Dunstan, a Cornish farmer, and his Irish wife Bridget, née Morrissey. 'Thrown early on the labour market', he led a roving life for nearly 40 years. He joined the Australian Workers' Union in 1892 as a shearer and in 1894 was a prominent militant in the Nelyambo strike camp in western New South Wales. From there he followed a gold rush to Mount Drysdale near Cobar, had no success and drifted in to Broken Hill. At the end of 1895 he went to the Bulloo River opal field in Queensland, but came back to Broken Hill and in 1899 was organizer for the Adelaide branch of the A.W.U. in the north of South Australia.

About 1901 Dunstan went to Western Australia. He was mining at Bonnie Vale in 1902-03 and at Black Flag in 1904-05. Returning to Broken Hill in 1906-09, he was president of the local branch of the Labor Party and the local representative of the A.W.U. In 1910 he became organizer then president of the Adelaide branch of the union; he was also active in the United Labourers' Union of South Australia.

After the merger of the Amalgamated Workers' Association and the A.W.U. in Queensland in January 1913, jealousy grew between their officials, and Dunstan was invited to become a neutral general secretary for Queensland. His appointment by the executive was questioned at his first convention and subsequently, but with the aid of the president, William James Riordan, and eventually, of E. G. Theodore [q.v.], he brought the union under firm bureaucratic control. Industrious, with a capacity for detail, he established an efficient and centralized organization that provided a base for the Labor Party to secure great influence over Queensland politics in 1920-52.

A pragmatist, Dunstan was anathema to the left wing led by E. H. Lane [q.v.], and is frequently pilloried in his *Dawn to dusk* (1939). Dunstan and Riordan were in the centre of battles over the One Big Union movement of 1916-21 and earned more opprobrium by their claim that the A.W.U. was already the O.B.U. Before 1915 the A.W.U. had been a leading and aggressive union, but good arbitration awards and access to political power later removed most of the need for militancy. As an advocate Dunstan tended to specialize in pastoral problems, but he also helped to secure many of the acceptable awards in other fields.

He was a delegate to every union convention but one in 1911-25, and was vice-president for Queensland on the national executive council of the union. In 1916-18 and 1920-26, Dunstan was a member of the Queensland Central Executive of the Labor Party; in 1920-23 he was a vice-president and a member of the executive committee of the Q.C.E. (the inner executive). He attended all interstate party conferences in 1915-25. Besides these multifarious offices he was a director of Labor Papers Ltd, and chairman of the board of directors of the *Worker*. Before leaving Broken Hill, he had been a director of *Barrier Daily Truth*.

In February 1920 Dunstan was appointed to the Legislative Council as one of those sworn to its abolition. In 1921 he was selected to contest the Federal seat of Maranoa. As a city machine official trying to replace a popular country man, he waged a defensive campaign throughout and he was defeated by 1422 votes. Nineteen months after the Legislative Council was abolished on 23 March 1922, Dunstan and W. N. Gillies [q.v.] were appointed as members of the Board of Trade and Arbitration. Here, too, Dunstan failed to satisfy some of his old colleagues. Accused of being too objective in the 1927 sugar and rail strikes, he was criticized in 1926 for abandoning the principle of equal pay for women; inquiry, he said, might show that 'neither males nor females are doing all the work they might do'. In 1930 he was appointed as conciliation commissioner for two years by the Moore [q v] government. A serious street accident in 1926 had permanently affected his health, and on 13 September 1930 he died, unmarried, of chronic nephritis. He was buried in Toowong cemetery with Anglican rites. His estate, valued for probate at £5720, was left to relatives.

E. Lane, *Dawn to dusk* (Brisb, 1939); *Government Gazette* (Qld), 31 Oct 1925, 25 Jan 1930; *Advocate* (Brisb), 15 Sept 1926; *Daily Standard*, 15 Sept 1930; *Worker* (Brisb), 17 Sept 1930; J. D. Armstrong, Closer unity in the Queensland trades union movement 1900-1922 (M.A. thesis, Univ Qld, 1976); G. M. Dalton, The Queensland labor movement, 1919-1929 (B.Econ. thesis, Univ Qld, 1974).
                                    BETTY CROUCHLEY
                                    H. J. GIBBNEY

DURACK, ERNEST (1882-1967), politician, accountant and storekeeper, was born on 10 August 1882 at Mutton Falls, New South Wales, son of Thomas Durack, storekeeper, and his wife Mary, née Webb; both parents were born in the colony. Educated at All Saints' College, Bathurst, he had some local farming experience and became an accountant. At his marriage on 18 November 1903 at Rydal to Cora Emmaline Armstrong, a butcher's daughter, he was described as a grazier.

Appointed a justice of the peace on 30 April 1913, Durack narrowly won the Bathurst seat for Labor in the Legislative Assembly elections of December. He was typical of the new breed of young, Australian-born politicians who were to replace the party founders in the coming crises; from August to November 1916 he was acting chairman of committees. Opposed to conscription, he was one of the Labor members who on 31 October withdrew support from W. A. Holman's [q.v.] ministry; he became their temporary leader. Next day he attempted to move a censure motion but Holman secured a postponement and eventually formed a Nationalist coalition. On 6 November Durack defeated John Storey [q.v.] for Labor Party leadership because he was 'the abler debater, and a much harder worker'. When the vote of no confidence was taken next day, he found himself leader of an Opposition comprising 21 against the government ranks of 53. Holman could afford to congratulate him on discharging 'his duties as the elected leader of the disaffected Labor members with undoubted ability'. Over the next few months he was an effective spokesman for Labor; in J. T. Lang's [q.v.] assessment Durack had modelled himself on Holman, proving a polished speaker with a good analytical mind.

But personal problems were to undo him. In August 1916 a child which he later acknowledged to be his was born to a woman not his wife. On 21 February 1917, four days after Holman had unexpectedly announced the date for a general election, Lang, as secretary of the parliamentary Labor Party, announced that he had received Durack's resignation, on grounds of ill-health. In H. V. Evatt's words he 'had mysteriously disappeared from the political scene'.

A few days later Durack withdrew from the forthcoming contest for Bathurst. He enlisted as a private in the Australian Imperial Force on 21 September, embarked for overseas service in December and was taken on strength of the 1st Training Battalion in the United Kingdom on 13 February 1918. But in April he was found medically unfit for active service; he returned to Australia and was discharged from the A.I.F. in August. He did not go back to his wife (d. 1956) and his movements for the next thirty-two years are not known.

In 1950 Durack was a storekeeper and postmaster at Wimbledon near Bathurst. He married Frederica Henrietta McNab in Sydney on 7 July 1959. In the 1960s they moved to Auburn. Survived by his wife and their daughter and by two sons and three daughters of his first marriage, Durack died in hospital at Lidcombe on 16 November 1967. His body was given to the University of Sydney.

H. V. Evatt, *Australian Labour leader...W. A. Holman* (Syd, 1940); J. T. Lang, *I remember* (Syd, 1956); *PD* (NSW), 1916, p 2439, 2667; *SMH,* 19 Aug, 8, 11, 16 Nov, 5 Dec 1916, 21, 23 Feb 1917.

CHRIS CUNNEEN

DURACK, MICHAEL PATRICK (1865-1950), pastoralist, was born on 22 July 1865, at Grabben Gullen near Goulburn, New South Wales, eldest of four sons and four daughters surviving infancy of Patrick Durack [q.v.4] and his wife Mary, née Costello. After a childhood on Thylungra station, Queensland, he was sent with his brother John Wallace (1867-1936) to St Patrick's College, Goulburn, and then worked on Thylungra. After his family's 1882-83 overlanding expedition to the Kimberleys in Western Australia, he was sent in 1886 to the head-station, Argyle Downs, arriving just in time for the Halls Creek goldrush. On his 21st birthday he made the first sale of Kimberley cattle to a Halls Creek butcher for £1200 in raw gold. After the field declined he and his relations found new markets by overlanding stock to Pine Creek, Northern Territory (1891) and Derby, Western Australia (1893).

New opportunities arose in 1894 when a shipping trade from Wyndham to Perth was started by Francis Connor (1857-1916) and Denis J. Doherty (1861-1935). The Duracks became the main suppliers for this market and, in 1897, overriding the misgivings of old Patrick Durack, they negotiated a merger with their shipping agents to form the firm of Connor, Doherty & Durack Ltd. Controlling properties totalling nearly 6000 square miles (15 500 km²) on the Western Australia-Northern Territory border, and largely dominating the Wyndham export trade, this firm would be a major influence in the Kimberley pastoral industry for the next half-century.

Troubles came immediately. Because of the spread of cattle-tick from the Northern Territory, quarantine restrictions were imposed on the export of East Kimberley cattle. Believing that the restrictions were imposed for the benefit of the rival West Kimberley firm of Forrest (Alexander), Emanuel [qq.v.] & Co. Ltd, Connor, Doherty & Durack pro-

tested vigorously but unsuccessfully before searching for overseas markets. In 1902 Durack negotiated the shipment of 3612 cattle to Natal; this was long claimed as a record overseas consignment of live cattle. In 1905-06, with Doherty, Durack investigated North America and in 1909 he was appointed an honorary commissioner by the South Australian government to examine possible Asian markets for Northern Territory livestock.

In 1910 he visited the Philippines to explore a demand created by the decimation of local herds by rinderpest. After a successful trial shipment the firm was blocked by a ban imposed for the benefit of American exporters. Connor went to Manila in 1911 and successfully negotiated the lifting of the ban, but his extravagance alienated the Durack brothers. Doherty had retired to England some years since and, especially after Connor's death in 1916, the effective decision-making in the firm lay with Michael and John Durack.

By now Michael was a leader of his community as justice of the peace and local magnate, and in 1917 he entered State parliament as a Nationalist member of the Legislative Assembly for Kimberley. An honourable and conscientious backbencher, never really at home with parliamentary cut and thrust, he concentrated on promoting northern development. In 1920 with E. H. Angelo [q.v.7] he joined the Country Party from discontent at the (Sir) James Mitchell [q.v.] government's alleged neglect of northern interests; in 1922 he moved for a separate financial administration for the northern part of Western Australia, but the measure was narrowly defeated. In 1924 he retired from politics, but in 1928 chaired a royal commission on the State's meat industry. Few of its recommendations were adopted because of the onset of the Depression. During the 1920s Durack gave keen support to the search for minerals, especially oil prospecting, in the Kimberleys; his investments were substantial but unsuccessful. He also took a lively interest in the development of aviation in the North-West.

The Depression, coming after a decade of poor beef-cattle prices, found the Connor, Doherty & Durack properties heavily in debt. Durack's old age was dominated by the struggle to win free of these burdens. In 1938-39 he was negotiating with Dr Isaac Steinberg for the sale of the firm's properties to form a settlement for Jewish refugees from Nazi Germany. Despite post-war prosperity and against the wish of his family, Durack effected the sale of almost all the family properties to Peel River Estates in 1950. He then, on his 85th birthday, erected a memorial at Argyle to his pioneering kinsmen and retired to Perth where he died on 3 September; he was buried in the Catholic section of Karrakatta cemetery. His estate was sworn for probate at £61 195.

An intellectual whose strong sense of family loyalty had bound him to a lifetime as a pastoral entrepreneur, Durack was a distinguished figure with a trim vandyke beard and the stamina to take part in prospecting expeditions on horseback even in his 82nd year. Under his guidance Argyle gained a reputation for benevolent paternalism towards its Aboriginal employees. On 22 September 1909 he had married Bessie Ida Muriel Johnstone (1883-1980) in Adelaide. Of their four sons and two daughters, Kimberley Michael (1917-68) was a notable pioneer of agriculture in the Kimberleys, while Dame Mary Durack Miller (b. 1913) has gained distinction as an author, and Elizabeth Durack Clancy (b. 1915) is a noted painter. M. P. Durack's uncle Jeremiah ('Galway Jerry') (1853-1901), had founded Rosewood and Dunham stations before being killed by Aboriginals while asleep on the verandah of his homestead; he was the father of J. P. Durack Q.C. (1888-1978), and grandfather of Peter Drew Durack, attorney-general in the Malcolm Fraser Federal government from 1977.

M. Durack, *Kings in grass castles* (Lond, 1959); L. Hunt (ed), *Westralian portraits* (Perth, 1979); *Univ Studies in History and Economics* (WA), 1954, p. 7; *Western Argus,* 5 Mar 1901; Durack diaries and correspondence 1886-1950 (held by Dame Mary Durack Miller, Nedlands, Western Australia).   G. C. BOLTON

DURACK, SARAH (FANNY) (1889-1956), swimmer, was born on 27 October 1889 at Elizabeth Street, Sydney, third daughter and sixth child of Irish parents Thomas Durack, publican, a relation of Patrick Durack [q.v.4], and his wife Mary, née Mason. Known as Fanny, she learnt to swim in the Coogee Baths and trained in breaststroke – the only style in which there was a championship for women. While still a schoolgirl, she won her first State title in 1906. Later she adopted the trudgen stroke and by 1911 had changed to the Australian crawl.

Although women had been forbidden by the New South Wales Ladies' Amateur Swimming Association to appear in competitions when men were present, such were her successes that there was public demand for her to go to the 1912 Olympic Games in Stockholm: debate among the clubs reversed the rule. It was argued that one event did not justify the inclusion of another swimmer, but the wife of Hugh McIntosh [q.v.]

launched a successful appeal for funds. Fanny sailed for Sweden via London, where she trained only half a mile a day. At Stockholm she swam a heat of the 100 metres free-style in 1 minute 19.8 seconds to break the world record. On 15 July she won the gold medal for the 100 metres, the only individual event for women, beating fellow Australian Wilhelmina (Mina) Wylie.

Her Olympic success led to tours with Mina Wylie in Europe and the United States of America, but Fanny's career continued to be dogged by controversy. In 1918 they arrived in America without official sanction to find themselves banned by the Amateur Swimming Union of Australia. Next year the Amateur Athletic Union of the United States threatened to suspend their amateur status, when they refused to swim until their manager's expenses were paid. After being defeated in two carnivals by American girls, she determinedly tried to limit her appearances until she had practised the new American crawl. Ordered by officials to swim at Chicago she jumped the starter's gun, swam half a length and got out – the tour was curtailed.

A week before the Australian team left for the 1920 Antwerp Olympics, Fanny Durack had an appendectomy (followed by typhoid fever and pneumonia) and withdrew. Between 1912 and 1918 she had broken twelve world records, including swims of 100 yards in 1 minute 6 seconds, 100 metres in 1 minute 16.2 seconds, and 1 mile in 26 minutes 8 seconds. Her successes did much to promote women's swimming. Determined and self-willed, she had long dark hair and a figure that showed 'no symptom of ropes of athletic muscles'. In America she was honoured by the International Swimming Hall of Fame at Fort Lauderdale, Florida, and received a Helms award.

Early in January 1921 Fanny Durack retired from competitive swimming and on 22 January at St Mary's Cathedral she married Bernard Martin Gately, a horse-trainer. She devoted herself to coaching young children and, a member of its executive, was made a life member of the New South Wales Women's Amateur Swimming Association in 1945. She died of cancer at her home at Stanmore on 20 March 1956 and was buried in the Catholic section of Waverley cemetery. Her brother Frank presented her Olympic gold medal to the Commonwealth government that year; it is held in the National Library of Australia, Canberra.

F. Mezo, *The modern Olympic games* (Budapest, 1956); D. Fraser and H. Gordon, *Gold medal girl* (Melb, 1965); K. Dunstan, *Sports* (Melb, 1973); P. Besford, *Encyclopedia of swimming* (Lond, 1976); NSW Ladies' Amateur Swimming Assn, *Annual*

Report, 1905-06, 1909-11 (ML); *Referee,* July, Aug 1919; E. S. Marks sporting collection, no 20, 24, 448, 455, 622 (ML).   HELEN KING

DWYER, CATHERINE WINIFRED (1861-1949), schoolteacher and Labor leader, was born on 13 June 1861 at Tambaroora, New South Wales, second daughter of Joseph Golding, an Irish-born gold-miner, and his Scottish wife Ann, née Fraser. Kate was educated at Hill End Public School and in January 1880 began teaching at Tambaroora Public School. She was transferred to Bathurst next year, Spicers Creek in 1884, Binnaway in 1885 and Coffey Hill and Blayney in 1886. She resigned next year and on 28 December 1887 at Hamilton, Newcastle, married a fellow schoolteacher Michael Dwyer.

In 1891-93 Michael was headmaster of the Broken Hill Public School and Kate came into close contact with working-people impoverished by severe drought and a prolonged strike, and developed a deep sympathy for them. In 1894 the Dwyers moved to Sydney where Michael was headmaster at Marrickville West until 1900, then at Camperdown and Redfern Public Schools.

Kate Dwyer was a member of the Womanhood Suffrage League of New South Wales and was prominent in the fight for female suffrage. She was a founder of the Women's Progressive Association in 1901 and worked for the right of women to enter the legal and other professions and to have a fair share of the accumulations of the marriage partnership. She wrote extensively on political, industrial and women's questions in the press, and was 'a fine speaker, with a gift of repartee'. From 1904 she was first president of the Women's Organizing Committee of the Political Labor League and next year was elected to the State Labor executive. She was a delegate to the Commonwealth Political Labor Conference in Brisbane in 1908 and Hobart in 1912.

Kate Dwyer worked tirelessly for improved working and living conditions for women and for a minimum female living wage. With Mrs Flanagan, she formed the Women Workers' Union for home and fringe factory workers to combat 'sweating'; as president from 1910, she was a delegate to the Sydney Labor Council. In evidence to the 1909 royal commission on the improvement of the city of Sydney and its suburbs, she had advocated model dwellings for working men with a weekly rental of one day's pay, and opposed the building of tenements. Next year the lord mayor Sir Allen Taylor [q.v.] paid tribute to her as 'one of our great workers'. In 1911 she assisted A. B. Piddington [q.v.] on the royal commission into the alleged shortage of labour and into the conditions of employment of female and juvenile labour; she visited over 100 factories and, as well as generally condemning conditions in them, stressed her abhorrence of piece-work which she believed was responsible for 'much sweated labour of women'. In 1911-13 she sat on the royal commission of inquiry as to food supplies and fish. Dignified, with wavy hair, she was an imposing figure.

During World War I Mrs Dwyer was a member of the committee organizing the 'no' vote for the 1916 conscription referendum. She opened a factory for unemployed needlewomen and procured a military contract as a start for them. For men, she organized a tent-housing scheme at Stannumville, known as Canvas Town. In 1915 she was selected to stand for the half-Senate election, due in 1916 but deferred. In 1921 she was a representative at the Commonwealth Political Labor Conference in Brisbane when she voted against the 'socialist objective'. Back on the executive, in 1923 she supported Jack Bailey [q.v.7] at the State conference in Sydney. During the war she had represented the Women Workers' Union on Wages Boards and in the 1920s was on conciliation committees. In 1925 she was defeated as one of five members for the Balmain seat in the Legislative Assembly.

Mrs Dwyer was a fellow of the Senate of the University of Sydney in 1916-24 and worked for the establishment of a chair of domestic science. From 1910 she was a director and in the 1940s a vice-president of the Benevolent Society of New South Wales. She was also a director of the Royal Hospital for Women, Paddington, and the Renwick Hospital for Infants, and a trustee of the King George V and Queen Mary Jubilee Fund for Maternal and Infant Welfare. In May 1921 she was one of the first female justices of the peace appointed in New South Wales.

Kate Dwyer lived at Annandale and remained a member of the local branch of the Australian Labor Party. She was a devout Catholic all her life and enjoyed gardening, reading and lecturing. She died in the Sacred Heart Hospice for the Dying, Darlinghurst, on 3 February 1949. Predeceased by two sons and a daughter, she was survived by a son and daughter. Her estate was valued for probate at £1473. Her sisters Annie and Belle Golding [qq.v.] were also active in the political and social reform movements.

Cyclopedia of N.S.W. (Syd, 1907); A.L.P. Golden Jubilee Committee, *50 years of Labor* (Syd, 1940); J. T. Lang, *I remember* (Syd, 1956); *Lone Hand,* Nov 1911; *Daily Telegraph* (Syd), 3 Mar 1915; *Aust Worker,* 12 Oct 1916, 3, 10 May, 4 June 1917;

Woman Voter, 18 Apr 1918; *SMH*, 5 Feb 1949; Senate minutes (Univ Syd Archives); R. Cookson, The role of certain women and women's organizations in politics in N.S.W. and Victoria between 1900 and 1920 (B.A. Hons thesis, Univ Syd, 1959); V. Gallego, Martyrs and martinets ... Mary Gilmore's women's page in the *Australian Worker*, 1914-1918 (B.A. Hons thesis, Macquarie Univ, 1977).   VIVA GALLEGO

DWYER, JAMES FRANCIS (1874-1952), author, was born on 22 April 1874 at Camden Park, New South Wales, fifth son of Michael Dwyer, farm labourer, and his wife Margaret, née Mahoney, both from Cork, Ireland. The family moved a few miles to Menangle in 1883 and next year to Campbelltown. James was educated in local public schools until, at 14, he was sent to relatives in Sydney, where he worked as a publisher's clerk. He became a letter-carrier at Rockdale in May 1892, and despite a brief meeting with Robert Louis Stevenson which turned his thoughts towards writing, he remained in suburban post offices, eventually becoming a postal assistant from 1895 at the Oxford Street branch. On 7 November 1893 he married Selina Cassandra Stewart, who bore him a son and a daughter.

In May 1899 Dwyer, with two associates, was convicted of forgery and uttering and received a seven years sentence. After serving nearly three years in Goulburn gaol, he was released in 1902. While he was in prison, one of his poems was sent to J. F. Archibald [q.v.3] of the *Bulletin,* who published it; on the day of his release two short stories appeared. As 'J.F.D.', 'Burglar Bill', 'D' and 'Marat', he wrote verse and 'pars' for the *Bulletin,* and worked consecutively as salesman, pigeon-buyer and signwriter. He was befriended by a coterie of writers, including Victor Daley, Roderic Quinn and Albert Dorrington [qq.v.] and turned to journalism, freelancing for *Truth* and *Sydney Sportsman.*

Throughout a long and eventually lucrative career, Dwyer believed that 'the Australian writer has no real chance in his own land'. Ignoring advice from Rudyard Kipling he sailed in 1906 to London, where he sold stories 'in insufficient quantities'. Next year he moved to New York, worked as a streetcar conductor and in other jobs, sold stories, and, after winning a contest, received a good commission to write for the *Black Cat* in Boston. Thereafter his stories, published in *Harper's Bazaar, Collier's* and other popular magazines, proved very profitable. The first of ten novels, mainly stories of mystery and adventure, period thrillers or romances, was *The white waterfall* (New York, 1912). To gather material for his set-

tings he travelled in America and Europe; he briefly revisited Australia (where one novel and several short stories are set) in 1913. In December 1919 he was divorced, and on 30 December married Catherine (Galbraith) Welch, his agent.

In 1921 they established the Dwyer Travel Letters to inform prospective American tourists about places in Europe. Dwyer settled at Pau, in the French Pyrenees, but his search for exotic settings and tourist information, and his wife's interests as a cultural historian, carried them through Europe, Asia and North Africa. Three of his later romantic novels, however, are influenced by Provençal traditions. When France fell in 1940 they escaped through Spain and lived at Dover, New Hampshire, United States of America, during World War II; they returned to Pau in September 1945 and Dwyer died there on 11 November 1952. In 1949 he had published his autobiography, *Leg-irons on wings* (Melbourne).

Described by Sir Frank Fox [q.v.] as 'a big sinewy fellow with the eagle look', and 'wildly generous, solidly faithful to his friends, aggressively indignant towards snobbery and pomposity', Dwyer could also be truculent and impetuous, and, he conceded, vain and obstinate and ill-tempered. Sensitivity about his imprisonment as a young man developed in him a determination to succeed and to achieve public recognition. Having abandoned Catholicism he adopted a faith which 'took in all forms of Christianity'. He believed, too, in extra-sensory perception, and claimed to have experienced prophetic visions. Throughout his expatriation he vigorously affirmed his Australian nationality.

Bookfellow, 1 Jan 1912; J. F. Dwyer letter, 6 Apr 1911, Ad 51 (ML)   KEN STEWART

DWYER, PATRICK VINCENT (1858-1931) and JOSEPH WILFRID (1869-1939), Roman Catholic bishops, were born on 21 August 1858 at Albury, New South Wales, and on 12 October 1869 at East Maitland, sons of William Dwyer, schoolteacher, and his wife Anastasia, née Dermody, both from Kilkenny, Ireland. In 1862 William became inspector of schools in the Bathurst district and in 1867 was transferred to Maitland.

Educated at St Stanislaus College, Bathurst, Vincent attracted the attention of Bishop James Murray [q.v.5], while working as a catechist at Maitland. Later the bishop persuaded Dwyer's father to send him to Holy Cross College, Clonliffe, Dublin, and then to Rome where he lived in the Pontifical Irish College and studied at the Pontifical

Urban University of Propaganda Fide. He was ordained in Rome on 4 March 1882 and immediately returned to Maitland.

Dwyer was Murray's protégé, even favourite: he became his secretary and diocesan inspector of schools, and was also given charge of the school adjacent to the cathedral. From 1888 he was president of the Sacred Heart College, West Maitland. When Murray asked for a coadjutor, Dwyer was appointed, despite the preference of the priests for Patrick Hand, the vicar-general. On 6 June 1897 he was consecrated titular bishop of Zoara and coadjutor-bishop of Maitland, becoming the first Australian-born member of the hierarchy. He succeeded to the see in 1909.

In many ways his episcopate was a continuation of Murray's. If less abrasive with the priests and religious of the diocese, Dwyer was just as inclined to impose his own will, even in minor matters. However, he broke with Murray's policy of having his priests educated in Ireland or Rome – instead he sent candidates to St Patrick's College, Manly – and he was a far better accountant. Possibly too concerned with financial problems, he did consolidate where Murray had been forced to rush. He was responsible for several major charitable institutions, and the buildings which he authorized were superior to anything Murray had been able to construct.

At Clonliffe Dwyer had formed a close friendship with Joseph (Columba) Marmion, one of the most influential Catholic spiritual writers of the twentieth century. Their correspondence formed the basis of his personal spirituality, which was described as 'other-worldly rather than this-worldly, monastic rather than apostolic'. Nevertheless his pastoral work was wide ranging. He was interested in the lives of his flock, a schoolmaster as well as a spiritual leader; and he believed in the need for Catholics to be political where 'the interests of the Faith' were involved, although Marmion often warned him against politics and finance.

Proud of his Australian birth, Dwyer nevertheless saw himself as an Irish-Australian. Though the coolness and imperturbability for which he was noted restrained him in the sectarian battles which raged for a decade after the World War I conscription referenda, he was clearly a supporter rather than a critic of Archbishop Mannix [q.v.]. When his health began to deteriorate in the late 1920s he obtained as his coadjutor an Irish-born Redemptorist who had also been a Murray protégé, Edmund Gleeson. Dwyer died of coronary vascular disease on 28 March 1931 and was buried in the Sacred Heart Church, Campbells Hill, which was attached to the orphanage he had founded as a memorial to Murray.

Joseph, after attending St Aloysius College, Sydney, and St Patrick's College, Goulburn, went to Clonliffe in 1888 and the Pontifical Urban College of Propaganda Fide in 1891. After ordination in Rome on 24 May 1894 he worked briefly in Ireland before returning to New South Wales. He went to Goulburn, teaching at St Patrick's College for two years; he then served at Gundagai and Wagga Wagga and became for a time diocesan inspector of schools. After working at Albury and Yass, he was appointed parish priest at Temora in 1912. When the Goulburn diocese was divided in 1917 Dwyer became first bishop of Wagga Wagga and was consecrated on 13 October 1918.

In July 1920, in the atmosphere of sectarian bitterness engendered by the recent State elections, a young Irish nun, Sister M. Ligouri [q.v. Bridget Partridge], left the Presentation Convent in Wagga Wagga in a distraught condition and took refuge with members of the local Orange lodge. Dwyer, as her religious superior and influenced by her wild allegations, sought a warrant for her apprehension on the grounds of lunacy; when this was refused by a nervous chamber magistrate at Wagga, he obtained one in Sydney by means which could be represented as wire-pulling. Miss Partridge was arrested, spent some days in the reception house, and was then certified sane. She later claimed £5000 damages for malicious detention. In July 1921 the jury found that, although Dwyer had not taken all reasonable care to ascertain the facts, he had not been actuated by malice: the action was dismissed. The affair roused great public excitement, and undoubtedly exacerbated sectarian disputes. Although Mr Justice Ferguson [q.v.] criticized the role of the Orange lodge, Dwyer was at least imprudent in his actions, but had been motivated by a sense of responsibility to the girl's parents in Ireland. For a time he became the great hero of Australian Catholics and the *bête noire* of militant Protestantism, supplanting even Mannix and Archbishop Kelly [q.v.].

Dwyer lacked his brother's sang-froid; he also 'held pronounced views on social, ecclesiastical and international questions, and did not hesitate to express himself plainly and forcibly on occasion', particularly with regard to Irish affairs, but the rest of his episcopate was uneventful. Including money given to support him in the Ligouri affair, he had raised enough to complete St Michael's Cathedral in 1925. That year he visited Rome, Lourdes (France), and Ireland with Mannix, a close friend, and in 1932 attended the International Eucharistic Congress in Dublin. Joseph also died of coronary vascular disease on 11 October 1939 at Wagga Wagga, and was buried in the cathedral.

Both brothers were men of wide culture; both were interested in music, sacred and profane, Vincent being an accomplished pianist. His other interests included history and archaeology. Joseph spoke fluent Italian and was a keen student of Australian botany and a member of the Linnean Society of New South Wales from 1920.

H. Campbell, *The diocese of Maitland 1866-1966* (Maitland, 1966); J. O'Brien, *The men of '38 and other pioneer priests* (Kilmore, Vic, 1975); K. T. Livingston, *The emergence of an Australian Catholic priesthood, 1835-1915* (Syd, 1977); P. J. O'Farrell, *The Catholic Church and the community in Australia; a history* (Melb, 1977); S. Walsh, *Dr. Joseph Wilfred Dwyer D. D.* (Wagga Wagga, 1978); Linnean Soc NSW, *Procs,* 65 (1940); *SMH,* 1-14 July 1921, 19, 20 June 1934, 12 Oct 1939; Dwyer papers (Diocesan Archives, Maitland).   W. G. McMINN

DWYER, SIR WALTER (1875-1950), lawyer, was born on 27 August 1875 at Carrick-on-Suir, Tipperary, Ireland, third son of Walter Dwyer, contractor, and his wife Mary, née Hartrey. He was educated at the local Christian Brothers' seminary and at 16 migrated to Victoria and taught at the Christian Brothers' College, East Melbourne, where some of his pupils were older than he. Attracted by gold discoveries, he then moved to Western Australia and from 1895 worked as a clerk in the Education Department for nine years. He also began studying law part time and in 1904 was articled to C. Lyhane at Kalgoorlie and Boulder. After a year he returned to Perth and completed his articles with Villeneuve Smith & Lavan. He completed his law course by external study with the University of London (LL.B., 1906), was admitted to the Western Australian Bar in 1907, and practised at Boulder and Kalgoorlie, and in Perth from 1910.

Dwyer was over six feet (183 cm) tall; handsome, with a resonant voice he had a slight Irish brogue which he used most effectively in public speaking. In 1911 he won the Perth seat in the Legislative Assembly for the Labor Party. In parliament he helped to draft the 1912 Industrial Arbitration Act and secured the passage of the Money Lenders Act (1912) which protected borrowers, and the Landlord and Tenant Act (1912). On 28 August that year, at St Mary's Catholic Church, Guildford, he married Maude Mary, daughter of Charles Smith, a pastoralist in the Murchison district. He lost his seat in 1914 — which he regarded as a blessing in disguise — but remained a 'behind the scenes' adviser to the party.

In his profession Dwyer specialized as counsel in civil and appeal cases before the Full Court of Western Australia and the High Court of Australia. In 1915 he took into partnership J. P. Durack and, in 1917, W. H. Dunphy, forming the firm of Dwyer, Durack & Dunphy. Dwyer was defence counsel for several of the defendants in the Perth Industrial Workers of the World trials of 1916. In 1919 as a leading member of the Celtic Club, and supporter of Irish nationalism, he led a prohibited march through the city on St Patrick's day. He was prosecuted, convicted and fined; having refused to meet the fine, he only escaped imprisonment because a supporter paid for him. To mark the occasion, the Celtic Club presented him with an illuminated address.

On the establishment of the new State Court of Arbitration in 1926, Dwyer agreed 'at a monetary sacrifice', to become its first presiding judge. He strongly opposed 'sweetheart' deals between unions and employers, in which both parties would combine over the question of over-award payments. He scrutinized such agreements closely and, if suspicious, would call the parties together to discuss the real meaning of the documents. Thus he controlled the economic situation and eliminated dealings not strictly in accordance with the public interest or the Arbitration Act. He fully understood industrial problems and gave all his judgments fairly and thoroughly. On his retirement in 1945 he left a record which his successors found hard to equal, and it was widely felt that the State's freedom from industrial trouble was largely due to the confidence in the court that he had created. In 1946 he advised and supported his successor in settling a major transport strike.

Dwyer was a charitable man, a gifted speaker and a lover of literature and the arts: he was one of the first trustees of the Public Library, Museum and Art Gallery of Western Australia in 1913 and president of the trustees in 1929-47. He remained faithful to Irish and Christian traditions. He enjoyed reading, particularly history and politics, and gardening and he was a tireless walker. Dwyer was knighted in 1949. After a long illness, he died from kidney failure on 22 March 1950 in St John of God Hospital, Subiaco. After a requiem Mass in Sacred Heart Church, Highgate Hill, he was buried in Karrakatta cemetery. He was survived by his wife (d. 1969) and their two daughters, Pauline Mary and Mollie Teresa.

J. S. Battye (ed), *Cyclopedia of Western Australia,* 1 (Adel, 1912); *Western Mail* (Perth), 17 July 1919; *SMH,* 4 Nov 1932; *West Australian,* 23 Mar 1950.   E. A. DUNPHY

DWYER-GRAY, EDMUND JOHN CHIS-
HOLM (1870-1945), journalist and politician, was born on 2 April 1870 in Dublin,
son of Edmund Dwyer Gray, M.P., and his
wife Caroline Agnes, elder daughter of Caroline Chisholm [q.v.1]. He was educated at
the Fort Augustus Benedictine monastery in
Scotland and the Jesuit Clongowes Wood
College, Naas, County Kildare, in 1884-1887.
He also studied law for a short period in
Dublin. Late in 1887 he began a tour of
Australia to improve his health, but he returned to Dublin after the death of his father
in March 1888 and next November was appointed to the editorial committee of the
Dublin nationalist daily *Freeman's Journal*,
of which his father and grandfather Sir John
Gray, an associate of Daniel O'Connell, had
been proprietors.

After a second visit to Australia, from
early 1889 to February 1891, Dwyer-Gray
returned to Ireland at the height of the
Parnell leadership crisis. At first like his
mother, to whom his father's interest in the
Freeman's Journal had passed, he supported
Parnell; later, however, because of vigorous
competition from a newly established anti-
Parnellite organ, he arranged, not without
difficulty, for its policy to be altered, a serious blow to the Parnellite cause. By 1893 the
Gray family had relinquished its interest in
the *Freeman's Journal*, and next year Edmund, apparently suffering from rheumatism, announced his intention to settle for
life in Australia. Apart from a visit home in
1898, following his marriage in Sydney on 2
February 1897 at the Woollahra Roman
Catholic Church to Clara Agatha Rose,
Dwyer-Gray now severed his direct connexion with Ireland. His youthful incursion
into Irish politics had been unsuccessful:
inconsistent and prickly, he was easily
outmanoeuvred.

On leaving Ireland, Dwyer-Gray appears
to have travelled through Australia, New
Zealand and Fiji, dabbling with some success in mining ventures. After his 1898 Irish
visit he settled down in the New Norfolk area
of Tasmania as an orchardist and farmer.
Little is known of his activities in the next
decade. He seems to have been unsuccessful
as a farmer and may have lost most of his
available capital. By 1912 he was in Hobart,
editing the Labor Party's *Daily Post*. Apart
from temporary demotions, sometimes the
result of his serious drinking problem, he
remained editor after the paper was taken
over in 1918 by the Australian Workers'
Union and renamed the *World*, but he lost
control in 1922 after a quarrel with the Labor
leadership. Briefly expelled from the party
and then reinstated, Dwyer-Gray went to
Sydney to work as a journalist for J. T. Lang
[q.v.]. In 1925, the *World* having failed, he
returned to Hobart to edit a new Labor
weekly, the *People's Voice* (subsequently the
Voice). He continued as editor till his death,
always emphasizing his independence of the
party in a journal representing the Australian Council of Trade Unions.

In 1915 Dwyer-Gray had stood unsuccessfully for the Legislative Council; in 1928,
hyphening his name to Dwyer-Gray, to gain
higher placement on the ballot paper and
hence more of the donkey vote, he was
elected for Denison to the House of Assembly. Deputy leader to Albert Ogilvie [q.v.] in
1932, he became treasurer and deputy
premier in the Ogilvie ministry two years
later, continuing in that office till Ogilvie's
death in June 1939 when, as the result of an
agreement with Robert Cosgrove, he held
the premiership for six months. On Cosgrove's assumption of office in December
Dwyer-Gray resumed as treasurer.

As an editor, a party politician and a
flamboyant local personality, Dwyer-Gray
played an important part in building the
Tasmanian Labor Party. His journalism was
lively, vitriolic and sometimes irresponsible.
He relentlessly attacked opponents within
and without the party. During World War I
he supported voluntary enlistment and acted as a member of the State Recruiting
Committee, but campaigned lustily through
the *Daily Post* against conscription. After the
war he took up the cause of Ireland, till the
Anglo-Irish Treaty of 1921, forming a Tasmanian branch of the Self-Determination for
Ireland League. Simultaneously, he waged
war on the local Labor right-wingers on
behalf of socialization and the One Big
Union. In the 1930s and 1940s Dwyer-Gray's
Voice was preoccupied with monetary issues,
vociferously demanding 'national credit', a
version of Major Douglas's theory espoused
by G. S. Carruthers [q.v.7]. In the 1940s it was
often outspoken in denunciation of John
Curtin and J. B. Chifley for their alleged
failure to implement party policy on national
credit. In such controversies, especially
during the Depression, Dwyer-Gray, like
Ogilvie, was strongly pro-Lang.

Inside the Labor Party he was frequently
elected as a Tasmanian delegate to the
Federal conference or Federal executive,
was active in the negotiations which led to
reform of party structure, and later, as a
defender of Tasmanian interests, battled
against party centralization and defended
Lang's breakaway party. In 1933 Dwyer-
Gray promoted a short-lived Tasmanian
breach with the Federal Labor Party which
had failed to reach an accommodation with
Lang. A devout Catholic, he strove in his
later years to reverse the party's state-aid
policy, his basic philosophy moving towards
a form of Catholic distributism. In office he

was regarded as a highly effective treasurer who managed to 'bring home the bacon' and laid the basis for Ogilvie's post-Depression reforms. By a mixture of bluff, moral blackmail and sheer gamesmanship, Dwyer-Gray obtained favourable treatment for Tasmania from the Commonwealth Grants Commission and the Loan Council. But, despite his inevitably long and involved budget speeches, his real financial competence, away from treasury advisers, is doubtful. His monetarist diatribes in the *Voice* are difficult to reconcile with economic responsibility.

There is, however, no doubt about Dwyer-Gray's colourful personality. His tall, stooping figure and his shock of white hair made him an ideal subject for cartoonists, while fads like anti-vivisection, erratic drinking habits, uncertainties of temper, fluent but inaudible speeches and his aura of great culture and erudition provided substance for countless anecdotes. Childless, survived by his wife (d. 1947), he died on 6 December 1945 in Hobart and was buried in Cornelian Bay cemetery.

Tas Hist Teachers' Assn, *Veritas*, July 1977; *PTHRA*, 25 (1978) no 4; *Mercury*, 6 Dec 1945; Aust Labor Party (Tas), Executive minute-book, 10 Dec 1930, 9 Nov 1942, *and* State Conference minutes, 1917-30, 1930-36, 1937-42 (TA).   R. P. DAVIS

DYASON, EDWARD CLARENCE EVELYN (1886-1949), company director, economist, mining engineer and stockbroker, was born on 8 April 1886 at Sandhurst (Bendigo), Victoria, son of Isaac Edward Dyason, property manager from Kent, England, and his wife Harriet Eastwood, née Mason, from Guernsey, Channel Islands. Dyason was educated at St Andrew's College, Bendigo, and the University of Melbourne, graduating B.Sc. in 1908 and B.M.E. in 1909. He began his very successful business career while still an undergraduate, taking up the first of many company directorships when 19. Enduring friendship at the university began with (Sir) David Rivett and (Judge) A. W. Foster [qq.v.]; later academic friends were to include Sir Harrison Moore, L. F. Giblin [qq.v.] and (Sir) Samuel Wadham. On 9 April 1914 at St Andrew's Church of England, Brighton, he married Anne Elizabeth McClure, who bore him a son and two daughters.

Dyason practised as a mining engineer at Bendigo and Melbourne before setting up his own stockbroking company, Edward Dyason & Co., in Melbourne in 1921. He kept up his mining interests: his *Report on the Bendigo goldfield central area* (Bendigo, 1916) had accompanied a letter to the Victorian minister of mines urging re-establishment of gold-mining in the area; it was later used by Dyason, G. Lindesay Clark and W. S. Robinson [q.v.] in setting up Bendigo mines Ltd in 1934. Dyason was also on the boards of Napoleon (B.M.L.) Mines and Derby and Carshalton Reefs. He owned the unprofitable Maude and Yellow Girl Mine at Glen Wills, which remained in operation until the last employee had reached retirement. Other firms with which he was associated included Melbourne Dry Docks, Kraft Foods Ltd, G. G. Goode Ltd, Pelaco Ltd, A. W. Allen Ltd and J. C. Hutton Pty Ltd. In 1918-22 Dyason was president of the Chamber of Mines of Victoria and in 1918-25 of the Gold Producers' Association of Australia. He joined the Melbourne Stock Exchange in 1921.

Describing himself as a 'militant pacifist' throughout the war, for the rest of his life Dyason supported 'peace through systems and regulations'. After the war he joined or contributed money to organizations such as the Australian Peace Alliance and the World Disarmament Movement, formed in 1928. His study of 'psychology of conflict' theory dated from the late 1920s.

Dyason was a 'valuable link between academic economists and the business world'. As an economist he was ahead of his time in favouring unorthodox rather than traditional solutions to the Depression. Politicians of all parties sought his advice, resulting in his membership of various unofficial committees set up by the Commonwealth government between 1921 and 1931 to deal with economic problems. In 1924 he reviewed the work of the Arbitration Court with Harrison Moore for Prime Minister S. M. (Viscount) Bruce [q.v.7]. In 1929, with Giblin, D. B. Copland and others, he reported to the prime minister on the costs and compensations of the Australian tariff; Melbourne University Press published their findings as *The Australian tariff* in the same year. Dyason, Copland and Giblin also issued two memoranda in 1930 which were used as a basis for the decision to depreciate the currency and in the formulation of the Premiers' Plan in 1931. Dyason and Giblin were called upon by E. G. Theodore [q.v.] to persuade the banks to agree to a compromise which would limit unavoidable deflation. Dyason himself advocated a liberal credit policy. Never a publicity-seeker, he rejected both a knighthood and attempts to get him into politics.

In 1924 Dyason was a founding member of the Economic Society of Australia and New Zealand, was president of the Victorian branch in 1926-28 and of its central council in 1930 and 1932. He was also on the editorial board of the *Economic Record* from 1925 to 1931, and contributed numerous articles to its pages. In the 1930s he set up a monthly digest known as the *Edward Dyason & Co. Economic Service*.

Always an internationalist, in search of the cause and treatment of international disharmony, Dyason helped to establish the Australian Institute of International Affairs in 1933 and was active in its Victorian branch. He chaired the Bureau of Social and International Affairs (Melbourne) in 1930-32 and 1934-39. In 1948 he gave £600 to the University of Melbourne to fund research in 'social conflict and prejudice'. He also provided money to bring F. S. C. Northrop to Australia on a lecture tour; as he intended, this was the first of an annual series made under the aegis of the A.I.I.A., later known as the Dyason Memorial Lectures. Speakers included Bertrand Russell, Julian Huxley and A. J. Toynbee.

Asia and its philosophies had always fascinated Dyason and he visited China and the Soviet Union in the 1920s. Zen Buddhism in particular caught his interest. In 1939 he set up the *Austral-Asiatic Bulletin*; this publication merged in 1947 with the A.I.I.A.'s *Australian Outlook*. The onset of war prevented Dyason from visiting Japan and the Far East to explore Zen Buddhism at first hand and instead he went to the United States of America in 1940 for a preliminary study of the Far East at the Rockefeller Institute, the Carnegie Foundation and the Institute of Pacific Relations. He had wanted for some years to leave Australia 'to shake myself free . . . from institutional and national involvement' in order to study the wider issues 'confronting our race and civilization'. When Australian monetary funds were blocked, Dyason moved to Buenos Aires at the end of 1940. His overtures in 1941 to Prime Minister Curtin over becoming Australia's representative to South America were considered but came to nothing.

Dyason was a trim, dapper man, and wore a Spanish grandee style beard. Full of verve and fun, he had, according to Copland, 'a flair for the paradoxical that at times shocked the more sober-minded of his hearers'. He enjoyed boating, bushwalking, squash and skiing and was a champion royal tennis player; he also collected art and appreciated the ballet, theatre and music (taking part in setting up the Melbourne Symphony Orchestra in the 1920s). While brought up as an Anglican, he did not belong in later years to any church. He was a member of the Athenaeum Club, Melbourne.

After the war Dyason moved to England. He died of coronary vascular disease at sea, aboard the *Queen Mary* on 3 October 1949 after leading the Australian delegation to the British Commonwealth Relations Conference at Bigwin, Ontario. His ashes were scattered over the property he had bought in Surrey. His estate in Victoria was valued for probate at £174 590.

E. M. Moore, *The quest for peace as I have known it in Australia* (Melb, 1950); C. D. W. Goodwin, *The image of Australia* (Durham, N.C., 1974); *Aust Outlook*, Dec 1949; *Economic Record*, June 1950, p 107; papers, E. Dyason, *and* Dyason Foundation (Univ Melb Archives). MAYA V. TUCKER

DYER, LOUISE BERTA MOSSON HANSON (1884-1962), patron of the arts and music publisher, was born on 19 July 1884 in Melbourne, daughter of Louis Lawrence Smith [q.v.6] and his second wife Marion Jane, née Higgins. In 1891 she began attending Presbyterian Ladies' College, East Melbourne, where her musical aptitude soon emerged. A talented pianist, she won the gold medal of the Royal College of Music, London, and afterwards went to Edinburgh to continue her musical studies.

Three years after returning, Louise married, on 27 December 1911, 54-year-old James Dyer, who as a young man had sung in the Liedertafel. He was now Australasian manager of Messrs Michael Nairn & Co. of Kirkcaldy, Scotland: contemporary gossip columnists referred to him as 'Jimmy Dyer, the linoleum king'. Louise's immediate sphere of social activity became the P.L.C. Old Girls' Association, which she served first as secretary and then as president in two double terms, 1919-21 and 1924-26.

After moving in 1922 from Hawthorn to Kinnoul, Toorak, Louise Dyer held regular *divertissements*. The prime mover in the foundation of the British Music Society of Victoria in 1921, she was in touch with the best performers offering, and paid them handsomely. Programmes were designed by leading artists, the hostess rising to the occasion with gorgeous dressing; flamboyance united the imperious and Bohemian aspects of her personality. She was also serious: before long she was mounting a production of Gustav Holst's *Savitri* and the Lully-Molière *Le mariage forcé*. Active in the Alliance Française, she extended her interest in literature to works being written around her: she underwrote the publication in book form of Shaw Neilson's [q.v.] *Ballad and lyrical poems* (1923) and, with characteristic energy, organized a deputation to the prime minister which sought an increase in the funding of literary pensions.

The Dyers were bound eventually to move to Europe: on a previous departure Louise told the press of the necessity to go to England to procure music unavailable in

Australia. Shortly after donating £10 000 to encourage the establishment of a permanent orchestra, they left Melbourne for England in April 1927 and a year later settled in Paris. There, after an initial period taking in galleries and concerts, she decided to complement the Lully edition then in progress by publishing a similar one of the music of Couperin le Grand, whose bicentenary was approaching. Thus was born the 'Editions de l'Oiseau-Lyre', the homage to her homeland spelt out in a photograph of tail feathers from a lyre-bird that adorned the front endpapers.

When the twelve volumes of the Couperin edition appeared in 1933, they created a sensation: material which had existed hitherto only in manuscript form, or in inaccurate nineteenth century editions, suddenly became available as the finest printed music most people had ever seen, impeccably edited. The edition was intended to be as permanent as possible, 'traversing time and space', as Louise wrote in her introduction; and to this end the best engravers and printers in Paris were set to work with the finest hand-made papers. By 1940, some forty volumes had been printed, including collections of sonatas by Purcell and Blow and the *Polyphonic Music of the XIIIth Century* (bound in Australian blackwood). Gramophone recordings were undertaken initially as Mrs Dyer's response to the earnest theorizing of a young musicologist, who was suddenly provided with the facilities to demonstrate his arguments about performance; but as the catalogue grew, the recordings became the means by which the Editions de l'Oiseau-Lyre became best known.

In the early long-playing era Lyre-Bird was the first to record the Monteverdi *Vespers*, Handel operas, the larger stage works of Purcell, and the complete *ordres* of Couperin; also works by Schönberg, Milhaud and Stravinsky. Such discs were often notable for the vivacity and freshness of the performance, often a direct result of Louise Dyer contacting the artists involved immediately after a particularly impressive radio broadcast. The publishing programme continued, though now overshadowed; as before, it catered for the needs of institutions and accredited scholars rather than the tastes of collectors.

Louise Dyer, along with the musicians Nadia Boulanger and Wanda Landowska, was a key figure in the revival of the serious performance of Baroque music in recent times: in consequence the French government appointed her a chevalier de la Légion d'Honneur in 1934, with promotion to officier of that order in 1957. Yet although she moved effortlessly in Parisian musical and social circles, Louise Dyer's attachment to Australia, while attenuated, was unassailable. The Editions de l'Oiseau-Lyre published works by Peggy Glanville-Hicks and Margaret Sutherland; Louise tried to interest Gallimard in publishing a translation of Furphy [q.v.]; and, at the moment of her greatest triumph, the appearance of the Couperin edition, she wrote of the presentation copy to the Public Library of Victoria, 'Number One went to the President of the French Republic; Number Two goes to my own homeland library'. She returned to Melbourne frequently, most notably to be lady mayoress to her brother (Sir) Harold Gengoult Smith in 1933.

James Dyer died in January 1938. On 6 April 1939 at Amersham, Buckinghamshire, England, Louise married 30-year-old Joseph Birch Hanson, an Englishman who had studied at the universities of Melbourne and Paris. They left Paris on the outbreak of war; Hanson taught at Balliol College, Oxford, until August 1945. Finding post-war conditions in Paris untenable, they moved to Monaco, where they carried on their music publishing business. Louise Hanson-Dyer died in hospital at Monaco on 9 November 1962; her ashes were brought back to Melbourne general cemetery. The greater part of her Australian estate, valued in Victoria for probate at £241 380, was bequeathed to the University of Melbourne. The principal beneficiary of her estate in Europe was her husband, who carried on the work of l'Oiseau-Lyre; his second wife Margarita continues it still.

Portraits of Louise by Tom Roberts and W. B. McInnes [qq.v.], are in the National Gallery of Victoria and at P.L.C.

K. Fitzpatrick, *PLC Melbourne* (Melb, 1975), J. S. Neilson, *The autobiography of John Shaw Neilson* (Canb, 1977); Record Soc, *Monthly Review*, July 1964; *The Times*, 17 Nov 1962; Kate Baker collection (NL); P. Serle papers (LaTL); information from Miss Sibyl Hewett, Brighton, and Mr James Craig, Ivanhoe, Melb.   JIM DAVIDSON

DYETT, SIR GILBERT JOSEPH CULLEN (1891-1964), ex-servicemen's leader, was born on 23 June 1891 at Bendigo, Victoria, third child of Benjamin Dyett, blacksmith, and his wife Margaret Frances, née Cullen, both Victorian-born. He was educated by the Marist Brothers at Bendigo, leaving school at 14 to work for J. H. Curnow [q.v.] & Son, estate agents. He was engaged in several business ventures on his own account in Victoria and Western Australia, and at the outbreak of the war in 1914 was in South Africa. He rushed back to Australia to enlist in September, qualified for an officers' school and in March 1915 was commissioned as lieutenant in the 7th Battalion, Australian Imperial Force. He embarked in April and fought on Gallipoli, but in August was so badly wounded at Lone Pine that he was reverently covered and left for dead. Rescued and repatriated, he was told that he would not walk again, but in later years was able to list 'walking' among his recreations.

While convalescing at Bendigo, Dyett took charge of the local recruiting campaign with such success that in May 1917 he was appointed secretary of the Victorian State Recruiting Committee, with promotion to temporary captain. He brought enormous energy to this job, combining opposition to conscription with a strong belief in military service. He initiated schemes such as a recruiting train and returned-soldier bands, but his attempt to introduce recruiting speeches during theatrical performances drew complaints about his over-zealousness.

After the war, Dyett became secretary of the Ocean Road Trust but resigned when the duties of the post clashed with his work as secretary for the successful Anzac Remembrance Appeal. In June 1919 he took up the part-time position of secretary to the Victorian Trotting and Racing Association, which was largely controlled by John Wren [q.v.]; he held the post for thirty years. Wren is said to have chosen him as a respectable front-man. Dyett did not smoke, drink or gamble, and knew little about the racing side of trotting, but he performed his duties with military precision, honesty and enthusiasm. He was on the Racecourse Licences Board of Victoria in 1930-51 and was central registrar of trotting names for Australia for many years. In 1950 he was caricatured as 'Captain Dwyer' by Frank Hardy in his novel *Power without glory*.

In 1916 Dyett had been elected a Federal vice president of the Returned Sailors' and Soldiers' Imperial League. By 1919 dissatisfaction was growing within the league about the 'law and order' policy of its national president, Senator W. K. Bolton [q.v.7]. A Victorian faction campaigned for Dyett who defeated Bolton for the presidency on 15 July. His immediate task was to turn wartime promises into legislation protecting the interests of returned soldiers. Despite the circumstances of his election, Dyett believed in a policy of 'patience, tact and diplomacy'; after an inauspicious clash with W. M. Hughes [q.v.] soon after assuming office, he maintained an almost daily contact with Federal ministers. This quiet diplomacy under his personal domination was at odds with the more aggressive tactics favoured by many branches and, with sharply falling membership fuelling opposition, Dyett several times only narrowly avoided defeat. In 1930 he announced his resignation due to pressure of business; he was persuaded to stand again but had to rely on his own vote and the casting vote of the federal secretary to survive when branches representing two-thirds of league membership voted against him. Thereafter a new emphasis on public lobbying emerged.

In the 1920s and 1930s Dyett was active in international ex-servicemen organizations; he represented Australia at several overseas conferences and in 1921-46 was dominion president of the British Empire Service League. From May 1932 he was a member of the Board of Management of the Australian War Memorial, and he was a trustee of the (Sir Samuel) McCaughey [q.v.5] bequest for the education of soldiers' children. He was appointed C.M.G. in 1927 and was knighted in 1934.

Dyett stepped down from the presidency of the R.S.L. in 1946. He maintained his racing interests until the early 1950s, and spent his retirement at his home at Olinda, in the Dandenongs. He died in hospital in East Melbourne on 19 December 1964 and was buried in Bendigo cemetery after a requiem Mass. Dyett never married. He took an interest in the welfare of children, and in the handicapped, especially the blind. Over the years he had bought and built a number of houses at Brighton and elsewhere which he let at low rentals to ex-servicemen; he left an estate valued for probate at £103 754. His friends spoke highly of his efficiency and tact, his magnetic personality and his ascendancy in debate.

L. Hills and A. Dene, *The RSSILA: its origin, history* . . . (Melb, 1927, 1938); G. L. Kristianson, *The politics of patriotism* (Canb, 1966); L. L. Robson, *The first A.I.F.* (Melb, 1970); N. Brennan, *John Wren* (Melb, 1971); M. J. Agnew, *Australia's trotting heritage* (Melb, 1977); E. H. Buggy, *The real John Wren* (Melb, 1977); *Reveille* (Syd), Apr 1933, Apr 1934, Aug 1944, Feb 1965; *Punch* (Melb), 3 Feb 1921; *Age*, 21 Dec 1964; *Bendigo Advertiser*, 21, 24 Dec 1964.

J. N. I. DAWES

DYMOCK, WILLIAM (1861-1900), bookseller, was born on 11 May 1861 at North Melbourne, fourth son of Scottish parents Walter Dymock, wheelwright, and his wife Janet, née McFarlane. About 1867 the family moved to Sydney and lived at Redfern. William was educated chiefly at Cleveland Street Public School. By 1878 he was employed in the book trade, working for John Andrews, James Reading & Co. and the Sydney branch of George Robertson [q.v.6] & Co.

After visiting England, where he established contact with Bernard Quaritch, Dymock set up his own business in Sydney in the early 1880s, being at 208 Pitt Street by 1884. The shop was called Dymock's Book Arcade and his trade was aimed not only at a broad popular market but at discriminating collectors like Alfred Lee [q.v.] and D. S. Mitchell [q.v.5]. He took over several other firms, notably the Picturesque Atlas Publishing Co. Ltd, as the Book Arcade expanded its activities and moved its premises, first to 142 King Street and then in December 1890 to 428 George Street; his new arcade was 200 ft. (60 m) by 30 ft. (9 m).

From 1884 Dymock issued regular catalogues and lists; that year the first of a series of publications containing views of Sydney appeared. Although he was to offer Sir Henry Parkes [q.v.5] £2000 in 1890 to write a two-volume autobiography, general publishing came second to bookselling. The absorption in 1896 of William Maddock's circulating library, with Maddock continuing as manager, added an important new dimension to the firm's place in the Sydney book world. Dymock proudly proclaimed himself Quaritch's agent and maintained an interest in valuable collections of antiquarian books, acquiring the libraries of Dr George Bennett and Sir Wigram Allen [qq.v.1,3]. His advertisements described the George Street arcade as 'the largest Book Shop in the world', holding 'upwards of one million books'.

At the Sydney Municipal Council elections on 1 December 1898 Dymock contested Macquarie Ward for the Citizens' Reform Committee and defeated Sydney Burdekin [q.v.3]. He campaigned strongly as a 'young Australian', 'broad and progressive in his views'. In September 1900 he gave evidence and appeared on his own behalf before the Legislative Assembly select committee on the working of the Free Public Library; he believed its principal librarian H. C. L. Anderson [q.v.7] was giving undue favour to Angus [q.v.7] & Robertson [q.v.]. Dymock died of a cerebral haemorrhage early on 5 October 1900 and was buried in Waverley cemetery with Presbyterian forms, although he had requested that no minister be present. He was a Freemason.

Dymock was unmarried and his sister Marjory, wife of John Forsyth, managing director of A. Forsyth [q.v.4] & Co. Ltd, was executrix, trustee and principal beneficiary of his estate, valued for probate at £10 399. She continued the business and her family still has a controlling interest in the company set up in 1913. In 1926 George Robertson (Sydney) recalled affectionately 'the somewhat erratic but wholly lovable William Dymock'; despite vigorous competition, relations remained good between two outstanding firms created about the same time by former employees of the other George Robertson. Dymock was a member of several clubs and sporting associations and perhaps less single-mindedly devoted to the book trade than his rival; but he retains the distinction of being the first native-born Australian to have launched an enduringly successful major book-selling business.

J. R. Tyrrell, *Old books, old friends, old Sydney* (Syd, 1952); J. Holroyd, *George Robertson of Melbourne, 1825-1898* (Melb, 1968); G. Ferguson, *Some early Australian bookmen* (Canb, 1978); *V&P* (LA NSW), 1900, 4, 583; *JRAHS*, 52 (1966), 228; *Daily Telegraph*, 18 Nov-2 Dec 1898, 6 Oct 1900; *SMH*, 2 Dec 1898, 6 Oct 1900; *Bulletin*, 13 Oct 1900; Parkes correspondence (ML); documents lodged under Companies Acts, no 4769 (NSWA); letters 1899-1908 (Syd Municipal Archives, Town Hall, Syd); information from Mr M. H. Forsyth, Dymock's Book Arcade Ltd, Syd.   WALLACE KIRSOP

DYSON, EDWARD GEORGE (1865-1931), writer, was born on 4 March 1865 at Morrison near Ballarat, Victoria, second child of George Arthur Dyson and his wife Jane, née Mayall. His father, a Londoner by birth, had arrived in the colony in 1852 and later worked as a miner and mining engineer in the Ballarat district. His mother, daughter of a Lancashire cotton-spinner, came, so Dyson said, 'from a life of refinement in England' and it was she, perhaps, who fostered the artistic inclinations of her three talented sons, Edward, William Henry and Ambrose [qq.v.].

Much of Dyson's boyhood was spent on the move as his father followed his employment from Morrison to Alfredton, Bendigo and Soldier's Hill. Shunted from school to school he recoiled from formal education with 'bewilderment and loathing'. He learned much more, as boy and writer, from the blighted landscape beyond the school yard. 'The deserted mines took hold of me', he later wrote, 'and I haunted them like a familiar spirit'. Scrambling across mullock heaps, hunting rats in worked-out shafts and yarning with old prospectors, he stored up the memories and anecdotes that fed his prolific literary career. Waddy, the grey weather-board township described in his later mining stories, is Alfredton, while many of his stock characters — the Wesleyan class-leader, the Irish saloon-keeper, the Chinese laundryman — were modelled on childhood acquaintances.

When he was 12 Dyson left school to help his father, who by then was working as a dry-goods hawker, another experience he used years later in his *Tommy the hawker* (1911). During his teens he worked in various jobs 'below and on top' at Ballarat, Clunes, Bungaree, Lefroy (Tasmania), Smeaton and Gordon. About 1883 the family settled in South Melbourne and Ted, the mainstay of the family since the death of his elder brother in 1879, went to work in his uncle's paper-bag factory.

Dyson had already contributed short pieces to the Ballarat and Melbourne press and in 1885 some paragraphs sent to the Sydney *Bulletin* drew an encouraging reply from J. F. Archibald [q.v.3]. After a short stint as sub-editor on the weekly *Life*, he struck out as a freelance writer and by the end of the decade material over his usual pen-name, 'Silas Snell', had appeared in *Australian Tit-bits*, Melbourne *Punch* and other papers. His first real success came in 1889 when his short story 'A golden shanty' was used as the title-piece in the *Bulletin*'s Christmas anthology.

The popularity of the *Bulletin* inspired Dyson and the artist Tom Durkin to begin their own two-man local version, the *Bull Ant* (later the *Ant*), which enjoyed a short but merry life until its closure in mid-1892. With creditors at his heels, Dyson resumed freelancing and in the mid-1890s he was among the most prolific of the *Bulletin*'s contributors. He produced his first and best book of verse, *Rhymes from the mines*, in 1896.

For Dyson writing was a trade as much as a vocation. In 1889 he reflected on his former life as a miner, comparing it favourably with 'the weary curse of slinging rhymes / When wages, not the will, impels'. To maintain his heavy work schedule, he evolved an elaborate system of literary book-keeping. He jotted down ideas, facts and phrases in his notebooks; then, as they were turned into finished stories, he entered the titles and proceeds in a ledger. From a trough in the mid-1890s, his earnings quickly rose to over £600 a year and by 1901 he could afford to turn down William Macleod's [q.v.] generous offer of a permanent job on the *Bulletin* at £10 a week.

In the late 1890s Dyson and his brothers, together with Lionel, Percy and Norman Lindsay [qq.v.], their fellow refugees from goldfields Methodism, founded the Bohemian Ishmael Club. In their company Dyson unleashed his humour in bawdy playlets, satirical speeches and mock liturgies that reveal how far he shared the enthusiasm of his younger confrères for Nietzsche, Ibsen and the *décadence*.

After 1900, as his brothers and sisters were launched on their own careers and marriages, Dyson's financial responsibilities eased. But he kept up his 'machine-like productiveness', writing jokes and captions for Melbourne *Punch*, attempting to break into the theatre with melodramas for the Bland Holt and Robert Brough [qq.v.4,3] companies, and keeping up a constant sup-

ply of stories, long and short. With *Below and on top* (1898), *The gold-stealers* (1901) and *In the roaring fifties* (1906) he worked through his reserves of goldfields material. Then, capitalizing on the vogue for larrikin literature, he turned his own adolescent factory experiences to account in his *Fact'ry 'ands* (1906), *Benno and some of the push* (1911), and *Spats' fact'ry* (1914). Dyson eschewed the gloomy realism of Arthur Morrison and Louis Stone [q.v.] and his 'comic sketches' celebrate the perennial gaucherie of youth rather than expose the problems of the slums.

On 9 September 1914 the inveterate bachelor was married to 22-year-old Dorothy Boyes, a music teacher, at St George's Church of England, Royal Park; in 1917 a daughter was born. Except for *Hello soldier!* (1919), a transparent attempt to emulate C. J. Dennis's [q.v.] brand of digger humour, he published little of consequence during the war period. With an income of some £800 a year from investments, royalties and occasional journalism he apparently looked forward to a secure and relaxed old age. Sadly, it was not to be. In the wake of the 1919 influenza pandemic, he contracted encephalitis, which left him drowsy, withdrawn and inarticulate. He died on 22 August 1931 at his home in Elwood and was cremated with Anglican rites.

In his life, as in his writings, Dyson was an essential product of the Victorian goldfields. In middle life he retained the sturdy build and brisk movements of a working miner. While he and his fellow Ishmaelites rejected the philistinism of goldfields Methodism, they retained the hard work-discipline and gritty determination to succeed that so often went with it. Dyson was the most professional Australian writer of his generation and, like his great contemporary Arnold Bennett, an habitual word-counter. Even with his natural fluency it took method and application to become 'the only writer to freelance a competence in Australia'. His was a lesser talent than Lawson's or Paterson's [qq.v.] and his brand of facetious humour has not worn well. But his goldfields stories and poems formed an authentic strand of the consciously Australian literature which the *Bulletin* had set out to create in the 1890s.

R. Bedford, *Naught to thirty-three* (Syd, 1944); N. Lindsay, *Bohemians of the Bulletin* (Syd, 1965); *Free Lance* (Melb), 14 May 1896; *Bulletin*, 21 Nov 1912; *Argus*, 24 Aug 1931; E. G. Dyson papers (LaTL).   GRAEME DAVISON

DYSON, WILLIAM HENRY (1880-1938), political cartoonist, was born on 3 September 1880 at Ballarat, Victoria, ninth child of George Arthur Dyson, then a hawker, and his wife Jane, née Mayall. When he was very young the family moved to South Melbourne; by then the Dysons were almost entirely supported by Edward (Ted) [q.v.]. Bill, or Will, as he later signed his work, attended Albert Park State School until 1892.

Although Will Dyson was to become one of the most influential satirists Australia has produced, he was known initially in Australia only by his illustrations to Edward's book *Fact'ry 'ands* (1906), and his caricatures of Commonwealth personalities published in the *Bulletin* and the *Lone Hand*. He first submitted his self-taught drawings to the *Bulletin* in 1897, struggling with both drawing style and making a living. At 18 he met Norman Lindsay [q.v.], with whom he formed a close friendship. The two went about the streets of Melbourne following likely types to draw; both were concerned with technical efficiency of draughtsmanship and the close observation of human character.

In 1903 Will succeeded his elder brother Ambrose on the Adelaide *Critic*, contributing coloured caricatures. Although he specialized at this period in caricature, he was developing his own style of satire, drawing political cartoons in 1908 for the coloured covers of Randolph Bedford's [q.v.7] *Clarion*. Black and white freelance work was badly paid and avenues for it were very few; the most Will Dyson ever received for a caricature in Australia was ten shillings. Naturally he longed for wider horizons.

In May 1909 an exhibition of his caricatures opened at Furlong's Studios in the Royal Arcade, Melbourne. On 30 September at Creswick, Dyson married Ruby Lindsay [q.v.], sister of Norman, herself a talented black and white artist. In 1910 they left for London accompanied by Norman, but the friendship was soon broken, partly at Ruby's insistence.

Dyson's big chance came in 1912 when he was appointed cartoonist-in-chief at £5 a week to the new labour newspaper, the *Daily Herald*, whose editor gave him *carte blanche* to express his own ideas. His work, published full newspaper size, was sensational. A convinced socialist, with a humanist outlook generated in his youth when the conflict between labour and capital was emerging as the dominating theme in Australian politics, Dyson hacked into the pomposity and humbug of pre-war England, championing the working man boldly and without reserve. 'In British cartooning Before Dyson', his friend Vance Palmer [q.v.] wrote, 'the working man had been depicted as a pathetic figure, a depressed person lacking any human dignity. Will Dyson drew him young, militant, an image of hope with fist upraised'. He at no time called for bloody revolution, but he was stronger in his demands for social justice than most progressive intellectuals of his day, fighting the slum landlords, courts, Labour renegades, the press, exploitation, and Tory reaction in all forms. His cartoons were graphically dramatic, and in tone bitter, attacking unemployment, hunger and suffering.

Dyson's cartoons were drawn in the 'grand manner', heavy with symbols. His devils represented war and destruction: he took the familiar labour symbol 'Fat', representing Capital, Finance and Power, and made a gross figure of large paunch, top hat, spats and a cigar, the image of greed in a world of ignoble advantages. Hackneyed now, the symbol was a notable creation in its day.

Like most supporters of the majority labour movements of Britain, France and Germany, Dyson accepted the war as just and necessary. In 1915 the most famous of his seven collected cartoons books was published: twenty large drawings titled *Kultur cartoons*, with a foreword by H. G. Wells. In December 1916 he was commissioned by the Commonwealth as the first Australian war artist. While living with the Australian soldiers on the Western Front, Lieutenant Dyson was twice wounded but returned to continue producing his compassionate drawings of humanity under fire. A collection of these water-colour wash and crayon drawings, each with Dyson's interpretative text, was published in *Australia at war* (1918).

Back with the *Daily Herald* in 1919, Dyson drew what was to be his most celebrated and reprinted cartoon. Remarkable for its astonishing prophecy, it depicted Woodrow Wilson, Lloyd George and Orlando of Italy leaving the Versailles peace treaty meeting with Clemenceau who is saying, 'Curious! I seem to hear a child weeping!' – the weeping child in the cartoon was labelled '1940 class'.

In 1919 Dyson lost his wife Ruby, aged only 32, when she became a victim of the influenza epidemic. The fire and sting went out of him from this time on. His utter grief was evident in his *Poems: in memory of a wife* (London, 1919). The next blow to his fortunes came in 1922 when the *Daily Herald* was taken over by the Trades Union Council: Dyson resigned, to become, in effect, unemployed for the next two years. For he was staunchly independent and would not work for a direct organ of a political party.

In this mood Dyson accepted the offer of a substantial salary to come back and work for the Melbourne *Herald* group; its weekly magazine *Punch* had secured the talents of the poet and journalist Kenneth Slessor, the writers Vance Palmer and Myra Morris [q.v.], the artists Percy Leason [q.v.] and 'Unk' White, the lyric poet Hugh McCrae [q.v.] and his firm friend to be, Jim Bancks [q.v.7]. In 1925 and for the next five years Dyson's cartoons appeared in the *Herald* and in *Punch* and its successor *Table Talk*. His original misgivings were realized, for he and (Sir) Keith Murdoch [q.v.] quarrelled incessantly. Murdoch insisted on a 'read-as-you-run' cartoon comment on local affairs, while Dyson preferred to take a god's-eye view of the broader international scene. But he was soon edged from his special field into turning out pleasant comic drawings of theatrical personalities, in addition to cartoon comment on local matters. Even so, his *Punch* work was distinguished from time to time by his typical admonishing satire on such issues as unemployment, the political neglect of education and science, and rearmament for war. Perhaps from frustration, he became interested in etching and dry-points, an exacting skill which he mastered brilliantly under the expert tuition of the Melbourne etcher Cyril Dillon.

In 1930, his *Herald* contract finished, Dyson returned to England via the United States of America, where he exhibited his satires of manners in a series of etchings and dry-points in several major cities, and then again in London. These satires demonstrated again that whatever Dyson did he did well. They were acclaimed, and were seemingly his last triumph.

In 1933 he published *Artist among the bankers*, a hostile judgment upon the economic conduct of the world and of 'banker-business'. He had rejoined the vastly changed *Daily Herald*, a paper now shy of socialism, with an eye towards advertisers.

Dyson's sudden death on 21 January 1938 at Chelsea from a long-standing heart condition made newspaper headlines around the world. His last cartoon, published on the day of his death, showed—despite an enforced editorial alteration—the old Dyson fire. He had drawn two vultures perched on a crag watching Franco planes bombing defenceless Barcelona. His caption read: 'Once *we* were the most loathsome things that flew!'

Will Dyson, pessimistic, often darkly depressed, concealing his inner feelings behind a sardonic mask, had a mordant wit that could be used with withering effect particularly in his brilliant after-dinner speeches; he was one of the robust minds of his time. In his irony and force he has not been approached as a cartoonist by any Australian, then or since. Most State and many regional galleries in Australia hold examples of his wartime drawings and lithographs. The largest collection of about 500 Dyson *Daily Herald* cartoons are preserved at the Cartoon Research Centre at the University of Kent at Canterbury, England.

Will's elder brother AMBROSE ARTHUR DYSON (1876-1913) was born on 13 April 1876 at Ballarat and like Will had no formal art training, developing his skills by sketching in the streets. Some of the rudiments were acquired from fellow artist Tom Durkin. In his teens Amb Dyson had his drawings published in Melbourne *Punch*, and later in the *Bulletin* while cartooning in 1898 for the Adelaide *Critic*. He went to Adelaide next year as the *Critic's* chief artist and worked there until 1903 when he returned to Melbourne to accept a staff position with the *Bulletin*, producing a full page of cartoons and comment on Victorian politics. Between 1906 and 1909 with Will and Ruby Lindsay, Ambrose contributed joke drawings to the *Gadfly* (Adelaide). Other work by him appeared in *Table Talk*, the *Clarion* and the Sydney *Worker*. His drawings are of important documentary interest in portraying the first indigenous Australian city type – the larrikin.

On 14 December 1912 Dyson married Mabel Norah Frazer; their son Edward Ambrose (1908-1953) was also a capable artist. Ambrose senior died on 3 June 1913 in a mental hospital at Kew. Although his pen drawing of the tonal school was orthodox in technique – and skilful at that – his individual, original, decidedly comic style presented a subsequent breakaway from the straight illustration-type drawing that went with a joke or political caption. It was his feeling for intelligent distortion – the problem for all true humorous draughtsmen – that places him not so much among the great, as among the innovators.

N. Lindsay, *My mask* . . . (Syd, 1970); V. Lindesay, *The inked-in image* (Melb, 1970); *Lone Hand*, Sept, Oct 1908; *20th Century Studies*, Dec 1975; *Worker* (Syd), 10 Dec 1908; *Punch* (Melb), 15 Jan 1925; *Daily Herald* (Lond), 21 Jan 1938; *Herald* (Melb), 22 Jan 1938; *Argus*, 24 Jan 1938; *SMH*, 25 Jan 1938; *Record* (Sth Melb), 28 Apr 1955; N. Lindsay letters to author, 1961.

VANE LINDESAY

E

EADY, CHARLES JOHN (1870-1945), sportsman, lawyer and politician, was born on 29 October 1870 in Hobart, son of George Eady, butcher, and his wife Jane Sarah, née Williams. Educated at F. W. Norman's Derwent School, Eady left at 13; next year his cricketing career commenced when he played in the junior team of the Lefroy Club; in 1890 he joined the Break O'Day Club. Playing for Tasmania against Victoria in Hobart in early 1895 he became the first Australian to make a century in each innings of a first-class match — 116 and 112 not out. This feat attracted great attention, but it was as a fast bowler that he was selected for inclusion in the Australian team which went to England in 1896 under G. H. S. Trott [q.v.].

Known as the 'genial giant', Eady was over six feet tall, with a magnificent physique; but on the tour he suffered at times from a heavy cold and minor injuries and did not find good form. However, he still received offers, which he did not pursue, from several English county teams. He played in the fifth Test in the 1901-02 series in Australia. He won the Tasmanian Cricket Association bowling average several times, twice taking ten wickets in a match; his 1902 score of 566 for Break O'Day Club v. Wellington still stands as a record in any grade of Australian cricket and is listed in *Wisden*. In 1908 he retired from first-class cricket. He had been involved with the administration of the game from 1890 and was elected president of the Tasmanian Cricket Association in 1926, holding the position until his death.

Eady was an all-round athlete, was president of the Amateur Sports Federation of Tasmania in 1910-33 and, for shorter periods, of the Tasmanian Amateur Boxing Association and the Tasmanian branch of the Royal Life Saving Society. A one-time member of Derwent Rowing Club he was also involved with racing, as secretary to the Tasmanian Amateur Jockey Club (1917-27), and judge for the Tasmanian Racing Club, Brighton Jockey Club and Hobart Turf Club. A first-rate footballer, renowned for his high marking, Eady captained the Holbrook Club in 1890, and represented southern Tasmania against Victorian teams several times. He held various positions in the Tasmanian Australian National Football League including the presidency in 1900-08 and 1925-41.

In 1890 Eady became an articled clerk in the firm of Finlay and Watchorn, and was admitted to the Supreme Court of Tasmania five years later. After two short-lived part-nerships, he became the senior partner in the firm of Eady and Bradford in 1913. For several years from 1912 he was chairman of various wages boards. Associated with the Civic Club from its inception in 1911 he was president in 1927-45.

Running as a member of a team of three Liberal League candidates, Eady failed in the 1914 Denison by-election for the House of Assembly. Nine years later he again lost, as an Independent, in a bid for the seat of Hobart in the Legislative Council, but won it in a 1925 by-election and held it until his death. While in the council he initiated several bills, none of which became law, served as one of the government representatives on the Hobart Public Hospitals Board, and was a member of the parliamentary standing committee on public works and chairman of committees (1937-44). In May 1944 he was elected president of the council.

Eady died on 20 December 1945 and was cremated after a state funeral. He was survived by his daughter; his wife, Florence Isobel, née Guesdon, whom he had married on 22 October 1903 at St George's Anglican Church, Battery Point, had predeceased him by nine months. A sociable man with a wide circle of friends, Eady was well liked, and respected for his sense of fair play and his integrity. There is a bronze tablet in memory of him and his wife in All Saints Church of England, South Hobart, and the C. J. Eady memorial cup has been competed for annually since 1947 by the country cricket associations of Tasmania.

R. Page, *A history of Tasmanian cricket* (Hob, 1957); R. K. Pinchin, *A century of Tasmanian football, 1879-1979* (Hob, 1979); *Mercury*, 9 Jan 1914, 9 May 1923, 24 June 1925, 21 Dec 1945; *World* (Hob), 2 Aug 1919; *Examiner* (Launc), 21 Dec 1945.   BARBARA VALENTINE

EAMES, WILLIAM L'ESTRANGE (1863-1956), medical practitioner and soldier, was born in 1863 at Neemuch near Poona, India, son of William Leslie Eames, an Anglican chaplain attached to an East India Company regiment, and his wife Henrietta, née L'Estrange. As a small boy he went to England and was educated at Oswestry Grammar School and Caius College, Cambridge, with the intention of entering the Church. When his mother died he altered his plans and became a medical student at Trinity College, Dublin. He was interested in soccer, rugby and rowing. In 1885, while he was still an undergraduate, the Sudan War broke out; he enlisted in a medical unit but the war ended and it did not embark.

In 1886 Eames graduated (B.A., B.Ch., B.A.O.) and applied to join the Army Medical Corps but although he passed the necessary tests there were no vacancies and he decided to sail for Australia. In August next year he arrived in Sydney and settled at Newcastle where he was associated with Dr J. L. Beeston in a busy general practice which was largely concerned with the shipping industry. On 19 November 1888, at Christ Church, Newcastle, he married Elizabeth Jane Lockhead; they had two daughters. He remained in practice at Newcastle until 1914 and was a foundation member of the Newcastle Club.

In 1891 Eames had joined the New South Wales Army Medical Corps (later part of the Australian Army Medical Corps) as a captain, and on the outbreak of the South African War volunteered for service. He left Sydney on 17 January 1900 as a major in the corps' second contingent and disembarked at East London on 22 February. After arrival he organized and commanded the No. 2 Bearer Company. The New South Wales A.M.C. distinguished itself throughout the war and was noted for its fine training, equipment and mobility.

Eames served during operations in the Orange Free State from February to May 1900, including actions at Vet River and Zand River; in the Transvaal in May and June including actions near Johannesburg, Pretoria and Diamond Hill; and east of Pretoria from July to November. He was taken prisoner by Boers, among whom were Generals Botha and Smuts. Smuts is reputed to have asked Eames, 'Why do you Australians come over here to fight us?' Eames said, 'When you have lived under Britain for ten years you will want to fight for her too'. To this Smuts replied 'Never'. Eames was released, resumed active service and for his work in South Africa was appointed C.B., awarded the Queen's Medal and mentioned in dispatches. By early 1901 he was back at Newcastle and in 1903, as a brevet lieut-colonel, was given medical responsibility for the army in the Newcastle area. He became a substantive lieut-colonel in the A.A.M.C. in 1909.

In 1914 Eames and his family visited England for a holiday. While he was there war broke out and he was keen to enlist, but at 51 was considered too old and was precluded by Commonwealth policy from enlisting in the Australian Imperial Force overseas. Lady Dudley [q.v.] decided to raise a voluntary hospital to be staffed by Australian medical officers and nurses visiting or resident in England, and Eames was appointed to command it, with the temporary rank of lieut-colonel in the Royal Army Medical Corps. By 29 August the Australian Voluntary Hospital was in France and on 5 September it opened at St Nazaire, near Boulogne, where it soon had a capacity of over 1000 beds, and at a later stage, 2000. Admirable pioneering medical work was done by this unit which was well equipped and maintained a high standard of efficiency.

As the war progressed it became increasingly difficult to staff the hospital from voluntary sources and in July 1916 it was absorbed into the British Army and renamed No. 32 Stationary Hospital. Eames continued as its commanding officer and in June 1918 was promoted brevet colonel. During the war nearly 74 000 cases passed through the hospital. For his service Eames was appointed C.B.E., awarded the Portuguese Order of Avis and twice mentioned in dispatches.

In April 1919 he resigned his command and returned to Australia. That year he retired from general practice but in 1920 became the principal medical officer of the 2nd Military District (New South Wales); he was placed on the retired list of the Australian Military Forces in 1921. He maintained an active retirement, with business interests in Sydney and Newcastle, and was a director of the City of Newcastle Gas and Coke Co. An ardent golfer, he was also keenly interested in horse-racing and seldom missed a meeting at Randwick or Warwick Farm. He was a driving force behind the North Australian White Settlement Association which aimed at settling over 100 000 British men and women in northern Australia.

Eames was disappointed when no suitable medical appointment could be found for him in World War II. Survived by his two daughters, he died at Rose Bay, Sydney, on 26 October 1956, and was cremated with Anglican rites. Tall and dignified, but possessed of endearing charm and dry humour, he was a distinguished professional man who radiated kindly benevolence.

F. Fremantle, *Impressions of a doctor in khaki* (Lond, 1901); Aust Defence Dept, *Official records of the Australian military contingents to the war in South Africa*, P. L. Murray, ed (Melb, 1911); A. G. Butler (ed), *Official history of the Australian Army medical services . . .* 1914-18 (Melb, 1930, Canb, 1940, 1943); H. Cushing, *From a surgeon's journal 1915-18* (Lond, 1936); *University of Sydney, Book of remembrance, 1914-18* (Syd, 1939); *MJA*, Dec 1956; *SMH*, 9 Feb 1920, 24 Jan 1922, 16, 18 May 1923; *Newcastle Morning Herald*, 27 Oct 1956.

D. M. HORNER

EARLE, JOHN (1865-1932), union organizer and premier, was born on 15 November 1865 at Bridgewater, Tasmania, son of Charles Staples Earle, a farmer of Cornish descent, and his Irish Catholic wife Ann Teresa, née McShane. Jack (as he was familiarly known) attended Bridgewater State School but, a determined self-improver, moved to Hobart where he became a blacksmith's apprentice in 1882 and enrolled in engineering and science classes. He also attended lectures on economics, rationalism, evolution, natural science and socialism at the Hobart Mechanics' Institute; he formed friendships with people such as the liberal-minded Hobart city librarian A. J. Taylor [q.v.6] and joined the Hobart Debating Club.

Towards the end of the decade Earle left Hobart for the new mining communities, moving from the Mathinna goldfield to Zeehan and then to the Corinna goldfield. He was a miners' representative at a government mining conference in Hobart in 1893. Returning to Zeehan in 1898 he assumed such leading positions as the chairmanship of the hospital board and presidency of the local branch of the Amalgamated Miners' Association. Concentrating on union affairs, he became an active organizer in spite of bitter opposition from the powerful Mt Lyell Mining and Railway Co. In 1903 when employed as a blacksmith in the South Lyell mine he headed a list, compiled by the Mt Lyell manager, of twenty-eight 'disloyal and treacherous men'. His 'disloyalty' was probably highlighted by his action in denouncing Britain's 'unjustifiable' Imperialistic involvement in the South African War.

As his frustration in union activities mounted, Earle took a more practical interest in parliamentary politics. Tasmania now had manhood suffrage and the time seemed ripe to follow mainland States in organizing a Labor party. In September 1901 Earle chaired a meeting at Zeehan to draw up a platform for the proposed Workers' Political League of which he became the first president. Their demands — adult suffrage, adequate payment of members of parliament, the eight-hour day, a graduated land tax, free education — were moderate. Their aim, to ensure fair and equitable legislation for all sections of the community, would be pursued by Earle at every opportunity and encouraged by contact with such Labor leaders as J. C. Watson [q.v.], who attended the 1903 Hobart conference to establish a State-wide organization.

Earle became first president of the Tasmanian Workers' Political League at this conference, having recently been only narrowly defeated in the State elections. In 1906 he won the west coast seat of Waratah, and

formed an Opposition of seven in the House of Assembly. In 1909 he campaigned successfully for the rural seat of Franklin, defining the purpose of the Labor party as the implementation of 'true progressive liberalism' rather than socialism. In October Earle led the first Tasmanian Labor government into office but, a minority ministry, it lasted only a week. During the pre-war years he was conducting a bookshop and was chairman of directors of the Labor *Daily Post*. The Anglican bishop, J. E. Mercer [q.v.] was a close friend.

Earle's return to office on 6 April 1914 as premier and attorney-general was controversial. Labor had won a no confidence motion against A. E. Solomon [q.v.] and Earle was commissioned by the governor to form a government on the understanding that he would immediately call a dissolution. Having formed his ministry Earle rejected these conditions, appealing successfully to the Colonial Office. In the House of Assembly Labor was hampered by its dependence on the capricious Independent J. T. H. Whitsitt, and the Legislative Council was dominated by conservatives. The government was able to increase bursaries for the children of the poor and extend secondary education; it established the first national park at Mount Field and completed the transfer of the Great Lake hydro-electricity scheme to state ownership.

Earle imported vast quantities of wheat to keep bread prices down in the drought year of 1914 and similarly made large investments in public works to alleviate war-caused unemployment. These measures earned him some popularity, but increasingly he alienated some of the more vocal and radical trade unionists in his party. He also advocated a 'party truce' during wartime, refused to adopt a policy of preference to unionists, and told the unemployed to enlist, thereby confirming for his opponents in the Labor movement his identity as a collaborator with the capitalists and Imperialists. His government was defeated in the election of April 1916 and when he finally resigned from his party over conscription in November, he was merely formalizing a division of many years.

Of his resignation, Earle remarked that it had been the most 'painful trial of his life'. Vilified as a 'time-server, a seeker after place and pay, a traitor to his class', he branded his former party as a 'worse enemy than the Hun' and embraced his old foes in W. M. Hughes's [q.v.] hastily formed National Party. In rapid behind-the-scenes manoeuvres he resigned from the House of Assembly in March 1917 to fill a Senate vacancy caused by the sudden retirement of Labor Senator R. K. Ready: Labor thus lost its Senate majority. On the crest of the wave of jingoism which swept Hughes's government into office in May, Earle topped the Senate poll in his State. He entered Hughes's ministry as vice-president of the Executive Council in 1921 but was defeated in the 1922 election. Three years later, repelled by the anti-union measures of the Bruce-Page [qq.v.] government, Earle stood for the Senate as an Independent, but was again defeated. He was also unsuccessful in 1928 when as an Independent he contested Waratah in the House of Assembly elections.

On 30 April 1914 at St Andrew's Church of England, Nugent, Earle had married Susanna Jane Blackmore, an ardent member of the Labor party. At the 1916 State conference, before Earle had committed himself to conscription, she had declared: 'In a fight like this it should be "one out all out" ', and she was arguably of some influence in persuading her husband to adopt the liberal principle of 'equality of sacrifice'. After 1922 the Earles retired to live at Oyster Cove. They had no children but took pleasure in country pursuits and drew spiritual comfort from the teachings of theosophy. Earle died of cancer on 6 February 1932 at Oyster Cove, and was cremated in Melbourne. His estate was sworn for probate at £3963. He became, in the memory of the Labor movement, a 'rat'. But in so many ways – in his background, education, union organizing, in his nationalism and liberalism – Earle was in fact the archetypal Labor man of his time.

G. Blainey, *The peaks of Lyell* (Melb, 1967); M. Lake, *A divided society* (Melb, 1975); D. J. Murphy (ed), *Labor in politics* (Brisb, 1975); Tas Public Service Assn, *Service*, Feb 1954; *Labour Hist*, Nov 1977, no 33, p 29; *PTHRA*, 23 (1976), no 4, p 149; *Zeehan and Dundas Herald*, 27 Sept 1901; *Mercury*, 27 Feb 1909, 8 Feb 1932; *Daily Post* (Hob), 28 July, 17 Oct 1916, 8 Sept 1917; P. Fagan, The Earle Labor government 1914-16 (B.A. Hons thesis, Univ Tas, 1975).   MARILYN LAKE

EARP, GEORGE FREDERICK (1858-1933), merchant and importer, was born on 24 January 1858 at Nottingham, England, son of George William Earp, railway clerk, and his wife Priscilla Martha, née Shetton. Educated at Derby Grammar School and Beaufort House Collegiate School, London, he was employed as a railway clerk when he decided to visit Australia for his health.

Reaching Western Australia in 1883 Earp saw the possibilities of trade in bunker coal. He formed a partnership with W. J. Gillam of Albany, then went to Newcastle, New South Wales, and bought a ship for £1100. He gradually extended his interests to include the export of coal, coke and timber and the import of timber and general merchandise. The partnership was dissolved in 1900 and in 1903 Earp Bros & Co. Ltd was incorporated with Earp as managing director. The firm helped open the South Maitland coalfields and he became a director of the East Greta Coal Mining Co. Ltd.

Earp visited England in 1893 and on 6 May in London he married Gertrude Mary Saddington; in 1903 he again went overseas, this time for health reasons, and attended the Congress of Chambers of Commerce of the British Empire; in 1908 he was a commissioner for the Franco-British Exhibition. On his return in 1904 he had formed Earp, Woodcock, Beveridge, & Co. Ltd by amalgamating three leading timber and joinery firms. Hardware, at first a sideline, became the main business of Earp Bros after they sold their coal interests to the John Brown [q.v.7] firm in 1931 to concentrate on the supply of tiles and bathroom fittings.

A director of the Central Trading Co. and of Edward Chapman [q.v.7] & Co., Earp was president of the Newcastle Chamber of Commerce in 1899-1901. In his annual address in February 1900 he praised the Protectionist Lyne [q.v.] government for improvements to Newcastle harbour, and in November, despite his free-trade views, was nominated to the Legislative Council; he was later a Nationalist. An infrequent speaker, he was keenly interested in matters affecting Newcastle and the coal trade. He supported female suffrage in 1901 because he believed women to be a conservative influence, but was willing to try industrial arbitration despite obvious qualms. In 1912 he opposed an eight-hour day in mines but supported a more practicable bill three years later.

In 1905 Earp moved to Sydney, leaving day-to-day management of his companies to his brother Charles. Support and fund-raising for charities was claiming more and more of his time: he was a director of the Benevolent Society of New South Wales, president of the Health Society of New South Wales and a vice-president of the National Association for the Prevention and Cure of Consumption; he was also a vice-president of the Geographical Society and president of the Association for the Protection of Native Races. He was a member of the Church of England Sydney Diocesan, General and Provincial synods, and served on the Council of The King's School, Parramatta, and the Home Mission Society (Church Society from 1911). During World War I he was active in many patriotic associations and was joint honorary treasurer of the Polish Relief Fund. In 1919 he was appointed honorary consul-general for Poland – he did not treat the position as a sinecure – and in 1921 knight of the Order of Polonia Restituta. He was a founder of the Empire Literature Society and vice-president in 1929.

In his prime Earp was described as 'tall, spare and aristocratic-looking'. He was appointed C.B.E. in 1920. Survived by his wife, three daughters and two sons, he died on 12 March 1933 at his home at Edgecliff. His estate was valued for probate at £44 144.

Newcastle Chamber of Commerce, *Annual Report . . .*, 1898-1901; *Newcastle Morning Herald*, 2 Oct 1903, 13 Mar 1933, 27 July 1961; *SMH*, 12 June 1919, 13 Mar 1933; papers and information supplied by Mr R. Earp, New Lambton, NSW.

L. E. FREDMAN

EARSMAN, WILLIAM PAISLEY (1884-1965), labour movement activist, was born on 16 March 1884 at Edinburgh, son of James McDonald Earsman, mason, and his wife Elizabeth, née Aitken. After education at a council school, Earsman completed an apprenticeship as a turner and a 'night-school' course. In 1908 he went to New Zealand. Two years later he came to Melbourne, and worked for the Camberwell Motor Works from June to September 1910, the Victorian Railways (to September 1914) and the Colonial Ammunition Co. (to July 1917), earning repute as a skilful tradesman.

In Edinburgh Earsman had been in the Amalgamated Society of Engineers, and he joined the Melbourne District branch — on its committee from March 1911, he was secretary in 1915-16 and was active in industrial disputes in 1917-19. A committed socialist and industrial unionist, from 1911 to 1916 he was a member of the Victorian Socialist Party, becoming director of the Socialist Sunday School (1912), acting secretary (1913) and trustee (1914-15). In 1913 he joined the Free Religious Fellowship and in 1915 the Anti-militarist and Anti-conscription League, being conspicuous in the referenda campaigns of 1916 and 1917.

In June 1917 Earsman initiated the Victorian Labor College, becoming secretary until mid-1919, when he moved to Sydney. He founded the New South Wales Labor College, acting as secretary and lecturer until April 1921. His pamphlet, *The proletariat and education*, was published in Melbourne in 1920.

A syndicalist with strong 'Wobbly' (Industrial Workers of the World) sympathies, Earsman appears to have been the single most important person involved in the formation of the Communist Party of Australia, and was elected secretary at its foundation meeting in Sydney on 30 October 1920. When the party split in December, Earsman led what became known as the 'Sussex Street' faction. Seeking recognition

for his group, Earsman went in April 1921 to the third Congress of the Third Communist International (Comintern) in Moscow. He was also at the Congress of the Red International of Labor Unions in July. In Moscow he abandoned his syndicalist position for official Comintern strategy which advocated political as well as industrial weapons in the revolutionary struggle.

When Earsman returned in December his papers were seized by the Commonwealth security service which had tracked him since early 1918. He became embroiled in the rivalry between the two Australian Communist parties before leaving in May 1922 for the fourth Congress of the Comintern in Moscow. He gained official recognition for the 'Sussex Street' party, became a member of the Comintern executive, met Trotsky (whom he greatly admired) and Lenin, and was made an honorary member of the Red Army. In London in January 1923 he learned that he was barred from Australia. After a few weeks in Edinburgh he went to Moscow to teach English at the Red Army Military Academy. Back in England in August 1924, he tested British machine tools for a Soviet importing agency.

In 1914 Earsman had revisited New Zealand to marry, on 8 April, at Leeston Presbyterian Church, his cousin Alison Lockhead Aitken. She joined him in Moscow in August 1923 but died in Edinburgh on 16 April 1925. On 29 October 1927 at St Vincent of Paul's Catholic Church, Sheffield, England, he married Margaret Ellen Killelea.

About that time Earsman left the Communist Party. He wanted to re-enter Australia but despite the support of Maurice Blackburn [q.v.7] and John Curtin, he was twice refused. In 1932 he returned to Edinburgh, joined the Labour Party in 1934, and in 1937-49 was secretary of the Edinburgh Trades Council. Now a moderate social democrat, he concealed his earlier affiliations. He was active in municipal affairs and a councillor of the Edinburgh Festival in 1946-62; in 1950 he was appointed O.B.E. He died of cancer in Edinburgh on 13 January 1965, survived by his second wife, their son, and the daughter of his first marriage. His widow believed that 'he was a man who wanted to leave the world a better place than he found it'.

A. Davidson, *The Communist Party of Australia* (Stanford, California, 1969); K. D. Buckley, *The Amalgamated Engineers in Australia, 1852-1920* (Canb, 1970); *Scotsman*, and *Edinburgh Evening News*, 14 Jan 1965; *Aust Left Review*, Oct-Nov 1970; Earsman papers (Special MSS Lib, Edinburgh Univ); F. Hancock papers (ML); Amalgamated Soc of Engineers, Melb District Cttee, Minutes, *and* Vic Labor College records (Univ Melb Archives); Vic Socialist Party records (NL); Military Intelligence and Investigation Branch records (AAO); information from Mrs M. E. Earsman, Edinburgh.

ANN TURNER

EAST, HUBERT (1862-1928) and HUBERT FRASER (1893-1959), drapers, were father and son. Hubert was born on 19 April 1862 at Ballyfarnon, Roscommon, Ireland, son of Henry East and his wife Margaret, née White. Educated at public schools, he was apprenticed to a Sligo draper in 1878-82 and then worked at Athy, County Kildare, until 1886. On 2 March that year at Sligo, he married Margretta Esther Greet and in June sailed from Glasgow in the *Cloncurry* for Queensland. Employed in various Brisbane drapery houses including Edwards & Chapman and Allan & Stark, he made a lifelong friend of a fellow employee Frank J. McDonnell [q.v.]. In November 1901, financed by Peter Murphy, a publican, he joined McDonnell in forming the new drapery house, McDonnell & East. They ran the company jointly as managing directors and occupied the chair alternately until East died on 26 May 1928. He was buried in Toowong cemetery and left an estate valued for probate at £14 959.

Hubert Fraser was born on 2 June 1893 in Brisbane and was educated at the Brisbane Normal School and privately. He and a brother joined the firm as shop assistants about 1908. He enlisted in the Australian Imperial Force in 1915, joined the Army Service Corps and served as a driver in motor transport from 1917 until his discharge in February 1920. He returned to McDonnell & East and, on the death of his father, joined the board, sharing the role of managing director and chairman with McDonnell's son. The firm proved remarkably successful and became one of Brisbane's major retail stores. It is the one major Brisbane store which has not succumbed to take-over from Sydney or Melbourne. East became the first president of the Brisbane Retailers' Association in 1933-37.

His deep involvement in the welfare of returned soldiers after World War I gained him award of the C.M.G. in 1937. He served as president of the Queensland branch of the Returned Soldiers and Sailors' Imperial League of Australia in 1923-30 and as vice-president in 1933-34. He was a foundation member of Legacy when it was formed in 1929 and active during its early years. During World War II he served as chairman of the Blinded Soldiers' Committee and as vice-chairman of the appeals committee of the Queensland Patriotic and Australian Comforts Fund (Queensland Branch). He was also prominent in other patriotic organizations and was vice-president of the Queensland Blinded Sailors and Soldiers' Association.

Fraser East devoted a large part of his life to helping others and especially former servicemen who were experiencing immense problems as a result of their wartime service. His major recreations were golf and tennis. A keen supporter of band music for many years, he was patron of the Queensland Band Association.

On 30 October 1930 at Toowong he married Enid Jeanette Howes; they had one son and two daughters. After an illness of several months, East died of cancer on 20 November 1959 in the Mater Private Hospital, Brisbane, and was cremated. He left an estate valued for probate at £32 458 in Queensland and £1016 in New South Wales.

M. G. Macdougall, *Notable men of Queensland – 1950* (Brisb, 1950); Syd Stock Exchange, Research and Statistical Section, *Company Review* (McDonnell and East), 18 May 1971, (copy held ANU Archives, Canb); *Courier-Mail*, 21 Nov 1959.

A. L. LOUGHEED

EASTERBROOK, CLAUDE CADMAN (1889-1975), soldier, was born on 25 May 1889 at Maitland, New South Wales, son of Elijah Easterbrook, cabinetmaker, and his wife Bridget, née Lynch, both native-born. His father later became a constable in the New South Wales Police Force and was stationed at Walgett and Murrurundi before moving to the lower Hunter where Claude went to the public schools at Waratah and Hamilton. On leaving school he joined the Postmaster General's Department but in November 1909, after some part-time military service, he enlisted in the Australian Military Forces (permanent staff) as a member of the 4th Infantry Regiment at Wallsend.

Before universal training could begin in 1911 competent instructional staff had to be found. To this end a special school was established at Albury. Among those on the first course in August 1910 was Staff Sergeant Major Easterbrook who in that rank had been appointed to the Australian Administration and Instructional Staff a month before. In January 1911 he returned to Newcastle and the 4th Northern Brigade. He stayed there until 6 October 1914 when he joined the Australian Imperial Force as staff sergeant major, serving briefly with the 6th Light Horse Regiment before going to the 7th. It was as a regimental sergeant major of that unit that he sailed for Egypt on 21 December. Five days earlier, at New Lambton, he had married Vivienne Muriel Nicholson (d.1965) with Methodist forms.

In August 1919 he was back in Australia,

a major who had been awarded the Military Cross and was about to receive the Distinguished Service Order and a mention in dispatches. He had been commissioned on Gallipoli in June 1915 and as a lieutenant was in command of the last detachment of the 7th L.H.R. to leave during the final hours of the evacuation. He was promoted captain on 26 March 1916.

After Gallipoli it was Sinai, Palestine and Trans-Jordan for the rest of the war, from Romani to the second action at Amman. Easterbrook served with the 7th L.H.R. until March 1917 when he was appointed staff captain, 2nd Light Horse Brigade. He was wounded at Wadi Ghuzze in April, resumed duty in June and on 5 October was promoted major; he then rejoined the 7th Regiment. Between June and September next year he commanded the 2nd Light Horse Training Regiment before being appointed brigade major, 2nd Light Horse Brigade, a post he held until the end of the war. His service was a blend of outstanding regimental and staff soldiering and was widely recognized as such.

When his A.I.F. service ended in October 1919 he reverted to his substantive rank of warrant officer in the A.M.F. In May 1920, on the permanent forces list once more, he became an area officer in Newcastle and adjutant and quartermaster of the 5th Battalion, 2nd Infantry Regiment. He was now quartermaster and honorary major, a rank he retained on appointment to the Australian Instructional Corps when it was formed in April 1921.

For the greater part of the next twenty years, during which there was to be no further advancement, Easterbrook served with the 1st Cavalry Brigade, the Army Service Corps and as assistant director of supplies and transport, 2nd Military District. In January 1936 he became quartermaster of the Royal Military College which was in its last year of exile in Sydney. He went home with it to Duntroon and stayed there until May 1940 when he was appointed assistant director of supplies and transport at Army Headquarters. Thereafter, as an assistant and then deputy director, he was a lieut-colonel and colonel. In 1948 he became chief instructor (R.M.C. Wing) at the Army Service Corps School and then chief instructor of the school itself.

When he retired on 6 September 1949 he was granted the honorary rank of colonel. Survived by his son, a graduate of Duntroon, and three daughters, he died in Melbourne on 8 May 1975 and was cremated with Anglican rites.

In appearance tall and spare (he was the light horseman of the picture books), in manner modest and unassuming, in standard of behaviour uncompromising, in character forthright, he was representative of the best in the Light Horse and later in the Australian Instructional Corps. Never one to force advice on others he gave it generously when asked. Young men making their way in the corps remembered it and were grateful. So too were those Duntroon cadets perceptive enough to realize that here was someone who on active service had been, and patently still was, the officer they hoped sometime to be. No one would have been more embarrassed than Claude Easterbrook to have heard that said.

H. S. Gullett, *The A.I.F. in Sinai and Palestine* (Syd, 1923); J. D. Richardson, *The history of the 7th Light Horse Regiment A.I.F.* (Syd, 1923); C. E. W. Bean, *The story of Anzac*, 2 (Syd, 1924); *London Gazette*, 1 Jan 1918, 12 Dec 1919, 3 Jan 1920, 8 June 1939; *Army J*, July 1975; Easterbrook papers, file 419/30/18 (AWM); family information.

G. D. SOLOMON

EATHER, RICHMOND CORNWALLIS (1888-1966), soldier, station-owner and manager, was born on 18 January 1888 at Goodooga, New South Wales, son of John Rowland Eather, storekeeper, and his wife Hannah Anne, née Crothers, both native-born. He was educated at Goodooga Public School but left at 13 to work in local shearing sheds. In 1907 he moved to Richmond, Queensland, and later to Muttaburra and Hughenden, to manage properties owned by his uncles, R., T. and H. Crothers.

Eather enlisted in the Australian Imperial Force as a private on 17 June 1915, embarked with reinforcements for the 15th Battalion in August and saw action at Gallipoli. In March 1916 he was transferred to the 47th Battalion which reached France in June and in August-September fought in the battles of Pozières and Mouquet Farm. Eather was awarded the Military Medal for personal bravery during this period. Promoted sergeant in September, he was posted to the 6th Officer Cadet Battalion at Oxford, England, and in March 1917 was commissioned second lieutenant in the 25th Battalion.

Early in June 1918 a series of minor counter-blows was made by British and Australian formations to relieve pressure on their French allies. On 10 June near Morlancourt the 25th took its objective in a twenty-minute assault. As the battalion's intelligence officer, Eather showed conspicuous gallantry by maintaining communications with the attacking companies after the signals officer had been wounded. He repeatedly passed through heavy enemy barrages to bring in the wounded as well as to maintain telephone lines to the forward companies, and for these actions was awarded the Military Cross.

In September the allied offensive against the Hindenburg line began, and on 3 October the 25th Battalion spearheaded its brigade's attack in a two-corps assault on the Beaurevoir line. Eather again showed great bravery and initiative for which he won a Bar to his Military Cross. The battalion attacked at 6 a.m. across three-quarters of a mile (1200 m) of open country and, after hard fighting, captured its objective. Eather then went across to the right flank under heavy fire and returned with information that the neighbouring battalion was unable to move forward. The 25th immediately established a flank defence to protect against an enemy counter-attack. Eather then went further forward towards the enemy line and brought back valuable information for guiding the next phase of this crucial operation. He was transferred to the 26th Battalion later in the month.

On 13 March 1919 at Knockbreda, Antrim, Ireland, Eather married Mary Jane McFarlane Longmore, a British Army nurse who had won the Royal Red Cross. They returned to Australia in May and until 1927 managed a family property at Muttaburra. Eather then managed Sylvania station near Hughenden and eventually bought the partners out; in 1954 he sold Sylvania and retired to Warwick. He was a prominent citizen in the Hughenden, Richmond and Muttaburra districts and served several terms on the Flinders Shire Council. His main hobbies were horse-racing and exhibiting hacks and hunters in shows. Survived by his wife and two daughters, he died on 21 April 1966 at Warwick.

C. E. W. Bean, *The A.I.F. in France*, 1916-18 (Syd, 1929, 1933, 1937, 1942); *London Gazette*, 8 Dec 1916, 24 Sept 1918, 8 Mar 1919; *North Queensland Register*, 23 Apr 1966; War diaries, 25th and 47th Battalions, A.I.F. (AWM); information from Mrs T. Keenan, Muttaburra, *and* Mr H. Eather, Maxwelton, Qld.   DARRYL MCINTYRE

EDDEN, ALFRED (1850-1930), coalminer and politician, was born on 24 December 1850 at Tamworth, Staffordshire, England, posthumous son of John Edden, labourer, and his wife Mary, née Thirlby. From 10 he worked in a colliery. On 20 February 1871 at Hucknall, Nottinghamshire, where he was working, he married Maria Brown; about 1879 they migrated to New South Wales and settled near Newcastle. By 1884 he was living at Adamstown and working in the nearby Waratah colliery. He became a Methodist lay-preacher and in 1887 was a founder of the Lay Methodist Church which rejected paid clergy. When Adamstown was incorporated in January 1886 he was elected alderman, later serving as mayor in 1889 and from February to July 1891.

Edden was president of the Waratah colliery lodge during the strike of 1888 when he was arrested in a confrontation with strike-breakers. In 1891 he became one of the first Labor members in the Legislative Assembly, representing Northumberland. A protectionist, he opposed the party solidarity pledge and won Kahibah as an independent Labor candidate in 1894, but next year he rejoined the party. In the assembly he took a particular interest in the welfare of coalminers. Though his own measures for an eight-hour day were defeated in the Upper House, he influenced the government's Coal Mines Regulation Act of 1896 – in particular a clause which guaranteed proper ventilation.

With J. R. Dacey and W. A. Holman [qq.v.] and others of the 'solid six', Edden helped to manoeuvre Labor into supporting (Sir) William Lyne's [q.v.] 1899 censure motion, thus ensuring its success. He expected more concessions from Lyne; he also welcomed the opportunity to regain the independence which he felt Labor had compromised by its support for (Sir) George Reid [q.v.] since 1894. W. M. Hughes [q.v.] described Alf Edden as a 'powerfully built man in his fifties, of medium height, grey-haired, red-faced, bubbling with energy and goodwill to all mankind'. Naturally eloquent, he spoke in a rich Staffordshire dialect.

Edden remained in State politics after Federation. He supported B. R. Wise's [q.v.] Industrial Arbitration Act (1901), served for some time on the Parliamentary Standing Committee for Public Works and, when Labor won office in October 1910, became secretary for mines. That year he became chairman of the Miners' Accident Relief Board and in 1913 carried an amending Coal Mines Regulation Act. However his expressed irritation with strikes which he considered unnecessary and unreasonable lost him support, even among the miners, and he was dropped from the cabinet after the election of December. He remained close to Holman and was expelled with him by the Political Labor League in November 1916 for supporting conscription. He won Kahibah in 1917 as a Nationalist, but in 1920, with the introduction of proportional representation, he decided not to seek re-election.

His wife had died on 1 June 1887; on 28 September that year he married a widow Mary Ann George, née Langley, at the Adamstown registry office. She died on 18 March 1929. Edden died at his daughter's home at Redfern, Sydney, on 27 July 1930, and was buried with Masonic rites in the Church of England section of Sandgate cemetery, Newcastle. He was survived by six of his nine children, two sons and a daughter of each marriage. His estate, valued for probate at £2156, was divided among them, his stepchildren and a grandchild.

Edden, though considered 'a forceful speaker' was well liked by his opponents, in parliament and in the party, among whom he enjoyed a reputation of being generous with his limited means.

W. F. Morrison, *The Aldine centennial history of New South Wales*, 2 (Syd, 1888); H. V. Evatt, *Australian Labour leader . . . W. A. Holman* (Syd, 1940); W. M. Hughes, *Crusts and crusades* (Syd, 1947); E. Ross, *A history of the Miners' Federation of Australia* (Syd, 1970); B. Nairn, *Civilising capitalism* (Canb, 1973); *Daily Telegraph* (Syd) 2 July 1891; *SMH*, 7 Nov 1916, 30 Mar, 2 Apr 1917, 28 Jan 1930; *Newcastle Morning Herald*, 28, 29 Jan 1930.

W. G. McMINN

EDDY, EDWARD MILLER GARD (1851-1897), railway commissioner, was born on 24 July 1851 in England, son of Edward Miller Eddy, marine engineer. After elementary schooling, he became a junior clerk in 1865 with the London and North Western Railway. Promoted in 1866 to the general superintendent's office, Eddy worked under G.P. Neele, a pioneer of the scientific construction of railway timetables. On 29 October 1874 at the parish of St Mary, Chester, he married a widow, Gwen Ellen Lowndes, née Roberts (d. 1882); they had a daughter and three sons. In 1875 Eddy became district superintendent of the Chester and Holyhead section of the railway. His success in improving the running of trains over this difficult area led to his promotion as Southern division superintendent in 1878. Assistant superintendent from 1885, he became involved in the famous 'railway races' to Scotland, valuing their publicity aspect and using them to gain money from his board to improve safety. Eddy introduced reforms designed to reduce costs and increase traffic. In 1887 he was seconded to the ailing Caledonian Railway as assistant general manager. Next year he accepted the position of chief commissioner of the New South Wales Railways at a salary of £3000 with a future increase left to the 'justice of the Government and Parliament'. He wrote: 'I take so much delight in my work, and I can see how, in a country which will owe much to the judicious management and extension of its railways, I could be of great service to the Colony, and also obtain credit for myself'. Described by the acting agent-general Sir Daniel Cooper [q.v.3] as of an 'open, clear countenance; six feet high;

nice firm manner', he arrived in Sydney in October.

The Government Railways Act of 1888, which established a board of three commissioners, was an attempt by the Parkes [q.v.5] ministry to create an efficient management structure for a system which had been bedevilled by political interference at every level. That political aspects, ostensibly removed by the Act, still lingered, became evident when the appointment of W. M. Fehon [q.v.] as second commissioner precipitated the fall of the Parkes government in January 1889. Although Eddy was not affected directly by the change of government or by the subsequent royal commission, the imbroglio made him wary of parliament. In this political and economic context the commissioners were expected to 'make the railways pay'.

One of Eddy's first acts was to arrange for a complete examination of locomotive and rolling stock by R.P. Williams and William Thow [q.v.] of the South Australian Railways. Major changes were recommended and Thow was appointed in May 1889 as locomotive engineer. An abortive attempt was made with Henry Hudson [q.v.4] and a consortium of British manufacturers to set up a local locomotive building plant. Eddy's administrative reforms were immediate and numerous, but his proposed staff changes and reductions were resisted. Parkes protected Eddy but by 1890 industrial relations were worsening. A series of disastrous accidents brought Eddy into conflict with William Schey [q.v.], general secretary of the Amalgamated Railway and Tramway Services Association. In 1891 Eddy had H. C. Hoyle, the association's president, dismissed for making an off-duty political speech. When Schey and, later, Hoyle entered parliament they subjected the chief commissioner to remorseless criticism. Schey launched a major attack in 1892, alleging nepotism and financial mismanagement. Completely exonerated by the subsequent royal commission, Eddy found that he was separated from the union movement.

But he was a benevolent employer, providing many educational and welfare programmes for railway workers and their dependents. Eddy was the driving force behind the establishment of the Railway Institute. The sense of identity which he encouraged among his employees may have contributed to the very spirit of the unionism that he opposed; it certainly led to the development of a mystique about him that railwaymen have nurtured to the present day.

Despite political obstruction and criticism and economic depression Eddy extended the railway system. He introduced more powerful locomotives, better rolling stock, improved facilities at stations, better public relations and an active advertising campaign which encouraged new traffic. While unsuccessful in bringing the railway to the centre of Sydney, he enlarged the tramway network, and permitted the first experiments in electric traction.

Before Eddy's term of office expired in 1895 he returned to England. At the International Railway Congress in London he read an important paper based on his Australian experience. His several offers to remain in England included the general managership of the South Eastern Railway, but the urging of the colonial government and demonstrations of public support determined him to 'sink all personal considerations' and accept re-engagement, even though his promised salary rise was not forthcoming.

The effects of the 1890s depression and the beginning of the long drought eroded finances and the volume of traffic and Eddy found himself with less parliamentary support. His health, indifferent for some years, began to deteriorate. Formerly a keen sportsman with an especial interest in cycling, he now had to abandon much physical activity. A painful condition diagnosed as a kidney complaint made even standing difficult for any long period. He collapsed on 21 June 1897 on Wallangarra station while journeying to Brisbane, where he died later that evening. His body was sent back to Sydney for burial in the Anglican section of Waverley cemetery. He was survived by his four children and by his second wife Ellen, née Wilkinson, whom he had married on 15 April 1886 at Walsall, Staffordshire, England.

Like Richard Speight [q.v.6] in Victoria, Eddy was essentially a railway manager rather than an engineer. A man of careful penmanship, and with an accountant's eye for figures, he was able to leave the mechanical side of the railways to those whom he recognized as technically competent. He nevertheless retained firm overall control and enlisted the complete loyalty of a wide range of subordinates, giving shape and form to a system which had grown irregularly in its first forty years. Between 1888 and 1897 a profit of nearly £3 million had been earned and the percentage of working expenses to gross earnings had declined from 66.69 to 54.47; the New South Wales railways were well prepared to face the challenges of the new century. The Eddy Memorial Railway, and Tramway Orphan fund was established in 1904.

G.P. Neele, *Railway reminiscences* (Lond, 1974); *V&P* (LA NSW), 1887-88,6, 625, 1892-93, 5, 159, 543, 1894-95, 1, 303, 341, 4, 623, 1895, 3, 595; *Engineering Review* (Lond), 21 Jan 1895, p 207; *Engineering* (Lond), 25 June 1897, p 860; *Australasian*, 26 June 1897; *Sydney Mail*, 3 July 1897; *SMH*, 15 Mar 1960; *Sun* (Syd), 21 Aug 1979; personal file, Chief Commisioner E. M. G. Eddy (Public Transport Commission Archives, Syd).

R. M. AUDLEY
K. J. CABLE

EDELFELT, ERIK GUSTAF and ISABELLE; *see* BEAN, ISABELLE

EDGAR, ALEXANDER ROBERT (1850-1914), Methodist minister and social reformer, was born on 8 April 1850 in County Tipperary, Ireland, second of five sons and four daughters of Edward Edgar, engineer, and his wife Mary, née Haslam. The family landed in Melbourne in February 1855, camping on arrival at Fitzroy, then residing at Windsor where Alexander went to All Saints' School. They moved in 1857 to St Arnaud, where he attended day school until he was 14. He was successively pupil-teacher, gold prospector, tutor, prospector again, and assistant to the district surveyor.

Although an Anglican, Edgar was influenced by Rev. Albert Stubbs to join the St Arnaud Methodist Church in June 1867. Finding employment difficult to obtain he left in August for Ballarat, Castlemaine and Warrenheip, before returning in March 1869 to join his father in working unsuccessfully a St Arnaud mine. He then moved to Pleasant Creek (Stawell), working manually at the mines. As a lay preacher, he gave his first sermon at Concongella Creek on 18 July.

Edgar was nominated in January 1872 to the Methodist Provisional Theological Institution attached to Wesley College, Melbourne. Completing two years training, he was appointed to Kangaroo Flat in April 1874, followed by Inglewood (1876-79) during, which time seventeen new churches were built. He was ordained at Wesley Church, Melbourne, early in 1878 and on 3 April married 29-year-old Katharine Haslam. He was appointed to Long Gully, Bendigo (1879-81); Sebastopol, Ballarat (1881-84); Port Melbourne (1884-87) where he opened a 'ragged school' in the slum area, was active in the temperance movement and became chairman of the local option campaign; Chilwell (1887-90); and Geelong (1890-93) where Christian Endeavour was introduced to Australia, and a mission established. A tall, broad-shouldered man with a magnetic personality, Edgar was a dynamic preacher and persuasive evangelist. His organizing ability and sympathetic understanding of and sincere activism in social problems extended his influence. Asked why he helped the undeserving, he replied, 'I spend my life in giving men another chance'. He was an excellent lecturer.

In 1893 the Methodist Conference established the Central Methodist Mission at Wesley Church, with Edgar as superintendent and A. J. Derrick as secretary. At this time there was great public concern over the exploitation of labour by many employers during the widespread unemployment of the early 1890s. In 1893 the government appointed a board of inquiry into the Factories Act, particularly the practice of sweating. Edgar joined a deputation of tailors and bootmakers to the chief secretary in 1894. Meetings on 'The sweating evil' were called at the Central Mission on the following Sunday afternoons and both were filled to capacity to hear Edgar, S. Mauger and Dr W. Maloney [qq.v.], who was an inquiry member.

This inaugurated Pleasant Sunday Afternoon services as a weekly feature; they continued as a major forum for social, political and religious leaders. Music of good standard was introduced and applause permitted. The Gaiety Theatre was rented in 1900 to hold crowded meetings. Old-age pensions and women's suffrage were advocated, and in May 1906 the fiery W. H. Judkins [q.v.] used the forum to launch the Forward Social Reform Movement to attack gambling, liquor, prostitution, corruption, and John Wren [q.v.]. It was said that 'services at Wesley were ritualistic in the morning, socialistic in the afternoon and evangelistic at night'.

As a result of his anti-sweating activities, Edgar was appointed chairman of the first Victorian wages board – the clothing – and later the coopers' and jam boards. On 19 September 1901, in giving evidence to the royal commission on the operation of the factories and shops law, he stated that as board chairman he had negotiated agreements without ever having to give a casting vote. He was also a member of the board of inquiry on unemployment (1899-1900).

Other social activities initiated by Edgar in the depressed 1890s included the village settlement at Kardella, Gippsland; free labour bureaus; unemployed committees; the Sisterhood and Sisters' Home; South Yarra Central Mission Rescue Home for women; Central Mission Hospice for men; Tally Ho boys' farm at Burwood; Bichloride of Gold Institute of Victoria for alcoholism and drugs; and the annual Old Folks' At Home gathering. Open-air meetings with a brass band and singing were a feature of Edgar's mission. When the 'move on' clause against street meetings was invoked Edgar

preached while striding down Bourke Street.

In a lecture on 'the need for good government' on 19 August 1894, Edgar was reported in the *Age* as having said: 'You have individuals in Parliament who are a disgrace to the community; men who are known to be liars and profligates; men who are prepared to tread under foot everything that is noble to attain their ends'. On 22 August he was called to the bar of the Legislative Assembly on a breach of privilege charge, but after debate, the House proceeded to the next order of the day.

In 1901 Edgar became president of the Wesleyan Methodist Church, and next year Methodist Union with the United Free Methodist, Bible Christian and Primitive Methodist churches was achieved. His health was affected by the strain of his many activities and he visited England three times to recuperate from breakdowns, and for eye treatment. In 1906 he visited British Methodist missions and North America. He preached in Wesley Church for the last time on 26 January 1912. Edgar died of heart disease on 23 April 1914 at Hawthorn, survived by his wife and two daughters of their eight children. He was buried in Melbourne general cemetery. A memorial tablet and a stained-glass window were placed in Wesley Church.

A brother William Haslam (1858-1948) was an estate agent and a member of the Legislative Council in 1904-13 and 1917-48 and of the John Murray and W. A. Watt [qq.v.] ministries in 1909-13.

L. Fison, *The Methodist history of Victoria and Tasmania 1898-1908* (Melb, nd); *Souvenir of a great historical event* (Melb, 1902); I. E. Watkin, *Jubilee history of Wesley Church ... 1858-1908* (Melb, 1908); A. J. Derrick, *The story of the Central Mission* (Melb, 1918); W. J. Palamountain, *A Methodist greatheart* (Melb, 1933); C. I. Benson (ed), *A century of Victorian Methodism* (Melb, 1935); *PD* (Vic), 1894, p 1403, 1446; R. Howe, 'Protestantism, Social Christianity, and the ecology of Melbourne, 1890-1900', *Hist Studies,* April 1980; *Age,* 20, 23, 25 Aug 1894, 24 Apr 1914; *Australasian,* 25 Aug 1894; *Punch* (Melb), 27 May 1909; *Argus,* 20 Apr 1914; E. M. Wilson, The campaign for national righteousness ... 1900-16 (B.A. Hons thesis, Univ Melb, 1957).

IAN F. McLAREN

EDGELL, ROBERT GORDON (1866-1948), civil engineer, farmer and manufacturer, was born on 6 February 1866 at Hunters Hill, Sydney, son of Henry Edgell, insurance clerk from England, and his native-born wife Charlotte Packer, née Gordon. In 1872 the family moved to northern Tasmania, where Gordon was educated privately and under John Clemon at

Evandale Public School. He joined the Mount Bischoff Tin Mining Co. as a cadet in 1882. Edgell returned to Sydney in 1885 and joined Mort's [q.v.5] Dock and Engineering Co. Ltd. On completing his apprenticeship he was appointed a draughtsman. He also studied mining-engineering and metallurgy and was briefly a consulting engineer to a chemical manufacturer.

In mid-1890 Edgell joined the roads and bridges branch of the New South Wales Department of Public Works as a temporary draughtsman, designing the lift bridge over the Murray River at Swan Hill, Victoria, the swing mechanism for the Pyrmont Bridge, Sydney, and bridges over many northern rivers in New South Wales. In 1895 he was in charge of the Wollombi district, and was transferred as road superintendent to Maitland in 1898 and to Bathurst in 1902.

At All Souls Anglican Church, Leichhardt, Edgell married Elsie Catherine Keep (d. 1939) on 20 August 1896. On retiring from the public service in 1906, he and his wife bought Bradwardine, near Bathurst, from Sir Francis Suttor [q.v.6]. He planted a hundred acres with apples and pears on the uplands, and asparagus on the flats, applying the latest technology to farming – including mechanical cultivation, elevated water channels fitted with irrigation gates, soil analyses and other innovations.

In 1925 Edgell sent his eldest son Maxwell to the United States of America to learn asparagus canning techniques; in September next year, in partnership with two sons Maxwell and Hampden, he opened his first cannery at Bradwardine in a galvanized iron shed, where the small staff made their own cans and sealed them with a hand-held soldering-iron. In 1930 he registered a public company, Gordon Edgell and Sons Ltd and was chairman of directors until 1948. Under Edgell's guidance the firm prospered despite the Depression: a new, larger factory was built in 1933, and extended with administrative blocks in 1938; a popular product was launched – the growing and canning of green peas; and additional farming land was bought and contracts entered into with private growers. The industry boomed during World War II as it supplied food to the Australian and American armed forces, as well as to the domestic market. Edgell began processing carrots, apples, cauliflowers, Brussels sprouts, potatoes, tomatoes, and a range of soups. He supervised the purchase of land at Cowra and in 1943 started another cannery there.

Edgell was sometime president of the Bathurst Fruit Growers' Association, bowling and Rotary clubs, and had become an associate member of the Institution of Civil Engineers, London, the Institution of Engineers and Shipbuilders in Scotland, the Royal Society of New South Wales and the Engineering Association of New South Wales in the 1890s. He bought his first car in 1903. For his services to Bathurst he was awarded King George V's silver jubilee medal in 1935 and King George VI's coronation medal in 1937. On 2 December 1948 Edgell died at Bradwardine, Bathurst, and was cremated with Anglican rites in Sydney. He was survived by his three sons. By that time Edgell's canned foods had become a well-established brand name with a reputation for quality throughout Australia. His estate was sworn for probate at £29 900.

G. Edgell and Son, *1930-1955, 25 years of achievement* (Bathurst, 1955); F. Clune, *Saga of Sydney* (Syd, 1961); B. H. Hillsmith (ed), *The first fifty years 1926-1976* (Crows Nest, nd); *National Advocate*, 3 Dec 1948.   K. L. FRY

EDGERTON, ERIC HENRY DRUMMOND (1897-1918), soldier, was born on 1 April 1897 at Moonee Ponds, Melbourne, third son and fifth child of James Edgerton (d. 1946), secretary of an iron-rolling mill, and his wife Florence Grace, née Shacklock (d. 1943), both Victorian-born. He was educated at Hawksburn State School and from 1911 at Wesley College, where he was very active in life-saving activities. In 1915 he passed the leaving certificate and on 14 April, describing himself as a student, enlisted in the Australian Imperial Force as a private.

Edgerton left Australia on 25 June with the 1st reinforcements to the 24th Battalion, 6th Brigade. After training in Egypt he saw active service at Gallipoli where, for daring patrol work in the defence of Lone Pine, he was promoted corporal in November and awarded the Military Medal. He served at Anzac until the evacuation and then, after a short time in the Suez Canal zone, embarked for France in March 1916. In August, amid the great confusion at Pozières Ridge, he again distinguished himself by his cool and courageous conduct; in November he was promoted sergeant. Next February, at Warlencourt on the Somme, he was awarded a Bar to his M.M. – the first in the 6th Brigade – for a daring and valuable patrol; on 8 March he was commissioned in the field.

In August 1917 Edgerton went to England to attend bayonet-fighting and physical-training schools. On 5 September he was promoted lieutenant and before rejoining the battalion in France in April 1918 went with his father and brother James on a short tour of Scotland and the English Lakes district. In May he led several patrols to the River Ancre and on the 19th he and his men – rushing and silencing enemy strong points – played a key part in the capture of Ville-sur-Ancre. For cool initiative, courage and brilliant leadership on this occasion he was awarded the Distinguished Service Order. On 14 July he commanded the Australian troops in the march through Paris.

Three days after the great advance on 8 August the battalion went into the front line between Rainecourt and Framerville. On the night of 11-12 August, while standing talking to his men on the post, Edgerton was killed by a stray bullet from out of the darkness. He was buried first at Blangy-Tronville and later in the military cemetery at Villers-Bretonneux: no man in the 24th was more deeply mourned. He was just 21 and unmarried. On 8 November he was mentioned in dispatches.

Very boyish-looking, lithe and powerfully built, Edgerton combined a sunny, generous and unassuming nature with extraordinary energy, courage and leadership. Clear-headed in danger, he quickly saw his duty which he performed with directness and singleness of aim; to his commanding officer, Lieut-Colonel W. E. James [q.v.], who had recommended him for the Victoria Cross, Edgerton was 'the "show" boy of the battalion'. According to a digger, he often carried up to three rifles and the packs of men who had knocked up on the march, and 'would have carried the burdens of the whole A.I.F. if he could'.

Edgerton's letters home reveal a sensitive nature, love of beauty and a strong Christian faith: a padre wrote that the war's effect was to deepen his character and make him 'a true representative of the Master'. He is commemorated by a stained glass window in the Cato Uniting Church, Elsternwick, Melbourne. Of his four brothers William became headmaster commander, Royal Australian Naval College; James was an industrialist and founder of the Australian Institute of Metals; and Clive, who joined the Royal Australian Air Force, was killed in a flying accident in 1935.

W. J. Harvey, *The red and white diamond* (Melb, 1920?); C. E. W. Bean, *The A.I.F. in France*, 1918 (Syd, 1942); G. Blainey et al, *Wesley College. The first hundred years* (Melb, 1967); *Wesley College Chronicle*, Easter 1911, Dec 1914, Dec 1915, Dec 1918, May 1919; *London Gazette*, 27 Oct 1916, 11 May 1917, 16 Sept, 31 Dec 1918; *Reveille* (Syd), May 1938; E. Edgerton diary, 1915-18, and letters (AWM); information from Mr I. R. E. Clarke, Balwyn North, Melb.   G. P. WALSH

EDKINS, EDWARD ROWLAND HUEY (1871-1939), pastoralist, and BOYD ROBERTSON HUEY (1882-1930), racing driver, were sons of Edward Rowland Edkins, pastoralist, and his wife Edwina Marion, née Huey, daughter of a pioneer Tasmanian doctor. The family had settled in the Gulf country managing Beamsbrook station on the Albert River, Queensland, in the early 1860s. Edward Rowland Huey was born on 30 January 1871 at Maryborough. Educated at Launceston Grammar School, Tasmania, and at Wesley College, Melbourne, he learned the pastoral business chiefly as a jackeroo on Kensington Downs, Queensland, under John Cameron [q.v.7].

In August 1890 Edward selected his own property, Bimbah, near Longreach, and lived there for the rest of his life. He soon became president of the Mitchell Selectors' Association and was president of the succeeding Graziers' Association of Central and North Queensland in 1918-22. He represented the latter in the United Graziers' Association of which he was vice-president in 1920-21 and an executive officer from 1921. Frequently president of the Longreach Pastoral and Agricultural Society, he helped to found the Longreach Shire Council, became its first chairman and occupied the position many times thereafter. As his business interests expanded, he became chairman of Edkins, Marsh & Co. Ltd, which owned a stock and station agency and a chain of wool-scours, and Edkins, Campbell & Co. which controlled seven large stations including Bimbah.

An enthusiastic sportsman, Edkins played tennis and cricket and chaired football, tennis and cricket clubs. His main love was the turf and besides being president of the Longreach Jockey Club for nearly forty years, he founded the Longreach Amateur Racing Club in 1912 and was its president for many years. His Snapshot won the Queensland Cup in 1908 and his Piastoon won the Sydney Cup in 1927. He is credited with having initiated the practice of positioning judges well back from the edge of race tracks. On 30 April 1894 at Rockhampton he married Lucy Elizabeth Rule; they had three children. Edkins died of cerebro-vascular disease at Longreach on 23 June 1939 leaving an estate valued for probate at £21 457. He was buried in the Anglican section of Longreach cemetery.

His brother Boyd was born on 12 December 1882 at Mount Cornish Station, Muttaburra, Queensland. Educated at The King's School, Parramatta, New South Wales, he managed the family's Malboona briefly, but country life had little appeal for him and he returned to Sydney about 1905. In August 1906, in the chapel of The King's School, he married Katherine Muriel Edwards: they had two children. Edkins was employed initially by Kinglec Ltd, selling farm machinery, but about 1908 he joined the motor dealer George Innes, agent for Vauxhall and Humber cars. Just before World War I he established an independent business called Motor House in Milford Street. After the war he floated this as a company, Boyd Edkins Ltd. To prove the worth of their cars, retailers often took a leading part in races and rallies. Edkins twice broke the speed record from Melbourne to Sydney, in 1914 and in March 1916. He held hill-climb records in both New South Wales and Queensland and in December 1922 broke the record from Sydney to Brisbane.

For four years Edkins was president of the Motor Traders' Association of New South Wales. He chaired the inaugural meeting in 1920 of the National Roads Association, was chairman of its provisional committee, and became one of its first vice-presidents. He negotiated for amalgamation with the equivalent Victorian association, was a leader of the 1923 reorganization as the National Roads and Motorists' Association, and was a councillor of the association until 1929. The police consulted him frequently on traffic policy.

Edkins was frequently under stress because of the need to pay for imported cars before they were unloaded from ships, a practice which often necessitated a scramble for funds when a cargo arrived. He died in Sydney of chronic nephritis on 23 January 1930 leaving an estate valued for probate at £14 644. He was cremated.

M. J. Fox (ed), *The history of Queensland*, 2 (Brisb, 1921); *Pastoral Review*, 15 Apr 1916, p 336, 16 May 1918, p 501, 14 Sep 1921, p 456, 15 July 1939, p 755; *Sea, Land and Air*, 1 Sept 1922, p 444; *Motor Trade J*, May 1927, p 33, 15 Dec 1929, p 28, 15 Feb 1930, p 52; A. Wilkinson, The NRMA story . . . (unfinished, held by NRMA,Syd).

A. I. McMurchy

EDMENTS, ALFRED (1853-1909), merchant and philanthropist, was born on 17 October 1853 at Whitechapel, London, son of James Edments, labourer, and his wife Ann, née Lyons. After brief schooling he worked for a firm of cork merchants but in his twentieth year sailed for Sydney, arriving virtually penniless. He joined his brother James, a contractor at Cowra, but soon returned to Sydney and was employed by a wholesale drapery firm for four years. To gain further experience he went to Wellington, New Zealand, to manage a dairy-produce store, but though the business thrived under his direction, in 1880 he went back to Sydney and became an auctioneer and commission agent in the firm of James Walker.

In 1888 Edments established himself as an auctioneer in Melbourne but soon founded the Melbourne Supply Stores at 82 Bourke Street. The firm became noted for its watches, clocks, jewellery, cutlery and fancy goods. Edments's hard work and intelligence brought prosperity and he established branch stores in several Melbourne suburbs and at Geelong; later two shops were opened in Hobart.

Edments made the first of three overseas buying trips in 1891-92 and established a buying office in London. In search of novelties he travelled through Europe and the United States of America and, with an ever-increasing trade, he employed English and Continental buyers to assist him. His fancy goods business was the largest in Victoria and became one of the largest of its kind in the Commonwealth. On 15 September 1896 he married Annie Fennell and they made their home at Goodwood, Canterbury Road, Surrey Hills. Edments was a strong-featured, good-looking man, with wide-apart blue eyes, short-cropped hair and a full moustache, a kind-hearted citizen who, though without a family of his own, loved children. He was also fond of animals, especially horses.

Edments established his main Melbourne store at 309-311 Bourke Street in a three-storied spacious building. He believed in the principle of 'spot cash' and conducted a large cash business through the post, inviting country shopkeepers to inspect his wholesale stock in the upper floors. To him, one satisfied customer was worth a page of advertisements. He trained his staff well and was ahead of his time in his consideration of them. He distributed a proportion of profits half-yearly in the form of staff premiums, and he gave full holiday pay; their salaries, and often their medical bills, were paid when they were ill. He made a substantial donation to the (Royal) Melbourne Hospital and his employees were obliged each to contribute one penny weekly towards its support.

Continual hard work caused Edments's health to deteriorate while he was still in his forties and, in the last nine months of his life, he managed his business from his home. There, on 13 July 1909, he died of heart disease, leaving an estate valued for probate at £107 594 and an enlightened will which enabled his trustees to expand his business should they wish to do so. In 1916 a store was set up in Adelaide and in 1928, also in Adelaide, a chain of stores was created where nothing was priced over 2s. 6d. (25¢). In the early 1930s there were twenty-three Edments stores, many in the Melbourne suburbs. An outstanding provision of his will was that made for charities in the Melbourne and metropolitan area by the establishment of the Alfred Edments Trust, formed in perpetuity. The splendid benefaction is a memorial to a vigorous yet unassuming merchant who, arriving destitute in Australia, built up a notable business and a considerable fortune.

J. Smith (ed), *Cyclopedia of Victoria*, 1 (Melb, 1903); J Allan (ed), *The Victorian centenary book* (np, 1936); *Aust Storekeepers' J*, 21 October 1904, p 11, 31 July 1909, pp 55, 57, 30 October 1909, p 31.
NEILMA SIDNEY

EDMOND, JAMES (1859-1933), journalist, was born on 21 April 1859 at Glasgow, Scotland, son of James Edmond, carpetmaker and cloth-cutter, and his wife Janet, née Dickson. His formal schooling lasted only until he was 12, but he supplemented it with assiduous reading in the Glasgow Public Library. After some years as an insurance clerk, he migrated in 1878 to New Zealand, where he worked in a sweets factory before moving to Victoria about 1884 and then to Queensland. By claiming experience he did not have, he became a proofreader and possibly also a reporter on the Rockhampton *Morning Bulletin*; he began sending paragraphs of comment on financial matters to the Sydney *Bulletin*. Its editor J. F. Archibald [q.v.3] was impressed by Edmond's ability to write about politics and finance not only lucidly and cogently, but also with a dry and pungent humour. He invited him in 1886 to join the small full-time staff, and commented later to others, 'Jimmy's the only man I know who can get fun out of a balance-sheet'.

Fun was an integral part of the *Bulletin*'s most serious business. Edmond's humour – discursive, sometimes ponderous, always erudite, inclining to grotesquerie – balanced Archibald's finer mischief in the orchestration of the journal, while his editorials gave it range and strength. From 1890 Edmond was associate editor, from 1892 financial editor and chief deviser of the celebrated 'Wild Cat' columns. He also contributed dramatic criticism, paragraph material throughout the paper – some of it carrying his pseudonym 'Titus Salt' – and occasional short stories. He was editor from 1903 until 1914, when he retired on the grounds of ill-health and exhaustion.

Much was claimed, both during Edmond's lifetime and after it, for his editorial influence upon the makers of the Australian Constitution and on the political leaders of the early Commonwealth. He argued untiringly against overseas borrowing, in favour of fiscal self-sufficiency and therefore also for protection; patiently, through the long campaign for Federation, he sorted out the problems of tariffs and national taxation *vis-a-vis* the competing interests of the un-

equally populated colonies. His 'A policy for the Commonwealth', first published as a series of *Bulletin* leaders between August and December 1900, and later re-issued as a pamphlet, brought together his principal arguments for a federated, protectionist White Australia. He also advocated Federal administration of the Northern Territory, particularly to prevent South Australia from permitting its control by overseas-based companies using black or coloured labour.

Elsewhere, he argued for Federal control of education, and also of all railways and rivers. The makers of the Constitution clearly did not always agree with him, and were not persuaded by the *Bulletin* on every relevant point; and the relations between them may not have been so much a matter of (unprovable) influence as of mutual reinforcement, shared participation in a common framework of pragmatic, liberal reformism. Edmond certainly drew the *Bulletin* from its early maverick role into the dominant areas of debate. In the course of developing its practical nationalism, he let its republican idealism drop into obscurity; he also prepared the ground for Australia's fortress-minded isolationists.

Little is known of Edmond's private life. His marriage to Nellie Wilson, at Woollahra, in Sydney on 1 September 1886, was evidently happy; they had four children, and he was regarded as a stable family man, by contrast with Archibald and other club-centred Bohemians. He opposed Archibald's misogynistic anti-feminism, at times strongly and publicly; their difference in that regard accounted for one of the most productive areas of contradiction within the complex, continuing text of the *Bulletin*.

His later travels in Africa, India and the Middle East confirmed his strong views on Australia's needs for self-containment and racial exclusiveness. He continued to express them, in the *Bulletin* and elsewhere, until shortly before his death.

Edmond was described by John Dalley [q.v.]: 'Viewing his gigantic head and towering forehead one was reminded of a portrait of Socrates! He had small short-sighted eyes, a broad nose, a chin that was Scottish stubbornness personified and a wide kindly mouth'. He spoke with a marked Glasgow accent. For most of his working years he struggled courageously with heart disease. Edmond died on 21 March 1933, and was cremated with Presbyterian forms. His estate was valued for probate at £16 920.

E. V. Palmer, *The legend of the nineties* (Melb, 1954); *Lone Hand*, 22 (1918), p 63; *Newspaper News*, 1 Apr 1933; *Punch* (Melb), 8 Jan 1925; *SMH*, 22 Mar 1933; *Bulletin*, 24 May 1961. SYLVIA LAWSON

EDMUNDS, WALTER (1856-1932), judge, was born on 6 January 1856 at Maitland, New South Wales, son of John Edmunds, saddler, a Welshman and non-Catholic, and his wife Rosina, née Smith, a Londoner and a Catholic. He was brought up as a Catholic. Educated at Lyndhurst College, and at Fort Street Training School in 1874, he later taught for two years at Wollongong. Teaching in Sydney, he lived at Lyndhurst and attended the University of Sydney (M.A., 1879; LL.B., 1881). From 1883 to 1893 he was a fellow of St John's College within the university.

Admitted to the Bar on 31 July 1882, he became a leading and affluent junior. His circle included Edmund Barton [q.v.7] and A. B. Piddington [q.v.] and was known as 'the Stable'. A protectionist, Edmunds represented South Sydney in the colonial parliament in 1889-91; in May 1891 he quoted from G. B. Shaw's (ed) *Fabian essays in socialism* (1889) and forecast revolution if trade unions were destroyed. On 9 February 1897 he married Mary Victoria Monica McGrath. He gained enough subscriptions for the publication of his friend C. J. Brennan's [q.v.7] *Poems* (Sydney, 1914).

In 1911 Edmunds became a District Court judge and chairman of Quarter Sessions, and in 1914 the Holman [q.v.] Labor government appointed him to the Court of Industrial Arbitration — he had previously been chairman of special mining tribunals. In 1914-19 he was also chairman of the Necessary Commodities Control Commission. In 1916, after H. B. Higgins [q.v.] had refused, Prime Minister Hughes [q.v.] appointed Edmunds, under national security regulations, a special coal tribunal — in December he granted shifts of 'eight hours bank to bank' and approved an agreement raising rates of pay. Next year it was alleged that Hughes had appointed Edmunds 'with instructions to concede the men's demands'. Both denied it. In the 1917 transport strike railwaymen's unions offered to return to work if Edmunds were appointed to arbitrate, and the card system withdrawn pending his decision, but it was refused. In February 1920 he replaced C. G. Heydon [q.v.] as president of the Board of Trade; in August the Storey [q.v.] Labor government made him senior judge of the Industrial Court, and (Sir) George Beeby [q.v.7] replaced him on the board. Storey also announced in August that Edmunds would conduct a royal commission into the railways (the 1917 strike).

He was closely involved in the settlement of the 1919-20 strike at the Broken Hill mines. The miners had sought a reduction of their 44-hour week underground and healthier conditions of work, and in May 1920 Edmunds was asked to act as conciliator. On 2 October 1919, when he was acting president of the Board of Trade, it had recommended that Professor H. G. Chapman [q.v.7] be appointed to chair the medical inquiry; it made its first report on 12 July, and on 30 August Edmunds issued his interim decision. He left underground hours at forty-four pending proceedings before the Commonwealth Arbitration Court, but he stated that compensation for occupational disease would be decided 'at an early date'. Hearings were resumed on 7 September and he re-opened the hours question, later announcing a fresh decision, in which he specified rates of compensation for incapacitated miners and provided for a 35-hour week underground. The strike ended in November.

The most likely explanation of Edmunds's volte-face is that Premier Storey, pressed by P. S. Brookfield [q.v.7], asked Edmunds to grant the thirty-five hours and he obliged, but not for any expectation of reward — in judicial preferment he was at the end of his hopes and fears, and he had already been chosen royal commissioner for the railways inquiry. His sympathies lay with the employees and he contributed much to the health and welfare of miners; but he was judicially impartial.

On 25 November 1920 Edmunds as royal commissioner recommended salary increases for members of the Legislative Assembly and for ministers. His report of 13 February 1922 on the transport strike did not question the finding of the H. R. Curlewis [q.v. Turner] commission of 1918 that the card system was reasonable, but he indicated injustices in the treatment of ex-strikers. In 1925-26 he chaired the royal commission on safety in coalmines; in 1926 he retired, but was chairman of a royal commission in 1927 which cleared Piddington of charges of biased decisions as industrial commissioner.

On 15 August 1932 Edmunds died at his home at Strathfield, and was buried in Rookwood cemetery; he was survived by his wife, his only son John, a solicitor who practised at Casino, and his five daughters, of whom Jean was her father's associate from 1919 until her marriage to Dr H. J. Daly. Edmunds left no will, and administration was not taken out. Dignified by a neat beard, he was approachable and witty as a barrister, reserved and scholarly as a judge. Fluent in Italian, he translated from Dante. He helped to organize Catholic graduates' activity in the 1928 Eucharistic Congress.

A. B. Piddington, *Worshipful masters* (Syd, 1929); G. Blainey, *The rise of Broken Hill* (Melb, 1968); H. T. E. Holt, *A court rises* (Syd, 1976); B.

Kennedy, *Silver, sin, and sixpenny ale* (Melb, 1978); *Barrier Daily Truth*, 26 May, 2, 5 June, 19, 31 Aug, 3, 8. 14, 17, 30 Sept, 13, 18-27 Oct 1920; *Barrier Miner*, 14 July, 5 Aug, 17 Sept, 10 Nov 1920; *Freeman's J* (Syd), 18 Aug 1932; R. J. Parsons. Lawyers in the NSW parliament 1870-90 (Ph.D. thesis, Macquarie Univ, 1972); E. Wetherell, The stormy years of 1910-21 (pc held by Broken Hill City Lib).   E. J. MINCHIN

EDWARDS, ALBERT AUGUSTINE (1888-1963), hotelier, philanthropist and politician, was born on 6 November 1888 in the West End of Adelaide; no record of his birth has been found, but his mother was a Mrs Miller. He attended St Joseph's Catholic primary school before working on stalls at the city's markets and racecourses; from 1915 he ran a tea-room. He became secretary of the West Adelaide Democratic Club and of the Adelaide Electorate Committee of the United Labor Party, and a controversial official of the West Adelaide II Football Club. In 1914-31 he held Grey Ward in the Adelaide City Council for the Labor Party. He was licensee from 1915 of the Duke of Brunswick Hotel. An anti-conscriptionist, he was member for Adelaide in the House of Assembly in 1917-31. In parliament Edwards belligerently defended persecuted Germans, the city's poor, bookmakers, underpaid teachers and police; in 1920 he campaigned with his friend John Wren [q.v.] against the deportation of the German priest, Charles Jerger [q.v.]. Described by an opponent as a 'Tammany Hall boss', Edwards nevertheless sought slum clearance and control of 'land sharks' and rack-renters. He supported the licensing of bookmakers and opposed a prohibition referendum. He was also an active prison reformer.

In 1924 Edwards sold his public house and leased the Newmarket; he also had a hotel at Second Valley where he and young footballers celebrated after Saturday's matches. He relished the pleasures of public life: from 1922 he sat on the Central Board of Health and following Labor's huge win in 1924 was government spokesman on prisons and reformatories. Next year he became visiting justice at Yatala Labour Prison and a member of the State Children's Council; he joined the board of the Public Library, Museum and Art Gallery. At Yatala he was an effective reformer, but in 1926 conservatives' suspicion precipitated a royal commission into the release of prisoners. Charges against Edwards were not substantiated; and it was stated that he had often 'raised prisoners practically from the dead'. Nevertheless he resigned in 1927 to the dismay of staff and prisoners. 'Bert', or 'the King', as he was known, resembled Hal

Gye's [q.v.] illustrations of the hero of *The songs of the sentimental bloke;* Gye also drew him for the *Bulletin*. He had also upset the State Children's Council. He told the 1926 law reform commission that the Magill Reformatory was filthy, vermin infested and did not rehabilitate, and that state wards were being used as a cheap labour force. He recommended a smaller board, and by the end of the year a new Act set up the Children's Welfare and Public Relief Board; in 1928 the old council was abolished. In 1927 Edwards had opened another hotel, at Victor Harbor.

As the Depression worsened, rifts between Labor factions deepened. Edwards, a member of the Australian Workers' Union, directed in August 1929 D. H. Bardolph's [q.v.7] bitter pre-selection campaign for a Legislative Council by-election; Edwards's tactics against the winner S. R. Whitford [q.v.] endangered his own position. In September he defied caucus and joined a march of unemployed. By the end of the month the party's council refused him pre-selection for Adelaide, but his electorate committee overturned this and in 1930 he won with the swing to Labor.

In October Edwards and Bardolph campaigned for J. T. Lang [q.v.] in New South Wales. In his absence the party refused endorsement for his City Council seat. Since he had already nominated, the council held that he could not withdraw and he defeated his Labor opponent in December.

Allegedly 'under the baton of Bill Denny [q.v.]', the attorney-general and one of Edwards's 'most bitter opponents' in the party, he was arrested on 13 December and charged with having committed sodomy in May. His trial lasted eight days in February 1931. Some of those who recall it allege that Edwards was 'framed', although it is not usually denied that he was a homosexual; he is said to have antagonized police by probing their fatal shooting of an escapee in 1930. The main evidence against him came from his ex-employee, John Gault Mundy, then an inmate of Magill Reformatory, who admitted that he had hoped to shorten his own sentence for a similar offence by informing. Edwards was sentenced to five years hard labour at Yatala. 'My enemies have succeeded . . . with loaded dice', he told the chief justice, Sir George Murray [q.v.]. The Edwards Defence Committee unavailingly arranged three appeals, including one to the High Court.

On 8 June 1933 Edwards was released; in 1937 he resumed hotel-keeping. Next year he was suspended from the Labor Party for alleged ballot irregularities. He failed in attempts to re-enter State parliament that year and in 1950, and the Federal parliament in

Edwards

A.D.B.

1940. In 1948 he won back his old seat on the City Council. He continued to donate to the party generously.

Edwards displayed his increasing wealth in characteristically truculent and flashy style; but he also retained his lifelong compassion for Adelaide's destitute. In 1961 he gave £13 000 for a men's refuge in Whitmore Square; in 1963 he provided an adjoining property as a rehabilitation centre for prisoners – the Frank Lundie [q.v.] Hostel. He supplied money to the Daughters of Charity for their Hutt Street meal centre, the hall of which bears his name, and he was a benefactor to numerous other denominations. Each week he collected surplus food from city shops and distributed it among the poor. He had a well-stocked library; and his home was used by needy country people seeking family members' medical treatment.

Between the wars Edwards drove a large Studebaker car. He dressed in white suits, with Homburg hat, bow tie and suede shoes, favouring silk pyjamas and gold-tipped cigarettes. One arm was tattooed with a heart. His dark, curling hair, parted in the middle, framed a large hooked nose over a receding chin. Following his death, on 24 August 1963 and a requiem Mass at St Francis Xavier's Cathedral, his body was embalmed and buried at West Terrace cemetery in a copper casket. His estate, divided among Adelaide's poor, was sworn for probate at £45 942.

PD (SA), 1920, p 662, 1926, pp 1063-1066; *PP* (SA), 1925 (38), 1926 (54) (75), 1927 (23) (38) (58); *Gay changes*, 2 (1979), no 4, p 11; *Daily Herald*, 29 Mar, 15 May 1917; *Advertiser* (Adel), 21 Feb 1919, 19, 21, 26 July, 5 Aug 1920, 10 Jan 1925, 2, 28 June 1926, 4 Apr 1927, 22 Dec 1928, 26 Sept, 18 Oct, 12, 29 Nov 1929, 14, 17 Nov 1930, 4-7, 11-14, 18 Feb, 11 May 1931, 8 July, 24 Mar 1933, 13, 14 Jan 1938, 26, 28 Aug 1963; *Bulletin*, 28 Aug 1929; *Southern Cross* (Adel), 2 June 1961, 30 Aug 1963; register no 35, 1931 (Supreme Court, SA); PRG54/33, 41 1931 (SAA); information from Messrs C.R. Cameron, Adelaide, C.L. Shea, Dulwich and N. Makin, Glenelg SA.   SUZANNE EDGAR

EDWARDS, GEORGE (1886-1953), pioneer of the radio serial in Australia, was born Harold Parks on 11 March 1886 at Kent Town, South Australia, elder son of Lewis Arthur Parks, grocer's assistant and later manager of Crawford & Co., Adelaide, and his wife Sarah Jane, née Turbill. After leaving North Norwood Public School at 11, Hal worked as an office boy with D. & J. Fowler, wholesale grocers and importers, and later with Wood, Son & Co. He joined the Appendrena Club of Dramatic Players; a talented mimic, he also performed comic duets with his brother Albert Lewis (Lew). In later years he recalled that a stutter, which vanished when performing, had been alleviated by Lionel Logue. The stammer was a reality, but the association with Logue, who had assisted King George VI with his speech, was a fiction, although Logue did come from Kent Town. At 18 Parks left for England, returning after three years to musical comedy with J. C. Williamson [q.v.6] Ltd at the Princess Theatre, Melbourne. On 6 August 1907 he married Margaret Rose Wilson with Congregational forms; they had one daughter.

Hal became an acrobatic dancer and patter artist in vaudeville and costume farce. He toured Australia, New Zealand, the United States of America and, during World War I, South Africa, but never achieved major success. In the late 1920s he married Mollie Hughes in Sydney, and in 1929 was a featured entertainer on the Sydney Show Boat. By this time vaudeville was dying and in 1927-31 he made a number of short films including *The haunted barn* (1931). He also acted as a theatrical agent with his brother.

In 1931, encouraged by Lew, Parks moved into radio, doing comedy sketches for the Australian Broadcasting Company, sometimes in partnership with his daughter Chandra. He changed his name to George Edwards, not bothering to dispel popular confusion with the celebrated George Edwardes, London theatrical entrepreneur. In October to December 1931 he broadcast with the A.B.C. Light Opera Co.; in December he and Chandra were among the A.B.C. Players whose repertoire included *The ghost train*, often cited as the play which drew public attention to Edwards. Early in 1932 he had a new partner for his comedy routines, a young soubrette, Helen Dorothy Malmgrom, who had worked with him on the Show Boat and who now took the name Nell Stirling. Early in 1933 George moved to the commercial radio station 2UE, and in May George, Nell and an enthusiastic writer, Maurice Francis, went to 2GB as the nucleus of the George Edwards Players, masters of the melodramatic and comic serial.

To save money Edwards played a variety of roles – and became known as 'The Man with a Thousand Voices'. It was a ventriloquial gift that encompassed small children, every variety of male voice, aged women and foreigners. The maximum number of voices Edwards produced for a single scene was six; in the course of a single episode he would often double it. By 1936 when he moved to 2UW Edwards led the list of the ten favourite Sydney radio personalities. Beginning at breakfast with *Darby and Joan*, George Edwards Productions, whose scripts Maurice Francis wrote with

416

extraordinary rapidity, would see the night out with *Famous Trials*. In between were historical dramas, detective thrillers and children's serials ranging from *Inspector Scott of Scotland Yard* to the popular *Dad and Dave*, begun in May 1937. Edwards's last radio serial, in 1953, was *Ralph Rashleigh*. At first performed live, the serials were later recorded without rehearsal under the Columbia imprint and sold throughout Australia and New Zealand.

George divorced his second wife in 1933 and married Nell on 29 March 1934 at St David's Presbyterian Church, Haberfield; many pieces of hand-knitted baby clothes were received through the mail when their daughter was born in 1942. The radio programmes netted them a large fortune, embodied in their luxury apartment house, Darjoa (short for Darby and Joan), at Point Piper, but much of this wealth was lost by George to horse-racing, alcohol and night club ventures. The Edwardses were divorced in 1948. Nell remarried next year and on 20 February 1953 George married Coral Lansbury. Edwards died of liver disease on 28 August, shortly after the sudden death of Nell; he was cremated. His estate was valued for probate at £32 766.

R. R. Walker, *The magic spark* (Melb, 1973); A. Pike and R. F. Cooper, *Australian film 1900-1977* (Melb, 1980); *Wireless Weekly*, 24 Apr, 9, 23 Oct, 6, 20, 27 Nov, 4 Dec 1931, 29 Jan, 12 Feb 1932, 5 May 1933, 20 Apr 1934, 4 Oct 1935; 10 Jan 1936, 29 Jan 1937, 29 Apr, 6, 13, 20, 27 May 1938; *Radio Pictorial*, 1 July 1935; *SMH*, 29 Aug 1953; *Bulletin*, 22 July 1980.   CORAL LANSBURY

EDWARDS, JOHN HAROLD McKEN-ZIE (1894-1942), soldier and superintendent of native labour in New Guinea, was born probably on 10 June 1894 at Terang, Victoria, son of Charlotte Edwards. Little is known of his early life, though before World War I he was a labourer at Brunswick, Melbourne.

On 9 April 1915 he enlisted in the Australian Imperial Force as a private, giving his name as Harold Edwards and his age as 24; throughout his military career his date of birth was therefore recorded as April 1891. He embarked in Melbourne on 8 May as a sergeant in the 21st Battalion, served at Anzac and left Egypt for France in March 1916. Wounded on 26 August 1916 during the battle of Mouquet Farm, he was awarded the Distinguished Conduct Medal for 'conspicuous gallantry and able reconnaissance work' in this action; he had been 'in command of a carrying party which made three endeavours to reach a post, under very heavy shell and machine-gun fire'. His

D.C.M. was gazetted on 20 October and seven days later he was awarded the Military Medal, the first to be won by the battalion. He received it for his part in a brigade raiding-party on the night of 29-30 June.

Edwards was taken on strength of the permanent cadre at No. 1 Command Depot in England on 12 May 1917 and in December was commissioned as second lieutenant and posted to general infantry reinforcements. He returned to the 21st Battalion on 12 January 1918 and was promoted lieutenant on 1 April. As a platoon commander he was involved in the fighting at Ville-sur-Ancre in May. On 6 July he was wounded again at Villers-Bretonneux and, for daring reconnaissance work resulting in the capture of a German trench-mortar and the destruction of several others, received the Military Cross. The combination of decorations he had won for individual bravery was very rare. He resumed duty with the 21st Battalion on 11 September.

Edwards was demobilized in Melbourne in August 1919 and next January became a lieutenant on the reserve of officers, Australian Military Forces. On 13 April 1921 he joined the permanent staff of the A.M.F. as a probationary staff sergeant major on the Queensland Instructional Staff. Four months later he was provisionally promoted warrant officer, class 2 and was confirmed in this rank in October. While a member of the Australian Instructional Corps he served with the 11th Mixed Brigade in Queensland. On 11 April 1923 he left the shrinking permanent army at his own request and later moved to New Guinea where he was employed by Burns [q.v.7] Philp [q.v.] & Co. as a native labour overseer at Rabaul. There, on 12 February 1930, he married Susan Jean McKenzie; there were no children of the marriage. On 13 October 1939 Edwards was appointed a lieutenant in the New Guinea Volunteer Rifles but was not called up for full-time duty. He was officially presumed to have died as one of about 200 Australian civilian prisoners of war on 1 July 1942 when the Japanese transport, the *Montevideo Maru*, on a journey from Rabaul to Hainan Island, was torpedoed by an American submarine off Luzon in the South China Sea. He was survived by his wife who had been evacuated to Australia the previous January.

C. E. W. Bean, *The A.I.F. in France*, 1918 (Syd, 1942); L. Wigmore, *The Japanese thrust* (Canb, 1957); *London Gazette*, 20, 27 Oct 1916, 26 May 1917, 24 Sept 1918; *Pacific Islands Mthly*, Jan 1946, supp, p vii; *Australian Territories*, 7 Feb 1961 p vii; B. O. C. Duggan, History of the 21st Battalion, A.I.F. (AWM); file A77/470, series A452, item 59/1337 (AAO, Canb).   C. NEUMANN

EDWARDS, LEWIS DAVID (1885-1961), public servant, was born on 14 October 1885 at Silkstone, Ipswich, Queensland, son of John Lewis Edwards, coalminer, and his wife Anne, née Morris. A typically Welsh home, rich in sound and faith, laid the foundation for his lifelong participation in the arts of the eisteddfod. A beautiful voice served him well, in small communities when he was a teacher, and later as a lecturer, trade union leader and advocate, and educational administrator. Fluent in recitation and song, he was said when young to be able to provide a complete school concert. After retirement he was president of the Art of Speech Association and of the Eisteddfod Council of Queensland.

Edwards was educated at the Newtown (later Silkstone) State School of which he was dux in 1898, winning the McGill medal. From 1899 he was a pupil-teacher and later assistant teacher at Spring Creek. He moved as an assistant teacher to Ipswich West (boys), Boonah, Petrie Terrace (boys) and Milton, all relatively large schools, then became head-teacher of very small schools at Silverleigh and Mount Cotton.

Without secondary education and while teaching, he matriculated in the new University of Queensland in 1911. Working entirely as an evening student, he eventually graduated with first-class honours in mental and moral philosophy in 1917 (M.A., 1919). G. E. Mayo [q.v.] had been his main teacher. During this period of intense study, Edwards married Mary McQueen on 8 July 1913 and settled in Brisbane as an assistant secondary teacher.

From August 1920 he was appointed a temporary lecturer at the university, first in ethics and metaphysics, later in logic and philosophy. From March 1922, during Professor Mayo's absence, he was acting head of the philosophy department. That year he was elected unopposed as president of the Queensland Teachers' Union. His term was noted for his eloquent and successful advocacy on behalf of secondary teachers before the Industrial Arbitration Court; during his later career he was a popular speaker at annual union conferences. In 1922 he was also assisting to inspect grammar schools. On 1 March 1923 he was appointed acting professor of philosophy and head of the department, but he resigned to take the post of chief inspector of schools from 12 April.

From 1923 until his retirement in 1951, Edwards was associated with the main features of educational development in Queensland. As chief inspector he devoted much attention to the creation of the new primary syllabus issued in 1930, and was especially interested in methods of educa-

tional psychology. In 1935 he visited the United States of America, England and Europe under a Carnegie Corporation programme to gain first-hand experience of educational trends of which he was already fully aware. He became director of education in 1937, and director-general in 1941 with the passing of the University Co-ordination Act. As director-general he was *ex officio* a member of the senate and chairman of the academic standing committee of the university, and chairman of the Library Board of Queensland, the National Fitness Council, the Board of Post-primary Studies and Examinations, the Board of Adult Education and the Schools Broadcast Advisory Committee.

Edwards was universally regarded as a successful administrator and a warm human being. However he served through a period of depression and war and under a succession of Labor governments for whom education was never a major political priority. The expansion of secondary education, dear to his heart, was limited by the government's narrow adherence to the scholarship system. Among other things he was able to encourage the growth of libraries and the introduction of audio-visual aids, to re-emphasize the importance of teaching music and art and — a particular triumph — to create the State String Quartet in 1942. He demonstrated in some fine annual reports and public addresses his awareness of innovations in public systems of education elsewhere, but he fundamentally adhered to the tradition of education created for Queensland in 1915 by J. D. Story [q.v.]. When Edwards received an honorary Ph.D. from the university in 1950, Story hailed him as a 'notable product of the National System of Education'.

His reputation rests on the personal qualities of intellectual ability, charm and humanity which he displayed throughout his career. He died in Brisbane on 10 February 1961 and was cremated after a Congregational service. His wife survived him, but their only son had died in 1954.

E. R. Wyeth, *Education in Queensland* (Melb, nd, c. 1953); R. Goodman, *Secondary education in Queensland, 1860-1960* (Canb, 1968); D. J. Murphy, R. B. Joyce and C. A. Hughes (eds), *Labor in power ... Queensland 1915-1957* (Brisb, 1979); *Qld Teachers' J,* 20 Nov 1951, p 1; Dept of Education (Qld) Archives; Univ Qld Archives.

J. LAWRY

EDWARDS, PERCY MALCOLM (1875-1958), soldier, public servant and costume manufacturer, was born on 5 December 1875 at Collingwood, Melbourne, son of William

Samuel Edwards, coachbuilder, and his wife Catherine, née Malcolm, both English-born. On leaving East Prahran State School at 15 he joined a firm of Melbourne warehousemen, Robert Reid [q.v.] & Co., with whom he worked for six years. He served with the volunteer artillery in 1893-97 and, in 1898, having moved to Western Australia to become a clerk in the Department of Railways, joined the field artillery in Perth.

On the outbreak of the South African War Edwards enlisted as a company sergeant major in the 1st Western Australian (Mounted Infantry) Contingent. He served in the Colesberg area, the advance to Bloemfontein and in the Transvaal. Near Pretoria, on 4 June 1900, he took part in what he later claimed to be the first mounted charge with fixed bayonets. He was twice mentioned in dispatches and was also awarded the Distinguished Conduct Medal for gallantry at Diamond Hill. Under cover of darkness he and two others broke through the Boer lines and blew up the Delagoa railway. Their action strengthened the British position and also enabled recovery of a trainload of British prisoners and two trainloads of merchandise. Edwards returned home in December 1900 and resumed his public service career. On 30 January 1901, at St Alban's Anglican Church, Armadale, Melbourne, he married Elena Danson; they had no children.

Edwards continued his militia service and was commissioned in the 18th Light Horse Regiment in 1908; he served with the 25th L.H.R. in 1912-13 and in October 1913 joined the Australian Field Artillery. In 1908 he had resigned from the public service and established a successful softgoods factory in Perth. Volunteering for active service in World War I, he was commissioned lieutenant in the 8th Battery, 3rd Australian Field Artillery Brigade, Australian Imperial Force, on 17 October 1914.

Edwards served throughout the Gallipoli campaign and was promoted temporary captain in July 1915 and adjutant of the 2nd A.F.A. Brigade in October. In Egypt, next February, he transferred to the 4th Divisional Artillery, leaving for France in June. He commanded the 112th Howitzer Battery from March 1916 to January 1917 and temporarily led the battery's parent unit, the 24th Brigade. He then transferred to the 11th A.F.A. Brigade, commanding the 111th Howitzer Battery for the rest of the war except for brief temporary commands. His main service was in the Somme and Passchendaele offensives. Promoted major in July 1916 and temporary lieut-colonel a year later, he was twice mentioned in dispatches and awarded the Distinguished Service Order in the New Year honours of 1918. He

returned home in September 1918 and was demobilized in November.

Little is known of Edwards's civilian life after the war. He and his wife moved to Sydney in 1920 and in 1929-42 ran a women's costume manufacturing and importing business in George Street. He rejoined the Citizen Forces, commanding the 14th A.F.A. Brigade in 1921-25, and was placed on the retired list as an honorary colonel in 1936. Survived by his wife, he died at Mosman on 23 July 1958 and was cremated with Anglican rites.

Aust Defence Dept, *Official records of the Australian military contingents to the war in South Africa*, P. L. Murray ed (Melb, 1911); J. S. Battye (ed), *Cyclopedia of Western Australia*, 1 (Adel, 1912); C. E. W. Bean, *The story of Anzac* (Syd), 1924); *London Gazette*, 27 Sept 1901, 1 June, 28 Dec 1917, 1 Jan 1918; *SMH*, 10 Nov 1923, 8 May 1929; War diaries, 3rd, *and* 4th Aust Field Artillery brigades AIF (AWM); information from the Dept of Veterans' Affairs, Canb and Melb.
RICHMOND CUBIS

EDWARDS, WILLIAM BURTON (1856-1925), public service inspector, was born on 26 May 1856 at Launceston, Tasmania, son of William Frederick Alexander Edwards, broker, and his wife Charlotte Mary, née Burton. The family lived in New Zealand in 1862-68 before moving to Melbourne where Edwards attended St Paul's School and Wesley College, his father operating a wood and coal yard at Windsor.

After working at the South Yarra post office from 1872 Edwards joined the Victorian Postmaster-General's Department in March 1875 as assistant telegraphist at Stawell; in 1878 he was transferred to the Melbourne central telegraph office. He became the first secretary of the Telegraph Operators' Association when it was formed in 1886 to combat the stifling of promotion opportunities for telegraphists by the 1884 reclassification of the public service; at least some of the grievances had been removed when he relinquished office in 1888. In 1891 'appointments' clerk in the correspondence branch, Edwards was made senior clerk and acting inspector of accounts in 1897, chief clerk under the Commonwealth, and in March 1907 chief inspector of the inspection and inland mail branch.

Dignified and quiet, 'W.B.' was a just man of keen perception and great efficiency. Lauded for his management of the model post, telegraph, and telephone office at the 1888 Melbourne Centennial International Exhibition, he also handled the distribution of 250 000 copies of the Commonwealth constitution bill, and proved equally able as a returning officer for the first election of the Public Service Association's divisional representatives and as Commonwealth electoral officer for Victoria in 1906-07. Throughout his departmental career he displayed marked ingenuity: in 1884 he conceived the idea, taken up with great success, of issuing a post office Christmas card; in 1890 he initiated a scheme for the appointment of a regular relieving staff and he later reorganized sick-leave arrangements.

On 1 July 1908 Edwards left the postal department to become Commonwealth public service inspector. In 1916 he was appointed acting public service commissioner on the retirement of D. C. McLachlan [q.v.]; he held the position until the formation of the Commonwealth Public Service Board in 1923, when he retired. Edwards's talent for innovation deserted him during his periods as acting commissioner: conscious that he lacked the calibre of McLachlan, he adhered rigidly to precedent, attributing the consequent decline in the authority of his office to the use of arbitration within the public service. He died of hemiplegia on 23 May 1925 at Elsternwick; the *Argus* wrote, 'There was no day in which his work was completed within 12 hours, and he practically lived for the service'. A Freemason since 1897, and at his death worshipful master of the Wesley Collegians' Lodge, Edwards was buried in St Kilda cemetery after a Masonic funeral. His first wife Ellen Elizabeth, née Henderson, whom he had married on 7 June 1882 according to Free Presbyterian forms at Windsor, died in 1892. He was survived by his second wife Mabel, née Mueller, whom he had married on 1 June 1893 at St John's Anglican Church, Windsor, and by three sons of this marrige and a son and a daughter of the first.

G. E. Caiden, *Career service* (Melb, 1965); Aust Cwlth Post and Telegraph Assn *Transmitter,* 18 July 1908; *Argus,* 25, 26 May 1925.

ANN G. SMITH

EDYE, SIR BENJAMIN THOMAS (1884-1962), surgeon, was born on 17 July 1884 at Orange, New South Wales, second son of native-born parents Andrew Edye, saddler, and his wife Harriet Jane, née Anderson. Educated at Orange, he was apprenticed to a pharmacist Alexander Durno in Sydney. In 1905 Edye completed pharmacy at the University of Sydney, winning a gold medal, then studied medicine, graduating M.B. with first-class honours and the university medal in 1910, and Ch.M. in 1913.

Appointed resident medical officer at Royal Prince Alfred Hospital in 1911, he became senior medical officer in 1912 and next year demonstrated pathology at the university. In 1914 he went to England for further studies and became a fellow of the Royal College of Surgeons in 1915. Unable to enlist in the Australian Imperial Force in London, from June he served as a captain at the Australian Voluntary Hospital, Wimereux, France, under Sir Alexander MacCormick [q.v.] until December 1917, then with the 56th Division and later with the 41st Casualty Clearing Station. In 1918 he returned to Australia to enlist but the war ended. On 28 June 1919 at Kogarah, Sydney, he married Jessie McLean (d. 1948).

From 1920 Edye was honorary assistant surgeon (honorary surgeon from 1928) at Royal Prince Alfred Hospital, demonstrated anatomy at the university and until 1929 assisted MacCormick in private practice at a salary of £350; he learnt much from the latter whom he held in the highest regard. In 1923 he became honorary assistant surgeon at St Vincent's when it became a teaching hospital. Next year he achieved senior status, but resigned in 1928 to become acting professor of surgery at the university until 1930. In the 1930s he developed a large consultant practice. When MacCormick retired, Edye became surgical consultant at the St George, Manly and Ryde hospitals. Later he developed the surgical unit at the Rachel Forster Hospital for Women and Children. In 1936 he visited Europe and the United States of America where he studied thoracic and plastic surgery.

During World War II, with the rank of lieut-colonel, Edye was senior visiting surgical consultant at the 113th Military Hospital, Concord. After the war he pioneered heart surgery and became an honorary consultant at the Royal North Shore Hospital, where much early work in this field was performed. A council-member of the New South Wales branch of the British Medical Association, he was president in 1938-39, and was a founder and council-member in 1949-59 of the Royal Australasian College of Surgeons. In 1945-58 he was president of the New South Wales Medical Defence Union Ltd. A gifted and skilful surgeon, he worked until the end of his life, despite increasing physical infirmities. Appointed C.B.E. in 1957, he was knighted next year.

As a young man Edye enjoyed rifle-shooting, but later took up golf and eventually bowls; he was a member of Royal Sydney Golf Club, and also of the Union Club. He regularly attended concerts and became enthusiastic about ballet through his daughter. Sincere and earnest, with simple tastes and high standards, he was conservative in his political outlook. He was rather slender in build with clean-cut features, and was noted for his courtesy and interest in people, and for his resulting lack of regard for the passage of time and punctuality.

Sir Benjamin died on 12 October 1962 in the Scottish Hospital, Paddington, and was cremated with Anglican rites. He was survived by a son and two daughters of his first marriage, and by his second wife Catherine Maclean Menzies, née Macdonald, a widow whom he had married at St Mark's Church, Darling Point, on 13 April 1955. His estate was valued for probate at £122 338.

MJA, 31 Aug 1963.   DOUGLAS MILLER

EGGLESTON, SIR FREDERIC WIL-LIAM (1875-1954), lawyer, politician, diplomat, writer and controversialist, was born on 17 October 1875 at Brunswick, Melbourne, eldest son of John Waterhouse Eggleston, lawyer, and his wife Emily, née Overend. His grandfather was Rev. John Eggleston [q.v.4]. His maternal grandparents were also Methodists. His mother died in 1884 and in 1887 his father married Ada Crouch. Frederic attended state schools at Brunswick and St Kilda, then Queen's College, St Kilda, and Wesley College, which his paternal grandfather helped to found. During a family tour of Britain and Europe in 1891, Eggleston spent two terms at the Leys School, Cambridge.

His hopes of entering a university, either at Cambridge or Melbourne, were disappointed. The family income suddenly declined in the early 1890s, caused by the financial crash in Victoria. On returning from England, Eggleston became a clerk in his father's legal firm, Eggleston & (T. P.) Derham, and studied for the articled clerk's certificate. In 1897 he jointly won the Supreme Court prize for the best results in the final examinations, and was admitted to the Victorian Bar.

In 1895 Eggleston won the University of Melbourne's Bowen [q.v.3] prize for an essay on 'History as treated by Shakespeare, Carlyle and Scott'. In 1898 his first published writing appeared in the *Summons*: a two-part essay on 'British Legal Development as a Representative Institution'. This essay revealed the influence of the legal historian Sir Henry Maine, whose ideas were taught by Professor (Sir) W. Harrison Moore [q.v.]. Eggleston expressed deep respect for the British legal tradition, but argued that future legal development would emerge from legislation rather than purely legal and judicial precedent; in the future the patriotic lawyer would play a wider role through parliament and politics. A further anticipation of his later career was a sociological approach to jurisprudence, which rejected John Austin's utilitarian conception of 'sovereignty'.

In his twenties Eggleston suffered from nervous depressions and breakdowns which were the product of a dutiful disposition, overwork, emotional incompatibility with his father and stepmother, and religious doubt. After his admission to the Bar, his problems began to diminish as he made friendships outside his family Methodist circle. Tendencies toward nervousness, personal shyness, and self-pity remained enduring features of his adult personality. By the time he was 25 he had rejected Methodism and denominational Christianity, but Christian social philosophy, expressed in the Sermon on the Mount, later reappeared as a central theme in his thought. In the 1890s and early 1900s he fashioned his own personal philosophical system, an eclectic mixture of personal (not absolute or Hegelian) idealism and social evolutionism. Although sympathetic towards the late Victorian decadent movement, locally represented by the musician, Professor G. W. L. Marshall-Hall [q.v.], Eggleston's strong literary and artistic interests remained fixed in a mould of Matthew Arnold, Robert Browning, and George Meredith. His early aesthetic interests were gradually projected upon the ideals of public life, statecraft as an art and a science, and upon the concept of 'citizenship'.

In 1897 Eggleston met Louisa (known as Lulu) Augusta, daughter of F. A. Henriques, a Melbourne grain and corn broker whose family were Jamaican Jews of Marrano extraction. After a protracted friendship and correspondence, they were married in Perth on 10 May 1904. She introduced him to artistic and intellectual circles close to Alfred Deakin [q.v.]. Although, unlike his wife, Eggleston did not play an active role in the People's Liberal Party, he absorbed a similar political outlook during his early married life. These years corresponded with the political and personal demise of Deakin and Deakinism, and Eggleston's later career in Australian public life was marked by a sense of alienation from the Australian political party system.

At the beginning and end of his public career Eggleston supported the Labor governments of Fisher [q.v.] (1910-13, 1914-15) and Hughes [q.v.] (1915-16), and then of Curtin (1941-45) and Chifley (1945-49). His generally anti-Labor political position in the years after the conscription referenda (1916-17) during World War I was modified by a highly critical attitude towards the Nationalists, the United Australia Party, and the Liberal Party of (Sir) Robert Menzies. Eggleston's prolific political writing in the Australian and British press was marked by wide sympathies and uncompromising criticism of both major Australian parties. His strongest contempt was reserved for the Country Party. His closest personal friendships, such as those with (Sir) John Latham [q.v.] and Maurice Blackburn [q.v.7], transcended conventional political boundaries. Eggleston's adult career alternated between elective or appointed public office, and the solicitor's practice which he shared with his next brother, John Bakewell, from 1904 to 1932, and thereafter with his son, Egan Moulton, until 1941.

In 1911-20 Eggleston was a municipal councillor in Caulfield, including a year (1914-15) as mayor. He advocated progressive reforms, such as the systematic adoption of British town planning principles in municipal government, the abolition of plural voting, and the enfranchisement of non-ratepaying residents. In the years before the war he was also active in the establishment of voluntary civic groups such as the Workers' Educational Association, and the Melbourne and Australian groups of the Imperial Federationist quarterly, *Round Table*. He combined his legal practice with both public work and writing for the local and British press on Australian politics and Imperial problems.

In 1914-15 Eggleston gave several lectures which defended Australian social and political experiments, but argued that such experiments should be subjected to social-scientific study and rationalization. The major product of this sympathetic, but sceptical, critical interest in Australian statecraft and social ideals was *State socialism in Victoria* (1932).

Eggleston enlisted in the Australian Imperial Force in March 1916, an act of conscience which expressed his lifelong dual loyalty to Australia and to the Empire. He served in 1917-18 in an administrative capacity, in the court martial section of the A.I.F. units on Salisbury Plain. While in England he strengthened his ties with the *Round Table* group and arranged to become post-war Australian correspondent for the *New Statesman* (1919-21), but his experience of the manners and ethos of British life convinced him of his fundamental Australianness. When the war ended, he hoped to enter politics or obtain a 'big administrative job'. He was commissioned in August 1918, and after the Armistice was transferred to the staff of W. M. Hughes to work at the Peace Conference with his friends Latham and Sir Robert Garran [q.v.]. He was too Wilsonian in his views to enjoy working for Hughes, however, and left Paris before the conclusion of the peace treaty.

After a brief return to municipal politics. Eggleston won St Kilda in the Victorian election of 1920. Although he had stood as an Independent Nationalist and Independent Liberal, he at first supported the Nationalist government of (Sir) Harry Lawson [q.v.]. In 1922-23, however, he joined with a faction of metropolitan liberals to demand a reconstruction of the ministry which would lead to greater concentration upon unsolved urban problems, including electoral redistribution, and a coalition of Nationalists and Victorian Farmers' Union members which would prevent Labor taking office. These irreconcilable demands structured Eggleston's political fortunes in 1924-27, when he was minister of railways and a vice-president of the Board of Land and Works in the Peacock [q.v.] ministry; and attorney-general, solicitor general and minister of Railways in the Allan [q.v.7]-Peacock ministry.

His ministerial career was complicated by narrow parliamentary majorities, and the need to rely upon a group of capricious Independents. The Railways portfolio was a source of constant trade union, budgetary and managerial problems, and Eggleston resigned it in August 1926, when his health broke down. The legislation which led to his defeat in the 1927 election was the Motor Omnibus Act, which regulated and rationalized the operations of small private bus companies. Eggleston was not personally responsible for it but he wholeheartedly supported it, believing that unregulated private competition would undermine the public investment in railways and tramways. He supported the drastic reduction of private bus routes which crossed his own electorate. Intense campaigns against him were mounted by local residents and representatives of the bus lobby. Burnett Gray, the Independent candidate, defeated him at every polling booth. He contemplated standing for the Federal seat of Balaclava, but did not do so.

Eggleston had been appointed to the Council of the University of Melbourne on 6 January 1921; he was replaced on 19 September 1927. In the aftermath of his parliamentary defeat, he returned to voluntary public work in the *Round Table* group, the Institute of Pacific Relations and the Victorian branches of the Australian Institute of International Affairs and the League of Nations Union. He was the leading intellectual figure in the internationalist organizations which were linked, largely through the skills of E. C. Dyason [q.v.], in the Bureau of Social and International Affairs. Eggleston also resumed writing for British and Australian magazines and newspapers, on a scale far larger than his pre-war or early post-war work. He began research on Victorian and

Australian public finance, and the political economy of statutory corporations. In addition to prolific newspaper articles and commentaries, he produced a major biographical work, *George Swinburne, a biography* (1931), to which E. H. Sugden [q.v.] contributed a short personal account, and *State socialism in Victoria*.

In 1933 Eggleston was appointed first chairman of the Commonwealth Grants Commission, a position he held until 1941. Although the technical problems facing the distribution of Commonwealth grants to the 'claimant States' of Western Australia, South Australia and Tasmania were largely solved by another commissioner, the economist L. F. Giblin [q.v.], Eggleston was a powerful and sophisticated chairman, dedicated to the revision of the Federal system. His writings and research on Australian public finance during the Depression, and his more sociological writings (often unpublished) on the modern conflict between the need for large administrative units and the need for self-government, constituted important independent influences upon the now famous early reports of the commission. In 1939 Eggleston visited Papua and New Guinea as chairman of a committee inquiring into the possibility of amalgamating their administration, and on the outbreak of war he became a member of the Capital Issues Advisory Board. He had become a trusted servant of the Commonwealth. In the late 1930s he also produced his most cerebral and audacious book, *Search for a social philosophy* (1941), an attempt to provide a conceptual apparatus for the unification of the discrete social sciences, and a powerful argument against specialization in the social disciplines. Considerably in advance of both academic and administrative thought at the time, it was the least successful and accessible of his five books.

In 1941 Eggleston was knighted and appointed first Australian minister to China. In the Chinese wartime capital, Chungking, he proved himself a natural diplomat and an acute analyst of political intelligence at the highest levels. He wholeheartedly supported the foreign policy of Dr H. V. Evatt. Although a relatively minor Australian diplomat by comparison with those in Canberra, Washington or London, Eggleston's enthusiasm for a 'Pacific first' allied strategy derived from his long-term intellectual work, begun before World War I, on Australia's specific regional and geographic strategic interests.

At the end of his diplomatic furlough in 1944, Eggleston was appointed to the temporary position of Australian minister to the United States of America, succeeding Sir Owen Dixon. He had expected to return to Chungking, where he had developed close ties with Chinese intellectuals, educationists and politicians, but agreed to go to Washington in order to participate in the peace conference. The hectic political atmosphere there at the end of the war, however, was not conducive to his natural style of quiet diplomacy, and at the San Francisco Conference in 1945 he collapsed and had to rest in hospital. His direct influence upon Australian diplomacy at San Francisco was negligible, although he enjoyed the contrasts and similarities with Versailles, and was one of a handful of individuals who had been present at both conferences. In 1946 he retired from active diplomacy and returned to Australia.

From 1946 to 1949 Eggleston was employed in a part-time capacity as an official adviser to the Department of External Affairs, and as lecturer to diplomatic cadets. Belatedly, his lecturing and advisory work constituted a satisfying opportunity to teach younger men, an ambition he had always cherished. He also served as a member of the Interim Council of the Australian National University and took a close interest in the planning, educational structure and personnel of the Research Schools of Social Sciences and Pacific Studies, for which his lifetime of private study and public work had prepared him. He saw the establishment of the A.N.U. as an attempt to develop more institutionalized centres for Australian creative social thought, yet his own intellectual life had been largely voluntary, detached from formal educational institutions. Although his views on the need for interdisciplinary studies based upon sociology, social philosophy and social psychology were in advance of contemporary opinion, the structure of the Research School of Social Sciences failed to reflect his priorities. The A.N.U. came too late in his life for Eggleston significantly to determine its ethos, and like his teaching of diplomatic cadets, was a measure of the ungainliness of his career as a whole.

Eggleston spent the last years of his life from 1949 to 1954, despite the onset of blindness, writing published and unpublished reminiscences and reflections upon his experience. At the end of 1952 his *Reflections of an Australian liberal* was published. It became his only best-selling book, and was widely read and quoted. Shortly before his death he completed a manuscript posthumously published as *Reflections on Australian foreign policy*, in 1957. During the early 1950s he also wrote or dictated unpublished reminiscences of which the most important were 'Melbourne memoirs. A social and cultural history of

Melbourne from the eighteen eighties to the present', and 'Confidential notes', a series of personal memoirs of historical figures he had known. The latter manuscript was deposited in the Australian National University Library, and the former in the Eggleston papers, National Library of Australia.

Despite the brief impact of *Reflections of an Australian liberal* and frequent articles for the Melbourne press, Eggleston's last years were lonely and relatively obscure. He died in hospital at Camberwell, Melbourne, on 12 November 1954 and was cremated. Two sons and a daughter survived him.

W. Osmond, F. W. Eggleston (1875-1954): portrait of an Australian intellectual (Ph.D. thesis, Univ Syd, 1980), and for bibliog.

WARREN OSMOND

ELDER, SIR JAMES ALEXANDER MACKENZIE (1869-1946), businessman, was born on 10 November 1869 at Elgin, Scotland, son of James Elder, parish clerk, and his wife Isabella, née Allan. He was educated at the Elgin Academy and completed his law articles in a local law firm. In 1891 he migrated to Melbourne and began work with the New Zealand Loan and Mercantile Agency Co., later moving to the Australian Mortgage (Mercantile), Land, and Finance Co. There he met John Cooke [q.v.], then Australian manager of the firm. In 1895, when Cooke started business as a frozen meat exporter in his own right, Elder left the firm to work for him. On 10 August 1898, with Presbyterian forms, he married Margaret Blyth Nicoll; they had a son and a daughter.

Elder's business fortunes prospered with those of Cooke. After a business trip to Britain in 1906 he was made a junior partner in what by then was one of the largest meat exporting businesses in Australia, operating in several States. In 1913, when the business was perhaps at a peak of its fortunes, Cooke finally established a company to run it. Elder was the largest shareholder after Cooke himself, holding 20 per cent of the shares, and was now managing director. As Cooke's health deteriorated, he played an increasingly dominant role in the company, becoming undisputed head when Cooke died in 1917.

Elder was unlucky to become managing director at the time when the fortunes of the meat export trade were about to decline. After World War I in particular, all exporters battled to survive and John Cooke and Co. Pty Ltd was only one of the ventures, if the largest, to wind up its affairs in the troubled 1920s. Notice of the company's intention to retire from the meat trade was given by

Elder in February 1924. While labour problems, higher wages, and fuel and transport costs were cited as some of the reasons why a firm 'so well established and with such wide ramifications' should voluntarily resign its business activities, it is evident that Elder lacked the entrepreneurial and organizational flair of the firm's founder, which alone perhaps could have held together its many far-flung interests. Privately, indeed, Elder was criticized by his competitors for lack of business judgment. Furthermore, from his other activities it would seem that he did not devote his attention single-mindedly to the affairs of a difficult business.

From the outbreak of war Elder began in effect a second career, as trade adviser to the Federal government. In 1914 he became the representative of the Associated Chambers of Commerce on the Commonwealth Board of Trade, holding that position for the next decade. In 1919 he accepted an invitation to investigate trade and investment problems between Australia and Britain. On this unpaid mission, he visited nearly one hundred British firms and subsequently several new enterprises were established by British firms in Australia. Elder was a commissioner of the British Empire Exhibition held in London in 1924 and 1925 and was for a time deputy chairman of its Australian section. In September 1924 he took up a two-year appointment as commissioner for Australia in the United States of America. There, he energetically promoted Australian trade interests, travelling widely, delivering lectures and making extensive use of the new wireless medium. In June 1925, while in the United States, in recognition of his services to Australian trade, he was knighted. He served as a member of the royal commission on wireless services in 1927, his last major activity for the Federal government.

Perhaps symbolic of his lifelong interest in Australian pastoral exports Elder was from 1916 a director of Goldsbrough Mort [qq.v.4,5] & Co. Ltd; when resident in Australia he rarely missed a meeting. He was also a director of the Union Trustee Co. of Australia Ltd until 1942, and a director, in 1932-43 chairman, of the National Bank of Australasia. In 1932 he was described as being tall and well built, with silver-grey hair, the 'glow of health in his cheeks' and a ready smile. He was a Presbyterian, a member of the Melbourne and Australian clubs, and described his recreations as motoring, fishing, golf and shooting. Elder had diabetes for some years before his death of coronary-vascular disease in hospital at East Melbourne on 30 May 1946. He was survived by his wife and son, and was buried in Brighton cemetery. His estate was valued for probate at £41 427.

Pastoral Review, 15 Mar 1924, June 1946; *Argus*, 23 Feb 1924, 3 June 1925, 31 May 1946; *Age*, 31 May 1946; E. A. Beever, A history of the Australian meat export trade, 1865-1939 (Ph.D. thesis, Univ Melb, 1968).   E. A. BEEVER

ELKINGTON, JOHN SIMEON (1841-1922), professor of history, was born on 22 November 1841 at Rye, Sussex, England, eldest son of John Elkington, then a wool-stapler, and his wife Marian, née Smith. He migrated to Victoria with his parents in 1848. He was educated at Melbourne Church of England Grammar School, matriculating in 1862, and at the University of Melbourne, where he graduated B.A. with first-class honours in history and political economy in 1866 (M.A., 1874; LL.B., 1884).

In July 1866 Elkington was appointed second-class inspector of schools under the Common Schools Act; he served in most parts of the colony for over a decade. In his reports he was critical of educational standards in country schools and strongly advocated compulsory education. In 1876 he joined the university as lecturer in history and political economy and, when Dr W. E. Hearn [q.v.4] became dean of the law school in 1879, was appointed for life as professor of history and political economy. He was the first Australian-educated scholar to be appointed to a chair. He retired by agreement on 1 March 1913.

In a small professorial board, Elkington's ebullience and sharp tongue caused occasional personality clashes, one of which led to his suspension for a month. He was elected for his only term as president in 1886. He was distinguished chiefly as a teacher, lecturing in ancient, British and constitutional history (his main subject), history of the British Empire and political economy. Most Victorian lawyers for a third of a century sat at his feet and were influenced by his views, for he was an intense political partisan and a 'Freetrader of Freetraders'. A gifted raconteur, he 'interspersed the dry facts of historical research and economic argument with anecdotes and stories' whose Rabelaisian quality had to be censored when women students entered the university. His lectures changed little after 1887.

Elkington was well read but his own research was minimal. 'I have work in hand, but I have not committed myself to anything very extensive in book form so far', he told the royal commission on the university in 1903. He published only a handful of articles, mainly on constitutional history. His opportunities for research were limited by his involvement in non-university affairs. He

practised law for eleven years and was active in civic matters, serving on the (Royal) Melbourne Hospital Committee in 1881-85. His interest in social problems arose partly from the physical handicap of a club-foot. Gregarious by nature, he attracted interesting people: 'he has known everybody and is full of anecdotes and incidents about the leading men in Victorian life'. Bankruptcies in 1892 and 1895 after speculating in land and mining, as well as his inordinate thirst, created problems for the university.

On 28 December 1867 at St Mary's Roman Catholic Cathedral, Sydney, he had married Helen Mary, sister of W. R. Guilfoyle [q.v.4]. She died in 1897 and on 13 April 1903 at St John's Church of England, Lilydale, Victoria, he married her sister Charlotte Corday Guilfoyle. Elkington suffered from diabetes for some thirty years before his death on 6 June 1922 at his Canterbury home. Buried in Melbourne general cemetery, he was survived by two sons of his first marriage, the elder being John Simeon Colebrook Elkington [q.v.].

G. Blainey, *A centenary history of the University of Melbourne* (Melb, 1957); Education Dept (Vic), *Vision and realisation*, L. J. Blake ed (Melb, 1973); Roy Com on Univ Melb, *PP* (LA Vic), 1903, 2 (20), p 83; *Alma Mater* (Univ Melb) 1 (1895), no 4, 7 (1962), no 2; *Table Talk*, 26 Dec 1889; *Punch* (Melb), 23 Sept 1909; register of careers (history section, Education Dept, Melb); Univ Melb Archives.   NORMAN HARPER

ELKINGTON, JOHN SIMEON COLEBROOK (1871-1955), advocate of public health, was born on 29 September 1871 at Castlemaine, Victoria, son of John Simeon Elkington [q.v.] and his wife Helen Mary, née Guilfoyle. After education at Melbourne Church of England Grammar School and Carlton College, Elkington studied medicine at the University of Melbourne from 1890, but crashed in finals and qualified as a licentiate at Edinburgh and Glasgow in 1896. That year on 27 August in Melbourne he married 29-year-old Mary Cassandra Parkinson; they were to have no children. Elkington mixed with the Lindsay brothers [qq.v.] in Melbourne's Bohemia and introduced Norman's work to the Sydney *Bulletin*. Nationalism in the *Bulletin* style attracted him, and he strove to write fiction under A. G. Stephens's [q.v.] tutelage. Other hobbies were boxing and hunting, appropriate to this man of fine, sometimes overbearing, presence.

Elkington found congenial work in assisting D. A. Gresswell [q.v.] of Victoria's Department of Public Health. In early 1902 he took a diploma of public health in London, bacteriology and tropical medicine being his particular interests. They intensified during a spell with the Imperial medical service in India.

The Elkingtons returned to Melbourne in mid-1903. Smallpox was then raging in Launceston, and the Tasmanian government sought help from Victoria. Gresswell nominated Elkington as the man it needed. Through August and September he worked in Launceston with panache and effect. His report on the epidemic began an *oeuvre* of bureaucratic prose, outstandingly pungent and skilful. On invitation, he became Tasmania's chief health officer in a newly established department.

Funding was always scanty, but Elkington achieved much. He exhorted local authorities to care about health, campaigned against tuberculosis and food adulteration, and fostered infant care. His greatest *coup* was a system of checking schoolchildren's health, which became a model throughout Australia. Two books, *Health in the school* (1907) and *Health reader* (1908), were published for the Empire and Australasian markets respectively. Elkington remained a champion of tropical medicine, insisting that with its aid Anglo-Saxons could settle northern Australia. Nationalism also led him to advocate a Federal quarantine service, achieved in 1908.

On 1 January 1910 Elkington took up his post as commissioner of public health in Queensland. There a larger staff allowed more vigorous crusades. One, again in the Australian van, was to treat venereal disease with public health care for its victims — rather than by moralist preaching and/or policing of prostitutes. Food and drugs came under close scrutiny, Elkington showing himself to be a pioneer of consumer protection. Above all, in Queensland he developed his tropical interests. He cherished the Australian Institute for Tropical Medicine, funded principally by the Commonwealth and sited at Townsville.

Meanwhile the Federal quarantine service had developed. In mid-1913 J. H. L. Cumpston [q.v.] became its director, and in November Elkington replaced him as its officer in Queensland. The two respected each other and stayed close for the present. From 1916 Elkington's responsibilities extended to the Northern Territory, although during the influenza epidemic of 1918-19 he managed Sydney's quarantine station. Expansion of the quarantine service into a Federal Department of Health owed much to his efforts, most importantly in persuading the Australasian Medical Congress of 1920 to back the scheme in order to foster tropical medicine.

After the department was established in March 1921 under Cumpston's direction,

Elkington led a division of tropical hygiene. It supervised the Institute of Tropical Medicine and a campaign against hookworm throughout Australia and its territories. With some colleagues, notably (Sir) Raphael Cilento, Elkington hoped that Australia might direct health care throughout the South Pacific. His pen continued brilliantly, for example in *Notes on quarantine practice for quarantine officers* (1925).

Overall, however, Elkington's impact declined in the 1920s. Jack Lindsay, their nephew, suggests that only Mary Elkington's fierce ambition kept her husband at the bureaucratic yoke. Certainly Elkington's passion for travel and the outdoors waxed strong, before and after Mary's death in 1925. Cumpston and Elkington lost their intimacy, and tropical medicine some standing within the department. Elkington resigned in July 1928.

World-wide travel, fellowship, reading, and writing for the *Bulletin* were Elkington's chief interests in retirement. He retained contact with Cilento, and so with public medicine. In Sydney on 13 April 1945 he married Ida Isabel Hood Elkington, née McBride, the divorced wife of his brother. They lived at Mooloolaba, Queensland, and his wife survived Elkington's death there on 8 March 1955.

J. Lindsay, *Life rarely tells* (Lond, 1958); R. Cilento (ed), *Triumph in the tropics* (Brisb, 1959); *MJA*, 23 July 1955, p 144; *Hist Studies*, no 67, Oct 1976, p 176; *Brisbane Courier*, 4 July 1928.

MICHAEL ROE

ELLIOTT, CHARLES HAZELL (1882-1956), soldier and clerk, was born on 19 August 1882 in Hobart, son of Robert Elliott, corn and produce merchant, and his wife Sophia, née Hazell. He was educated at The Friends' School, Hobart, and joined the clerical staff of the Australian Mutual Provident Society on 21 December 1898. In 1906 he joined the Derwent Regiment, Australian Military Forces (militia), was commissioned as a second lieutenant in July 1907 and promoted captain in 1911.

With the outbreak of World War I Elliott enlisted in the Australian Imperial Force on 14 August 1914 and in October embarked as captain in command of 'A' Company, 12th Battalion. He was promoted major in Egypt in January 1915. Within hours of the landing at Gallipoli on 25 April he took command of the battalion following the wounding of Lieut-Colonel S. Hawley and the death of Colonel L. F. Clarke. Then Elliott too was wounded in the left shoulder and arm, and after treatment in the field was eventually invalided to England in June. He returned in September and was temporarily promoted to lieut-colonel in command of the battalion. His rank and command were confirmed on 1 March 1916 and he led the 12th Battalion for the rest of the war.

On 29 March the battalion left Egypt for the Western Front and in July and August fought at Pozières and Mouquet Farm. In November-December the unit was engaged in trench warfare on the Somme and in April 1917 saw action at Bullecourt. On 15 April the Germans launched a surprise attack at Lagnicourt which threatened the battalion's headquarters. Elliott quickly organized the defence, showing 'a wonderful example of leadership, sangfroid and enthusiasm'. The *London Gazette* wrote: 'Although the enemy had penetrated our line, and were within 500 yards of Battalion Headquarters, he took up a position with batmen, cooks and signallers and checked the enemy's advance, thus enabling the counter-attacking to come forward and drive the enemy back. His action at a most critical time turned what might have been a defeat into a victory'. He had been wounded in the head and did not resume command until 10 May.

Other operations that Elliott took part in during 1917-18 included Hill 60, Polygon Wood, Strazeele, Zonnebeke and Broodseinde. In August 1918 he was wounded again at Lihons, suffering gun-shot injuries to the left arm and chest. Many times between May 1917 and February 1919 he temporarily commanded the 3rd Infantry Brigade for short periods. For his war service he was mentioned in dispatches three times and was awarded the Distinguished Service Order in the New Year honours of 1917 and a Bar next June for his work at Lagnicourt. He was also appointed C.M.G. and received the Légion d'honneur. His A.I.F. appointment ended in August 1919.

Elliott was appointed commander of the 2nd Battalion, 40th Infantry Regiment, A.M.F. (militia) in 1920 and the 12th Infantry Brigade in 1922 with the temporary rank of colonel; he was placed on the reserve of officers in 1930. After the war he continued to work for the A.M.P. Society as a cashier and later as a claims officer until his retirement in 1945. In London on 20 December 1917 he had married Alice Gordon King, a sister in the Australian Army Nursing Service. They had one son, Charles Gordon (b. 1925).

In private life Elliott was devoted to home and garden. He was also a keen sportsman and after the war held executive positions with the Hobart Harrier Club, the Tasmanian Amateur Athletic and Boxing associations and the Derwent Rowing Club. He was a Freemason from 1911. Survived by his wife and son, he died at his home in New Town, Hobart, on 27 April 1956 of cerebro-vascular disease and was cremated.

Elliott was a gallant soldier, always concerned for the well-being of those under his command. A schoolmate wrote of him in the April 1919 edition of The Friends' School journal: 'The best of Charlie is that, however many decorations he gets, he alters not a bit. Each time a fresh decoration is presented to him he lines the whole battalion up, shows them the medal and says, "Here you are, boys; have a look at this. *You* won it, not I". What more could men expect of their commander?'

C. E. W. Bean, *The story of Anzac*, 1, 2 (Syd, 1921, 1924); L. M. Newton, *The story of the twelfth* (Hob, 1925); *Cyclopedia of Tasmania* (Hob, 1931); C. E. W. Bean, *The A.I.F. in France*, 1916-18 (Syd, 1929, 1933, 1937, 1942); W. N. Oats, *The rose and the waratah* (Hob, 1979); *London Gazette*, 29 Dec 1916, 2 Jan, 18 June, 28 Dec 1917, 28 May, 3 June, 17 Aug 1918; *Mercury*, 28 Apr 1956; C. H. Elliott papers (TA); personal information. RODNEY K. QUINN

ELLIOTT, GILBERT CHARLES EDWARD (1872-1934), British regular soldier, was born on 8 October 1872 at East Stonehouse, Devonshire, son of Gilbert Elliott, physician, and his wife Harriott, née Druitt. He was educated at Clifton College, Bristol, and at the Royal Military Academy, Woolwich.

Elliott was commissioned as a second lieutenant, Royal Engineers, on 22 July 1892, and was promoted lieutenant in 1895 and captain in 1903. He served in Canada in 1897-1903, and again in 1906-08 as a major with the Royal Canadian Engineers at Halifax. His majority in the Royal Engineers, however, was not gained until 22 July 1912. Pleased with his Canadian experiences, Elliott volunteered for special duty with the Australian Military Forces and, from 23 October 1913 to 15 April 1918, was employed by the Commonwealth government. Hardly had he become chief engineer, Royal Australian Engineers, in New South Wales, when World War I began. Believing that 'the best training for war was war', he volunteered for service on 18 August 1914 and was appointed to raise and command the engineers of the 1st Division, Australian Imperial Force, as lieut-colonel from 16 October.

After training his engineers at Mena Camp, Egypt, Elliott landed at Anzac on 25 April 1915. He was wounded on 15 May and resumed duty two months later. On 26 July he was appointed commander of the 2nd Australian Divisional Engineers whom he trained in Egypt then brought to Anzac. On 30 October he was gassed by poisonous fumes after the explosion of an Australian mine in a tunnel; this left him unfit for duty until early 1916.

Elliott's capacity and thoroughness were recognized by the decision that he should organize and command the engineers of the 4th Division from 26 February. From June 1916 to March 1918, as commanding royal engineer (the first time this designation was used), 4th Australian Division, he was engaged in operations in France and Belgium, mainly in the Ypres sector. He was awarded the Distinguished Service Order and the French Croix de Guerre, appointed C.M.G. and mentioned in dispatches three times. In June 1917 he commanded the engineers in holding operations after the battle of Messines, then moved forward for the 3rd battle of Ypres where his men distinguished themselves at Polygon Wood in September. Next March, having suffered poor health since being gassed at Anzac, he was granted leave to England and was then pronounced unfit for further active service. His A.I.F. appointment ended in April. Known in the A.I.F. as 'Snowy', Elliott was 'a man of kindly nature, often distressed by the ravages of war and in all circumstances just and honourable'. He should be remembered in Australia as the officer who first mobilized and led into battle the Royal Australian Engineers.

Elliott was returned to the British Army in April 1918 and was promoted lieut-colonel in 1920 and colonel in 1924. In 1920-24 he served as C.R.E. with British forces in Ireland, in Turkey and at York. While in Turkey he met Helen Muriel Cox, whom he married in 1924. He was placed on the retired list in 1926 and, survived by his wife, died of coronary vascular disease at his home at Beaconsfield, Buckinghamshire, on 1 September 1934.

C. E. W. Bean, *The story of Anzac* (Syd, 1921, 1924), and *The A.I.F. in France*, 1916-17 (Syd, 1929, 1933); *London Gazette*, 22, 25 Sept, 21 Nov, 8 Dec 1916, 2, 4 Jan, 11 Dec 1917, 20 May 1918; *Roy Engineers J*, supp, Nov 1934; *Reveille*, (Syd), Dec 1934; War diaries, 1st, 2nd and 4th Divisional Engineers, A.I.F. (AWM).   C. NEUMANN

ELLIOTT, HAROLD EDWARD (1878-1931), soldier, lawyer and politician, was born on 19 June 1878 at West Charlton, Victoria, son of Thomas Elliott, farmer, and his wife Helen, née Janvrin. He was educated at Ballarat College and at Ormond College, University of Melbourne, where he joined the officers' corps. In 1900 he interrupted his studies to enlist in the 4th Victorian (Imperial) Contingent, serving in South Africa in 1900-02. He was awarded the Dis-

tinguished Conduct Medal for an audacious night exploit and was commissioned in the 2nd Royal Berkshire Regiment. However, he remained with the Australians as acting adjutant. Later he served with the Border Scouts and was specially congratulated by Lord Kitchener for his successful defence of a post. Elliott was also mentioned in dispatches.

Returning to the university in 1903, he won many scholarships and prizes (LL.B, 1906; LL.M., and B.A., 1920); he was also a champion athlete. In 1907 he was called to the Bar of Victoria and the Commonwealth; he also set up a firm of solicitors, H. E. Elliott & Co. He had returned to the army in 1904 as a second lieutenant in the 5th Infantry Regiment (militia). In 1913 he became lieut-colonel commanding the 58th Battalion in the new universal training scheme. As C. E. W. Bean [q.v.7] observed, 'his whole heart and interest were in the Army' and this meant not only parades and camps but also the study of textbooks and military history. On 27 December 1909 at Northcote he had married Catherine Frazer Campbell with Presbyterian forms. They had a daughter and a son.

When the Australian Imperial Force was being raised in August 1914, Elliott was appointed to command the 7th Battalion in the 2nd Brigade. His massive frame – he had been a good footballer and university champion weight-putter – his energy, strength of character and explosive temper quickly established him as one of the characters of the force. His men called him 'Pompey', a nickname which did not please him but clung to him to the end. Hard training and stern discipline were the foundations on which he built the 7th at Broadmeadows and in Egypt.

On the day of the Gallipoli landing, 25 April 1915, Elliott was wounded and evacuated, not returning until early June. He soon won a reputation for cool courage in the fighting for German Officers' Trench. At Lone Pine on 8 August he relieved part of the 1st Brigade and in the next twenty-four hours repulsed the Turkish counter-attacks by furious close-quarter fighting and bombing. Of the seven Victoria Crosses awarded for Lone Pine, four went to Elliott's battalion but his own work was not recognized. His divisional commander, Major General H. B. Walker, had told him that his name had been at the head of his list of recommendations. This was the beginning of an irritation for Elliott, which, before the end of the war, had become an obsession.

He was evacuated sick in August, returning in November but, on the eve of the evacuation of Anzac, a sprained ankle caused him to be sent off ahead of his unit. In

February 1916 Elliott was made commander of the 1st Brigade but on 1 March he was given the congenial task of organizing the 15th (Victorian) Brigade in the new 5th Division and promoted brigadier general.

In July Elliott began his service on the Western Front where he fought in most of the great battles of the A.I.F. He trained his brigade as he had trained his battalion and made it 'a magnificently effective instrument'. This he did in spite of the appalling losses in battles such as Fromelles, their first action, when his two assaulting battalions suffered 1452 casualties in less than twenty-four hours. Elliott had protested about the hopelessness of the task; he was in the front line at zero hour and visited his troops before they were withdrawn. Next morning, A. W. Bazley, Bean's assistant, saw him greeting the remnants: 'no one who was present will ever forget the picture of him, the tears streaming down his face, as he shook hands with the returning survivors'.

Although he could himself be foolhardy, Elliott tried to avoid taking risks with his soldiers. He visited his front line daily about dawn. He thrived on battle and was exhilarated by the achievements of his men. 'It is beautiful to see them fight', he wrote in March 1917, 'and then it is fine to see the old Bosches jump out and run . . . and our guns open on them and smash them. It is just the fun of the world'. After the capture of Péronne in September 1918 he found a punt and took a friend onto the moat while German shells splashed into the water nearby. 'A great game, isn't it!' said 'Pompey', smiling at his anxious companion.

It has been said of Elliott that he could do some things with Australian troops no other commander could do. Elliott knew it and was humble about it. After Polygon Wood he wrote to his wife: 'It is all due to the boys and the officers like Norman Marshall [q.v.] . . . It is wonderful the loyalty and bravery that is shown, their absolute confidence in me is touching – I can order them to take on the most hopeless looking jobs and they throw their hearts and souls not to speak of their lives and bodies into the job without thought. You must pray more than ever that I shall be worthy of this trust, Katie, and have wisdom and courage given me worthy of my job'.

Part of Elliott's success lay in his careful selection of officers, but it was over the appointment of his battalion commanders that he first clashed with Lieut-General Sir William Birdwood [q.v.7] and Brigadier General (Sir) Brudenell White [q.v.] in March 1916. Elliott was given officers who were obviously, to him, unsuitable. When told that they must remain and that their reputations were sacred he replied that the lives of his men were more sacred. His frankness was understood within his brigade and provided countless anecdotes but it was little relished at higher headquarters. Worse still, he sometimes wrote reports sharply critical of senior commanders and the failures of troops on his flanks. One, after Polygon Wood, was so outrageous and inaccurate in its strictures on a neighbouring British division that Birdwood ordered all copies to be destroyed.

'Pompey' could be a difficult subordinate especially when the safety of his men was involved. At least twice after Fromelles he protested so vehemently against attacks ordered by 5th Division headquarters that the operations were cancelled. His objections were always based on knowledge of the ground obtained from personal reconnaissance and on a profound grasp of the tactical possibilities.

In the brief period of open warfare which marked the advance to the Hindenburg line in March 1917, Elliott was in his element as commander of one of the Australian advanced guards. With a small force of all arms and a degree of independence impossible in trench warfare, he probed for weak spots and turned the German rearguards out of their positions by encircling movements. It was during this phase that he made a rash misjudgment when he ordered an attack in daylight in retaliation for a German counter-attack. His instruction that 5th Division headquarters was not to be notified was resisted by his brigade major, G. F. G. Wieck [q.v.], and Elliott gave way. Major-General (Sir) J. J. T. Hobbs [q.v.] cancelled the attack and hurried forward to Elliott's headquarters. He could hardly have survived this affair had word of it reached Birdwood who had already reprimanded him for occupying a village outside his boundaries.

No impulsive actions marred his tactics in the battle of Polygon Wood on 25–26 September 1917, when his grasp of the situation and capacity for quick, decisive action was supreme. As usual, Elliott was up with his foremost battalions soon after dawn. Bean attributes the outcome to the way in which Elliott's troops 'snatched complete success from an almost desperate situation . . . the driving force of this stout-hearted leader in his inferno at Hooge . . . was in a large measure responsible for this victory'. During this battle his brother Captain G. S. Elliott, a Military Cross winner, was killed, and a letter from home revealed the collapse of his firm leaving him with a debt of £5000.

After Polygon Wood, Elliott was confident that if a divisional command became vacant he would get it. Ambitious and utterly self-reliant, it was a hope he had long cherished. His work in the defensive battles of March 1918 and his part in the famous counter-attack at Villers-Bretonneux in April must have reinforced his optimism. It had been a desperate time in which Elliott's measures were not always approved by his superiors. Under his orders, a British staff officer had been arrested for looting wine at Corbie after which Elliott made it known that looters would be publicly hanged. The looting stopped but the aggrieved officer complained to General Headquarters. In another written instruction, officers rallying British stragglers in his sector were ordered to shoot any who hesitated. This was quickly withdrawn on the orders of Hobbs.

In May 1918 the promotion of Brigadier Generals (Sir) J. Gellibrand and (Sir) T. W. Glasgow [qq.v.] to major general and to command divisions was a shattering blow to Elliott. In an intemperate letter to White he complained, *inter alia*, of being superseded which, as an experienced officer, he knew was fallacious, for such promotions were by selection. White gave him the opportunity of withdrawing his letter so that it did not reach Birdwood. For the rest of the war Elliott nursed his grievance while leading his brigade with all his old fire. He was wounded again in August but remained on duty. When, owing to lack of reinforcements, seven battalions were to be disbanded in September, all refused. Only the 60th obeyed after Elliott had addressed them.

Elliott spoke to his brigade for the last time to thank them in January 1919. Afterwards all the battalions paraded voluntarily and marched around his headquarters cheering him. 'So I had to go out and give them one more speech and then they cheered again'. Since 1915 he had been appointed C.B. and C.M.G. and had been awarded the Distinguished Service Order, the Russian Order of St Anne and the French Croix de Guerre. He was mentioned in dispatches seven times and in a special order of the day by the commander of the French 31st Corps.

When he returned to Melbourne in June 1919 Elliott began to rebuild his firm but by September he was back in the militia as commander of the 15th Brigade. In the elections of 1919 he stood for the Senate as a Nationalist and topped the Victorian poll; he was re-elected in 1925. Elliott never attained office but he spoke on a wide range of topics especially on the Federal capital and defence. He made full use of his position to publicize and seek redress of his wartime grievances.

In February 1921 he asked to be placed on the unattached list and for his alleged supersession to be placed before the minister for defence. Besides, he disliked serving under White who was now chief of the General Staff. His position was aggravated by reports that Gellibrand and Glasgow would become divisional commanders in the new organization. This, he claimed, was a further supersession. The Military Board rejected his claims and refused, as it was bound to do, his request for a judicial enquiry. When his grievances were debated in the Senate, his arguments were firmly rebutted by the minister for defence, G. F. Pearce [q.v.].

Elliott engaged in a sporadic campaign in the press in which he aired his grievances, attacked Birdwood and White and was contemptuous of the British high command whom he blamed for the grievous casualties amongst the Australian infantry. This attracted little sympathy and some sharp criticism. Fortunately he had much to occupy him. He had become city solicitor for Melbourne and a director of the National Trustees, Executors & Agency Co. in 1919. He was involved in the affairs of returned soldiers and was chiefly responsible for redrafting the constitution of the Returned Sailors' and Soldiers' Imperial League of Australia. For his help during the police strike in 1923 he was specially thanked by the premier of Victoria, (Sir) H. S. W. Lawson [q.v.].

In 1926, under Sir Harry Chauvel [q.v.7] as C.G.S., Elliott again commanded the 15th Brigade and next year the 3rd Division. He was promoted major general in August 1927 but, in a sense, this was too late. Although he threw himself into training with the old enthusiasm, his disappointments still gnawed at him. In 1929 he corresponded with Generals Sir J. W. McCay [q.v.], Hobbs and Sir J. Monash [q.v.] about his 'supersession' and the reasons for it. To Hobbs he admitted: 'The injustice of the position as I conceive it has actually coloured all my post war life'. Neither the generosity nor the wise advice of the replies he received mitigated his frustration. He turned to White in 1930 but White refused to discuss the past and a second unfortunate attempt to obtain his views was curtly rejected.

Elliott's deep and abiding sense of injustice combined with the strain of his war service and his ceaseless activity to undermine his health. Early in 1931 he was in hospital under treatment for blood pressure. When discharged he did not return to the Senate. Soon afterwards he was found with a wound in the arm and was rushed to hospital where he died on 23 March. An inquest returned a verdict of suicide. 'Pompey' Elliott was buried with full military honours in Burwood cemetery. His wife and children survived him. His portrait by W. B. McInnes [q.v.] hangs in the Australian War Memorial.

Aust Defence Dept, *Official records of the Australian military contingents to the war in South Africa*, P. L. Murray ed (Melb, 1911); C. E. W. Bean, *The story of Anzac*, 1, 2 (Syd, 1921, 1924), and *The A.I.F. in France*, 1916-18 (Syd, 1929, 1933, 1937, 1942), and *Two men I knew* (Syd, 1957); G. Blaikie, *Remember Smith's Weekly?* (Adel, 1975); *PD* (Cwlth), 1921, p 7727; *Reveille* (Syd), Mar 1931, Aug 1937; *Punch* (Melb), 13 Nov 1919, 6 Aug 1925; *Age*, 28 May 1921, 24 Mar 1931; *Argus, Herald* (Melb), and *SMH*, 24 Mar 1931; H. E. Elliott papers (AWM).   A. J. HILL

ELLIOTT, HELENA SUMNER LOCKE; *see* LOCKE

ELLIOTT, JAMES FREDERICK (1858-1928), industrial chemist and businessman, was born on 8 November 1858 at Balmain, Sydney, third son of London-born George Robinson Elliott, surgeon, and his Calcutta-born wife Anne, née Mackay. George had migrated to Sydney in the late 1840s with two brothers Frederick and James and in 1859 they bought Edward Youngman's importing, wholesale druggist and dry-salting business. They expanded into the manufacture of drugs and chemicals, packaging and the sale of surgical implements, and in 1873 formed a private company, Elliott Brothers Ltd; it was registered as a public company in 1885.

After attending Sydney Grammar School, James Frederick was sent abroad to study chemistry in London and Germany. At Berlin he studied under Professor Hoffmann, graduated Ph.D. from the Albert Ludwigs University at Freiburg, Germany, and then taught chemistry under Hoffmann. On 23 February 1879 at Pimlico, London, he married Clara Martha Boelke. He was recalled to Australia by his father and in 1884 began working for Elliott Bros as a pharmaceutical chemist and chemical engineer, and later designed their laboratories at Rozelle. He made many visits overseas to investigate developments in pharmaceutical manufacturing and, as he drew closer to the commercial heart of the firm, in search of raw materials. In 1912, after the death of his elder brother George, he became chairman and managing director of the firm.

Elliott was also a director of the Australian Alliance Assurance Co. and the Automatic Bread Baking Co. Ltd, and of Taylors & Elliotts Ltd, Brisbane. During World War I, when Australia's dependence on overseas chemical supplies, especially German, became clear, Elliott extended and improved his company's ability to manufacture bismuth (then much used in medicine), various fertilizers and mineral acids.

A noted yachtsman, Elliott raced *Magic*, bought from (Sir) James R. Fairfax [q.v.] in 1891, and later *Meteor*. He was rear-commodore of the Royal Sydney Yacht Squadron in 1893-94 and 1900-02 and vice-commodore in 1902-04, and was a director of the private company formed to buy the club's premises, Carabella, Milsons Point, in 1904. He was reputedly 'a man of liberal ideas, keen judgment, happy disposition'. From childhood he suffered from recurring throat and chest complaints which often prompted him to travel north in the winter. In 1905 Elliott had legally separated from his wife and endowed her with £400 a year for life. Predeceased by his two sons, he died at his home, Lahane, Wunulla Road, Point Piper, on 9 September 1928 and was buried in the Anglican section of South Head cemetery.

At the time of Elliott's death Evelyn Elizabeth Evans was living at Lahane: in his will Elliott provided handsomely for her, and also for Margaret Jackson and Alice Taylor. His estate was valued for probate at £126 335; of the final residue, two-sixths went to John Jackson, Katoomba, and one-sixth was left to each of the four children of Elliott's two nephews. In 1929 Elliott Bros became part of Drug Houses of Australia Ltd.

P. R. Stephensen (ed), *Sydney sails* (Syd, 1962); G. Haines, *The grains and threepenn'orths of pharmacy* (Melb, 1976); Elliott Bros Ltd, *Aust Pharmaceutical Notes and News*, 1 July 1920, 10 Feb 1926, 10 Sept 1928, 10 Oct 1930, 10 June, 10 Dec 1931; *SMH*, 11 Sept 1928.   GREGORY HAINES

ELLIOTT, ROBERT CHARLES DUNLOP (1884-1950), businessman, newspaper proprietor and senator, was born on 28 October 1884 at Kyneton, Victoria, fourth surviving child of Robert Cochrane Elliott, a grocer from Northumberland, England, and his wife Maria Jeanette, née Williamson, from Inverness, Scotland.

His early years are variously reported. He began to earn his living after local state primary school education. In 1905-11 he served in the militia as a lieutenant. By then he had set up as a business agent. On 5 April 1913 at Balaclava, Melbourne, he married Hilda, daughter of Theodore Fink [q.v.]; Dr Charles Strong [q.v.6] officiated.

Known as 'R.D.' he acquired proprietorships and directorships. By 1924 these included the Arabic Co. Pty Ltd, roofing manufacturers; lime works at Curdie's River; Stoddart, Fitcher & Millist, millinery specialists; Watters & Sons Pty Ltd, seedsmen; Spicers & Detmold, wholesale stationers and manufacturers; and the Yorkshire Insurance Co. As a leading influence with Armstrong Whitworth Pty Ltd and its successor (1927), the Civil Engineering Construction Co. Pty Ltd, he undertook bridge-building, notably at Mildura, and hydro-electric schemes at Sugarloaf-Rubicon (Eildon) in Victoria, Shannon in Tasmania, and Grafton in New South Wales.

In 1924 with Ethel, wife of (Sir) Earle Page [q.v.], and P. G. Stewart [q.v.], he purchased the recently constituted New Sunraysia Daily Pty. Ltd. which acquired *Sunraysia Daily* from the receivers; he virtually controlled the paper although he was not proprietor until the early 1930s. Elliott acquired other country newspapers, including the *Castlemaine Mail* (1932) *Shepparton Advertiser* (1935), Swan Hill *Guardian* and Wentworth *Western Evening News* (1938), *Albury Banner* (1940), *Yarrawonga Chronicle* (1943), *Cobram Courier* (1944), *Maryborough Advertiser* (1945), *Cohuna Farmers' Weekly* (1947) and *Wangaratta Chronicle* (1949). He also controlled radio 3MA (Mildura) from 1932. He was director of Western Newspapers Group and of Australian United Press, and a foundation director of the Australian Provincial Daily Press Association (Regional Dailies of Australia Ltd). He followed his father-in-law as delegate at Imperial press conferences in London in 1930 and South Africa in 1935.

Narrowly defeated on 2 June 1928 for the Victorian Legislative Council (North-Western Province), Elliott was elected as senator for Victoria on 17 November and sworn in on 14 August 1929. With all Victorian Federal Country Party members, including W. G. Gibson [q.v.], he rejected the State executive's demand for a conformity pledge for the election of 15 September 1934. Elliott was dropped from the United Australia Party-Country Party Senate team which, however, included Gibson. Prime Minister Lyons [q.v.] had objected to charges of dishonesty and corruption against his government in Elliott's *Castlemaine Mail* of 19 August 1933. Elliott observed that 'the political team did not want in Parliament any independent who had a mind of his own'. He was defeated by Gibson but held his seat under the Constitution until 30 June 1935. He had chaired the Senate select committee on the standing committee system and served on Senate library and disputed returns committees.

Elliott admired and tried to model himself on Lord Beaverbrook. He joined Beaverbrook's fervent 'crusade', beginning in 1929-30, for 'Empire Free Trade'. Beaverbrook regarded him as Australia's voice. They promoted dominion food supplies for Britain, and British capital and manufactures for dominions and colonies

with some concession to dominion manufacturers. Zeal obscured the practical difficulties. Elliott's pamphlet, *The Empire crusade; plain facts for Australians* (1930), made well-calculated appeals to economic advantage and Empire patriotism. Sinister competition appeared: 'the East Prussian farmer' and the 'Argentine Meat Octopus' with its 'propaganda of the most insidious and subtle nature'.

In 1940 he went to Britain to serve as special assistant to Beaverbrook in his effective and effervescent wartime ministries (aircraft production, 1940-41, and supply, 1941-42). Elliott was appointed C.M.G. in 1942. His role is not clear. The Beaverbrook spotlight and smoke-screen still dazzle and obscure. One Beaverbrook personal secretary fancifully suggested that, 'Like a St Bernard dog he followed his master around, a barrel of adulation round his neck, from which Beaverbrook could drink at need. He was very kind but rather stupid'. Beaverbrook preferred to recall to Elliott's widow that, 'whenever I, as a Minister was faced by some tiresome and recalcitrant problem, sometimes a problem which Mr Churchill had asked me to tackle, I always turned to your husband. I knew that he would never rest or relax and never allow himself to be deflected. He probably annoyed a great many people as he swept on. But he did the job. I was indeed a fortunate man to have his services then and to get so much credit which belonged to him'. After his return to Australia, Elliott chaired the Commonwealth Advisory Panel on Munitions Contracts and Annexes, and the War Investigation Committee (Navy).

He promoted civic endeavours, crying 'develop, develop, develop'. He supported as he clashed with the Murray Valley Development League. He borrowed slogans like 'Don't pray for rain: dam it'. Originality was not his strongest suit. In the 1920s he helped the Melbourne Symphony Orchestra to present shilling concerts for a wider public. He initiated (1925) and paid for guided lectures at the National Gallery of Victoria. His artistic legacy, notably Orpens and Brangwyns, led to the foundation of the Mildura Art Gallery, where his portrait by his friend Sir William Orpen now hangs. His wife called their Toorak house 'The Orpenage'.

From 1924 Elliott was a trustee of the Public Library, Museums and National Gallery of Victoria, and sometime treasurer to 1940. In the 1944-45 reorganization he became a trustee of the gallery. Differences about gallery policy and administration sharpened with Sir Keith Murdoch [q.v.] in the chair from 1939 and with (Sir) Daryl Lindsay [q.v.], director in 1941-55. Elliott could be vain, personal and obstructive. J. D. G. Medley, Murdoch's deputy, reputedly referred to 'a tale told by an Elliott, full of sound and fury'. Murdoch used his wide influence against Elliott. One pettiness was the Murdoch press's insistent reference to 'ex-senator Elliott' when he characteristically continued to claim his earlier title.

He had no children. His wife, a strong personality, helped to control his newspaper group after his death. 'With him', she said, 'there was never a dull moment. His only idea of Heaven would have been activity'. Elliott died of cerebro-vascular disease at Toorak on 6 March 1950. His estate was valued for probate at £79 848. At his funeral at Toorak Presbyterian Church Rev. Dr A. C. Watson commented, 'Many of those with whom he was associated could not share all his opinions on matters of public policy, but all of us covet his spirit'.

H. W. Malloch, *Fellows all* (Melb, 1943); U. R. Ellis, *A history of the Australian Country Party* (Melb, 1963); D. Farrer, *G-for God almighty* (Lond, 1969); L. B. Cox, *The National Gallery of Victoria, 1861 to 1968* (Melb, 1970); *Art in Aust*, Feb 1935, p 23; *People* (Syd), 13 Jan 1954, p 27; *Argus*, 4 June, 7 Nov 1928, 10, 20, 21, 23 Aug 1934, 7 Mar 1950; *Sunraysia Daily*, 30, 31 May, 1, 2, 4, 5 June 1928, 23 Sept 1944, 7, 8, 10, 11 Mar 1950; *Table Talk*, 8 Nov 1928; *Bulletin*, 28 Dec 1949; *Age*, and *The Times*, 7 Mar 1950; Catalogue of paintings from Hilda Elliott bequest and R. D. Elliott collection (Mildura Gallery, Vic); Fink papers (Faculty of Education, Univ Melb); information held by author.

L. R. GARDINER

ELLIS, CONSTANCE (1872-1942), medical practitioner, was born on 2 November 1872 at Carlton, Melbourne, sixth child of Louis Ellis, deputy sheriff and later sheriff of Victoria, and his wife Lydia Constance, née Phillips; both parents were born in New South Wales of Jewish stock. 'Connie' herself never married. In 1886 she entered the Presbyterian Ladies' College, where she completed a brilliant scholastic career in 1890. She enrolled for the medical course at the University of Melbourne in 1894, and from 1896 to 1898 attended the Janet Clarke [q.v.3] hostel, Trinity College, as a non-resident. She gained honours in every year of the course, and at the final examinations in March 1899 came second in surgery and third in medicine. This entitled her to a residentship at the (Royal) Melbourne Hospital, and after a year there she spent a further two years residency at the (Royal) Children's Hospital. She took up general and obstetric practice in Wattletree Road, Malvern.

In March 1903 Dr Ellis obtained the degree of M.D. (by examination), the first woman graduate of the University of Melbourne to do so. She had joined the honorary staff of the Queen Victoria Hospital in 1902, where she organized the pathology department and was honorary pathologist from 1908 until 1919. During this period she was appointed demonstrator and lecturer at the university department of pathology, and deputized for Sir Harry Allen [q.v.7] during his absence. The Victorian Baby Health Centres Association was one of her main interests; she was a council-member from its inception and a vice-president in 1920-42. As president of the Medical Women's Society, Dr Ellis acted as its delegate on the council of the Victorian branch of the British Medical Association, and was the first woman doctor in Australia to become a councillor of the B.M.A. She lectured frequently to women's groups, and in girls' schools, on the care of babies and expectant mothers, and was closely associated with the College of Domestic Economy (later the Emily McPherson College) in its early years.

Dr Ellis maintained a continuing interest in her old school: in 1911 she was president of the Old Collegians' Association and in 1925 she took part in the school's jubilee congress, a two-day discussion on social and welfare matters. She was a founder and vice-president in 1912 of the Lyceum Club and its president in 1918-19. In July 1925 she became a member of the first committee of the Melbourne Business and Professional Women's Club. She was exceptionally widely read and was an excellent violinist. Her many community activities left her little time for writing, and she made only two small contributions to medical literature.

Dr Ellis died at South Yarra on 10 September 1942, after a lingering illness (Paget's disease), and was cremated. She left her large collection of books and pictures to Janet Clarke Hall and the University Women's College. Her personality is well described by M. O. Reid: 'she was the soul of kindness, with great human understanding, a keen sense of fun, and an enormous capacity for making friends'.

G. H. Swinburne, *Queen Victoria memorial hospital* (np, 1934); M. O. Reid, *The ladies came to stay* (Melb, 1960); K. Fitzpatrick, *PLC Melbourne* (Melb, 1975); J. M. Gillison, *A history of the Lyceum Club Melbourne* (Melb, 1975); *MJA*, 24 Oct 1942, p 391; *Argus*, 11 Sept 1942.

A. S. ELLIS

ELLIS, HENRY AUGUSTUS (1861-1939), physician and politician, was born on 24 July 1861 at Omagh, Tyrone, Ireland, fourth son of Colonel Francis Ellis and his wife Louisa, née McMahon. He was educated at St Columba's College, Dundrum, and privately at Stratford-upon-Avon, England, before studying medicine at Trinity College, Dublin, from 1879 (M.B., 1884; Ch.B., 1885). He migrated to Sydney in 1885, practised at Double Bay and was honorary surgeon at the Sydney Hospital in 1891-92. He had studied the growth of germs and collaborated with Dr Herbert Butcher in experiments designed to exterminate rabbits by spreading disease among them. In Sydney he married a Miss Spear.

In 1894 Ellis went to Perth. From 1897 he was a health officer and superintendent of the government sanatorium on the Coolgardie goldfield. He drew up a code of by-laws which was later copied on other goldfields, and gained a reputation as a kindly, effective practitioner who was also a learned if at times abstract conversationalist over a wide range of literary and political thought.

In 1899-1900 he led a campaign to separate the goldfields from Western Australia, if the Perth government should refuse to join the Federation. He was the prime organizer, draftsman and propagandist for the Federal League, whose motto was 'Separation for Federation'. In 1901 Ellis was an unsuccessful candidate for the first Senate elections, but in 1904 he won the Coolgardie seat in the Legislative Assembly for the Labor Party: he supported equal pay for women, old-age pensions, compulsory arbitration and the White Australia policy. In parliament he advocated an eight-hour day for nurses and was briefly chairman of committees: his long-winded speeches usually covered a mass of detailed analysis. Disenchanted with Labor's premier, Henry Daglish [q.v.], he led the attack in August 1905 on government proposals to buy the Midland Railway, thus precipitating the government's defeat and resignation. That year he left the party after a pre-selection wrangle; in the election he stood as an Independent, but lost. He resumed practice in Coolgardie and served on the Municipal Council in 1912.

On 4 April 1914 he married Kassie Gordon Wylie, a young schoolteacher, and they went to Britain. Ellis represented the Western Australian government at the International Congress on Medical Electrology and Radiology at Lyons, France. He worked through World War I as a tuberculosis officer at Middlesbrough Hospital, Yorkshire, and was a commandant of the Red Cross Society. From 1919 he was assistant physician at Margaret Street Hospital for Diseases of the Chest, London. He then practised privately in Harley Street as a specialist in tuberculosis, having studied miners' phthisis. His publications displayed an awareness of psychological factors in sickness. His main

work involved a talented elucidation of constitutional types from a chemical point of view: he was imaginative and inventive and his analyses of urine were unusually elaborate.

Ellis was also an inventor, a good draughtsman and amateur photographer. His flowing moustache and beard contributed to an 'uncommonly commanding appearance' and while he expressed himself whimsically, his thought was unconventional. After a long illness he died at Crowborough, Sussex, on 3 October 1939, survived by his second wife. A brilliant and versatile pioneer on the Western Australian goldfields, he was remembered affectionately despite, or perhaps because of, the high-mindedness which had limited his success in politics.

J. S. Battye (ed), *Cyclopedia of Western Australia*, 2 (Adel, 1913); *V&P (LA NSW), 1887-88, 8, 962, 1890, 5, 37; British Medical J*, 4 Nov 1939, p 932; *Morning Herald* (Perth), 11, 12 Jan 1901; *Western Argus*, 17, 24 Oct 1905; *West Australian*, 24 Feb 1940.   G. C. BOLTON

ELMSLIE, GEORGE ALEXANDER (1861-1918), politician, was born on 21 February 1861 at Lethbridge, Victoria, son of Henry Elmslie, a stonemason from Kent, England, and his Irish-born wife Catherine, née Ryan. The family later moved to Carlton, Melbourne. It was intended that George should be a schoolteacher, but at 16 he decided to follow his father's trade. He worked on several major buildings in Melbourne including Wilson [q.v.6] Hall for three years and St Patrick's Cathedral for twelve. On 7 April 1887 at St Jude's Church of England, Carlton, he married Clara Ellen Williams, daughter of a stonecutter; they had a son and a daughter.

Like his father, Elmslie was a diligent and dedicated member of the Operative Stonemasons' Society, from 1888 holding various offices on its central committee including that of president in 1892. He represented the union on deputations, on the Trades Hall Council, the Political Labor Council and on wages boards, notably the Stonecutters' Board in 1900-01. When in October 1902 he won the Legislative Assembly seat of Albert Park for Labor he acknowledged modestly that 'as far as any ability he possessed was concerned, it was largely due to his connection with the Society'. Melbourne *Punch* described him as 'careful, deliberate, patient and reliable', as befitted his painstaking trade; a man whose radical political beliefs evolved from careful reasoning over many years. J.W. Billson [q.v.7] remembered him as 'slow to make up his mind, but very determined when he came to a decision'.

Elmslie served as secretary of the Victorian Parliamentary Labor Party in 1904-12 and deputy leader in 1912-13, and became leader in September 1913 when George Prendergast [q.v.] resigned after illness. At that time the Liberal ministry of W.A. Watt [q.v.] proposed to enlarge the assembly, increasing the disparity between quotas for metropolitan and country seats, and this aroused much controversy. On 4 December, when thirteen Liberals voted with eighteen Labor members to defeat a clause of the electoral districts bill, Watt resigned, and Lieut-Governor Sir John Madden [q.v.] invited Elmslie to form Victoria's first Labor government. On 9 December Elmslie was sworn in as premier and treasurer. At this time salaried ministers were required to resign and recontest their seats on appointment, usually a mere formality. Elmslie remained outside the parliament for the entire fourteen days of his ministry although he was an interested spectator in the public gallery during debates. Conscious that he was in a sense 'a sort of locum tenens' while Watt played his political game, Elmslie did not attempt to initiate policies or amend legislation during this period. On 16 December a censure motion was carried by 40 votes to 13 and, after Madden refused to grant Elmslie a dissolution, Watt was recommissioned as premier on 22 December.

During the war Elmslie staunchly supported the war-aims of the Empire. He was a hard-working politican and a frequent and lengthy speaker, regarded by many as merely a 'decent plodder'; his aversion to self-advertisement left him virtually unknown to the Victorian public. He took an interest in local sporting and social bodies: he was president of the South Melbourne Football Club and a member and ex-president of the Middle Park Bowling Club. He was also an active supporter of the South Melbourne Technical College. In his later years, he suffered from poor health and in 1916 went on a voyage to Hawaii. However, his death of uraemia on 11 May 1918 at his Albert Park home was unexpected. His wife died of cancer three months later; their son survived them. After a state funeral Elmslie was buried in Melbourne general cemetery — all evidence of his grave has now disappeared.

PD (Vic), 1918, 2nd S, v 149, p 4, 18; Labor Call, 31 Aug 1911, 7, 14 June 1914, 14 May 1918; Punch (Melb), 12 Mar 1914; Argus, 13, 14 May 1918; Aust Worker, 16 May 1918; Operative Stonemasons' Soc of Aust, Vic branch, Deposit no E 117 (ANU Archives).
                                    BARRY O. JONES

ELPHINSTONE, AUGUSTUS CECIL (1874-1964), businessman and politician, was born on 13 September 1874 in London, son of Henry Walker Elphinstone, clerk, and his wife Harriet Ann, née Eldred. Educated at Forrest House College, Woodford, he joined the staff of the Bank of England and in 1892 spent a year at Charters Towers, Queensland. Returning to England in 1894, he was fourteen years in insurance, becoming general manager of the Welsh Insurance Corporation, and serving seven years in the Territorial Army.

Elphinstone returned to Queensland in 1912 and was briefly a tobacco farmer near Bowen. He moved to Brisbane in 1914 as one of the founders of the Queensland Cement and Lime Co. at Darra, first as general manager in difficult formative years, and then on the board. In 1917, when the entry of the United States of America into the war created potential shortages of motor car parts, Elphinstone acquired a large shipment of Bosch magnetos and began selling motor accessories from a basement in Queen Street. Elphinstone Pty Ltd, which he launched in 1918, later became public and is still trading. In August-November 1918, he served in the Australian Imperial Force.

He also entered politics in 1918 as Nationalist member for Oxley in the Legislative Assembly. In 1921 he joined the Country Party, announcing that he hoped to provide it with 'strong leadership and administrative ability'. He was one of the main figures in the creation of the United Party in November 1922 and was asked to resign from the Country Party. Despite frequent quarrels, he stayed in the renamed Country and Progressive National Party. But, infuriated by internal feuds and what he saw as unfair business competition by a party member, he resigned in 1929, tried to form a small centre party and, standing as an independent, lost his seat.

According to Bernays [q.v.3], Elphinstone was tall, clean-shaven and pleasant looking with the cultivated manners of an English public school boy. Able and fluent, he could speak on many topics, but was at his best in destructive analysis of government economic proposals. He had the capacity to be a great premier but, through vanity and his ability to make enemies even in his own party, 'he ended up by being nothing'.

Besides maintaining his business interests, Elphinstone became a grand master of the Royal Society of St George, president of the Empire Marketing League and president of the Wholesale Automotive Suppliers Association of Queensland. He was one of the original trustees and sometime president of the Graceville Bowling Club. On 5 October 1897 at Chingford, Essex, he had married

Louisa Dinah Lloyd; they had five children. When he died in Brisbane on 24 March 1964, he was cremated with Anglican rites. His estate, valued for probate at £18 372, was left entirely to his family.

C. A. Bernays, *Queensland – our seventh political decade 1920-1930* (Syd, 1931); Aust Hist Publishing Co., *Queensland and Queenslanders* (Brisb, 1936); *PD* (Qld), 1922, p 40, 1927, p 49, 432, 706; *Brisbane Courier*, 18 Nov 1921, 13 June 1923, 24 Aug 1928, 20 Feb 1929; *Daily Mail* (Brisb), 4 Sept 1923; *Courier Mail*, 25 Mar 1964; Z. Abidin, The origins and development of the Queensland Country Party 1909-32 (M.A. thesis, Univ Qld, 1958).   A. L. LOUGHEED

EMANUEL, ISADORE SAMUEL (1860-1954), pastoralist, was born on 4 February 1860 at Goulburn, New South Wales, son of Solomon Emanuel junior (d. 1898), merchant and pastoralist, and his wife Sarah, née Myers; he was a grandson of Samuel Emanuel (1803-68) member of the Legislative Assembly for Argyle in 1862. Isadore and his brother Sydney Phillip (1861-1919) were educated locally and worked in the family business, including a Sydney livery stable. When the Kimberley district of Western Australia was opened for pastoral settlement in 1880 Solomon Emanuel joined with Patrick and Michael Durack [q.v.4] in applying for large tracts of country on the Ord River, but following a reconnaissance in 1882, the Emanuels decided to concentrate on the Fitzroy valley in West Kimberley. Isadore arrived there in January 1884 with 2860 sheep, and during the next five years established a major sheep station at Noonkanbah and cattle-runs at Margaret Downs (Gogo) and Lower Leveringa. They were efficient pastoralists who chose good managers and earned high returns, though at the risk of overstocking. Although Isadore advocated the segregation on reserves of Aboriginals who interfered with his enterprise, in practice Aboriginals comprised a major part of their workforce, and were used as shearers on Noonkanbah at least until 1916.

In 1894 Isadore and Sydney entered into partnership with Alexander Forrest [q.v.], obtaining a virtual monopoly as agents for the trade in live cattle between Derby and Fremantle. The Emanuels were responsible for the purchase of stock from other Kimberley pastoralists, and expanded the firm's station interests by acquiring shares in Jubilee Downs and Meda. After Forrest's death in 1901 they bought out his share of the firm, and in 1902 together with (Sir) Sidney Kidman [q.v.] acquired Australia's largest pastoral property, Victoria River Downs in the Northern Territory. Either solely or in partnership, the Emanuel brothers held an interest in over 20 000 square miles (51 800 km²) in the Kimberleys and the adjacent part of the Northern Territory – the largest pastoral empire in the district. They also held a substantial investment in the wholesale and retail meat trade in Western Australia. Press and politicians condemned them as leaders in a 'meat ring' but a royal commission into the industry in 1908 found little cause for criticism.

After travelling to Europe in 1900, as Western Australian commissioner to the Paris Universal International Exhibition, Isadore Emanuel settled in Perth. On 24 August 1902 he married Muriel Urella O'Meehan; they occupied one of Perth's finest houses, close to King's Park, of which Emanuel became a trustee. A well-known character in Edwardian Perth, Emanuel was considered a shrewd, reserved personality, very knowledgeable about horses and a keen racing man, an *habitué* of the Weld Club, and never seen in public without an umbrella in his hand. He donated a prize for the best carriage horses to the Royal Agricultural Society of Western Australia and a shield for competition among the squadrons of the local Light Horse unit; he also consistently supported the Liberal League with donations.

In 1909 the Emanuels and Kidman sold Victoria River Downs to Bovril Australian Estates Ltd for £170 000 (the purchase price in 1902 had been £20 000). After the return of a Labor government in Western Australia Emanuel decided in 1912 to move to London where he remained for the rest of his life. He kept a vigilant eye on the family's pastoral interests in the Kimberleys until his death aged 93 on 5 January 1954. He was survived by his wife and three sons. His gross estate in England and Australia was valued at over £1 million.

Univ Studies in History and Economics, 2 (1954), no 2, p 1; *Pastoral Review*, Feb, Mar 1954; *West Australian*, 8 Jan 1954; *SMH*, 22 Oct 1957.
                                            G. C. BOLTON

EMBLEY, EDWARD HENRY (1861-1924), anaesthetist, was born on 28 February 1861 at Castlemaine, Victoria, younger son of Richard Edward Embley, baker, and his wife Mary, née Smith, both from Gloucestershire, England. Embley showed early promise in chemistry and mathematics at Castlemaine Grammar School and at 14 was apprenticed to a local pharmacist. He later went to Bendigo and while working in a chemist's shop attended Bendigo High School. He was registered as a pharmacist in 1882 and took on a small business in Melbourne. On 27 December 1883 at Carlton he married Lydia Matilda Jane Cox, by whom he had a son, who died in infancy, and two daughters.

In 1884 Embley began a medical course at the University of Melbourne, supporting himself by pharmacy. He graduated M.B., B.S. in 1889, proceeding M.D. by thesis in 1901. Entering general practice in La Trobe Street, he was soon in demand as an anaesthetist. He was honorary anaesthetist at the (Royal) Melbourne Hospital in 1895-1917, an honorary consultant in 1917-24, and lectured on the subject at the university from about 1900 to 1919.

Embley is remembered for his study of chloroform. This anaesthetic was known to depress the respiration and circulation, and to damage the liver and kidneys. It could also cause sudden death in the induction stage. Embley rejected the Hyderabad Commission's findings of 1889-91 that these deaths were due to respiratory failure, a view which ignored the sudden deaths. In 1899 he went as a week-end volunteer to the university's physiology department, to work under (Sir) Charles Martin [q.v.]. The upshot was his classic paper of 1902. Embley proved sudden death under chloroform to be due to cardiac, not to respiratory failure. His paper aroused world-wide interest. Henceforth, chloroform was to be given progressively, with close watch upon the pulse and avoidance of surgical interference until anaesthesia was complete.

Discovery rarely springs complete from a single brain. Speculation thus arose as to Martin's share in the paper. Professor W. A. Osborne [q.v.], Embley's close friend, wrote that he had been ignorant of laboratory methods at first, but soon became a first-class experimental physiologist. While Martin admitted that he had, understandably, helped Embley, he praised the latter's insatiable curiosity, perseverance and fine qualities.

Embley believed chloroform over-stimulated the vagal nerve-centre in the brain, thus leading to cardiac arrest. This view was mistaken: he had quite missed ventricular fibrillation which A. G. Levy in 1911-13 proved could be induced by chloroform. Embley was sceptical at first but soon assented. Neither man had used the electro-cardiograph which reached Australia only in 1912 and was perhaps unusual in English laboratories in 1911. Later electro-cardiograph studies bore out Levy's view. Withal, Embley in 1902 deserved full credit for refuting the Hyderabad Commission, for proving the cardio-toxication of chloroform, and for proposing a safer method of administration.

Embley studied ethyl chloride, showing it to affect the heart much as does chloroform, but in minor degree: ether was even less toxic. Initially, he had used the unphysiological 'closed' ether-inhalers of his day. He was converted about 1909 by R. W. Hornabrook to 'open-mask' administration. If Australian anaesthetists in 1909-45 had unusual skill with 'open' ether, they owed it to the precepts of Hornabrook and Embley. The latter published one paper upon anaesthesia with nitrous oxide-oxygen, but probably had no great experience with it.

Embley published some twenty-four papers: clinical, pharmacological and chemical. He received the first David Syme [q.v.6] prize for scientific research in 1906. He sent papers to two international congresses (London, 1913; San Francisco, 1915), but apparently never travelled himself. In 1920 he retired because of ill health. He died of cerebro-vascular disease at his Camberwell home on 9 May 1924, survived by his wife and daughters, and was buried in Melbourne general cemetery.

In his lifetime Embley was better known abroad than at home. Recognition came in 1929 when the International Anaesthesia Research Society held a memorial dinner in Chicago, and presented a scroll of honour to the University of Melbourne. In that year the triennial Embley Memorial lecture and the annual Embley medal were endowed by the British Medical Association (Victorian Branch), members of his family and others; in 1930 the association erected a memorial plaque in its own hall, and a duplicate in the University of Melbourne.

Something of Embley's personality has survived the years. Osborne spoke of him as 'a gentle spirit' and 'a dedicated man'. Sir William Upjohn, once his pupil, describes him as having been slow speaking, kindly and a fine teacher; he himself used Embley, whenever possible, as his anaesthetist. His manner inspired confidence, and his colleagues held him in the highest esteem.

J. Smith (ed), *Cyclopedia of Victoria* 1 (Melb, 1903); H. K. Beecher, *The physiology of anesthesia* (New York, 1938); R. M. Waters et al (eds), *Chloroform, a study after 100 years* (Madison, 1951); *Heart* (Lond), 5 (1913-14), p 299; *MJA*, 12 July 1924, p 47, 28 May 1932, p 755, 11 Feb 1939, p 209; *Anaesthesia and Intensive Care*, 7 (1979), p 114; *Table Talk*, 22 Sept 1904; Embley papers (Dept of Medical Hist, Univ Melb, *and* Roy A'sian College of Surgeons, Melb).   GEOFFREY KAYE

EMERY, GEORGE EDWIN (1859-1937), bank officer, was born on 15 November 1859 at Castlemaine, Victoria, son of Francis Emery, carpenter, and his wife Fanny, née Hancock, both natives of Somerset, England. Emery was educated at Castlemaine, at the National School and privately. In July 1874 he began work in Castlemaine as a clerk with the Commissioners' Savings Bank and in June 1879 moved to the head office in Melbourne. On 5 May 1880 with Baptist forms, he married Ada Heley at Castlemaine. He was promoted chief clerk in January 1886, accountant in June 1892 and secretary in January 1893. In 1897 when the Commissioners' Savings and Post Office Savings banks amalgamated as the State Savings Bank of Victoria, Emery became its first administrative head, and was formally appointed in January with the title of inspector-general.

Emery's leadership of the bank at only 37 reflected a combination of total dedication to the savings bank cause, enormous capacity for hard work, and an innovative, entrepreneurial spirit that was relatively rare in a savings bank officer. As secretary in the troubled years of the 1890s, he was in close touch with the Victorian government and other colonial banks, and contributed significantly to his institution's successful weathering of the storm. More important in the long run, he saw that savings banking in Victoria could play a key role in assisting agriculturalists, upon which general economic recovery largely depended. With others, notably the Austrian consul, Carl Pinschoff [q.v.], he was an enthusiastic advocate of *crédit foncier*, in essence long-term low-interest loans on the security of land. In May 1894 he instituted a pilot scheme in Victoria, which proved to be the forerunner to the more general and permanent system of *crédit foncier* provided for under the Savings Bank Act of 1896. Although significantly different from such schemes operating in Europe, notably in using depositors' funds for loans, the Victorian scheme became one of the key sources of farm finance in the State, and overall was highly successful.

Retaining his enthusiasm for this type of finance throughout his life, Emery extended it in 1910 to loans on houses and shops. In 1920 largely through his efforts, the Victorian parliament legislated to liberalize the terms on which such loans could be made to low-income earners. In 1926 he visited England to study low-cost housing, and there became a convert to garden and model city schemes. On his return to Melbourne, he recommended the purchase of some forty-five acres (18 ha) of crown land at Fishermans Bend. This became the basis for the bank's own semi-detached garden city, in which the houses built by the bank were sold on liberal credit terms to less affluent members of the community.

Emery retired in 1929 after thirty-two years as head (the title of inspector-general

was changed to general manager in 1923) and is rightly regarded as the most influential figure in its history. He was fortunate both in leading the bank during the long upswing in Victoria's economic fortunes when there was so much scope for successful innovation, and in having an exceptionally able deputy in Alexander Cooch [q.v.].

Emery was a prominent Freemason. He was grand master of the United Grand Lodge of Victoria in 1907-08 and was deeply involved in the higher branches of the craft and Christian degrees. A devout Anglican, he was a lay canon at St Paul's, and also member of the vestry at St Andrew's, Brighton. Particularly after his retirement from the bank, he served on the boards of several companies, including Colonial Mutual Life Assurance, Brighton Gas, and the Mutual Store of which for a time he was chairman of directors. Among his physical recreations were bowls and gardening. He was an active Rotarian. In 1924 he was appointed C.M.G. He died on 18 February 1937 at his home in Middle Brighton after a long illness and was buried in St Kilda cemetery. His wife, four daughters and three sons survived him.

C. A. Grant, *500 Victorians* (Melb, 1934); T. Craddock and M. Cavanough, *125 years . . . the State Savings Bank of Victoria* (Melb, 1967); *Age*, and *Argus*, 19 Feb 1937; R. F. Middelmann, Victoria's credit foncier and rural lending on long-term mortgage (Ph.D. thesis, Univ Melb, 1971).   E. A. BEEVER

EMMETT, EVELYN TEMPLE (1871-1970), tourist director, bushwalker and writer, was born on 18 May 1871 at Launceston, Tasmania, youngest of four sons of Skelton Buckley Emmett, farmer, and his wife Maria Evelyn, née Smith, and grandson of Henry James Emmett [q.v.1]. He was educated at the Stanley State School and Scotch College, Hobart, where he also taught for a short period. On 14 April 1903 at St Paul's Church of England, Stanley, he married Sophie Margaret Maguire; they had three sons and three daughters.

In 1888 Emmett joined the Tasmanian Main Line Railway Co., before it was taken over by the government in 1890, and was appointed chief clerk in 1902. Proficient in shorthand, he occasionally took evidence at government inquiries. In 1913 he was sent to Melbourne to open a Tasmanian Government Railways tourist office; next year he returned to Hobart as director of the Tasmanian Government Tourist Bureau which was separated from the Railway Department in 1934.

Always an outdoor man, in his youth

Emmett excelled in cycling, road races and walking matches. He acquired an extensive knowledge of the State and a deep appreciation of its scenic and historic attractions, enabling him to assess its tourist potential accurately. Gentle and courteous, he exercised a moderating influence in committee debate.During the 1920s he regularly lectured in other States, using lantern slides to illustrate Tasmanian scenic highlights; later he made full use of film and radio. In 1923, after visiting Mount Kosciusko, New South Wales, where he learnt the rudiments of skiing, he publicized the sport in Tasmania and arranged skiing weekends at the National Park Reserve (Mount Field National Park). In 1929 he established the Hobart Walking Club. He was a foundation executive member of the Scenery Preservation (1915) and National Park (1917) boards and for several years from December 1931 personally led parties of mainland bushwalkers on the 65 mile (105 km) track through the Cradle Mountain – Lake St Clair Reserve. Mount Emmett, near Cradle Mountain, and a lake in the Mount Field National Park are named after him.

Emmett also had considerable literary ability. He wrote with humour and gentle irony, sometimes under the pseudonyms 'Orion' or 'Ah Wong', on a variety of topics for Tasmanian journals, and gained top awards in Tasmanian and Victorian literary competitions. A member of the Royal Society of Tasmania from 1921, he spoke on historical subjects and in 1937 published *A short history of Tasmania* (Sydney). He also wrote much early departmental publicity, including *Tommy's trip to Tasmania* (Hobart, 1913) and is said to have walked over 1000 miles (1600 km) while researching his later *Tasmania by road and track* (Melbourne, 1952).

After his retirement in 1941, Emmett continued his activities as bushwalker and Rotarian, became acting secretary of the Royal Autocar Club of Tasmania, and re-established a skill as a ballroom dancer. In 1918 Emmett was deputy director of the committee which hosted a French mission to Tasmania; in recognition of his work the French government conferred upon him the Palmes d'Officier d'Académie. In 1959 he was appointed O.B.E. He died on 9 December 1970 at New Town and was cremated after a Congregationalist service.

Tasmanian Tramp, Dec 1949, p 9, Dec 1961, p 4, Dec 1972, p 20; *Mercury,* 23 May 1961, 14 Oct 1967, 10 Dec 1970.   JOHN B. THWAITES

ENRIGHT, WALTER JOHN (1874-1949), solicitor and scientist, was born on 10 March 1874 at West Maitland, New South Wales, eldest of seven children of John Enright, a dealer (auctioneer) from Limerick, Ireland, and his locally born wife Julia, née Maher. Educated at West Maitland at St Mary's Dominican Convent and at the Sacred Heart College under Fr P. V. Dwyer [q.v.], he went on to St John's College, University of Sydney (B.A., 1893). At the university he studied modern languages and geology; Professor (Sir) Edgeworth David [q.v.] made a lifelong impression on him.

On completing his articles of clerkship, Enright was admitted as a solicitor on 22 August 1896. He successfully practised at Maitland and throughout the Hunter valley until the end of his life; he found a knowledge of geology very useful in coal-mining cases. Active in local affairs, he was elected to the West Maitland Municipal Council in 1899, was mayor in 1906 and president of the hospital board in 1914. He was a member of the Maitland French Circle and fluent in German and Italian. On 31 December 1914 at St Mary's Catholic Church, Clermont, Queensland, he married Adelaide Abelia Appleton.

Enright's absorbing interest was in his total environment. An 'amateur scientist of distinctly high calibre', he gladly assisted those 'seeking information in local geology, entomology, forestry, ichthyology and anthropology'. He helped to organize visits to the Maitland area of sections of the British Association for the Advancement of Science in 1914 and the second Pan Pacific Science Congress in 1923. From his youth he had associated with local Aboriginals and his interest in anthropology was stimulated by R. H. Mathews [q.v.5], and later by A. P. Elkin, who became a close friend. He contributed many notes to such journals as *Mankind* and *Oceania.* He was a member of the Royal, Linnean and Geographical societies of New South Wales, the Royal Australian Historical Society, the Royal Australasian Ornithologists' Union, the Australasian (Australian and New Zealand) Association for the Advancement of Science, the Numismatic Society of New South Wales, the Royal Anthropological Institute of Great Britain and Ireland and the Royal Geographical Society of London.

In his youth Enright played cricket and Rugby football and belonged to the Maitland Rowing Club; later he enjoyed tennis and bowls. Throughout his life a practising and reasoning Catholic, he had strong ecumenical leanings; he was a lay fellow of St John's College in 1916-28. Enright died at his Maitland home on 27 September 1949 and was buried in Campbell's Hill cemetery. He was survived by his wife and two sons. His estate was valued for probate at £22 702.

Mankind, 4 (1950), no 4, p 162, and for publications; Roy Soc NSW, *J*, 84 (1950), p xxv; St John's College records (Univ Syd Archives); letter, 21 Sept 1938, from Director Aust Museum, *and* 8 Feb 1939, from Mr L. E. Stachelin to Mr W. J. Enright (held by author, Maitland, NSW).

W. A. G. ENRIGHT

ESSEX EVANS, GEORGE; *see* EVANS, GEORGE ESSEX

ESSON, THOMAS LOUIS BUVELOT (1878-1943), dramatist, was born on 10 August 1878 at Leith, Edinburgh, only child of Thomas Clarence Esson, marine engineer, and his wife Mary Jane, née Paterson. When he was 3 his recently widowed mother joined her two sisters and a brother in Melbourne; the artist John Ford Paterson [q.v.5] was another brother. Louis Esson was raised by his aunts in Carlton, and attended Carlton Grammar School.

In 1896 Esson began an arts course at the University of Melbourne but left without completing a degree. At university he had chatted with fellow students about socialism and literature and was soon to begin his own experiments as an Australian dramatist. In 1905 he visited Paris with Leon Brodsky (Spencer Brodney [q.v.7 M. Brodzky]) and in Dublin he met the Irish dramatist, J. M. Synge, who urged him to create a national theatre in Australia.

From 1904 Esson had published verse and topical paragraphs in the *Bulletin*; his first contributions included vicarious evocations of Melbourne's low life and the conventional warnings about Australia's vulnerability to Japan, a country he visited in 1908 on a trip through south and east Asia. By 1906 Esson had grown dissatisfied with the *Bulletin* and increasingly sceptical of claims that the journal continued to be a positive influence on Australian literature. He felt that it had degenerated into a formula and that the insistence on brevity was a sterile obsession. After 1910 his *Bulletin* contributions were infrequent. In 1906 Esson joined the Victorian Socialist Party as a foundation member and soon contributed articles to the *Socialist*. Bernard O'Dowd [q.v.] was a regular contributor and a revered example of literary dedication and high-mindedness to a rising generation of writers, including Esson. The *Socialist* gave him scope to air his views and in 1911, under the sympathetic co-editorship of Frederick Sinclaire and Marie Pitt [qq.v.], he contributed a jauntily Bohemian series of articles on Australian institutions. His first full-length play, *The time is not yet ripe*, a Shavian comedy in four acts, was completed and staged in Melbourne in 1912 before a large and appreciative audience. Esson had also published *Three short plays* (including *The woman tamer, Dead timber,* and *The sacred place*) and two slim volumes of verse, *Bells and bees* and *Red gums and other verses*, enough to secure a reputation as a promising young writer.

Esson's personal life had been less successful. He had no memory of his father and was unflattering about his mother whom he considered flighty and economically irresponsible. She married twice in Australia to Victorian graziers before her death in 1932 at Shepparton. The only child of these marriages and her favourite son, Francis (Frank) Paterson Brown (d. 1928), became a sporting journalist and an aspiring dramatist. On 22 January 1906 at Queen Street Melbourne Esson married with Presbyterian forms Madeleine Stephanie Tracy. According to family tradition, she had talked the unworldly young writer into the marriage. The union appeared shaky from the outset and ended in divorce in November 1911. The only child of the marriage, James Paterson Esson (d. 1971), was raised by the Paterson aunts and eventually became editor of newspapers at Shepparton.

Esson's second marriage, on 15 December 1913, to Hilda Wager Bull proved to be a better match. The marriage was celebrated by Dr Charles Strong [q.v.6] of the Australian Church. Their only child, Hugh, was born in 1918. Hilda Bull was born in the Sydney suburb of Waverley on 2 July 1886. The family moved to Melbourne where her father left his vocation as a gentleman to become a herbalist. She was educated at Presbyterian Ladies' College, matriculated in March 1906 and completed a medical degree with distinction at the University of Melbourne in 1913. She was a foundation member of the Melbourne University Dramatic Society. After interrupted work as a medical practitioner, in 1927 Hilda Bull became assistant to Dr John Dale [q.v.], health officer to the City of Melbourne; she married him in March 1951 after his divorce. She died in Melbourne on 29 June 1953.

Hilda was a gifted, strong-minded woman with broad interests. Her economic, intellectual and emotional support enabled Louis to pursue his career as a dramatist and freelance writer at a time when writing was a poorly rewarded and disheartening pursuit. Indeed, the outbreak of war in August 1914 appeared to make a literary career in Australia even more remote. After Louis had been rejected for military service on medical grounds, the Essons left Australia in 1916 for New York. The city overwhelmed them, while American civilization struck them as vulgar, commercial and pushy. Their attitude softened a little, but not before they had left America. London was more congenial; there were old friends, familiar cultural associations, new contacts with Irish dramatists, but Louis found writing difficult. W. B. Yeats, however, encouraged him again to attempt to create a national theatre. In July 1921 the Essons returned to Melbourne, where they renewed their friendship with Vance and Nettie Palmer [qq.v.] and laid the basis for the Pioneer Players, an organization dedicated to performing Australian plays; Hilda acted in these productions.

The Pioneer Players' first performances were in 1922: Esson's *The drovers*, a spare, atmospheric bush play in one act, was staged in 1923. Their last production, after a two-year gap, was Esson's *The bride of Gospel Place*, performed in June 1926. The movement was not the success for which Louis and Hilda Esson had hoped, but their expectations had been high. They had exposed Melbourne audiences to local drama and given local dramatists a chance to have their work staged. While press response was favourable and the audiences, though small, were appreciative, Esson was angered at Melbourne's stuffiness and sought consolation at Mallacoota inlet. Rural simplicity proved to be an inspiring literary ideal, but a tedious and uncomfortable reality. The Essons soon found themselves back in Melbourne, where Louis became Melbourne drama critic for the *New Triad* from 1924 to 1927.

Esson's last collection, *Dead timber and other plays*, had appeared in 1920. He was already slowing down and by the late 1920s his career as a dramatist had ended. He tinkered with some of his old plays and toyed with some new themes, but without believing that his efforts would come to anything. Ever suspicious of Melbourne's deadening atmosphere, he moved to Sydney late in his life, but there was to be no literary rejuvenation.

Louis Esson's instincts were essentially urban. He loved theatre, night-life, cafés and talk. *The time is not yet ripe* gave his talents some scope, for the play was set in Melbourne and his characters ran the gamut from socialist idealism to a constipated liberalism, with several shades of topical political nincompoopery in between. There was snappy dialogue, playful humour and some neat satire. Esson's bush plays too often relied upon evocative scenes and a handful of sombrely inarticulate bush folk caught in the toils of a great life experience. There were plays to be written about the bush, but it is a pity that Louis Esson, a small, verbal, unworldly urbanite should have attempted them.

Esson died in Sydney on 27 November 1943. Hilda arranged the publication of *The*

Southern Cross and other plays in 1946, which included *The bride of Gospel Place* and *Mother and son*, along with memories of Esson and the Pioneer Players; in 1948 Vance Palmer published a selection of his letters in *Louis Esson and the Australian theatre*.

L. Esson, *The time is not yet ripe*, P. Parsons ed (Syd, 1973); L. Rees, *The making of Australian drama* (Syd, 1973); D. R. Walker, *Dream and disillusion* (Canb, 1976); *Meanjin Q*, Winter 1947, p 93, Dec 1972, p 417; S. Brodney papers (LaTL); Palmer papers (NL); A. G. Stephens papers (ML); Univ Melb Archives; family information.

D. R. WALKER

ESTELL, JOHN (1861-1938), coalminer and politician, was born on 20 June 1861 at Minmi, near Newcastle, New South Wales, third surviving son of English parents Robert Estell, coalminer and later railway sub-contractor and publican, and his wife Rebecca, née Thompson. Frequent moves by his family meant Estell was educated at Rydal, Wallerawang and Bathurst public schools. At 17 he began work as an engine-cleaner for the railways, but by 1882 he had returned to Minmi, where he was an engine-driver at the collicry. He was working as a miner when he married Alleshia (Alicia) Jane Kirk at the Minmi Primitive Methodist Church on 10 September 1885.

On marrying Estell moved to near-by Plattsburg. Working at the Wallsend colliery, he earned enough to build his own home, joined the co-operative society and became a Freemason. These were hallmarks of respectability. He was an alderman on the Plattsburg Municipal Council in 1887-1900 and mayor in 1891, 1897 and 1899, president of Wallsend and Plattsburg Fire Brigade, patron and president of Plattsburg Mechanics' Institute and a member of the committee of management of the Wallsend Mining District Hospital. A 'lover of good sport of all kinds', he played cricket for several clubs and was a member of the Wallsend Jockey Club. He sported a luxuriant moustache.

President of the Wallsend and Plattsburg Labor and Protection League in 1891, in 1894 Estell joined the Labor Electoral League, which required that the fiscal question of protection versus free trade should be sunk; but he lost the parliamentary pre-selection ballot to David Watkins [q.v.]. He was secretary of the Wallsend miners' lodge from 1894 and president of the Colliery Employees' Federation in 1897-99. In 1899 he was nominated to the Legislative Council on the advice of (Sir) George Reid's [q.v.] ministry, and continued to work in the mines for eight months until he secured a post as assistant superintendent with Citizens' Life Assurance Co.

In June 1901 Estell resigned from the council and in July was elected to the Legislative Assembly for Wallsend; he represented Waratah in 1904-13, Wallsend again in 1913-20 and Newcastle in 1920-22. Although he was an infrequent speaker in parliament, when he did speak he was blunt and direct. What was important for his constituents and his party was his capacity for hard work on their behalf: he was party whip in 1904-14, minister for labour and industry from 1914 and also secretary for mines from March 1915 in W.A. Holman's [q.v.] government. Estell, an anti-conscriptionist, resigned his portfolios on 31 October 1916. In 1920-22 he was secretary for public works and minister for railways in the Storey and Dooley [qq.v.] ministries. On 13 February 1922 he resigned his seat and next day was re-nominated to the Legislative Council.

Estell died at his home at Hamilton on 18 October 1928 and was buried in the Methodist section of Wallsend cemetery. He was survived by his wife, three daughters and four of his five sons. Two of his sons served with the Australian Imperial Force.

J.P.Osborne, *Nine crowded years* (Syd, 1921); *PD* (NSW), 1928, p 1124; *T&CJ*, 28 Apr 1908; *SMH*, 19 Oct 1928.   ELLEN McEWEN

ETHERIDGE, ROBERT, junior (1846-1920), palaeontologist and museum director, was born on 23 May 1846 at Cheltenham, Gloucestershire, England, only son of Robert Etheridge (1819-1903), palaeontologist to the Geological Survey of England and the British Museum, and his wife Martha, née Smith. He was educated at the Royal School of Mines, South Kensington, under T. H. Huxley [q.v.1] and John Tyndall (though he did not take his associateship), and was trained as a palaeontologist by his father.

On 15 March 1866 Etheridge was appointed assistant field geologist to the Geological Survey of Victoria under the direction of A. R. C. Selwyn [q.v.6] at a salary of £250. In 1868 he contributed to Selwyn's *A descriptive catalogue of the rock specimens and minerals in the National Museum* ... When the survey was discontinued in 1869 he went gold-mining with his colleague R. A. F. Murray [q.v.5], before returning to England in 1871. At St Philip's Church, Kensington, London, he married Harriet Emily Ewen on 26 October that year. In 1873, after working as underground manager in a coal-mine in south Wales, he became palaeontologist to the Geological Survey of

Scotland, and in 1874 an assistant in the geology department of the British Museum (natural history) under his father and Henry Woodward, who became a lifelong friend.

In 1873-86 Etheridge published over a hundred notes and papers, including many relating to the geology of eastern Australia especially on the fossils of Palaeozoic and Tertiary rocks. He contributed abstracts of literature relating to 'the stratigraphical and descriptive Geology of Australasia' to the *Geological Record* (1874-78). From 1877 he worked on Queensland fossils sent him by R. L. Jack [q.v.4]. With Jack he published *Catalogue of works, papers, reports, and maps, on the geology, palaeontology, mineralogy, mining and metallurgy, etc. of the Australian continent and Tasmania* (London, 1881), and with P. H. Carpenter, *Catalogue of the Blastoidea in the geological department of the British Museum (natural history)* (London, 1886).

Persuaded by his old Victorian colleague C. S. Wilkinson [q.v.6] Etheridge returned to Australia, and on 13 April 1887 became palaeontologist to the Geological Survey of New South Wales and to the Australian Museum, Sydney, working month and month about. In 1887 he led a collecting expedition to Lord Howe Island, and next year explored the caves at the junction of the Murrumbidgee and Goodradigbee rivers. In 1889 he founded a new serial, *Records of the Geological Survey* and next year, at his suggestion, the *Records of the Australian Museum* appeared. In the 1890s he served on the councils of the Royal and Linnean societies of New South Wales.

In 1892 he and Jack published their monumental *Geology and palaeontology of Queensland and New Guinea* (Brisbane), the basis of all subsequent geological work in Queensland. Etheridge had earlier introduced the term Permo-Carboniferous as a way around difficult problems of late Palaeozoic classification: he and Jack now applied it to the coal measures and associated marine beds of Queensland and New South Wales. By 1895 Etheridge had published a further hundred notes and papers on subjects ranging from Palaeozoic invertebrata to ethnology. As well as his annual progress reports to the Survey, he began a series of official contributions to the palaeontology of South Australia.

On 1 January 1895 Etheridge, who had acted in the position in 1893, was appointed curator of the museum on the retirement of E. P. Ramsay [q.v.6]. His term was distinguished despite serious quarrels with senior staff – including Charles Anderson [q.v.7], Sutherland Sinclair and Charles Hedley [q.v.] – and his aversion to publicity and to public gatherings. To be fair, Etheridge faced more difficulties than most incumbents; but the museum building was enlarged, the collections renovated, enriched and better displayed; and a fine library was built up, public lectures and demonstrations were resumed and cadetships introduced to train future staff.

Etheridge enlarged his interest in ethnology and published widely on the art, artifacts and customs of the Australian Aboriginals. In 1906 he set up a separate department of ethnology headed by his assistant W. W. Thorpe: he regarded the large collection of ethnological objects from Australia and the Pacific region as his greatest work for the museum. In 1914 Etheridge wrote an *Elementary guide to the exhibited zoological collections* and later two papers on the museum's history. Honorary consultant to the Geological Survey from 1895, Etheridge continued to publish widely in his prime field.

Shy, aloof and austere with a sardonic sense of humour, Etheridge had few intimate associates, but to those who won his liking he was a staunch friend. He had no hobbies and few interests outside his work from which he seldom allowed himself any respite, even though in later years he suffered from chronic nephritis. A thorough scientist and conservative by nature, he had little sympathy with speculation and directed his attention mainly to exact observation and the recording of facts: he was author of over 355 publications and co-author of about 60 others. His contribution to Australian stratigraphy was considerable and, according to Sir Edgeworth David [q.v.], 'the classification and correlation of the coalfields, goldfields, artesian water basins, oilfields, and other mineral deposits of the Commonwealth are based essentially on . . . [his] work'.

The honours he received were not commensurate with his large output of valuable work: however, he benefited under the Wollaston 'Donation Fund' of the Geological Society, London, in 1877 and received the [W. B.] Clarke [q.v.3] memorial medal of the Royal Society of New South Wales in 1895 and the Mueller [q.v.5] medal of the Australasian Association for the Advancement of Science in 1911.

Predeceased by his wife, Etheridge died suddenly of pneumonia on 5 January 1920 while on holiday at his son's residence, Inglewood, Colo Vale, New South Wales, and was buried in the Anglican section of Fitzroy cemetery, Mittagong. He was survived by two of his three sons. Numerous species of animals, both fossil and recent, were named in his honour and his name was also given to a river and gold-field in Queensland, a high range on the Kosciusko

plateau and a glacier in Antarctica.

R. Strachan et al (eds), *Rare and curious specimens* (Syd, 1979); Geological Soc of Lond, *Quarterly J*, 60 (1904), lxviii, 76 (1920) lix; Vic Geological Survey, *Bulletin*, 23 (1910); *Geological Mag* (Lond), 57 (1920), no 5, p 194, 239; Roy Soc Vic, *Annual Report*, 1919, p 5; Linnean Soc NSW, *Procs*, 45 (1920), p 5; *Nature* (Lond), 26 Feb 1920, p 700; Roy Soc NSW, *J*, 54 (1920), p 28, 76 (1942), p 96; Roy Soc SA, *Trans*, 44 (1920), p 379; Aust Museum, *Records*, 15 (1926), p 1; T. G. Vallance, 'Pioneers and leaders . . .', *Alcheringa*, 2 (1978); *Daily Telegraph* (Syd), 9 Jan 1920; H. Deane papers (NL); Etheridge letters (Dixson Lib, Syd).

G. P. WALSH

EVANS, ADA EMILY (1872-1947), barrister, was born on 17 May 1872 at Wanstead, Essex, England, youngest daughter of Henry Griffiths Evans, foreman at stoneworks and later architect, and his wife Louisa, née Cansdell. She received her early education at a private school at Woodford and in 1883, with her parents and some members of her family, arrived at Sydney. She attended Sydney Girls' High School, and later the University of Sydney (B.A., 1895). She was proficient in music and art and intended making teaching her career. With her sister she established a small private school, Cheltenham College, Summer Hill, but ill health forced her to abandon it.

Her mother came from a legal family, and Ada Evans was convinced that there was a need for women trained in the law to counter the prejudices of an all male legal system. Although aware, as the law then stood, she would not be permitted to practise, in 1899 she enrolled in the Sydney University Law School. Her entrance was made possible by the absence on leave of the dean, Professor Pitt Cobbett [q.v.], who would not have accepted a woman law student. She applied to the Supreme Court to be registered as a student-at-law but was rejected on the ground that the admission of barristers and solicitors did not apply to women. In 1902 she became Australia's first woman to graduate LL.B. Her next step was to seek admission to practise, but she was again refused. She canvassed the possibility of being called to the English Bar, but there too she was told there 'was no precedent'.

Numerous letters to successive governments requesting that the law be altered brought no result, although enabling Acts were passed in other States and a woman was admitted to the Victorian Bar in 1905. Women's organizations supported her endeavours but it was not until the passing of the Women's Legal Status Act in 1918 that the legal profession in New South Wales was opened to females. Ada Evans then served the required two years as a student-at-law and on 12 May 1921 was the first woman to be admitted to the New South Wales Bar. Although immediately offered a brief she declined, deterred by the lapse of time since her graduation, indifferent health and compelling family commitments. Under the nom-de-plume 'A.L.B.' in 1903 she had edited a weekly page for women in the newspaper, the *Australian Star*, and contributed articles ranging from the philosophical to the flippant, but always with an underlying theme that truth and kindness were essential ingredients for human happiness.

In 1909 Ada Evans, with her brother, bought Kurkulla at Bowral; keen gardeners, they made it their home and developed the sixteen-acre (6 ha) property into a self-supporting farm for herself and several members of her family. Taught by a visiting English nephew, she was also an expert pistol shot. After moving to Bowral she retained, for a time, her flat at Potts Point, and was a member of the Royal Sydney Golf Club, Rose Bay. She died at Kurkulla on 27 December 1947 and was cremated in Sydney with Anglican rites.

Physically attractive, intelligent, confident and compassionate, Ada Evans was well equipped to take her place as a member of the legal profession, but was frustrated in doing so by the law itself. Like many pioneers she was unable to reap the reward of her labours, but as Professor W. Jethro Brown [q.v.7] had predicted when encouraging her to persevere with her legal studies, her reward would be 'the glory of the pioneer'.

T. R. Bavin (ed), *The jubilee book of the law school of the University of Sydney* (Syd, 1940); J. M. Bennett (ed), *A history of the New South Wales Bar* (Syd, 1969); J. Mackinolty and H. Radi (eds), *In pursuit of justice* (Syd, 1979); *Aust Law J*, 20 May 1948; *SMH*, 13 May 1921, 29 Feb 1936; *Bulletin*, 21 May 1921; family papers held by Miss Ida Kyngdon, Bowral, NSW.   JOAN M. O'BRIEN

EVANS, ALEXANDER ARTHUR (1881-1955), soldier, accountant and politician, was born on 3 November 1881 at Launceston, Tasmania, son of Alexander Evans, soap manufacturer, and his wife Elizabeth Grace, née Groom. He was educated at Launceston Grammar School and became a clerk.

Evans served in the South African War with the 2nd Tasmanian Imperial Bushmen from March 1901 to May 1902 and was wounded, mentioned in dispatches and promoted from private to sergeant. For part of his service he was 'galloper' (mounted orderly) to the commander-in-chief, Sir Redvers Buller. On returning home he retained his interest in the army, serving for

five years with the Launceston artillery, and was appointed lieutenant in the senior cadets in 1912 and second lieutenant in the field artillery, Australian Military Forces (militia) in February 1914. By this time he had distinguished himself as a sportsman; he rowed for Tasmania, won major cycling events and represented the State in road races, sailed and played club football. In 1902-14 he worked for Massey-Harris & Co. Ltd and for Sir Philip Fysh [q.v.] & Co. as area manager at various towns in northern Tasmania. On 7 July 1910, at St John's Anglican Church, Launceston, he married Gladys Jeanette Luttrell.

When war began in 1914 Evans was appointed as a second lieutenant in the 3rd Artillery Brigade, Australian Imperial Force, and embarked in October with the first contingent. He was promoted lieutenant in February 1915 and reached Gallipoli on 25 April, though his battery's guns were not taken ashore until early May. He served with the 9th Battery at Razorback Ridge and Lone Pine; he was wounded on 7 August, mentioned in dispatches and also received special mention in divisional orders for conspicuous gallantry in May-June. He was awarded the Military Cross for his action when a Turkish shell struck a gun-pit, setting fire to ammunition and surrounding scrub. Dazed by the explosion, and at great personal risk, he organized survivors and extinguished the fire. He continued to serve as an artillery officer in France and Belgium in 1916-18, his units including the 9th, 103rd and 110th batteries. He also served briefly as an artillery staff officer at 4th Division Headquarters. He was promoted captain in July 1916, major in September 1917 and at the close of hostilities commanded the 10th Field Artillery Brigade as a temporary lieut-colonel. He was awarded the Distinguished Service Order in the King's birthday honours in 1918, was twice mentioned in dispatches and wounded several times.

Evans returned to Australia in November 1919. He rejoined the Citizen Forces and was awarded the Volunteer Officers' Decoration in 1931. At the beginning of World War II he returned to full-time duty with the army recruiting staff and was finally demobilized in 1945 as a temporary lieut-colonel.

Between the wars Evans played a significant part in the business and political life of Tasmania. After farming at Mangalore, Victoria, and in the Derwent Valley, Tasmania, he turned to accountancy in Launceston, becoming in 1922 a founding member of Evans & Garrott, accountants and secretaries. He was an alderman in 1922-31 and became mayor of Launceston in 1925. He entered parliament in 1936 and remained a member of the Legislative

Council for Launceston until 1942. He was also secretary to major racing and trotting clubs in northern Tasmania and on retiring to Hobart continued his interest in these sports. Known as 'Mr Racing', he was usually portrayed on a horse when members of the Legislative Council were caricatured. Survived by his wife, two sons and two daughters, he died of coronary vascular disease on 3 June 1955 in Hobart and was cremated.

Aust Defence Dept, *Official records of the Australian military contingents to the war in South Africa* P. L. Murray ed (Melb, 1911); L. Broinowski (ed), *Tasmania's war record 1914-1918* (Hob, 1921); *London Gazette*, 14 Mar 1916, 1 June 1917, 28 May, 3 June 1918; *Weekly Courier* (Launc) 21 Apr 1921, 17 Dec 1925; *Examiner* (Launc) 4-6 June 1955; *Mercury*, 4 June 1955; Evans file, War records section (AWM); records, State Library of Tasmania; family information.   D. V. GOLDSMITH

EVANS, DANIEL EDWARD (1885-1951), shipbuilder and soldier, was born on 8 May 1885, at Geelong, Victoria, fifth son of Charles Herbert Evans, described as a mariner, and his wife Jean, née Millard. A jack of all trades, Charles Evans was a foreman on the building, both of Princes Bridge, Melbourne, and of Mort's [q.v.5] Dock, Sydney. When Charles went to Bundaberg, Queensland, to manage a dredge, Daniel attended the Bundaberg Boys' Central School, which he left at 14 to become an engineer-apprentice at the Bundaberg Foundry.

The family moved to Adelaide where Daniel became a draughtsman for the Outer Harbour Construction Co. but soon shipped as an engineer on the cable-ship *Restorer*; he spent his nineteenth birthday on her in Singapore. Promoted to second engineer when the ship was transferred to an American company, he studied for his chief engineer's certificate and gained a second-class Board of Trade certificate at 21. He then returned to Adelaide and gained his chief engineer's certificate in 1908 while working for the Adelaide Steam Ship Co.

Evans had called frequently at Brisbane and saw a need for an enterprising firm of engineers there. In 1910 he and the 23-year-old Arthur Deakin opened a small business in Edward Street as suppliers of engineering equipment. They acquired their first workshop in 1913.

In December 1912 Evans was commissioned as second lieutenant in the Australian Military Forces (militia). He joined the Australian Imperial Force as a lieutenant in the 2nd Divisional Engineers in July 1915 and served in Egypt and France. By the time his active service was terminated by wounds in February 1918 he was a major,

had been mentioned in dispatches and awarded the Distinguished Service Order in the New Year honours of 1917. Contacts made while on leave in England later secured his appointment as a non-exclusive surveyor in Brisbane for Lloyds. He also joined the Institution of Engineers and Shipbuilders in Scotland.

In 1924 Evans became lieut-colonel commanding the 5th Division, Australian Engineers, and in 1930 colonel commanding the 11th Infantry Brigade. He was awarded the Volunteer Officers' Decoration in 1931 and in 1936 was placed on the unattached list.

The business, carried on during the war by Deakin, had prospered, although the workshop had been lost. Evans started a new workshop making small pieces of equipment in an outbuilding of his Coorparoo home in 1919. He pioneered the introduction in Queensland of both oxy-acetylene and electric arc welding. A larger establishment was bought in 1922. One of their first contracts was for 300 wagons for the Queensland Government Railways. A new large workshop built at Rocklea for structural steel and railway-engine repairs in 1926 was ready to manufacture the steel work for the Story [q.v.] Bridge in 1933. Joining M. R. Hornibrook, he chaired a new construction company which erected the bridge.

Evans was in uniform again at the outbreak of World War II as chief engineer, Northern Command. He was also appointed chairman of the Board of Area Management, Queensland, under the Ministry of Munitions; this work won him an M.B.E. In addition he established the Evans Deakin shipyard at Kangaroo Point. A 1200-ton lighter commenced on 27 July 1940 was the first of seventeen naval and merchant ships built in wartime. The last of eighty-one ships built in the yards was launched in 1971. Evans personally supervised much of the work and served also as a director for Mt Isa Mines Ltd, Cossey Motors (Pty) Ltd and Tableland Tindredging (NL). Energetic, forceful and gregarious, he liked whisky and frequented the United Services and the Johnsonian clubs. An old trade unionist, he was apolitical, joined the Australian Institute of Marine and Power Engineers, looked after the welfare of his men and had little industrial trouble.

A member of the first council of the Institution of Engineers, Australia, in 1921, Evans was one of the first members of the Professional Engineers Registration Board, and also belonged to the Institution of Naval Architects, London, and the American Society of Mechanical Engineers. He was on the board of the faculty of engineering of the University of Queensland from 1921 till his death; he left a substantial bequest to the university, and is commemorated by an annual memorial lecture.

Evans retired in 1948, died of cancer in Brisbane on 1 December 1951, and was buried in Nudgee cemetery with Anglican rites. His wife Kathleen Mary, whom he had married in Sydney on 4 November 1908, was the daughter of the Kimberley pioneer Michael (Stumpy) Durack. They had one son and four daughters. His estate, valued for probate at £183 158, was left principally to his family. Other bequests included a memorial to the Royal Australian Navy and the Merchant Navy, funds for Legacy, the Red Cross and the Spastic Children's Welfare League, an engineering bursary in memory of his old Bundaberg foreman, William Parry, and funds to commemorate himself in the University Faculty of Engineering and at Evans Deakin Ltd.

Qld Digger, Jan 1952; *Qld Maritime Bulletin*, Dec 1972, Apr, May, Aug, Sept 1973; *Courier Mail*, 3 Dec 1951; L. H. McDonald, unpublished paper, Daniel Evans memorial lecture, Faculty of Engineering, Univ. Qld.   L. H. McDONALD

EVANS, GEORGE ESSEX (1863-1909), poet, journalist and public servant, was born on 18 June 1863 at Regents Park, London, youngest son of John Evans, Q.C., Liberal M.P. for Haverfordwest, Pembrokeshire, 1847-52, and his wife Mary Ann, née Owen. Evans's father died in 1864 and the family returned to Wales where George entered Haverfordwest Grammar School. When he was 10 the family moved to Jersey where he attended St James College. He excelled at sport but was considered a rather dull student. Increasing deafness precluded an intended career in the army, and the family's depleted fortunes caused him, his brother John and two sisters to migrate to Queensland in 1881.

The brothers acquired a farm at Allora on the Darling Downs but George was injured in a riding accident and worked as a teacher and an agricultural reporter for the *Queenslander*. In 1883 he joined a surveying expedition to the Gulf country, then resumed farming before finally joining the public service in 1888 as a bailiff in the Lands Department. He was a clerk in the Patents Office in 1891-93, then became registrar for births, deaths and marriages at Toowoomba. While still in the public service he contributed poetry, criticism and articles to many Australian, and to some British, newspapers and journals. He wrote a regular column in 1902-05 first for the *Darling Downs Gazette* and then for the *Toowoomba Chronicle*. In 1892 and 1893 he had edited a literary annual, the *Antipodean*, with John Tighe Ryan [q.v.]. Published in London, it aimed to win an English as well as an Australian audience; many of Australia's best-known authors and public men contributed. Although it sold over 13 000 copies of its first issue it proved to be uneconomic. Evans revived it in 1897, bringing out another annual with A. B. Paterson [q.v.] as first editor, but again the venture proved unsuccessful and no more issues appeared. In 1905 he tried his hand at publishing his own weekly newspaper, the *Rag*, which was circulated in southern Queensland. It lasted for some fifty issues.

On 6 November 1899 at Drayton he married Blanche Hopkins, née Eglinton, a widow with two children; he ran a small dairy near Toowoomba, part time, and delivered milk. Evans found it a constant struggle to make a living and in 1905 was incapacitated for six months by a major operation.

Evans's first volume of poetry, *The repentance of Magdalene Despar and other poems*, was published in London in 1891. *Loraine and other verses* appeared in 1898 and *The secret key and other verses* in 1906. A collected volume of his poems was published posthumously in 1928. Descriptive, reflective, narrative and patriotic poems predominate in his work, but the poet's concern with a moral and physical law as part of a 'universal system' is reflected throughout.

His patriotic poems brought Evans to national attention. He commemorated in verse the Federation movement, Queensland's golden jubilee, Australia's statesmen and the work of the pioneers. The award of a £50 prize for a poem to celebrate Federation was the occasion for a biting critique from A. G. Stephens [q.v.] who found the ode to be 'a statement of the trite, a re-iteration of the obvious'. Alfred Deakin [q.v.] on the other hand demonstrated genuine admiration for the poet in a long correspondence. There is some evidence for Evans's claim that his Federal song helped materially in the Queensland and Western Australian Federation campaigns. In reviewing *Loraine* in 1898 Stephens said 'the Red Page opinion of Mr Evans' verses is that considered as poetry with a P they are readable and regular enough but essentially uninspired. Often neatly didactic or pleasantly descriptive they have no wings'. His publications were, however, generally well received in Australia and England and he was one of the best-known and most popular poets of the day. When Evans died in Toowoomba on 10 November 1909 after an operation for gallstones, his passing was mourned throughout the country. He was survived by his wife and son. Deakin described him as Australia's 'national poet'.

Evans's poetry was appreciated most by those who knew him personally and his reputation has lasted longer in Queensland than in any other State. A monument to his memory was erected at Toowoomba and a pilgrimage and memorial lecture are held each year in his honour.

H. A. Kellow, *Queensland poets* (Lond, 1930); K. Lynch, Cultural developments in Queensland, 1880-1930 (B.A. Hons thesis, Univ Qld, 1955); R. M. Fiddes, A minor public poet . . . (B.A. Hons thesis, Univ Qld, 1965); D. Birchley, The life and works of George Essex Evans (1863-1909) (M.A. thesis, Univ Qld, 1978); Deakin papers (NL); G. E. Evans papers (Fryer Memorial Lib, Univ Qld, Brisb).   M. D. O'HAGAN

EVANS, SIR JOHN WILLIAM (1855-1943), seaman, businessman and politician, was born on 1 December 1855 at Liverpool, England, son of George Matthew Evans, merchant seaman, and his wife Mary Ann, née Fisher. In 1859 the family migrated to Battery Point, Hobart. After an education at Alexander Ireland's Collegiate School, and a year-long voyage with his parents to Eastern ports, Evans became an apprentice on his father's part-owned barque *Helen*, trading to China and Japan. He then worked as second mate on the *Wynaud* and *Harriet McGregor*. In 1878-85 he served the Tasmanian Steam Navigation Co. and was in command of *Tasman* when she was wrecked in 1883. He lost a second ship *Esk* in 1886 and, although exonerated from blame, left the sea to go into the ironmongery business with James Harcourt, ex-mayor of Hobart, whose daughter Emily Mary he had married on 20 October 1883 at the Davey Street Congregationalist Church. Two years later he took charge of the river and channel steamer *Huon*. In 1891 he became traffic manager for Huddart [q.v.4] Parker Ltd and from 1894 until his death was manager of the firm's Hobart branch.

From the time he began to live ashore Evans took a practical interest in public welfare. A director of the International Exhibition in Hobart in 1894 he supported the Tasmanian Tourist Association from its inception next year. He was for many years president of the Tasmanian Consumptives' Sanatorium and of the St John Ambulance Society, and for shorter periods of the King George's Fund for Sailors, the Tasmanian section of the League of Boy Scouts and the Royal Life Saving Society. He was a magistrate from 1909, a Rotarian and Freemason. In 1891 he was elected to the Hobart Marine Board and was master warden eight times before 1939. He was a member of the Technical School Board in 1899-1900 and actively supported football and cricket.

Sometime president of the Southern Tasmanian Licensed Victuallers' Association and chairman of the Liberal League and National Federation, Captain Evans was elected to the House of Assembly for Kingborough in 1896. When in 1903 the premier Sir Elliott Lewis [q.v.] lost not only the State election but his own seat, Evans became leader of the Opposition facing the government of W. B. Propsting [q.v.]. In July 1904 Propsting, refused a dissolution by Lieut-Governor Dodds [q.v.4] when his finance bill was rejected by the Legislative Council, resigned and Evans was commissioned. In October 1905 he took the treasurer's portfolio on the resignation of C. L. Stewart.

More prosperous conditions in the State helped Evans win the election of 1906, after which he reconstituted his ministry with himself premier and chief secretary. With Propsting as his attorney-general in the Legislative Council he tried in vain to reach a constitutional settlement of differences between the Houses, but he did succeed in establishing a new electoral system with large districts, common rolls for State and Commonwealth elections, and the Hare-Clark [q.v.3] method of voting. He legislated to provide free education in state schools and gave the Complex Ores Co. the right to begin the development of hydro-electric power.

Evans survived in the 1909 election when he won Franklin with a narrow majority over Labor, but his health was deteriorating and in June 'the little skipper' relinquished the premiership to Lewis. In 1913 he became Speaker and held office, except for two brief periods, for the next twenty years, making a mark by his sense of fairness, amiability and salty humour. Appointed C.M.G. in 1906 he was knighted in 1926 and retired from parliament in 1937 on his appointment as lieut-governor of Tasmania. He published *The life story of Sir John Evans K.B., C.M.G.* (Hobart) in 1934, and died on 2 October 1943 in Hobart. He was given a state funeral after a Congregationalist service and was buried in Cornelian Bay cemetery, survived by a son and daughter, his wife having died in 1941. His estate was valued for probate at £8432.

Cyclopedia of Tasmania, 1 (Hob, 1900); *PP* (Cwlth, Senate), 1901-02, 1, 769; *Table Talk*, 28 Aug 1902; *Weekly Courier* (Launc), 4 Aug 1921, 6 Aug 1925, 7 Jan 1926, 29 Feb, 21 Nov 1928; *Examiner* (Launc), 19 Feb 1937; *Mercury*, 6 Aug 1941, 4 Oct 1943.   W. A. TOWNSLEY

EVERGOOD, MILES (1871-1939), artist, was born Myer Blashki on 10 January 1871 at Carlton, Melbourne, eleventh child of Philip Blashki, jeweller, and his wife Anna, née

Imergud; his Polish parents had married in Manchester, England, before migrating. Little is known of Blashki's early education. He was commissioned a lieutenant in the 2nd Victorian Regiment in September 1890 and served for four years. His main interest, however, was art, and in the early 1890s he studied at the National Gallery School, Melbourne, under George Folingsby [q.v.4] and Bernard Hall [q.v.]. He was a member of the Bohemian student group, the Prehistoric Order of Cannibals, which included Max Meldrum, Will Dyson, George Coates and the Lindsay brothers [qq.v.]. His satirical cartoons on political events appeared in Melbourne *Punch* and the *Champion*.

After unsuccessfully competing for the travelling scholarship in 1896, Blashki worked in Sydney for two years before leaving Australia in 1898 accompanied by a fellow student, Frank McComas. *En route* for New York, he worked on the Honolulu *Evening Bulletin* and the *San Francisco Examiner*. He went on to London where on 10 February 1900 at St Martin-in-the-Fields he married Flora Jane Perry; their son Philip was born in New York next year. About that time Blashki changed his name to Miles Evergood. His work received critical recognition, and as well as being elected a life member of the New York Lotos Club, he exhibited at the National Academy of Design. A retrospective exhibition was held in 1909 at the Salmagundi Club, New York.

Evergood had left Australia as an admirer of Whistler. While in New York he was struck by the works of the French Impressionists and in London by those of later masters in Roger Fry's Post-Impressionist exhibitions in 1910 and 1912. He probably also worked at this time in Paris. In London he exhibited with the International Society of Sculptors, Painters and Gravers and the New English Art Club. After the outbreak of war he enlisted for service and worked in the War Office.

About 1930, after the death of his first wife, Evergood married in New York Pauline Konitzer, a rug-designer many years his junior. In 1931 he returned to Australia with his wife and lived in Brisbane, where he was a member of the Royal Queensland Art Society, and later Sydney; he arrived in Melbourne in 1935 and established a home at Kalorama in the Dandenongs. In Sydney (1933) and Melbourne (December 1935) he held exhibitions of landscapes, portraits and flower subjects. Fundamentally an Impressionist, his robust style was characterized by an exuberant sense of colour and vigorous, expressive brush-strokes and use of palette knife. The bold impasto effects reflected the influence of the English artists Walter Sickert, Wilson Steer and Duncan Grant, rather than Pierre Bonnard or André Dunoyer de Segonzac with whom he has been linked.

Evergood died of cancer on 3 January 1939 in a Melbourne hospital and was cremated. He was survived by his second wife and his son who, after education in England at Eton College, the University of Cambridge and the University of London Slade School, became a leading social realist painter in America before his death in 1973.

Art in Aust, 15 Apr 1933, p 17; *SMH*, 5 Jan 1933; *Herald* (Melb), 19 Nov 1935; *Bulletin*, 20, 25 Nov, 11 Dec 1935; *Argus*, 4 Dec 1935, 4 Jan 1939; Melville Haysom's art exhibitions original book, Fryer MSS 51/13 (Fryer Lib, Univ Qld, Brisb).

RICHARD HAESE

EWART, ALFRED JAMES (1872-1937), botanist, was born on 12 February 1872 at Toxteth Park, Liverpool, England, second of four sons of Edmund Brown Ewart and his wife Martha, née Williams. His father, of Scottish (Dumfriesshire) descent, was lecturer in chemistry and director of the chemical laboratory of the Liverpool Institute and School of Art.

Alfred was educated at the Liverpool Institute, whence he matriculated with first-class honours in the University of London examination (1888), passed the intermediate science examination (1889), and attained honours in physics (1890); he entered University College, Liverpool, graduating B.Sc. with first-class honours in botany in the University of London examination. He was appointed a demonstrator in botany at University College, Liverpool, and it was at this time that he made his earliest original researches in plant physiology, publishing two papers in the *Transactions* of the Liverpool Biological Society — 'Observations on the vitality and germination of seeds' (1894), and 'Observations upon the pollen-tube' (1895). He was awarded an 1851 Exhibition Research scholarship, worked under the leading European plant physiologist Wilhelm Pfeffer at the University of Leipzig, and graduated Ph.D. (Leipzig) in 1896. This research on 'Assimilatory inhibition in chlorophyllous plants' was published in the *Journal* of the Linnean Society, London, in 1896.

An extension of the scholarship enabled him to travel to Java (Indonesia) and to visit Ceylon (Sri Lanka) and Singapore. In Java he worked at the Buitenzorg (Bogor) Botanical Garden under Melchior Treub studying 'The effects of tropical insolation' (published in *Annals of Botany*, 1897), and 'Contact irritability' (published in 1898 in the *Annals* of the botanic garden, Buitenzorg). He also published studies on tropical bacteria.

Ewart returned to England in 1897, was awarded the degree of D.Sc., London, and appointed deputy professor of botany at Mason College, Birmingham (which became the University of Birmingham in 1900). From mid-1898, having matriculated at Oxford, he spent two years as an extension lecturer and research scholar there, continuing his researches on the physiology of plants, and translating into English Pfeffer's classic three-volume work *Physiology of plants*. This was published between 1900 and 1906 by the Clarendon Press. At St Paul's Church of England, Oxford, on 17 December 1898, he married Florence Maud Donaldson [q.v. Ewart]. In 1900 the couple returned to Birmingham, where Ewart was appointed science master at King Edward's School, and from 1902 he also held the position of lecturer in botany at the Municipal Technical School until 1904, when he was appointed lecturer in botany and plant physiology at the University of Birmingham, a post which he occupied for just over one year, before he left for Melbourne. During this year he continued his association with the department of botany and the Botanic Gardens at Oxford, graduating B.Sc. in 1906. He was awarded an Oxford D.Sc. in 1910. Possibly the most important contribution to botanical literature from this early part of his career was a book *On the physics and physiology of protoplasmic streaming in plants*, published at Oxford in 1903 following a four-page abstract in the *Proceedings* of the Royal Society, London, 1902.

In 1906 Ewart took up the foundation chair of botany and plant physiology at the University of Melbourne, the first chair of botany in an Australasian university. In recommending Ewart's appointment, Professors Marshall Ward of Cambridge and F. W. Oliver of London stressed his extensive knowledge of physiological botany and the advantage that this would be in agricultural teaching. Further, in 1902-05 Ewart had been a tenant at Hurst Green Farm near Birmingham, and had gained some experience of commercial and experimental farming operations. He came to Melbourne with extensive teaching experience also, having already, in 1902, published a botany textbook for matriculation students. The Melbourne appointment was a joint one – by the university as professor of botany, and by the Victorian government as government botanist. This was not without its difficulties in terms of salary, small classes but heavy teaching responsibilities, increasingly crowded teaching and research conditions shared with other departments, and, especially, the geographical separation of the university and the National Herbarium

in the Botanic Gardens. Ewart spent half of each day at the herbarium and the other half at the university.

For the first eight years after the chair was established, botany was not regarded as equivalent to other sciences. Although this was rectified in 1914, another seven years elapsed before the chair of botany was made a full-time appointment. Ewart's exceptional energy and his activity as a teacher and a scientific researcher (both plant physiologist and systematic botanist) contributed to his building a botany school from humble beginnings to a major department in the University of Melbourne. The present botany school main building was planned by him, and it is said that the building and equipping of it were 'supervised by him in every detail'. At the time of opening in 1929 he had built up a department from six students in 1906 to 229, from one staff member to six academics and five technical assistants.

Although primarily a physiologist, Ewart found it necessary to teach the whole field of botany, and his work as government botanist immediately involved him in a research field in which he had not previously published – plant taxonomy. Even in his first year in Melbourne he published short papers on Australian flora, both of native and introduced species, and he soon became a leading authority on Victorian flora. At the same time, several of his major works on his earlier physiological researches were also published. His series of contributions on the flora of Australia continued for most of his working life, with No 36 appearing in 1930. By 1909 he was also contributing papers on agricultural botanical problems (germination of cereals, seed testing, nitrogen fixation), and in 1909 he produced, after only five years in this country, a semi-popular book on *Weeds, poison plants, and naturalized aliens of Victoria*. Even after his resignation as government botanist in 1921 he maintained an active interest in Australian, and especially Victorian, flora. He had by then published, in collaboration with O. B. Davies, *The flora of the Northern Territory* (1917), but undoubtedly his greatest contribution to floristic botany was his *Flora of Victoria* published by Melbourne University Press in 1930. His name has been commemorated in taxonomic botany by the genus *Ewartia*, a small group of the Compositae, and he is also remembered by a number of specific names in other genera.

Throughout his working life Ewart maintained a high level of research activity. He published some 154 scientific papers, mostly botanical, but some related to agricultural and veterinary problems. He was the author of six books, as well as the translator of Pfeffer's work. Undoubtedly, apart from this translation, the early work on protoplasmic streaming and the later work on the flora of Victoria are the most notable. However, many of his other papers represent pioneering contributions to botanical science over a wide range of topics.

Ewart was frequently consulted by governments on botanical matters, often associated with agriculture and especially with problems of stock poisoning, weed biology and forest conservation and management. He was a foundation member in 1908 and chairman in 1928-37 of the committee of management of Wilson's Promontory National Park which he often visited. Some of his services necessitated extensive travelling through inland Australia. His enquiries into stock poisoning on the overland stock route required of him, in 1924, some months in central and northern Australia at times under considerable hardship. Again, in 1927, when he investigated a disease of horses known as 'walkabout', his journey to the remote Kimberley area of north-western Australia was both arduous and demanding. His findings were published in collaboration with D. Murnane of the Council for Scientific and Industrial Research in *Bulletins* Nos 36 and 50. Ewart was active in forestry and the education of foresters in Victoria from 1908. This interest probably culminated in 1925 with the publication by the Victorian Forests Commission of his *Handbook of forest trees for Victorian foresters*. He took an active interest in the establishment of the Forestry School at Creswick in 1910, and as chairman of the examination board for over twenty-nine years had a major influence on the curriculum.

Ewart was elected a fellow of the Royal Society, London, in 1922. He was president of Section D (Biology) of the Australasian Association for the Advancement of Science meeting in Melbourne in 1921, and of Section M (Botany) at the Perth meeting in 1926. When the British Association had visited Australia in 1914 he was the local secretary of the botanical section. He was also a foreign member of the Czechoslovak Botanical Society, Prague, and fellow of the Linnean Society, London, for almost forty years. In the university he held a number of important posts – dean of the faculty of science, 1920-25 and 1929; of veterinary science, 1916, 1917, 1932-37; and of agriculture, 1917-18. It has been said by some that he might have been even more involved in university government, as well as leading Australian botany, but for some protracted controversies with the administration: reputedly he had a 'somewhat choleric disposition'.

Ewart's first marriage was dissolved in

1929. On 9 February 1931 he married a 34-year-old teacher, Elizabeth Bilton. He died of coronary vascular disease at East Malvern on 12 September 1937 and was cremated, survived by his second wife and the two sons of his first marriage. His Victorian estate was sworn for probate at £7168.

Alfred James Ewart 1872-1937 (Melb, nd); *DNB*, 1931-40; *Vic Naturalist*, 22 (1905-06), p 143; Linnean Soc Lond, *Procs*, 1937-38, p 314; *Obituary Notices of Fellows of the Roy Soc*, 2 (1939), p 465; recollections of the Ewarts by Mrs E. M. Warwood Birmingham, (typescript held by author, Botany Dept, Univ Melb).   T. C. CHAMBERS

EWART, FLORENCE MAUD (1864-1949), musician, was born on 16 November 1864 at Kentish Town, London, daughter of Frederick William Donaldson, accountant, and his wife Elizabeth, née Lewis. A brother, Frederick Lewis Donaldson, became a canon of the Church of England.

Florence made her début as a violinist at the Albert Hall, London, at the age of 14. Taught by John Carrodus, she was one of the first twelve to win a Birmingham scholarship to the South Kensington National Training School (Royal College of Music). She went on to study at Leipzig and at Berlin where she was a pupil of Joseph Joachim, paying for her instruction with her earnings as a coach for Dr Adolph Brodsky of Leipzig. By 1894 she had established a reputation in Birmingham as a conductor, recitalist and lecturer. On 17 December 1898 at the parish Church of St Paul, Oxford, she married Alfred James Ewart [q.v.] whom she had met in Leipzig. The couple lived at Birmingham; their two sons were born in 1900 and 1902.

In February 1906 the Ewarts moved to Melbourne. In 1907 Florence was co-conductor for the first Australian Women's Work Exhibition, winning first prize for an ode, 'God guide Australia', which was performed by the all-women orchestra at the exhibition. A rheumatic condition was the reason she gave for curtailing her appearances as a violinist from that time and she turned more to composition; her music was performed before such groups as the Musical Society of Victoria, at the Melbourne University Conservatorium, and occasionally at private vice-regal parties.

Unhappy and unsettled in her domestic life, Florence went abroad in 1910, 1916, and in 1920-21 when she visited Italy and Paris and first came under the influence of Debussy's music. After this trip she asked for a separation from her husband. In Europe again from late 1924 until June 1928, she studied with the composer Ottorino Respighi, working ten hours a day for nearly three years. In March 1925 Alfred petitioned for divorce. A decree absolute was granted on 24 December 1929.

Florence Ewart began work on the opera *The courtship of Miles Standish* in mid-1928, at Olinda, near Melbourne. It was performed in 1931, first at the New Conservatorium of Music and in May at the Melbourne University Conservatorium, a piano reduction being used in place of the orchestral setting; excerpts were broadcast on 3LO. Altogether Florence Ewart composed six operas of which the four-act *Ekkart* is thought to be the first, probably completed about 1909 though dated 1926; the prologue was first performed in 1923. *Mateo Falcone* (two acts) and *Nala's wedding* (one act) followed. *A game of chess* exists only in fragments, under the pseudonym of 'Sonia Aldon'. *Pepita's miracle* is dated November 1945. She wrote five works for voice and orchestra, forty-six songs and a body of instrumental works. All these are housed at the Grainger [q.v.] Museum at the University of Melbourne. Totally dedicated to composition, she had no chance to hear her major works or to grow through experience in performance, while the social and domestic duties expected of her left her no time to produce a large body of tested work.

Florence Ewart died at her home in South Yarra on or about 8 November 1949 and was cremated. She was survived by her sons.

Women Individual Arts Collective, *Lip*, 1978-79, p 97; *Argus*, 13, 14, 17, 18 Sept 1929; Florence Donaldson Ewart collection (Grainger Museum, Univ Melb).   MAUREEN THÉRÈSE RADIC

EWEN, JOHN CARR (1892-1951), farmer, soldier and businessman, was born on 25 October 1892 at Didsbury, Manchester, England, son of Frederick William Ewen and his wife Marion Eastwood, née Carr. After attending Cheadle Hulme (Warehousemen and Clerks) School, he worked for the marine superintendent of the Lancashire and Yorkshire Railway at Fleetwood. He was a keen cricketer and served for six months with the Territorial Army. In 1912 he migrated to Australia and became a farmer at Bellingen, New South Wales.

Ewen enlisted in the Australian Imperial Force on 21 October 1915 and next January embarked for Egypt with reinforcements for the 2nd Divisional Ammunition Column. From there he went to France in March as a gunner in the 22nd Howitzer Battery. In May he transferred to the 105th Howitzer Battery of the 5th Field Artillery Brigade, and during the fighting at Pozières on 3 August displayed gallantry and self-sacrifice by mending and keeping open two lines of communications under constant enemy fire. For this action he was appointed bombardier on 23 August and awarded the Military Medal. Promoted corporal on 24 November 1916 and sergeant on 17 March 1917, Ewen won the Distinguished Conduct Medal at Bullecourt on 30 April for conspicuous gallantry and devotion to duty. After heavy shell-fire had caused many casualties in his battery and wounded all the officers, he took command and completed the task of bringing the guns into position. In June he was sent to the Royal Artillery Cadet School at St John's Wood, London, and on 30 November was commissioned.

He arrived back in France in December 1917 and joined the 11th Battery of the 4th Field Artillery Brigade; he was promoted lieutenant on 28 February 1918. At Herleville in August he was in charge of the communications of an observation party when the forward observing officer was killed. Ewen immediately took his place, and for sending back valuable tactical information of enemy batteries engaging Australians holding a newly captured position, he received the Military Cross. The award of this honour made his combination of decorations for individual bravery extremely rare. Wounded on 3 October, he was evacuated to England and did not rejoin his unit until the end of March 1919. On 10 April he left for Australia and his A.I.F. appointment ended on 24 July.

On 30 October 1919 Ewen married Gladys Hamson at St Peter's Anglican Church, Neutral Bay, Sydney. He started a pest control business in Sydney about 1925 and later expanded into building renovations and contracting. He volunteered for service during World War II and in June 1941 was appointed to the militia field artillery in New South Wales as a temporary captain. He transferred to the A.I.F. in 1942 and was promoted captain in the 17th Australian Field Regiment in September. After great insistence he was sent to New Guinea, where he commanded the 53rd Battery with rank of major. He returned to Australia in 1943, serving in training appointments in Queensland, and was finally placed on the retired list in August 1951.

Ewen spent a period of time after the war re-establishing his building business, J. C. Ewen & Co., before returning to farming at Moss Vale. Survived by his wife, twin sons and two daughters, he died of cancer at the Repatriation General Hospital, Concord, on 20 November 1951 and was cremated.

London Gazette, 20 Oct 1916, 17 July 1917, 1 Feb 1919; *SMH*, 22 Nov 1951; records (AWM*); family papers held by Mr K. C. Ewen, Roseville, NSW.
                                        REX CLARK*
                                C. D. COULTHARD-CLARK

EWING, JOHN (1863-1933), politician and surveyor, was born on 6 October 1863 at Wollongong, New South Wales, son of Thomas Campbell Ewing, Anglican clergyman, and his wife Elizabeth, née Thomson. After attending The King's School, Parramatta, he was apprenticed to his brother, a surveyor, and practised at Wollongong. For about five years he organized the surveying of the Berry [q.v.3] estate in southern New South Wales. On 28 July 1888 at Bowral, Ewing married Beatrice Maud Swinson.

He moved to Western Australia in 1896 where he worked at land and mining-surveying on the Murchison and eastern goldfields. Next year he went to Collie where the colony's first coalfield was being explored. Ewing made the early surveys of the town site and discovered and developed coal-seams. The first local justice of the peace to be appointed, he was also chairman of the progress association and of the health and road boards. In 1901 he won the South-West Mining District seat in the Legislative Assembly with a large majority. An anti-ministerialist Liberal, he favoured old-age pensions, votes for women, government-subsidized workmen's insurance, free trade, taxation of unimproved land values, liberalizing of the land laws to encourage population and the breaking up of large landed estates, trade unionism and higher wages for railway workers. He saw the government as the greatest sweater in the colony.

In parliament Ewing vigorously urged improved working conditions in the coal-mines, a subject which he knew well. As a private member he introduced the Coal Mines Regulation bill, chaired a 1901 select committee on it, and saw its enactment next year. Also in 1902 he secured the appointment of a government inquiry into the need to stimulate the coal industry: the trade-unionists and other residents of Collie recorded their gratitude by presenting him with a gold watch.

Ewing soon became one of the most active of a small group working for wider acceptance of Collie coal, then regarded as inferior to that imported from Newcastle, New South Wales, and for economic incentives for its greater use. Largely through his promotion, in 1902 a railway-line, which considerably shortened the haul to the goldfields, was built from Collie to Narrogin. That year he gave evidence to a select committee on the Collie-Boulder line, and successfully repudiated accusations that he had used his parliamentary position to further his own financial interests. He was involved in the commercial development of the coalfield in the Griffin Coal Mining Co. and the Collie-

Cardiff series of mines. Ewing lost his seat in 1904, regained it under its new name of Collie in 1905, and lost it again in 1908. He then became involved in the mapping and classifying of land, particularly as a contract surveyor for the Midland Railway Co., around the Carnamah lakes and along its route between Midland Junction and Walkaway.

Still a Liberal, Ewing entered the Legislative Council in 1916 as a member for South-West Province. He held the seat until his death and again used it to harry governments, both State and Federal, on the need to use Collie coal on their railways. He consistently criticized the management of the State railways for failure to modernize equipment in order to use the local coal. By 1920 he was successful. Next he pressed the Western Australian government to use Collie brown coal to establish 'a super power scheme at the source of supply', to generate electricity to power the whole State; 'it is a fetish of mine', he admitted in 1928.

Ewing had been chairman of committees in 1920-23 and minister for education, the North-West and justice in the Mitchell [q.v.] government in 1923-24. He introduced the Amendments Incorporation Act and a Friendly Societies Amendment Act. In this same period he was a member of the Senate of the University of Western Australia. Colleagues described Ewing as gentle and generous with a buoyant and optimistic outlook: his debating was never bitter and he made no enemies. A keen punter, Ewing was penniless when he died. He rarely sat in the council during his last three years, due to illness. This was compounded in his final months by partial blindness.

Survived by his wife, two daughters and two sons, Ewing died of cerebro-vascular disease on 30 November 1933 at Guildford and was buried in Upper Swan cemetery. His brothers (Sir) Thomas Thomson and Norman Kirkwood [qq.v.] were also politicians. Between the three they served for sixty years in seven houses of four parliaments.

P.W.H. Thiel & Co., *Twentieth century impressions of Western Australia* (Perth, 1901); J.S. Battye (ed), *Cyclopedia of Western Australia*, 1 (Adel, 1912); *V&P* (LA WA), 1902, 2 (A9); *PD* (WA), 27 Sept 1916, 19 Feb 1918, 26 Sept 1918; *Western Mail* (Perth), 4 Nov 1905; *Univ Studies in History and Economics*, 3 (1957) no 1; *Morning Herald* (Perth), 24 Apr 1901; *West Australian*, 1, 6 Dec 1933.

PETER EWING
SUZANNE EDGAR

EWING, NORMAN KIRKWOOD (1870-1928), politician and judge, was born on 26 December 1870 at Wollongong, New South

Wales, tenth child of Rev. Thomas Campbell Ewing, Anglican clergyman and rural dean, and his wife Elizabeth, née Thomson. His uncle R. K. Ewing was an early moderator of the Presbyterian Church in Tasmania. Educated at Illawarra College (Wollongong), Oaklands (Mittagong) and later at night-school in Sydney, Ewing was articled to M.A.H. Fitzhardinge, and was admitted a solicitor in 1894. After practising at Murwillumbah he moved to Perth where, admitted to the Bar in 1897, he established the firm of Ewing & Downing.

Like his older brothers (Sir) Thomas and John [qq.v.], Ewing was attracted by politics. An unsuccessful Protectionist candidate for the Tweed in the New South Wales Legislative Assembly elections of 1895, he was Independent member for Swan in the Western Australian parliament from 1897 to 1901 when he became a Free Trade senator. However, a dwindling practice necessitated his resignation two years later. In 1904 he unsuccessfully contested the State seat of Canning.

On 15 October 1897 at St George's Cathedral, Perth, Ewing married Maude Louisa, daughter of (Sir) Edward Stone [q.v.]. About 1905, in a search for climatic conditions to ease her asthma, they moved to Hobart. Admitted to practice in March 1906 Ewing became a partner in Ewing & Scager, and made a name as a forceful barrister. He was narrowly defeated for the Senate in 1906, helped establish the Progressive League next year, and in April 1909 won the House of Assembly seat of Franklin as an anti-socialist. In October he led a successful revolt against the Lewis [q.v.] government although, after John Earle's [q.v.] Labor government failed, a re-fusion of the Liberal factions secured Lewis's return to power. In October 1914 Ewing's political flair earned him the leadership of the Opposition following the sudden death of A. E. Solomon [q.v.]. But Ewing was not in politics long enough to make a lasting mark. Next year he was made King's Counsel and in September was elevated to the bench as the third judge. Cynics suggested that the Earle ministry made the appointment to prevent Ewing from becoming premier, but the legal profession made no protest. It was the crowning achievement of his distinguished legal career. In 1919 he moved to Launceston where it was considered one of the judges should reside. From November 1923 until June 1924 he was administrator of Tasmania.

A distinguished-looking, bespectacled man, with marked aquiline features, Ewing was author of *The practice of the local courts of Western Australia* (Perth, 1897) and as chairman of a committee appointed by the government was associated with the drafting of the Tasmanian Criminal Code, 1924. Within Tasmania he sat on royal commissions into the public debts sinking fund (1915), the Hobart Licensing Bench (1916), the charges made against V.R. Ratten (1918), and the Tasmanian Institution for the Blind, Deaf and Dumb (1925). However he is best remembered for work performed outside the State. In 1919-20 he investigated the administration of the Northern Territory, and in 1920 conducted the royal commission into the case of the imprisonment of Industrial Workers of the World members in Sydney. His decisions in these controversial matters earned him some notoriety, especially his liberal findings on the I.W.W. 'twelve'.

In 1924 Ewing suffered a stroke. With his son acting as amanuensis he continued his work spasmodically until his death on 19 July 1928 at Launceston. Survived by his wife, his son and one of his two daughters, he was buried in Carr Villa cemetery. Ironically, poor legal management by others of his considerable land holdings left his wife in straitened circumstances: his estate was valued for probate at £2761.

PTHRA, 18 (1971), no 4, p 137; *Examiner* (Launceston), and *Mercury*, 20 July 1928; *Morning Herald* (Perth), 2 Apr 1901; *Aust Worker*, 25 July 1928; Deakin papers (NL).   SCOTT BENNETT

EWING, ROBERT (1871-1957), taxation commissioner, was born on 31 August 1871 at East Maitland, New South Wales, son of Robert Ewing, engineer, and his wife Elizabeth, née Cunningham. Educated at Sydney High School, he did some junior reporting for the *Sydney Morning Herald*. In September 1896 he joined the New South Wales public service as a temporary officer in customs, Colonial Treasurer's Department, and for a time acted as secretary to the commissioners of taxation. In 1901 he was transferred to the central staff of the new Federal Department of Trade and Customs in Melbourne where he became confidential clerk to the comptroller-general of customs, (Sir) Nicholas Lockyer [q.v.]. In 1911 Ewing joined the land tax branch of the Department of Treasury as secretary and in 1916-17 he served as deputy commissioner of taxation in Victoria. After a brief spell as acting commissioner of taxation, he was appointed commissioner in 1917, holding the place until his retirement in 1939. From 1925 he also held the separate position of commissioner of land tax. His influence was far-reaching: on his death most of the senior

Commonwealth taxation officials had been trained by him.

The three decades during which Robert Ewing was associated with the Federal taxation office and for the greater part of which he was its commissioner, were years during which the Commonwealth substantially increased its powers over Australian taxation. Between 1916-17 and 1938-39 total Federal taxation collections rose from £24.5 million to £74.1 million (or from 4.8 to 8.1 per cent of gross domestic product) which effectively doubled per capita Federal tax burdens. During the first decade of Federation, the Commonwealth had raised all its financial requirements from customs and excise revenue. It then entered other areas of taxation, frequently in direct competition with the States. The Fisher [q.v.] Labor government introduced the land tax in 1910 and followed this in 1914 with a Federal estate duty. In 1915, largely to finance the growing expenditure requirements of Australia's participation in World War I, a Federal income tax was introduced which in 1917 was supplemented with a special wartime profits tax. An entertainment tax came into force the same year. Shortfalls in customs revenue during 1930 were compensated for by the introduction of a sales tax at a rate of two and a half per cent, raised to six per cent in 1931.

Ewing was closely associated with all these measures, but more particularly with the introduction of income tax, the wartime profits tax and the sales tax. The last two resulted in his publications, *War-time profits tax* (1917) and *Sales tax* (1932). These were in fact official handbooks prepared under his auspices as taxation commissioner. His third publication in this area, *Taxes and their incidence* (1926), provided an historical overview of the development of taxation in Australia, particularly the more recent developments at the Federal level, and was given originally as a lecture to the Melbourne University Commerce Society. Although the title suggests a theoretical discussion of the incidence of specific tax instruments, the contents provide little more than a descriptive account of developments and problems in Federal income tax, land tax and estate duty, the emphasis being on 'the many details associated with taxation in practice, and the general reasons for taxation'.

Appointed C.M.G. in 1933, Ewing was described on his retirement as a man whose mild demeanour and frail appearance concealed outstanding administrative efficiency and a determination to uphold the integrity of his office. His more interesting publications, written in retirement, emphasize Christian socialist principles. The first, *A plan of economic reconstruction* (1941), contains a Utopian scheme for the reconstruction of post-war Australia. The second, *Money pitfalls in Labor's socialism, the cure*, was privately printed in 1947, and supplements the previous work on certain issues. Both booklets were followed by a spate of shorter pamphlets in the 1950s; they raise intriguing questions about the economic ideas of Australia's commissioner of taxation — because so much of their economic content was influenced by 'currency cranks' such as the Victorian L.G. de Garis, as well as by the more well-known heretical ideas of Major Douglas and Henry George [q.v.4].

Ewing's *Plan for economic reconstruction* is based on the simple premise that post-war reconstruction provided a unique opportunity 'to establish . . . the Kingdom of God on Earth within the Nation and the Empire'. The spiritual foundations of this kingdom lay in the two commandments to 'love the Lord thy God' and to 'love thy neighbour as thyself', that is, in the principles of mutual co-operation and ownership in common. Its economic basis rested on the propositions that 'production of all goods essential to the best possible standard of living should be secured; and that the distribution of the goods should be effected in the simplest possible manner'. The plan was to be implemented by replacing ownership of the means of production with 'a compensated tenant-trusteeship', by paying a basic standard of living to all, by regulating wages in terms of this living standard, by the abolition of interest and by central control over international trade. His *Money pitfalls in Labor's socialism* compared this plan with the Australian Labor Party's 'socialistic' platform of reconstruction, attacking the latter as a half measure which left the 'money power' untouched. Although Ewing's plan was enthusiastically endorsed by the Melbourne journalist and writer, Ambrose Pratt [q.v.], no reviews or serious discussions of its proposals appear to have been published.

Ewing's first wife, Alice Mary Church, whom he had married on 9 May 1900 at St Aidan's Anglican Church, Annandale, Sydney, died in 1904. On 16 January 1909 at Upper Hawthorn, Melbourne, he married her sister, Maude Olivia (d. 1945), according to Methodist forms. There were no children of either marriage. Ewing died on 15 October 1957 at East Camberwell and was cremated. His estate was valued for probate at £12 533.

Roy Com on taxation, Report, *PP* (Cwlth), 1932-34, 4, p 2249, 1934-37, 3, p 1917; *Argus*, 3 June 1933; *SMH*, 3 June 1933, 21 Oct 1957; *Age*, 16 Oct 1957; *Canb Times*, 18 Oct 1957.

P. D. GROENEWEGEN

EWING, Sir THOMAS THOMSON (1856-1920), politician, was born on 9 October 1856 at Pitt Town, New South Wales, son of Rev. Thomas Campell Ewing, Anglican clergyman, and his wife Elizabeth, née Thomson. After receiving a good education he was intended to study for the Bar but at 17 he joined a surveyor's party. In June 1877 he became a licenced surveyor with the New South Wales Department of Lands; he was appointed a second-class surveyor in 1882 at a salary of £530 and did much work in the Richmond River Valley. On 1 October 1879 at St Michael's Church of England, Wollongong, he married Margaret Russell MacCabe; they had three sons and two daughters.

Ewing resigned from the department on 15 October 1885 to stand, successfully, for the Legislative Assembly. Setting aside his 'theoretical' free trade convictions, he supported a policy of moderate protection, favoured extension of technical education, female suffrage and payment of members, and opposed the current land Act and non-European immigration. In 1887 he published a pamphlet on the natural resources of the Richmond electorate which he represented until 1894; from 1894 to 1901 he held the new nearby seat of Lismore. Energetic, popular and independent, he quickly broadened his interests from merely local matters to include hydro-electricity for Sydney, fiscal policy and Federation. He held Sir Henry Parkes [q.v.5] in high regard, supported Sir George Dibbs and Sir Patrick Jennings [qq.v.4], and did good work as chairman of the parliamentary Public Works Committee.

In 1901 Ewing moved into Federal politics, winning the seat of Richmond in the House of Representatives. By now a staunch Liberal-Protectionist, he soon attracted the attention of Alfred Deakin [q.v.] who valued his judgment highly. In Deakin's second administration Ewing was vice-president of the Executive Council in 1905-06, minister for home affairs, 1906-07, and minister for defence, 1907-08. In the latter portfolio Ewing did his most notable political work. He had long been an extreme exponent of the 'Yellow Peril' doctrine and a supporter of universal military training, and his examination of Australia's military preparedness in 1907 confirmed him in his views. Using the report of Colonel W. T. Bridges [q.v.7] on the Swiss military system, Ewing and Major J. G. Legge [q.v.] worked out a scheme for compulsory military training for young men. This became the basis of the Defence Act of September 1909 and after further modification by the Fisher [q.v.] government the basis of Australia's pre-war 'citizen army'. In 1910 Ewing retired from politics because of ill health and devoted himself to farming on the Tweed River.

Amiable, humorous and well-liked, Ewing was a good debater and captivating spinner of yarns. 'There are two well-defined sides to his character', said Melbourne *Punch* in 1905, 'one emotional, the other practical. In business the man of the world comes uppermost; in politics the ideals which he still cherishes most often guide his words. Now and then the dual forces come into conflict while he is on his feet, and the result is a mixture of sense and sentiment. His quickness of wit is astonishing. His speeches are always relieved by delicious paradoxes and quaint conceits, and his humour never scarifies ... Altogether he is a most engaging personality'. Ewing's wide interests included history, science and literature; he enjoyed writing short stories. In 1903 with (Sir) T. A. Coghlan [q.v.], he published *Progress of Australasia during the nineteenth century,* and in 1913 his *Review of the rival railway schemes for the connection of the tableland of New England with a deep sea port on the north coast.*

Ewing was appointed K.C.M.G. in 1908 even though what he called the 'titled mediocrities' of parliament had often been the butt of his wit. According to a parliamentary colleague, R. A. Crouch [q.v.], Deakin knighted him as a joke and Ewing took it as such.

Ewing died of heart and kidney disease in a private hospital at Darlinghurst, Sydney, on 15 September 1920 and was buried in Wollongong cemetery. His estate was valued for probate at £54 975. Two younger brothers, John and Norman Kirkwood [qq.v.], also had distinguished political careers.

J. A. La Nauze, *Alfred Deakin* (Melb, 1965); N. K. Meaney, *A history of Australian defence and foreign policy, 1901-23,* 1 (Syd, 1976); *PD* (Cwlth), 1908, p 437 ff, 1920, p 4726; *SMH,* 13 Oct 1885, 16 Sept 1920; *T&CJ,* 26 May 1887, 11 Nov 1908; *Punch* (Melb), 10 Aug 1905, 19 Nov 1908; L. D. Atkinson, Australian defence policy ... 1897-1910 (Ph.D. thesis, ANU, 1964); Crouch memoirs (LaTL).

G. P. WALSH

F

FAHEY, JOHN (1883-1959), Catholic priest and military chaplain, was born on 3 October 1883 at Rossmore, Tipperary, Ireland, son of Michael Fahey, farmer, and his wife, Catherine, née Ryan. Educated by the Cistercians at Mount Melleray and at the Brignole Sale Seminary, Genoa, Italy, he was ordained priest in May 1907. Leaving almost immediately for the Australian mission he worked briefly in Perth at the cathedral and was then appointed to the parish of York and of Yarloop-Pinjarra in the south-east. Fahey was a manly type of priest well suited to the timberworkers he served. He was an excellent sportsman, a fine shot and lived a rough unconventional life. Bush experience provided him with an excellent preparation for the Australian Imperial Force which he joined on 8 September 1914 as a chaplain, 4th class (captain). He was assigned to the 11th Battalion.

Fahey reached Gallipoli on 25 April 1915 and although chaplains were ordered not to disembark because every available space was reserved for combatants, he disregarded this, asserting his duty to go with his men. His work, consoling the wounded, burying the dead and encouraging the living, was widely appreciated and he became a very popular figure; he typified the active, robust priesthood so admired in Australia. From Gallipoli he wrote that he 'was shot twice through my overcoat without the skin being touched. I had a book shot out of my hands, the jam tin I was eating out of was shot through'. Evacuated sick in July, he resumed duty in September and remained at Gallipoli until 7 November. He was mentioned in dispatches and awarded the Distinguished Service Order for 'gallantry under fire'.

Rejoining the 11th Battalion in March 1916 Fahey left for France in April. Here a new battle experience awaited him; to the horrors of Gallipoli were added the might of heavy artillery. 'For an hour or so', he wrote, 'shells of all calibres, mostly high explosive, simply rain on a small sector of the front . . . It is appalling, it is diabolical, and it is wonderful how anyone escapes'. He remained in France until 14 November 1917, becoming the longest-serving front-line chaplain of any denomination, although he only won promotion to chaplain 3rd class (major). He left for Australia on 16 March 1918. Against his wishes, he was fêted on his return to Perth. War service had aroused in him a deep admiration for Australian soldiers: he explained that 'the more I knew them the more I loved and admired them . . . Their bravery has been written in deeds that will live to the end of the world'.

Fahey was stationed at Cottesloe in 1919-32, at Kellerberrin in 1932-36 and at various Perth parishes in 1936-39, after which he was parish priest at Cottesloe until his death. He was a faithful pastor, kept up his A.I.F. and sporting contacts and occupied a number of minor diocesan positions. He died at the St John of God Hospital, Subiaco, on 28 April 1959 and was buried in Karrakatta cemetery. About 2000 people attended his funeral.

J. T. McMahon, *College, campus, cloister* (Perth, 1969); M. McKernan, *Australian churches at war* (Syd, 1980); *London Gazette*, 14, 28 Jan 1916; *Advocate* (Melb), 31 July 1915; *West Australian*, 29 Apr 1959; *West Australian Record*, 30 Apr, 7 May 1959; *Geraldton Guardian*, 30 May 1959; information from Catholic archives office, Perth.

M. McKernan

FAIRBAIRN, Sir GEORGE (1855-1943), pastoralist, politician, company director and oarsman, was born on 23 March 1855 at New Town, Geelong, Victoria, eldest son of George Fairbairn [q.v.4] and his wife Virginia Charlotte, née Armytage. His brothers were CHARLES (1858-1925), pastoralist and oarsman, FREDERICK WILLIAM (1865-1925), pastoralist, Red Cross director and sportsman, James (1856-1891), medical practitioner, Thomas (1860-1918), pastoralist, and Stephen [q.v.].

George was educated from 1864 to 1871 at Geelong Church of England Grammar School; Charles attended in 1868-75 and Frederick in 1880-84. All six brothers became captain of cricket, and the four who were there after the institution of a senior prefect in 1875 all held that office. On these four, too, the influence of J. L. Cuthbertson [q.v.3] was added to that of the headmaster J. B. Wilson [q.v.6]. Generosity to their old school was a conspicuous trait of the brothers' lives.

George represented the school at football, but did not, like most of his brothers, row at school, as the boat club was not founded until 1874. After a period at Edinburgh, where he was taught by his uncle Patrick Fairbairn, a Free Church moderator and biblical scholar, he had two years at Jesus College, Cambridge, where he gained his university trial cap and rowed for the college in the first two of the eleven successive years (1875-85) in which Jesus went head of the river. In 1878, two years after returning to Australia, George rowed for Victoria in the first inter-colonial boat race. In 1903 he founded the Henley-on-Yarra regatta, with A. R. Black-wood [q.v.7 R. O. Blackwood] and W. C. Rivett, and became the first president of the Melbourne Amateur Athletic and Rowing Club.

For some years George managed Peak Downs and Barcaldine stations in Queens-land for his father; at the former, in 1878, he pioneered the use of wire-netting to keep out kangaroos. On 24 November 1880 at St John's Church of England, Toorak, Mel-bourne, he married Jessie Kate Prell; they had a son and a daughter. In the early 1880s he returned to Victoria and joined William Sloane & Co., stock and station agents, and in 1886 became manager of the Union Mortgage & Agency Co. of Australia Ltd. In 1890 he took over the family property of Lara, where he at once established a merino stud and in 1900 a Shropshire stud. Later he acquired Benarca, near Deniliquin, New South Wales, and Greenlaw, Mount Martha, Victoria. His business interests increased, and he was a director of the Union Trustee Co. of Australia Ltd for more than forty years, chairman for more than thirty of the British & Foreign Marine Insurance Co. Ltd., chairman until 1925 of the Victorian board of advice of Dalgety [q.v.4] & Co., a director of the Australian Mutual Provident Society and head of the family firm of G. & C. Fairbairn. He was president for six years of the Employers' Federation of Australia, a trustee of the estate of Edward Wilson [q.v.6] and in 1936-37 a director of the Argus and Australasian Ltd. In 1931 he was president of the National Union, a political fund-raising body. He was a member of the committee of management of the Alfred Hospital, active in the Big Brother movement from its in-ception, and a churchwarden of St John's, Toorak. President of a short-lived associa-tion of Old Geelong Grammarians in 1883, in 1904 he became third president of the con-tinuing body, founded in 1900. He was president of the Melbourne Club in 1890 and 1902.

In 1903 Fairbairn was elected to the Legislative Assembly seat of Toorak which he held until 1906 when he resigned to con-test the newly created seat of Fawkner in the Federal House of Representatives. He lost that seat in the redistribution of 1913, but in 1917 was elected to the Senate. As one of Forrest's [q.v.] corner group he had worked for the fusion of non-Labor in 1909 and was active in arranging for the financing of the Liberal Party. His parliamentary speeches were numerous, wide-ranging, and marked by native eloquence, robust common sense, and a 'tolerant and even sympathetic atti-tude to liberal and progressive movements'. Perhaps his best epitaph as a public figure is contained in a speech which he made in parliament on 23 October 1912: 'I do not often speak strongly, but, when there is ty-ranny in the air, my old Scotch blood arises, and I must say what I think'. He did not seek re-election in 1923, and in 1924 was ap-pointed agent-general for Victoria in Lon-don, holding the office with distinction until 1927. In 1926 he was knighted.

Fairbairn's first wife died in 1921 and on 20 February 1924 at the Presbyterian Church, Mornington, he married Lorna Bessie, daughter of G. P. Robertson of Co-ragulac, Colac. Sir George died in Mel-bourne on 23 October 1943, survived by his second wife and his son, Clive Prell, grazier and Cambridge rowing blue. His estate was valued for probate at £164 170 in Victoria and £49 394 in New South Wales.

The third brother, Charles, was born on 12 August 1858 at Kelso, Scotland. He ma-triculated at Cambridge in October 1877 and rowed in the university crew which defeated Oxford in 1879. Later he was joint manager with George of the family interests in Queensland, where with his brothers he played a leading part in breaking the shearers' strike of 1891. In 1897 he acquired Banongill, near Skipton, Victoria, and in 1918 Wooloomanata, near Lara, where he spent his final years. In 1911 he presented the Fairbairn Challenge Cup for the headship of the river among the associated public schools of Victoria. Charles had married Elizabeth Osborne on 15 July 1891 at St Stephen's Church of England, Elsternwick. He died in Melbourne on 27 October 1925 of cerebro-vascular disease, predeceased by his wife and survived by two daughters and three sons, one of whom was James Valen-tine [q.v.].

Frederick Fairbairn was born on 21 July 1865 at Richmond, Melbourne. After studying at Cambridge he acquired Logan Downs station, near Clermont, Queensland, and subsequently Woolbrook, near Teesdale in Victoria. During World War I he worked in London for the Australian Red Cross Society as an honorary colonel and director for Victoria, and visited France and Swit-zerland in the interests of Australian pri-soners of war. He was appointed O.B.E. in 1918. He remained a keen sportsman, being captain of the Geelong golf club, playing cricket, and serving on the committee of the Victoria Racing Club. On 30 September 1891 at Clermont he had married Rhoda Jane McLeod, who survived him, with two daugh-ters and a son, on his death of cancer in Melbourne on 22 February 1925.

The six Fairbairn brothers — 'my thirty-seven feet of sons', as their father called them — were natural leaders and legendary athletes, clannish yet individual, shrewd yet generous, spacious yet straightforward in their mode of living. They had an eye for quality and a great capacity for enjoyment. Always somewhat larger than life, they bestrid the worlds they conquered, epitomizing the vigour, independence, and carefree spirit of many of the first generation of Australian native-born.

F. Brittain and H. B. Playford, *The Jesus College Boat Club, Cambridge* (Cambridge, 1928); S. Fairbairn, *Fairbairn of Jesus* (Lond, 1931); A. Henderson (ed), *Early pioneer families of Victoria and Riverina* (Melb, 1936); *Geelong Grammar School*, (1) *Annual*, 1875-76, and (2) *Q*, 1877-84, Dec 1891, and (3) *Corian*, May 1925, Dec 1925, Dec 1943, Mar 1977; *Pastoral Review*, 16 Nov 1943; *Punch* (Melb), 18 Jan 1911; *Age*, and *Argus*, 25 Oct 1943; Geelong Grammar School Archives; family information.

MICHAEL D. DE B. COLLINS PERSSE

FAIRBAIRN, JAMES VALENTINE (1897-1940), pastoralist, aviator and politician, was born on 28 July 1897 at Wadhurst, Sussex, England, second son of Charles Fairbairn [q.v. Sir George Fairbairn] and his wife Elizabeth, née Osborne. He grew up on his father's station, Banongill, near Skipton, Victoria. Educated at Geelong Church of England Grammar School in 1908-15, he was remembered as a boy who overcame natural shyness and won many friends, including Charles Hawker and (Sir) Hudson Fysh [qq.v.].

On leaving school he went to England to enlist for active service; he was accepted by the Royal Flying Corps and commissioned as a flying officer in July 1916. On 14 February 1917 he was shot down and captured by the Germans while helping to escort a squadron taking photographs between Cambrai and St Quentin. An account of the incident and his fourteen-month captivity until he was released on exchange was published in the *Corian*. His right arm had been badly damaged and was to remain largely disabled despite repeated operations; but he refused to be diverted from an intention to continue flying.

Fairbairn returned to Australia in 1919 and, after further treatment, took over the management of Peak Downs, in Queensland. On 21 March 1923 at St John's Church of England, Toorak, he married Daisy Olive (Peggy) Forrester. In 1924 he acquired Mount Elephant station, near Derrinallum, in Victoria, where he built an airstrip.

After his election in 1930 to the Hampden Shire Council, he played an increasing part in public life. He was a member of the council of the Anglican diocese of Ballarat, though

brought up a Presbyterian; in 1932-33 he was president of the Old Geelong Grammarians' Association, and from 1932 a member (and from 1937 chairman) of the school council. He was a director of the Commercial Banking Co. of Sydney and of the Union Trustee Co. of Australia Ltd. He played polo, golf, lawn tennis and squash, being president of the Australian Squash Racquets Association.

In 1932, as a United Australia Party candidate, Fairbairn was elected to the Legislative Assembly seat of Warrnambool, but he resigned in 1933 to contest successfully the House of Representatives seat of Flinders in a by-election caused by the resignation of S. M. (Viscount) Bruce [q.v.7]. He regularly flew himself between his property and Canberra, where he was recognized as an authority on aviation. In 1935 he flew around Australia, and in 1936, after going to England in an airmail plane, flew himself back to Australia in his own newly acquired machine.

On 26 April 1939, at the outset of the first Menzies government, Fairbairn joined the cabinet as minister for civil aviation and vice-president of the Executive Council; he also assisted the minister for defence. On the outbreak of war in September 1939 he went to Canada to help inaugurate the Empire air scheme whereby airmen from Britain and the dominions were to be trained in Canada. In an historic ceremony in November 1939 he was sworn in at Ottawa as Australian minister for air by Lord Tweedsmuir, governor-general of Canada; this portfolio involved all Royal Australian Air Force matters. Fairbairn was subjected at times to fierce press criticism but he refused to be deflected into useless controversy. Those who worked with him bore witness to his energy, enthusiasm, and tireless, single-minded dedication.

In July 1940 he flew himself around Australia in his D.H. Dragonfly in order to review all R.A.A.F. stations. On 13 August he was killed, together with two other cabinet ministers, G. A. Street and Sir Henry Gullett [qq.v.], and the chief of the general staff, General Sir Brudenell White [q.v.], and others, when the R.A.A.F. bomber in which he was travelling crashed on approaching Canberra airport. 'Jim Fairbairn', (Sir) Robert Menzies said in parliament next day, 'added lustre to his family name. His mind and character were strong, and he displayed an unusual combination of cheerful fellowship with, perhaps, a hint of Scottish dourness. He was slow to speech, but, once engaged, he was gifted in exposition and resolute in advocacy of what he believed to be true'. He was survived by his wife, a daughter, and a son Geoffrey Forrester

(1924-1980) who became reader in history at the Australian National University and an authority on insurgency movements in Asia. Fairbairn is remembered, not only as an appropriate eponym of Canberra's airport, but for public service given freely and from a sense of duty.

A. Henderson (ed), *Early pioneer families of Victoria and Riverina* (Melb, 1936); R. G. Menzies, *Afternoon light* (Melb, 1967); H. Fysh, *Qantas at war* (Syd, 1968); *Geelong Grammar School Q,* 1909-13, and *Corian,* 1914-1915, Aug 1916, Dec 1916, Dec 1917, Dec 1918, Aug 1933, Aug 1936, Dec 1938, Aug 1939, Aug 1940, Dec 1940; *Aircraft* (Melb), 1 July 1939, 1 June 1940, 2 Sept 1940; *Age, Argus,* and *Geelong Advertiser,* 14 Aug 1940; Geelong Grammar School Archives; family information. MICHAEL D. DE B. COLLINS PERSSE

FAIRBAIRN, STEPHEN (1862-1938), oarsman, rowing coach and pastoralist, was born on 25 August 1862 at Toorak, Melbourne, fifth son of George Fairbairn [q.v.4], and his wife Virginia Charlotte, née Armytage. Like his brothers, who included (Sir) George [q.v.], he was educated at Geelong Church of England Grammar School. In his earlier years, after frequent thrashings by a Calvinistic aunt, he was so wild that several schools found him too hot to hold; but at Geelong the headmaster, J. B. Wilson [q.v.6], won his undying respect, having by trust tamed his unruly spirit. During seven years at Geelong, 1874-80, he excelled at cricket, football, and rowing; was champion athlete, swimmer, and gymnast; helped J. L. Cuthbertson [q.v.3] to edit the school *Quarterly*; and was librarian, dux in mathematics and English, and senior prefect.

In 1881-84 he read law at Jesus College, Cambridge (B.A., 1884; M.A., 1898), being admitted at the Inner Temple in 1882 and called to the Bar in 1886, though he never practised. At Jesus his fame as an oarsman eclipsed even that of his brothers and his Armytage cousins. He rowed in the university crews of 1882, 1883 (both defeated by Oxford), 1886, and 1887 (both victorious), in college crews at the head of the Cam four times, and in crews which won the Grand Challenge Cup (the blue ribbon of amateur rowing in England), the Stewards', and the Wyfold at Henley, all the while – in his own phrase – winning 'hundreds of Regatta races'.

Fairbairn visited Australia in 1884-85, and from 1887 to 1904 was mostly there, pursuing his family's pastoral interests in Victoria and western Queensland, notably at Beaconsfield, near Longreach, whence derived a fund of frequently unprintable stories to be told with characteristic gusto to generations of friends. On 18 November 1891 at St John's Church of England, Toorak, he married 17-year-old Ellen (Eleanor), daughter of Sydney Sharwood, of Aramac, Queensland, by whom he had two sons. Visiting England, he competed at Henley (to the general astonishment) in 1897 and 1898, and was captain of the Thames Rowing Club. In 1899 he rowed for Queensland. While settled at Meltham, near Gheringhap, in Victoria, he coached Geelong Grammar and, while visiting England, Cambridge University crews. In 1904-38, with little interruption, he lived in England, dividing his time between London – where he was a director of Dalgety [q.v.4] & Co. – and Cambridge, in both places pursuing his great love, rowing.

He coached the Jesus boats for part at least of every year except one during that third of a century. More often than not the college went head of the river, and never was it lower than fourth. Steve's genius as a coach and his masterful and overpowering yet sympathetic personality were felt throughout the club, benefiting awkward novices and lower crews as well as first boats. 'Fairbairn of Jesus', the title of his autobiography, published in London in 1931, is no mere vainglorious phrase. A new style – Fairbairnism – was often, but erroneously, attributed to him: his innovation, if innovation it was, was to concentrate the oarsman's mind on the oar and on moving the boat rather than on the supposedly correct motions of the body. He was prepared to experiment, as with long slides and swivel rowlocks. He was full of aphorisms: 'If you can't do it easy, you can't do it at all'; 'It has all got to come from inside you, laddies'; 'Enjoy your rowing, win or lose'; 'Mileage makes champions'. He described the best action for moving a boat as 'an exact imitation of the Heave Ho of eight sailors heaving at a rope, a perfect loose and easy elastic action' – elsewhere described as 'swan-like' and 'dreamy-looking'. There was something of the mystic in his search for perfection in rowing.

In 1926 he founded the annual race for the headship of the Thames Tideway over a course from Mortlake to Putney – the winning crew holds for a year a bronze bust of Steve cast by G. C. Drinkwater. By the proliferation of similar races, by his writings, and above all by his personal influence, he increased the popularity of rowing and has some claim to be called its greatest figure.

Steve Fairbairn died in London on 16 May 1938, survived by his wife and two sons. Appropriately, his ashes rest beneath the shadow of Jesus College chapel. A portrait by James Quinn [q.v.] is held by the college.

F. Brittain and H. B. Playford, *The Jesus College Boat Club, Cambridge* (Cambridge, 1928), and *The Jesus... Boat Club 1827-1962* (Cambridge, 1962); *DNB*, 1931-40; A. Gray and F. Brittain, *A history of Jesus College, Cambridge* (Lond, 1960); *Geelong Grammar School* (1) *Annual*, 1875-76, and (2) *Q*, 1877-80, and (3) *Corian*, May 1921, May 1926, Dec 1932, Aug 1938, Oct 1974, June 1975; Jesus College Cambridge, *Chanticlere*, Easter 1925; *The Times*, 17 May 1938; Geelong Grammar School Archives; family information.

MICHAEL D. DE B. COLLINS PERSSE

FAIRBRIDGE, KINGSLEY OGILVIE (1885-1924), Imperialist and idealist, was born on 2 May 1885 at Grahamstown, South Africa, son of Rhys Seymour Fairbridge, mining engineer and land surveyor, and his wife Rosalie Helen, née Ogilvie. His great-grandfather Dr James William Fairbridge, in 1824 in Capetown, had helped set up a Children's Friend Society. Kingsley briefly attended St Andrew's College before, at 11, he moved with the family to Mashonaland, Rhodesia (Zimbabwe). He suffered severe malaria and at 12 had the vision that he would like to bring farmers to this fertile but empty land — it was reinforced by his exposure to the slums of England in 1902. He educated himself and went as a Rhodes scholar to Oxford in 1908.

He was awarded a diploma in forestry at Exeter College (1911) and a boxing blue as a middleweight. Next year with friends he formed the Child Emigration Society (later Fairbridge Society). He planned to initiate a series of farm schools for orphaned and underprivileged children, which would relieve overcrowded English slums and, within an agricultural setting, provide training in the underpopulated areas of the world. He chose Western Australia for his first experiment and on 14 December 1911 married Ruby Ethel Whitmore, who had some nursing training, at Felbridge, Surrey.

They arrived in Perth next year with idealism but little financial expertise or practical agricultural knowledge. They acquired a small mixed farm near Pinjarra where they built accommodation, initially in tents, for the first thirty-five orphans who arrived in 1913. World War I stopped further migration and dried up most of the society's funds. The State government helped with a subsidy and in 1919 the Fairbridges went to England where he raised the money for a 3000-acre (1200 ha) uncleared property north-east of Pinjarra. Next year this farm was laid out and separate cottages built for the boys and girls, each family-sized group with its own garden, designed to avoid an institutionalized approach. The government belatedly provided a formal school, and by 1924 there were 200 children being educated, gradually raised to 400.

The struggle had been justified and the farm school was a success. But the founder, weakened by malaria, died of lymphatic tumour in Perth on 19 July 1924 and was buried at his school. He was survived by his wife (d. 1966), two daughters and two sons who all returned to England. The farm school continued under a principal. While Fairbridge's orphans were undeniably given a happy, kindly start in life, for various reasons their training was inadequate and led to their being fitted for only a range of semi-skilled occupations. Lack of finance always limited the founder's dream of 'Great Colleges of Agriculture' and the final result hardly reduced either Britain's over-population or increased Australia's sparse inland settlement.

He wrote *Veldt verse* (1909) and an autobiography which was published in 1927. The story of the farm school, *Pinjarra*, was published by his widow in 1937. A painting of Fairbridge hangs in Rhodes House, Oxford, and there is a statue of him as a boy at Christmas Pass, Umtali, Zimbabwe. The society expanded the farm schools, with branches in other Australian States and Canada. But by the 1970s only the original school survived. An important part of the society's activity became the provision of Fairbridge scholarships for British students to Commonwealth universities.

Aust Q, 1929, no 4, p 74; *Aust Rhodes Review*, Mar 1934, p 97; *RWAHSJ*, 1948, p 21; *SMH*, 14 Sept 1921, 24 Mar 1923, 26 Nov 1930, 21 Mar 1936; *Western Mail* (Perth), 9, 16 Mar 1922, 24 July 1924.

FAIRFAX, SIR JAMES READING (1834-1919) and SIR JAMES OSWALD (1863-1928), newspaper proprietors, were father and son. James Reading was born on 17 October 1834 at Leamington Spa, Warwickshire, England, second son of John Fairfax [q.v.4], newspaper proprietor, and his wife Sarah, née Reading. On 26 September 1838 the family reached Sydney in the *Lady Fitzherbert*. Fairfax attended St Phillip's Church infants' school and W. T. Cape's [q.v.1] Sydney College. At 16 he was apprenticed as a printer at the *Sydney Morning Herald*, then owned by his father and Charles Kemp [q.v.2]. He entered the *Herald* office in George Street aged 18 and worked in various departments. In December 1856 he became a partner in John Fairfax & Sons, with his father and elder brother Charles (d. 1863). On 12 March that year at the Pitt Street Congregational Church he married Lucy, daughter of John Armstrong, surveyor, and granddaughter of Francis

Oakes [q.v.2]. They lived at Trahlee, Bellevue Hill, until moving to his father's nearby house, Ginahgulla, in 1877. In the 1880s he built Woodside at Moss Vale.

With important business interests Fairfax was a founder and director of the Perpetual Trustee Co. and a director of the Australian Mutual Provident Society, the Bank of New South Wales, the Commercial Banking Co. of Sydney and Burns [q.v.7], Philp [q.v.] & Co. Ltd. He was active in the Congregational Union of New South Wales and, among many charitable interests, president of the Young Men's Christian Association, a founder and director of the Boys' Brigade, the Sydney Ragged Schools, Royal Prince Alfred Hospital and was first president of the New South Wales Bush Nursing Association. He was also closely connected with the establishment of the Mission to Seamen, Goodenough [q.v.4] Royal Naval House and the Volunteer Rifles; in 1860-64 he was captain of No. 3 Company, Sydney Battalion. He was knighted in 1898.

In 1871 Fairfax helped to set up the short-lived New South Wales Academy of Art and in 1874 was one of five trustees appointed to administer a vote of £500 to establish an art gallery: he was a trustee, vice-president and fourth president of the National Art Gallery of New South Wales — to promote it he offered valuable prizes for pencil drawings. Confident in his staff at the *Herald* he travelled widely with his family, enjoying the art galleries of Europe. At Ginahgulla his furnishings included a fine painted ceiling in the aesthetic style of the 1890s. A music-lover, he helped to found the (Royal) Philharmonic Society of Sydney in 1884 and, later, the Sydney Amateur Orchestral Society; he was a guarantor of Sydney Symphony Orchestra.

His keen perception and extensive reading gave Fairfax a wide grasp of world affairs, which enlarged the *Herald*'s outlook. He retained a firm grip on the paper's policy and supervised the introduction of 'first-rate technical equipment'. Believing in irrigation, he sent A. B. Paterson [q.v.] on tour to report on feasible schemes; their enthusiasm contributed to the construction of Burrinjuck Dam. In 1918 he wrote 'Recollections of old Sydney' for the journal of the Royal Australian Historical Society. He was a member of the Royal Society of New South Wales in 1868-1919. A keen yachtsman, he was commodore of the Royal Sydney Yacht Squadron in 1884-89, 1893-95 and 1904-13; in 1912 he presented the squadron with the Fairfax Cup, engraved with his famous yacht *Magic*, in which he won many races. He was also a member of the Union Club and president of Royal Sydney Golf Club.

Sir James died at Ginahgulla on 28 March

1919 and was buried in South Head cemetery after a service at Woollahra Congregational Church, where a memorial window was installed in 1924. He was survived by his wife, daughter and by five of his six sons, of whom the three eldest joined John Fairfax & Sons Ltd.

His third son James Oswald was born on 26 April 1863 at 189 Macquarie Street. Educated at Sydney Grammar School and Balliol College, Oxford (B.A., 1885), he was called to the Bar of the Inner Temple on 26 January 1886 and admitted to the colonial Bar on his return to Sydney on 14 February 1887. In 1889 he entered John Fairfax & Sons. On 22 November 1892 at St Andrew's Anglican Cathedral he married Mabel Alice Emmeline (1871-1965), second daughter of Francis Hixson [q.v.4].

In June 1909 Fairfax represented the *Herald* at the first Imperial Press Conference held in London, which led to the formation of the Empire Press Union; he was chairman of its Australian section until 1920 and in 1925-28. He led the Australian delegation at the third Imperial Press Conference in Melbourne in 1925. He was a director of John Fairfax & Sons Ltd from 1916, when it was registered as a public company, and of the Perpetual Trustee Co., the United Insurance Co. and the A.M.P. Society. In 1927 he participated in the first Empire wireless and telegraph and telephone concert from Sydney to London, organized by Amalgamated Wireless (Australasia) Ltd, radio station 2FC and the *Herald*.

From 1914 Fairfax was foundation chairman of the New South Wales division of the Australian branch of the British Red Cross Society, and during World War I devoted himself to its affairs and fund-raising activities. In May 1918 he and T. W. Heney [q.v.] represented the *Herald* on a delegation of Australian journalists invited to visit the Western Front by the British government. C. E. W. Bean [q.v.7] found him 'one of the most human of the party' and 'a bit of a sport'. He described with feeling his experiences in the *Herald* from December. That year he was appointed C.B.E. and in 1926 was knighted.

An ardent motorist from about 1903, Fairfax acquired a 6 h.p. Dion; he competed in several reliability trials organized by the (Royal) Automobile Club of Australia. He also enjoyed sailing and golf. Interested in education, he was chairman of the Boys' Brigade and president of the Sydney Grammar School Old Boys' Union. His wife was well known in Sydney as 'Lady Jim'; she was a person of forthright character and wit. An excellent golfer, she won the Royal Sydney Golf Club's associates championship in 1899, 1903, 1906 and 1916. She created lovely gardens at her homes, Fairwater on Seven Shillings Beach, Double Bay, and Sospel at Leura in the Blue Mountains.

Sir James died suddenly from heart disease on the links at Royal Sydney on 18 July 1928 and was buried with Anglican rites in South Head cemetery. He was survived by his wife and son, Warwick Oswald Fairfax. Remembered for many useful and kindly acts associated with charitable and philanthropic organizations, carried out in his quiet but authoritative way, he bequeathed £10 000 each to Sydney Grammar School and to the University of Sydney and presented to the university the Red Cross bell for its carillon.

A portrait of J. R. Fairfax by Tom Roberts [q.v.] and one of J. O. Fairfax by W. A. Bowring are held by John Fairfax & Sons; one of J. O. Fairfax by John Longstaff [q.v.] is held by the family.

C. B. Fletcher (ed), *Sir James Reading Fairfax* (Syd, 1920?); J. Fairfax & Sons Ltd, *Century of journalism* (Syd, 1931); J. F. Fairfax, *The story of John Fairfax* (Syd. 1941); G. N. Griffiths, *Point Piper, past and present* (Syd, 1947), and *Some houses and people of New South Wales* (Syd, 1949); P. R. Stephensen (ed), *Sydney sails* (Syd, 1962); C. W. Semmler, *The Banjo of the bush* (Melb, 1975); C. Simpson, *John Fairfax, 1804-1877* (Syd, 1977); G. Souter, *Company of heralds* (Melb, 1981); *Art and Aust*, 10 (1972), no 1; C. E. W. Bean, Diaries (AWM); Fairfax family papers, 1846-47, 1873-1945 (ML); Parkes correspondence (ML).

CAROLINE SIMPSON

FAIRFAX, RUTH BEATRICE (1878-1948), a founder of the Country Women's Association, was born on 8 October 1878, at Lue, near Rylstone, New South Wales, second surviving daughter of native-born parents Vincent James Dowling [q.v.4], and his wife Frances Emily, daughter of T. C. Breillat [q.v.3]. She was mainly educated by governesses at Lue and briefly attended the Sydney Church of England Grammar School for Girls under Miss Badham [q.v.7]. On 2 February 1899 at the Anglican Church, Dungarey, near Rylstone, she married JOHN HUBERT FRASER FAIRFAX (1872-1950).

The Fairfaxes went to live at Dalmore station near Longreach, Queensland, where she loved the outdoor life. In 1908 they moved to Marinya, near Cambooya on the Darling Downs, where their only child was born in 1909. While at Marinya, Ruth Fairfax regularly taught in the Sunday School and supported the Bush Brotherhood and other Anglican organizations. For her local war work she was awarded the Belgian Medal 'de la Reine Elizabeth'.

At a meeting at the Albert Hall, Brisbane, in August 1922, Mrs Fairfax was appointed first State president of the Queensland Country Women's Association, which was to prove 'her heart's great love'. She embarked on a strenuous six months tour in an open car of outback Queensland, organizing branches and holding some meetings on the banks of creeks. In 1926 she resigned as president of the southern division but remained as State president until 1931; she was appointed a justice of the peace in 1927.

The Fairfaxes visited England from March 1929 to December 1930. Ruth attended many gatherings of the similar Women's Institutes and represented Australia at the International Conference of Rural Women's Organizations in London in 1929, and on the Liaison Committee of Rural Women's and Homemakers' Organisations.

On their return to Australia the Fairfaxes lived in Sydney, at Elaine, on Seven Shillings Beach, Double Bay, that Hubert had bought from the estate of his uncle Geoffrey Fairfax. Ruth continued to work for the C.W.A. as New South Wales State secretary until 1946, a vice-president from 1934 of Associated Country Women of the World and as co-editor with Dorothy Catts [q.v.7 J. H. Catts] of the *Countrywoman in New South Wales*. As well she served on the boards of the Adult Deaf and Dumb Society of New South Wales and St Luke's Hospital, Darlinghurst, and on the State executive and general council of the Girl Guides' Association; she was a life governor of the Benevolent Society of New South Wales, a trustee of the Public Library of New South Wales from 1937 and chairman of the council of the Australian Board of Missions. In June 1935 she was appointed O.B.E.

Ruth Fairfax loved music and her gardens at Marinya, Elaine and Wanawong. She enjoyed entertaining and often lent Elaine for fêtes, pageants, meetings and entertainments for patriotic and charitable causes. Among her many activities during World War II, she helped to provide sheepskin vests and other comforts for the Australian Comforts Fund. Her friends remarked on 'her deft, capable hands'. Her 'dark brown eyes were strong and friendly, her gait was busy and purposeful; her voice and ready laughter made her presence cheerful and dynamic'. A diabetic for many years, Ruth Fairfax died from chronic nephritis in St Luke's Hospital on 1 February 1948 and was cremated with Anglican rites.

Her husband, always known as Hubert, was born on 11 May 1872 at Trahlee, Bellevue Hill, Sydney, fifth son of (Sir) James Reading Fairfax [q.v.] and his wife Lucy, née Armstrong. He was educated at Sydney Grammar School and Bath College, England, then returned to Australia and joined Dalgety & Co. Ltd. After practical experience under his future father-in-law at Lue, he bought Dalmore station in Queensland in 1897 and Marinya in 1908. He bred Ayrshire cattle and Corriedale sheep, which he successfully exhibited, and later often acted as judge at Australian shows. He was sometime president of the Ayrshire Association of Queensland, the Australian Corriedale Sheepbreeders' Association, the New South Wales Sheepbreeders' Association and a vice-president of the Royal Agricultural Society of New South Wales.

After he returned to Sydney in 1931 he bought Wanawong, 70 acres (28 ha) at Castle Hill. He was a director of John Fairfax & Sons Ltd in 1931-45, the Bank of New South Wales in 1932-50, the Australian Mutual Provident Society (1932-48), the Royal Insurance Co. and the Walter and Eliza Hall [qq.v.] Trust. He was also president of the Young Men's Christian Association from 1935, of the Boys' Brigade from 1945, and of the Australian Air League and a council-member of the British Empire Society and was involved with the Legacy Club of Sydney.

Fairfax was a keen golfer and a member of the Oriental Club, London, and of the Union and Australasian Pioneers' clubs, Sydney. He died in St Luke's Hospital on 10 June 1950 and was cremated with Anglican rites. He was survived by their son (Sir) Vincent.

Qld Country Women's Assn, *Fifty years 1922-72* (Brisb, 1972?); *Pastoral Review*, 16 Mar 1948, 15 July 1950; *SMH*, 28 June 1920, 29 Aug 1929, 3 June 1935, 7 Apr 1936, 17 June 1937, 15 Nov 1938, 2 Feb 1948, 11 June 1950; E. A. V. Sterne, Ruth Beatrice Fairfax, O.B.E., J. P. (MS, Oxley Lib, Brisb); information from Sir Vincent Fairfax, Syd.

MARTHA RUTLEDGE

FAIRLEY, SIR ANDREW WALKER (1884-1965), businessman, was born on 28 January 1884 at Grangemouth, Scotland, fifth son of James Fairley, draper, and his wife Mary Agnes, née Walker. The family arrived in Melbourne in 1886 and settled at Shepparton in 1887. Andrew was educated at Shepparton and later at Devon College, Launceston, Tasmania, where the principal was a family friend.

On arrival at Shepparton, James Fairley worked in a grocery store, which he later purchased and expanded. When he died in 1907 the business, a prosperous department store, continued under the control of his sons John Frederick, William and Andrew. Fred and Andrew also formed a separate business partnership which dealt in land subdivision, operated a large orchard and a grazing property, and built retail premises for leasing. Andrew became well known in Shepparton for his drive and business ability.

In 1921 he was asked to act as financial adviser to the Shepparton Fruit Preserving Co. Ltd (later the Shepparton Preserving Co. Ltd or S.P.C. Ltd) and was made a director. The co-operative canning company had been established with government assistance in 1917 but after some successful years was facing financial difficulties. Until it again became profitable, Fairley refused to accept salary or expenses. In 1924 he became chairman, and in 1926 managing director; under his guidance, S.P.C. became one of the largest co-operative fruit-canning plants in Australia. By 1929 all government loans and interest had been repaid. The company began to pay substantial annual bonuses to grower-shareholders, and plant and buildings were fully modernized and expanded. Fairley took a keen interest in operations on the factory floor, as well as in financial and managerial problems; he walked through the plant morning and afternoon. His fairness, as well as his firmness, was recognized by employees, and he established good relations with the trade-union movement. In his will, Fairley left a legacy for each S.P.C. staff-member of five years standing.

In December 1926 the Commonwealth government set up the Canned Fruits Export Control Board to implement quality control and the orderly marketing of exports, and Fairley was appointed as representative of co-operative and state-owned canneries. In 1931 he was appointed to the Fruit Industry Sugar Concession Committee. During World War II he was made a member of the Commonwealth Tinplate Control Board, and was commissioned to organize a scheme of vegetable production and canning in the Shepparton district. He was a member of the State Electricity Commission of Victoria for over twenty years. In 1947 he was appointed C.M.G. for his services to the fruit industry and the State of Victoria, and K.B.E. in 1951.

In 1927 Fairley became first mayor of the Borough of Shepparton, and in 1948-49 the first mayor of the city. He was also mayor in 1931, and for many years was chairman of the council's public works committee. He made donations to the municipal art gallery, and in his will bequeathed for investment £10000, the income to be used for the acquisition of works of art. The permanent collection gallery in the Shepparton Arts Centre has been named after him, and his portrait in oils by William Dargie hangs at the entrance.

On 18 April 1934 at Canterbury, Melbourne, Fairley married Mineta (Minnie) Lenore Stewart; there were no children. One of the many local organizations to benefit from his philanthropy was the Baptist Church; he worshipped regularly, and his fellow directors became accustomed to his biblical quotations. 'Ab' Fairley's favourite recreation was field shooting, and he was a keen fisherman. He played golf and bowls, and in 1927 won the Victorian Country Singles Bowls Championship. He was a member of the Melbourne Cricket and Victoria Racing clubs.

Survived by his wife, Sir Andrew died in Melbourne on 15 April 1965 and was cremated. He left an estate valued for probate at £421 462, the bulk of which was used to establish the Sir Andrew and Lady Fairley Foundation for the benefit of registered charities in Victoria.

Age, and *Herald* (Melb), 17 Apr 1965; *Shepparton News*, 21 Apr 1965; SPC, *Annual Report*, 1964-65, *and* F. J. Pick, Our golden valley (held by SPC, Shepparton, Vic); information from Mr N. Dennis, Shepparton, Vic.   A. McLEARY

FALK, LEIB AISACK (1889-1957), rabbi, was born on 31 January 1889 at Bauska, Russia (Latvia), son of Abraham Falk, commercial traveller, and his wife Hannah, née Hillkowitz. Leib studied at various *yeshivot* including those in Lithuania at Kovno (Kaunas) and Telsch (Telshyay); one of his early teachers was Rabbi Kook, later chief rabbi of Jerusalem. In 1911 Falk moved to Scotland and in 1912-15 was minister at Dundee, Forfarshire (Angus-shire) where he married Fanny Rosen, daughter of a local pawnbroker, on 2 May 1915. After serving from 1915 at Plymouth, England, he was chaplain in 1918-21 to the 38th-40th Royal Fusiliers (First Judeans) in Egypt and Palestine. In September 1922 he was inducted as second reader at the Great Synagogue, Sydney.

Inspired by his experiences in Palestine Falk was an 'ardent, militant' Zionist. He enjoyed a close friendship with V. E. Jabotinsky and became honorary president of the Sydney Revisionist movement. In the 1920s he was co-editor of the *Australian Jewish Chronicle*. At the same time he was an admirer of Britain and, until 1948, hoped that Palestine would become a dominion.

Falk's relations with his chief ministers were chequered. He clashed with Rabbi F. L. Cohen [q.v.] over Zionism but respected him for his learning. In 1936 he visited Palestine and received his rabbinical diploma. He failed to establish a working relationship with Rabbi E. M. Levy in 1935-38 and in February 1938 asked to be relieved from the Sydney Beth Din. During the controversy over Levy's forced resignation an untenable situation developed when both Falk and Levy tried to act as chief minister. Falk acted as chief minister until the arrival of Rabbi Dr I. Porush in 1940; again relations were

strained and he was eased out of the Beth Din. Falk also encountered difficulties with the synagogue board of management, which felt that he lacked respect for its authority and interfered with administrative policies. In the 1930s he had been forbidden to speak from the pulpit on political matters such as Zionism and was asked not to make public statements without the board's permission; nevertheless he continued to act and speak according to his principles.

In 1935 Falk was commissioned as chaplain to the Australian Military Forces and in 1942 to Eastern Command; he became well known for his Anzac Day addresses. He was also chaplain to the State prisons and to Jewish internees in World War II; although he worked hard to secure their release, he was criticized for lack of sympathy. He believed that refugees should integrate quickly and opposed setting up institutions that maintained their culture. However he became renowned for his sympathetic visits to the sick and for his love of children and animals. He was a devoted family man.

Despite limited financial resources, Falk built up a fine library of Anglo-Judaica, Australiana Judaica and Jewish folklore. It was bought by the Great Synagogue in 1959 and named the Rabbi L. A. Falk Memorial Library. He was also an excellent bookbinder, cabinetmaker and Hebrew calligrapher and, later in life, a talented silversmith. He contributed to various periodicals and was foundation vice-president of the Australian Jewish Historical Society and a vice-president of the New South Wales branch of the League of Nations Union.

Falk died of hypertensive cardio-vascular disease in St Vincent's Hospital, Sydney, on 6 May 1957 and was buried in Rookwood cemetery. He was survived by his wife, daughter and three sons. A portrait by M. Nathan is owned by his daughter, and one by Valerie Lazarus is in the Rabbi L. A. Falk Memorial Library.

M. Freilich, *Zion in our time* (Syd, 1967); I. Porush, *The house of Israel* (Melb, 1977); Aust Jewish Hist Soc, *J*, 5 (1962), pt 6, p 281; *Hebrew Standard of A'sia*, June, Sept 1922, Dec 1935, Jan 1936; *SMH*, 7 May 1957; *Aust Jewish Times*, 10 May 1957; S. D. Rutland, The Jewish community in New South Wales, 1914-1939 (M. A. thesis, Univ Syd, 1978); minute-books 1922-39 (Great Synagogue office, Syd).   SUZANNE D. RUTLAND

FALKINER, FRANC BRERETON SADLEIR (1867-1929) and OTWAY ROTHWELL (1874-1961), sheep-breeders, were born on 17 June 1867 and on 16 December 1874 at Ararat, Victoria, eldest (after four girls) and third sons of Franc Sadleir Falkiner [q.v.4], a sheep-farmer from Tipperary, Ireland, and his wife Emily Elizabeth, née Bazley, who had been born at sea. In 1878 Otway's asthma prompted the family to move to the Riverina, where their father bought Boonoke North and its merino stud from the Peppins [q.v.5]. Franc was educated at Geelong Church of England Grammar School and Otway at St Kilda Grammar School and privately. Franc managed Moonbria from January 1885, then Tuppal from 1891 for his father, gaining much practical experience; from 1890 Otway became studmaster. On their father's death in 1909 Franc became managing director of F. S. Falkiner & Sons Ltd, formed in 1899, while Otway continued as stud-master until 1953.

Known as 'Bert', Franc was a foundation member of Conargo Shire Council in 1906. His interest in politics was aroused by the 1910 Federal land tax; in 1913 he entered the House of Representatives for Riverina, defeating J. M. Chanter [q.v.7], who turned the tables next year. In 1917-19 Falkiner held Hume for the Nationalists, but was defeated for the Senate in the 1919 elections. A large man, balding, with a bristling moustache, he was an impatient parliamentarian, brusque and humorous; he coined the phrase 'bangle bonus' for Andrew Fisher's [q.v.] 1912 maternity allowance.

After losing Riverina, Franc had sold his shares in F. S. Falkiner & Sons to his brothers in 1914 and in 1916 bought Haddon Rig near Warren and its Wanganella-based stud flock from James Richmond [q.v.6]. Falkiner sold the outside block, improved the homestead's water-supply and consolidated an 80 000-acre (32 000 ha) property. His concentration on burly, robust, plain-bodied merinos was rewarded with successes at the Sydney Sheep Show (1922, 1923) and the Sydney ram sales in 1924. At Foxlow, Bungendore, bought as drought relief pasture in 1920, and at Haddon Rig, he also bred Red Poll Hereford cattle and Percheron horses.

A growers' representative on the Central Wool Committee from 1917, Falkiner was a member of the British Australian Wool Realisation Association Ltd in 1920-26. He was also president of the Southern Riverina Pastoralists' Union (representing it on the Pastoralists' Federal Council of Australia in 1915) and the New South Wales Sheep-breeders' Association (1919-1926), a founder of the *Australian Stud Merino Flock Register* and a director of the Bank of New South Wales 1919-29, Pitt, Son & Badgery [qq.v.5,3] Ltd, and the Commercial Union Assurance Co. Ltd.

Falkiner died of intracranial haemorrhage at Foxlow on 30 October 1929 and was buried with Anglican rites in the churchyard of St Thomas, Carwoola, on the eve of the dedication of the Falkiner Memorial Chapel at Geelong Grammar School. Survived by his wife, Edith Elizabeth, née Howat, whom he had married at Scots Church, Melbourne, on 5 May 1902, two sons and two daughters, he left an estate valued for probate at £434 438. In 1954 his son George gave £50 000 to the University of Sydney to establish the F. B. S. Falkiner laboratory in the Physics-Nuclear Research Foundation.

At Deniliquin on 14 June 1899 Otway married Elizabeth McLaurin, daughter of a grazier; she died after the birth of their third child in 1909. On 15 November 1910 at St John's Church, Toorak, Melbourne, he married Una Caroline, daughter of A. A. C. Le Souef [q.v.5]. In 1914 he succeeded Franc as managing director of F. S. Falkiner & Sons. He and his brother Leigh formed a close, harmonious partnership operating from Boonoke North and Wanganella Estate (bought in 1910 from the executors of Thomas Millear). The firm continued to buy properties, selling off the wheat lands; it was reputed to be the world's largest merino stud, selling rams all over Australia and to South Africa and New Zealand from the early 1900s. The 1920 ram sales inaugurated its golden decade: Otway's stiffest competitors were Haddon Rig and Charles Mills [q.v.5] (Uardry) Ltd. In 1927 he bought Zara and next year sold its stud, a large number of sheep going to Fritz Hirschhorn's Smart Syndicate in South Africa. Falkiner severely criticized the 1929 embargo on stud merino exports.

Boonoke ram sales were severely hit by the Depression. In 1934 Falkiner made his greatest contribution to stud merino breeding: the Poll Boonoke. To offset wartime transport disruption he established a ram depot at Cleeve, near Longreach, Queensland. A formidable octogenerian, he surrendered the stud to Basil Clapham in 1953 (but remained chairman of directors); presided over the record ewe sale in 1957; and, next year, achieved his lifelong ambition by reuniting all Peppins' original studs with the purchase of Wanganella from the descendants of Albert Austin [q.v.3]. By 1957, 70 million of Australia's 150 million sheep were descended from his rams.

A playboy and a strange mixture of authoritarianism, gruffness, crudity and kindness, Ottie was keen on breeding Clydesdale horses and racehorses. His greatest success, David, won the Sydney Cup in 1923. In 1944 he donated 1500 acres at Deniliquin to the Commonwealth Council for Scientific and Industrial Research, to establish the Falkiner Memorial Field Centre.

Falkiner died in his sleep at Boonoke on 23

October 1961, and, after a service at St Paul's Church of England, Deniliquin, was cremated in Melbourne. He was survived by a son and daughter by his first wife and by a daughter of his second wife; their son John was killed in World War II flying for the Royal Australian Air Force. Falkiner's estate was valued for probate at £357 659 in New South Wales and £192 788 in Victoria.

NSW Sheepbreeders Assn, *The Australian merino* (Syd, 1955); B. F. Short and H. B. Carter, *Statistical abstract of the records of the registered Australian merino stud flocks* (Melb, 1956, copy Univ NSW Lib); T. E. P. Hewat, *Golden fleeces* (Syd, 1980); *Pastoral Review*, 15 Nov 1910, 16 June 1913, 16 Mar, 16 June 1922, 16 Nov 1948, 16 May 1952, 18 Nov 1961; *New Nation Mag*, Apr 1935; *Punch* (Melb), 15 Jan 1914; *Australasian*, 24 June 1922; *SMH*, 31 Oct, 1 Nov 1929, 16 Dec 1954, 24 Oct 1961; *Queenslander*, 7 Nov 1929; *Farmer and Settler*, 26 Aug 1955; *Bulletin*, 12 Aug 1980; information from Mrs J. Oppenheimer, Walcha, NSW.

JOHN ATCHISON

FALLON, CYRIL JOSEPH (1887-1948), physician and politician, was born on 18 April 1887 at Surry Hills, Sydney, second son of native-born parents John Fallon, tailor, and his wife Katherine, née Macken. His father died when Fallon was still a boy. Educated at St Mary's Cathedral High School, he won a Cardinal's scholarship to St Joseph's College, where he played in the first cricket and Rugby teams and was dux in 1904. He won an exhibition to the University of Sydney where he studied French, Latin, and English, graduating B.A. in 1908. He then enrolled in medicine, supporting himself by tutoring in classics at St John's College. Graduating M.B. in 1913, he was resident medical officer at Sydney Hospital before becoming a medical officer with the Department of Public Instruction, a position which required considerable travel throughout the State. After a year at Prince Henry Hospital studying infectious diseases, and a time as locum in Surry Hills, he commenced his own practice in Avoca Street, Randwick. On 28 September 1915 he had married Mildred Mary Hunt of Randwick; two years later the first of five children was born.

From a poor background, with parents of Irish stock, educated in the classics as well as a profession, handsome and with an eloquence practised in debating at school, university and the Waverley Catholic Debating Society, Fallon was well placed to become favoured son of Sydney's embattled Catholic society. A delegate to the 1919 Irish Race Convention in Melbourne, he was an active committee-member of the Self-Determination for Ireland League of Australia, formed in 1920. That year he defended Fr

Jerger [q.v.] against deportation.

A member of the New South Wales branch of the Catholic Federation, Fallon helped its leader, P. S. Cleary [q.v.] form the Democratic Party in 1919 and was its vice-president during its unsuccessful election campaign in 1920. In the 1922 elections he led the party and was elected to the Legislative Assembly as fifth member for Eastern Suburbs. He embraced a wide range of social policies close to Labor's (in 1923 he joined the council of A. C. Willis's [q.v.] Industrial Christian Fellowship), but his main concern was to obtain government assistance for Catholic schools and charities. He attended parliament infrequently, but when he did, spoke with cool aplomb, attacking the Fuller [q.v.] ministry for its refusal to countenance child endowment almost as often as for its refusal to aid Catholic schools. It was a government in which Orangemen were prominent and Fallon's last speech was an attack on the marriage amendment (ne temere) bill, designed to prevent Catholic clergy from saying that Catholics who had contracted only a civil marriage were not properly married. The Democratic Party did not survive long and, after some indecision, Fallon stood unsuccessfully in 1925 as an Independent Catholic candidate.

Henceforth Fallon devoted his attention to his practice and to being a model Catholic layman; he became immensely popular. For a time in the 1920s he was an assistant physician at St Vincent's Hospital, but found teaching had little appeal. He helped persuade the archdiocese and Sisters of St Joseph take over from Gertrude Abbott [q.v.7] St Margaret's Hospital, Darlinghurst. In 1933 he helped found the Catholic Medical Guild of St Luke; its master until 1936, he remained a council-member until 1948. Long active in the St Joseph's College Old Boys' Union, he assisted the Marist Brothers at every opportunity. He was president of the Marist Medical Mission Society and honorary physician to Marcellin College, Randwick. Active on many Catholic committees and societies, he was constantly in demand as a public speaker and in that role frequently extolled the life and works of his cynosure G. K. Chesterton.

In 1940 Fallon was appointed knight commander of the Order of St Sylvester by Pope Pius XII. On 20 April 1948 he died of lung cancer in St Vincent's Hospital and was buried in Waverley cemetery. His wife, three sons and two daughters survived him. He left an estate valued for probate at £7 302.

Catholic Medical Guild of St Luke, *Transactions*, Dec 1947; *Catholic Press*, 23 Feb 1922, 21 May 1925; *Catholic Weekly* (Syd), 6 May 1948.

MARK LYONS

FARBER, HENRY CHRISTIAN (1880-1965), equestrian showman, was born on 2 September 1880 at Waverley station, Broadsound, Queensland, son of Frederick William Farber, station-hand, and his wife Elizabeth, née Schneider. On cattle-stations Harry helped break horses for Cobb [q.v.3] & Co. and developed into an outstanding bareback rider; when thrown, he would land on his feet and vault back on to the horse. He became known through Queensland as an equestrian and showman.

Farber trained horses for the South African War, then for about ten years specialized in breaking in horses near Rockhampton. In 1912 he took 200 horses from Charters Towers to Halls Creek, Western Australia. After a nine-month journey he sold the horses and drove a mob of cattle from the Kimberleys to Meekatharra, more than a thousand miles (1700 km) to the south. Here he joined the Ireland family in organizing a travelling buckjump show. With Harry as bareback rider, they drew big crowds at Broome, Kalgoorlie, Boulder, Southern Cross, Meekatharra and Perth. He was tall, sun tanned, wiry and handsome and wore tough trousers under leather pants strapped on around the waist, a long scarf knotted at the neck, high-heeled boots, gun-belt and slouch hat.

Because of bunions, Farber spent World War I breaking in remounts for the Australian Light Horse regiments. Afterwards he resumed droving. He always put his stock's protection before his own or his men's comfort and would sing to the cattle at night to soothe them; a tough boss, he was nicknamed 'The Murderer of Men and Mules' and 'Farber the Bastard from the back of B[o]urke'.

In Perth on 24 March 1921, with Anglican rites, he married Rita Arnold. He then managed Mount Fraser station; after a year his wife persuaded Farber to return to Meekatharra for the birth of their first child. But Harry preferred the free outback life. He kept horses at Mount Padbury until 1927: for six months of the year he would leave them and go droving. Towards Christmas he would rejoin his family in Meekatharra and stage a rodeo in the open-air picture-theatre: he was described by an onlooker 'as lithe, nimble and tigerish in his agility.

In 1928 Harry retired from the show-ring, his body kicked and bitten and with broken ribs and a crooked arm. His last drive was in 1936. During this, two-thirds of the sheep broke free and were lost. It left him in debt which, coupled with the scarcity of droving work, led him to take a job carting water for the Comet mine; he and his family settled nearby. Farber's last official horse-race was at 68 when he won an event on Pebremas at Marble Bar. From 1959 he worked there as a licensed scrap-dealer. He applied for a pension at 79; but even when old, he regularly enjoyed Saturday race meetings and dancing at the balls which followed them.

In 1960 Farber became ill with asthma and went to Port Hedland hospital. Next year he was transferred to Nazareth House, Bluff Point, where he remained until his death on 27 June 1965. Farber was survived by two daughters and two sons; he was buried in Utakarra cemetery.

L. Hunt (ed), *Westralian portraits* (Perth, 1979); *RWAHSJ (Early Days)*, 6 (1969), pt 8; Harry Farber scrap-book, held by Mrs C. McGregor, Port Hedland, WA.
                                                        EDNA WARD

FARLEIGH, JOHN GIBSON (1861?-1949), manufacturer and politician, was born in County Sligo, Ireland, son of Edward Manicom Farleigh (d. 1909), and his wife Elizabeth, née Gibson. He arrived in Victoria in 1865 with his father and uncle John Farleigh (d. 1885); in 1874 all moved to Sydney where his father set up a tannery at Canterbury. In 1876 John senior, with W. C. Nettheim and the Melbourne firm Michaelis [q.v.5], Hallenstein & Co., set up a tannery at Concord and later a boot upper factory in Kent Street, Sydney. 'King of Mimosa' leather soon became well-known and in 1901, when the tannery was treating 500 hides a week, a new trade mark 'Australian Leather' was widely promoted.

In 1875, after attending Cleveland Street Public School, John junior worked as office boy, clerk and salesman and in 1877 began as a junior clerk in Farleigh, Nettheim & Co. Always well prepared for the next promotion, Farleigh rose through bookkeeper, accountant and manager to partner and senior partner, attributing his success to 'hard work with a steady attention to duty'. He qualified as a fellow of the Institute of Incorporated Accountants of New South Wales; in 1906 he became a justice of the peace and in 1903-08 was an alderman on Rockdale Municipal Council.

A free trader, Farleigh was founding president of the Liberal and Progressive League in 1909. A council-member of the Liberal, National and United Australia parties, he was a member of the New South Wales Legislative Council from July 1908 until its reconstruction in April 1934. His speeches, usually on industrial and social questions, were short, direct and fair minded, although as a councillor of the Employers' Federation of New South Wales he was always careful to protect that particular interest. From September 1920 to June 1923 he served on the Commonwealth royal commission on taxation chaired by W. W. Kerr [q.v.].

Prominent in manufacturing organizations, Farleigh was a councillor of the New South Wales Chamber of Manufactures (president 1907-10) and the Associated Chambers of Manufactures of Australia and president of the Master Tanners' and Leather Manufacturers' Association; he was also a member of the Pure Food Act (1908) advisory committee. A great believer in the application of scientific research to industry and technical education, he established a tannery school and night classes so that his workers could better understand 'the routine of their daily duties'. A Freemason, he was a member of the Loyal Orange Institution of New South Wales, the Millions and National clubs, Sydney, and the Prisoners' Aid Association of New South Wales of which he was president in 1928-34. In 1926 he became a director of Rubber Moulders Ltd.

Farleigh died on 5 May 1949 in Royal Prince Alfred Hospital and was cremated after a service at Arncliffe Methodist Church. At St Peters, Sydney, he had married Alice Elizabeth Howard on 13 November 1883; they had three sons and two daughters. His estate was sworn for probate at £54 612.

E. Digby (ed), *Australian men of mark*, 2 (Syd, 1889); *T&CJ*, 6 Apr 1878, 6 Oct 1909; *Clarion* (NSW), 25 May 1901; *Newcastle Morning Herald*, 9 July 1908; *Daily Telegraph* (Syd), 17 Apr 1922; *SMH*, 4 Sept 1920, 6 May 1949; *Labour Daily*, 17 Jan 1934.   G. P. WALSH

FARNELL, FRANK (1861-1928), politician and public administrator, was born on 10 September 1861 at Ryde, New South Wales, second son of James Squire Farnell [q.v.4] and his wife Margaret, née O'Donnell, both native-born. Educated at Newington College, Farnell worked as clerk for William Wolfen & Co., commission merchants, and in 1880 with the Railway Department where he advanced to pay clerk in 1883-85. Business ventures with the tea, wine and spirits firm, Allen, Bowden & Farnell, resulted in bankruptcy, first in 1889 (discharged 1891) and again in 1899 (discharged 1899).

Unsuccessful in the election of 1885, Farnell was returned to the Legislative Assembly for Central Cumberland in 1887 as a supporter of (Sir) Henry Parkes [q.v.5]. He represented this electorate until 1891 and Ryde in 1894-98 and 1901-03. Party whip in the ministries of Parkes (1890) and (Sir) George Reid [q.v.] (1894), he was deputy chairman of committees in 1894-96, and a member of the Public Works Committee in

1896-98. He was on thirty-two committees of inquiry in 1887-97, and his public appointments included those of justice of the peace, commissioner to the International exhibitions at Melbourne (1888) and Chicago (1891), and honorary visiting magistrate to Lord Howe Island (1900-13).

As a political figure he was a solid, pragmatic local man, successfully avoiding the clashing loyalties of rival faction politics. One could view him as an archetypal fence-sitter, as when he kept silent during the divisive censure motion in 1894 by Parkes on his party leader Reid; whilst supporting Reid he privately assured Parkes of his wish for him 'to continue nobly to discharge those duties which have made you prominent ... throughout Australia'. Though he professed a liberal disposition, his conservative instincts appeared on issues involving social change; he counselled caution in the women's suffrage debate of 1894 and warned of women 'losing the arts of washing and dressing a baby'. However, as a practical-minded man preferring to avoid party conflict in favour of compromise, he may well have represented the solidifying component in colonial politics during a period of impermanent and futile fiscal alignments.

From this perspective Farnell had a special commitment to two practical areas of politics — the reform and administration of the Fisheries Act (1881) and the development of the (Royal) National Park. Chairman of a select committee (1889) and a royal commission on fisheries (1894-95), he was also chairman of the Fisheries Board (1903-10), resigning from parliament in December 1903 in order to carry out his duties. His support of fishermen in netting, trawling and oyster farming in coastal estuary and river catchment areas would now be unpopular with conservationists, but at the time did advance the interests of coastal fisheries.

A member of the Intelligence and Tourist Bureau in 1904-10 he was a trustee of the National Park from 1888 and chairman in 1907-29. To Farnell the park was a reserve for the recreation and enjoyment of a growing city population, a policy promoted by the State's tourist publicity in agreements with private interests, and helped by the extension of the railway to the park. Though Farnell's dedication to the park and its welfare is undoubted, recent evaluation by historians presents him as 'a man with few ideas and an easy mark for those who wished to put sections of the park to their own personal or financial use'.

Captain of St George's Rifles in 1896, Farnell was president of the Sailors and Soldiers' Fathers' Association, a member of the Proportional Representation Society and of the United Grand Lodge of New South Wales. He unsuccessfully contested the elections of 1913 (Bondi) and 1916 (Drummoyne) as an Independent Liberal, and 1920 (North Shore) as a Progressive. He died of cerebro-vascular disease on 16 July 1928 at North Sydney, survived by his wife Amy Briscoe, née Cox, whom he had married on 12 August 1889 at St Andrew's Cathedral, and by two sons. He was cremated.

W. Goldstein (ed), *100 years of national parks* (Syd, 1979); Roy Com ... Lord Howe Island, Report, *PP* (NSW), 1911, 2, p 945; *Annual Report*, 1903-10, Board of Fisheries (NSW), *and* 1903-25, National Park Trust (NSW); *Daily Telegraph* (Syd), 5 July 1894, 6 July 1901, 16 May 1917, 3 Mar 1920; *SMH*, 17 July 1929; *Worker* (Syd), 24 July 1929; bankruptcy file 1598/1, 1636/1, 13 397/8 (NSWA).   J. A. RYAN

FARRAR, ERNEST HENRY (1879-1952), trade unionist and politician, was born on 3 February 1879 at Barnsley, Yorkshire, England, son of Henry Farrar, ironmoulder, and his wife Mary Elizabeth, née Buckley. Brought to Australia as an infant, he was educated at Granville and Petersham Superior Public schools, Sydney, and attended Methodist Sunday schools. He became a shearer and later a saddler and wool-presser, working in New Zealand and Tasmania for a time and on H. E. Kater's [q.v.5] Mumblebone station, New South Wales, about 1904; at 17 he joined the Australian Workers' Union.

In 1902 Farrar helped to found the Saddle and Harness Makers' Union, becoming its State secretary, and was foundation president of the Australian Saddlery Trades Employees' Federation in 1907-12. A member of the executive of the Political Labor League of New South Wales from 1908, he was vice-president in 1909-10, 1911-12 and 1915-16, and president in 1912-14. He was also president of the Labor Council of New South Wales in 1910. In 1912 he was nominated to the Legislative Council and in 1915-22 served as president of the Board of Fire Commissioners of New South Wales.

Although in September 1915 Farrar protested against the unauthorized attachment of his name to the Universal Service League manifesto, when conciliation proved impossible and voluntary enlistment seemed insufficient, he later campaigned vigorously for conscription. He attacked the expulsion from the Political Labor League of W. A Holman [q.v.] and his followers, pointing out months after the split that, since no one could get his job, he had not been expelled although he had travelled the State sup-

porting Holman. At State and Federal levels, Farrar helped to draft the constitutions of the new National Party, was a State vice-president in 1917-32 and regularly attended interstate meetings.

Minister for labour and industry in Sir George Fuller's [q.v.] ministry in 1922-25 and under (Sir) Thomas Bavin [q.v.7] in 1927-30, Farrar was in a 'hot seat'. Despite his impressive industry, Fuller had to defend him in May 1922 against rumours that cabinet colleagues were critical of him. However by 1924 registered unemployment had declined from 14500 in April 1922 to a monthly average of 8790 in 1924. Occasional deputations which became offensive or violent had to be ordered out of his office. He was also singled out for Labor abuse: in 1926 the *Labor Daily* called him 'a conceited and shallow but ambitious . . . political renegade . . . ever the most venomous enemy of those he has betrayed'.

Farrar could claim ministerial credit for some major public works, for dedicated effort and accessibility as a minister and for personal generosity to and concern for the unemployed, yet he fully shared his contemporaries' failure of comprehension and vision at the outset of the Depression. By April 1930 there were 50000 registered unemployed in New South Wales. Although the numbers employed on public works did increase, the early measures of the Council for Prevention and Relief of Unemployment (of which Farrar was deputy chairman) were restricted and heavily dependent upon private initiatives and support.

Although as late as September 1931 Farrar was still strongly non-Labor, he saw himself as still in some way a union man. In 1932 he became honorary chairman of the Employment Council of New South Wales and chaired sessions of the first State convention of the United Australia Party; in 1933-34 he sat on its council. On the reconstruction of the Legislative Council in 1934 and in 1946 he was elected for twelve-year terms. With the waning of the J. T. Lang [q.v.] threat, Farrar moved towards the final phase of his career – the 'above politics' parliamentary officer. From May 1934 until April 1946 he was chairman of committees in the council, besides being acting-president for almost six months in 1938 and deputy-president for three months in 1941. Unanimously chosen president in 1946, he continued in office after Labor won control of the council in 1949. Both sides respected his fair and efficient management of debates and his scholarly study of procedural authorities and traditions. In 1946 his casting vote defeated the Legislative Council abolition bill.

Throughout his career, Farrar was active

in the Empire Parliamentary Association and his feeling for the Empire remained strong. After playing an active part in its planning from mid-1922, he went to England as an executive commissioner for the British Empire Exhibition at Wembley in 1924. On his return he promoted British immigration. He was also a Freemason, a trustee of Ku-ring-gai Chase, the Australian Museum, Sydney, and Sydney Grammar School, a founder and president of the National Club, and a member of Manly Bowling Club.

On 6 February 1911 at Forest Lodge he had married Susan Priscilla Whitfield with Baptist forms; they lived at Manly. Farrar died in hospital at Manly with coronary occlusion on 16 June 1952 and was cremated with Anglican rites. He was survived by his son.

J. Roe (ed), *Social policy in Australia* (Syd, 1976); *PD* (NSW), 1952-53, p 7, 19; *Aust J of Politics and Hist*, Aug 1964, p 205; P. D. and E. H. Farrar papers (ML).   KEN TURNER

FARRELL, JOHN (1883-1955), teacher and soldier, was born on 20 March 1883 at Hamilton, Scotland, son of Joseph Farrell, coalminer, and his wife Mary, née McLaughlan. His father migrated to Australia in 1886 and next year his wife and three children joined him at Eidsvold, Queensland. Farrell completed his primary education there and remained as a pupil-teacher. In 1901 the family moved to Howard where he was a pupil-teacher and an assistant teacher in 1903-11. In 1901 he had joined the Wide Bay Infantry Regiment (militia) as a private; he was commissioned in 1905 and promoted lieutenant in 1908 and captain in 1910.

In 1911-14 Farrell taught at Rockhampton Central School. On 19 December 1912, at Rockhampton, he married May Watson Williams, a teacher, with Presbyterian forms. He was transferred to Charters Towers as acting headmaster in April 1914 and later that year became an assistant teacher at Leichhardt State School; in 1915 he was headmaster at Mackade. On moving to Rockhampton he had joined the Port Curtis Infantry Regiment, first as quarter-master and then as company commander and adjutant, and in September 1915 the Department of Education released him for full-time military duty. Until his appointment as a captain in the Australian Imperial Force on 1 April 1916 he was a company commander at Brisbane training camp, then quartermaster and assistant adjutant at Enoggera. Promoted major in May, he was appointed second-in-command when the 42nd Battalion was formed, and reached

Armentières, France, in November. In 1917 he fought at Ploegsteert Wood, the battle of Messines and at Warneton and in October commanded the battalion in its successful attack at Zonnebeke. He again held command from December to 12 January 1918 at Bois Grenier and Le Biset.

In February 1918 Farrell was promoted lieut-colonel and transferred to the 43rd Battalion as commanding officer, a post he held until the end of the war. Under his leadership the 43rd distinguished itself in actions at Sailly-le-Sec and Villers-Bretonneux, in the battle of Hamel in June, and in the August offensive at the capture of Méricourt-sur-Somme and operations near Bray-sur-Somme. On 1-2 September the battalion saw action near Mont St Quentin and captured Haut Allaines. Farrell was mentioned in dispatches in December and awarded the Distinguished Service Order for his leadership in the capture of Hamel.

In August 1919 he returned to Australia and resumed teaching at Wooloowin State School, Brisbane. After transfer to Ascot as an assistant teacher he was promoted to head-teacher at Woodford. He was head-teacher at Barcaldine in 1921-23 and Mount Morgan in 1924, then next year was appointed an assistant district inspector and in 1926 a district inspector; he was based in Brisbane from 1934. Though he retired in 1949, in 1950-53 he was officer-in-charge of special schools for recent migrants. Survived by his wife, two sons and a daughter, he died on 9 December 1955 at Windsor, Brisbane, and was cremated.

Farrell was largely responsible for moulding the 42nd Battalion into an exceptional fighting unit with an excellent *esprit de corps*. His able administration and efficient leadership was recognized by his appointment as commander of the 43rd Battalion. He was a leader who took a strong personal interest in the welfare of his men and who understood and tolerated their exuberant spirits when out of the line. He never sought popularity but his fine example won him the respect of those he led.

E. J. Colliver and B. H. Richardson, *The Forty-Third* (Adel, 1920); V. Brahms, *The spirit of the Forty-Second* (Brisb, 1938); *London Gazette*, 31 Dec 1918, 1 Jan 1919; Department of Education, Qld, Records (Brisb); records (AWM); information from Mrs E. M. Mostyn, Weetangera, Canb, and Mrs L. M. Story, Bundaberg, Qld.   BARRET J. CARR

FARRELLY, MARY MARTHA (1866-1943), social worker and diet reformer, was born on 18 June 1866 at Greenough, Western Australia, one of fourteen children of John Stephen Maley [q.v.5] and his wife Elizabeth

Kniest, née Waldeck. Although her maternal grandparents were pioneer Methodist missionaries, she married, on 2 April 1889 at Rudd's Gulley, a young Catholic solicitor, Alfred William Gresswell Farrelly; they had no children. After a serious illness she helped herself to regain her health by a self-chosen diet of wholemeal grains and fresh fruit and vegetables. When her husband's mental faculties deteriorated she decided to live apart from him.

Kindly but determined, and interested in the welfare of women and children, she joined the Women's Service Guild soon after its foundation in 1909, held several senior offices in it, and helped to establish the State's Kindergarten Union and girl guide movement. From 1915 she was also a committed member of the Theosophical Society. In 1916 she fought for attempted assault on children to be reclassified as a crime rather than a misdemeanour; for raising the age of consent to 18; and for the teaching of 'scientific physiology' in schools. She was a justice of the peace from 1921 and became a vice-president of the Western Australian Women Justices' Association. Believing that alcoholism was the root of many evils, she headed the social purity department of the Woman's Christian Temperance Union. In this capacity, and as a feminist, she put up a 'most strenuous fight' against government proposals in 1917 to amend the Health Act (1915) to give the commissioner of public health power to order anyone to be medically examined for venereal disease, merely upon the suspicion of an informer. She also organized the Prison Gate Committee to rehabilitate ex-prisoners. When Mrs Farrelly approached parliamentarians on deputations they were often daunted by her tall commanding presence. But this square-jawed, serious woman had an endearing personality and a latent roguish humour which won her many friends, particularly among countrywomen.

Country Circles were formed, by the Service Guild, for isolated women in 1912. She also organized rural household science courses to teach domestic efficiency to such women. It was there that the seed of the Country Women's Association in Western Australia germinated. A splendid speaker, at her lectures Mrs Farrelly demonstrated the virtue of wholemeal flour with home-made loaves and platters of wheaten biscuits. Her 34-page booklet, *How to cook wheat*, offering recipes for 'Wholesome, Nutritious, Appetising and Economical Dishes', was published in the Depression; at sixpence a copy it sold well, running to many editions. Its author was in great demand as a speaker in the country. Train travel meant loss of sleep and infrequent meals, but she fortified herself with a seemingly inexhaustible supply of puffed wheat, carried in her well-worn large handbag, along with pamphlets, recipe books and nomination forms. She munched, even while talking animatedly, and her listeners grew prepared to be wary of the shower which fell their way.

She was one of the four prime movers in founding the (Royal) Western Australian Historical Society in 1926, and eventually became a senior vice-president. Towards the end of her life her work was recognized at a reception at Government House when friends presented her with a large new handbag and a purse filled with much-needed sovereigns. Mary suffered from arthritis; she died on 28 August 1943 and was buried in Karrakatta cemetery's Methodist section in her brother's grave. Her estate was sworn for probate at £46.

B. M. Rischbieth, *March of Australian women* (Perth, 1964); R. Erickson, et al (eds), *Her name is woman* (Perth, 1974); *JRWAHS*, 8 (1977), pt 1, p 21; *Western Mail* (Perth), 30 Jan 1936; information from Mrs I. Greenwood, Shenton Park, WA.

RICA ERICKSON

FARRER, WILLIAM JAMES (1845-1906), wheat-breeder, was born on 3 April 1845 at Docker, Westmorland, England, son of Thomas Farrer, tenant farmer, and his wife Sarah, née Brunskill. He gained a scholarship to Christ's Hospital, London, where he won a gold and a silver medal for mathematics. Another scholarship took him to Pembroke College, Cambridge, (B.A., 1868). He began medicine, but soon contracted tuberculosis and migrated to Australia at 25.

Farrer was first a tutor at George Campbell's sheep station, Duntroon (Canberra), New South Wales. Unable to buy a pastoral property as he had planned, because of financial problems, he qualified as a surveyor in July 1875, and until 1886 worked in the Dubbo, Nyngan, Cobar and Cooma districts with the Department of Lands. On 11 September 1882 at St Philip's Anglican Church, Sydney, he married Nina Henrietta Sophia Fane de Salis, daughter of Leopold de Salis [q.v.4]. They were childless.

Farrer's pamphlet, *Grass and sheep farming* . . . (1873) showed his early thinking on agriculture. But his continuing interest became fixed on wheat-growing, and he concluded that the industry's problems were based on the unsuitability under Australian conditions of the types sown. As early as 1882 he started to formulate specific plans for producing improved wheats. His ideas began with the concept of selecting individual plants which showed superior qualities. But he soon included foreign wheats and the systematic cross-fertilization of suitable parents prior to selecting promising plants. The possible use of cross-breeding to improve wheat was then only being attempted in Europe and America, and Farrer was forced to rely on overseas correspondence for his information.

In July 1886 he resigned from the Lands Department, settled on Lambrigg on the Murrumbidgee River near where Canberra now stands and intensified his experiments. In 1889, the year of his first crude attempts at cross-breeding, the colonies' crop was one of the worst in Australia's history, and flour-millers had to import wheat. Such was the disaster that an Intercolonial Rust in Wheat Conference was convened in 1890 by the Victorian minister for agriculture – losses due to rust had been estimated to be over £2.5 million. By letter Farrer emphasized his belief that cross-breeding would improve not only resistance to rust, but baking quality of the grain. His concern for the latter as well as for agronomic attributes distinguished Farrer from his contemporaries overseas.

At Lambrigg he devised and improvised, culling suitable introductions, cross-pollinating one to another using hairpins until forceps were available, and producing hundreds of crossbred plants to be further culled and selected. The evaluation of milling and baking quality was beyond his resources, but in 1892 F. B. Guthrie [q.v.] set about devising procedures that reproduced the flour-mill and bakehouse in miniature, providing a quantitative assessment of the yield of flour from the mill and its behaviour on baking. Farrer was able to choose parents and progeny by results rather than by repute or appearance. He worked assiduously throughout the 1890s, although he was not robust and a riding accident in 1878 had left him with one shoulder a little lower than the other and with impaired eyesight.

Until his appointment as wheat experimentalist to the Department of Agriculture in September 1898 at a salary of £350, Farrer, his wife and her father had been living on their own means. At one stage, a wealthy uncle in England offered him the alternative of returning to inherit a fortune there or of being disinherited. He chose to stay, despite being to many people 'a crazy faddist', who wasted time on 'pocket handkerchief wheat plots'. He kept faithful to himself and was convinced of the value of his work.

Farrer made annual visits to the Rust in Wheat Conferences. Guthrie paid tribute to him, 'It was this knowledge of the usefulness of the work he was doing that kept his enthusiasm undiminished to the end. He loved his work . . . Simple and frugal in his personal habits, he was equally direct and straightforward in his habit of thought, and was incapable of . . . self-seeking. Of a highly sensitive disposition, he was by nature extremely reserved and reticent towards comparative strangers. Widely read and of broad culture and sympathies, his conversation was always suggestive and invigorating, and it can be quite truly said of him that no one could enjoy an intimate conversation with him without feeling a better man'.

The first successes came from selecting outstanding individuals from introduced wheats. Blount's Lambrigg, the name given by Farrer to one of these, was selected in 1889 from Professor Blount's Hybrid No. 38, Gypsum. It was not widely grown but was an important breeding parent. Bobs, the first Farrer wheat to be commercially grown, was in turn directly derived from Blount's Lambrigg. Not only did it yield well, but it also met his high ideals for grain quality, particularly in its superior blending ability. Continuing observation of the range of introduced wheats convinced him that the prospects for disease resistance and drought tolerance lay in the Indian wheats, which largely escaped rust and the hot, dry winds of summer because of their early maturity. On the other hand, Guthrie's studies pointed to the Canadian Fife wheats as the basis of milling and baking quality, but they were late maturing. The answer was to hybridize the two types and to select individuals that combined the advantages of both. In addition, the Fifes offered stiff straw, and the Indian wheats promised shorter straw and an ability to hold the grain in the ear. Early in the 1890s the variety Yandilla came from crossing Improved Fife with Etawah. Comeback (with Improved Fife, Indian G and Indian A in its pedigree) was a further improvement on the grain quality of Bobs, yielding flour 'better than the best imported Manitoba' according to the report of 1914 of the manager of the Adelaide Milling Co.

However, before the turn of the century, the flour-millers preferred the soft Purple Straw types with which they were familiar. But the final Rust in Wheat Conference in Melbourne in 1896 reported that the millers' opposition to the new generation of wheats 'has no legitimate foundation, but arises either from misconception or from conservatism'; in the same year the harvest was poor, and hard wheat from North America of the same quality as that produced by Farrer had to be imported. In altering their machinery and their attitudes to accept the imported grain, the millers saw the advantages that his wheats offered.

Farrer's 'strong' wheats were still being

out-yielded in many districts by older types, such as Purple Straw, in seasons when disease was not a problem. He and Guthrie came to realize that more stress was needed on the yield of grain by including as breeding parents the older wheats that had established reputations. Federation, named in 1901, was the product of this combination – the result of crossing the Fife-Indian wheat Yandilla with 14A, a Purple Straw, in 1895. Seed from this cross was planted next year and the last seed in the plot produced a plant noted as 'specially fine with good brown heads and strong straw'. Further selection produced Federation, the Farrer variety that became by far the most widely grown of his wheats. Its rapid spread was 'the result of sheer ability to yield well, despite an unattractive appearance in the field'. Although Federation compromised his idealistic wish never to release any wheat that was not of top grain quality, it did fulfil his aim to produce a wheat with a short, strong straw suited to Australian methods of harvesting. From 1910 to 1925 it was the leading variety for the whole continent.

Farrer named a large number of the more promising of his crossbreds and selections – of the twenty-nine varieties recommended for growing in the various districts of New South Wales in 1914, twenty-two were Farrer wheats. Of greatest importance was the impressive effect that they had on overall production. Farrer-bred wheats were largely responsible for the extension of wheat-growing (a four-fold increase for the State between 1897 and 1915) into drier or rust-prone districts, while in established areas yields and quality were improved. In addition, because he conducted his introduction of foreign wheats on an exchange basis, many of his varieties spread to other wheat-growing countries where some of them proved to be widely grown and popular in commercial production. His wheats were subsequently replaced by newer varieties, although Florence was still the second leading wheat in Queensland as late as 1938, and their contribution continues to the present day because of their extensive use as parents in the breeding of modern varieties. The famous Waterhouse wheat Gabo, which quickly became popular in the 1950s with farmers facing ruin from losses due to rust, can be seen as an extension of and justification for the Farrer breeding philosophy.

Farrer was not so successful in producing rust-resistant varieties as popular legend credits him. Rather, his varieties were rust escaping, due to their early maturity. However a degree of specific rust resistance, as now understood, was achieved in his wheats Florence and Thew. He was more successful in breeding for bunt resistance, largely because in the case of this seed-borne disease he achieved artificial inoculation. Florence was also resistant to flag smut.

Farrer's contributions extend beyond the provision of new wheats, since his systematic experimentation also added to scientific knowledge. Many years before the rediscovery of Mendelian principles of genetics, Farrer became aware of, and investigated, the heritable nature of disease resistance, of maturity and of grain-quality factors. He also discovered that they segregate independently, but that segregation only occurs in the second and subsequent generations after crossing.

For most of his life Farrer was not so involved in scientific publication, or with scientific societies, as would be a comparable professional scientist. However, a full account of his aims and experimental work is provided in a paper he read before the Australasian Association for the Advancement of Science in January 1898 (reprinted in the 1898 *Agricultural Gazette of N.S.W.* 9, 131-168, 241-260). During his term as wheat experimentalist he was a regular contributor to the *Agricultural Gazette*.

Farrer continued his work until his death, of heart disease, on 16 April 1906. He and his wife (d. 20 February 1929) are buried on the hilltop behind their house at Lambrigg. The grave is now marked with a granite column, erected by the Commonwealth Government and unveiled on 16 January 1939.

A Farrer Memorial fund was opened in Sydney in 1911. Currently it administers the annual award of the Farrer Memorial medal for outstanding service to agricultural science in research, administration and education, and the Farrer Memorial research scholarship, awarded for postgraduate research in agriculture. Australia has remembered Farrer well. In addition to a place on currency and stamps, he is perpetuated in the names of schools, streets, a suburb of Canberra, a flour-mill and several institutions. There is a bronze bust of him at Queanbeyan.

A. Russell, *William James Farrer, a biography* (Melb, 1949), and for bibliog; E. J. Donath, *William Farrer* (Melb, 1970); *Lone Hand*, Sept 1910, p 419; Dept of Agriculture (NSW), *Science Bulletin*, 1922, no 22, and for bibliog; *RAHSJ*, 22 (1936-37), p 406; Aust Inst of Agr Science, *J*, 21 (1939), p 208; *Records of the Aust Academy of Science*, 4 (Nov 1978-Apr 79), no 1, p 7, and for bibliog.

                                        C. W. WRIGLEY

FATNOWNA, JOHN KWAILIU ABEL-FAI (1866?-1906), sugar-plantation labourer and community leader, was born about 1866, son of Luifera and Sauroro of the Rakwane descent group on Malaita, one of the

Solomon Islands. He was educated in the customs of his island, which in his youth had barely been visited by Europeans. In common with other Solomon Islanders, Malaitans propitiate their ancestors through elaborate rituals controlled by priests who generally claim descent from a mythical founder. Traditionally Malaitans live in small cognatic descent-groups in the mountains or on artificial islands in the lagoons around the coast. Kwailiu lived on mountain slopes overlooking Fakanakafo Bay in the dialect area of Fataleka.

Kwailiu was recruited twice to Queensland: on the first occasion he was probably kidnapped but the second time he went willingly. Little is known of the first period except that he served out the customary three-year indentured term; he would have received the statutory payment of £6 a year plus food, accommodation and a limited supply of clothes. On his return to Malaita he married Orrani from West Fataleka. Soon afterwards the couple were recruited for Queensland. As an experienced labourer, Kwailiu would have received a higher cash payment, perhaps as much as £10, but in other respects the conditions of his service would not have changed. Probably the couple worked for three years in the Innisfail district; their first two children were born on the Johnstone River in 1891 and 1893. Having served their indenture, Kwailiu and his wife elected to remain in Queensland. As time-expired labourers they had much greater freedom of movement and their earnings, though much less than those of Europeans or Chinese wage-labourers, would have been greater than those serving their first indenture. As a female, Orrani would always have earned less than Kwailiu.

By 1895 Kwailiu and Orrani had moved to Mackay where their next three children were born in 1895, 1897 and 1901. There they lived for the remainder of their lives, working on plantations and farms. Oral testimony from the present day Islander community leaves no doubt that Kwailiu was one of the most important Malaitan leaders in the Mackay district, a conclusion confirmed by the unprecedented scale of his funeral in 1906. This pre-eminence depended entirely on descent and on force of character: he remained pagan all his life and held no position recognized by Europeans, unlike other leading Islanders who gained status from positions in a Christian Church or the Pacific Islanders Association. Kwailiu's grandfather Dedeana had been a powerful leader of the Rakwane; if Kwailiu had returned to Malaita as he was often urged, he would have assumed the position of Fataabu (priest) among the Rakwane.

After Kwailiu's death of malaria on 25 March 1906 at Pioneer, Orrani married Luke Logomier, another Fataleka man and lay preacher at St Mary's Anglican Church at Farleigh outside Mackay. They both died in the influenza epidemic in 1919. Kwailiu's daughters married other Solomon Islanders at Mackay, as did their son, who adopted the surname Fatnowna. Their families are prominent in the present day Islander community.

H. Reynolds (ed), *Race relations in North Queensland* (Townsville, 1978); *Mackay Mercury*, 28 Mar 1906; registers, Holy Trinity Anglican Church, Mackay, Qld; oral history supplied by members of the Fatnowna, Quaytucker, Bobongie and Mooney families, Mackay, Qld, and by Ishmael Itea and Charles Luiramo, Malaita, Solomon Islands.

CLIVE R. MOORE

FAWSITT, CHARLES EDWARD (1878-1960), professor of chemistry, was born on 8 May 1878 at Govan, Lanark, Scotland, son of Charles Albert Fawsitt, a chemist's manager, and his wife Mary, née Pollock, whose uncle founded the local shale oil industry. Educated at a Glasgow high school and the University of Edinburgh, he did doctoral work in physical chemistry under Ostwald at Leipzig on an 1851 Exhibition scholarship. After further research at Aachen, London and Birmingham, Fawsitt returned to Edinburgh to assist Crum-Brown, his former teacher, and to take a D.Sc. degree. In 1904 he moved to Glasgow to lecture in metallurgical chemistry and to further his research into corrosion and the reaction between iron and sulphuric acid. When several British universities were requested by the University of Sydney to suggest candidates for its chair of chemistry, vacant on the retirement of Archibald Liversidge [q.v.5], Glasgow nominated Fawsitt. In October 1908 he was appointed by the senate and took up the position in the next year. At St Stephen's Presbyterian Church, Sydney, on 16 December 1909 Fawsitt married Lena, daughter of Rev. Dr Matthew Gardner of Hyndland church, Glasgow; there was one daughter of the marriage.

On his arrival Fawsitt found a department modest in membership but well off for equipment and buildings. It was a time of concern for the expansion of chemistry into industry and the practical application of science. In 1910 Fawsitt expanded his courses to include the newly popular physical chemistry and made organic chemistry compulsory. Two years later funds were provided to found a chair in organic chemistry, pure and applied – a compromise between Fawsitt's emphasis and the official policy of encouraging industrial chemistry.

Research took little of Fawsitt's personal attention. He published papers on corrosion and allied topics in local journals but he had a greater talent for encouraging the research projects of his colleagues and students. Despite friction, in the 1930s and later, with the second organic chemistry professor, Fawsitt built up a distinguished group of lecturers, setting the scene with his own lucid, precise mode of teaching. Dean of the faculty in 1923-29 he pressed for the expansion of science; late in World War II, past the usual retiring age, he was preparing successfully for the post-war influx of students and the creation of an extended school of chemistry. He retired on 31 August 1946 and was made emeritus professor.

Fawsitt's concern for chemistry extended beyond the university. From his arrival, he served on the New South Wales Pure Food Advisory Committee. He supported the Commonwealth Institute of Science and Industry, as an effective means of co-ordinating academic and industrial work in World War I. Membership of the National Research Council followed in 1919. He served as president of the Royal Society of New South Wales (1919-20), the Royal Australian Chemical Institute (1924-25) and the National Committee of Pure and Applied Chemistry. Courteous and dignified, impressive in stature and manner, Fawsitt was a highly effective chairman. An accomplished pianist, with a Scotsman's devotion to golf and Presbyterianism, Fawsitt had few personal foibles, though his fear of possible contagion led him to sterilize the coins he carried with him. He died at the Scottish Hospital, Sydney, on 16 November 1960 and was cremated. His estate was sworn for probate at £22 573.

Univ Syd, *Union Recorder*, 28 Nov 1946, 16 Mar 1961; Roy Aust Chemical Inst, *Procs*, Jan 1961; *SMH*, 8 May 1919, 17 Nov 1960; Senate and Professorial Board minutes, 1908-60 (Univ Syd Archives).   K. J. CABLE
                                        URSULA BYGOTT

FEAKES, HENRY JAMES (1876-1950), rear admiral, was born on 16 March 1876 in London, son of John James Feakes, civil servant, and his wife Jane, née Chappell. After overcoming his father's opposition to a naval career he entered the Thames Nautical Training College, H.M.S. *Worcester*, as a cadet. Although he was appointed chief cadet captain in his final year he failed to receive a warrant as a midshipman in the Royal Navy but was admitted to the Royal Naval Reserve. After leaving the *Worcester* he spent four years in sail to qualify as an officer in the merchant marine and in 1896 joined the renowned Peninsular & Oriental

Steam Navigation Co.'s Far Eastern service.

Feakes kept up his naval training, spending as much time as possible with the Royal Navy, and when he learned in 1904 that the infant Commonwealth Naval Forces of Australia needed officers he applied for an appointment; he was accepted in 1906. He was precisely the sort of man who was needed. With the arms race against Germany under way and the Royal Navy undergoing great expansion there were few R.N. officers willing to come to Australia on loan. Feakes, with his long experience in the R.N.R. and the merchant service, was a very good second best. On reaching Australia he found that parliament had not yet approved the plans of Captain (Sir) William Creswell [q.v.], director of the Commonwealth Naval Forces, to begin construction of a destroyer flotilla and personnel recruiting on a large scale. However, he remained, possibly because he was courting an Australian girl, and on 17 June 1907 was gazetted a navigating sub-lieutenant in the C.N.F.

Feakes's first months, spent in H.M.A.S. *Cerberus*, were disappointing but he soon learned that he was earmarked to commission one of Australia's first torpedo-boat destroyers, then under construction in England. On 25 September 1907, at Scots Church, Melbourne, he married Corona Patterson and next year was promoted lieutenant. By this time he was on his way to England with nucleus crews for the new destroyers, H.M.A.S. *Parramatta* and H.M.A.S. *Yarra*. The next eighteen months were among the most rewarding of his career; apart from training the crews of the two ships and acting as Australian naval liaison officer in London, he also undertook gunnery and torpedo courses to fit himself for command. His efforts were commended by the Australian high commissioner, Sir George Reid [q.v.], and British naval authorities as well as the senior officer of the Australian flotilla, Commander C. L. Cumberlege [q.v.]. When the *Parramatta* arrived in Australia he was lieutenant-in-command.

In June 1912 Feakes returned to England to do a navigation course before being posted to the dreadnought H.M.S. *Orion* to gain experience in heavy ships. Next February he joined the new light cruiser H.M.A.S. *Sydney* as navigator, to commission the ship and bring her out to Australia. He served in the *Sydney* for over eighteen months, leaving her as a lieut-commander after operations against German possessions in the Pacific in 1914. In mid-1915 he was appointed captain as an acting commander of the old cruiser H.M.A.S. *Psyche* for patrols on the East Indies and China stations, and later became senior naval officer of the Burmese coastal patrol. Conditions were appalling but, despite the ship's aged machinery and the strain of the tropical climate, *Psyche's* efficiency and Feakes's keenness earned excellent reports from successive British commanders-in-chief. On 1 October 1917, after his return to Australia, Feakes was promoted commander, Royal Australian Navy.

He was successively appointed to the training ship H.M.A.S. *Tingira*, the battle cruiser H.M.A.S. *Australia* as executive officer, and the light cruiser H.M.A.S. *Melbourne*, before being promoted captain on 1 July 1921. Although gratifying, this promotion was to have unfortunate consequences. To maintain efficiency it was decided at this stage that all R.A.N. officers should do a period of exchange service with the R.N. at least once in each rank and be recommended for promotion to the next rank by a senior R.N. officer. Feakes had done no service with the R.N. as a substantive commander and this meant that the Admiralty would not accept him for command of a British ship. He therefore had no chance of becoming a flag officer on the active list. In the 1920s he held a succession of the highest Australian commands: he was captain superintendent at Flinders Naval Depot, Victoria, in 1925-27; he represented the R.A.N. at the 1927 Naval Disarmament Conference as well as serving as Australian naval liaison officer in London in 1927-29; and was second naval member of the Australian Naval Board in 1930-33. By the late 1920s, however, he realized that he could go no further in the service.

By 1930, with the reductions which were being effected in the R.A.N., Feakes was faced with the prospect of unemployment until he retired. He was reprieved by the request of Rear Admiral E. R. G. R. Evans (of Antarctic fame) that he be appointed to the seaplane-carrier H.M.A.S. *Albatross* under Evans's command in the Australian Squadron. He accepted the post with delight and spent a year in command in 1930-31 before going to his last appointment as captain superintendent of naval establishments at Sydney and captain-in-charge, New South Wales, in 1931-33. Though he was considered for temporary command of the Australian Squadron as a commodore after Evans's return to England, the first naval member, Rear Admiral (Sir) Francis Hyde [q.v.], and the Admiralty rejected his appointment because of his lack of sea service with the R.N.

Feakes retired in February 1933 and was placed on the retired list in September as a rear admiral; that year he was appointed C.B.E. The rest of his life was spent largely in the study of naval strategy and history. In the 1930s he was among those who warned against Japanese expansionism and the inadequacy of Australian and British reaction. He travelled extensively in the Far East and, as a senior officer of great experience and journalistic ability, was able to express his views on defence not only in professional circles but in the Australian press.

Feakes's second major interest after retirement was the writing of a popular history of the navy's part in the development and defence of Australia. This task took up most of his time after World War II. By then his health had begun to fail but his *White ensign – Southern Cross* (1951) was accepted for publication before he died in Sydney on 24 April 1950. He was cremated with Anglican rites. His wife survived him; their only child, a daughter, had predeceased him.

A. W. Jose, *The Royal Australian Navy* (Syd. 1928); *Australasian*, 9 Apr 1927; *SMH*, 18 Apr 1929, 22 Jan, 14 Feb 1930, 23, 27 July 1931, 25 July 1932, 12 Jan, 11 Feb, 3 June 1933, 4 Aug 1936, 25 Apr 1950, 18 Aug 1951; *Queenslander*, 30 Jan 1930.

                                    J. V. P. GOLDRICK

FEETHAM, JOHN OLIVER (1873-1947), bishop, was born on 27 January 1873 at Penrose, Monmouthshire, England, fourth son of William Feetham, vicar of Penrose, and his wife Mary, née Crawley. Of his five brothers, the eldest became a general, two became priests, one a poet and the other a judge. Through schooling at Marlborough in 1886-92, John Oliver came to admire the British Public School education: it served as his ideal in establishing schools in North Queensland. At Trinity Hall, Cambridge, in 1892-95 he continued his studies in mathematics, graduating senior optime. At Oxford House, Bethnal Green, in the slums of London, he carried out a lay ministry for eighteen months before entering Wells Theological College. Ordained deacon in 1899 and priest in 1900, he stayed in Bethnal Green as curate at St Simon Zelotes. The influence of his colleagues in the East End remained with him thoughout his life.

Frederick Campion [q.v.7], a fellow curate, came to Australia in 1902 and founded the Brotherhood of the Good Shepherd, based in Dubbo, New South Wales, in 1904. Feetham was interested in the work and followed him in 1907 as the second principal. Love of the Australian bush and its people and belief in the importance of the Brotherhood became distinctive marks of his episcopate in North Queensland. While he was in the Brotherhood, the bishop of North Queensland, G. H. Frodsham [q.v.], invited him to Townsville to conduct the clergy retreat. Feetham was unanimously elected to the see in October 1912, when Frodsham resigned. Consecrated on St Mark's Day (25 April) 1913 in St John's Cathedral, Brisbane, by Archbishop St Clair Donaldson, assisted by Bishop White [qq.v.] of Carpentaria, he was enthroned on 4 May 1913 in St James Cathedral, Townsville.

Feetham was bishop of North Queensland from 1913 to 1947. His episcopate spanned crucial years in the development of North Queensland. In both world wars he was a vigorous exponent and supporter of the allied cause. In fighting for what he believed, in church and state, there could be no half measures, and like many other public figures, he was a pro-conscriptionist in 1916 and 1917. He was favourable to the Labor Party at first, but by the end of the 1920s was critical of it.

Feetham contributed much to the maintenance and vivifying of the Bush Brotherhood, and to the spread of religion in the outback. He inspired the Brothers to see country people as epitomizing the virtues of an Australian character partly formed by the bush itself. The success of his appeals for financial support from the pastoral companies indicates the influence of this outlook. He left a permanent imprint on the churchmanship of the diocese. As a priest, he had been at loggerheads with the evangelical Archbishop Wright [q.v.] of Sydney, and under Feetham's guidance the diocese of North Queensland became one of the most uniformly catholic in Australia. Far from being 'high and dry', the North Queensland Church was very much alive. He infected others with his own enthusiasm, and his personality, into which his Christianity was fully integrated, was colourful, attractive and eccentric.

His outstanding achievement was the foundation of schools. They were primarily 'the bishop's schools', and he devoted tremendous effort to them, leaving a powerful imprint on them: All Souls and St Gabriel's, Charters Towers, and St Anne's, Townsville, are flourishing still, while St Mary's, Herberton, closed in 1966. His aim was to bring up the children of North Queensland in the best Imperial and church traditions. The patriotism of past and present pupils during World War II reflected his success — 'Church and Empire' were his watchwords. He believed in the Anglican Church and in the British race which produced it, and despite post-war changes the vitality of this ethos remains: the Church identified with him. It is probably this personal influence for which he is most remembered.

The immense number of letters and telegrams at the time of Feetham's death show the regard in which he was held. The clergy write in glowing terms of his effects upon them, and the enthusiasm still present in the diocese is unmistakable. The anecdotes of his exploits and eccentricities stress his remarkable impact: with a long neck and big clerical collar, he was 6ft. 2ins. (188cm) tall; his trousers usually showed an expanse of white socks and enormous feet in large shoes. He drove an early model Ford, 'Ermintrude', with panache, and usually refused to sleep in a bed.

On 20 July 1947 Feetham announced his resignation from 30 September. He had been ill for some time and in 1946 had gone to Brisbane for surgery. He returned to Townsville, where, unmarried, he died on 14 September 1947. He was cremated.

J. Norman, *John Oliver. North Queensland* (Melb, 1953); R. Fraser, *A historical sketch of the diocese of North Queensland* (Townsville, 1958); R. Feetham, *The commemoration of John Oliver Feetham* (np, 1964); A. Hayhoe, John Oliver Feetham (B.A. Hons thesis, Univ Qld, 1968); K. Rayner, The history of the Church of England in Queensland (Ph.D. thesis, Univ Qld, 1962).

ALISON MOORE

FEEZ, ADOLPH FREDERICK MILFORD (1858-1944), surveyor and solicitor, and **ARTHUR HERMAN HENRY MILFORD** (1860-1935), barrister, were sons of Lieut-Colonel Albrecht Frederick Robert John Feez, a Rockhampton merchant born in Bavaria, and his wife Sophia, daughter of Mr Justice S. F. Milford [q.v.5]. Born on 29 May 1858 in Brisbane, Adolph began his education at Rockhampton, went to The King's School, Parramatta, New South Wales, then sought the experience necessary to join his father in business at Rockhampton. He rapidly abandoned business, took up surveying and spent eighteen months with a survey party in the Riverina. He was then for two years second-in-charge of a survey camp in the far west of Queensland, and accomplished the first surveys of the Diamantina and other rivers.

When he returned sick to Rockhampton, C. S. D. Melbourne, solicitor and family friend, persuaded Feez to take up law. Articled to Melbourne, he worked subsequently at Charters Towers and Cairns and completed his articles in Brisbane with Peter MacPherson and L. F. Bernays; he was admitted as a solicitor on 1 December 1885 and on 1 January next year commenced practice as a partner in MacPherson, Miskin & Feez. After Miskin retired, MacPherson & Feez was involved in some of the major litigation of the 1890s, including two Privy Council appeals on behalf of the Brisbane City Council, Martin's case and the Clark and Fauset case over the Victoria Bridge. They were also retained in the celebrated

Robb [q.v.6] arbitration case. When the partnership was dissolved at the turn of the century, Feez carried on under his own name until 1905 when Arthur Baynes joined him. In 1912 Adalbert Friedrich Theodor Ruthning came into the firm which became Feez, Ruthning & Baynes. After Baynes died in 1923, it became Feez, Ruthning & Co. in January 1927. Feez retired on 31 December 1942, but the firm still continues under the same name.

When young, Feez represented Queensland several times at Rugby Union. He founded the Brisbane Hunt Club, was master and hunted regularly until lack of support caused the club to collapse after eight years. He was also a founder of the Queensland Polo and the Queensland Lawn Tennis associations. A keen judge and breeder of horses and cattle, he always maintained some rural interests. On 11 October 1888 at Brisbane, Feez had married Kate Elise Molle. She and their three children survived him when he died on 13 October 1944; he was cremated. His estate was valued for probate at £4973.

Arthur Feez was born on 4 March 1860 at Rockhampton. Matriculating from The King's School to the University of Sydney, he graduated in law and was admitted to the Queensland Bar on 6 September 1881. He was a leader in establishing on 7 November 1907 the Incorporated Council of Law Reporting for the State of Queensland, and from 1912 until he left Queensland he was its chairman. By 1900 Feez was the colony's leading barrister, retained in major cases like the Tyson [q.v.6] succession case and *Regina* v. Queensland Trustees Ltd (1900). He stood unsuccessfully for Rockhampton against William Kidston [q.v.] in 1908. When he took silk late in 1909, he filled a long-standing gap in the Queensland Bar. Domineering, determined but always correct, he was known for his dislike of any hint of smart tactics.

As leader of the Bar, Feez was senior counsel in many of the bitter anti-socialist constitutional actions brought against the T. J. Ryan [q.v.] government. Ryan was a capable constitutional lawyer but he and his party, after his death in 1921, developed an antipathy to Arthur Feez because of his dogged resistance to their socialist plans. His opposition to the appointment of T. W. McCawley [q.v.] as a Supreme Court judge helped fuel this antipathy. Consequently Feez, although leader of the Bar, had the humiliation of seeing bench vacancies filled several times by lesser lights. When F. T. Brennan [q.v.7] was made an acting judge of the Supreme Court on 13 March 1925, a brief item in the *Brisbane Courier* announced that Feez had presented his commission as K.C.

to the Supreme Court of New South Wales on 22 April. He lived in Sydney until he retired in 1934. In 1889 Feez had married Fanny Lloyd Hart by whom he had one daughter. He died in London on 8 April 1935 while on a world tour.

Feez was chancellor of the diocese of Brisbane in 1897-1910. He had been best man at the wedding of Nellie Melba [q.v.] to Charles Armstrong, and his interest in the arts lead to friendships with Anna Pavlova and the Carandini family [q.v.3]. During his lifetime he made many philanthropic gifts, but he left his estate, sworn for probate at £139 620 in New South Wales and £34 223 in Queensland, largely to his daughter and granddaughter.

Alcazar Press, *Queensland, 1900* (Brisb, nd); J. Hetherington, *Melba* (Melb, 1967); D. J. Murphy, *T. J. Ryan* (Brisb, 1975); W. R. Johnston, *History of the Queensland Bar* (Brisb, 1979); QSR, *Memoranda*, 1908-09, 1910-11, 1925; *Brisbane Courier*, 7 Sept 1881, 23 Apr 1925; *Telegraph* (Brisb), 19 May 1934; *Courier Mail*, 9, 11 Apr 1935.

J.C.H. GILL

FEGAN, JOHN LIONEL (1862?-1932), coalminer and politician, was born at Chelmsford, Essex, England, son of John Lionel Fegan, labourer, and his wife Alice Maud, née Hazel. He began work in coalmines in Lancashire and on 3 February 1883 at Eccleston he married Ann Saggerson. Arriving in New South Wales alone about 1886 he worked briefly in several northern mines before moving to the Wickham and Bullock Island (Carrington) colliery, where he became check inspector and delegate for his lodge.

In 1891 Fegan, representing Newcastle, was one of the first Labor members elected to the Legislative Assembly; he was a free trader in a protectionist district. Refusing to take the solidarity pledge, he lost Labor Electoral League endorsement and was returned for Wickham in 1894 as an independent. That year he secured and chaired a select committee on working of collieries and in 1897 served on the royal commission on city railway extension. He joined Labor in supporting (Sir) George Reid's [q.v.] free trade ministry and shared their criticism of the Federation bills and the government's lack of interest in industrial reform. In August 1899 he was involved in the defeat of Reid, moving the key amendment, in the form of censure for the payment to J. C. Nield [q.v.].

Fegan was thus an appropriate choice as secretary for mines and agriculture in W. Lyne's [q.v.] government. He carried the Miners' Accident Relief Act and an Act limiting the hours worked in mines to eight.

After Lyne became Federal minister for home affairs, he offered the post of under-secretary in his department to Fegan, who resigned his portfolio in March but was prevented from accepting the post by opposition in the Federal cabinet and from Reid. Later Fegan served as minister without portfolio in the See [q.v.] government in 1903-04 and under T. Waddell [q.v.] as minister of public instruction and for labour and industry from June to August 1904. He had recognized the declining importance of the fiscal issue, and from 1901 held his seat as a Progressive until he was defeated in 1907 after 'fusion' with the Liberals. After several abortive efforts he re-entered parliament in 1920, as one of the five members elected – he was the only Nationalist to represent Newcastle. He was defeated in 1922 and 1925.

In his youth Fegan had sung to waiting audiences during Gladstone's Midlothian campaign and so participated in one of British liberalism's great triumphs. A prominent Methodist lay-preacher and temperance advocate, he was grand chief templar in New South Wales of the International Order of Good Templars in 1902-04. Elected to Wickham Municipal Council in 1917, he was mayor in 1924 and 1931; he was a member of the Newcastle Board of Health in 1909-32 and the (Royal) Newcastle Hospital Board, superintendent and secretary of the Newcastle and Northumberland Benevolent Society and served on other local bodies. In a wider sphere he was chairman of the New South Wales Miners' Accident Relief Board in 1901-10, a trustee of the Public Library of New South Wales in 1903-12 and a member of the State Children's Relief Board from 1908.

Fegan died on 29 December 1932 at his home at Wickham and was buried in Sandgate cemetery. He was survived by a daughter, and by his second wife Edith Louisa, née Edwards, whom he had married on 27 October 1897 at Newtown, Sydney; they had no children. Fegan concealed his first marriage and two children for many years. His son Donald later lived with his father and stepmother, enlisted in the Australian Imperial Force and was killed in action at Gallipoli.

A.B. Piddington, *Worshipful masters* (Syd, 1929); H.V. Evatt, *Australian Labour leader* ... *W.A. Holman* (Syd, 1940); V&P (LA NSW), 1896, 3, p 621; *PD* (NSW), 1899, p 1076; *Newcastle Morning Herald*, 17 June 1891, 5 July 1894, 8 Sept 1899, 30 Dec 1932; *Methodist* (Syd), 14 June 1933.

L. E. FREDMAN

FEHON, WILLIAM MEEKE (1834-1911), railway administrator, was born in March 1834 in London, son of John Fehon, printer, and his wife Sarah, née Greenhaus. Educated at Brixton school, he entered a commercial firm and in 1851 joined the Eastern Counties Railway Co. as a clerk and was later in the engineer's office. He worked for the Great Western Railway Co. of Canada from 1856 until his brother invited him to come to Australia. Arriving in Melbourne in April 1858, on 1 May Fehon married Ann Gumm (d. 1907). He was employed by the Victorian Railways Department and rose to be traffic manager in 1870. Two years later, he became a partner in William McCulloch [q.v.5] & Co., a large carrying organization and, when it was made a limited company about 1876, managing director. From 1880 the company expanded by its association with the New South Wales firm of Wright [q.v.6], Heaton & Co. Ltd. Fehon became a public figure in Victoria as a member of the Central Board of Health, a justice of the peace and a licensing magistrate.

Fehon resigned from McCulloch's in 1883 and visited Europe. He reported on railways for the Service [q.v.6] government and assisted in the selection of Richard Speight [q.v.6] to head the Victorian railways. On his return Fehon went in for sugar-growing and pastoral pursuits, but with little success. Badly shaken, he found an opportunity to return to railway work when the Parkes [q.v.5] ministry removed the New South Wales railways from direct political control. Under the Government Railways Act of 1888, Fehon was appointed second commissioner on 22 October, under E. M. G. Eddy [q.v.]; C. N. J. Oliver [q.v.] under-secretary for lands, was the third.

His appointment aroused a storm: J. H. Want [q.v.] declared that Fehon had shown partiality to McCulloch's before leaving the Victorian railways and had later been involved in land and wool scandals associated with Wright Heaton. Parkes's reluctance to take the charges seriously contributed to his loss of office in January 1889. The Dibbs [q.v.4] government appointed a royal commission which, somewhat dubiously, exonerated Fehon. The railway commissioners faced bitter criticism. The railways system needed major reconstruction. Labour relations deteriorated and political criticism grew as Eddy's vigorous reforms were pushed forward. Fehon, who greatly admired Eddy and supported him loyally, acted as a moderating influence, especially with the unions.

Reappointed in 1895 Fehon, not unwillingly, became third commissioner at a lower salary. After 1897 Oliver, unable to maintain Eddy's (d. 1897) professional primacy, fell out with the abrasive David Kircaldie [q.v.], second commissioner, on policy and personal issues: Fehon, though anxious to keep the peace, tended to side with Kircaldie. By 1905 the situation had aroused such service and political disquiet that the royal commission into railway administration was appointed, partly to inquire into 'inharmonious relations between the commissioners'. Its divided report generally placed least blame on Fehon, who was portrayed as a conciliator.

His appointment ended on 11 April 1907 and he retired with only a years salary, being ineligible for a pension. He served on the royal commission of inquiry on forestry in 1907 but resigned in January 1908 because of increasing deafness. After a visit to Britain, Fehon lived in retirement mainly at the Warrigal Club. He died at his son's Homebush residence on 4 February 1911 and was buried in Rookwood cemetery with Anglican rites. He was survived by a son and daughter and left an estate sworn for probate at £3283 in New South Wales and £500 in Victoria.

Cyclopedia of N.S.W. (Syd, 1907); *V&P* (LA NSW), 1889, 5, 121; *PP* (LC & LA, NSW), 1906, 4, pt 1; *PD* (NSW), 1888, p 1065, 1511, 1889, p 1856, 1906, p 845; *NSW Railway and Tramway Mag*, 1 Dec 1920, p 750; *SMH*, 6 Feb 1911; Carruthers papers, *and* Parkes letters (ML).   K. J. CABLE

FELL, WILLIAM SCOTT (1866-1930), shipping merchant, and DAVID (1869-1956), accountant, were born on 20 July 1866 at Elleray Villa, Rosneath, Dunbartonshire, Scotland, and on 9 March 1869 at Montrose Lodge, Langside, Glasgow, third and fourth sons of John Wilson Fell, ship-broker, and his second wife Jessie McKinley, née Power. They were educated at Dollar Academy and Graham's Academy, Greenock, Scotland. After their father's death, they migrated with their mother, reaching Sydney in the *John Elder* on 21 March 1879.

William worked for F. Lassetter [q.v.5] & Co. Ltd and Potts & Paul, ship-chandlers; he set up as a broker in 1882 and later as a general commission agent. In financial difficulties in 1888 and 1891, he was bankrupted in 1895. He discharged his debts in full on 23 March 1903; meanwhile he had been managing W. Scott Fell & Co. then owned by O. G. S. Lane. In 1903 Fell floated W. Scott Fell & Co. Ltd, shipping and coal contractors, as a public company and was managing director. In 1908 he and the firm were bankrupted. His discharge was suspended for twelve months because he had committed misdemeanours under the Bankruptcy Act. He won an appeal to the High Court. After his discharge in August 1911 Fell chartered coastal ships. In 1914 he

formed and was managing director of the Interstate Steamship Co. and was later also managing director of Maitland Main Collieries Ltd. He prospered during World War I.

As an Independent Liberal, Fell had failed in bids for the Legislative Assembly seats of Middle Harbour in 1907 and Mosman in 1913. In 1922 he won North Shore as an independent coalition candidate. In 1926 he slandered a fellow-politician Alfred Reid and had to pay £30. He resigned in 1927 to contest a Federal by-election for Warringah but lost. He was described by the *Bulletin* (10 September 1930) as 'a go as-you-please Nationalist, with stubborn views of his own on most subjects'.

On 17 September 1889 at Newcastle he had married Emma Catherine Bain. Fell was a Freemason, a fellow of the Royal Geographical Society of London, and president of the British Empire Union in Australia until ousted by H. D. McIntosh [q.v.] in 1928. He died of cerebro-vascular disease on 7 September 1930 at his home in Macquarie Street, Sydney, and was buried in the Presbyterian section of Manly cemetery. He was survived by his wife, two sons and three daughters. His estate was valued for probate at £54 601.

On completing his education at Fort Street Public School, David worked for R. Little & Co. Soon he was a clerk with Davenport, Miles & Co., accountants. In 1893 he set up as a public accountant and in 1898, with W. Horner Fletcher as partner, established David Fell & Co. He soon acquired two important overseas clients, Whinney, Smith & Whinney, chartered accountants of London, and the Equitable Life Assurance Society of the United States, and later was attorney for Great Cobar Ltd. Branches of David Fell & Co. were opened in Melbourne in 1907, Brisbane in 1914 and Adelaide in 1920. In evidence before the 1912 royal commission of inquiry as to food supplies and prices, Fell refused to disclose the names of members of a meat cartel or information about the American Beef Trust, despite being threatened with proceedings for contempt of court. He was also chairman of the Illawarra and South Coast Steam Navigation Co. Ltd and of Thomas Elliot & Co. Ltd, a director of many companies including Lysaght Bros & Co. Ltd and the Commonwealth Oil Corporation Ltd and auditor of the University of Sydney and the Royal Agricultural Society of New South Wales. He was a founder, fellow and later vice-president of the Australasian Corporation of Public Accountants.

In the 1890s he helped (Sir) James Graham [q.v.4] in his early political campaigns. In 1904-13 as a Liberal, Fell represented Lane

Cove in the Legislative Assembly. Although he held some radical ideas, he was staunchly conservative in economic and financial matters, but never achieved his ambition of attaining the treasury portfolio. He did not seek re-election in 1913.

Active in many diverse activities, Fell was honorary treasurer of Sydney Hospital in 1901-12 and vice-president in 1912-15, a founder in 1895 and honorary secretary of the Women's Hospital, Crown Street, a founder of the New South Wales Wine Association and for many years vice-president of the New South Wales Rowing Association. A talented singer, he was vice-president of the (Royal) Philharmonic Society of Sydney, a foundation council-member of the North Sydney Orphans' Society and chairman of the government's advisory committee for the establishment of the State Conservatorium of Music.

Retiring from the active management of his firm in 1914, Fell went to England with his family; he had married Mabel Bryce (d. 1915) at Balmain on 18 September 1895. He was asked by Governor Strickland [q.v.] to explore prospects for State government loans on the London market. During World War I Fell made several visits to Australia and the United States of America where he negotiated war loans. In Sydney in 1916 he was a founder and honorary secretary of the State branch of the Federal National Party. Later at the request of the British government and the Victoria League he lectured to soldiers in France.

After the war Fell lived in England and in 1925 retired as senior partner in David Fell & Co. An ardent supporter of White Australia, Fell was involved in several societies that aimed at settling British ex-servicemen on the land in the Empire. His co-founder in these activities was Alice Florence, daughter of Viscount Elibank, whom he married at Holy Trinity Church, Brompton, on 24 July 1919; her first marriage had been annulled in 1910.

Fell devoted his later years to ex-servicemen's organizations from his home at Bledlow, West Wycombe, Buckinghamshire. He died at Hove, Sussex, on 6 January 1956 and was buried beside his first wife in Kingston cemetery, Surrey. His Australian estate was valued for probate at £21 216. He was survived by two of his four sons, and by two daughters of his first marriage, and by his second wife. His eldest son David, Royal Field Artillery, was killed in action in France in World War I.

Cyclopedia of N.S.W. (Syd, 1907); *PP* (LC & LA, NSW), 1913, 4, 265; *Cwlth Law Reports*, 13 (1911-12), p 230; *Scottish A'sian*, Nov 1917, p 5905; *Daily Telegraph* (Syd), 10 Aug 1904, 5 Apr 1912, 30 Dec 1919, 13 May 1925, 7 Oct 1926; *SMH*, 26 Feb, 13, 18 Apr 1912, 18 Nov 1916, 6 Nov 1917, 8 Sept, 6 Oct 1923, 13 May, 4 Dec 1924, 23 May 1927, 8 Sept 1930; *The Times*, 30 Jan 1919, 8 Oct 1921, 9, 16, 18 May 1929; *Sun* (Syd), 2, 3, Sept 1926; *Labor Daily*, 6 Oct 1926; *Truth* (Syd), 6 June 1954; notes on history of David Fell & Co. (held by Messrs Ernst & Whinney, Syd; Fell papers (ML); Bankruptcy files 3543, 10, 287/7, 17, 906/11 (NSWA); information from Commander R. A. Fell, Inchture, Perthshire, Scotland, Mr C. A. Hardwick, Wollstonecraft, NSW, Mr M. R. Hardwick, Sydney, and Mr W. D. Scott Fell, Darling Point, NSW.

R. G. DRYEN

FENNER, CHARLES ALBERT EDWARD (1884-1955), educationist, geographer and author, was born on 18 May 1884 at Dunach, Victoria, fifth of eight children of German-born Johannes Fenner, poultry-farmer, publican and miner, and his wife Mary, née Thomas, from Adelaide. He remained at the local school as a monitor until he was apprenticed to the printer of the *Talbot Leader*. After five years he joined the Victorian Education Department as a pupil-teacher and in 1903 became principal of two part-time bush schools. Two years later he won a scholarship to Melbourne Teachers' College whence he matriculated to the University of Melbourne (B.Sc., Hons I, 1912; Dip. Ed., 1913).

Fenner resumed teaching at Sale High School and Mansfield Agricultural High School, where he was headmaster. On 4 January 1911 he had married Emma Louise Hirt, a teacher, at Christ Church Cathedral, Ballarat. From 1914 he lectured in geology and mineralogy at the Ballarat School of Mines, where he was later principal, and completed research for the degree of D.Sc. (1917). In 1919 his work 'Physiography of the Werribee River area' won the Sachse [q.v.] medal and ten years later he won the David Syme [q.v.6] research prize, an honour also awarded in 1949 to his second son Frank.

From 5 November 1916 Charles Fenner was superintendent of technical education in South Australia. The *Register* introduced him as 'a leading educational authority . . . a grand organizer and teacher' with 'fine powers of lucid expression'. Although theoretically in an ideal position to influence the department's activities, he was frustrated by having to work within a pre-established framework, by the financial constraints of a world war and the Depression, by political procrastination, by opposition to his proposed reforms and by ill health. His plans for a unified technical education system were undermined by the autonomous South Australian School of Mines and Industries and by delays, until 1940, in expanding secondary technical education on the model of Thebarton Technical School (opened 1924).

Fenner encouraged innovation, an example being an individual freedom scheme of learning introduced in 1927 at Thebarton. Details of this were outlined by him and the headmaster A. G. Paull in their publication, *Individual freedom* (1928). Fenner's criticisms of traditional schooling, summarized in his *Individual educational requirements for modern citizenship* (1940), were also influential in liberalizing the primary school curriculum. He supported the teaching of technical subjects in high schools and liberal subjects in technical schools. He established a vocational guidance and placement scheme and argued for raising the school leaving age. He was also responsible for technical training courses for unemployed youths during the Depression, and for reconstruction schemes following both world wars. He helped draft the 1917 Technical Education of Apprentices Act which, with its concept of compulsory, part-time, technical study for apprentices, set a precedent for other States. His own experience of the conditions and limitations of traditional apprenticeship provided a valuable guide for this Act, and he always retained 'a soft spot for the lad in overalls'.

Fenner was a figure of his time in stressing the views of education for citizenship, and technical education as a means of providing skilled labour to develop South Australia's industrial base. In other respects he was forward thinking: his proposals and educational articles were based on research on overseas and interstate trends, appraised in the light of local needs and conditions. In 1931 he was a delegate for Australian geographers at the centenary meeting of the British Association for the Advancement of Science in London. In 1937 he investigated education on a world tour sponsored by the Carnegie Corporation of New York. While superintendent of technical education, Fenner had established a course in geography at the University of Adelaide in 1930, retiring to honorary lecturer in charge when he became director of education in 1939.

His directorship coincided with World War II. This exacerbated Fenner's impatience at being unable to effect changes that he had advocated for two decades; he increasingly sought refuge in writing. When he retired in 1946, on grounds of invalidity, he was disappointed to receive no token of his long service; although respected, and nicknamed 'Doc', he never commanded the affection in Education Department circles which his predecessor W.J. Adey [q.v.7] had. When Fenner was first appointed superintendent, regret had been expressed that no South Australian was considered suitable for the job. Local prejudice no doubt contributed both to his difficulty in having his ideas accepted, and to Adey's appointment to the directorship in 1929, despite Fenner's broader and longer experience of high-level administration and his superior intellectual standing.

In retirement Fenner assisted the South Australian Museum in the study of tektites – a field in which he became an authority: he undertook the morphological classification of 10 000 specimens. He belonged to the Adelaide University Theatre Guild, the Dual Club and the Wongana circle. His friend Ivor Hele painted a portrait of him, now held by his eldest son; a second portrait is at Croydon Park College of Further Education. He had always worked for the Royal Society of South Australia and the local branch of the Royal Geographical Society of Australasia of which he was president in 1931-32; he edited the *Proceedings* for many years and inaugurated its Historical Memorials Committee. In 1947 the society awarded him its John Lewis [q.v.] gold medal.

Fenner's publications, collated in the *Proceedings* (1962), include nearly forty educational, historical and scientific research papers. His book *A geography of South Australia and the Northern Territory* (1956) is a revision of two earlier volumes. He also published collections of essays, wrote articles in the *Australasian* under the pseudonym 'Tellurian', and was a contributor to and joint editor of *The centenary history of South Australia* (1936). He died of hypertensive cerebro-vascular disease at Rose Park on 9 June 1955 and was buried in the Centennial Park cemetery. He was survived by his wife, their daughter and four sons.

PP (SA), no 44 for 1917, 1918, 1922, 1924, 1930, 1932, and no 54 for 1946; *Education Gazette* (SA), 17 July 1917, 15 June 1946, 15 July 1955; *SA Teachers' J*, 3 (1917), no 2; *PRGSSA*, 56 (1955), 63 (1962); *Advertiser* (Adel), 6, 22 Sept 1916; *Observer* (Adel), 22 Sept, 21 Oct 1916; K. Karim, The development of government-directed apprentice training in South Australia, 1917-1940 (B.A. Hons thesis, Univ Adel, 1964); L. Trethewey, Post-primary technical education in South Australia, 1915-1945 (M.Ed. thesis, Flinders Univ, 1977); Education Dept (SA), Correspondence files, no 909, 1926, no 1594, 1929 (SAA); information from Prof F. Fenner, ANU, Canb.

LYNNE TRETHEWEY

FENTON, JAMES EDWARD (1864-1950), printer, journalist and politician, was born on 4 February 1864 at Nette Yallock, near Avoca, Victoria, son of John Philip Fenton, a publican originally from Suffolk, and his Scottish wife Catharine, née Taylor.

Fenton was educated at a state school and at 13 became a printer's apprentice with the *Avoca Mail*. When 21 he moved to Melbourne and, after a brief period in Sydney, became a compositor in the Government Printing Office, losing his job in the depression in 1893. He was on the board of management of the Melbourne Typographical Society in 1888-89 and 1891-94. From 1894 until 1903 he was editor and printer of the *Broadford Courier* and in 1904-10, when he travelled the State for the Victorian Butter Factories Co-operative Co., manager-editor of the *Co-operative Dairyman*. On 5 April 1887 at West Melbourne he married Elizabeth Jane Harvey. He was a Methodist lay preacher, and for a time was a member of the Australian Natives' Association.

Fenton failed in three attempts from 1897, as a Liberal, to obtain election to the Victorian Parliament. In 1908 he stood as a Labor candidate, then in 1910 won the Federal seat of Maribyrnong. He soon became well known for his loquacity in the House, as he spoke on a wide range of topics; Melbourne *Punch* in 1911 made much of this 'fault'. Fenton retained his seat easily at succeeding elections, except in 1917 and 1919; he lost votes because he opposed conscription, though he agreed on holding a referendum on the issue. In 1921 he became party whip in the Lower House and was elected to caucus executive, holding both posts until the Scullin [q.v.] ministry was formed. For some years he was a member of the Parliamentary Committees of Public Works and of Public Accounts.

When Labor won the general election of October 1929 Fenton was an obvious choice for cabinet. A champion of the claims of Australian industry, he became minister for trade and customs. With Scullin, his long-standing friend, he was responsible for greatly increasing the scale of protective tariffs through a sequence of new schedules, beginning in November. In December Fenton left Australia to attend the London Naval Conference of January-April 1930. Though he supported the limiting of naval armaments he had little impact on the conference; indeed, like Scullin, he viewed his journey, which extended to North America, as an exercise in trade promotion as much as one in disarmament diplomacy.

Fenton returned just as the immensity of the problems facing the government, including steeply rising unemployment and a growing budgetary deficit, was becoming apparent. In July the cabinet was weakened by the resignation of the treasurer, E. G. Theodore [q.v.], following allegations of corruption while he had been Queensland premier. So in August it was Fenton, not Theodore, who became acting prime min-ister during Scullin's nineteen-weeks absence attending the Imperial conference in London.

Scullin had not intended parliament to meet while he was overseas. However, Fenton and J. A. Lyons [q.v.], the acting treasurer, soon had to recall parliament to consider further cuts in government expenditure so as to reduce the budget deficit. These sittings caused fierce, widely publicized dissension between radical and conservative groups in caucus over anti-Depression policy. Fenton could not quell the argument. 'I find it a way of thorns', he said in September. His stand was conservative. He often spoke to Scullin by telephone, and felt he was defending his views against radical critics. Scullin, on his return, reinstated Theodore as treasurer; he had been active amongst the radical critics in recent months. This apparent act of ingratitude, and the fear that Scullin was about to adopt radical and inflationary financial policies, caused Fenton — and Lyons — to resign their portfolios on 4 February 1931.

Fenton remained in caucus until, in mid-March, he voted against the government on an unsuccessful no-confidence motion. Early in May he joined the newly created United Australia Party led by Lyons, and in November he helped to bring down the Scullin government. The opening of his local election campaign, in the Moonee Ponds town hall, was rowdy, but he held his seat, narrowly. In January he became postmaster-general, ranking fourth in Lyons's ministry. He introduced into parliament in March the legislation which set up the Australian Broadcasting Commission. In June he campaigned in southern and central New South Wales in the State election caused by J. T. Lang's [q.v.] dismissal from office. Four months later he ended several weeks of speculation by resigning his portfolio in protest at cabinet's acceptance of the Ottawa Agreement which he believed threatened Australia's high protectionist policy. He voted against the bill ratifying the agreement.

In 1933 Fenton was still quite prominent in debate, though his range of interests narrowed and he tended to concentrate on the tariff. He lost his seat to Labor's A. S. Drakeford next year. Fenton then lived on his farm near Frankston and for about ten years was a director of Commonwealth Oil Refineries. He was appointed C.M.G. in 1938. He died at Frankston on 2 December 1950 and, after a state funeral, was buried in the Methodist section of Mornington cemetery. His wife had died over twenty-five years earlier; a daughter, also, had predeceased him. He was survived by a son and a daughter.

A burly man, Fenton looked to one newspaper reporter rather as if he ought to have been a senior army officer. In 1911 he was termed a 'wowser'. Socially, he was conservative, politically he was no radical. Though a Labor renegade he was a man of some principle who twice resigned from a cabinet post. He was stolid, an undistinguished if talkative debater, hard-working but of limited talent; he had a weak grasp of parliamentary procedure. He was thrown into a national prominence his abilities did not warrant because of a series of unfortunate accidents which plagued the Labor Party, and because of its shortage of parliamentary talent.

J. Robertson, *J. H. Scullin* (Perth, 1974); *V&P* (LA Vic), 1893, 1(8), p 25; *Argus*, 15 Oct 1900, 18 Dec 1908; *Punch* (Melb), 21 Sept 1911; *Table Talk*, 26 Dec 1929; *SMH*, 31 Jan, 5 Dec 1931, 6, 7 Oct 1932.   J. R. ROBERTSON

FERGUSON, SIR DAVID GILBERT (1861-1941), judge, was born on 7 October 1861 at Muswellbrook, New South Wales, second son of John Ferguson (d. 1862), storekeeper from Scotland, and his native-born wife Elizabeth, née Johnston. He was educated at the Scone national and Church of England schools and finally at Fort Street Model School, Sydney. He returned to Scone for two years and learned shorthand.

Back in Sydney he worked as a clerk in the copyrights office, then was employed by Want & Johnson [qq.v.6,4], solicitors, as a shorthand writer. In 1882 he entered St Andrew's College, University of Sydney (B.A., 1886), and financed his studies by reporting for the *Sydney Morning Herald* and the *Daily Telegraph* and, while living in Brisbane for several months of the year, for Queensland Hansard.

At Woollahra, Sydney, on 16 March 1887 Ferguson married Alice Rosa Annie Curtis. They settled in Sydney to allow him to read for the Bar with Edward Scholes and Cecil Stephen [qq.v.], while working part time for New South Wales Hansard. He was admitted to the Bar on 8 March 1890. While practising, and a member of the Bar Council, Ferguson in 1901-11 was Challis [q.v.3] lecturer in the law of procedure, evidence and pleading at the Sydney University Law School. In 1902 he was a founding vice-president of the Sydney University Law Society (president in 1913). He was a member of the university senate in 1913-34 and was vice-chancellor in 1919.

Appointed as acting judge of the Supreme Court of New South Wales in 1911, Ferguson was confirmed in office in March next year. His judgments were noted for their lucidity and clarity, and he was regarded as an expert in the law of evidence. In 1926 he presided over the action brought by Sister Ligouri [q.v. Brigid Partridge] against Bishop J. W. Dwyer [q.v.]. For much of 1929 he was acting chief justice; he took final leave from the Bench on 6 October 1931.

During World War I he did much for returned soldiers and German prisoners of war and was chairman of the Amelioration Committee. He was royal commissioner inquiring into the Wheat Acquisition Act in 1915, and into the cost of production and distribution of gas in 1918. In his spare time he made a raised model of the entire Anzac area at Gallipoli: it was so accurate that C. E. W. Bean [q.v.7] in his second volume of *The story of Anzac,* used it as an illustration. In 1932 he chaired the Commonwealth royal commission on taxation, which sat for three years; its findings were largely accepted by all Australian governments. In 1934 he was knighted and next year was appointed chairman of the Returned Soldiers and Sailors' Employment Board.

Ferguson divided his time between his Sydney home and his much-loved garden at Bowral. He never completely retired, and early in 1941 was on a committee to study various aspects of law reform. Sir David died in hospital at Woollahra, Sydney, on 2 November and was cremated with Presbyterian forms. He was survived by his wife, daughter and one of his three sons, (Sir) Keith, who became a Supreme Court judge in 1955. His second son Arthur was killed in action in France in 1916.

Cyclopedia of N.S.W. (Syd, 1907); A. B. Piddington, *Worshipful masters* (Syd, 1929); T. R. Bavin (ed), *The jubilee book of the law school of the University of Sydney* (Syd, 1940); M. and E. Macfarlane, *The Scottish radicals* (Syd, 1975); *Aust Law J,* 15 (1941-42), p 213; *State Reports* (NSW), Obit, 1941; *SMH*, 19 May 1921, 7 Oct 1931, 27 May 1932, 4 June 1934, 3 Nov 1941; D. G. Ferguson papers (ML)   J. L. ARTHUR

FERGUSON, EUSTACE WILLIAM (1884-1927), pathologist and entomologist, was born on 24 October 1884 at Invercargill, New Zealand, third son of Scottish parents Rev. John Ferguson [q.v.], Presbyterian minister, and his wife Isabella, née Adie. In 1894 the family moved to Sydney; Eustace completed his education at James Oliver's school at Glebe and at the University of Sydney (M.B., 1908; Ch.M., 1909). He was junior resident medical officer and pathologist at Sydney Hospital in 1908-10. In 1911 he set up in private practice with Dr Walton Smith, but suffered a severe attack of nephritis. At Timbriebungie, near Narromine, on 14 December he married Jessie

Perry, daughter of a grazier. In August next year he became medical officer at Rydalmere Hospital for the Insane and on 18 June 1913 transferred to the Department of Public Health as assistant microbiologist.

Like many entomologists, Ferguson's interest in insects was a passion that became a profession. As a medical student, he was stimulated by the Macleay [q.v.5] Museum at university and its curator George Masters [q.v.5], and within a year of graduation had published his first paper on Amycterides (Coleoptera); it received high praise. He was a gifted collector: H. J. Carter [q.v.7] claimed that among his companions on bush rambles 'I have never met his equal for close observation of natural objects, his vision apparently combining certain telescopic, as well as microscopic qualities'.

In August 1915 Ferguson enlisted in the Australian Imperial Force and, as a captain in the Australian Army Medical Corps, went to London with No.10 Australian General Hospital, then with No.1 Australian Auxiliary Hospital, Harefield. He returned to Australia briefly early next year. In June 1917 he was transferred to No.3 A.G.H. at Abbeville in France, but was sent to Egypt. Promoted major in October, he was in charge of the Anzac Field Laboratory in Palestine from August 1918 until March 1919; he returned to Sydney and was demobilized on 1 September. Overseas he was chiefly engaged in bacteriological work while his knowledge of mosquitoes helped in the control of malaria. He was also interested in the history and archaeology of the old world, studying Roman remains in France, and Egyptology and Assyrian relics in the Middle East.

Ferguson returned to the Department of Public Health in 1919, and succeeded (Sir) John Cleland [q.v.] as principal microbiologist in June 1920. His capacity for systematic observation and morphology were readily applied to microbes. His work on tests for susceptibility to diphtheria and his report on dengue fever were notable. However he made his mark scientifically in medical entomology by his study of fleas, ticks, biting flies and mosquitoes. In 1923 he addressed the second Pan Pacific Science Congress on the distribution in Australia of insects capable of carrying disease, summarizing the state of medical entomology in Australia. He published numerous papers on Amycterides (Coleoptera), Diptera, medical entomology and parasitology, in scientific journals and in the *Reports* of the director-general of public health. In 1926 he received a diploma in public health from the university.

Ferguson's scientific curiosity extended to ornithology and botany: he often sur-prised his friends with his wide knowledge of birds. He was a member from 1908 and president in 1926-27 of the Linnean Society of New South Wales, president of the Royal Zoological Society of New South Wales in 1922-23, a member of the Royal societies of New South Wales and South Australia and of the Royal Institute of Tropical Medicine, London, an associate member of the Australian National Research Council and a member of the Great Barrier Reef Committee. In 1922 he ably pressed for a biological survey of Australia based on the work done by the United States Bureau of Biological Survey.

On 18 July 1927 Ferguson died from nephritis at his home at Wahroonga and was buried in the Presbyterian section of Northern Suburbs cemetery. He was survived by his wife, five sons and an infant daughter.

Aust Museum Mag, 3 (1927), no 4, p 131; *Aust Zoologist*, 5 (1927), p 114, and for publications; *Emu* (Melb), 1 Oct 1927, p 131; Linnean Soc NSW, *Procs*, 53 (1928), p iv; Roy Soc SA, *Trans*, 51 (1927), p 426; *SMH*, 9 Jan 1926.   PETER VALLEE

FERGUSON, JOHN (1830-1906), builder, contractor, mining investor and politician, was born on 15 March 1830 at Kenmore, Perthshire, Scotland, son of John Ferguson, weaver and lead-miner, and his wife Janet, née Ferguson. After a limited education he worked as a ploughboy on the estates of the marquess of Breadalbane. He then trained as a carpenter, working in that trade in Killin and Glasgow before sailing to Sydney at the end of 1855. Over the next five years he was a miner and carpenter at the Mudgee and Ararat, Victoria, goldfields. He also worked as a carpenter in Sydney, before moving to Rockhampton, Queensland, probably in 1862. On 1 March 1862 he had married Eliza Frances Wiley in Sydney.

In Rockhampton Ferguson became a builder in his own right. He constructed a number of buildings, including the first meatworks and cottages at Lakes Creek. He became a member of many public and semi-public bodies and served as a deacon in the Congregational Church. In 1884 he purchased a large share in the Mount Morgan mine. This was a lucrative investment which added greatly to his wealth and he was able to retire from the building trade in 1888.

Ferguson served on the Rockhampton Municipal Council from 1878 until 1890; he was mayor in 1880-81 and 1882-83. In 1881-88 he represented Rockhampton in the Legislative Assembly, at first supporting McIlwraith [q.v.5], then Griffith [q.v.], and in 1894-1906 was a member of the Legislative

Council. Though a poor speaker and not widely read, he worked hard for Rockhampton.

During the 1890s he travelled extensively throughout the world. As president of the Central Queensland Separation League, he visited England as a delegate in 1892. He believed strongly that the Queensland government was neglecting the region, but gossip averred that his elaborate mansion was built on the Athelstane Range in 1890 in expectation of becoming governor of a new colony.

While overseas in 1901 Ferguson, who had long been a supporter of Federation, was nominated as a candidate for the Senate. As he did not return until after the poll, his supporters campaigned for him on the platform of support for free trade and White Australia. Once elected he achieved some prominence as the only Queensland senator to oppose the Pacific islands labourers bill, pleading for a longer period during which the islanders could be phased out of the sugar industry. But old age and illness prevented him from being an active parliamentarian. On 13 October 1903 the Senate declared his seat vacant after he had been absent without permission for two consecutive months during a session. The Commonwealth Electoral Act of 1902 would in any case have prevented his renomination while he held his Legislative Council seat.

Ferguson died of cancer in Sydney on 30 March 1906, survived by his wife, one son and five daughters. He was buried at Waverley cemetery with Congregational forms. His estate, valued for probate at £218319 in Queensland and £12179 in New South Wales, was left to his family. One of his daughters married J. T. Bell [q.v.7], the Queensland politician.

Ferguson was remembered as honest and unassuming. Despite his status and wealth, he was always mindful of his humble origins. His main achievements were at a local level and he was much less successful in colonial and national politics.

V&P (LA, Qld), 1894, 1, p 503; *T&CJ*, 4 Apr 1906; *Morning Bulletin*, 31 Mar 1906, 29 Nov 1924; *Capricornian*, 7 Apr 1906; V. R. de V. Voss, Separatist movements in Central Queensland in the nineteenth century (B.A. Hons thesis, Univ Qld, 1952).

DAVID CARMENT

FERGUSON, JOHN (1852-1925), Presbyterian minister, was born on 27 December 1852 at Shiels, Aberdeenshire, Scotland, third son of William Ferguson, farmer, and his wife Elizabeth, née Mitchell. In 1862, with his parents, he migrated to Otago, New Zealand. On leaving school at 14, he became a pupil-teacher, and also acted as laboratory assistant in the chemistry department at the University of Otago.

Realizing his desire to enter the ministry, the congregation of Knox Church, Dunedin, gave Ferguson a bursary to complete the full course at New College, Edinburgh. Licensed as a probationer by the Free Church presbytery of Deer at Stuartfield, Old Deer, Aberdeenshire, he returned to Otago and was ordained to the ministry on 20 May 1880 and sent to work among the miners at Tuapeka in the Central Otago goldfields. On 4 February 1881 at Dunedin he married Isabella Adie, from Old Deer. Soon he became colleague and successor to Rev A. Stobo at Invercargill, where he remained for fourteen years in full charge. In August 1894 Ferguson was inducted to St Stephen's, Phillip Street, Sydney, the largest Presbyterian congregation in Australia. His ministry in Sydney was very successful.

Ferguson took a full part in Australian religious and public life. He was moderator-general in 1909 and his inaugural address, published as *The economic value of the Gospel*, raised a storm in Melbourne and praise from trade union leaders. W. M. Hughes [q.v.] said, 'The new moderator preaches a gospel all sufficient, all powerful. He grapples with the problems of poverty... he insists on justice being done, though the heavens fall. I advise every citizen to read every word of it'.

Ferguson was a tall, dark-haired man, with a drooping moustache and a commanding presence. An attractive preacher, with a genial and informal friendliness, he seldom forgot a face or a name and few entered St Stephen's without a warm personal greeting. He was admired and respected by all the Churches. His ecumenical interests led him to seek an audience with the Pope on a visit to Rome in 1914, an action that evoked much hostile criticism in Sydney.

As senior Presbyterian chaplain in New South Wales, he preached on many special occasions such as the arrival of H.M.A.S. *Australia* and the memorial services at the end of the South African War and World War I. He was first chairman of the board of the Australian Inland Mission, chairman of the council of the Presbyterian Ladies' colleges at Croydon and Pymble, a member of the councils of Scots College and St Andrew's College, University of Sydney, and vice-president of the Highland Society of New South Wales.

In October 1924 Ferguson collapsed in the pulpit of St Stephen's and died at his house, Atherton, Bayswater Road, on 1 March 1925; he was buried in South Head cemetery. He was survived by his wife, three sons including (Sir) John, judge of the New South Wales Industrial Commission and bibliographer, and Eustace [q.v.] and by two daughters. There is a memorial hall and tablet in St Stephen's, Macquarie Street, Sydney.

Aberdeen Weekly J, 1 May 1925; *Scottish A'sian*, 1925, p 439; *Daily Telegraph* (Melb), 2 Mar 1925; *SMH*, 2, 3 Mar 1925; *Aust Christian World* (Syd), 6 Mar 1925; Ferguson papers (Ferguson Memorial Lib, Syd); Minutes of NSW General Assembly of Presbyterian Church, 1925 (Presbyterian Lib, Assembly Hall Syd).   ALAN DOUGAN

FERGUSON, SIR RONALD CRAWFORD MUNRO; *see* MUNRO FERGUSON

FERGUSON, WILLIAM (1882-1950), trade unionist and Aboriginal politician, was born on 24 July 1882 at Waddai, Darlington Point, New South Wales, second of seven children of William Ferguson, shearer and boundary rider from Scotland, and his wife Emily, née Ford, formerly an Aboriginal housemaid in a prosperous station homestead – she died in childbirth in 1895. Ferguson's brief education (1895-96) came from nearby Warangesda mission school. Working in Riverina shearing sheds from 1896, he later became shed organizer for the Australian Workers' Union. On 18 February 1911 at Narrandera Presbyterian Church he married Margaret Mathieson Gowans, domestic servant of Carrathool, whom he had known as a station-manager's daughter at Darlington Point; they lived at Santigo near Narrandera, but travelled about for shearing work. The family settled in 1916 at Gulargambone, where Ferguson re-formed the local branch of the Australian Labor Party, being its secretary for two years. In 1920-24 he worked as mailman between Quambone and Gular, but returned to shearing. From 1928 he took labouring jobs, speaking in his union on reform of government relief work. He settled his wife and twelve children at Dubbo permanently in 1933.

Ferguson had been aware since the early 1920s of the control imposed on the Aboriginal people by the New South Wales Aborigines Protection Board, which expected Aboriginals of mixed descent to 'absorb' into society, and others to die out. Young men expelled from reserves by managers became bushworkers. Inspectors took girls away for training as domestic servants; 'pocket-money' was held in trust. When parliament amended the Aborigines Protection Act (1909) in 1936 to increase the powers of the board, Ferguson began organizing the 'dark people'. On 27 June 1937 he launched the Aborigines' Progressive Association at Dubbo, opening branches later on reserves. In November he was a witness before the Legislative Assembly's select committee on the administration of the Aborigines Protection Board; when the proceedings failed to initiate reform Ferguson, with two Aboriginal leaders, William Cooper and John Patten [qq.v.], organized a 'Day of Mourning' conference for Aboriginals, on Australia Day, 1938. That year Patten and Ferguson wrote the pamphlet, *Aborigines claim citizen rights!*, and petitioned the prime minister J. A. Lyons [q.v.], for a national Aboriginal policy.

From 1938 Ferguson organized the A.P.A., conducting five annual conferences in country towns, formulating its policies, arranging publicity and welfare work. Among his assistants were Pearl Gibbs, Herbert Groves and William Onus, and a few white people. The Aborigines Welfare Board, replacing the old Protection Board, in 1940, was concerned with 'assimilating' Aboriginals to European ways, in nuclear families. Responding to A.P.A. demands for democratic rights, the government in 1943 had two Aboriginal representatives elected to the board. Against many candidates Ferguson won easily, but could not sit at first because officials vetoed Walter Page's nomination; but Aboriginal voters later confirmed Page in office.

Ferguson was with the Welfare Board in 1944-49. Listening to complaints from reserve residents, he was astounded at the poor conditions. He demanded an inquiry into Menindee Aboriginal station, and though the board exonerated the manager, it recommended finding a better site. In July 1946 board members resolved to ask Ferguson to resign but next month reinstated him. Despite better housing, state school education in reserves and welfare work, segregation remained, and Ferguson denounced individual exemption from the Act as conditional citizenship.

By February 1949, Ferguson was vice-president of the New South Wales branch of the Australian Aborigines' League, a national body with Onus as president. In June it sent a deputation to Canberra, asking for many administrative reforms drafted by Ferguson. Ben Chifley's minister for the interior, H. V. Johnson, was unresponsive; Ferguson, furious, left for Sydney intending to stand for parliament. Both political parties, he felt, ignored Aboriginal welfare; resigning from the Labor Party, he stood as Independent for Lawson, the Dubbo seat, in the December elections. The United Nations Declaration of Human Rights inspired his policy of civil rights for all people; but he won only 388 votes. He collapsed after his final speech, and died of hypertensive heart disease on 4 January 1950 in Dubbo Base Hospital.

Ferguson habitually checked his facts with reserve residents before attacking official policies on land, housing and control, and he inspired young Aboriginals to take up politics. The A.P.A. resolutions, mostly Ferguson's work, were ahead of their time. He stood tall, with a calm and reliable manner, and his strong Presbyterian faith supported his pride in Aboriginal people.

J. Horner, *Vote Ferguson for Aboriginal freedom* (Syd, 1974); NSW Public Service report, Aug 1938, *and* Sel cttee on administration of Aborigines Protection Board, Procs . . . *PP* (NSW), 1938-40, 7; *Abo Call*, 1 (1938), no 2, p1, no 3, p2; *SMH*, 27 Jan, 18 Apr 1938, 14, 15 Feb, 26 Nov, 3 Dec 1949; *Smith's Weekly* (Syd), 18 June 1949; A. T. Duncan, A survey of the education of Aborigines in New South Wales . . . (M.Ed. thesis, Univ Syd, 1970); Aborigines Protection Board, Minutes (NSWA).

JACK HORNER

FERRY, MICHAEL AUGUSTUS (1872-1943), pioneer racing commentator, was born on 24 November 1872 at Albury, New South Wales, second son of Irish parents Bryan Ferry, servant and later grazier, and his wife Bridget, née Ferry. By 1894 he was a grazier at Bullenbong, near Hanging Rock; defeated by the long drought, he was working as a labourer in Sydney in 1898-1900. About 1900 he went to Perth and in May next year his appointment as a racecourse detective, at a guinea ($2.10) a meeting, was confirmed by the West Australian Turf Club. In 1904 he was employed as a wool-classer. He later claimed to have been a steward and handicapper in the West and the Riverina. He was associated with A. E. Cochran, owner of the Belmont Park racecourse, who in 1905 sent him to France, Britain and the United States of America looking for bloodstock.

By 1908 Mick Ferry had set up as a horse-dealer at Wagga Wagga, New South Wales, and bought and sold horses for the Indian market. In 1911 he gathered together a team of rough-riders and buck-jumpers which he took to England, probably for the Festival of Empire. About 1923 Ferry left Wagga and moved to Randwick, Sydney where he worked as a labourer. At his own suggestion, in 1925 he began early morning broadcasts of the training gallops for radio station 2FC (then a private company). They proved so popular that he was asked to do race commentaries — his first big race broadcast was the Australian Jockey Club Easter meeting in 1925.

At first commentators were not allowed on racecourses. At Canterbury Ferry broadcast from a fowlyard, often feeding the birds to keep them quiet, and at Moorefield his stand was outside the course at the top of the straight — in the final drive to the winning post he could see only the horses' rumps, which made it difficult to pick the places, especially in big fields. By October 1926 2FC had a private stand at Randwick. Ferry spoke in 'clear incisive tones' and allowed 'a little of the excitement . . . to creep into his voice'. He often called a horse during the race as '100 to 1 on' to win, and was never nonplussed if it failed. From 1932 he continued his broadcasts for the Australian Broadcasting Commission.

In addition to actual race broadcasts, Ferry clocked the training gallops and reported back on form over 2FC long before the newspapers appeared. He attended and reported on the annual yearling sales, took part in ball-to-ball descriptions of Test matches and was racing correspondent for several Queensland newspapers. Until his last illness he supplied the A.B.C. with acceptances and results as well as assisting with race commentaries.

Ferry died from cancer at the Sacred Heart Hospice, Darlinghurst, on 5 April 1943 and was buried in the Catholic section of Botany cemetery. He was survived by his wife Julia née Condon, whom he had married in Sydney on 25 October 1927; she celebrated her hundredth birthday in 1972 and died on 6 November 1975.

Wireless Weekly, 22 Oct 1926; *Listener In*, 10 Sept 1932; *ABC Weekly*, 24 Apr-5 May 1943; *Radio Active*, Nov 1972; *SMH*, 6 Apr 1943, 26 Jan 1972.

MARTHA RUTLEDGE

FERRY, THOMAS ARTHUR (1877-1963), public servant, was born on 14 March 1877 at St George, Queensland, son of Thomas Ferry, grazier, and his wife Margaret, née Ward. After a state school education, Ferry entered the public service on 21 September 1898 as fisheries clerk in the Marine Department at Thursday Island, where on 8 November 1902 he married Gertrude Elizabeth Maude Collis; they had two children.

Transferring the same year to the office of the clerk of petty sessions on the island, Ferry served later at Charleville, Brisbane, Chillagoe, Mackay, Cairns and Townsville before being appointed police magistrate at Ingham on 1 July 1914. While clerk of petty sessions at Mackay in March 1909-March 1911, he had the unusual distinction of being also a director of the North Eton Central Sugar Mill. He went to Cairns in 1916 as police magistrate and, from 1 January 1917, was also both industrial magistrate and chairman of the northern Railway Appeal Board from mid-1919. His ability in industrial negotiation was highly commended by Chief Justice T. W. McCawley [q.v.] after settlement of the Fairymead sugar-workers' strike in 1919. Ferry's skill in assessing evidence soon led to the first of a long series of appointments to conduct special inquiries, when in 1916 he investigated charges made against his predecessor in Cairns by the local police. In 1918 with H. I. Jensen [q.v.], he investigated government expenditure at Croydon on a search for a lost gold reef.

In March 1920 the Theodore [q.v.] government appointed Ferry commissioner of prices under the Profiteering Prevention Act 1920, a move which annoyed certain sections of the commercial world. Appointed an electoral redistribution commissioner in 1921, he became acting under-secretary of the Chief Secretary's Department on 23 November 1922, permanent from 20 April 1923. From August 1924 he was a member of the State Stores Board. Ferry was appointed a full-time member of the Board of Trade and Arbitration on 5 March 1928 but retained his prices post till 15 December 1938. In the meantime he had become a conciliation commissioner on 23 January 1930, and served in industrial arbitration until his retirement from the bench on 31 January 1947.

Throughout his career the special tasks recurred. In 1925-26 he conducted a royal commission on the social and economic effects of the increase of aliens in North Queensland; although naive in many respects, his report was in general fair to the Italian migrants. Further royal commissions followed in 1926 on unemployment among waterside workers and in 1929-30 on the mining industry. He investigated the disposal of sapphires at Anakie in February 1928 and chaired a royal commission on the mining industry in 1929-30. In 1935-36 he chaired another royal commission − into racing and gaming. From 11 January 1934 Ferry chaired the Central Coal Board. He was an electoral redistribution commissioner in the same year as well as chairman of the Licensing Commission from 1935. An opposition member disclosed in parliament in 1936 that, because of his many offices, Ferry earned £52 more in the current year than did the chief justice. At his farewell from the service, his 'fair and conscientious work' on the bench was noted. He died in Brisbane Hospital on 26 May 1963 and was buried in Nudgee cemetery with Roman Catholic rites.

W. D. Borrie, *Italians and Germans in Australia* (Melb, 1954); *Queenslander,* 16 Apr 1921; *Brisbane Courier,* 3 Mar 1928, 24 Jan 1930; *Courier Mail,* 27 May 1963.

FETHERSTON, RICHARD HERBERT JOSEPH (1864-1943), medical practitioner, was born on 2 May 1864 at the Melbourne Lying-in Hospital (now Royal Women's Hospital), son of Gerald Henry Fetherston (1829-1901), resident surgeon, and his wife Sarah Ellen, née Harvey, who had been matron. His father, born in County Roscommon, Ireland, had settled in Melbourne in 1860 after several years as a ship's surgeon.

'Bertie' Fetherston was educated at Wesley College and the Alma Road Grammar School. In 1881 he went to Dublin, where he was admitted as licentiate of the Royal College of Surgeons in Ireland (1884) and licentiate in medicine and midwifery, King and Queen's College of Physicians in Ireland (1885). He then went to the University of Edinburgh where he graduated (M.B., Ch.M., 1886). His thesis for M.D. was accepted by that university in 1888 and he received the M.D., Melbourne (*ad eund*) the next year.

Returning to Melbourne in 1887, Fetherston joined his father in Prahran. However, he soon accepted appointment as resident medical officer at the Women's Hospital. His father was a member of the honorary staff there and when he retired in 1891, Fetherston succeeded him, serving until 1914 when he resigned to accept appointment as the first honorary gynaecologist to the (Royal) Melbourne Hospital. He retired from there in 1924. At both hospitals he was a successful clinical teacher and lecturer and was an examiner for the University of Melbourne. In 1891 he had recommenced working in Prahran. He took in a partner, R. N. Wawn, in 1911, started in Collins Street specializing in obstetrics and gynaecology the following year, and left the Prahran practice in 1913.

As had his father, Fetherston served Prahran well as medical officer and as local councillor. In 1921 he was elected to the Legislative Assembly, but found politics not to his liking and retired in 1924. He was also medical officer to the Blind and Deaf and Dumb asylums and to Wesley College. His many posts in the British Medical Association included president in 1911 of the Victorian branch, founder-member in 1912 of the federal committee, and director of the Australasian Medical Publishing Co. He remained a councillor of the Victorian branch and a trustee of the Medical Society of Victoria until his death − in 1935 he was elected a vice-president of the parent body when it held its annual meeting in Melbourne, a signal honour. He was a fellow of the College of Surgeons of Australasia (1927).

Fetherston's contributions were perhaps greatest in the military sphere. He was gazetted surgeon with the relative rank of captain in the Victorian Militia in 1887 and had attained the rank of lieut-colonel at the outbreak of World War I. He volunteered for active service but on 15 August 1914 was appointed director-general of medical services, based in Melbourne, with the task of raising the medical service for the Australian Imperial Force. In 1915 he made a tour of inspection and reorganization of the Australian Army Medical Corps, visiting Egypt, Gallipoli and England. He was promoted major general in 1916 and made another inspection tour in 1918. He was retired at his own request shortly after the end of the war.

Despite a meagre staff, small salary and frustration at not being released for active service, Fetherston worked with remarkable energy and enthusiasm. Official historian A. G. Butler [q.v.7] paid tribute to his 'absolute impartiality' and wholehearted devotion to duty. Fetherston had urged the appointment of (Sir) Neville Howse [q.v.] as director-general of medical services overseas and continued to support him, though obliged to implement government policies such as acceptance of lower standards of fitness for recruits, which Howse strenuously opposed. Major General Rupert Downes [q.v.] remembered Fetherston's decisiveness, hatred of humbug, and fearlessness 'both moral and physical'.

Fetherston was short, compact in build, and bearded. Imperturbable and shrewd, he was ready to give sound advice and sensible help. He was a follower of outdoor sports and a member of the Melbourne Cricket and Victoria Racing clubs. On 4 July 1894 he had married Victoria Amelia Gourlay at South Yarra Presbyterian Church. He died at his St Kilda home on 3 June 1943, survived by two sons and a daughter. He is remembered by the medical profession by the triennial Fetherston Memorial Lecture on a subject relating to maternal welfare.

A. G. Butler (ed), *Official history of the Australian Medical Services . . . 1914-18,* 1, 2, 3 (Melb 1930, Canb 1940, 1943); C. E. Sayers, *The Women's* (Melb, 1956); *MJA,* 21 Aug, 11 Sept 1943, 12 Jan 1957; *Age* and *Argus,* 4 June 1943; Fetherston papers (Roy Women's Hospital, Melb, Archives), *and* (AWM).   FRANK M. C. FORSTER

FEWINGS, ELIZA ANN (1857-1940), schoolteacher, was born probably on 28 December 1857 at Bristol, England, daughter of Charles Fewings, boot-closer, and his wife Sarah, née Twining. Registered as Ann, she adopted Eliza later. Trained as a teacher by her brother, then head of King Edward VI Grammar School, Southampton,

she worked as an assistant in the Roan School, Greenwich, in 1876-86 and became a successful head of Dr Williams's Endowed High School for Girls, Dolgelly, Wales.

Miss Fewings was appointed head of the Brisbane Girls' Grammar School in 1896. Early in 1899 she was charged with academic and managerial incompetence by the school's board of trustees, largely on the unsupported accusations of her first assistant, Maud Sellers, a woman of some academic distinction. Miss Fewings was questioned in private by the board's chairman Sir Samuel Griffith and John Laskey Woolcock [qq.v.], both experienced barristers; her request for an independent inspection was refused and she was dismissed. Despite meetings of parents, censuring Griffith and the board, appeals to the minister and accusations of injustice in the *Brisbane Courier,* the trustees refused to change their verdict. The dismissal gave impetus to existing moves for closer government control of the grammar schools; the Grammar Schools Act Amendment Act (1900) introduced inspection by the Department of Public Instruction.

A new headmistress was appointed to the deeply divided Grammar School and Miss Sellers in her turn was dismissed, allegedly for insulting and insubordinate conduct — she left Queensland for a distinguished career in teaching and scholarship in New South Wales and England.

Urged by some parents, Miss Fewings established the Brisbane High School for Girls (Somerville House) with thirty-one students in October 1899. Based on English models, it became the largest girls' secondary school in Queensland in three years with 150 students. She was a committee-member of the University Extension Movement, was on the board of the School of Arts and was a foundation member of the Field Naturalists' Club. As a councillor of the Brisbane Technical College, she played an active part in a conflict with the Board of Technical Education over college staffing policies. She visited England in 1900, and in 1905 inspected educational institutions in North America as well as England. While visiting Wales in 1908 she was appointed warden of Alexandra Hall, a women's residential establishment in University College, Aberystwyth, and returned to Brisbane only to dispose of her school.

After establishing the first Young Womens' Christian Association centre in Wales, Miss Fewings retired in 1914 but remained on the Court of Governors and the Council of the University College. She was also a governor of Dr Williams's School at Dolgelly. She visited Brisbane in 1921, received an honorary M.A. from Aberystwyth in 1931 and died at Bristol on 11 October 1940.

Small with a firm jaw, Eliza Fewings was an able speaker whose determined views were strengthened by her financial independence. Despite her absence of academic qualifications she earned the respect and affection of students and colleagues.

P. G. Freeman, *History of Somerville House* (Brisb, 1949); *Brisb High School for Girls Mag*, 1902-08; *Dr Williams's School Mag*, July 1941, p 3 (copy Gwynedd Archives, Wales); *Brisbane Courier*, 20 Sept 1899; *Queenslander*, 7 Oct 1899, 9 July 1921; MS 4531, Fewings papers (NL).

E. CLARKE

FIASCHI, THOMAS HENRY (1853-1927), surgeon, and PIERO FRANCIS BRUNO (1879-1948), medical practitioner, were father and son. Thomas was born on 31 May 1853 at Florence, Italy, son of Lodovico Fiaschi, a professor of mathematics at the University of Florence, and his English-born wife Clarissa, née Fisher, who had tutored the children of Prince Corsini of Florence. He enrolled at the university as a medical student and at 21 left for Australia, where he was on the north Queensland goldfields before becoming a 'house surgeon' at St Vincent's Hospital, Sydney. At Bethel House, George Street, Sydney, on 17 February 1876 he married with Congregational forms Irish-born Catherine Ann Reynolds, a nun from St Vincent's. They returned to Florence where in 1877 he graduated M.D. and Ch.D. (Pisa and Florence). Their first son, Lodovico (d. 1944), who was mentally retarded, was born there. In 1878 Thomas was licensed to practice medicine and surgery in Italy and, after a short time in London, reached Sydney with his family in the *Garonne* in February 1879.

Fiaschi practised at Windsor, and in 1883 moved to Sydney, where he was active in the New South Wales branch of the British Medical Association (president 1889-90). In 1890 he published *A viso aperto* . . . on the Italian community and the maritime strike. In March 1891 he became honorary surgeon captain in the New South Wales Lancers and in 1894 honorary surgeon to Sydney Hospital. He served with the Italian Army in Abyssinia in 1896, was made a knight of the Order of St Maurice and St Lazarus, and commander of the Order of the Crown of Italy; he wrote about the war in *Da Cheren a Cassala. Note di viaggio* (Florence, 1896) and about the mutilation and eviration of Italian prisoners of war in the *British Medical Journal*. After visiting Italy, he returned home through the United States of America,

where he studied advances in aseptic and abdominal surgery. In 1897 he moved to 149 Macquarie Street.

During the South African War Fiaschi was promoted major, commanded the New South Wales 1st Field Hospital and was senior medical officer with General (Sir) Edward Hutton's [q.v.] brigade. In February 1900, while searching for wounded in the Boer trenches, he received the surrender of Cronje's forces. For conspicuous bravery and devotion to duty he was awarded the Distinguished Service Order, and was twice mentioned in dispatches. On his return he was promoted lieut-colonel in the Commonwealth forces, was honorary surgeon to the governors-general in 1902-09, and in 1911 became principal medical officer of the 2nd Military District with the rank of colonel. In 1909 he was chairman of the board of medical studies at Sydney Hospital, and in 1911 became honorary consulting surgeon.

On 25 April 1910 his third son, Carlo Ferruchio, a medical practitioner, died from a self-administered overdose of morphia. In March 1910 Carlo and a nurse had been acquitted on a charge of manslaughter of a patient on whom he had operated; his death and burial with Anglican rites revived the sectarian bitterness surrounding his mother's past and marriage. Fiaschi was asked by the superior general of the Sisters of Charity to withdraw from St Vincent's private hospital pavilion. He did so and gave the correspondence to the *Daily Telegraph*, protesting against 'mere religious rancor'.

On 10 August 1913 Fiaschi's wife died in Sydney, and on 19 August 1914 he married with Anglican rites Amy Curtis, a nurse, at Christ Church, Bundaberg, Queensland. In May 1915 Fiaschi left Sydney for Lemnos, where he commanded the 3rd Australian General Hospital before being invalided to England with beriberi in November. On recovery he went to Italy, where in July 1916 he temporarily resigned his commission in the Australian Imperial Force, to be surgeon in a military hospital at Schio in the Trentino; he was accompanied by his wife who worked as a nurse in the Italian Red Cross Society. They returned to Australia in October 1917 and he joined the Australian Army Medical Corps Reserve as colonel, retiring in January 1921 as an honorary brigadier-general.

Fiaschi was a bold and enterprising practitioner and a good teacher; his keenness did not fade with the years. He did pioneering work in Listerian surgery, the treatment of exophthalmic goitre, hydatid disease and in bone surgery which, according to Dr Archie Aspinall, was his best work. He translated Bassini's text on hernia, and published several papers. He was a president of the Australasian Trained Nurses' Association.

Tall and handsome with keen, searching eyes, fine physique and erect military bearing, Fiaschi was a dignified and imposing figure. Though quick-tempered, he readily forgave and never bore a grudge. He had a keen sense of humour and anecdotes about him abound. A man of wide culture, he was well read in both the general and medical literature of Italy and France. On his professional jubilee in July 1926 he was honoured by a wide section of the community; he was presented with a portrait of himself by Dattilo Rubbo [q.v.], a gold medal from the Dante Alighieri Art and Literary Society (of which he was a founder and president) and a book of autographs illuminated by W. Hardy Wilson [q.v.].

Also an expert viticulturist, Fiaschi was a firm believer in wine as a medicament; he planted the Tizzana vineyard on the Hawkesbury, another near Mudgee and had cellars in Little George Street, Sydney. He was president of the Australian Wine Producers' Association of New South Wales in 1902-27, a councillor of the Royal Agricultural Society of New South Wales and an active member of the local Royal Society.

Fiaschi died at his son's home at Darling Point on 17 April 1927 and was buried in the Anglican section of Waverley cemetery. He was survived by two sons and two daughters of his first marriage and two daughters of his second; his daughter Clarissa (d. 1975), became the Marchesa Torrigiani. His estate was valued for probate at £11 137.

His second son Piero, born on 5 March 1879 at Windsor, went to the United States, where he graduated from the New York College of Dentistry in 1903 and M.D. in 1905 from Columbia University; in 1906 he qualified M.R.C.S. (England) and L.R.C.P. (London) and next year returned to practise in Sydney. In 1909 he became a part-time officer in the A.A.M.C. and, serving in Egypt, Gallipoli, France and England during World War I, rose to lieut-colonel, was mentioned in dispatches and was appointed O.B.E. Discharged in February 1919, he spent some time in the United States before returning home. On 31 January 1917 at All Souls Parish Church, Marylebone, London, he had married Grace Horwood Thompson.

Fiaschi set up a highly successful practice at 178 Phillip Street, became a genito-urinary specialist and an authority on venereal disease: 'the *condottiere* of Phillip Street', he refused to move when Macquarie Street became fashionable for the profession. He was clinical assistant at Sydney Hospital in 1936-46.

From March 1921 to April 1935, when he was placed on the retired list, he held a number of medical appointments in the militia: he commanded the 9th Field Ambulance, 1927-28, the 4th Cavalry Field Ambulance, 1928-30, and in 1930-32 was acting director of medical services of the 1st Cavalry Division of 2nd Military District. In 1939-48 he was honorary medical officer to the South African War Veterans' Association of New South Wales and in 1941-42 senior member of the mixed medical commission inspecting prisoner of war camps. He was a familiar figure in Sydney's Anzac Day march.

Tall, lanky with an aquiline face, dark, sad eyes and booming voice, Piero was a strange mixture of bluntness and sensitivity. His war experience had affected him deeply. Although outwardly abrupt, he was inwardly shy; with many lovable qualities, he combined the hospitableness and stubbornness of the northern Italian with the generosity and impetuosity of the Irish. He was full of contradictions: to his friend H. M. Moran [q.v.] he was 'the stormy one'; to E. Haslett Fraser, in Goldoni's words, a *'burbero benefico'* (a repiner with a heart of gold). Piero was intensely fond and proud of his father, and like him the subject of many anecdotes.

He died in Sydney Hospital on 15 June 1948 from burns received when a spirit heater he was lighting exploded. He was survived by his wife and child, a daughter, and buried in the Anglican section of Waverley cemetery.

Father and son are commemorated by a life-sized bronze replica of the famous Florentine *Porcellino* monument outside Sydney Hospital, which was donated to the city by the Marchesa Torrigiani in 1967.

H. M. Moran, *Viewless winds* (Lond, 1939), and *Beyond the hills lies China* (Lond, 1945); *MJA*, 14 May 1927, 30 Dec 1933, 15 Apr 1939, 4 Sept, 16 Oct 1948; *Windsor and Richmond Gazette*, 7 Mar 1891, 4 June 1926; *SMH*, 13 Oct 1896, 29 Jan, 22, 23 Mar, 28 Apr 1910, 30 Oct 1917, 27 May, 14, 21, 22, 25 July 1926, 18 Apr 1927, 12 Jan 1940, 18 June 1948, 22 Aug 1967; *Daily Telegraph* (Syd), 3-7 May 1910; information from Mrs P. N. Morison, Canb.

G. P. WALSH

FIDLER, ISABEL MARGARET (1869-1952), tutor to women students, and MABEL MAUDE (1871-1960), headmistress, were born on 21 March 1869 in Sydney and 2 March 1871 at Wollongong, New South Wales, second and third of five children of William Fidler (d. 1874), Wesleyan minister, and his wife Alice Maude Bedford (formerly Brennand). William Fidler, son of a Wesleyan missionary, was born in Trinidad and arrived in Australia in 1857. Isabel and Mabel were educated to matriculation level at Emily Baxter's Argyle School in Surry Hills. Isabel won the Fairfax [q.v.4] prize at the junior public examination in 1884 and was first *prox. acc.* at the senior examination in 1887. Mabel shared the senior Fairfax prize in 1889.

Isabel entered the University of Sydney in 1895 and graduated B.A. in 1898 with first-class honours in English, French and Latin. Two years later she took up duties as tutor to the women students. Although at first she offered tutorial assistance in Latin and French, she increasingly tried to improve the conditions for women students, promoting their awareness of the opportunities and obligations of university life. She was president of the Sydney University Women's Association (Union) in 1903 and 1908. The senate's decision in 1914 to provide a building for women's activities within the university led to the reorganization of the women's union. The years 1915-21, when Isabel Fidler was its president, saw the building of (Sir W. M) Manning [q.v.5] House and the organization of its administration under the women's union. She was president again in 1923-25 and 1927-28. Thereafter as vice-president, with her office located in Manning House, she provided administrative guidance until she retired in 1939. Her services were recognized when its reading room was named the Isabel Fidler Room.

A foundation committee-member of the Sydney University Women Graduates' Association, Isabel was president in 1928 and later a vice-president. In 1946 she was appointed an honorary life vice-president. Her concern for the status of women in public and social life led her to support the National Council of Women of New South Wales. She was convenor of its education committee in 1912-37 and vice-president for about twenty years. A vice-president of the Sydney University Women's Society (Sydney University Women's Settlement) 1900-21, chairman of committees (1921-32) and president of the reorganized and renamed Sydney University Settlement (1932-45), and a vice-president (1945-52) she was active in the acquisition and maintenance of the centre in Edward Street, Chippendale, and the development of its clubs for the children and women of the area. Her recognition of the need for professional training in social work led her to support the Board of Social Studies and Training from its inception in 1928; she was a member of the executive committee (1928-33) and vice-president 1934-40.

Small in stature, composed in manner, Isabel Fidler enjoyed the formal life of the university. She was appointed M.B.E. in 1939. She died on 5 June 1952 in hospital at Lindfield and was cremated with Baptist forms. Her portrait by W. A. Bowring, painted in 1931, hangs in Manning House, and a memorial garden is located nearby.

Mabel Fidler was a governess for some years. This experience and the example of Emily Baxter encouraged her· to open a school when she and her sisters built a house at Gordon in 1899, which they named Ravenswood. The school, opened in 1901 on land adjacent to the house, shared its name and grew rapidly as a non-sectarian, private day place for girls. By 1924, when it was sold to the Methodist Church, it was the largest of its type in Sydney, with an enrolment of 180, and was highly regarded for the quality of its teaching and its achievements in sport. Mabel Fidler took a personal interest in the pupils from kindergarten to leaving certificate. A quiet woman, restrained and firm in manner, she attracted well-qualified and enthusiastic teachers; she was a vice-president of the Classical Association of New South Wales. She retired from Ravenswood in 1925.

Both sisters then moved to Pymble where Mabel kept house and cultivated the garden which they both loved. Her last years were spent with her sister-in-law at Chatswood where she died in hospital on 25 February 1960 and was cremated with Presbyterian forms.

W.C.O'R., *Ravenswood in retrospect* (Syd, 1952); A. G. McGrath, *A short history of the N.S.W. Association of University Women Graduates* (Syd, 1970); National Council of Women of NSW, *Seventy five years, 1896-1971* (Syd, 1971); Univ Syd Union, *Union Recorder*, 16 Apr 1931, 30 Mar 1939, 19 June 1952, 27 Nov 1952, 9 July 1964; Univ Syd Women's Settlement, *Annual report*, 1932-53 (ML); Board of Social Study and Training, Annual report, and minutes, 1928-1940, *and* Senate minutes, *and* Univ Syd Women's Union, Minutes of Board meetings (Univ Syd Archives).

MARJORIE JACOBS

FIELD, EDWARD PERCY (1855-1928), barrister and evangelist, was born on 7 October 1855 in the Mahableshwar Hills, Bombay Presidency, India, second son of General Sir John Field (d. 1903), hero of the Abyssinian war of 1867-68, and his wife Aletta Hendrina, née Faure, daughter of a Dutch clergyman of Huguenot descent. Field had a good classical education at Clifton College, Bristol, and Repton School, Derbyshire, ending with a year at Corpus Christi College, Cambridge. In August 1876 he left Gravesend, England, by the sailing ship *Lady Allen* for New Zealand where he worked for a time in the Public Works Department and afterwards as a teacher. On 8 June 1879 he arrived in Sydney, sailing before the mast in a small barque with dreadful food and quarters. After working briefly as a docker and as a free-lance journalist, he became an assistant master at Sydney Grammar School, under A. B. Weigall [q.v.6], who was a friend of General Field. On 25 January 1883 at St John's Anglican Church, Darlinghurst, Field married Edith Bell Cox, daughter of a Mudgee grazier and a descendant of Edward Cox [q.v.3] and Archibald Bell [q.v.1]; she bore him three sons and a daughter.

To obtain funds to study law, Field gave scientific lectures and wrote for newspapers. He published a rather critical report on Sydney Technical College in 1883; its president Judge (Sir) William Windeyer [q.v.6], published a gross libel of Field's motives and Field sued. The case aroused a great deal of interest in the press. Field won the action defending his own case but the chief justice, Sir James Martin [q.v.5] intervened and annulled the decision. The *Bulletin* on 15 December published a large cartoon over the caption, 'Two to one against the Field!'.

Despite this difficult start Field was admitted to the Bar on 11 February 1884 and was soon successful; but he was stricken down with suspected cancer of the throat. This dramatic experience brought him to Christ. In 1890 he left Sydney with his family to consult a famous surgeon Sir Felix Semon, who told him 'But you have been operated on already!'. Field believed God had cured him. Returning to Sydney he preached in the open air, mainly at Martin Place, Moore Street and Coogee Beach; he visited the sick at Sydney Hospital regularly. A fellow barrister (Sir) George Reid [q.v.] warned him that his activities would interfere with his legal work but Field went ahead with greater zeal, attracting large crowds. Ministers and laymen of various denominations regularly assisted him and Archbishop Saumarez Smith [q.v.] once attended a meeting at Coogee Beach.

Field was an Anglican and a committee-member of the Church Society for the Diocese of Sydney. He preached in churches in various cities and towns and converted the sculler Ned Trickett [q.v.6]. Doctor's orders concerning his health caused his return to England with his family in 1897; he was briefly with Mutual Life Association, then as its secretary he led the Evangelical Alliance in open-air preaching. His wife, who had long resented their loss of income and 'the curtailment of all theatre-going, dances, etc.', left him and returned to Australia in 1908; Field found her departure 'a spiritual blessing'. He also worked as a canvasser of advertisements with the *Westminster Gazette* and in 1912-23 with the *Law Times*. In 1912 he moved with his youngest son to a cottage at Dunton Green, Kent, where he had a 'museum' of geological specimens and a telescope in the garden for his astronomical observations.

Field died of heart disease at Dunton Green on 13 March 1928; his son Archibald, a captain in the Royal Engineers, was killed in action in France in 1916. Field's work in Australia lapsed for a short time but was revived by some of his associates as the 'New South Wales Evangelistic Prayer Band', which in 1922 became Open Air Campaigners, an international and interdenominational organization.

C. H. A. Field, *Sir John Field K.C.B., soldier and evangelist* (Lond, 1908); W. R. Angus, *Truceless warfare* (Melb, 1941); J. A. Duffecy (ed), *Another 'Sherlock Holmes' in England* (New Jersey, USA, 1970); *Bulletin*, 15 Dec 1883; *SMH*, 5 Dec 1883; E. P. Field, Diaries and papers (ML).

JAMES A. DUFFECY

FIELD, ERNEST (1875-1947), agrarian activist, was born probably on 17 September 1875 at Canowindra, New South Wales, son of Albert Thomas Field and his wife Susannah, née Gordon. Educated briefly at Canowindra Public School, he worked as a farm labourer before joining his brother working on a station near Carcoar in 1888. After some years he took to the road, working and shearing in New South Wales and Queensland and gathered sufficient skill to 'ring' the Burra Burra shed in 1897.

After two years in New Zealand Field returned to Australia and took up a leasehold property near Orange. There he met a schoolteacher, Mary Ann Maneary; in accordance with his Plymouth Brethren upbringing, they eschewed a church marriage, and were wed at the Orange registry office on 7 September 1899.

After the expiry of Field's lease and the arrival of rabbits, he worked as a railway navvy for a year until he drew a closer settlement block near Marrar in 1906. Now a bona fide farmer on his own land, Wave Hill, he joined the Marrar branch of the Farmers and Settlers' Association. In 1907-23 he was secretary of the branch. For over a decade from 1912 he was on the council of the Murrumbidgee Pastoral and Agricultural Society and served twice as its vice-president.

During World War I he worked on the Wheat Pool, and by 1919 he was a member of the executive of the F.S.A. and the Wagga Wagga Pastures Protection Board. Next year he was elected to Coolamon Shire

Council. He was involved in drafting the Progressive Party's constitution and in 1921 protested against it joining in the coalition with the National Party. With his wife's counselling and assistance, he stood as a Progresssive for the Legislative Assembly but was defeated for Murray in 1922 and Cootamundra in 1925.

Following the death of 'Mum', his wife, in 1931 Field farmed at Forbes in partnership with H. K. Nock [q.v.]. After disagreements he bought out Nock's share of Tarlemara and succeeded him as president of the F.S.A. in 1933-36. In 1934 in evidence before the royal commission on the wheat industry, he argued against bounties and for the equitable treatment of the wheatgrowing industry. In 1936 he joined the board of the association's newspaper, the *Land*. He was appointed to the Farmers' Relief Board in January 1935 and was in a position to see that the thousands of farmers who applied for government relief got a fair deal. He was regarded as a 'particularly good bloke, but inclined to be a bit heavy handed'.

On the outbreak of World War II Field was appointed to the Australian Wheat Board in his capacity as president of the Australian Wheatgrowers' Federation and served for eight years. His position on the Wheat Board was the culmination of his lifelong dedication to the belief that the farmer could only benefit from orderly marketing. While his experiences in farming, and his single-minded approach to issues led him to expect the same effort in his associates, he thought that farmers collectively should be given assistance they failed to demand.

Field died in hospital at Forbes from coronary vascular disease on 24 July 1947 and was survived by his daughter. He was cremated after a Presbyterian service.

SMH, 18 Nov 1921, 26 Oct 1926, 10 Aug 1933, 1 Mar 1934, 1 Jan, 8 Aug 1935, 14 Sept 1939, 11, 25 July 1947; *Land* (Syd), 3 Mar 1922, 19 Aug 1932, 1 Aug 1947.   S. W. DYER

FIHELLY, JOHN ARTHUR (1882-1945), public servant and politician, was born on 7 November 1882 at Timoleague, Cork, Ireland, son of Cornelius Fihelly, customs officer, and his wife Anne, née McCarthy. The family arrived in Brisbane in September 1883 as migrants on the *Duke of Westminster.* John was educated at the Petrie Terrace State School and St Joseph's College, Gregory Terrace, until October 1895 when he joined the Post Office as a telegraph messenger. He transferred later to the Department of Trade and Customs and in 1908 was a junior clerk in its State office on £60 a year.

Handsome and well-built, Fihelly was an enthusiastic Rugby footballer. An aggressive forward, he represented Queensland against New South Wales in 1905-07, and in 1907 both Queensland and Australia against New Zealand. A founder of the Rugby League code in Queensland and a Queensland and Australia representative player, he was also assistant manager of the first Australian team to visit Britain in 1908-09. He became a referee later. He was president of the Queensland Amateur Rugby League in 1914-16.

Widely read, Fihelly also wrote well, and regularly contributed to the *Worker* from about 1906. He won Paddington for Labor in the Legislative Assembly in April 1912 and in May, with Roman Catholic rites, married Marguerite Agnes, daughter of Peter Murphy [q.v.]. The attorney-general Thomas O'Sullivan [q.v.] wrote that Fihelly added much to the debating strength of the Opposition; 'aggressive, personal and witty, he attacked the man rather than the subject'. Confident, ambitious and a protégé of E. G. Theodore [q.v.], Fihelly became secretary of the party caucus in 1914; with Theodore he was also its principal writer of campaign literature. He was minister without portfolio in the Ryan [q.v.] government in 1915-18. As assistant minister for justice, he was an innovator who revitalized the department. With Ryan and McCawley [q.v.] he drafted the workers' compensation bill; both it and the Insurance Act, 1916, were piloted through parliament by him.

Fihelly's outspoken support of Irish dissidents offended many. After his impassioned denunciation of the British government in September 1916 at a Queensland Irish Association meeting, Governor Goold-Adams [q.v.] refused to speak to him; and Fihelly was suspended from Executive Council meetings until he apologized. Ryan was determined to keep him in the ministry and persuaded caucus to withdraw a censure motion; but colleagues registered their dismay at Fihelly's lack of tact by preferring the junior member J. H. Coyne [q.v.] as secretary for railways. Because of his anti-conscription activities, the pejorative term 'Fihellyism', signifying disloyalty and support for Germany and the Sinn Fein rebels, gained some currency.

Fihelly was so competent, nevertheless, that in April 1918 he was made secretary for railways. He travelled in North America and Europe on departmental business in 1918-19 and instituted a number of important reforms but critics claimed he had no genuine working-class sympathy. Northern unionists particularly found him arrogant and without sympathy for Charters Towers railway men suspended in 1919. It was known that he held shares in several businesses including Cummins [q.v.7] & Campbell of Townsville.

Easily defeated by Theodore in the October 1919 election of a new party leader, Fihelly still won the deputy-leadership. After October 1919 he added the ministry of justice to his railways portfolio and in August 1920, both the treasury and public works. Even for a man of his energy, it was an enormous work-load. In 1919-21 he was also on the senate of the university. Despite his alleged disloyalty, his reception as acting premier of the prince of Wales in 1920 was impeccable.

Fihelly's personal behaviour was becoming embarrassing to the government by 1921 and in June he was defeated by W. J. Dunstan [q.v.] in pre-selection for the Federal seat of Maranoa. In February 1922 he accepted appointment as agent-general. When Theodore decided to negotiate personally in London about maturing loans, Fihelly was furious. Beset also by domestic and emotional problems, he left London early in February 1924 without advising his government, met Theodore in New York and handed him his resignation. It was accepted from 31 March.

Making no further attempt to enter parliament, Fihelly retired into relative obscurity. He won the Paddington ward for Labor in the first 'Greater Brisbane' council elections in February 1925 and held it until 1930; he had defeated E. M. Hanlon in the selection ballot. Late in 1925 he stood unsuccessfully against (Sir) D. C. Cameron [q.v.7] for the Federal seat of Brisbane. In September 1926 his skull was fractured in an accident at Sandgate and from then he steadily deteriorated. In 1930-33 he was employed for short periods in minor capacities by the Queensland government. After several terms in the Dunwich Benevolent Institution, he died of a cerebral thrombosis in Brisbane on 2 March 1945, survived by his wife, their daughter and two sons, one of whom was a prisoner of war. He was buried in Toowong cemetery after a state funeral.

D. J. Murphy, *T. J. Ryan*, and with R. B. Joyce (eds) *Queensland political portraits 1859-1952* (Brisb, 1978); *Daily Standard*, 6 Jan 1913, 20 May, 9 July 1915; *Punch* (Melb), 20 July 1920; *Worker* (Brisb), 9 Feb 1922, 5 Mar 1945; CO 161/165 193/331, 351 418/221/5.   BETTY CROUCHLEY

FINDLEY, EDWARD (1864-1947), compositor, publisher and politician, was born on 8 September 1864 at Sandhurst (Bendigo), Victoria, son of Timothy Findley, engine driver, and his wife Mary, née Toohey. After serving an apprenticeship as a compositor and working on the *Bendigo Independent*, Ted Findley moved to Melbourne in the early 1880s where he was employed as a journeyman compositor on the *Daily Telegraph*. When this closed in 1892 he worked on an evening paper and became active both in the trade union movement and in newspaper publishing. He was elected president of the Australasian Typographical Union in 1897, representing it on the Melbourne Trades Hall Council of which he was president in 1896-97. He served also as president of the Melbourne Eight Hours' Committee and the United Labour Party, and was a councillor of the Melbourne Working Men's College from 1896 to 1900.

In 1894 Findley, with G. M. Prendergast [q.v.] and others, established the *Boomerang*, 'a real live weekly paper run on democratic lines'. Only eight issues appeared, between August and October. He was more successful when in 1896 he was part of the group, including J. P. Jones, Bernard O'Dowd [qq.v.], Prendergast and others, which established the labour weekly *Tocsin*. Findley, with Prendergast, was responsible for the technical and printing aspects of the publication, and at various times he was nominally manager or printer and publisher.

Late in 1900 Findley entered the Victorian Legislative Assembly as Labor member for Melbourne, his election being aided by a split vote among his three Liberal opponents. But on 25 June 1901, soon after he had taken his seat, he was expelled from the assembly for seditious libel. *Tocsin*, on which Findley's name appeared as printer and publisher, had reprinted on 20 June, as part of an article on the freedom of the press, an item libelling King Edward VII which had first appeared in the Dublin *Irish People* and had led to that newspaper's suppression. Findley was held by the assembly to be responsible for the content of *Tocsin* and was accordingly expelled by a vote of 64-17. He soon stood for the recently vacated seat of Melbourne East but was defeated, largely because the number of Liberal candidates was reduced to avoid a split vote. He was again unsuccessful in the 1902 election for the same seat.

In 1903 Findley was elected as a senator for Victoria, gaining during the election a reputation as a vigorous, resourceful and tenacious campaigner. He was defeated in 1917, but re-entered the Senate in 1922. In his three terms as senator he sat on several select committees and royal commissions, including those investigating the tobacco monopoly (1905-06), press cable services (1909) and beam wireless links with England (1929). Between 1910 and 1913 he served as an honorary minister in the Fisher [q.v.] government, taking responsibility in the

Senate for the areas of home affairs and postmaster-general.

On 11 January 1911, at St Mary's Catholic Church, West Melbourne, he married Lilian (Lily) Foyle, a 29-year-old photographer of Warrnambool.

Following his defeat in the November 1928 election, Findley was appointed as a government director of Commonwealth Oil Refineries Ltd, a post he held from 1930 until his death on 26 October 1947 at his home at Caulfield. He was survived by his wife and one of his two daughters, and was buried in Coburg cemetery. His estate was sworn for probate at £15 982.

PD (Vic), 1901, p 108; *A'sian Typographical J,* Mar 1898, p 3; *Tocsin*, 20, 27 June 1901; *Punch* (Melb), 12 May 1910; *Age*, and *Argus*, 27 Oct 1947; *Labor Call*, 30 Oct 1947; files on G. M. Prendergast, *Tocsin* and labour newspapers (Merrifield Collection, SLV).   TONY MARSHALL

FINK, THEODORE (1855-1942), solicitor, politician, newspaper proprietor and educationist, was born on 3 July 1855 at St Pierre, Guernsey, Channel Islands, youngest son of Moses Fink, storekeeper, and his wife Gertrude, née Ascher. Benjamin Fink [q.v.4] was his eldest brother; while Theodore lacked Benjamin's unrestrained panache in business dealings and the academic brilliance of his brother Wolfe (b. 1853) he had a touch of the family audacity and an astute, cultivated intelligence.

Moses Fink and his family arrived at Geelong, Victoria, in April 1861. There, Theodore attended the Flinders National grammar school and then Geelong College, but the single most stimulating influence on him was the family's move to Melbourne in 1871. He entered Melbourne Church of England Grammar School, where he was a class-mate of Alfred Deakin [q.v.], an admired friend from that time, matriculated, and won the school prize for poetry. The company of his brother Wolfe's friends, his membership with Deakin of discussion societies such as the Eclectic Association of Victoria, and a course of reading at the Public Library, all heightened his interest in the arts and politics. Like Deakin, and under his influence, he was to become an ardent worker for Federation.

In 1872 Theodore Fink joined the reputable firm of Henry J. Farmer as an articled clerk, studying law part-time at the University of Melbourne. He was soon initiated into various branches of the profession especially mercantile law, including insolvency proceedings and conveyancing. This later proved a most apt apprenticeship. In 1874 he became Farmer's managing clerk and three years later was admitted to practice as a solicitor. He steadily improved his knowledge of mercantile and constitutional law and in 1886 entered a legal partnership with (Sir) R. W. Best [q.v.7] and P. D. Phillips. He also led an active social life. A writer of occasional verse from boyhood, Theodore became a well-known writer and public speaker, contributing to Melbourne *Punch* and other papers, and writing the occasional serious essay as readily as he composed topical verses for George Musgrove's [q.v.5] pantomimes. He delighted in the company of artists, writers and intellectuals and gained a reputation as a wit and as a very practical patron of the arts.

In 1879 Fink became the youngest member of the Yorick Club. His close associates, then and later, included writers and journalists such as Marcus Clarke and J. F. Archibald [qq.v.3] and artists such as Conder [q.v.3], Longstaff, Streeton, McCubbin, MacKennal, Tom Roberts [qq.v.] and Phil May [q.v.5] – to whom he was particularly helpful. He was a long-standing member of the Victorian Artists' Society. While enjoying Bohemian company, his own habits were temperate; he liked his garden and long walks in the countryside. On 6 July 1881, according to the rites of the Hebrew faith, Fink married Kate Isaacs at her father's home in South Yarra.

His varied and increasingly secure life was shattered by the collapse of the land boom. In 1886 land values were already high. The partnership flourished, but he began to speculate and by 1891 owed £70 000. Falling values made nonsense of his assets. Fink's speculations had largely been in ventures started by Benjamin, yet he defended his brother (and other land boomers) against accusations of culpably reckless speculation, preferring an explanation which stressed impersonal international factors as much as local greed for unrealistically high returns on investment. Theodore resolved his own financial difficulties by taking advantage of a procedure which avoided the scandal of a public bankruptcy. Such private compositions were in principle legal, but open to misuse. He himself made two private compositions of his debts, in January and July 1892. Furthermore, as a partner in the restructured firm of Fink, Best & Hall he arranged compositions for many of the major speculators.

In 1893 Fink showed both his resilience and his ability. In an address to the Bankers' Institute of Australasia, entitled 'Foreign Loans and a Young Democracy', he warned that it could not be assumed 'that the influx of capital into a colony is an unmixed blessing', and suggested that indirect taxation which pressed 'unfairly on the smallest incomes' should be replaced by direct taxation, and that the capital so raised, rather than foreign capital, should be the major source of government spending. In that same year his lengthy, complex, and successful defence of Sir Matthew Davies [q.v.4] of the Mercantile Bank was greatly praised.

Another set of events was eventually to give Theodore Fink a different career. In 1889, on the death of J. B. Halfey [q.v.4], joint-owner of the *Herald*, Fink bought three £1000 shares in a new company, the Herald and Sportsman Newspapers Co. Ltd. At the time of his secret compositions he had paid only £400 of this sum; these shares, which carried a directorship with them, would certainly have been lost to Fink had his insolvencies been public. In the event, their possession strengthened his interest in journalism and public affairs.

Fink's parliamentary career began in 1894, with his election to the Legislative Assembly as member for Jolimont and West Richmond. He held the seat until 1904, when he withdrew from State politics. He unsuccessfully contested the Federal seat of Kooyong in 1901. While in parliament he worked intelligently and tirelessly in a number of public causes. In 1899 he was appointed chairman of the royal commission on technical education. Interpreting the terms of reference very comprehensively, Fink began an extensive review not only of technical education but of the Education Department itself. The commission's findings led to two bills (February 1900 and December 1901) which initiated basic reforms, including an extension of the period of compulsory schooling and the freeing of the department from public service control. Throughout his chairmanship of this commission and the later commission on the University of Melbourne in 1902-04 he took a liberal and professional stance. The University Act of 1904 was more cautious than he had hoped, but the university grant was increased and new courses were offered. On his retirement from political life Fink was thanked by parliament for the work of these two commissions. Subsequently he served on the university council and the Council of Public Education, chaired conferences on apprenticeship (1906 and 1913) and an inquiry into the Working Men's College (1910), and helped to found the Victorian Council of Legal Education. He recognized Frank Tate's [q.v.] worth and strongly supported him.

During World War I Fink devoted his time to the *Herald*, of which he was then chairman of directors, and to the war effort. Ties formed during his trips to Europe, par-

ticularly that of 1909 when he was Australian delegate to the Empire Press Conference, were strengthened by the war (in which his eldest son was killed). As vice-chairman of the State War Council and later chairman for Victoria of the Commonwealth repatriation scheme, he defended the rights of ex-servicemen. In 1920 he appointed (Sir) Keith Murdoch [q.v.] as editor of the *Herald* and supported him strongly. Later, however, he resisted Murdoch's attempts to gain a directorship and hence access to the chairmanship. That position Fink intended for his youngest son Thorold, already a director. Ironically, Thorold was fatally injured in an accident only months after his father's death.

Although Fink's prolonged chairmanship of the *Herald* press group was in later life his main interest he continued to write the occasional humane but often politically conservative article. A youthful admirer of Herbert Spencer, he valued success but interpreted it broadly, resenting the vulgar error of equating success for those of Jewish origin with the mere making of money. He died at his Toorak home on 25 April 1942, survived by two sons and two daughters, the elder of whom, Hilda, was married to R. C. D. Elliott [q.v.]. He was cremated after a funeral service conducted by Rabbi Danglow [q.v.]. Fink's estate was valued for probate at £55 266.

M. Cannon, *The land boomers* (Melb, 1966); E. L. French, *Theodore Fink: public educationist* (Melb, 1966); T. Fink papers and autobiographical notes (Dept of Education, Univ Melb).

WILMA HANNAH

FINLAY, MARY McKENZIE (1870-1923), matron, was born on 28 January 1870 at Kilmore, Victoria, eldest child of James Finlay, station manager and later land valuer, from Coleraine, Londonderry, Ireland, and his native-born wife Elizabeth, née Hill. Mary and her eleven brothers and sisters spent their childhood on a pastoral property at Towaninnie in north-western Victoria and were educated by a governess. In 1890 the family moved to Melbourne.

On 16 December 1896 Mary Finlay began training as a nurse at the (Royal) Melbourne Hospital and completed her certificate on 16 February 1900. She remained at the hospital as sister-in-charge of surgical ward 22 until she completed her matron's certificate of technical fitness in December 1907 and accepted the position of matron at the Melbourne Church of England Grammar School. As hospital sister and school matron she was regarded as a first-class nurse who was much loved by her patients and noted for her kindness, devotion and perennial good temper. At the Exhibition of Australian Women's Work held in Melbourne in October 1907, she was awarded the essay-prize for surgical nursing.

Mary Finlay had been among the first enlistments in the Australian Army Nursing Service in 1904. When war began in 1914 she volunteered for overseas service with the A.A.N.S.; joining the Australian Imperial Force on 11 October, she embarked on the transport *Shropshire* nine days later and was one of the first six Victorian nurses to be sent on active service. On arrival in Egypt Sister Finlay was attached to the staff of the 1st Australian General Hospital, then in July 1915 she became matron-in-charge of Ras-el-Tin Convalescent Home at Alexandria.

On 25 March 1916, before embarking for France, she was appointed matron of the 1st A.G.H. which was to be stationed at Rouen. Working under primitive and arduous conditions she established this large military hospital and was its matron for almost two years. In her first winter at Rouen there was a shortage of such basic necessities as water and stoves with which to keep patients and staff warm. In recognition of her services at Rouen she was awarded the Royal Red Cross (1st class) in December 1916. She left France in February 1918 to become matron at the 2nd Australian Auxiliary Hospital, Southall, England, which had been established for the treatment of limbless servicemen. She remained there until January 1919 when she embarked for Australia.

Matron Finlay was demobilized on 26 July and resumed her position at Melbourne Grammar School. The demands of war service had seriously undermined her health and in 1922 she resigned. She died, unmarried, at Warrandyte of cancer on 21 March 1923 and was buried in St Kilda cemetery after a special service in the school chapel.

Sister Finlay had been an early member of the Royal Victorian Trained Nurses' Association, honorary secretary of its council in 1910-22 and vice-president in 1920-22. In these capacities she had shown a keen interest in her profession and in the maintenance of high standards of nursing training and practice.

A. G. Butler (ed), *Official history of the Australian Army Medical Services . . . 1914-18*, 1, 2, 3, (Melb, 1930, Canb, 1940, 1943); K. S. Inglis, *Hospital and community* (Melb, 1958); Melb C. of E. Grammar School, *Liber Melburniensis,* centenary ed (Melb, 1965); *London Gazette,* 29 Dec 1916; *Una,* June 1904, Dec 1907, July 1909, Sept 1914, July 1915, Sept 1916, Oct 1920, Oct 1921, May 1922, April 1923; *V.H.M.,* Dec 1942; *Herald* (Melb), 29 July 1919; *Argus,* 23, 24 Mar 1923; War diaries, 1st Australian General Hospital, 1916-18, *and* 2nd Australian Auxiliary Hospital, 1916-19 (AWM); information from the Royal Melbourne Hospital, *and* D. L. Finlay, Croydon, Vic. SUSAN KENNY

FINN, HENRY (1852-1924), soldier, was born on 6 December 1852 at Tenterden, Kent, England, son of Samuel Finn, tailor, and his wife Elizabeth Frances Austen, née Hilder. He was educated at Tenterden and joined the British Army on 11 May 1871 as a private in the 9th (Queen's Royal) Lancers at Aldershot. During the Afghanistan War o 1878-80 he participated in severe fighting, was mentioned in dispatches, and was awarded the Distinguished Conduct Medal for bravery.

After almost ten years in the ranks, Harry Finn was commissioned second lieutenant in the newly formed 21st Hussars in March 1881 and promoted lieutenant next July. In 1882 he was appointed instructor of musketry to the regiment and on 1 July 1884 became adjutant. He married in 1886 Catherine Scott in Dublin. He was still adjutant when the regiment was sent to India in November 1887, when he was promoted captain. From 1890 he filled several general staff appointments at Bangalore in the Madras command, and in Burma, and was promoted major in 1894 before returning to his regiment in 1898.

Finn's regiment was that year converted to the 21st (Empress of India) Lancers and sent to Egypt, where it took part in the Nile Expedition into the Sudan in August. Finn commanded the Lancers' left wing during their famous charge at Omdurman on 2 September and was mentioned in dispatches and promoted brevet lieut-colonel in November. In 1899 he accompanied his regiment to Newbridge, Ireland, but was there only three months before he was offered, and accepted, the post of commandant of the Queensland Defence Force with local rank of colonel. He arrived to take command on 11 April 1900. During his tenure in the post the Australian colonies were federated, and Finn was selected to preside over a Commonwealth Defence Pay Committee which met in Sydney in 1901 to consider rates of pay and allowances for the forces.

Finn was soon offered the post of commandant in New South Wales with local rank of brigadier general, and began duty on 1 January 1902. In terms of seniority he was second-in-command of the Commonwealth Military Forces following the arrival in 1902 of another British officer, Major General Sir Edward Hutton [q.v.], as general officer commanding. Hutton considered Finn 'an experienced and valuable officer' and specifically named him to the membership of a board of advice which he proposed in 1904 be established to co-ordinate the functioning of the Defence Department under the minister.

In other respects Finn's association with Hutton was not so happy. In April 1904 Senator Lieut-Colonel J. C. Neild [q.v.] complained that, following speeches made by him in the Senate, Hutton and Finn had attempted to have him retired from his militia appointment. A select committee called Finn to give evidence on 17 May; its report in October exonerated him but not Hutton. Finn was also called to give evidence in June 1904 before another Senate select committee inquiring into whether an officer retrenched by Hutton had been justly treated.

He was granted brevet rank of colonel in the British Army in February 1904. In October he was a member of the Commonwealth Defence Committee which assembled in Melbourne and, after Hutton's departure for England at the expiration of his appointment on 15 November, Finn assumed temporary command of the Commonwealth Military Forces. On 24 December he was appointed inspector general, the Commonwealth's new senior military post, but retained powers of the G.O.C. pending the establishment of a military board of administration. He was given local and temporary rank of major general from February 1905.

As inspector general, in 1905 Finn became chairman of the promotions board, and president of the Commowealth Defence Committee charged with drafting a Commonwealth defence scheme. He also sought to discharge conscientiously his duties of examining the condition of the country's defence works, the efficiency of the troops and preparedness for war, by undertaking extensive visits to all States. Although allotted a staff officer, he had no aide-de-camp and no clerical staff; none the less he produced detailed and comprehensive observations concerning the efficiency of the forces for 1905.

Finn's efforts went largely unappreciated by the government of the day, although in the Senate in 1906 he was described as 'the ablest military man in the Commonwealth' and a man possessing 'grit, determination, ability, and backbone'. Defence minister Thomas Playford [q.v.], however, spoke disparagingly of Finn's endeavours, criticizing him for constant travel to visit corps in the 'backblocks' instead of inspecting State commandants and their staffs. Playford later asserted that Finn 'disapproved of everything that had been done — the Council of Defence, the Act of Parliament we had

passed, the objection to the appointment of Imperial officers and so on'. Reports submitted by Finn in 1906 speak of the disabilities under which he laboured, particularly the continuing inadequacy of his staff and the futility of having an inspector general if the Military Board was not a competent body to grasp and implement his recommendations. It seems probable that frustration and animosity with the minister were behind Finn's decision to retire, ostensibly on grounds of ill health. He left for England on 3 September 1906 on leave in anticipation of the expiry of his appointment at the end of the year. He was appointed C.B. in 1907 and upon his retirement that year after a brief period of half-pay, he engaged in commerce in London.

In 1912 Finn was nominated by Mrs Walter Hall [q.v.] as secretary of the Walter and Eliza Hall Trust in Sydney, and he held this post from December 1912 until his death. He was also private secretary to Sir Gerald Strickland [q.v.], governor of New South Wales in 1913-17, and in 1923-24 to the lieut-governor, Sir William Cullen [q.v.]. Finn died in St Luke's Private Hospital, Sydney, on 24 June 1924. He was survived by his wife, two daughters and a son.

Finn was buried with full military honours in South Head cemetery. The funeral cortège was so large that it took two and half hours for the last mourners to arrive at the cemetery following the service at his Point Piper home. A beautifully sculptured white marble Celtic cross, funded by public subscription, was erected over his grave.

Coming to Australia in the prime of his life, Finn made a strong impression as a professional soldier; among British officers who served in the Commonwealth his influence was second only to that of Hutton. Remarkable at the time as one of the few men to have risen through the ranks of the British Army — he could claim to have served in all ranks from private to major general — Finn's breezy, informal and direct manner made him well liked by the men he commanded. He did much to infuse enthusiasm into young and inexperienced troops and set an example of soldierly bearing and conduct. In this way he was prominent among the small group of professional officers who did much to lay the foundations upon which the reputation of the Australian Imperial Force was built.

Cyclopedia of N.S.W. (Syd, 1907); *PD* (Cwlth), 1906, p 628, 6352; *PP* (Cwlth), 1901-02, 2, 77, 1904, 2, 297, (Senate), 1904, 1, 305, 1906, 2, 117; *British A'sian*, 16 Jan 1902; *London Gazette*, 4 May 1880, 30 Sept 1898; *Australasian*, 5 Oct 1901, 29 Nov 1902, 18 July 1903, 5 July 1924; *Sydney Mail*, 11 Jan 1902; *Table Talk*, 24 Aug 1905; *Punch* (Melb), 18 Jan 1906; *SMH*, 13 Oct 1923, 25-27 June, 4 July, 14

Aug 1924; A8, files 01/30/24, 02/30/4 (AAO, Canb); records (AWM).

C. D. COULTHARD-CLARK

FINNERTY, JOHN MICHAEL (1853-1913), mining warden and magistrate, was born on 31 January 1853 in Limerick, Ireland, third son of Charles Finnerty, army officer, and his wife Elizabeth, née Mathews, who were Anglicans. The family arrived in Western Australia in 1859 where the father was staff officer of enrolled military pensioners at Fremantle. In 1867-72 John attended Rugby School in England, where he was a mediocre scholar and a top Rugby player. He returned home in 1873 and worked as clerk to Sir Archibald Burt [q.v.3].

He then went pearling and traded to Malaya. In 1878-82 he worked a pastoral lease on the Gascoyne River with John H. Monger [q.v.5] and built there the first brick house in the north. After two visits to England, in 1886 he was inspector of police at Derby when the Kimberley goldfield was proclaimed. Next year he was warden and resident magistrate at Halls Creek to cope with the colony's first gold rush. In 1889 he moved to Southern Cross on the Yilgarn goldfield as warden and, from 1891, resident magistrate again. Here, on 10 December, he married Bertha Mary Oats (d. 1911) from Cornwall, whose father William was the town's first mayor. Next year Finnerty ruled against leaseholders who applied for exemption from the labour clauses of the Goldfields Act, 1886, which required manning of leases while awaiting capital and company development; this caused unemployment and tied up possibly rich country. The Act was amended to allow the minister to grant exemptions.

On 17 September 1892 Arthur Bayley [q.v.7] rode in to Southern Cross and applied to Finnerty for a reward claim. Riding to inspect the find, it is said that Finnerty visited a near-by rock-hole and wrote down its Aboriginal name, Coolgardie, which the goldfield was later named. It started Western Australia's greatest gold rush. Finnerty saved lives when water was short by persuading the government to provide tanks along the road and by ordering diggers back to Southern Cross, allowing them to resume their claims after the winter rains. In an outspoken community he used common sense to interpret the regulations of an Act which gave wide supervisory powers to wardens. On Coolgardie when newcomers broke specimens from Bayley's Reward lease, Finnerty ruled that a lease could be entered for alluvial gold, but not within fifty feet (15.24 m) of the reef or lode. This was the origin of the famous dual title, part of the 1895 Act. Giving a title to the alluvialist as well as the lessee was an important cause of the following mining boom. The immediate granting of leases aided the investment of British capital and the extension of company mining; the dual title allowed the simultaneous mining of alluvial and reef gold on the leases.

Finnerty helped plan the town of Coolgardie where he was warden from 1894; it rapidly became the third largest town in the colony but then the field declined. In 1900 he was appointed to Kalgoorlie, the main centre of the eastern goldfields. In 1911 he retired to a property near Geraldton where he died of diabetes with infection on 8 December 1913, survived by two daughters and a son. He was buried in the Urch Street cemetery with a gravestone erected by goldfields friends.

He had been a fellow of the Royal Geographical Society, a Freemason and president of the Coolgardie Liedertafel. With the rank of lieut-colonel he commanded the Goldfields Regiment of the Volunteer Defence Force. A great raconteur, he wore a full beard with a 'walrus' moustache and had a commanding but genial presence. He was a big man, physically and officially, good at his job. For twenty-five years Finnerty interpreted the mining acts with discretion and his decisions were respected. As a bushman, his authority and leadership were accepted in the camps: no officer of the Crown was held in higher regard in the mining community.

M. Uren, *Glint of gold* (Melb, 1948); A Reid, *Those were the days* (Perth, 1933); J. Kirwan, *My life's adventure* (Lond, 1936); G. Casey and T. Mayman, *The mile that Midas touched* (Adel, 1964); *Univ Studies in History and Economics*, 2 (1955), no 3; *RAHSJ*, 43 (1957); *Western Argus*, 11 Mar 1902; *West Australian*, 22 May 1935; D. Mossenson, Gold and politics ... (M.A. thesis, Univ WA, 1952).

TED MAYMAN

FISHBOURNE, JOHN WILLIAM YORKE (1843-1911), medical practitioner, was born in December 1843 at Coalkenno Rectory, Wicklow, Ireland, fourth son of Rev. Robert Fishbourne and his wife Anne, née Greene. He was educated at Cullaghmore, Carlow, and later at Kilkenny. At 16 he entered Trinity College, Dublin (B.A., 1863; M.B., 1864; Ch.M., 1865). He studied briefly in Brussels, then became a ship's surgeon aboard the *Avoca* before settling in Victoria in 1869. On 13 January 1870 at Wickliff Church of England, Learmonth, he married Marian Isabella, daughter of Rev. Richard Radcliff of County Meath, Ireland. The couple had one son and six daughters, one of whom seems to have been epileptic.

Fishbourne's chief medical interest was in

'diseases of the mind' and this led him to work in mental asylums at Ararat (1872-77) where he was resident medical officer, and Kew (1877-82) where he was deputy medical superintendent. He then entered private practice at Moonee Ponds. About 1886 he became health officer for Essendon. In 1885 he had been a witness to the Zox [q.v.6] royal commission on asylums for the insane and inebriate, where he supported Dr J. W. Springthorpe's [q.v.] criticism of Victoria's existing mental insitutions; he urged that, if no psychiatric medicine could be crammed into Melbourne's medical course, doctors at asylums should be empowered to provide some lectures and training. The establishment of the Victorian Lunacy Department in 1903 was largely due to Springthorpe and Fishbourne persuading the British Medical Association (Victorian branch) to put pressure on the government. Fishbourne was also a founder, in 1906, of the Talbot Colony (now the Royal Talbot Centre), a residential centre for epileptics. In September 1911 he wrote for the Australasian Medical Congress in Sydney a paper on the care of the feeble-minded: 'his last and splendid effort to the cause to which he devoted his life'.

In 1893, during the depression, Fishbourne resigned as municipal health officer and his abundant energy was channelled back into his chosen field. With his daughter Laeta, he made over his home, St Aidan's in Puckle Street, Moonee Ponds, as a school or day-centre for mentally retarded children, and showed that some at least were educable, and that some of the uneducable were trainable. In 1907 the Education Department recognized St Aidan's as a primary special school; unfortunately it did not long outlive its founder and closed in 1913. It may rightly be regarded as the forerunner of Victoria's schools and centres for mentally handicapped children.

Fishbourne died of cerebro-vascular disease at his home on 26 September 1911, survived by his wife, son, and five of his daughters. He was buried in Fawkner cemetery after a service conducted by the vicar of St Thomas Church, Essendon, where Fishbourne had for many years sung in the choir. He is best remembered for his services to and compassion for the mentally afflicted. In the Essendon area he was a well-known figure who 'never flinched from the task of unburdening his mind in public'. This pioneer of both residential and day care for the mentally ill was revered for his kindness, probity and 'upright bearing' as a 'friend of the poor' who treated many without fee or hope of fee.

J. Smith (ed), *Cyclopedia of Victoria*, 2 (Melb, 1904); C. R. D. Brothers, *Early Victorian psychiatry*

1835-1905 (Nelb, 1962); *A'sian Medical Gazette*, Sept 1882, p 167, 20 Oct 1911, p 619, 630; *MJA*, 2 (1977), p 255; *Age*, and *Argus*, 27 Sept 1911; *Essendon Gazette*, 28 Sept 1911.

LYNDSAY GARDINER

FISHER, ANDREW (1862-1928), prime minister, was born on 29 August 1862 at Crosshouse, near Kilmaurs, Ayrshire, Scotland, second son of Robert Fisher, coalminer, and his wife Jane, née Garvin. Robert Fisher, a sober, temperate Presbyterian, was one of ten men who established a co-operative store in Crosshouse in 1863. The co-operative, later part of the Scottish Co-operative Wholesale Society, developed a library and reading room which Andrew used. Despite a law prohibiting boys under twelve from working in the pits, Andrew seems to have begun work at about 10, his father having developed pneumoconiosis. Andrew's education was limited to the local public school, supplemented by evening classes at Kilmarnock.

In 1879 Fisher was elected secretary of the Crosshouse district branch of the Ayrshire Miners' Union. Keir Hardie, whom Fisher admired, became secretary of the central body. A ten weeks strike in 1881 wiped out the union. Fisher again represented the local miners when it was reformed in 1884. But there were slim prospects at Crosshouse. With his younger brother James, he considered migrating to New Zealand or Australia, torn between his responsibilities at home, where his father's health had worsened, and his ambition to better himself. After long family discussions he was persuaded to go.

The brothers arrived in Queensland on 17 August 1885 in the *New Guinea*. Finding no work on the Ipswich coalfields they moved to the Burrum field, where Andrew obtained work with the Queensland Colliery Co. at Tornbanlea. Two months later he directed the sinking of a new mine for the company and then became a manager. In 1887 he was a shareholder in the Dudley Coal & Investment Co. Rejected as manager of a mine owned by Isis Investment Co. of Queensland, he left Burrum for the goldfields at Gympie. Here he worked at North Phoenix No. 1 field until the end of 1890 when he went on strike and was dismissed. As in blacklistings in Scotland, Fisher's ability gained him work in other mines. Obtaining his engine driver's certificate, he went to work on the surface for the South Great Eastern Extended mine.

At Gympie Fisher was active in the Royal True Friendship Lodge of the Manchester United Independent Order of Oddfellows, a superintendent of the Presbyterian Church Sunday School, a shareholder in the Gympie

Industrial Co-operative Society and for a period a member of the local unit of the Colonial Defence Force. He joined the Amalgamated Miners' Association which, with a general advance in Queensland unionism, began at Gympie in 1886. He became secretary and then president of the branch in 1890 and 1891, before its collapse towards the end of the latter year.

In June 1889 the Australian Labor Federation was formed in Brisbane; its Wide Bay and Burnett district council, centred on Maryborough and extending its influence to Gympie, was formed the following May. W. H. Demaine [q.v.], who was to become a lifelong friend of Fisher, was one of its organizers. Inter-city jealousy and the distance delegates had to travel caused the Gympie unions to break away in mid-1891 to form a Gympie Joint Labor Committee; George Ryland was president and Fisher secretary. Out of the A.L.F. came Workers' Political Organizations, local branches of the new Labor Party. In July 1891 a branch was formed at Gympie, with Fisher president. He was now one of the most significant members of the Gympie labour movement. Tall and well-built, with a long black moustache and sandy hair, he was confident and determined to succeed, but his manner was quiet and his approach conciliatory.

Fisher drafted the welcome to Thomas Glassey [q.v.] when the Labor leader visited Gympie in July 1891, and he represented Gympie at a Labor-in-Politics Convention in Brisbane in August next year. He topped the poll for Labor at Gympie in the 1893 Legislative Assembly elections. The first three years in parliament provided Fisher with valuable experience for the future. He witnessed the scandals associated with the collapse of the Queensland National Bank; his own ideas on a state bank, included in the Labor platform, were forming. He developed ideas on the role and ownership of state railways; Sir Thomas McIlwraith's [q.v.5] scheme to finance a trans-colonial railway through land grants to the builders was opposed by Fisher and the other Labor members; they emphasized that railways should open up land and not be profit-making enterprises. In 1894, following the second long pastoral strike, the government introduced a peace preservation bill which the Labor members dubbed a 'Coercion Bill'. Fisher favoured a system of arbitration tribunals established by the state. His view during 1894 and 1895 was that Labor should co-operate with the Liberals in trying to defeat the government, but should retain its separate identity.

Fisher's political philosophy contained no concept of class warfare; nor was he attracted to William Lane's [q.v.] Utopian settlement in Paraguay. His ideas were based on his background in Ayrshire, his experiences as a miner and his habits of reading and study. In 1908 he was to identify society as having a labouring class 'and a speculating class'. His solution to this division was to provide parliamentary reforms in banking, industrial safety, workers' compensation, land and employment, and so elevate the living standard of the labourer. A graduated income tax, control of monopolies and state ownership of certain enterprises would conversely lessen the power of the speculating class.

Fisher lost at the 1896 elections, because of the strong opposition of the *Gympie Times* and a weak campaign by Labor. He obtained work as an engine driver and, for a time, as auditor to the municipal council. To counter the anti-Labor influence of the *Gympie Times*, Fisher and other leading Laborites in Gympie established the Gympie *Truth*. A company with 5000 shares at 5s. was floated on 15 April 1896. Fisher, who was chairman and treasurer, Ryland and the editor, Henry Boote [q.v.7], largely wrote and produced the paper which first appeared in July. Following an attack of typhoid in 1897, Fisher concentrated on the financial management of the company.

In June 1898 Fisher represented Gympie at the Labor Party convention in Brisbane but declined election to the Central Political Executive. Although Labor was able to mount a better campaign in 1899, there remained problems with Glassey's leadership and disharmony had emerged between the A.L.F. and sections of the parliamentary party. Fisher did not seek formal endorsement by the executive, but chose to fight the election locally in Gympie. Both he and Ryland were elected. His three years absence had lost Fisher some seniority; Anderson Dawson [q.v.] replaced Glassey as leader. But Fisher was trusted and remained one of the caucus leaders. In 1899 he introduced the first workmen's compensation bill and, when debate was abandoned by the government, he reintroduced it in 1900, again without success. He was one of the negotiators in the formation of the minority Dawson Labor government on 1 December 1899; Fisher insisted that, in any coalition with the Liberals Labor should have a majority, otherwise a minority Labor government should be formed. He was appointed secretary for railways and for public works, but as the government lasted only six days he had little opportunity to demonstrate any ministerial capacity.

Fisher opposed sending Australian troops to the South African War, but supported and campaigned for the new Commonwealth, against the anti-Federation campaign of Boote in the *Gympie Truth*. In the referendum of 1899 Gympie strongly supported Federation. Fisher was endorsed as the Federal Labor candidate for Wide Bay, and won with 55 per cent of the votes. In May 1901 he met with the other Labor parliamentarians to form the Commonwealth Labor Party. It was a year of mixed personal fortunes. In July his brother John, chief constable at Grimsley, was killed; James had been killed in a mining accident in India in 1893 and another brother, Robert, in a railway accident in Canada in 1895. The year ended on a happier note on 31 December when Fisher married the 27-year-old Margaret Jane Irvine, his Gympie landlady's daughter.

The new party had few precedents to assist it in determining its role. There was no agreement on the fiscal question, or on a possible alliance with the Liberal Protectionists. J. C. Watson [q.v.] favoured a formal alliance with Alfred Deakin [q.v.], whereas Fisher, and eventually the Labor Party itself, was against political alliances, though Fisher was prepared to support Deakin where the government's programme agreed with broad Labor policy. In April 1904, in the debate on the conciliation and arbitration bill Fisher moved an amendment, unacceptable to Deakin, to include State employees in the bill. The amendment was carried, Deakin resigned, the caucus rejected a proposal to form a coalition with Deakin, and Watson formed the first Federal Labor government. Fisher was allotted trade and customs and listed fifth in the ministry after Watson, W. M. Hughes, H. B. Higgins [qq.v.] and E. L. Batchelor [q.v. 7].

The Watson government fell in August on the same conciliation and arbitration bill. Much of its time was taken up on debate about an alliance with the Liberal Party and with granting electoral immunity to some sympathetic Liberals. Fisher accepted the caucus majority view supporting an alliance, while insisting that the Labor Party remain independent. When the Inter-State (Federal) Conference was held in July 1905 Fisher and Watson were on opposite sides. Fisher said he opposed alliances generally; he also opposed electoral immunities but raised no objection to the caucus electing the ministry. The conference decided that the Labor Party should enter no alliance which would last beyond the life of the parliament, and recommended that caucus elect the ministry. Watson submitted his resignation ostensibly on health grounds, but was persuaded to withdraw. The caucus, on 9 August, elected Fisher deputy leader to ease Watson's work-load. Fisher's promotion from fifth to second reflected not only his

ability but also the trust in which he was held. He attended the 1907 Queensland Labor-in-Politics Convention to support Boote and Albert Hinchcliffe [q.v.] in their contention that Queensland Labor, also, should reject any coalition promise.

Although Labor won twenty-six seats at the 1906 Federal elections to Deakin's seventeen, it continued to support Deakin in office as the best means of achieving the Labor priorities of aged pensions, anti-trust laws and New Protection. When Watson resigned in October 1907, Fisher defeated Hughes and W. G. Spence [q.v.6] for the leadership. More competent than Hughes in economic matters and in handling caucus, Fisher was closer to the extra-parliamentary organizations, and a better judge of rank and file Labor opinion. He did not share the passion of Hughes for free trade or that of Watson and Hughes for defence.

While some contemporaries claimed to see a certain vanity in Fisher, his most notable characteristic was an innate modesty. In political terms he was a radical, on the left of his party, with a strong sense of Labor's part in British working-class history. At the 1908 Federal Conference he argued for the place of women in the Australian parliament: 'I trust that not another Federal election will take place without their (*sic*) being a woman endorsed as a Labour candidate for the Senate'. Not a brilliant orator, he nevertheless projected a sense of security to the electorate and, to his colleagues, an assurance that he would not deviate from Labor policy. Due to the entry of Labor into politics, socialism, he said, had moved from

> being tabooed, sneered at and scouted [and had been] brought to a first place in public discussion... We are all Socialists now and indeed the only qualification you hear from anybody is probably that he is "not an extreme socialist". I do not think that the ideas of the originators have altered one jot.

By early 1908 the Labor caucus had become restive about continuing to sustain the Deakin government. With his ministry in jeopardy, Deakin talked to Fisher and Watson about a possible coalition and, following their report, the caucus agreed to a coalition providing that Labor had a majority in cabinet, that there was immediate legislation for old-age pensions, that New Protection was carried and that at the following election the government would promise a progressive land tax.

Although no coalition was formed, Labor pressure on Deakin was productive: the government agreed to hold a royal commission into the post office, old-age pensions were to be provided from the surplus revenue fund and £250000 set aside for ships for an Australian navy. New Protection was declared invalid by the High Court in June; Fisher found the tariff proposals of Deakin unsatisfactory; caucus was also dissatisfied with the old-age pension proposals. Without Labor support the Deakin government fell on 10 November.

Fisher became both prime minister and treasurer in the second minority Labor government, whose ministers were elected by caucus. There was little possibility of Labor introducing its more important legislation, but Fisher felt that it was important for Labor to be seen as a party government. Ramsay MacDonald and Keir Hardie wrote to congratulate him. The new government amended the Seat of Government Act (1904) to provide that the new Federal capital should be in the Yass-Canberra area. It also passed the Manufacturers' Encouragement Act to provide bounties for iron and steel manufacturers who paid fair and reasonable wages. It accepted responsibility for local naval defence and placed the Australian Navy at the disposal of the Royal Navy in wartime. In February 1909 three torpedo boat destroyers were ordered. In March Fisher proposed a military defence scheme involving compulsory military training for youths up to age 20.

Fisher was now confident that Labor could govern in its own right. At Gympie on 30 March 1909 he committed Labor to amending the Constitution for more Commonwealth power in labour, wages and prices, to expanding the naval forces and providing compulsory military training for males up to 21, to increased Commonwealth expenditure on pensions, to a land tax, a transcontinental railway, a Commonwealth note issue and to protection of the sugar industry. Although he had jumped ahead of caucus where some members wanted such policy speeches approved first, he was in command. It was clear that the days of Liberal-Labor alliances were over.

On 27 May the new Fusion Party of Deakin and (Sir) Joseph Cook defeated Fisher's government in parliament. He failed to obtain a dissolution and went back into Opposition. In the following nine months, he welded the parliamentary party into an effective Opposition working through specialist committees. Fisher's area was finance and he sought per capita grants to the States but wanted this incorporated in Commonwealth legislation, not in a Constitutional amendment.

Labor went into the 1910 election with confidence and Fisher gave the appearance of trust, competence and stability and reflected the values implicit in widespread national hopes. On 13 April it won forty-three of the seventy-five House of Representative seats and all eighteen Senate seats, giving it twenty-three of the thirty-six Senate positions. At the first meeting of the new caucus Fisher was re-elected leader unopposed. The Fisher government of 1910-13 represented the culmination of Labor's involvement in politics; it was a period of reform unmatched in the Commonwealth until the 1940s. Fisher was not responsible for all the legislation, but whether it was preference to unionists, construction of the Kalgoorlie (Western Australia) to Port Augusta (South Australia) railway, lowering the criteria for pensions, establishment of the Commonwealth Clothing Factory, or the Commonwealth Bank, he had a fine understanding of what caucus and the electorate wanted. His royal commission into the sugar industry provided the basis for later legislation by the T. J. Ryan [q.v.] government in Queensland, which stabilized and expanded the most important tropical agricultural industry. His judgement proved sound in the Brisbane general strike of 1912 when he refused a request by the Queensland premier, Digby Denham [q.v.], to use Commonwealth troops against the strikers.

In October 1910 Fisher went to South Africa for the inauguration of the Union. In May next year he proceeded to London for the Imperial Conference and the coronation of George V. Visiting Kilmarnock and Crosshouse he was given a hero's welcome and returned to his birthplace after the conference to be made a freeman of the burgh. At the conference, Fisher, as the only Labor prime minister, was an object of some curiosity. He followed Deakin's 1907 arguments in trying to have the British government consult the Dominions on matters of relevant foreign policy, and supported unsuccessfully the establishment of a standing committee to consider matters arising out of the conference. Despite his assessment that 'many important subjects were dealt with in a satisfactory manner' Fisher had been overwhelmed by the British officials. Britain had conceded nothing to the Dominions. Fisher returned to Australia in August a reluctant privy councillor, having accepted the office only in order to avoid an open breach with the new king. He did not like decorations of any kind and adhered to this view throughout his life.

During the 1910 session of parliament, Labor's legislation fell into two parts: that of a distinctively reformist nature and that of continuing the development of a national government. In the former were amendments to the Conciliation and Arbitration Act (1904) to provide greater authority for the court president, and a Land Tax Act to tax unimproved land values in excess of £5000 with the intention of breaking up big estates into farms for 'small men'. In the latter were the Surplus Revenue Act providing an annual per capita grant of £15s. to the States and the Commonwealth acquisition of the Northern Territory from South Australia.

One of Labor's major goals had long been the establishment of a state bank. At the 1908 Federal Conference a 'Commonwealth Bank' had been written into the fighting platform. During the 1910 session Fisher passed an Australian Notes Act to provide for a Commonwealth note issue and to exclude private banks' notes. At the first meeting of the 1911 session he outlined the government proposals for a 'National Bank'. Legend later ascribed a key role in the creation of the Commonwealth Bank to King O'Malley [q.v.], but it is clear that it was Fisher, as treasurer carefully implementing a cabinet recommendation and an important Labor policy, who was responsible.

During the 1911 session the Conciliation and Arbitration Act was again amended to allow for Commonwealth employees' industrial unions, registered with the Arbitration Court; compulsory enrolment was provided for Commonwealth elections, and Labor attempted to amend the Constitution to give the Commonwealth the same power as the States over labour laws, to regulate monopolies and to nationalize industries. To Fisher the restrictions of the Constitution, shown by the High Court's rejection of New Protection, nullified 'the people's will'. He wanted additional Commonwealth power for national health and welfare, and for broader bases of fixing wages and working conditions. These referendum proposals were defeated, but he told the 1912 Federal Labor conference that they would be reintroduced.

In the final session of the 1910-13 parliament, Fisher retained overall control of legislation. Maternity allowances and a Workers' Compensation Act for Commonwealth employees were provided; the Inter-State Commission was established; invalid and old-age pensions were liberalized, the recommendations of the sugar royal commission were implemented, and the High Court was increased from five to seven judges. Six proposals were put to the electorate at the 1913 referendum held with the elections. All were lost by narrow margins and Labor lost government by one seat. Following the loss Fisher defeated challenges to his leadership from Hughes and W. G. Higgs [q.v.].

Fisher had moved permanently to Melbourne by 1906 and, as a successful investor, was able to purchase Oakleigh Hall, East St

Kilda, in 1912, a mansion compared with his Crosshouse and Gympie residences. Following the 1913 election he gave the first indication that he was feeling the strain of being the father of six children, all under twelve, and leading a Labor Party, jealous of its own collective decisions, through the formative period of the Commonwealth. The 1913-14 session of parliament was among the most hectic of his career. Both government and Opposition sought a double dissolution issue. In October 1913 the government chose the postal voting restoration bill and the government preference prohibition bill as their grounds. After visiting several electorates during March and April 1914, Fisher sensed a return of support for Labor and concluded that his party should use its power in the Senate to force an election. On 5 June the governor-general granted a double dissolution. Fisher and Hughes were delegated the writing of the party manifesto for the election on 5 September.

Fisher delivered his policy speech in Bundaberg on 6 July: it was largely a restatement of what he had said in 1913. The tenor of the campaign changed towards the end of July when the likelihood of a European war increased. At Ballarat, Victoria, on 31 July Cook pledged the resources of Australia to the Empire if war broke out. On the same night at Colac, Fisher made an equally unqualified promise. His 'last man and last shilling' pledge was to become the core of the conscriptionists' arguments two years later. It did not receive great prominence in 1914 and was essentially political rhetoric, though Fisher's support to Britain was never lacking. He saw no advantage in the war to Australia; concepts of martial glory were totally absent from his character. His immediate commitment to Britain, however, and to co-operation with Cook on war plans removed any possibility of the war becoming an election issue. Hughes, whose enthusiasm for the war outran his political judgement, frantically urged the cancellation of the election, but Fisher along with Cook rejected this and Labor, in a resounding personal victory for Fisher, routed the government.

It now became Fisher's responsibility to dispatch the first Australian troops overseas and to provide the foundations for financing the war. Since there were reports of German cruisers in the Pacific and Indian oceans, he refused to allow the convoy to sail until it was fully assembled and protected, over-riding the protests of Major General (Sir) W. T. Bridges [q.v.7]. Fisher informed the British government that Australia would meet the cost of its own troops. Initially he hoped to raise the money by increasing Commonwealth land tax and providing succession duties, but this was not possible. He negotiated an £18 million loan from Britain and insisted that all State borrowing during the war, limited to a total of £10 million, had to be through the Commonwealth. Early in 1915 he passed legislation enabling the Commonwealth to raise war loans in Australia.

The Australian soldiers were better paid than their British counterparts and, as the first wounded men returned from Gallipoli, Fisher instituted preference to returned soldiers in the public service irrespective of whether they were unionists or not. His 'last man and last shilling' promise, however, did not extend to conscription. The humanitarianism that lay behind his political philosophy prevented his taking that step. Moreover, unlike Hughes, he was not carried away by the emotional demand for troops but retained his cooler judgements about conscription. The decision to have Australian forces participate in the Gallipoli landing had not been Fisher's. It was the first example of a continuing problem about the British use of Australian forces. Fisher knew that the Australian Imperial Force had been moved from Egypt but was ignorant of the actual operation until after the landing, although it is doubtful that he would have opposed it.

Although Fisher should have been at the height of his political career after the 1914 election, the strains of leading a restive parliamentary party led to further decline in his health and a desire to resign as leader. In October a grant of £100 000 to assist the Belgians brought an attack on the government by some of its own supporters. After a torrid budget session Fisher retreated to New Zealand, ostensibly for war talks, but really to regain his health. Throughout 1915 he faced Labor pressure for the control of prices and the reintroduction of the constitutional referenda. He was criticized over the War Precautions and War Census Acts and after Gallipoli he was burdened with demands for conscription. The exclusion of Australia from policy-making on the war worried him. In April 1915 he sent Watson to England to report on operations. Although aware of his personal strain, Watson thought that Fisher should remain prime minister and press for a conference of the Dominions. However, on 30 October he resigned. While Hughes had increasingly accepted extra work, it had been Fisher who had borne the final responsibility: the stress had finally become unbearable. He succeeded Reid as high commissioner in London, and prior to leaving for England made Oakleigh Hall available as a convalescent home for soldiers.

As high commissioner Fisher became a member of the Dardanelles Commission; he visited the Australian troops in France and established a good relationship with General Birdwood [q.v.7]; he handled Australian representations in London but on matters of high policy Hughes made the decisions himself. When Fisher refused Hughes's request to sign a public statement supporting conscription, (Sir) Keith Murdoch [q.v.], rather than Fisher, became the trusted source for Hughes's British intelligence. For his service on the Dardanelles Commission and in recognition of Australia's part in the war the French government awarded him the Légion d'honneur, which he declined.

In 1921 Fisher returned to Australia. There were attempts to secure him a seat in the Federal parliament and to have him lead the Labor Party once more. His heart, however, was no longer in active politics though he attempted to obtain Labour selection for a Scottish seat in the House of Commons. He returned to London in 1922 where he lived a quiet life in declining health until his death on 22 October 1928 at South Hill Park. He was survived by his wife, a daughter and four sons.

Fisher was one of the most successful Australian politicians even though his career was overshadowed by the war, the turbulent prime ministership of Hughes and the split in the Labor Party over conscription. His contemporaries saw him as honest and trustworthy, but surpassed by Hughes in wit, oratory and brilliance. Fisher's record however reveals a legacy of reforms and national development which lasted beyond the divisions that Hughes left in the Labor Party and in Australia.

C. E. W. Bean, *The story of Anzac*, 1, 2 (Syd, 1921, 1924); J. A. La Nauze, *Alfred Deakin* (Melb, 1965); R. Gollan, *The Commonwealth Bank of Australia* (Canb, 1968); D. J. Murphy et al (eds), *Prelude to power* (Brisb, 1970); P. M. Weller (ed), *Caucus minutes*, 1-3 (Melb, 1975); L. F. Fitzhardinge, *William Morris Hughes*, 1-2 (Syd, 1964, 1979); *Aust J of Politics and Hist*, May 1963; G. Marginson, Andrew Fisher. The colonial experience, 1885-1901 (B.A. Hons thesis, Univ Qld, 1967); Fisher papers (NL).   D. J. MURPHY

FISHER, MARY LUCY (LALA) (1872-1929), poet and editor, was born on 27 January 1872 at Rockhampton, Queensland, daughter of Archibald John Richardson, surveyor, and his wife Lucy Knox, née D'Arcy, sister of William Knox D'Arcy [q.v.]. With limited education but a cultured family background, she went to England, probably in 1892, returned and on 7 August 1893 at Rockhampton married Francis

George Fisher, her father's assistant; they had two sons.

On 9 June 1897 the family left for England again. Living at Bembridge on the Isle of Wight, she was frequently in London and won some small fame as a writer, songwriter, lecturer and long-distance swimmer. In 1898 she published a book of verse, *A twilight teaching*, and in 1899 edited *By creek and gully*, an anthology, chiefly of prose by expatriate Australian writers. She became a member of the Writers' Club, was a fellow of the Anthropological Society of London and was president for Queensland in the International Congress of Women. Before she left England, she had been presented to Queen Victoria at Windsor.

The family returned to Australia in 1901 when, or a little later, a temporary estrangement occurred. In Queensland until 1906 Lala Fisher lived in Charters Towers, Rockhampton and Brisbane and wrote for various papers, including the radical *New Eagle* of Charters Towers, edited by Frank Hill, and *Steele Rudd's Magazine*. In May or June 1906 the family moved to Sydney. In financial difficulties, she worked for some time as a canvasser for the Colonial Mutual Life Assurance Co. and took a position as housekeeper at a hotel in the Blue Mountains. Her two sons returned to Rockhampton to live with her father's family. They and their cousins went to England for technical training in 1911 and both served in World War I. In 1909 Lala bought the *Theatre Magazine* in Sydney. When Frank Hill became a partner in 1912 she probably continued editing until about 1918; the magazine was sold in 1923.

Her second book of verse, *Grass flowering*, was published in 1915 and the third, *Earth spiritual*, in 1918; a second (revised) edition followed the next year. Since 1894 or even earlier she had corresponded with A. G. Stephens [q.v.] of the *Bulletin*, asking for advice on her poetry. In 1917 she was able to reciprocate, and to offer him a page in the *Theatre Magazine* for a fee of £5.5.0. From about 1920 she began to suffer some emotional or mental affliction and for two years, according to a letter to Stephens in 1922, she had been unable to work, and said that her husband 'insists that I have been mentally ill for some months'. Probably in 1923 she entered Gladesville Hospital, where she died of heart disease on 27 February 1929. She was buried in South Head cemetery.

Fisher's life and writings suggest a vigorous and active young woman, independent and even unorthodox; then a wife and mother on whom responsibilities begin to weigh; and last a woman whose physical powers fail under incessant demands. She was a poet with early submission to 'romantic' diction — a tendency never completely outgrown — but with a developing awareness. Some of the verse in her last volume has an almost metaphysical response to obscure inner promptings.

H. A. Kellow, *Queensland poets* (Lond, 1930); *British A'sian*, 11 Aug 1898, 23 Mar 1899, 25 Oct 1900; *Bulletin*, 2 Sept 1926; M. L. Fisher letters (Fryer Lib, Univ Qld); information from Mr F. W. Fisher, Leicester, U.K.   CECIL HADGRAFT
                                    LORNA L. McDONALD

FISK, SIR ERNEST THOMAS (1886-1965), radio pioneer and businessman, was born on 8 August 1886 at Sunbury, Middlesex, England, second child of Thomas Harvey Fisk, builder, and his wife Charlotte Hariette, née Halland. He was educated at local schools, St Mary's and Sunbury Boys'. Although he later enrolled at the United Kingdom College, a private London coaching college, and, in 1917, in the diploma course in the department of economics and commerce at the University of Sydney, he sat for no examinations.

From selling newspapers on Sunbury railway station, Fisk 'graduated in engineering' in the works of Frederick Walton, before joining the British Post Office as one of their earliest wireless telegraphists. In June 1906 Fisk joined the Marconi training school. At Liverpool and Chelmsford he learned morse and wireless telegraphy, qualifying as a radio engineer and operator. From 1909 he worked for American Marconi, demonstrating wireless to the Newfoundland sealers and on the St Lawrence, before returning to Marconi's administrative headquarters in London.

When Fisk first visited Australia in mid-1910 in the *Otranto* to demonstrate Marconi's apparatus for the Orient Steam Navigation Co., wireless was still largely the preserve of amateur enthusiasts. That year the government let the contract for the construction of two land stations for ships to Australasian Wireless Ltd, a Sydney firm with rights to the patents of Marconi's German rival, Telefunken. In 1911 he returned to Australia as resident engineer to represent the interests of the English Marconi's Wireless Telegraph Co. Ltd, trading under several names. His mission was to persuade shipowners to fit Marconi equipment, which he installed and trained telegraphists to operate. He established service depots in Australia and New Zealand. The sinking of the *Titanic* in 1912 gave business a boost.

In 1912 when the English Marconi company sued the Australian government for infringing their patent (and A.W.L. issued writs against firms using Marconi equipment), the government decided in future to use circuits designed by John Balsillie [q.v.7]. Eventually the two settled their differences and in July 1913 formed a new company, Amalgamated Wireless (Australasia) Ltd, with exclusive rights throughout Australasia to the patents, 'present and future', of both Marconi and Telefunken. The first chairman was (Sir) Hugh Denison [q.v.]; Fisk, a foundation director, was general and technical manager. In 1916 he became managing director and in 1932 chairman.

At St John's Anglican Church, Gordon, Sydney, Fisk married Florence, second daughter of Samuel Chudleigh, music teacher, on 20 December 1916. Earlier that year, on one of his regular visits to England, he had arranged for a series of test transmissions from the Marconi long wave station in Caenarvon, Wales. With Australia then dependent on underwater cables for its contact with the world, Fisk obtained official permission to use a receiver in his home. In September 1918 he arranged for the transmission of messages to Australia from the prime minister W. M. Hughes [q.v.] and Sir Joseph Cook [q.v.] and established that direct wireless communication between Britain and Australia was practicable. In August 1919 Sydney received its first public demonstration of radio telephony.

In 1921 Hughes took Fisk as an adviser to the Imperial Conference in London. Against the recommendation of the Imperial Wireless Committee, which envisaged an Empire linked by short distance relays, Hughes promoted Fisk's scheme for direct communication between Britain and the Dominions. In 1922 the Australian government, insisting that it was not prepared to settle for anything less, commissioned A.W.A. to create the service, boosted the company's capital and became its majority shareholder. A beam service between Australia and Britain, undercutting the cable companies, was inaugurated in April 1927; that between Australia and Canada in 1928. In September 1927 A.W.A. pioneered Empire broadcasting; in April 1930 an Empire radio-telephone service. In 1931 Marconi was godfather to Fisk's fourth son David Sarnoff Marconi.

Fisk promoted wireless as integral to the Empire; 'No scientific discovery offers such great possibility for binding together the parts of our far-flung Empire, and for developing its social, commercial and defence welfare'. He became a member of the New South Wales branch of the Royal Empire Society in 1934, and was its president in 1941 and 1944. Awarded King George V's Silver Jubilee Medal in 1935, Fisk

was knighted in the Coronation honours of 1937; he went to England for his investiture. In 1933 he had been appointed to the Order of the Crown of Italy.

At the same time Fisk was proudly Australian. He promoted the professional organization of the wireless industry: he was president of the State division of the Wireless Institute of Australia in 1914-22, founding its journal, *Sea, Land and Air*, and of the Institution of Radio Engineers, Australia, in the 1930s. He was a member of the Institute of Radio Engineersn United States of America, from 1915, a fellow from 1926, and a fellow for life from 1951m In 1o23 he had published 'The application and development of wireless in Australia', in the *Proceedings* of the Pan-Pacific Scientific Congress.

As head of a major manufacturer, heavily protected after 192on Fisk promoted the case for local industry and worked to sustain the political, industrial and moral organizations conducive to its prosperity. He contributed to the National Party and its successors. He published 'Ideals in modern business', in *Business Lectures for Business Men*, no 6, 1933. In the early 1920s he had been a member of the local Royal Society. From 1939 he was president of the Electrical and Radio Development Association; in 1934-36 and 1938-40 vice-president of the New South Wales Chamber of Manufactures, and in 1939-42 a member of the Road Safety Council of New South Wales. A Freemason since early manhood, Fisk was a member of the Electron Chapter founded among A.W.A. employees in 1937. His favourite recitation at 'smokos' was said to be Kipling's 'If'. He was also a long-time member of the Millions Club in Sydney and the Australian in Melbourne, a member of Rotary, and in 1939 inaugural chairman of the New South Wales State Council for Physical Fitness (later National Fitness Council of New South Wales); that year he chaired the Young Men's Christian Association's appeal.

Once knighted, Sir Ernest was asked to join a number of boards. He became an Australian director of the Royal Exchange Assurance of London and a director of York Air Conditioning and Refrigeration Australasia Pty Ltd, Standard Portland Cement Co. Ltd and Sargents Ltd. Another company, of which he was chairman, Great Pacific Airways Ltd, formed in 1934 to run an international air service, did not get off the ground. Fisk subsequently used it as a company for private investments. In November 1939 (Sir) Robert Menzies appointed Fisk secretary of the economic cabinet and director of economic co-ordination: the job of co-ordination was 'a fantastic assignment', with Fisk by 'background and experience . . . not the man to do it'. In October 1941 (Sir) A. Fadden terminated the position.

While the demands of business meant that Fisk's grasp of electronics was quickly being overtaken, the future he painted for wireless was boundless: lighting lamps, cooking the roast, even driving cars. Wireless raised hopes for an international language and Fisk saw the possibility of communicating with the dead, especially after the death of his son, Thomas Maxwell, on active service in World War II. He showed a continuing interest in spiritualism.

For years Fisk kept a laboratory in his home and had many patents to his credit. Among the best known were the Fisk solariscope, which distinguished daylight from darkness around the world for users of shortwave radio; and the Fisk soundproof windows which were incorporated into Wireless House, the then tallest building in Sydney which A.W.A. built for its head office at the end of 1939.

By 1944, from 'a cloud no bigger than a man's hand', said Hughes, A.W.A. had grown to cover 'the whole heavens'. With a turnover in excess of £4 million and 6000 employees it had become one of Australia's largest organizations. Fisk that year stepped down to become managing director and chief executive of the Electrical and Musical Industries (His Master's Voice) group in London. In addition to a salary of £10 000 plus 1½ per cent net annual profits (compared with £A4500 plus 2¼ per cent from A.W.A.), Fisk was paid £50 000 for the rights to fourteen of his British letters patent. He restructured E.M.I. While profits rose in some areas, including the group's Australian interests, net profits declined in 1949 and 1950 and again after 1951 and he had weakened the firm's long-term prospects. In 1952 E.M.I. decided not to renew Fisk's contract: on top of a life pension of £5000 a year, he was retained, nominally, as a consultant for five years at £3000 a year. He returned to Sydney as 'a consultant in commerce, industry and technology', with his business interests now centred on the share market. His views were sought on the future of television, but his main concern was the future of solar, hydro and nuclear power. He still read and while he no longer swam daily, he cycled. The inscription on his coat of arms, *mens sana in corpore sano*, he rendered as 'fit but not stupid'. He continued to enjoy champagne for lunch and was a member of the Union and Australian clubs, Sydney, and the Royal Sydney Yacht Squadron.

In younger days Fisk declared an interest in landscape garden design: in 1931 A.W.A.

had promoted its new works at Ashfield as 'An Australian Factory in an Australian Garden'. He had also been a 'speed demon', establishing 'business driving records' between Sydney, Melbourne and Canberra. In the early 1920s he was a member of the New South Wales section of the Australian Aero Club; and later vice-president of the Australian Air League. No longer patron of the Music Teachers' Alliance or the Royal Philharmonic Society of Sydney, Fisk in retirement still enjoyed singing. One of the great entrepreneurs of his time, he was good company and in demand as a speaker. A personal magnetism and feel for public relations earned for A.W.A. and for Fisk himself an enviable press. Even without his high-domed head, the Fisk radiola, or A.W.A.'s Victorian establishment, Fiskville, his name in Australia would have been synonymous with the development of radio.

Fisk died at his Roseville home on 8 July 1965 and was cremated with Anglican rites. He was survived by his wife and three sons. His estate was valued for probate in Sydney at $354 628 and for $11 102 in England; he had settled substantial sums on his children and members of his wife's family after the war. A portrait of Fisk is held by Dr Graham Fisk of Sydney.

S. J. Butlin, *War economy, 1939-42*, 1 (Canb, 1955); R. R. Walker, *The magic spark* (Melb, 1973); *Rydges* Apr 1929; *Radio Pictorial*, 1 June 1937; *Radio Retailer of Aust*, 21 Sept 1939; *Scope* (Lond), Apr 1946; *AWA Technical Review*, 15 (1974), no 4; *Electronics Australia*, May-Aug, 1974; *Table Talk*, 10 Feb 1927; *Surrey Comet* (Eng), 20 Apr 1931; *Sun* (Syd), 31 May 1931; *Middlesex Chronicle* (Eng), 20 May, 29 July 1939; *Age*, 26 Nov 1931; *Truth* (Syd), 11 Dec 1939; AWA papers (held by Mr E. Fisk, Canberra, ACT); information from Mr and Mrs E. Fisk, Mr P. Geeves, AWA, Syd, Mr L. Petts, EMI, Hayes and Harlington, England.

MURRAY GOOT

FITCH, ALGERNON SYDNEY (1881-1972), shipmaster and businessman, was born on 30 January 1881 in London, son of Dr Robert Owen Fitch, chemist, and his wife Jemima Susannah, née London. Indentured as a cadet on a windjammer, he served on a hospital ship in the South African War before joining the Hooghly Pilot Service at Calcutta. In 1914 he settled at Bagdad, Tasmania, as an apple-orchardist. Despite three years in the Royal Naval Reserve, he joined the Australian Imperial Force in October 1916, but was discharged as medically unfit the following April.

As a member of a syndicate salvaging a wreck off King Island in Bass Strait, he became master of its elderly steamer, *Queenscliffe*, in 1919. When the wreck proved beyond recovery the syndicate, now styled Steamships Pty Ltd, permitted Fitch to take his ship to Papua where a war-created shipping shortage might make her profitable. Because of his perseverance in an unpromising trade and his skill in navigating hazardous waters, the company began a regular shipping service along the south coast. A store, mainly for urban Papuans, was soon opened in Port Moresby; it was expanded in 1925 and a branch was opened at Samarai in 1927.

When Fitch arrived in Papua the planting and business community was violently hostile to the pro-Papuan policy of (Sir) Hubert Murray [q.v.]. In April 1920 Fitch alleged in the *Sydney Morning Herald* that the Catholic Murray had favoured the Catholic mission by exempting its imports from duty. After chairing a meeting of a Citizens' Association on 28 September, he cabled to the King suggesting that white settlers in Papua might rebel. His cable was repudiated by most of the dissidents and was ridiculed by Murray's supporters.

Shunned by the élite in the Papua Club because of his connexion with the 'native' trade, he abandoned politics henceforth, stuck to business and prospered. By the late 1930s his Steamships Trading Co. (renamed in 1924) had become second in Papua only to Burns [q.v.7] Philp [q.v.] Ltd in trading and to the British New Guinea Development Co. in plantations. The Depression ruined most planters and the company was able to pick up cheaply several largely developed estates. It established subsidiaries including the Coral Sea Insurance Co. Ltd (1924), and in 1937-38 two very profitable rubber companies.

Fitch was evacuated in 1942 with other civilians in the face of the Japanese advance in New Guinea. With the formation of the Australian New Guinea Administrative Unit, he was permitted to return to Papua to keep his company's rubber plantations in production. Trading in the company's stores started again in November 1945. War damage compensation payments and a new share issue in 1946 facilitated a quick recovery and in November that year Fitch was able to retire.

Bluff, hard-working and pragmatic, Fitch attracted the loyalty of subordinates. After the missions, he was the first employer to appoint Papuans as masters on his coastal boats. He lived his long retirement at Kirribilli, Sydney, gambled on the stock exchange, travelled overseas and joined both the Royal Automobile Club and the Royal Sydney Yacht Squadron. He died in Sydney on 30 May 1972 and was cremated.

His first wife was a divorcee Jessie Elaine Goodeve, née Crovett, whom he had married in Sydney on 27 May 1930. On 4 July 1951 he married another divorcee Celia Josephine Smith, née McKenzie. Both marriages were civil ceremonies and were childless but there was a stepchild in each. His estate was valued for probate at $271 177.

F. West, *Hubert Murray* (Melb, 1968); Second Waigani Seminar, *The history of Melanesia* (Canb and Port Moresby, 1968); *Pacific Islands Mthly,* July 1972; *Papuan Courier,* 1, 8, 15 Oct 1920; *SMH,* 14 Apr 1920.   D. C. LEWIS

FITCHETT, WILLIAM HENRY (1841-1928), clergyman, writer and educator, was born on 9 August 1841 at Grantham, Lincolnshire, England, third son of William Fitchett and his wife Hannah, née Hubbard. His father, a perfumer, hairdresser, clog and pattenmaker and toy-dealer, was a Wesleyan local preacher who came to the Port Phillip District with a land order for 65 acres (26 ha) under J. D. Lang's [q.v.2] migration scheme. He arrived at Geelong in the *Larpent* with his wife and five children on 20 June 1849 and died in December 1851. Of William's brothers, Alfred Robertson became dean of Dunedin and Frederick solicitor-general of New Zealand.

William's formal schooling at a Wesleyan denominational school was brief and — while legend claims that he learnt Latin declension and translated Molière when pushing trucks in a Geelong quarry — he actually furthered his self-education by voracious reading and by participation in mutual improvement groups at Lydiard Street Wesleyan Church, Ballarat.

When interviewed in 1892 he referred to being 'Placed in business' in Geelong, 'Placed upon a farm', perhaps at nearby Ceres, where he first considered becoming a local preacher, and later, probably in 1862, going to Queensland as a jackeroo. By 1863 he was 'engaged in business on his own account' at Ballarat and taught at Lydiard Street Sunday School with James Campbell, a lifelong friend. By January 1865 he was an accredited local preacher. The following year he entered the Wesleyan ministry and was stationed at Mortlake (1866-67), Echuca (1868-69), South Yarra (1870-72), Lonsdale Street, Melbourne (1873), Carlton (1874-75), Bendigo (1876-78), and Hawthorn (1879-81). On 24 March 1870 at Mortlake, he married Jemima (Cara), daughter of Thomas Shaw [q.v.2]. In July 1872 he matriculated at the University of Melbourne, graduating B.A. in 1875.

After his appointment to Methodist Ladies' College, Kew, as founding president in 1882 he was withdrawn from the rigours of the itinerant ministry, although, as a forceful and fervent preacher who saw Methodism as 'intensely evangelical', he preached frequently. He saw his journalistic and educational work as part of his ministry and subservient to it. He applied his considerable business acumen to the financial and administrative affairs of his church and was on many committees. During the boom of the late 1880s he indulged in speculation on his own behalf.

In 1886 Fitchett was elected president of the Wesleyan Methodist Conference of Victoria and Tasmania, and in 1902 first president of the United Methodist Victorian and Tasmanian Conference. In 1904, in recognition of his contribution to the reunification of Methodism's five branches, he was elected first president of the General Conference of the Methodist Church of Australasia, holding the position until 1907. He also became a popular figure in world Methodism, addressing the Methodist Conference in London in 1899 and attending various British Conference meetings in 1905, when he gave the 35th Fernley Lecture on 'The Unrealised Logic of Religion'. He was a delegate at the Ecumenical Conference in Toronto in 1911.

His career as a journalist and writer began with a weekly column, 'Easy Chair Chat', in the *Methodist Spectator and Wesleyan Chronicle* (Melbourne) under the penname 'XYZ' (1875-79). His comments were witty, outspoken and controversial. He left the *Spectator* board and his 'Easy Chair' on a matter of principle when it was decided, in the interests of economy, no longer to pay contributors.

In 1882 Fitchett became editor of the *Southern Cross*, a weekly religious paper; in April 1900 his son, Thomas Shaw Fitchett, printer and publisher, became manager. In 1883, when James Balfour [q.v.3] bought the *Daily Telegraph* to establish a secular daily sympathetic to Christian interests, Fitchett became consulting editor until it was sold to the Herald and Weekly Times Ltd in 1892. In July that year the Australasian edition of W. T. Stead's *Review of Reviews* was launched under Fitchett's editorship; a 32-page supplement of local matter was added to the English edition. Fitchett was replaced in 1903, after having, as an Imperialist, fallen out with Stead regarding the South African War. In 1902 T. Shaw Fitchett published the *New Idea*, a women's magazine which, in 1911, became *Everylady's Journal*. Fitchett wrote occasional articles for this as well as becoming editor in 1904 of his son's companion publication, *Life*.

The books which made W. H. Fitchett a household name throughout the British Empire were 'in a sense a literary accident', arising from his journalism. Sir Cyprian

Bridge, commander of the Australian Station in 1896, asked Fitchett to write commemorative sketches on anniversaries of notable events in British history. These became an *Argus* Saturday feature running for sixteen months under the pen name 'Vedette'. The articles were pirated in India, republished in a London weekly, published in shilling form in Australia and finally, as *Deeds that won the Empire* (1897). The book was placed by the Admiralty in all warships' libraries, adopted as a holiday-task book in some great English public schools and printed in Braille. 100 000 copies of the sixpenny edition were sold.

This was followed by *Fights for the flag* (1898); *The tale of the great mutiny* (1899); *Wellington's men* (1900); *Nelson and his captains* (1902); *How England saved Europe* (1899-1900), a four-volume story of the war of 1793-1815 written for *Cornhill Magazine*; *The great duke* (2 vols, 1911); *The new world of the south* (2 vols, 1913); and articles on Australian identities collected and published in 1938 as *From convict to bushranger*. He said of his stories that 'the art which produced them was simply the barrister's art of getting up a case quickly and easily ... There was no attempt at fine writing, no pretence of original research ... with short words and short sentences, always seizing on the most picturesque incidents and translating the whole story, as far as possible, into personal terms'.

His novels, *The commander of the Hirondelle* (1904); *Ithuriel's spear* (1906); *A pawn in the game* (1907); and *The adventure of an ensign* (1917), reprinted from *Blackwood's Magazine*, were less successful. His religious publications include *Wesley and his century* (1906); *The beliefs of unbelief* (1908) and *Where the higher criticism fails* (1922).

In his *Forty years at the M.L.C.* ... (1921) Fitchett gave his account of the school's founding and growth from an enrolment of 111 at the end of 1882 to 721 (including 117 boarders) in 1928. Four headmasters served under him. Except when overseas in 1886, 1889, 1891, 1899, 1905 and 1911, he supervised the spiritual life of the college and boarding-school, assisted by his wife. After her death on 15 September 1918 he wrote: 'She was the governing mind of the Methodist Ladies' College on its domestic side'. On 31 March 1920 at Queen's College chapel he married Edith Skelton, née Wimble, widow of Rev. William Williams. His niece, Ada Fitchett (1859-1945), was on the school staff from 1883 to 1921, serving as lady superintendent for twenty-four years. His elder daughter, Elsie, while at school was amanuensis for *Deeds that won the Empire*, and taught there before marriage. His sons Frank, Thomas and William were school solicitor, publisher and medical officer respectively. His second son, Alfred, was also a solicitor. The school's first assembly hall, built in 1917, was named in his honour and has a stained-glass window to the memory of his younger daughter Nellie who died of meningitis in 1897. Fitchett Chapel, opened in 1959, and one of the school houses also commemorate him. There are portraits in the new assembly hall and in the chapel entrance. Strongly opposed to secular, state-controlled education, he contributed to the school his talent for public relations and advertisement. He attracted devoted service from those who worked with him on the staff and generous donations from fellow Methodists who were school council-members, including Henry Berry, F. J. Cato [qq.v.3, 7] and the Nicholas brothers [qq.v.].

In 1899 he was awarded an honorary LL.D. by Queen's University, Kingston, Canada, 'for his great literary achievement'. He was a trustee of the Public Library, Museums, and National Gallery of Victoria for thirty-five years. He listed his recreations as 'golf and hard work' and had an interest in cricket. He was a passionate son of the British Empire whose greatness was the theme of much of his writing. 'In dinnertime talk he was brilliant, in private conversation witty, in debate devastating', 'an autocrat – with an autocrat's virtues and faults'. A gracious friend, he could be an implacable foe. Writing in 1904, Fitchett admitted to 'a memory, loose-fibred and inexact as to dates and details of facts and verbal forms' but 'curiously susceptible to every touch of picturesque description'. He was so much a man of his time that it is difficult to appreciate his greatness in an age when certainties are unfashionable.

He died at the school on 26 May 1928 after suffering a haemorrhage of a duodenal ulcer and was buried in Boroondara cemetery. His estate, valued for probate at £14852, included a large library.

P. L. Brown (ed), *Clyde Company papers*, 5 (Lond, 1963); *Table Talk*, 12 Aug 1892; *Spectator* (Melb), 8, 29 Mar 1895; *Life* (Melb), Dec 1904-Mar 1905; *Methodist Recorder* (Lond), 3 Aug 1899, 27 July 1905; *Age*, 7 Dec 1904; *Argus*, 7, 8, 10, 12 Dec 1904, 8-11 Apr 1905, 26, 28, 29 May 1928; *SMH*, 26 May, 18 Aug 1928; *Southern Cross* (Melb), 8 June 1928; Fitchett travel notes, 1891, *and* MLC, Kew, Vic, Council minutes (held at school); Sir Samuel Way letter book, Nov 1897-Aug 1898, PRG 30/5/4 (SAA); personal information held by author.

A. THOMSON ZAINU'DDIN

FITZGERALD, JOHN DANIEL (1862-1922), compositor, journalist, barrister and politician, was born on 11 June 1862 at Shellharbour, New South Wales, son of John Daniel Fitzgerald, schoolteacher, and his wife Mary Ann, née Cullen, both from Limerick, Ireland. He was educated at the local public school, then at Fort Street and St Mary's Cathedral schools, Sydney. Apprenticed as a compositor at Bathurst, by 1885 he was working on the *Evening News* in Sydney and active in trade unionism and radical politics. He joined the Typographical Association, was president in 1887-88 and its delegate on the Trades and Labor Council, where he was elected to the executive and became a leading exponent of advanced political and social reforms. He was a member of the Socialist League and the founder of a republican league. An insatiable reader of progressive literature, he was a keen student of British socialism and trade unionism. In 1891 he was a foundation councillor of the Womanhood Suffrage League.

Jack Fitzgerald was in the forefront of the maritime strike of 1890. In September he went at his own expense to England on behalf of the Labor Defence Council to publicize the dispute; he also wanted to 'foster the spirit of kinship which has so recently developed between the old world workers and the new', following the Australian donation of about £38000 to London dockers in their 1889 strike and his own awareness of the similarity of gross squalor in London and Sydney slums. He travelled widely, addressed many meetings and gave impetus to the 'hands across the sea' concept which, in English-speaking countries, was modulating the grim doctrine of the class war. He met prominent radicals and liberals, including Mr Gladstone, John Burns, Keir Hardie, Tom Mann [q.v.], George Shipton and R. B. Cunninghame Graham; he studied municipal socialism and urban renewal in London and elsewhere, also visiting France, Germany and Italy. He later corresponded with several of his overseas friends. In March 1891 he published in the *Nineteenth Century* 'A reply' to H. H. Champion's [q.v.7] attack on the leaders of the maritime strike.

Fitzgerald returned to Sydney in time to take an important part in the final stages (March) of the founding of the Labor Electoral League (Labor Party) by the T.L.C. He was one of the four party members elected for West Sydney at the June general election, and became a member of the five-man committee of advice that attempted to lead thirty-five Labor parliamentarians. A confirmed protectionist, he was not happy with the party's support of the Parkes [q.v.5] Free-Trade ministry. In October the more suitable Dibbs [q.v.4] government took over, by which time the Labor Party was in disarray. In December a split occurred and Fitzgerald became one of the protectionist

Labor members keeping Dibbs in office.

A more serious party conflict broke out in September 1892 during the Broken Hill strike: (Sir) George Reid [q.v.], the new Free-Trade leader, moved a simple censure motion, but would not bring the government down on a Labor amendment condemning the handling of the strike; Fitzgerald voted for the latter but, with ten other Labor protectionists, refused to support Reid's censure, and Dibbs remained in office. Of the eleven, only four, including Fitzgerald, were still regarded as belonging to the party; they were execrated by all sections of Labor and were formally expelled at a conference in November 1893. By then Fitzgerald's radicalism had acquired firmer ideological bases, influenced by the British Fabians, and by the middle-class reformism of Alfred Deakin and C. C. Kingston [qq.v.], with whom he corresponded. He had lost some of his trade union, Labor pragmatism and now sought social and political improvements by democratic, knowledgeable, alert and concerned professionals, operating at various levels of government.

Fitzgerald was of medium build, handsome, with a style and assurance complemented by a well-trimmed moustache and Vandyke beard. He had returned to England in 1892 and, on 26 May at Chelsea registry office, married Octavie Camille Clara Ernestine Roche: John Burns was a witness. Fitzgerald's wife was a cultivated Frenchwoman; she fostered his growing cosmopolitanism and interest in music (he played the piano), literature, art and architecture. In 1893, when registering the birth of his only child, Maria Galatea (Ara), he described himself as a painter. The same year he was a commissioner for the Chicago exhibition.

W. M. Hughes [q.v.], the 'solidarity' Labor candidate, beat him at the 1894 general election. Fitzgerald lost again in 1895, at Bathurst, where he had Catholic connexions. He went back to journalism, contributed to radical papers, and edited *Fairplay*, the journal of the liquor trade. He worked for a time at Rockhampton, Queensland, and was editor of the Sydney *Freeman's Journal* in 1899-1904. In 1897 he was in London again. With the help of his brothers Tom and Dan, who had made a success of Fitzgeralds' circus (wound up in 1906), he studied law and was admitted to the New South Wales Bar on 30 April 1900. Supporting (Sir) Edmund Barton [q.v.7], Fitzgerald was a Federationist and contested the seat of Robertson in 1901, but lost. He was an alderman of the Sydney Municipal Council in 1900-04, and in the latter year failed as an independent to win the State seat of Belmore. In 1903 he became a member of Central Board for Old Age Pensions.

The Sydney council had not been responsive to Fitzgerald's views on the role of local government in the modernization of cities but, probably more than any other individual, he prepared public opinion for improvement in New South Wales. In 1899 he had published his Toynbee lecture, *Municipal statesmanship in Europe, what municipal reform has done*. He refreshed his ideas with a trip to Japan in 1903; in 1906 he stimulated discussion with *Greater Sydney and greater Newcastle*; and next year 'Sydney, the cinderella of cities', in the *Lone Hand*, exposed some unpalatable facts. His hope that (Sir) Joseph Carruthers [q.v.7] would be able to pass appropriate legislation was unfounded. He respected and remained loyal to Deakin, but Federal politics offered no solutions for town-planning. With the Fusion of the conservative parties under Deakin in 1909, Fitzgerald returned to the Labor Party, but was beaten by (Sir) Daniel Levy [q.v.] for the middle-class State seat of Darlinghurst next year, when Labor won office for the first time.

He again became active in the party and was a member of its executive in 1911-16 and vice-president in 1912. He revisited Europe in 1913 and attended the funeral of August Bebel. Fitzgerald was Labor Party president in 1915-16, marking the temporary retention of party control by the premier, W. A. Holman [q.v.], and the remaining precarious influence of intellectual socialism opposed to the syndicalism and trade unionism of the 'industrialists'. He was appointed to the Legislative Council in 1915, and was vice-president of the Executive Council (until July 1919) and representative of the government in the council (until June 1918). Feeling keenly the plight of France and Belgium in World War I, and with his wife and daughter in Rome, he was a founder in 1915 of the Universal Service League, which sought total commitment to the war. With many others he was again expelled from the Labor Party in 1916 for supporting conscription.

In Holman's National government of that year Fitzgerald also became minister for public health and for local government. The conservatism of his new colleagues, his heavy work-load, his declining health, and wartime exigencies retarded his still-vital reformism, but he improved his departments and, building on the work of F. Flowers [q.v.], facilitated progress in mother and child welfare and in the treatment of tuberculosis and venereal disease. He was president of the Health Society of New South Wales and founded the Society for the Prevention and Cure of Consumption. He provided effective leadership in the State campaign against the influenza pandemic in 1918-19.

On the death of J. R. Dacey [q.v.] in 1912, Fitzgerald had become chairman of the Housing Board; he helped to initiate and, with the aid of (Sir) John Sulman [q.v.], controlled the early building of the 'garden suburb', Daceyville. In 1913 he was on the royal commission for a greater Sydney. A foundation member and vice-president of the Town Planning Association of New South Wales that year, he was chairman of the first interstate conference in Adelaide in 1917 and of the second in Brisbane next year. Against increasing difficulties — which included six months sick leave in 1917 when he visited the United States of America — he managed to work on a local government bill; passed in 1919, it remains a landmark in its field, although, in the end, it was a pale projection of Fitzgerald's ideas and aspirations. In 1919-20 he was solicitor-general and minister of justice.

For his assistance to French charities and to Frenchmen passing through Sydney, Fitzgerald was awarded the Légion d'honneur in 1919. He was close to Archbishop Kelly [q.v.], especially in the war years. Secretary of the local Irish National League, after years of work for Home Rule — he kept in touch with John Redmond [q.v.6] — he was isolated by the Dublin Easter rising in 1916. He was a trustee of the Public (State) Library of New South Wales in 1912-22. In 1915 he published *The rise of the N.S.W. political Labor Party*; in 1922, a novel, *The ring valley*; in 1923, stories of circus life, *Children of the sunlight*, and next year, *Studies in Australian crime*. He also chanced his arm at poetry and play-writing.

Fitzgerald died of cancer in his home at Darling Point, Sydney, on 4 July 1922 and was buried in the Catholic section of Waverley cemetery. He was survived by his daughter who, as Maria Galatea Clarke, achieved some notice in America for her singing. His estate was sworn for probate at £904. A portrait by Longstaff [q.v.], his close friend, is in the Sydney Town Hall. Fitzgerald Avenue, Maroubra, is named after him.

B. Nairn, *Civilising capitalism* (Canb, 1973); P. Spearritt, *Sydney since the twenties* (Syd, 1978); J. Roe (ed), *Twentieth century Sydney* (Syd, 1980); *Advertiser* (Adel), 11, 12 Mar 1891; *Punch* (Melb), 23 Sept 1915; *SMH*, 9 May, 6 June 1916, 23 Nov 1917, 18 June 1918, 25 Feb 1919, 5 July 1922; Papers of Barton, *and* Deakin (NL), *and* Carruthers (ML), *and* Fitzgerald (Dixson Lib, Syd).

BEDE NAIRN

FITZPATRICK, JOHN CHARLES LUCAS (1862-1932), journalist and politician, was born on 15 February 1862 at Moama, New South Wales, son of John James Fitzpatrick, a Dublin-born police constable, and his native-born wife Elizabeth, née Lucas. In 1869 the family moved to Windsor. Educated at a denominational school, at 14 Fitzpatrick began an apprenticeship in the *Australian* office at Windsor and at 18 was a compositor on Melbourne *Punch*. He worked on newspapers at Gunnedah, Narrabri, Walgett and Parramatta, New South Wales, and in 1885 became a reporter on Hugh Mahon's [q.v.] *Southern Argus* at Goulburn. On 11 January 1886 at St Patrick's Roman Catholic Church, Parramatta, he married Agnes Clare Kelly. About 1888 he established the *Windsor and Richmond Gazette* which he managed and edited until 1899. In 1890 he was a founder of the Provincial Press Association. In 1905 he bought the *Molong Argus* and sold it in 1907.

In 1895 Fitzpatrick was elected to the Legislative Assembly for Rylstone as a free trader. The election was invalidated but two months later he was re-elected. He held the seat until 1904 when he was defeated for Northumberland; in 1906 he was defeated for the Federal seat of Calare by Thomas Brown [q.v.7]. Next year he returned to the Legislative Assembly, representing Orange until 1920 and in 1927-30. In 1920-27 he was a member for Bathurst.

A good debater, Fitzpatrick was always alert and wide awake in the House even at 5 a.m. He was closely associated with the testator's family maintenance and the unclaimed money bills and with one to regulate the taking of evidence in select committees. In the early 1900s he supported the right of women to stand for parliament but towards the end of his career claimed that politics seduced them from their homes. He believed that rural interests could best be served by limiting government control of such matters as abattoirs and wheat sales, and in 1916 recommended the completion of country railways before the erection of the Sydney Harbour Bridge.

From 1900 Fitzpatrick was a trustee of the Public Library of New South Wales. His love of Australian history lay behind his support of the term of David Scott Mitchell's [q.v.5] bequest. While in parliament he compiled several books of local reminiscences, mostly of Windsor and the Hawkesbury district. He also published two books of poetry, *Various verses* (Parramatta, 1895, 1907) and two travel books about a visit to the East, *Eastward ho* (1905) and *A jaunt to Java* (1908).

Fitzpatrick was one of six Liberals chosen by W. A. Holman [q.v.] to form his Nationalist ministry on 15 November 1916; he became secretary for mines and on 30 October 1918 treasurer also; the government lost the March 1920 election. During a serious strike in 1917 he carried the controversial Coal Mines Regulation (Amendment) Act which permitted inexperienced men to work in the mines. Labor branded the measure as retrograde and anti-unionist and Fitzpatrick as a murderer, but the strike ended soon after the Act was enforced. His conviction that Australia had a strong obligation to support the British Empire was strengthened by his son's service with the 1st Light Horse Regiment in Gallipoli and Egypt. On 20 December 1921 he was secretary for mines and minister for local government in (Sir) George Fuller's [q.v.] seven-hour ministry and held the same posts in his ministry in 1922-25. Fitzpatrick was also chairman of the Lord Howe Island Board.

Although he was forceful and independent, often claiming to speak for himself rather than for his party or electorate, Fitzpatrick was never malicious; he proudly maintained friendships despite party differences. Known as 'Fitz', he conducted elections with good-humoured bluster, gaining Protestant support by criticizing Rome, but keeping his friendships with local priests. He had no sympathy for criminals and voted against the abolition of capital punishment in 1925. He was a 'mercurial little man' with a luxuriant moustache, and was noted for his witty speeches, 'racy jokes', dapper clothes and fresh buttonholes, worn with the pride of a keen gardener.

Fitzpatrick retired from politics in 1930. Survived by a son and daughter, he died on 7 August 1932 at his Roseville home and was cremated with Methodist forms. His estate was valued for probate at £11 657.

PD (NSW), 1917, 2S, p 590; *Western Post*, 24 Dec 1895; *T&CJ*, 4 Dec 1907; *Fighting Line*, 14 Aug 1913; *Bulletin*, 23 Aug 1917, 10 Aug 1932; *SMH, 8 Aug 1932*; *Molong Argus*, 12 Aug 1932; Carruthers, *and* G. E. Reeve papers (ML).

JILL WATERHOUSE

FITZSIMMONS, ROBERT (1863-1917), professional boxer and sometime actor, was born on 26 May 1863 at Helston, Cornwall, England, twelfth child of James Fitzsimmons, policeman (but formerly an Irish soldier), and his wife Jane, née Strongman, of Truro. The Fitzsimmons family migrated to Timaru, New Zealand, in 1872, where James became a veterinary shoeing-smith. Robert and an older brother became blacksmiths.

Bob Fitzsimmons was boxing with bare knuckles as an amateur at 15. He first drew attention by knocking out four opponents in one afternoon in an 1880 Timaru tournament staged by Jem Mace, the visiting British ring hero. In 1883 he went to Sydney seeking the tutelage of Larry Foley [q.v.4]. He enjoyed some success there as a pugilist, but mainly supported himself as a blacksmith. On 14 October 1885 he married an English girl Louisa Johns; of their three children a son survived. In eight years in Sydney Fitzsimmons boxed 27 times, for 16 wins, 4 losses and 7 no-decision bouts. On 12 February 1890, he was knocked out in four rounds by Jim Hall, contesting the Australian middleweight championship, but had knocked out Hall in one round two days earlier. There is some suggestion that these two results were prearranged.

Leaving Sydney for San Francisco, United States of America, on 16 April 1890, Fitzsimmons won three fights within two months. On 14 January next year at New Orleans, he knocked out Jack Dempsey, 'The Nonpareil', in fourteen rounds to win the world middleweight championship. His greatest success came on 17 March 1897, at Carson City, Nevada, when he knocked out James (Gentleman Jim) Corbett in the fourteenth round with his 'solar plexus punch' to gain the heavyweight championship of the world. Two bouts and two years later, he lost this title by knockout to James J. Jeffries, and lost a return bout in 1902. A twenty rounds points decision over George Gardner at San Francisco on 25 November 1903 won him the newly recognized world light heavyweight championship, which he lost to Jack O'Brien at Philadelphia in 1905. His last championship contest was for the Australian heavyweight title on 27 December 1909 in Sydney, where he was knocked out by Bill Lang. He had a further two no-decision bouts in Pennsylvania in 1914 aged 50.

In a professional career extending from 1881 to 1914, Fitzsimmons had 81 bouts for 53 wins, 11 losses, 1 draw, 12 no-decisions and 4 exhibitions. His feat, winning world titles in three divisions, has been equalled only once, by Henry Armstrong some forty years later. While powerful in the shoulders and arms, Fitzsimmons weighed only 160 lbs. (72 kg), was spindly-legged, pale and freckled, and balding — he was sometimes known as 'Ruby Robert' or the 'Freckled Freak'.

In 1893 Fitzsimmons was divorced from his wife and on 24 July at San Francisco married his manager's sister, Rose Julian, an Australian acrobat, who bore him two sons and a daughter. On Rose's death in 1903, he married on 24 July a young actress, Julia May Gifford, also at San Francisco. They were divorced in 1915 and on 16 March at Newark, New Jersey, Fitzsimmons wed another actress, Temo Ziller of Portland. Like most heavyweight champions of his time, Fitzsimmons capitalized on his fame and appeared in several stage plays. His book *Physical culture and self-defence* (Philadelphia) was first published in 1901. In the final months of his life, he became an evangelist. He died of pneumonia at Chicago on 22 October 1917. Born in Cornwall, raised in New Zealand, but serving his boxing apprenticeship in Sydney, Fitzsimmons is claimed as a British, New Zealand, or even Australian, champion. However before winning a world title he became an American citizen.

Dictionary of American Biography, 6 (New York, 1931); B. F. O'Brien, *Kiwis with gloves on* (Wellington, NZ, 1960); K. Roberts, *Captain of the push* (Melb, 1963); G. Odd, *The fighting blacksmith* (Lond, 1976).   A. F. COLLINGS

FITZSIMONS, WILLIAM ROBERT (1870-1926), dentist and politician, and HERBERT PATON (1898-1970), politician, were father and son. William was born on 26 November 1870 at Greencastle, near Moville, Donegal, Ireland, son of Samuel Fitzsimons, of the constabulary, and his wife Isabella, née McCloy. After the death of her husband, in about 1887 Isabella moved her five sons and two daughters to Sydney, where William joined the National Bank of Australasia. At Chatswood, on 21 January 1898 he married Bessie Amy Louisa, daughter of Henry Clifford Love, and became a director of Clifford Love & Co. Ltd, eastern merchants. They lived at Gordon. About 1901 William qualified as a dentist and practised in Macquarie Street.

In 1910-22 Fitzsimons served on the Kuring-gai Shire Council and was its president in 1917-21. At the same time he acted as honorary secretary in their electorates for (Sir) Charles G. Wade [q.v.] and (Sir) Joseph Cook [q.v.7]. As a Nationalist Fitzsimons won Cumberland in the Legislative Assembly in 1922 and held his seat in 1925. An infrequent and unimpressive speaker in the House, he was extremely popular, and assiduous, in his electorate; in 1924-26 he was a member of the Public Accounts Committee.

Fitzsimons died in Sydney Hospital on 20 March 1926 from injuries received when knocked down by a car while leaving a tram in Hunter Street, and was buried in the Presbyterian section of Northern Suburbs cemetery. He was survived by his wife, son and daughter.

His son Herbert Paton was born on 25 November 1898 at Gordon, Sydney, and was educated at Abbotsholme College with F. G. Pratten. A senior cadet in the 18th Battalion, after army service in World War I he enrolled in first-year medicine at the University of Sydney in 1920. After working for Boswell & Co., manufacturers, in 1925 he joined the sales staff of Pratten Bros. Ltd, printers, and became a director. On 2 April 1927 at the Presbyterian church, Pymble, he married Eleanor Margaret Brown.

In the 1920s Fitzsimons had been campaign director for H. E. Pratten [q.v.] and was a councillor of the National Association of New South Wales in 1929-31 and 1936-37. In July 1930 he won a by-election for the State seat of Lane Cove. Rising rapidly to cabinet rank, he became an honorary minister under (Sir) Bertram Stevens [q.v.] in February 1933 and minister for health from August 1935. He carried important amendments to the Medical Practitioners and Pharmacy Acts in 1939 and 1940. Early in 1939 he visited Europe and the United States of America to study later developments in hospital design and the treatment of tuberculosis and cancer.

Soon after the outbreak of World War II Fitzsimons got leave from his ministerial duties and, as a temporary captain in 1940 became staff officer, medical services, and established military hospitals. Seconded to the Australian Imperial Force, in August 1942 he was registrar of the 114th Australian General Hospital, Goulburn, until 1943. Promoted major on 17 July 1943, he was registrar of the 2/5th A.G.H., Port Moresby, in 1943-44. Returning to Australia in 1944 he did not seek re-election because of his military duties; he was assistant registrar of the 113th military hospital, Concord, until 1947.

Meanwhile Fitzsimons had held his seat in the 1941 elections that brought the Labor Party to office. In 1944-55 he served on the Kuring-gai Shire Council. He was elected to the Legislative Council in September 1955 where he continued to take an interest in health affairs and chaired its select committee on public hospitals in 1961. Afraid that the Liberal Party could support a proposal for the council's abolition, in September 1959 he joined the Country Party; he was government whip in 1967-70.

Fitzsimons died on 31 January 1970 at Wamberal, near Gosford, and was buried in the Presbyterian section of Northern Suburbs cemetery after a service at St John's Anglican Church, Gordon. He was survived by his wife, son and daughter.

Aust National Review, 20 Mar 1926; *SMH*, 22 Mar 1926, 30 Sept 1959, 2 Feb 1970.
                                               JOHN MCCARTHY

FIVEASH, ROSA CATHERINE (1854-1938), botanical aritist, was born on 22 July 1854 in Adelaide, youngest child of Robert Archibald Fiveash, businessman and supe-

rintendent of the Blinman and Yudanamu-
tana copper-mines, and his wife Margaret,
née Rees. She was trained by Miss A. Benham and at the Adelaide School of Art and
Design in 1881-88, and then taught art
privately and at Tormore House School in
North Adelaide for many years. In 1882 Rosa
was invited to illustrate *The forest flora of
South Australia* by John Ednie Brown
[q.v.3]. Nine parts of this work, which was
never completed, were published in 1882-90.
Each one contained five attractive lithographs of native plants and Rosa drew 32 of
the 45 published; they were drawn as
specimens came to hand, in no particular
botanical order.

Her services were increasingly sought as a
versatile illustrator of scientific papers. She
provided seven of the coloured plates accompanying (Sir) Edward C. Stirling's
[q.v.6] description in 1891 of the newly discovered marsupial mole, as well as 322 clear,
bright illustrations of toas (Aboriginal direction signs), for a later paper by Stirling
and E. R. Waite [q.v.]. Fiveash pioneered
china-painting in Adelaide, attending to all
stages of the process, including the firing.
Her main love was flower-painting; a portfolio of these pictures so impressed the
governor, Lord Tennyson [q.v.], and Robert
Barr Smith [q.v.6] that they bought them in
1900 as a gift to the colony. She collaborated
with Dr R. S. Rogers [q.v.] for thirty years,
illustrating his publications on orchids, including his section on them in J. M. Black's
[q.v.7] *Flora of South Australia* Part I (second
edition). Fiveash was so meticulous that she
would wait for weeks for a rare orchid bud to
open fully before recording it.

Apart from two years overseas, Rosa lived
all her life in the family home, Gable House,
North Adelaide, with her sister. They were
both unmarried and devout Anglicans. Rosa
worked steadily until failing eyesight
supervened four years before she died. In
1937 she presented many of her paintings to
the Public Library of South Australia. Most
of her life's work — beautifully drawn flower
portraits in glowing water-colours — is now
in the State Library and the South Australian Museum.

Rosa Fiveash died on 13 February 1938
and was buried in West Terrace cemetery.
Rogers described her as the foremost Australian botanical artist of her day; this was
well-merited praise, for her scientific illustrations had been rather inconspicuously
acknowledged in her lifetime. She is
remembered as a little lady of quiet dignity
and with a zest for work. *Australian orchids*,
a book of her pictures from the museum
collection, edited by Noel Lothian, was
published in Adelaide in 1974. It demonstrates her ability to capture the beauty of a
flower without departing from botanical
accuracy.

R. Biven, *Some forgotten, some remembered*
(Adel, 1976); Roy Soc SA, *Trans*, 14 (1890-91); *Lone
Hand*, May 1915; Sth Aust Museum, *Records*, 1
(1919), no 2; *Vic Naturalist*, 49 (1932-33), 54
(1937-38); *South Aust Naturalist*, 49 (1974-75), 55
(1980-81); Hunt Inst biogs (Basser Lib, Canb).
                                          ERIC B. SIMS

FIZELLE, REGINALD CECIL GRAH-
AME (RAH) (1891-1964), painter and
teacher, was born on 4 September 1891 at
Baw Baw, near Goulburn, New South Wales,
second son of Hubert George Fizelle, a Victorian-born schoolteacher, and his native-
born wife Agnes Elizabeth, née Marsden.
After training at Teachers' College, Sydney,
he joined the Department of Public Instruction and was teaching at Goulburn
when he enlisted in the Australian Imperial
Force in January 1916. He fought with the
22nd Battalion in France, was promoted to
lance sergeant and was wounded three
times.

Fizelle returned to Australia in 1919 with
the after-effects of gas and a badly damaged
left arm. Back at the Teachers' College, he
specialized in art, under May Marsden, and
in 1921 won a scholarship to Julian Ashton's
[q.v.7] Sydney Art School. In 1922-26 he
taught at Darlington Public School, and
continued evening classes with Ashton and
also studied under Will Ashton [q.v.7].
Known as 'Rah', he chiefly painted pleasantly airy landscape water-colours and exhibited with the Society of Artists, Sydney,
from 1923 and the Australian Water-Colour
Institute from 1925. His teaching was progressive, introducing creative expression as
opposed to representation.

In 1927 Fizelle studied in London at the
Polytechnic School of Art, Regent Street,
and the Westminster School of Art under
Bernard Meninsky. In Italy in 1928-30 his
landscape paintings and water-colours
became simplified, stylized and geometric.
He was further influenced by the early
Renaissance painting of Giotto and Piero
della Francesca: El Greco remained his
favourite artist. He travelled widely in Europe, and exhibited at the Royal Academy of
Arts, London, and the Salon de la Société des
Artistes Français, Paris.

Back in Sydney in 1931, Fizelle held one-
man shows there and in Melbourne, and next
year painted at Dorrit Black's [q.v.7]
Modern Art Centre. In 1932-37 he and Grace
Crowley conducted joint classes: their
studio, at 215a George Street, was the most
advanced centre of modern art in Australia.
The week-day students were few, but at
evenings and on Saturdays, colleagues such

as Ralph Balson and Frank Hinder worked there. In 1939 the group held a long-planned manifesto exhibition, 'Exhibition 1', at David Jones' [q.v.2] Art Gallery. Fizelle's characteristic paintings and drawings of the 1930s are semi-abstract figure compositions, but he also showed a special interest in the dignity of labour with a series of pea-pickers.

In 1939 Fizelle became the first president of the New South Wales branch of the Contemporary Art Society of Australia, and for some years was a regular exhibitor. He was president of the Australian Water-Colour Institute in 1948-51, constantly exhibiting with it until 1962. In 1938 he had returned to teaching, at Balgowlah Public School (whose 6 to 10-year-olds' work he presented at the Grosvenor Galleries – an unprecedented context for children's art) and then at Redfern. He lectured at Teachers' College, Sydney, in 1947-57. His art in the 1940s and early 1950s included near-abstract figures in carved wood, sandstone and pottery. Most later water-colours are realistic studies of natural abstract structures, like eroded rock or tree forms, found near the homes he had at Palm Beach and Kulnura – the George Street studio remained as a city *pied-à-terre*.

On 28 November 1942 at North Sydney registry office he had married Edith Agnes Watson, née Collins; an artist, known as Michael Collins, she had been one of his early students. On 25 October 1964 he died in Royal Prince Alfred Hospital, Sydney, and was cremated without religious rites. He was survived by his wife. His collection of Italian majolica pottery and woven fabrics was given by his widow to the Museum of Applied Arts and Sciences, Sydney.

Enthusiastic, wide-ranging and cultivated in his artistic sympathies, Rah Fizelle ultimately gave less energy to his own art than to his fellow artists and their causes, to his students, to children and the underprivileged. Modern art was perhaps one of many good causes to be supported by a man who best loved art-history and natural beauty.

R. Free, *Balson, Crowley, Fizelle, Hinder* (Syd, 1966); *Art and Aust*, 3 (Sept 1965), no 2; *Art Gallery of NSW Q*, Oct 1966; Fizelle papers (Art Gallery of NSW Lib, Syd).   DANIEL THOMAS

FLACK, EDWIN HAROLD (1873-1935), athlete and accountant, was born on 5 November 1873 at Islington East, London, son of Joseph Henry Flack, accountant, and his wife Marian, née Smith. In 1878 the family migrated to Melbourne where Joseph established an accountancy firm. After education at Melbourne Church of England Grammar School, Teddy joined his father,

then a partner in the firm of Davey, Flack & Co. In March 1895 he went to London to gain experience with Price, Waterhouse & Co., chartered accountants (whom he later represented in Australia), and graduated F.C.P.A. and F.S.A.A. (England). He returned to Melbourne in 1899. With his father and later his brother Henry he built up the firm of Flack & Flack, accountants, with branches in Sydney, Brisbane, Adelaide and Perth, and Auckland and Wellington in New Zealand.

Flack was a director of several companies including (William) Howard Smith [q.v.6] Ltd, Robert Harper [q.v.] & Co. Ltd, and Australian Iron and Steel Ltd. At his Burnbank stud farm near Berwick, he bred Friesian cattle. Following his father, Flack was on the committee of management of the Alfred Hospital from 1918 to 1935. He was a member of the Melbourne, Australian and Royal Melbourne Golf clubs. After suffering from heart trouble for a long time, he died after an operation on 10 January 1935, leaving an estate valued for probate at £43 855. He was unmarried.

Flack is remembered as the first Australian to win a gold medal at the Olympic Games. Before going overseas he was well known as an amateur athlete. In 1892 he founded the Melbourne Hare and Hounds Club. He was the one-mile champion of Australasia in 1893 and 1894, and had won several colonial championships. In England he joined the London Athletic Club and the Thames and the Hampton Court hare and hounds clubs. He ran often and quite successfully. Nevertheless newspaper reports of his presence in Athens for the revived Olympic Games in 1896, at which Australia was not officially represented, came as a surprise to his family who learned that he had taken a months holiday.

Flack decided to run both the 800 and 1500 metre races, and, even more enthusiastically, put his name down for the marathon. The favourites for the first two events were Lermusiaux of France and the American, Blake. Flack won his heat of the 800 metres convincingly. Next day was the 1500 metre race. Because of the roughness of the track and the tight corners, the pace soon slackened but as they started down the last straight Blake came like fury and almost levelled. But the Australian had his measure, pulling up fresh and strong in 4 minutes 33.2 seconds. The victory was popular because the Americans had been dominating the competitions. Two days later Flack became the favourite for the 800 metres final because Lermusiaux had withdrawn to concentrate on the marathon, and won easily in 2 minutes 11.9 seconds.

Later that afternoon he was in a coach

travelling the dusty, stony road to Marathon; the journey took four hours. He fancied less and less the idea of returning on that track the next day, yet he knew he would regret it forever if he missed it. The longest distance he had previously run was ten miles on a grass surface.

The marathon started under a very hot sun in front of a huge and enthusiastic crowd. Lermusiaux bounded out in front; Flack at first chose to stay with the Greeks who had had most experience, but found the pace too easy. By the ten kilometre mark he had passed everybody but the leader. At thirty kilometres he passed Lermusiaux, who soon after quit the race; Blake had already done so. With six kilometres to go he was still in front but finding it very hard. A figure swept by. A Greek. He could not win now, but neither could he stop. He swayed from one side of the road to the other and eventually sagged to the ground. He was taken to the stadium by ambulance and was able to watch the finish; it was impossible to grudge the Greeks their victory.

For the rest of the week Flack was treated like royalty. A friend said, 'Why, you're the lion of all Athens'. He left to the accompaniment of bands and waving flags, returning by himself to London. His athletic career had culminated in those seven wonderful days when the Olympic spirit was resurrected in Athens that hot summer of 1896.

R. Clarke and N. Harris, *The lonely breed* (Lond, 1967); *Argus*, 11 Jan 1935.   RON CLARKE

FLANNERY, GEORGE ERNEST (1872-1945), barrister, was born on 13 March 1872 at Albury, New South Wales, fifth son of Irish parents Edmund Hayes Flannery, inspector of schools, and his wife Ellen, née Mac-Sweeney. He was educated at Sydney Boys' High School and from 1886 at St Ignatius College, Riverview, where he won many prizes. At the University of Sydney he graduated B.A. in 1892, winning the (Sir G.) Wigram Allen [q.v.3] scholarship for law, and LL.B. in 1894, with first-class honours and the university medal. Professor Pitt Cobbett [q.v.] urged other students to emulate Flannery's industry and mental clarity, but Flannery recalled that Cobbett served all students 'with a large dose of brimstone and a minimum of treacle'. Admitted to the Bar on 23 July 1894, he read with A. G. Ralston [q.v.].

One of the bright young men surrounding (Sir) Edmund Barton [q.v.7], Flannery campaigned energetically for Federation. Much influenced by Senator R. E. O'Connor

[q.v.], he became his private secretary in 1901. Next year he accompanied Barton to England for the coronation of Edward VII; he met many prominent people, visited Ireland and returned through North America. In 1903, when O'Connor was appointed to the High Court of Australia, he became his associate.

Returning to the Bar in 1904, Flannery acquired a large, varied practice especially in appeals before the Full Bench of the Supreme Court and the High Court. He combined a mastery of legal principle with an orderly mind and the gift of lucid argument. His early High Court cases dealt mainly with patents, land tax and arbitration. He was increasingly briefed by the Commonwealth and New South Wales governments in cases involving constitutional law. He recognized the need for amendments to the Constitution. In 1916 under the War Precautions Act he was appointed by the Commonwealth government chairman of a board to try to determine issues relating to the coal strike. On 5 May 1920 he took silk. He kept abreast of the 'changing face of litigation' brought about by the financial development of the State, new commercial relations and the growing importance of constitutional law and taxation, which resulted in a more restrained class of advocacy. In 1931 he was retained by the Incorporated Law Institute of New South Wales to address the Legislative Assembly on the demerits of a controversial bill to reconstitute the legal profession; the bill was dropped. He retired in 1937; Mr Justice F. S. Boyce [q.v.7] observed that he had 'resisted all endeavours to lift him to a more serene atmosphere [the bench]'.

With great affection for his old school, Flannery was a foundation member of the Old Ignatians' Union and its second president. In 1901-41 he was a fellow of St John's College, within the university. He found his recreation following the turf and regularly attended Randwick racecourse.

Flannery lived at Centennial Park, and later nearby at Ocean Street, Woollahra, where he died from coronary occlusion on 28 January 1945; he was buried in the Catholic section of Waverley cemetery. He was survived by his wife Susan Teresa, née O'Donnell, whom he had married at St Joseph's Church, Woollahra, on 17 January 1914, and by one of their two sons. His estate was valued for probate at £44 335.

T. R. Bavin (ed), *The jubilee book of the law school of the University of Sydney* (Syd, 1940); J. M. Bennett (ed), *A history of the New South Wales Bar* (Syd, 1969); St Ignatius College, Riverview (Syd), *Our Alma Mater*, 1893, Christmas 1896, 1900, July 1904, July 1905, 1920, 1945; *Aust Law J*, 18 (1945); *SMH*, 16 Apr 1937; A27, Boys' Ledger 1885-89 (St

Ignatius College, Riverview, Syd, Archives).

JOHN KENNEDY MCLAUGHLIN

FLEGG, HENRY (JERSEY) (1878-1960), football administrator and sewerage engineer, was born on 6 April 1878 at Bolton, Yorkshire, England, son of Henry Flegg, engine-man, and his wife Ann, née Willis. About 1888 the family came to Sydney where his father worked as a labourer for the Metropolitan Board of Water Supply and Sewerage. As a carrot-headed lad, Flegg was nicknamed 'Jersey' after the red-haired governor [q.v.]. He attended St John's and William Street schools, Darlinghurst. After his father's death in 1894 'Jersey' Flegg was in turn employed as labourer by the water board, beginning on 16 October. At his marriage, with Congregational forms, to a dressmaker, Margaret, late O'Mara, née Delohery, on 26 February 1908 he described himself as electrician. In 1910 he was appointed assistant inspector, sewerage maintenance, in 1930 general superintendent and engineer in 1936, because of his 'outstanding knowledge of and contribution to sewerage maintenance' (though he had no formal qualifications). He retired from the water board on 6 April 1946, and was awarded the Imperial Service Medal.

Spare-time energies Flegg devoted to football. A hard-working and strong-tackling Rugby Union forward, he had played for the Adelphi club in the 1890s, then for Sydney. In 1902 he represented the State against Queensland. When a players' revolt led to the foundation of the New South Wales Rugby Football League, in January 1908 he was elected secretary of the Eastern Suburbs club and founding delegate to the league, of which he was made a life-member. In the 1908 and 1909 seasons he captained an Easts team that included 'Dally' Messenger and Sid Pearce [qq.v.], then retired to become State selector, holding the position for a record nineteen years. He was also sometime metropolitan and Australian selector, and in 1922 managed the State team which toured New Zealand.

In 1925 Flegg became a vice-president of the league and member of its judicial committee. Sir Joynton Smith's [q.v.] elevation to position of patron in 1929, after Fred Flowers' [q.v.] death, led to Flegg's election as president. Joynton Smith's had been a nominal presidency, Flegg's was to be an active and guiding role for the next thirty-one years. The Depression reduced the league's gate receipts from £24 487 in 1928 to £15 500 in 1931 and for the next fifteen years revenue remained low. A man of 'inflexible determination ... a rugged and likeable character, forthright in his utter-

ances', Flegg managed the league's affairs shrewdly. In 1937-58 he was a director of the New South Wales Leagues' Club, and for seventeen of those years was chairman. As chairman of the Australian Board of Control from 1941 he was noted for exercising his casting vote without State favouritism.

Long a resident of Paddington, childless and from 1945 a widower, he later lived in the premises of the Leagues' Club, Phillip Street, which he had helped to build. He remained president of the State league and chairman of the Australian board until his death in hospital at North Sydney on 23 August 1960. After an Anglican service he was cremated. His estate was sworn for probate at £2228.

Arrow, 2 June 1906; *Rugby League News*, 5 June 1920, 27, 28 Aug 1960; *SMH*, 23 Aug 1960; information from Metropolitan Water Sewerage and Drainage Board.   CHRIS CUNNEEN

FLEMING, JOHN WILLIAM (1863?-1950), anarchist and agitator, was born at Derby, England, son of an Irish father; his English mother died when he was 5. Both his father and grandfather had been involved in militant worker movements. At the age of 10 he went to work in a Leicester boot factory; as a youth he attended free-thought lectures by Bradlaugh and others. Invited by an uncle to come to Melbourne, Fleming arrived in 1884 and obtained work as a bootmaker. Known as 'Chummy', he soon embarked on a career of agitation for freedom of choice in industrial and personal spheres, acting as an irritant to conservatives and reformers alike. He joined the Victorian secular movement, and in October 1884 attended the second Australasian Freethought Conference in Sydney. In early 1885 he was arrested for speaking on the North Wharf and taking part in an unemployed demonstration. Discharged, he worked in Ballarat for a few months as a bootmaker and became secretary of the local branch of the Australasian Secular Association.

Fleming joined the Melbourne Anarchist Club, becoming a close friend of J. A. Andrews [q.v.7]. In 1889, after the break-up of the club, he helped to establish the Melbourne branch of the Australian Socialist League, its successor the Social Democratic League, and the semi-secret Knights of Labor. He agitated for the Sunday opening of libraries and museums and for free speech, and supported the single-tax movement; he is credited with arranging the first Victorian collection for the London dock-strikers in August. He was often in gaol or threatened with arrest.

As a bootmaker, 'Chummy' campaigned

for better work conditions and the right to organize. He was elected as delegate of the Victorian Operative Bootmakers' Union to the Trades Hall Council in 1890. Next year he was president both of the bootmakers' union and of the Fitzroy Progressive Political League. His union activities were important to him but it was only in the early 1890s that he was not considered an outsider by the dominant protectionist group of union officials. In 1890 he helped to organize the first Victorian May Day meeting and in 1892 chaired the first public May Day meeting. For his part in the growing militancy of the unemployed, Fleming was beaten up by paid thugs and isolated from mainstream politics. He continued to support co-operatives and the village settlement movement.

Particularly after the death of Andrews in 1903, Fleming publicly emphasized his anarchism. No theoretician, he left few written statements, but corresponded with overseas journals until late in life. In 1904 he was expelled from the T.H.C. for his attacks on Labor politicians. He was active in the anti-conscription movement during World War I but afterwards his public activities declined.

Fleming continued to march on May Day and to address the public from his Yarra Bank stand. A gentle man, affectionately regarded by later generations, he looked forward to a millenium in which happiness and brotherly love would prevail. He suffered from a duodenal ulcer before his death some time on 25 or 26 January 1950 at his home in Carlton, where he had carried on his own bootmaking business for many years. He was cremated.

B. Walker, *Solidarity forever* (Melb, 1972); *Hist Studies*, 5 (1952), no 19, p 258; *Recorder*, 1 (1964), no 1, p 3; *Tocsin*, 17 Oct 1901; *Age*, 25, 26 June 1902; *People's Daily*, 25 Feb 1904; *Daily Telegraph*, 4, 9 Apr 1904; *Argus*, 8 Dec 1945; *Freedom* (Lond), 23 July 1977, 16 June 1979; F. B. Smith, Religion and freethought in Melbourne, 1870 to 1890 (M.A. thesis, Univ Melb, 1960); K. J. Kenafick, Life of Maurice Blackburn and John Curtin (MS, NL).

BOB JAMES

FLEMING, WILLIAM MONTGOMERIE (1874-1961), grazier, politician and writer, was born on 19 May 1874 at Avon Plains in the Wimmera district of Victoria, third son of John King Fleming, grazier from Scotland and his Tasmanian-born wife Helen, née Hastie. Educated by tutors at his father's station, Ulah, near Walgett, New South Wales, he entered Cooerwull Academy, Bowenfels, at 15 and won many academic and sporting prizes, passing the junior public examination in 1892. He spent a term at the University of Sydney, where his capacity for disputation terrified his lecturers. On 21 March 1900 at Aberdeen near Scone, Fleming married Caroline Benn; they both loved horses, and he won many amateur races, riding in the family colours of pink and grey, inspired by the galah. They settled at Russley, near Aberdeen, and had three children, William, Helen and Beatrix.

In 1901 Fleming defeated R. G. D. Fitzgerald for Robertson (Upper Hunter) and became the youngest member of the Legislative Assembly. An idealist, 'the kid' as he was nicknamed, saw merit in Labor policies, but by temperament and education was a consistent Liberal. He opposed the Labor solidarity pledge and alone spoke out in 1901 against the compulsory clauses in the arbitration bill. When he resigned in 1910 to contest a Federal seat he was convinced that State parliaments were outmoded.

Endorsed by the State Farmers & Settlers' Association, Fleming won the Federal seat of Robertson in 1913 from W. J. Johnson. He was a member of the Commonwealth Prices Regulation Board in 1916-17. After Johnson was killed in action, Fleming, an ardent patriot, felt duty-bound to volunteer for the Australian Imperial Force. Enlisting on 6 October 1916, he embarked on 31 October 1917 and served as a driver with the Australian Army Service Corps; he was promoted sergeant; gassed at Péronne, he was demobilized in London on 27 December 1918.

On his return to Australia Fleming was temporary chairman of committees in 1920-22. In 1921, when offered the treasury by W. M. Hughes [q.v.], he said 'I would not work under [him] if he would give me Sydney'. In March he crossed to the Progressive Party, creating a furore which the prime minister attempted to quell with the canard that he deserted when not offered a cabinet seat. Fleming's nemesis was his membership from 1920 of the Parliamentary Joint Committee of Public Accounts which resolved to investigate Hughes's transactions. To avert this he secured a dissolution in November 1922, and campaigned himself in Fleming's electorate, avowing that he 'must be destroyed' — Fleming lost. He was later defeated three times for the House of Representatives and once for the Senate. He remained chairman of the Metropolitan (Sydney) branch of the Country Party until 1934.

Writing was always Fleming's chief passion. Introduced to journalism by Harry 'The Breaker' Morant [q.v.], he wrote verse, prose sketches, and serials for numerous newspapers including the *Sydney Morning Herald*, the *Bulletin*, and the *Pastoral Review* — which he edited briefly in World War II. His permanent place in Australian literature is as a writer of children's stories, told originally to his own children. *Bunyip says so* (Melbourne, 1923) and *The hunted piccaninnies* (London, 1947) were fantasies based on animal lore and Aboriginal insight into 'the friendship of all living things'. He made a number of radio broadcasts on rural topics in the 1930s and his novel, *Broad acres* (Sydney, 1939), was serialized by the Australian Broadcasting Commission in 1940.

Fleming died on 24 July 1961 at Terrigal, and was cremated with Presbyterian forms. His manuscript autobiography is held by the family. A political opponent once complained of him: 'He is a possum out of a hollow log somewhere in the bush. He don't drink, don't smoke, don't swear and writes poetry — this baby politician'. In malice he remained a child, but in his understanding of Australia's first citizens, the bush and development, 'the kid' was always an elder statesman.

A.A.A., All About Australians, 1 Dec 1902, p 146f; *Punch* (Melb), 30 Oct 1913; *Newcastle Morning Herald*, 31 July 1961. STUART PIGGIN

FLETCHER, CHARLES BRUNSDEN (1859-1946), surveyor and journalist, was born on 5 August 1859 at Taunton, Somerset, England, third of thirteen children of Charles Fletcher, silk throwster, and his wife Ruth, née Bloor. In 1864 his father followed his eldest brother, Joseph Horner Fletcher [q.v.4], to New Zealand aboard the *Surat* to assist in the Wesleyan world mission service; he moved on to Sydney in 1872. Charles junior attended Newington College, where Joseph Horner was then principal and another uncle, John, a teacher, and the Fort Street Model School. He became a cadet in the Survey Department of New South Wales, progressing to supernumerary draftsman in 1879 and field assistant in 1881, after which he worked on the Detail Survey of the City of Sydney. Moving to Brisbane to assist in his father's real estate business in 1884, he obtained his Queensland survey licence next year, began private practice, and served on the Board of Examiners of Licensed Surveyors in 1888-93.

In 1893, when the land boom in Brisbane was ended by floods and bank crashes, Fletcher chose journalism as an alternative profession, having previously written for William Lane's [q.v.] *Boomerang* and been secretary of the Brisbane Literary Circle. He joined the *Brisbane Courier* as leader-writer and was also appointed Queensland correspondent of the Melbourne *Argus*. A member of the Ithaca Shire Council in 1892-98 and president in 1894, he succeeded F. W. Ward [q.v.], his lifelong friend and fellow Wesleyan, as editor of the *Courier* in

1898. On 13 November 1899 he and Florence Mary Macleay, daughter of (Sir) Arthur Rutledge [q.v.] were the first couple to be married in the Albert Street Wesleyan Church.

Fletcher's success in journalism was due to a vigorous and incisive style of writing and certain attitudes he hammered home in his articles — his unswerving beliefs in the qualities of the Anglo-Saxon people; in Imperialism; and in the prospect of a magnificent future for Australia. In 1903 he returned to Sydney as associate editor of the *Sydney Morning Herald* and capped his journalistic career with the editorship in 1918-37. He was a member of the Australian delegation to the coronation of King George V and Queen Mary in 1911, and in 1930 represented his paper at the fourth Imperial Press Conference in London. President of the New South Wales Institute of Journalists in 1923-27, it was through his efforts that the course of diploma in journalism was introduced at the University of Sydney, on the senate of which he served in 1923-39.

Fletcher became recognized as an authority on Pacific affairs on which he wrote three books, *The new Pacific: British policy and German aims* (1917), *The problem of the Pacific* (1919) and *Stevenson's Germany: the case against Germany in the Pacific* (1920), all inspired by World War I and Germany's expansionism. He urged a greater interest in the area by Australian legislators, and co-operation between businessmen and missionary bodies in its further development. This concern and, no doubt, his memory of the enterprise of his father, his uncles Joseph Horner and John, and his uncle William, who had been a missionary on the Island of Rotumah, inspired his writing of *The black knight of the Pacific* (1944) on the life and work of the famous Methodist missionary, Dr George Brown [q.v.3]

Fletcher also wrote books on the Coolah (1927) and Murray (1926) valleys, in New South Wales; the latter was followed up in *Water magic: Australia and the future* (1945), an examination of the need for water conservation. His autobiography, *The great wheel: an editor's adventures* (1940), contains journalistic reminiscences and memoirs of public figures and newspaper colleagues such as Ward, C. E. W. Bean [q.v.7] and F. M. Cutlack [q.v.]. His personality, by all accounts, was an attractive one; acquaintances recalled his 'charming old-world courtesy . . . keen powers of appreciation and a broad, kindly outlook'. He was made a lay member of Wesley College council in 1919. At his death, on 17 December 1946 at Kirribilli, the Sydney *Bulletin* described him, for his 'constant mind' and 'honesty of purpose', as one who 'would go down in history as the last

Sydney editor able to carry on the old dignified tradition of the great dailies'. He was survived by two daughters and a son, his wife and another son having predeceased him; his estate was valued for probate at £6329.

J. Fairfax & Sons Ltd, *A century of journalism. The Sydney Morning Herald* (Syd, 1942); Gavin Souter, *Company of Heralds* (Melbourne, 1981); *Newspaper News*, 1 Sept 1930, 2 July 1945; *SMH*, 14 Nov 1923, 11 Aug 1927, 19 Dec 1946.

CLEMENT SEMMLER

FLETCHER, JAMES LIONEL (1890-1977), soldier, teacher and farmer, was born on 4 December 1890 at Warwick, Queensland, son of English-born George Frederick Fletcher, apiarist and storekeeper's assistant, and his native-born wife Matilda, née Roper. He attended Sandy Creek State School until he was 14, then in 1906-09 was a pupil-teacher at Sandy Creek and at Warwick. He taught at Warwick as an assistant teacher for the next two years and at Cunnamulla in 1912-15. He served for two years in the Junior Cadets and as a lieutenant in the Senior Cadets, Universal Training Scheme, in 1911-12.

After enlisting in the Australian Imperial Force on 14 February 1915, Fletcher was promoted sergeant and then commissioned as a second lieutenant on 29 March before being posted to the 25th Battalion. He was promoted lieutenant on 1 June and embarked for Egypt on the *Aeneas* at Brisbane on 29 June. He landed at Gallipoli with the 25th on 11 September and served there until the evacuation.

The battalion reached Marseilles, France, on 20 March 1916, moved into the Armentières sector and was in action at Pozières Heights from 3-4 August. Fletcher, responsible for moving the troops to the front, was wounded in action at Pozières. He was awarded the Military Cross for laying telephone wires under heavy machine-gun and shell-fire. Although he was wounded, and had severe casualties among his men, he continued to maintain communications and rally his troops. He was promoted captain on 12 August while recuperating from his wounds. He rejoined his unit on 22 October but was detached to the 7th Infantry Training Battalion from January to June 1917.

After his return the 25th Battalion took part in the battle of Broodseinde on 4 October and suffered heavy losses, Fletcher being one of the wounded. He returned to his unit on 20 December but was again wounded on 5 June 1918. He was awarded a Bar to his Military Cross for displaying conspicuous gallantry when his company was held up during an attack by heavy machine-gun fire from the right flank. Rallying his men, he rushed an enemy trench, killing six Germans with his revolver.

Fletcher was awarded the Distinguished Service Order for his untiring efforts during an attack near Mont St Quentin on 2 September 1918: he personally captured a machine-gun post and took command of his unit after the commanding officer was wounded. He was promoted temporary major on 26 September and posted to the 26th Battalion on 12 October. He was mentioned in dispatches in 1919 before returning to Australia in September; his A.I.F. appointment ended that month and he was placed on the reserve of officers as a captain in January 1920.

After demobilization, Fletcher bought a pineapple and citrus farm at Palmwoods, Queensland. On 18 April 1920 he married Leila Barnett Warner at St Albans Anglican Church, Cunnamulla; they had one son and three daughters. He moved to Belmore, Sydney, in 1973 and died at Campsie on 18 August 1977; he was cremated. His four children survived him.

C. E. W. Bean, *The A.I.F. in France*, 1916-18 (Syd, 1929, 1933, 1937, 1942); *London Gazette*, 26 Sept 1916, 24 Sept 1918, 31 Jan, 1 Feb, 11 July 1919; 25 Battalion AIF, Brief summary of events 1915-18, *and* F. S. Rosensjkar, With the 25th Battalion AIF, *and* war diary, 25th Battalion AIF (AWM); information from Mrs J. R. Torrington, Belmore, NSW.

A. W. HAMMETT

FLETCHER, JOHN WILLIAM (1884-1965), pastoralist, was born on 25 January 1884 in Sydney, son of John Walker Fletcher, schoolmaster and later a magistrate, and his wife Ann, née Clark. Leaving Sydney Grammar School in 1899, he joined the shipping and export firm G. S. Yuill & Co. In 1906-07 he was in Manila as assistant manager of Philippines Cold Stores Ltd. Returning to Queensland in November 1907, he worked for the Queensland Meat Export & Agency Co. Ltd in which Yuill had a controlling interest, first as a book-keeper and later as secretary and chief accountant. With two partners, he bought the Torrens Creek meat preserving works near Hughenden in 1910, and on 25 October married Evelyn Barbara de Winton in Brisbane; they had one son and four daughters.

Fletcher bought out his partners in 1912 and formed a new company. In 1915 it processed a record 119000 sheep. However, the works did not reopen after that year. Swift Australian Co. (Pty) Ltd had entered the field and early in 1916 Fletcher became general manager of its Gladstone meatworks. He also became a member of the town council and the Harbour Board, and vice-president of the local Chamber of Commerce and Turf Club. In October 1920 he won Port Curtis as a Nationalist in the State election but failed to hold the seat in May 1923. In 1924 he bought several properties totalling more than 230 000 acres (93 000 ha) near Mitchell. He was chairman of Booringa Shire in 1927-32 and in 1930 served under W. L. Payne [q.v.] on a royal commission on dingo and rabbit boards and stock route administration.

After his wife died on 28 November 1931 Fletcher decided to turn Bonus Downs, his principal property, into a wether station and to become a stock-dealer. After having 120 000 sheep on the road or on agistment in 1932, he bought Authoringa near Charleville in 1933 and formed a family company for his children. Through other transactions in 1934, 1938 and 1942, he secured vast and widespread areas of pastoral land in Queensland controlled by at least three family companies; most of these properties were ultimately sold in 1947-50. He became president of the Maranoa Graziers' Association and a councillor of the United Graziers' Association of Queensland. On 4 April 1934 in Brisbane he married Amy Muriel Cribb; they had no children.

On the recommendation of Payne, Fletcher was appointed on 23 March 1937 as one of a two-man committee to report to the Commonwealth government on land development policy in the Northern Territory. After travelling 10 000 miles (16 000 km) and examining 150 witnesses, they submitted their report on 10 October. It is still considered one of the better examinations of Territorial affairs but few of its recommendations were adopted. Fletcher refused any fee for the work because 'the successful outcome of enquiry would mean more to me than remuneration'. He was appointed O.B.E. in 1941.

Chairman of the Queensland Primary Producers Co-operative Association Ltd in 1953-55, Fletcher held other directorships and chaired the Queensland division of the Australian Comforts Fund in 1940-43. He stood unsuccessfully for the Federal seat of Brisbane in 1940 and 1943, was a member of the royal commission on abattoirs and the meat industry in 1945, helped raise £240 000 for St John's Cathedral, Brisbane, in 1946 and was on the Commonwealth Bank Board in 1951-52. He has been described as among the best-informed of representatives of the northern cattle industry.

An accurate judge of sun-time, Fletcher carried neither a watch nor, relying on an excellent memory, a notebook. In youth a notable cricketer and later an intelligent commentator, he had been secretary of and played for the Paddington (Sydney) club in 1902 with Victor Trumper and M. A. Noble [qq.v.]; he also represented Queensland. All his life, he divided his income into three, allotting a third to improving his properties, a third to the care of his family and a third to worthy causes. He died in Brisbane on 13 March 1965. A typescript autobiography is in the Fryer Library, University of Queensland.

J. H. Fingleton, *The immortal Victor Trumper* (Syd, 1978); *Qld Country Life*, 18 Mar 1965; *Courier Mail*, 1 Jan 1941; Payne-Fletcher cttee (AAO).

W. C. SKELSEY

FLETCHER, JOSEPH JAMES (1850?-1926), biologist and editor, was probably born at Auckland, New Zealand, eldest son of English parents Rev. Joseph Horner Fletcher [q.v.4], Methodist clergyman, and his wife Kate, née Green. He arrived in Australia with his parents in 1861 and was educated at Ipswich Grammar School, Queensland, Newington College, Sydney, where his father was president, and the University of Sydney (B.A., 1870; M.A., 1876). He taught briefly at Wesley College, Melbourne, where he developed an interest in natural science. As no science degree was offered in Australia, from 1876 he studied at the Royal School of Mines and University College, University of London (B.Sc., 1879). Specializing in biology, he studied for a time at Cambridge and in 1881 published his first paper.

From his return to Australia that year Fletcher taught at Newington until 1885; he introduced an elementary course of anatomy and physiology and was acting headmaster. He was one of the first to investigate closely the embryology of marsupialia; carrying out field work around Bathurst he published three papers in 1881-83 on the genito-urinary organs of the kangaroo, and in 1884 a paper in the *Proceedings* of the Linnean Society of New South Wales, 'Catalogue of papers and works relating to the mammalian orders, marsupialia and monotremata'. He had joined the society in 1881, its council in 1883 and in January 1886, at the invitation of the society's founder (Sir) William Macleay [q.v.5], became librarian — as Macleay's executor he was later involved in the legal and financial difficulties arising from his will.

Director of the society from 1893, for thirty-three years Fletcher guided its affairs and meticulously edited its *Proceedings* from Elizabeth Bay House. He published thirty-eight important papers in the *Proceedings*, the majority on earthworms, land planarians, peripatus and the Amphibia, on which he was a world authority. In January 1900 he made a notable contribution to the history of natural science in Australia in his presidential address to the biology section of the Australasian Association for the Advancement of Science.

On his retirement as director in 1919 Fletcher turned his attention to the sandstone flora around Sydney, published on the phases of eucalyptus and acacia seedlings and intensively investigated the Proteaceae and Loranthaceae. He was president of the society in 1919-20 and 1921; in his first presidential address he stressed the scientific need to study drought; in his second he attacked the university over its trust in regard to the Macleay Museum. On the centenary of Macleay's birth in June 1920 he gave an important address, 'The Society's Heritage from the Macleays', which contained much of biographical, historical and zoological interest. He gave his own zoological collection to the Australian Museum, Sydney, of which he was an elected trustee. He also gave over 300 books and pamphlets to the Mitchell Library. In 1921 he was awarded the (W. B.) Clarke [q.v.3] medal by the Royal Society of New South Wales.

Fletcher was an original and successful teacher, dedicated scientist and, as editor, he was as modest and tactful as he was helpful. He relished field excursions, where according to J.H. Maiden [q.v.] he was 'a charming companion, always bright and full of clever wit'. His simple observations and lucid descriptions reminded Sir Baldwin Spencer [q.v.] of the famed Gilbert White of Selborne. Poetry, especially the poetry of nature, was one of his great loves. He died suddenly on 15 May 1926 at his home, Ravenscourt, Woolwich Road, Hunters Hill and was buried in the Methodist section of Field of Mars cemetery. Childless, he was survived by his wife Emma Jane, née Spencer, whom he married in the Newington College Chapel on 9 April 1884.

Linnean Soc NSW, *Procs*, 45 (1920) 1, 46 (1921) 1, 52 (1927), v, xxiii, 54 (1929), 185, 686, 55 (1930), 738; *Nature* (Lond), 3 July 1926; *SMH*, 1, 2 Apr 1921, 17, 18 May 1926; *Daily Telegraph* (Syd), 17 May 1926.   G. P. WALSH

FLETCHER, LIONEL BALE (1877-1954), Congregational minister and evangelist, was born on 22 May 1877 at Maitland, New South Wales, eighth child of John Fletcher, teacher and Methodist lay preacher, and his wife Eliza, née Bale. Three of their sons became ordained Methodist ministers, including Michael Scott Fletcher (1868-1947), professor of philosophy at the University of Queensland in 1923-38; all seven sons were preachers.

After completing his schooling at Newington College, Sydney, Fletcher when 16 went to sea as an apprentice hand on the sailing-ship *Macquarie*. After the return voyage from England he worked on a brother's property, near Peak Hill. Here, in July 1896, he was converted. In December 1897, attending a meeting of the annual Petersham evangelical conference, he had a second decisive religious experience. This convinced him that a full Christian life was only possible in the power of the Holy Spirit. Fletcher was a clerk when he married Maude Harris Basham on 24 January 1900. She was an able speaker and musician and a partner in all his subsequent work, but the marriage temporarily blocked entry to the ministry. After working as a miner and journalist at Charters Towers, in 1905 he was accepted by the New South Wales Congregational Union as a home mission agent and extramural theological student. He was ordained on 24 March 1908 and served briefly at Kurri Kurri.

Fletcher had three highly successful pastorates: at Port Adelaide (1909-15) where he followed Rev J. C. Kirby [q.v.5]; at the Wood Street church, Cardiff, Wales (1916-22); and at the Beresford Street church, Auckland, New Zealand (1923-32). In all three he preached to convert and, beginning in South Australia, became increasingly involved in wider evangelism. He was active in South Australia's campaign for six o'clock closing and in New Zealand, for prohibition. He also denounced drink, gambling and lipstick. Another abiding interest was the Christian Endeavour Union, of which he became world vice-president. In 1922-23 he and his wife conducted the successful 'New Life Campaign' in Britain.

In 1931 Fletcher returned to England to lead a six-month youth evangelical campaign which drew in thousands and, he claimed, was 'the greatest and most inspiring religious movement England has known in this generation'. In September 1932 he became 'Empire Evangelist' for the Movement for World Evangelization, newly formed in London. He broke with this group in 1935, but continued full-time work in England with the National Council of the Evangelical Free Churches. Probably his greatest campaigns were in South Africa in 1934 and 1936. In 1941 he returned to settle in Sydney. He retained his commitment to evangelism, but had by now lost much of his former energy and believed that he saw about him a new religious indifference. He died in hospital at Mosman, after a short illness, on 19 February 1954, survived by his wife, a son and a daughter.

Fletcher was influenced in his evangelistic work by American revivalists such as Dwight L. Moody and J. Wilbur Chapman. His preaching was unsensational in style, direct, forceful and humorous, with a fund of stories drawn from his wide experience of life. He employed his gift for writing on occasional journalism, and on evangelism and the Christian life; as 'Uncle Leo' he ran a children's programme on radio station IYA Auckland.

C. W. Malcolm, *Twelve hours in the day* (Lond, 1956); *Congregationalist* (Syd), Apr 1954; *Register* (Adel), 2 Feb 1924; *SMH*, 7 Apr 1923, 26 Apr 1924, 27 May 1929, 17 Aug 1931, 18 June 1932.

HUGH JACKSON

FLIERL, JOHANN (1858-1947), missionary, was born on 16 April 1858 at Buchhof, parish of Furnried, Bavaria, son of Johann Konrad Flierl, farmer, and his wife Kunigunda, née Dannhauser. He was determined to become a missionary but with parents too poor to send him to university a missionary seminary was his only hope. After completing primary school he worked for four years on his father's farm, until he was old enough to enter the seminary in Neuendettelsau. It had been founded in the 1850s, primarily to train pastors to serve communities of Lutheran emigrants, but Flierl hoped that a small mission among the American Indians, abandoned some years before, would soon be reopened. He was told instead that a missionary was wanted for work among the Australian Aboriginals; he volunteered, and left for Australia shortly after his consecration at Easter 1878.

Flierl spent seven years working on Bethesda station at Cooper's Creek. In 1882 he married Beate Maria Louise Auricht, daughter of a Lutheran pastor in the Barossa Valley, South Australia, and seemed ready to settle down to a quiet life in a remote desert reserve. Early in 1885 he heard about the founding of a German colony in New Guinea and decided to go there as a pioneer missionary to help the local people 'that the white settler may not drive them, too, from the land of their fathers, as he has done with the American Indian and Australian native'. It was July 1886 before Flierl, a tall, strong, determined young man, landed in Finschhafen, the capital of the new colony, having founded another mission station (Hope Valley) among the Aboriginals during an enforced stay in Cooktown, Queensland.

His first station in New Guinea, Simbang, near Finschhafen, seemed discouraging. The local people were hostile and Flierl and his first colleagues battled with health, language and supply problems. Having started a second station on Tami Island, the local trade centre, in 1889 they were just finding their feet when an epidemic wiped out almost half the European population; Finschhafen was abandoned in 1891 but Flierl resolved to stay in Simbang, perhaps most of all because he felt too old to make yet another start and live to see 'the harvest ripening' – which he knew would be slow. Spurred on by an ultimatum from his wife, who was worried about their baby daughter, Flierl embarked upon a determined push into the mountains to avoid the effects of the climate. He devoted much time during the next years building a station on Sattelberg and a road to Finschhafen, which cut the travelling time from three days to five hours.

Until 1899 when the first baptisms were performed, the mission progressed slowly. Subsequent doubling of the stations was still consolidation rather than expansion. Yet it was clear that rapid development was possible – as well as necessary if competing missions were to be kept out of the area, but heavy financial and logistic problems had to be faced. A supply station was founded at Finschhafen in 1903 and next year Flierl moved down to Heldsbach on the coast where, besides starting a commercial coconut plantation, the mission acquired its first substantial vessel in 1907. By 1914 the entire coast, from Sio in the west to the Papuan border, had been occupied and major inroads into the interior had been made. Flierl, now in his late fifties, thought of withdrawing into the background.

The 'end of an era' atmosphere was reinforced by a visit from Superintendent Steck from Neuendettelsau. Intended as a fundamental review, it would have led to conflict but, with the outbreak of World War I, reforms were out of the question and a different kind of struggle for survival began. Under the eye of a distrustful Australian military occupation, Flierl steered the mission carefully, strengthening connexions with Lutheran churchmen in Australia and the United States of America, to secure supply of goods and personnel. These connexions became even more important after the war, when it seemed as if the German missions would be expropriated and their staff deported. It was 1925 before this threat had passed and 1929 before the reorganization of Protestant mission activity had been completed.

Honoured with a doctorate of divinity from Wartburg Seminary, Iowa, Flierl retired in 1930 with his wife to her hometown, Tanunda, South Australia. Four years later, after his wife's death, he returned to Neuendettelsau with his daughter, who died before him; he died there on 30 September 1947. Of his four children, Wilhelm and

527

Johannes became ordained mission pastors, Dora was a mission teacher and nurse and Elise married the missionary Wilhelm Kelhofer.

Some believe that Flierl was too preoccupied with the external side of mission work, that he was a planter of crops rather than shepherd of souls. There is some truth in this criticism but it does not do him justice. Though not an inspired theologian he was humble, pious and knew the bases of his faith. He did not take a deep interest in the alien cultures he met but, nevertheless, he founded a mission, that, more than any other external force, gave a sense of community to the previously divided peoples of the Morobe peninsula. Though paternalistic to the local people, he always aimed at putting them on their own feet and was prepared to stand up for them before both the German and Australian administrations. In such confrontations, his gaunt features, gruff voice, penetrating blue eyes and patriarchal beard were assets. A prolific writer, his main publication in English is *Forty years in New Guinea* (Chicago, 1927).

E. A. Jericho, *Seedtime and harvest* (Brisb, 1961); G. Pilhofer, *Die Geschichte der Neuendettelsauer Mission in Neu-Guinea* (Neuendettelsau, 1961-63); *Neue Deutsche Biographie*, 7 (Berlin, 1966).

P. G. SACK

FLOWER, WILLOUGHBY (1858-1914), Anglican clergyman, was born on 22 January 1858 at Matlock Bath, Derbyshire, son of Thomas Simpson Flower, chemist and druggist, and his wife Jane, née Keeling. Although baptized as a Wesleyan Methodist, he received an Anglican schooling. At 20 Flower entered the University of Cambridge with non-collegiate status, a new category designed for impecunious students. With help from the Cambridge Clerical Education Society and his stipend as a lay assistant at St Matthew's, Cambridge, Flower put himself through the university (B.A., 1881; M.A., 1884). After attending the requisite divinity lectures, he was made deacon on 12 June 1881 and ordained priest on 4 June next year by Bishop Woodford of Ely. He remained at St Matthew's as curate until 1885 when he became curate of St Mary's, Twickenham. The parish was in sequestration and Flower was virtually in charge. For an able young man without patronage, the position was a useful opportunity. Flower impressed Bishop Thornton [q.v.6] of Ballarat who invited him to come to Australia. On 7 May 1885 he had married Emily Sarah George (1855-1936). They left for Australia late in 1886.

For more than ten years, Flower was a leading country clergyman. He served no apprenticeship but was given at once positions of importance, becoming in 1887 vicar of St Peter's, Ballarat, and, four years later, a canon and a diocesan delegate to General Synod. When Archdeacon A. V. Green [q.v.] of Ballarat was elected bishop of Grafton and Armidale, he requested Flower's aid. Flower, as vicar and archdeacon of Grafton, was virtually in charge of one part of the joint diocese. In 1897 he acted as diocesan administrator but, in the same year, abandoned his prospects of becoming a country bishop by moving to St Mark's, Darling Point, Sydney, which was then at its height as an upper-class area.

Flower had matured into a capable minister with courtly manners and intellectual tastes, including church music, without losing his strong personal piety. His incumbency was successful, although he failed to sub-divide his parish. A moderate High Churchman, he preserved good relations with the predominantly Evangelical diocese of Sydney, becoming archbishop's chaplain in 1910 and a canon of the cathedral in 1913. At the same time, he kept his connexions with the wider Church, being commissary for the bishops of New Guinea and Bathurst, examining chaplain and commissary for Grafton and Armidale, acting registrar in 1911-13 of the Australian College of Theology (of which he had become a fellow in 1896) and, from 1901, a fellow of St Paul's College within the University of Sydney. As honorary chaplain to the New South Wales Corps of Engineers, he developed a military link.

By the end of 1913 Flower was at the peak of his reputation. But his health and temperament had deteriorated and he went back to England in search of recovery. He returned on the *Demosthenes* greatly depressed, in pain and suffering from sleeplessness. On 21 July 1914, the day after his arrival in Sydney, he died at the rectory at Darling Point from the effects of a self-inflicted bullet wound while suffering from temporary mental derangement.

Flower was buried at South Head cemetery and is commemorated by a stained glass window at St Mark's. He was survived by his wife, two sons and two daughters.

Cyclopedia of N.S.W. (Syd, 1907); H.W.A. Barder, *Wherein thine honour dwells* (Syd, 1949); *Church Standard*, 31 July 1914; *Guardian*, 17 Sept 1914.

K. J. CABLE

FLOWERS, FRED (1864-1928), house painter and politician, was born on 4 March 1864 at Dilhorne, Staffordshire, England, son of William Flowers, gardener, and his wife Dorothy, née Robinson. He migrated to

Sydney with his family about 1882. Joining the United Painters' Trade Society (he also worked as a plasterer), he became its delegate on the Trades and Labor Council of which he was vice-president in 1892. He played a part in the council's founding of the Labor Electoral League (Labor Party) in 1890-91, and as a Labor candidate ran unsuccessfully for the seats of South Sydney, 1891, Newtown-St Peters, 1895, and Waterloo, 1898. He was prominent in the extraparliamentary work of the party and in June 1892, with J. C. Watson [q.v.], represented the T.L.C. in discussions with the central executive committee of the L.E.L. which restored the role of the council within the league.

In 1894 the T.L.C. was temporarily disbanded because of financial problems, and its president, Watson, won a country parliamentary seat. Flowers replaced him as the efficient and popular city industrial leader needed to maintain the essential trade union base of the Labor Party. By the end of the year he was chairman of the L.E.L. In 1895 he presided over negotiations that settled the competing interests of the L.E.L. and the Australian Labor Federation, an industrial-political organization dominated by the Australian Workers' Union, which had sought to assume the position of the T.L.C. in the party. In May the Political Labor League emerged from the discussions – it remained the official name of the Labor Party in New South Wales until 1918, when it became the New South Wales Branch of the Australian Labor Party. Flowers became the first president of the P.L.L. He widened his community status by work for temperance, heading a campaign in Newtown in 1892. He had married Annie Foster at St Peter's Anglican Church, Sydney, on 26 January 1888.

Flowers' leadership of the Labor Party helped to consolidate its structural growth in the 1890s. He chaired successive annual conferences in 1896-98, firmly upholding the sovereignty of conference over the parliamentarians and the powerful role of the executive. At the 1897 meeting he stressed the educative role of the party, remarking that even some workers identified Labor with anarchy. That year he was one of the ten top Laborites who ran on a specific Federation platform for the Australasian Federal Convention. None was elected. Defeated for the party presidency in 1898, he took the set-back urbanely. Next year the parliamentary Labor Party precipitated the downfall of the (Sir George) Reid [q.v.] government, and in 1900 the new premier, (Sir) William Lyne [q.v.], had Flowers appointed to the Legislative Council. The Labor Party, which planned to abolish the council, then had five members in a house of sixty.

The measured pace of the Upper House suited Flowers' style. He developed as a tactful and skilful politician, with a mastery of procedure. Meanwhile, he remained near the head of affairs in the party. He was a delegate to its Federal conference in 1900 and was on the State executive in 1900-12, president in 1906-07. He was the president of the premier Rugby League club, South Sydney, in 1908-28; as the patron of the New South Wales Rugby Football League in 1910-28, he contributed much to its survival in the difficult early years. In 1924 he became first chairman of the league's Australian Board of Control.

In October 1910 the Labor Party formed its first government in New South Wales. In the McGowen [q.v.] ministry (1910-13) Flowers was appointed vice-president of the Executive Council and representative of the government in the Legislative Council (until 1915). In 1911-12 he had short terms as chief secretary, minister for public instruction and secretary for lands. In the Holman [q.v.] Labor ministry (1913-16) Flowers acted as colonial secretary from June 1913 to April 1914, and became the State's first minister of public health, from April 1914 to April 1915 – he had been one of the originators of the Labor Party's health policy in 1897 when it sought the nationalization of medicine. His interest and knowledge in the field were extended in 1900-11, when various annual party conferences sought wider and improved medical and hospital services. The Labor pressure complemented informed professional opinion. As acting chief secretary in 1911, and later as health minister, he energetically and efficiently effected reforms and paved the way for further improvement by J. D. Fitzgerald [q.v.] in 1916-19. Flowers was a director of Royal Prince Alfred Hospital in 1916-18.

He shared the enthusiasm of N. R. W. Nielsen [q.v.] for the preservation, as parks, of the remaining Sydney Harbour public waterfronts. When he took over from Nielsen as secretary of lands in 1911, (Sir) Charles G. Wade [q.v.] asked whether a housepainter was up to the job. Flowers encouraged the building of a new zoological gardens at Taronga Park, on Bradleys Head, and became chairman of the controlling trust next year. In 1915-16 he arranged the transfer of animals and birds from their inadequate location in Moore Park to their new harbour site. The zoo became known internationally.

The Legislative Council proved a bugbear for the Labor Party, especially for Holman. Abolition was unrealistic; Labor appointments were necessary, but would confirm its power and affront party members; a Labor majority seemed impossible. In 1911 Holman had 11 put in, including 4 who were not in the party; next year he appointed Fitzgerald, giving Labor 13 in a House of 70. Sir Francis Suttor [q.v.6], president of the council, died on 4 April 1915, and Flowers succeeded him on 27 April with salary of £750.

Flowers combined deep patriotic feelings for both England and Australia. Visiting England early in 1916, he noted the sacrifices trade unionists were making to help defeat the 'ultimate barbarian', Germany. With two sons at the war (one was killed), he joined the Universal Service League and was on W. M. Hughes's [q.v.] platform when the pro-conscription campaign was opened in September 1916 in Sydney. Because of his membership of the Upper House he was not directly involved in the Labor Party spasms over conscription. But he separated from the party, although he did not join Holman's National Party. He co-operated with the Storey-Dooley [qq.v.] Labor governments in 1920-22. Storey appointed him to the Tramway Construction Advisory Board in 1920. Flowers was not so friendly with J. T. Lang [q.v.] in 1925-27.

He had long suffered from diabetes and died of its complications on 14 December 1928; he was buried with Anglican rites in South Head cemetery, survived by his wife, two daughters and a son. Flowers' estate was sworn for probate at £9826. There is a memorial tablet to him at Taronga Park.

Flowers was a good example of the many intelligent young men, socially and educationally deprived, who were active in radical circles in Sydney in the late 1880s and early 1890s; who, many of them, were delegates at the T.L.C.; who joined the Labor Party and whose lives became inextricably mixed with its growth in New South Wales, with mutual benefits, as the party took the lead in social and administrative improvement, holding office in 1910-16. Trade unionism matured Flowers' reforming insight, and through him and others modified New South Wales society. His interest and advancing expertise in medical and hospital development gave depth and form to party policy in 1897-1911, and his administrative flair conditioned practical progress in 1911-15. His contribution to environmental betterment was also noteworthy. As a successful, experienced and popular politician he was poised in 1916 to help Labor to resolve its embarrassment over the Legislative Council. But the party was convulsed by the war and the conscription split.

H. V. Evatt, *Australian Labour leader... W. A. Holman* (Syd, 1940); B. Nairn, *Civilising capitalism* (Canb, 1973); *NSW Rugby League Annual*, 1928; B. Dickey, 'The Labor government and medical services in N.S.W., 1910-1914', *Hist Studies*, no 48, Apr 1967; *SMH*, 10 June 1918, 23 July 1920, 15 Dec 1928; *Aust Worker*, 19 Dec 1928. BEDE NAIRN

FLOYD, ALFRED ERNEST (1877-1974), musician, was born on 5 January 1877 at Aston, Birmingham, England, son of Charles Hulme Floyd, Methodist minister, and his wife Annie Maria, née Maggs. In 1890 the family moved to Cambridge, where Floyd attended the Leys School. He was accepted as an organ pupil by Dr A. H. Mann, organist of King's College in the University of Cambridge; from Mann came elements of his later style both in extemporization and in accompanying the psalms. After leaving school he worked as a chemist in his brother-in-law's sulphuric acid works. He kept up his music and was accepted as assistant at Winchester Cathedral to Dr G. B. Arnold, who had been a favourite pupil of S. S. Wesley.

Floyd left Winchester to gain experience as a parish organist and choirmaster and held posts at Llangollen in Wales and at Oswestry, Shropshire, where on 11 January 1913 he married Frances Mary Griffiths (Daisy), daughter of Dr Aylmer Lewis. Meanwhile he completed his bachelor of music degree (Oxford) in 1912; J. C. Bridge and C. H. Kitson were among his mentors, and C. H. H. Parry one of his examiners.

In February 1915 Floyd arrived in Melbourne to take up the position of organist and choirmaster of St Paul's Cathedral; he had been appointed from a field of two hundred applicants. In September 1917 the degree of Mus. Doc. was conferred on him by the archbishop of Canterbury on the recommendation of a group of leading English church-musicians who had visited Melbourne. Floyd's interest in Melbourne schools is witnessed by a string of school songs. He was in constant demand as an adjudicator at music festivals throughout Australia and in 1916-56 from time to time as examiner for the Melbourne University Conservatorium of Music. For many years he lectured in music for the Workers' Educational Association and until 1963 for the Council of Adult Education. Precise, but with an impish humour, he quickly established an empathy with his listeners. In 1933-34 he made a foray into musical journalism as music critic of the *Argus*, enjoying the spate of concert-going despite its excessive demands on his time.

During Floyd's thirty-two years at St Paul's, his influence permeated the musical life of the cathedral. The superb standard maintained by the choir in daily and Sunday services was recognized as equal to that of the best English cathedrals. He introduced annual choral services before 1920, while his other special excellences were his extemporizations, much in the Wesley style, before service, and his accompaniment of the psalms which paralleled the light and shade of the words. He wrote several anthems, which were widely performed in Australia, and some organ music.

Floyd had a wide impact through his radio sessions for the Australian Broadcasting Commission. From 1944, at first in Victoria only and then nationally, he broadcast at 4 p.m. on Sundays; from March 1948 his 'Music Lovers' Hour' was played at 8 p.m. on Sundays, continuing, apart from a brief suspension, for twenty-four years. His approach was uncomplicated; his frail voice belied his essential vitality. Lindley Evans described him as the kindly elder statesman of musical broadcasting: 'He could charm the last sixpence from the canniest Scot, had he chosen to do so. In common with thousands of listeners I am filled with affection and admiration for this gentle man and fine musician'.

Dr Floyd's work received official recognition in 1948, when he was appointed O.B.E., and in 1971 when he was awarded an honorary D.Litt. from Monash University. He died at Armadale on 13 January 1974, predeceased by his wife and survived by two sons. His body was willed to the Department of Anatomy, University of Melbourne.

People (Syd), 15 Mar 1950; *Aust J of Music Education*, Oct 1973; *Table Talk*, 14 Mar 1929; *Herald* (Melb), 27 Dec 1947; *Age*, 15 Jan 1974; L. Evans, Memoirs (MS, copy held by ADB).

W. F. CHAPPELL

FLYNN, JOHN (1880-1951), Presbyterian minister, founder and superintendent of the Australian Inland Mission of the Presbyterian Church of Australia, was born on 25 November 1880 at Moliagul, Victoria, second son of Thomas Eugene Flynn, schoolteacher, and his wife Rosetta Forsyth, née Lester. Educated at Snake Valley, Sunshine and Braybrook primary schools, he matriculated from University High School, Carlton, aged 18. Unable to finance a university course, he became a pupil-teacher with the Victorian Education Department and developed interests in photography and first aid. In 1903 he began training for the ministry through an extra-mural course for 'student lay pastors', serving meanwhile in pioneering districts of Beech Forest and Buchan. His next four years in theological college were interspersed with two periods on a shearers' mission and the publication of his *Bushman's companion* (1910).

On completion of his studies for ordination Flynn volunteered for appointment in 1911 to the Smith of Dunesk Mission in the northern Flinders Ranges, South Australia. This parish extended to the rail head at Oodnadatta where the mission had placed a nursing sister and planned a nursing hostel; under Flynn's practical assistance, it was opened on 11 December. Next year Flynn surveyed the Northern Territory and on receiving his two long and detailed reports, one on the needs of Aboriginals and one on the needs of white settlers, the Presbyterian General Assembly that year appointed him superintendent of its Australian Inland Mission, which, in principle, it established at the same meeting. The South Australian, Western Australian and Queensland assemblies transferred their remote areas adjoining the Northern Territory to Flynn's care, and his new charter was initiated at Oodnadatta Nursing Hostel. The mission he was to direct for another thirty-nine years commenced operation with one nursing sister, one padre, a nursing hostel and five camels. It began as it continued 'without preference for nationality or creed', to become a great mantle of safety composed of a network of nursing hostels and hospitals each in close association with a patrol padre.

It took another seventeen years before Flynn's caring service to remote homesteads and communities was completed with the establishment of the A.I.M. Aerial Medical Service at Cloncurry in 1928 and Alfred Traeger's [q.v.] invention of the pedal radio in 1929. Flynn's writings in the *Inlander* indicate that this fourfold concept was his goal almost from the beginning. In his understanding of community development, he was ahead of his time, for the service he envisaged was to be a framework within which outback communities might 'structure and co-ordinate' their own 'canopy' of safety. By 1918, although World War I impeded development, in addition to the first nursing hostel and patrol based on Oodnadatta Flynn had established patrols based on Port Hedland and Broome in Western Australia, Pine Creek in the Northern Territory and Cloncurry in Queensland. He had also appointed nursing sisters to Port Hedland and Halls Creek in Western Australia and Maranboy and Alice Springs in the Northern Territory, though the latter appointment soon lapsed because of lack of a suitable building. Five years later, Flynn had twenty-three nursing sisters in the field.

The nursing hostel designs were usually prepared by Flynn himself after consultation with architects, engineers and local people to ensure that the design was suitable to climatic conditions and available building material. His design for the Alice Springs hostel, published in 1920 in the *Inlander*, illustrates his research, having ducted air-cooling via a tunnel under the ground floor where wet bags filtered the dust and cooled the air drawn by convection through the wards to the lantern roof. This massive stone building with wide verandahs was completed in 1926.

Between 1913 and 1927 Flynn's magazine, the *Inlander*, led his battle for a 'brighter bush'. His photographs, documents, statistics, maps and articles publicized the needs of the people and northern Australia's potential for development, which he argued could only be effected by providing security for women and children. He did not overlook Aboriginals, and devoted the first issue of the 1915 *Inlander* to photographs and stories of the plight of the fringe-dwellers in particular: 'A blot on Australia is shown on our frontispiece . . . There is no call for sensation. Sensation is too cheap. We need action'. He confessed that everyone was ignorant of how to help but that 'it is up to us to educate ourselves and mend our ways'. He claimed that Aboriginals were neither incompetent nor 'beneath the practice of self-help' and noted also the care that they gave their old men. He continued: 'We who so cheerfully sent a cheque for £100 000 to Belgium to help a people pushed out of their own inheritance by foreigners—surely we must just as cheerfully do something for those whom we clean-handed people have dispossessed in the interests of superior culture'.

There were few in that time who were as outspoken or perceptive as Flynn on this subject—a fact rarely recognized by either Church or public. Within his own Church, another department was responsible for the care of Aboriginals, but Flynn's A.I.M. hospitals were then, as now, open to Aboriginals who were encouraged to seek the medical care offered. Long after Flynn's death, however, allegations mainly by Dr Charles Duguid in his book *Doctor and the Aborigines* (1972), that A.I.M. hostels had refused to treat Aboriginals and that Flynn had become indifferent to their plight, roused heated controversy.

Flynn's strategy for the location of his nursing hostels and associated patrols was to choose what he called the 'port', whether inland or on the sea front, serving the surrounding outback, and then ensure that the need was confirmed and the hostel supported by the local people who were encouraged to 'take over the entire management wherever they desired and when they were able to bear the burden'. This was not only true of the nursing hostels or homes, for in 1933 when the A.I.M. Aerial Medical Service was transferred to the national Australian Aerial Medical Service, all radios and other equipment went as a gift to the people and communities concerned.

The second phase of Flynn's strategy was marked by his concentration on radio and the 'flying doctor'. As early as 2 May 1925, he declared that 'the practicability of the Flying Doctor proposal depends almost entirely on the widespread adoption of wireless by bush residents' to provide the link between doctor and patient. The press responded to Flynn's ready use of publicity. Later that month he was in Adelaide with George Towns, a returned soldier radio technician, to take delivery of his specially designed Dodge Buckboard for their first inland experiment in radio transmission. They drove to Alice Springs via Beltana, Innaminka, Birdsville, Marree and Oodnadatta conducting test transmissions as they travelled, using a pulley drive from the jacked-up back wheel to generate electricity for radio transmission. The following year Flynn persuaded Alfred Traeger [q.v.], whom he had met in Adelaide, to come to Alice Springs for further experiments, this time using a Lister engine to generate power at their nursing home base and heavy copper-oxide batteries at Hermannsburg and Arltunga. Their success, including the transmission of the first radio telegram, was only partial, for the type of battery used was unsuitable for remote homesteads.

Meanwhile Flynn had been working on his other project, the aerial medical service. This vision had been inspired in 1917 through a letter to Flynn from Lieutenant Clifford Peel of the Australian Flying Corps, Australian Imperial Force. Later, Flynn's friendship with (Sir) W. Hudson Fysh [q.v.], a founder of Queensland And Northern Territory Aerial Services Ltd (QANTAS), brought him further technical information and encouragement, as did Hugh Victor McKay [q.v.]. When McKay died in 1926 he left £2000 to finance Flynn's experiment on the proviso that the Presbyterian Church doubled that. The Church assembly approved the experimental Aerial Medical Service on condition that Flynn raised £5000, which he obtained with modest help from the civil aviation branch of the Department of Defence and the Wool Brokers' Association. QANTAS leased on very favourable terms a De Havilland 50 aircraft, the first machine available and suitable for aerial medical work. History was made and Flynn's vision became a reality on 17 May 1928 when Dr St Vincent Welch, with pilot Affleck at the controls of *Victory*, answered the first call received by the A.I.M. Aerial Medical Service. Next year Flynn was a delegate to the first world conference on aviation medicine in Paris. Fysh later wrote, 'Flynn the Dreamer . . . who saw a vision of a Flying Doctor well before the days of practical flying, but kept it firmly fixed in his mind', was a 'practical man when the time came for action'.

This second period also marked Flynn's recognition of the role the two-way radio was to play in the socialization of people in remote areas as they developed a community that is 'heard' but rarely seen. Later he gained Adelaide Miethke's [q.v.] support for the establishment of the Alice Springs Aerial Medical Service: on a visit, she recognized the potential the 'flying doctor' network offered for a 'school of the air' which she later inaugurated. In Sydney on 7 May 1932 Flynn, aged 51, married his devoted secretary, Jean Blanch Baird. 'Thus for the last nineteen years of his life' wrote Scott McPheat, 'the man who championed home-life in two-thirds of Australia himself enjoyed the "glow of a fireside"'.

The final phase of his work began with his merging his A.I.M. Aerial Medical Service into a national community service having resources far greater than any Church could provide. Flynn's dealings with members of State and Commonwealth parliaments now made him a representative for the scattered settlers in two-thirds of Australia for whom he had become the advocate for an adequate aerial medical service. He had made his first move in 1931 but the Depression not only kept the matter from the agenda of the premiers' conference that year, but, without Flynn's indefatigable publicity, it would have put his flying doctor out of the air. By 1933 he judged the time opportune and made his major overtures through W. Forgan Smith [q.v.], Queensland's premier. At the same time he maintained a flow of correspondence with key State and Federal parliamentarians. In 1933 the premiers resolved that 'this Conference approves a general co-operation of the Governments of the Commonwealth and States with a view to furthering the Australian Aerial Medical Service'.

Flynn still needed the approval of his Church whose General Assembly was meeting later that year. In a letter to his friend and confidant J. Andrew Barber [q.v.7], he revealed something of what this move was costing him personally, yet knowing that he and the Church could act in no other way to be true to the A.I.M.'s vision, 'For Christ and the Continent'.

If we do not become a national body the A.I.M. will be in danger of losing revenue . . . I mean we must either shrink back into a mere preaching agency, or, as a dynamic partner in a national enterprise to help the frontier people, we establish ourselves as a power greater than when

we had the isolated areas to ourselves . . . If the Assembly baulks at the hurdle and refuses to invite everybody interested to join the A.M.S. adventure, I believe the A.I.M. will shrivel into a selfish little runt . . . I repeat my fears, that our colleagues do not realise that our conditions are being completely changed.

Flynn's arguments inspired his Church assembly and he won the day on his terms. That year he was appointed O.B.E.

Much of his time was now spent in setting up the State sections of the National Aerial Medical Service of Australia. (The name was changed in 1942 to the Flying Doctor Service of Australia and the designation of 'Royal' was added in 1954). Flynn's concept of the structure of the N.A.M.S. demonstrated his concern for community partnership through a series of State sections and local committees 'unified by their common Articles of Association' which he described as 'Multiple Heads – one Heart'. Throughout Australia he addressed public meetings, and held press interviews and consultations until the N.A.M.S. became a reality with the constitution that he envisaged.

In 1939 Flynn was elected to the three-year term as moderator-general of the Presbyterian Church of Australia. In 1940 and 1941 the degrees of D.D. were conferred on him by the University of Toronto and the Presbyterian College at McGill University, Montreal, Canada. The war and post-war period inhibited any new work until his closing years when the Old Timers' homes in Alice Springs, and Warrawee, the Far North children's holiday and health scheme in Adelaide, were established.

Survived by his wife, Flynn died of cancer in Sydney on 5 May 1951 and his ashes, at his request, expressed through his widow, were interred at the foot of Mount Gillen, Alice Springs. At this service his senior padre, Kingsley Partridge, said, 'Across the lonely places of the land he planted kindness, and from the hearts of those who call those places home, he gathered love'. In 1956 the John Flynn Memorial Church was opened in Alice Springs.

Flynn enjoyed a remarkable range of friendships and from them his fertile imagination drew concepts that enriched people and places. His letters reveal his dry sense of humour and irony, but above all his compassion. He was an inveterate talker, holding listeners far into the night, but he was also a good listener. His ecumenicity was shown by his being one of the founders of the United Church in North Australia. He accepted a specific charter and refused to be side-tracked into other areas of his concern, believing that a given task must receive total commitment. The same standard was expected from those who served in the A.I.M. with him. When he said 'A man is his friends', he expressed something akin to Martin Buber's philosophy that 'All real living is in meeting'. His meeting with other people often revealed a compulsive humanism which gave meaning to his own life as an ordained minister of his Church and to the faith by which he lived and served.

W. S. McPheat, *John Flynn, apostle to the inland* (Lond, 1963); M. F. Page, *The flying doctor story, 1928-78* (Adel, 1977); Aust Inland Mission, *Inlander*, 1913-14, 1915, 10 Dec 1972; Presbyterian Church of SA, *Minutes of Procs*, Mar 1942; *MJA*, 14 July 1951; *SMH*, 21 May 1940, 2 Sept, 2 Oct 1972; *Canb Times* and *Herald* (Melb), 1 Sept 1972; *Age*, 2, 6 Sept 1972; *Advertiser* (Adel), 2, 6, 12, 13 Sept 1972, 10 Jan 1973; *National Times*, 16-22 Nov 1980; J. G. Bucknall and R. V. Guthrie, Conquest of distance (MS held by authors, Alice Springs; Bulleen, Vic); MS 3288, Flynn papers, *and* MS 812, G. Simpson papers, *and* MS 5574, Commission on National Mission, Uniting Church (NL).

GRAEME BUCKNALL

FLYNN, JULIA TERESA (1878-1947), educationist, was born on 24 January 1878 at West Melbourne, youngest of six children of Daniel Flynn, grain and corn merchant, and his wife Bridget, née Burke, both Irish-born Catholics. Julia was educated first in Carlton, then at South Melbourne College and later at Presbyterian Ladies' College, where she came under the influence of a brilliant mathematics master, J. P. Wilson [q.v.] She matriculated in 1893. Three years later she again took the examination, this time with first-class honours in geometry and trigonometry.

On 25 January 1897 she was appointed monitor to Brunswick South State School. In 1900 she entered the newly re-opened Training College, with Frank Tate [q.v.] as principal. Unlike her two elder sisters, who were very successful primary teachers, Julia went on to gain a university degree, due partly to the vision of Tate, who had persuaded the government to allow some college students to stay on to pursue the first year of a degree course. Nine students were chosen initially, among them Julia Flynn. She left college at the end of 1901, having completed a Trained Teachers' Certificate course and first year arts. The degree, undistinguished, was not accomplished till March 1912. Clearly the demands of teaching were great.

On leaving the college, Julia Flynn taught first at Christmas Hills and then at Bright. In 1907 she was appointed to the Continuation School (later Melbourne High School) and was soon recognized as an outstanding teacher of mathematics and a person of

'unselfish disposition and wide sympathies'. In 1914 she was appointed to one of the three newly created positions of inspector of secondary schools, at a time when all senior education posts were held by men. Through long hours, hard work and dedication she rose to senior inspector in 1924, then assistant chief inspector early in 1928. When M. P. Hansen [q.v.] succeeded Tate as director of education in June of that year, Julia Flynn became acting chief inspector of secondary schools. No woman had ever reached so high a level in the Victorian Public Service.

Hansen attempted to block her progress in July 1928, with an advertisement for the vacant chief inspectorship deliberately captioned '(Male Required)'. When pressed, Hansen admitted that he could not conceive of a woman chief inspector. Immediately, powerful women's groups rallied, appeals were made to the 1926 Women's Qualification Act, questions were asked in parliament and the *Age* took up the cause of women's rights. She finally won the position on appeal from J. A. Seitz [q.v.], but held it for only a six months probationary period, as Hansen refused to recommend confirmation of the appointment, claiming that she lacked vision and imagination. Not until 1936, with Seitz as director, was she finally appointed chief inspector, a position she held until her retirement on 25 January 1943.

As an inspector and administrator, Miss Flynn was considered formidable, but just. The high standard she required of others was a reflection of her total commitment to the welfare of children and the cause of education. In retirement she worked indefatigably as secondary schools advisory officer to the Catholic Education Office, thereby serving the Church she held so dear. On 14 October 1947, two days after suffering a heart attack, she died at Mount St Evin's Hospital, East Melbourne. She was buried in Melbourne general cemetery.

Education Dept (Vic), *Vision and realization*, L. J. Blake ed (Melb, 1973); *PD* (Vic), 1929, 3rd S, v 179, p 102, 222, 734, 1133; *Vic Education Gazette and Teachers' Aid*, Sept 1901, Feb 1902, Jan 1928, July 1928, Mar 1943, Oct 1947; Aust NZ Hist of Education Soc, La Trobe Univ, *J*, Nov 1975; *Age*, and *Argus*, 15 Oct 1947; *Advocate* (Melb), 22 Oct 1947; Vic Dept of Education Archives (Melb); MDHC Archives; Julia Flynn (unpublished paper by C. R. T. Mathews, Nth Oakleigh, Melb).

IMELDA PALMER

FLYNN, THEODORE THOMSON (1883-1968), zoologist, and ERROL LESLIE (1909-1959), film actor, were father and son. Theodore was born on 11 October 1883 at Coraki, New South Wales, son of John Thompson Flynn, cordial manufacturer, and his wife Jessie, née Thomson. He received his education at Fort Street High School, Sydney, the Sydney Training College for Teachers and the University of Sydney (B.Sc., 1907) where he gained the university medal and the Johns Coutts scholarship in biology. His first teaching post was as science master at Newcastle and Maitland High schools in 1907; later he was appointed to the Newcastle and West Maitland Technical colleges, lecturing in chemistry and physics. His main interest remained in the natural sciences and in 1909 he became lecturer in biology at the University of Tasmania. On 23 January of that year at St John's Church of England, Balmain North, Sydney, he married Lily Mary (Marelle) Young, a descendant of one of the *Bounty* mutineers.

Flynn's lectureship was initially temporary, but he soon showed his worth, and in 1911 withdrew from an appointment as Macleay [q.v.5] research fellow of the Linnean Society of New South Wales to accept the first chair of biology in Hobart as the Ralston professor. The terms of his appointment included liberal provision for research and he pursued a vigorous study of the marsupials of Tasmania and also did original work on megapodes. The Australian Antarctic Expedition of 1912 attracted his interest and he took charge of some research during the *Aurora*'s summer cruise. He also devoted considerable time to fishery research and in 1915 was appointed royal commissioner to enquire into Tasmanian fisheries. He was a fellow of the Royal Society of Tasmania (1909) and in 1913-19 a trustee of the Tasmanian Museum and Botanical Gardens. He gained his D.Sc. at the University of Sydney in 1921 for work on marsupial embryology.

In September 1930 Flynn left Hobart for London to continue his research on marsupial embryology, and also to seek funds on behalf of the Australasian Association for the Advancement of Science for scientific and economic exploration of the south-west coast of Tasmania. Next January he was awarded a Rockefeller Foundation grant to carry out research with his former mentor, Professor J. P. Hill [q.v.], on the development of monotreme ovum. In June he took up the chair of zoology at Queen's University, Belfast, Northern Ireland; he also became director of the marine station at Portaferry.

Flynn, who held attention during his lectures by a theatrical manner as well as by his subject matter, liked to take part in community affairs – debating, theatre and adult education. He was appointed M.B.E. in 1945. A fellow of the Linnean and Zoological societies, London, he was also a fellow of the International Institute of Embryology,

Utrecht, and a member of the Royal Irish Academy. After his retirement in 1948, as emeritus professor, he resided in Surrey, England. He died in a nursing home at Liss, Hampshire, on 23 October 1968, survived by a daughter. His estate was valued for probate at £519.

Errol was born on 20 June 1909 in Hobart. During a rebellious childhood he attended several Hobart schools, in none of which he lasted long, as well as South Western London College, while in London with his father, and Sydney Church of England Grammar School (Shore), from which he was expelled. In 1927, after a short period of office work with a Sydney shipping company, he began training as a district officer in New Guinea, but moved on to become in rapid succession copra plantation overseer, partner in a charter schooner business and gold prospector. He purchased the cutter *Sirocco* in Sydney in 1930; his seven-month journey back to New Guinea, where as manager of a tobacco plantation at Laloki he wrote columns on New Guinea life for the Sydney *Bulletin*, became the subject of his first book *Beam ends* (1937). Sailing remained a lifelong hobby.

In 1932, back in Sydney and notorious for unpaid debts in New Guinea, he played the part of Fletcher Christian in the film *In the wake of the Bounty* directed by Charles Chauvel [q.v.7]. Next year he went to England where he acted with the Northampton Repertory Company until signing a contract with Warner Bros. After *Murder at Monte Carlo*, made at the Teddington studio, he moved to California, where in 1935 he shot to stardom as the swashbuckling hero in *Captain Blood*. He proceeded to make some sixty films, his heyday as one of Hollywood's most handsome and agile actors being 1936-42. *The adventures of Robin Hood*, *The dawn patrol* and *The sea hawk* date from this period. Granted American citizenship in 1942 he never returned to either New Guinea or Australia. In his later years he was a wanderer aboard his schooner *Zaca* and addicted to drink and narcotics.

On 19 June 1935 at Yuma, Arizona, Flynn married actress Lilliane Marie Madeleine Carré (Lili Damita). Divorced in 1942 he married Nora Eddington in 1943 or 1944 at Acapulco, Mexico. Nora divorced him in 1949 after which, on 23 October 1950 at Monte Carlo, Monaco, he married Patrice Wymore. Apparently a playboy all his life, Flynn, according to his most recent biographer, Charles Higham, was a friend to the Nazis during World War II. He died on 14 October 1959 at Vancouver, Canada, survived by his wife, a son of his first marriage and two daughters of his second. His novel *Showdown* was published in 1946 and his autobiography *My wicked, wicked ways*, ghosted by Earl Conrad, in 1960.

T. Thomas, R. Behlmer and C. McCarthy, *The films of Errol Flynn* (NY, 1969); J. H. Moore, *The young Errol* (Syd, 1975); C. Higham, *Errol Flynn* (NY, 1980); *Industrial Aust and Mining Standard*, 4 Sept 1930; *Who was who*, 1961-70; *Weekly Courier* (Launceston), 4 Feb 1931; *New York Times*, 21 July 1946, 15 Oct 1959; *The Times*, and *SMH*, 16 Oct 1959; *North Shore Times* (Syd), 25 Aug 1976; *Sun-Herald*, 15 Apr 1979, 6 Jan 1980; *Canb Times*, 6 Jan 1980; MS 55, J. P. Hill papers (Basser Lib); information from Mr D. Norman, Lauderdale, Hob.
WILLIAM BRYDEN

FOLEY; *see* GRIFFEN-FOLEY

FOLLETT, FRANK WILLIAM (1892-1950), aviator and aerial surveyor, was born on 27 March 1892 at Marrickville, Sydney, son of English parents William Follett, warehouseman from Devonshire and his wife Ada, née Dodridge. Educated at Sydney Boys' High School, he joined the firm of Simpson Bros, engineers, in Sydney, and in May 1910 then joined the engineering department of the Metropolitan Board of Water Supply and Sewerage as a cadet draftsman and by 1916 was a compiling draftsman.

Enlisting in the Australian Imperial Force in January 1916, Follett saw active service in France with the Australian Field Engineers and was later promoted sergeant and assistant technical warrant officer. After training with No. 29 Training Squadron, Royal Flying Corps, at Fern Hill, England, he was commissioned second lieutenant in the A.I.F. on 18 November 1917 and lieutenant in the Australian Flying Corps on 18 February 1918.

In July 1918 in France with No. 2 Scouting Squadron operating out of Reclinghem (south-west of Aire) with S.E.5s, Follett saw much action harassing the enemy over the Lys in poor flying conditions. During the August Somme offensive his squadron helped reinforce British scouts in the Fourth Army and took part in the air-raids on Lille. In September he went back to No. 6 Training Squadron in England.

Returning to Australia in June 1919, he resumed his pre-war job. On 24 April 1920 at St Paul's Catholic Church, Dulwich Hill, he married Helen Gertrude Molloy. On 2 February Follett was appointed superintendent of aircraft in the civil aviation branch of the Department of Defence under H. C. Brinsmead [q.v.7] with headquarters in Melbourne; his work included the inspection of aircraft all over Australia and flight-testing new models. At Richmond, New South Wales, in December 1924, during Australia's first flying week for testing

locally built low-powered aircraft, Follett flew departmental aeroplanes; he gained the highest number of points in the trials in a P.H.53 (but failed to beat Bert Hinkler's [q.v.] mileage record), and won the aerial Derby in a D.H.37. He resigned from the Defence Department in June 1929 and from July 1929 to August 1930 was manager and chief instructor of the (Royal) Aero Club of New South Wales at Mascot.

In 1930 Follett founded Adastra Airways Pty Ltd which specialized in aerial surveying. In 1939, aware of the enormous potential in Australia and the lag in Australia's aerial mapping programme, he studied the latest techniques in England, the Netherlands, Switzerland and Germany, arriving home just before the outbreak of World War II. After the war the firm expanded. By 1949 it had the most sophisticated stereo-plotting equipment in Australia and received large government contracts including an 8000-square mile (21 000 km²) survey of the entire Darling River.

Quiet, retiring and somewhat dour, Follett played a leading part in the development of aerial surveying and photogrammetry. His outside interests included tennis, boating, growing orchids and Legacy. He was a member of the Imperial Service Club of New South Wales and of the Royal Society of Arts, London. In 1935 he received the silver medal of the Royal Humane and Shipwreck Society.

Follett died of heart disease at the wheel of his car outside his Vaucluse home on 25 October 1950 and was cremated with Presbyterian forms. He was survived by his wife; a daughter had predeceased him.

F. M. Cutlack, *The Australian Flying Corps...1914-1918* (Syd, 1938); *SMH*, 21 Feb 1921; 4, 8, 9 Dec 1924, 22 July 1926, 26 Aug 1932, 18 Aug 1939, 20 Apr, 9 May 1949, 27 Oct 1950; information from Dr W. B. Molloy, Middle Cove, NSW.
G. P. WALSH

FOOTT, CECIL HENRY (1876-1942), regular army officer, was born on 16 January 1876 at Bourke, New South Wales, son of Irish-born Thomas Wade Foott, stock inspector and station-owner, and his Scottish-born wife, Mary Hannay Foott [q.v.4], née Black, teacher, poet and journalist. After his father's death in 1884 he was educated at Toowoomba and Brisbane Grammar schools and later qualified as a mechanical engineer.

Foott was commissioned second lieutenant in the Queensland Militia Garrison Artillery in March 1895 but joined the Queensland Permanent Artillery in September 1896 as a lieutenant. In March 1901 the military forces of the Australian States were transferred to Federal control and in July Foott was promoted captain in the Royal Australian Artillery; that year, on 15 October, he married Isobel Agnes McDonald at Moorooka, Queensland.

In 1902 Foott transferred to the Royal Australian Engineers but remained in Queensland as staff officer, engineer services. He went to England for technical training in 1908 and on returning was staff officer and commander, R.A.E., in Victoria in 1909-10. Promoted major in August 1909, his next posting was to Army Headquarters, Melbourne, where in 1910-11 he was director of works and in 1911-12 director of engineers. He attended the staff college at Camberley, England, in 1912-13 and in 1914 was attached to the British Army in England for further training.

In January 1915, in the rank of major, Foott joined Major General (Sir) William Bridges's [q.v.7] 1st Division, Australian Imperial Force, as deputy adjutant and quartermaster general. After the Gallipoli landing Bridges was mortally wounded in May and in August Foott, who had been promoted lieut-colonel in June, was re-posted within the division as assistant adjutant and quartermaster general, an appointment he held for the next two years. During this time the division withdrew from Gallipoli, reorganized in Egypt and then served on the Western Front, Foott was appointed C.M.G. and awarded the Serbian Order of the White Eagle (4th class) in 1916.

He was transferred to A.I.F. depots in Britain as deputy adjutant and quartermaster general in July 1917, and in March 1918 was posted to Lieut-General Sir William Birdwood's [q.v.7] Australian Corps in France as chief engineer. Although Foott was an engineer officer this was his first appointment as such during the war and he retained it after Lieut-General Sir John Monash [q.v.] took command of the Corps on 1 June. After the Armistice, when the A.I.F.'s Department of Repatriation and Demobilization was established in London, Foott became its deputy director general with Monash as director general. For his war service he was mentioned in dispatches seven times and in 1919 was appointed C.B. His only brother, Private Arthur Patrick Foott, was killed in action at Passchendaele.

Foott returned to Australia in November 1919 after an eight-year absence and his A.I.F. appointment ended in February 1920. The post-war era which he faced as a regular officer in the Australian Military Forces was one of economy in defence, with few prospects of promotion. In October 1920, as a colonel and honorary brigadier general, he joined the newly formed Australian Staff Corps, then in 1922-25 served as a colonel in various posts at Army Headquarters in the quartermaster general's branch. In 1926 he was posted to Queensland where he was given, concurrently and temporarily, for the next four years three command appointments including that of base commandant, 1st Military District. By late 1929 the Depression had forced further cuts in military spending. In August 1930 Foott was transferred from Queensland to Victoria to be temporary commander of the 4th Australian Division as well as temporary commandant and base commandant of the 3rd Military District. In these circumstances, at the age of 55, he was transferred to the reserve of officers in July 1931; his army career ended then although it was not until February 1936 that he was officially placed on the retired list as an honorary brigadier general.

Foott's wife had died in 1926 and on 6 September 1934 he married Agnita Regnier Cogan at St James Anglican Church, Pakenham, Victoria. Survived by his wife and the son and two daughters of his first marriage, he died of a coronary occlusion on 27 June 1942 at Upper Beaconsfield, and was buried in Berwick cemetery with Anglican rites. His estate was valued for probate at £975. C. E. W. Bean [q.v.7] described him as 'a man of educated tastes and fine intellect' and 'an officer of great ability' who became 'one of the notable figures in the Australian Imperial Force'. His portrait, by George Coates [q.v.] is in the Australian War Memorial.

C. E. W. Bean, *The story of Anzac* (Syd, 1921, 1924), and *The A.I.F. in France*, 1916-18 (Syd, 1929, 1933, 1937, 1942); *London Gazette*, 5 Nov 1915, 3 June, 11 July 1916, 2 Jan, 15 Feb, 1 June, 28 Dec 1917, 31 Dec 1918, 1 Jan, 11 July 1919; *Reveille* (Syd), July 1931; *SMH*, 6 Nov 1915, 3 June 1916, 16 Feb 1917, 2 Apr 1920, 23 Dec 1925, 29 Nov 1929, 1 July 1931, 16 Sept 1940, 29 June 1942; *Courier Mail*, 1 July 1931; *Argus*, 29 June 1942; records and letters (AWM); information from Mrs B. Ogden, Gloucestershire, U.K.   WARREN PERRY

FORAN, MARTIN HENRY (HARRY) (1850?-1908), schoolteacher, journalist, Domain and Yarra Bank orator, was born about 1850 at or near Kilkee, Clare, Ireland, son of James Forhen. The family had been peasant freeholders but had turned to fishing. A precocious student at the local elementary school, Foran contemplated training for the priesthood, but in 1871 was appointed trainee teacher at the Kilkee Boys National School. Resigning on grounds of ill health, he became locally prominent in tenant reform and Home Rule agitation, but trouble with the police induced him to migrate to Victoria in 1876.

Chastened by Irish misadventures, he returned to teaching; first in Catholic schools and from 1879 as a permanent state-school teacher. Fairly successful at first but unable to hasten promotion by political patronage, he embarked on a sustained war of complaint. He did not receive his licence to teach until 1885, and correctly suspected that department heads wished to be rid of him. In September 1888, upon complaint by his headmaster, Joseph Derrick, Foran was suspended and brought before the Public Service Board on a charge of disciplinary and sexual misconduct. Although he was substantially cleared, the board was induced by the government to reopen Foran's case in April 1889, and this time ordered his dismissal. An appeal to the Supreme Court failed. By 1890 the case had become a minor *cause célèbre*, but Foran's parliamentary friends, such as C. F. Taylor, were unable to institute a select committee of inquiry. In 1892 Foran sued Derrick for libel but had to adandon the case when the Crown, successfully pleading privilege, refused to produce Derrick's report.

Next year Foran was in Sydney, earning a living by freelance journalism and as a salesman of Catholic books. A regular and popular Sunday afternoon speaker on the Domain, his chief appeal was to the Irish Catholics among the unemployed. His main political stamping-ground was the street corners and open public spaces of the inner city. Publicly, he scorned the self-serving machinations of all parties; but, in practice, linked himself with fellow Catholics among the radical Protectionists – notably E. W. O'Sullivan [q.v.].The Labor Leagues he saw as dangerously tainted by atheistic socialism, opportunism and Protestant bigotry. Foran initiated or dominated many ephemeral protest groups including the Anti Humbug League (1894), the New Labour Organisation (1895), the Christian Socialists (1895), the Protectionist Labour Party (1895), the Unemployed Organisation (1896), the Republican League (1896-97), and the Patriotic Vigilance Committee (1897). In 1894-95 he edited the *Sydney Irish World*. In 1894, 1895, 1898 and 1901 he was an independent, flamboyant and drastically unsuccessful candidate for the New South Wales parliament. However he polled better in the 1897 election of delegates to the Federal convention, and in the 1901 Federal election for East Sydney against (Sir) George Reid [q.v.]. Witty, verbally and sometimes physically violent, attracting derisory but affectionate nicknames such as the 'Domain Demosthenes' and the 'Mayor of Hyde Park', Foran in these years gained a foothold on the margins of respectable State politics.

He returned to Melbourne in 1902 and established himself as a Yarra Bank identity. In 1903, according to Melbourne *Truth* he drew larger crowds than any other speaker. A founding director in November 1903 of Australia's first daily labour newspaper, the *People's Daily*, he broke with the paper in December, angered by its decision to support the endorsed Federal Labor candidate for Melbourne Ports instead of himself.

In his last years the pattern of Foran's public activity began to alter. About 1904 he joined the Labor Party and served for a time on the Metropolitan District Council; he was a sporadic contributor to the populist Catholic weekly, the *Tribune*; in 1905 he became vigorously involved in the bishops' crusade against atheistic socialism; in 1906 he took part in the Wren [q.v.] machine's fight to keep open the Collingwood tote – at one stage reviving the Christian Socialists for the purpose. He gave up his Yarra Bank meetings early in 1908 when his health failed, and died of jaundice and hydatids on 25 April at St Vincent's Hospital, Fitzroy, unmarried and virtually penniless. He was buried at Boroondara cemetery in a plot belonging to a Labor Party friend, Alderman J. T. Street of Richmond.

A 1906 writer in *Truth* declared, dismissively, that Foran 'had a variable career as a political failure'. An obituarist in the *Tribune* praised his defence of Catholic doctrine and principles, and hinted that despite eccentricity, he was as worthy a 'knight of the Southern Cross' as some recently honoured by the archbishop. A *Bulletin* obituarist declared that Foran 'probably was the most fluent public speaker in Australia – not even excepting Deakin ... as a claptrap orator he stood supreme'. These judgments are extravagant, but not absurd.

P. Ford, *Cardinal Moran and the A.L.P.* (Melb, 1966); *Hard Up*, 28 Mar, 4 Apr 1896; *Age*, 20 June 1892; *Truth* (Syd), 17, 24 June, 1 July 1895, 7 Mar, 12, 19 Sept, 3 Oct 1897; *Freeman's J* (Syd), 13 Feb 1897, 14 May 1908; *Catholic Press*, 6 Apr 1901; *Argus*, 11 June 1906; *Truth*, 2 May 1908; *Bulletin*, 7 May 1908; Minute-book, Metropolitan District Council of the Political Labour Council, Vic (LaTL); R. G. Ely, The trouble with Harry . . . (Univ Tas, Lib).   RICHARD ELY

FORBES, ARTHUR EDWARD (1881-1946), soldier, minister of religion and military chaplain, was born on 4 December 1881 in Brisbane, son of William Joseph Kirnshaw Forbes, butcher, and his wife Martha, née Barrett, both London-born. He was educated locally.

At 19 Forbes enlisted for service in the South African War as a bugler with the 3rd (Queensland Mounted Infantry) Contingent and reached Cape Town in April 1900. After a skirmish at Koster River on 22 July his commanding officer reported: 'The most notable act of bravery . . . was that of Bugler Forbes . . . [He] took my horse and his own to what was supposed to be cover . . . and held these horses until they were both shot . . . During that trying time he had a bullet sent through his haversack'. He then took refuge in a farmhouse with others of his unit and when 'ammunition commenced to run short, Forbes under fire went out amongst the shot horses and ransacked the saddle wallets' for bullets. For this action he was awarded the Distinguished Conduct Medal and mentioned in dispatches.

His unit returned home in June 1901 and in September the people of Brisbane presented Forbes with a silver-mounted bugle and a purse of sovereigns. He went back to South Africa in March 1902, serving with the 1st Australian Commonwealth Horse as a bugler until August. During his two periods of active service he served in the Transvaal, Rhodesia, Cape Colony and the Orange Free State.

Conscious of a call to a ministry in the Church, Forbes studied at the Glasgow Bible College, Scotland, in 1907-09 and, on being ordained a Baptist minister, returned home for mission work with the Queensland Evangelization Society. Based at Beaudesert, he worked amongst shearers, miners and Melanesian cane-cutters and in 1910-11 also studied part time at a Baptist Union theological college. He married Ruby Loloma Ruddle on 1 March 1911 at Bundaberg Methodist Church. In August 1912 he transferred membership from the Baptist Union to the Churches of Christ denomination, remaining with the latter for the rest of his life. That year he became pastor at Albion, Queensland.

In 1914 Forbes moved to the parish of Belmore, Sydney, and when war began, volunteered for service as a military chaplain. On 1 March 1915 he was commissioned as a chaplain (4th Class) but, chafing at the delay in being posted overseas with the Australian Imperial Force, resigned his commission and enlisted as a gunner in a medium trench-mortar battery, rising to the rank of sergeant. Just before embarkation he was discharged from the battery and attested as a chaplain in June 1917. He sailed for England in August and from October served in A.I.F. depots in England and France; he returned to Australia in May 1919 and was discharged in June. Of his war service a Lieutenant L. Price wrote from England: 'he is having a great time. The fellows leave the other services and come to his. Forbes gives them the stuff they like — bed-rock principles and not orthodoxy'.

After demobilization Forbes took charge of the Auburn Church, Sydney, applying himself with typical zeal. While stationed there he was a part-time chaplain with the Australian Military Forces and in 1919-22 held appointments as chaplain 1st Class and senior chaplain, 2nd Military District; he reverted to chaplain 4th Class in 1922. He moved to Croydon parish, South Australia, in January 1923 and three years later was appointed the evangelist for the Churches of Christ. In 1923-27 he was also a chaplain with the 4th Military District. Late in 1927 he transferred to Brighton Church, Melbourne, and was pastor there until 1931. For the next four years he was engaged in commerce but then returned to Brighton, again as pastor. While living in Victoria he held the rank of military chaplain, 2nd Class, from 1930 and was awarded the Efficiency Decoration in 1938. In 1940 he was posted to Mile End Church, South Australia, ministering there until September 1941 when he became a full-time military chaplain. A veteran of three wars, he was placed on the retired list, A.M.F., on 16 January 1944 and that year became pastor of the Hamilton Church, Victoria.

A year later, after suffering from nephritis and a coronary occlusion, he retired to Sandringham. Survived by his wife and three daughters, he died there on 19 April 1946 and was buried in New Cheltenham cemetery.

Aust Defence Dept, *Official records of the Australian military contingents to the war in South Africa*, P. L. Murray ed (Melb, 1911); *London Gazette*, 27 Sept 1901; Churches of Christ (Bris), *Australian Christian*, 22 Aug 1912, Apr-May 1946; *Brisbane Courier*, 2 Mar 1900, 13-17 June 1901; family information from Mrs. E. L. Charlesworth, Sandringham, Melb.   A. E. E. BOTTRELL

FORBES, CATHERINE ELLEN (1874-1946), religious sister and educationist, known as Mother Mary Elizabeth, was born on 18 July 1874 at Carlton, Melbourne, eldest daughter of Alexander Forbes, accountant, and his wife Jane Mary, née Costello, both Australian-born.

Catherine was educated at home; her matriculation entry, 1892, signed by her father and by a private tutor, L. D. Brouard, listed French, geography, English honours, Latin, geometry, algebra, arithmetic and physiology. In 1893 she began an arts course at the University of Melbourne and graduated B.A. in March 1897. At the university she was an active member of the Princess Ida Club. Her address after 1897 was Loreto Abbey, Mary's Mount, Ballarat. On 2 February 1900 she was received as a postulant into the Institute of the Blessed

Virgin by Mother Gonzaga Barry [q.v.3] and given the name Elizabeth.

Her first appointment after profession in 1902 was to the newly founded Loreto Convent in Adelaide. The small school, poorly equipped, was a challenge to test new methods in primary classes and her experience there proved invaluable. The 1905 Victorian Registration of Teachers and Schools Act opened the way to her specific educational career. As a result of the Act, the Central Catholic Training College at Albert Park, Melbourne, was founded with Mother Hilda Benson as principal and Barbara Bell [qq.v.7] as mistress of method. Mother Elizabeth took the necessary education subjects at the university to secure her diploma of education and in 1906 was ready for her post as collaborator with Mother Hilda. The college, essentially for the training of primary teachers, religious and secular, was also a residence for those students taking university courses. Students armed with 'registration' went out to all States; they bore in mind the prudent guidance given them by Mother Elizabeth and remembered too the salt of wit in her criticism lessons.

Reports of the training college led to a request from Western Australia for a summer school. Accordingly, Mother Elizabeth and the artist, Mother Catherine, conducted a 'school' at Loreto, Claremont, in the Christmas vacation of 1915-16, inaugurating what was to become a feature of Catholic education in Western Australia. Earlier, in 1912, Mother Elizabeth had given support and guidance to the opening of the Loreto Free Kindergarten at South Melbourne; she was anxious to involve past students in this service.

In 1918 St Mary's Hall at Parkville, a residence for Catholic university women students, was opened. Mother Elizabeth was the obvious choice as administrator. She loved the work, despite its responsibilities. In 1924 she went to Sydney where she held administrative positions at Loreto, Kirribilli, and later became superior and administrator of Loreto Boarding School, Normanhurst, during the Depression. Finally she was principal of Loreto Convent, Adelaide.

In each post she was beset by exam-oriented systems that taxed all her courageous experimentation, tact, and integrity of principle. Alternative 'courses' were examples of her care for the individuality of the person. She was essentially the teacher. A 'contemplative in action', she saw God in everything: she was a keen nature-lover and gardener, and knew every bird call. Her death at Loreto Convent on 1 March 1946 came after a period of retirement forced on her by failing health. After a requiem Mass she was buried in West Terrace cemetery, Adelaide. But she lives on in the annals of Loreto education.

E. Scott, *A history of the University of Melbourne* (Melb, 1936); M. Oliver, *Love is a light burden* (Lond, 1950); J. G. Murtagh, *Australia: the Catholic chapter* (Syd, 1959); S. Murray-Smith (ed), *Melbourne studies in education* (Melb, 1976); J. Brownfoot and D. Scott, *The unequal half* (Syd, 1976); G. O'Hagan, *Ballarat to Broome* (Ballarat, 1977); Loreto in development of secondary education in Victoria (typescript, Mary's Mount Archives, Ballarat).   M. BORGIA TIPPING

FORGAN SMITH: *see* SMITH, WILLIAM FORGAN

FORREST, ALEXANDER (1849-1901), explorer, politician and investor, was born on 22 September 1849 at Picton, near Bunbury, Western Australia, fourth of nine sons of William Forrest, miller, and his wife Margaret Guthrie, née Hill. His older brother was (Sir) John Forrest [q.v.]. After education at Bishop Hale's [q.v.4] School in 1863-65, he worked at his father's mill until in 1868 he advertised himself as a surveyor. This somewhat premature move was followed by a further period of training, but by 1870 he was experienced enough to serve as second-in-command of John's first transcontinental expedition, along the edge of the Great Australian Bight. On 1 January 1871 he was appointed to the Survey Department as surveyor-in-charge of the Albany district; but, following a reorganization later that year, he became an independent licensed surveyor working by contract for the department. This kept him constantly at work during the pastoral expansion of the 1870s until his marriage on 15 January 1880 to Amy Eliza Barrett-Lennard (1852-1897).

Old colonists considered that Alexander was a better bushman than John, quicker to accept and persevere with risks, though a less careful surveyor. In August-September 1871 he had led a six-man expedition for pastoral country on the Hampton Plains, forming a favourable impression which did not survive a second reconnoitre in 1876. In 1874 he was second-in-command of John's second transcontinental expedition, frequently acting as advance scout and proving himself a loyal confidant. Following an important survey of the North-West in 1875, he planned an examination of the remaining unoccupied area in the far north of Western Australia. In March 1879, accompanied by his brother Matthew (1857-1884) and six other men, he began a six-month exploration which resulted in the discovery and naming of the Kimberley district, the Margaret and Ord rivers, the

King Leopold ranges, and a vast tract of well-watered pastoral country on the Fitzroy and Ord rivers. There were privations; much valuable time was spent in fruitless attempts to penetrate the Leopolds, so that the expedition ended in a desperate dash to the security of the Overland Telegraph Line. Yet Forrest could boast the discovery of a land of good grass and water, promising prospects for gold and tropical agriculture, and Aboriginals who showed no hostility. It became a magnet for squatters and investors.

Survey Department officials were not expected to profit from their finds and the Forrest brothers had already been criticized for their investments in North-West station properties. Alexander Forrest turned from surveying to set up as a land agent specializing in the Kimberleys. He was consulted by the Duracks [q.v.4] and Emanuels [q.v.], the MacDonald brothers [q.v.5] and many more who swarmed to take up over 51 million acres (21 million ha) of Kimberley pastoral leaseholds by 1883. Between 1883 and 1886 he also acted as local agent and adviser to Anthony Hordern [q.v.4], the Sydney investor who constructed a land-grant railway from Albany to the terminus of the government system at Beverley. The line was opened in 1889. During its construction Forrest acted as local agent for other speculators with proposals for land-grant railways, but none came to fruition. He was principal shareholder in the timber company supplying the colony's second land-grant railway, the Midland, and during its financial difficulties of 1888-91 assisted its contractor Edward Keane [q.v.5] in his negotiations with the government.

In 1887 Forrest entered the Legislative Council as first member for Kimberley. He soon identified himself as a headstrong partisan of his brother John and the chief justice (Sir) Alexander Onslow [q.v.5] in their feuds with Governor Broome [q.v.3]. For a time he was involved with the more radical wing of the responsible government movement, being one of the speakers at a mass meeting in September 1887 when Broome's effigy was burnt by a working-class crowd. During the 1887-88 tariff debates he led the protectionist lobby, successfully moving for increases in the duties on imported meat, livestock, and grain, thus insulating local producers against competition from the eastern colonies. As a local member his main concerns were the acquisition of public works and the strengthening of police protection for Kimberley pastoralists against Aboriginal raids on their stock and property. When responsible government came in 1890 he represented

West Kimberley in the Legislative Assembly, easily retaining the seat until his death. He never held cabinet office, but as government whip he wielded such influence during Sir John Forrest's premiership that he was popularly known as 'the sixth minister'.

When (Sir) Stephen Henry Parker [q.v.] joined the Forrest ministry late in 1892 Alexander Forrest succeeded him as mayor of Perth, holding office for six years (1892-95; 1897-1900). These gold-rush years saw the city's most rapid expansion and placed great strains on municipal services. Forrest's main achievements were the establishment of Perth's first tramways; improvements in the paving of the city streets; the creation of several important parks and reserves; and the maintenance of a generous record of civic hospitality. He was adept at winning subsidies from Sir John Forrest's government. Public health was less satisfactory. A smallpox epidemic early in 1893 was followed by persistent typhoid, and counter-measures were inadequate. Forrest initiated negotiations for the purchase of the privately owned Perth waterworks; they were vested in 1896 in a government board of which he was an *ex officio* member from 1898, but he took little part in its proceedings and was singled out as a heavy consumer in times of shortage. During his second term of office he had too many irons in the fire to give satisfactory civic leadership and had to stave off a strong challenge at the 1899 mayoral election. However he deserved credit for his last action as mayor, the appointment as acting town clerk of the young and able W. E. Bold [q.v.7].

Forrest was quick to seize the investment opportunities created by the Western Australian gold rushes. He was one of the first speculators in 1888 to float a company on the Yilgarn goldfield and, for the rest of his life, played the stock market zestfully if at times lucklessly. His greatest coup came in 1894 when he grub-staked John Dunn in the discovery of the Wealth of Nations mine north-west of Coolgardie, which was sold to British investors for £147 000. He was also a partner in the Londonderry syndicate which Sir John Forrest's government indemnified against accusations of claim-jumping. Forrest's profits went into further speculations. He was a partner or shareholder in several northern sheep stations, and owned a farm at Cubbine, east of York. He was a prolific investor in real estate and led the syndicate which in 1895 subdivided Peppermint Grove, now Perth's most affluent suburb. He invested substantially in the timber industry, and was sleeping partner in a chain of retail butchers' shops. From 1890 he held a major investment in the *Albany Advertiser*, though without attempting to influence its anti-Forrest political stance. When in 1896 a Perth company published the *Morning Herald* as an avowedly 't'othersider' daily, he found no difficulty in serving as chairman of directors. By 1895 his business reputation stood high enough for the *Coolgardie Pioneer* to flirt with the notion of him as a potential supplanter to Sir John, capable of running the colony on sound commercial lines; but before long the goldfields press saw him as Western Australia's arch-capitalist squeezing profit from family connexions.

Forrest came most under attack as creator of the 'meat ring', a combination of local suppliers battening on goldfields consumers. Between 1893 and 1898 he was the staunchest defender of the protective stock tax, despite repeated pressure by consumers for its reduction or abolition. Following the negotiation in 1893 of a satisfactory contract with the Adelaide Steamship Co. for serving the North-West ports, Forrest formed a partnership with Isadore and Sydney Emanuel for the shipment of Kimberley cattle to the Perth and goldfields markets. Through retail contacts Forrest, Emanuel & Co. came to dominate, though never to monopolize the livestock trade, especially after their main rivals, the Wyndham firm of Connor, Doherty & Durack Ltd, were disadvantaged by the imposition in 1897 of quarantine regulations against tick-infested East Kimberley cattle. Long and spirited controversy over the tick regulations gave rise to accusations that they were imposed partly to favour Forrest, Emanuel & Co. Anxious to parry the impression of the Forrest brothers as a self-seeking clique, the government halved the food duties in 1898. Complaints about the 'meat ring' continued nevertheless and controversy intensified during 1899 and 1900.

Unlike his brother, Alexander was a convinced opponent of Federation. As a delegate to the 1891 National Australasian Convention, his sole comment had been in opposition to payment of members and since then he had grown to fear the impact of eastern Australian competition on the young industries of the West. With Charles Harper he led the anti-Federationists in the Legislative Assembly and stumped the goldfields in a futile attempt to stem the Federal tide. In May 1900 Richard Robson, the newly elected member for Geraldton, accused the Forrest government of bribery and corruption, alleging that at least four members on the government side were financed by Alexander. A select committee found the charges unsubstantiated and Robson resigned in June and went into obscurity. In fact several members of parliament were then in debt to Forrest, his open-handed munificence making him an easy touch for those in financial trouble. There is, however, no evidence that he ever tried to influence his debtors' votes, or that he ever needed to. At the time of the Robson inquiry the Kalgoorlie *Sun* alleged a series of freight frauds by the Perth Ice Co., of which Forrest was briefly acting chairman of directors. Another select committee exonerated the directors of any knowledge of these frauds.

Constant criticisms took their toll of Forrest's health. The pressure lifted a little after Sir John's resignation to enter Federal politics in February 1901 and in May Alexander was delighted with his appointment as C.M.G. in recognition of his services as mayor. Later that month he was shattered by news of the death in action in the South African War of his 17-year-old son Anthony. On 20 June Alexander died at Perth of complications arising from kidney trouble. He was buried in Karrakatta cemetery. Probate was assessed at £195 238, one of the largest estates hitherto amassed in Western Australia, though probably diminished by unfortunate mining investments. In 1903 a statue of him was erected in a small reserve near his former home at the west end of St George's Terrace. This was later moved to a more prominent site at the intersection of St George's Terrace and Barrack Street.

Forrest was a man of stalwart physique, though in middle age he carried less weight than his brother. Although fully bearded as a young man, after his marriage he was clean shaven except for a moustache. He was a keen patron of sport, and as a committeeman of the Western Australian Turf Club was responsible for the establishment in 1887 of the first Perth Cup, which was won by his own horse First Prince. As a capitalist he was an uncomplicated believer in the development of Western Australia's natural resources, enjoying the gamble of speculative investment, generous in prosperity and uninterested in the acquisition of power beyond the extent necessary to serve his immediate interests. But he was careless of appearances and failed to realize that the casual practices of a small-town business community, linked by kinship and connexion, could be interpreted unkindly in a more sophisticated commercial and political milieu. Extremely kind-hearted to those in need, he tended to be imperceptive about the need for government initiatives in social welfare. On issues such as Aboriginal policy and women's suffrage he was a conservative paternalist. To his daughter and his four sons he was a devoted family man, especially after his wife's early death.

Forrest's next brother, David (1852-1917) managed the family's North-West sheep stations, was member for Ashburton in 1900-01 and later strongly supported the State's Liberal party organization; David's son (Robert) Mervyn (1891-1975) was M.L.C. for North Province, 1946-52. Another nephew, Percival Dicey Forrest (1890-1960) pioneered the use of subterranean clover in the south-west. Of Alexander Forrest's sons, the third, John (1887-1960) succeeded to the management of the family's interests, and was for many years on the committee of the Pastoralists' Association of Western Australia.

G. C. Bolton, *Alexander Forrest* (Melb, 1958); F. K. Crowley, *Forrest: 1847-1918*, 1 (Brisb, 1971); C. T. Stannage, *The people of Perth* (Perth, 1979); A. Forrest papers (Battye Lib).   G. C. BOLTON

FORREST, EDWARD BARROW (1838-1914), company director and politician, was born in February 1838 at Windermere, Westmoreland, England, son of John Forrest and his wife, née Barrow. In 1842 the family migrated to Sydney where his education was completed at The King's School, Parramatta. Leaving school at 14, he became a clerk in the office of the Colonial Sugar Refining Co. and was sent to Brisbane in 1860 as the company's agent. He became managing partner in 1872 for Parbury Lamb [q.v.5] & Co., merchants. One of the first directors of Perkins & Co. and later of Castlemaine brewery, he was a director of the Queensland Investment & Land Mortgage Co., the Brisbane Gas Co., the North British and Mercantile Insurance Co., a local director of the Colonial Sugar Refining Co. in Queensland, and was on the Queensland board of the Australian Mutual Providence Society.

Regarded as a careful and efficient businessman, Forrest was appointed in 1873 to a commission of inquiry into the system of keeping the public accounts. An active supporter of the (Sir Thomas) McIlwraith [q.v.5] party in elections of the early 1880s, he was appointed to the Legislative Council in August 1882; in 1896, although a shareholder in the bank, he was chairman of the committee selected by the government to investigate the Queensland National Bank. He was also a member of the Marine Board of Queensland.

In March 1899 Forrest stood for North Brisbane in the Legislative Assembly. As a ministerialist he was unopposed, but when his election was challenged on the ground that he was on the Marine Board, he resigned and was re-elected. For most of his parliamentary career he was junior in the two-member electorate to John Cameron [q.v.7]. Primarily motivated by commercial concerns, as in his enthusiasm for Federation,

he does not seem to have had any particular aspirations in his political life, but he played a significant role on two occasions. In November 1899 he led a group of malcontents who crossed the floor and brought down (Sir James) Dickson's [q.v.] government. Both Andrew Dawson and James G. Drake [qq.v.] suggested that Forrest should form a ministry, but he would not agree to their conditions, and Dawson then formed the first Labor government. In September 1903 Forrest helped to defeat the Philp [q.v.] government by opposing his proposed extension of the Stamp Duties Act to tax all bank deposits. In 1905 Forrest's Railway (Employees' Appeal) Act became law. He lost his seat in 1912, probably as a result of the new forces released by the Brisbane general strike of that year. He was appointed again to the Legislative Council on 14 June 1913 but became ill shortly afterwards.

Sturdily-built and vigorous, with a powerful booming voice which earned him the nickname 'Pom Pom', Forrest was kindly, bluff and genial. He was a liberal supporter of philanthropic and social institutions, particularly the Brisbane General Hospital. President of the Brisbane Musical Union, a collector of paintings, including many Queensland works, he was a member for forty years of the Queensland Club, president of Brisbane Tattersall's Club, and patron of the Commercial Rowing Club. He was fond of sailing and was for many years commodore of the Royal Queensland Yacht Club. He also served as vice-consul for France.

Forrest died in a Brisbane hospital on 30 March 1914 and was buried in Toowong cemetery with Anglican rites. His estate, valued for probate at £13 232, was left to his family. On 29 April 1861 in Sydney he had married Elizabeth Leary, who predeceased him. He was survived by six of their eight children.

R. S. Browne, *A journalist's memories* (Brisb, 1927); D. J. Murphy and R. B. Joyce (eds), *Queensland political portraits 1859-1952* (Brisb, 1978); *Qld Heritage*, Nov 1978; *Brisbane Courier*, 30 Nov 1899, 15 Apr 1907, 31 Mar 1914; J. McCormack, The politics of expediency. Queensland government in the eighteen nineties (M.A. thesis, Univ Qld, 1974); A. Jenkins, Attitudes towards Federation in Queensland (M.A. thesis, Univ Qld, 1979); Broadbent cutting book (Oxley Lib).   BETTY CROUCHLEY
H. J. GIBBNEY

FORREST, HAUGHTON (1826-1925), artist, was born on 30 December 1826 at Boulogne-sur-Mer, France, youngest son of Thomas Arthur Forrest, equerry to Queen Victoria, and his wife Mary Lowther, both parents being of distinguished family. Forced to flee to Jersey, England, on the commencement of the French revolution in 1830, the Forrests later travelled throughout France and Germany before returning to their country home Forest Lodge in Berkshire. Young Haughton was subsequently educated in Jamaica, where his father had extensive sugar plantations, and at a military college at Wiesbaden, Germany. In 1852 he obtained a commission in the Honourable Artillery Company of London; he later joined the 31st Royal Monmouth Light Infantry, but resigned after attaining the rank of captain to work for the Post Office in London. On 30 September 1858 at the Plymouth parish church, Devon, he married a widow, Susan Henrietta Bunce, née Somerville (d. 1893). Their early married life was spent on the Isles of Wight and Man and in southern England where Forrest spent much time yachting and painting marine subjects, some of which were reputedly commissioned by the Prince of Wales (King Edward VII).

In 1875 Forrest took up a grant of sixty acres (24 ha) in Kittoland, Parana, southern Brazil, but finding conditions unsuitable returned to London. Next year he migrated with his family in the *James MacDuff* to take advantage of a grant of 100 acres (40 ha) in north-eastern Tasmania. Later he moved to Sorell where he obtained municipal appointments as bailiff of crown lands and of the court of general sessions, inspector of nuisances, of weights and measures, of thistles and of stock. He was also superintendent of police. All these positions he relinquished in March 1881 when he moved to Wellington Hamlets, near Hobart. In 1889-90 he was chairman of the Wellesley Road Trust.

Forrest spent the rest of his life after 1881 fully devoted to his art, painting many fine marine subjects and landscapes. His output, which spanned some seventy years, was prolific, and varied from small oils, painted on board, to large canvases. The marine paintings were usually of stormy scenes in which the vessels were meticulously detailed and the foam-crested breakers remarkably green and translucent. By contrast, his landscapes were peaceful, with mystical backgrounds of hazy blue or purple mountains. In 1899 Forrest's views of Mount Wellington and Hobart, in conjunction with the photographs of J. W. Beattie [q.v.7], formed the first set of pictorial stamps produced in Australia. He is also known to have painted New Zealand scenes, an occasional still life, a hunting scene and a brood of chickens. The extreme detail and exactitude of Forrest's technique gave his works a photographic quality which, in earlier years,

some art critics strongly deprecated. It is only recently that there has been a strong demand for his paintings.

Forrest died on 20 January 1925 at Melton Mowbray, leaving only a modest estate and survived by two daughters and one of his two sons. Many of his paintings hang in Tasmanian and other Australian art galleries. A self-portrait, in military uniform, undertaken in his early years, is in a private collection in Hobart.

Univ Tas Fine Arts Cttee, *Captain Haughton Forrest* (biog by G. D. Brown and exhibition cat) (Tas, 1976); *Hobart Town Gazette*, 25 June, 23 July 1877, 28 May 1879, 15, 29 Mar 1881; *Art and Aust*, 14 (Spring 1976), no 2; *Mercury*, 21 Jan 1925; *Argus*, 22 Jan 1925; *Australasian*, 24 Jan 1925; *Canb Times*, 17 Jan 1974.   G. R. GARROTT

FORREST, SIR JOHN, 1ST BARON FORREST OF BUNBURY (1847-1918), surveyor, explorer and politician, was born on 22 August 1847 at Preston Point, near Bunbury, Western Australia, fourth child and third son of the ten children of William Forrest and his wife Margaret Guthrie, née Hill. William was from Birnie, near Stonehaven, Kincardineshire, Scotland; Margaret came from a Dundee shopkeeping family related to the Black Campbells of Ayrshire. They had migrated to Western Australia in December 1842 as servants to Dr John Ferguson [q.v.1]. In 1846 William Forrest completed his engagement and settled at Picton as a farmer and millwright, where they shared in the general advance of the colony after the introduction of nearly 10 000 British convicts in the years 1850-68. John and his eight brothers were taught to help with chores, and he early became a splendid rider. The boys were enrolled at the government school in Bunbury, and in 1860 he followed his eldest brother William to Bishop Hale's [q.v.4] School in Perth. John did well particularly in arithmetic, and in November 1863 was apprenticed to T. C. Carey, the assistant surveyor at Bunbury. He completed his training successfully in December 1865, and was appointed a temporary government surveyor. Thereafter, until 1890, he was on the staff of the Surveyor-General's Office.

Forrest worked in most parts of the south-west, and in March 1869 was offered appointment as second-in-command and navigator to Dr Ferdinand Mueller [q.v.5] on an expedition from Perth in search of clues to the fate of Leichhardt [q.v.2]. When Mueller could not manage the trip, Forrest was chosen to succeed him. From 15 April until 6 August he successfully led six men and sixteen horses over 2000 miles

(3200 km), much of it in uncharted wilderness around Lake Moore and Lake Barlee, and inland almost as far as the later site of Laverton. He found no trace of Leichhardt, and no good pastoral land. He had, however, systematically surveyed his route using the most up-to-date methods of stellar observation, and he had brought back specimens for botanists and geologists.

Later that year the governor of Western Australia, (Sir) Frederick Weld [q.v.6], proposed an expedition to make a proper survey of the route between Western Australia and South Australia taken thirty years earlier by Edward John Eyre [q.v.1]. Since Eyre's hasty trip on foot along the coast from the head of the Great Australian Bight to Albany on King George Sound nobody had reached Western Australia except by ship. Forrest was appointed leader of the party, again six men and sixteen horses. They left Perth on 30 March 1870 and reached Adelaide on 27 August. The tangible results were not impressive. It was the first west-to-east crossing of Western Australia by land, and it showed that a telegraph line could readily be erected along the coastline. This was done, and the line, completed in December 1877, put Perth into telegraphic contact with London. But Forrest found only one new pastoral region, in the neighbourhood of the Hampton Range, far from any existing settlement and practically waterless.

However, the expedition brought widespread publicity to its leader and to his brother Alexander [q.v.], and also confirmed Forrest's own confidence in his ability and in his style of command. His objectives were boldly conceived, but cautiously executed. He was rarely compelled to go forward without knowing what lay ahead; nor was he obliged to advance merely because he could not retreat. As a surveyor he could not get lost, and his occasional gamble in the daily search for drinking water and feed for his horses was always calculated well in advance.

In 1871 the newly appointed surveyor-general, (Sir) Malcolm Fraser [q.v.4], appointed Forrest government surveyor for the northern district. In 1872 he was nominated to lead an expedition from Champion Bay eastwards across the central desert country. However, because expeditions were already being organized by Ernest Giles, W. C. Gosse [qq.v.4] and P. E. Warburton [q.v.6] from the South Australian side, the proposal was deferred. Only Warburton reached the western coast.

This left Forrest the opportunity to take a central route, and on 1 April 1874 he led an expedition of six men with twenty horses out from Geraldton. Moving by careful stages from waterhole to waterhole, he made a crossing of the western interior, arriving at Peake Hill on the north-south overland telegraph line on 30 September, after experiencing several hairbreadth escapes from death by thirst and some violent encounters with hostile Aboriginals. Sixteen horses died before 3 November when the men reached Adelaide, to be given a public reception rather resembling a Roman triumph. Forrest had led the first west-to-east expedition through the western centre of Australia; but he readily confessed that the practical results had not been great. Most of the country traversed was never likely to be settled.

Forrest's reputation spread rapidly throughout Australia, and press accounts of his courage and endurance attracted attention in Britain. In 1875 he was given leave to visit London, and was acclaimed as 'The Young Explorer' by a generation that fed on the glories of Antarctic, Arctic and African exploration. His leave was extended, and he was allowed to select a free grant of 5000 acres (2000 ha) of Crown land when he got home. He gave several public lectures in London, and arranged for the publication of his journals as *Explorations in Australia* (1875). He visited the birthplaces of his parents in Scotland, and arranged for his family to be registered with a coat of arms and a motto — *Vivunt dum Vivent* (They live while they flourish).

In 1876 Forrest was promoted to deputy surveyor-general and received the founder's gold medal of the Royal Geographical Society of London. On 29 February at St George's Cathedral, Perth, he married Margaret Elvire, eldest daughter of Edward Hamersley of Guildford, who stood in the front rank of Western Australia's territorial and social élite. Margaret, at 31, was tiny, lively and abundantly accomplished; she was a talented water-colourist, and her social aplomb was as important an asset to the marriage as the financial security she inherited from her father.

During the next four years Forrest was involved in four large-scale trigonometrical surveys, and in 1878, when he served for a time as acting surveyor-general and commissioner of Crown lands, he was the first colonial-born Western Australian to be admitted to the Executive Council. From May 1880 until August 1881 he served as acting superintendent of convicts, and in May 1882 was appointed C.M.G.: he was also elected a fellow of the Linnean Society of London in recognition of his work in collecting Australian flora on behalf of Mueller.

In January 1883 Forrest became surveyor-general and commissioner of Crown lands with a seat in the Executive and

Legislative Councils. This appointment was a landmark in his career. By perseverance and leadership he had by then overcome his triple disadvantage – he was colonial-born, rough-hewn, and lacked family connexions in Britain. As an administrator, he had a clear personal pattern of approach, which ensured his success in his new position. He was strong, thorough and punctilious. He made sure that the constant flow of settlers' inquiries and requests was attended to expeditiously, and often answered difficult inquiries personally. He watched expenses carefully, and his bureaucratic competence in handling official business was a rare quality in colonial Australia. His style of writing was direct, straightforward and lucid, and he was quick to reply in detail to anything he perceived as an aspersion. His characteristic mode was to write whilst he thought, and he was at his best when instructing his field staff on surveying techniques, or assessing the cost of various proposals, or explaining a complicated land transaction. In short, he carried over into his day-to-day administration of the Lands and Survey Department all those habits of thought, expression and command which he had developed as a field surveyor and inland explorer over twenty years.

After 1883 Forrest became involved in the higher levels of the colony's administration and politics, and he developed a strongly adverse opinion about the existing system of government, and the dictatorial manner in which he believed it was being managed by the newly arrived governor, (Sir) Frederick Napier Broome [q.v.3]. As time passed, it became clear that Forrest and the other top officials enjoyed quarrelling among themselves, and were not much given to compromise or to temperate statements; indeed, in 1884-86 the proceedings of the Executive Council came to resemble a 'bear-garden' – the colonial secretary's phrase. The climax came in September 1887 when the governor suspended Chief Justice A. C. Onslow [q.v.5] from duty. In the consequent imbroglio, which wasted much time and energy, Forrest's part did him little credit.

In 1883 Forrest organized the first large-scale survey of the Kimberley district, which had been explored by his brother Alexander in 1879, and accompanied the party for several months: it was his last field survey work. Next year he published a small booklet, *Notes on Western Australia, with statistics for the year 1883*, which, after several issues, was replaced by the *Western Australian year book*. He also visited the eastern colonies. In 1885 he was involved in a lengthy investigation into the Crown land regulations, and in 1886 toured the newly discovered Kimberley goldfield and selected the site of

the port of Wyndham. He piloted through the Legislative Council a new set of land regulations, designed to do equal justice to pastoral tenants and the 'bold peasantry' whose arrival the colony was hopefully awaiting: residence, with 'improvement', was made a *sine qua non* of alienation from the Crown. In 1887 he again visited London to represent the colony at the first Colonial Conference and at Queen Victoria's jubilee celebrations. The following year he arranged for the administration of the Pilbara and Yilgarn goldfields, and also drew up a report on a proposed government railway route from Perth to Bunbury.

As a government officer, Forrest did not take a very active part in the public debate on responsible government which agitated the colony in the late 1880s, but he strongly supported the proposal to establish a local parliamentary system in place of Crown Colony government. He did, however, take part in the Legislative Council debates on the new Constitution, and was disappointed not to be a delegate in London when the Constitution was being considered by the Imperial parliament. He had seen himself, from the outset, as the prime contender for appointment as first premier, being the only member of the old Executive Council who wished to continue in public life after the introduction of the new system; and he had manoeuvred successfully to frighten away his only possible competitor, (Sir) Stephen Henry Parker [q.v.]. He was elected unopposed as member for the Legislative Assembly electorate of Bunbury, and on 29 December 1890 was sworn in as colonial treasurer: the title 'premier' which he assumed was a courtesy title conferred not by the Constitution, but by usage and common consent. His experience and ability were uncontested; nobody else in Western Australia enjoyed the same sort of personal support. Head and shoulders above the others by force of personality, he also stood nearly six feet tall (183 cm) and weighed almost sixteen stone (102 kg).

Forrest was appointed K.C.M.G. in May 1891, the first native son to be so honoured, and held office as premier and treasurer until 15 February 1901. From December 1894 until April 1898, he was also colonial secretary. He thus established a record for longevity in Australian colonial politics. During these ten years his original cabinet's personnel changed completely, apart from himself. None of them achieved the same influence as Septimus Burt [q.v.7], his attorney-general. Parker resigned in 1894 when he found that cabinet was a one-man band, and Harry Venn [q.v.] was sacked in 1896 when he disagreed with the premier in public and refused to resign.

While he was not a good parliamentary speaker or debater – he had no gift for repartee, subtlety or blandishment – Forrest relied on being taken for what he was, a man of forthright rectitude, robust common sense, and homely hard-headedness. He never doubted that he knew what was best for his audience, and he based both policies and language on his perceptions of practical ways to solve practical problems. As a public speaker he had an earnest persuasiveness founded on a command of the situation as a whole, and he tended to view politics very much as he had surveyed the Australian bush – from above, from horseback or an elevated trig station. He tended also to think that political solutions were discovered easily enough if the correct levels had been taken and the right angles measured. If things turned out the wrong way, he started again. He was sensitive to public opinion, especially when it had been fully expressed on an important issue. He never lagged far behind it, but allowed it to mature, so as to enable him to give effect to demands in deliberate and calculated fashion. Thus he could forestall opposition in parliament, and claim that he was governing on behalf of the whole community. When convinced of the soundness or urgency of a proposal, he expected unwavering support from colleagues in his efforts to meet it, and subsequently full public appreciation. For a decade he usually enjoyed both.

At no time during the 1890s was Forrest challenged as premier; there was not even an heir-apparent. His government was stable, though it survived numerous defeats on individual measures; he withdrew items when the situation looked unpromising. He won the 1894 and 1897 Legislative Assembly elections, but with the increase in the number of metropolitan and goldfields seats and voters, he had to put more effort into ensuring that his supporters were voting his way. To some extent Forrest had himself created the situation, by abolishing the property qualification for electors of the assembly in 1893, and by adding three goldfields electorates that year and six in 1896.

Forrest never created a political party, or extra-parliamentary organization, or even a faction of his supporters within the parliament. From time to time he called together a caucus when drumming up support for a particular 'patriotic' or 'national' proposal. But the social round centred on his wife and his home in Perth was much more important in securing the personal loyalties on which he depended. The Forrests had a legion of relatives by birth and by marriage, many of whom were influential in parliament and business. Forrest could count on the support of his brother Alexander, a member of parliament and mayor of Perth for most of the 1890s, and also on that of (Sir) John Winthrop Hackett [q.v.], editor of the *West Australian*. Nor was there ever a fully effective parliamentary Opposition, even when a succession of leaders emerged in the 1890s: there was no Labor Party and no party system until after 1900. Forrest had more difficulty disciplining his own supporters and preventing them from forming competing regional and interest groups. He also had some trouble with the Legislative Council, both as a nominated house and, after 1893, as a house elected on a property franchise from an electoral system very heavily weighted to favour the agricultural districts.

Forrest's main political problems arose in the later 1890s because of friction between alluvial miners and the mining companies. Under legislation of 1895 both were permitted to use the same ground, but when alluvial gold became scarce the miners began to sink shafts, and there were several serious riots when police tried to prevent them. In March 1898 Forrest was mobbed by unruly diggers at Kalgoorlie, who were protesting at the situation and later that year the government abolished the dual title, but ensured that no leases would be granted unless they contained reef gold only. The government's administration of mining was never popular. But while mining members opposed the government in parliament, they never constituted a serious threat to it.

Forrest proposed to provide Western Australia with those public works which were lacking because the previous unrepresentative government had been unable to pay for them. He expected that thereby much new land would be opened up for settlement; that the population (only 46 000 in 1890) would be increased by immigration; that ex-goldminers would settle on farms or take jobs in shops, quarries and timber yards; and that the government would have money to spend for the good of the community at large. To achieve all this he raised loans in London, and for as long as the population continued to increase, so did the colony's ability to pay the annual interest. During the ten years of Forrest's premiership, the public debt rose from £1.4 million to £12.2 million.

Forrest saw himself as the broker who decided which public works would be given to which districts by receiving deputations at his office, or else by travelling during parliamentary recesses to meet the people and learn directly about their needs. Nevertheless, he had some overriding policies. First and foremost, he believed that there should be an apportionment between the needs of the metropolitan, agricultural, pastoral and mining regions, so that provision for railways, water-supplies, hospitals, harbours, schools and other public buildings were made with a view to long-term needs. In that view, the goldfields would decline before long in their relative importance. Forrest wanted to make the prosperity of the present pay for the hoped-for success of the future; the floating population of the goldfields would help those who had a permanent stake in the country.

This did not endear him to goldminers. His policy meant high railway freights and high tariffs. The goldminers were also annoyed because whilst they got their own railways, they did not get the one they really wanted from Kalgoorlie to Esperance on the south coast.

This complaint illustrated the second major Forrest policy, which was to develop Perth as the colony's only major rail terminus and Fremantle as the port-of-call for all overseas mail and passenger services. The dredging of a new harbour on the mouth of the Swan was begun in 1892 and completed in 1898, and mail-steamers on the England-Australia run began to call regularly in 1900. By the time Forrest resigned as premier, every major goldfield was connected by telegraph or railway to Perth and all the big towns had been provided with essential services. So, too, had the south-western farming districts and their local centres.

The Forrest government was extraordinarily lucky. While the eastern colonies were suffering from droughts, depression, unemployment, financial crises and bank crashes, one new goldfield after another was discovered in Western Australia, especially after the discovery of Coolgardie (1892) and Kalgoorlie (1893). Hundreds of companies were formed in the eastern colonies and in London to exploit the gold deposits, and much capital flowed in for investment in mines, business and property. The spectacular boom reached its peak in the years 1898-1903. The population rose from 59 000 in 1892 to 180 000 in 1900. Most came from Victoria, New South Wales and South Australia. Annual gold production rose to 1 million ounces in 1900, and trade and commerce increased rapidly. The increased demand for foodstuffs on the goldfields greatly benefited the farmers and pastoralists. In fact Forrest rode on the crest of the boom and took the political credit for it.

He also made several bold decisions from which the development of the colony benefited greatly in the long run. By the Homesteads Act (1893), the Land Act (1898), and the Agricultural Bank Act (1894) he used the credit of the government to provide for the well-being of the next generation of farmers. The Coolgardie Water Scheme, begun in 1895 and completed in 1903, not only provided water for the mines and short-term employment, but also met the needs of a generation of farmers who pioneered a new wheat-belt between the western coastal districts and the eastern goldfields. And the government's purchase of the Great Southern Railway in 1896 quickly opened up much new farming land in the south-western districts, and illustrated Forrest's preference for government rather than private enterprise in the main public utilities.

The Forrest government also initiated significant industrial, social and political reforms which brought Western Australia into line with the other colonies. Notable among these was a change in the law in 1892 which enabled married women to own personal and real property in their own right, and another which gave servants greater protection and independence from their employers. Workers' compensation for injury was granted by law in 1894, and trade unions were legalized and an Arbitration Court established in 1900. Other industrial legislation of the late 1890s laid down rules for the hours and conditions of work to be observed in gold-mines, factories and in the Collie coal industry. It ensured that all workmen were paid wages owing to them, and paid in money not in goods, and it compelled employment agencies to be registered. Hours of work in shops were limited, and there was to be no work in mines on Sundays apart from maintenance. Female shop assistants and factory hands were to be provided with chairs and stools. State aid to religion and to church schools was abolished in 1895, and an Immigration Restriction Act (1897) established a dictation test so as to exclude the Chinese; Forrest was proud that he had never allowed miners' rights to be issued to Asians. Finally, women were given the vote in 1899, and from the following year members of parliament were to be paid.

To many observers Forrest appeared to be a reluctant Federalist when in 1899 Australian Federation was becoming a reality. However, he was in a difficult position, which required all his skills as a broker of competing interests. From the outset he had participated in all Federal activities. He supported the idea in a speech at the first Science Congress in Sydney in 1888. He attended the meeting of the first Federal Convention in 1891 and, as premier, all meetings of the Federal Council of Australasia. He attended all three sessions of the Conventions of 1897-98, consistently supported a political Federation and the establishment of interstate free trade in principle, and tried to ensure a strong Federal Senate to protect State rights. He also wanted to make sure that Western Australia would not suffer financially from joining the Federation. He was sympathetic yet cautious, an attitude mainly resulting from his local parliamentary situation. The settled farming areas provided the core of his support in the Legislative Assembly, yet they were most apprehensive of the financial and economic effects of Federation; they were especially worried about the likely high cost of farm equipment if eastern manufacturers were given tariff protection. The Legislative Council was strongly opposed to Federation in any form. Forrest's tactic was to resist being rushed into it by the eastern goldfields population of newcomers — who then comprised one-third of the colony's population — and yet educate his supporters in the coastal districts into accepting Federation if the conditions of entry could be improved.

In this situation Forrest was criticized from both sides. The 'Sandgropers' accused him of selling out to 't'othersiders'. The goldfields accused him of nepotistic government supported by a gerrymandered electorate, and early in 1900 started a Separation movement, aiming to make the eastern goldfields a separate colony which could then federate with the rest of Australia. Forrest tried very hard to secure last-minute concessions — in particular, the retention of the local tariff for five years; the right to divide the colony into electorates for the election of senators; and a guarantee for the construction of an east-west railway. But he secured none of these concessions. He therefore persuaded his supporters to take what was offered, lest the terms should be even more unpalatable later on. In that sense only, Forrest was a reluctant Federalist: he had, however, long since learned to make the best of a hard bargain. When the Legislative Council finally decided to allow the referendum to be held, Forrest led the 'yes' campaign, which was successful in the pastoral and metropolitan regions, as well as on the eastern goldfields.

When the Commonwealth of Australia was inaugurated, Forrest was elected unopposed for the electorate of Swan in the House of Representatives. He was by then a big man by achievement, by reputation, and by personality. He also now weighed almost twenty stone (127 kg), with a 54-inch (137 cm) waist. He was one of the wealthiest of the first generation of Federal politicians, and when in Melbourne on ministerial and parliamentary duties hired a large suite of rooms in the Grand Hotel and entertained on a princely scale. He was successively postmaster-general (for a few weeks), minister

for defence (1901-03), home affairs (1903-04), and treasurer in five ministries (1905-07, 1909-10, 1913-14, 1917-18, 1918). A remark commonly heard in Perth during the fifty years after his death was that Forrest was a back-number in Federal politics, that his colleagues had either obscured him or else had never taken him seriously. This view was cultivated by Labor politicians who disliked his declamations against caucus domination, and by Western Australians who were either ignorant of events occurring east of Kalgoorlie, or who (as secessionists) had a vested interest in proving that Forrest was chiefly responsible for dragging Western Australia into the Federation, and later was unable to rectify the alleged 'losses' which resulted. However, the Federal parliament was required to create new national policies and institutions, rather than public works, and Forrest's achievements during his eighteen years in Commonwealth politics cannot be measured by the miles of new roads and railways built, or by the number of new wharves, schools, hospitals and other public buildings completed.

Nevertheless, they are impressive. In 1901-03 as minister for defence he coped successfully with Australia's involvement in the last stages of the South African War. He helped to raise the first Commonwealth overseas contingents, and was involved in the early plan of integrating the six colonial forces into a unified Commonwealth Military Force, and arranging for the continuance of the British Naval Squadron in Australian waters. He also showed that in matters of national and Imperial policy and long-term planning he had as responsible and as broad a view of Australia's future responsibilities as his chief military advisor, Major General Sir Edward Hutton [q.v.], though he was more of an Imperialist than most of his nationalist-minded cabinet colleagues desired. He was both Imperial-minded and an Australian nationalist, and he saw no contradiction in the dualism of his loyalty. At the Colonial Conferences of 1887 and 1897 and when in London in 1902, he supported the view that Australian defence was ultimately a question of Imperial strategy, not of colonial or dominion initiative.

While serving as treasurer in the Deakin [q.v.] government in 1905-07, Forrest successfully balanced the competing claims of Australia's seven treasuries under the tight Federal book-keeping system, and initiated the discussions which led to the creation of a separate Australian currency, and the subsequent adoption of the *per capita* system of distributing Federal revenue among the States. Under his administration the original concept of limited Federation was protected, and the States continued to be regarded as partners, though this caused his political opponents to accuse him, unjustly, of being a narrow States-righter. From March until June 1907, he also acted as prime minister and minister for external affairs whilst Deakin was at the Imperial Conference: this was the pinnacle of his career.

Meanwhile, ever since he had declined a portfolio in the short-lived Reid-McLean [qq.v.] government of 1904-05, he had worked hard to bring about a fusion of all members of Federal parliament opposed to the new Labor party, resigning his seat in cabinet in 1907 when unable to persuade Deakin to form and lead such a coalition. From the time of the inauguration of the Labor Party in Western Australia in 1901, he had no sympathy with the 'caucus socialists', who seemed to want to found a utopia in Australia and give the spoils to those who had no real 'stake in the country'. Forrest believed that Labor members were entirely subservient to outside organizations. During the exciting times of 1908-09, when the first fully protective tariff was enacted, and while there was a short-lived Labor government, he was the leading negotiator, emissary and spokesman for the 'Corner Group' in the manoeuvres which led to the successful linking of most non-Labor members of both Houses into a new party. By 1909 Forrest was back in office as treasurer, and held third place in the cabinet. When he brought down his thirteenth parliamentary budget in August 1909, he had the distinction of being the first Federal treasurer to budget for a deficit. As treasurer in 1909-10 he paved the way for the financial arrangements between Commonwealth and States which lasted until 1927. He was appointed G.C.M.G. in 1901.

Forrest and his 'Fusion', soon renamed Liberal Party, colleagues were out of office in 1910-13, when the Fisher [q.v.] Labor government made effective use of its majority in both houses. However, the closely contested Representatives election of 1913 returned the Liberals to power with a one-seat majority, and Forrest was second in the cabinet led by (Sir) Joseph Cook [q.v.] who had succeeded Deakin as party leader, defeating Forrest by one vote in the party meeting. Forrest's budget of 1913 continued Fisher's policy of presenting his successor with a substantial reserve. Then war broke out in Europe, and Forrest and his colleagues unhesitatingly offered all of Australia's resources to help the mother country. His last act as treasurer was to authorize the payment of money for the raising of the Australian Imperial Force. Shortly afterwards his party was soundly defeated at the double dissolution election of 1914, and Forrest returned once more to the Opposition.

Thereafter, the character of Federal politics underwent a profound change, which arose particularly from the demands of the war and the controversy over overseas military conscription. In 1917, after the defeat of the first conscription referendum, a second fusion took place between W. M. Hughes [q.v.] and his ex-Labor group and the Liberals. Forrest was disappointed that he did not secure the leadership of the new National Party and, reluctantly, once more became treasurer, this time in a government led by Hughes, and committed to the introduction of compulsory overseas military service to reinforce the troops on the Western Front. It is difficult to make a clear judgement on the fifteenth budget of Forrest's career in 1917, which was designed for a nation at war with a vastly changed internal balance of power between Federal and State authorities. The nation was also at odds with itself, because it had again narrowly rejected conscription. However, in the same year Forrest gained great personal satisfaction from being a passenger in the first train to cross on the East-West Trans-continental Railway, a project which had formed an important plank in his first policy statement in 1890, and which had been part of his conversational repertoire ever since.

In January 1918, during the discussion between party leaders and the governor-general which followed the defeat of the second referendum, Forrest pressed his claim to be prime minister in place of Hughes. But he did not have the numbers, and he reluctantly took office in Hughes's cabinet as treasurer, for the fifth time. By then, illness and old age were against him. Late in January he attended a treasurers' conference, and soon soon afterwards had a second operation on his temple for a cancerous growth. On 9 February it was announced in the press that Forrest had been recommended for a barony, the first native-born to be so honoured. He was delighted, and thereafter signed only his surname, but was more than a little aggrieved that he was not also prime minister. In March, much weakened by the recent operation, he resigned from the ministry, and late in May left Melbourne with the intention of seeking further medical aid abroad, if and when war conditions would allow it. He had no intention of resigning from parliament, though he was hoping that when the legal formalities had been completed, he might sit for a time in the House of Lords as an elder statesman of the Empire.

On 30 July he left Albany with his wife and a nurse in the troopship *Marathon*, bound for London with A.I.F. reinforcements. He was very ill and suffering much pain when he celebrated his seventy-first birthday at sea on 22 August, whilst sailing up the west coast of Africa. He died on 3 September 1918, when the ship was anchored off Sierra Leone. He was buried in Karrakatta cemetery, Perth. His estate was sworn for probate at £45 160.

Forrest was the first professional politician in Western Australia, and also the most successful and influential public man in his home State during the whole of his career. As a surveyor and civil servant he was never denied a promotion, and as a State and Federal politician he never lost his seat at an election. He was well rewarded for his efforts by public esteem, titular and other honours and awards, high official salaries, and by business opportunities which made him a wealthy man. When asked to name his most significant contributions to Western Australia's development, he liked to mention his Homestead Act and Agricultural Bank, with the construction of the Coolgardie Water Scheme, Fremantle harbour, and the East-West Transcontinental Railway. Had he been asked to name his failures and disappointments, he might reluctantly have mentioned that his efforts on their behalf were not adequately appreciated by the eastern goldfields population of the 1890s; that too many of his Federal electors were ungrateful for his previous efforts as their State's premier; that his colleagues in the Federal Liberal Party did not elect him as their leader, and thereby enable him to become prime minister; and that he had no children. Nor had he received, before his death, the official document which would have legally confirmed the recommendation that he be made a peer of the United Kingdom. However, by then it was the year 1918, and the administrative style and personal-loyalty strategies which had done so much to bring him success and public acclaim were no longer suited to the conditions of Australian politics. He had been a successful political broker and gardener in a small colony, but he lacked the vision or the ideology to become a statesman in the national scene, and in his wealthy old age he appeared to be more concerned with the conservation of Empire and privilege than the betterment of Australian society. Nevertheless, when he died, he was one of the last surviving heroes of Australian exploration, and one of the last of the founding fathers of Federation. His portrait, by E. Phillips Fox [q.v.], hangs in the Western Australian Art Gallery, and his statue, by Bertram Mackennal [q.v.], is in King's Park, Perth.

J. S. Battye, *Western Australia* (Oxford, 1924); G. C. Bolton, *Alexander Forrest* (Melb, 1958); J.A. La Nauze, *Alfred Deakin* (Melb, 1965); F. K. Crowley, *Sir John Forrest*, John Murtagh Macrossan lecture (Brisb, 1967), and *Forrest: 1847-1918* (Brisb, 1971), and *Western Australia's Lady Forrest* (Perth, 1977); N. Meaney, *A history of Australian defence and foreign policy, 1901-23*, 1 (Syd, 1976); P. Loveday et al (eds), *The emergence of the Australian party system* (Syd, 1977); L. Hunt (ed), *Western portraits* (Perth, 1979); *Univ Studies in History* (WA), 1966; *Aust Economic Hist Review*, Mar 1968.   F. K. Crowley

FORREST, WILLIAM (1835-1903), pastoralist, company director and politician, was born on 11 January 1835 at Ballykelly, Ireland, son of James Forrest, farmer of Dromore, Londonderry, and his wife Margaret, née Sherrard. Educated privately, he studied engineering at Glasgow. In December 1853 he arrived in Melbourne by the *Ravenscraig*, subsequently working as a goldminer and engineer in the New Chum and other Bendigo Golden Gully mines. Successful in mining, he joined the rush to pastoral Queensland in 1860, first managing an out-station for the Mt Hutton Pastoral Co. in the Dawson district and later (1867) purchasing the head-station with (Sir) Simon Fraser [q.v.4].

This venture prospered. In 1877 Forrest joined his old Bendigo chum, (Sir) Thomas McIlwraith [q.v.5], with William Collins [q.v.3] and Patrick Perkins [q.v.5], in floating the North Australian Pastoral Co., an enterprise designed to lease vast tracts of land in the Northern Territory, fatten store stock in the Kennedy area and promote sugar-growing and land speculation in the Burdekin delta. He was the key figure in floating the company's securities in Melbourne, allaying the fears of Victorians about McIlwraith's grandiose schemes and shrewdly negotiating with conservative South Australians worried about their virgin incubus, 'the Territory'. Although difficulties were great and dividends small, the concern survived. This was a not inconsiderable achievement and the credit must go to Forrest.

Although Forrest had 'no special taste for public life', McIlwraith saw his ability, appointed him to the Legislative Council for life in March 1883 and twice offered him a portfolio. Running McIlwraith's northern campaign, Forrest 'frightened the overconfident and indolent into activity and stimulated the jealous to further exertions'. In 1893 he was gazetted Queensland's agent-general in London. Alas, although he had purchased an ornate court uniform and gilt sword, the financial problems of the Brisbane mercantile and pastoral community, of which he was a pre-eminent technician, pulled him back. A shrewd director and consolidator, he resigned as agent-general without taking office, to restructure the stock and station firm, B. D. Morehead [q.v.5] & Co. and, most significantly, ensure the progress of the refrigerated meat export trade as both the chairman of directors of the Queensland Meat Export & Agency Co. and the chief public advocate for wholesale processing. He did, however, represent Queensland at the 1894 Ottawa Conference and discreetly, through business lubrication, facilitated the colony's entry into the Australian Federation.

In his pamphlet, *The present depression: its causes and cure* (Brisbane, 1893), Forrest advocated an export-led economic recovery for Queensland based on new technology, control of the rabbit plague, and sound business management. This would free his world from the curse of experimental legislation and allow 'natural forces and laws to defeat all agitators and political misleaders'. Well might T. Macdonald-Paterson say in 1895: 'He put his shoulders to the wheel at a time when finance was depressed ... the position of the meat export trade is largely due to [his] enterprise'. Business, in short, was his passion—'he loved it and expected others to feel the same'. 'Dogged perseverance and thrift leads', he said, 'to prosperity'. Brusque, yet lavish with advice and money to his friends, he was, if socially conservative, a more than competent representative of a somewhat discredited section of Queensland society. Most commodities Forrest measured in £.s.d. He was more tolerant of the Aboriginals than most, however, acknowledging their need for custom and movement, but this was like his advocacy of coloured labour to develop the north: he saw virtue in it because it was cheap, or, in the case of Aboriginals, both cheap and docile.

William died of heart disease at his brother's house, St Magnus, Bowen Terrace, on 23 April 1903. Unmarried, he left, after previous discreet disbursements, a mere £5490. His Anglican funeral, attended by the governor and the Brisbane Establishment, saw 'his old cabman drive an empty hansom, and four old servants of the Queensland Club (he was twice president) join in a common wreath and follow the hearse to the Toowong grave'.

His younger brother, JOHN (1848-1911), born at Ballykelly on 18 October 1848, was less of an entrepreneur and more of a manager, reflecting shifts in Queensland's economic and political life. He migrated in 1868, joining William at Mount Hutton. Between 1875 and 1880 he managed Gin Gin station near Bundaberg for Thomas McIlwraith. Financed by McIlwraith he established Avoca sugar plantation in 1880 but failed through a combination of 'bad seasons, floods and dear kanakas'. Forrest acted as McIlwraith's constituency manager, Bundaberg political organizer and local government figure. Patronage plus ability secured him the post of pastoral inspector for the Queensland National Bank. In 1902 he succeeded William as chairman of Moreheads and managing director of the North Australian Pastoral Co. A local director of the Australian Mutual Provident Society and the North British Insurance Co., Forrest, like his brother, was offered but declined the agent-generalship in 1909.

A pioneer Brisbane golfer and president of the Brisbane Golf Club in 1902-09, he was also an enthusiastic horse-breeder and a committee-man of the Queensland Turf Club. Personally kind and generous, he was an active supporter of the Boy Scouts. On 11 May 1881 he married Edith Irene Hanford, a great-niece of Hamilton Hume [q.v.1]; by her he had three sons of whom two survived him. Forrest died with coronary vascular disease at St Magnus on 29 September 1911 and was buried in the Church of England section of Toowong cemetery. A bust by Harold Parker is in the Queensland Club and his name lives in Forrest's mouse *Leggadina forresti* Thomas 1906, a short-tailed rodent found in the arid regions of northern Australia.

J. Connelly, *John Drysdale and the Burdekin* (Syd, 1964); *Sydney Mail*, 31 Mar 1883; *Maryborough Chronicle*, 28 May 1889; *Brisbane Courier*, 24 Apr 1903, 30 Sept 1911; *Telegraph* (Brisb), 24 Apr 1903; *Queenslander*, 7 Oct 1911; Palmer-McIlwraith papers (Oxley Lib, Brisb).

                                          D. B. WATERSON

FORSTER, SIR HENRY WILLIAM, 1ST BARON (1866-1936), governor-general, was born on 31 January 1866 at Southend Hall, Kent, England, son of Major John Forster, late 6th Dragoon Guards, and his wife Emily Jane, née Case. Educated at Eton and New College, Oxford (B.A., 1889), he excelled at tennis and fencing, played cricket for Eton, Oxford and Kent, captained Hampshire, and represented the Gentleman against Players. Over six feet tall, he was of the spare, typical sportsman's build. On 3 June 1890 he married Rachel Cecily, daughter of the first Lord Montagu of Beaulieu. A Unionist, in 1892-1918 Forster represented Sevenoaks and in 1918-19 Bromley in the House of Commons. He was a junior lord of the Treasury in 1902-05, Conservative whip 1902-11 and financial secretary to the War Office 1915-19. Appointed privy councillor in 1917, next year he became president of the Marylebone Cricket Club and in 1919 he was created Baron Forster of Lepe.

In June 1920, of three men suggested to the Australian government as suitable governors-general, W. M. Hughes's [q.v.] cabinet chose Forster, who was appointed G.C.M.G. Succeeding Sir Ronald Munro Ferguson [q.v.] he was sworn in at Melbourne on 7 October. Earnestly attentive to the social duties of the office, Lord and Lady Forster travelled tirelessly around Australia, often dedicating war memorials; their two sons had been killed in the war. In 1924 Forster visited Papua and New Guinea. A founder of Toc H in Australia, he was also chief scout; his charitable interests included the Big Brother Movement. Lady Forster was keenly interested in music, art, social questions, and women's movements. Among the numerous sports the vice-regal family patronized was yachting – the governor-general won several races and in 1920 presented the Forster cup for inter-State competition in 21-foot class yachts.

No political crises disturbed his tour of duty. Hughes's overthrow caused His Excellency no problems as on resigning the prime minister advised that S. M. (Viscount) Bruce [q.v.7] be commissioned. Although he had intended to stay only two years, and despite his dissatisfaction at being forced to draw more than £2000 annually from his private income, Forster was prevailed on to remain until 1925. He left Australia on 7 October.

Diffident, though popular, Forster had less influence than either his predecessor or his successor, Lord Stonehaven [q.v.]. He reflected the less active role British governors-general were to play in Australia after World War I. In May 1925 he wrote, 'the work of a G.G. and his wife is just like the work of looking after a big constituency'. Forster was survived by his wife and two daughters when he died of coronary-vascular disease in London on 15 January 1936. His portrait by John Longstaff [q.v.] hangs in Parliament House, Canberra.

SMH, 13 Oct 1920, 17 Jan 1934; *The Times*, 16 Jan 1936; *Argus*, 17 Jan 1936; C. Cunneen, The role of governor-general in Australia 1901-1927 (Ph.D. thesis, ANU, 1973); Hughes papers, MS 1538, box 155 folder 2, *and* Stonehaven papers, MS 2127, series 3, *and* CO 418/190, 202, 218 (NL).

CHRIS CUNNEEN

FORSTER, THOMAS RICHMOND (1862-1951), pastoralist and benefactor, was born on 13 January 1862 at Richmond, Melbourne, sixth child of Christopher Brooks Forster, stationmaster, from Cornwall, and his Tasmanian-born wife, Catherine, née Marzetti, and grandson of Captain G. B. Forster, R.N. He was brought up in Sydney, attending The King's School in 1875-77, and entered the Commercial Banking Co. of Sydney which posted him to Armidale in 1887. On 31 January 1891 he married Kate Sarah (1864-1949), eldest daughter of Frederick Robert White, and niece of James White [q.v.6]. Kate grew up in the large houses of her family in the Hunter valley, was educated in Sydney, travelled extensively in Britain in 1884-85 and moved in 1888 into the huge new mansion, Booloominbah, designed by Horbury Hunt [q.v.4] on the outskirts of Armidale.

Upon the marriage F. R. White bought the 40 000-acre (16 000 ha) property, Abington, near Bundarra and settled it in trust on his daughter and son-in-law. Forster resigned from the bank and devoted himself to improving his property. In the 1890s much of it was converted to freehold, it was consolidated to 20 000 acres (8000 ha), fences were erected, a fine merino stud established from White stock, and a new house built. His meticulous diaries, letter-books and business records reveal an able and hard-working businessman, and a devoted husband and father. Much business and family life was focussed on Booloominbah, the White home; and when F. R. White died in 1903 Forster partly took over his role as leading Anglican layman and benefactor – from 1904 he was a member of the Armidale Diocesan Synod. He was determined to honour the debt he believed all Australians owed to their pioneer forebears, and wrote that Labor's Federal victory in 1910 showed that Australians would permit only 'the Aristocracy of Brains'. By the 1920s the Forster family was the largest shareholder in The Armidale School; Thomas was a member of its board and was also a founder of Cranbrook School in Sydney. Forster insisted that the wealthy landed and professional classes should be prepared to pay heavily for the privilege of a private school education.

In 1936 Forster offered to buy Booloominbah from the trustees of the White estate and give it to the University of Sydney, if it would agree to establish a university college. The large home stood in 183 acres (74 ha) and was valued at £30 000. His offer rekindled the local movement which since 1924 had been campaigning for a university for Armidale. He remained the anonymous donor for much of the hectic eighteen months it required to obtain government and university support, but was a determined and significant figure in the negotiations, working closely with the local member and minister for education, D. H. Drummond [q.v.]. Once classes began in February 1938 Forster became a member of the Advisory Council and at its first meeting took the lead in pledging that the council members would have 'no sectarian or political bias or interests of any kind'.

The loss of his eldest son Frederick, who won the Military Cross, in France in 1917 was a terrible blow to the close-knit family. Another son, Norman Lachlan Forster (d. 1949), though crippled by infantile paralysis from boyhood, became one of Australia's leading breeders of Aberdeen Angus cattle, and was a founder and president of the Aberdeen Angus Society of Australia. Forster had a quick mind and strong opinions. Although not popular, he was respected; he never quite became a bushman and was always more comfortable in the Union or Australian clubs in Sydney. He died on 11 May 1951 at Abington and was buried in the Anglican section of Armidale cemetery. He was survived by a son and a daughter. He left £10 000 and the residue of his estate, valued for probate at £35 846, to provide scholarships at The Armidale School.

G. N. Griffiths, *Some northern homes of NSW* (Syd, 1954); D. H. Drummond, *A university is born* (Syd, 1959); *Pastoral Review*, 16 Dec 1949, 16 June 1951; A. Harris, Abington: the history of a station and its people (MS held by author, Neutral Bay, Syd); Abington papers (Univ New England Archives).   BRUCE MITCHELL

FORSYTH, JAMES (1852-1927), company director and politician, was born in 1852 at West Plean, Stirling, Scotland, son of John Forsyth, farmer, and his wife Janet, née Munnock. Leaving the county school early, he worked with Henderson Bros, merchants in Stirling, and then spent five years with Arnott & Co. in Glasgow.

Forsyth stayed almost a year in Sydney after arriving early in 1875, then moved to Brisbane on Christmas eve. Employed by James Burns [q.v.7] & Co. as their manager at Normanton from 1880, he was mainly responsible for the expansion of the firm's business in North Queensland. By 1884 he was paid more than any other employee and in 1883, when the business interests of Burns and (Sir) Robert Philp [q.v.] were amalgamated, he and his brother Adam became directors of Burns Philp & Co. Ltd. As the only director resident in Queensland from about 1893, he became very influential.

Forsyth's heavy investment in North Queensland mining started with the financing of a ten-head stamper battery on the Hodgkinson goldfield in 1876. His negotiations in Sydney with T. H. Kelly [q.v.5] and G. S. Caird [q.v.3], in an attempt to establish Burns & Co.'s smelting works at Watsonville near Herberton, were indirectly responsible for excluding Kelly from the field as a competitor to John Moffat [q.v.].

Forsyth was a director of the Wild River Tin Mining Co. Ltd at Herberton in 1881 and was associated with Burns in financing Baker, Daniels and Denny's Monarch tin battery at Herberton in 1882-84. With J. V. Mulligan [q.v.5], he acquired the Mount Molloy copper-mine in 1896 when it was abandoned by its discoverer. They sold it to a Melbourne syndicate financed by (Sir) Alexander Peacock [q.v.]. The syndicate paid £6000, obtained a geologist's report indicating meagre copper reserves and, after sinking the shaft to 180 feet (55 m), abandoned the mine. As the property had not been legally transferred, Forsyth regained control and sold it again in 1902 to John Moffat for £1500.

Forsyth won Carpentaria in the Queensland Legislative Assembly in 1899 as a ministerial supporter. He was defeated in 1907 but won Moreton at a by-election in 1909; in 1912 he transferred to Murrumba and held it until his retirement in 1918. Lucid but not brilliant, he spoke rapidly in a broad Scots accent, judged all proposals by possible profit and relied for effect on the constant reiteration of simple ideas. Though an intimate friend of Philp (he was later an executor of his will) and an acknowledged authority on finance, Forsyth was never in a ministry. He and Philp invested together after 1911 in Thylungra and Kyabra consolidated runs in the Eromanga district west of Charleville. With Philp, Simon E. Munro, J. M. and P. L. Tully, solicitors, and John Cordner, manager of Kyabra, Forsyth formed the Kyabra Pastoral Co. in 1911 to take over the leases from Bodkin and Pepper. The lease of Thylungra was transferred from the Union Bank of Australia to Forsyth, Philp and Munro on 10 December 1913 and taken over on 13 November 1919 when the Thylungra Pastoral Co. was formed. Forsyth was a director of the North Queensland Insurance Co. (later the Queensland Insurance Co.). In 1919-27 he was honorary consul for Japan in Brisbane.

On 13 January 1882 Forsyth had married Helen Morrison Campbell; they had no children but after the death in 1918 of Philp, they adopted one of his daughters. He was a member of the Toowong Bowling Club and Indooroopilly and Stanthorpe golf clubs. He worshipped regularly at St Paul's Presbyterian Church and was a member of both the Queensland and Brisbane clubs.

Forsyth died at his Toowong home on 14 October 1927 and was buried in Toowong cemetery. His estate, valued for probate at £154 546 in Queensland and £103 044 in New South Wales, provided bequests for some of Burns Philp staff, war-widows and their children, the Brisbane Children's Hospital, Presbyterian homes and the Young Women's Christian Association. The University of Queensland received a bequest of £5000 towards endowment of a chair of agriculture. After his death the family gave the university a further £10000 towards a building for its central library. The library now has a James Forsyth Reading Room and the librarian is officially designated 'the James Forsyth Librarian'.

G. C. Bolton, *A thousand miles away* (Brisb, 1963); *Queenslander*, 28 Oct 1876, 17 Sept 1881; *Cairns Post*, 23 Oct 1884, 28 June 1907; *Brisbane Courier*, 15 Oct 1927; Letters 3/404-526, 902, Philp papers (Oxley Lib); Company file, 26 of 1911, 45 of 1919, *and* LAN/N148, p 114, *and* SCTP/1591, file 851/1927 (QA).   RUTH S. KERR

FORSYTH, JOHN KEATLY (1867-1928), soldier, was born on 8 February 1867 in Brisbane, son of William Forsyth, builder, and his wife Elizabeth, née Hood, both Irish-born. Educated at Fortitude Valley State School and the Normal School, Brisbane, he joined the clerical staff of a sawmill and later a solicitor's office. Enlisting in the Queensland Mounted Infantry as a trooper in November 1885, he served in all non-commissioned ranks and received his commission on 18 July 1892. He reached the rank of captain in the militia before appointment on 1 August 1897 as a lieutenant on the headquarters staff of the permanent Queensland Defence force; that year, on 10 November, he married Catherine McMaster in a Brisbane Wesleyan Methodist church.

In February 1901 Forsyth was promoted captain and in 1901-02 served as adjutant to the 1st and 2nd Queensland Mounted Infantry and the 4th Infantry Regiment. After three years as staff officer with the 1st and 2nd Queensland Mounted Infantry he became in 1905 secretary to Major General Henry Finn [q.v.], inspector general of the Commonwealth Military Forces in Melbourne. He joined the Victorian Administrative and Instructional Staff in 1907, was promoted major in May 1908 and in 1909-10 was an exchange officer in India and brigade major to the Amballa Cavalry Brigade; he was then deputy assistant adjutant general for instruction and later served as a general staff officer before being appointed director of equipment, Army Headquarters, in July 1912.

In March 1914 Forsyth was promoted lieut-colonel and just before the outbreak of war appointed quartermaster general and third member of the Military Board. He joined the Australian Imperial Force on 15 August in the same rank and raised and organized the 1st Light Horse Brigade and the 4th Light Horse Regiment of the 1st Division, A.I.F.; in temporary command of these units he embarked from Melbourne on 21 October. As arranged, he handed over command of the 1st Light Horse Brigade to Colonel (Sir) H. G. Chauvel [q.v.7] on arrival in Egypt, retaining command of the 4th L.H.R. until May 1915 when, as assistant adjutant and quartermaster general with divisional headquarters, he reached Gallipoli. In July he was appointed commander of the 2nd Infantry Brigade with the temporary rank of brigadier general and planned the assault by the 6th Battalion on German Officers' Trench on 7 August. He remained at Gallipoli until just before the evacuation when his brigade went to Lemnos for a rest period.

In January 1916 Forsyth's brigade reached Tel-el-Kebir, Egypt, and then moved to Serapeum where they constructed and occupied six miles of entrenchments. On 27 March Forsyth, his headquarters and brigade troops, comprising the 5th, 6th, 7th and 8th Battalions and a machine-gun company, embarked for France. After training in the Bailleul area the brigade had four months action in the Fleurbaix sector where it was detached from the 1st Division and served in the line at Messines with the 7th (British) Division; it then rejoined the 1st Australian Division for the attack on Pozières and subsequent actions in July and August. After suffering a breakdown in health on the Somme late in August, Forsyth was evacuated to London and on discharge from hospital became commanding officer of Group 'B' A.I.F. Depots at Rollestone, Salisbury Plain, in October. Ill health forced his return to Australia in December 1916. He had been mentioned in dispatches and was appointed C.M.G. in 1917.

Forsyth became commandant of the 4th Military District (South Australia) on 16 February 1917 and in April left the A.I.F. In July 1918 he was appointed quartermaster general, Australian Military Forces, and third member of the Military Board; he was made a colonel in 1920. Although promoted to temporary major general in January 1921, he relinquished this rank in July 1922 when placed on the unattached list. He retired with the honorary rank of major general on 9 February 1925. On retirement he became secretary and later field superintendent to the National Federation of Victoria and then, after transferring to the National Union, was selected in 1928 as the second candidate in the Victorian National Party's Senate team. He contracted influenza while electioneering at Sea Lake and died of lobar pneumonia nine days later on 12 November 1928 at his Auburn home.

At the time of his death 'Dad', as Forsyth was affectionately called by soldiers in the 4th Light Horse, was president of the Light Horse Association and a devout member of the Auburn Methodist Church. Both S. M. (Viscount) Bruce [q.v.7] and J. H. Scullin [q.v.] paid him tribute. He was survived by his wife, one of his two sons and three daughters. He was buried in Boroondara cemetery, Kew, with full military honours.

C. E. W. Bean, *The story of Anzac* (Syd, 1921, 1924), and *The A.I.F. in France*, 1916 (Syd, 1929); *Reveille* (Syd), July 1929, Dec 1936; *Sabretache*, July 1967; *Argus*, 17 Feb, 28 Sep 1917, 13-15 Nov 1928; *SMH*, 27 June 1918, 2 Apr 1920, 29 June, 9 Aug 1922, 13, 24 Nov 1928; *Age* (Melb), 14, 15 Nov 1928; *Herald* (Melb), 14 Nov 1928; *Queenslander*, 15 Nov 1928; *Bulletin* (Syd), 21 Nov 1928; Piesse papers (NL); Forsyth file, war records section, and War diary, 2nd Infantry Brigade A.I.F. (AWM).

J. G. WILLIAMS

FORSYTH, SAMUEL (1881-1960), Methodist minister, was born on 1 May 1881 at Aghyaran, Tyrone, Ireland, fourth child of Samuel Forsythe, farmer, and his wife, devout Methodists. After primary education at Carricoughan National School, Forsyth was apprenticed to a draper in Castlederg. In 1901 he migrated to Brisbane to stay with his uncle William, father of Major General J. K. Forsyth [q.v.]. Samuel junior went to New Zealand in 1902 where he helped with open-air gospel meetings.

Forsyth spent 1905 studying mission work at Rev. W. L. Morton's Hope Lodge at Belair, South Australia. He and fellow student Tom Willason then became successful freelance evangelists on Yorke Peninsula: Forsyth's preaching was loving, he never denounced or scourged.

At Minlaton on 2 October 1907 he married Ida Rosely Nankivell who shared his work as gospel soloist; they had a daughter and a son. Next year Forsyth was accepted as a candidate for the Methodist ministry at Maitland. At Moonta in 1914 he influenced Lionel Bale Fletcher [q.v.] to take up evangelism. Forsyth was ordained in the Kent Town Methodist Church in 1912, when a minister at Broken Hill.

From October 1916 he served as a chaplain with the 10th Training Battalion for a year in Britain. Later South Australian Church appointments took him to the country and suburbs. After the death of his first wife, Forsyth married Ida Muriel Brummitt, a returned army nurse and writer, at Medindie on 29 March 1923; they had one son. In 1929, after a six-month tour of British central missions, Forsyth was appointed superintendent minister of the Adelaide Central Methodist Mission.

As a result of the Depression Forsyth was soon haunted by the tramp of single unemployed men on the dole: he envisaged a scheme to start a farm-training settlement to

help them gain jobs. He personally raised 5000 by public subscription and obtained land at a low rent from the government near Willunga. In June 1930 he opened Kuitpo Industrial Colony where men could work for their board and lodging, 'thereby retaining their self-respect, and a sane outlook on life until they could find a job'. It was run on good-humoured, non-militaristic lines. His Church was dubious about it and never backed the undenominational colony, but after financial struggles it flourished and over 7000 men were helped. An employment agency was set up in the city to help 'colonists' find work. Next year Forsyth formed the South Australian Council of Charitable Relief Organizations; he was its chairman. In 1937 he was appointed O.B.E. and next year became president of the South Australian Methodist Conference. The Kuitpo Colony became a rehabilitation centre.

In 1943 Forsyth negotiated for the mission to run the Adelaide radio stations 5KA and 5AU, and was chairman of directors of the companies involved. He saw the radio as an outlet for the Christian message and the source of much-needed additional income to finance the mission's social work. Next year he initiated a Central Mission Old Folks' Home (Aldersgate Village) at Felixtowe. Forsyth retired in 1952 and died of cerebro-vascular disease at the home on 24 August 1960. His second wife had predeceased him and he was buried in Payneham cemetery.

I. Forsyth, *He came from Ireland* (Adel, 1952); Methodist Church of A'sia (SA), *Conference minutes*, 1960; *Advertiser* (Adel), 8 Apr 1933, 23 Feb 1954, 25 Aug 1960; N. Hicks, Kuitpo colony (MS, prepared for Uniting Church in SA Hist Soc, Adel, 1978); information from Mr A. Scholes, Findon, SA.

A. E. VOGT

FORTH, NOWELL BARNARD DE LANCEY (1879-1933), soldier, was born on 22 December 1879 at Dwaroon, near Warrnambool, Victoria, son of De Lancey Forth, farmer, and his wife Annie Thompson, née Ware, both native-born. After attending Geelong Church of England Grammar School he enlisted as a private in the 4th (Queensland Imperial Bushmen) Contingent and embarked in the *Manchester Port* for South Africa on 18 May 1900. Promoted sergeant in June and twice recommended for a commission, he was gazetted to the 3rd Manchester Regiment, British Army, a promotion which was made effective from 19 May. He saw action in the Orange River Colony, and near Pretoria in the Transvaal. After this service which included fierce action at Zilikat's Nek, he was invalided to Australia.

In July 1901 Forth was promoted lieutenant in the Manchester Regiment and in 1901-06 served with the British regular forces. Seconded to the Egyptian Army in March 1907, he spent the next nine and a half years as a member of the Sudan Camel Corps and took part in campaigns in the Jebel Nyiama district in 1908, southern Kordofan in 1910, the Nuba Mountains in 1914 and general operations in the Sudan in 1914-16. Promoted captain in the Manchester Regiment in 1912, he was mentioned in dispatches, attained his majority and was awarded the Military Cross for his service in the Nuba Mountains. In 1917 he commanded the 3rd Battalion, Imperial Camel Corps, and remained with it in Sinai and Palestine, leading it in two particularly notable engagements. In the first, a charge against Tank Redoubt during the 2nd battle of Gaza, he was wounded but continued to direct the fight until the battalion withdrew. On the second occasion his battalion was ordered to protect the right flank of the British 53rd Division at Tel-el-Khuweilfe by occupying a hill after it had been supposedly captured by a British regiment. While leading his troops out before dawn on 6 November 1917 Forth realized that the hill was still held by Turks and that his battalion was isolated and within a few yards of enemy lines. With a quick command he retired his men in perfect order under heavy fire to the cover of a spur, thereby saving them from annihilation. They held on under severe fire all day and through the night and withdrew only after receiving artillery support. For his decisive and courageous action Forth received a Bar to the Distinguished Service Order he had won in a previous engagement.

The 3rd Battalion next held a portion of the line at Auja River before it retired to the Canal Zone for reinforcements. Once up to strength, the battalion returned to Palestine mounted on horses and Forth, now an acting lieut-colonel, was transferred in June 1918 to command the 7th Battalion, Essex Regiment, also in Palestine. As well as his M.C., D.S.O. and Bar he also received three mentions in dispatches for his war service. Promoted temporary lieut-colonel in December, he was stationed until 1920 at Sollum, on the Egyptian-Cyrenaica frontier, in command of the Western Desert Forces. In April 1920 he was employed by the Egyptian Government as commander of the Camel Corps and Light Car Patrols, Frontiers Districts Administration. Stationed mainly in Cairo he remained in command of this unit until 1924. He was awarded the Order of the Nile, the Order of the Mejidieh and was made a fellow of the Royal Geographical Society for his explorations in the Libyan Desert in search of the lost oasis of Zehzura.

Forth gave distinguished service during his association with the Camel Corps and brought to his command a thorough knowledge of the operation of mounted troops in desert warfare. He maintained close links with the Australians who served under him during the war and was planning to visit Australia when he died at Alexandria, Egypt, on 5 March 1933.

Aust Defence Dept, *Official records of the Australian military contingents to the war in South Africa*, P. L. Murray ed (Melb, 1911); H. S. Gullett, *The A.I.F. in Sinai and Palestine* (Syd, 1923); G. McMunn and C. Falls, *History of the great war – military operations: Egypt and Palestine*, II (Lond, 1930); G. F. and E. M. Langley, *Sand, sweat and camels* (Kilmore, Vic, 1976); *London Gazette*, 25 Oct 1916, 28 Dec 1917, 1, 12 Jan, 26 Mar 1918; *Reveille* (Syd), June 1933; *Sabretache*, July 1971; *SMH*, 27 Nov 1919, 9 Mar 1933; *Argus*, 7, 17 Mar 1933; records (AWM).   J. G. WILLIAMS

FOSTER, ALFRED WILLIAM (1886-1962), judge, was born on 28 July 1886 at Beechworth, Victoria, eldest of the three surviving children of Alfred William Foster, tobacconist and commission agent, and his wife Sarah, née Brown, daughter of a Jewish draper. In the 1850s Foster's paternal grandfather, a Yorkshire man, had left his post as a police magistrate in Tasmania to bring his family to the gold diggings, near Beechworth. Alfred was educated there and matriculated from the Beechworth College at 14. As a youth he became interested in spiritualism and rejected Christian beliefs for which he claimed his studies revealed no scientific evidence.

In 1906 Foster went to Melbourne to study law and there he joined the Victorian Rationalist Association. As a member of a conservative debating society he was chosen to debate socialism against a team from the Victorian Socialist Party which included John Curtin. Not only was Foster badly beaten in the debate but he was converted to socialism and subsequently joined the V.S.P.

Foster signed the roll of the counsel of the Bar in June 1910 and spent the next few years as a struggling barrister. He became politically prominent with the outbreak of war in August 1914 as an outspoken opponent of Australia's involvement. When conscription became an issue Foster wrote articles and pamphlets, lectured, addressed street-corner rallies and defended fellow anti-conscriptionists charged with offences under the War Precautions Act. In 1917 he too faced charges for a fiery anti-conscription speech but escaped conviction. Much of his opposition to the Hughes [q.v.] government during the war years was directed at 'unjust and suppressive' censorship provisions.

During the war Foster joined the Australian Labor Party. In 1917, following the split in the party over conscription, he was elected to the Victorian central executive; that year he stood unsuccessfully as the Labor candidate in the strongly Nationalist Federal electorate of Balaclava.

In 1918 Foster founded the Y Club for 'sociable socialists'. Through this he became involved in campaigning for the One Big Union until the movement lost impetus. Seeking a broader base for his political ambitions, he joined the Food Preservers' Union and became its president and delegate at the annual conferences of the Victorian branch of the A.L.P. and a member of the Trades Hall Council. In 1922 and 1925 he stood as the endorsed Federal Labor candidate for Fawkner but was defeated.

Advancement in Foster's legal career came with his appointment as union advocate to the 1920 royal commission on the basic wage. He demonstrated that the basic wage was quite inadequate to meet the cost of living, but the commission's recommended increase was so high that it was not implemented. Another valuable brief came his way in 1924 with his appointment as counsel assisting the royal commission inquiring into the 1923 police strike in Melbourne. Then in 1926 he was appointed as counsel to represent the Labor governments of New South Wales and Queensland in the Commonwealth Court of Conciliation and Arbitration's main hours case which reduced standard hours from forty-eight to forty-four a week in the engineering industry.

When Foster became a judge of the County Court of Victoria in 1927 he had to give up all political party positions, including that of senior vice-president of the Victorian branch of the A.L.P. His work as a judge spanned the Depression years and many of the defendants in his court were victims of economic hardship. Foster enforced the laws but at the same time canvassed the need to reform many outdated provisions, calling also for medical assessment and treatment for sex offenders. He provoked a public outcry in 1934 when he told a boy witness, 'There is no hell, sonny'.

Throughout the 1930s Foster worked for peace with an increasing sense of urgency. As president of the Victorian branch of the League of Nations Union he sought to publicize the need for support of the league as a force for peace. When war came he became Victorian president of the Sheepskins for Russia appeal and joined the Australia-Soviet Friendship League.

In October 1942 the Curtin government set up a wartime Women's Employment Board and appointed Foster to head it. For the next two years the board set the wages, hours and conditions for more than 70 000 women, in most cases awarding 90 per cent of the male wage rate instead of the standard 54 per cent.

Foster was transferred to the Commonwealth Arbitration Court in October 1944. In 1945 he conducted an inquiry into the troubled stevedoring industry and recommended changes which were incorporated into the Stevedoring Industry Act of 1947. His first major case was the standard hours hearing which spanned the twenty-two months to September 1947. During that time he became the senior puisne judge with the task of writing and delivering the judgment which awarded the 40-hour week. In assessing his arbitration work he always remained proudest of this decision. In the 1950 basic wage case he was dominant in awarding a huge £1 increase to the weekly wage of £7 per week to enable workers to share in the post-war prosperity. His participation in the 1959 basic wage case was notable for his suggestion that the legalistic 'burden of proof' was inappropriate in arbitration cases.

At first the unions regarded Foster as their champion. But in 1949, during the crippling seven-week national coal strike, he gaoled eight officials and imposed heavy fines on their unions for their defiance of the Chifley government's emergency legislation to stop union funds from being used to assist the strikers.

In 1956 the arbitration system was overhauled and the functions of the court were split between the newly established Commonwealth Industrial Court and the Commonwealth Conciliation and Arbitration Commission. Foster, although the senior remaining arbitration court judge, was not appointed to head either body but became senior deputy president of the commission.

He remained in charge of the maritime industry to which he had been assigned in 1952. His direct approach and availability at all times resulted in a speedier turn around of ships and a reduction of time lost through disputes. He instituted a 'hard-lying' allowance to encourage shipowners to modernize or replace dirty, old and obsolete vessels, and this was virtually achieved by 1958. He conducted an inquiry into seamen's conditions and in 1955 made a new seamen's award, the first since 1935. The award pleased seamen but shipowners complained of a double payment effect in the leave provisions. When in 1960 Foster made a new award to correct this anomaly, seamen were indignant. Demonstrations against him marred the last years of his arbitration work and obscured the substantial gains made by seamen during his administration of their industry.

Foster's interests included tennis and golf, at which he excelled, the repairing of old and valuable clocks, carpentry – he made his own golf clubs – gardening and the study of mathematics. On 12 January 1916 he had married Beatrice May Warden, a fellow member of the Victorian Socialist Party. A son was born before her death from cancer in 1925. On 25 January 1927 Foster married Ella Wilhelmina Jones. He died at his San-dringham home on 26 November 1962, sur-vived by his wife and their two sons and daughter. To the end of his life he described himself as a socialist, a pacifist and a ra-tionalist. In accordance with his wishes there was no religious service before his cremation. Instead his friend, Sir John Barry, spoke of his tenacity, courage and unshakable integrity in the pursuit of truth.

Economic Record, 39 (1963), no 85, p 107; *Age*, 29 Nov 1962; C. Larmour, Judge Foster – a socialist judge: aspects of his life and work (M.A. thesis, Monash Univ, 1973), *and* Rebel judge – a bio-graphy of Judge Foster (MS held by author, Weetangera, Canb).   CONSTANCE LARMOUR

FOSTER, HUBERT JOHN (1855-1919), army officer, was born on 4 October 1855 at Biggleswade, Bedfordshire, England, son of John Nathaniel Foster, coal and wine mer-chant, and his wife Frances Mary, née Wedd. Educated at Harrow, he entered the Royal Military Academy, Woolwich, in 1873 and on graduating two years later gained the academy's most coveted awards, the sword of honour for 'exemplary conduct' and the Pollock prize for 'the most distinguished cadet of the season'. He was commissioned lieutenant in the Royal Engineers in January 1875 and joined the school of military en-gineering at Chatham for two years tech-nical training.

Foster was then posted to the 31st Com-pany, R..E., which was sent to Cyprus when a British force occupied the island in 1878. He served in the Egyptian War of 1882 with the Telegraph Troop, R.E., and took part in the battle of Tel-el-Kebir on 13 September and the occupation of Cairo. Next year he qualified for admission to the staff college at Camberley, graduating in December 1885. Promoted captain in January 1886, he served from November 1886 to June 1890 as brigade major, R.E., on the staff of the commander of the Land Forces in Ireland. His next posting was to the War Office, London, where he worked in the military intelligence division in 1890-95; in September 1894 he became a major.

Later Foster went to Canada where, from August 1898 to April 1901, he was quarter-master general of the Canadian military forces. In this post he was directly concerned with the preparation and movement of Canadian troops to South Africa where war began in October 1899. In April 1901 he resumed duty with the British Army, was posted to the district of Guernsey and Al-derney in August as commanding royal en-gineer and in October was promoted lieut-colonel. However, he soon returned to ex-tra-regimental duties and in 1903-06 held the dual appointment of British military attaché in Washington and Mexico City. He married Mary Agatha Gough, née Tobin, at the British consulate, Venice, Italy, on 16 Jan-uary 1904. In January 1906 he returned to the War Office – which had been reorgan-ized since his earlier posting there, with military intelligence becoming a function of the War Office general staff.

That year Foster's career was changed radically when he was offered and accepted the newly created appointment of director of military science at the University of Sydney; he was initially appointed for three years from September 1906. The programme which he organized and directed was a three-year diploma course and began in March 1907. In an address to officers in April Foster said he did not propose 'to give in-struction in the details of the military profession. The scope of the course was wider and more suited to the university spirit'. The War Office had placed Foster on half-pay in October 1906; earlier, in October 1904, he had become a brevet colonel and in December 1907 a substantive colonel. On 4 October 1912 he was placed on the British Army's retired list.

When World War I began Foster was al-most 59. The war reduced attendances in his department and in 1915 he had no students. For the previous nine years he had lectured at the university and in addition had con-ducted special courses of instruction each year for permanent and militia officers of the Australian Military Forces, many of whom held senior commands and staff appoint-ments during the war. The importance of all his instructional work can only be fully ap-preciated if it be recognized that, when Foster assumed duty in 1906, Australia had neither a military college for the training of cadets nor a staff college for the post-graduate training of officers. Apart from teaching he contributed to journals and newspapers on military subjects and in 1911-15 published four books and pamph-lets: *Organization: how armies are formed for war* (London, 1911), *Staff work: guide to command and general staff duties with small forces of all arms in the field* (London, 1912), *War and the empire: the principles of imperial defence* (London, 1914), and *The war in Europe: a sketch of the main operations up to August 1915* (Melbourne, 1915).

From January 1916 to September 1917 Foster was chief of the Australian general staff; he had become a temporary brigadier general in the A.M.F. in March 1916. From October 1917 to October 1918 he was director of military art at the Royal Military College, Duntroon, but the severe winter climate affected his health and led to his resignation. He was placed on the retired list, A.M.F., as an honorary brigadier general on 19 October 1918. He died on 21 March 1919 at Carlaminda, near Cooma, New South Wales, and was buried in Cooma cemetery with Anglican rites. He was survived by his wife and their son, (Sir) John Galway Foster, who later became a member of the British House of Commons.

Foster's work at the University of Sydney was highly praised by the chancellor, Sir Normand MacLaurin [q.v.], and by Lieut-General Sir J. W. McCay and General Sir John Monash [qq.v.]. Likewise his work as chief of the general staff had met the exacting demands of his minister, G. F. Pearce [q.v.]. Major General R. E. Williams [q.v.] said of Foster as C.G.S. that his 'services were of unusual value, but little known outside the Defence Department' and that 'to wide knowledge, long experience, and assiduous training were added unwearying patience and a gentleman's charm of manner'.

Royal Military College of Aust J, Dec 1918; *Royal Engineers J*, May 1919; *Reveille* (Syd), Nov 1937; United Service Inst (NSW) *J*, July 1954; *Call* (Perth), May 1907; *Manaro Mercury*, 24 Mar 1919; Univ Syd Archives.   WARREN PERRY

FOSTER, RICHARD WITTY (1856-1932), storekeeper, farmer and politician, was born on 20 August 1856 at Goodmanham, Pocklington, Yorkshire, England, son of William Foster, farmer, and his wife Rachel, née Witty. Educated commercially at Prospect House, Tockwith, he was then apprenticed to a draper and trained in the London softgoods trade. He migrated to South Australia in 1880 and after serving as a Wesleyan ministry probationer, he settled at Quorn as a grocer and general provider. Here on 25 September 1884 he married Elizabeth Lees.

In 1887 Foster was elected to the Quorn council becoming mayor in 1890-93, when he was elected to the House of Assembly for Newcastle. From 1902 he was member for

Flinders. He was influenced by Hugh Price Hughes's ideas on social Christianity and in 1893 he espoused policies that he never abandoned: parliamentary reform, closer land settlement, progressive land taxes, reduced duties on the necessities of life, and increased intercolonial trade. Although committed to free enterprise, he supported government action to control monopolies.

Foster generally supported the Liberal faction: he was commissioner for public works (1899-1904) and minister for industry (1902-04) in the (Sir) F. W. Holder and J. G. Jenkins [qq.v.] ministries. On 4 July 1904, desiring 'to draw closer together the parties in the House, thereby putting an end to the unseemly and unjustified plotting and scheming for personal advancement', he resigned his portfolios, but supported Jenkins until his ministry fell next year. Foster was commissioner for public works and minister for agriculture in (Sir) Richard Butler's [q.v.7] 1905 ministry. He was appreciated by colleagues for his 'breezy and approachable personality', but next year he lost his seat.

In 1909 Foster won the Federal electorate of Wakefield. He was implacably opposed to Labor and socialism and was a member of the 1914 commission on electoral law. In World War I he supported W. M. Hughes [q.v.], favoured conscription and demanded harsh penalties for those disloyal to King and Empire. In 1921, after a cabinet reshuffle and as a sop to the South Australian Liberals, Hughes appointed him minister for works and railways, but he was not included in the 1923 Bruce [q.v.7]-Page [q.v.] ministry. Suspecting that Page planned to destroy the power of the States, he refused to join the Country Party. At the 1928 election, he was defeated by one of their candidates.

In Federal politics, although blunt and outspoken, Foster remained a lack-lustre back-bencher who placed independence above political advantage. In 1913-26 he served on the Joint House Committee. On 5 January 1932 he died at St Peters, Adelaide, and was buried in Payneham cemetery. He was survived by his wife, three daughters and a son.

Pictorial Aust, Apr-May 1893; *PP* (SA), 1897 (94), 1898-99 (77), 1902 (22), 1903 (23, 32), 1904 (20); *Advertiser* (Adel), 25 Jan 1893; *Quorn Mercury*, 3 May 1895; *Register* (Adel), 7 Apr 1902, 30 Oct 1906, 17 Aug 1909; *Observer* (Adel), 4 Feb 1922; *Chronicle* (Adel), 7 Jan 1932.   D. I. McDONALD

FOSTER, ROLAND (1879-1966), singer and teacher, was born on 12 July 1879 at Dundalk, Louth, Ireland, son of William Edward Foster, described variously as merchant and commercial traveller, and his wife Margaret, née Gilholy. His English father came of a military family, that of his Irish mother contained much music, including a minor composer. Educated mainly in northern England, Foster entered a wholesaler merchant's office when his father died in 1894 and became a senior clerk; but he longed to sing. He began to take lessons as a bass from Eugène Goossens senior, and later from Frederick Austin. In 1902 he won a scholarship to the Hampstead Conservatoire of Music and went on to the Guildhall School of Music in 1904-07. After miscellaneous professional work round England, he turned to concert promotion and teaching because of ill health.

In 1912 Foster was invited to become secretary-manager to (Dame) Clara Butt and Kennerley Rumford on a world concert tour. The party arrived in Sydney on 10 May 1913. The principals left after seventy-eight Australian concerts on 2 January 1914, but Foster stayed behind at Clara Butt's suggestion and began teaching in Sydney. When Henri Verbrugghen [q.v.] arrived as the director of the new State Conservatorium of Music, he invited Foster, whom he had met in England, to become the first teacher of singing. He commenced work on 6 March 1916 with fifty-five students.

During the next forty-six years, Foster trained hundreds of singers including Rosa Alba, Essie Ackland, Raymond Beatty [q.v.] and Geoffrey Chard. In 1925 he began a regular annual stint as adjudicator for the Queensland Eisteddfod: he occasionally officiated also at South Street, Ballarat, and at Wellington and Invercargill in New Zealand. His busy life also included direction of the conservatorium's opera school from 1934 and the production of broadcast operas. In 1929 he launched the Music Advancement Guild in Sydney to counter the incursions of mechanical music; it developed into the Music Week Movement of which Foster was president in 1932-35. In 1933-36 he was director also of the City of Sydney Eisteddfod and in 1950-63 president of the Sydney Royal Philharmonic Society. He wrote two popular books *Vocal success* (1934) and *Competitive singing* (1941). On return trips to Europe he was appointed an honorary member of the Society of English Singers (1919), an honorary fellow of the Guildhall School of Music (1927) and in 1954 O.B.E.

Foster married his assistant teacher Jessica Cummins at St Philip's Church of England on 30 December 1918; they had no children and were divorced in September 1937. On 14 December 1939 he married another assistant, Thelma Irene Houston, with Methodist forms at a private house in Croydon. She died before him without issue.

His autobiography *Come listen to my song* was published in 1949.

Foster retired from the conservatorium in December 1962. A lifelong sporting enthusiast, prone to gambling and high living, he fared badly in retirement. Rescued from penury by friends, he spent his last years in a nursing home at Hunters Hill where he died on 1 November 1966; he was cremated.

Aust Musical News and Musical Digest, 1 Aug 1957; *SMH*, 4 June 1932, 4 Nov 1966.

H. J. GIBBNEY

FOSTER, WILLIAM JAMES (1881-1927), soldier, was born on 8 December 1881 at Warwick, Queensland, son of Henry Lamb Foster, an English-born civil servant, and his Irish-born wife Ellen Frances, née Ahern. After qualifying as a teacher he taught for several years at Warwick. He began his military career as lieutenant and adjutant of the 3rd Queensland Battalion, Commonwealth Cadet Corps, in July 1906 but resigned this appointment in November 1907 and was immediately commissioned as a second lieutenant in the 14th Light Horse Regiment (militia). His aspirations, however, were for a regular army commission and he was appointed a lieutenant on the Administrative and Instructional (permanent) Staff, Australian Military Forces, on 1 July 1910 and allotted to New South Wales.

Foster's progress in the next few years was steady but unspectacular. He was promoted temporary captain on 1 February 1912 and next October went to New Zealand on exchange duty; while there he was appointed brigade major, 4th Brigade (Newcastle). When World War I broke out he joined the Australian Imperial Force as a captain and aide-de-camp (to Major General (Sir) William Bridges [q.v.7]) and camp commandant, 1st Division. He sailed for Egypt in October 1914.

During training in Egypt his daring horsemanship almost certainly saved his divisional commander from serious injury. While returning from a training exercise, Bridges's horse caught its foot in a tram rail, stumbled, and might have bolted with the general out of the saddle and his foot still caught in the stirrup, when Foster, who was riding behind him at a canter, leapt off and had the reins in his hand before the horse had regained its feet. This incident, with its evidence of competence and cool resourcefulness, was to epitomize Foster's subsequent conduct in trying conditions, frequently under fire, during the remainder of the war.

As aide-de-camp to Bridges on Gallipoli,

Foster was wounded in action on 13 May 1915, not long before Bridges himself was fatally wounded. After recuperating, Foster was appointed brigade major of the 2nd Light Horse Brigade commanded by Colonel (Sir) Granville Ryrie [q.v.]. The personalities and attributes of the two men complemented each other and, in the words of the official war historian, 'between them, they made of the 2nd Light Horse Brigade one of the most trusted corps on Gallipoli'. Foster was wounded a second time on 13 October.

Like most of his contemporaries in the permanent forces, Foster's appointments – except for a short time in 1919 when he commanded a column during the Egyptian rebellion – were exclusively on the staff. After Gallipoli, he became successively general staff officer of the Anzac Mounted Division in Egypt, of the 1st Yeomanry Mounted Division, and of the 4th Cavalry Division, before becoming G.S.O.1, 1st Australian Mounted Division, immediately after the Armistice. As G.S.O.1 of the 4th Cavalry Division, his acute reading of the situation greatly assisted his commander to forestall a Turkish rearguard attempt to block the pass at Mus Mus. In the circumstances it would have blunted, and might have halted, the brilliant night move of the cavalry to debouch onto the Esdraelon plain at Megiddo after General Sir Edmund Allenby's infantry had broken the Turko-German forces at the battle of Sharon. For his services and personal courage during the war, from which he emerged with the reputation of a brilliant young staff officer, Foster was awarded the Distinguished Service Order and the Order of the Nile, was appointed C.B. and C.M.G. and was four times mentioned in dispatches.

By November 1918 he was a major on the Administrative and Instructional Staff, A.M.F. He elected to remain in the permanent army, soon to be reduced to a nucleus force. On 8 October 1919, at St Mary's Cathedral, Sydney, he married Margaret Ann Woods, a nurse who had served with the A.I.F. in Egypt and England and had been awarded the Royal Red Cross; she died in childbirth in 1920. That year Foster attended the staff college, Camberley, and later went on to hold a series of increasingly important staff appointments including director of military operations and training (1925), and temporarily, 2nd chief of the general staff, a post created in 1924. He was conscious that, as a professional soldier, his staff experience needed to be broadened by experience in command. To advance this he was chosen in 1926 to command a brigade in the British Army, an unprecedented appointment. He commanded the 2nd Cavalry Brigade at Aldershot from early 1927 until

his untimely death from chronic nephritis on 15 November 1927 in London. He was buried in Tidworth cemetery with full military honours. He was survived by a son.

Had he lived, there was every likelihood that Colonel Foster would have served the Australian Army in positions of great responsibility. General G. Barrow, under whom he had been G.S.O.1 in the 4th Cavalry Division, said of him that 'there never was a better staff officer of a mounted division than Foster . . . He was absolutely reliable, loyal and self-effacing'.

C. E. W. Bean, *The story of Anzac* (Syd, 1921, 1924); G. McMunn and C. Falls, *History of the great war – military operations: Egypt and Palestine*, 2, pt 2 (Lond, 1930); *London Gazette*, 2 May, 11 July, 1 Dec 1916, 12 Jan, 11 Apr 1918, 3, 5, June, 26 Nov 1919; *Reveille* (Syd), Dec 1932; *SMH*, 12 Apr 1918, 25 Oct 1926, 17, 18 Nov, 24 Dec 1927; *Queenslander*, 8 Jan 1921, 24 Nov 1927; *The Times*, 17 Nov 1927; Aust Defence Dept, Military Board, Proceedings, 1926-27.   H. J. COATES

FOWLER, ELIZABETH LILIAN MAUD (1886-1954), alderman and politician, was born on 7 June 1886 at Cooma, New South Wales, third daughter of Charles Gill, farmer and later coach driver, and his wife Frances Rebecca, née Gaunson, both native-born. Lilian was educated at the local public school and as a young woman assisted her father, who was a Labor League organizer and alderman for Cooma. She was working as a waitress in Sydney when she married a widower Albert Edward Fowler, bootmaker, on 19 April 1909 at Whitefield Congregational Church.

A woman of strong character and an outstanding organizer, Fowler became secretary to the Newtown-Erskineville Political Labor League. She made the branch her personal fief. From 1917, when F. M. Burke, the anti-conscriptionist Labor candidate won Newtown, she managed his electorate for him for over twenty years. She was elected to the central executive of the Australian Labor Party in 1920-21 and 1923-25. At the boisterous 1923 conference, Fowler initiated the move to admit J. Dooley [q.v.] and helped mount the attack on Jack Bailey [q.v.7] and corruption, which led to the exposure of the sliding-panel ballot boxes.

In 1926-27 Fowler was president of the Labor Women's Central Organising Committee which brought pressure on J. T. Lang [q.v.] to institute widows' pensions and child endowment, and an investigation into the administration of the Child Welfare Department. She led a deputation to the governor requesting appointment of women to the Legislative Council and organized the first interstate conference of Labor Women's Organizing committees.

In 1921 Fowler was amongst the first women appointed justices of the peace. She had separated from her husband shortly before her election in 1928 to Newtown Municipal Council – the first woman alderman in the State. She was re-elected in 1935-37, 1938-40, 1941-44, 1948; in 1938-39 she was the first woman mayor in Australia. She was especially interested in establishing playgrounds and obtaining assistance for the unemployed, and later claimed responsibility for extending the forty-hour week to all council employees. In 1939-40 she was an executive member of the Women's Voluntary National Register.

Unsuccessful in 1941, Fowler defeated Burke for Newtown in 1944 as a Lang Labor candidate. Lang's loss of the Labor Party leadership in 1939 may have been the reason for her decision to stand against Burke, but she also condemned the party's centralist tendencies and by 1944 was a fierce critic of bureaucratic direction from Canberra. Her singular achievement in parliament was the 1945 amendment to the Lunacy Act which secured the release of Boyd Sinclair who had been committed to Morisset criminal asylum in 1936 and held without trial. She fought tenaciously the local government amendment bill of 1944, which in its proposal to regroup municipal councils, typified the bureaucratic expansion which she abhorred. She ceased to be an alderman in 1948 when Newtown was absorbed into the City of Sydney; in 1950 she was defeated at the State elections. She was unsuccessful in the 1953 elections for Sydney Municipal Council.

Survived by a daughter, Fowler died on 11 May 1954 in King George V Memorial Hospital from coronary occlusion; she was buried with Methodist rites in Rookwood cemetery. She was a large woman, blunt in speech and remembered for that confidence, force and capacity to control which is alleged to be 'mannish'.

L. G. Norman, *Historical notes on Newtown* (Syd, 1963); *Labor News*, 2 June 1923; *Labor Daily*, 18-25 Feb, 23 Mar 1927; *SMH*, 29 May 1944.

HEATHER RADI

FOWLER, HUGH LIONEL (1891-1946), psychologist, was born on 5 October 1891 at Hemel Hempstead, Hertfordshire, England, elder son of Henry Silas Fowler, tailor, and his wife Rosetta, née Stone. He arrived in Western Australia aged 5 and was educated at state schools, the High School (now Hale [q.v.4]) and the Teachers' Training College at Claremont. He taught until 1913 when he began studying philosophy and English at the new University of Western Australia (B.A., 1916). He enlisted in the Australian Imperial Force in 1915 as a private in the 44th Battalion, was commissioned in May 1916 and in January 1918 was promoted captain; he was wounded twice.

Fowler remained in England after the war; by 1920, when he returned to an appointment as lecturer in psychology at his old teachers' college, he had obtained first-class certificates in general and experimental psychology from University College, London, and experience in clinical and industrial psychology. On 6 April 1922 at the Wesley Church, Bunbury, Western Australia, he married Winifred Vicary Finch, a teacher. He completed an M.A. in 1924 and, restless and ambitious, returned to England. In 1927 he obtained a teacher's diploma from the University of London and a diploma of education from the University of Oxford. Next year he was awarded a Ph.D. in psychology from London.

Fowler then returned to Western Australia as principal lecturer at Claremont and part-time lecturer in psychology within the philosophy department at the university. In 1930 this department was split and he became lecturer in charge of the independent psychology department. He built a department with facilities and equipment for practical work 'far in advance of most other Psychology departments in the British Commonwealth at that time'. It offered a degree in psychology available in both arts and science faculties, and required practical work to be taken in all undergraduate courses. It was the first Australian psychology department with these two characteristics. In 1936 a Carnegie Corporation travel grant enabled Fowler 'to see how psychology was taught and applied' in the United States of America and Britain. In 1934-35 and 1940-41 he was warden of convocation at the university where he sought to play an active part in university politics, but he was easily ruffled by colleagues who did not share his faith in psychology. In 1943 he became a fellow of the British Psychological Society and from 1938 he was associate professor.

Soon after the outbreak of World War II Fowler enlisted in the army but in 1941, while serving in Australia, he was discharged due to acute bronchitis and asthma. He re-enlisted in May 1942 to establish the Australian Army Psychology Service in Melbourne as deputy assistant adjutant general (psychology) with the rank of temporary major and was promoted to major in September. In November ill health again obliged him to retire. He returned to academic work until his death on 27 May 1946. Fowler was survived by his wife, two daughters and a son and buried in the Anglican section of Karrakatta cemetery.

D. P. Mellor, *The role of science and industry* (Canb, 1958); F. Alexander, *Campus at Crawley* (Melb, 1963); *Aust J of Psychology*, 10 (1958), p 7; *West Australian*, 29 May 1946; personal file 2393, Univ WA Archives; information from Mr F. Finch, Dalkeith, Perth.   ALAN RICHARDSON

FOWLER, JAMES MACKINNON (1863-1940), politician, was born on 20 June 1863 at Strathaven, Millholm, (anciently Evandale), Lanark, Scotland, son of James Fowler, farmer, and his wife Mary, née McKinnon, who was thought to be related to Lachlan Macquarie [q.v.2]. After education locally and at the Athenaeum, Glasgow, he entered a counting-house in 1884. There is a rumour that he served in the Black Watch (Royal Highland) Regiment, and he worked in drapery warehouses in Glasgow and Manchester before migrating to Australia in 1891. He prospected in Victoria and Western Australia, helped found the Victorian Socialist League, and settled in Perth in 1898. A widower, that year on 2 December he married Daisy Winifred Bastow at Subiaco; they had a daughter and three sons.

A propagandist and secretary of the Western Australian Federal League in 1899-1900, in 1901 Fowler won the Perth seat in the House of Representatives in the first Commonwealth parliament, as a revenue tariff candidate. He joined the Labor Party. One of its main spokesmen on finance, he served on the royal commission on customs and excise tariffs in 1904-07. He spoke in 'a high-pitched voice of great penetrating power and great Scotchness', but his speeches were often 'of criticism and complaint'. Within the party he opposed W. M. Hughes [q.v.] and helped to thwart his ambitions when Andrew Fisher [q.v.] became prime minister.

In June 1909 after the fall of Fisher's first ministry, partly because of his distrust of Hughes, Fowler left the party. He claimed that it was becoming too centralist and he refused to join it in opposing the Liberals' proposed financial arrangement, discussed in 1909. Critics alleged that he was vexed at failing to achieve ministerial office, but Fowler's version fitted his opinions throughout his career. Having joined the Liberals, he retained Perth at the 1910 elections despite a swing to Labor; but he was critical of Sir John Forrest's [q.v.] style. Fowler was chairman of committees in 1913-14, a member of the joint committee of

public accounts 1914-17 and chairman 1920-22. In 1916 he was involved in a brawl in Collins Street, Melbourne, with Henry Chinn [q.v.7].

Fowler was an early advocate of a Commonwealth literary fund. A freelance journalist, in 1919 he published a polemic against Hughes, now prime minister — *Statesman or mountebank: an Australian study*. He posted a copy to every Nationalist member of parliament outside the ministry, suggesting that they read it instead of attending the party meeting. He was embittered by attempts to deny him pre-selection at that year's elections and broke formally with Hughes early next year. Fowler particularly resented increased tariff protection. In 1921 the *Bulletin* commented that he would have 'achieved Ministerial rank long ago if he hadn't been such a good hater'. He lost party endorsement and was defeated at the 1922 elections.

Fowler's creed had been consistent: the Scottish free-trade radicalism of his youth, adapted to a Western Australian mistrust of the centralizing and protectionist tendencies of a Commonwealth dominated by Victoria and New South Wales. Yet he was never thoroughly assimilated into the West. Earnest, short-sighted, with a heavy moustache, he was too prickly, and his political manner too stand-offish and philosophical, to command widespread affection, although he showed solid qualities as a local representative and skill in financial argument.

After his defeat he lived in Melbourne and built up a private library of 4000 volumes. He continued writing: novels, short stories, newspaper articles and a film synopsis, often on the subject of his goldfields experiences. Sometimes he used the pseudonyms 'Hamish Mackinnon' and 'James Evandale'. He published *Australia's perils, real and imaginary* (Melbourne, 1926) warning of the dangers of Asian immigration, and *False foundations of British history* (Melbourne, 1943, edited by his son Richard), a study of the origins of the Anglo-Saxon race. He contributed to the *Age*, the *Australasian* and other journals in Britain and Australia and was associated with Sands [q.v.6] & MacDougalls's. After fighting 'cruel pain and blindness' in his last years, Fowler died in Melbourne on 3 November 1940 and was buried in Springvale cemetery. His wife survived him.

J. S. Battye (ed), *Cyclopedia of Western Australia*, 1 (Adel, 1912); *Bulletin*, 5 Jan 1905, 14 Apr 1921; *Punch* (Melb), 1 Aug 1912; *Daily Standard* (Brisb), 5 Jan 1916; *Morning Herald* (Perth), 4 Apr 1901; *Argus*, 4 Nov 1940; MS 1540, Deakin papers, *and* MS 2280, Fowler papers (NL).   B. K. DE GARIS
                                          G. C. BOLTON

FOWLER, THOMAS WALKER (1859-1928), civil engineer, was born on 23 November 1859 at Blaris Lodge, near Hillsborough, Down, Ireland, son of James Barrington Fowler, farmer, and his wife Deborah, née Bulmer (Boomer). He received secondary education at the Royal Academical Institution, Belfast.

In November 1876, with his widowed mother and two brothers, Fowler joined two other brothers already in Melbourne. Next year he began the course for a certificate in civil engineering at the University of Melbourne; he completed it in 1879 and graduated M.C.E. in 1885. In 1880-81 he worked in the survey branches of the Victorian and New South Wales railways.

In January 1882 Fowler was appointed engineer to the Shire of Huntly, near Sandhurst (Bendigo), the first of similar posts in the northern, north-eastern, central Gippsland and southern districts of Victoria. As a qualified engineer of water-supply under the Irrigation Act of 1886, he was responsible for directing conservation schemes on the Broken River, near Benalla, and for the Shepparton, Yarrawonga and Gisborne town supplies. On 12 March 1884 at St Stephen's Church of England, Richmond, he married Sarah Edith Warnock, daughter of a surgeon.

About 1887 Fowler made his home in Melbourne, living in Hawthorn, and later at Kew, with an office in the city. From 1891 to 1903 he lectured in surveying at the university, acting also as demonstrator in engineering from 1896 to 1903. In 1905-09 he lectured in civil engineering. Returning to full-time private practice, he carried out water-supply schemes for Warragul, Colac and Kerang, and electric light works at Kilmore, Camperdown, Terang and Deloraine (Tasmania). In 1909 he was a member of the special board of inquiry into the Melbourne water-supply and of the royal commission appointed by the Western Australian government to report on the sewerage of Perth and Fremantle.

In July 1913 Fowler was appointed engineer-in-chief of Tasmania and permanent head of the Public Works Department, at a salary of £500. He resigned this position on 31 December 1918 and returned to Melbourne.

Fowler was a member of the Institution of Civil Engineers, London, and was active in the local institutions of civil, mechanical, electrical and municipal engineers. He was president of the Victorian Institute of Surveyors in 1892. In 1908-13 he was chairman of the Municipal Surveyors' Board of Victoria. He was secretary and later vice-president of the Royal Geographical Society of Australasia (Victoria) and author of sundry papers in the society's proceedings, those of the Victorian Institute of Engineers and various scientific societies. A highly esteemed Freemason, he had been a representative of the English Constitution at the inauguration of the United Grand Lodge of Victoria in March 1889. He had attained the rank of past deputy grandmaster of the craft and was prominent in several associated Masonic orders.

Quietly spoken, with a studious and self-disciplined manner and distinguished bearing, Fowler was a tall man, some 6 ft. 5 ins. (196 cm) in height, with a neat grey beard and rimless spectacles. Reading and photography were his main relaxations: his library contained books mainly on science, engineering, philosophy, religion and Freemasonry. During summers spent with children and grandchildren at his holiday home at Sorrento (Blairgowrie), he kept careful meteorological records.

Fowler died of cerebro-vascular disease at Kew on 23 November 1928, survived by his wife, three sons and two of his three daughters. He was buried in Boroondara cemetery.

V&P (LA Vic), 1891, 2 (11), 1903, 2S, 2 (20); Inst of Engineers, Aust, *Transactions*, 1928, p 270; *Mercury*, 27 Nov 1928; *Argus*, 6 Dec 1928; CSD 22/206/151-32, 177/35A-21, 195/110-30, *and* public service record (PSC24/8) (TA); family information.   SALLY O'NEILL

FOWLES, EDWIN WESLEY HOWARD (1871-1945), barrister and politician, was born on 17 June 1871 at Oxley Creek, Queensland, son of William Fowles, schoolteacher, and his wife Nancy, née Whittle. Educated first by his father and then at the Brisbane Normal School, he won a government scholarship in 1884 to Brisbane Grammar School where he gained the Lilley [q.v.5] medal in 1887. A Queensland scholarship took him to Ormond College, University of Melbourne, in 1889 (B.A., 1893; M.A., LL.B.,1895). As an undergraduate he was prominent in student life, played cricket for the university and twice captained the colony in tennis. He became doubles champion of Queensland in 1906-08.

Fowles began teaching in 1895 as a resident master at Cumloden, Melbourne. He was briefly at Maryborough Boys' Grammar School, Queensland, then went back to Victoria for a spell at Geelong College. He was admitted to the Victorian Bar in 1901, and in February 1902 was admitted and commenced practice in Queensland. For over thirty years he was examiner for the Barristers' Board. On 2 November 1904 he married Janet Mary, daughter of John Archibald [q.v.7]; they had no children.

Fowles was a prolific writer. Apart from legal texts he published a matriculation Latin grammar in 1897, and wrote many articles for the Queensland readers put out by the Department of Public Instruction for use in state schools. Besides numerous general newspaper articles under the nom de plume 'Remanet', he produced leaders for the *Brisbane Courier* and was associate editor of the *Daily Mail* in 1903-07. In 1917 he was believed to have used his talents to launch a campaign of spurious anti-government letters to the editor.

A foundation senator of the University of Queensland in 1910-16, and first chairman of the library committee, Fowles was deeply involved in establishing the university as secretary of the finance committee in 1906-11. Associated closely, too, with the setting up in 1912 of the Methodist Kings College in the university, he was its bursar and a fellow in 1916.

Like many contemporary lawyers Fowles had political aspirations. In the general election of April 1912 he failed to win Fortitude Valley in the Legislative Assembly for the United Party against David Bowman [q.v.7], but in July was appointed by the Denham [q.v.] ministry to the Legislative Council. A brilliant debater who always prepared his brief carefully and was blessed with a ready wit to squash interjectors, he became after 1915 the unofficial leader of the Opposition in the council; he frequently obstructed the policy of the Ryan [q.v.] government. After the abolition of the Upper House in March 1922, he unsuccessfully sought a Legislative Assembly seat at Fortitude Valley in 1923 and Merthyr in 1925.

For some years Fowles was a leading temperance advocate and was on the executive of the Queensland Temperance League. Like his father-in-law Archibald, he was a fervent Methodist and gave unstintingly of body, mind and spirit to the work and worship of his church – as choirmaster, youth leader and lay preacher. In annual and general conferences and on many committees, his advice was respected. He was a foundation member of the Presbyterian and Methodist Schools Association.

Fowles wrote many hymns, revealing poetic gifts, spiritual insight and the evangelical tradition in which he had been reared. A member of the committee for the preparation of an Australian and New Zealand supplement to the *Methodist Hymn Book* of 1933, he worked very hard and contributed two of his own hymns to it. He prepared a 'Methodist Hymn Book Companion' to facilitate the introduction of the new book. In many Brisbane churches he conducted community hymn-singing and explained the origin of both words and tunes.

Fowles died at home on 29 December 1945 and was cremated. His estate, valued for probate at £9189, was left to his widow, relatives, friends and various Methodist foundations.

A'sian Methodist Hist Soc, *J and Procs*, Oct 1955, p 931; *Qld Methodist Times*, 10, 17 Jan 1946; *Brisbane Courier*, 12 Feb 1902; *Courier Mail*, 30 Dec 1945, 12,17 Jan 1946.   J. C. H. GILL

FOWLES, HERBERT JAMES (1889-1947), soldier and lighthouse-keeper, was born on 1 April 1889 at Albany, Western Australia, son of James Fowles, seaman, and his wife Sophia Elizabeth, née Simmons. Educated at the Christian Brothers' College, Albany, he left to join the Albany Pilot-Marine Ships Crew where he remained until 1910. He was next employed by the Commonwealth Lighthouse Service. His first appointed lighthouse was Cape Naturaliste and he was relieving at the Breaksea Light, Albany, when he enlisted as a private in the 11th Battalion, Australian Imperial Force, on 17 February 1915.

Fowles embarked from Fremantle on 19 April in the troopship *Argyllshire* with the 4th Reinforcements for the 11th Battalion and joined his unit at Gallipoli on 4 June. Wounded in action late that month, he resumed duty in October and left Gallipoli for Lemnos on the night of 16-17 November. The battalion reached Egypt in January 1916 and Fowles was promoted lance corporal in March; by 5 April the battalion was in France. On 23 July he was wounded in action during the battle of Pozières. He returned to his unit in September and was promoted corporal in October. In January 1917 he was wounded a third time when a sector of the front trenches at Flers was struck by a shell. Rejoining the battalion in February, he was promoted sergeant in March and warrant officer (Class II) and company sergeant major in April.

'Chook' Fowles won the Military Medal on 15 April at Louverval for his courage and determination in holding a valuable picquet post on the right flank of the battalion until reinforcements were brought up to the line. One month later, during the 2nd battle of Bullecourt, he was awarded the Distinguished Conduct Medal for organizing an immediate counter-attack in a trench which had fallen into enemy hands. His company quickly ousted the enemy, killing over thirty men. During the attack on Mont de Merris, near Strazeele, on the night of 2-3 June 1918, he captured a machine-gun post single handed and in the mopping-up phase which followed, brought in fifty prisoners. For this action he received a Bar to his D.C.M. Before returning to Australia he was promoted temporary warrant officer (Class I) and made regimental sergeant major.

Fowles returned to Australia in May 1919 and shortly before his discharge from the A.I.F. married Winifred Scott at St Alban's Anglican Church, Highgate, Perth, on 31 July. On returning to Western Australia he had resumed his job in the lighthouse service. He was head-keeper at Point Cloates, Cape Naturaliste (for twenty-one years), Cape Leeuwin and Point Moore, Geraldton. At Point Moore, on 12 January 1947, he was drowned while fishing alone from a small dinghy. His body was never found. He was survived by his wife, one son and two daughters.

C. E. W. Bean, *The A.I.F. in France*, 1917 (Syd, 1933); W. C. Belford, *Legs-eleven . . . the 11th Battalion A.I.F.* (Perth, 1940); *London Gazette*, 15 June, 14 Aug 1917, 30 Oct 1918; *Geraldton Guardian and Express*, 14 Jan 1947; records (AWM); information from Mrs D. Donald, Innaloo, W.A.

J. G. WILLIAMS

FOX, EMANUEL PHILLIPS (1865-1915), artist and art teacher, was born on 12 March 1865 at Fitzroy, Melbourne, seventh child of Alexander Fox, a Jewish photographer from London, and his Sydney-born wife Rosetta, née Phillips. Fox matriculated at 15 and took early drawing lessons from John Carter. Between 1878 and 1886 he trained at the National Gallery schools under O. R. Campbell and G. F. Folingsby [qq.v.3,4], together with Rupert Bunny [q.v.7], McCubbin, Longstaff and Tudor St George Tucker [qq.v.]. He won awards for landscape painting at the gallery students' exhibitions in 1884 and 1886.

In February 1887 Fox left for Europe. He studied in Paris at the Académie Julian, in Gérome's atelier at the Ecole des Beaux-Arts and with the American artist T. Alexander Harrison; in the summer he painted in *plein air* artists' communities at Etaples and in Brittany and visited Giverny. In 1890 he settled at St Ives in Cornwall, one of the key centres of *plein air* painting in England, and next year in Madrid copied Velazquez' works. These contacts modified his French training.

Fox returned to Melbourne in October 1892. He joined the Victorian Artists' Society and was a vocal council-member and exhibitor between 1893 and 1900. He launched one-man shows in 1892 and 1900-01, contributed to major displays in Sydney, Adelaide and Bendigo and was represented in the Australian Exhibition at the Grafton Galleries in London in 1898. Although his art was held in esteem, patronage was largely confined to portraits. In 1893 he and Tucker established the Melbourne School of Art where students were introduced to French academic practices; at its summer outdoor school, held from about 1894 at Charterisville, near Eaglemont, he taught *plein air* painting, incorporating some aspects of Impressionist practice. It was the most vital art school in Melbourne in the 1890s.

In 1900 the trustees of the National Gallery commissioned Fox to paint 'The landing of Captain Cook at Botany Bay', which, under the terms of the Gillbee [q.v.4] bequest, he was required to paint overseas; he departed in March 1901. After a visit to Paris he stayed at St Ives and later London. He exhibited at the Royal Academy from 1903, having previously shown there in 1895, and sent works elsewhere in Britain.

On 9 May 1905 at St Peter's Church, Ealing, London, Fox married Ethel Carrick; they then lived in Paris until 1913, travelling widely in Europe and northern Africa. These were fertile years in Fox's career, and his art celebrated a way of life that was leisured and elegant. From 1890 he had contributed works to the Old Salon, and in 1894 won a gold medal with his portrait 'My Cousin'; in 1906 he began exhibiting at the New Salon and elsewhere. He became a member of the International Society of Sculptors, Painters and Gravers, an associate of the Société Nationale des Beaux-Arts in 1907 and its *sociétaire* in 1910.

Phillips Fox and his wife came to Australia in 1908 and 1913, exhibiting and painting in Melbourne, Sydney and Adelaide. The outbreak of war brought them back to Melbourne from a trip to Tahiti, and in 1915 they helped to organize an art union in aid of war funds and the French Red Cross. On 8 October 1915 Fox died of cancer in hospital at Fitzroy, and was buried in Brighton cemetery.

A modest painter by European standards, Fox is among Australia's most gifted colourists and figure painters. Celebrated for his painting of sunlight effects, he combined Impressionist-oriented vision with an academic training. Apart from portraits and landscapes he mainly painted elegant female figures and family groups; his repertoire extended to market and Arab scenes and rural subjects. He is represented in the Australian National Gallery, all State and various regional galleries, and the Louvre, Paris.

Fox was an unassuming and reserved person. Perhaps absence of strong leadership qualities prevented him from exerting as powerful an influence as did Tom Roberts and later Max Meldrum [qq.v.]. However, his use of colour led artists of the younger generation such as Roland Wakelin [q.v.] to further experiment.

His wife ETHEL CARRICK FOX (1872-1952) was born on 7 February 1872 at Uxbridge, Middlesex, daughter of Albert William Carrick, a well-established draper, and his wife Emma, née Filmer. After education at home she joined the Guildhall School of Music, and later trained with Francis Bate and at the Slade School of Fine Art under Brown and Tonks. After her husband's death she remained in Melbourne until 1916, then lived mostly abroad, travelling extensively in Europe, the Middle East and Asia. She returned to Australia in 1925, 1933, 1940, 1948 and 1952, arranging exhibitions of their work and painting in several of the cities and along the rivers of northern New South Wales.

She first showed her work in London in 1903 and later exhibited widely in Britain, France and Australia. She was one of a group of Australian women artists who sought to establish themselves in Paris and London through joint exhibitions in Europe in the 1920s. By 1908 Carrick Fox was a member of the Union Internationale des Beaux-Arts et des Lettres; in 1911 she became *sociétaire* of the Salon d'Automne, later an associate of the Société Nationale des Beaux-Arts and prior to 1913 was the vice-president of the International Union of Women Painters. In 1928 she won the diploma of honour at the International Exhibition of Bordeaux.

Apart from her energetic organization of various artistic undertakings in Australia during both world wars, she fought for the recognition and placement of her husband's art in major Australian galleries and criticized the limited inclusion of Impressionist works in the National Gallery of Victoria. Her works are lively and colourful: she painted market scenes, parks and flower gardens, beach and Arab scenes, genre interiors and especially flower pieces. Interesting and urbane, Ethel Carrick Fox possessed a strong and independent personality. She was an Anglican, but in the 1940s joined the Theosophical Society in Sydney. Before her death in a Melbourne hospital on 17 June 1952 she had lived at the Lyceum Club in Melbourne. Her marriage was childless.

L. P. Fox, *E. Phillips Fox, notes and recollections* (Syd, 1969); C. B. Christesen (ed), *The gallery on Eastern Hill* (Melb, 1970); Geelong Art Gallery, *Ethel Carrick: a retrospective exhibition* (Cat, Geelong, 1979); A. Bradley and T. Smith (ed), *Australian art and architecture* (Melb, 1980); *Art in Aust*, 1 (1918), no 5; *Table Talk*, 23 Jan 1891, 9 Dec 1892; *Age*, 22 Oct 1932, 28 May 1949, 8 Nov 1958, 4 June 1974; *Argus*, 24 May 1952; Carter papers, letters received 1902-60 (ML); Fox letters (National Gallery, Vic); McCubbin papers (MS 8525, LaTL); Roberts papers, V3 (ML).

RUTH ZUBANS

FOX, SIR FRANK IGNATIUS (1874-1960), journalist and Imperialist, was born on 12 August 1874 at Kensington, Adelaide, second son of Charles James Fox, journalist, and his wife Mary Ann, née Toole. He moved to Hobart in 1883, when his father became editor of the *Tasmanian Mail*, and was educated at Christ's College. At an early age he wrote paragraphs for his father's paper.

Stranded in Sydney about 1891, Fox abandoned the idea of reading for the Bar, and became an office-boy on the *Australian Workman*. He became a shareholder in the staff co-operative that took over ownership from the Trades and Labor Council; as its editor in 1893-95 Fox opposed the efforts of the 'outside' Labor men to impose on the parliamentary party 'an impossible & silly pledge'. On 13 June 1894 he married, with Congregational forms, Helen Clint (d. 1958); they had a son and two daughters.

Next year Fox became editor of the Bathurst *National Advocate* and supported Federation. In 1898 he could not pay debts incurred by the illness of his wife and himself; he was released from bankruptcy in July 1900. Meanwhile he had returned to Sydney and worked for the *Daily Telegraph* and *Truth*. Fox joined the staff of the *Bulletin* in 1901. Next year, as 'Frank Renar', he published *Bushman and buccaneer*, a memoir of Harry 'the Breaker' Morant [q.v.].

A 'Radical-Protectionist' and Deakinite liberal, Fox cautioned Alfred Deakin against (Sir) George Reid [qq.v.], urged him to reach an understanding with J. C. Watson [q.v.], warned him against 'fusion' in 1909, and above all advocated a citizen army and an Australian navy. Fox was commissioned in the Australian Field Artillery on 1 September 1905 and was an early member of the Australian National Defence League; with G. R. Campbell [q.v.7] he edited its quarterly journal, the *Call*. He was influenced by Imperialist writings of Richard Jebb, whom he met in Sydney about 1906.

While still working for the *Bulletin*, Fox was appointed in 1907 first editor and manager of the *Lone Hand*. Deakin told him of his surprise at the 'variety and general excellence' of the first two numbers. Fox published a volume of political essays, *From the old dog* (Melbourne), in 1908. He was a keen horseman; but Norman Lindsay [q.v.] found him an 'equine exhibitionist'.

Fox dreamed of editing an independent daily newspaper. In 1909, after visiting Canada, he went to London where he sought financial backing. Meanwhile he wrote for the *Morning Post*, *The Times*, the *Daily Mail* and 'a swarm of other papers', and spoke on behalf of the National Defence League from Plymouth to Middlesbrough, warning of the menace of war. 'A man of strikingly handsome appearance and great enthusiasms', he was accepted in London as a 'wild young Australian'. He visited All Souls College, Oxford, and found it 'very charming to get into the inner political circle'. He discovered that 'one must be a Unionist [Conservative] even if it involves keeping political company with Dukes & other disgraceful people'.

Appointed assistant editor on the *Morning Post* in December, Fox late in 1910 was promoted news editor. His wife and family had joined him, but he confessed to Deakin: 'I still look on life here as an exile: but must stick it out until my big plan is achieved'. A prolific writer, he published *Ramparts of Empire* (1910) about the navy, *Australia* (1910), illustrated by P. F. S. Spence [q.v.], *Problems of the Pacific* (1912), *The British Empire* (1914) and many travel books.

In 1912 the *Morning Post* sent Fox to the Balkans; he accompanied the Bulgarian Army through Turkey and covered the Balkan peace conference. He was with the Belgian Army during the first stage of World War I. On 13 December 1914 he was commissioned in the Royal Field Artillery and served in France and was twice wounded in the battle of the Somme. In 1917-18 he was at the War Office, then served as staff captain at the quartermaster general's branch, General Headquarters, in France and in October returned to the War Office as a general staff officer with the temporary rank of major. Demobilized in January 1919, he had been mentioned in dispatches, and appointed O.B.E. (1919) and to the Belgian Order of the Crown. During the war he still managed to write: his books included *The agony of Belgium* (1915), *The British Army at war* (1917) and *G.H.Q., Montreuil-sur-Mer* (1920) under the pseudonym 'G.S.O.'.

After the war Fox returned to the *Morning Post* and writing. In 1923 he published a novel, *Beneath an ardent sun*, with an Australian background, and in 1928 *The mastery of the Pacific*. He also wrote the histories of *The Royal Inniskilling Fusiliers* (1928 and 1951) in the two World Wars. He continued to advocate Imperialist causes including Empire trade preferences. In 1923 he was secretary of the Fellowship of the British Empire Exhibition and was knighted in 1926. He organized the British Empire Cancer Campaign in northern England in 1927-29 and the Empire Rheumatism Council in 1936-46. Sir Frank visited Australia and New Zealand in 1935.

A member of the Savage and the Overseas clubs in London, Fox spent his last years in Sussex, at Broom Cottage, West Wittering, near Chichester. He died in hospital at Chichester on 4 March 1960.

L. W. Matters, *Australians who count in London* ... (Lond, 1913); N. Lindsay, *Bohemians of the Bulletin* (Syd, 1965); *Southern Sphere*, Jan 1911; *British A'sian*, 26 Oct 1916; *Biblionews*, May 1960; *Aust Worker*, 6 Aug 1908, 11 Feb 1909; *SMH*, 5 July 1926, 15 Apr 1935, 22 Apr 1936; *World* (Syd), 10, 17 Sept 1932; *Bulletin*, 19 Apr 1935; *The Times* (Lond), 11 Mar 1960; Deakin, *and* Jebb papers (NL); Bankruptcy file 13094 (NSWA).

MARTHA RUTLEDGE

FOXTON, JUSTIN FOX GREENLAW (1849-1916), politician, barrister and soldier, was born on 24 September 1849 in Melbourne, son of Captain John Greenlaw Foxton, accountant and former naval officer, and his wife Isabel Elizabeth, née Potts. Captain Foxton had been navigation officer of the *Hopewell* during an 1833-34 expedition to the Antarctic and had settled in Port Phillip in 1841. Educated privately and at Melbourne Church of England Grammar School (1859-62), Justin went in 1864 to Queensland and after jackerooing was articled to J. M. Thompson [q.v.6] of Ipswich, being admitted to the Bar in 1871. Next year he went to Stanthorpe, establishing a lucrative tinfield practice before moving to a Brisbane partnership with Thompson in 1878. He built The Priory, Indooroopilly, and afterwards lived at Bulimba.

Foxton held the Legislative Assembly seat of Carnarvon from 1883 until 1904 when he refused to support the Morgan [q.v.] coalition. His electioneering 'ploys' included persuading a coach driver to 'lose' his passengers — all political opponents — on the way to the polls, and smashing railway gates, deliberately closed against a trainload of his Brisbane supporters at Stanthorpe station. He served as secretary for public lands in 1896-98 during the Nelson [q.v.] and Byrnes [q.v.7] ministries, and again from April to September 1903; he was home secretary under Dickson and Philp [qq.v.] from October 1898 to April 1903. Federal member for Brisbane in 1906-10, he was honorary minister for ten months in Deakin's [q.v.] third government.

When lands minister, Foxton consolidated the complex Queensland land laws in the Land Act of 1897. The two most significant pieces of Queensland legislation which he initiated, however, were the Factories and Shops Act of 1900, which regulated conditions of employment, hours of work and child labour, and, more importantly, the 1901 Aboriginals Protection and Restriction of the Sale of Opium Act. This Act, the first effective such measure in Queensland, implemented a system of policed missions and reserves and stopped some female exploitation. Foxton had come to believe that 'as a matter of strict morals our obligations to the Aboriginals ... are of a higher, more exacting nature than those we owe to our own

... We are the interlopers, not they'; he also believed in the 'civilizing' influence of religious instruction.

In the Commonwealth parliament Foxton was a staunch anti-socialist, a fervent States-righter, a keen advocate of black labour for developing northern Australia, and a shrewd representative of the Brisbane mercantile community. Although in favour of a restricted franchise — 'there should be a distinct line drawn between those who have a stake in the country and those who have not' — he supported female enfranchisement. His role in the creation of the Australian fleet remains his greatest claim to remembrance. A faithful and effective conduit of Deakin's ideas and wishes, he, together with (Sir) W. T. Bridges [q.v.7] and (Sir) W. R. Creswell [q.v.], represented Australia at the 1909 Imperial Defence Conference in London when the principle of a separate Australian unit within the Empire's projected Pacific Fleet was agreed to. Foxton was an outspoken defender of Empire, with fear of an Asian invasion always at the back of his mind. Deakin was generous in his praise of his loyal colleague, but he did not recommend him for the K.C.M.G. which he sought. After his defeat in 1910 Foxton continued his law practice with the firm Foxton, Hobbs & Macnish.

Foxton was usually known, both formally and satirically, as 'Colonel' Foxton, a title he gained by over thirty years service in the militia; he ended his military career in 1912 as commandant of the Queensland Brigade of the Field Artillery with the C.M.G. (1903) and the Volunteer Officers' Decoration. He once routed his own troops when he drove on to the parade ground at Lytton in Queensland's first motor car. The horses bolted when the car backfired. In 1909 he was aide-de-camp to the governor-general. Although never smelling gunpowder, Foxton was a brave man. In 1884 he was awarded the Royal Humane Society's certificate of merit for saving a woman from drowning at St Kilda pier, Melbourne. Seven years later his attempt to rescue two sisters from the flooding Brisbane River gained him the society's bronze medal.

Foxton, whose other sobriquet 'Chinese' Foxton referred to his employment of Chinese tobacco-workers at his Texas property, was a handsome, upright, nattily dressed figure, with thick drooping black moustache, receding hairline and domed forehead. Aloof and legalistic, he irritated his political opponents with his caustic cynicism. Nevertheless he was a first-class administrator at a time when innovation was at a discount and strict economy the political virtue.

Keenly interested in cricket and yachting,

he was president of the Queensland Cricket Association and from 1907 a member of the Australian Cricket Board of Control. He helped found the Historical Society of Queensland and was grand registrar of the United Grand Lodge of Queensland.

Foxton died of cerebro-vascular disease at South Brisbane on 23 June 1916, and was buried in Toowong cemetery after Church of England rites. He was survived by his wife, Emily Mary, née Panton, whom he had married at Ipswich on 19 November 1874, and by two sons serving in the Australian Imperial Force and a daughter. Unwise speculations, including a directorship of the failed Metropolitan Land and Building Society, reduced his estate at probate to only £2040.

C. A. Bernays, *Queensland politics during sixty (1859-1919) years* (Brisb, nd, 1919?); N. Meaney, *A history of Australian defence and foreign policy, 1901-23*, 1 (Syd, 1976); *PD* (Cwlth), 1909, p 6665, 6735; *PD* (Qld), 1894, p 727, 1900, p 1950, 1901, p 201; *JRQHS*, 5 Oct 1918, p 32; *Brisbane Courier*, 7 Apr 1910, 24 June 1916; *Queenslander*, 1 July 1916; L. D. Atkinson, Australian defence policy: a study of empire and nation (Ph.D. thesis, ANU, 1964); Deakin papers (MS, 1540/15/833-1381, NL); A. Foxton, The Foxton family papers (MS, Oxley Lib, *and* Qld Women's Hist Assn, Brisb).

D. B. WATERSON

FOY, FRANCIS (1856?- 1918) and MARK (1865-1950), businessmen and sportsmen, were the eldest and third sons of Mark Foy [q.v.4] and his first wife Mary, née Macken: Francis was born at Kingstown, near Dublin, and Mark junior on 15 February 1865 at Bendigo, Victoria. Francis reached Melbourne with his mother about 1860. A high-spirited boy, he drove a bullock-team from Bendigo to Melbourne and back without mishap. At 18 he ran away to sea and returned to Ireland, where he was a counter-hand with Arnott & Co. Ltd, drapers, in Dublin. After three years he came home and, reconciled to his father, became a partner in his drapery shop at Collingwood. In November 1882 his father settled the business on him and brought in William Gibson [q.v.] as his son's partner. On 21 June 1883 at St John's Catholic Church, Heidelberg, Francis married Mary Maud Flanagan (d. 1900).

The partnership was dissolved in August 1884 and Francis and Mark moved to Sydney where in 1885 they set up shop in Oxford Street under the style of Mark Foy's, in memory of their late father. Francis established a colourful reputation as a buyer in England and on the Continent by a combination of shrewdness and unorthodoxy: he always bought without a book, later accurately recalling hundreds of transactions to his clerk at his London office. Business flourished and a new store near Hyde Park, modelled partly on Bon Marché in Paris, was opened in 1908: its piazza, chandeliers, marble and sumptuous ballroom made it a Sydney institution and one of Australia's foremost fashion stores. Always the innovator, Foy introduced Sydney's first escalator and motor delivery service. In November 1909 Mark Foy's Ltd was registered as a public company with an authorized capital of £600 000.

A popular, flamboyant turf identity, Foy imported many racehorses from Ireland and England and sent mares to stud in France. His Irish sense of humour showed in his equine nomenclature; at his stud, The Monastery, near Parkes, His Reverence stood as chief stallion and he called a foal by Something Irish, The Christian Brother. He raced for pleasure: it was said he gave away all his prize money and winnings, and he delighted in donating cups to racing clubs big and small. Each year he went to the Melbourne Cup meeting where he entertained at champagne luncheons – his horse, Voyou, ran second in the 1899 Melbourne Cup. In ill health, suffering for many years from diabetes, in 1918 he went to Melbourne as usual; he said to a bookmaker that he would bet three to one he would not return to Sydney alive. He won that bet, dying in the Melbourne-Sydney express near Goulburn, New South Wales, on 12 November 1918.

Foy was survived by his second wife Mary Ann, née Clark, whom he had married on 3 September 1912 at St Patrick's, Church Hill, and by four sons and four daughters of his first marriage; three sons saw active service in World War I.

Kind and generous, if a little impetuous, Foy was the subject of numerous stories. A prominent Catholic, he was buried in his French-style chapel vault in South Head cemetery which bears a punning epigraph: 'In Dieu foi aux amis foyer' (For God faith, for my friends hearth). His estate, which included his residence Auteuil, Killara, and a property of the same name in Queensland, was valued for probate at £149 271.

His brother Mark was a keen sportsman. As a young man he won several medals for rifle-shooting in the United States of America. In 1890 he founded the Sydney Flying Squadron to popularize and brighten up sailing on Port Jackson. His efforts resulted in the faster, cheaper, skiff-class 18-footers (unique to Australia), and in making sailing a public spectacle with big prize money and colourful boats which could easily be identified by supporters. When banned from participating in the Anniversary Day Regatta he started a rival one. In 1898 he took his 22-foot Irex to England, but lost all three races on the Medway to the Maid of Kent. On 19 September 1900 at St Mary's Cathedral, Hobart, Tasmania, he married Elizabeth Dominica Tweedie. Also interested in motor racing and boxing, in 1904 he presented a silver cup for a Sydney-Melbourne road race.

In July that year Foy opened the Hydro Majestic Hotel at Medlow Bath in the Blue Mountains as a hydropathic resort, complete with Swiss doctor and spa water from Baden Baden, Germany. With characteristic flair Foy provided a wide range of recreation facilities and amusements with excellent cuisine and made it one of the most fashionable resorts in Australia. Many international celebrities patronized it: Melba [q.v.] and Clara Butt sang in the casino and Bertha Krupp donated one of her grand pianos; in 1908 Tommy Burns trained there for his fight with Jack Johnson, and that year and 1925 it was host to visiting American fleets.

Foy retired from active participation in the retail business in 1908 and travelled extensively in Europe, Asia and the Pacific. Survived by two sons and two daughters, he died on 15 November 1950 after a fall in his garden at Bay View and was buried in the Catholic section of South Head cemetery. His estate was valued for probate at £68 981. The family were released by the Equity Court from a direction in his will that he be reburied in an elaborate tomb to cost £32 000 built in an acre of bushland at Medlow Bath.

Mark Foy's Ltd, The romance of the house of Foy, 1885-1935 (Syd, 1935); S. W. Davies, Foy's saga (Perth, 1946); British A'sian, 22 Sept 1898, 2 Feb 1899; SMH, 13, 15 Nov 1918, 17 Nov 1950, 30 Oct 1951, 10 Apr 1976; Sydney Mail, 20 Nov 1918; Freeman's J (Syd), 21 Nov 1918; Truth (Syd), 23 Mar 1952; Sun (Syd), 26 Dec 1975; Australian (Syd), 22 Jan 1980; Daily Telegraph (Syd), 24 Jan 1980.
                                          G. P. WALSH

FRANCIS, LEONARD (1866-1947), choral conductor and singing teacher, was born on 1 April 1866 at Exeter, Devon, England, second son of a manufacturer of footwear. Early experience as a choirboy in Exeter Cathedral bred in him an urge to make music his livelihood. After some demur his parents allowed him to finish his studies at the Pusey-Keith Conservatoire and with Isadore de Solla. He then embarked on the career of a concert baritone.

After visiting Australia on other business, he decided about 1900 to return permanently. Under the name Leonard Francis he came first to Melbourne but by 1903 was singing and teaching in Sydney; the Brisbane Courier of 5 June described his performance (as guest artist for the Brisbane Musical Union) in the name part of

Mendelssohn's *Elijah* as 'a thoroughly good reading'.

He was teaching in Brisbane by August 1905 and in 1906 was offered the conductorship of the Blackstone-Ipswich Cambrian Choir whose members came mainly from the Ipswich Welsh community. Although the post involved travelling from Brisbane and back twice a week, acceptance marked a turning point in his career. In 1908 under their new leader the Cambrians became the first Queensland choir to win the major choral event in the South Street competitions at Ballarat, Victoria. In 1910 they repeated their success at a similar Australia-wide competition festival in Sydney.

The impetus thus given to competitive choral singing in Queensland was immense. Almost unchecked by World War I, it reached its peak in 1922-39. During this heyday of the Queensland eisteddfod movement at least ten other large choirs existed in Brisbane and other cities with the Ipswich Cambrians always prominent.

Francis was in demand as a teacher and adjudicator of singing but his reputation rested on his outstanding skill as a choral conductor; the Cambrians were famed for their unforgettable lambency of tone and delicacy of expression. To the audience his beat, though clear, was undemonstrative. 'I will not turn myself into a semaphore', he said, but the choir faced a pair of compelling blue eyes, capable of infinite shades of musical meaning. Although from time to time he also conducted the choir of St Stephen's Catholic Cathedral, Brisbane, the Brisbane Apollo Club and the Metropolitan Choral Society, the Cambrians were always his first love. He was eight times president of the Musical Association of Queensland. Genial and quick witted, he was a member of the Johnsonian Club and played golf from a handicap of 7.

His first wife Kate, née Bland, died in March 1903. On 5 February 1935 at St Andrew's Anglican Church, Indooroopilly, Francis married Winnie Dunoon who survived him when he died on 6 April 1947. He was cremated. There were no children of either marriage.

Men of Queensland (Brisb, 1929); W. A. Orchard, *Music in Australia* (Melb, 1952); *Brisbane Courier*, 5, 20 June 1903, 12 Aug 1905; *Telegraph* (Brisb), 12 Apr 1941; *Qld Times*, 7 Apr 1947; Percy Brier Collection (Fryer Memorial Lib, Univ Qld); information from Mrs W. Francis, Chermside Nth, Qld.   JOHN VILLAUME

FRANKI, JAMES PETER (1843-1924), engineer and shipbuilder, was born on 27 November 1843 at Coglio, Switzerland, son of Martin Franki, builder and farmer; he came to Sydney aboard the *Ledunia* in 1855, and was educated at St Philip's School, Church Hill. Apprenticed for five years in the engineering and shipbuilding firm of P. N. Russell [q.v.6] & Co., Darling Harbour, he then worked with the Fitzroy Ironworks Co. at Mittagong and on railway construction projects with Mark Faviel. On 9 January 1867 he joined Macarthur & Co. which was then operating at Waterview Bay, Balmain; he started as chief engineering draughtsman, was promoted to manager on Thomas Macarthur's death in 1869, and appointed general manager when the dockyard became a public company in 1872 under the name Mort's [q.v.5] Dock & Engineering Co. Ltd. He was naturalized in 1875.

The spectacular development of shipbuilding at Mort's Dock (the largest privately owned dry dock in the southern hemisphere) continued from 1878 under the able control of Franki. When he joined it, about 200 men were employed; by 1915 the company's three docks — Waterview dock, Woolwich dock and Jubilee dock — and its engineering establishment at Woolwich, had more than exceeded 1000, sometimes up to 1500. Franki was managing director from 1915 until his retirement in 1923 when he was made an honorary director.

Fiery, known for his 'keen brain and far-seeing eye', he deplored the introduction of the arbitration system and stressed that friendliness and understanding were the essential ingredients for industrial peace. He was an early advocate, with Mort, of worker participation: in 1873 foremen at the dockyard became shareholders in the company, but the rank and file found it impossible to take up shares, and his experiment was a failure. He was also a constant advocate of the policy that Australia should build and man its own ships, both mercantile and naval.

Commissioner for New South Wales for the 1888 Melbourne Centennial International Exhibition, Franki was for over thirty years president of the New South Wales Iron Trades Employers' Association, and a member of the Employers' Federation, Chamber of Manufactures and Chamber of Commerce. A member of the Institution of Mechanical Engineers, London, he was a founding member of the Engineering Association of New South Wales (1870) and of the Institution of Engineers, Australia, and a fellow of the Royal Colonial Institution. He was chairman of the Commonwealth Munitions Committee before 1917.

A resident of Balmain for over fifty years he was an alderman in 1883, a justice of the peace from 1886 and a generous benefactor of local sporting and community associations. A Mason, he belonged to the Millions Club of New South Wales and the National Club. He married first Priscilla Scoles on 23 December 1869 at St Philip's Church of England, Sydney, and after her death in 1881, Bessie Johnson, on 4 October 1882 at Christ Church, Castlemaine, Victoria. Franki died at Balmain on 24 January 1924 of arteriosclerosis, and was buried in the Anglican cemetery at South Head. He was survived by one son and six daughters of his first marriage and one son of his second. Three sons predeceased him including Stirling Napier who died at Pozières in 1916. His estate was valued for probate at £50 146. The J. P. Franki memorial gold medal was initiated at the Sydney Technical College in 1923.

Cyclopedia of N.S.W. (Syd, 1907); J. A. Barnard, *Visions and profits (Melb, 1961);/JRAHS),* 24 (1938); *T&CJ,* 3 Jan 1917; *SMH,* 9 Jan 1917, 25 Jan 1924.

J. M. ANTILL

FRANKLIN, RICHARD PENROSE (1884-1942), schoolmaster and educationist, was born on 28 November 1884 at Surbiton, London, son of Samuel Franklin, solicitor, and his wife Julia Reed, née Gould. He was educated at Borlase School, Marlow, and at St Paul's School, London, where he distinguished himself both in the schoolroom and on the playing field. He was captain of the school in 1903-04 and played in the cricket and football teams. In 1904 he became an undergraduate at Pembroke College, Cambridge, where he obtained a first-class honour in the classical tripos. He won a blue for athletics. In 1908 he migrated to Victoria to join the firm of Dalgety [q.v.4] & Co. Ltd. Finding that his interests lay elsewhere he decided to try his hand at schoolmastering. In the last term of 1910 he joined the staff of the Geelong Church of England Grammar School. In the following year he became the senior housemaster and senior classical master of the Sydney Church of England Grammar School (Shore), where his brother Charles was also a teacher. In 1915 he applied for and was appointed headmaster of the Melbourne Church of England Grammar School.

In February 1917 Franklin enlisted in the Australian Imperial Force, and became a lieutenant in the artillery. He returned to Australia on 6 May 1919. He received a most enthusiastic welcome on resuming his duties as headmaster. By then he was known to the boys of the school as 'Lofty' because of his tall, slim figure. By then many boys had been privileged to get to know the inspiring teacher, and the warm friend behind the reserve which he presented to the world. The

1920s was to be the flowering time of his life.

A passionate believer in education in Greek and Latin as the foundation of a career in the professions, or public life or the Church, he urged all talented boys to study both those subjects. To assist him he was fortunate to have on the staff such brilliant teachers of the classics as Karl Kaeppel [q.v.] and H. A. K. Hunt, later professor of classics at the University of Melbourne. Whether this policy was beneficial to the other pupils remains one of the unanswerable questions. The policy produced results both at school examinations and at the university. The Franklin argument was that classics was the foundation for success in medicine, law, natural sciences, and the humanities. The Franklin argument was that boys must learn to decide for themselves what was right and wrong, what was true and what was false.

Under his direction the school enjoyed a similar success on the sporting field. Franklin's idea of the good man had been influenced more by Greek ideas than Christian teaching. Believing in the Greek maxims of 'Know thyself', 'Moderation in all things' and 'Avoid excess', he taught generations at the school the Greek idea of harmony, of balance between the Dionysian and the Apollonian elements in a human being. Discipline and restraint came, in his opinion, as much from the playing fields as the classroom. In his own field as a coach of high jump, long jump and hurdles he produced outstanding performers.

Franklin became prominent in the public life of education, notably as president of the Headmasters' Association and of the Headmasters' Conference of Australia. He was vice-chairman of the Soldiers' Children Education Board, and an active member of the Council of Public Education.

During a visit to Scotland in 1935 to attend an educational conference he contracted a severe chill. On his return to Melbourne he was granted six months leave of absence. As his health did not improve during that convalescence in June 1936 he accepted medical advice that he should resign the headmastership of the Melbourne Grammar School. He died on 12 October 1942 at Toorak. He did not marry. He was cremated after a memorial service in the school chapel.

Estimates of Franklin's work at the Melbourne Grammar School have differed rather sharply. Those in a position to benefit from his belief in the classics, and those privileged to get to know the man behind the forbidding exterior never lost their enthusiasm, their gratitude or their affection. Others believed it was a mistake to put such emphasis on the classics when education was moving so swiftly towards the sciences and the social sciences. Even those not in a position to benefit from any educational policy realized that they had the good fortune to grow up in the presence of a mighty spirit.

Melb C. of E. Grammar School, *Liber Melburniensis* (Melb, 1965); *Table Talk*, 9 June 1927; *Age*, and *Argus*, 13 Oct 1942; Melb C. of E. Grammar School Archives.   MANNING CLARK

FRANKLIN, STELLA MARIA(N) SARAH MILES (1879-1954), writer, was born on 14 October 1879 at Talbingo, New South Wales, eldest child of native-born parents John Maurice Franklin, of Brindabella station, and his wife Margaret Susannah Helena, née Lampe, who was the great-granddaughter of Edward Miles (or Moyle) who had arrived with the First Fleet in the *Scarborough* with a seven years sentence for theft. *Childhood at Brindabella* (1963) illuminates Stella's first decade amongst pioneering families of the Monaro. She was educated at home and at Thornford Public School after 1889, when her family moved to Stillwater, an unrewarding small holding near Goulburn. About 1902 the family took up unspecified farming enterprises at Cranebrook, near Penrith, and later at Chesterfield, and finally by 1915, giving up the land altogether, went to the modest south-west Sydney suburb of Carlton: her much diminished inheritance.

Downward mobility heightened Stella Franklin's pride and self-awareness, and contributed much to the making of Miles Franklin, nationalist, feminist and novelist. She readily appreciated her father's loss; shared hardships suffered especially by her more vigorous mother; and surmounted her own educational disadvantages proving thereafter an enterprising aspirant to literature. Her bush-bred talents were fostered by Charles Blyth, tutor at Brindabella, Thomas Hebblewhite of the *Goulburn Evening Penny Post*, and, after governessing near Yass in 1897, the example of Charlotte Brontë. Writing, rather than teaching, nursing and E. W. O'Sullivan's [q.v.] testimonials, delivered independence.

Completed by 1899, her marvellously rebellious *My brilliant career*, rejected locally and published with the aid of Henry Lawson [q.v.] by William Blackwood & Sons, Edinburgh and London, in 1901, brought instant acclaim. The ambiguities of publication were soon impressed on an otherwise resourceless 22-year-old female. As translated into the contemporaneous *My career goes bung* (unpublished until 1946), the self-styled 'Bushwacker' recoiled from rural notoriety and social-cum sexual patronage in Sydney, including A. B.

Paterson's [q.v.] sporting offer of collaboration in 1902. She struggled towards a literary niche, sheltered by the O'Sullivans and from 1902 Miss Rose Scott [q.v.], who introduced her to sophisticated feminist circles. For a year in 1903-04, disguised as 'Sarah Frankling', she worked in domestic service in Sydney and Melbourne seeking literary material. In Melbourne she met Joseph Furphy [q.v.], a mutual and lasting inspiration, Kate Baker [q.v.7] and the Goldstein [q.v.] women who encouraged her to Christian Science and, more effectively, emigration.

Without rejecting a marriage proposal from her relative Edwin Bridle in 1905, Franklin boldly embarked in the *Ventura* for the United States of America on 7 April 1906, intending to work as a 'Mary Ann', and publish at least one of the three manuscripts written since 1901, maybe *Some everyday folk and Dawn* (Edinburgh, 1909), set near Penrith. She arrived to the debris of the San Francisco earthquake. Her ill-documented first months in California appear to have been determined by a shipmate nurse of Seventh Day Adventist persuasion and letters of introduction to feminists from Vida Goldstein.

Reportedly set for New York, she had traversed America as far as Chicago by late 1906. There she stayed until October 1915. Directed to Jane Adams's Hull House, she was welcomed by fellow-Australian Alice Henry [q.v.], and impressed the philanthropic Margaret Dreier Robins, president of the fledgling National Women's Trade Union League of America, who in October 1907 offered her a post as personal secretary. Edwin Bridle's correspondence ceased.

Franklin's responsibilities grew steadily: in 1908 she was, unofficially, part-time secretary to the league, from 1910 secretary at a salary of $25 a week, in 1912 unofficially assistant editor to Alice Henry on its monthly journal, *Life and Labor*, in 1913-14 co-editor and, briefly, editor in 1915. In her limited spare time she took singing and piano lessons. Something of those dynamic years on Dearborn Street, Chicago, may be gleaned from her little-known romance, *The net of circumstance*, published in London in 1915 under her pseudonym 'Mr and Mrs Ogniblat L'Artsau'. Of feminist and biographical significance, it was her only American-based creative work to be published. Miles Franklin now had two careers, both pursued full-pelt. Her ever-worrying health collapsed in 1912, shortly after her first visit in 1911 to England and France. Then in her early thirties, she redoubled her literary and political efforts. But she was increasingly unsettled, partly by the attentions of bright young men.

Declaration of World War I in Europe clarified some things for Franklin: she finally rejected marriage, which she considered 'rabbit' work and, unnerved by American chauvinism, she reasserted her nationality. Faced by mounting ideological or personal conflict within the league, she took three months leave and sailed for England on 30 October 1915, vaguely envisaging war-work. From London she resigned, severing links with Chicago, although not her many friendships or affection for America.

Exhausted, Franklin worked briefly at Margaret McMillan's crèche at Deptford, and 'kept the wolf from the door' as a cook at the Minerva Café, High Holborn, meanwhile ineffectually negotiating under male noms de plume with publishers or dabbling in journalism. In June 1917 she joined as a voluntary worker the 'American' Unit of the Scottish Women's Hospitals for Foreign Service stationed at Ostrovo, Macedonia, and commanded by Dr Agnes Bennett [q.v.7] and Dr Mary De Garis [q.v. E. L. De Garis], a stimulating but debilitating experience for 'Franky Doodle', orderly. She returned unwell to London in February 1918, apparently not enticed to stay by the possibility of a paid post as cook on a twelve month contract. An inquiry about joining the Women's Royal Air Force foreshadowed her enthusiasm for the air-based defence of Australia.

Miles Franklin remained in London another eight years, punctuated by visits to Ireland in 1919 and 1926 and Australia, via America, in 1923-24. From 1919 she was employed as secretary with the influential National Housing and Town Planning Council in Bloomsbury, until wearied with male madness at the office in 1926. She had accumulated manuscripts, including many plays, but post-war malaise in London plus renewed Australian contact and refreshing companions like the Victorians, Mary Fullerton [q.v.] and yarner P. S. Watson, re-ordered her literary priorities. Her transition to nativism was symbolized by the completion of *Prelude to waking* in December 1925 (published 1950, but the first work under her new pseudonym, 'Brent of Bin Bin').

Family pressure, health and hope of 'Brent' brought her home in 1927, where she pursued her vocation by hiring a Hurstville hotel-room for typing, and eschewed 'tuft-hunters'. Between 1928 and 1931, Blackwoods published three of a projected nine-volume pastoral saga by 'Brent of Bin Bin'. The novels were well received and the little mystery of authorship exuberantly sustained until after her death by the author, her intimates and her publishers.

Dissatisfied with home and Australian literary life by late 1930, and in pursuit of publishers, Franklin left for London via America, returning late 1932. During that time her father died (1931); her finances dipped alarmingly; and *Old Blastus of Bandicoot* (London, 1931) appeared under her own name, the first such since 1909. In 1933 she published a pot-boiler, *Bring the monkey* and completed the six 'Brent' novels. Also the splendid, opinionated chronicle, *All that swagger*, which won the S. H. Prior [q.v.] Memorial Prize in 1936, was published by the *Bulletin* and, especially through the characterization of Danny Delacey, restored her Australian name.

Franklin worked long and hard for that, despite being 'diverted by sociology' and the pains of expatriatism, as unpublished writing indicates. Ironically she returned a writer at an unsustainable zenith, to draining, uneventful domesticity at Carlton. Exulting in her native land, whilst opposing its sectarian politics (voting Social Credit in 1934), oppressive censorship and parochial pomposities, she devoted herself to an Australian literature — for which she received King George V's Silver Jubilee medal in 1935 — and intellectual work. Spanning two literary generations, strengthened by knowledge of American parallels, also by the welcome of sensitive women writers and the esteem of C. Hartley Grattan, whose second tour in 1936 she helped to organize, she entered literary life with customary vigour: insofar as carefully controlled resources, a demanding mother who died in 1938 aged 88, and an expansive correspondence enabled, joining the Fellowship of Australian Writers (1933) and the Sydney P.E.N. Club (1935).

The largest hope faded first, with the demise of P. R. Stephensen's [q.v.] publishing projects, first mooted in London in 1932. Franklin thereafter promoted her own causes: Mary Fullerton's poetry; Lawson; reminders of *Joseph Furphy* (1944) in painful collaboration with Kate Baker (an earlier essay on Furphy had won them the Prior Memorial prize in 1939); protection for 'the last literary frontier'; and such promising young writers as Jean Devanny [q.v.], Sumner Locke Elliott, Ian Mudie, David Martin and Ric Throssell. She supported new literary journals, *Meanjin* and *Southerly,* the United Associations of Women, Mary Booth's [q.v] nationalistic projects, and various fellowship schemes to nurture Australian writers, including Commonwealth Literary Fund lectures (though later doubting 'the Government Stroke'). Indeed, her contributions to Australian literary history and appreciation culminated in lectures delivered at the University of Western Australia (1950), published posthumously as

Laughter, not for a cage (1956).

The bungled Australia First Movement (1941) confused cultural nationalists. Franklin condemned the exploitative Stephensen's politics as 'silly and reactionary', and his internment in 1942. Play-readings for troops, aid to the Soviet Union and the publication of outstanding manuscripts engaged her anxious wartime energies. She endeavoured to uphold 'our best traditions', dissociated from ideology. It was a passionate partisan stand, nonetheless, defensive of an Anglo-Saxon and Celtic inheritance.

Miles Franklin openly feared death, which came with coronary occlusion on 19 September 1954 in hospital at Drummoyne. She was cremated with Anglican rites (she had been confirmed at All Saints Anglican Church, Collector, in 1894); busybodies removed relatives' wildflowers from her coffin. Her ashes were scattered on Jounama Creek, Talbingo. She left the residue of her estate, valued for probate at £8922, to found an award for Australian literature. Her vision survives in the annual Miles Franklin award (first won by Patrick White for *Voss* in 1957), her published work, the international screen success of *My brilliant career* (a development she anticipated for Australian novels in the 1930s), and in her voluminous papers, willed to the Mitchell Library, Sydney – a select archive of the paradoxes of Australian history and culture, of which she was a proud and challenging, but elusive, expression. She had proved 'a real hard doer', as they used to say up country.

M. Barnard, *Miles Franklin* (Melb, 1967); *Guide to the papers and books of Miles Franklin* (Syd, 1980); *Meanjin Q*, 24 (1965), no 4; National Women's Trade Union League of America records (Lib Congress); Scottish Women's Hospitals collection (Mitchell Lib, Glasgow); S. M. Franklin papers (ML).

J. I. ROE

FRASER, SIR COLIN (1875-1944), geologist and company director, was born on 14 May 1875 at Coromandel, New Zealand, son of John Cameron Fraser, mining manager, and his wife Elizabeth Stuart (Stewart), née McKay. Fraser was a graduate of Auckland University College where he obtained a master of science in geology in 1906, while working as a clerk at the Bank of New Zealand. He joined the New Zealand public service as a geologist. In 1911 he moved to England where he was engaged as a consulting geologist by Lionel Robinson and William Clark, Australian-born stockbrokers with world-wide mining interests. Robinson Clark & Co. sent Fraser to Cornwall and Canada to investigate tin and nickel projects before requesting him to conduct a geological survey of the famous Mount Morgan mine in Queensland in 1914. On the completion of this report Fraser made his home in Melbourne; he had married on 20 March 1913 at St George's Church, Hanover Square, London, Mary Helen MacNamara, a Canadian.

Fraser's subsequent career was closely associated with W. S. Robinson [q.v.], Lionel's younger brother. In the early months of the war Robinson and W. L. Baillieu [q.v.7] founded Broken Hill Associated Smelters Pty Ltd (B.H.A.S.), a company which acquired a silver-lead smelting plant at Port Pirie, South Australia. With the support of Baillieu, Robinson secured Fraser's election to the board of B.H.A.S. in July 1915; a year later, Fraser was promoted to joint managing director. These appointments marked the beginning of his career as a company director.

B.H.A.S. was the first of a series of joint ventures undertaken by three large Broken Hill mining companies: Broken Hill South Ltd, North Broken Hill Ltd and Zinc Corporation Ltd, the parent companies of the loosely integrated but powerful Collins House group. As joint managing director of B.H.A.S., Fraser was a leading figure in the group from the outset, and as it expanded to embrace a wide range of activities, his directorships multiplied swiftly to include: Broken Hill South Ltd (1916, chairman 1926), British Australian Lead Manufacturers Pty Ltd (1918), Electrolytic Zinc Co. of Australasia Ltd (1919, chairman 1933), Zinc Corporation Ltd (1927), Electrolytic Refining and Smelting Co. of Australia Pty Ltd (managing director 1928), Metal Manufactures Ltd (chairman 1928), Austral Bronze Co. Ltd (1929), Associated Pulp & Paper Mills Ltd (1936), Commonwealth Aircraft Corporation Ltd (1936) and North Broken Hill Ltd (1937). Fraser emerged as effective head of the Collins House group in Australia in the 1930s. Outside the group, he was appointed a director of Dunlop Rubber Australia Ltd in 1926 and a string of mining companies including Western Mining Corporation Ltd in 1933. Eventually, he held forty directorships, many of them in major companies. He ranked high among Australia's business élite in the inter-war period.

Reflecting his prominence in mining and manufacturing, Fraser was the official government representative for the Australian non-ferrous metals industry at the Ottawa Economic Conference in 1932. In 1935 he was knighted for his services to mining and industry. He was one of the select circle of leading businessmen appointed to senior positions in the Department of Munitions during World War II. As director of materials supply his task was to procure essential raw materials.

Fraser had outstanding managerial ability. A dedicated man with enormous reserves of energy, he could handle a vast and strenuous work-load. Pragmatic and endowed with a talent for mastering complex and minute details of a company's operations, he had a reputation as a problem-solver, the director to whom the most difficult tasks were allocated. In his entrepreneurial outlook, he tended to be cautious, but his clear-headed assessments of the potentialities and pitfalls of an enterprise made him a valuable foil to more flamboyant colleagues, while a deep concern for attaining economic and technical efficiency rendered him receptive to innovation. He strove to introduce improvements in administrative techniques, machinery and processes and was an ardent advocate of research. In labour relations his name was connected with avowedly radical managerial initiatives to defuse tension at the turbulent centre of Broken Hill.

Equipped with this business aptitude, Fraser was important in bringing to fruition several significant developments in the Australian economy between the wars, such as the founding of the zinc-refining, hardwood pulp and paper, and aircraft industries, the revival of gold-mining in the 1930s and the extension of the silver-lead smelting, copper products and paints industries. His greatest achievement was at Port Pirie where, under his guidance, B.H.A.S. was transformed into the world leader in its branch of metallurgy. Fraser was president of the Australian Mines and Metals Association Inc., Melbourne, from 1932, represented Australia on the council of the Institution of Mining and Metallurgy, London, for seven years, and was a council-member for fifteen years and in 1923-24 president of the Australasian Institute of Mining and Metallurgy.

A tall, trim man, Fraser was polite and genial yet distant in his personal relationships, rarely revealing his emotions. Shy of publicity and conservative in dress, he projected an image of modesty and restraint. In business he was satisfied with discreet power and prestige while socially he was an unobtrusive member of the Establishment in Melbourne. He had little time for social activities or recreation although he enjoyed golf and racing and was a collector of antique furniture, often attending auction sales. He was a member of the Melbourne, Australian and Athenaeum clubs, Melbourne, and of the Union Club, Sydney. A firm believer in the work ethic, Fraser sought fulfilment and security almost solely from his work. He did not accumulate a large fortune.

Fraser died of cancer at his home in Toorak on 11 March 1944 and was cremated. His wife and two daughters survived him.

L. J. Hartnett, *Big wheels and little wheels* (Melb, 1964); W. S. Robinson, *If I remember rightly*, G. Blainey ed (Melb, 1967); *Aust J of Science*, 6 (1944), p 176; A'sian Inst of Mining and Metallurgy, *Procs*, Mar 1944, no 133, p 26; *Herald* (Melb), 11 Mar 1944, and *SMH*, 13 Mar 1944; Sir Colin Fraser papers (Univ Melb Archives).   JOHN KENNETT

FRASER, JOHN EDWARD (1877-1934), clerk, soldier and company director, was born on 16 August 1877 in Sydney, son of Scottish-born Donald Fraser, accountant, and his Irish-born wife Margaret Jane, née Armstrong. He attended Fort Street School, then joined the Sydney glass merchants, James Sandy & Co., as a clerk.

In 1894 Fraser began a long association with the militia when he enlisted in the 1st Regiment, New South Wales Scottish Rifles, later attaining the rank of colour sergeant. He served as a private in the South African War from November 1899 to January 1901 with the New South Wales Infantry Contingent (later known as 'E' Squadron, 1st New South Wales Mounted Rifles). The unit took part in the relief of Colesberg and the battles of Bloemfontein, Diamond Hill, Heidelberg, Elands River and Pretoria. He was awarded the Queen's South Africa medal. After the war he resumed work as a clerk and on 12 March 1902, at Waverley, Sydney, married Jessie Isabelle Ross with Presbyterian forms.

In 1906 Fraser transferred to the Australian Corps of Signals, Australian Military Forces (militia), as a company sergeant major and two years later was commissioned second lieutenant, rising to lieutenant in 1909. In 1911 he transferred to the Senior Cadets but in July 1913 rejoined the 24th Signal Company (Engineers) as captain in command. When war broke out he was mobilized for duty under the officer commanding Sydney Defended Port. On 11 August 1914 he was awarded the Colonial Auxiliary Forces Long Service Medal.

Fraser enlisted in the Australian Imperial Force on 22 March 1915 as a captain and brigade signal officer, 4th Light Horse Brigade. The unit embarked for Egypt on 31 May and was reorganized as part of the 2nd Australian Division Signal Company with Fraser second-in-command. Part of the company, led by Fraser, embarked for Gallipoli on 30 August on the transport *Southland*. On 2 September the ship was torpedoed but most of the men aboard were rescued by allied ships and landed at Anzac Cove on 4 September; there Fraser established the divisional signal office at Rest Gully and served at Gallipoli until the evacuation.

On 9 March 1916 he was appointed to command the 4th Division Signal Company and was promoted major on 1 May. Next month the company moved to France and assisted in all major divisional operations in 1916-18. Fraser was mentioned in dispatches in January and June 1917 and on 4 June was awarded the Distinguished Service Order. On 31 August 1918 he was transferred to the Australian Engineer Training Depot (signal section) in Britain. He returned to Australia in June 1919 and was demobilized next month.

Back in civilian life, Fraser became a salesman and later a director of Glass Products Ltd, Sydney. He retained an active interest in military affairs through his association with ex-servicemen's clubs and as an officer in the A.M.F. He was promoted lieut-colonel on 31 March 1921 and commanded the 2nd Divisional (Signal Services) Australian Engineers until March 1927. In 1921 he was awarded the Volunteer Officers' Decoration.

Fraser suffered from diabetes. Survived by his wife, two sons and a daughter, he died at his Petersham home on 3 June 1934 and was buried in Waverley cemetery. At his funeral a wreath was dropped from an aeroplane on behalf of Sir Charles Kingsford-Smith [q.v.], previously a signaller in Fraser's company.

Aust Defence Dept, *Official records of the Australian military contingents to the war in South Africa*, P. L. Murray ed (Melb, 1911); *London Gazette*, 1, 2 Jan, 4 June 1917; *Reveille* (Syd), July 1934; *SMH*, 5 June 1934; 2nd Australian Division Signal Company, AIF, A brief history, M95, Box 7/4, *and* War diaries, 2nd, *and* 4th Australian Division Signal Company, AIF (AWM).

KEVIN J. FEWSTER

FRASER, SIMON ALEXANDER (1845-1934), stockrider, whipmaker and bagpiper, was born on 13 February 1845 at Port Arthur, Van Diemen's Land, eldest son of the twelve children of Hugh Archibald Fraser (1796-1895) and his wife Mary, née Anderson (1827-1899). Hugh Fraser, a Scottish magistrate, migrated to New South Wales in 1828, later becoming an overseer in the penal settlement at Port Arthur where he earned a reputation for fairness and humanity. When Simon was a boy the family moved to Barwite, near Mansfield in Victoria; this district was Simon Fraser's home for much of his life although in 1908-09 he lived at Warrnambool, teaching and making and repairing bagpipes and fiddles.

The Frasers were all musical and Simon played the violin, flute, concertina, accordion and bagpipes. His mother, who claimed descent from the MacCrimmons, traditionally hereditary pipers to the clan MacLeod, taught him the piobaireachd (pibroch) vocables, secretly handed down by word of mouth and by lilting from mother to eldest son. These vocables are known as 'canntaireachd'. He also taught the secret language of the pipers in which by inserting extra notes a warning could be given. About 1816 Simon's father had written down the canntaireachd direct from Iain Dubh Mac-Crimmon and these he handed on to his son. When an appeal came from folklorists in Scotland, seeking lost piobaireachd vocables, Simon Fraser sent tunes; many of these letters and manuscripts are now in the National Library of Scotland, Edinburgh.

Fraser thought nothing of riding from Mansfield to Benalla and back to take lessons from the famous piper Peter Bruce. When droving sheep to Melbourne he would dismount from his horse, leave his brother William to control the flock, and walk ahead playing. He made his own bagpipes and was reputedly the first to use kangaroo-skin in preference to the traditional sheep-skin. He won championship contests throughout Australia.

He learned the craft of making stockwhips from Nangus Jack, an Aboriginal stockman whose whips were treasured by pioneer stockmen. Fraser could plait sixteen strands of leather into a whip supple enough to pull through a ¼ in. (6 mm) auger-hole. He wove forty-four strands into the longest whip that had been made in Australia. Don Hassell of Benalla was the only man able to crack this whip and he performed the 'triple crack' before the duke and duchess of York in Melbourne in 1901. Fraser whips made by Simon and his son were taken by John Rymill [q.v.] in the early 1930s for sledge-team work on his polar expeditions.

Simon Fraser was an outstanding buckjumper and steeplechase rider, winning many events. He once challenged any man in the world to compete with him in a triple event; playing the pipes, riding a buckjumper and plaiting the longest whip. No one took up the challenge. A student of both Bible and Koran, he was a great reader and a radical thinker, always ready to enter a debate — which was frequently fiery.

On 25 November 1872 at Mount Battery station, Mansfield, he married Florence (Flora) MacMillan, a skilled Scottish dancer. With five of their eight children Fraser formed a band, touring Victoria and once playing on request at Government House. Two daughters played clarinet and piccolo; three sons, piano, second violin and harp; Simon played first violin. His son Hugh was a champion piper of Australia and, taught by his father, also made excellent stock-whips; both men declared that plaiting kept their fingers supple for fingering the pipes.

Described at 84 as lean and clear eyed, with a shock of snow-white hair, Simon lived in old age with his son and grandchildren in Melbourne. He died in hospital at Mansfield on 17 April 1934, survived by three sons and three daughters.

J. Gillison, *Colonial doctor and his town* (Melb, 1974); B. Orme, *The piobaireachd of Simon Fraser with Canntaireachd* (priv print, Edinburgh, 1979); *Mansfield Guardian*, 13 October 1883; *Herald* (Melb), 11 Apr 1929.   JOAN GILLISON

FRATER, WILLIAM (1890-1974), artist and stained-glass designer, was born on 31 January 1890 at Ochiltree Castle, near Linlithgow, Scotland, son of William Frater, factor to Lord Rosebery [q.v.5, Primrose], and his wife Sarah, née Manson. His father died shortly after, leaving four children to be brought up by an uncle at West Ochiltree Farm. After education at Kingscavil Primary School and Bridgend Public School, Frater studied for a year at Linlithgow Academy. Late in 1905 he accepted a three-year apprenticeship in the Glasgow glass studio of Oscar Patterson, who encouraged him to enrol at the School of Art. He won the Haldane Scholarship for drawing in 1906 and remained at the school until 1909.

His ambition to become a painter was quickened by the local milieu, especially the Glasgow school's vigorous brushwork stemming from French Impressionism and the transition to the Glasgow Colourism of J. D. Ferguson and S. J. Peploc. Frater absorbed their protest against established fashion, and their dislike of niggling finish and superfluous facts. However he was prevented by his guardian from entering the final painting classes at the school.

Family discord caused him to migrate to Australia in the *Norseman*, arriving in Melbourne in September 1910. He was refused admission to the National Gallery School of Art by Bernard Hall [q.v.], accepted a five-year contract to be in charge of stained-glass design at Brooks, Robinson & Co. Ltd, and enrolled in the Victorian Artists' Society life class. After ten months he returned to Britain and in 1912-13 completed his training at Glasgow in the senior painting classes at the School of Art. In 1914 he returned to Melbourne and on 15 May 1915 at West Hawthorn Presbyterian Church he married Winifred Dow, a tailoress.

In the next twenty-five years 'Jock' Frater built up a high reputation as a craftsman and stained-glass designer: at first with Brooks, Robinson, where he resumed his earlier post, and then with E. L. Yencken [q.v.] & Co. Pty Ltd. The west window of Wesley Church, Lonsdale Street, Melbourne, he regarded as his most significant design. His contribution to art in Australia was, however, as a painter who introduced Post-Impressionist principles and challenged the notion that art was an imitation of nature.

Frater's *oeuvre* developed between 1915 and 1920 towards a simplification of design, an interplay of massed lights and shadows, and sonorous low-keyed colour that reflected his interest in the classical seventeenth century painters in interaction with the analytical tonal theory of Max Meldrum [q.v.]. Notable examples of his predominantly figure and portrait paintings are 'The artist's wife reading' (1915) and 'Portrait of artist's wife' (1919). An experimental Colourist phase followed in the next decade. His first solo exhibition was held in May 1923 at the Athenaeum, Melbourne, and he exhibited with the Twenty Melbourne Painters from the late 1920s, and the Contemporary Group of Melbourne in the 1930s.

In a lecture on modern art in 1925, Frater stated the basic position from which the rest of his *oeuvre* stems. 'Copying nature is not an art; ... to copy effects of light tends to destroy form and colour'. His approach in the 1930s was markedly indebted to Cézanne, especially in the portraits which predominated until his retirement from stained-glass designing in 1940. In the next years his exploration of coastal, bushland and mining areas of Victoria provided themes for landscapes exhibited at the Contemporary Art Society, and in his solo shows at Georges Gallery, Melbourne, and the Macquarie Galleries, Sydney, in 1946. He visited Central Australia in 1950 and Port Douglas, North Queensland, in 1952. His view that great art always had qualities of disturbing strangeness was outlined in an article in *Art in Australia* (March 1941) and in *Daub* (1959-60). His later major exhibitions were at the Australian Galleries, Melbourne, in 1958, the Victorian Artists' Society in 1963, and a retrospective at the National Gallery of Victoria in 1966. Frater was a revered president of the Victorian Artists' Society from 1963 until 1972, exhibiting annually with the society during the last decade of his career and filling three galleries at his final exhibition in July 1973.

Frater gave aggressive leadership to the small group of modernists in the 1920s. His example, teaching, lecturing and crusty style of polemic did much to disrupt the academic style as the arbiter of pictorial values and to pioneer a change of taste in the community.

In 1974 Frater was appointed O.B.E. for his services to art. His work is represented in galleries and private collections throughout Australia as well as the Glasgow Art Gallery. He died at his home at Alphington on 28 November 1974 and was buried in Arthurs Creek cemetery. He was survived by four sons and a daughter.

A.J.V. Shore, *40 years seek and find* (Melb, 1957); Bernard Smith, *Australian painting 1788-1960* (Melb, 1962); J. Hetherington, *Australian painters* (Melb, 1963); L. Course, 'Tradition and new accents . . .', *The gallery on Eastern Hill*, C. B. Christesen ed (Melb, 1970); *Meanjin Q*, 1948, no 1; *Studio* (Lond), 1953, no 145; *Herald* (Melb), 28 Nov. 1974.

                                                    L. J. COURSE

FRAZER, CHARLES EDWARD (1880-1913), politician, was born on 2 January 1880 at Yarrawonga, Victoria, son of James Bannerman Frazer, farmer, and his wife Susan née Atkinson. He attended the local school until he was 15 when the lure of gold attracted him to Western Australia. Employed on arrival in Perth in the Railways Department, he qualified as a first-class engine driver in 1899 before settling on the goldfields at Boulder as a mine-engine driver.

His ability and interest in local and union affairs were soon apparent. Frazer was elected president of the Boulder branch of his union early in 1902 and was secretary next year of the Goldfields Trades and Labour Council. He became active in the local Australian Natives' Association and was president in 1902; in November he was elected to the Kalgoorlie Town Council. When a Labor candidate was sought for the Federal seat of Kalgoorlie in 1903 to oppose the free trader, (Sir) John Kirwan [q.v.], Frazer easily secured the nomination. Despite a cyclone on election day that kept voters away, he was rewarded with a majority as convincing as it was unexpected. The miners appreciated his fierce advocacy of White Australia as much as his relish for drinking, smoking and gambling. Tall, handsome and confident, he was equally popular with women voters.

Frazer rapidly gained a reputation as a dedicated radical. Initially 'a Parliamentary larrikin', he worked so assiduously at improving his political skills that he was soon regarded as leadership material. He studied law, frequently reading textbooks during parliamentary debates, but did not qualify. He campaigned successfully to provide caucus with the power to select Labor ministries, formerly the prerogative of the parliamentary leader, then J. C. Watson [q.v.] who resigned temporarily as a result. Frazer also urged that Labor should withdraw its support from the minority Protectionist government: with his 'caustic, bitter tongue', he led the way in parliament by subjecting the government to 'rhetorical assault and battery'. Eventually, on his motion in November 1908, caucus decided to sever relations with the Protectionists, and in the ensuing short-lived Labor government Frazer was assistant government whip. After Labour's 1910 election victory a closely contested caucus ballot elevated him to the ministry. He was 30 years and 4 months: in eight decades after Federation there has been no younger minister. On 31 August 1904 at St Peter's Church of England, Melbourne, he had married Mary Kinnane, a Kalgoorlie shop assistant; her family disapproved of her marriage to a non-Roman Catholic.

Initially Frazer was honorary minister, twice serving capably as acting treasurer; on the death of E. L. Batchelor [q.v.7] in October 1911 he hoped to secure the treasury portfolio but became postmaster-general instead. His administration was again competent, and he was proud of the increased constructions and installations he had authorized. Privately he was contemptuous of the postal employees who were 'unreasonable', 'far too well paid' and like 'spoilt children'; he regretted cabinet's insistence that their demands be met. After Labor narrowly lost the election in June 1913, the new government replaced the design of the penny stamp Labor had introduced, although it lasted for most other values for many years; Frazer had originated the design which featured a kangaroo 'rampant upon a purely White Australia'.

Despite periodic ill health his death from pneumonia after a brief illness on 25 November 1913 was totally unexpected. His great capacity, energy and promise were unquestioned. The particularly glowing tributes reflected his general popularity and Labor's great loss. Frazer was better equipped to fill the leadership void after the conscription split than either F. G. Tudor [q.v.] or M. Charlton [q.v.7], and might have led Federal Labor out of the political wilderness earlier. He had the requisite ambition for leadership. Shortly before he was promoted to the cabinet he confided that if he were not a minister soon and prime minister within ten years he would quit politics. The first minister to be flown in an aeroplane, he was also one of the few to have a racehorse, Charlie Frazer, named after him. 'A brilliant life spoilt by too quick success and too much leisure', concluded R. A. Crouch [q.v.]. Leaving an estate sworn for probate at £1168 and survived by his wife, Frazer was buried in Melbourne general cemetery.

P. M. Weller (ed), *Caucus minutes*, 1 (Melb, 1975); *Southern Sphere*, 1 July 1910; *Univ Studies in History*, 4 (1966); *Punch* (Melb), 2 Sept 1909, 19 May 1910; *Argus*, 26 Nov 1913; *Aust Worker*, 27 Nov 1913; Crouch memoirs (LaTL); Frazer papers (NL).   ROSS MCMULLIN

FREAME, WYKEHAM HENRY KOBA (1885?-1941), adventurer, soldier, orchardist and interpreter, is believed to have been born on 28 February 1885 at Osaka, Japan, though on his enlistment in the Australian Imperial Force he gave his birthplace as Kitscoty, Canada. He was the son of Henry Freame, sometime teacher of English at the Kai-sei Gakko in Japan, and a Japanese woman, Shizu, née Kitagawa. As he was fluent in Japanese and spoke English with an accent it is likely that he was brought up in Japan. In 1906 he was a merchant seaman and on 19 July of that year married Edith May Soppitt at St John's Anglican Church, Middlesbrough, England.

Freame probably came to Australia in 1911 and on enlisting in the A.I.F. on 28 August 1914 described himself as a horse-breaker of Glen Innes, New South Wales. Posted to the 1st Battalion as a private, he embarked for Egypt on the troopship *Afric* on 18 October and was promoted lance corporal on 7 January 1915. On 25 April he landed at Anzac and after three days of heavy fighting was promoted sergeant. He was awarded one of the A.I.F.'s first Distinguished Conduct Medals for 'displaying the utmost gallantry in taking water to the firing-line although twice hit by snipers'. He was mentioned in dispatches for his work at Monash Valley in June when C. E. W. Bean [q.v.7] described him as 'probably the most trusted scout at Anzac'.

Having served in the Hottentot rising of 1904-06 in German East Africa and in the Mexican wars, Freame was an accomplished scout before joining the A.I.F. He had an uncanny sense of direction and would wriggle like an eel deep into no man's land, and at night even into the enemy trenches, to pick up information. His dark complexion and peculiar intonation of speech had led his companions to believe that he was Mexican — an impression which he reinforced at Anzac where, in cowboy fashion, he carried two revolvers in holsters on his belt, another in a holster under his armpit and a bowie knife in his boot pocket. On 15 August he was wounded during operations at Lone Pine and was evacuated to Australia. He was discharged as medically unfit on 20 November 1916.

Freame settled on the Kentucky estate in New England, New South Wales, when the estate was subdivided for a soldier sett-lement scheme, and was appointed government storekeeper. He eventually acquired a Kentucky block and·was a successful orchardist. His wife died in 1939 and on 16 August 1940 he married Harriett Elizabeth Brainwood, nurse and divorced petitioner, at St John's Anglican Church, Milson's Point, Sydney. With the outbreak of World War II he offered his services to the Australian Military Forces and in December 1939 was planted among the Japanese community in Sydney as an agent by military intelligence. In September 1940 he was appointed as an interpreter on the staff of the first Australian legation to Tokyo.

Early in April 1941, however, Freame returned to Australia because of ill health and was admitted to North Sydney Hospital. He died on 27 May and was buried in Northern Suburbs cemetery with Anglican rites. His death certificate records the cause of death as cancer though on his return to Australia he had severe throat injuries which greatly impaired his speech. His throat condition combined with his repetition of the words 'They got me' suggested that he had been the victim of a garrotting in Japan. He considered that the attack was the consequence of the injudicious wording of the announcement in the Australian press of his posting to Tokyo. He had been described as employed by the Defence Department at a time when he was telling his Japanese acquaintances another story. Medical evidence affirmed that his throat condition was not inconsistent with attempted strangulation.

C. E. W. Bean, *The story of Anzac*, 1, 2 (Syd, 1921, 1924); B. V. Stacy, F. J. Kingdom & H. V. Chedgey, *The history of the 1st Battalion, A.I.F. (1914-1919)*, Syd, 1931); *Reveille* (Syd), Sept 1931; *SMH*, 28, 29, 30 May 1941; *Northern Daily Leader*, 5 June 1941; Japan gazette hong list and trade directory, 1876; Dept of Army, Classified general correspondence 1937-45, MP 729/6, 15/403/16, *and* Dept of External Affairs, Correspondence files 1901-43, CRS' A981 (Aust) 186 (AAO).   JAMES W. COURTNEY

FREEDMAN, DAVID ISAAC (1874-1939), rabbi, was born on 17 April 1874 at Budapest, Austria-Hungary, son of Moses Freedman, merchant, and his wife Esther. Two years later the family went to London where he was educated at the Bell Lane School, Jews' College (1891-97) and the University of London (B.A., 1894). He was encouraged to write by the author Israel Zangwill and contributed to journals; in 1889 he was naturalized.

In 1897 Freedman arrived in Western Australia on the *Ophir* to minister to the Perth Hebrew congregation. He was a bearded, curly-haired, handsome young man. Joined by his fiancée, Anne Florence

(Mollie) Cohen, he married her on 22 December; they had two sons. He became a Freemason, established the Perth Hebrew Philanthropic Society and in 1899 wrote a report stressing the value of Hebrew education and the need to foster pride in the history and traditions of Judaism. He became headmaster of the Perth Hebrew School where he improved teaching methods by writing and setting to music over 150 songs covering the major teachings of the Jewish religion. In 1903 he set up a fund to aid victims of the Kishineff pogrom. From 1904 he edited the *West Australian Craftsman*, Scottish Freemasonry's official organ in the State. Next year he and his wife visited England. Freedman was a keen cricketer and tennis player and he encouraged by his membership a wide range of cultural and charitable activities within the Jewish congregation and in the wider Perth community. He became well known as a lecturer on literary and historical subjects. In 1910-11 he joined a delegation urging the State government to appoint a commission on the establishment of a university for Perth.

On 1 October 1915 Freedman was appointed as a chaplain in the Australian Imperial Force and he served briefly on Gallipoli and in Egypt and France. Throughout it was his policy to write home to the family of every Jewish soldier whom he met. In February 1916 the British War Office appointed him chaplain to all Jewish men in the Mediterranean Expeditionary Force. In France, for two years he took no leave and in December 1917 was mentioned in dispatches. Next year he returned to Perth, his war appointment terminated. During his absence the title of rabbi had been conferred on him by the London authorities of his faith. Perth Jews were relieved to have him back and they protested so vociferously.when he was offered a promotion in Sydney in 1920 that he remained with them for the rest of his life. Freedman had visited Palestine and on his return he became president of the Western Australian Zionist Association. He also became active in the Returned Sailors' and Soldiers' Imperial League of Australia and was its State president in 1924. Among the organizations to benefit from his membership were the Soldiers' Children Scholarship Trust, Jewish Returned Soldiers' Circle, Australian Jewish Welfare Society, Jewish and non-Jewish dramatic societies, Children's Protection Society, Victoria League, Institute for the Blind, Prison Gate Committee and the Home of Peace for the aged.

In 1932-38 Freedman was a member of the Senate of the University of Western Australia. In 1933 he went to London as a delegate to the British Empire Service League's sixth biennial congress; from there he went with the Australian delegation to the fourteenth assembly of the League of Nations at Geneva and spoke on the German-Jewish question which dominated the proceedings. Next year in Perth he spoke out against the 'good deal of anti-Jewish feeling in Australia' and called on the Federal government to make it a criminal offence to circulate racial propaganda. In 1936 he was appointed O.B.E.

As a pastor Freedman was orthodox yet understanding, benign and good-humoured. He possessed phenomenal energy and 'had his own methods of facing difficulties — sometimes with superb diplomacy and tact, at other times with a direct vigour that proved him to be a man of courage'. Until late in life he wore a monocle and a neatly waxed moustache. He never owned a car and enjoyed playing golf with the leaders of Perth's other religious denominations. Survived by his wife and sons, Freedman died on 24 June 1939 from a coronary occlusion suffered while at a hospital committee meeting. Two thousand mourners attended his burial in Karrakatta cemetery. The Jewish Centre and Perth's Hebrew congregation are now located in Freedman Avenue, Mount Lawley.

J. S. Battye (ed), *Cyclopedia of Western Australia*, 2 (Adel, 1913); H. Boas (comp), *The Australian Y.M.C.A. with the Jewish soldier of the Australian Imperial Force* (priv pub, Lond, 1919); P. Masel, *The story of the Perth Hebrew congregation* (Perth, 1946); *Western Mail*, 12 July 1918, 22 Jan 1920; *Westralian Judean*, 1 Apr 1937, 1 July 1939; Aust Jewish Hist Soc, *J*, 1 (1939), pt 2; *West Australian Craftsman*, 8 July 1939; *West Australian* (Perth), 18 Jan 1905, 24, 26, 27 June 1939; *SMH*, 6 Nov 1934.

O. B. TOFLER

FREELEAGUS, CHRISTY KOSMAS (1889-1957), businessman and honorary consul, was born Christos Frilingos on 16 November 1889 at Frilinganika on the island of Kythera, Greece, one of twelve children of Kosmas Frilingos, farmer, and his wife Irene, née Panagitapolou. He was educated at Potamos College on Kythera. As that island lacked opportunity, inspired by stories of sailors returning from Australian goldfields, with his elder brother Peter he left for Sydney rather than the usual goal, America; they arrived in October 1901. He stayed there until 1903 attending Fort Street Public School.

When he joined Peter in Brisbane, they first established a small restaurant, then added the Paris Café in Queen Street and later, the larger Astoria Café, a Brisbane landmark in Edward Street. The remaining eight brothers arrived over the next decade and in 1911 the family established Fresh Food and Ice Co. Ltd. Until his death Freeleagus remained managing director of what became one of the State's biggest wholesale and retail food chains; it provided the first employment over the years for hundreds of Greek migrants.

Freeleagus believed that Australia and Brisbane had a future and was determined to share it and to encourage fellow migrants to share it also. He read widely and, in spite of long working hours, took part in competitive sport, particularly swimming and lawn bowls; he represented Queensland at lawn bowls. Although an enthusiast for Australia, he desired passionately to make his Greek heritage better known and respected among Australians. On the recommendation of his friend Lockhard H. Spence, who retired in 1919 as first honorary consul for Greece in Queensland, Freeleagus was then appointed consul-general, the first of that rank any country had appointed to Queensland. In 1925 the post was reduced to a Queensland consulate. He was dean of the consular corps in 1954-57.

Freeleagus sailed for Europe in January 1921 and served in the Greek army during the Greek-Turkish war. In Greece he urged migration to Australia, and on 22 May 1922 delivered a lecture on Australia to the Athens Literary Society; the National Library of Greece holds a copy. While visiting London, he met Venezilos and sought assistance for Greek migration from the high commissioner Sir Joseph Cook [q.v.]. Passing through Melbourne in January 1923, he met Ariadne Kokonis, daughter of a Greek refugee from Smyrna who had settled in Melbourne after the Greek-Turkish war. They were married in January 1925 and had three children.

Encouraged by Freeleagus, the first Greek communities in Queensland outside Brisbane were formed at Biloela and Home Hill in the 1920s and 1930s. When royal commissioner T. A. Ferry [q.v.] attacked the behaviour of Greeks in the north in 1925, Freeleagus defended them in the Sydney press. During World War II and particularly after the Italian attack on Greece he led patriotic fund appeals, culminating in the highly successful Greek Day on 19 November 1941. That year he was awarded the silver cross of George I, the gold cross came in 1951. An appeal for victims of the 1953 earthquake in western Greece raised the largest amount sent from Australia.

A high-ranking Freemason and a member of various choral societies, Freeleagus was a founding member of the Royal Automobile Club of Queensland and a leader of the Chamber of Commerce. A founder of the first Greek Association, he was prominent in the religious and political life of the community. He died of a heart attack on 16 May 1957 and was buried in Toowong cemetery after a large funeral.

Queensland and Queenslanders (Brisb, 1936); *SMH*, 21 Jan 1921, 27 Jan 1923, 19 June 1925; *Queenslander*, 22 Jan 1921, 24 Jan 1929, 4 Apr 1935; *Brisbane Courier*, 26 Nov 1921, 5 Jan 1925; *Daily Standard*, 5 Jan 1925; M. P. Tsounis, Greek communities in Australia (Ph.D. thesis, Univ Adel, 1971).   ALEX FREELEAGUS

FREEMAN, AMBROSE WILLIAM (1873-1930), mining engineer, and **WILLIAM ADDISON** (1874-1956), solicitor and businessman, were born on 13 February 1873 and on 6 October 1874 in Sydney, second and third sons of native-born parents William Freeman, draftsman in the Surveyor-General's Office and later president of the Land Court, and his wife Lucy Rose, née Fisher. They were educated at Newington College and William also at Sydney Boys' High School. Ambrose was a clerk with James Moir & Co., stock and station agents, in 1889-92 and on the staff of the Australian Mutual Provident Society Ltd until 1895, while studying as an evening student from 1893 at the University of Sydney (B.A., 1896). William was articled to solicitors C. J. Ross at Tamworth and D. W. Roxburgh of Norton [q.v.5], Smith & Co., Sydney.

In 1896 the brothers went to the Western Australian goldfields at Coolgardie. Ambrose became part-owner with T. W. Horton [q.v.] of the Lancefield mine which they later sold through the agency of Herbert Hoover [q.v.]. Back in Sydney, William was admitted solicitor in the Supreme Court on 3 March 1900 and, on 28 August 1901 at St Andrew's Cathedral, he married Edith Hannah Palmer. They had no children. In 1903 he set up his own practice, specializing in company law.

After five years in the west, Ambrose returned to the university to study mining and metallurgy; he graduated bachelor of engineering in 1904. He had become an associate member of the Institution of Mining and Metallurgy, London, in 1903 (member, 1912). After visiting Britain, Europe and the United States of America in 1904-05, in September 1905, with Horton and William, he was a director and general manager of the Harden Gold Mine Ltd in New South Wales and from 1907 all three were directors of the Lobb's Hole Copper Mine (N.L.), near Kiandra, which William managed. At the same time Ambrose ran an office in Sydney as a mining consultant. On 22 June 1915 at Potts Point he married Dr Jessie Strahorn Aspinall [q.v.7].

In 1911 the brothers with H. E. Pratten, A. W. Palfreyman and Robert Cran [qq.v.] had formed the Malaysian Syndicate to obtain tin-mining concessions in the Federated Malay States and Burma. Next year Ambrose became chairman and managing director of Austral Malay Tin Ltd; William and Pratten were the other directors. Ambrose devoted his energies henceforward to tin-mining in Malaya and Burma, and divided his time between his office in Challis House, Sydney, and Taiping, Perak. His wife accompanied him on several visits. In an industry of which investors generally were wary, his loyalty and devotion to his companies reflected his energy, determination, probity and strict sense of justice. He provided career opportunities for Australian graduates. Until 1930 he remained chairman and managing director of Austral Malay Tin Ltd and four subsidiary tin dredging companies in the Federated Malay States and Burma, including Thabawleik Tin Dredging Ltd. He enjoyed golf and was a member of the Australian Club, Sydney.

Returning to Sydney from Penang, Ambrose Freeman died from heart failure in the *Nieuw Holland* on 1 October 1930 and was buried at sea with Anglican rites. He was survived by his wife, two sons and two daughters. His estate was valued for probate at £18 464.

In April 1918 William had enlisted in the Australian Imperial Force, in 'Carmichael's [q.v.7] Thousand'; he attended a non-commissioned officers' school in September and was discharged in November. Already a director of Austral Malay Tin Ltd and its subsidiaries, he took over as chairman after his brother's death and successully guided them through World War II. In 1928 he and C. A. Banks, a New Zealander, had founded the versatile international mining group, Placer Development Ltd in Canada; for many years Freeman was its president and also chairman of its first big offshoot, Bulolo Gold Dredging Ltd. In 1931 he made a six-month tour of Canada, the United States and Britain.

Freeman was active from the 1930s in the search for minerals, oil and natural gas in Australia and New Guinea. He was chairman of Drillers Ltd, Gas Drillers Ltd, Kamilaroi Oil Co. Ltd, and Oil Search Ltd, which was working in Papua and New Guinea in partnership with the Anglo-Iranian Oil Co. Ltd and the Standard-Vacuum Oil Co. He was also chairman of Jantzen (Australia) Ltd, and a director of the Australasian Petroleum Co. Pty Ltd and Ready Mixed Concrete Ltd. An innovator with a rare blend of adventurousness, sagacity and integrity, he firmly believed that Australia should use her managerial and financial

expertise to establish successful overseas enterprises. Not all his speculations were successful (like the search for natural gas near Sydney), but he took his failures philosophically. He was expert in company law and insisted on correct English usage in commercial documents.

Outside business his chief interests were the turf and golf. Freeman was owner and part-owner of many racehorses including Silver Standard (second in the Melbourne Cup, Caulfield Cup and Metropolitan in 1936), a member of the Royal Sydney Golf Club and founder of the Lakes Golf Club and the Elanora Country Club. He was a member of the Australian Club in Sydney and the Athenaeum Club im Melbourne.

He died at his home in Kent Road, Rose Bay, Sydney on 2 April 1956 and was buried from St Michael's, in the Anglican section of South Head cemetery. His estate was valued for probate at £640 194.

Cyclopedia of N.S.W. (Syd, 1907); Inst of Mining and Metallurgy (Lond), *Trans*, 40 (1930-31), p 450; *SMH*, 15 May 1916, 25 Mar 1925, 1, 9 Oct 1930, 22 Jan, 18 July 1931, 14 Jan, 22 Dec 1933, 6 Feb 1934, 8 Feb, 19 Dec 1935, 11 Sept, 1 Oct 1937, 20 Dec 1946, 4 Apr, 4 Sept 1956; *Daily Telegraph*, 4 Apr 1956; *Bulletin*, 11 Apr 1956.   G. P. WALSH
ARTHUR CORBETT

FREEMAN, JESSIE STRAHORN; *see* ASPINALL

FREEMAN, PAUL (1884?-1921), deportee and Comintern functionary, was probably born in Germany but registered as an American citizen in 1916. After working as a miner in Pennsylvania and Nevada, United States of America, he arrived in New South Wales in 1911 and found work at Broken Hill. There he joined the Marxist Australian Socialist Party but later advocated the activist anarcho-syndicalist doctrines of the 'Chicago' Industrial Workers of the World. He campaigned against the conscription referenda of 1916 and 1917. After the proscribing of the I.W.W. in 1917 Freeman worked in a copper mine at Cloncurry, Queensland, and later became a prospector. He continued to propagate anti-war views and eventually attracted attention from Commonwealth and police authorities.

On 8 January 1919 Freeman was arrested outside Cloncurry under the War Precautions Act, was sent to Sydney, put aboard the *Sonoma* and deported to America. On reaching San Francisco he was refused admission to that country. After crossing the Pacific four times he began a hunger strike and when the *Sonoma* next berthed in Sydney his plight aroused the sympathy of many members of the labour movement. An angry crowd estimated at over 10 000 tried to board the ship to force his release; his case was also taken up by the Labor Council of New South Wales and the Australian Workers' Union. A second large demonstration led the government to remove Freeman from the *Sonoma*. The acting prime minister, W. A. Watt [q.v.], disclosed 'that Freeman refused to naturalise in Australia ... was an advocate of I.W.W. doctrines, and had made a statement to the effect that anyone going to the war was lower than a dog'. Despite protests he was deported to Germany in October 1919.

Freeman entered the Soviet Union on 30 April 1920 and visited Leningrad, Kiev and Murmansk. Converted to Soviet Communism, he unsuccessfully sought to represent the Australian I.W.W. at the second congress of the Communist International (Comintern); he was later a candidate for the executive committee of the Communist International at its third congress in Moscow in 1921.

In late 1920 Freeman was sent on a secret mission to Australia where he conducted propaganda for the first congress of the Red International of Labor Unions, held in Moscow in July 1921. He failed to bring together the feuding factions of the newly formed Communist Party of Australia. He arrived back in Moscow in time to attend the third Comintern congress but died of injuries sustained in the crash of an experimental monorail train on 24 July 1921. Freeman was travelling with his friend the prominent 'Commissar Artem' [q.v. F. A. Sergeev]; they were buried in a common grave by the Kremlin wall.

A. Davidson, *The Communist Party of Australia* (Stanford, California, 1969); B. Walker, *Solidarity forever* (Melb, 1972); F. Farrell, *International socialism and Australian labour* (Syd, 1981); *PD* (Cwlth), 1919 p 10022, 10328, 10491, 10661; *International Communist*, 28 May, 4, 11 June, 1 Oct 1921; *Aust Worker*, 5, 12 June, 17 July, 25 Sept, 9, 16 Oct 1919; *Worker's Weekly*, 30 July 1926; *Tribune* (Melb), 27 Mar, 3 Apr 1963; PM's correspondence files, item 1919/2012 (AAO, Canb).

FRANK FARRELL

FRENCH, CHARLES (1842-1933), horticulturalist, naturalist and entomologist, and CHARLES HAMILTON (1868-1950), naturalist and entomologist, were father and son. Charles senior was born on 10 September 1842 at Lewisham, Kent, England, son of John French, jeweller, and his wife Ellen, née Tucker. After the death of his father in 1848 and the remarriage of his mother, the family migrated to Victoria, arriving on 6 April

1852 and settling at Cheltenham. Busy with clearing land and assisting bullock-wagons transporting supplies to the goldfields, young French was unable to spend much time pursuing his interest in natural history, particularly the collection of insects, which he had developed in England.

In 1858 he was apprenticed to nurseryman James Scott of Hawthorn, who specialized in the growing of trees. Later he transferred to the nurseries at South Yarra of Alex Bogie, a rose specialist, and of Joseph Harris who was a general nurseryman with pot plants as a specialty. There he met (Sir) Ferdinand Mueller [q.v.5], director of the Botanic Gardens, with whom he formed a life friendship. His outstanding horticultural expertise appealed to Mueller and in 1865 French was appointed to the nursery and gardening staff of the gardens. After his marriage with Presbyterian forms on 23 May 1867 to Janet Callander he lived in one of the lodges attached to the gardens.

On the appointment in 1873 of W. R. Guilfoyle [q.v.4] as curator of the gardens, French was transferred to the nursery complex in charge of the propagation of ferns and tropical plants. Guilfoyle in his first annual report in 1874 praised him for his 'aptitude and attention'; he had over 250 species of ferns in cultivation at that time. In 1881 he was transferred to the Phytological Museum of Melbourne, later the National Herbarium, under Mueller's control. By 1886 he had become first herbarium assistant at a salary of £225.

French had taken up his interest in insects again in 1860. In 1874 he contributed an article on timber-boring insects to the Department of Agriculture's annual report: this is now considered to be the first article on economic entomology published in Victoria. In 1889 French was made government entomologist, a post created to investigate the increasing ravages of native and introduced insects. Apart from routine identifications and inspections, his major work was the *Handbook of the destructive insects of Victoria*; Volumes I-V were published in 1891-1911; Volume VI, with text and coloured plates, was prepared but never published. At his suggestion an intercolonial departmental conference considered uniform vegetation diseases legislation and, following the passing of the Victorian Act in 1896, he was appointed chief inspector and was responsible for a standardized spraying and fumigation programme for fruit-trees. In 1907 he attended an International Conference of Entomologists in London, a prelude to his retirement in 1908. He is now generally regarded as having laid the foundation of economic entomology in Victoria. He published twenty-two articles on the subject between 1889 and 1912. He was a fellow of the Linnean Society of London, of the Royal Horticultural Society of England and of the Society of Isis, Dresden, Germany.

French was a foundation committee-member in 1880 of the Field Naturalists' Club of Victoria. He wrote extensively on Victorian ferns in the *Southern Science Record* in 1884-87, information that was incorporated in Mueller's two-volume *Key to the system of Victorian plants* (1885-88). During his life he made three major collections of Australian Coleoptera, one of which went to the Dutch East Indies (Indonesia), one to Holland and the other to the National Museum in Melbourne.

French's first wife had died in 1890; on 6 April 1891 at Christ Church, South Yarra, he married 28-year-old Emma Charlotte Merchant. After her death in 1908 he married Rachel De Lany on 28 June 1911 at St John's Church, Camberwell. He died at his home at Malvern on 21 May 1933, survived by his wife, his son and a daughter of the first marriage, and a daughter of the second.

Charles Hamilton French was born on 10 June 1868 at the Botanical Reserve. He was educated at the local state school and later entered the Melbourne offices of a solicitor and a doctor as a junior clerk. Assisting his father on collecting expeditions, he acquired a wide knowledge of Australian plants, birds, insects, reptiles and Aboriginal artefacts. On 1 July 1883 he joined the staff of the herbarium as a junior assistant, later rising to third herbarium assistant. For thirteen years his work required him to travel throughout Victoria collecting plant specimens; he also gathered insect specimens for his father.

On 5 September 1891 at South Yarra, French married Ada Crook, 19-year-old daughter of a drawing-master. In 1896 he was appointed to the Department of Agriculture as an inspector under the Vegetation Diseases Act; later, as this work developed in the direction of insect control, he became assistant government entomologist. In 1907-27 he contributed thirty-one articles on entomological studies to the monthly *Journal of Agriculture* as sole author and nine as joint author, writing as Charles French junior. From 1931 until his retirement in 1933 he was biologist to the Department of Agriculture and officer-in-charge of the science branch at Burnley Gardens.

With his father, French had attended informal meetings of naturalists which led to the formation of the Field Naturalists' Club of Victoria, but because he was a junior his admission as a member was delayed until July 1883. His association through the club, with (Sir) Baldwin Spencer [q.v.] led to a large collection of Aboriginal artefacts and skulls going to the National Museum, and his interest in native orchids resulted in the discovery of many new species in the State. He was elected an honorary member of the club in August 1937. His few articles in the *Victorian Naturalist* were on orchid localities and on native insects and birds of economic importance.

French lectured on entomology at the University of Melbourne for some years, and also to horticultural students at Burnley Gardens. In retirement he found much satisfaction in growing orchids, begonias and ferns in his glasshouses at Canterbury. He died in a private hospital at Deepdene on 17 July 1950 and was buried in Burwood cemetery, survived by three of his four sons and two of his three daughters.

J. H. Willis, *Botanical pioneers in Victoria* (Melb, 1949); R. T. M. Pescott, History of the Royal Botanic Gardens, Melbourne (MS held by author, Camberwell, Melb and Oxford Univ Press).

R. T. M. PESCOTT

FRENCH, SIR GEORGE ARTHUR (1841-1921), soldier and commissioner of police, was born on 19 June 1841 at Roscommon, Ireland, son of John French of Mornington Park, Dublin, and his wife Isabella, née Hamilton. Educated at the Royal Military College, Sandhurst, and the Royal Military Academy, Woolwich, he was commissioned as a lieutenant in the Royal Artillery on 19 June 1860. He married Janet Clarke, née Innes, of Kingston, Canada, in 1862. In 1862-66 he was adjutant, Royal Artillery, at Kingston, and was appointed inspector of warlike stores in Quebec in 1869. In December 1870, shortly before the withdrawal of British troops from Canada, he was made available on loan to the Canadian Army and appointed inspector of artillery, and chief instructor of the school of gunnery at Kingston, with local rank of lieut-colonel. On 11 December 1872 he was promoted captain, R.A.

In view of the Red River Rebellion of 1869-70, the problem of American whisky pedlars and the need to protect the building of a railway west to the Pacific Ocean, the Canadian prime minister, (Sir) John Macdonald, decided to establish a mounted police force. French became the first permanently appointed commissioner of the North West Mounted Police (now Royal Canadian Mounted Police) on 1 December 1873. In November Macdonald's government had fallen and in spite of little support from the new administration French set about raising his force. In July 1874 they set out on their famous march from the Red

River in Manitoba over 400 miles (650 km) west to the Rocky Mountains. Under his command the mounted police established a reputation for honesty, justice and fair play but friction between French and the new government became acute and in July 1876 his appointment was terminated. For his services in Canada he was appointed C.M.G. in 1877. He returned to England for duty with the Royal Artillery and in July 1881 was promoted major.

On 1 September 1883 French was appointed commandant of the Queensland Defence Force, with the local rank of colonel. Shortly after, he submitted a special report on the poor state of the colony's army, recommending the establishment of a permanent battery of artillery and a militia force, and the downgrading of the volunteer force to rifle club status. In 1885 the Queensland Defence Force was reorganized under the 1884 Defence Act, framed by French and based mainly on the Canadian system. He was also largely responsible for obtaining the agreement of the Australian colonies for the construction of fortifications on Thursday Island and King George Sound from 1891 to 1893. In 1891 he employed over 1400 troops to help break the shearers' strike, on one occasion personally controlling an advance with bayonets fixed against the strikers. His appointment in Queensland was twice renewed; in August 1891 he left for England.

In October 1887 French had been promoted lieut-colonel, R.A., and in August 1891 was appointed commander, R.A., Dover. In June 1892 he was appointed chief instructor, school of gunnery, Shoeburyness, and in November was promoted colonel for 'distinguished services other than in the field'. He was appointed colonel, R.A., Bombay, in January 1894 and in April next year officiating brigadier general, R.A., Bombay Command.

French was appointed commandant of the New South Wales Military Forces with the local rank of major general in March 1896. Despite his attitude towards the volunteers in Queensland the strength of the volunteer movement in New South Wales almost quadrupled under his command. The Australian Horse, Australian Rifles, National Guard and the Railway Corps were formed and the existing regiments greatly increased in strength. Although bitterly disappointed that he was not released for service in the South African War, French's energetic training programme was largely responsible for the high regard held for the New South Wales contingents serving in South Africa. In May 1900 he was promoted major general, R.A., and in 1901 Sir John Forrest [q.v.], minister for defence, appointed him

president of the Federal military committee to draft a defence act for the Commonwealth. He was an active president of the United Service Institution of New South Wales in 1896-1901. In January 1902 he handed over command to Brigadier General H. Finn [q.v.] and next month sailed for England where he retired on 3 September; that year he was appointed K.C.M.G. French died on 7 July 1921 at Kensington, London, and after a service at St Luke's Church, was buried with full military honours in Brompton cemetery. He was survived by two sons and three daughters.

French played a significant part in organizing the mounted police in Canada, in reorganizing the military forces of Queensland and New South Wales and in drafting the legislation for the establishment of the Australian defence forces. Somewhat intolerant of politicians, he was a vigorous professional army officer who, despite his not having had active service in the field, served with distinction in whatever appointment he held.

E. J. Chambers, *The Royal North-West Mounted Police* (Montreal, 1906); D. H. Johnson, *Volunteers at heart* (Brisb, 1974); L. M. Field, *The forgotten war* (Melb, 1979); *V&P* (LA NSW), 1900, 4, 37; *London Gazette*, 30 May 1877, 9 Nov 1902; *Brisbane Courier*, 23, 27 Jan, 3, 6 Feb, 14, 15 Apr, 1 Oct 1885, 18, 19 May 1888, 27, 28 Mar, 23 July 1891; *The Times*, 11 July 1921; North-West Mounted Police, Canada, Commissioner's report 1874 (ML); Privy Council cttees reports, 22 July, 7 Oct 1876 (Roy Canadian Mounted Police headquarters, Ottawa); correspondence with R.C.M.P., 11 July 1979 (held by author, Coogee, Syd); letter to author from D. J. French, Newbay, Wexford, Ireland, 11 Nov 1979.

R. SUTTON

FRENCH, SIR JOHN RUSSELL (1847-1921), banker, was born on 5 March 1847 at Mirzapore, Bengal, India, son of Major John French, 14th Bengal Native Light Infantry, and his wife Mary, née Forster. John French brought his family to New South Wales in 1858 and took up land at Kameruka in the Bega district. John was educated in England at Cheltenham College and in the colony under Rev. George Fairfowl Macarthur [q.v.5] at St Mark's Collegiate School, Macquarie Fields. He joined the Bank of New South Wales in Sydney in 1863, and after experience locally and in New Zealand, he was recalled to Sydney in 1887 and appointed inspector. At Christchurch, New Zealand, he married Margaret Annie Hawkins on 3 October 1872. Promoted chief inspector early in 1891 he acted for the general manager George Miller for most of the year. Over the next few years of economic depression and financial crisis French took on much of the detailed burden of managing the bank and on 1 July 1894 succeeded Miller as general manager.

Under French the Bank of New South Wales expanded after a period of consolidation and strengthening of its reserves. Conservative in banking principles and regarded as autocratic towards his staff, he nevertheless built up an efficient administration and delegated a great deal of responsibility, particularly in later years. Under his guidance the bank extended its activities to Fiji and Papua, and opened branches to service the growing export-oriented wheat, dairy and sugar industries. He was also responsible for expanding the bank's trade finance and exchange business; and was an early and lonely advocate of quoting the exchange rate of the Australian pound as a distinct currency rather than as a premium or discount on sterling.

A well-respected leader among bankers, French encouraged the spread of banking education. Moreover, through his reluctance to meddle in political affairs he was trusted and consulted by leading politicians of divergent views. Considering the financial questions raised by Federation, he was surprisingly apolitical. He did not strongly oppose a Commonwealth note issue monopoly as long as the notes were adequately backed by gold, though he was apprehensive of the issue getting into irresponsible hands, and he took a softer line than his colleagues on losing the right of banks to issue their own notes. He considered the Commonwealth Bank legislation of 1911 unnecessary but, relieved by its moderation, was prepared to co-operate in setting it up. He was reassured by the appointment of (Sir) Denison Miller [q.v.] as governor of the new bank, and probably had a hand in the decision, for Miller was one of his own trusted officers. French took pains to maintain good relations with the Commonwealth Bank, no doubt in part to prevent it straying into radical directions, and to urge a similar attitude on his banking colleagues.

Appointed K.B.E. in October 1918, French preferred to assist government through friendships with ministers rather than through official committees. But he was no stranger to public responsibilities. A foundation member and sometime president of the Institute of Bankers of New South Wales, he shared in its activities 'with zeal and energy'. He was an active president of the Sydney Chamber of Commerce (1900-01) and of the Associated Chambers of Commerce of Australia. He was also a member of the council of The King's School, Parramatta, a trustee of Sydney Grammar School, a foundation member of the Walter and Eliza Hall [qq.v.] Trust, and a director of the Royal Prince Alfred Hospital. A devout Anglican, he was elected a lay canon of the St Andrew's Cathedral Chapter.

French died at his Bellevue Hill home on 30 June 1921 and was buried in the Anglican section of South Head cemetery. He was survived by his wife, two sons and a daughter. His estate was valued for probate at £52 993. A distinguished public committee organized an endowment fund for the Royal Alexandra Hospital for Children in his memory.

R. F. Holder, *Bank of New South Wales: a history* (Syd, 1970); *A'sian Insurance and Banking Record*, and *Daily Telegraph* (Syd), and *SMH*, 1 July 1921; Bank of NSW Archives (Syd).   R. F. HOLDER

FREWIN, KENNETH MORETON (1905-1959), aviator and inventor, was born on 31 August 1905 in Melbourne, second son of John Henry Frewin, Anglican clergyman, and his wife Maria Eleanor, née Patterson. After attending Melbourne Church of England and Caulfield grammar schools, he served from 1923 to 1926 as a midshipman in the Royal Australian Naval Reserve.

In 1926 Frewin joined the Royal Australian Air Force as an air cadet. He resigned later that year and obtained first a private pilot's licence in October 1927 then a commercial licence in July 1928. He worked for a time with Mandated Territory Airways, New Guinea. On returning to Australia Frewin flew airmail runs and was personal pilot to Osment Howard Jolley, a flamboyant insurance salesman with a liking for making quick sales to wealthy graziers on outback stations. After an air circus tour of the Darling Downs Frewin co-founded Downs Air Service Ltd, Toowoomba, then became manager and chief instructor of the Air Schools and Taxi Co., Brisbane. Late in 1933 he moved to Melbourne to become senior captain for Tasmanian Aerial Services (renamed Holyman's [q.v.] Airways Ltd in July 1934 and later to become Australian National Airways Pty Ltd). He obtained a special aircraft radio-telegraphy licence when Holyman's became the first airline in Australia to use radio on a routine basis. Two Holyman De Havilland 86 aircraft crashed over Bass Strait late in 1934 killing all aboard. Frewin became the airline's chief pilot after the accidents. The airline dismissed him in July 1936 after he was convicted of drunken driving. In November that year he went to the United States of America as a guest of the Douglas Aircraft Corporation, spending five months studying American aircraft and airline operation.

Before the war Frewin was an instructor at Cambridge aerodrome, Tasmania. He enlisted in the R.A.A.F. in January 1940 and served as flying instructor at Point Cook, Camden and Wagga Wagga. In July 1941 he became a test pilot for the Commonwealth Aircraft Corporation and from August 1941 acted as aeronautical consultant to the Army Inventions Directorate. After the war he was appointed senior instructor and manager of the Geelong Aero Club then moved to the same positions at the Tasmanian Aero Club, Launceston.

In the early 1950s Frewin's restless spirit brought him back to Melbourne to concentrate on marketing various inventions he had patented over the years. These included a suitcase which allowed large items of clothing to be carried with minimum chance of creasing; the 'storpedo', a watertight cylindrical container with parachute, devised for dropping supplies to troops; and the Frewin arometer, a device permitting continuous mixing of a predetermined portion of liquid with a flowing body of water or other liquid. The 'storpedo' was used extensively during World War II and later in Malaya. His inventive mind visualized many other projects, including a flying car, which did not reach fruition.

Frewin had married Patricia Sarah Davies in Melbourne on 5 March 1936. They had one son before their divorce on 10 September 1942. On 30 August 1957 in Melbourne he married Joan Alison Beaumont. After a period of illness Frewin died of pneumonia on 2 December 1959 at his South Yarra home. He was cremated and his ashes were scattered over Bass Strait by pilots from the Victorian Aero Club.

Melb C. of E. Grammar School, *Liber Melburniensis* (Melb, 1937); *Aircraft*, Oct 1927, p 336, July 1928, p 36, Mar 1932, p 46, Apr 1932, p 18, Dec 1933, p 11, Mar 1934, p 11, Nov 1934, p 31, Jan 1948, p 32; *People* (Syd), 16 Oct 1957; *Herald* (Melb), 17 Mar 1932, 5 Mar 1936; *Argus*, 10 Nov 1936; *Sun News-Pictorial* (Melb), 3 Dec 1959; Aust patents and patents applications records, 117830, 119846, 167788.
                                          KEVIN J. FEWSTER

FRISTRÖM, CARL MAGNUS OSCAR (1856-1918), artist, was born on 16 January 1856 in the parish of Sturko, Blekinge, Sweden, son of Claus August Friström, schoolteacher and his wife Christina, née Carlson. Oscar is first described as a sailor in the household records of Torhamm in 1870-76. He probably came to Australia in a ship's crew and jumped ship in Brisbane in 1883. In 1884 he exhibited in the fine arts section of the annual Queensland National Association Exhibition. There is no evidence of any training before his arrival in Australia, and the academic studies exhibited suggest that he may have studied part time at the Brisbane Technical College, or privately.

Entering a partnership, the Elite Photo Co., in 1885 with the Brisbane photographer D. H. Hutchison, Friström became responsible for the colouring and over-painting of photographic portraits much in vogue at the time. He was also painting some of his first portraits, and beginning to gain repute as a professional artist. Using the name of his company, he exhibited landscapes and portraits, both photographic and painted, at Q.N.A. exhibitions. His youngest brother Claus Edward, first a photographer and then a painter, later in New Zealand, was also employed by the company in 1888. Oscar retained his interest in photography all his life and taught colouring and retouching. On 22 June 1885 in St Stephen's Roman Catholic Cathedral, he married Caroline Johnston, a gifted musician who taught for many years at All Hallows Convent where Friström was art master during the 1890s; the first of their two children was born in 1887, when he was naturalized.

At the Centennial International Exhibition, Melbourne, in 1888 Friström exhibited an oil portrait of the Aboriginal 'King Sandy' of Brisbane. He later produced a number of similar studies, especially during the 1890s, often done from photographs. He left Brisbane in 1891 apparently intending to go overseas, but did not go beyond Adelaide, where he set up for a short time as a portraitist, painting more Aboriginals. He was back in Brisbane in 1895.

As one of the few professional artists in Brisbane in the late 1880s, Friström had been involved with Isaac Jenner [q.v.] and Lewis Wirth in the formation of the Queensland Art Society, the earliest of its kind in Queensland. He was on the first committee in 1887 and in 1889. He exhibited with the society in the 1890s, but he and others gradually became disaffected, and withdrew from it. In June 1904 they formed the New Society of Artists. Among the leading professionals who joined him were the architect G. H. M. Addison and the sculptor James L. Watts; Edward Colclough, a civil servant and amateur painter, was secretary for twelve years. When the position of president was created in 1907 Friström became the first incumbent. Although attempts to amalgamate the two societies had begun seriously by 1910, they did not succeed until 1916. Friström played a prominent part in the negotiations and was elected to the council of the new body, the Queensland Art Society. He became president in 1918 but did not complete his term, dying of cancer on 26 June; he was buried in South Brisbane cemetery with Anglican rites.

Friström painted many subjects in several mediums but his reputation rests on his portraits. He painted some of Queensland's leading parliamentarians, professional men, Freemasons and members of prominent Brisbane families. Some of his many Aboriginal portraits are in private collections, art galleries, museums and libraries both in Australia and overseas. The Queensland Museum has a notable collection.

J. K. Brown and M. Maynard, *Fine art exhibitions in Brisbane 1884-1914* (Brisb, 1980); *Swedish-A'sian Trade J*, June 1931; *Brisbane Courier*, 27 June 1918; Roy Qld Art Soc Minutebooks, 1901-19 (held by Soc, Brisb); biographical files on Friström (Qld Art Gallery, Brisb).

JULIE K. BROWN

FRODSHAM, GEORGE HORSFALL (1863-1937), bishop, was born on 15 September 1863 at Sale Moor, Altrincham, Chester, England, son of James Frodsham, insurance surveyor, and his wife Jane, née Horsfall. When his father later became a Manchester architect, George was educated at Birkenhead and later at University College, Durham (B.A., 1888; M.A., 1895; D.D., honorary, 1903). During two years with a firm of shipbrokers and underwriters, he studied at St Aidan's theological college, Birkenhead, and became deacon in 1889. Ordained at Ripon in the same year, he served curacies in Leeds and elsewhere in Yorkshire until 1896, then accepted appointment as rector of St Thomas' Church, Toowong, Brisbane. Before sailing, he married Fannie Swinburne at Harrogate on 8 April 1896; they had five children.

At Toowong he was revealed as a dynamic personality with an insatiable appetite for work. He saved the parish from grave financial difficulties and persuaded many to work for the church. His term as rector saw an increase in giving, the beautification of the church and the ceremonial elaboration of its services. Musical recitals became a feature of the parish and he founded the Church of England Cricket Association. Chaplain to the bishop in 1900-02, his editing of the *Church Chronicle* was lively and he played a major part in diocesan and civic affairs and committees. He served on the committee to promote the establishment of the University of Queensland. He vigorously promoted the cause of religious instruction in state schools and the creation in 1905 of the ecclesiastical province of Queensland, ably supporting Bishop Webber [q.v.] on this issue. During the South African War he was chaplain to the Queensland Defence forces.

Frodsham visited North Queensland in 1901 and next year was unanimously elected bishop of that diocese. The primate, Saumarez Smith [q.v.], refused confirmation until the financial plight of the diocese was clearly explained to Frodsham. The failure of industries and droughts had produced financial disaster and the diocese needed to be founded afresh. Frodsham did this with vigour and came to be known as 'the Restorer Bishop'. He was consecrated in Sydney on 17 August 1902 and enthroned at Townsville on 3 September.

A cyclone in March 1903 wrecked his cathedral but funds raised on a series of trips to England repaired the damage and endowed the see. In 1909 he founded the North Queensland Auxiliary in England. Devoted to missionary work, he encouraged the work of the community of St Barnabas, founded in 1902, which later became the Bush Brotherhood of St Barnabas, and raised funds in England for it. Though a supporter of British and European migration, he spoke against narrowly racist views and encouraged evangelistic work within the diocese among Aboriginals, Polynesians, Chinese and Japanese. He visited Asia several times to study missionary problems. With his wide-ranging interest in education, Frodsham was one of the prime movers in the Institute of Tropical Medicine in Townsville; he visited England in 1911 to raise funds for the project.

Constant travel and the difficulties of his diocese took their toll. He began to appear more and more autocratic because of his wide vision and his faith in his own judgment. In October 1912 he said that he had tried to be 'a faithful administrator rather than a popular man'. In 1913 he resigned and returned to England. There he became resident canon of Gloucester Cathedral in 1914-20, rector of Halifax in 1920-23 and then canon of Wakefield. He was known as a friend and adviser of the parochial clergy whose needs he faithfully represented in the Church assembly. A governor of various church schools, he was chairman in 1914 of a War Office advisory committee on the employment of women in place of men. He wrote constantly but, apart from theological texts, his one substantial published work *A bishop's pleasaunce* (London, 1915) was a collection of published journal articles. He died at Halifax on 6 March 1937.

Frodsham had a wide vision for Australia and spoke and wrote against the legal nexus which bound the Anglican Church in Australia to the Church of England. Later bishops of North Queensland claimed that what they were able to achieve depended almost entirely on his work.

J. O. Feetham and W. V. Rymer (eds), *The North Queensland jubilee book 1878-1928* (Townsville,

1929); R. Fraser, *A historical sketch of the diocese of North Queensland* (Townsville, 1958); E. C. Rowland, *The tropics for Christ* (Townsville, 1960); H. Gregory, *A church for its times* (Brisb, 1977); Church of England (Syd), *Procs of General Synod*, 1905, *and* Diocese of Brisb, *Church Chronicle*, 1 Apr 1906; *Church Times* (Lond), 12 Mar 1937; *Northern Churchman*, 1 Apr 1937; K. Rayner, Attitude and influence of the churches in Queensland . . . (B.A. Hons thesis, Univ Qld, 1951) *and* The history of the Church of England in Queensland (Ph.D. thesis, Univ Qld, 1962).

JOHN CHARLES VOCKLER

FROGGATT, WALTER WILSON (1858-1937), entomologist, was born on 13 June 1858 in Melbourne, son of George Wilson Froggatt, and his wife Caroline, née Chiosso, both born in Yorkshire, England. Educated at the Corporate High School, Sandhurst (Bendigo), he was encouraged to study nature by his friend Richard H. Nancarrow, a bush naturalist. After leaving school, Froggatt spent four years on the land in Victoria before moving in 1880 to the Mount Brown goldfield near Milparinka, New South Wales, where he collected specimens. Two years later he collected on the Flinders River, Queensland, sending material to Sir Ferdinand Mueller [q.v.5] and Charles French [q.v.]. Although his scientific knowledge was slight, through observation and fieldwork he developed a sound knowledge of botany.

In 1885 with the assistance of Mueller, Froggatt was appointed special zoological collector and assistant zoologist, and later taxidermist, to the New Guinea expedition organized by the New South Wales branch of the (Royal) Geographical Society of Australasia. His work was widely acclaimed and his competence and devotion to duty was praised by J. W. Haacke, chief scientist to the expedition. In 1886 (Sir) William Macleay [q.v.5] proposed Froggatt for membership of the Linnean Society of New South Wales. He took an active part in the affairs of the society and in 1898-1937 he was a member of its council, serving as president in 1911-13. He was also a member and later a fellow of the Linnean Society of London.

Employed by Macleay as collector for his private museum, in 1886 Froggatt was in Queensland and in 1887-88 worked in the Kimberley region of north-western Australia. Arising from that experience, he prepared a paper 'Note on the Natives of West Kimberley', his first contribution to the Proceedings of the local Linnean Society. From 1892 until 1896 he was geological collector to the Technological Museum, Sydney, where he worked with J. H. Maiden [q.v.]. Froggatt edited a manuscript in which Maiden had made a study of the history of the Sydney Botanic Gardens, and published it in part in the *Journal and Proceedings* of the Royal Australian Historical Society, of which he was a member from 1928 until 1937.

In October 1896 Froggatt was appointed entomologist in the Department of Mines and Agriculture. He published the results of his research and observations, frequently in the *Proceedings* of the local Linnean Society, the *Agricultural Gazette of New South Wales* and the *Australian Forestry Journal* (nearly 400 in all). At the request of Lever's Pacific Plantations Ltd, he investigated coconut palm pests in the Solomon Islands in 1901 and two years later, on behalf of the French Planters' Association, he studied the palm leaf beetle. In 1907-08 he travelled overseas on behalf of the governments of New South Wales, Victoria, Queensland and South Australia to investigate problems of insect pests, particularly the fruit fly. In 1911-21 he lectured on entomology in the department of agriculture at the University of Sydney. Froggatt retired from the State Department of Agriculture in 1923, but was appointed forest entomologist by the Forestry Commission. At the request of the Commonwealth government he made a report, 'of great value', on timber borers and other insects. He finally retired in 1927 and that year sold his collection of insects to the Commonwealth Council for Scientific and Industrial Research.

Froggatt also contributed significantly to the popular study of natural history. He was a founder in 1891 and later president for a record eleven years of the Naturalists' Society of New South Wales, a council-member from 1910 of the (Royal) Zoological Society of New South Wales, which elected him a fellow in 1931, and a founder of the Australian Wattle League, the Gould [q.v.1] League of Bird Lovers of New South Wales and the Wildlife Preservation Society of Australia. He was a member of the Australian National Research Council in 1921-32.

In addition to scientific papers and official reports, Froggatt published newspaper articles on popular science, especially economic entomology. He wrote six books: the first, *Australian insects* (1907) was for many years a standard text. In 1933 he began a series of elementary 'nature books' for children with the *Insect book*. In his garden at Croydon, Sydney, he grew many Australian trees and shrubs, which he generously gave to local municipal bodies for planting in parks and streets. At the reserve at Balls Head, his work was commemorated in a look-out.

Froggatt died in his residence at Croydon on 18 March 1937 and was cremated with

Anglican rites. He was survived by his wife Anne Emily, née Lewis, whom he had married at Long Gully, Victoria, on 15 January 1890, and by a son John Lewis, an entomologist in New Guinea, and by two daughters, Joyce, a schoolmistress, and Gladys, the author of the *World of little lives* (1916) and *More about the world of little lives* (1929).

Roy Geog Soc of A'sia (NSW), *Trans and Procs*, 3 (1885), 4 (1886); *Aust Naturalist*, 1 (1906-09), 10 (1937); Gould League of Bird Lovers of NSW, *Gould League Notes*, 1937; *SMH*, 10 June, 24 Dec 1885, 22 June 1923, 19 Mar 1937; *Mosman Daily*, 15 July 1937; Roy Geog Soc (NSW), Diary, New Guinea exploration expedition, 1885 (ML); ML printed cat.   D. I. McDONALD

FROST, FREDERICK CHARLES-WORTH (1891-1971), soldier and plasterer, was born on 11 April 1891 at Redfern, Sydney, son of Thomas Frost, sawyer and later machinist, and his wife Rosetta, née Charlesworth, both from Leicestershire, England. He spent his childhood in the Redfern area and on leaving school worked as a plasterer for the firm of Bowering & Pratt of Marrickville. On 18 May 1912 he married Adelaide Jane Wickham at St Thomas Anglican Church, Balmain.

On 15 November 1915 Frost enlisted in the Australian Imperial Force and embarked for France in April 1916 with the 11th reinforcements for the 20th Battalion. In October he joined the battalion in the Ypres salient and soon after went into billets for a rest period at Steenvoorde. Transferring to the 61st Battalion in March 1817, he was promoted lance corporal in August. On 24 October he returned to his old battalion, then in billets at La Temple near Steenvoorde; he was promoted corporal in July 1918.

During the attack on Mont St Quentin on 31 August 1918 he won his first Distinguished Conduct Medal. Early in the day he and four men brought in twelve prisoners and two machine-guns. After the battalion had secured its objective by clearing the village of Feuillaucourt there was a withdrawal and it was then that Frost, normally in charge of a Lewis-gun section, remained behind alone and protected the movement of his company. Although the enemy were close at one stage he withdrew slowly, yard by yard, and killed four Germans who called on him to surrender. On 3 October, in operations against the Hindenburg line at Beaurevoir, he received a Bar to his Distinguished Conduct Medal for a single-handed daring attack against a heavily protected enemy machine-gun. Next day he was promoted lance sergeant.

Frost returned to Australia on 26 June 1919 and was discharged on 10 August. He resumed his former occupation and lived at Croydon Park, Sydney. He was retrenched during the Depression and worked at various jobs, including one with the water board. During World War II he and his wife worked at the Email munitions factory at Waterloo. After a second period of employment at Pratt's he became a maintenance officer with the Hospitals Contribution Fund and remained working until he was into his seventies.

He died at Newtown on 7 October 1971, survived by his wife and two daughters; one daughter had predeceased him. He was cremated with Anglican rites. Frost was typical of the many for whom the war was a great adventure in an otherwise routine life.

C. E. W. Bean, *The A.I.F. in France*, 1918 (Syd, 1942); *London Gazette*, 18 Feb, 12 Mar 1919; *SMH*, 9 Oct 1971; War diary, 20th Battalion, AIF (AWM); records (AWM); information from Mrs. O. Rix, Birrong, NSW.   J. G. WILLIAMS

FUHRMAN, OSMOND CHARLES WILLIAM (1889-1961), public servant and diplomat, was born Otto Carl Wilhelm Fuhrmann on 29 July 1889 at Richmond, Melbourne, elder son of Heinrich August Fuhrmann, a carpenter from Hamburg, Germany, and his wife Agnes, née O'Connor, a Tasmanian. Nothing is known of his education. He was a storekeeper in the country town of Alexandra before obtaining a position as an assistant in the library of the Supreme Court of Victoria.

Active in the Victorian militia between 1907 and 1910 and from 1913, Fuhrman enlisted as a second lieutenant in the 14th Battalion, Australian Imperial Force, in August 1914, serving with distinction at Gallipoli and on the Western Front. He was promoted captain in January 1916 and major in February. At Pozières he thwarted an attack on his sector by manning a machine-gun and killing some fifty Germans, for which he was awarded the Croix de Guerre. Accidentally injured in France late in 1917, he served with a training brigade in Britain in 1918-19, returning to Melbourne in December 1919. He had been appointed O.B.E. On 13 September 1917 at Acton, London, he had married Mildred Flora Mackay, a Queensland violinist. In 1918 he formally anglicized his name.

After demobilization Fuhrman returned to the Supreme Court Library where he deputized for the librarian and served as acting secretary to the Board of Examiners for Barristers and Solicitors. In 1921 he published *The High Court Procedure Act,*

1903-1915 and rules of the High Court of Australia ...

In April 1921 Fuhrman succeeded P. E. Deane [q.v.] as private secretary to the prime minister W. M. Hughes [q.v.]. Hughes was not an easy master and seven months later Fuhrman was faced with the option of a low-paid clerkship in the public service when Sir Joseph Cook [q.v.], about to leave for London as high commissioner, took him on as his private secretary.

Fuhrman served at Australia House in London from 1922 to 1938, until 1927 as private secretary to Cook and subsequently as a clerk attached to the external affairs branch of the Prime Minister's Department. Because Cook as a rule led Australian delegations to meetings of League of Nations bodies in Geneva, Fuhrman had opportunities to develop valuable expertise as a specialist on league matters, serving as secretary to most delegations to meetings of the assembly and of the International Labour Organization. Australia did not yet have a diplomatic corps, but in the 1920s and 1930s Fuhrman exercised useful diplomatic functions in dealings with other countries' delegations and especially with members of the league secretariat. His reputation had become so high that, by the late 1930s, he was virtually submitting in advance the kinds of questions he wanted put to Australian representatives by the Permanent Mandates Commission in its annual examinations of Australia's administration of New Guinea and Nauru. S. M. (Viscount) Bruce [q.v.7] as high commissioner in 1934 described Fuhrman as 'a zealous and capable officer'.

He returned to Australia late in 1938 to take up a position in Canberra with the National Insurance Commission but soon transferred to the Commonwealth Investigation Branch and then to the Department of Supply and Development. From 1940 to 1945 he served with the Eastern Group Supply Council in India. After the war he joined the Department of External Affairs, serving as official secretary in Pretoria in 1946, consul-general in Shanghai in 1947-48 and chargé d'affaires in Nanking in 1948. He concluded his career as minister in Tel Aviv from 1949 until 1953, retiring to Devon in England in 1954.

Fuhrman died at Tiverton, Devon, on 10 November 1961, survived by his wife and a daughter in England, and by a son, Colonel L. H. R. Fuhrman of Canberra. He will be remembered principally as one of the half-dozen or so men who, in the half-light of the years of dominion status, helped take Australia from behind Imperial walls into the politics and diplomacy of the world community.

Punch (Melb), 14 Apr 1921; *Argus*, 16 July 1922; CP 268/3, Prime Minister's Dept, Non-current personal files, 1920-54 (AAO).   W. J. HUDSON

FULLER, SIR BENJAMIN JOHN (1875-1952) and JOHN (1879 1959), theatrical entrepreneurs, were born on 20 March 1875 and on 20 April 1879 in London, second and third sons of the seven children of John Fuller (d. 1923), compositor and later theatrical entrepreneur, and his first wife Harriett, née Jones. From December 1884 Ben appeared for three months at the Savoy Theatre in a juvenile production of Gilbert and Sullivan's *The pirates of Penzance*. Two years later he played in London and the provinces with Montague Robey's Midget Minstrels, then joined Warwick Gray's Juvenile Opera Company. He returned to school, and at weekends as 'End Man' played in London clubs in his father's minstrel troupe.

In 1889 his father, who had a fine tenor voice, went to Australia with a theatrical company. After working briefly in an engineer's office for a year, where he learnt shorthand, Ben toured England as Harry Liston's dresser, then joined a troupe of 'waxyhommics' (or busking nigger minstrels) at Herne Bay. He played the piano and double-bass by ear. About 1894 he worked his way to Melbourne as a pianist in the *Austral*, then joined his father in Adelaide.

Meanwhile John junior, who had performed in his father's minstrel troupe and remained in London, arrived in Melbourne on 31 July 1891 and went to school at Collingwood. In February 1892 he was engaged by J. C. Williamson [q.v.6] for *La Cigale*. After several other engagements, he spent nearly three years as call-boy in Williamson's Royal Comic Opera Company. He played any juvenile parts going and occasionally deputized as stage-manager for Henry Bracy [q.v.7].

In 1894 the family settled at Auckland, New Zealand. While he was still at school, John sang at his father's Wednesday night popular concerts and Sunday night choir music. In 1898 John senior started waxworks displays and lantern shows, worked by John junior, interspersed with vaudeville, with Ben as comedian. About 1899 they took the show to Dunedin. Ben remained there when the rest of the family went to Melbourne. He was so successful that he soon opened at Christchurch and Wellington as well. The others returned to help. Gradually they built up a vaudeville circuit, regularly changing the items and the waxworks, and began to buy the houses they were showing in.

At Dunedin on 6 October 1900 Ben Fuller married a widow Jessie Elizabeth Burton, née McDonald; she bore a son in Sydney in 1902 and died in May 1903. Living at Auckland, he married Elizabeth Mary Thomson, a music teacher and singer, at the Sacred Heart Church on 8 November 1905. John, who was in charge in Wellington, married with Anglican rites Alice Gertrude Mary Fraser on 5 July 1902 in Hobart; they had a daughter and were divorced in December 1913. He served on the Wellington City Council in 1911-16. There he married Lavina Moar on 28 September 1916.

The Fullers went into the moving picture business in New Zealand in 1907 and gradually extended their vaudeville circuit, featuring 'Stiffy' and 'Mo' [q.v. H. Van Der Sluice], throughout Australia. In 1914 Ben and John became joint governing directors of John Fuller & Sons Ltd and Ben was based in Sydney, at Haughley, Elizabeth Bay. Reputedly he was 'the originator of the ideas but John developed them'. Prospering during World War I, they ventured into pantomime and melodrama and in 1916 presented a season of Italian grand opera. After Ben announced that he had volunteered for active service late in 1916, John moved to Sydney, leaving their brother Walter (d. 1934) in charge of the Fullers' and Hayward's Pictures Ltd. in New Zealand.

In 1920 Ben gave £1000 to Vernon Treatt to enable him to take up a Rhodes scholarship. Over the next year he gave two sums of £5000 for educational purposes and established the Fuller Trust to provide scholarships for overseas training in agriculture. He was knighted in 1921 and next year contested the Sydney seat in the Legislative Assembly as an independent but lost.

In partnership with Hugh Ward [q.v.] from 1923 to 1926, the Fullers moved into musical comedy; in December 1923 they opened with *The O'Brien Girl* at the Princess Theatre in Melbourne. In Sydney the Fullers built the St James Theatre and building on the site of the Sydney Girls' High School and opened on 26 March 1926 with *No, no, Nanette*; Sir Benjamin scored a hit in 1928 by paying Gladys Moncrieff [q.v.] £150 a week, despite John's protests, to star in *Rio Rita*. In 1929 John, with Frank Albert [q.v.7], became a director of the Australian Broadcasting Co. By the 1930s vaudeville had largely given way to cinema and in 1930 'talkies' apparatus was installed in most Fullers' theatres. They survived the Depression better than most, backed by their solid theatre freeholds in all the State capitals except Hobart.

By 1934 John was tired of travelling, and the brothers divided their assets, John taking the St James Theatre and building as the major part of his share. Henceforth he devoted himself to real estate. Sir Benjamin sold off his New Zealand interests, remained governing director of Fullers' Theatres Ltd and returned with gusto to the legitimate theatre. He tried to establish a permanent opera company, to sing in English, but the Melbourne season was a financial loss and he was forced to disband the company in 1935 when he failed to get a government subsidy. From 1939 he was associated with Garnet-Carroll and from 1946 governing director of the Carroll-Fuller Theatre Company Pty Ltd. They sponsored the tour of the Old Vic Theatre Company with Sir Laurence (Lord) Olivier in 1948. In 1950 the picture interests of Fullers' Theatres Ltd and Hoyts Theatres Ltd were merged.

Among other charitable activities Fuller was chairman of the Howard Prison Reform League and a vice-president of the Sydney Industrial Blind Institution. As president of the Australian Council for International Social Service, he raised money (contributing generously himself) to bring refugee children to Australia from Europe in 1950. He lived at Ardendraught, Point Piper, and decorated the hall with a massive stuffed gorilla. A large man, bluff, warm-hearted and genial, he enjoyed billiards, walking and reading. Generous in private, he was a hard-headed businessman, who never lost his love for 'the whole mocking illusion of the stage'.

Sir Benjamin died in St George's Hospital, London, on 10 March 1952. He was survived by a son of his first marriage, and by his second wife and their two daughters. His estate was valued for probate at £173 180.

John, always shy, retired from active business in 1944 and lived at Caerleon, Bellevue Hill. One of his 'best time-wasters' was bowls. He died in St Luke's Hospital, Darlinghurst, on 26 September 1959 and was cremated with Anglican rites. He was survived by his wife, two sons and two daughters. His estate was valued for probate at £163 406.

V. Tait, *A family of brothers* (Melb, 1971); *Theatre Mag* (Syd), 1 Nov 1913, 1 Apr 1915; *Punch* (Melb), 20 July 1916; *SMH*, 3 June 1921, 22 Nov 1922, 10 May 1923, 30 Apr, 2, 5 May, 29 Aug 1934, 2 Feb, 30 Mar 1935, 31 Oct 1950, 22, 28 Sept 1959; *Auckland Star*, 10 May 1923, 22 Mar 1952; *Table Talk*, 4 Mar 1926; *Evening Post* (NZ), 3 Apr 1952, 7 Feb 1956; *Christchurch Star*, 30 Sept 1960; Fuller trust records (ML).   MARTHA RUTLEDGE

FULLER, COLIN DUNMORE (1882-1953), farmer and soldier, was born on 10 February 1882 at Kiama, New South Wales, ninth surviving child of Irish-born George Lawrence Fuller, farmer, and his native-born wife Sarah Cunningham (Conyhame), née Miller. One of his elder brothers was Sir

George Fuller [q.v.]. He was educated at the Sydney Church of England Grammar School (Shore) and Sydney Grammar School and then worked on his father's property, Dunmore, in the Illawarra district, where he was known as a dashing and accomplished horseman.

At 23 Fuller joined the local militia unit, enlisting as a private in the 1st Australian Light Horse Regiment (New South Wales Lancers). He was commissioned lieutenant in 1906 and promoted captain in 1908. As militia service became more popular a new unit, the 28th L.H.R., was raised locally and given the territorial title of the Illawarra Regiment. Fuller was appointed its commanding officer in 1912. With the outbreak of World War I he joined the Australian Imperial Force on 28 September 1914 and was posted to the 6th L.H.R. as captain commanding 'A' Squadron. After a brief period as acting adjutant he was promoted major and second-in-command of his regiment and embarked for Egypt on the troopship *Suevic* in December.

The 6th L.H.R. fought unmounted at Gallipoli from June 1915. In November he became commanding officer and his unit remained at Anzac until the evacuation in December, with Fuller characteristically seeing off all his men before he left the beach. He was made a substantive lieut-colonel in February 1916. In Egypt and Palestine he led his regiment at Gaza-Beersheba, El Mughar, Jerusalem, Katia (where he was wounded) and Megiddo, until 15 December 1918. His soldiers found him 'always approachable and always . . . a sport'. The 'unerring accuracy of his always rapid decisions' led to a special mention in dispatches by General Murray, commander-in-chief of the Egyptian Expeditionary Force. He was awarded the Distinguished Service Order in the New Year honours of 1917 and in January 1920 received the Order of the Nile, conferred by the sultan of Egypt for 'distinguished services rendered in the course of the [Egyptian] campaign'. He held temporary command of the 2nd Light Horse Brigade from December 1918 until June 1919 when the unit returned to Australia. He remained with the militia, Australian Military Forces, as a lieut-colonel on the reserve of officers until 1926 when he was placed on the retired list.

On 10 March 1920 Fuller married Amy Elsie Blanche Rea at St Luke's Anglican Church, Mosman, Sydney. After the war he managed Dunmore, the family property, before retiring to Beverly Hills, Sydney; survived by his wife and two daughters, he died there of cancer on 19 September 1953 and was cremated. His estate was sworn for probate at £6835.

G. L. Berrie, *Under furred hats* (Syd, 1919); H. S. Gullett, *The A.I.F. in Sinai and Palestine* (Syd, 1923); R. J. G. Hall, *The Australian Light Horse* (Melb, 1967); *London Gazette*, 1, 22 Dec 1916, 16 Jan 1920; *SMH*, 21 Sept 1953; War diary, 6th Light Horse Regiment, A.I.F. (AWM).

RICHARD J. HALL

FULLER, SIR GEORGE WARBURTON (1861-1940), barrister and politician, was born on 22 January 1861 at Kiama, New South Wales, son of George Lawrence Fuller, storekeeper, and his wife Sarah Conyhame (Cunningham), née Miller. He was a brother of C. D. Fuller [q.v.]. A gifted scholar, he was educated at Kiama Public School, Sydney Grammar School and the University of Sydney (B.A., 1879; M.A. 1882). After reading law with Sir William Manning [q.v.5], he was called to the Bar in 1884 and was crown prosecutor on many occasions. On 23 March 1892 at Woollahra he married Ada Louisa King.

Politics and business interested Fuller more than law, and he never practised. A Federationist, Free Trader and supporter of Sir Henry Parkes [q.v.5], he entered the Legislative Assembly as member for Kiama in 1889. Re-elected in 1891, he was defeated in the 1894 swing against Parkes and again in 1898 although he had won a name for intelligent conservatism, stolidity and good temper. He entered the first Commonwealth parliament as Free Trade member for Illawarra in 1901, and held the seat until narrowly defeated by G. M. Burns (Labor) in 1913. As minister for home affairs (1909-10) under Alfred Deakin [q.v.], he introduced the bill to make Canberra the seat of Federal government. In 1911 he was a member of the Australian delegation to the coronation of George V.

Fuller re-entered State politics in 1915 as member for Wollondilly, following the death of F. A. Badgery. The Opposition leader, (Sir) Charles Gregory Wade [q.v.], welcomed him as a pragmatic conservative and experienced former minister, likely to promote that association of rural-minded Progressives and urban-minded Liberals to which Wade was committed. Fuller quickly became deputy leader of the Liberals. Then, when W. A. Holman [q.v.] formed his National ministry in November 1916 and Wade left politics, Fuller became colonial secretary, second only to Holman in the cabinet, and Liberal leader.

With Holman overseas in 1917 Fuller had a memorable acting premiership from 18 April to 30 October. In July, at a critical stage of the war, an apparently minor issue threw State transport into confusion: job time cards were introduced into the workshops of the Railways and Tramways Department and the Labor Council of New South Wales informed the government that the unions would strike rather than use them. Although talks with the union leaders nearly succeeded, Fuller came to see the strike as a politically motivated and disloyal attempt to incite a general strike in wartime. He proposed to dismiss men who did not return to work in seven days and to deprive them of seniority and superannuation; men who remained at work, and volunteers, would be rewarded. A. W. Buckley, member for Surry Hills and a former member of the Industrial Workers of the World, was arrested on charges of conspiracy to incite a strike. Attempts at mediation, even by the lord mayor and the Anglican dean of Sydney, were rebuffed. When the strike was settled in September, men returning to work were treated less liberally than the government appeared to have promised. Fuller's actions aroused lasting bitterness among unionists who charged that he had campaigned vindictively, hypocritically and sometimes illegally against unionism. But many people thought him a strong, resourceful leader, who had preserved law and order without violence and put victory in war ahead of other objectives.

Throughout 1918-19, while Holman's popularity declined, Fuller supported him loyally and gave no support to Liberal attempts to criticize or overthrow him. Late in 1919, the year in which he was appointed K.C.M.G., Fuller extended the government trawling enterprise by ordering new ships in order, he said, to provide cheap fish for the mass of the population. From 9 to 27 February he was vice-president of the Executive Council. The elections of 1920, the first held under the Proportional Representation Act (1918), ended the Holman government when the Progressives deprived the Nationalists of much rural, non-Labor support by campaigning alone.

In the new parliament Fuller was leader of the Opposition. Freed of his obligations of loyalty to Holman, he set about promoting the co-operation of Progressives and Nationalist Liberals. By late 1920 he was sure that some Progressives would rejoin the Nationalists if opportunity offered and harassed the ministry with two no-confidence motions. John Storey [q.v.] died on 5 October, so removing Labor's majority, and when the Liberal Speaker, Sir Daniel Levy [q.v.], resigned on 8 December Labor, now led by James Dooley [q.v.], having to find a Speaker, was defeated. Fuller shrewdly declined to form a ministry without full support from the Progressives. The resulting Nationalist-Progressive government formed on 20 December 1921 included as leading Progressives W. E. Wearne [q.v.] and (Sir) Thomas Bavin [q.v.7], together with the former premier, Sir Joseph Carruthers [q.v.7]. But the ministry lasted only seven hours. Some 'True Blue' Progressives, led by (Sir) Michael Bruxner [q.v.7], were antagonistic. Fuller, refused a dissolution, resigned. Labor returned to power while Levy, as Fuller wished, resumed the Speakership.

The general election of April 1922 was won by a coalition of Nationalists and Wearne's Progressives. Fuller's ministry again included Wearne, Bavin and Carruthers, but not Bruxner. At first Fuller did nothing to conciliate Bruxner, but in 1923, with the ministry in trouble over wheat pool finances and defeated in a debate over the estimates, he turned to him for help. After the passage of the Federal Main Roads Development Act (1923) Bruxner persuaded Fuller to increase work on rural communications; in April 1924 Fuller was constrained by Country Party pressure to appoint a royal commission into proposals, which eventually failed and which he himself opposed, for carving new States out of New South Wales.

The Fuller ministry passed the Sydney Harbour Bridge Act (1922) and the Monopolies Act (1923) giving the Supreme Court power to impose penalties on combinations in restraint of trade. Fees for high school education were reintroduced in 1922. The Marriage (Amendment) Act (1924) was passed in response to the Papal decree ne temere, concerning the claims of the Catholic Church to exclusive rights to marry Catholics, although the sectarian issues were raised against the wishes of Fuller, a Presbyterian. The forty-eight hour week was reintroduced; rural workers and public servants were removed from the jurisdiction of the Arbitration Court. As public servants had already had their salaries reduced by the State Arbitration Court, on the application of the Fuller government, the ministry became unpopular with its own employees. The railway strikers of 1917 were refused a settlement on seniority along the lines laid down by a royal commissioner, Judge Edmunds [q.v.], in 1922 while the ministry honoured Fuller's electoral promises to the 1917 loyalists. He failed in attempts to minimize possible conflicts of Federal and State arbitration jurisdiction although the Federal prime minister, S. M. (Viscount) Bruce [q.v.7], was sympathetic.

He had help from Carruthers, as vice-president of the Executive Council, in making government policy. As Fuller never much liked the detail of administration, however, execution was often left to Bavin. Fuller was sorry to have to take over the Treasury in February 1925, when Sir Arthur

Cocks [q.v.] became agent-general. The government provided the sound, economical administration that he had promised at the 1922 elections and was conservative to the point of reaction; strong bridges were built between Nationalists and the Country Party. Little had been done, however, to prevent a swing to Labor by a public weary of less money for more work; at the elections of June 1925 Labor campaigned on a programme of social welfare and Fuller lost. After ensuring that Bavin succeeded him, he retired from the Nationalist leadership. He remained member for Wollondilly until 7 February 1928 when he became agent-general. Returning to New South Wales in 1931, he was in time to support Holman at the Federal elections of that year.

Fuller's last years were spent in retirement at Bowral. He remained a member of the Australian Club and kept up his interest in cricket, fishing, gardening and billiards. A kindly, portly man of great courtesy, he enjoyed wide respect and popularity. He was made a councillor of St Andrew's College, University of Sydney, in 1895. Fuller, like his father, invested shrewdly in real estate. Although never a farmer, he had a good eye for rural land values, and also for company investments. He died on 22 July 1940 at Darlinghurst, and was buried with Presbyterian forms in the Anglican section of Porter's Garden Beach cemetery. His wife, a daughter and a son survived him.

H. V. Evatt, *Australian Labour leader ... W. A. Holman* (Syd, 1940); D. Aitkin, *The colonel* (Canb, 1969); *Daily Telegraph* (Syd), 7 July 1894; *Punch* (Melb), 9 Apr 1908, 26 Apr 1917, 19 Feb 1925; *Fighting Line*, 19 May, 19 June 1913, 18 Aug 1914, 15 Apr 1915, 26 Aug 1920; *T&CJ*, 11 June 1919; *Australasian*, 26 Sept 1925.   JOHN M. WARD

FULLER, SIR JOHN MICHAEL FLEETWOOD (1864-1915), governor, was born on 21 October 1864 at Neston Park, Corsham, Wiltshire, England, eldest son of George Pargiter Fuller, landed gentleman, and his wife Emily Georgina Jane, daughter of Sir Michael Hicks Hicks-Beach, eighth baronet. He was educated at Winchester College and Christ Church, Oxford; in 1887 he obtained third-class honours in history (B.A.; M.A., 1900), and was a polo blue. On a world trip in 1891 he spent a few weeks in Australia, moving in vice-regal circles. In 1894-95 he was aide-de-camp to the viceroy of India. On 5 July 1898 at Holy Trinity Church, Dilton Marsh, Wiltshire, he married 19-year-old Norah Jacintha Phipps. After three unsuccessful parliamentary bids, in 1900-11 he was Liberal member of

parliament for the Westbury division of Wiltshire. He was a junior lord of the treasury in 1906-07, vice-chamberlain of the Royal household in 1907-11 and a government whip for five years. He was created baronet in 1910 and appointed K.C.M.G. in 1911.

In February 1911 Fuller was appointed governor of Victoria to succeed Sir Thomas Gibson Carmichael [q.v.7]. He arrived in Melbourne on 24 May with his wife, two sons and four daughters. *The Times*, 14 January 1913, declared of Australians that 'A Governor of the right sort educates them, widens their views, eliminates their provincialism, keeps them in touch with the Empire and the world. As long as Great Britain sends out Governors who can do this, the most benighted and thrifty Australian will not grudge the expense or chafe at the ceremonialism'. Fuller, however, admitted 'I went to Melbourne much in the manner the "new boy" approaches his public school. I knew practically nothing of Australian life. When I got there I found it was impossible to know anything from merely English experience'.

Fuller had described himself to an Australian interviewer as 'just an ordinary type of English country gentleman and a good sportsman ... fond of hunting, shooting, stalking and the rest'; he had a reputation as an active politician, and a 'cheerily stubborn Liberal'. While he performed his duties amiably, there were minor controversies in office. In April 1913 he was reprimanded by the minister for external affairs for supposedly interfering in Federal matters by publicly suggesting the dispatch of an expedition to rescue (Sir Douglas) Mawson [q.v.] in the Antarctic. In July 1913 the *Argus* replied to Fuller's disappointment that his speeches were not proving good newspaper copy: 'His sense of humour' was more developed than 'his gift of humour'.

Fuller had difficulties with the Colonial Office over permission to escort his wife back from England where she had settled three daughters at school. Three months leave was later allowed and Fuller left Melbourne on 27 August 1913. An accident prevented him from returning to Melbourne with Lady Fuller, and on 24 November his resignation for health and family reasons was announced. He died at his home, Cottles Park, Atworth, Wiltshire, on 4 September 1915.

British A'sian, 18 May 1911; *Argus*, 6 Feb, 8 Mar, 17 May 1911, 8 Apr, 30 July, 6, 28 Aug, 3, 19, 24, 25 Nov 1913, 6, 13, 14 Jan 1914, 7 Sep 1915; *The Times*, 14 Jan 1913, 6, 7, 9 Sept 1915; Fuller file (news cuttings, 1911-13, LATL); CO 418/116/158-163, 196-211.   L. R. GARDINER

FULLERTON, MARY ELIZA (1868-1946), writer, was born on 14 May 1868 at Glenmaggie, Victoria, second surviving child of Robert Fullerton, born in Belfast of Presbyterian Scot extraction, and his wife Eliza, née Leathers, from Suffolk, England. Her father 'didn't know a plough from a handsaw' before he took up a selection in the Gippsland bush and built the bark hut where Mary was born. Mary was educated at home by her mother and at the local state school. She read avidly as a child: by the age of 11 she had read *Paradise lost* three times; she knew long passages of Shelley and Byron by heart and was steeped in the Bible. She also began to compose verse of her own.

After leaving school Mary helped on the farm but continued her reading. In her early twenties she moved to Melbourne. By 1899 she was living with her parents and sisters at Prahran; about 1907 they moved to Hawthorn. Overcoming a natural shyness, she became vocal in the women's suffrage movement of the late 1890s and early 1900s. She gained election to the Prahran School Board of Advice in 1899-1902, addressed women's progressive league meetings and joined the Women's Organizing Committee of the Political Labor Council of Victoria. During World War I she contributed articles on feminist issues and the case against conscription for publications such as *Ross's Monthly* and the Victorian *Socialist*.

At the same time she wrote stories, articles and verse for magazines and periodicals, sometimes under the pseudonym 'Alpenstock'. She was a member of the local literary and debating society and won several prizes for her work. In 1908 she published *Moods and melodies*, a collection of thirty-seven sonnets and nine lyrics. In 1921 she published more verse, *The breaking furrow*, and a collection of delightful reminiscences of childhood entitled *Bark house days* (reprinted in 1931 and 1962).

Mary had visited England in 1912; in 1922 she returned there, sharing a house with a friend and patron, Mrs Mabel Singleton. She met Miles Franklin [q.v.]; their rapport is evident in their voluminous correspondence between 1927 and 1946. Though weakened by asthma and heart trouble in later life, Mary wrote three novels under her own name – *Two women* (1923), *The people of the timber belt* (1925) and *A Juno of the bush* (1930) – and two under male pseudonyms, as well as a descriptive piece, *The Australian bush* (1928). Sensitive about her lack of university education and convinced that her sex prejudiced recognition of her work, she insisted that her authorship remain anonymous as 'E' when Miles Franklin arranged for her verse to be published as *Moles do so little with their privacy* (1942) and *The*

wonder and the apple (1946). Her identity was revealed only after her death.

Mary Fullerton never married: 'My nature really intended me to be the "go alone" that I've been', she wrote in her unpublished memoirs. Miles Franklin described her as 'sensitive, fastidious, reticent, self-mastered'. She died on 23 February 1946 at Maresfield, Sussex, and was buried in the local cemetery. While her novels have little lasting merit, some of her poems, and certainly her *Bark house days*, deserve a place in Australian literature.

Aust Woman's Sphere, 15 Mar 1904; *Age*, 11 Feb 1904; *Argus*, 4 July 1905; *Bulletin*, 15 May 1946; *Tribune*, 24 May 1946; S. M. Franklin papers (ML); Mary Fullerton papers (ML, *and* LaTL).

SALLY O'NEILL

FULLWOOD, ALBERT HENRY (1863-1930), artist, was born on 15 March 1863 at Erdington, Birmingham, Warwickshire, England, son of Frederick John Fullwood, jeweller, and his wife Emma, née Barr. From 15, Henry, as he was known, attended Birmingham Institute on a scholarship. On completing his studies he migrated to Sydney in 1881.

Employed first by John Sands [q.v.6] Ltd, Fullwood worked as a black and white artist for the *Picturesque atlas of Australasia* in 1883-86. He travelled extensively, including visits to Thursday Island, Torres Strait, Palmerston (Darwin), Port Moresby, New Guinea, and later New Zealand. His illustrations were workmanlike but diverged little from those of other staff artists such as Julian R. Ashton [q.v.7]. In the 1880s he shared a studio with Frank Mahony [q.v.]; with Ashton they spent the weekends painting. For a time he lived with friends Tom Roberts and Arthur Streeton [qq.v.] at their camp at Sirius Cove in Sydney. Fullwood, encouraged by Livingston Hopkins [q.v.4], also returned to etching. He contributed drawings to the London *Graphic* and *Black and White* as well as to the *Australian Town and Country Journal*, the *Bulletin*, *Illustrated Sydney News* and the *Sydney Mail*. In the centennial issue of the *Sydney Mail* (21 January 1888) he made a large wood-engraving of the city.

A member of the Art Society of New South Wales from 1884, Fullwood, with Roberts and others who were dissatisfied with the influence of laymen on its committee, was active in setting up the breakaway Society of Artists, Sydney, which was confined to professionals; he served on its council. On 13 October 1896 he married Clyda Blanche, daughter of J. H. Newman [q.v.], a photographer; she bore him two sons. In 1900 he auctioned his work and took his family first to New York for a year, thence to London. He visited Capetown in 1903. He found plenty of black and white work in London, exhibited at the Royal Academy of Arts from 1906 and the Salon de la Société des Artistes Français, Paris. A member of the Chelsea Arts Club, he was a friend of English artists and Bertram Mackennal [q.v.].

Soon after the outbreak of World War I Fullwood joined the Allied Arts Corps. From April 1915 to November 1917, when he was discharged as medically unfit, he served as a sergeant in the Royal Army Medical Corps, and was posted to No. 3 London General Hospital, Wandsworth, with fellow Australian artists, Roberts, Streeton, George Coates and Miles Evergood [qq.v.]. In 1918, with the rank of honorary lieutenant in the Australian Imperial Force, he went to France as official artist to the 5th Division and painted scenes of the Western Front, mainly water-colours, for the Australian War Memorial, Canberra.

Demobilized on 31 December 1919, Fullwood embarked for Sydney in February next year. In 1920 with John Shirlow [q.v.] he was a founder of the Australian Painter-Etchers' Society and in 1924 served on the first committee of the Australian Water-Colour Institute.

Fullwood died from pneumonia in the War Memorial Hospital, Waverley, on 1 October 1930 and was buried in the Anglican section of Rookwood cemetery. He was survived by a son. His estate was valued for probate at £844. Fullwood's work in oil, water-colour and etching is equally significant. His monotypes are also of interest. His earliest landscapes, dark in tone, reflected the influence of Ashton and were consciously Australian in spirit; from the late 1880s his work was lighter in mood. In England the illustrative qualities of his Australian oils and water-colours gave way to painting rather more rich and academically Impressionist. His portrait by James Quinn [q.v.] is in the Art Gallery of New South Wales.

Fine Art Soc Gallery, Melb, *A. H. Fullwood*, memorial exhibition cat, June 1936; Institute of Architects of NSW, *J*, 3 (1906), no 1, p 2; *Art in Aust*, no 8, 1921; *British A'sian*, 4 June 1914; *A'sian Antique Collector*, 19 (1979), p 75; *SMH*, 3 Oct 1930; T. W. Pring letters (ML).   MARTIN TERRY

FURBER, THOMAS FREDERICK (1855-1924), surveyor and lecturer, was born on 13 May 1855 at St Pancras, London, son of Augustus Frederick Furber, bookbinder, and his wife Mary Ann Forwood, née Bartlett. His father migrated to Sydney and in November 1860 became foreman of the bookbinding branch of the Government Printing Office. Thomas attended Fort Street Public School; in September 1869 his appointment as supernumerary draftsman in the survey branch of the Department of Lands over candidates much his senior was regarded as a school triumph. In 1875 he qualified as a licensed surveyor, and in 1877 was appointed to the triangulation staff as draftsman and computer. He became draftsman in charge of the General Survey of the Colony in 1880 and in 1890 chief computer. In 1904 he was appointed director of trigonometric surveys and metropolitan district surveyor; on his retirement in 1914 he was elected an honorary member of the New South Wales Institution of Surveyors, having been a founding member (1891), councillor, secretary, journal editor and several times president.

Furber was largely responsible for raising the standard of education in surveying; he joined the Board of Examiners of Licensed Surveyors in 1881 and was secretary from 1890. In 1892 with (Sir) George Knibbs [q.v.] he represented the Institution of Surveyors at the Intercolonial Conference of Surveyors in Melbourne. This led to reciprocity in the issue of certificates in all Australian States and New Zealand and stimulated the adoption of the zone system of time.

Furber's ability in mathematics was frequently noted and he contributed several papers, mainly didactic, to the *Surveyor*. With Joseph Brooks [q.v.7] in the field and Furber based in Sydney a high standard of accuracy was attained in the General Survey; Furber's reports compared well with the best of those of the great surveys in other parts of the world. He was concerned to add to knowledge of the figure of the earth; his valuable discussions of trigonometrical survey in Australia, published in reports of the Australasian (1898) and British (1914) Associations for the Advancement of Science and in proceedings of the Pan-Pacific Science Congress, Australia (1923), include discussion of deflection of the vertical in eastern areas. In December 1882 he went to Lord Howe Island to observe the transit of Venus.

Furber's appointment as actuary to the Public Service Board in 1903-14 and as secretary to the royal commission on sites for the seat of government of the Commonwealth in 1903, indicate the recognition of his abilities. In 1906 appointment as lecturer in geodosy and astronomy in the University of Sydney, continued until 1924, enabled him to extend his influence and education.

Furber's influence may well have reflected his personality rather than his status. He was energetic and devoted in his work, a 'no-nonsense' character described, apparently with some understatement, as incisive rather than conciliatory. His interest in reservation of areas on the Sydney foreshores and in the Blue Mountains is commemorated in Furber Steps at Katoomba. A fellow of the Royal Astronomical Society and a member of the Royal Society of New South Wales, he was keen on sailing and, in later years, on golf. On 17 May 1876 at St Benedict's Catholic Church, Sydney, he married Catherine Lee; after her death he married Blanche Osborne Wilkinson on 20 February 1883 at Albury with Anglican rites. He died with amyloid disease on 7 October 1924 at Sydney and was buried in the Anglican section of South Head cemetery. His second wife, a son and daughter from his first marriage and two sons from his second, survived him.

Surveyor (Syd), Dec 1904, p 221, Nov 1924, p 80; Syd Univ Union, *Union Recorder*, 30 Oct 1924; Roy Soc NSW, *J*, 59 (1925), p 5; *SMH*, 10 Oct 1924.

HARLEY WOOD

FURPHY, JOSEPH (1843-1912), writer, was born on 26 September 1843 at Yering, near Yarra Glen, Port Phillip District, son of Samuel Furphy, a tenant farmer, and his wife Judith, née Hare, who had migrated from Northern Ireland in 1841. John Furphy [q.v.4] was an elder brother. Joseph was educated by his mother who introduced him at an early age to the Bible and Shakespeare. In 1850 the family moved to Kangaroo Ground, where Joseph briefly attended the local school, and in 1852 to Kyneton, where Samuel Furphy ran a corn and hay business. Later he leased a farm and acquired a threshing plant, and Joseph became his agent in the district. At Glenlyon he met Leonie Selina Germain, of French descent. They were married at Christchurch, Daylesford, on 27 May 1867; Leonie was 16. His wife was to remain an enigma to him and a mystery to both her contemporaries and to later observers of the human scene.

After his marriage Furphy purchased a selection in the district of Colbinabbin. For the next six years he strove unsuccessfully to establish himself as a farmer. By 1872 he had decided that the land he was working was not suitable for farming. In 1873 he sold the farm, bought a team of bullocks, and set up business as a carter in the Riverina district of New South Wales. There he established a reputation as a Sterne in moleskins or a Munchhausen among the bullock-drivers. Nature had planted in him a vast fund of cheery optimism. All his life he was a stranger to the pessimism and the melancholy which weighed down Henry Lawson [q.v.] and other bush writers. During his years in the Riverina his literary talents blossomed in the long, bantering, half-humorous, half-serious letters which he wrote to his mother.

By then he was a self-professed believer in the gospel of work, self-discipline and self-education. In conversations with his fellow bullock-drivers out on the Lachlan Plains, and in the district round Hay he began to have the 'vision splendid'. It was to be a more serious-minded, non-Dionysian view of the fate of being a man in Australia. Furphy spurned the wild drinking-bouts with which the itinerant bushworkers consoled themselves for being deprived of creature comforts, and a woman's tender care. He was never the Bohemian either of the heart or the bar-room in the bush shanty. When his fellow bullock-drivers drank deeply of the waters of stupefaction Furphy was reading by a slush lamp in a tent pitched by some river bank on those inhospitable plains. His relations with his wife became even more tenuous.

He was changing slowly from the cheery optimist into the self-taught man who believed he had a message for his fellow Australians. He had acquired some of the doctrine he would preach when the time came to put pen to paper. He shared the Psalmists' condemnation of putting money upon usury. He went further and chided himself for making too much money. He seemed to accept the Pauline teaching that the love of money was the root of much evil. He told his father in February 1882 that the man who pursued money had made a 'compact with the evil one'. At the same time he preached the benefits of temperance to the bushworkers. While the Bohemians of the *Bulletin* were looking into the wine cup when it was red, Furphy was counselling remittance men and others out on the plains of desolation who had been 'imbibing the accursed thing for about a week' to promise to abstain until at least the following Sunday.

The drought of 1883 ended abruptly his life as a bullock-driver. In 1884 he began to work with his father in the family iron foundry at Shepparton. There by night Furphy continued to read voraciously in an endeavour to find the meaning of life and the probable future of society in Australia. From the few of his observations which have survived from that period he emerges as a man who did not whine, or wail, scowl or snarl. He had a religion. He called it a proud, humane religion that had no Thirty-nine Articles or surpliced flummery about it. He saw himself as a kind-hearted man. His friends said of him at the time that a kinder-hearted man never aimed a hammer at an anvil, or thrust a pen at an ink-bottle.

By the time of the depression of the 1890s Furphy was chewing over ideas for a work which would convey his vision of life. He already had some practice as a writer. In 1867 the Kyneton Literary Society had awarded him the first prize for some verses on the death of President Lincoln. It was perhaps significant that he should have taken as his principal character a man of heroic proportions, and a moralist. For Furphy was by nature a prophet, albeit a very humorous prophet denouncing the sins of the members of his own generation. In January 1893 he wrote to a friend about 'the hideous depression brought on by the unbridled greed of vile men in high places'. By then he was contributing stories and sketches to the *Bulletin*.

His friend was Kate Baker [q.v.7], a school teacher in Shepparton. She was encouraging Furphy to put his ideas on life down on paper. He had already tried to do just that, but was still agonizing over the medium he should choose. At that time he told Kate Baker that the only duty he recognized both in his life and in his writing was 'the very momentous one of forwarding the New Order'. That was the subject over which he laboured in the shed in the backyard at Shepparton.

At the end of March 1897 he wrote the last words of the manuscript:

Such is life, my fellow-mummers — just like a poor player that bluffs and feints his hour upon the stage, and then cheapens down to mere nonentity. But let me not hear any small witticism to the further effect that its story is a tale told by a vulgarian, full of slang and blanky, signifying — nothing.

Using the pen-name 'Tom Collins,' Furphy believed he had written a moral for his age and, he hoped, a moral for all times and places about the human situation. Like all great confessions about life it had come out of his own experiences, as a bullock-driver in the Riverina.

The next task was to get it published. On 4 April 1897 he wrote to the *Bulletin* for advice. Characteristically he asked for a reply of two or three words only. He asked A. G. Stephens [q.v.] to recommend a publishing firm. Stephens sent a reply Furphy would relish: 'Send the animal for inspection'.

The first response by Stephens summed up what subsequent readers were to find.

Rather long-winded, yet *Such is Life* is good. It seems fit to me to become an Australian classic, or semi-classic, since it embalms accurate representations of our character and customs, life and scenery which in so skilled and methodical a form occur in no other book I know. I think the book ought to be published and would find a sale.

Stephens offered to edit the work for Furphy.

When Furphy arrived in Sydney to discuss publication, the Bohemians of the *Bulletin* found him a very naive man. An anonymous wit published this description of him

Tom Collins
Who never drinks and never bets
And loves his wife and pays his debts,
And feels content with what he gets.

While the Bohemians of Sydney were mocking at conventional morality Furphy was writing high-minded letters to his mother about the 'possible righteousness of the human race', or telling her that 'the day of carousal' was past, and 'the day of work' had begun.

On the advice of Stephens Furphy agreed to take out of his original manuscript two huge slices. He then took the manuscript back to Shepparton where he laboriously rewrote it in long hand. In 1903 it was published in Sydney by *Bulletin* publications.

The reception of the work was very much as Stephens had predicted. Critics sensed Furphy was a formidable man: they perceived that the work was by a man inspired by a great moral passion: they agreed that the aim of the author had been to assist the Australian reading public to get both wisdom and understanding, but they were not able to agree on precisely what that wisdom consisted of. Some called Furphy the 'sage of Riverine', and left it at that. The reading public was also slow to respond. The sales of the work disappointed both Stephens and the author.

There was an equally indifferent response to the publication of the two deleted sections of the original manuscript of *Such is life*. Chapter V, after suitable revisions by Furphy, was published first as a serial in the *Barrier Truth*, Broken Hill, in 1912. As *Rigby's romance* it was first published as a book in an abridged form in 1921, and complete in 1946. Chapter II was revised and published as *The buln-buln and the brolga* in 1948. There was a second edition of *Such is life* with a preface by Vance Palmer [q.v.] in 1917, an abridged edition with an introduction by Vance Palmer in 1937, another edition of the full text in 1944, and a reissue of that text in 1948. That year Chicago University Press published the 1903 text with a biographical sketch and commentary by the American literary critic and historian, C. Hartley Grattan.

The critics both in Australia and the United States of America had insisted that the work was a minor classic, or that, at the least, it enjoyed a very special position in the history of Australian literature. Yet by an odd irony the only words by Furphy which lingered on in the memory of subsequent generations were the words he tossed off in his brief letter to the *Bulletin* on 4 April 1897: 'temper, democratic; bias, offensively Australian'. Critics such as Vance Palmer, Arthur Phillips, John Barnes, Guy Howarth and Ian Turner have endeavoured to detect deeper purposes, and subtleties in the development of the story.

What is clear is that Furphy held very passionate opinions on human behaviour in Australia. He had called his work 'offensively Australian'. He certainly believed in the virtues and capacities of the Australian bushman. He believed in a meritocracy: 'I acknowledge no aristocracy except one of service and self-sacrifice, in which he that is chief shall be servant, and he that is greatest of all, servant of all'. He believed in moral enlightenment. He believed that by a blending of the teaching of the Sermon on the Mount and the Enlightenment, humanity would move out of the darkness in to the light. He believed that by such moral persuasion a good time would come for the whole of humanity. Yet, paradoxically, the good time would not be accompanied by the pleasures which appealed to the Australian bushman such as drinking and general profanity. Furphy went on believing that 'honest water never left men in the mire'. Also he did not have much faith in love between man and woman. For him, it would seem, the great personal pain was his failure to know happiness with a woman. On why this was so, he remained silent all his life. Joseph Furphy was a private man, who never risked showing his heart in any public place.

He was also a very witty man. Possibly the two most memorable passages in his work were the section in *Rigby's romance* in which the bullock-drivers out in the Lachlan Plains described their reactions on first reading the story of Moses in the Old Testament, and the section in *The buln-buln and the brolga* where the honest bushman recounted his reactions to a Shakespeare play. But through all these works this boisterous humour lived side by side with a dignified melancholy, and a sadness about woman's love. Furphy remained possibly as much a mystery to himself as to his critics and readers.

The year after the publication of *Such is life* Furphy and his wife joined their two sons at Claremont in Western Australia. Survived by his wife, sons and a daughter, he died there on 13 September 1912, and was buried in Karrakatta cemetery after a Church of Christ service. After his death Kate Baker devoted the remainder of her life to keeping his name alive for Australian readers. In 1916 she collected and edited *The poems of Joseph Furphy*. In 1944 she published in collaboration with Miles Franklin [q.v.] *Joseph Furphy: The legend of a man and his book*. Extracts from the letters of Joseph Furphy were published in the *Bulletin* on 16 January 1935. But the devotion of his admirers, and the praise of some critics have not upset his standing as the author of a classic which few were to read and no one was ever to establish clearly what it was all about.

A. L. Archer, *Tom Collins (Joseph Furphy) as I knew him* (Melb, 1941); J. Barnes, *Joseph Furphy* (Melb, 1963); Furphy papers (ML).

MANNING CLARK

FYSH, Sir PHILIP OAKLEY (1835-1919), politician and merchant, was born on 1 March 1835 at Highbury, near London, son of John Fysh and his wife Charlotte. He was educated at the Denmark Hill School at Islington until 13, when he began work in a London stockbroker's office. Two years later he secured a subordinate position with the London shipping firm of L. Stevenson & Sons. After ten years service the firm offered him the charge of their Hobart agency. Fysh arrived in Melbourne on board the *Bombay* in August 1859, and settled in Tasmania at the end of that year. Accompanying him were his wife Esther Kentish, née Willis, whom he had married on 14 October 1856 at the Union Chapel, Luton, according to the rites of the Protestant Dissenters, and their new-born son. In 1862, amid widespread depression, Fysh purchased his employer's wholesale agency, and within a few years, trading as P. O. Fysh & Co., general merchants, became the leading wholesale businessman in Hobart. Later in his political career he found it difficult to establish his credentials as a reformer for, as one radical newspaper expressed it, he was still 'the representative of the old order of things'. He retired from the management in 1894.

In June 1866 Fysh won election to the Legislative Council on a progressive policy of economic development. Throughout the 1860s and 1870s parliament was torn with factional fighting; political alliances shifted constantly, making it difficult for any government to survive. Fysh represented Hobart in the council until 1869 and Buckingham in 1870-73, when he was also chairman of the board of directors of the Van Diemen's Land Bank. During this time he advocated railway development and taxation on incomes, and came to be regarded as one of the most promising politicians of the day.

Fysh moved to the House of Assembly in August 1873, winning the seat of East Hobart, and served as treasurer in the Alfred Kennerley [q.v.5] ministry. This experience broadened his political outlook, for the administration placed some emphasis on social reform. Fysh's main task was to secure the passage of an income tax bill through parliament, but, although a 'fluent and ornate speaker' and a clever tactician, he was defeated by the dominant landowning group.

In August 1877 Fysh formed his first government: it was not especially noteworthy. In March next year ill health forced him to resign. He served in the W. R. Giblin [q.v.4] ministry without portfolio until November, and spent the next eighteen months holidaying in England with his family. While there he studied the liberal movement and returned to Tasmania an advocate of classical liberalism.

After several years expanding his business, Fysh in 1884 re-entered the Legislative Council as member for Buckingham when a local liberal movement began to flourish. He was constructive in identifying platforms which the liberals could adopt, and in stimulating public debate; his main concern was manhood suffrage. In March 1887 Fysh again became premier. His cabinet, with himself as chief secretary, included Andrew Inglis Clark [q.v.3] and (Sir) Edward Braddon [q.v.7]; in their efforts to reform the social and political structure of the colony they brought a new character to Tasmanian politics. Legislation was introduced to regulate health, employment and charitable institutions. In addition, trade unions were legalized, a technical education scheme established and provision made for the creation of a university. Payment of members and triennial parliaments were introduced. However, the government lacked the resolve to press parliament to pass manhood suffrage, and was unable to deal with the onset of economic depression. It fell in August 1892.

Despite the defeat of his government, Fysh continued in politics. When the liberal faction returned to power in April 1894 under Braddon's leadership Fysh, newly elected to the Legislative Assembly for North Hobart, served until December 1898 as treasurer and postmaster-general. During the 1890s, also, he was active in the Federal movement. In May 1892, while still premier, he visited mainland colonies to discuss intercolonial customs reciprocity. His commitment to Federation at this time and later was motivated by his belief that it offered the only solution to Tasmania's economic problems. He represented the colony at the Federal conventions of 1891 and 1897-98 and was a member of the Federal Council of Australasia in 1895 and 1897. Moreover, while in London as Tasmania's agent-general in 1899-1901, Fysh joined with Barton [q.v.7], Deakin and Kingston [qq.v.] in securing final British approval for the Commonwealth Constitution bill.

With the establishment of the Commonwealth, Fysh entered Federal politics as minister without portfolio in 1901-03, and postmaster-general in 1903-04. As member for Denison during the last years of his political career he was forced into the role of a conservative in response to the growing influence of the Labor Party, whose creed he abhorred. He retired from politics in 1910 and farmed in the Derwent Valley.

Tall and willowy, Fysh was an impressive figure with his flowing white beard. Always a private man, he left very little of a personal nature on record. His keen sense of public responsibility, however, is shown in his involvement with numerous community organizations. Appointed justice of the peace in 1867, he was a city alderman in 1868-69, and later president of the Central Board of Health and chairman of the Metropolitan Drainage Board. Co-founder and sometime president of the Hobart Working Men's Club, he also supported the Ragged Schools Association, the council of Hobart High School, the Hobart Benevolent Society and the Tasmanian Political Reform Association. He held the rank of major in the Tasmanian Volunteer Rifle Regiment. He was appointed K.C.M.G. in 1896, an honour he had declined in 1891; he received an honorary Oxford D.C.L. in 1901. He died on 20 December 1919 at Lower Sandy Bay, survived by five sons and four daughters, his wife having predeceased him in 1912. A Congregationalist, he was buried in the family vault at Cornelian Bay cemetery. Over many years he had had few equals as a democrat and reformer in Tasmanian politics.

F. C. Green (ed), *A century of responsible government 1856-1956* (Hob, 1956); *Sydney Mail*, 20 Mar 1897; *Punch* (Melb), 7 Sept 1905; *Argus*, 23 Dec 1919; Q. J. Beresford, The evolution of a colonial liberal (Litt. B., Univ New Eng).

QUENTIN BERESFORD

FYSH, SIR WILMOT HUDSON (1895-1974), airline director, was born on 7 January 1895 at Launceston, Tasmania, son of Frederick Wilmot Fysh, merchant, and his wife Mary, daughter of Henry Reed [q.v.2]. His great-uncle Sir Philip Fysh [q.v.] was twice premier of Tasmania. After education at various schools including Launceston Grammar School and Geelong Church of England Grammar School, Victoria, he became a jackeroo and woolclasser, but on the outbreak of war enlisted as a trooper in the 3rd Regiment of the 1st Australian Light Horse Brigade. Serving on Gallipoli and in Egypt and Palestine he was commissioned lieutenant in 1916 in the brigade's machine-gun squadron before transferring to the Australian Flying Corps as an observer. He won the Distinguished Flying Cross, and graduated as a scout pilot at Heliopolis on 28 February 1919.

After his return to Australia that year Hudson Fysh, with Pat McGinness, another ex-service airman, and Arthur Baird, an engineer, planned to enter the Australian government's £10000 prize contest for a flight from England to Australia. Unable to proceed because of the death of their financial backer, Sir Samuel McCaughey [q.v.5], Fysh and McGinness were instead commissioned by the government to survey the Longreach (Queensland)-Darwin section of the route: their T-model Ford was the first car to journey overland to the Gulf of Carpentaria. On 16 November 1920 Fysh and McGinness with western Queensland graziers Fergus McMaster [q.v.], Ainslie Templeton and Alan Campbell formed the Queensland and Northern Territory Aerial Services Ltd (QANTAS). Operating with an Avro Dyak and an old BE2E war-disposals aircraft the company moved its head office from Winton to Longreach in 1921 and engaged in taxi, ambulance and stock inspection services, and joy-riding.

Through the second half of 1921 the company, backed by Federal politicians such as D. C. Cameron [q.v.7], A. S. Rodgers, J. A. J. Hunter, Sir T. W. Glasgow and (Sir) W. Massy Greene [qq.v.], worked to persuade the government to back a regular Charleville-Cloncurry passenger service. In February 1922 QANTAS tendered successfully and the service, with its invaluable mail-subsidy, opened on 2 November with 87-year-old Alexander Kennedy as its first passenger. Two surplus war-disposals Armstrong Whitworth aircraft were used.

A poor student at school, Fysh now tried to make up for lack of training; he read voraciously, studied economics and took a course in Pelmanism (memory-training). A shy, quiet man, he had nevertheless great political acumen and a hard head for business and soon established a reputation as a stern, uncompromising taskmaster. He became managing director of QANTAS in 1923, remaining a regular pilot until 1930 when the company registered its first million miles (1.61 million km) and moved its head office to Brisbane.

By this time QANTAS had begun flying schools in Longreach and Brisbane, had constructed seven of its own aircraft, operated Australia's first daily air-service (between Brisbane and Toowoomba in 1928-29) and had had the Charleville-Cloncurry route extended to Brisbane. In 1921 Fysh had advised John Flynn [q.v.] on the practicalities of a flying-doctor service and in 1928-47 QANTAS piloted an ambulance airplane for the Australian Inland Mission.

In April 1931 Fysh flew the Brisbane-Darwin section of an experimental airmail service between Australia and England. In 1933, as a passenger in the British Imperial Airways monoplane *Astraea*, he made a survey of the route to Karachi and on 18 January 1934 QANTAS in equal partnership with Imperial Airways founded Qantas Empire Airways Ltd (QEA), with Fysh as managing director; in the face of fierce competition from other local airlines and Royal Dutch Airlines (KLM), the new company secured the Australian government airmail contract between Australia and England. With the opening of the England-Australia flying boat service in 1938 headquarters were moved to Sydney. In 1940 Fysh was a founding director of Tasman Empire Airways Ltd (TEAL) which established the first air service to New Zealand.

During World War II Fysh, a squadron leader in the R.A.A.F. reserve, oversaw the use of QEA equipment and expertise against the Japanese; in 1943 the company ferried equipment and troops to New Guinea and evacuated casualties. In July that year QEA reopened the Middle East air route to England by flying via Perth and Ceylon; the trip to Ceylon took twenty-seven hours, the longest non-stop regular air service ever established.

In December 1946 the Australian government acquired the original half-interest of Imperial Airways in QEA and next year became the company's sole owner. Unlike his colleagues, Fysh accepted the inevitability of the government purchase; he conducted the negotiations, remained managing director and at the same time succeeded McMaster as chairman. He became chairman of the newly formed hotel company Qantas Wentworth Holdings in 1951. Appointed K.B.E. in 1953, he retired as managing director of QEA in 1955, in which year also the old QANTAS went into liquidation. In the past Fysh's single-mindedness had led to some bitter clashes; in 1934-35 his insistence on the use of the unreliable DH86 had caused a falling-out with the distinguished aviator P. G. (Sir Gordon) Taylor [q.v.]. He was in frequent conflict with other members of the QEA board and eventually relinquished chairmanship in 1966.

In retirement Fysh wrote an autobiographical trilogy, *Qantas rising* (1965), *Qantas at war* (1968) and *Wings to the world* (1970). He also published *Taming the north* (1933),

The Log of the Astraea (1933?), *Round the bend in the stream* (1968), a treatise on trout fishing, and *Henry Reed: Van Diemen's Land pioneer* (1973). An original committee-man (1945) and later president of the International Air Transport Association, he was a prominent member of the Australian Early Birds' Association, the Australian National Travel Association, the Australasian Pioneers Club, and the Institute of Transport. He was a fellow of the British Interplanetary and of the Royal Aeronautical societies.

Fysh died on 6 April 1974 at Paddington, Sydney, survived by his wife, Elizabeth Eleanor Dove, whom he had married at St James Church of England, Sydney, on 5 December 1923, and by a son and daughter. His estate was valued for probate at $95 817.

T. Hall, *Flying high* (Syd, 1979); *Australasian,* and *Aust Financial Review,* and *Canb Times,* and *The Times,* 9 Apr 1974.   J. PERCIVAL

G

GABRIEL, CHARLES JOHN (1879-1963), conchologist and naturalist, was born on 28 May 1879 at Collingwood, Melbourne, son of Joseph Gabriel, from Wales, and his wife Elizabeth Lovatt, née Baker, from Worcester, England. His father, a pharmacist, was a very early member and office-bearer of the Field Naturalists' Club of Victoria and an honorary collector for the National Museum of Victoria; his reports on marine expeditions to the Bass Strait islands were a major part of the twenty-one papers he published in the *Victorian Naturalist*.

Charles Gabriel was registered as a pharmacist in February 1902, and had a retail shop in Victoria Street, Collingwood. He married Laura Violet Marian Vale, daughter of a pharmaceutical chemist, at Holy Trinity Church, Kensington, on 20 April 1910; they had two sons.

From an early age Charles was a keen shell collector and, under the influence of his father, he arranged and classified that collection in a scientific manner. In 1900 he became a member of the Field Naturalists' Club and in 1908 published his first paper, 'Marine molluscs found near Stony Point, April 1908', in the *Victorian Naturalist*. At that time Gabriel began a twenty-three-year collaboration with J. H. Gatliff [q.v.] on additions and alterations to the latter's *Catalogue of the marine shells of Victoria*. In all they wrote twenty-seven joint papers in which they proposed forty-five new taxa and recorded many species for the first time for Victoria. After Gatliff's death in 1935, Gabriel continued this work alone. In 1936 he published a handbook on *Victorian sea shells* and in 1962 with J. H. Macpherson, the definitive *Marine molluscs of Victoria*.

Gabriel was the first Victorian conchologist seriously to study and describe the land and freshwater molluscs of the State. J. C. Cox [q.v.3] and C. Hedley [q.v.] in 1911 had published a preliminary paper on the land snails of Victoria but Gabriel devoted much time to documenting the fauna in a series of nine papers including a twenty-six-page *Catalogue of the land snails of Victoria* in 1930, a paper on *The freshwater Mollusca of Victoria* in 1939 and additions to his *Catalogue* in 1947. These still form the basis for the study of non-marine molluscs in Victoria. He described twenty-three new non-marine taxa and made many new records and observations on the fauna. Altogether Gabriel published fifty papers on molluscs in which were erected 110 new taxa.

Gabriel was appointed honorary curator of shells at the National Museum of Victoria in 1933 and later honorary associate in conchology. He was awarded the Australian Natural History medallion in 1958 for his outstanding contribution to Australian malacology. Survived by his sons, he died on 19 June 1963 at his Toorak home and was cremated. Gabriel's estate was valued for probate at £28 961. His very extensive shell collection and library were bequeathed to the National Museum of Victoria. The collection, housed in four magnificent glass-fronted cabinets, contains items of incalculable value because it includes many secondary types obtained on exchange from such early workers as Sir Joseph Verco, W. L. May [qq.v.], Hedley, T. Iredale and many others.

Vic Naturalist, 80 (1963-64), p 227; Malacological Soc of Aust, *J*, 1 (1969), no 12, p 32.

BRIAN J. SMITH

GABRIEL, CHARLES LOUIS (1857-1927), medical practitioner and photographer, was born on 25 June 1857 at Kempsey, New South Wales, eldest son and third of thirteen children of Charles Louis Gabriel, surgeon, and his English wife Rhoda Emma, née Rudder. Dr Gabriel senior, born at Martinique, Lesser Antilles Islands, West Indies, had visited Sydney as a surgeon with a French expedition to the South Pacific and later returned to settle at Kempsey. Young Charles Louis was educated there, and matriculated at the University of Sydney. From 1878 he studied at the School of Medicine of the Royal Colleges, Edinburgh (L.R.C.P., L.R.C.S., 1885). Copies of testimonials from Edinburgh paid tribute to his broad education, general culture and humanity.

By 1886 Gabriel had returned to Australia and next year went to Gundagai, New South Wales. In July he became medical officer to the Independent Order of Oddfellows' lodge, a post he held for more than thirty-five years. In 1888 he was appointed government medical officer to the Gundagai District Hospital and maintained a private practice. He quickly became one of the liveliest members of the community: the leading influence in the fledgling literary institute, president of the football club and patron of the swimming club. At the same time, and involuntarily, he became one of the principal actors in a public and prolonged dispute revolving around the hospital, its staff, administration and facilities. Gabriel repeatedly argued that improvements, particularly in hospital finances and general hygiene, must be effected. He was successful and at the same time earned for himself the reputation of the hospital's chief fund-raiser.

Of a number of pastimes, photography was his favourite — Gundagai and its citizenry were his subjects. Gabriel left a legacy of some 900 negatives which record the town in which he lived for 40 years. His main photographic preoccupation was people and in particular women. He managed to capture with warmth and intimacy the lazy life of the country town at the turn of the century. He photographed such events as the flood of 1900, the erection of the memorial to the men of the Bushmen's Contingent who fought in the South African War, the opening of the new hospital in 1904 as well as sporting activities such as tennis, fishing and chess. His films were processed by C. E. Weston, a draper and an amateur photographer. His photographs show a notable sense of composition and visual dynamics and represent a fine blend of art and documentary history.

Unsubstantiated folklore suggests that Gabriel had two wives; but he never alluded to an earlier marriage. On 30 March 1891 he married a widow, Jessie Violette Walton, née Young, at St Patrick's Church; they had no children. He died in Tumut hospital on 10 February 1927 after surgery for appendicitis and was buried in the Catholic section of Gundagai cemetery. An obituarist described Gabriel as 'Gundagai's most talented man'.

P. Quartermaine (ed), *Gundagai album* (Canb, 1976); *Gundagai Independent,* 10 Feb 1927; J. Gormly, Newspaper articles on Gundagai and Wagga, 1902-18 (NL); Gabriel family papers (NL).

CATHERINE SANTAMARIA

GABY, ALFRED EDWARD (1892-1918), soldier and labourer, was born on 25 January 1892 at Springfield, near Ringarooma, Tasmania, seventh son of Alfred Gaby, farmer, and his wife Adelaide, née Whiteway. Little is known of his early years other than that he was educated at Scottsdale and worked on the family farm after leaving school. He then spent some time in southern Tasmania. While working on his father's farm he had joined the militia and served for three years with the 12th Infantry Battalion (Launceston Regiment). Two elder brothers had seen active service in the South African War.

Before the outbreak of World War I Gaby followed one of his brothers to Western Australia where he worked as a labourer at Katanning. On 6 January 1916, after having been twice rejected for active service, he enlisted in the Australian Imperial Force as a private, and after training at Blackboy Hill camp was posted to the 10th reinforcements of the 28th Battalion. He sailed on the troopship *Ulysses* in April and joined his battalion in France on 6 August. His previous military experience brought him rapid promotion: from lance corporal on 13 August through all the ranks to sergeant on 30 December. On 7 April 1917 he was commissioned second lieutenant; he was promoted lieutenant on 26 September and was wounded in action (gassed) on 29 October.

Gaby was acting as commander of 'D' Company when, as part of the 2nd Division, his battalion was engaged in the great allied offensive of 8 August 1918. The 28th Battalion attacked German positions east of Villers-Bretonneux and in the course of this action Gaby showed conspicuous bravery and dash in leading and reorganizing his company when it was held up by barbed wire entanglements. He found a gap in the wire, and single-handed, approached an enemy strong point in the face of machine-gun and rifle fire. 'Running along the parapet, still alone, and at point-blank range, he emptied his revolver into the garrison', driving the crews from their guns and capturing fifty men and four machine-guns. He then reorganized his men and captured his objective. On 11 August 1918 in another attack near Lihons, during which he again showed bravery and coolness in engaging an enemy machine-gun position, he was killed by sniper fire.

In recording his death the war diary of the 28th Battalion paid special tribute to this gallant officer. He was awarded the Victoria Cross posthumously and was buried in Heath cemetery, Harbonnières. Lieutenant Gaby was unmarried.

K. R. Cramp, *Australian winners of the Victoria Cross . . . 1914-19* (Syd, 1919); C. E. W. Bean, *The A.I.F. in France,* 1918 (Syd, 1937, 1942); L. Wigmore (ed), *They dared mightily* (Canb, 1963); *London Gazette,* 30 Oct 1918; *Mercury* (Hobart), 8 Jan 1919, 30 Jan 1956; records (AWM).

D. ELLIOTT

GADSDEN, JABEZ (1858-1936), businessman, was born on 29 November 1858 at Blisworth, Northamptonshire, England, son of Elijah Gadsden, flour-miller, and his wife Harriet, née Allen. Jabez was employed in London in the boot manufacturing trade, and after migrating to Australia in 1879 he worked for three years for a Melbourne boot manufacturer. He began to keep accounts for Joseph Joyce, who had set up a bag-making business. Bags for rice were cut and sewn at Joyce's home, and sent out to be printed. As business grew, the firm obtained premises in William Street, Melbourne, and later moved to King Street, where the machinery consisted of a sewing-machine and a printing-press for printing the bags.

In 1884 Gadsden was made a partner in the business and, when Joyce moved to Sydney in 1889, became sole proprietor. The company now owned a litho-printing machine, and for a time undertook general printing work. Of an innovative turn of mind and interested in mechanical matters, Gadsden began in 1889 to experiment with the processes of printing on tinplate; it is claimed that he was the first man in Australia to practise the art. In 1896 he imported a flatbed lithographic press from England, and established a tinprinting and decorating works. The company produced the first printed can in Australia — a tea caddy commemorating the diamond jubilee of Queen Victoria. During the South African War, printed butter tins were supplied to the army, and the increase in trade made it necessary to import a second machine. In 1917 the first rotary machine to be brought to Australia was introduced.

Gadsden took over the business of a local tinsmith, and began to make tin canisters of all descriptions. The company had moved to Lonsdale Street, and in 1927 moved again to larger premises in West Melbourne. As well as textile bags and tin containers, the firm now produced canvas goods, wire mattresses and bedding, blinds and blind-rollers. By 1936 it had twelve factories spread throughout Australia and New Zealand.

Jabez had married Georgina Wilkinson, a milliner, on 24 December 1885 at Richmond, and they had three sons and a daughter. Georgina died in 1900. On 23 July 1902 he married Alice Strickland, principal of a girls' school and daughter of a Geelong clergyman. A member of a Plymouth Brethren sect, Gadsden attended church regularly. Always careful with his money, his philosophy was that every man should earn his keep, but he would help anyone genuinely in need. He took great interest in the well-being of his employees and staff. His interests were medicine, dentistry and biology, and in later years his hobby was making glass slides of insects and other objects, which he studied under his microscope.

Gadsden died at his home at Hawthorn on 12 December 1936 and was buried in Boroondara cemetery; his wife predeceased him. His estate was valued for probate at £62 107. In his will he left money to a number of his staff, to hospitals, charities and technical schools. He made provisions to ensure the preservation of family interest in the company, and although it is now a public company, it still bears his name and is managed by members of the third generation of the family.

A. Pratt (ed), *The national handbook of Australia's industries* (Melb, 1934); O. White, *The saga of the canmaking industry in Australia* (Melb, 1956); *Age*, and *Argus*, 14 Dec 1936; *Canb Times*, 7 June 1961; R. Gadsden, personal information, *and* F. Hodge, History of the firm of Gadsden and Company (MS, held by Mr R. Gadsden, J. Gadsden Aust Ltd, Melb).   A. McLeary

GALE, CHARLES FREDERICK (1860-1928), civil servant, and WALTER AUGUSTUS (1864-1927), parliamentary clerk, were the sons of William Gale, merchant and collector of customs, and his wife Mary Ann, née Scott. Charles Frederick was born on 26 November 1860 at Geraldton, Western Australia. He was educated at the Bedford Commercial School in England and later at Bishop Hale's [q.v.4] College (Hale School), Perth. He was a squatter in the Gascoyne district in the early 1880s, but was ruined by drought and went prospecting. From 1893 he was an assistant inspector of stock at Geraldton and from 1897 inspector of pearl-shell fisheries at Shark Bay. Two years later he became chief inspector of fisheries at Perth and in 1906 gave the joint select committee on the fishing industry valuable information on the western fishing grounds, gathered while leading a trawling expedition in 1904. From 1908, after an amalgamation, Charles was also chief protector of Aboriginals.

His first report recommended the establishment of reserve stations which the natives of each tribal district 'could look upon as a home'. Gale suggested that this could be done by splitting up some of the large pastoral holdings. He anticipated the 'strong opposition and protestation' of the squatters, but during his term, Moola Bulla, the first Aboriginal cattle-station, was begun. In 1909 he also persuaded pastoralists to ration free of charge Aboriginal indigents on their properties, by pointing out that they were, after all, 'born in the country from which in many instances large profits are yearly made'.

On 22 July 1914, in Melbourne, he married a widow, Flora Marie Farquhar, née Blackman. He then took long service leave in Japan. After resuming work in February 1915, he was retrenched in March, 'owing to the re-organisation of certain departments'. This was probably due less to differences over policy than to a clash of personalities.

R. H. Underwood, the minister, held a low opinion of Gale's 'ability and energy'. The dismissal upset public servants and a select committee of inquiry was appointed on the motion of Gale's friend, (Sir) Walter Kingsmill [q.v.]. All witnesses attested that Gale's work had been satisfactory and the committee reported that his dismissal was 'illegal'; it recommended reinstatement. This was not done and further intimidatory measures forced him to accept retrenchment. In 1917-19 he was secretary of the Civil Service Club.

Gale was a committee member of the Western Australian Turf Club and a justice of the peace. Childless and survived by his wife, he died of pneumonia, in the Armadale hospital on 24 September 1928. His estate was sworn for probate at £500.

Walter was born on 22 November 1864 at Geraldton, Western Australia, and was educated at the High School, Perth, and the Collegiate School of St Peter, Adelaide. He won a scholarship to Exeter College, Oxford, England, where he spent a year in 1884, excelling in cricket and football, but did not graduate. He returned home next year to teach at the High School, Perth. A protégé of (Sir) John Forrest [q.v.], in 1886 he became an assistant registrar in the colonial secretary's office for two years. He then became secretary to the Central Board of Education. In 1890 he was acting registrar-general and registrar of patents and next year became clerk and librarian of the Legislative Assembly. On 18 November 1896 at Busselton he married Georgiana Kennedy Richardson-Bunbury; they had a daughter and two sons.

On 1 May 1901 Walter became the second clerk-assistant to the Federal House of Representatives in Melbourne and, soon after, clerk-assistant. He wrote poetry and songs and published a booklet of war verse, *Are we downhearted? NO NO* (1915), from which over 10000 copies of the urging, patriotic 'Play the game' were circulated by the Commonwealth to aid recruiting. In 1917 he succeeded Charles Gavan Duffy [q.v.] as clerk of the house and in 1920 he was appointed C.M.G. From that year he was also honorary secretary of the Empire Parliamentary Association and in 1924 toured South Africa, as guest of their association, with members of the Australian parliament.

After eight years of failing health, Walter collapsed at work, in the new Parliament House, Canberra, and died from heart disease on 27 July 1927. He had been esteemed by members of all parties for his thorough parliamentary knowledge and after his burial in the churchyard of St John's Anglican Church, Canberra, a memorial holly tree was planted below his old office.

J. S. Battye (ed), *Cyclopedia of Western Australia*, 1 (Adel, 1912); P. Biskup, *Not slaves, not citizens* (Brisb, 1973); *PP* (LA WA), 1902, 2 (A8), 1909, 1 (2); *Western Mail* (Perth), 10 Apr 1914, 3 Aug 1917; *Table Talk*, 11 July 1901; *SMH*, 7 May, 3 June 1920, 11, 30 July 1924, 28, 30 July, 24 Sept 1927; *Herald* (Melb), 23 Mar, 3 May, 27, 28 July 1927; *Australasian*, 6 Aug 1927.   J. G. WILLIAMS

GALE, WALTER FREDERICK (1865-1945), banker and astronomer, was born on 27 November 1865 at Paddington, Sydney, son of Henry Gale and his wife Susannah Gordon, widow of F. F. Phillips and daughter of Charles Windeyer [q.v.2]. He was educated at Paddington House School. After five years working in insurance and commercial offices, he joined the Savings Bank of New South Wales in 1888. In 1897 he was appointed accountant at the Newcastle branch, in 1914 manager at Newtown (after it was amalgamated with the Government Savings Bank of New South Wales), in 1916 manager at Barrack Street, Sydney, and in 1917 manager and chief inspector at the head office. After retiring in 1925 he was manager of Hoskins Investments Ltd until 1938.

Gale's interest in astronomy was stimulated by his father and firmly established by the appearance of the Great Comet of 1882. About 1884 he built a telescope with an 18-cm mirror, the first of many that he owned. Elected a fellow of the Royal Astronomical Society, London, in 1893, that year he visited Chile with a Lick Observatory eclipse expedition, and observatories in the United States of America. He valued the contacts then made.

Back in Australia, Gale was a founder and organizing secretary in 1894 of the New South Wales branch of the British Astronomical Association and then secretary for several years. Later he was president for twenty years. He formed the habit of sweeping the sky on every clear night and discovered independently seven comets. In three cases, 1894 II, 1912 II and 1927 VI, priority was recognized by attaching his name to the comet. He also discovered some double stars which bear his name and a ring nebula. He was leader of a party to observe the eclipse of 1922 at Stanthorpe, Queensland.

An assiduous observer of the planets Mars, Jupiter and Saturn, Gale published drawings in the *Journal* and *Memoirs* of the British Astronomical Association. He examined surface features of Mars, being first to note some, and was an ardent supporter of the suggestion of life on the planet. On the other hand, he was one who held that the great turbulent activity in the atmosphere of

Jupiter must be evidence of an internal energy source — this is now recognized.

When the Government Savings Bank of New South Wales closed in 1931 Gale became chairman of a committee formed to protect depositors, and had to control several turbulent meetings, one by getting the Town Hall organist to drown the noise. His interests included coins, stamps and handwriting; he regularly played cards, solo and poker. In all his fields he was prepared to assist and advise others, particularly the young, and was a frequent and able public lecturer on astronomy.

Gale twice received awards from the (Thomas) Donovan [q.v.] Trust and in 1935 the Jackson-Gwilt medal of the Royal Astronomical Society 'for his discoveries of comets and his work for astronomy in New South Wales'. He was chairman of the board of visitors of Sydney Observatory and a trustee of the Public Library of New South Wales in 1913-37.

Gale's usual sweep of the sky was frustrated by cloud on 1 June 1945; later that night he died in a few minutes from a heart attack; he was cremated. He was survived by his wife, Violet Marion, née Birkenhead, whom he had married on 28 June 1899 at St Mary's Anglican Church, West Maitland; and by two sons and four daughters. A portrait of Gale by G. F. Harris is held by his descendants.

Aust J of Science, 8 (1945), p 73; A. W. W. Gale,'Life and work of W. F. Gale', British Astronomical Assocn, *J*, 56 (1945), p 18; Roy Astronomical Soc, *Monthly Notice*, 106 (1946), p 29; British Astronomical Assocn (NSW branch), *Bulletin*, 1964, no 441; Cwlth Bank Archives, Syd.; family records.   HARLEY WOOD

GALL, WILLIAM (1867-1938), public servant, was born on 13 May 1867 at Ipswich, Queensland, son of William Davidson Gall, builder and contractor, and his wife Isabella, née Stewart. Educated at West Ipswich Primary School, he won a scholarship to Ipswich Grammar School. Despite winning a trustee's scholarship in 1883, he left school and joined the public service as clerk in the Colonial Secretary's Department on 27 February 1885. He married Louise Wohlgemuth at Rosewood on 24 May 1893.

He transferred to the Audit Office in October 1894 after keeping accounts of government operations in the 1891 shearers' strike, and in 1899 became an inspector. Responsible from July 1901 for all South African War accounting, he became accountant in the Home Secretary's Department on 13 January 1903 and chief clerk and accountant in July 1904. After successfully centralizing the department's financial procedures, he was in charge of pension administration in 1908-10.

On 26 November 1913 Gall was appointed under-secretary for home affairs and protector of Aborigines. An unsuccessful candidate in 1915 for the position of auditor-general, he was acting comptroller-general of prisons from June 1926. Despite his expressed wish to complete fifty years in the public service, he was retired on 31 February 1934. State parliamentary redistribution commissioner in 1910 and 1931 (chairman), and a Commonwealth commissioner in 1911, he was State returning officer in the 1917 referendum for the abolition of the Legislative Council. In 1903-15 he was a trustee for the Queensland Patriotic Fund. He was appointed C.M.G. in 1930.

Fair-haired, handsome and efficient, Gall was a success in the Home Secretary's Department under the Denham [q.v.] Liberal government. Under the Ryan [q.v.] Labor ministry in 1915, he felt strongly that his job was at stake. Accused by the premier in September 1917 of antagonism to the government, he won some friends by his unswerving support of his ministerial head, the ailing David Bowman [q.v.7]; Gall survived the hostility of John Fihelly [q.v.] whom he saw as his worst enemy. Although he lost responsibility for electoral administration and was attacked in 1920 by W. J. Riordan, 'the reputed Tory under secretary' had witnessed the signature of his departmental head John Huxham [q.v.] on the Labor Party pledge in 1918. By the time Gall retired, he had become a trusted confidant of his minister Edward Hanlon.

Gall particularly enjoyed working, and was regarded as a skilled negotiator, in the area of local government. He was less happy as protector of Aborigines, and was involved in a number of controversies about reserves; he supported J. W. Bleakley [q.v.7] in his policies of regulation and control. Pressed by James Stopford [q.v.] into accepting oversight of prisons in 1926, he had to cope with a prisoners' mutiny at Brisbane (Boggo Road) prison shortly after his appointment; he supported a prison farm system for first offenders, and played a considerable part in the opening of Palen Creek Prison Farm.

Despite his high government office, Gall was an enthusiastic if mostly unsuccessful speculative investor. He was a director of the Holbourne Island Syndicate formed in 1917 to exploit guano deposits off Bowen. With Stopford and Spencer Browne [q.v.7], he bought forty acres of land at Keperra near Brisbane as a development speculation; this later became the Keperra Country Golf Club. With police commissioner W. H. Ryan, he held joint shares in Bowen Salt Ltd and, by accepting a parcel of shares in Yellow

Cabs Queensland Pty Ltd, again with Ryan, he risked serious complaint – the shares were accompanied by a note thanking the two men 'for what you have done on our behalf'. After retirement Gall served as a company director. He concentrated on gold exploration but had other interests ranging from the Australian Patent Potato Farmer Pty Ltd to the Queensland Electric Coursing Association Ltd.

Intensely interested in Queensland history and toponymy, Gall served on the Oxley Memorial Library Committee in 1936-38 and on the quasi-official Queensland Place Names Committee. A block of State archives, borrowed by him in pursuing his private interests, was only returned to official custody in 1969. A keen shooter and fisherman, he collected Australian literature and was an enthusiastic gardener.

Gall died on 14 May 1938 and was cremated after a Presbyterian service. His estate, valued for probate at £7074 in Queensland and £328 in New South Wales, was left to his wife and their three surviving children.

Daily Mail (Brisb), 3 June 1930; *Courier Mail*, 16 May 1938; *Queenslander*, 18 May 1938; Gall papers (Fryer Lib, Univ Qld); Ecclesiastical file 831/1938 (QA).   PAUL D. WILSON

GALWAY, SIR HENRY LIONEL (1859-1949), soldier and governor, was born on 25 September 1859 at Alverstoke, Southampton, England, son of Lieut-General Sir Thomas Lionel Gallwey and his second wife, Alicia Dorinda Lefanu, née MacDougall. Educated at Cheltenham College and the Royal Military College, Sandhurst, he was commissioned in 1878. He was aide-de-camp to the governors of Bermuda in 1882-89 and was promoted captain in 1887. Appointed deputy commissioner and vice-consul in the Niger Coast Protectorate in 1891, he championed the overthrow of 'fetish rule', relished punitive expeditions and sent to the British Museum 2800 looted bronze and ivory sculptures. He tricked the King of Benin into accepting a treaty, which was savagely enforced in 1897. Often mentioned in dispatches, he was rewarded with the Distinguished Service Order (1896), appointment as C.M.G. (1899) and promotion to major (1897). Given the rank of lieutcolonel when placed on half-pay in 1901, he retired from the army in 1902 to become governor of St Helena, where he revived capital punishment. Appointed K.C.M.G. in 1910, he was transferred to Gambia in 1911. That year Gallwey changed his surname to Galway and on 26 August 1913 in London he married Baroness Marie Carola Franciska

Roselyne D'Erlanger, née Blennerhasset, a widow.

Galway then became governor of South Australia. He was ill-chosen and resented the limits to a constitutional governor's freedom. At his welcome in 1914 he upset people by praising the River Murray Waters Agreement, awaiting parliamentary debate, and compulsory military training. His support of gambling, and of minimal restrictions on liquor trading, angered puritans. He abhorred Australian egalitarianism, remarking that 'the people are ruled by the coolies'. He criticized women's enfranchisement and the State's educational system; when he called for an end to the White Australia policy, opining that the Northern Territory needed Asian labour, the prime minister Andrew Fisher [q.v.] demanded and obtained a full withdrawal and apology.

His frankest speeches were to the South Australian Caledonian Society. Thus in 1915, deploring the 'crooked' minds of the 'well-paid' Islington ironworkers who had demanded higher wages, he said 'he would have liked to put all those men in khaki and discipline and ship them to the front'. This drew fire from the premier C. Vaughan [q.v.] and gave cartoonists a field day.

The Colonial Office disapproved of his callousness towards the unemployed, his hysteria about South Australians of German ancestry and his disregard of instructions: he refused to send the governor-general copies of his dispatches and repeatedly disobeyed Imperial requests to consult the Commonwealth before making consular appointments.

His superiors began to think that he should be recalled, but World War I saved him. He became 'the most effective voluntary recruiting agent in Australasia' and before each conscription referendum called for a 'yes' vote. Consequently he was allowed to retain office. But his 1917 declaration that 'It must have been a joyful day for Germany when Australia turned down conscription', drew abusive rejoinders from J. H. Scullin [q.v.], the *Daily Herald* and the Ballarat *Evening Echo* and prompted a State Opposition motion for the abolition of his office. When this was debated the Speaker refused to allow Labor members to make personal remarks; the motion failed. But it was at the governor's insistence that Sir Richard Butler [q.v.7] was dropped from A. H. Peake's [q.v.] ministry in 1919 and when cabinet adopted recommendations that a war memorial be built on the site of Government House and a new vice-regal residence be purchased in the suburbs, Galway dissuaded Peake from the scheme.

Lady Galway was a compassionate woman of culture, liberal opinions and charm. Her public talks on history and poetry and her lectures on modern languages at the universities of Adelaide and Melbourne were popular, though the *Bulletin* observed: 'Sassiety is getting brain fag in the effort to keep up to the intellectual standard of Lady Galway'. She was tireless in her war work and founded South Australia's Red Cross Society.

While Galway's tactlessness made him South Australia's most controversial governor since F. H. Robe [q.v.2], he was admired by Adelaide's establishment; but all Labor parliamentarians boycotted his farewell. The Colonial Office refused him another post. They considered him 'impertinent' and 'incorrigible'. He left South Australia in 1920 and in retirement continued an active interest as chairman of the Big Brother committee, an emigration scheme to settle British youths as farm labourers in Australia. He died in London without issue on 17 June 1949 and Lady Galway died in 1963.

M. C. Galway (ed), *Lady Galway Belgium book* (Adel, 1916); P. Gosse, *St Helena 1502-1938* (Lond, 1938); M. C. Galway, *The past revisited* (Lond, 1953); P. A. Howell, 'More varieties of vice-regal life', *JHSSA*, 9 (1981), and for bibliog; *SMH*, 17 Feb 1936.   P. A. HOWELL

GAME, SIR PHILIP WOOLCOTT (1876-1961), governor, was born on 30 March 1876 at Streatham, Surrey, England, son of George Beale Game, a merchant of Broadway, Worcestershire, and his wife Clara, née Vincent. Educated at Charterhouse and the Royal Military Academy, Woolwich, he was commissioned in the Royal Artillery in November 1895. Promoted captain in 1901, he was mentioned in dispatches during the South African War. He served in India and Ireland and passed through the Staff College at Camberley in 1910. On 11 August 1908 he married Gwendolen Margaret, daughter of Francis Hughes-Gibb of Dorset.

In 1914 Game went to France as a major. In the war he was awarded the Distinguished Service Order, the Légion d'honneur and the Order of the Crown of Italy and was five times mentioned in dispatches. In 1916 he was seconded to the Royal Flying Corps, subsequently transferring to the Royal Air Force on its inauguration. Game's ability in staff work led to his appointment as director of training at the Air Ministry and, after a tour of duty as air officer commanding, India (1922-23), as air member for personnel on the Air Council. Appointed K.C.B. in 1924, he retired at the beginning of 1929 with the rank of air vice marshal. Later in the year he was promoted G.B.E. and next year was appointed governor of New South Wales.

The new governor arrived in Sydney in May 1930. The problems of the Depression were compounded by bitterness arising from the desire of the Labor Party, led by J. T. Lang [q.v.] to abolish the nominated Upper House, and from Lang's radical socio-economic views. These seemed to Game to be highly dangerous. When the election of 25 October returned Lang, the governor privately expressed his regret to the Nationalist Party leader (Sir) Thomas Bavin [q.v.7], but for the next eighteen months his official and even personal relations with Lang were not unfriendly. Game was conscious that it was very difficult for him to get an unbiassed point of view, his social engagements bringing him in contact with 'ninety-nine Nationalists for every one Labour man'.

On 5 November Game demurred when asked for a number of appointments to the Legislative Council, in order to abolish that chamber. The Bavin government had in 1929 obtained an act providing that the council might not be abolished without a referendum. Game urged the premier to wait until the council had rejected an abolition bill; but when Lang pressed him he agreed to appoint twenty-five new members. Lang, however, presented a much larger list to which Game refused assent, and the premier dropped the matter. Lang was by now aware that the council was prepared to pass a bill for abolition, relying on the 'entrenchment' of its position under Bavin's act.

The issue arose again in March 1931 when the council blocked two of Lang's most controversial legislative proposals, an arbitration bill and the reduction of interest bill. Game refused to swamp, and was accused by some of Lang's supporters of acting in the interests of bond-holders. There is, however, no evidence of pressure from London, and Game quite properly ignored approaches from people in New South Wales hostile to Lang. He rejected a similar request in June after the political situation had been further complicated by a split between the premier and the Federal Labor Party and the economic situation aggravated by the closure of the Government Savings Bank. By this time the council had built up a formidable list of bills rejected or blocked, and political tension had increased amid growing economic depression. Lang was particularly concerned about his emergency taxation bill. The secretary of state in London refused Lang's request to intervene.

But the question whether the governor was entitled to discretion in the matter of advice concerning Upper-House appointments remained unresolved. In September Lang, standing on the principle that such advice should be followed, refused an offer of twenty-one new council members because he wanted seventy. But Game was becoming alarmed by the activities of Eric Campbell's [q.v.7] New Guard and the reactions of some of Lang's supporters to it. When the premier asked for a modest twenty-five appointments in November he assented. Game was attacked by the press, accused of accepting bribes from Lang and subjected to a snubbing campaign by some of the leaders of Sydney society for giving way. There seems little likelihood that he was influenced by such unjust and improper treatment. Circumstances, rather than pressure of this kind, were pushing him unwillingly into confrontation with his premier.

The most important of these circumstances was the confrontation which had already developed between Lang and the Commonwealth government. Lang effectively defaulted in the payment of overseas debts. The Commonwealth sought to ensure payment by passing a series of Financial Agreement Enforcement Acts, which in April 1932 were found valid by the High Court, and the Commonwealth proceeded to seize the State's balances at the banks. Lang resisted, and Game, who up to this time had refused to take any action against the government, believing, properly, that such action would be unconstitutional, now felt that the situation had changed and demanded Lang's compliance with the law or resignation. Lang refused and on 13 May Game dismissed him. Parliament was dissolved and in the election which followed Lang's party was heavily defeated. The bitterness of the controversy was lessened by a split in the Labor Party which isolated Lang from much of his natural support. The furore died down rapidly and the rest of Game's term was uneventful. He had some sympathy for Lang's position, and remained unhappy that he had felt forced to dismiss his premier, whose humanitarian instincts he sincerely admired.

In January 1935 Game left Sydney and in December became commissioner of the London Metropolitan Police. There was considerable discontent in the force over some of the changes made by his predecessor; and he was forced to deal with Fascist and Communist demonstrations, an Irish Republican Army bombing campaign, and, a little later, the organization of the police role in air-raid precautions and relief. He dealt effectively with those problems and the consequent improvement in police morale was an important factor in the survival of London during the concentrated German air attack of 1940-41.

Game retired in 1945; he had been ap-

pointed K.C.M.G. on his departure from New South Wales and G.C.V.O. for his organizational work at the 1937 coronation, and was now promoted G.C.B. He died at his home, Blackenhall, Sevenoaks, Kent, on 4 February 1961, survived by his wife, daughter and by his elder son, who had married Vera, daughter of Sir Charles Bickerton Blackburn [q.v.7]. His second son had been killed in action at Taranto, Italy, in 1943.

Few Australian governors were asked to solve the kind of problems which faced Game. His English liberal background, the clear-headedness which made him a first-rate staff officer, and a sympathy for human misery which prompted him to return one-quarter of his gubernatorial salary to a hard-pressed Treasury and spend a significant part of the rest on private charity made it possible for him to surmount them. Few even of Lang's strongest supporters really hated him. Perhaps his qualities were best summed up in the weeks following the dismissal of Lang. While the Opposition rejoiced and the electors approved he lamented the fate which made him strike what he called 'my assassin's stroke'. A real success as both staff officer and police commissioner, he was far from a failure as a governor.

H. V. Evatt, *The king and his dominion governors* (Lond, 1936); B. Foott, *Dismissal of a premier* (Syd, 1968); H. Radi and P. Spearritt (eds), *Jack Lang* (Syd, 1977); *The Times*, 6 Feb 1961; A. H. Chisholm correspondence, *and* Game papers (ML).

W. G. McMINN

GANT, TETLEY (1853-1928), lawyer and politician, was born on 19 July 1853 at Manningham, Yorkshire, England, son of James Greaves Tetley Gant, solicitor, and his wife Sarah Ann, née Gaunt. He was educated at Rugby School and St John's College, Oxford, (B.A., 1877; M.A., 1879), where he rowed and played cricket for the college. At the Inner Temple he formed a close friendship with Tasmanian-born (Sir) Elliott Lewis [q.v.] before being called to the Bar in 1883. Next year he migrated to Hobart where he was admitted to the Supreme Court of Tasmania and in 1888 entered into partnership with Lewis. On 19 July 1882 at St John's Church of England, New Town, he married Frances Amy Roope, daughter of a well-to-do Hobart merchant, whose fine New Town residence, Wendover, was for a time the Gants' family home.

In May 1901 Gant was elected to the seat of Buckingham in the Legislative Council, a position he retained until ill health forced his resignation in August 1927. In 1904 he was appointed chairman of committees and from

July 1907 was president of the council for a record nineteen years; none of his rulings was ever challenged.

Like Lewis, Gant took a deep interest in the University of Tasmania. Appointed to the university council in 1905, he succeeded Lewis as vice-chancellor in 1909 and was chancellor in succession to Sir John Stokell Dodds [q.v.4] in 1914-24. His speeches at the annual commemoration gatherings were invariably marked by a keen desire to encourage the spread of higher education throughout the community. In 1909 he represented the university at the inauguration of the University of Queensland in Brisbane. He was a member of the Tasmanian Club from 1898 and president in 1913, the year he was appointed C.M.G. He was president of the Amateur Horticultural Society of Hobart from 1902 until his death.

Gant died on 7 February 1928 at Lower Sandy Bay. His obituarist in the *Mercury* described him as 'an ideal English gentleman . . . He had a fine personal presence, was debonair, affable and courteous in manner, liberally disposed, [and] was highly respected and esteemed by all classes'. He was survived by his daughter, his wife having died in 1926, and was buried in St John's cemetery. His estate was valued for probate at £4876.

J. Foster, *Men at the Bar* (Lond, 1885); *Mercury*, 20 Mar 1924, 8 Feb 1928; *SMH*, 2 Aug 1927, 8 Feb 1928.   PETER STOPS

GARDEN, JOHN SMITH (1882-1968), clergyman, trade union leader and politician, was born on 13 August 1882 at Nigg, Kincardine, Scotland, second son of Alexander Garden, whitefisher, of Lossiemouth, and his wife Ann, née Smith. Both his parents came from fisherman stock from the north of Scotland. He went to the state school at Lossiemouth, was apprenticed as a sailmaker to his cousin W. Cormack and read evangelical literature. His elder brother James, also a sailmaker, migrated to Australia in the 1890s; the rest of the family joined him in Sydney in 1904.

In 1906 Garden was a Church of Christ minister at Harcourt, Victoria. Next year on 6 May in Melbourne, with the forms of that Church, he married Jeannie May Ritchie, from Leith, Scotland. By 1909 he was a member of the Labor Party and was a Baptist preacher at Maclean, New South Wales; at the 1910 State elections it was reported that he would contest the local seat, Raleigh, as an independent Labor candidate against the official Laborite, who labelled him 'an Orangeman' and a 'member of the "no-

licence" party', but Garden withdrew. He was in Sydney for the 1913 elections and was mentioned as the Labor candidate for Petersham, but again did not run. Next year he was living at Paddington and working intermittently at his trade; he became the president of the Sailmakers' Union and its delegate on the Labor Council of New South Wales, which was to be his power base until 1934. In 1916 he was elected assistant secretary of the council, and in 1918 became its secretary. He failed as a Labor candidate at Parramatta in the 1917 State elections.

In the meantime 'Jock' Garden was employed from 1915 by the Department of Defence at its ordnance store at Circular Quay. In 1916 he was fined £10 for improperly accepting a gift from a supplier to the department; he was dismissed on 14 March next year after admitting that he had destroyed an important voucher. Garden was an ardent fundamentalist, who remained attached to Christianity as a deacon of the Church of Christ, at least to the early 1920s. His belief in the 'lowly Nazarene' was a vital part of his populist radicalism, and in 1918 he defended 'the workers' against Presbyterian charges that they were 'steeped in infidelity and disloyalty'. His early opposition to gambling and smoking decomposed but not his aversion to drinking. His oratorical style, seasoned by a ripe Scots burr, ranged from beguiling to ranting, adaptable to the pulpit, the Trades Hall and the Sydney Domain: often his speeches were incoherent harangues, but seldom ineffective. He was a great reader of non-conformist and radical writing, including Marx and Lenin especially after the 1917 Russian revolution. He was courageous, generous and romantic. His ideas reflected his enthusiasm and eclectic longings, and nourished his determination to succeed; if he could not make people pious, he would make them better off. The unfriendly J. Bailey [q.v.7] called him 'an addle-headed Pommie'.

The times were propitious for Garden on the Labor Council in 1916-18. The Labor movement was deeply split over World War I and conscription. In 1916 the Labor Party premier, W. A. Holman [q.v.], and other politicians were expelled and formed the conservative National Government; the victorious industrial wing, led by the Industrial Vigilance Council, became more radical. In the ferment some moderate unions left the Labor Council, and the Industrial Vigilance Council attempted to make the Labor Party the political creature of the One Big Union – a grandiose, revolutionary scheme. The Australian Workers' Union exacerbated the turmoil by seeking to make itself a non-revolutionary O.B.U. with some co-operation from politicians, moderate unions and conservative Labor groups.

At the 1919 Labor Party conference the A.W.U. faction, led by Bailey, had the numbers to expel the extremist proponents of the O.B.U.; John Storey [q.v.], leader of the parliamentary Labor Party, took every opportunity to condemn Garden in 1919-20. But he consolidated his position on the truncated industrial wing, and at the Labor Council led an activist majority of its executive, soon known as 'The Trades Hall Reds'. He was a member of the Socialist Party of Australia and of the Industrial Socialist Labor Party. In November 1920 he announced the formation of the Communist Party of Australia, which he had initiated with W. P. Earsman [q.v.]. Garden was prominent in 1921 at the All-Australian Trade Union Congress in Melbourne, which wanted to impose a positive socialist policy on the Australian Labor Party.

In 1922 the Labor Council was affiliated with the Red International of Labor Unions (Profintern). That year Garden attended the Second Profintern and Fourth Comintern congresses in Moscow, and euphorically claimed that '1000 Communists were influencing 400 000 members of Australian trade unions, and could even direct the Labor Party'; less imaginatively, he said that 11 out of 12 executive members of the Labor Council were communists. He was elected to the Executive Committee of the Communist International (Comintern). While overseas he provoked his European communist comrades by taking an active part in a Christian revivalist meeting in Scotland.

In Sydney in April 1923 Garden said that he was not impressed by 'the slow Slavonic mind', and argued that 'Australia must formulate a policy to suit her own needs'. He said that Lenin and Trotsky were well informed on the country, and that the former wanted unity in the Australian Labour movement. Following Lenin's advice, Garden and other communists rejoined the Labor Party in order to 'whiteant' it, and at the June State conference the balance of factional forces saw him elected to the executive. Next month he discussed the theme that the Labor Party was 'rotten, corrupt and bourgeois', which annoyed the party's president, A. C. Willis [q.v.]. But Garden kept his militant reputation intact by serving fourteen days in gaol in August 'for the right to free speech'.

J. T. Lang [q.v.], the new parliamentary Labor leader, also resented Garden's attacks on his colleagues, and in October alleged that he 'had been nearly everything in turn, and nothing very long, and those who know him best regard him as a rather exotic brand of political mountebank'. The Labor Party executive ruled that no communist could be a member of the party and in November expelled Garden. The 1924 State conference confirmed the ban. He continued to meddle in the party's kaleidoscopic factional disputes, weakening the Labor Council (affiliations fell to 42 in 1926), and diluting his own ideals. Lang remained the butt of Garden's frustration, with Sir George Fuller [q.v.], the National Party premier, taking advantage of the crossfire. Garden organized a special trade union conference in September which proposed to run industrial 'Labor candidates at the 1925 State elections, a decision which was compounded in December 1924 when the Communist Party resolved to run separate candidates. The end of his machinations was his humiliating defeat as a Communist against Labor in the seat of Sydney in May 1925. Labor won the elections and Lang became premier. Garden had become a conspicuous target of the Nationalists, as personifying the 'red menace' of the Labour movement. Prime Minister S. M. (Viscount) Bruce [q.v.7] used him astutely in beating Labor at the 1925 Federal elections.

· By 1926 Garden could appreciate the advantages of coming to terms with Lang, who was not so enthusiastic, but could see him as a trade union ally in his leadership troubles. In January Garden praised the premier for his work for the forty-four hour week. In September, living at Maroubra, he announced his resignation from the Communist Party and his application to rejoin the Labor Party – his religious feelings had always made him an imperfect communist, and he had concluded that the party had little political future. Lang loomed as a replacement for Lenin in his pantheon. He remained associated with the Pan-Pacific Trade Union Secretariat, the executive of the Red International of Labor Unions and was editor of the *Pan-Pacific Worker*. More than anyone else, he was responsible for the foundation of the Australasian (Australian) Council of Trade Unions in Melbourne in 1927.

E. G. Theodore [q.v.] increased A.W.U. pressure on Lang as his caucus disputes with P. Loughlin, T. D. Mutch [qq.v.] and V. M. Goodin intensified: but a conference in March in 1927 adopted the so-called 'Red rules' which effectively excluded the A.W.U. from controlling the Labor Party. Lang reconstructed his cabinet in May, and next month the central branch of the union withdrew from the Labor Council. The Lang-Garden front was consolidated, while the A.W.U. added to conservative propaganda that the Labor Party under them was revolutionary and anti-Australian.

On 13 June 1928 Garden was arrested and

charged with incitement to murder. It was alleged that in a speech on tactics in the marine cooks' strike he had said the 'scab cooks . . . may lose their balance. In which case the water is damp, the sea is deep, and dead men tell no tales'. He was acquitted in August. In January 1929 he rejoined the Labor Party. At a Labor Council meeting in February an attack on Garden by communists was frustrated when a girl rushed to play 'The Red Flag' on a piano and they all joined in singing. He was active in the timber strike that year and debated trade unionism with barrister R. Windeyer [q.v.] at the University of Sydney; he also spoke on the strike at the Constitutional Club, 'with sirs on the right of me, sirs on the left . . . and sirs in front of me'. In July he was accused of conspiracy in connexion with the strike, but was discharged. He was granted continuity of membership in the Labor Party in April 1930 to enable him to contest the Sydney Municipal Council elections; he won and sat for Flinders Ward in 1930-34. At the 1930 State elections he committed himself further to Lang; he said that 'There is one man, and only one man, who can save you and that man is John T. Lang'. Lang's win tightened the shackles.

In March 1931 he was 'counted out' by communists at a meeting of the unemployed in the Domain. He was in the thick of Lang's struggle with the Labor prime minister J. H. Scullin [q.v.] to enforce the half-baked 'Lang Plan' which Lang's devotees saw as a nostrum to cure the Depression: Garden debated it with D. R. Hall [q.v.] in August. In April his absence from a meeting of the Labor Council, because of his political work for Lang, was criticized. In June violence broke out at a council meeting when unemployed factions demonstrated. Next month he ran as the Lang Labor candidate for the Federal seat of Cook, but lost narrowly. On 6 May 1932 he was assaulted at his home by eight men, and was rescued by his two sons and two dogs. His attackers belonged to an unbalanced group, known as the Fascist Legion, within the New Guard; they trained in black-hooded gowns. In November the communists made another unsuccessful attempt to defeat Garden as secretary of the Labor Council.

Labor politics in the early 1930s had become even more Byzantine than in the 1920s, with State and Federal factions in conflict. Garden's vision of a strong industrial movement, aware of its international obligations, was fading fast. Lang's 'inner group', including Garden, was in control of the 1933 State Labor conference. He was Lang's hatchet man in the demolition of the party's 'socialisation units'. After quoting Lenin on the nationalization of banking, he said 'Our leader (Lang) is ahead of the God they bend their knee to. Our report goes further than the policy advocated by Lenin. Mr Lang is the greatest leader the country has ever produced'. This has come down the years as Garden saying that 'Lang was greater than Lenin'. Early in 1934 he was campaigning interstate for the Lang group to take over the Australian Labor Party. In another debate with Windeyer, his style was still described as 'fervent, declamatory, thunderous'.

In May 1934 there were signs that some Sydney trade unions were waking up to Lang, and Garden again had the job of pulling them into line. His influence had waned, but he was still secretary of the Labor Council and through it controlled radio station 2KY. Lang was now losing elections. In the 1934 Federal elections the United Australia Party prime minister, J. A. Lyons [q.v.], used Garden effectively as the communist-red spectre haunting the Labor Party. Garden won Cook for Lang Labor. He resigned from the Labor Council, received a gold medal and became a life member; but he left a vast rehabilitation task for his successors. From Canberra Garden had a clearer view of Lang's defects. He could see the advantages of Labor unity and worked for it as he became an efficient and popular parliamentarian. His relations with Lang deteriorated, exacerbated in 1936 by a struggle to control 2KY and, as Lang was still in command of the State Labor machine, Garden was once more expelled. He was vulnerable in a variety of ways. His black hair, brushed back, was now greying, his face was lengthening and a dewlap was forming.

In 1937 John Curtin, the new Federal Labor leader, intervened to seek unity in New South Wales. Garden was readmitted, but Lang arranged that he should lose preselection for Cook. In October he became a tariff consultant and began a business, Dengar Publications. He ran again for Cook in 1940 as an official Labor candidate, but the Lang Labor man beat him. In 1942-47 he was employed, at the instigation of E. J. Ward, the Federal minister for labour, as liaison officer between him and the trade unions. Garden had known Ward for a long time as a fellow participant in the frantic Labor politics of Sydney. He also took up racing, running horses under the name of 'Mr Leo', after his zodiac sign.

In January 1948 Garden was charged with his son Harcourt and others, with forgery and falsification in connection with certain 1944-45 financial dealings in New Guinea timber — £50000 was involved. He was found guilty on one charge and was sentenced to three years. In November Garden,

Harcourt and others were charged with conspiracy in connexion with the affair. Garden implicated Ward and alleged that Harcourt Garden was his dummy in the transaction. In December all were acquitted, and in June 1949 Ward was exonerated by a royal commission. In March 1957 Garden and his son were charged with fortune-telling; they were joint proprietors of the astrology weekly magazine, *Review*; the case was dismissed after it had been said that a client had paid £3 3s. for a horoscope he had not received.

Garden died in hospital on 31 December 1968. Cremated with Church of Christ forms, he was survived by his wife, one of his two sons and one of his two daughters.

I. Turner, *Industrial labour and politics* (Canb, 1965); A. Davidson, *The Communist Party of Australia* (Stanford, USA, 1969); R. Cooksey, *Lang and socialism* (Canb, 1971); J. Robertson, *J. H. Scullin* (Adel, 1974); M. Dixson, *Greater than Lenin?* (Melb, 1977); H. Radi, P. Spearritt (eds), *Jack Lang* (Syd, 1977); F. Farrell, *International socialism and Australian labour* (Syd, 1981); *SMH*, 21 Jan 1920, 21 May 1921, 16 Apr 1923, 8 Sept 1924, 27 May 1927, 29 Aug 1928, 25 Apr 1930, 24 Feb 1933, 27 Apr 1937, 17 Sept 1940, 13 Apr 1946, 29 Jan 1948, 6 May, 23 Dec 1948, 4 July 1950, 7 May 1957, 5 Jan 1969; I. Young, Conflict within the New South Wales Labor Party 1919-1932, (M.A. thesis, Univ Syd, 1961), *and* The impact of J. T. Lang on the N.S.W. Labor Party, 1929-1943 (M.A. thesis, Univ NSW, 1963); Labor Council of N.S.W., Minutes, 1916-34 (ML).   BEDE NAIRN

GARDINER, ALBERT (1867-1952), politician, was born on 30 July 1867 at Orange, New South Wales, seventh son of William Gardiner, wheelwright, and his wife Charlotte, née Davis, both native-born. Educated at the local public school, he was apprenticed at 15 as a carpenter. In 1890 he moved to Parkes to build the Hazlehurst gold battery, stayed to work as a feeder and in the 1891 election stood for Forbes as the newly formed Labor Electoral League's candidate. He was an Anglican and a total abstainer; the Protestant temperance movement had afforded him debating practice. He was also well known as a cricketer, footballer and amateur boxer. Despite his youth, he topped the poll. In 1894 he won the new single-member electorate of Ashburnham. Although he had refused to agree to the 1893 solidarity pledge, claiming later that it might compromise his temperance principles, he was endorsed by four of the five local leagues. In parliament he was not accepted by official Labor, and voted mainly with the Free Traders. He was defeated in 1895.

Out of parliament, he put some of his energies into rugby football and, known as

'Jupp' Gardiner, played in the forwards for New South Wales against New Zealand and Queensland in 1897 and against England in 1899. An organizer for the Australian Workers' Union in 1898 he was an unsuccessful Free Trade candidate for Ashburnham next year and Independent candidate for Orange in 1901; in the absence of official Labor candidates he received union support.

His first marriage ended in divorce, and on 3 April 1902 Gardiner married Theresa Alice Clayton at Parramatta, taking a job in Fiji with the Colonial Sugar Refining Co. Dissatisfied with conditions, he resigned and after visiting New Zealand returned to Orange to join the Labor Party, emboldened by the inclusion in its platform of local option. He won Orange in the 1904 election and not long afterwards, when a royal commission sought to investigate land scandals attributed to W. P. Crick and W. N. Willis [qq.v.], he attracted State-wide publicity with charges implicating the premier Sir Joseph Carruthers [q.v.7] in other land scandals and for having links with Willis. He revived these charges during the 1907 campaign which he lost. He then became a State political organizer for the A.W.U.

Gardiner was impressive for his size and weight of some eighteen stone (120 kg) and his forceful delivery, 'rapid in utterance, fiery in tone'. In 1910 he was one of the team of three successful Labor Senate candidates. A member of the parliamentary delegation to the coronation in 1911, he was made vice-president of the Executive Council in 1914. In 1915-16 as assistant minister for defence he took a close interest in the conditions of military camps. He opposed conscription and resigned from cabinet on the eve of the first conscription referendum in October 1916. In the much smaller Labor Opposition, he became Labor leader of the Senate (for three years he was the only Labor senator) and subsequently deputy leader of the party. In 1918 he achieved some fame by delivering an overnight speech lasting twelve hours forty minutes, the longest ever in Federal parliament; this forced the introduction of a time limit on parliamentary speeches.

Although he never discarded his free-trade opinions, loyalty to the Federal Labor Party characterized Gardiner's remaining years of political activity. In 1923 he joined Matthew Charlton [q.v.7] and the State parliamentary leader, James Dooley [q.v.], in attacking the executive of the New South Wales branch of the party as corrupt and in bringing about Federal intervention when the State executive expelled Dooley and appointed J. J. G. McGirr [q.v.] as parliamentary leader. Late in 1925 he lost his Senate seat. In 1927, with the New South

Wales party again split, Gardiner supported the A.W.U. faction against Jack Lang [q.v.]. His criticism of the Lang faction earned his expulsion from the party. Next year, after nomination by the anti-Lang leader T. D. Mutch [q.v.], Gardiner was elected to a Senate vacancy created by the death of John Grant. As it was a casual vacancy, he filled the position for only five months. Without party endorsement, it was futile for him to stand again for the Senate. Instead, in the 1928 Federal election, he contested Dalley, against E. G. Theodore [q.v.], as an Independent Labor candidate. In 1931, when the Federal Executive of the A.L.P. expelled the New South Wales branch, Gardiner joined the official branch set up in opposition to Lang's party. He worked loyally for the branch and contested the State seats of Waverley (1932) and Canterbury (1935) but polled badly both times. He then retired from active politics and resumed his trade as a builder. He died on 14 August 1952 at his home at Bondi Junction, and was cremated. He was survived by his wife, a son and a daughter.

B. Nairn, *Civilising capitalism* (Canb, 1973); D. J. Murphy (ed), *Labor in politics* (Brisb, 1975); AWU, *Official report of annual convention*, 1910; *Daily Telegraph* (Syd), 23 July 1895, 10 Aug 1904; *Western Champion* (Parkes), 1 July 1898, *Orange Leader*, 9 Aug 1904, 20 Aug 1907; *Punch* (Melb), 22 Aug 1912; *Argus*, 18 Sept 1914; *Smith's Weekly* (Syd), 13 Nov 1937; *SMH*, 15 Aug 1952.

MARK LYONS

GARDINER, JAMES (1861-1928), land agent, auctioneer and politician, was born on 12 June 1861 at Papakura Valley near Auckland, New Zealand, son of George Gardiner, farmer, and his wife Mary, née Craig. In South Australia from 1867, he was educated at Saddleworth Public School before finding work with a carrying company. In 1882-93 he worked for William Hamilton, a Victorian stock and station agent and married Emily Louisa Browne on 22 April 1889 at Northcote, Melbourne. They migrated to Western Australia in 1895 when Gardiner was sent by Gordon & Gotch [q.v.4] Ltd to manage a new branch. In 1900 he established his own auctioneering firm.

Following association with liberals on the Federal League's executive in the campaign for Federation, he was elected for the State seat of Albany next year. A Liberal government under (Sir) Walter James [q.v.] emerged in July 1902. To the surprise of many, the inexperienced Gardiner was appointed colonial treasurer and was soon seen as the 'iron headed man of business'. Luckily the economy was buoyant: gold production peaked in 1903 and the State had not yet felt the full impact of Federation. Gardiner represented Western Australia at the Federal-State Treasurers' Conference of February 1904, where it was ironic that he found himself arguing States' rights.

Gardiner was comfortable with the pragmatic liberalism of the James government, but personal financial difficulties forced him to resign from Cabinet in April 1904 and to withdraw from the mid-year elections. He left with considerable bitterness, engendered by Labor's co-operation with arch-conservatives to turn out a Liberal government. In 1906-18 he managed the land-grant Midland Railway Co. As successive subdivisions were made of the company's grants between Perth and Geraldton, Gardiner worked in the field classifying land and supervising sales and he initiated a scheme to settle British migrants on partially cleared blocks. He acquired 5000 acres (2023 ha) at Moora and settled his eldest son there.

Gardiner's financial interests now prospered: he also held directorships in the Commercial Union Assurance Co. (W.A. branch) and the South Perth Ferry Co. He helped found the Perth Club and was president of the Western Australian Cricket Association in 1908-24 — frequently entertaining visiting cricket teams out of his own pocket.

In 1909 Gardiner was president of the National Political League and next year travelled to Britain where he advocated emigration and promoted Western Australian fruit exports. In 1914 he won the wheat-belt seat of Irwin under the banner of the Country Party, which he had been active in establishing. His experience gained him leadership of the eight-man party and he promoted an independent stance for it, balanced in a potentially powerful position between John Scaddan's [q.v.] Labor government and the conservative Liberals. Gardiner's Country Party opposed Labor's platform of land resumption and the replacement of freehold by leases, but he felt at home with their moderate reformist tone. His party supported Scaddan's agrarian socialism: government credit, services, transport and marketing and Labor's other state enterprises designed to benefit metropolitan workers. A consensus politician, he could see little sense in defeating an energetic government's programme to alleviate the effects of the 1914 drought. This was reinforced by his close personal friendship with Scaddan. These views placed him out of step with the conservative elements of his party's backers, the Farmers' and Settlers' Association, which voted in March 1915 to secure a new parliamentary leader. Gardiner resigned six days later and the

Country Party voted with the Liberals to oust the Scaddan government next year.

Gardiner now found himself out of the political arena as Speaker of the Legislative Assembly in March-June 1917; deafness forced his resignation. But out of the reorganization of political factions after the conscription crisis of World War I, and the split in the Labor Party, Gardiner emerged in mid-1917 as treasurer in a composite National government under (Sir) H. B. Lefroy [q.v.]. Despite criticism from the F.S.A., Gardiner was happy in the National government with its conservative, Country Party and ex-Labor elements. However he resigned in April 1919 because he was irked at his colleagues' failure to cut spending and he disagreed with their influenza epidemic regulations. Gardiner retired from parliament in March 1921. He had always swum against the political tide in seeking agreement based on private capital, practical socialism and moderate social reform. Following three years illness, he died of cardiac failure on 27 October 1928 in Perth and was buried with Church of England rites in Karrakatta cemetery. He was survived by three sons and three daughters, his wife having predeceased him.

R. Pervan and C. Sharman, *Essays on Western Australian politics* (Perth, 1979); *Univ Studies in History* (WA), II (1955), no 3, IV (1965), no 3, IV (1966), no 4; *Hist Studies*, no 43, Oct 1964; *West Australian*, 1, 2, 3 Apr 1919, 28 Oct 1928; MS 1540/16/108, Deakin papers (NL).

GARDNER, ROBERT (1837?-1915), merchant, was born at Bannockburn, Stirlingshire, Scotland. As a young man he migrated to Victoria with his brothers William and John. In 1864 he obtained from the Tasmanian Survey Office a lease of the 480000 acre (194000 ha) Flinders Island in Bass Strait for £400 per annum, a rent which was decreased to £112 10s. 6d. in 1871-77. Gardner had tenants on the island until 1886 when the government decided against giving the lease to one individual. Hummock Island, known as Prime Seal Island in the Furneaux group, was also leased by Gardner from 1864 and in 1866 he purchased 40 acres (16 ha) of Roydon Island. Gardner and his tenants mainly engaged in sheep farming.

In 1872 he began operating in Launceston as a wool and grain broker, general merchant and tanner, in partnership with Richard John Stevenson McKenzie. With offices initially in St John Street, a Wellington Street tannery and a leather and grindery store in Charles Street, Gardner and McKenzie expanded to become shipping agents trading around the north-east coast

to George's Bay in the St Helens district. In 1879 the partners established a smelting works at Wharf Esplanade acting as agents for the Tasmanian Tin Smelting Co., but failed in a bid to undercut the Mt Bischoff Tin Mining Co.'s smelters. When the partnership was dissolved in January 1883 Gardner carried on the various businesses himself. About 1901 he joined Thomas McKenzie in a separate venture as the Tasmanian Manufacturing and Importing Co., and in 1909, with his nephew George Duncan Gardner, registered a public company, Robert Gardner Ltd, with headquarters in Cameron Street.

Over the years Gardner became an extensive landowner with pastoral and agricultural interests in various parts of Tasmania, always including the Bass Strait islands. One of the largest exporters in Launceston, he was a principal of the Launceston Shipping Co., established in 1909, trading in the River Tamar to the Furneaux group of islands. He was a warden of the Marine Board of Launceston in 1889-97. An early shareholder in the National Bank of Tasmania, he was a director in 1885-1912 and chairman for several years. He was a local director of the South British Fire and Marine Insurance Co. of New Zealand, an investor in the Glasgow Engineering Co. and a director of the auctioneering firm of W. T. Bell & Co. Ltd. His mining interests included directorships of the Hercules Gold and Silver Mining Co. and the Red Hills Silver Mining Co.

Gardner was a generous patron of the Launceston Rifle Club from its inception, but was reputed to be mean in business and frugal in his manner of living. In his later years a chronic sufferer from a 'bronchial affection', he died on 31 July 1915 at St Margaret's Hospital, Launceston, and was buried with Presbyterian forms. Gardner never married. His estate was valued for probate at £90460. In 1916 Robert Gardner Ltd was acquired by Allan Stewart and wound up in 1920.

Cyclopedia of Tasmania, 2 (Hob, 1900); E. A. Bell, *An historic centenary—Roberts, Stewart & Co Ltd, 1865-1965* (Hob, 1965); *Examiner* (Launceston), 16 Nov, 21 Dec 1872, 28 Apr 1879, 9 May 1884, 20 May 1895, 2 Aug 1915; SC 337/1, LSD 16/18, 19, 20, 64 (TA).   ALAN WARDEN

GARLAND, DAVID JOHN (1864-1939), clergyman, was born on 4 October 1864 in Dublin, son of James Garland, librarian, and his wife Mary, née Saunders. Trained for the law, he migrated with his parents to New South Wales, and in 1889 joined the Church of England ministry. As a deacon he served in Grafton, Quirindi and Narrandera, then was sent to Perth in 1892 and ordained there as missionary priest for the diocese. Because of his success in launching and financing scattered bush parishes, he was also made diocesan registrar and secretary in 1895-1902, chaplain to the bishop in 1894-1902 and canon of Perth in 1900-02. His crusade for religious education in state schools led to the incorporation of a permissive clause in the Elementary Education Act of 1893. Before leaving for Perth he had married a widow, Mary Hawkins, née Hadfield, at Christ Church St Laurence, Sydney, on 29 October 1892. They had one son.

In 1902 Garland became rector of Charters Towers, Queensland, and a canon of St James Cathedral, Townsville. He was appointed archdeacon of North Queensland in 1903, administered the diocese in 1903-04, and in 1904-07 was its registrar. Unhappy under Bishop Frodsham [q.v.], he resigned in 1907 to devote his full attention to the Bible in State Schools League in Queensland. A referendum on religious instruction in state schools was carried on 15 April 1911 by a large majority. In July 1912 he was asked to testify to a New Zealand government inquiry into religious instruction. His advice accepted, in 1914 he published relevant testimonies given to the inquiry in *Religious instruction in state schools.*

A chaplain to the volunteers in Western Australia and Queensland from 1896, Garland volunteered at the outbreak of World War I. Senior army camp chaplain in Queensland in 1914-17, in 1915 he founded and was director of the Soldiers Help Society. Co-founder with Colonel A. J. Thynne [q.v.] of the Compulsory Service League, he was also honorary organizing secretary for recruiting in Queensland. He served in 1918-19 in the Middle East where he founded eight clubs for Australian troops. After the expulsion of the Turks from Jerusalem he was the first chaplain to celebrate the Eucharist in the Anglican chapel of the Church of the Holy Sepulchre. During the 1919 rebellion in Egypt he provided liaison between the British military authorities and the Coptic Church, and was awarded the knighthood of the Gold Cross of the Holy Sepulchre by the patriarch of Jerusalem. Returning to Queensland in 1920, Garland became rector of Ithaca; director of immigration for the Church in 1911-33, he was president of the New Settlers' League from 1926. From 1927 until his death he broadcast Sunday services on public radio from his parish church, St Barnabas. When in 1937 the Australian Broadcasting Commission barred politicians from broadcasting for three months before the Federal election, Garland challenged what he called the commission's 'dictatorship of opinion'. He invited the Queensland premier, W. Forgan Smith [q.v.] to be the principal speaker at a communion breakfast and, when the A.B.C. objected, enlisted the private station 4BC. The result was a full press coverage and questions in parliament. Garland was never loath to mix the spiritual and the secular.

As an important architect and originator of Anzac Day ceremonies and rituals, Garland was described in 1924 by acting premier W. N. Gillies [q.v.] as the 'life and soul' of the Anzac Day Commemoration Committee, although he later shared the post of honorary secretary of the committee with Captain E. R. B. Pike. With the support of the various Queensland premiers who chaired the committee *ex officio*, Garland ensured that, as Anzac Day was a civilian tribute, the committee should remain civilian. The Returned Sailors' and Soldiers' Imperial League of Australia under (Sir) Raymond Huish only gained control of the committee and thereby of Anzac Day in Queensland in 1935.

Garland initiated the Anzac Day march, the returned soldiers' luncheon, the two minutes silence, the wreath-laying ceremonies at memorials and the special church services. He also began a trust to use money raised from Anzac Day badges for the care of soldiers' graves at home and abroad. The royal blue silk badges devised by Garland include the winged lion of St Mark, because St Mark's Day coincided with Anzac Day. The badge and ceremonies, vigorously backed by Garland, were taken up in other States and to a very large extent in New Zealand and Great Britain.

Garland was overpoweringly energetic with a distinctive flair, if not genius, for organization. He was appointed O.B.E. in 1934. An enthusiastic Jacobite, he bore various titles in the Order of King Charles the Martyr. Widowed in 1933, he died on 9 October 1939 and was buried in Toowong cemetery. His estate was valued for probate at £3660.

Anzac Day Commemoration Cttee (Brisb), *Anzac day sermons and addresses* (Brisb, 1921), *and* Minute-books, 1916-22, 1923-37 (Oxley Lib); Church of England, Diocese of Nth Qld, Year book, 1904-05; W. M. Mansfield, Anzac day 1915-1937, its origin, its culture and its political mythology … (B. A. Hons thesis, Univ Qld, 1979); Wilson family papers (held by author); Obit by Rev. L. J. Hobbes, radio station 4QR, 12 Oct 1939 (held by Rev. N. Jackson, St Paul's C of E, Ashgrove, Brisb).   WENDY M. MANSFIELD

GARLAND, JOHN (1862-1921), barrister and politician, was born on 17 September

1862 at Cowhythe near Fordyce, Banffshire, Scotland, son of Robert Garland, farmer, and his wife Isabella Whyte, née Neill. He was educated at Fordyce Academy and the University of Aberdeen (M.A., 1882) and received his legal training at the University of Edinburgh (LL.B., 1886).

Garland arrived in Australia in 1887, was admitted as a student-at-law in July and to practice at the Colonial Bar on 30 November 1888. Within a few years he had established a large junior Crown practice, particularly at common law, and was retained in important land law cases. He was a founder and elected member of the Council of the Bar of New South Wales and its legislation committee in 1902-05. He became a K.C. in 1910.

Elected to the Legislative Assembly for Woollahra in July 1898, Garland was a loyal and active supporter of (Sir) George Reid [q.v.]. He strongly advocated Federation and diligently scrutinized proposed legislation for technical defects. Defeated in June 1901, he won a by-election for Tamworth in April 1903 but lost again in July next year and failed in a bid to win Phillip in 1907. Garland was a prominent member of the Liberal and Reform Association, and was among twelve members appointed to the Legislative Council by (Sir) Charles Gregory Wade [q.v.] in July 1908. He served as minister of justice and solicitor-general from December 1909 until October 1910.

In Opposition at the beginning of World War I, Garland strongly criticized Labor's approach to the war effort and the restrictions which this placed on his friend, the premier W. A. Holman [q.v.]. In 1915 and 1916 he served on the executive of the Universal Service League. When Labor split over conscription in 1916, Garland energetically promoted the formation of the National Party. He became minister of justice and solicitor-general in Holman's new National ministry on 16 November 1916. In office Garland vigorously supported every facet of the war effort and accused the Labor movement and, particularly, the Industrial Workers of the World, who opposed conscription and encouraged strikes, of treason. He also acted as leader of the government in the council and displayed considerable ability in guiding legislation through that chamber. In July 1919 he succeeded D. R. Hall [q.v.] as attorney-general, a post he held until the resignation of the ministry in April 1920.

As a politician, Garland won respect from all sides for his conviction that the national interest must override party considerations. He was described by the *Bulletin* as 'a most lovable little man; and though he hit trenchantly both at the Bar and in politics – he had the stentorian declamatory manner of

the Edmund Burke school – he never made a real enemy'.

An active Presbyterian, Garland was procurator of the Presbyterian Church of New South Wales from 1894, of the Presbyterian Church of Australia from 1901, and for many years lecturer on ecclesiastical law and procedure and in 1898-1920, a councilmember of St Andrew's College, University of Sydney. He was a fellow of the senate of the university in 1915-21 and a director of Sydney Hospital in 1910-21. He 'cared little for sport and less for Society, and had most frugal tastes', but was a member of the Australian Club and active in the Highland Society of New South Wales.

Garland died at his Bellevue Hill home on 23 February 1921 following a strenuous term in parliament. He was survived by his wife Isobel, née Chisholm, whom he had married in Sydney on 21 December 1896, and by their only daughter. His intestate estate was valued for probate at £5451.

J. Cameron, *Centenary history of the Presbyterian Church in New South Wales* (Syd, 1905); *Cyclopedia of N.S.W.* (Syd, 1907); Newspaper Cartoonists' Assn of NSW, *Sydneyites as we see 'em 1913-14-15* (Syd, 1915?); J. M. Bennett (ed), *A history of the New South Wales Bar* (Syd, 1969); *Scottish A'sian*, Aug 1913, 14 Mar 1921; *SMH*, 16 Nov 1916, 23 Mar, 16 July, 23 Nov 1917, 7 June 1918, 23 July 1919, 25 Feb 1920, 24 Feb 1921; *Fighting Line*, 24 Feb 1921; *Bulletin*, 3 Mar 1921; Council of the Bar of NSW, *Annual Statement*, and Minute-books (held by Bar Assn of NSW, Syd).

STEWART J. WOODMAN

GARNSEY, ARTHUR HENRY (1872-1944), Anglican clergyman, was born on 3 December 1872 at Windsor, New South Wales, son of Rev. Charles Frederick Garnsey [q.v.4], from Gloucestershire, England, and his first wife Mary Emma, daughter of Rev. H. T. Stiles [q.v.2]. In 1876 the family moved to Sydney where Garnsey senior was rector of Christ Church, St Laurence. Arthur was educated at Sydney Grammar School and the University of Sydney (B.A., 1894; M.A., 1896). He captained the university cricket team, also won a 'blue' for tennis and graduated with first-class honours in Greek.

Garnsey was made deacon in 1897 and ordained priest next year by Bishop Stanton [q.v.6] of Newcastle, who appointed him curate of Muswellbrook. In 1899-1905 he was chaplain at Melbourne Church of England Grammar School, where he also taught classics. At Croydon, Sydney, he married Bertha Edith Frances Benn (d. 1919) on 9 July 1901; her sister Caroline married W. M. Fleming [q.v.]. In December 1905 Garnsey became sub-dean and precentor of Christ Church Cathedral, Newcastle, New South

Wales. Next year he was warden of St John's Theological College, Armidale. He secured the Th.Schol. in 1908. Made canon of St Peter's Cathedral in 1914, he was examining chaplain to the bishops of Armidale in 1916-29.

In June 1916 Garnsey was appointed warden of St Paul's College, University of Sydney. In that volatile community he won the affectionate respect of the students by his fairness, his respect for their freedom and his pastoral concern. He loved nature, literature, history and music. Keenly interested in university affairs, he was a member of the senate in 1919 and in 1934-44. He was largely responsible for the establishment of the board of studies in divinity in 1936 — a notable departure from the prevailing secular assumptions about the nature of the university. A leader in the Australian Student Christian Movement, he worked for church union, and was a founder with Rev. Samuel Angus [q.v.7], of the interdenominational Heretics' Club, and of the Sydney Theological Society. He was also president of the New South Wales branch of the League of Nations Union in 1925-29 and a vice-president of the Friendship with Russia League in 1941-44.

Garnsey came into conflict frequently with other churchmen and political conservatives whenever he felt that truth or freedom was being attacked. He defended the academic freedom of radical students and professors and in 1938 led forty-five senior clergymen in 'A plea for liberty', seeking the representation of points of view other than the dominant Evangelicalism of the Sydney Diocese, but Archbishop Mowll declined to meet them.

From his father Garnsey had inherited the austerity and reverence of the Oxford Movement. His theology was based on the Broad Church radicalism of F. W. Robertson, Charles Kingsley and F. D. Maurice. He welcomed the results of proved biblical scholarship and stressed the humanity of Jesus Christ and the need to relate His teaching to contemporary problems. Although not a profound theologian, Garnsey was a good scholar and teacher: his *A study of Jesus* (1927) was widely used and *How the gospels grew* (1935) was one of the earliest expositions in Australia of 'Form-Criticism'. He was examining chaplain to the archbishops of Sydney from 1918 and a canon of St Andrew's Cathedral from 1928.

Garnsey died from cancer on 21 June 1944 in Royal Prince Alfred Hospital, nine days before he was due to retire, and was cremated. He was survived by two sons and a daughter from his first marriage and by his second wife Ann Stafford Smairl, daughter of Bolton Stafford Bird [q.v.3], a widow whom he had married at Bruny Island, Tasmania, on 28 August 1922. His portrait by Arthur Murch is held by St Paul's College.

SMH, 22 June 1944; *Union Recorder*, 6 July 1944; E. R. Garnsey, History of the Garnsey family (MS; and family papers held by author, Dickson, ACT).

D. A. GARNSEY

GARRAN, SIR ROBERT RANDOLPH (1867-1957), lawyer and public servant, was born on 10 February 1867 in Sydney, sixth and youngest child and only son of Andrew Garran [q.v.4] and his wife Mary Isham, née Sabine. Educated at Sydney Grammar School and the University of Sydney (B.A. 1888, M.A. 1899), Garran was admitted to the New South Wales Bar on 28 August 1891 and practised mostly in the equity jurisdiction.

Throughout the 1890s Garran was active in the Federation movement, as one of (Sir) Edmund Barton's [q.v.7] youthful helpers, as a councillor of the Australasian Federation League of New South Wales, and as an organizer of and league delegate to the unofficial conferences supporting Federation at Corowa (1893) and Bathurst (1896). He published *The coming Commonwealth*; and *Australian handbook of Federal government* (1897), outlining the history of federalism as backdrop to the arguments for and against the 1891 draft constitution. Garran attended the official Federal Convention of 1897-98 as secretary to (Sir) G. H. Reid [q.v.], New South Wales premier. There he became secretary to the convention's drafting committee, at Barton's request. He went to the 1899 Premiers' Conference which further amended the bill as Reid's 'counsellor upon legal and constitutional matters'.

During the 1898 and 1899 referendum campaigns Garran organized a small team of lawyers and journalists who disseminated a spate of pro-bill propaganda, largely through New South Wales country newspapers. He collaborated with (Sir) John Quick [q.v.] in preparing an *Annotated Constitution of the Australian Commonwealth* (1901) to usher in the Federal era. The book remains a classic history of the federating process and commentary on the constitution.

At the request of Alfred Deakin [q.v.], first attorney-general, Garran became the first, and briefly the only, Commonwealth public servant on 1 January 1901 as secretary, Attorney-General's Department, and parliamentary draftsman. On the same date his services to the Federal movement were recognized by his appointment as C.M.G. On 7 April 1902 at St John's Church of England,

Darlinghurst, Garran married a schoolmistress, Hilda Robson: they had four sons.

Garran set out to make the Attorney-General's 'as far as possible a professional department with as little as possible of administrative work'. He was mainly responsible for establishing the first Federal departments, getting the first parliament elected without Federal electoral law or machinery, and designing legislation for the administration of defence, customs, the public service, posts and telegraphs, future parliamentary elections, and a Federal judicial system. In opening a new statute book Garran strove for 'clear, straightforward language, free from technical jargon'. He also introduced a mode of drafting statutes that facilitated incorporation of future amendments without wholesale reconstruction. The department's functions included legal advice to governments and to other departments, and the conduct of litigation for the Commonwealth. Garran appeared personally in some important cases, and made his first visit to England, in 1907, in order to appear before the judicial committee of the Privy Council in a constitutional appeal.

During World War 1 W. M. Hughes [q.v.], as attorney-general and then prime minister, drew heavily upon Garran's skill and sagacity, and a bond of mutual regard grew between the two men, who were superficially incongruous in every respect. In 1916 Hughes appointed Garran to a new statutory office of solicitor-general, thenceforth delegating to him most of his powers and duties as attorney-general. Echoing wartime journalistic sallies, Hughes is supposed to have said a few years later that 'the best way to govern Australia was to have Sir Robert Garran at his elbow, with a fountain pen and a blank sheet of paper, and the War Precautions Act'.

Knighted in 1917, Garran next year accompanied Hughes and (Sir) Joseph Cook [q.v.] to London for meetings of the Imperial War Cabinet and Conference, and went to Paris as a member of the Australian division of the British Empire delegation at the Peace Conference (1919). He worked on various drafting committees, provided Hughes with ingenious arguments, especially on reparations, and helped to formulate the mandates provisions of the League of Nations Covenant, including the proposal for the 'C' class mandate which Hughes insisted should apply to New Guinea. Appointed K.C.M.G. in 1920, he accompanied S. M. (Viscount) Bruce [q.v.7] to the Imperial Conference of 1923, and in 1930 was a member of the Australian delegations led by J. H. Scullin [q.v.] and Attorney-General Frank Brennan [q.v.7] to the 11th Assembly of the League in Geneva and the Imperial Conference in London where he was made chairman of the drafting committee.

Garran at times undertook tasks of a quasi-political kind. In 1919, for instance, he was appointed, with Professors Harrison Moore [q.v.] and Jethro Brown [q.v.7], to formulate more precisely the powers over profiteering and industrial relations which State parliaments were being asked to refer to the Commonwealth. During some serious industrial disputes in the 1920s he was deputed to obtain the views of union leaders and State governments. He gave forthright public testimony to select committees and commissions of inquiry, notably to the royal commission on the Constitution in 1927.

Garran retired from the public service on 9 February 1932 after thirty-one years as a permanent head – a record unlikely to be broken. He had been the trusted confidant and counsellor of all eleven attorneys-general and sixteen governments, irrespective of party. The reasons lay partly in his unrivalled knowledge of the Constitution and his professional competence as draftsman and opinion writer, partly in his unusual combination of political flair and detachment. Contemporaries anticipated Sir Frederic Eggleston's [q.v.] verdict of the early 1950s that 'Sir Robert Garran was the greatest of all the Commonwealth Public Servants'. As a lawyer Garran was in general far sighted and meticulous rather than inventive. He was thoroughly aware that 'constitutional law is not pure logic, it is logic plus politics', and he favoured a pragmatic, commonsensical approach to its interpretation. He was convinced of the durability of federalism in Australia but he advocated periodic review of the Constitution, prefer ably by elected conventions.

Upon retirement Garran expanded and added to his already considerable range of personal interests and commitments. Taking silk in New South Wales within a month, he resumed private practice, mainly supplying advisory opinions to public authorities and private clients, and keeping a watching brief for business firms on government policies and legislation both Federal and State. He occasionally appeared in court, at least up to 1951, and once (in 1936) before the bar of the New South Wales Legislative Council to argue on behalf of public service staff organizations against the continuance of Depression salary cuts.

He was also in demand for official assignments. In 1932, on the recommendation of (Sir) J. G. Latham [q.v.], the British government appointed him chairman of the Indian Defence Expenditure Tribunal to advise on the resolution of a decades-old dispute about the apportionment of the costs of Indian defence between Britain and India. In 1934 he was made chairman of the Commonwealth's advisory Book Censorship Board and, after its reconstitution in 1937, continued as appeal censor. In 1934 he was commissioned, with three others, to prepare *The Case for union: a reply to the case for the secession of the State of Western Australia* (1934). Governments sought his counsel on various issues during World War II. Typical among services rendered to private organizations was his work as chancellor (formal legal adviser) of the Anglican diocese of Goulburn in 1939-56.

A number of Garran's personal interests found expression through his devotion to Canberra as the infant national capital. One of the first officials to move his household from Melbourne to Canberra in 1926-27, he worked to alleviate the trauma of that move for the rank and file, both through official measures such as adequate provision for housing and costs of transfer, and through private hospitality and the promotion of social activities in Canberra, in which Lady Garran was equally active. As he had done in Melbourne, Garran presided over a Society of Arts and Literature for the *cognoscenti*, whom he told in 1927 that there was 'no reason why Canberra should not become the centre and the focus of the artistic life of Australia'. Garran was for many years a vice-president of the Canberra Musical Society; he sang in its choir and played second clarinet in its amateur orchestra.

To Garran it was 'unthinkable' from the beginning that there should not be a university at Canberra, first because transferred public servants and their offspring had a right to tertiary teaching, second because a modern central government needed 'to have at hand all the aids that science and learning can give'. His influence on governments, bolstered by forming the Canberra University Association in 1929, secured as an interim measure the Canberra University College (teaching for University of Melbourne degrees), whose council he chaired from its inception in 1930 to 1953. But from the middle 1920s through the 1930s Garran consistently advocated the establishment of what he prophetically called 'a National University at Canberra', 'distinctly different, in character and function, from any [existing Australian] institution', 'first and foremost . . . for post-graduate research and specialized higher study', on 'Oriental matters, Pacific relations, . . . international relations generally, public administration, . . . economics'. Inevitably, Garran served on the Interim Council of the Australian National University from 1946 to 1951 when on the award of an honorary LL.D. he became the university's first graduate. His con-

tributions to university education, the city and the public service were also recognized in the naming of a Canberra University College chair of law (now in the National University), of one of the university's halls of residence, a road on campus, a Canberra suburb, and an annual oration of the Royal (Australian) Institute of Public Administration. He received honorary doctorates of laws from the universities of Melbourne (1937) and Sydney (1952).

Garran was president of Canberra Rotary Club upon its founding in 1928-29 and also in 1934-35, and governor of Rotary International's 76th District (comprising eastern Australia from Cape York to the Murrumbidgee) for 1937-38. He was appointed G.C.M.G. in 1937. In 1940-41 he made a three-month private goodwill lecture tour in the United States of America and Canada, with the organizing help of Rotary. He had been active in the foundation and leadership of the League of Nations Union and its successor the United Nations Association in Australia. He was patron, president or chairman of many national bodies for promoting intellectual co-operation and the arts.

'The cultivated son of a cultivated father', Robert Garran showed a lifelong predilection for the literary arts, especially those associated with music. He read widely in several languages. He wrote entertaining light verse for all occasions; his serious verse was, at the least, respectable. He published a complete translation of Heine's *Book of songs* (1924) and, in old age, *Schubert and Schumann: songs and translations* (1946). His versions were used by professional singers, and Paul Hindemith published an edition of his own *Four songs* (Op. 43, No. 2) with Garran's translations. Garran was, especially after his retirement, a prolific contributor of correspondence and special articles to the press, and of scholarly pieces to learned journals and books, mainly on constitutional questions, historical and topical.

Despite Garran's impressive physical stature of 6 ft. 4 ins. (193 cm), lean and erect to the last, his personality, like his prose, was devoid of pedantry and pomposity and, though dignified, was laced with a quizzical turn of humour. He was capable of strong and decisive administrative action when required; what people of all kinds most remembered were charity, modesty, courtesy and charm. A few weeks after completing his memoirs, published posthumously as *Prosper the Commonwealth* (1958), he died in Canberra on 11 January 1957, Lady Garran having predeceased him in 1936. After a state funeral (the first for a Commonwealth public servant) he was buried at St John's Anglican Church, Canberra. There are portraits in oils at Government House, Canberra, at Garran Hall, Australian National University; and in the possession of Mrs Winifred Garran, Canberra. There is also a bust in bronze by May Barrie at the law library, Australian National University, and a bronze bas-relief by Dora Ohlfsen, also owned by Mrs Winifred Garran.

Of Garran's sons, Richard Randolph (b. 1903) became an industrial chemist; John Cheyne (1905-1976) a grazier; Andrew (1906-1965) a Rhodes Scholar, parliamentary draftsman and chairman of the Victorian Public Service Board; and (Sir) Isham Peter (b. 1910) an ambassador in the British Foreign Service.

J. A. La Nauze, *Alfred Deakin* (Melb, 1965); *People* (Syd), 6 June 1951; *Aust Law J*, 22 Feb 1957; *Aust Q*, Mar 1957; *Canb Times*, and *SMH*, 12 Jan 1957; ABC, Commonwealth public servant number one (biog files, NL); F. W. Eggleston, Confidential notes: some great public servants (Menzies Lib, ANU); R. R. Garran papers (NL).

R. S. PARKER

GARRATT, CHARLES CLEMENT (1892-1918), soldier and labourer, was born on 21 July 1892 at Islington, London, son of Charles Edward Garratt, book publisher's clerk, and his wife Maggie Constance, née Brown. Clem Garratt was tall, fair, strong-looking, brave, honest and forthright. He was also reserved and secretive, and left for posterity virtually no record of his pre-war days. In 1915 he was educated, single, a labourer with the Co-operative Mineral Waters & Brewing Co., boarding in Church Terrace, Walkerville, Adelaide, and he claimed to have served four years in the British Army. He probably reached Australia in 1913 and possibly some grievance had led him to migrate, for during the war he would not speak of his past and he visited his mother and sister in London only rarely.

Garratt joined the 5th Reinforcements of the 16th Battalion at Oaklands, South Australia, on 11 January 1915, and held the temporary ranks of corporal from 16 January and sergeant from 6 March. He left Australia on 20 April, and joined his unit at Anzac on 13 July, reverting to private on that date. Five days later he was evacuated with a slight wound in the hand, but returned on 13 November, and for the rest of his life remained with 'D' Company, 16th Battalion. He served at Anzac until the evacuation and was promoted corporal on 24 December. On 7 June 1916 his unit reached France where he took part in the fierce fighting before Mouquet Farm in August and on 11 April 1917, as a sergeant, in the 1st battle of Bul-

lecourt. In this murderous trench battle almost 80 per cent of his brigade were casualties; in the German trenches Garratt organized a party which repulsed a counter-attack, then captured and held 300 yards (275 m) of trench, and finally, when ordered to withdraw, made a skilful retreat. He won the Distinguished Conduct Medal, the award second to the Victoria Cross for non-officers.

On 8 June Garratt was promoted company quartermaster sergeant and on 26 September, at Polygon Wood, led a charge under heavy fire to destroy a pillbox, capturing its guns and killing their crews. During the consolidation he 'displayed the greatest coolness and disregard of danger under intense fire'. For this he won a Bar to his D.C.M., one of only about thirty Australians so decorated in the war. His comrades especially admired the consistency of his leadership and daring: on at least three other occasions he might easily have won decorations, and become a well-known war hero. He was gazetted second lieutenant on 1 May 1918, served with his battalion throughout the remainder of its front-line service, and on 9 November 1918 died of Spanish influenza. He was buried in Abbeville Communal Cemetery Extension in France. His passing went unremarked in Australia: his estate was settled by the Public Trustee, and the Walkerville honour-roll does not include his name. Yet his mates did not forget, and sixty-one years after his death his name brought an old comrade to tears. 'He was a magnificent soldier', he said. He was indeed.

C. Longmore, *The old Sixteenth* (Perth, 1929); C. E. W. Bean, *The A.I.F. in France*, 1918 (Syd, 1942); *London Gazette*, 15 June, 5 Feb 1918; *Advertiser* (Adel), 7 Dec 1918; War diary, *and* records, 16th Battalion, A.I.F. (AWM); information from Mr H. Pitman, Myrtle Bank, S.A.

BILL GAMMAGE

GARRETT, THOMAS WILLIAM (1858-1943), cricketer and civil servant, was born on 26 July 1858 at Wollongong, New South Wales, second son of Thomas Garrett [q.v.4], newspaper proprietor and politician, and his first wife Mary Ann Elizabeth, née Creagan. He was educated at Newington College, where his ability as a cricketer and sprinter was encouraged by the assistant master Joseph Coates [q.v.3]. In 1873 he matriculated at the University of Sydney and attended lectures for several terms. In January next year his father secured for him a clerkship in the Department of Lands; he transferred to the Supreme Court in 1876 and was admitted as a solicitor on 25 February 1882. He became registrar of probates, in 1890, curator of intestate estates as well in 1896, and public trustee in 1914. When he retired in 1924 his staff had increased from 14 to 67 and some 25 000 estates involving over £10 million had passed through his office. That year he returned to practise as a solicitor and at 81 still attended his office daily.

A promising young all-rounder, Garrett was chosen as a bowler in the 'Grand Combination Match' against James Lillywhite's professional team in Melbourne in 1877. In what was to be recognized as the first Test Match he made the second highest score of 18 not out to Charles Bannerman's [q.v.3] monumental 165. He was a member of the 1878-79 overseas tour and played for over fourteen months in Britain, North America and at home. With only eleven regular members, he did much bowling, taking 291 wickets (146 in England). He played in the match in which the Australians defeated the Marylebone Cricket Club in a single day. A strict amateur, he found that his civil service duties and prospects for promotion restricted his opportunities in international cricket, but he visited England with the third touring side in 1882, participating inconspicuously in the famous 'Ashes' Test at the Oval. On the fifth Australian tour in 1886, an injury to F. R. Spofforth [q.v.6] obliged Garrett to take a heavy bowling load. He was able to represent Australia more often at home, playing in fifteen of the first nineteen Test matches. In all Tests he scored 339 runs with a top score of 51 and took 35 wickets, half of these in three matches in the 1881-82 summer.

From the 1894-95 season to that of 1897-98, Garrett captained the New South Wales team, achieving success as a batsman. His best year was 1897 when, aged 38, he scored 131 against South Australia and its great fast bowler, Ernest Jones [q.v.]; some months afterwards, he top-scored in his colony's second innings against A. E. Stoddart's visiting English team. His tactful and experienced leadership gave his side the Sheffield Shield on two occasions. More important, Garrett was the mentor of many young players, including Victor Trumper [q.v.]. He led the university cricket club for many years until a dispute about eligibility for membership led to his break with the officials.

After retiring from the field, Garrett gave time to the administration of the game and became a life member of the New South Wales Cricket Association. He was also a prominent golfer. He was something of a legend when he died at Warrawee, Sydney, on 6 August 1943; he was cremated with Anglican rites. He was survived by his wife Helen Alice Maude, daughter of John Applewhaite, a sea captain, whom he had married on 25 March 1879 at St James' Church, Sydney, and by four sons and three daughters. On his diamond wedding anniversary, Garrett received a congratulatory message from the M.C.C. on behalf of all cricketers in England.

A tall, lean man, with a neat beard, Garrett was a fierce hitter who later steadied down. A fine cover fieldsman, he was best known as a bowler. He bowled above medium pace, with a high action, and could turn the ball either way. *Wisden* reported that 'on hard ground many good judges regarded him as more effective than Spofforth or Boyle' [q.v.3].

Cyclopedia of N.S.W. (Syd, 1907); S. M. W. Brogden and J. Arlott, *The first test match* (Lond, 1950); *John Wisden's Cricketers' Almanack*, 1944, p 314; *SMH*, 27 June, 1 July 1924, 7 Aug 1943; *The Times*, 11 Aug 1943; Univ Syd Cricket Club, Minutes, 1874-1900 (Univ Syd Archives).

K. J. CABLE

GARSIA, RUPERT CLARE (1887-1954), naval officer, was born on 9 October 1887 at Christchurch, New Zealand, son of Captain Christopher Garsia, 79th Cameron Highlanders, and his wife Elizabeth Parker, née Watson. He was educated at Christchurch High School and later in England at H.M.S. *Britannia*, the Royal Navy's training ship. Appointed a midshipman in H.M.S. *Russell* in the Channel Fleet in July 1904, he became a sub-lieutenant in September 1907 and a lieutenant in April 1910. He served in the cruiser H.M.S. *Psyche* on the Australian Station in 1909-11 and then in battle cruisers in the Home Fleet.

Garsia resigned from the Royal Navy on 15 April 1914. He joined his family in Tasmania, but when war was imminent offered his services to the Royal Australian Navy and went on board H.M.A.S. *Australia* in Sydney on 4 August 1914 as lieutenant on the R.N. emergency list (on loan to the R.A.N.). He was transferred on 12 August as prize master to the *Zambesi*, a small vessel carrying material for the German wireless station at Bitapaka, New Britain. Garsia took the *Zambesi* to Sydney, arriving there on 26 August; he left the same day to go north again and served in H.M.A.S. *Sydney* from 14 September until the end of the war. The *Sydney* escorted the first convoy of troops from Australia to the Middle East and, en route, destroyed the German light cruiser *Emden* at Cocos Island on 9 November 1914; in this engagement Garsia was in charge of a group of guns. From Colombo he sent his father in England a description of the fight and this was published in the London *Times* ahead of the official account.

In 1915-16 the *Sydney* patrolled in the West Atlantic and in June 1916 joined the Grand Fleet in the North Sea. She suffered casualties in action in December 1916 and engaged the Zeppelin, L43, in May 1917. Her aeroplane, operated from a launching-platform, was in action on 1 June 1918. This was soon after Garsia's promotion to the rank of lieut-commander, R.N., on 1 April 1918; he returned to Sydney in July 1919. On 31 January 1919 he had been appointed a lieut-commander in the R.A.N. He served in H.M.A.S. *Tingira*, the boys' training ship in Sydney, from August 1919 until April 1921 when he went to command H.M.A.S. *Penguin*, the depot ship in Sydney. Promoted commander on 1 July 1921, he served in H.M.A.S. *Brisbane* from July 1921, and in the flagship *Melbourne* from March until November 1922 when he took command of the sloop *Marguerite*.

Garsia was sent to England in 1924-25 to study training and education in the R.N. On his return in August 1925 he took command of the *Tingira* where he remained until April 1927 when, to his acute disappointment, boys' training was abandoned and the *Tingira* was paid off. The Naval Board had refused his politically naive submission that it should once more seek the government's permission to reintroduce caning as the form of punishment which had been abolished after parliamentary debate. Garsia then commanded H.M.A.S. *Platypus*, a depot ship. In April 1928 he returned to the *Penguin* in command until August 1929 when he moved to H.M.A.S. *Brisbane* in command and as senior officer, reserve ships. In June 1930 he again took command of the *Penguin*.

Garsia ceased duty with the navy when he was appointed administrator of Nauru in December 1932, remaining there until October 1938. This phosphate island in the Pacific gave scope to his naval predilections for efficiency, paternalism, correctitude and a taste for intrigue. At the age of 46 he surprised everyone at Nauru by marrying. His wife was Dorothea Lloyd, a teacher of Hunters Hill, Sydney; the wedding took place at the Anglican church, Bong Bong, New South Wales, on 28 April 1934. There were no children of the marriage. In 1939 Garsia settled in Canberra, and in 1940 was appointed acting captain and served as commodore of convoys until 1943. He commanded H.M.A.S. *Leeuwin*, the navy's main depot in Western Australia from October 1943 until September 1945 when his naval service finally concluded.

Survived by his wife, Garsia died of a cerebral haemorrhage in Canberra on 18 February 1954 and was cremated with Anglican rites. He was tall and well built and had a commanding presence; he made a significant contribution both as naval officer and administrator. He was public spirited, strong on the dignity of his naval rank and on his vision of the navy as the unchallengeable safeguard of the nation.

A. W. Jose, *The Royal Australian Navy 1914-18* (Syd, 1928); G. H. Gill, *Royal Australian Navy, 1939-42* (Canb, 1957); P. Adam-Smith, *The ANZACS* (Melb, 1978); *Reveille* (Syd), Mar 1933; *SMH*, 20 May 1918, 14 Apr 1925, 25 May 1928, 2 Feb 1933, 6 Mar 1934, 24 Mar 1936, 20 May, 11, 18 Oct 1938; *Canb Times*, 20 Feb 1954; R. C. Garsia, Diaries & letter (AWM); Aust Naval Bd, Minutes, 6 Jan 1926 (AAO).   ROBERT HYSLOP

GARVAN, SIR JOHN JOSEPH (1873-1927) financier, was born on 17 January 1873 at Hill End, New South Wales, eldest son of the six sons and six daughters of James Patrick Garvan [q.v.4], insurance entrepreneur and politician, and his wife Mary Genevieve, née Glissan. Educated at Sydney Boys' High School and St Ignatius College, Riverview, Sydney, he spent some of his early life on St Helena, a family property near Byron Bay. Garvan followed his father into the insurance business. In 1897 he became general manager and a director of the Citizen's Life Assurance Co. Ltd, and in 1899 was appointed managing director. He helped the Australian Widows' Fund and the Mutual Life Association of Australasia by amalgamating them with the C.L.A. to form the Mutual Life and Citizens' Assurance Co. Ltd in 1908.

At a time when theoretical training in economics and allied subjects was meagre, Garvan proved a skilful, prudent and successful businessman, excelling in financial management. He kept the expenses of the M.L.C. low and strengthened policy reserves; his control helped to turn the company into one of the main insurance groups in Australia. In the early 1900s he perceived a weakening of values in real estate and began the process whereby those assets were changed into public securities – by 1915 real estate represented only 0.43 per cent of company assets. At his instigation a branch was established at Montreal, Canada, in 1913.

In World War I, and after, Garvan concentrated on public service, although he continued to participate in major company decisions. With a strong faith in the gold standard, in 1914 he was appointed to the Federal Finance Council which organized war loans and, through the treasurer, advised the government on war finances. The first war loan was for £5 million and the M.L.C. contributed £1 million. Garvan became a member of the Commonwealth Bank of Australia's Note Issue Department in 1920, and next year was chairman of the inquiry into the break of railways gauge. He resigned from the royal commission into the incidence of Federal taxation in 1921. On his return from overseas the same year he criticized presciently the financial terms of the treaty of Versailles. In 1924 he became a director of the Commonwealth Bank and was elected chairman, rendering expert service as it assumed central bank functions. Ill health caused his resignation in 1926, and he was knighted next year.

'Retiring almost to the point of shyness', Garvan was tall and well built. He was a benefactor of several charities, including the St Vincent de Paul Society. Like his father, he was a keen sportsman, expecially interested in tennis and polo. Sometime vice-president of the New South Wales Polo Association, in the 1900s he played a reliable game at full back and was a member of a team that twice won the Countess of Dudley [q.v.] Cup; he donated the J. J. Garvan Cup which is still played for. He had a string of racehorses, including Braehead and The Pied Piper, but they had little success.

Garvan died of coronary vascular disease on 18 July 1927 at his home in Darling Point and was buried in the Catholic section of South Head cemetery. He was unmarried. His estate was sworn for probate at £156 558. The prime minister, S. M. (Viscount) Bruce [q.v.7], described him as 'an outstanding figure in the business life of Australia, and one of its leading financial authorities'.

A. C. Gray, *Life insurance in Australia* (Melb, 1977); *A 'sian Insurance and Banking Record*, 1927; *SMH*, 19 July 1927; *The Times*, 21 July 1927; information from D. McCorquodale, North Sydney.

BEDE NAIRN

GARVIN, LUCY ARABELLA STOCKS (1851-1938), headmistress, was born on 28 January 1851 in England, daughter of Frederick Wheatley-Walker, gentleman, and his wife Catherine, née Stocks. She was probably partly brought up on the Isle of Man. According to tradition she trained as a governess in England and came to Australia under the patronage of Professor Charles Badham [q.v.3]. She was living in Sydney when she was chosen by Badham from twenty-two applicants, and appointed headmistress of the new public High School for Girls in Sydney, at a salary of £400, on 20 August 1883.

The new school shared the premises of the old St James Denominational School in Elizabeth Street with the new Boys' High School under Joseph Coates [q.v.3]; the boys

moved out in 1892 and the girls took over the whole building. In October 1883 Miss Wheatley-Walker started with 39 pupils; they had increased to 87 by January 1884 – among them were Ethel Turner and Louise Mack [qq.v.]. At first her relations with the Department of Public Instruction were not always smooth: she was reprimanded for minor inaccuracies in remitting fees and for being seen outside the school in school hours. She had a continuing feud with Dr Thibault, the visiting French master, which resulted in a flurry of letters to the department. Meanwhile Miss Wheatley-Walker besieged the department with requests, not always granted, to make the old building more satisfactory for staff and girls. After raising £10 at a cake and apron fair, she asked for another £10 to start a library – books of reference and 'a large number of good storybooks, and standard authors, which may encourage a taste for literature and induce a love of reading'. The request was granted.

At St Jude's Anglican Church, Randwick, on 23 June 1891, Lucy Wheatley-Walker married William Charles Garvin, a 30-year-old draftsman. As Mrs Garvin she continued as headmistress: she had brief accouchement leave for the births of her sons – in 1892, 1895 and 1897. On 27 February 1898 her husband died.

As the years passed Mrs Garvin became an institution at the Sydney Girls' High School. Distinguished-looking, with wavy hair, she had great presence and was quietly formidable, not needing to raise her voice to exert her authority. She dressed well and 'always loved rings'. Her older girls discovered her kindness and humour. She always expected the best from her pupils and 'taught them what it meant to be a citizen of the British Empire. Again and again during the war she rallied them to the call', raising money for war charities. In 1919 she was appointed 'officier d'Académie' by the French government. Keenly interested in her old girls, Mrs Garvin encouraged them to take an active interest in the school.

In 1911 Mrs Garvin admitted to the department that she had been born in 1851 not 1855; henceforth her appointment was renewed annually until January 1919, despite a petition from her staff that Mrs Garvin had lost none of 'her enthusiasm and energy' and that the influence of her strong personality is 'still the source of inspiration that it has so long been to a large number of the most highly educated women of this State'. Over 4000 girls had passed through her hands; various presentations were made to her.

In December 1919 Mrs Garvin was appointed principal of St Chad's Church of

England Girls' School, Cremorne (later Redlands). She resigned late in 1922 and next year went to England where her eldest son was living; she visited Sydney in 1928. Lucy Garvin died at Meols, Wirral, Cheshire, on 20 January 1938. She was survived by her eldest son; the youngest had been killed in action in France while serving with the British Army.

P. Poole (ed), *The diaries of Ethel Turner* (Syd, 1979); *SMH*, 2 June 1919, 21 Dec 1933, 10, 15 Feb 1938; school files, *and* special high school files 20/12749, 12750 (NSWA); S.G.H.S. Archives; information from Old Girls, S.G.H.S.

JENNIFER ROWSE

GASCOIGNE, STEPHEN HAROLD (YABBA) (1878-1942), 'rabbito' and barracker, was born on 19 March 1878 at Redfern, Sydney, son of Amos Gascoigne, a dealer from Oxfordshire, England, and his native-born wife Catherine, née Bingham. As a child he was nicknamed 'Yabba' because he 'was a bit of a talker'. He described himself as a groom when he married Ada Florence Rogers at 471 Pitt Street in 1899. He later claimed to have fought in the South African War. However for the greater part of his life he was a 'rabbito', selling dressed rabbits door-to-door in Balmain and adjacent suburbs.

It was as 'Yabba', 'the world's greatest barracker', that Gascoigne became first a local, then a national figure. He seldom missed a Sheffield Shield or Test Match at the Sydney Cricket Ground. A big man, with close cropped hair, a cap and pipe, always wearing dark trousers and a white shirt, he habitually arrived early and took a seat on the 'hill' in front of the scoreboard. He watched the game intently, making comments with a wit which became legendary and in a voice that could be heard outside the ground. He was genuinely interested in the game, and very knowledgeable about it. He rarely drank more than the two bottles of beer he brought with his lunch, and never shouted irrelevant advice or abuse. Some of his expressions, such as his comment on a spell of wild bowling, 'Your length's lousy but you bowl a good width!' passed into the vernacular of the game. Others were too appropriately tailored to the circumstances to be pirated. Gascoigne was particularly hard on slow batsmen – when Charles Kellaway, after a long period of stodgy defence, opened his score by stealing a single, he shouted: 'Whoa there! he's bolted'; and in 1932 when the Nawab of Pataudi (whom he called 'Pat O'Dea') batted for half an hour without scoring, he advised the umpire, a gas-meter inspector, to 'Put a penny in him George, he's stopped registering'.

For over a generation, Gascoigne was an attraction in his own right for those who watched cricket in Sydney, and also a favourite with players, especially visitors. When (Sir) Jack Hobbs, on his last appearance in Sydney, was presented with a testimonial, he walked around the ground, asked for 'Yabba' and shook hands with him. In 1937 he commented on the Fifth Test for radio station 2SM.

Gascoigne died of heart disease in the State Hospital, Lidcombe, on 8 January 1942, and was buried in the Anglican section of Rookwood cemetery. He was survived by his wife, a son and two daughters. The members of the New South Wales Cricket Association stood in silence before their first meeting after his death. Inevitably legends became current about his generosity during the Depression but nothing is known of his business or private life.

Wireless Weekly, 26 Feb 1937; *SMH*, 9, 20 Jan 1942, 26 Feb 1955, 31 July 1969; *Sun* (Syd), 30 Jan 1976.

W. G. McMINN

GATLIFF, JOHN HENRY (1848-1935), conchologist and naturalist, was born on 17 May 1848 at Leeds, Yorkshire, England, son of John Gatliff, broker, and his wife Eliza, née Beaumont. The family migrated to Victoria in 1857 and settled at Geelong. He is reported as having joined the Bank of Victoria in Ballarat at the age of 18, but no further details have been found of his early life. He joined the Commercial Bank of Australia in 1880 and was appointed manager in 1885, first at Heathcote, then at Collingwood (1889) and Carlton (1895). As inspector for the bank from 1910 until his retirement in 1912, he travelled widely in Australia. He had married 20-year-old Emma McLean at Christ Church, St Kilda, on 9 June 1879 and they had nine sons and two daughters.

Gatliff became interested in natural objects and natural history early in life. He joined the Field Naturalists' Club of Victoria soon after its founding in 1880 and published his first scientific paper on 'The Pecten' in the *Southern Science Record* in 1883. From the start he was a serious shell collector and quickly developed an interest in Victorian marine molluscs, few species of which had previously been studied or recorded. He published a two-part list of marine molluscs of the Victorian coast in 1887 and 1888, and described his first new species of Victorian molluscs, *Conus segravei*, in 1891. This was the start of his lifelong scientific contribution of documenting the Victorian marine mollusc fauna, during which he published sixty-one papers, either alone or in collaboration, describing ninety-three new genera and species and recording many others from Victorian waters for the first time.

From 1898 to 1906 he published with G. B. Pritchard [q.v.] a *Catalogue of the marine shells of Victoria* (in nine parts) and a companion series of papers giving details of the new records, including descriptions of thirty-five new taxa. After the *Catalogue* was completed Pritchard returned to his work on fossils and Gatliff continued the work on the Victorian marine molluscs. He published additions to the *Catalogue* alone in 1907 and then began twenty-three years of collaboration with Charles Gabriel [q.v.] on additions and alterations to the *Catalogue*, again with a companion series of papers to describe the new species. Together Gatliff and Gabriel wrote twenty-seven papers and erected forty-five new taxa.

Gatliff also had an interest in Australian shells generally: he described a new species of volute, *Voluta (Amoria) spenceriana*, from North Queensland in 1908 and sent another species, to be described by J. B. Sowerby as *Voluta (Amoria) gatliffi*, from Port Keats, Northern Territory, in 1910.

Gatliff was appointed honorary conchologist to the National Museum of Victoria in 1933. Survived by his wife, six sons and a daughter, he died on 14 September 1935 at South Yarra and was cremated. His collection of marine molluscs, consisting of 35000 specimens including forty Holotypes, was purchased for £200 from his estate by the museum and forms the basis for its reference collection of Victorian marine molluscs.

Vic Naturalist, 52 (1935-36), p 117, 64 (1947-48), p 247; Malacological Soc of Aust, *J*, 1 (1969), no 12, p 32.   BRIAN J. SMITH

GATTY, HAROLD CHARLES (1903-1957), air navigator, naturalist, adventurer and writer, was born on 5 January 1903 at Campbell Town, Tasmania, son of James Gatty, schoolteacher, and his wife Lucy Fitzjohn, née Hall. With his three brothers and two sisters, Harold attended the state primary school at Zeehan where his father was headmaster. In 1916 with a bursary he attended St Virgil's College, Hobart, and next year won a place as cadet-midshipman at the Royal Australian Naval College, Jervis Bay, Federal Capital Territory. He withdrew from the college in May 1920 to serve for three years as an apprenticed ship's officer with the Patrick steamship company of Sydney.

After gaining his certificate of competency in 1923, he joined the Union Steamship Co. of New Zealand. Dissatisfied with conditions he returned to Tasmania, then went to Lakes Entrance in Victoria to earn a meagre living from fishing, interspersed with rabbiting in the Gippsland hills. Later in Sydney, he acquired a small launch carrying goods to the Garden Island Naval Dockyard and to ships at anchor in Sydney Harbour, but his launch sank and he returned to Patrick's. On 3 June 1925 at Mosman, with Presbyterian forms, he married a divorcee Elsie Louise Boyd, née Limmex (known as Vera McCulloch), a pianist.

In October 1927 Gatty took his family to California where for a short time he was chief mate on a schooner, the *Goodwill*, owned by sporting-goods millionaire, Keith Spalding. Next year, keenly aware of the limitations of existing methods and instruments for aerial navigation, he opened a laboratory repairing navigation instruments, including aircraft compasses, and making air-route maps for the Pioneer Instrument Co.'in Los Angeles; this developed into a small navigation school. His work attracted the attention of P. V. H. Weems, inventor of a system of air navigation. To work in conjunction with the 'Weems curves', Gatty devised his ground-speed and drift indicator. This instrument formed the basis of the automatic pilot which later came to be standard equipment on most aircraft.

In 1929 Gatty flew as navigator with Roscoe Turner in a record nineteen-hour non-stop flight from Los Angeles to New York. He followed this with two demonstrations of navigational skill which brought him universal acclaim. In September 1930 he accompanied the Canadian airman, Harold Bromley, in an attempt on the first flight across the Pacific, from Honshu in Japan to Tacoma in Washington State. After flying 1200 miles (1900 km) the plane was forced to return because of fuel tank trouble. With fog all the way, with no radio and using only his dead reckoning techniques, Gatty navigated Bromley back to their starting point on Honshu Island — perhaps one of the greatest air navigational feats.

In an immediate sequel, Gatty's assistance was sought by the one-eyed stuntman, oil rigger and air adventurer, Wiley Post, to fly around the world. They set off from Roosevelt airfield, New York, on 23 June 1931 in the *Winnie Mae*, a Lockheed Vega monoplane powered by a single Pratt and Whitney Wasp engine, and re-landed there on 1 July. They had covered 15000 miles (24900 km) in eight days, fifteen hours and fifty-one minutes, with actual flying time of one hundred and six hours, eight minutes. The easterly route across the North Atlantic, Siberia, the Bering Sea and Alaska called for pin-point navigational accuracy. The airmen were accorded a tumultuous ticker-tape reception in New York City. Next year he was co-author with Post of *Around the world in eight days*.

Despite his refusal of American citizenship, Gatty in 1931-34 served in the United States Army Air Corps as senior air navigation engineer. His plans to engage in the 1934 Melbourne Centenary air race fell through, as did a brief try at passion-fruit farming in Alabama. In 1935 he joined Pan American World Airways and was sent to Australia and New Zealand to obtain support from both governments for a trans-Pacific passenger service. Because of British opposition he had no success in Australia, but in New Zealand agreement was reached, and in 1937 he surveyed a route from San Francisco to Auckland. However, plans for a regular flying-boat service were interrupted by World War II. In 1936 Harold and Vera Gatty were divorced, and in July 1937 in New York, Gatty married Allerdina Fenna Bolderhey. From 1942 he served in Java, Australia and New Guinea as director of air transport for the United States Army Air Corps in the South West Pacific and was honorary group captain with the Royal Australian Air Force until May 1943 when he began work on polar navigation with the United States Navy. That year he published, privately, a safety manual, *The raft book*, which explained the zenith star navigation methods of the ancient Polynesians. The book, an immediate best-seller, was standard equipment in U.S. Army Air Force life rafts.   Soon after the end of the war Gatty returned to Pan American Airways as South Pacific regional manager. He bought the beautiful Fiji island of Katafanga, where he worked a copra plantation. In 1948 he started a tuna fishing industry, South Sea Marine Products Ltd, at Suva, but losses forced its closure. On 1 September 1951 he founded Fiji Airways Ltd, a successful three-plane airline operating out of Nadi among the inhabited islands.

Gatty served two terms in the Legislative Council of Fiji. A fellow of the Institute of Navigation, England, he was writing of ocean currents and the migratory habits of birds when he died of a cerebral haemorrhage on 30 August 1957, survived by his wife and the three sons of his first marriage. *Nature is your guide* was published posthumously in 1958; the foreword referred to him as the 'foremost navigator of his time'. A monument commemorating Gatty's round the world flight was erected at his birthplace in 1961.

P. V. H. Weems, *Air navigation* (Annapolis, US, 1955); B. Hilder, *Gatty memorial lecture* (Syd, 1958); *Air Legion Weekly* (Washington), 4 Dec 1931; *Pacific Islands Monthly*, Nov 1948, Sept 1957, Feb 1961; *Sun* (Syd), 8 Feb 1947; *Herald (Melb)*, 31 Mar 1937, 22 June 1958; family papers held by Mrs D. Nolloth, Pendle Hill, NSW; information from Capt. A. L. Wilkinson, Kororo, NSW.

ALAN WARDEN

GAUNT, CECIL ROBERT (1863-1938), army officer, SIR ERNEST FREDERICK AUGUSTUS (1865-1940) and SIR GUY REGINALD ARCHER (1869-1953), admirals, were born in Victoria, sons of William Henry Gaunt [q.v.4] and his wife Elizabeth Mary, née Palmer. Mary Eliza [q.v.] was their sister.

Cecil was born on 1 October 1863 at Woodlands, Chiltern, where his father was then police magistrate. After education at Melbourne Church of England Grammar School in 1876-81, he entered the Union Bank of Australia. In 1887 he went to England and enlisted in the 13th Hussars; in June 1891 he was commissioned as second lieutenant in the 4th Dragoon Guards. He served on the Indian North-West Frontier and was twice mentioned in dispatches. A fine horseman, he became well known as a polo player. He fought in the South African War and was mentioned in dispatches at Ladysmith. From March 1901 to November 1902 he was seconded to the South African Constabulary.

In May 1904 at Bombay, India, Captain Gaunt married Helen Maud Beatrice, daughter of Major General C. J. Moorsom of Rawalpindi. Retiring to Bangalore in 1913, he devoted himself to racing. After the outbreak of World War I he returned to service and in June 1915 arrived at Mesopotamia as major in the 4th Dragoon Guards. He was commandant of the base depot at Basra in 1916-17, was promoted brevet lieut-colonel (reserve of officers) in March 1916, and was awarded the Distinguished Service Order for his part in the relief of Kut-el-Amara in February 1917. In 1919 he commanded the Rawalpindi area and for service on the North-West Frontier was mentioned in dispatches and appointed O.B.E. In April next year he was demobilized. He retired to St Mary Bourne, near Andover in Hampshire, England. Predeceased by his wife, he died in hospital at Andover on 4 May 1938; he had no children.

Ernest Gaunt was born on 25 March 1865 at Beechworth. After a year (1876) at Melbourne Grammar he went to England to join H.M.S. *Britannia* as a naval cadet. He served on the Australia Station from 1880 to 1884; as sub-lieutenant in H.M.S. *Nelson*, he hoisted the British flag when the British Protectorate over New Guinea was proclaimed. In 1896 he was promoted first lieutenant of the armoured cruiser *Narcissus*, and in China in 1898-99 served in administrative posts; he was thanked by the

Austrian and German commanders-in-chief for his services during the Boxer Rebellion. In early December 1903 he was severely wounded when he commanded a landing party to avenge the death of an Italian naval officer in Somaliland; on 31 December he was promoted captain and subsequently commanded the battleships *Majestic*, *Queen* and *Superb*. From October 1914 he held the rank of rear admiral and commanded the 1st Battle Squadron of the Fleet in the Battle of Jutland. He was promoted vice admiral in February 1919 and admiral in June 1924 before retiring in March next year. He was appointed K.C.B. in 1919 and K.B.E. in 1922. In 1899 he had married Louise Geraldine Martyn (d. 1934) of County Clare, Ireland. He retired to Monte Carlo and later London, where he died on 20 April 1940 at Westminster Hospital, survived by a son and two daughters.

Guy Gaunt was born on 25 May 1869 at Ballarat West. A boarder at Melbourne Grammar in 1881-83, he was intended for the law but pleaded to go to sea. His father could only afford to send him to H.M.S. *Worcester*, the training ship for officers of the merchant navy; he soon transferred to the Royal Naval Reserve and was rated a midshipman on 17 December 1886. In October 1895 he joined the Royal Navy under the provisions of a special Order-in-Council.

In February 1896 Guy Gaunt became navigating lieutenant of the gun vessel *Swift*, then on the China Station, and took part in operations in the Philippines in 1897. Serving in H.M.S. *Porpoise* in 1897, he commanded the British Consulate at Apia, Samoa, during a rebel attack, and in subsequent uprisings raised and commanded a native force, dubbed 'Gaunt's Brigade', and was mentioned in dispatches. In June 1901 he was promoted commander. He served in the battleship *Vengeance* in China during the Russo-Japanese war and later in *Cressy* and *Glory*. In 1904 at Hongkong he married a widow, Mrs Margaret Elizabeth Worthington, daughter of Sir Thomas Wardle.

Promoted captain in 1907, Guy Gaunt commanded the cruiser *Andromeda* and subsequently the cruisers *Niobe* and *Challenger* (on the Australia Station) and the battleships *Majestic* and *Thunderer*. In June 1914 he was appointed naval attaché in Washington; his success in counteracting the effects of German propaganda in North America brought him prominence. He was appointed liaison officer with the United States of America on its entry into the war. In 1918 he was employed in convoy service across the Atlantic and in June was appointed to the naval intelligence staff at the Admiralty. He was promoted on the retired list to rear admiral in October 1918, vice

admiral in July 1924 and admiral in February 1928. He was appointed C.M.G. in 1916 and C.B., K.C.M.G., in 1918, and was elected a younger brother of Trinity House.

In 1922 Sir Guy was elected to the House of Commons as Conservative member for the Buckrose Division of Yorkshire but resigned in February 1926. In July he was cited as co-respondent in the divorce case between Sir Richard Cruise and his wife. Sir Guy's wife divorced him in December 1927. He retired to Tangier, and on 1 December 1932 married a 35-year-old widow, Sybil Victoria Joseph, née Grant White; they had two daughters. His autobiography, *The yield of the years*, was published in 1940. Sir Guy visited Australia in ·1925, 1931-32 and in 1951. He lived at Cobham, Surrey, England, before his death in hospital at nearby Woking on 18 May 1953; he was cremated.

C. E. Lyne, *New Guinea* (Lond, 1885); Melb C. of E. Grammar School, *Melburnian*, 29 Aug 1938, 14 May 1940; *Argus*, 31 July 1926, 22 Dec 1927, 22 Apr 1940; *The Times*, 20 May 1953.

SALLY O'NEILL

GAUNT, MARY ELIZA BAKEWELL (1861-1942), novelist and traveller, was born on 20 February 1861 at Indigo, Victoria, daughter of William Henry Gaunt [q.v.4], police magistrate and later judge, and his wife Elizabeth Mary, née Palmer. Cecil, Ernest and Guy [qq.v.] were her brothers. Known as 'Minnie' to her family, she was educated at Grenville College, Ballarat, where her facility in writing was noted.

Mary Gaunt believed that a woman had the right to follow her own career and be financially independent, even if married. On 19 March 1881 she was one of the first women to sign the matriculation roll of the University of Melbourne; she began an arts course but did not continue after poor results in her first year. She turned to writing: 'It was never my ambition to be a writer', she recalled, 'I wrote merely because I wanted to make money', and money was 'a means of locomotion'. Drawing on childhood memories of goldfield towns and her brothers' yarns of exotic places, she contributed articles and stories to Australian and overseas papers and magazines. One of her earliest pieces was an article on gold for *Cassell's picturesque Australasia*. Her earnings enabled her to travel to England and India.

Her first novel, *Dave's sweetheart*, was published early in 1894. On 8 August that year at St George's Church, Malvern, she married a widower, Dr Hubert Lindsay Miller of Warrnambool who supported her desire to continue writing under her maiden name. A collection of short stories (1895) and two novels were published in the years before his death on 30 October 1900. Left with an income of some £30 a year she decided to go to London to be near the literary market; she left Melbourne on 15 March 1901.

Lodging at first in two rooms in a 'dull and stony street' in Kensington, Mary Gaunt struggled to establish herself as an author. As her stories began to sell, she travelled in France, Italy and Spain. Successful collaboration with John Ridgwell Essex in adventure tales set on the west coast of Africa led to a trip to the Gold Coast (Ghana) in 1908 and in 1910 to a commission from her publisher to explore the old west-coast forts. Setting out with a 'cabin trunk of pretty dresses, rose trimmed hats, gloves', photographic equipment, and a retinue of bearers, she was the only white woman on what proved an often dangerous journey. Her account of it was published in London in 1911 as *Alone in West Africa*.

She next determined to visit China, taking advantage of an invitation from George ('Chinese') Morrison [q.v.] and his bride, and arrived in Peking in February 1913. She travelled north by mule cart to visit the Hunting Palace of the Manchus at Jehol (Chengde). On her return, she rented a small temple in the hills west of Peking and wrote the greater part of *A woman alone in China*. To leave China, she had hoped to follow the old caravan route to Asiatic Russia but instead she had to return the way she had come, across Siberia, to Finland. Meanwhile war had broken out and she reached England with difficulty. Her experiences provided her with material for two travel books and several novels and stories. In 1919 she spent some months in Jamaica.

From the early 1920s Mary Gaunt settled at Bordighera, Italy, where a devoted housekeeper cared for her. In the next twelve years she wrote ten books and worked on her memoirs. In 1940 she had to abandon most of her belongings and flee to France, settling at Vence. Her health became weaker (she was asthmatic) and on 19 January 1942 she died at Cannes.

Mary Gaunt was not a great writer but she knew her limits and within them she wrote with economy, directness, imagination and energy. She told a story well and though she did not study character deeply, she was convincing. Six of her novels are set in Australia and these include her best, notably *As the whirlwind passeth* (begun in 1898 and finally published in 1923) and *Joan of the Pilchard* (1930). Her research for all her writing was thorough. Short and stout, with determined features and an imperious manner when the occasion demanded, she was a strong character, often in conflict with

authority when she wished to travel in dangerous places. She invariably won her point.

J. Gillison, 'Two invincible ladies', *VHJ*, no 200, May 1980; *British A'sian*, 18 June, 17 Sept 1908, 17 Nov 1910.
                              E. ARCHER*

GAVAN DUFFY; *see* DUFFY, CHARLES GAVAN

GAY, WILLIAM (1865-1897), writer, was born on 2 May 1865 at Bridge of Weir, Renfrewshire, Scotland, eldest child of William Gay and his wife Jane née Tagg. His father, an engraver for textile printing machinery, was apparently fond of his son but the two were far apart in their religious beliefs and so mutually uncongenial that young William twice ran away from home to London. He briefly studied Greek and English literature at the University of Glasgow and nursed an ambition to become a professor of philosophy, especially in the Hegelian tradition, but, tubercular before the age of 20, he went to sea for his health. After arriving in April 1885 at Port Chalmers, New Zealand, he worked for two years on intercolonial steamers as an assistant purser, until forced into convalescence.

Gay arrived in Melbourne in May 1888. Befriended by Dr Charles Strong [q.v.6] of the Australian Church, he became a steady contributor to Strong's publication *Our Good Words* (later the *Australian Herald*). Professor E. E. Morris [q.v.5], whom Gay had met in 1886, engaged him to write chapters on New Zealand for *Cassell's picturesque Australasia*. For a few months he was resident master at Scotch College, but had to resign in April 1889. In June he went to Sandhurst (Bendigo), attempted a tutoring post in Melbourne and spent some time in Deniliquin, New South Wales, before returning to Bendigo in August 1893. He spent the rest of his life mainly confined to bed, living in a cottage hospital kept by the Misses Sampson. For a short time he was engaged to one of the sisters, Mary Elizabeth.

Gay was able to make a little money by his pen, but was mostly supported by friends. For the *Australian Herald* and its predecessor he wrote a serial story, numerous poems, and critical articles on such subjects as 'Marcus Aurelius', 'Miracles' and 'Modern spiritualism'. In 1892 the paper carried his three-part critique of Whitman which with revisions and additions became the 1893 pamphlet, *Walt Whitman, the poet of democracy*. Two years later he produced, for a meeting in Brisbane of the Australasian

Association for the Advancement of Science, *Walt Whitman: his relation to science and philosophy*. These two booklets, taken together, form a substantial, well-balanced treatment of the American poet. In them we see Gay's first love, philosophy, blended with the interest in, and practice of, poetry. He achieved minor fame with his three slight volumes of poems published between 1894 and 1896; a collection of his verse was published in Melbourne in 1911.

Within the limits of his frail health and meagre means, Gay was an ardent proponent of Federation. In 1895, with Mary Sampson, he edited *The Commonwealth & the Empire*, a compilation of statements he had solicited from leading colonial and Imperial writers and statesmen on the subject of Australasian Federation. Alfred Deakin [q.v.], with whom Gay corresponded from 1895, described Gay's famous sonnet on Federation (first published in 1896) as 'the strongest and shapeliest poem inspired by the movement since Brunton Stephens' [q.v.6] Ode'.

Gay's optimism, as expressed in the poem 'Thanksgiving', made him thankful not only for 'birds and flowers,/For radiant suns, reviving showers', but also for 'the cheerful gale,/The curious frost, the dancing hail', and it would not be too much to say that his life experienced a full share of rough weather. The photo-portrait published in *Sonnets* (Bendigo, 1896), shows a slight, sensitive face with moustache and light beard, high forehead, serious eyes and lips. He died on 22 December 1897 and was buried in Bendigo cemetery.

J. G. Oliphant (ed), *Complete poetical works of William Gay* (Melb, 1911); R. Ingamells, *William Gay, Australian man of letters (1865-1897)* (Melb, 1952); J. A. La Nauze, *Alfred Deakin* (Melb, 1965); *Argus*, 13 Feb 1932; Deakin papers (NL); Gay papers (Fryer Lib, Univ Qld).   JOSEPH JONES

GEACH, PORTIA SWANSTON (1873-1959), artist and feminist, was born on 24 December 1873 at 28 Swanston Street, Melbourne, fifth surviving child of Cornish parents Edwin Geach, warehouseman and later draper, and his wife Catherine, née Greenwood. She studied design in 1890-92 and painting from 1893 to 1896 at the Melbourne National Gallery schools. As a student she 'rode through the Gippsland wilds *en cavalier* in national costume'. Late in 1896 she won a scholarship to the schools of the Royal Academy of Arts in London, where she studied for four years. She also worked in Paris and exhibited in England, Paris and New York.

Back in Melbourne, Portia held an ex-

hibition in January 1901 in her Collins Street studio, including a portrait of Donald Macdonald [q.v.]. Portraits became her specialty and she later painted Edith Cowan and (Sir) John Quick [qq.v.]. She also painted murals and was a member of the Victorian Artists' Society. About 1904 her family moved to Sydney, where in 1914 she exhibited mainly oils and water-colours of the shores of Sydney Harbour and Victorian rural scenes, with some portraits.

On her return to Sydney from a visit to the United States of America in 1917 Portia, influenced by a meeting of a housewives' association she had attended in New York, founded and was president of the New South Wales Housewives' Association. It aimed to educate women in the principles of proper nutrition and to aid them in their struggles against profiteering and rising food prices. In 1928 she reorganized the association as the Housewives' Progressive Association. For many years she was also president of the Federated Association of Australian Housewives. In the *Sydney Morning Herald* and over the radio she frequently expressed her views on such subjects as buying Empire goods, the use of preservatives in foodstuffs, the date-stamping of eggs, the marking of lamb and the high price of milk and bread.

Active on the committee of the National Council of Women of New South Wales, Miss Geach was a delegate to the International Council of Women's conference in Washington in 1925. She believed in equal pay for men and women and the right of women to hold public office. In 1926, while overseas, she exhibited at the salon of the Société Nationale des Beaux-Arts, Paris.

In 1938 the Housewives' Progressive Association was incorporated under the chairmanship of Eleanor Glencross [q.v.]; Portia became a director. Their rivalry led to the expulsion in 1941 of Portia and four others, who alleged that the association had been working in co-operation with the Meadow-Lea Margarine Co. Pty Ltd. In 1947 she formed the breakaway Progressive Housewives' Association and was president until 1957. She also served on the council of the Australian Women's Movement against Socialization from 1947.

Comfortably off, Portia was diminutive and always fashionably dressed. She lived in the Astor Flats, Macquarie Street, enjoyed frequent overseas holidays, and belonged to the Women's Club, Sydney, and the Lyceum Club, Melbourne. With a strong personality, she fought for better conditions for women in the home and campaigned against the closed front that she claimed had faced her when she had tried to exhibit her paintings. She died at her home on 5 October 1959 and was cremated with Anglican rites. Her estate, valued for probate at £56 582 in New South Wales and £9744 in Victoria, was left to her sister Florence Kate, who died in 1962 and provided in her will for an annual £1000 prize, known as the Portia Geach Memorial Art award, for a portrait by a woman artist.

Alma Mater (Univ Melb), Mar 1901; *Wireless Weekly,* 29 Apr 1938; *Australasian,* 6 Aug 1896; *Table Talk,* 10 Jan 1901; *Daily Telegraph* (Syd), 3 July 1914; Progressive Housewives Assn, Portia Geach – the champion of the housewife (nd. copy ML).   ANDRÉE WRIGHT

GEAKE, WILLIAM HENRY GREGORY (1880-1944), research engineer and service officer, was born on 23 February 1880 at Earley, Berkshire, England, son of John Venning Sandercock Geake, tea merchant, and his wife Sarah Ann, née Gregory. He was educated at All Souls College, Reading, and as a young man migrated to Australia.

Geake had a remarkably inventive mind. While employed as a buyer and agent for a Sydney wholesale firm he constantly sought ways to improve its merchandise. In 1906 he lodged his first application for an Australian patent and during the next thirty-five years applied for patents for over 120 industrial and household devices. Shortly before World War I he opened his own importing and wholesale business in Pitt Street, Sydney. He married Sybilla Isabella Charlotte Marsh at Christ Church, Springwood, on 18 March 1909.

On 18 January 1916 Geake enlisted as a private in the Australian Imperial Force and was posted to reinforcements for the 13th Battalion. He was promoted acting sergeant in April and in July was sent to the officer training school, Royal Military College, Duntroon. During training he displayed his inventiveness and, working with Mr Alfred Salenger, developed a bomb-thrower. Plans of this were sent to London and the two Australians were invited to present their ideas to the Ministry of Munitions. Geake sailed for England on the troopship *Kaiser-I-Hind* in December. In March 1917 he joined A.I.F. Administrative Headquarters in London and in August was promoted lieutenant and appointed commander of a new inventions research section with its own facilities and experimental ground. The A.I.F. Research Section was responsible for assessing inventions submitted to it and for designing special equipment and weapons to order. The latter was particularly important work which was performed successfully. The section often worked with dangerous explosives and under conditions and deadlines which would have been unacceptable in peacetime.

On 26 September 1917 Geake was outside an explosives packing shed when an explosion occurred. Ignoring the danger from fire and igniting ammunition, he rushed into the building and helped out an injured man. He then returned and dragged out a mortally injured soldier and, although suffering from burns, went back a third time to check that no one was left behind. For his action in saving life he was awarded the bronze Albert Medal. The day after the rescue Geake himself was severely injured during a weapons demonstration and did not resume duty until 17 December. In the New Year honours for 1918 he was appointed M.B.E. for his contribution to the war effort. He continued to head the research section and to produce valuable inventions. Among those attributed to him were a message-carrying rocket, a floating naval flare shell and a rod gun. The message rocket was his most successful military invention; it was in use on the Western Front at the time of the Armistice.

Promoted captain in January 1919, Geake embarked for Australia in August and was demobilized in December. After the war he was employed as a refrigeration representative and later as an industrial research engineer. Royalties from his many inventions supplemented his income. His work was affected by the Depression and he tried a number of ventures including a small manufacturing business in partnership with his son. During World War II, by concealing his age, he enlisted in the Royal Australian Air Force and was commissioned as a flying officer in July 1940, and promoted flight lieutenant in 1941 and squadron leader in 1942. From October 1940 he was stationed at R.A.A.F. Headquarters, Melbourne, and was involved in assessing inventions and carrying out inspections. He died of cancer in the R.A.A.F. Hospital, Richmond, New South Wales, on 14 March 1944 and was buried in the war cemetery at Rookwood.

William Geake was a man of energy and imagination who also displayed rare courage. His Albert Medal was one of only three such decorations awarded to Australians in World War I. He was survived by his wife, a son and two daughters.

London Gazette, 22 Nov 1918; *Sabretache,* Apr 1978; *North Shore and Manly Times,* 19 Jan 1918; *Daily Mirror* (Lond), 23 Nov 1919; *SMH,* 18 Mar 1944; information from Mr G. O. Geake, Lane Cove, NSW.   PETER BURNESS

GELLATLY, FRANCIS MEPHAN (1872-1919), journalist and publicist, was born on 13 November 1872 at Ballarat, Victoria, eldest son of James Gellatly, a London-born lithographer, and his Scottish wife Christian, née Ferguson. He was educated at the Church of England Grammar School, Ballarat, and at The King's School, Parramatta, New South Wales.

In 1891 Gellatly joined the New South Wales Forestry Department as a cadet working in the Gosford district. Within twelve months he resigned to work on the *Sydney Morning Herald*. In 1896, under the pseudonym 'Yarrowee', he published a slight novel, *Back from the jaws of death*, in which he examined injustice within the legal system as a result of 'maladministration of the Law, the perversity of judges, or the stolidity of juries'. He was, for a short period, a member of the actuarial staff of the Equitable Life Assurance Society of the United States. In 1912 he travelled abroad to study economic and financial journalism.

As financial editor of the *Herald* from 1905, Gellatly frequently warned a gullible public against wild-cat financial ventures. In World War I he used his columns to explain economic and legal problems arising from transactions with former overseas trading partners. Later, he provided concise explanations of wartime legislation, examined the financial proposals of the government and, in attempts to whip up support for war loans, engaged in jingoistic language which was in marked contrast to the lack-lustre prose of his commercial reports.

In a short series of articles published in 1917 in the *Trustees' Quarterly Review*, Gellatly supported the government's financial policies and argued that inflation was inescapable in time of war; its control should be tackled in the post-war era. He also condemned widespread industrial unrest and believed that industrial legislation should bear equally upon all parties. From 1908 he studied law part-time at the University of Sydney (LL.B., 1912; LL.D., 1916). Although admitted to the New South Wales Bar on 22 November 1912, he never practised. He was also vice-president of the New South Wales Institute of Journalists, chairman of the New South Wales Journalists' Board of Advice (1917-1918) and a member of the War Savings Council.

In April 1918 Gellatly, whom W. M. Hughes [q.v.] often consulted on financial matters, agreed to become director of the proposed Commonwealth Institute of Science and Industry and, in June, he was also appointed to the Commonwealth Advisory Council of Science and Industry. His appointment as director met with some criticism: his education and training scarcely fitted him to head a scientific institution, while Hughes's patronage won him few friends among the Labor Party.

Although enabling legislation was not enacted during his lifetime, Gellatly took up duty on 1 June and for the next fifteen months worked tirelessly to establish the institute. More importantly, with great tact he set out to win over those State politicians and scientists who felt that the organization would be a threat: to that end, he travelled throughout Australia in a successful campaign. An early venture was to publish a monthly journal, *Science and Industry*. It was said of Gellatly that 'he addressed himself to the task assigned to him with characteristic zeal and energy . . . and gave promise of great usefulness in his new sphere'.

On 24 September 1919 Gellatly died of pneumonic influenza at his home at Neutral Bay and was buried with Presbyterian forms in the Congregational section of Gore Hill cemetery, Sydney. He was survived by his wife Agnes Mary, née Jones, whom he had married at North Sydney on 30 March 1899, and by two sons and three daughters.

G. Currie and J. Graham, *The origins of CSIRO* (Melb, 1966); *PD* (Cwlth), 1917-19, pp 3726, 4295, 11547, 11552, 11562, 11572, 11577, 12766; *Science and Industry*, 1 (1919), no 6, p 1; Qld Trustees Ltd, *Trustees' Quarterly Review*, Oct 1919; *Sydney Mail*, 29 Apr 1899; *SMH*, 23, 25 Sept 1916, 26 Apr, 29, 30 May, 8 Aug, 30 Dec 1918, 24, 25, 26 Sept 1919; Minutes, Advisory Council Cwlth Inst of Science and Industry, (CSIRO Archives, Canb).

D. I. McDONALD

GELLIBRAND, SIR JOHN (1872-1945), soldier and farmer, was born on 5 December 1872 at Lleintwardeine, Ouse, Tasmania, son of Thomas Lloyd Gellibrand, grazier, landowner and parliamentarian, and his wife Isabella, née Brown, and grandson of Joseph Tice Gellibrand [q.v.1].

Soon after her husband's death in 1874 Mrs Gellibrand took her seven children to England. John was educated at Crespigny House, Aldeburgh, Suffolk, at Frankfurt-am-Main, Germany, where the family lived for a time, and at the King's School, Canterbury, England, in 1888-89. At 17 he passed the Royal Indian Engineering College entrance examination but bank failures in Australia prevented his taking the course. He decided on a military career and, after entering the Royal Military College, Sandhurst, in September 1892, gained the highest marks in the aggregate at the final examinations a year later. Commissioned as a second lieutenant in the South Lancashire Regiment on 21 October 1893 and posted to its 1st Battalion, he was promoted lieutenant in 1895, having the previous year qualified as an interpreter in German and French. On 27 July 1894, at the parish church, Ilkley, Yorkshire, he had married Elizabeth Helena Breul with Anglican rites.

In the South African War Gellibrand commanded a company in the operations of February 1900 leading to the relief of Ladysmith, and in March served in Natal. Transferred next May as a captain to the 3rd Battalion, Manchester Regiment (then being raised at Aldershot), he was in 1902-03 stationed at St Helena as adjutant of the garrison responsible for Boer prisoners of war. Then, with the two companies which had been left with him on the island, he rejoined the rest of the battalion in South Africa.

In December 1906, soon after its return to England, the 3rd Battalion was disbanded. Gellibrand was selected to attend the staff college at Camberley; he graduated in 1907 and was posted next year to Ceylon as deputy assistant adjutant and quartermaster general. Before his four-year term ended, he was placed on half-pay. Greatly disappointed, he resigned his commission and was gazetted out of the army on retired pay — after World War I, C. E. W. Bean [q.v.7], in the official history of the Australian Imperial Force, was to comment that it was 'a constant wonder . . . how a man with his qualities and with staff college training could have been allowed — much less almost compelled — to slip out of the British Army'.

He returned to Tasmania in June 1912 with slender means and few prospects, but grimly determined to succeed. He bought an orchard at Risdon and settled there with his wife and young family in February 1913, working assiduously. He also had a tenth share in Cleveland, the property his father had owned. On the outbreak of war in August 1914 he met with difficulty in obtaining a military appointment in Tasmania. Within a fortnight, however, as the War Office had intimated that it did not then require his services, Army Headquarters, Melbourne, offered him employment 'without conditions'. He was appointed on 20 August by General (Sir) W. T. Bridges [q.v.7] to the administrative staff of the 1st Australian Division as deputy adjutant and quartermaster general and was promoted major on 23 September.

At the Gallipoli landing on 25 April 1915, Gellibrand organized the work of the beach parties and the sending of ammunition and other supplies to the hard-pressed troops on the spurs and ridges, and was constantly seen in the forward areas, rounding up stragglers, supervising the burial of the dead and the landing of reinforcements. A tremendous worker, with a keen sense of humour and a quick understanding of men, he was, according to Bean, 'one of those officers whose bravery was conspicuous even according to the standards by which gallantry was judged in the early days at

Anzac'. Twice in three weeks he was wounded by shrapnel and was evacuated to Egypt on the second occasion. Before the end of May he was back on the peninsula.

In August 1915 Gellibrand was transferred as deputy assistant adjutant and quartermaster general to the headquarters staff of the 2nd Division, and in December was given command of the 12th Battalion and promoted lieut-colonel. Three months later, in Egypt, during the reorganization of the greatly expanded A.I.F., he was appointed commander of the 6th Infantry Brigade, which he took to France, having meanwhile been promoted colonel and temporary brigadier general in March 1916. On 21 May he was again wounded, but returned to duty late in June. He took part in the heavy fighting at Pozières and Mouquet Farm in July-August, followed by operations in the Bapaume sector in March-April 1917, and in the battle for the Hindenburg line near Bullecourt in May.

About this time, because of misunderstandings between himself and the staff of the 2nd Division, Gellibrand asked to be relieved of the command of the 6th Brigade and posted 'for such other employment as may be available'. General Sir William Birdwood [q.v.7], after trying unsuccessfully to settle the difficulty, granted his request and sent him temporarily to the A.I.F. depots in the United Kingdom, where he overhauled the entire organization and recommended drastic changes in the training syllabus of the several arms. The task completed, he returned to France in November 1917 to command the 12th Brigade. At the end of May 1918, when Lieut-General Sir John Monash [q.v.] became general officer commanding the Australian Corps, Gellibrand was promoted major general and succeeded him in the 3rd Division, which he commanded with outstanding success in the final operations along the Somme from Hamel to the Hindenburg line.

With every new appointment he had enhanced his reputation as a leader, although he was not always popular with some of his superiors. Birdwood recognized the extraordinary influence Gellibrand had over officers and men but disliked his outspokenness and unconventional dress. Monash looked on him as 'more a philosopher and student than a man of action', yet conceded that his personal bravery and high sense of duty compensated for 'some tendency to uncertainty in executive action', that his command of the 3rd Division in 1918 was 'characterised by complete success in battle', and that he held to the last the confidence of his troops. Bean stated that there was 'at least one great battle now to the credit of the A.I.F. [Bullecourt, May 1917] which, if ever a fight was won by a single brain and character, was won by John Gellibrand'. The historian of the 12th Battalion wrote that he not only possessed a thorough knowledge of infantry training, but was 'gifted with a wonderful understanding of human nature, and was able to get the maximum amount of work out of his Battalion without apparent effort'.

For his work at Anzac Gellibrand was awarded the Distinguished Service Order and mentioned in dispatches; in France he received a Bar to the D.S.O. for his service at Bullecourt, was appointed C.B. and later K.C.B., and was several times mentioned in dispatches. He was also awarded the American Distinguished Service Medal, the French Croix de Guerre and the Légion d'honneur.

The war over, he returned to his farm at Risdon but was hardly back there, when in August 1919 the Tasmanian government offered him the post of public service commissioner, which he accepted 'with reservation'. In characteristic fashion Gellibrand made a point of personally looking into the conditions of the service. Twelve months later he resigned when the government rejected his proposals for the reclassification of the public service. Shortly before this the Victorian government invited him to become chief commissioner of police in that State. He took up the appointment in August 1920, but resigned in February 1922 when the reforms he recommended were shelved.

As, according to Bean, Gellibrand had been regarded in the A.I.F. as the 'finest trainer of young officers', the post that would unquestionably have suited his talents on his return from the war, and would also have been in Australia's interest, was that of commandant of the Royal Military College, Duntroon: but he was passed over. He remarked to a friend years afterwards, 'I would have walked to Canberra barefoot for that post'. In 1921, when the Australian Military Forces were being reorganized, Gellibrand, then living in Melbourne, accepted the Military Board's invitation to command the 3rd Division, based in Victoria. Next year, however, he relinquished that appointment on returning to Tasmania after resigning from the Victorian police force.

At the end of 1925 Gellibrand was elected to the House of Representatives as the Nationalist member for Denison, but was defeated at the general elections of 1928, and again in 1929. For the next eight years he worked diligently and quietly at Risdon, and in running Garth, a foreclosed property near Smithton he had bought from the Australian Mutual Provident Society, of which he was a director. In 1936, at the age of 63, he decided

to settle in Victoria, mainly to be near his son who was then on the land at Yea. Selling Risdon and Garth, he bought Balaclava, at Murrindindi, near Yea, to which he moved early in 1937 – '100 years after my grandfather's intention to do the same', as he noted in his diary.

From the time he left the A.I.F. in 1919 Gellibrand had taken a deep interest in public affairs, and particularly in Australia's defence. But perhaps his finest monument was his untiring work for the Legacy movement, the formation of which he inspired when he founded the Remembrance Club in Hobart in 1922. From its original aims, mainly to guard the interests of ex-soldiers, the Legacy clubs extended their activities to caring for widows and children of deceased ex-servicemen. In his foreword to the *History of the Legacy Club of Sydney* (Sydney, 1944), Bean says: 'And, coming back to the great and good man from whose original work it all sprang – there was a time when some of us thought that the best monument to John Gellibrand might be the story of Second Bullecourt. Now I feel there will be an even better – the record of Legacy'.

From 1938, when the Australian government began to think seriously of rearmament after years of neglect of defence, Gellibrand was consulted several times by prime minsters Lyons [q.v.] and Menzies, and various cabinet ministers; in the next eighteen months he prepared a series of papers, wrote articles for the press in a nation-wide campaign to double the size of the militia, and spoke at recruiting meetings. For some months after the outbreak of war he contributed articles to the daily press and other journals – including 'Defence in dreamland', under the pseudonym 'A General of the A.I.F.' in four issues of *Reveille* (January-April 1940), as well as articles for the newly formed Department of Information. Recurrent ill health forced him to give up this work in 1940.

Survived by his wife, a son and two daughters, Gellibrand died of cerebro-vascular disease at Balaclava, Murrindindi, on 3 June 1945 and was buried in Yea cemetery. A portrait by James Quinn [q.v.] is in the Australian War Memorial, Canberra.

J. Monash, *The Australian victories in France in 1918* (Lond, 1920); C. E. W. Bean, *The story of Anzac*, 1, 2 (Syd, 1921, 1924) and *The A.I.F. in France*, 1916-18 (Syd, 1929, 1933, 1937, 1942); L. M. Newton, *The story of the twelfth* (Hob, 1925); C. Blatchford, *The story of the Melbourne Legacy Club* (Melb, 1932); E. Hilmer Smith, *History of the Legacy Club of Sydney*, 1 (Syd, 1944); M. Lyons, *Legacy: the first fifty years*, 1 (Melb, 1978); *Reveille* (Syd), Dec 1930; *Stand-To* (Canb), Apr 1950; *Argus*, 20, 21, 28, Dec 1921; *Herald* (Melb), 17 Nov 1922; *SMH*, 4, 6

June 1945; J. Gellibrand, Diaries and papers (AWM); family information.   A. W. BAZLEY*

GEORGE, MADELINE REES (1851-1931), headmistress, was born on 25 May 1851 at Lewisham village, Kent, England, daughter of Francis George, gentleman, and his wife Ann Fell, née Rees. In 1866-69 Rees George attended boarding-school in Wiesbaden, Germany. Proficient in German and French, she became a governess in Kissingen and Munich; in 1875, holding an impeccable reference, she joined her family in South Australia.

In Adelaide, after teaching in several families, she was appointed in 1880 as part-time German and French mistress at the new Advanced School for Girls, South Australia's only state secondary school. Leaving in 1885 to conduct her own private school in North Adelaide, she returned in 1886 as headmistress of the Advanced School. Working with inspector-general John Anderson Hartley [q.v.4], she maintained high academic standards, encouraged *esprit de corps* and increased enrolments. In 1892, following the opening of a substantial new building in Grote Street, 180 students enrolled. Emulating English girls' high schools, Rees George provided higher education for girls equal to that in the best private boys' schools.

In 1900, after an educational tour abroad, she introduced the school motto, *Non scholae sed vitae*, presented a wide-ranging report on girls' education to the South Australian government, added Greek and chemistry to the syllabus and introduced inter-school tennis matches. The Advanced School influenced girls' private schools in attitudes to academic standards and public examinations. Those schools and State primary schools were increasingly staffed by its old scholars and former staff, including Caroline Jacob [q.v.] and Ellen Benham [q.v.7]. Until 1898 all University of Adelaide female graduates were former Advanced School students. Rees George herself passed several university subjects between 1880 and 1902.

She set state school teachers' and public examination papers, assisted in training pupil-teachers, and was committee-member of the Teachers' Guild of South Australia and the Collegiate Schools' Association. In 1904 she became foundation secretary of the League of the Empire in South Australia, cultivating a vigorous patriotism among her pupils; in 1907 she attended the league's first Imperial conference on education in London. She worked through the league to have a bronze statue of Charles Sturt [q.v.2] made in England and erected in Victoria Square, Adelaide, in 1916.

In 1908 the Advanced School for Girls provided the model for the State's secondary schools when it was incorporated into the new Adelaide High School. Miss George remained headmistress of the girls' section, advising the headmaster, until her retirement in 1913 when she travelled in Italy. In 1915-22 she taught at the Methodist Ladies' College; interrupted only by an overseas trip in 1926, she remained the school's weekly visitor on behalf of the League of the Empire and in 1928 was acting headmistress for a term. In 1923 she had been president of the Women Teachers' Association.

A staunch Anglican, her thin, erect figure, sharp features and often tart comments masked generosity and kindness. Her pupils regarded her as 'stern but fair'. In 1916 she had adopted a new interest: after attending lectures, she established a model 'scientific' poultry farm in the backyard of her Childers Street, North Adelaide, home. Her aim was to demonstrate to women and war invalids how they might easily and practically supplement their incomes. Miss George died at Eastwood Mental Hospital on 15 June 1931; her name is commemorated by the M. Rees George Memorial Prize for French at the University of Adelaide.

P. Twynam, *To grow in wisdom* (Adel, 1977); *Education Gazette* (SA), June 1889, p 47, Mar 1890, p 21, Sept 1891, p 87; *Lone Hand*, 1 June 1916; H. Jones, 'Pinnacle of the state school system . . .' *J of the Aust and NZ Hist of Education*, 4 (1975), no 1; *Register* (Adel), 23 Dec 1898, 21 Dec 1900; *Advertiser* (Adel), 16, 17 June 1931; Education Dept (SA), Correspondence files Inspector-General of Schools, 2861/1879, *and* Teachers' Guild of SA and Collegiate Schools' Assn, Minute Book, 1891-1905 (SAA).   HELEN JONES

GEORGE, WILLIAM JAMES (1853-1931), engineer and politician, was born on 26 January 1853 at West Bromwich, Staffordshire, England, son of Henry Wellington George, draper, and his wife Eleanor, née Sheldon. He studied mechanical engineering at the Birmingham and Midland Counties Institute and later worked as an iron merchant and bicycle maker. In 1884 he travelled widely and settled in Victoria where, next year, he joined Neil McNeil & Co., public works contractors. He helped build several Tasmanian and Victorian railways and sections of the Watts River aqueduct, Victoria. At Casterton, on 3 June 1891 he married Mary Ann Nelson.

George had moved to Western Australia in December 1890 to manage the firm's Jarrahdale timber station and Perth waterworks. Later general manager, he built the Jarrahdale Junction to Bunbury and the Mullewa railways and Victoria reservoir. In

1894, with William Smith, he established in Perth the Black Swan Foundry, which flourished. He was elected to the Perth Municipal Council in 1894. From 1899 he was chairman of the Chamber of Manufactures; he chaired the campaign committee for the National Political League in 1900 and was secretary of the National Liberal League of Western Australia in 1910.

In 1895 George had won the seat of Murray in the Legislative Assembly and held it for three terms. He opposed Sir John Forrest's and George Leake's [qq.v.] governments, undermining them by constant, well-publicized criticisms of railway policy. George felt that he was the only one fighting against the whole House, and that this had been 'as hot a time as any man ever had', an experience he 'would sooner die' than repeat. He had been on two royal commissions on the government railways. Retiring from parliament and the foundry in 1902, after considerable controversy he became commissioner of railways.

Energetic, able, and strong-minded, George was well suited for the post and the (Sir) W. H. James [q.v.] ministry believed that, as a self-confident outsider with strong local connexions, he would prove an impartial adviser at a time when the State's financial policy was in the balance. But George was harried by subordinates and the government failed to relinquish, as planned, the power to make important policy decisions, creating an uneasy position of dual control. Nor would cabinet determine whether railways should be run on commercial principles (at least meeting interest repayments) or, as in the past, as a medium for development. George was unpopular because of tactlessness and 'a disposition to autocracy' and some mistrusted him because of the allegations of fraud over the carriage of goods for the Perth Ice Co. Criticisms were constant in parliament and the press. Despite lack of power to make substantial reforms, he managed to improve railway administration: traffic grew, mileage increased from about 1356 (2182 km) to over 1800 (2900 km), working expenses fell and a start was made in reconciling the commercial and developmental role of railways.

In 1907 George retired and took up farming but two years later returned to parliament, again representing Murray. In 1916-17 he was minister for works and trading concerns under Frank Wilson [q.v.] and in 1917-24 held works and water supply. His experience and independent judgment were valued and, as departmental head and chairman of various committees, his contribution to the State's expansion proved invaluable. With Sir James Mitchell [q.v.],

he saw an active entrepreneurial role for the State – unlike their more conservative colleagues. In 1920 George organized the prince of Wales's tour, and ensured that he received maximum political benefit in his own constituency from the royal visit. He was appointed C.M.G. next year but in 1922 the mayor of Perth complained publicly of his 'despotic attitude' and use of 'bluff, bounce and bluster'.

George left parliament in 1930. He died on 10 March 1931 and was buried in the Anglican section of Karrakatta cemetery. His estate was sworn for probate at £17888. He was survived by his wife, a daughter and two sons – a third had been killed at the landing at Gallipoli. There is a rose window in memory of the Georges in Christ Church Anglican church, Claremont.

P. W. H. Thiel & Co., *Twentieth century impressions of Western Australia* (Perth, 1901); Truthful Thomas, *Through the spy-glass* (Perth, 1905); J. S. Battye (ed), *Cyclopedia of Western Australia*, 1 (Adel, 1912); Duke of Windsor, *A king's story* (NY, 1947); *V&P* (LA WA), 1902, 2 (25); *A'sian Hardware and Machinery*, 1 Sept 1902; *West Australian*, 11 Mar 1931; *Sunday Times* (Perth), 15 Mar 1931; *Advertiser* (Adel), 19 Mar 1931; *SMH*, 24 Mar 1922; T. Manford, A history of rail transport policy in Western Australia, 1870-1911 (Ph.D. thesis, Univ WA).   TOBY MANFORD

GEPP, SIR HERBERT WILLIAM (1877-1954), mining metallurgist and manager, public servant, industrialist and publicist, was born on 28 September 1877 in Adelaide, eldest son of William John Gepp, clerk, and his wife Marian, née Rogers. His grandfather, a veterinary surgeon, was a pioneer settler of 1836. 'Bert' Gepp was educated at state schools and won a scholarship to Prince Alfred College but family indigence prevented him from proceeding to the University of Adelaide. In 1893 he became a junior chemist with the Australian Explosives and Chemical Co. at Deer Park, near Melbourne, soon taken over by Nobel's Explosive Co. of Glasgow, Scotland. During this period he rode a bicycle, three nights a week, from Deer Park to the University of Melbourne to attend (Sir) David Masson's [q.v.] chemistry lectures. Such early trials gave him the disciplined toughness of the self-made man and, less commonly perhaps, a sympathy for the underdog. In 1896 he went to Nobel's Glasgow factory for two years; throughout his life he benefited much from regular trips to Europe and North America and always insisted on the broadening effect of 'sabbaticals' for businessmen. At Hawthorn, Melbourne, on 5 July 1905, with Congregational forms he married

Jessie Powell Hilliard; they had a son and four daughters.

Gepp's long and fruitful association with the Collins House group began in late 1905 when he joined the staff of the Zinc Corporation Ltd and went to Broken Hill to help solve the 'sulphide problem'. In 1907 he became manager of the de Bavay's [q.v.] Treatment Co. Ltd and played an active part in the development of the flotation process. Gepp demonstrated an early interest in the industry's more serious labour problems and took steps to improve the safety and welfare of his men. He urged the companies to increase their subsidies to the local hospital and in 1913, after an overseas trip, initiated the Broken Hill Progress Association in order to ameliorate living conditions in the neglected town. In spite of the opposition of militant unions and apathy of company boards, Gepp's organization built some playgrounds, spent money on gardens, and arranged a seaside holiday for miners' children. More importantly, it laid the groundwork for the welfare schemes pursued by the companies after World War I.

An ardent nationalist, Gepp enlisted in the Australian Imperial Force at the outbreak of war and went into camp at Fort Largs near Adelaide. Early in 1915 he was released from the army on the initiative of W. M. Hughes [q.v.] and W. L. Baillieu [q.v.7] and went with his family to the United States of America to sell zinc concentrates and to investigate the manufacture of munitions on behalf of the government. The experience of these two years greatly stimulated him and he remained a fervent admirer of American business efficiency. While in North America he met many industrial 'experts' and recruited Charles Warner, Guy Riddell, and Gilbert Rigg for the new smelters at Port Pirie; his knowledge of the electrolytic zinc process developed by the Anaconda Copper Co. also proved to be a major asset when Collins House moved into the manufacture of refined zinc after the war. But it was the evident success of American companies in labour relations that most impressed Gepp, and on his return to Australia he persuaded (Sir) Colin Fraser [q.v.] to launch the first concerted attempt to tackle labour unrest on the Barrier. Gepp's own contribution stressed the importance of housing, co-operation with management, and the role of industrial 'experts'.

In 1917 Gepp became general manager of the Electrolytic Zinc Co. of Australasia Ltd and, with the support of W. L. Baillieu, led that company through its difficult early years. The venture was comparable in scale to the creation of the Newcastle steel industry and Gepp figured prominently in the mastery of its metallurgical problems. In six

years at Risdon, Tasmania, he was responsible for the design and supervision of a pilot plant, then a ten ton (tonne) plant, and finally a 100 ton (tonne) plant to produce zinc of 99.95 per cent purity from Broken Hill and Port Pirie zinc tailings using hydro-electric power. In 1924 Gepp was elected president of the Australasian Institute of Mining and Metallurgy and with Gilbert Rigg received the gold medal of the London parent institution. That year he represented Australia at an Empire congress of the institute in London, and served as a commissioner for the British Empire Exhibition at Wembley.

Bored and restless after his return from abroad Gepp began a new career in 1926 as a public servant. S. M. (Viscount) Bruce [q.v.7] appointed him chairman of the Development and Migration Commission, which, like the Council for Scientific and Industrial Research, formed the same year, was to apply scientific methods to economic and political problems in the interests of national development and efficiency. The new role provided ample scope for Gepp's boundless energy, inventive mind, and commitment to industrial growth. Incessant daily work, constant travel, continual conferences, lengthy reports written and redrafted and drafted again preceded his recommendations to the government on a variety of national problems. In 1930 the Scullin [q.v.] government terminated the commission but Gepp was retained as a part-time consultant on development. In 1933 he was knighted. He chaired the royal commission on the wheat, flour, and bread industries which reported at length in 1934-36, and in 1934 he became director of the North Australian Aerial Geological and Geophysical Survey.

Gepp was also an effective publicist and in lectures, articles, and broadcasts promoted the cause of science in industry and agriculture: reafforestation and soil erosion were two of his major concerns. At this time he read J. M. Keynes and turned increasingly to national economic planning as the solution to many of Australia's problems. He regarded *laissez-faire* as a policy of 'drift'; it was the lack of social responsibility which was 'the root cause of political unrests and upheavals, wars and rumours of wars, exploitations and economic distress'. When war came Gepp made a significant contribution. A friendship with John Curtin contributed in part to his influence as an advocate of central planning and an architect of post-war reconstruction. From 1942 to 1945 he served as chairman of the Central Cargo Control Committee.

Meanwhile he had returned to private industry. From 1931 he was technical consultant to Australian Paper Manufacturers Ltd and in 1936 became its general manager:

the Maryvale pulp mill in Gippsland came into production in 1939 under his direction, and the housing scheme for the mill-workers was his conception. He retired in 1950.

While not tall — he was 5ft.8½ins. (174 cm) — Gepp had a dominating and impressive presence. He had a 'large-featured, rather lowering visage', penetrating dark brown eyes and thick, wavy dark hair which was hardly touched with grey at his death. He never wore a hat, and would dress unconventionally if he felt like it. He was proud of his children but his work habits left little time for family, who according to one who knew him, felt the strains of his driving energy more than most. Farming, reading and golf were his major recreations. He died suddenly on 14 April 1954 at his farm at Kangaroo Ground where he had spent many happy hours indulging his passion for improvements. He was buried in the local cemetery. Survived by his wife and children, he left an estate valued for probate at £91 702.

Gepp made significant contributions to the solution of the great metallurgical problems of the mining industry in the 1900s; he was a pioneer in the application of enlightened labour policies in industry; he was an apostle of the role of science in industry, government, and the economy, and helped to established the C.S.I.R., the Royal Australian Chemical Institute, the Australian Institute of Management, and the Institute of Public Affairs; and he was an influential transmitter of advanced British and American ideas to an Australian public. His selected addresses were published as *Democracy's danger*, 1939, and *When peace comes*, 1943. Promethean in abilities and interests, Gepp was driven by a 'divine discontent' which made few concessions to the softer side of his nature or to the complacency of his generation.

C. D. Kemp, *Big businessmen* (Melb, 1964); B. Kennedy, *Silver, sin and sixpennny ale* (Melb, 1978); T. Rowse, *Australian liberalism and national character* (Melb, 1978); Gepp papers, MS390, *and* miscellaneous papers, MS1548 (NL).

B. E. KENNEDY

GERARD, ALFRED EDWARD (1877-1950), merchant and Aboriginal welfare worker, was born on 11 August 1877 at Aberdeen, South Australia, son of William Gerard, labourer, and his wife Emily, née Russell. After schooling at Burra, Gerard worked with a local coachbuilder. He then worked in Western Australia, at Broken Hill, New South Wales, and in Salisbury, South Australia, as an engineer and driver for the millers, Edwin Davey & Sons [q.v.]. On 26 March 1902 in Salisbury Methodist Church, he married Elsie Maria Goodman.

In 1907 Gerard started an electrical merchandizing business in Adelaide, Gerard & Goodman. In 1921 he erected a substantial show-room and factory in Synagogue Place. Then, electrical conduit and cast fittings were imported: many had conflicting size tolerances. His solution was to manufacture conduit fittings for sheet metal so that they could expand or contract. He joined the Chamber of Manufactures, Chamber of Commerce, the Electrical Employers' Association of South Australia and the Standards Association of Australia. The business prospered with his four sons, A. H., W. G., K.E., and J. H. Gerard managing two registered companies, and Alfred, chairman of directors of both. In 1936 a factory was built at Bowden where Gerard Industries Pty Ltd, produced the nationally known Clipsal products.

Gerard was interested in the welfare of Aboriginal children and gave them city holidays and employment when possible. At an Australasian Christian Endeavour convention in Adelaide in 1924, T. E. Colebrook, a leader of the Australian Aborigines' Mission, influenced him. A local council was formed with Gerard as a foundation member. Amalgamations with similar bodies led to the creation in 1929 of the United Aborigines' Mission; Gerard was local president and a federal delegate until his death.

In collaboration with the South Australian Aborigines' Protection Board, the U.A.M. supported many mission stations: Finnis Springs at Marree; Colebrook Home at Eden Hills, near Adelaide; Nepabunna at Copley; and others at Oodnadatta, Ooldea, Quorn and Swan Reach. Gerard financed a project at Winkie, which began in 1944, with leasehold land covering 5800 acres (2300 ha) and a River Murray frontage. It included a small chapel and was called Gerard Mission. He wrote of it, 'I was standing on the "Land of Promise" . . . ours for the natives to the glory of God . . . to assist in redeeming our great debt to the Aborigines'. He anticipated the popularization of the Aboriginals' cause, 'land rights' and the 1967 constitutional amendment and believed that he had 'learned a lot from the natives'. In 1946 a government grant of £1500 was received and the mission was ultimately taken over by the State protection board.

A Freemason, for forty-four years Gerard was a staunch member and lay preacher of Highbury Street Methodist Church, Prospect. His book, *Ears of corn* (1944), was a collection of his sermons and next year he published a short history of the U.A.M. He died on 13 October 1950 and was buried in

Payneham cemetery. His estate was sworn for probate at £7660. The Gerard manufacturing business is still in the family in 1981.

PP (SA), 1947 (20); *Ipad*, Aug 1947, p 43; *Hardware J*, 17 May 1948, p 66; *SA Freemason* (Adel), Oct 1952, p 6; *Advertiser* (Adel), 14 Oct 1950, 14 Nov 1980.   ALAN WARDEN

GERARD, EDWIN FIELD (1891-1965), war balladist, soldier and farmer, was born on 22 May 1891 at Yunta, South Australia, son of Frederick Gerhard, blacksmith, and his wife Catherine, née McKenzie. The family moved in 1896 to the Kalgoorlie area, Western Australia, where Edwin was educated. He appears to have left school at 16, starting work, according to one account, as a coachmaker and signwriter, and according to another as a coachpainter. Employment as an underground trucker on the Kalgoorlie and Coolgardie goldfields may have been followed by a spell as a gold prospector. In 1912 or 1913 he worked his way to the eastern States, arriving in Sydney during the first half of 1914. Here he took up art studies, later to be relinquished in favour of writing verse. It was probably about this time, when anti-German feeling was rife, that he changed his surname to Gerard.

Enlisting in the Australian Imperial Force on 6 January 1915, Gerard saw active service as a dismounted trooper with the 7th Australian Light Horse Regiment at Gallipoli from August until the evacuation in December and as a mounted trooper with the 12th Light Horse in Sinai, Palestine, Jordan, Syria, and Lebanon. His published poems about the war appeared over the pseudonyms 'Gerardy' and 'Trooper Gerardy' in periodicals such as the Sydney *Bulletin*, the Kalgoorlie *Sun* and the *Kia Ora Coo-ee* (Egypt), and in two volumes, *The road to Palestine and other verses* (Melbourne, 1918) and *Australian Light Horse ballads and rhymes* (Melbourne, 1919). His 'The road to Palestine' (holograph) is in the Mitchell Library.

After the war Gerard pursued an indifferent career as a journalist in Sydney but in 1921 he obtained under the War Service Land Settlement Scheme a property of 850 acres (344 ha), The Pinnacle, near Grenfell, New South Wales, which he farmed until 1957 when he retired to Parkes.

During the 1920s and early 1930s he turned, at the suggestion of S. H. Prior [q.v.], editor of the *Bulletin*, to the writing of verses on peacetime topics, most of them being published in that journal. 'Denman's reef', 'The tropical frog', 'Tinned-dog camp' and 'Old Bluey' are some of his better ballads about gold-prospecting and gold-mining camps; 'The horsey man', 'Cycling days',

and 'The old buckboard' are typical of his nostalgic laments for the passing of old days and ways; and 'Fallow song', 'Header song' and 'Harvest song' are lyrical pieces celebrating farming life. Gerard also contributed to periodicals such as *Reveille* and *Aussie* more directly didactic verses commemorating Anzac Day or propounding the need for a more confident and courageous approach to life. All these post-war verses remain uncollected. Though in May 1950 the *Bulletin* announced that 'a collection of his best verses, now with the publishers, is awaiting book covers', the publisher, Frank Johnson, failed to bring out the projected volume, which Gerard had intended to call 'Rhymes of the restless years'.

Gerard writes best when working within the broad traditions of the Australian literary bush ballad; his ballads of war constitute his best group of writings. In these – notably 'Lofty Lane', 'Riding song', 'The horse that died for me', 'Two scouts', 'El Maghara', 'North of Jerusalem', 'South of Gaza', 'Garden post', 'Es Salt' and 'Esch-Scham' – he writes as the poet laureate of the Australian light horsemen, although not as their uncritical panegyrist. These poems are more firmly embedded in the shared experiences of historical events than are most literary bush ballads, but what they sacrifice in narrative particularization and inventiveness they gain in representativeness and realism. Gerard vividly recreates actual incidents of the desert war, and at the same time conveys the common sensations and feelings experienced – the constant movement, the harsh conditions, the hard fighting, the bloodshed, the successive moods of exhaustion, depression, mourning, and exaltation. His style, at its best, is vigorous, swift moving, vivid, and musical.

Throughout the war ballads we are conscious of Gerard's personal sensitivity and sincerity, his desire to pay tribute to the Australian dead, his respect for courage and endurance, his quiet patriotism, and a cautiously optimistic nature that sets him apart from the many disenchanted war writers. In his later years he showed himself as a gregarious, generous and modest person.

Gerard died at Parkes on 19 January 1965 after suffering from Parkinson's disease and rheumatic arthritis. He had married in 1921 and was survived by a son.

J. D. Richardson, *The history of the 7th Light Horse Regiment A.I.F.* (Syd, 1923); C. E. W. Bean, *The story of Anzac*, 2 (Syd, 1924); *Aussie*, 15 (1920); *Reveille* (Syd), Feb 1944; *Bulletin*, 10 May 1950; *Champion Post*, 22 Jan 1965; Keesing papers, *and* F. Johnson papers (ML); Gerard papers (SLSA); History of the 12th Australian Light Horse Regiment (AWM); information from Mr E. H. Gerard, Parkes, NSW.   J. T. LAIRD

GIBB, WILLIAM (1890-1960), soldier and plumber, was born on 14 March 1890 at Waimataitai, near Timaru, New Zealand, son of David Duke Gibb, fireman, and his wife Jane, née Deavoll. He was educated at Timaru, became a plumber there and in 1909-14 served as a volunteer in the City Rifles. On the outbreak of World War I he sailed for Sydney where he enlisted in the 1st Field Company, Engineers, Australian Imperial Force, on 20 August 1914. He embarked on the troopship *Afric* on 18 October for overseas service. On arrival in Egypt his company undertook training in desert warfare, bridging and fortifications, and in February 1915 occupied a defensive position on the Suez Canal, south of Kantara.

In March his unit embarked for Lemnos and undertook dredging, well-sinking and the construction of accommodation, roads and floating landing-stages. On 25 April he was present when his company landed with the 3rd Brigade near Ari Burnu on the Gallipoli peninsula as the covering force for the 1st Australian Division. As the Turkish resistance increased the engineers became heavily committed to offensive sapping, tunnelling and demolition of enemy trenches. Gibb was evacuated temporarily on 30 July with influenza. During the withdrawal from Gallipoli on 20 December he was a member of a rear-party responsible for tunnel patrolling and mine demolition despite his unit's departure some weeks before. When the A.I.F. returned to Egypt the engineers moved into camp at Tel-el-Kebir and then in January 1916 the 1st Field Company again occupied a defensive position on the Suez Canal. On 22 January Gibb was promoted lance corporal.

With the expansion of the A.I.F. to five divisions in 1916, Gibb was transferred to the 15th Field Company, 5th Division, and promoted corporal on 25 April. In June the division moved to the Western Front in northern France and Gibb's company again became involved in offensive sapping under heavy fire; at Fromelles in July the division suffered over 5000 casualties. Gibb then served in the Armentières area and on 6 December was promoted sergeant. Following the German withdrawal to the Hindenburg line he participated in the Bullecourt and Messines operations in 1917 during which the engineers suffered heavy casualties. For his exemplary service in these operations he was awarded the Military Medal. On 23 February 1918 he was commissioned second lieutenant, and on 23 May promoted lieutenant. In June he was attached to the 567th Army Troops Company, Royal Engineers, which was supporting the 5th Australian Division.

At the battle of Hamel on 4-5 July 1918,

Gibb commanded a section of sixty engineer troops who constructed a sap forward under heavy enemy fire near Ville-sur-Ancre, thus allowing a continuous firing line to be formed to the 15th Brigade objective. For his outstanding effort he was awarded the Military Cross. In the British offensive which followed he constructed a motor transport bridge at Péronne on 3 September under heavy enemy fire. Two days later at Flanucourt, east of Péronne, he daringly reconnoitred sites, then in full view of the enemy constructed a field artillery bridge. For these two actions he was awarded a Bar to the Military Cross.

In September 1918 Gibb went to Australia on leave and was demobilized on 23 January 1919. He resumed plumbing, working in Japan and then Canada where he married a Canadian widow with one child. There were no children of his marriage. When the Japanese bombed Pearl Harbour in World War II Gibb was in Honolulu working for the navy as an engineer plumber. Between the wars he had become an American citizen and settled at Portland, Oregon, where he died in 1960. One of his brothers had served with the New Zealand forces at Gallipoli.

A. D. Ellis, *The story of the Fifth Australian Division* (Lond, 1920?); C. E. W. Bean, *The story of Anzac* (Syd, 1921, 1924), and *The A.I.F. in France 1916-18* (Syd, 1929, 1933, 1937, 1942); R. R. McNicoll, *The Royal Australian Engineers 1902 to 1919* (Canb, 1979); *London Gazette*, 14 Dec 1917, 24 Sept 1918, 31 Jan 1919; War diaries, 1st *and* 15th Field Companies, Australian Engineers A.I.F., *and* 1st Field Company, Australian Engineers 1914-15, a brief history, *and* T. Slee (ed), 1st Field Company, Engineers, 1914-18, *and* W. E. Turnley, 1st Field Company, Australian Engineers, *and* 15th Field Company, Australian Engineers, brief record (AWM); information from the Dept of Veterans' Affairs, NSW, *and* Miss M. & Mr R. Gibb, Temuka, NZ, *and* Mrs A. Mee, Christchurch, NZ, *and* Mr C. Cheetham, Bundaberg, Qld.   R. SUTTON

GIBBS, HERBERT WILLIAM (1852-1940), public servant and artist, and CECILIA MAY (1877-1969), author, were father and daughter. Herbert was born on 21 November 1852 at Alverstoke, Southampton, England, eldest of seven children of William Gibbs, merchant, and his wife Eliza, née Emery. He was educated by his father (who became a private tutor at Singleton, Sussex, about 1871), then at a grammar school until, at 14, he lost an eye, and finally by Rev. Edward Cole, rector of St Peter's, Brighton. In 1870 he joined the civil service, working as a clerk in the General Post Office in 1877, and studied art at the School of Design, South Kensington, and with Philip Sydney Holland. On 24 October 1874 at

Sydenham, Kent, he married Cecilia Rogers, a fellow art-student.

In June 1881, with his brother George, Gibbs arrived in South Australia in the *Chimborazo*, and was followed in October by his wife and three children. After an unsuccessful farming venture at Franklin River, he moved to Norwood and worked as a surveyor. In 1885 with George and two others he formed a company to take up the Stirling estate at Harvey in Western Australia. After two years the brothers sold out and moved to Perth. Herbert worked as a newspaper cartoonist in 1889 and next year was drawing master at Perth High School. In April 1891 he joined the Lands and Survey Department as a draftsman and clerk; he was clerk in charge, information, from 1894 until he retired in December 1917.

Active in the artistic life of Perth, Gibbs was a founder in 1890 with B. H. Woodward, H. C. Prinsep and G. Temple Poole [qq.v.] of the Wilgie Club, and of the West Australian Society of Arts and Crafts, exhibiting with them in 1896-97 and 1902-03. He painted landscapes in oils and water-colours and was interested in printmaking, sculpture and wood-carving. He and his wife were also active in the Musical Union and the Amateur Operatic Society which presented Gilbert and Sullivan operas.

Gibbs died at his home in South Perth on 4 October 1940 and was cremated with Anglican rites. He was survived by his wife, daughter and two sons.

His only daughter Cecilia May was born on 17 January 1877 at Sydenham, Kent, England, and reached Adelaide with her mother and brothers in the *Hesperus* on 31 October 1881. She was educated at Amy Best's [q.v.3] girls' school in Perth. From 1901 to 1904 she studied art in England at the Cope and Nichol school, the South Western Polytechnic, Chelsea, various night schools and the Henry Blackburn School of Black and White Art.

Returning to Perth, in 1904 May Gibbs supplied the *Western Mail* with articles, illustrations and cartoons, but, restless, she went to England again in 1909 where she pursued her studies, completed assignments as an illustrator for George G. Harrap & Co., published a fantasy about London chimneys, *About us* (1912), and drew cartoons for the *Common Cause*, published by the suffragettes.

Ill health forced May Gibbs to return to Australia in 1913 and she settled at Neutral Bay, Sydney. She earned her living by doing quick sketches of soldiers departing for World War I, illustrating for the New South Wales Department of Public Instruction, contributing to *Lone Hand* and the English *Tatler*, and designing covers for the *Sydney Mail*. In 1916 she published *Gumnut babies*, the first of the Gumnut books she had written and illustrated. She also wrote other books, sold book-marks, small calendars and other novelties with gumnut and blossom babies. Her readers reacted to her 'sense of fun' and surprised her publishers, Angus [q.v.7] & Robertson [q.v.] Ltd, by scooping up 17 000 copies of *Snugglepot and Cuddlepie* (1918) on its first release.

On a visit to Perth in 1919 May met Bertram James Ossoli Kelly, a mining agent, and married him on 17 April. They returned to Sydney to live and built a Spanish-type house, Nutcote, on the shores of Neutral Bay surrounded by gum trees. About this time she was described by 'Pixie O'Harris' (Mrs B. Pratt) as 'fairly tall, medium weight, with dark hair, a lean artistic face and keen eyes. Her voice was firm and refined'. May collected Spode and willow-pattern china and enjoyed gardening, camping, music and theatricals. She pursued her career as an author and illustrator, publishing *Little Ragged Blossom* (1920) and *Little Obelia* (1921). Her gumnuts, blossom babies and bad 'banksia men' were to delight generations of children. On 3 August 1924 the first 'Bib and Bub' cartoon strip was published in the Sydney *Sunday News*: the comic strip survived sundry newspaper mergers to run until September 1967. In 1925-31 the rival *Sunday Sun* published her second comic strip 'Tiggy Touchwood', under the pseudonym, 'Stan Cottman'. She also wrote a weekly column, 'Gumnut Gossip'.

Until the 1930s May Gibbs was very successful. She published *Nuttybub and Nittersing* (1923) and *Two little gum-nuts* (1929). All her books were reissued and five cartoon books of *Bib and Bub* appeared. However, she never recovered financially from the Depression, which disrupted negotiations for selling her work in England and the United States of America and for screen rights. After her husband died in 1939, she lived on at Nutcote with her dogs (usually Scotch terriers) and published *Scotty in gumnut land* (1941), *Mr. and Mrs. Bear and friends* (1943) and her last book *Prince Dande Lion* in 1954. In 1955 she was appointed M.B.E..

May Gibbs died in Sydney, on 27 November 1969 and was cremated with Anglican rites. Childless, she willed all her papers and copyrights to the New South Wales Society for Crippled Children and the Spastic Centre of New South Wales and the residue of her estate, valued for probate at £42 532, to the United Nations International Children's Emergency Fund.

H. Anderson (ed), *The singing roads* (Syd, 1965); B. Chapman, *The colonial eye* (Perth, 1979); *Aust*

Home Beautiful, 12 Mar 1926, p 16; *West Australian*, 11 Dec 1889; *SMH*, 12 Nov 1953, 9 June 1955, 29 Nov 1969; 'Pixie O'Harris', A memory of May Gibbs (MS 1661, ML); May Gibbs papers (ML); 3 illustrated letters to H. C. Prinsep from Butlers Swamp, 1887, *and* articles of partnership in land in Western Australia, 24 Mar 1894 (553 A, *and* 1773 A, Battye Lib); information from Mrs J. Moyes, Claremont, Perth.   MAUREEN WALSH

GIBBS, SYBIL ENID VERA MUNRO; *see* MORRISON

GIBLIN, LYNDHURST FALKINER (1872-1951), political economist, was born on 29 November 1872 in Hobart, son of William Robert Giblin [q.v.4], barrister, and his wife Emmely Jean, née Perkins. Educated at The Hutchins School, Hobart, and University College, London, he entered King's College, Cambridge, in 1893, graduating senior optime (mathematics and science) in 1896 (M.A., 1928). He rowed for King's but excelled at Rugby Union, representing not only his college and university but All-England too. Revisiting King's in 1938, an extraordinary career behind him, he was elected to an honorary fellowship and given the use of Keynes's rooms. When Giblin died the college established a studentship in his name.

After coming down from Cambridge he and a fellow Kingsman joined to prospect for gold in the Cassiar-Stickine district of North British Columbia. The isolated life, if at times adventurous, was always harsh and ultimately meagre of reward; it was essential to work as lumberman, teamster or boatman to help pay one's way. Giblin's correspondence from this period conveys the deprivation, the routine and the eccentric acquaintance of his mining existence. In 1904 he joined the crew of a schooner bound for Australia, but the same year found him once again in London, where *inter alia*, he helped to teach ju-jitsu. After visiting a Solomon Islands plantation in 1905 he returned to Hobart and set about establishing an orchard. He also taught mathematics and explored Tasmania's high country, measuring more precisely certain peaks. In April 1909, bristling with criticism of his State's recent financial past, Giblin unsuccessfully contested the seat of Franklin as a Liberal Democrat. He then joined the Labor Party, gave elementary lectures to branches on economic subjects, and made his way to the State and Federal executives. In 1913 he won the State seat of Denison. When Labor took office Giblin gained a reputation for independence. He became unofficial adviser to the treasurer J. A. Lyons [q.v.], persuading him of the need for an inquiry into the public debt. Upon the dissolution of the assembly in 1916 he did not seek re-election.

From March 1909, when he had been commissioned a lieutenant of the Intelligence Corps, Giblin had been active in the citizen forces. In January 1914 he became captain and during 1916 transferred to the 40th Battalion of the Australian Imperial Force. He was wounded at Armentières and Messines, and won the Military Cross in August 1917. Recovered, and promoted major, he fought in the third battle of Ypres, Passchendaele and on the Somme. He received the Distinguished Service Order on 3 June 1918, but a third wounding on 24 August at Bapaume removed him from the war.

Late in 1919 Giblin was appointed Tasmanian government statistician. He enlarged the office, extended the range of its data gathering, and became a protagonist of uniformity in State collections. Resuming the role of adviser to Lyons, he also drew close to two economists, (Sir) D. B. Copland and J. B. Brigden [q.v.7], and in 1924 helped form the Economic Society of Australia and New Zealand. He had Brigden's support in preparing Tasmanian claims for special grants under Section 96 of the Constitution. In 1927 these two, with Copland, E. C. Dyason and the Commonwealth statistician, C. H. Wickens [qq.v.], were appointed by Prime Minister (Viscount) Bruce [q.v.7] to investigate the Australian tariff. Their report, which attracted international notice as a major work in applied economics, appeared in 1929, when Giblin also took up the new Ritchie Chair of Economic Research at the University of Melbourne. Although Giblin was without formal economic learning, his intellect, varied experience and mathematical background ensured him prominence in a local profession which had yet to mature.

In the second half of 1930 he joined with Copland and Dyason to present the 'Melbourne' approach to Depression policy. Always closely in touch with Labor politicians, particularly Lyons and E. G. Theodore [q.v.], in 1931 Giblin became an observer at government-bank talks and Loan Council meetings. From April 1931 to December 1932 he acted as Commonwealth statistician in Wickens's absence, prepared the census of 1933 and served upon various advisory bodies — most notably the Copland Committee, whose report underpinned the Premiers' Plan; the Unemployment Secretariat Sub-Committee; and the (Sir) Wallace Bruce [q.v.7] Committee. In 1933 Giblin became a founding member of the Commonwealth Grants Commission, which he left in 1936, having accepted, in October 1935, a seven-year appointment to the board of the Commonwealth Bank. His sojourn abroad in 1938 was followed, in December, by the chairmanship of a small informal committee, with (Sir) R. Wilson and (Sir) L. G. Melville as its other members, which examined certain economic implications for Australia of early Japanese participation in the conflict then threatening. After war with Germany broke out, this body, now designated the Commonwealth Advisory Committee on Finance and Economic Policy, was augmented first by Brigden and Copland, then by H. C. Coombs, E. R. Walker and (Sir) Harold Brown among others. It filled a brains-trust role in relation to economic aspects of the war effort, and did much to create the intellectual framework within which post-war economic problems were considered. From the close of 1941 an elaborated departmental structure absorbed its tasks, but it survived formally into 1947. Then Giblin turned more fully on his history of the Commonwealth Bank, published posthumously in 1951.

He achieved eminence in Australian political economy as a relatively old man. Acquaintances were to recall a large, sagging figure of quiet presence, the head close cropped, the cheeks high, the attire eccentric — homespun trousers and jacket, improvised tie, stout boots dubbined rather than polished — and the mouth clamping an ancient pipe. Friends remembered a man sane, reposed, vastly commonsensical, wryly humorous. Giblin's writings, plain of style but leavened occasionally by a striking image, reveal two characteristics: first, a disdain for pure 'theory'; and second, an alertness to those economic distortions likely in a democracy — with which, in turn, was associated a keen sense of the politically possible. Although a fine intuition and feeling for relevant magnitudes took him far, it is arguable that he might have accomplished even more had he been less self reliant, less confident of teasing coherences from a commonsensical purview of the facts.

Giblin won professional renown in the fields of Federal finance, tariff policy, employment analysis, Depression diagnosis, and post-war economic management. He resisted the idea that Federal assistance under section 96 of the Constitution be rationalized in terms of 'disabilities' imposed upon underpopulated rural States by Federal tariff, wage and navigation policies. Aside from noting the difficulty of measuring usefully the costs of Federal policy, he argued that claimant-State disabilities were more general anyway and that the criterion for special grants should, accordingly, be relative financial need. But in relation to raising and spending money a claimant State should exhibit, by the standards of the Federation, a better-than-average record.

Giblin's ideas achieved their fullest expression in Appendix J to *The Case for Tasmania, 1930*. Before this he had touched upon Federal finance in his presidential address to the Economic Society of Australia and New Zealand (1926) and, with Brigden's assistance, in a memorandum to the royal commission on the Constitution (1929). He had also estimated differences in the taxable capacities and fiscal efforts of the States and regularly updated the figures. By 1936 the Grants Commission was pursuing principles much along the lines he had advanced in 1930. Moreover, in 1938 he presented to the Rowell-Sirois Commission in Canada evidence which influenced post-war arrangements there for fiscal equalization.

Whatever the burden of tariff policy upon rural States, Giblin followed Brigden in claiming that it had bestowed advantages upon the great bulk of the Federation's citizens: it had reconciled two apparently inconsistent ambitions, to grow in population and to preserve the real wage. Thus the 1929 tariff report maintained that protection had supported real wages at the expense of rural rents, thereby sparing labour the normal consequence of its own increase. In contrast with the loose *a priori* reasoning with which Brigden had earlier defended protection, the report relied upon an empirical-statistical approach owing much to Giblin, and hinged upon the idea of protected activities being more labour intensive than those promoted by free trade. The argument, in places unsatisfactory, provoked debate about the tariff and income redistribution which culminated in the Stolper-Samuelson theorem of 1941. Giblin drew attention to the growth of certain rural assistance which in contrast with aid to manufacturing was not monitored by a board responsible to parliament, and he wrote with irony of a future which dispensed 'protection all round'. He also observed that the efficiency cost of the manufacturing tariff would fall with any sustained deterioration of the terms on which Australia sold its major rural exports. In 1930 he forecast such a decline, and in 1936, after several years of low export prices, claimed that Australia's contrived industrial development of the 1920s had in proportion (if accidentally) paid off.

In 1930, about a year before the 'multiplier' article by Kahn which was to contribute so vitally to Keynes's *General Theory* of 1936, Giblin applied a geometric series to the analysis of fluctuations in income and employment. He showed how the repercussions of dwindling export income and capital inflow would not, as intuition suggested, ramify without cease; rather they would, owing to leakages from the expenditure stream, sum to a finite value. His multiplier, expressing the ratio between initial change in external receipts and ultimate change in real income, was a function of spending leakages into imports and exportables. Certainly Giblin's exposition, confined to the foreign-trade variant of the multiplier, was less sophisticated than Kahn's; but it did portray an income mechanism of trade-balance adjustment which Kahn was to miss and which foreshadowed extensions of Keynes's 'closed system' of 1936 to the open-economy case. In any event his concept informed 'Melbourne' economic advice through 1930-31, and Theodore exploited it in his policy recommendations. Only slowly did Giblin draw upon Kahn's insights and he showed little interest in the more general implications of multiplier analysis for contemporary monetary debate.

Addressing himself to the collapse of Australia's external income in 1929-30, and presuming that overseas debt obligations would be met in full, Giblin argued that the only way of avoiding secondary effects upon income and employment was to modify appropriately the distribution of national expenditure between home and foreign goods. Early in 1930 he favoured a broadly goldstandard solution in which the domestic wage-price level, not the exchange rate, bore the burden of expenditure-switching. Accordingly, he sought to persuade workers that a wage-cut was in order. But then, as the Depression deepened, he came to share Copland's and Dyason's liking for domestic price stability and joined them in articulating a 'middle course' which comprehended 'inflationary' as well as 'deflationary' initiatives. Now, from exchange depreciation, credit creation and money-wage cuts, was to flow relative cost improvement in a setting of domestic price stability, while special taxation would ensure that rentiers shared in national loss. Such a policy, it was believed – along with a hoped-for improvement in export prices and an effort to lift efficiency all round – would promote recovery. Although direct action to reduce budget deficits was seen as integral to the task of keeping national spending within national means, it was also appreciated that fiscal balance must be in some degree a function of recovery itself. Inevitably Giblin approved the exchange and wage adjustments of early 1931, and the premiers' mid-year budgetary plan; but he also, as the Depression persisted, came to take a softer line on government spending. Here, however, an appreciation of Australian realities tempered a developing intellectual conviction, and he remained wary of bold proposals.

After 1941 the Finance and Economic Committee gave increasing attention to the post-war prospect. In particular it deliberated Australia's response to Article VII of the Mutual Aid Agreement. A central idea was that full employment would be compromised by balance of payments problems should major industrial countries not be committed similarly; Australia must at once urge the objective upon other countries and retain her freedom of action in relation to the exchange rate and the tariff. In 1943-45 Giblin wrote more generally upon the problems of reconstruction. Unlike some others he anticipated high employment as a result of delayed spending plans, and was apprehensive of related inefficiencies. He doubted the will of politicians not only to discriminate among investment projects but also to eschew inflationary finance; and he was fearful, too, of intransigent income bargaining by organized interests. Moreover, even if the employment ideal were spared such domestic follies the external constraint would remain. Failing, with many others, to anticipate the strength of post-war demand for Australian exports, he became anxious about the wherewithal for imports needed to keep domestic industries going. Finally, his opinion reputedly was influential in the adoption first of the 'special accounts' arrangement for controlling trading bank liquidity, and second, of two per cent a year as a realistic estimate of population growth upon which to premise reconstruction policy.

Giblin died on 1 March 1951 in Hobart, survived by his wife, Eilean Mary, née Burton, whom he had married on 29 July 1918 in London. He had no children. His estate was valued for probate at £9897 in Tasmania and £4408 in Victoria. A portrait by William Dobell hangs in the University of Melbourne.

S. J. Butlin, *War economy, 1939-42*, 1 (Canb, 1955); D. B. Copland (ed), *Giblin. the scholar and the man* (Melb, 1960), and for bibliog; C. B. Schedvin, *Australia and the great Depression* (Syd, 1970); R. L. Mathews, *State and local taxation* (Canb, 1977); S. J. Butlin and C. B. Schedvin, *War economy, 1942-45*, 2 (Canb, 1977); W. Prest and R. L. Mathews (eds), *The development of Australian fiscal Federalism* (Canb, 1979); *Economic Record*, Nov 1952; *Stand-To* (Canb), Aug-Sept 1952; *Aust Economic Papers*, June 1973; *Aust Economic Hist Review*, Mar 1980; Giblin papers (MS 366, NL).

NEVILLE CAIN

GIBLIN, RONALD WORTHY (1863-1936), surveyor and historian, was born on 3 January 1863 in Hobart, son of Thomas Giblin, banker, and his wife Mary Ann, née Worthy. He was grandson of Robert Wilkins Giblin, who had arrived in Van Diemen's Land in 1827, and cousin to L. F. Giblin [q.v.]. Educated at The Hutchins School, he received the Tasmanian Council of Education's associate of arts degree in 1879. He then travelled and worked on the land in Tasmania and Queensland until 1884 when he joined the Lands Department in Hobart. Remaining there for less than a year, he went to New South Wales where, becoming a licensed surveyor in 1889, he worked briefly for the Public Works Department and then in the Department of Lands. His surveying work was apparently highly regarded, as in 1894 he was nominated by G. H. Knibbs [q.v.], then lecturer in surveying at the University of Sydney, to be one of two Australian surveyors engaged to work in the Royal Survey Department of Siam. He left for Bangkok in October. He was director of the department from 1901 until 1910, retiring with a pension and the Order of the White Elephant. In 1906 he was a founding director of the Kombok Rubber Co. Ltd which, initially Singapore based, moved its headquarters to London in 1911.

After leaving Siam, Giblin went to England and settled in Cheltenham, Gloucestershire. In 1915 he was registrar at the Cheltenham Red Cross Centre for wounded soldiers, and in September next year obtained the position of indent officer in the London office of the Tasmanian agent-general. Giblin's knowledge and interest in Tasmania's past had been recognized by the agent-general as early as 1914 when Giblin had provided advice on matters relating to Tasmanian history. It was not surprising that when, in 1921, the Tasmanian government requested detailed information on the first fifteen years of Tasmanian settlement, Giblin was chosen for this task. He finished in November 1922 and was highly praised for both his research work and historical analysis.

This work provided the impetus for Giblin's proposed three-volume history of Tasmania (1642-1853); in November 1924 he resigned from the agent-general's office to devote his time to research and writing. By late 1926, with the first volume almost completed, he attended celebrations in Tasmania to mark the centenary of the Giblin family's settlement there, using the opportunity to work on local records for his second volume, although most of the research was done on material held in London supplemented by correspondence with acquaintances in Tasmania. He returned to London in May 1927. Next year, with the help of a Tasmanian government grant of £300, *The early history of Tasmania*, volume one (1642-1804) was published, to favourable reviews. While his rather wordy style is somewhat difficult to read and perhaps at times reflects too much the preoccupations

of a professional surveyor, Giblin is concerned both to describe the early exploration within the context of European expansion into Australasia and to provide a detailed account of the early visitors' explorations and impressions of Tasmanian geography, flora, fauna, and particularly Aboriginals. The quantity of information has ensured that the volume has remained the definitive work on this subject even though his interpretation of some events may be challenged.

Giblin's research for volume two (1804-36) progressed very slowly, partly because of sickness; by 1935 when his health began to deteriorate rapidly it became apparent that he would be unable to complete it. When he died, on 13 March 1936, in London, leaving a wife and two sons, his partially completed manuscript and notes were forwarded to J. D. A. Collier, librarian of the Tasmanian Public Library. These were edited by Collier and published in 1939 as volume two (1804-18) although some material up to 1836 was included. Although the volume as a whole is less cohesive and comprehensive than volume one, the completed sections reflect the immense amount of research undertaken by Giblin and his efforts to immerse himself in the ethos of the period. He was a fellow of the Royal Geographical Society and of the Royal Colonial Institute. A member of the Royal Society of Tasmania from 1926, he also published articles on Tasmanian history in its *Papers and Proceedings* (1925 and 1929).

Mercury, 16 Mar 1936; Giblin papers, correspondence *and* Premier's Dept, Correspondence, 1914-28 (TA); Col Sec, In-letters (NSWA).

IAN PEARCE

GIBNEY, MATTHEW (1835-1925), bishop, was born in November 1835 at Killeshandra, Cavan, Ireland, son of Michael Gibney, farmer, and his wife Alice, née Prunty. He studied for the priesthood at the preparatory seminary at Stillorgan and from 1857 at the Catholic Missionary College of All Hallows, Drumcondra, Dublin. He was ordained priest in 1863 and arrived in Perth later that year.

Gibney had a kindly personality and plenty of drive and in 1873 he was appointed vicar-general to Bishop Martin Griver [q.v.4]. He had a large physique and massive shoulders and his energy gave rise to many legends: his resilience when riding for days without water; his swimming flooded rivers to administer the sacraments; almost dying from arsenic poisoning when a farmer's wife mistook it for carbonate of soda. In 1868 Gibney had opened the Catholic Girls' Orphanage in Perth and in 1871 the Clontarf

Orphanage for Catholic boys at Subiaco. As a result of damage to the boys' orphanage, he set off for the eastern colonies to collect funds for rebuilding. In Victoria on 28 June 1880, while travelling by train from Benalla to Albury, he learned that Ned Kelly's [q.v.5] gang had been surrounded at Mrs Ann Jones's Glenrowan hotel and were shooting it out with police. Gibney left his train and tended the seemingly seriously wounded Kelly, heard his confession and gave him the last rites. Although advised against it by the bushranger, Gibney entered the now burning hotel to minister to the remainder of the gang, only to find their dead bodies; Martin Cherry received the last rites from Gibney before he too died. The priest returned to Perth in a blaze of glory and resumed work under Griver's appreciative gaze.

In 1886 he became coadjutor bishop of Perth, in November Griver died and next year Gibney was consecrated bishop. During his episcopate the diocese increased from 12 churches, 11 primary schools, 2 orphanages and 3 superior schools, to 31 churches, 43 primary schools, 2 orphanages, 21 superior schools, 1 college, a wayward women's asylum, 2 hospitals and a monastery. In 1898 he divided the diocese and created the diocese of Geraldton. Gibney stalwartly defended the Aboriginals in the North-West; he claimed to have been 'the first to take a practical interest' in them at a time when they were receiving scant sympathy. He had first gone there in 1878, admired their culture and was horrified at their treatment by white pearlers. He was concerned at the diminution of the black population since the arrival of Europeans and resolved to open a mission. By 1890 he secured from the government land at Beagle Bay and missionaries from the Trappist Order, whom he accompanied and helped to settle in. Ten years later the missionaries' departure caused a crisis. He had 10 000 acres (4050 ha) of freehold land, on condition that £5000 worth of improvements be made. These had not materialized. In 1900, with Canon Martelli and Daisy Bates [q.v.7], he went to the mission and, in his mid-sixties, dug, hoed and cleared paddocks to retain the mission for the Aboriginals. Next year the Pallottine Order took it over.

Gibney identified himself closely with the political and social aspirations of his fellow Irishmen: he had been partly responsible for the 1871 Elementary Education Act by which the subsidization of religious education was extended to Catholic schools. In the Perth by-election of 1888 Catholics voted en bloc for John Horgan [q.v.], Gibney's solicitor. But Gibney deplored the property qualifications and restricted franchise of the Electoral Act operating at the first general

election held under responsible government in 1890. He condemned it publicly: 'the advancement of the country ... has been retarded for twenty years by the opposition of the Upper Class and now they have hampered the Constitution with conditions which will render the new Constitution nugatory for the vast majority of the people'. Later, when the subsidy system was threatened, he wrote to Bishop Salvado [q.v.2]: 'if we can only succeed to draw our Catholic body together in every district we will make our enemies quail ... ways are devised to baffle us in our good intentions'. In the 1894 elections the principle of government aid to Catholic schools was defeated, despite the bishop's efforts to mobilize votes for candidates supporting it. Next year the ecclesiastical grant was abolished; he requested £50 000 for the church in compensation and received £15 000.

Probably because of a need to replace these lost funds, Gibney then involved himself in some financial dealings which were ill advised. From the late 1890s the Church bought many shops, offices, houses and a hotel in the city of Perth. In 1905 he acquired control of the Morning Herald. He banned horse-racing information from it, circulation dropped and the paper went into liquidation in 1909. Another dubious venture was his partnership in the Greenbushes Development Co. The company operated ineffectively and returns were meagre. By 1908 the Church's debts were over £216 000 and his vicar-general was found to have been signing documents with Gibney's signature.

Word travelled to the Pope and to Cardinal Moran [q.v.] in Sydney who instigated an inquiry into Gibney's financial management by Archbishop O'Reily [q.v.] of Adelaide and Bishop P. V. Dwyer [q.v.] of Maitland. In 1910 O'Reily suggested that Gibney resign. Dissatisfied, Gibney prepared a statement to go directly to Pius X. This was considered, but he was requested to stand down. On 14 May he resigned and Father Patrick Clune [q.v.] succeeded him.

Matthew Gibney went into seclusion. A few days before his death at his North Perth home from cancer on 22 June 1925, he received a message granting him a papal benediction. He was buried in the Cathedral of the Immaculate Conception, Perth.

W. B. Kimberly, History of West Australia (Melb, 1897); J. T. Reilly, Reminiscences of fifty years residence in Western Australia (Perth, 1903); P. Hasluck, Black Australians (Melb, 1942); M. Durack, Kings in grass castles (Lond, 1959); D. F. Bourke, The history of the Catholic Church in Western Australia (Perth, 1979); C. T. Stannage, The people of Perth (Perth, 1979), and J of Religious History, 6 (June 1971); PP (LA WA), 1895, 2 (A10); Freeman's J (Syd), 4 Dec 1919, 11 Nov 1920, 28 Feb

1924; *Australasian*, 27 June 1925; D. Bates, MS 2300/11 (NL).   V. E. CALLAGHAN

GIBSON, ALEXANDER JAMES (1876-1960), engineer, was born on 18 December 1876 at Hanover Square, London, son of Edward Morris Gibson, articled clerk and later solicitor, and his wife Martha, née James. He was educated at Alleyn's College of God's Gift (Dulwich College) and served an apprenticeship with the Thames Iron Works, Ship Building & Engineering Co. at Blackwall, London. An associate member of the Institution of Civil Engineers, London, from 1899, he went that year to Shanghai, China, with S. C. Farnham & Co., where he was again involved in shipbuilding and marine work. He served with the Shanghai Volunteers during the Boxer Rebellion.

Arriving in Sydney late in 1900, Gibson became a fitter at Mort's [q.v.5] Dock & Engineering Co. On 11 March 1902 at St John's Church of England, Gordon, he married Marion Ellen Florence Hitchman (d. 1947). Encouraged by Professor W. H. Warren [q.v.6], in 1903 he applied successfully for the post of assistant lecturer in engineering building and design at the University of Sydney. In 1910 he was appointed foundation professor of engineering in the University of Queensland; he designed and built the engineering laboratories, then the finest in Australia.

Commissioned in the Corps of Australian Engineers in 1904, Gibson transferred to the Australian Intelligence Corps in 1908 and was promoted captain in 1910. From August 1914 he was assistant censor and temporary censor in Brisbane. In 1917 he served in England as temporary major working on Professor (Sir) Henry Barraclough's [q.v.7] munitions scheme for the Commonwealth Department of Defence. Returning to Australia he was acting general manager and chief engineer of the Australian Arsenal in 1918.

In January 1919 Gibson resigned his chair at the University of Queensland to become superintendent of construction at the Broken Hill Proprietary Co. Ltd's steelworks at Newcastle, New South Wales. In 1922 he went into partnership with Sir George Julius [q.v.] and William Poole, to form the consulting engineering firm of Julius, Poole & Gibson, Sydney; he was senior partner for many years. In 1933-34 he chaired the technical education commission appointed by (Sir) Bertram Stevens [q.v.], and in 1938 visited London to discuss safety measures for Burrinjuck Dam. He was later chairman of the Advisory Council of Sydney Technical College. He helped D. H. Drummond [q.v.] with the Technical Education Act, 1940; it

was nullified by the (Sir William) McKell government the following year.

In February 1931 Gibson had founded and was president of the All for Australia League, which aimed at 'purging politics' and called for unity; it attacked political parties and 'inept Parliaments'. After the dismissal of the premier J. T. Lang by Governor Sir Philip Game [qq.v.] in 1932, the league merged with the United Australia Party. Ten years later Lang described Gibson as 'a sinister figure', who had 'sold out' to Stevens at the price of becoming consulting engineer to the government, and accused him of having put the government to unnecessary expenditure on Burrinjuck Dam. The charges were never substantiated.

Awarded an honorary M.E. by the University of Queensland in 1919, Gibson was a member of the Institution of Engineers, Australia, its president in 1932, and P. N. Russell [q.v.6] medallist in 1940. In 1934-39 he was a fellow of the Senate of the University of Sydney and in 1940-48 chairman of the Standards Association of Australia. He also served on the council of the Commonwealth Scientific and Industrial Research Organization and on the board of Prince Henry Hospital, Sydney; he was honorary consultant to Sydney Hospital and the Royal Alexandra Hospital for Children. He was a member of the University and New South Wales clubs.

On 12 October 1954 Gibson married at Chatswood, Sydney, Ann Muriel Dent of Rockhampton, Queensland. Predeceased by her he died at Cammeray, Sydney, on 2 December 1960 and was cremated with Anglican rites. He was survived by two sons and two daughters of his first marriage. His estate was valued for probate at £38 000.

Univ Syd, School of civil engineering, *Acta Structorum*, Mar 1960; *JRAHS*, 50 (1964), pt 4, p 277; *JRAHS*, 57 (1971), pt 2, p 160; *SMH*, 13, 17 Feb, 10, 21 Mar 1931, 13 May, 5, 6, Nov 1942, 3 Dec 1960; MP 1044/1, 18/0458 (AAO).   J. M. ANTILL

GIBSON, ELIZABETH (BESSIE) DICKSON (1868-1961), artist, was born on 16 May 1868 at Ipswich, Queensland, daughter of James Gibson, bank manager, and his wife Anne, née Blair, who had been twice married. Bessie was a sister of John Lockhart Gibson [q.v.]. When her father retired as bank manager in Ipswich, the family moved to Manly, from where she studied art at Brisbane Technical College in 1899-1905 under Godfrey Rivers [q.v.]. In 1901-02 she visited relatives in Scotland and was inspired to study abroad.

A remarkably open-minded family financed what was meant to be only a three-year study trip to Paris. She sailed in September 1905, visited Edinburgh and was settled in Paris by May 1906. She lived in Montparnasse to 1939, except for frequent trips to Britain and one to Algeria. Never part of the *avant-garde*, she maintained close friendships with fellow expatriates and remained firmly in the conservative world of the Royal Academy and Salon exhibitions. Studying principally at the Castelucho and Colarossi ateliers under Frances Hodgkins and the American Edwin Scott, she also briefly studied miniature painting, at which she excelled, under Mlle Debillemont-Chardon.

Gibson's work included miniatures of family or friends, formal portrait studies in oils, Whistlerian études on wooden panels of Paris, Honfleur and Cherbourg; and water-colours of portraits, landscapes or interiors. Dating is difficult because she showed little stylistic or technical development. Her miniatures gained early recognition but when fashion changed in the 1920s she concentrated on oil-on-canvas portraits which are largely unsuccessful — these form the bulk of her Royal Academy and Salon entries. Her *pochades* on small panels do have considerable charm, but the tonal application of paint does not reflect nineteenth-century French experimentation after the late 1860s. Her work suggests a conservative application of the Whistler manner.

Gibson's fresh and individualistic water-colours are her most successful works although they are indebted to Frances Hodgkins. Unfortunately, the long-established and then-decaying system of Salon and Royal Academy Exhibitions, in which she achieved reasonable, if unspectacular success, worked against their due recognition. A miniature was 'hung on the line' in the 1905 Royal Academy exhibition and she was exhibited there at least fifteen times between 1905 and 1923. After 1913 Bessie Gibson exhibited almost annually at either the Société des Artistes Français or the Salon d'Automnes until 1939. She won an honorable mention from the former in 1924 and a bronze medal at the International Exposition for Miniatures, 1937.

Despite recognition of the work of contemporary female expatriates, Gibson's work remained almost unknown in Australia. This is probably because of her shyness and her Queensland background. After spending the war years in England, she returned to Australia in 1947 and began to exhibit in Sydney and Melbourne. Her work is now in several State galleries, the Australian National Gallery and in private collections. A more historical approach to Australian art and interest in women artists in the late 1970s has made her better known.

She died in a Brisbane convalescent home on 13 July 1961 and was cremated. Her estate was valued for probate at £10361.

N. D. H. Underhill, *Bessie Gibson* (Brisb, 1978); J. Burke, *Australian women artists 1840-1940* (Melb, 1980).   NANCY D. H. UNDERHILL

GIBSON CARMICHAEL; *see* CARMICHAEL, SIR THOMAS

GIBSON, JOHN LOCKHART (1860-1944), ophthalmologist, was born on 17 July 1860 at Ipswich, Queensland, eldest son of James Gibson, bank manager, and his wife Annie Bush, née Blair. Bessie Gibson [q.v.] was his sister. He was educated at Ipswich Grammar School and the University of Edinburgh (M.B., 1881; M.D., 1885) where he won first-class honours and a gold medal; he later studied in Vienna, Berlin and London. Rejecting an academic career in Britain, in 1886 he commenced general practice in Brisbane, then a small city without a medical school or university. The new Hospital for Sick Children appointed him its first visiting physician later in that year, and in 1895 its ophthalmologist. After an illness Gibson's practice was restricted to diseases of the eye and ear, nose and throat, and two years later to ophthalmology. He was president of the Queensland Medical Society in 1892, of the British Medical Association (Queensland Branch) in 1908 and was on the association's federal committee. He was also active in the medical congresses at this time.

At the 3rd Intercolonial Medical Congress in Sydney in 1892, of which he was vice-president, Gibson and Jefferis Turner [q.v.] pointed out that anemia in children could be caused by hookworm. It was not until the Rockefeller Foundation's hookworm survey 1917-19, and the Australian Hookworm Campaign 1919-23, revealed the magnitude of the problem in tropical and sub-tropical areas that eradication began. At the 1892 congress, Gibson, Turner and others also reported ten cases of lead-poisoning in Brisbane children. Overseas, this ailment affected adults; in Queensland, children. The source of the poison was unknown until, in 1904, Gibson had the powdered paint from his own house analysed and lead carbonate was found. The paint on wooden Queensland houses dried and powdered in the hot sun. Most of the affected children were nail-biters or thumb-suckers who carried it on sweaty hands to the mouth. Gibson led the campaign to have lead paint replaced in the vulnerable parts of buildings; this was legally required by the Health Act of 1922. Gibson joined the Australian Imperial

Force on 1 May 1915. As a major that year he was in charge of the ophthalmic department of the 3rd Australian General Hospital on Lemnos. It was well equipped with instruments obtained from London and paid for with £200 sent to him by the Australian Red Cross Society, Queensland Division. Because of its efficiency, his unit had all eye casualties from Gallipoli directed to it. When his appointment terminated in August 1916, he served on a district medical committee on exemption from military service. Gibson was a fellow of the College of Surgeons of Australasia in 1927 and president of the Ophthalmological Society of Australia in 1940-44. A strong supporter of the Presbyterian Church and the Brisbane Grammar School, he was a senator of the University of Queensland in 1920-35. For his sympathetic interest in returned servicemen, the Returned Sailors' and Soldiers' Imperial League of Australia conferred life membership on him.

Gibson's home life was happy. He had a good share of Scottish stories which he loved. His was a familiar figure in Brisbane, short, with a brisk walk, helmet and little crooked cane. He was dogged in pursuit of scientific truth and painstaking in his medical work. His stubborn, uphill fight against lead paint showed the born fighter. Described as 'a man of strong and emphatic opinions, he acquired enough enemies to make life interesting, but he also made deep and lasting friendships'.

Gibson died in Brisbane on 30 September 1944 and was cremated. His wife Mary Florence, née Burkitt, whom he had married in Brisbane on 3 March 1887, and their three children inherited his estate valued for probate at £15 576. In 1960 the Jefferis Turner-Lockhart Gibson memorial oration was instituted by the Australian Paediatric Association (Queensland) in recognition of their achievement.

Alcazar Press, *Queensland, 1900* (Brisb, nd); Guy's Hospital (Lond), *Reports,* 70 (Jan 1922), p 63; *MJA,* 2 (1944), p 649, 1 (1961), p 841.

RONALD WOOD

GIBSON, ROBERT (1855-1936), farmer and land agent, was born on 19 May 1855 at Stephen Street, Melbourne, eldest of six sons of John Gibson, shoemaker, and his wife Marion, née Gemmell, both from Ayrshire, Scotland. The family moved to Colac in 1856 where John followed his trade; in 1875, after inspecting the Riverina, New South Wales, he selected part of Gunbar station which he named Narringa. The Gibsons, with six sons, were prominent in the Hay district closer settlement. Robert was educated at Colac and, after teaching at Daylesford Grammar School for a year, gained business experience with Alexander Hamilton, Colac flour-miller and architect. He married Isabella McLeod at Ovens Bank near Peechelba on 16 November 1882. While acquiring farming expertise Robert revealed organizing skills as secretary of the Gunbar Free Selectors' Association.

About 1889 at Hay Gibson set up as a land, stock and general commission agent: his business gave him an unrivalled knowledge of the western lands and he frequently appeared for clients before the Land Board. The *Selectors Guide,* his companion to the 1884 and 1889 Crown Lands Acts, became the settlers' vade-mecum. He was a director of the Hay butter factory, a partner of the boiling-down works, a committee-member of the local Pastoral and Agricultural Society, secretary of the Federation League, an elder of the Presbyterian Church and mayor of Hay in 1892, 1902 and 1903.

After supporting John Andrews, originator of the experimental Hay irrigation scheme, Gibson took up land in the area and was president of the Hay Municipal Irrigation Trust in 1902-06. He believed that irrigation was essential to the survival of closer settlement west of Narrandera, and in 1901 was convinced by Hugh McKinney, chief engineer of the water conservation, irrigation, and drainage branch of the Department of Public Works, that irrigation would never be adequatley developed by government. Gibson promoted the Murrumbidgee northern water supply and irrigation bill as a commercial undertaking. He adapted McKinney's northern scheme and drew heavily on government data.

Backed by Victorians William Cain, M.L.C., and Sir Malcolm McEachern [q.v.], London guarantors and community enthusiasm, Gibson approached parliament in 1903 but his efforts to get legislation were frustrated. After standing, unsuccessfully, as an independent for the State seat of Murray in 1904, he was guaranteed action by (Sir) Joseph Carruthers [q.v.7], but an emasculated bill was dropped after lobbying from Hay. At a 1905 conference Gibson's standing was acknowledged, and a compromise resolution favoured government or private enterprise launching Murrumbidgee irrigation scheme, with government right of resumption. In 1905 an amended bill was referred to the Parliamentary Standing Committee on Public Works, but an accompanying departmental scheme was approved, breaking Gibson's health and finances; he was denied claims for expenses. He never received due recognition, with McKinney, for proposing the first extensive irrigation scheme in New South Wales.

In 1908 Gibson moved to Harden and opened Robert Gibson & Sons, a stockselling agency. He continued to make land evaluations and helped with the evaluation of Yarralumla station for the Federal Capital Territory. In 1913 he was again defeated for Murray by R. Scobie. Through the Farmers and Settlers' Association he fought for a fair price for wheat.

Gibson died in his sleep at Young on 3 September 1936, and was buried in the Presbyterian section of Murrumburrah cemetery. He was survived by his wife, two of his six sons and two daughters, one of whom, Jessie, married Albert David Reid, later senator.

R. Clark, *The Family of John and Marion Gibson, of Narringa, Gunbar, 1854-1974*, and A. and B. Gibson, *John and Marion Gibson and their descendants in Australia 1854-1974* (Hay, NSW, 1974); *PP* (LC & LA, NSW), 1904, 1 (21) p 321, 1906, 5 (531) p 40 15; Sel cttee on Murrumbidgee North . . . Bill, *V&P* (LA NSW), 1903, 1905; *PD* (NSW), 1906, p 40 15; Hay Hist Soc, *Procs,* Jan 1977; *Riverine Grazier,* 24 July 1903; *Colac Herald,* 18 May 1917; *SMH,* 4 Sept 1936; *Harden Express and Galong Reporter,* 10 Sept 1936; information from Messrs E. A. Eldridge, 'Berangerine', *and* J. B. Gibson 'Keringal', Hay, *and* R. Reid, Epping, *and* J. I. McIntosh, Colac, Vic.   JOHN ATCHINSON

GIBSON, SIR ROBERT (1863-1934), businessman and financier, was born on 4 November 1863 at Sunnyside near Falkirk, Scotland, third son of John Edward Gibson, metal manufacturer, and his wife Harriette, née Hicks. Robert's father had worked his way from employee to managing partner in the Camelon Iron Co. at Falkirk. An elder of the Presbyterian Church, he was described as retiring, reliable and steadfast. Robert's mother, who came from an impoverished English gentry family and had been obliged to teach in a Scottish ladies' seminary, was a woman of striking appearance and strength of purpose. She instilled in her children an intense sense of duty, the need for discipline, and the obligation to help those in need.

Educated at Falkirk High School, Robert left school at 15 to join his father's firm. In 1883 he was apprenticed to Robert Gardner & Co., lithographic draughtsmen of Glasgow, to develop his outstanding gift for drawing and design. He also studied at the Haldane Academy (subsequently the Glasgow School of Art). Robert rejoined the Camelon Iron Co. in 1887 as designer, and soon after was appointed manager of the company's London office.

With only a few pounds in his pocket, Gibson sailed for Melbourne on 22 March 1890, the day of his marriage at Trinity Congregational Church, Croydon, Surrey, to Winifred Margaret Moore. His prospects at the Camelon Iron Co. were clouded because his father neither possessed a controlling interest nor chose to exercise his influence. Robert's brother Henry sailed ahead of him, and another brother John (1861-1929), an industrial chemist who had migrated to New Zealand in 1888, moved to Melbourne in 1890 to manage David Mitchell's [q.v.5] cement works. He became Mitchell's right-hand man and with (Sir) John Monash [q.v.] they formed the Reinforced Concrete and Monier Pipe Construction Co. Pty Ltd, which before World War I monopolized building in reinforced concrete in Victoria and dominated concrete pipe construction; John Gibson remained managing director through the 1920s. Robert's mother and several sisters visited him in Melbourne, and he assisted his family in Scotland when able to do so. Mostly, however, kin were kept at a distance and he never returned to Scotland.

In Melbourne Gibson worked as a draughtsman and designer and steadily accumulated savings despite highly unfavourable economic conditions. In 1897 he started his own business in North Melbourne: the Austral Manufacturing Co. which specialized in metal bedsteads mainly for hospital use and met with only moderate success. A second venture, the Lux Foundry Pty Ltd, incorporated in 1906, helped to lift Gibson to a senior position in the Victorian Chamber of Manufactures and from there to national prominence. The Lux Foundry manufactured fuel stoves, metal grates, baths and other products of the light casting industry. By World War I he had established himself as a man of means.

Gibson was a man of high sensitivity and broad accomplishment with a personal style far removed from the ordinary self-made, power-seeking industrialist. A craftsman in all he attempted, he was also a perfectionist with an intense desire to impose stringent control on his physical surroundings and the emotional content of his life. His slight figure and full forehead, sculptured beard and moustache, prominent eyebrows and deep sunken eyes combined to give him a distinguished though slightly distant appearance. Fine hands with tapered fingers were used eloquently, yet he spoke slowly and deliberately, almost reluctantly. His advice was sought on many matters because of his sound judgment, clarity and simplicity of expression, and the objective manner of his pronouncements. His own supreme self-control reassured and instilled confidence in other people.

Gibson lived at a pace and level of intensity exceeded by few others. As a child he attracted attention because of his inventiveness in building toys from improbable materials. In manufacturing business he designed his own products. As a husband and father he refurbished the interior of a large house on the banks of the Yarra in Toorak, built and largely maintained an extensive garden, designed Christmas cards, fixed the plumbing, turned his own shirt-cuffs, attended to his ironing when needed, acted as counsel for his five daughters and two sons, but rarely gave himself time for a full family life. Other interests reflected his preoccupation with the material world. As a motorist he most enjoyed taking the machine apart and putting it together to discover the secrets of its design. As a photographer he developed his own still-life prints which revealed his depth of perception and sensitivity to form; with his close friend and medical adviser, Julian Smith [q.v.], he helped create the Victorian Salon of Photography in the 1920s.

The restless energy, great need for independence and highly developed sense of duty were limited by Gibson's frail constitution. From childhood he suffered many long periods of illness and several times in his fifties and sixties he was believed to be close to death. Uninterested in food he much preferred coffee. He smoked incessantly, one of the few indulgences he allowed himself. He slept poorly and was not easy to sedate; often he worked far into the night devising new schemes and planning for improvements in administrative efficiency. His undemonstrative style and tight control were disturbed only occasionally, but at such times his temper could be explosive. Much of his energy was directed towards the anticipation of threat, particularly illness, and towards building for a more secure future. Thus, his economic philosophy placed a high valuation on thrift, saving, giving to those in genuine need, and steady improvement in material conditions; he disliked speculation, waste, indulgence for its own sake, and the overt exercise of power.

Before World War I Gibson persuaded the Victorian Chamber of Manufactures to establish its own insurance company of which he was chairman in 1914-28. Membership of the chamber's council from 1911 gave him the opportunity to expand his interests. He was nominated by the chamber to be the Victorian representative on the Central Coal Board in 1916 because of his knowledge of coal-using industries. He was a member of the short-lived Luxuries Board in 1917, and deputy chairman of the original Repatriation Commission, 1917-20. He attracted considerable attention and earned a reputation as a martinet in some circles for his forthright criticism of waste and inefficiency in the public service, particularly the Post-master-General's Department, as chairman of the royal commission on public expenditure (the 'Economy Commission') in 1918-21. He was the Commonwealth government's representative on the board of Commonwealth Oil Refineries from 1920, and joined the Victorian State Electricity Commission in 1919; he worked harmoniously with Monash and remained a commissioner until his death. His involvement with private industry was less extensive, but he served on the board of the National Mutual Life Association, the Union Trustee Co., and Robert Harper [q.v.] & Co., and as president of the Victorian Chamber of Manufactures, 1922-25, and of the Associated Chambers of Manufactures, 1924-27. For a time he was a member of the Council of the University of Melbourne. He was appointed C.B.E. 1918, K.B.E. 1920, and G.B.E. 1932.

In 1924 Gibson was gazetted an original member of the Commonwealth Bank Board following the decision to substitute a seven-man board for one-man control by the governor. He was elected chairman in 1926 following the retirement through ill-health of (Sir) John J. Garvan [q.v.]. Gibson brought to the position the craftsman's dedication to perfection and precision, and a firm conviction that his prime legal and moral responsibility was to serve as senior trustee of the nation's currency. Money was interpreted as currency and bullion in its tangible form and excluded those balances which were the result of credit creation. 'Real' money was seen as the outcome of thriftiness and the steady accumulation of savings. Gibson believed, with many of his contemporaries, in the strict separation of monetary management and government policy. His view was that governments could not be trusted with other people's money.

Although the chairmanship of the Commonwealth Bank was a part-time and non-executive position, Gibson assumed tactical responsibility for the bank's policy during the early 1930s. Already he had withdrawn from business and reduced his other commitments to concentrate on the bank. Initially he was concerned to maintain the gold standard in Australia, and spoke as if the standard would be still operating well after gold payments were abandoned in January 1930. Next he sought to retain exchange parity between the pound sterling and the pound Australian, but this was being undermined by Australia's poor credit standing in London which was linked with past profligacy of governments. The only way to stabilize the value of the currency was to ensure that governments balanced their budgets. Accordingly Gibson was responsible for the invitation to a representative of the Bank of England, Sir Otto Niemeyer, to visit Australia to help devise a plan for rapid budget-balancing. When this failed and 30 per cent devaluation was forced on the country, he refused a moderate request in April 1931 for further credit expansion to permit unemployment relief expenditure and wheat industry assistance. Before the bar of the Senate the following month he gave contradictory evidence about the desirability of selling off the remaining gold reserve. His immediate objective was to force governments to balance budgets within an agreed period; his wider purpose was to maintain external financial solvency and the sanctity of contracts.

Gibson was alternatively idealized and vilified for his tough stand. Conservative and liberal groups saw him as a figure of reason and responsibility in a world that seemed to be falling apart. He was remembered vividly for his radio broadcast on 3 May 1932 in which he used his soft Scots burr to evoke a sense of strength and security in a successful attempt to reassure depositors about the safety of the Commonwealth Bank. Indeed, he liked to see himself as guardian and defender: his favourite cartoon depicted him as the little Dutch boy with his finger in the dike preventing inundation by the raging sea. The Labor Party and radicals saw him as a ruthless representative of the capitalist class interest. Both views have some merit but they miss the essence of the man. Gibson was a gifted craftsman whose personal need for order, stability and control led to over-rigid reliance on a set of simple axioms which were inadequate to negotiate the turmoil of the Depression. The judgment applies to nearly all his contemporaries in similar positions of authority.

Gibson disliked publicity, and the strain of the early 1930s took a heavy toll of his frail body. He had several long bouts of illness during 1932 and 1933, and, survived by his wife and children, died on 1 January 1934 at South Yarra. On 3 January, the day of his state funeral and burial at Box Hill, the Commonwealth Bank closed during the afternoon as a mark of respect. A bronze bust to stand in Parliament House, Canberra, was commissioned by the Victorian Chamber of Manufactures, a small University of Melbourne scholarship was endowed, and a biography was to be written by (Sir) Ernest Scott [q.v.]. The biography lapsed probably because few personal papers were available: the tasks that Gibson imposed on himself gave him little time for expressive rather than functional communication. His estate in Victoria was valued for probate at £85811.

L. F. Giblin, *The growth of a central bank* (Melb, 1951); G. E. Caiden, *Career service* (Melb, 1965); C.

B. Schedvin, *Australia and the great Depression* (Syd, 1970); *Bank Notes*, Jan 1934; *Victorian Chamber of Manufactures Gazette*, 30 Jan 1934; *Aust Q*, Mar 1934; *SMH*, 11 May 1929, 2 Jan 1934; *Table Talk*, Sept 1930; *Herald* (Melb), 1 Jan 1934; Gibson papers (LaTL); Reserve Bank Archives (Syd); family information.

C. B. SCHEDVIN

GIBSON, WILLIAM (1842?-1918), draper and importer, was born at Glasgow, Scotland, son of James Gibson, clothier, and his wife, née Dick. As a boy, he entered the firm of Mann, Byars & Co. He had risen to the position of cashier, with the reputation of 'honest, steady and industrious habits' at the time of his marriage to Mary Hislop in 1881 at St Andrew's Presbyterian Church, Glasgow. Later that year he resigned from the firm and in February 1882, with his wife and infant son, he sailed for Australia.

From his early twenties Gibson had cherished hopes of setting up a drapery business; but once in Melbourne he did not rush into putting his plans to action. By the end of May 1882 he had obtained a position as New Zealand representative for the wholesalers Beath, Schiess & Co. Late that year a chance to buy into a drapery business came when Mark Foy [q.v.4] was looking for a partner for his son Francis [q.v.]. The agreement setting up Foy & Gibson, drapers of Collingwood, was signed on 6 March 1883 with Gibson and Francis Foy each putting in £5000. Francis Foy continued to act as manager, controlling both the buying and selling, while Gibson took charge of the office and routine work. While naturally reserved, Gibson had a genial manner and excellent memory for names and faces, and soon established good relations with customers and clients. However, as the business prospered, he began to resent Foy's control over the buying and general management of the store. Matters came to a head after a disagreement in mid-1884, and when tempers had cooled, it was decided to dissolve the partnership. In August 1884 Foy went to Sydney where he established Mark Foy's Ltd, and Gibson became sole proprietor of the Collingwood shop; they agreed not to set up in opposition.

Gibson now set out to improve his overseas buying organization, and established the practice of sending departmental buyers to Britain. Growth was rapid and he soon brought others into the firm: first William Dougall and later his nephews Samuel Gibson and John Maclellan. A huge four-storey hardware department was built next door to the Collingwood store. In March 1889 Gibson went overseas to take on the firm's buying himself. He visited Paris, where he was particularly impressed by the Bon Marché department store. He toured the main manufacturing centres of Britain and bought £100 000 worth of merchandise before returning to Australia in March 1890. He left again for Glasgow at the end of 1891 and in 1893 was in London when news reached him of the bank crashes in Melbourne. He hurried back and by hard work and 'dogged determination' kept the business going in the depression that followed.

In 1895, after a preliminary investigation of the business situation in Perth, Gibson arranged to set up a branch of the firm there. Undeterred by the problems of scarce building supplies, he had a prefabricated corrugated iron structure sent from Melbourne to Perth to serve as temporary premises. In 1897 he transferred his overseas buying office from Glasgow to London. About the same time he began the manufacture of articles such as men's clothing and shirts, ladies' underclothing, millinery, furniture, bedding and hardware to supply the Perth and Melbourne stores. His large 'Gibsonia' woollen and hosiery mills developed from a few hand-knitting machines for producing men's socks. In 1902 a new store was completed in Prahran, known as Maclellan & Co. or 'The Big Store'; Gibson was senior partner. On a visit to South Africa he bought a site in Johannesburg, but never went ahead with his plan to set up a branch there. He opened a store in Brisbane in 1903 and in Rundle Street, Adelaide, in 1907.

Gibson went to London for a six months visit in 1914 but war conditions detained him there. In 1917 a son was killed in action and in August 1918 another died in London. On 5 November that year Gibson died. He was survived by five sons and four daughters. His estate in Australia was valued for probate at over £1 850 000. His nephew John Maclellan carried on the business, which survived until 1967.

S. W. Davies, *Foy's saga* (Perth, 1946); *Industrial Aust and Mining Standard*, 14 Nov 1918; Foy and Gibson Ltd collection, *and* William Gibson estate papers, *and* P. Howson collection (Melb Univ Archives).   SALLY O'NEILL

GIBSON, WILLIAM ALFRED (1869-1929), film producer and businessman, was born in London, son of William Gibson, soldier, and his wife Matilda, née Day. He attended Ilford College, Essex, and migrated to Australia while a teenager. With Presbyterian forms on 17 November 1898 at Albert Park, Melbourne, he married Annabella Kirk; they had a son and a daughter. Gibson worked as a chemist in the firm of William Johnson & Son of St Kilda, and supplied

chemicals to some of the first film exhibitors in Melbourne. In 1900 he bought a projector and films from one of his clients, and in partnership with William Johnson's son, Millard, he began to screen films for the public. Huge crowds were attracted and soon the firm of Johnson & Gibson bought other 'biograph' machines, engaged staff, and expanded their operations until they were presenting some forty shows in and around Melbourne. Except for some local scenic items, all their films were imported.

In 1906 Johnson and Gibson joined the theatrical entrepreneurs, John and Nevin Tait [q.v. Tait family], to produce a dramatic film, *The story of the Kelly gang*. By this time, Johnson and Gibson had become experts in photography and film processing, and they were responsible for technical aspects of the production. Directed by another Tait brother, Charles, the film was staged mainly at Heidelberg near Melbourne. When completed, it was over 4000 feet (1219 m) in length and ran for well over an hour, and claims have been made that it was in fact the world's first 'feature' film. It was certainly the first such film to be made in Australia. It opened at the Athenaeum Hall, Melbourne, on 26 December 1906, and was an immediate commercial success.

Johnson and Gibson continued to photograph films for other producers until March 1911, when they merged with the Tait family in a greatly expanded company, Amalgamated Pictures Ltd. This new company, based in Melbourne, produced a series of profitable feature films, including in 1911 *The mystery of a hansom cab* and *The bells*.

In November 1912, in the context of increasingly fierce competition between rival film exhibitors and film importers, Amalgamated Pictures joined a cluster of companies centred around Australasian Films Ltd for film distribution, cinema equipment and production, and Union Theatres Ltd for cinema ownership and film exhibition. The combine dominated the Australian film trade as a monopoly until after World War I, when American production companies began to set up branches in Australia to market their own films. Australasian Films and Union Theatres continued, however, to be major forces in the Australian trade, and became the foundation for the present-day Greater Union Organization. Gibson held positions as joint managing director of Union Theatres and as director and then general manager of Australasian Films until his death. He also served on the management boards of several subsidiary companies in the combine.

A highly astute businessman, Gibson early realized that it was safer to import films than to produce them, and Australasian

Films only occasionally ventured into feature film production; its substantial technical resources were used mainly for newsreels and short films. Although sometimes referred to as the 'father' of Australian film production, because of his part in making *The story of the Kelly gang*, Gibson rarely associated himself directly with production after 1912, and ironically found his companies becoming the target of many critics who saw them as the instrument by which production had been suppressed in Australia. The companies were investigated by a royal commission into the film industry in 1927, but no action resulted against them.

Hollow-cheeked and grey-faced, even when young, Gibson was tirelessly hard working, and had few outside interests, although he was president of the Dandenong Agricultural Society, in the vicinity of his home, Oakwood Park. For business he travelled extensively around Australia, to Europe and America. In 1920 he was appointed O.B.E. for his services to the community, especially for patriotic work and fund-raising activities during World War I.

Survived by his wife and children, Gibson died from broncho-pneumonia aged 60 on 6 October 1929 in Melbourne. He was buried in Brighton cemetery. His estate was valued for probate at £41 976.

A. Pike and R. Cooper, *Australian film 1900-1977* (Melb, 1980); Roy Com on the moving picture industry in Australia, Report, *PP* (Cwlth), 1926-28, 4, 1371; *Theatre Mag* (Syd), 1 June 1920; *Everyone's* (Syd), 7 Feb 1923, 27 July 1927; *Film Weekly* (Syd), 10 Oct 1929; *Table Talk*, 6 Jan 1927; *Argus*, 7 Oct 1929; *Sunday Herald*, 9 Oct 1949; *SMH*, 27 Oct 1962.   A. F. PIKE

GIBSON, WILLIAM GERRAND (1869-1955), storekeeper, farmer and politician, was born on 19 May 1869 at Gisborne, Victoria, second son of David Gibson, farmer, and his wife Grace, née Gerrand. His parents had migrated to Victoria from Scotland in 1860 to pioneer land at Riddells Creek, Wild Dog Valley and Tarnagulla before settling at Gisborne. 'Billy' worked with his father, then on his own land, before turning to trading. On 4 November 1896 at Riddells Creek he married Mary Helen Young Patterson with Presbyterian forms. For thirteen years he kept general stores at Romsey and Lancefield, returning to the land in 1910 when he bought a substantial subdivision of J. C. Manifold's [q.v.] Gnarpurt estate near Lismore in the Western District for cropping and grazing. A younger brother, David Havelock (Harvey), bought a subdivision in the neighbouring Cressy district.

Gibson was typical of a small group of men who united farmers to gain political and financial recognition in keeping with their increasing numbers and their contribution to national development. Though of slight build and gentlemanly mien, he had a lively, inventive and determined disposition. To minimize settlers' costs for their machinery and supplies, he organized and managed the Cressy Co-operative. In 1911 he became secretary of the Lismore Branch of the People's Party but although its original purpose was to represent the farmers' interests it fell under the domination of the city-based Liberal Party. In 1916 price-fixing under the War Precautions Act caused farmers to suspect that merchants in the Liberal Party were manipulating the price of wheat at the growers' expense. Farmers' Union branches were raised up in protest and Gibson was elected secretary of the Lismore branch and a councillor of central executive. His brother, president of the Cressy branch, was the successful candidate for the assembly seat of Grenville when Farmers' Union men stood for State parliament in 1917.

In 1918 Gibson became the first member of the Farmers' Union Party (Country Party from 1921) to be elected to Federal parliament when he defeated J. H. Scullin [q.v.] on preferences at a by-election for Corangamite. Both dairy and wheat growers benefited from Gibson's influence over price-fixing processes until the return of the open market in 1921; their gratitude enabled him to hold his seat. However, even during this period, Gibson's commitment to individual enterprise led him to lean noticeably towards Nationalist Party policies.

A member of the select committee appointed to inquire into the proposed agreement with Amalgamated Wireless (Australasia) Ltd in 1921-22, and deputy leader of the Country Party from January 1923, Gibson made his most positive contribution to the welfare of country people as postmaster-general in the Bruce- [q.v.7] Page [q.v.] government of 1923-29. It was a role in which he could combine his interest in technology with his commercial and political skills. Viewing the post as a mission to decrease the isolation of country dwellers, he pursued four different approaches: construction of more telephone lines; extension of the network of roadside mail deliveries; building of post offices in country districts; and encouragement and regulation of the infant radio broadcasting services. The appointment of the able (Sir) Harry Percy Brown [q.v.7] as a member of the Postal Advisory Committee in 1922 and next year as head of the department contributed to Gibson's success. Gibson represented Australia at the International Postal Convention in Stockholm in 1924 and from December

1928 he was also minister for works and railways.

Gibson's defeat in 1929, though part of the general rout of the Bruce-Page government, may have reflected his lack of support for the marketing control favoured by many Corangamite farmers. He returned to his property, Cluan, and applied his ingenuity to developing a Corriedale sheep stud, harvesting subterranean clover seed, and experimenting with charcoal-powered tractors. He was returned again for Corangamite in 1931 but Prime Minister Lyons [q.v.] reserved the postmaster-general's portfolio for J. E. Fenton [q.v.]. In 1934 Gibson stood for the Senate. Consistent with his political beliefs, he joined a combined United Australia Party-Country Party team, so preventing the Country Party candidate, R. D. Elliott [q.v.], from being elected. As a sanction he was excluded from the federal party rooms for some time. In spite of failing health Gibson remained a senator until 1947 when he retired to Cluan. In 1941-42, possibly in belated recognition of his work for radio broadcasting in the twenties, he chaired the parliamentary committee whose major recommendations were embodied in the Broadcasting Act of 1942.

Gibson died on 22 May 1955 at Lismore and was buried in the local cemetery. He was survived by a son and daughter; his wife and his daughter Grace, who acted as his secretary, predeceased him.

U. R. Ellis, *A history of the Australian Country Party* (Melb, 1963); B. D. Graham, *The formation of the Australian Country Parties* (Canb, 1966); A. W. Thomas, *Broadcast and be damned* (Melb, 1980); L. G. Lomas, The western district farmer 1914-27 (Ph.D. thesis, Monash Univ, 1979); information from Mrs W. E. Long, Ocean Grove, *and* Mr I. D. Gibson, 'Cluan', Lismore, Vic.   L. LOMAS

GIBSON, WILLIAM RALPH BOYCE (1869-1935), philosopher, was born on 15 March 1869 in Paris, son of William Gibson, Methodist minister there, and his wife Helen Wilhelmina, daughter of William Binnington Boyce [q.v.3]. He was educated in England at Kingswood School, Bath. At the Queen's College, Oxford, (B.A., 1892; M.A., 1895; D.Sc., 1911) he studied mathematics which he subsequently taught at Clifton College, Bristol. Having become interested in philosophy, he went to Jena in 1893 where Rudolf Eucken was teaching. He later studied philosophy at Paris and Glasgow. From 1898 he lectured in logic, psychology and ethics at Hackney, Regent's Park and New colleges, and from 1900 at Westfield College, University of London. In 1909, on being elected external examiner in philosophy for the University of London, he re-

signed all teaching engagements, but in June next year he accepted a post as temporary lecturer in philosophy at the University of Liverpool. He was appointed to the chair of mental and moral philosophy at the University of Melbourne in 1911, arriving in Victoria in February 1912.

By then Boyce Gibson had written a great deal. Papers of his had appeared in the *Revue de Métaphysique et de Morale, Mind* and the *Proceedings* of the Aristotelian Society, London. He contributed an essay to *Personal Idealism* (1902), a collection edited by Henry Sturt, which reflected and promoted an important trend in Idealist philosophy. Personal Idealism — in its day very popular with philosophers in Australia — engaged itself in the defence of the metaphysical autonomy of personality against opposite adversaries: against Naturalism which made personality merely an outcome of 'the mechanism of Nature', and against a form of Idealism which made it merely an 'adjective' of the Absolute. He had also written *A philosophical introduction to ethics* (1904) and, with the co-operation of Augusta Klein, *The problem of logic* (1908; reprinted as late as 1930). Two other books, published in 1906 and 1909, expounded Eucken's philosophy, a very inspirational form of Personal Idealism which held (in Gibson's words) that 'the measure and standard of our thought is fixed by the measure and standard of our life'.

Gibson's philosophical principles and his character alike would not allow him to impose in any way his strongly held metaphysical beliefs upon his students. He was 'completely open-minded', one of his last students said of him. He was remembered for his power to convey enthusiasm, and for the way he brought students to a resolution of their difficulties, enabling them to see what *they* were groping towards. He held up exacting standards to his classes.

Between 1910 and 1935 there was a strong awareness, especially in Melbourne, of contemporary Continental philosophy. Gibson shared with his colleagues a considerable interest in Henri Bergson. He was also interested in the relation between physics and philosophy and in 1928 had published a survey of the ideas of the Hungarian Melchior Palágyi whom he read in German. These two interests came together in his presidential address, 'Relativity and first principles' to Section J of the Australian and New Zealand Association for the Advancement of Science conference in 1931.

Gibson's most important concern with Continental philosophy was his attention to the Phenomenological movement, and he is accorded some prominence by its historian, Herbert Spiegelberg (writing in the 1950s). Gibson's translation, published in 1931, of

Husserl's *Ideen zu einer reinen Phäno-menlogie und phänomenologischen Philoso-phie* pioneered the rendering of Husserl's thought into English. He wrote a set of articles for the *Australasian Journal of Psychology and Philosophy* (1933-35) on the ethical thought of Nicolai Hartmann, who was associated with the movement.

Gibson died at Surrey Hills on 2 April 1935 and was cremated. He had retired from the chair the year before. At Liverpool, England, on 8 September 1898 he had married Lucy Judge Peacock (1872-1953). They had met when she was sent to stay at the Methodist parsonage in Paris to improve her French. She studied classics and then oriental languages at Girton College, Cambridge, and Sanskrit at the Sorbonne and at Jena. She collaborated with her husband in translating two of Eucken's works and singly translated another one. In Melbourne she was celebrated for the liveliness of her mind. There were five children of the marriage: Alexander became third professor of philosophy at Melbourne; Keith was killed in a climbing accident; Ralph became a leading member and functionary in Victoria of the Australian Communist Party; Colin became a Unitarian minister; and Quentin began the teaching of philosophy in what was then Canberra University College.

H. Spiegelberg, *The phenomenological movement* (The Hague, 1969); *A'sian J of Philosophy*, June 1935; *J. of the British Soc of Phenomenology*, 2 (1971).

S. A. GRAVE